INTRODUCTION TO COACHING SPORTS

DR. THOMAS E. REED.,
CHAD EARL,
AND
ACIE EARL

First Edition

PAGE PUBLISHING, INC.
Conneaut Lake, PA

First originally published by Page Publishing 2021

ISBN 978-1-64544-321-6 (pbk)
ISBN 978-1-6624-3713-7 (hc)
ISBN 978-1-64544-322-3 (digital)

Printed in the United States of America

CONTENTS

PREFACE

Today, the term *coach* invokes many different emotions and opinions compared to several decades ago. Coaching has become extremely stratified in modern society. Low-level coaching includes volunteer roles in community and recreational organizations often because an interest of one's child. Moderate-level coaching includes participation in travel sports or AAU programs driven by personal experience with the game and a desire to share competitive knowledge in a relaxed atmosphere. High-level coaching includes varsity sports, prep schools, college, or national AAU teams. Coaches at this level seek compensation, a more committed athlete and stronger competitive environment. Professional coaching is either working at the division one, two, or three college or professional franchise level. The professional coach seeks the most lucrative pay, highest competitive environment, and greatest social visibility available in the profession. To be successful at any level, the coach must possess a set of character traits coupled with an adequate knowledge base to lead their athletes and positively represent their school, organization, or community. We therefore feel and understand that coaching is a tremendous privilege and opportunity to make a difference in the minds and hearts of athletes, their families, alumni, fans, and vested stakeholders.

Qualitative research provides several motivations for those individuals who desire to coach, irrespective of gender, level, or type of sport. The primary one being creating and contributing to an environment of fairness and self-worth through equitable competition. Ultimately, successful coaching is effective leadership that starts with the individual and then is duplicated by all the members of team, thus becoming reflective and transformative at an organizational and community level. To develop a successful athlete, the coach must also develop a positive teammate, a productive student, and a responsible citizen. Sports, therefore, can serve as a tremendous platform for positive life experiences, self-esteem, self-sacrifice, discipline, accomplishment, and other positive virtues. The decision to become a coach is exciting. We are delighted to join in the journey.

Topics Covered

The text is organized by five demarcations of content:

Section 1 (chapters 1, 2, and 3): **Effective Coaching Communication**—this section discusses various personality structures, player motivation, and establishing a coaching philosophy.

Section 2 (chapters 4, 5, and 6): **Practical Athletic Development**—this section addresses athletic mindset, physical assessment, and athletic muscular development.

Section 3 (chapters 7 and 8): **Nutrition Guidelines for Athletes**—this section provides coaches a framework to recommend both healthy and performance-based nutrition recommendations. In addition, chapter 8 provides information to help coaches advise athletes on how to discern the difference between low- and high-quality supplement products.

Section 4 (chapters 9, 10, and 11): **Elite Sport Participation and Recruitment**—coaches need athletes that can successfully compete in the athletic, social, and academic environment, their organization, or school demands. Locating and identifying the players that successfully meet these challenges can be incredibly difficult. This section explains the differences in personal criteria and athletic ability between the various college levels, semiprofessional, and professional environments a coach will need to be mindful of when recruiting their target athlete.

Section 5 (chapter 12): **Coaching Certification**—the final chapter (12) addresses the general coaching requirements and certifications in the following states: Illinois, Iowa, California, New York, Ohio, Pennsylvania, Texas, and Florida.

Our Target Reader

This book is for individuals who have an aspiration to coach, advise, or manage athletes in competitive sports. Our assumption is that the reader is passionate, has some level of personal experience with sports, and has a fundamental understanding of coaching. The primary audience for this text includes:

- Laypersons who is interested in learning various dimensions of coaching
- Undergraduate or graduate students who lack in formal coaching experience
- Current coaches who have coached under five years
- Past and present coaches who are looking for strategies to maintain a level of success
- Administrators who oversee athletic programs in recreational, elementary, middle school, high school, and college

ACKNOWLEDGMENTS

The authors of this book have each expressed their gratitude to those individuals who encouraged, inspired, and gave their continued support throughout this process. Here are their reflections:

First and foremost, I would like to thank God for giving me the wisdom, patience, and insight to write this book. I would also like to thank my wife, Makeda Lewis-Reed, for her insight, love, and support throughout this project and to both Chad Earl and Acie Earl for their expertise and writing contributions to this book (Dr. Thomas E. Reed).

I would like to thank my wife, Tabia Earl, for her love and support throughout this process. I would also like to thank my father, Acie Earl Sr., and uncle, Glenn Earl Sr., for their insight and invaluable feedback. Lastly, a special thank you and measure of a gratitude to Dr. Thomas Earl Reed and my oldest brother, Acie Earl II, for their contributions to this project (Chad Earl).

I would like to thank my brothers, Chad Earl and Dr. Thomas E. Reed, for bringing me on board with this unique and groundbreaking project. I would also like to thank my mentors and professors at Iowa University, Dr. Mike Teague and Dr. Ben Hunnicut, as they inspired me to teach, write, and dream big. I also give gratitude to the Sports and Recreation program at Iowa University where I was an instructor and course designer for seven years. In closing, I want to give a special thanks to the many fans who have supported me for my previous six books I have written over the years. I am truly grateful (Acie Earl).

CHAPTER 1

DIMENSION OF COACHING

Understanding the Dimensions of Coaching Young Athletes

The dimension of coaching is far more than blowing a whistle between the lines or on one half of the court or field. There are many *aspects of coaching* that need to be considered when one decides to take on the role of a coach. In the United States alone, it is estimated that millions of children under the age of eighteen participate in school and extracurricular programs. These programs range from all types of sports (Ewing and Seefeldt 2002).

There are multiple interpretations regarding youth sport, which include children who cheat, fight, and disrespect opponents and officials, coaches who encourage such behavior, and parents and fans who act inappropriately. Although these perspectives may be rare as we take a global look at youth participation, they are prevalent. Ultimately, it is the coach's responsibility to curtail these behaviors by taking on a leadership role and understanding the various dimensions of coaching in today's society. It is important that coaches should have an understanding of the framework, which provides guidelines, rules, regulations, organizing practice, and incorporating a fun environment. It is a coach's responsibility to provide a safe place to practice, decrease the possibility of injury, increase enthusiasm, encourage prolonged participation, reward the effort in place of the outcome, where being competitive does not supersede an overall joyful experience for youth sport participation. Some data has pointed out that the traditional concept of coaching, teaching, and encouraging youth participants (O'Rourke, Smith, Smoll, and Cumming 2011) has been replaced by the concept of gaining victories, collecting trophies, and establishing a higher winning percentage, which is a reflection that the coach is better and claims modern wisdom. This ideology has caused some coaches to solely focus on winning and recruiting the best athletes regardless of their sportsmanship demeanor, which minimizes the concept of positive youth development and participation.

Please read the scenario below and make a decision how you would handle the situation?

> Adam, your star forward, was involved in a loose ball, whereas he and the opponent were battling for the possession of the ball during a crucial point in the game. Adam was not only frustrated that his opponent gained possession of the ball but that he was not playing well and his team was losing. Adam, several plays later, throws an elbow and catches his opponent, who gained possession of the ball during the loose ball play, on the chin with his elbow. The officials miss the play and there is no call, and you, the coach, are so wrapped up in the game that you miss the elbow Adam landed on the opposing player. The next day, the opposing coach gives you a call and states that his player received a deliberate elbow from your player and the rules state that although an official may miss the play, if it is noticed in game video, the player initiating the elbow could be suspended. The statute of limitation for this non-sportsman demeanor is two days after the contest. The opposing coach calls and says that he will leave it up to you to enforce the penalty on your player. Upon viewing the game video, you clearly see the "cheap shot" Adam displayed. Do you suspend Adam the next game, or do you let him play?

Developing a Coaching Philosophy

The scenario described is one of many reasons why developing a coaching philosophy with clear-cut objectives is key criteria to establishing rules and bylaws that allow you to make informed decisions. You will be faced with challenging decisions as a coach, and your philosophy in conjunction with established coaching objectives allows you to address the type of issue above with a clear conscious.

There are many tough decisions you will need to make when you coach, particularly young sport participants. One dimension of coaching that I think is very important is establishing a coaching philosophy, which lays a foundation of how you will facilitate the team as a whole.

Establishing a coaching philosophy was one of my toughest challenges as a young coach. I was fragmented in my ideologies about structuring a practice, keeping the young participants engaged throughout practice, recruiting strategies, hiring practices, managing a budget, system of play, and implementing rules that govern the program. Your coaching philosophy should be based on the values and morals you hold and knowing the conditions of your own mind (Martens 2012). Uncertainty of your philosophy can lead to inconsistency of how you manage the team, which can destroy personal relationships and create chaos within a team. Ralph Sabock (1985, pp. 49–50) illustrated a good story, where a boy and an old man not having their own philosophy about an appropriate etiquette created uncertainty and criticism.

There was an old man, a young boy, and a donkey. They were going into town, and it was decided that the boy should ride. As they went along, they passed some people who exclaimed that it was a shame for the boy to ride and the old man to walk. The man and boy decided that maybe the critics were right, so they changed positions. Later, they passed some more people who exclaimed that it was a real shame for the man to make a young boy walk. The two, not having a philosophy, decided that maybe they both should walk. Soon they passed some other people who exclaimed that it was stupid to walk when they had a donkey to ride. The man and boy decided that maybe the critics were right, so they decided that they both should ride the donkey. They soon passed other people who exclaimed that it was a shame to put such a load on a poor little animal. The old man and the boy decided that maybe the critics were right, so they decided to carry the donkey. As they crossed a bridge, they lost their grip on the animal, and the donkey fell into the river and drowned. The moral of the story is that without a philosophy, you may try to please everyone which could cost you your ass.

One dimension of coaching is that "coaching" in and of itself is challenging due to the many difficult decisions and dilemmas that come with the job. Developing a philosophy helps making the difficult decisions a little easier as opposed to not having one and problem solving on the fly. As one author stated, your philosophy, in conjunction with your knowledge of the sport, will save you from losing your ass. *A coaching philosophy* should describe your system of play, how you will train your participants, rules, code of conduct, short- and long-term objectives, and other aspects of coaching. If you participated in sports, you may have some philosophical ideal of how you live your life, how you play, the roles of teammates, coaching, and an overall subconscious perspective about playing the game. When you assume a coaching role, it is imperative that you have a coaching philosophy, and although they are lifelong and ever changing, it's important to establish one.

Most youth, high school, college, and professional coaches have coaching philosophies that vary in dimensions as noted above. I would assume that after taking on a leadership role in a sport program and embracing all the responsibilities that come with running a program, a coach will have a concept of a philosophy or develop one in a hurry and the dimension thereof.

- *Shaka Smart*, one of the best upcoming college basketball coach, emphasizes that being able to find meaning in your participation is critical. As a player, you choose to be in a program, and as a coach, you are chosen to run the program. Philosophically, as the player or coach, you are striving to become a better person. Coach Smart's perspective is a part of a coaching philosophy.

- One of William Brown's past head men's basketball coach for University of California at Pennsylvania and Division II men's basketball Hall of Fame recipient's philosophy is that "emphasis must be placed on defense and at the end of the game it comes down to making stops in any sport. Defense travels with you on the road, and it requires great effort and mental toughness."

One's coaching philosophy can have several objectives. One objective to consider is the skill of motivating participants, whereas you are trying to influence the direction and intensity of one's effort (Clutterbuck and Megginson 2011). The ability to motivate people, coupled with implementing the technical or tactical knowledge of a sport or physical activity, is what separates the very good coach from the average one. Another objective to meet is instilling a competitive attitude within participants. Competitiveness is defined as "a disposition to strive for satisfaction when making comparisons with some standard of excellence in the presence of evaluative others" (Martens 1976, p. 3). Martens's view on competitiveness is based on achievement behavior in a competitive context, with social evaluation as a key component.

Meeting specific objectives can be challenging, particularly when you find yourself in a situation where you cannot get your team to be motivated about competition or display a competitive demeanor. However, this is not the time to discard this part of your coaching philosophy principle. It may be an indicator that you need to search for a different protocol or way you would meet the objective of motivating or creating a competitive spirit within participants when issues arise. Below are some issues you could face as a coach:

- Team is tired of practicing because it's been a long season
- Certain players are struggling academically and need more study time
- You have young players that do not understand the work ethic needed to be competitive
- You notice that your team has other agendas outside of the sport that seem to distract from motivation and competitiveness in practice and competition

Addressing these issues could cause you to evaluate your coaching philosophy and develop objectives that can be used to deal with these issues if and when they arise. You need some flexibility when establishing your coaching philosophy to ensure that it is not incongruous with values that participants and family members may deem important. One other important note is that your coaching philosophy will most likely change over the years if you stay in the coaching profession for a period of time.

Tubby Smith Coaching Personified

Tubby Smith, the legendary college basketball coach, was a recipient of the John R. Wooden "Legends of Coaching" award in 2016. This award recognizes the lifetime achievement of coaches who exemplify Coach Wooden's high standard of coaching success and personal achievement. When selecting the individual, the Wooden Award committee considers a coach's character, success rate on the court, graduating rate of student athletes, one's coaching philosophy, and his identification with the goals of the John R. Wooden Award (Krista Pirtle, Oct. 2016 lubbuckonline.com). Coach Smith has demonstrated through his coaching the importance of meeting these criteria with his teams, and that is why he is one of the most successful coaches in the business.

I had a brief conversation with Coach Smith when I took him to the airport after he presented at a Nike Coaches Clinic at College of DuPage. I could tell from our brief conversation that Coach Smith is a man with high integrity, and I believe that his coaching illustrates "being a teacher." If you have watched him coach over the years, you can see that his players display good sportsmanship, which guides athletes in learning technical, tactical, and life skills. I also believe that his ideologies of "life" shape his coaching philosophy.

Coaching Personality

Understanding who you are and the uniqueness you bring to the coaching professions also helps young athletes understand who they are. Have you ever tried to describe your own personality as it relates to coaching? If you have, you probably listed adjectives, such as outgoing, funny, player's coach, upbeat. Maybe some of these self-descriptive adjectives are based on how you reacted in various situations. When participants see you act with respect and a demeanor that is appreciated by others, there will be a tendency for your athletes to behave the same way. If you demonstrate good character in guiding your athletes through competitive experiences, you will likely build character in those you guide and mentor.

Many theorists have attempted to define personality, and many have come to an agreement on one concept: "uniqueness." In essence, personality refer to a blend of characteristics that make a person unique. You can think of personality in various structures that are divided into separate but related levels (Hollander 1967, Martens 1975). Three personality levels that coaches can define that may bring a deeper understanding of their own uniqueness are psychological core, typical responses, and role-related behaviors.

Personality Structures (Dr. Thomas E. Reed Photo)

The most basic level of one's personality is the *psychological core*. It includes your attitudes, interests, values, motives, and beliefs about yourself and your self-worth. It is the centerpiece of your personality. It's who you really are, not who you want others to think you are. One question you may ask yourself is, are your basic values shaped by your family morals, do your friends influence these values, and how does religion play a part in your ethics and moral (Weinberg 2015 and Gould 2015)?

Typical responses are ways that we learn to adjust to the environment, or how one respond to the world around them Typical responses and your psychological core coincide with each other.

Typical responses can be a good indicator of your psychological core. For example, being calm and non-expressive on a consistent basis could be a sign that one is introverted and shy. However, although you have a calming demeanor during certain activities could be mistaken that you are introverted. It may have been that the particular situation caused you to be calm and non-expressive; the calm demeanor may not be a typical response in other situations.

One of the changeable aspects of personality, whereas your behavior changes as your perception of the environment changes, is termed *role-related behavior*. You may play a different role based on the situation. On any given day, you may play a different role of AAU travel team coach, graduate student, employee, husband, or wife. Each one of these situations cause you to act differently. For example, you may exert a more passive personality if you are sitting in the classroom as a graduate student as opposed to being on the sideline or field coaching.

Do I Know Who I Am?

Now is a good time for self-reflection. As you read each of the following questions, reflect for a few moments and then answer in the spaces. Take your time to clearly think about who you are. These questions may assist you in understanding your self-concept (how you perceive yourself). Your beliefs about yourself may not be realistic because it could be based on how you perceive other people responding to you.

- Do I truly know who I am?

- What do I want to do?

- Where am I destined to go?
- Does my behavior align with my goals and objectives?
- Can I be proud of myself?
- Do I enjoy what I do?

As you evaluate the questions above, take some time to answer them. Here are five additional questions specific to coaching and note what you think:

- What are my purposes for coaching?
- Am I coaching for the right reason?
- Are my goals and objective clear?
- How do I measure being a good coach?
- How do I become a better coach?

Form 1.1: Knowing Your Personality Structures

Instructions:

1. For the first role listed, rate yourself based on your attitude, values, interest, motives, and beliefs about yourself and your self-worth (psychological core).
2. Then rate yourself as you respond to the world around you (typical responses).
3. Next, rate yourself as your behavior changes as your perception of the environment changes (role-related behavior).

4. Use the rating scale (negative self, neutral self, positive self) and rate each item as it relates to the personality structure (psychological core, typical response, role-related behavior).

Rating scale –3 –2 Negative self	–1 0 Neutral self	+1 +2 +3 Positive self	
Item	**Psychological core (beliefs about yourself and self-worth), the real Self as you perceive your self**	**Typical responses (the way you learn to adjust to the environment and how you respond), the public self as you believe you are seen by others**	**Role-related behaviors (behavior change as your perception changes of the environment), the ideal self as you would like to be**
Knowing yourself as...			
an athlete			
a coach			
a mother or father			
successful			
honest			
anxious			
empathic			
domineering			
loyal			
humble			
needing recognition			
respected			
stubborn			

Permission granted from R. Martens, 2012, *Successful Coaching 4th ed.* (Champaign, Illinois: Human Kinetics). Available on line at www. Humankinetics.com Successful Coaching.

Part of your coaching philosophy may entail developing athlete's skills mentally and physiologically. However, your success as a coach can be strongly related to the perception you have of yourself. The knowing your personality scale can be helpful in identifying some characteristics that possibly can assist you in identifying and changing ineffective patterns of behavior.

Insight Personality Discovery

Part of building a coaching philosophy may be utilizing several concepts, in conjunction with knowing your personality is your insight personality discovery. How much of yourself will you share with your athletes? At the very start of the self-awareness journey is *Insight Personality Discovery*, a psychometric tool based on the psychology of Carl Jung. This concept could help coaches understand themselves, understand others (athletes), and make the most of the relationships building as a whole.

I personally believe that coaches should be somewhat transparent and not be detached from the athletes. *Building trust* and respect is a key component of a coaching philosophy, and if the goal is to produce the best product, athletes need to have confidence in you and themselves. Athletes should know how you feel about what they say and do. Sometimes, you need to take risks in your relationship with your athletes, and it is difficult to do that if you do not understand your own personality and more challenging to develop your coaching philosophy.

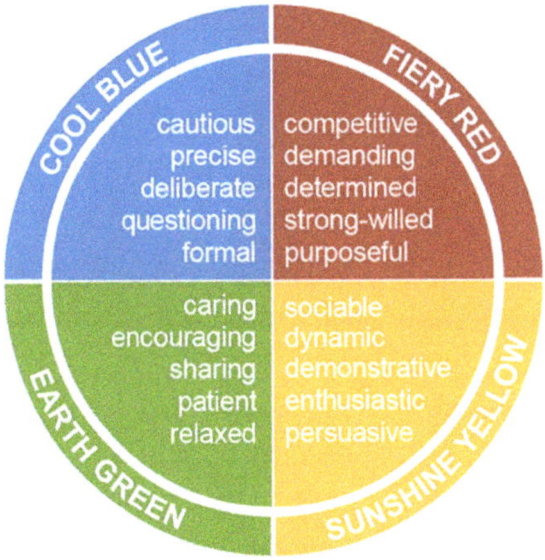

Some of psychologist Carl Young work was based off Hippocrates's ideologies. Carl defined four temperaments based on colors: cool blue, earth green, sunshine yellow, and fiery red. As I describe the meaning of each energy colors based on Carl's ideologies, I will make a connection on how they can help you develop your coaching philosophy.

Color Blue: Coaches with high levels of color blue live their lives according to facts and logic in reality. They analyze various possibilities to ensure that they don't make uninformed decision. They are planners and organizers.

Establishing a plan, organizing your system of play strategies, and highlighting values and objectives you want to achieve within your program is key to developing your coaching philosophy. Individuals who have *cool blue* characteristics may identify these criteria a little easier as opposed to others who have different temperaments.

Earth Green: Coaches with *earth green* characteristics are concerned about feelings and relationships. They are sensitive to the values behind people's actions and remain calm and patient in stressful situations. When establishing your coaching philosophy, you may ponder regarding being an athlete-centered coach or coach-centered. Athlete-centered coached involve their athletes making decisions about the team goals and season activities. Individuals who uniquely show more characteristics as *earth green* may highlight in their coaching philosophy that they are more athlete-centered and embrace a participatory democratic philosophy.

Sunshine Yellow: Coaches who fall into the category of *sunshine yellow* have a tendency to race toward their dreams of the future. They move from one idea or activity to the other, and their behavior can be fun and others may embrace this demeanor. They may be perceived as more imaginative and creative than the other colors. In establishing your coaching philosophy, one question that you may consider addressing is the objective of making athletes have fun. Coaches who fall into the *sunshine yellow* category may be more prone to create a fun environment for participants in sport programs.

Fiery Red: Coaches with a high level of *fiery red* energy know what they want and have little difficulty in stating their conclusions.

Concerned primarily with action, they deal quickly with the present situation and appear to have little concern for the past. Their responses are efficient and focused; they know what they want and tend to be impatient with delays. Coaches who have a tendency to be "*fiery red*" know what they want. Coach-centered coaches believe that they know what is best, and as the leader of the program, they have the right and responsibility to make all decisions.

Dimension of Motivation

Billy is the best athlete on the elementary school soccer team. His team is not very good, but if they all give maximum effort and play as a team, they could be successful with the potential of winning 50 percent of their games. Basically, all the teams in the conference have about the same skill level, and winning is dependent upon who exerts the most motivation and seek out challenges of overcoming adversity.

Billy's frustration, with some of his teammates', centers around the fact that they don't play very hard and or exert the type of motivation and effort he does. Some of his teammates are more skilled than he is, which makes it more frustrating for Billy. Billy wonders what he can do to motivate some of his teammates.

Many coaches and teachers scratch their heads, wondering why some individuals are more motivated, excited about participation, appreciate the notion of competing while other participants avoid displaying these characteristics. One of the many challenges all coaches face is incorporating motivation tactics to keep athletes engaged.

Often, the ability to motivate sport participants is as important as the coaching knowledge of a sport or physical activity. Embracing this concept separates good instruction from average or mediocre instruction (Weinberg and Gould 6th edition, 2015). It is important that you develop some effective motivation techniques and recognize the importance of player motivation. *Motivating players* can produce successful outcomes, not just winning but enhanced play, enthusiasm, and skill improvement. Some coaches do not devote the time needed to understand how to motivate sport participants nor do they spend enough time doing the things necessary to learn motivating tactics.

Keep in mind that coaching is teaching, and with that mindset, the priority is the athletes learning, not winning and losing. This is a simple and profound concept that coaches need to embrace. When the coach treats the player as a student, players and the team show tremendous improvement.

Explain the Reason Why

A good coach (or salesperson) explains the reason why you are doing a certain drill. A good coaching dimension that should be included in your coaching philosophy from a conceptual perspective is being that salespersons; you definitely need it when you recruit participants to your program. Having said that, players will most likely want to know why they are practicing certain drills. If you don't explain why you are doing the drill and get them to buy in, they will not be motivated. Frankly, they will not believe that the drill has any purpose to their development. This is why you need to explain "the reason why" you implement the fundamental and drills in practice.

Participants Need to See Growth and Improvement

The *best motivation* that participants experience is when they can see growth and improvement throughout the season. The beginning of the season is always exciting, drills are fresh, some participants are very enthused and may feel that they are making improvement. As the season goes on, drills become repetitive, excitement wanes, and there may be a feeling of staleness. So, make sure that there is progression and development, and the more feedback they receive is important for their self-esteem, especially the players that don't get to play much. Make sure that practices evolve as the season progresses. In other words, continue to refine your drills and routines so that there is an element of challenge and growth present at all times.

Be organized (the importance of establishing a coaching philosophy) because it helps with player's growth and improvement from the standpoint of utilizing your drills and practice efficiently. A disorganized and unbalanced training session can de-motivate players from giving their best. Plan well ahead and cater for the individual group's and team's needs. Remember, variety is the spice of life! Training should be both mentally and physically stimulating. For players who are substitutes, incorporate a practice and scrimmage where you as the head coach are working with them exclusively. You can have one of the assistant coaches work with the starters while you work with the nonstarters. This will make the substitutes feel like you care about them and boost their motivation and self-esteem.

Highlight Success Both Individual and Team

Put players in a position where they can be rewarded about other successes. For example, when you work on free throws in basketball, chart player's free throw percentage and discuss their improvement during practice. Although these successes seem small, make sure you celebrate them. Charting statistics and showing improvements can be a positive motivating tactic.

Sports participants definitely want to be successful, but not everyone or team can win. Finding ways to show appreciation of other successes is key. Below are some examples:

- Celebrate finishing first in a drill
- Celebrate meeting a goal
- Celebrate accurate execution of skills
- Celebrate when they learn a new skill
- Celebrate when the team shows solidarity
- Celebrate when they learn specific offense strategies
- Celebrate when the team or a player breaks a tough habit

Frequency of Feedback and Praise

Positive reinforcement should not be a once in a while thing; the more you provide positive reinforcement, the more sport participants will feel good about your coaching. Here is a technique that was used by a soccer coach. Upon going to practice, there would be four paper clips and a marble in the right pocket. One clip would be moved to the left pocket whenever there was a positive remark. However, the marble would be moved to the left pocket whenever a negative remark is made. The point is that you can only move the marble back to the right pocket when all the paper clips from the left pocket are in the right pocket. This can be repetitive throughout the practice. You can use your own variation of this technique, and it does not have to be with marbles and paper clips or four-to-one ratio. You can do this periodically throughout the season. It is a good way to get back into the habit of praising your athletes and showing them that you appreciate them.

Be Specific When Giving Feedback and Praise

It is extremely important that when you give praise to young participants, be specific with words. Making comments like "great hustle or "nice shot" is much better than not saying anything. However, specifics comments help to keep motivation high, promote positive behavior, and as the coach, you should really like when participants demonstrate good sporting behavior. The players usually respond well and feel like you are paying attention to how they perform when you are specific with your praise. Although "great hustle" is a positive comment, "excellent job hustling for the ball" is even better. "Good job squaring up, extending, and following through on your shot" is better than "nice shot." There should be no misconception in how you praise and give feedback to sport participants.

Do Not Run at the End of Practice

This could ruin practice because participants may not give 100 percent during practice, knowing that there will be conditioning at the end of practice. Incorporate conditioning in your regular practice scheme.

Explain the Reason Why

A good teacher explains the "reason why." Quite often, players don't understand why they are doing certain drills and can lose motivation or interest. This is why you need to explain the "reason why" the fundamentals and drills you run are important. Don't assume the players know that they are because most likely they don't.

Measure Performance

Measuring performance might sound the same as goal setting. But it's not the same. Here's a business fact that carries over into all sports: *"When performance is measured, performance improves. When performance is measured and reported back, the rate of improvement significantly accelerates."*

Simply showing the right statistics and metrics to your players will boost their performance. Posting reports in the locker room and talking about them will make players more aware of how they are performing. Only share the critical numbers or data that are most important to the team and your players.

Show You Care and Improve Relationships

One of the best ways to motivate participants is to show that you care about them outside of sports. For example, you could attend their choir concert or whatever other extracurricular program they participate in. Provide assistance with schoolwork and postacademic achievements as well as athletic accomplishments in the locker room.

Take a Break

Another important way to keep players motivated is to encourage them to get away from sports several times a year. In today's society, sport participants are going year around without taking necessary breaks from sports. Sport participants need time to recover mentally and physical from participating in competitive sports. I can recall when sport participants took breaks to reenergize themselves and enjoy activities not related to sports. This is no longer the norm, and sport participants are encouraged to practice and condition year around. Taking a break to allow the mind and body to recover is good for all sports participants.

Discussion Questions:

1. The dimension of coaching is far more than blowing a whistle between the lines or on one half of the court or field. Do you believe this statement is true? Explain your position.
2. Has the concept of coaching, teaching, and encouraging changed in today's society? If so, give examples.
3. In the example of "Adam, the star basketball player," displaying unsportsmanlike conduct, would you suspend him the next game?
4. Why is it important to develop a coaching philosophy?
5. Explain the philosophical view of Division II Hall of Fame Basketball Coach William Brown's statement: In any sport, defense travels with you on the road and it requires great effort.
6. How does "uniqueness" regarding personality coincide with psychological core, typical response, and role-related behavior?
7. What motivation tactics would you use to help Billy with his frustration of his teammates?
8. Do you believe sport participant motivation is dependent upon progress and development? If so, explain why.
9. When giving praise, why is it important to be specific with words?
10. Explain the concept that coaching is teaching.

CHAPTER

DIMENSION OF PLAYER CHARACTER

Introduction

As a sport coach, *building character* is very important, and understanding the various dimension of a participant's character exhibited throughout a season becomes very important information that can help you nurture the type of character you deem important to each individual in your program.

Youth Sport Justification and Building Character

One primary justification of organized youth sports in the United States has been to develop participant's character (Power and Sheehan 2014). There have been many discussions regarding the benefit of *adult-supervised sports*. Some theorist believe that it has saved the lives of youth and gave them a pathway to a different style of living as opposed to influences of the streets in their neighborhoods. Others feel that it teaches youth the virtues of discipline, teamwork, character development, trust, and partnerships, which are vital to success in life and the workplace (Chudacoff 2007). There is a belief that one dimension of character building of participating in youth sports is achieving personal perseverance and self-confidence. However, contrary to some ideologies about the positives of sport participation and *character development* is the question that youth sports are losing moral resonance, and although the thriving youth sport industry is booming (Koba 2014), should there be concerns about the perception of sports, where winning supersedes fostering character development.

We have seen some of our popular sport role models behave badly, and the Internet can be used to display poor character behavior by these role models. Can we really say that sport participation build character? Research regarding this topic revealed that 13 percent of youths report trying to hurt an opponent, 31 percent argue with officials, and 27 percent display bad characteristics after losing (Shields, Lavoi, Bredemeier, and Power 2005). High school athletes also feel that *gamesmanship* is just part of their sport, and research has revealed that some high school athletes put morals aside in order to win (Camire and Trudel 2010). Defining character is difficult, and although there may be a general idea what the term mean, rarely is it defined precisely or agreed upon with an exact meaning. Sport psychologists Shield and Bredemeier contend that *morality* in sport comprise three related concepts: fair play, good sporting behavior, and character.

Most coaches should want participants to develop good sport character that can be developed by sport participation. Some coaches espouse the character-developing benefits of sport participation and contend that participants learn to overcome obscurity, embrace the concept of team, better understand themselves (self-control), and persist in the face of competition (Ewing, Seefeldt, and Brown 1996).

Philosophical View of Building Positive Morals and Character

Does research regarding sport participant's moral character development substantiate the notion that playing organized sports build character and enhance a positive moral dimension? Or has it been the notion of coaches who witnessed remarkable change of personality, character, and moral development of participants in various sports programs, who initially portrayed negative personality traits; however, because of sport participation became prominent citizens in their respected societies. Both the research and the coach's notions have merit, and based on Lickona and Davidson research (2005), they stated that *moral character* is marked by oriented virtues, such as respect of others and their welfare, positive personality traits, and positive learned behavior as it relates to growth and development. You can see a correlation of all these ideologies regarding sport participation and positive moral character development given that sport participant is given appropriate guidance and mentoring.

There is widespread interest in character development as a whole through youth and adult sports (e.g., Character Counts, Gold Medal Standards Campaign, CHARACTER COUNTS, 2006). The view of character defined by some theorist differentiate moral from performance character (Weiss 2008). In the study by Kant (Kant, Schneewind, Baron, and Kagan 2002) and Kohlberg (1981), their argument is that achievement-related virtues, such as self-discipline, courage, and perseverance, are sometimes viewed as independent virtues but should be coupled with the character and moral virtues, which are rooted in principles of justice and benevolence. Building these character, *moral obligations* begin with the coach. If participants in your program experience indifferences, such as favoritism or the coach allow uncharacteristic behavior, then negative moral issues can develop and curtail the concept of building positive moral character through sport participation.

Perspective on Moral Issues in Sports (Insert borders here to highlight this point of view, "Foundation of Sport," 572)

Sport Psychologist Moria Stuart (2003) recorded a qualitative assessment identifying what *moral issues* children aged ten to twelve years experienced in sport. The children reflected such things as:

> A problem with our coach is that his daughter is on the team, and he (coach) lets her play most of the game, and there are other players who are better and they don't get to play as much as his (coach) daughter. He should not play favorites because other player don't get to play as much and that's not fair (p. 451).

> The opponent know they are supposed to shake hands after the game, win or lose, so when we went to shake their hands after the game, our opponent spit on their hands before they shook our hands. That isn't right, and that's not how you act after a game (p. 451).

These and other statements that the children made were classified into three general categories of moral issues. These include concerns about

- the fairness of adult actions (e.g., unfair decisions by officials, coaches playing favorites, parents pressuring them to play or win);
- negative game behaviors (e.g., verbal intimidation by opponents, intentional fouls, violations of the spirit of the game); and
- negative team behavior (e.g., selfish teammates, dishonesty, teammates misbehavior).

In another study, elite athletes were interviewed, and the results of those interviews revealed that respect for and *transgressions of competitive rules* were based on the athletes' individual characteristics (e.g., desire to win), the social environment (e.g., team norms and pressure from the coach), sport values and virtues (e.g., fair play), and sport rewards (e.g., media recognition). Most interesting were the findings of *moral disengagement* (Long, Pantaleon, Bruant, and D'Arripe-Longueville 2006), where the athletes justified rule breaking in the name of defending sport values, such as team moral, winning record, and perception being labeled as a smart team.

These findings confirm and extend various perspectives regarding moral issues as it relates to sport participation. Displaying negative moral and ethical behavior can be directly related to poor practice protocols, before and after game participant demeanor strategies, and how sport participant's home upbringing is managed.

Moral development of participants in youth programs should be a part of a coach practice and PST (Psychological Skill Training) plan. The age-related changes in thoughts and emotions that guide ideas of right and wrong and ultimately how participants in sport should act are crucial in the whole development of the young athlete, and although research point out many views of moral development, youth coaches can look at some examples of these various views and adopt a philosophical approach of developing morality of participants in sport programs. Youth sport programs as a whole, coupled with coaches that facilitate those programs, should review the format of the *Cognitive Moral Education Program*, where adolescents discuss a broad range of issues in the hope of developing strategies for positive moral reasoning. The character education approach encourages participants to learn and follow a specific moral code that guide behaviors in and out of school. This concept can be beneficial in developing successful programs.

Preparing coaches to be *character educators* requires the right training so that emphasis is placed on values, maintaining discipline, participant's education success, and controlling players' behavior. The coaches' role is critical in shaping how athletes participate in sports and how they play the game. Coaches develop a special relationship with players that is not solely based on the time they spend with athletes but also the intensity of the experience they share. This special bond gives coaches the opportunity for significant influence, whereas they can provide direction and positive modeling for the athlete.

Most coaches may view themselves as character educators because they do practice teaching life lessons, demanding that their players accept the discipline, rules, and regulations required to achieve athletic success, which are key components to character education, coupled with other oriented virtues, like respecting coaches, teammates, and opponents. However, these tenets may be based on how well the season is going or success the team is experiencing (winning). True convictions to these terms can be tested when you are losing or both the participants and coach feel unsuccessful. I have witnessed countless scenarios where a sport team has not had a successful season from a win-loss perspective and the coach and participants lost concepts of displaying good sporting behavior.

The foundation of this model should also be grounded in the organization philosophical view. As Coakley (2015) pointed out that community-based youth sport organizations, parks and recreation leagues, YMCA, and other programs should focus on sports as a means of serving all children, particularly those in needs, by promoting not only character education but health development.

Private youth sport and elite sports clubs place high emphasis on recruiting the most talented athletes for elite competition and a "compete-to-win orientation," with some emphasis on developing character education skills.

Some high school and middle school sport programs often straddle the two orientations, where character development is important to their missions, in conjunction with the pervasive *play-to-win culture*, which can lead coaches to lose sight of their roles as character educators. Power and Sheehan, who have studied coaches at all levels but particularly youth sport coaches (Power and Sheehan 2012), pointed out that coaches typically understand the value in all their players attaining playing time. However, they also feel that they must play the "best" athletes to win. If coaches are to become character educator, they must find the balance of all Sport Participant Character Education concepts. Fraser-Thomas, Cote, and Deakin's (2005) research suggest that coaches who place a priority on winning rather than on the athletes' development are perceived as exploiting their players or engaging in exhortation, where they motivate athletes to act based on "whatever it takes to win" strategies. These points of view can influence non-sensitivity to negative moral issues and reasoning of participants in sports and physical activity (Berkowitz and Bier 2005, Power Higgins and Kohlberg 1984, Power and Power 2012). All stakeholders have a responsibility to educate athletes to embrace a holistic view of sport competition as it relates to positive character education, positive moral demeanor, and reasoning. In my humble opinion, becoming a character educator requires an understanding of principles related to building good character and moral behavior, coupled with commitment, sacrifice, and making critical decisions.

For example, in my *Introduction to Coaching* course, where emphasis was placed on character education and preparing students to become youth coaches and/or attain coaching certification, I can reflect on one assignment in particular where the students are presented a scenario, where they need to make a decision from a coach perspective about the star running back who has committed an unsportsmanlike act during the game to the opposing player (he spit on the opposing player because he tackled him, hit him in the stomach, and the player he attacked needed medical attention). This unsportsmanlike act warrants the star player to sit out the remainder of the game. However, if the coach chooses to have him sit out, it may diminish the team opportunity to win the game and make it to the playoffs. If the team wins, it would be the first time in school history that the football program made it to the playoff. One hundred replies were evaluated, and 58 percent indicated that they would sit the star player out of the game, and although this is more than 50 percent, there is concern that the other 42 percent placed winning, or their perception of letting the team down if the star player has to sit out, or feeling that the coach job would be in jeopardy if he did not allow the player who committed the unsportsmanlike conduct to finish the game. Despite the character education protocols discussed in the class, these students (42 percent) thought that allowing the player to remain in the game was the appropriate thing to do.

Parent Implementing Moral and Character Education for Their Children

Parents also play a major role in developing their child's moral behavior. Extensive research has demonstrated that positive moral development is embraced by sport participants when parents love and support their children, provide opportunities for their children to learn about other people's views and feelings, and the parent display good moral thinking and behavior themselves (Baumeister and Vohs 2007). This process of *induction* makes it easier for parents to explain to their child why particular behavior is right or wrong and its impact to others. Research also conveys that parents who use "induction principles" (as it relates to moral development and sport participation), their children display higher levels of empathy and pro-social behaviors and lower levels of antisocial behavior, as opposed to children whose parents rely on physical punishment or withdrawal of love and attention as their primary approach to discipline.

Dimension of Developing Good Sporting Behavior

In this chapter, there has been discussion regarding moral and character behavior and the responsibility of coaches and parents to navigate pathways for athletes to embrace these ideologies and strategies to ultimately display good sporting behavior.

Canadians sport psychologist Robert Vallerand and other sport psychologist (Vallerand, Briere, Blanchard, and Provencher 1997) conducted an extensive study of over one thousand athletes from different sports and derived from the research five factors that these athletes highlighted as good sporting behavior protocols:

1. Be fully committed toward participation (consistency in work ethic, show up to all practices and games, be conscientious of other's mistakes and how they try to improve)
2. Consistently respect the rules and officials (if the officials are incompetent, show respect anyway)
3. Respect social aspects (shaking opponents' hands, acknowledging good performance of opponents and teammates' losing with dignity)
4. Showing concerns for opponents (do not take advantage of an injured opponent, possibly lend equipment, play the contest if the opponent shows up late)
5. Don't display poor attitude (avoid a win-at-all-costs approach, displaying a good temperament after a mistake, compete for the love of the game)

So, to summarize the research, the athletes that participated in this research define good sporting behavior as "respect for others, including rules and officials, social concerns, full commitment to your sport and caring for the opponent, and no negative approach toward sport participation" (Vallerand et al., 1997, p. 198). There is no universal definition of good sporting behavior. However, good sporting behavior should be identified with situation-specific definitions, and each coach, parent, or stakeholder that is involved in the program should be mindful of this concept.

Social Learning Theory, Modeling, and Observational Learning

Aggression and character development is linked in many ways to what sport participants view on and off the playing field, courts, and social media. According to Albert Bandura's (1977) theory, one can assume that certain sporting behavior attitudes can be learned from modeling or observational learning. If behavior is displayed in a negative or positive demeanor, it can be internalized by observers or participants and mimicked. This contends that sport participants social learning history can determine their sporting behavior. However, behavior can also be determined by an interaction or personal and situational factors (Bandura 1991).

During sport competition, everyone is observing interactions and behavior of parents and coaches in particular. If the coach is acting inappropriately, his or her behavior can be internalized by the sport participant on their team. The same can be true of sport participants modeling the behavior of someone doing something wrong and receiving praise. An example given by Weinberg and Gould (2015) is that by participants observing other children reporting false sit-ups scores to the PE instructor and receiving praise spearheaded the same behavior of the observing participants. Participants learn in physical education class that it is acceptable to cheat on a fitness test in hopes of getting praise and attention from the teacher. The same can be said for sport participants who witness that their coach displaying very poor behavior and act the same way.

Bandura (1961) conducted a study to investigate if aggression (in the sense of negative behavior) can be acquired by observation and imitation or modeling and mimicking behavior. Bandura, Ross, and Ross (1961) tested thirty-six boys and thirty-six girls from a nursery school at Stanford University. The ages of the boys and girls were three to six years old, and the method used was termed a match pair design, where the children had similar levels of aggression in their everyday behavior. The experiment was based on the type of model the children were exposed to.

- Aggressive model is shown to twenty-four children
- Nonaggressive model is shown to twenty-four children
- No model is shown (control-condition) twenty-four children

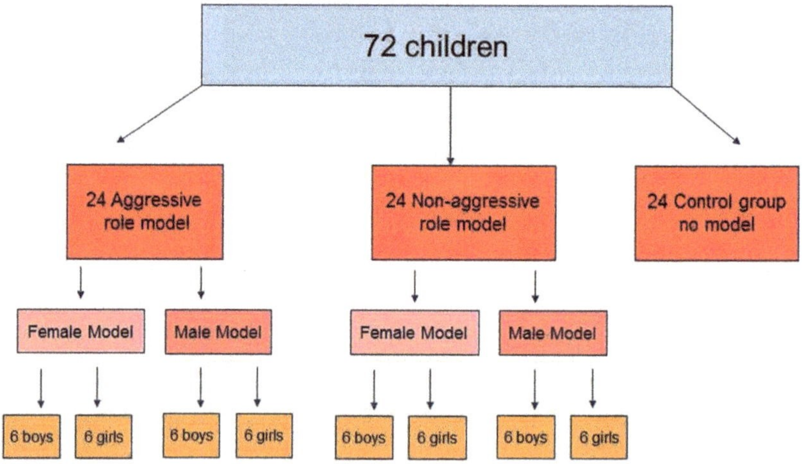

A majority of the children that were exposed to negative behavior of the BoBo doll mimicked the negative behavior, particularly the boys who imitated the same aggressive behavior as the male adult model. The girls' negative behavior was not as strong when they witness the negative behavior of the BoBo doll by the female adult model. However, the girls did display more negative behavior when they witness the male adult model display negative behavior on the BoBo doll.

The nonaggressive role models displayed a nonaggressive behavior toward the BoBo doll, and that behavior was mimicked from a majority of the twenty-four boys and girls in the nonaggressive group observing their behavior. All groups were burdened with a frustrating task before they were allowed to play with the BoBo doll. How they handled their frustration was somewhat determined on how aggressive or nonaggressive the model's behavior was against the BoBo doll. Although this was not an epidemiological study, there is some merit to the notion of sport participants mimicking the negative behavior of coaches and parents during frustrating times of sports participation, which gives some credence to social learning theory, modeling, or observational learning, where participants who witness negative behavior may display those negative behaviors in similar settings.

Game Reasoning and Aggression

Although there is some debate about David Shield and Brenda Jo Bredemeier's studies regarding *game reasoning* and aggression, where participants (college athletes) use a less mature form of *moral reasoning* than their nonathletic peers and that children participation in high-contact sports is associated with less mature game reasoning and greater self-reported tendencies to aggress, can evoke the notion that sport participation induces players to an egocentric arrogance that diminish a feeling of empathy and produces this evil of militarism attitude. This concept may not be warranted from a holistic perspective. However, I believe that there are some tenets of this study that deserves to be observed and taking into consideration when coaching. Most coaches believe that aggressions could produce a positive outcome in competition and that developing this aggressive demeanor within a team or individual is a norm and belief that breeds success.

There are many classic examples of coaches from the professional, college, high school, and lower levels who would attest that the success of their team started with the mentality of being aggressive and dominating their opponents both physically and psychologically. For instance, Kermit Washington, an ex-NBA player, stated that "being mean helped him from being pushed around on the court," and Jack Tatum, an ex-HFL football player who was known for his aggressive play, stated "that his team had a greater likelihood of succeeding if he punished his opponents on every play" (Papanek 1977). Although these examples are from professional athletes who may have had higher stakes in their performance because they were paid to play and it was there job to perform at a high level does not negate to some degree that aggressive acts coupled with negative game reasoning ideologies are not appropriate in the sport environment, particularly at the lower levels.

A more important question may be how do coaches and sport participants find a balance in bracketed morality (or game reasoning) and aggression in sports? Certainly, the relation between sport performance and aggression is complex, and there have been cases in which aggressive acts have "paid off" regarding positive outcome. Some sport psychologist agree that aggression facilitates performance outcomes (Widmeyer 1984), whereas others believe it does not (Gill 2000).

In my humble opinion, Bredemeier and Shield's studies may need to be reviewed more closely, and although some of the tenets of their ideologies may have some merit, measuring athletic aggression, game reasoning, and moral maturity may require more research. If coaches consider what they know of aggression and develop strategies for participants to control it in sports at all levels may be a step in the right direction to safer play and less injuries. Having said that, we may need to discuss strategies for understanding when aggression is most likely to occur, modifying aggressive actions, and teach appropriate behavior.

When Aggression Is Most Likely to Commence

History has revealed that certain situations provoke aggressive behavior. Aggression usually occurs when participants are frustrated because they are losing, feel officiating is poor, are injured and cannot participate in games or practice, experiencing low self-esteem due to poor performance, and playing below their capabilities (Widmeyer, Dorsch, Bray, and McGuire 2002).

A specific situation that illustrate this point is during one of my colleagues' (William Anderson) basketball practice; an athlete who is very passionate about the sport of basketball was injured and not able to participate in team drills. One of his teammates preceded to make a negative comment to him regarding his inability to participate in the practice due to his injury. The injured player immediately became defensive due to his perceived failure of his identity as a key figure to the team due to his injury and displayed aggression toward his teammate by using negative verbal words and threats. He was immediately dismissed from practice and reprimanded on negative comments, which stemmed from him not being able to participate in practice.

On a study of over 400 athletes, Maxwell and colleagues (2009) stated that athletes who can control their aggression tend to be less aggressive and do not feel that aggression is legitimate to enhancing performance. Some other intervention studies revealed that youth hockey players were taught cognitive and emotional skills as well as on-ice routines designed to decrease aggressive acts (Lauer and Paiement, 2009). Overall results revealed that most of the young athletes showed decreased aggression. However, greatest reduction was found in retaliatory and major aggressive acts, which is important because these more serious aggressive actions can lead to injuries and suspension.

It is difficult to control situations that may cause frustration. However, observing participants more closely and making substitutions or immediately commenting when a situation arises may curtail some aggression displayed during competition. Teaching skills that will assist participants in controlling their emotions and minimizing their frustration will most likely keep them on the playing fields and court as opposed to being on the sideline or bench. Athletes tend to be motivated and ambitious, and when they see something amiss, their reaction is to respond, and it may not be the appropriate response.

Not every problem that participants encounter during competition is the coach's problem to fix. However, training participants to focus on tangibles that they can control may help them deal with aggression. It is important that coaches teach emotional control strategies to athletes and simulate frustrating conditions in practice so that participants have an opportunity to work on emotional control strategies under pressure. Coaches and other stakeholder should have a sense when aggression can occur and be mindful in detecting and controlling aggression in frustrating situation. It is important that coaches teach emotional control strategies to athletes and simulate frustrating conditions in practice so that participants have an opportunity to work on emotional control strategies under pressure.

Sport Participant Knowledge of Aggressive Behavior

It may be to a coach's advantage to test participants' knowledge of what is deemed aggressive and nonaggressive. Below are examples of aggressive and nonaggressive acts. See if you and your participants can decipher between aggressive and nonaggressive acts.

Aggressive or Nonaggressive

Circle A or N to indicate whether you consider the behavior in each of these situations to be aggressive (A) or nonaggressive (N).

(A N) 1. A hockey player delivers an extremely vicious but legal "check" to an opposing player and indicates to his teammates that he wanted to send a message so that he and his teammates would think twice about skating freely.

(A N) 2. A basketball player delivers a hard foul to an opponent driving to the basket.

(A N) 3. A volleyball coach breaks a chair in protesting a disputed call.

(A N) 4. Tina, during a double match, return a forehand shot to the thigh of her opponent because the opponent's partner nailed her teammate several plays before.

(A N) 5. A race car driver kills a fellow competitor by running into the competitor's stalled car coming out of a turn.

(A N) 6. Trying to make a field goal kicker on the opposing team worry and think about the negative ramification of a game-winning field goal, the opposing coach calls a time-out.

(A N) 7. John knows that Kevin is sensitive and self-conscious about his ability to kick extra point field goals, so he tells Kevin that the coach said that if he misses this field goal, he will not renew his scholarship next year. The coach never made this comment.
(A N) 8. Rebecca hits Francis with a fastball that got away from her.

Answers:

1. Aggressive (Although "checking" is legal, the intent was to inflict harm.)
2. Nonaggressive (There was no intent to inflict harm.)
3. Nonaggressive (The action was not directed at a human being.)
4. Aggressive (Although her teammate was hit first, the intent was to inflict harm.)
5. Nonaggressive (Although the other driver was killed, there was no intent to do harm.)
6. Aggressive (Although many would consider this a tactical smart move, the intent was to inflict psychological harm on another in the form of fear and anxiety.)
7. Aggressive (The intent was to inflict psychological harm.)
8. Nonaggressive (Although harm resulted, there was no intent to harm.)

(Adopted from R. Martens, 1982a, "Kids Sports: A Den of Iniquity or Land of Promise." In children in sport, edited by R.A. Magill, M.J. Ash, and F.L. Smoll. Champaign, Illinois: Human Kinetics. 204–218.)

Establishing Team Norms

Establishing team norms is a strategy that could decrease *sport aggression*. This involves discussing with athletes and your team leaders about the difference between aggression and assertive behavior. Your team captains can help with this by monitoring team members' actions so that participants' actions can be discussed at the first sign of aggressions. It is also important that you choose the right team captains who display good social learning characteristics. In addition to learning appropriate behavior, physical activity, participants should know how to resolve conflict and disputes in a nonviolent fashion. Here are some intervention strategies that can be used by captains or peer leaders to resolve conflict that can happen within the team structure of the sport or activity program.

1. Agree to meet. Have disputants agree to meet with the mediator (team captain or peer leader). However, make sure that the disputants do not sit together at the meeting.
2. Make sure facts are recorded, whereas each disputant is given an opportunity to tell their account of the event. The mediator listens but does not take sides.
3. Express feelings. Each disputant expresses their feelings regarding the conflict, and the mediator repeats what is said to ensure clarity of meaning.
4. Look for resolution. The outcome you want is to resolve the conflict, and the disputants should come up with strategies to do so. The mediator emphasizes areas of agreement relative to the benefits of resolving the conflict.
5. Outline necessary changes. The disputants list what they each can do to resolve the conflict.
6. Develop an action plan. A plan of action is developed, and each disputant signs it, indicating commitment to the action plan and resolving the conflict cooperatively.
7. Follow up on the plan after a short time. The disputants are asked if the problem still exists.

There are many conflict resolution models, and this is not to say that this model would work. However, it should demonstrate the value and importance of teaching sport participants how to resolve conflict nonviolently.

Discussion Questions:

1. Does organized sports build character in youth participants?
2. Some theorist believe that youth sport participation has saved the lives of some youth and gave them a different perspective on life as opposed to influences of the streets in their neighborhood. Do you believe this statement to be true or false? Please explain your answer.
3. Explain why developing good morals in sports begins with the coach.
4. Do you believe that private and elite sports programs have a compete-to-win orientation? If so, please explain why.
5. Explain how you think parents should build good moral and character behavior.
6. How does "uniqueness" regarding personality coincide with psychological core, typical response, and role-related behavior?
7. Do you believe that displaying an aggressive demeanor as a team or individual make you more successful during competition?
8. Give some examples when aggression could surface during practice or a game.
9. List some intervention strategies that can be used by team leaders or the coach to resolve conflict.
10. What type of skills can you incorporate in practice to help participants manage frustration from competition?

CHAPTER

DEVELOPING SYSTEM OF PLAY

System of Play

In chapter 1, we discussed the importance of developing your coaching philosophy. However, developing a system of play is equally important, and regardless if you coach a travel team, middle school, high school, or recreation park program, it is essential that you establish a system of play. In preparation of implementing your system of play, you should consider the type of approach you will take in teaching your sport participants the technical and tactical skills needed to understand your system.

According to Martens (2012), considering a game approach to teach your system of play may be beneficial to sport participants in today's society. Games approach teach athletes how to play the game while retaining the joy of participation. Learning the system of play thorough game, like practice activities that create realistic and enjoyable learning situations, is very appealing to sport participants.

Holistic Approach

Many coaches use a part-whole-part teaching protocol when teaching their system of play. I also have used this approach with many of my teams. However, what was more enjoyable for my athletes was the holistic approach, and two of my NJCAA National Championship Women's basketball team enjoyed this approach more so than the *part-whole-part approach*. The games approach is more holistic approach to leaning the sport. The athlete has the opportunity to learn what your system is all about in conjunction with learning the game and how to play it.

(Stock Images/Photo Image Girls Soccer Player)

The games approach help athletes learn the system of play within the context of gamelike situations. Players learn how to implement your system (without you telling them) by experiencing it in gamelike situations. As the coach, you help them understand what they've experienced (meaning, your system of play and how it works in the game). Implementing an *athlete-centered guide discovery* method of teaching your system of play empowers your athletes to figure out the nuances of the system, and this is a big part of the fun of playing sports.

System of Play Development or Developing System of Play

As you start to develop your system of play, try to imagine how sport participants can learn the playing style. You do not want a throw-out-the-ball-and-let-them-play approach. The games approach requires skillful analysis of the offense and defense so that players learn what they need to know to play well.

Rainer Martens (2012) discusses three methods that I think are applicable to not only developing system of play in sports but teaching sport participants key tools to learning your offense and defense strategies.

Shaping Play

As you develop your offense and defense strategies within your system of play, the coach should consider how you will teach the athletes by using the gamelike experience approach. Ultimately, the athlete has to play the game, and it is important that you develop learning protocols to enhance an understanding of your system of play. There are four aspects of the game approach that you can implement to create a variety of learning situations.

1. We know that rules are used to dictate what players can and cannot do in a game. When considering your style of play, think how you can "modify the rules" in practice to create the learning environment you want.
2. Alter player participation and active learning time. For example, diminishing the number of player's involved, whereas only a few of the players are participating and minimizing time of participation to enhance learning strategies. This approach will not only increase the opportunity for participants to learn technical and tactical skills but will allow you to reflect on the system of play and its appropriateness for the players you have in your program.
3. Spacing is critical in both individual and team sports, and creating certain angles depending on the sport can be very advantageous both from the offense and defense perspective. Altering the size of the playing area or change the size of the goal can help your athletes focus on learning a particular concept of the game.
4. Shaping how players play by using modifications such as the goal and scoring.

As you think about player movement, spacing, angles, offense, and defense concepts as it relates to the style of play, redesign the game so that your athletes have the opportunity to practice what is relevant in the real game.

How Players Use the Term "Focus Playing" in Your System

Athletes will have questions learning your system, and although you may modify the variables as described earlier, you will need to focus their attention on key elements of the game that you want them to learn about so that the system of play is beneficial. Master coaches excel at getting their players to focus their attention on critical elements of learning the system in practice. Clock management, player isolation, two-or-three-person game, where you isolate two or three players against your opponent's two or three players (if applicable), understanding opponent mental state are just a few examples of focus playing. This vital process of learning focus playing is developed by having practices that are structured and helps athletes transfer what they learn in practice games to real games. A critical concept that players can focus on is developing game IQ, which coincides with learning the system of play, understanding patterns of player movement, both on offense and defense, so that when the participant is playing offense or defense, they develop an advantage to offset the opponent, using the system of play you implement as the coach.

The following are several examples of sports and what a coach could take into consideration when developing a system of play. There are many different sports that could have been used as examples. However, I choose only a couple to illustrate the strategies and philosophical constructs needed to develop a system of play.

Soccer System of Play

Soccer is a complex game where the possibilities are endless. Your proficiency in learning the system of play depends on your skill with and without the soccer ball and your ability to read the game. Although dribbling, defending, passing, and shooting are essential, it's all useless without an understanding of soccer strategy, understanding patterns of movement, knowing where to pass the ball, when to dribble, and just a general understanding of the game. It's important that as you develop the system of play, you are mindful of these basic skills that are key to player efficiency. From the offense concept, what can you do in the short term to allow your team to move the ball upfield and score? As you think about the development of the system of play as it relates to soccer, how do you structure corner kicks, maintain possession of the ball, try to win a throw-in, switching the ball to the other side of the field where you have more space? These are a few concepts to think about when developing offense system of play (Coerver Coaching 2018).

In today's modern era of soccer, there are several offense systems of play utilized by coaches in the game of soccer today. I will focus on the 4-4-2, which is based on partnership through the middle of the field to create balance. One center back tries to win the ball, the other is dropping back to cover the space behind. Two midfielders are either attacking or in a defensive role. The strikers can be paired to offer different threats. Although this attack is considered a little old-fashioned and rigid and could be offset with other defense tactics, the speed and power that can be employed with this system makes it appealing to coaches for implementation.

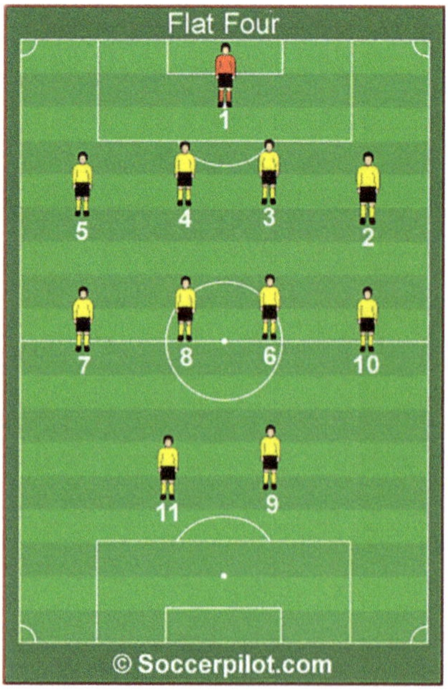

1 The Goalie

Here is a little more detail about the 4-4-2 alignment. The goalie is a key factor in this scheme and is integrated into the passing game. There are times he plays the role of the missing sweeper. "The goalie is the game decider."[1]

The First 4 (Defenders)

In front of the goalie is a back four alignment. The players are standing wide (2 to 5). Players 2 and 5 are the left and right fullbacks, and players 4 and 3 are the center backs ("Back Four—Structured Exercises—Shifting"[2]).

The Second 4 (Midfielders)

The uniqueness of the *Flat Four* is found in the midfield. These players are positioned in front of the center of defense. There are two players in front of the back four. Known as the "double pivot" in other systems, there are two players displayed in the diagram (8 and 6). Players 7 and 10 are located at midfield, with two wingers.

The 2 (Strikers)

Here is how the strikers come into play (9 and 11). They basically close the gap. Meaning, one striker falls forward midfield to create a "station" to face off. The other striker is playing high up the field, which allows him to hold the ball up and lay it off to his partner (Ottmar Hitzfeld).

In conjunction with good offense tactics, the 4-4-2 "Flat Four" allows for a very strong defense wall, which makes it possible to double up on the opponents of the sidelines and close the center. The opponent can be attacked at the wings. Passing lanes can be easy to predict.

To learn more:

1 https://www.soccerpilot.com/soccermagazine/articles/how_the_modern_goalie_plays.html

2 https://www.soccerpilot.com/tactic/articles/back-four-1wa.html

From an offense perspective, the strength lies clearly in the wing positions. The fullbacks (5 and 2) as well as the two midfielders (7 and 10) provide offensive pressure on the sidelines. A sideline defender can attack over the wing and the corresponding midfielder. Of the two central midfielders (8 and 6), one takes the offensive role and the other takes the defense, which allows the gap between the two strikers to be further closed, which could result in the defense midfielder to become a third attacker ("The Foundations of the 4-4-2 (Diamond Midfield)"[3]).

Single Tennis System of Play

When determining a system of play for your tennis player, there are several criteria that are important.

First, it is important that a player have the strokes that will get the ball over the net. Making sure that you have depth on your shots is the second necessity. Limiting the number of options is the third.

Although there are so many strategies to playing the game of tennis, here are five things your players can do to an opponent from the baseline:

1. hit to the opponent's left
2. to their right
3. over their head
4. at their feet
5. through them

You must devise a realistic plan for your players, which will allow them to evaluate their own game, scout their opponent, and learn how to play against them. Unlike team sports, tennis requires a lot of *self-strategic play*. You lay the foundation as the coach, but the player must be able to navigate and think critically during the match. If you have beginner players, your most basic rule is to get it down

[3] https://www.soccerpilot.com/tactic/articles/foundations-of-the-4-4-2-diamond-midfield.html

the middle and place the ball deep. This strategy is applicable on any surface or conditions. It maximizes success by (1) keeping your opponent from hitting behind the baseline; (2) the net is lower in the middle then at the singles sideline, giving less chance for error; (3) players can concentrate more on stroke mechanics because you are not gambling with the sidelines; (4) by hitting down the middle, you reduce the length of the diagonal available to your opponent if they want to hit crosscourt. It is important to keep the ball going deep, which improves your chances of staying ahead regarding stroke efficiency.

Attacking the net is the next step in understanding system of play. More advance players use this tactic frequently because they learn how to hit the ball deep and approach the net because they have confidence in the shot. Most players hit the ball, back up, wait, or hesitate too long when getting the opponent in trouble or sensing when a ball will be short. This is a good opportunity to get to the net. Good tennis system of play is teaching a variety of tactics, how to close out a point, coming in behind a deep shot, and not letting your opponent keep playing. If you can develop the confidence to take the short ball and hit an approach shot, volley, and come in, you will to start to anticipate always moving forward rather than staying back.

The system of play for tennis is to remain consistent and to reduce errors, understanding that more points are lost than won in a match, so you must simplify your strategy. When challenged by a tough shot, hit a ball that has the highest percentage of staying in the court and keeping you in the point. Incorporating hitting drills that require keeping the ball in play is a good teaching strategy to build on as players develop this particular system of play.

As you develop your system of play, you should incorporate *psychological skill training*. Although this is mentioned in another chapter, it should be implemented in your system of play so players can learn how to function under pressure.

Pressure has a way in tennis of making players play a safe ball by throwing off the *biomechanics* of stroke production and control, which could cause the ball to sit-up and the point could be over for your player. Teaching your players as they learn your system that they should not think about winning the match but knowing the pressure of the match or the game. The key is basically being consistent and aggressive.

There are many key strategies to developing a system of play for tennis. Breaking down an opponent's rhythm, overplaying to your opponent's strong shot, hitting crosscourt ground strokes, hitting with purpose, and playing with an overall game plan.

Basketball System of Play

Developing a basketball system of play requires understanding player's positions, offense and defense schemes. The coach needs to realize that each player has a specific strength that needs to be considered when you put in your system of play. In addition to universal skills, all five players' positions require somewhat different secondary skills and attributes (Morgan Wooten and Joe Wooten). In today's game, these positions are exchangeable, and some coaches no longer identify these positions by number or name. However, below is a simplified description of the *five positions for the sport of basketball.*

1. Point guard (1)
2. Shooting guard (2)
3. Small forward (3)
4. Power forward (4)
5. Center (5)

Most system will have a position that is critical in running the offense. The point guard usually referred as the "1 player" runs the offense, should be able to defend, should be able to get everyone involved in the offense, and should have the intelligence to influence both offense and defense. You should think about this position and the role this person will play in your offense and defense system.

The shooting guard sometimes referred as the "2 player" could be one of your better shooters and could be the second-best ball handler, is equally as good of a defender like the point guard. Must be a good passer and ideally a good rebounder and possess the ability to run the offense.

The small forward referred as the "3 player" should be versatile to play both outside and inside, depending on the situation and your system of play. This player should ideally be a little taller than both the 1 or 2 guard but may or may not possess the quickness of the 1 or 2 guard but should be able to handle ball if called upon to help with ball-handling duties. Depending on your system of play, I like to refer this player as my utility person, possess the ability to rebound during offense possessions and guard both guards and small forward.

The power forward referred as the "4 player" should be one of the biggest and strongest players on the team and have the versatility to bring the ball up the floor, rebound on both the defense and offense end of the floor, shoot the three, play facing the basket and with their back to the basket as well. The person that plays this position could be the primary screen role person and is a primary rebounder on both ends of the floor.

The center referred as the "5 player" is in my opinion the second most important player in your system of play. This person is the heart of the team and should be the best rebounder, be able to play facing the basket and with their back to the basket. This position is also heavily involved in the screen roll options of the offense. This position is primarily responsible for rebounding and protecting the basket on defense. Because the center could primarily shoot shots in traffic or drive to the basket and potentially could draw fouls, the person playing this position should be a good free-throw shooter, in fact all the players should be good free-throw shooters. Shots that are taken near the basket are the highest percentage, and although today's style of play embraces the three-point shot, I would encourage that you contemplate an inside-outside approach.

Perimeter and Post System of Play

As you design both your offense and defense system, it may be useful to designate players by groups: perimeter players and post players (Wooten 2013). This allows for versatility of players that basically can play a variety of positions, particularly 4 and 5 who can handle the ball and guards who can play inside on offense and defense; your 4 and 5 player who is athletic enough to guard a perimeter player and a 1, 2, or 3 player who is strong enough to guard an inside player. As players have become multidimensional, using the entire court to create space for offense and minimize space when you play defense, has allowed coaches to be very creative on how they use their players.

Fast Break with Offense Concepts

We discussed the positions of the various players. However, coaches need to consider if you will use the break, implement various offense and defense sets. These are basic concepts that are critical to system of play. In any offense, you want to establish a numbers advantage. One way of doing this is establishing a fast break into your system of play. There are many examples of *running a fast break*; the center or power forward can *rim run*, meaning sprinting directly to the rim on the fast break. The other players can fill various positions on the floor, and the key is to advance the ball up the floor as quickly as possible, hopefully giving the offense an advantage. Below is an example of a fast break alignment that I used with two of my NJCAA National Championship Division III Women's basketball teams. Over the years, we changed the options but maintained the same alignment. We called this *Freelance Break* with "Kansas" options.

The 1st option is for 1 to pass the ball to 2 and 2 looks to score. It can be done once player 2 is in position or as they run up the court. 1 man can pass it up as early as he can, and the ball then is dribbled into position.

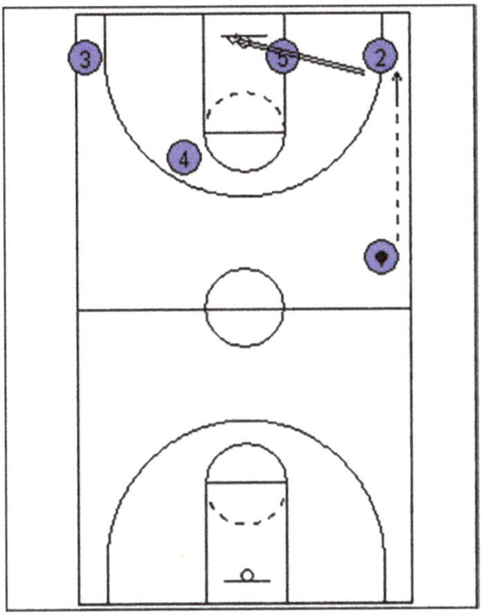

2nd option is after the ball is passed to 2, he passes to the post trailer (5) as he fills the block.

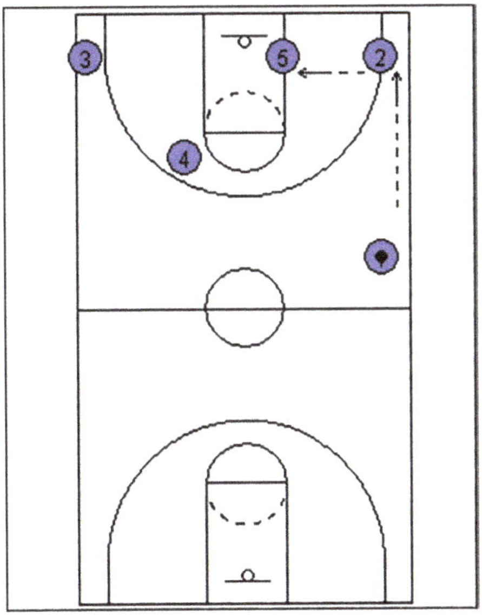

3rd option, 2 passes to the high trailer (4), 5 ducks in, and 4 can either look to score or pass high low to the 5 man.

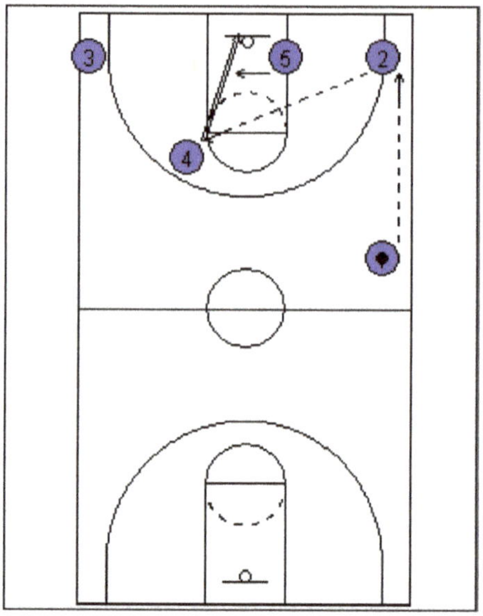

4th option is 1 passes to 2 in the corner.

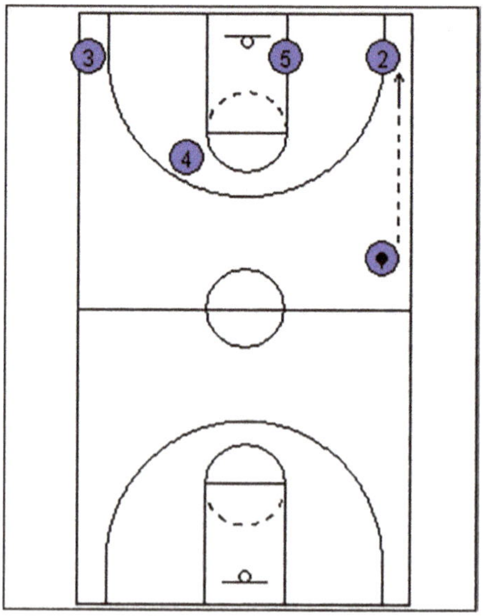

After screening, 2 steps outs. If 3 has no shot, pass to 5 in post; look to penetrate; pass back to 2.

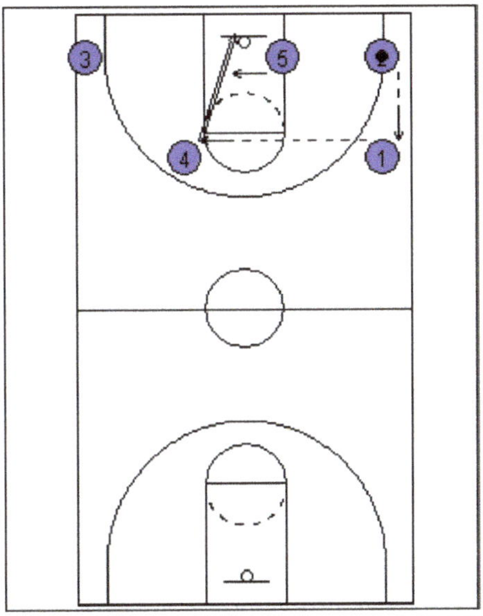

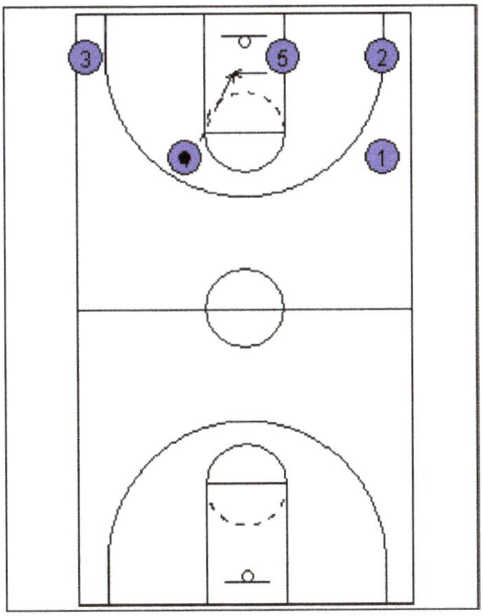

5th option

High trailer cannot score or pass inside, so he reverses to 3. After ducking in, 5 continues his cut to the block. 3 can look to score.

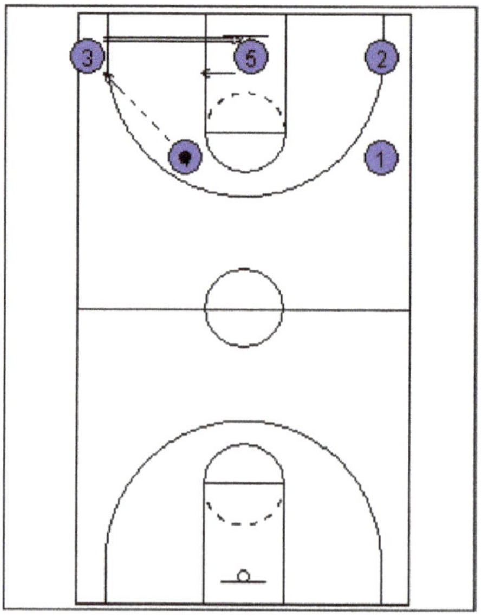

3 can also look to the block to 5.

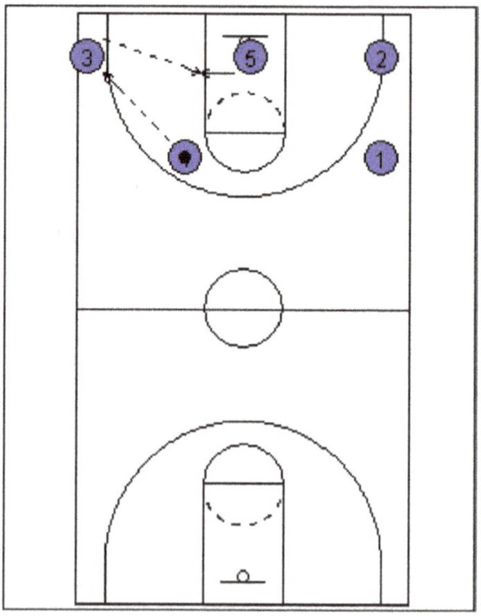

6th option

After reversing the ball to 3, 2 steps to the middle and then up to backscreen for 4, 4 cuts off the backscreen, and 3 looks for the lob and pass to 4.

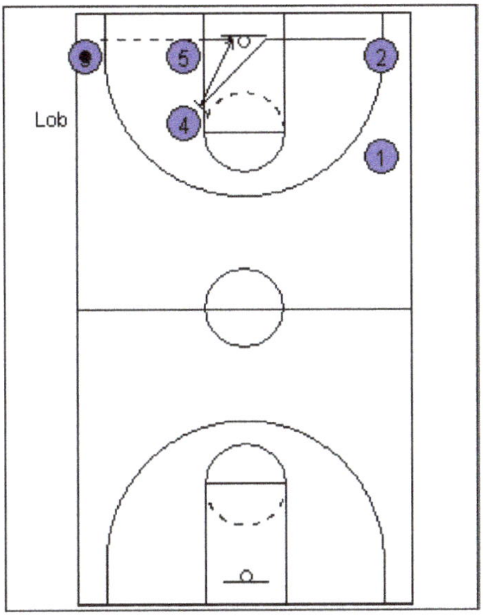

After screening, 2 steps out.

If 3 has no shot, pass to the post or lob to 4 opportunity; he passes back out to 2.

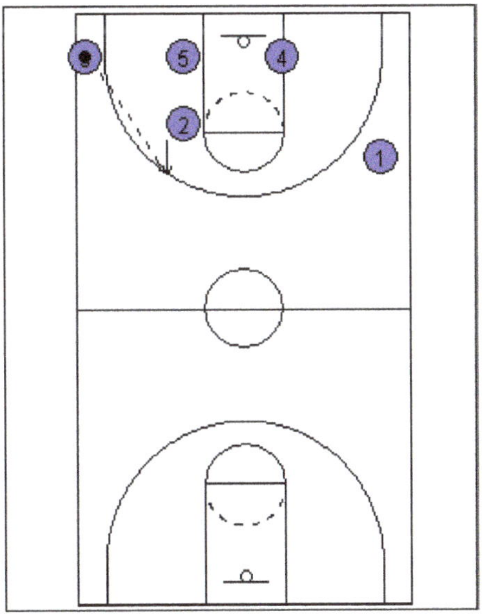

7th option

5 ducks in and 2 can look to score or looks high-low to 5.

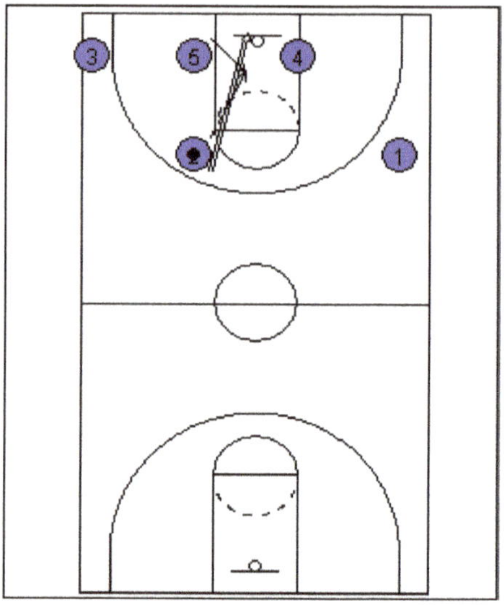

8th option

2 reverses the ball to 1. 1 looks low to 4.

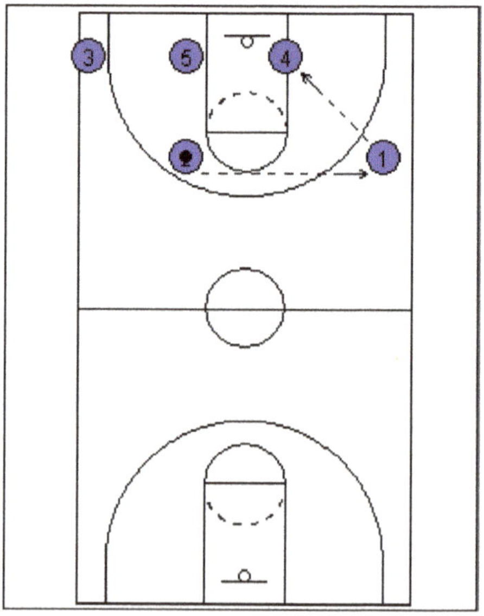

9th option

If there is no pass into the low post, 4 cross screens for 5.

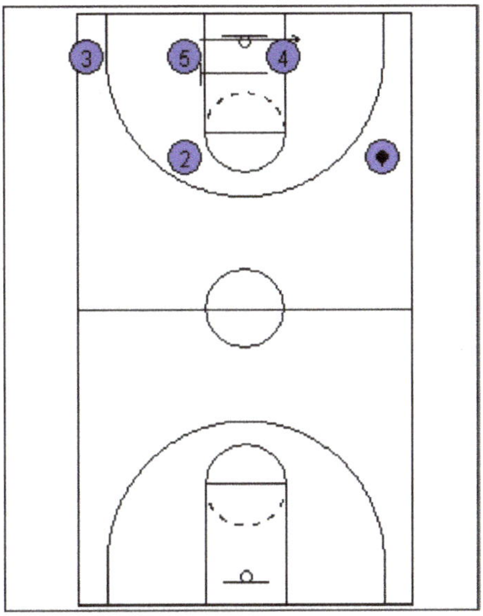

1 looks into the low post for 5, and 2 down screens for 4.

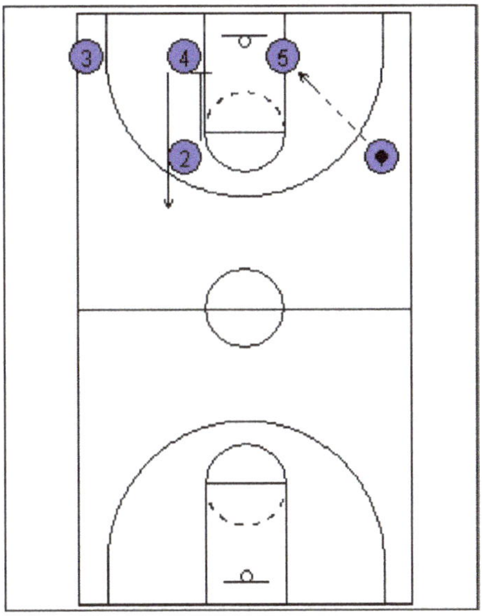

1 passes to 4, and players use appropriate spacing for motion offense.

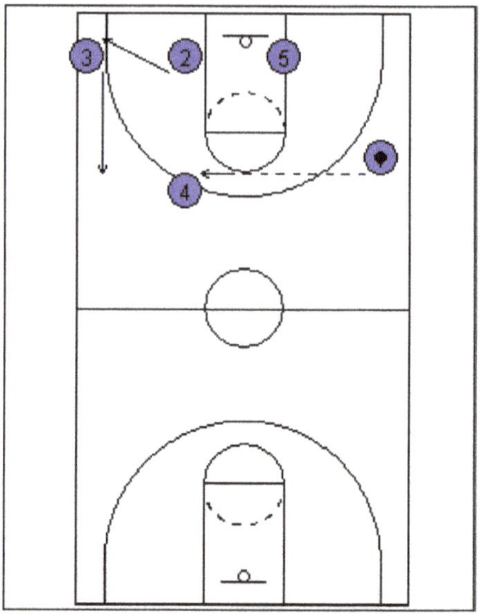

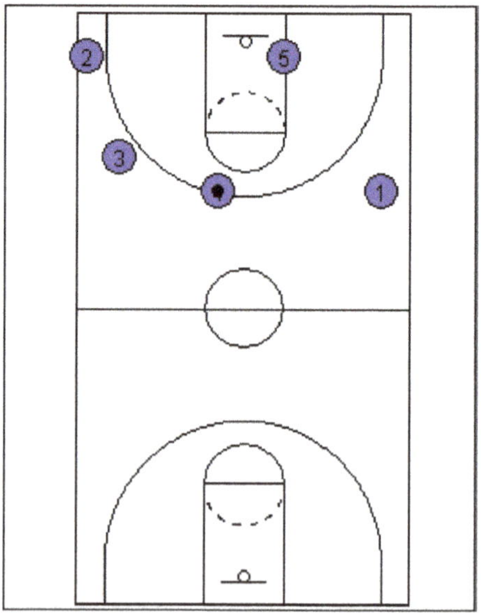

Here are a couple of wrinkles[4] you can throw in for ball reversal.

1 makes a direct pass to the high trailer (4).

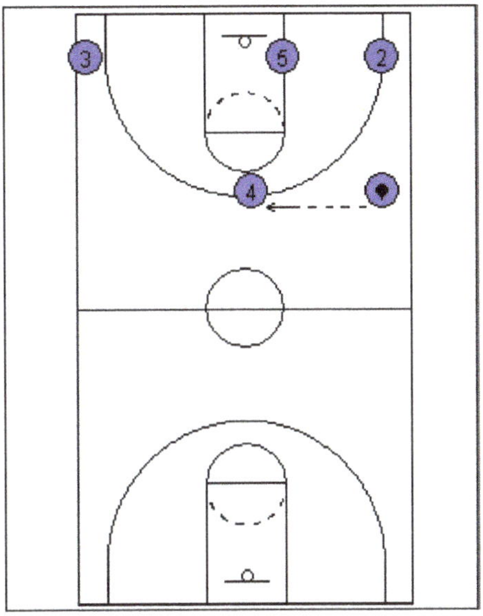

1 then cuts and takes a handoff from 4.

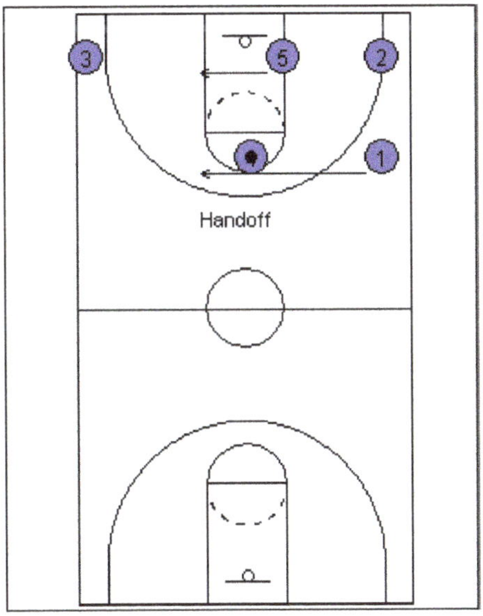

4 To learn more: https://www.breakthroughbasketball.com/offense/fast-break-offense-carolina.html

As the handoff is made, 2 cuts middle and then up to back screen for 4. 4 cuts off the backscreen. 1 looks to pass to 4 on back door or lob.

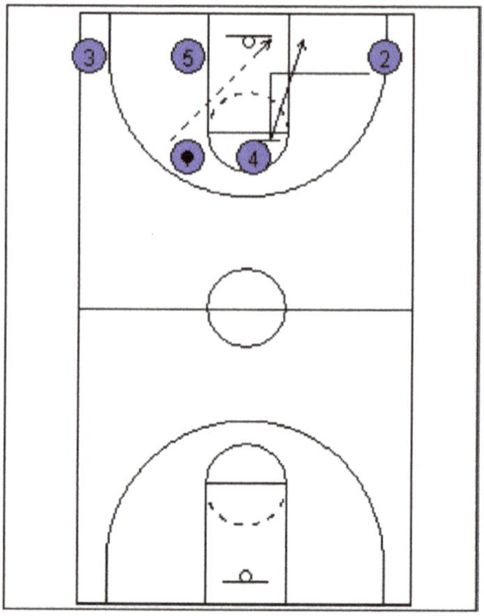

The second wrinkle[5] is this: 1 keeps his dribble alive. The high trailer (4) fills his spot and then ball screens for 1. 1 dribbles off the ball screen, and 5 cuts to the opposite block.

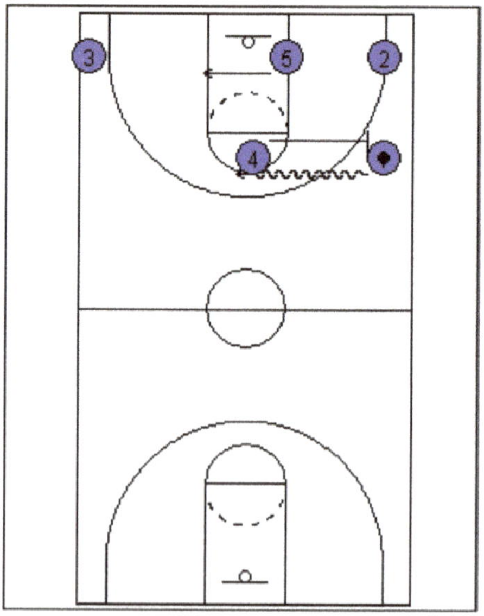

[5] To learn more: https://www.breakthroughbasketball.com/offense/fast-break-offense-carolina.html

2 cuts in and to back screen for 4; 1 looks to 4 for back door or lob pass.

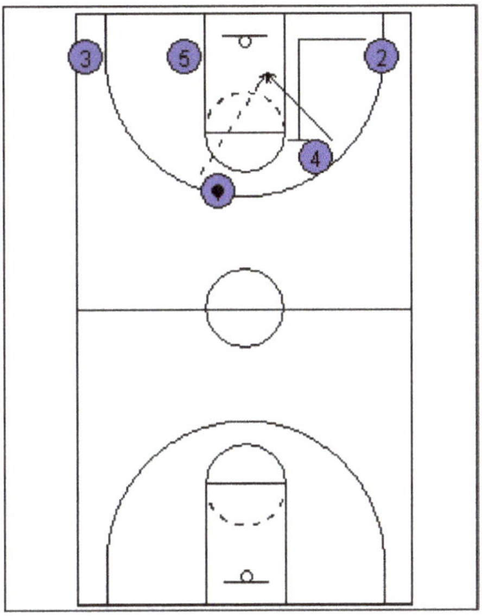

Many of the patterns used in these diagrams can serve as offense plays even though there are part of the fast break system of play. Some coaches would use the term as preliminary offense or secondary break because they have the same patterns and player movement of offense set plays. Other options from these diagrams are screen and roll options, player slipping to basket off screens, dribble "at" where player with the ball dribbles at his opponent's defense player, creating confusion for the player on defense and flicks where you flick the ball to your teammate when dribbling at them.

Developing Team Defense System of Play

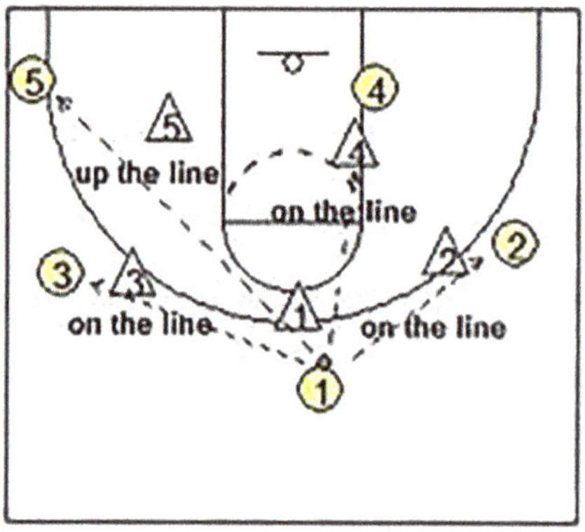

Figure 3.1. Man-to-Man

There are various numbering systems you can use when designing your defense system. I believe that the primary defense to use is man-to-man because it is the foundation to all other defense strategies. When players learn the basic concepts of man-to-man, it makes teaching other defenses a little easier. Below is a diagram that shows basic defense positioning. The concept of "on the ball line and up the ball line" references where the defender (triangle cones) is in relationship to the ball.

As the offense players and ball moves to different positions, the defense makes the proper shifts. This defense style is utilized to apply pressure and deny offense passing lanes and good help side defense.

The diagrams below are a basic defense setup for *2–3 zone*. This defense is primarily used to stop the offense from penetrating to the basket and entice the offense to shoot the ball from the outside. Diagram A is your basic setup and uses the same premise as man-to-man defense. However, in zone, you are responsible for guarding a space and the player that occupies that space. Diagram B shows how the defense shifts depending on where the player and ball is in relation to a player (red dot). Diagram C demonstrates how you can trap the ball if it is in the corner. You can see how the defense would shift according to the placement of the player and ball.

There are so many defense strategies you can use when developing your defense system as it relates to basketball. The key is to assess your player personnel and make a decision on what type of style you will play.

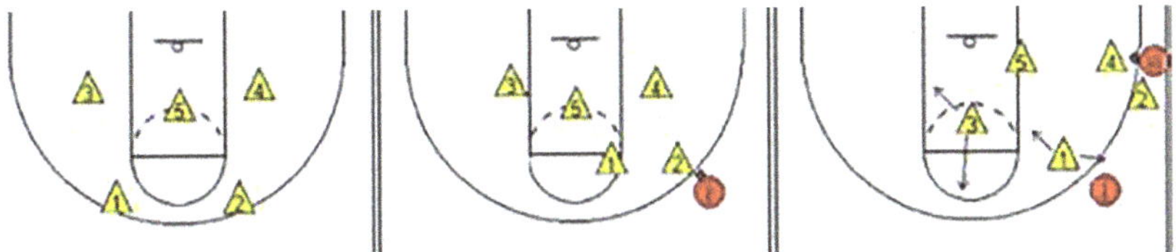

Diagram A.
2-3 Zone set up.

Diagram B.
2-3 zone, ball on the wing.

Diagram C.
Trapping the corner.

Football System of Play

There are many systems of play regarding football, both on defense and offense, and depending on the system of play you are implementing, some basic concepts become important when implementing a strategical approach. The diagram below demonstrates a basic setup for both the defense and offense. Understanding the various positions is critical to designing a system of play.

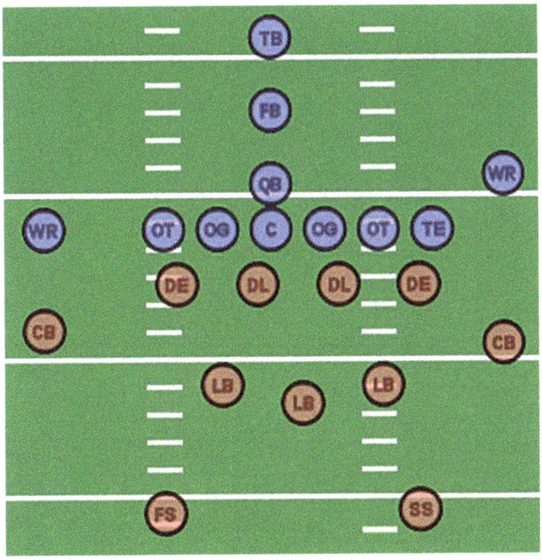

The quarterback (QB) is a key position. This person is responsible for handing off the ball, passing, or running. The fullback or tailback's (FB or TB) primary responsibilities are running, blocking, and on rare occasions could also pass the ball. The offense line, offense tackles (OT), offense guards (OG), center (C) are responsible for protecting the quarterback, providing running lanes for the fullback and tailback. The tight end (TE) may have multiple responsibilities, receiving a pass or blocking. The wide receivers (WR) have multiple responsibilities as well. However, the primary responsibility is to catch the ball. The persons that play this position could have some blocking assignment as well.

The responsibility of the defense positions is key in developing your defense system of play. The defense line has multiple responsibilities. The defensive ends (DE) and defensive tackles or defense line (DL or DT) apply the rush to attack the quarterback; they protect against the run and disrupt the offense system as a whole. The cornerbacks (CB) are responsible for covering the wide receivers, secondary line of defense against the run, and occasionally can rush the quarterback. The linebackers (LB) have multiple responsibilities: protecting against the run, rushing the quarterback, and providing coverage against the pass. The free safety and strong safety (FS and SS) have the responsibility of protecting against the pass and could be the last line of defense if the running back, wide receivers, quarterback, or tight end break free.

Having an understanding of these positions, both on offense and defense, gives you the latitude to be very creative in your system of play. You can shift players around and provide a variety of schemes that can be used to develop a football system of play.

Discussion Questions:

1. Please explain the "game approach" as it applies to teaching a system of play in sport activity.
2. How would you define a "part-whole-part" teaching approach?
3. Give an example of how "modifying the rules" during practice could be beneficial to sport participants.
4. Explain the term "spacing" as it relates to system of play of your favorite sport.
5. Discuss how "Game IQ" coincides with knowing the system of play in a sport.
6. Why would developing good stroke mechanics in tennis be beneficial?
7. Why is the goalie a key component in the 4-4-2 scheme in soccer?
8. What player takes on the role as a "coach" on the floor in the game of basketball, and, please, explain why this position is important.
9. Please explain the term "system of play" as it relates to offense and defense in sports.
10. List the name of sports that use a "fast break" in their system of play strategy.

CHAPTER 4

DIMENSIONS OF MENTAL SKILLS TRAINING

Introduction

In coaching, *mental skills methods and training* can take on several different meanings, and its application to sport participant can vary from understanding arousal, using anxiety to enhance performance, developing mental toughness, developing *conflict resolution strategies*, increasing self-efficacy, and dealing with stress. Developing a systematic and consistent practice of *mental or psychological skills* to enhance performance can increase enjoyment, curtail aggression, and allowing athletes to achieve greater sport and physical activity. To use this training methodology, one must have an understanding of the benefits coupled with the experience of using mental skills methods and training.

Some sport psychologist believe that psychological skill training can contribute 50 to 90 percent of improved performance of sport participants performance. To develop skills of *goal setting*, *self-talk*, *mental imagery*, and *mental rehearsal*, coaches can review four prominent PST methods used by athletes. Each method enables the athlete to work on developing more than one psychological skill, improve and maintaining mental cues, such as commitment, concentration, attention, and motivation as they build up their skill weak area (Hardy et al., 1996; Gould, 1996).

Why PST Training Is Important

Sport and exercise participants experience mental letdowns and mistakes consistently. Have you experienced or knew an athlete who has experienced mental issues or performance disappointments? Below are some examples:

- Walking off the playing field disappointed after losing the game you believed you should have won
- Not coming through at a critical point in a competition
- Having an injury and the recovery period is taking too long
- Lacking the desire or motivation to exercise
- Focus disruption or your mind wandered during a competition
- Being upset and frustrated with your performance and put yourself down

You may have experienced or the participants in your program fell victim to at least one of the mental breakdowns on the list above. Developing the methods and skills to improve *PST* training is important and beneficial. However, participants as well as coaches may neglect this type of training because they lack knowledge, have misunderstanding about PST, or do not take the time to implement it in the practice routine.

Psychological Myths Surrounding Skills Training

Research has pointed out that some coaches and exercise specialist have myths about using PST training protocols. Below are four myths about the use of PST in maximizing sports performance (Gould and Eckland, Petlichkoff, Peterson, and Bump1991):

1. It is more advantageous for those "sport participants" that have problems.
2. Psychological Skill Training is for experienced and elite athletes only.

3. If you want a "quick-fix," PST training will provide that need.
4. It is not useful (Weinberg and Gould, 1999).

Psychological Skills Training focuses on developing skills of all types of athlete, younger or order athletes and those who are experienced or inexperienced, looking to develop their skills (Hellstedt, 1987). Sport participants that have "special needs" can also benefit from PST training (Asken, 1991, as cited in Weinberg and Gould, 1999; Clark and Sachs, 1999). There are many dimensions to PST methods and training protocol. Let's review four practices in order to establish a systematic framework of how these methods can be utilized by coaches and sport participants.

Goals

When coaches think about sport participant's goal setting strategies or trying to help them establish them as they relate to sport activity and PST methods, it is important to define the meaning of goals and the subcategories that people in sport and exercise may look at. Goal setting, according to Locke, Shaw, Saari, and Latham, 1981, p. 126), is what an individual is trying to accomplish; it could be the objective or subjective aim of an action or statement. Sport participants that identify *objective goals* are looking to attain a specific standard of proficiency or a task within a specified time (Locke and Latham, 2002, p. 705). Attempting to attain a specified level of participation within a certain period of time (making the varsity team) or attaining a specific goal percentage by the end of the season are a few examples of objective goals. *Subjective goals* are general statements of intent (e.g., "I want to improve my performance," "I want to enjoy the experience of competing") that are not measurable or objective. Establishing a PST methodology for sport participant to use to address both objective and subjective goals could be beneficial.

In the sport and exercise psychological literature, the belief is that it is important that all stakeholders have goals, and there are many aspects to goal-setting ideology. Identifying the types of goals one wants to achieve, be it *outcome performance* or process goals, is crucial. Coaches should understand and convey to sport participants the effectiveness of goal setting and why goal setting works. Establishing some principles for setting goals and providing the correct application of these principles (Gould, 2005; Murphy, 1996) to provide a strong foundation for designing a goal-setting program is a good coaching strategy.

Setting practice and competition goals are good because of the large amount of time athletes spend practicing and competing. Setting long- and short-term goals is very beneficial. However, it is important that these goals be linked to provide a progression of goal accomplishment, starting with some that can be achieved immediately and others that lead to more difficult and future objectives. There are many different goal-setting systems, but according to Weinberg and Gould, most include three stages: (a) preparation and planning, (b) education and acquisition, and (c) implementation and follow-up.

Self-Talk

Although *self-talk* can be both positive and negative in terms of an internal distractor to deal with distractions when performing, I feel that sport participants should learn to use the technique to enhance performance and concentration. Anytime you think about something, you are in a sense of talking to yourself. The process of self-talk, preparing to execute, or executing a skill, in which self-talk functions as a mediator between action and a response, is displayed in figure 1.4. As the relationship shows, self-talk can play a key role in how participants react to situations, and these situations affect future actions and feelings.

My setup is good, I should be able to drive the ball with accuracy (positive).

or

I don't want to overthink this shot like I did on the last hole, it was a disaster (negative).

My form is good, I just need to maintain this pace throughout the race (positive).

or

I don't feel strong, and my strokes are not fluid, I can see my competition catching up to me (negative).

Figure 4.1. Two examples of the self-talk process.

Self-talk has cognitive and motivational functions (Hardy et al. 1997; Hardy et al. 2004). The *motivational functions* address a variety of things, one being self-confident, relaxation and arousal control, and maintaining and increasing drive. In the positive self-talk statement (see above), the sport participants give positive *verbal cues* that allow confidence in executing the skill. On the other hand, negative self-talk increases anxiety by being critical, which has generally been associated with poor performance. It has been documented that positive self-talk techniques, that is, cognitive restructuring, countering, and thought stopping enhance performance more than negative self-talk. Positive self-talk enhances self-esteem and attentional focus.

Mental Imagery

Mental imagery when used in conjunction with goal setting and positive self-talk can enhance performance. However, it is important to discuss the mental or cognitive concept of mental imagery as it applies to enhancing performance. Driskell et al. (1994) suggest that mental imagery entails cognitive rehearsal of an activity without physical movement. In other words, participants visualize the movement or activity in their mind before performing the task. Acquiring the knowledge of phenomenal mental images entail cognitive rehearsal, and participants must practice this technique with the intentions to perform competencies covertly without implementing the required movement.

Sport coaches may need to take an elementary approach when implementing this PST method. Something as simple as having the participant visualize completing a simple task, one that is realistic for them to imagine doing prior to physically attempting the skill.

Imagery Use by Athletes

There are many studies to support that mental imagery and practice is a viable instrument in enhancing sport performance. Murphy (2005) stated that the effectiveness of imagery in cultivation sport performance is maximized only through a controlled systematic practice. Synthesizing mental imagery, relaxation, and behavioral modeling (Hall and Erffmeyer, 1983) may also have substantial improvement of those skills that require *visuomotor behavior* (free throwing shooting, putting a golf ball, or bowling). Monroe et al. (2000) in a qualitative assessment of imagery use—where, when, why, and what—highlighted enlightening details about imagery utilization by sports persons. With reference to "where," sports persons documented using imagery extensively in both training and contest and described doing so before, throughout, and after each event, be it practice or a contest.

With regard to "what," they imaged and described a variety of features such as the frequency with which they use imagery. It is essential to note that a few scientific researchers assume that participants should physically practice a new skill first before endeavoring to practice it using imagery (Richardson, 1967; Smith, 1987) although this is contradictory to some scientific beliefs. This is to ensure that the participants comprehend the adequate strategies required to obtain an interior sense of how they are expected to perform that skill. Avoiding this type of comprehension, participants may visualize incorrect techniques, which could result in physically performing the skill using inaccurate techniques that would have minimal impact on enhancing their performance.

Supplementary research has found that athletes may also reap the benefit of the usage of mental imagery immediately after a successful performance, enabling them to reexperience the positive aspect of their performance, enhancing their feeling of self-confidence and competence for the next performance (Hodges, Huys, and Starkes 2007, MacIntyre and Moran 2007).

Imagery Skill Level Assessment

It's important to set up imagery training with the athlete to assess their current level of understanding and using imagery as a skill that will be beneficial to improving their sport performance. Individuals will differ in how they image, and measuring one's ability in imaging is not easy. Most sport psychologist prefer using questionnaires to discern the various aspects of imagery content. The *Sport Imagery Questionnaire* below has various frequency items, and results from this questionnaire when used pointed out that athletes found the particular imagery and strategies effective (Weinberg, Butt, Knight, Burke, and Jackson 2003).

Other researcher found that the function, not the content, was the most critical (Short, Monsma, and Short 2004). Basically, if an athlete use imagery to improve self-confidence, it doesn't matter what the image is, the end result is that it improves self-confidence. Williams and Cumming (2011) presented a development of the Sport Imagery Ability Questionnaire, whereas sport-specific images as opposed to general movement images assess image ability. Various questionnaire can be used by the practitioner and based on the most appropriate instrument for a specific use and situation.

Student-Athlete Name:______________________________Date:__________________________

Sport Imagery Questionnaire

This questionnaire, developed by Rainier Martens, PhD, author and pioneer in sport psychology, was designed to help you pinpoint how you experience imagery. Follow the instructions and then add your final score at the end to determine if you more intensely experience the sights, sounds, feelings, or moods of an image. This knowledge will help you individualize your mental training program. You'll learn to concentrate on those areas you experience the most vividly as you work on controlling or altering your mental images.

Read the questions below and rate each one using the following scale:

1 = no image present
2 = not clear or vivid, but a recognizable image
3 = moderately clear and vivid
4 = clear and vivid
5 = extremely clear and vivid

1. **Practicing Alone**

Pick one skill in your sport and imagine yourself doing this wherever you normally practice—but with no one else there. Close your eyes for a minute; try to see yourself, hear the sounds, feel your body perform the movement, and be aware of your state of mind.

a. ______How well did you see yourself doing the activity?
b. ______How well did you hear the sounds of doing the activity?
c. ______How well did you feel yourself making the movements?
d. ______How aware were you of your mood?

2. **Practicing with Others**

You're doing the same thing, but practicing with the coach and your teammates present. This time you make a mistake that everyone notices. Close your eyes for a minute and imaging making the error and the situation afterward.

a. ______How well did you see yourself in this situation?
b. ______How well did you hear the sounds?
c. ______How well did you feel yourself making the movements?
d. ______How well did you feel the emotions of the situation?

Student-Athlete Name:______________________________Date:___________________________

3. **Watching a Teammate**

Think of a teammate making a mistake in a critical part of a game or competition, such as missing a goal or falling.

a. ______How well did you see your teammate?

b. ______How well did you hear ths sounds?

c. ______How well did you feel your own physical presence or movement?

d. ______How well did you feel the emotions of the situation?

4. **Competing**

Imagine yourself performing the same or similar activity in a game or competition, but imagine yourself doing it skillfully with the spectators and teammates showing their appreciation. Close your eyes for about a minute and imagine this situation as clearly as possible.

a. ______How well did you see yourself in this situation?

b. ______How well did you hear the sounds in this situation?

c. ______How well did you feel yourself making the movements?

d. ______How well did you feel the emotions of the situation?

Scoring

Add up your total score for each a answer, b answer, and so on. Then add all four figures for a total score.

a. Visual (what you saw) ______

b. Auditory (what you heard) ______

c. Kinesthetic (what you felt) ______

d. Mood (how you felt) ______

Total ______

Factors Affecting the Effectiveness of Imagery

There are factors that could determine the extent to which imagery could or could not be beneficial to sport participants. With younger athletes, it may be difficult for them to grasp the concept of "nature of the task," whereas the performer practicing mentally can think about what to do and how to overcome potential barriers, using temporal and spatial regularities of a skill. For instance, to make the right decision based on the visualization of what they might see. In basketball, it could be finishing off a fast break, note the changing positions of the offense and defense players, results in a successful decision by the ball handler to make the appropriate pass. Although research on both discrete and serial tasks (e.g., golf) and continuous tasks (e.g., swimming) shows positive effects of imagery, the coach has to able to teach or use these imagery concepts in developing their athletes.

How does a coach who has young participants start to embrace and teach the concepts of imagery strategies? Imagery needs to be added to one's normal physical practice. However, it should not take the place of the physical practice but implemented in what I consider part of the "practice package," which is both mental and physical practice. For example, during the practice session, take a pause and have participants visualize doing various tasks before the tasks is practiced. This can be any movement or mental action that is required to perform the tasks with efficiency. For example, with inexperienced and experienced athletes, just thinking about jumping over the high bar, hitting a perfect tennis serve, healing an injured arm, or sinking a golf putt could actually help athletes accomplish these things, but it has to be implemented into the "practice package."

Inexperienced and experienced athletes can generate information from memory that is essentially the same as an actual experience; consequently, imaging events can have effects on our nervous system similar to that of the real or actual experience. According to Marks (1977), "Imagined stimuli, perceptual, or real have a qualitatively similar status in our conscious mental life" (p. 285). Additional research has resulted in the belief that not one theory can really explain all the different findings surrounding imagery research and practice; each theory can shed light on the mechanism, driving imagery and why it can enhance performance.

Below is another example of using imagery with a simple self-awareness techniques called guided imagery. Although this technique requires practice with both inexperienced and experienced sport participants, coaches may be able to use the video or guided imagery script (below) to start using imagery to enhance performance, health-related, physical, and emotional benefits. It can help you feel less nervous or upset, be less bothered by pain, or achieve a goal, such as an athletic or academic achievement.

Try watching this video: https://www.youtube.com/watch?v=35ch88kmlls or enable JavaScript if it is disabled in your browser.

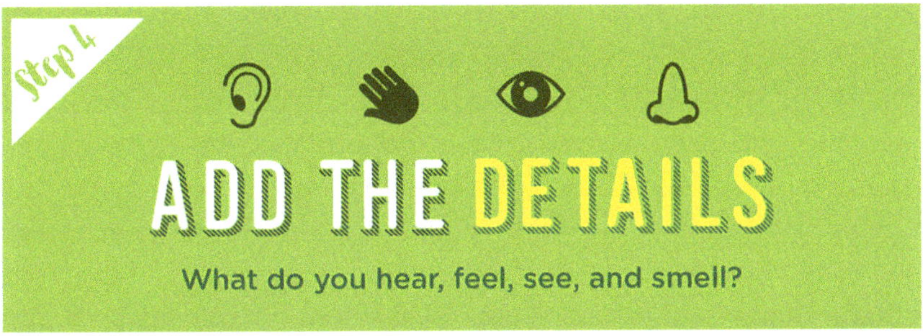

Both the coaches and players can determine which area to incorporate into an athlete's daily training regimen. It's not necessary to make the process complex or cumbersome, and it should be complimentary to the participant's daily training routine. Athletes may want to practice imaging in a quiet setting with few distractions. However, as they become proficient in imagery, they should practice it in different settings (on the field, during practice, in the locker room, at the pool, in the gym). As skill developed, it is hoped that athletes learn to use imagery amid distractions and in competition.

Dimension of Concentrating

We have explored several concepts that address mental skills training protocols. However, at the core of these concepts mentioned in this chapter is the ability to concentrate or focus. Developing the ability to concentrate is essential to mental skills training and development.

Coaches, parents, and educators use this word religiously to get sport participants, children, and students to maintain focus on relevant environmental cues. Most of us have experienced environmental changes in various ways, and when this happens, it is crucial to our attentional focus change. If we do not make this change mentally, *irrelevant cues* can lead to performance errors, be it poor sport performance, failure to execute, successfully taking an exam, or completing day-to-day tasks. William James (1890) perhaps had one of the best descriptions of concentration (attention): "Everyone knows what attention is. It is taking possession by the mind, in clear and vivid form, of one out of what seems several simultaneously possible objects or trains of thought. Focalization, concentration of consciousness are the essence. It implies withdrawal from some things in order to deal effectively with others" (pp. 403–404).

There are various aspects of concentration, and James's definition refers to selective attention. However, a more contemporary definition of concentration refers to a person's ability to exert deliberate mental effort on what is most important in any given situation (Moran 2004). Researchers have compared successful and less successful athletes, and they contend that attentional control is important. From my own personal experience of coaching hundreds of student-athletes, those who were more successful performing had the ability to become less distracted by irrelevant stimuli; their task-oriented focus was more defined as opposed to their competitors and teammates. Optimal performance states are closely related to the ability to concentrate, a special state of involvement or awareness of and absorption in the task at hand. Although this research is questioned by other researcher, Nideffer and colleagues (Nideffer 1976a, b, 1981; Nideffer and Segal 2001) view *attentional focus* along two dimensions: width (broad or narrow) and direction (external or internal). Page 89 displays pictures of athletic participants that display some aspect of the theoretical framework described by Nideffer and colleagues.

This participant is demonstrating *external attentional focus.*

She is concentrating outward to an object (the ball) as she also realizes that her opponents are moving as well.

This participant is exhibiting a *narrow attentional focus* as she responds to only one or two cues as she prepares to hit The ball that the coach is presenting it to her.

A *broad attentional focus* is demonstrated when a participant has to perceive several occurrences simultaneously. This athlete view opponents, teammates, space, and concentrate on his next move.

This athlete is displaying an *internal attentional focus,* whereas she is directing inward to thoughts and feelings as she prepares to receive the tennis ball from her opponent.

Discussion Questions:

1. What are some benefits of mental skill training that athletes can use to improve performance?
2. Name at least one Psychological Skills Training strategy you would use on an athlete who has an injury.
3. Least one Psychological Skills Training protocol for an athlete who is trying to establish a subjective and objective goal. You can choose the sport and the subjective and objective goal.
4. Do you think incorporating self-talk strategies are beneficial to sport participants?
5. Please describe a mental imagery strategy that could be effective for a sport participant. You choose the sport you would use this mental imagery technique.
6. Please describe what attentional focus (concentration) means to you in relationship to sports participation.
7. Explain the concept "nature of the task" as it relates to imagery effectiveness.
8. Go to an Internet browser and type in the YouTube video "Guided imagery create the state you want." Practice one of the guided imagery exercises and discuss if you think the exercise could be beneficial in helping sport participants or coaches relax.
9. Explain why an athlete in any sport would be less successful if they could not comprehend some aspect of attentional control.
10. Explain the concept of narrow attentional focus.

CHAPTER 5

TRAINING FOUNDATIONS

Key Terms	Page
Neuromuscular Control—the ability of the central nervous system (CNS) to control the muscles during multi-limb movement patterns	
Sport Performance—training that is designed to improve an individual's physical capacities to a level that allows the body to maximally compete and express technical skills in a competitive environment.	

Anthropometrics—a set of measurements and proportions of the human body used to classify growth, conditioning level, daily behaviors, and the impact of stress. Some of which include: height, weight, lean mass, fat mass, waist circumference, hip circumference, neck circumference, and shoulder circumference.	
Skill Expression—the set of specific coordinated movement patterns that are necessary to master to achieve a competitive advantage in a sport	
Bio-Motor—the six expressions of physical capacity: strength, endurance, speed, flexibility, balance, and coordination	
Division One—used to illustrate the standard of physical capacity required to participate in a top fifty NCAA collegiate sports program	
Periodization—the strategic implementation of distinct training phases for developing specific aspects of performance, most commonly endurance, strength, hypertrophy, power, and recovery	
Absolute Strength—The maximal amount of force that can be exerted against an object or person regardless of one's muscle or body size.	
Relative Strength—The maximal amount of force that can be exerted against an object or person at a given weight.	

Introduction

"Bigger, faster, stronger" is an old sports adage, common to both coaches and fans alike. This is so because these characteristics when maximized lead to a competitive advantage for an athlete (Poliquin 2001). The undersized, hardworking athlete, devoid of physical talent makes for a great story and post-game interview but in truth does not translate into success in the athletic environment. Coaches need to understand this sobering reality: elite sport *bio-motor ability* cannot be developed with current exercise, nutrition, and recovery practices. Elite expression of speed, jumping, and strength is reserved for the genetically gifted or induced by pharmaceutical aids and hard work. However, what can occur with a professionally designed *sports performance* program is that most athletes can development their physical traits from average to excellent standards (Poliquin 2001). The below figure depicts the sports and performance ranges of a limited set of metrics to improve individual understanding.

Approximate Bio-Motor Expression in the United States Population						
Healthy to Wellness Ranges			Fitness to Varsity Sports		Division 1 to Pro	
Poor	**Fair**	**Average**	**Good**	**Excellent**	**Superior**	**Elite**
<20%–39%	40%–49%	50%–59%	60%–79%	80%–94%	95%–99%	1%
Muscular Endurance Examples (performed consecutively, expressed as repetitions)						
Push-Up	Push-Up	Push-Up	Push-Up	Push-Up	Push-Up	Push-Up
<20	21–35	36–49	50–64	65–74	75–99	>100
Cardiovascular Endurance Examples						
1 mile	1 mile	1 mile	1 mile	1 mile	1 mile	1 mile
>20 min	15 min	10 min	8 min	6 min	5 min	<5 min
(Male) **Muscular Strength Examples (expressed as pounds)**						
Bench Press	Bench Press	Bench Press	Bench Press	Bench Press	Bench Press	Bench Press
50–74	75–100	101–150	151–200	201–250	251–299	300–350
(Male) Muscular Power Examples (expressed as inches)						
Vertical Jump	Vertical Jump	Vertical Jump	Vertical Jump	Vertical Jump	Vertical Jump	Vertical Jump
<12	12–16	16–20	20–24	25–29	30–35	>35
(Male) Speed Examples (expressed as seconds)						
40-Yd Dash	40-Yd Dash	40-Yd Dash	40-Yd Dash	40-Yd Dash	40-Yd Dash	40-Yd Dash
7	6.5	6.0	5.5	5.0	4.5	4.3 sec

Figure 5.1. Training Expectations
(Data taken from ACSM Guidelines 2016, "Essentials of Strength Training and Conditioning," 2008)

Therefore, the following chapters are critical for providing coaches with the framework to train and develop youth sport participants into competitive high school athletes and division one scholarship candidates. As a coach, the ability to win games and dominate opponents is most heavily influenced by the athletic attributes, mindset, and physical characteristics of your players (Poliquin 2001, Haff 2016).

To begin an athletic training plan, one must have a clear understanding and direction of how to develop athletic ability. Phase one (postseason): muscular endurance and muscular symmetry; phase two (off-season): strength and hypertrophy; phase three (preseason): muscular power and cardiovascular conditioning; and phase four (in-season): strength maintenance and injury prevention. This thus leads to bio-motor optimization (Poliquin 2001, Haff 2016). This type of cyclical seasonal development is termed *periodization* and will be discussed in greater detail in chapter 6. The physical development program we recommend develops these four areas of conditioning over time to avoid injury, prioritize skill practice, increase mental resiliency, and decrease sport burnout. Many sport coaches concentrate on increasing performance metrics solely, leaving strategic goal setting, player health, injury potential, and psycho-emotional resiliency disproportionally open to random chance. This nearsighted focus we feel is not optimal or required to create a high achieving and more durable athlete.

Training Basics

The head coach in any organization has a lot to manage and is given the wide-ranging responsibility of developing his or her athletes. Physical development is only one component of athletic improvement, and a sport coach does not have to be an expert in human physiology or sport performance to manage this process effectively. However, a coach should understand the two fundamental questions when implementing a sport performance program. Question one: what combination of anthropometric traits (height, weight, muscle mass, fat mass, etc.) are most significant for success in my sport?

Question two: what type of physical capabilities (strength, flexibility, endurance, balance, etc.) must my athletes optimally develop to create the greatest advantage in my sport?

The following tables are averages of arguably the most successful athletes in sport history (Hall of Fame members respectively in each sport), and therefore provide a practical, theoretical framework for projection of success in each sport category. Figure 5.1 is used to answer the first question we posed, and figures 5.2 and 5.3 are used to answer the second. A coach only has two options when attempting to create a physically imposing and dominant team: one, enhance their current team's athletic ability through implementing an annual strength and conditioning program or two, recruit the most gifted athletes from within their surrounding available communities.

Average Height Above Six Feet Three Inches					
Sport (Male)	**Avg. Height Ranges**	**Weight Ranges**	**Pounds per Inch**	**Lean Mass Pounds**	**Fat Mass Pounds**
Basketball	6.3 to 7.2 ft.	185 to 250	2.5 to 2.9	164 to 212	19 to 38
Volleyball	6.4 to 6.10 ft.	185 to 238	2.4 to 2.9	166 to 202	19 to 36
Swimming	6.2 to 6.7 ft.	178 to229	2.4 to 2.9	160 to 194	18 to 35
Average Height Above Six Feet and Below Six Feet Three Inches					
Tennis	5.7 to 6.9 ft	147 to 202	2.2 to 2.5	132 to 171	15 to 31
Football	5.11 to 6.5 ft.	178 to 254	2.5 to 3.3	160 to 216	18 to 38
Hockey	5.8 to 6.9 ft	170 to 235	2.5 to 2.9	153 to 200	17 to 35
Baseball	5-6 to 6.11 ft	190 to 290	2.6 to 3.3	171 to 246	19 to 44
Track & Field	6.0 to 6.5 ft	172 to 195	2.4 to 2.6	155 to 165	17 to 30
Average Height Above Five Feet and Eight Inches, Below Six Feet					
Soccer	5.8 to 6.5 ft	122 to 210	2.5 to 2.75	110 to 178	12 to 32
Cross Country	5.0 to 5.11 ft	126 to 170	2.1 to 2.4	113 to 144	13 to 26
Golf	5.5 to 6.2 ft	162 to 185	2.5	146 to 157	12 to 28
Bodybuilding	5-5 to 6.2 ft	208 to 259	3.2 to 3.5	197 to 233	11 to 26
Wrestling	5.0 to 5.8 ft	132 to 163	2.2 to 2.4	125 to 147	7 to 16
The Average Height for General Sport Success >6 Feet and <6 Feet 8					
General Athlete	6.0 to 6.5	180 to 223	2.5 to 2.9	162 to 190	18 to 33

Figure 5.2. (A) Male Competitive Athletic Frame

Average Height Above Six Feet					
Sport (Female)	**Height**	**Weight Ranges**	**Pounds per Inch**	**Lean Mass**	**Fat Mass**
Basketball	5.3 to 6.8 ft.	116 to 184	1.85 to 2.3	99 to 152	17 to 32
Volleyball	5.5 to 6.8 ft.	120 to 184	1.85 to 2.3	102 to 152	18 to 32
Above Five Feet Seven Inches					
Softball	5.4 to 6.0 ft.	118 to 176	1.85 to 2.45	100 to 145	18 to 31
Swimming	5.3 to 6.0 ft.	116 to 155	1.85 to 2.15	99 to 128	17 to 27
Tennis	5.3 to 5.10 ft.	116 to 154	1.85 to 2.2	99 to 127	17 to 27
Above Five Feet Five Inches					
Track & Field	5.3 to 5.10 ft.	116 to 147	1.85 to 2.1	99 to 121	17 to 26
Soccer	5.2 to 5.9 ft.	114 to 152	1.85 to 2.2	97 to 125	17 to 27
Lacrosse	5.2 to 5.8 ft.	114 to 156	1.85 to 2.3	97 to 128	17 to 28
Golf	5.2 to 5.9 ft.	114 to 159	1.85 to 2.3	97 to 131	17 to 28
Below Five Feet Five Inches					
Sport (Female)	Height	Weight Ranges	Pounds per Inch	Lean Mass	Fat Mass
Bodybuilding	5.0 to 5.4 ft.	106 to 154	2.1 to 2.4	90 to 127	16 to 27
Cross Country	5.0 to 5.4 ft.	106 to 118	1.65 to 1.85	90 to 97	16 to 21
Cheerleading	4.11 to 5.4 ft.	98 to 118	1.67 to 1.85	83 to 97	15 to 21
Above Five Feet Five Inches					
The General Athlete	5.5 to 6.2 ft.	120 to 166.5	1.85 to 2.25	102 to 137	18 to 29

Figure 5.3. (B) Female Competitive Athletic Frame

The above figures assist a coach in identifying participants that can best naturally succeed in the various sporting environments. The tables reveal physical attributes of a male and female elite-level athlete who participate in the most popular high school sports in the United States. Recall the opening statement, "bigger, faster, stronger," is an old sports adage. Height and weight compromise the first component, muscular power is the second, and muscular strength is the third when formulating the three-part sport success equation. The better suited the body is for the given sport played, the greater skill development and athletic success a coach can expect. Refer to figure 5.1 and compare the successful basketball and football athletic stature to that of a successful cross-country athlete.

Sport (Male)	Avg. Height Ranges	Weight Ranges	Pounds per Inch	Lean Mass Pounds	Fat Mass Pounds
Basketball	6.3 to 7.2 ft.	185-250	2.5 to 2.9	164 to 212	19 to 38
Football	5.11 to 6.5 ft.	178 to 254	2.5 to 3.3	160 to 216	18 to 38
Cross Country	5.0 to 5.11 ft	126 to 170	2.1 to 2.4	113 to 144	13 to 26

Figure 5.4. (C) Truncated Comparison by Competitive Frame

One can quickly conclude that on average, tall athletes (those greater than six feet and two inches tall) or heavily muscled athletes (those greater than 2.8 pounds per inch) do not run at competitive championship levels for long distances. In contrast, short, thin athletes (those less than five feet and eight inches tall and 2.4 pounds per inch) are not well suited for one-on-one spatially compressed competitive situations such as basketball or football. A successful coach understands these competitive truths and what physical form best optimizes specific advantages in their sport. As a coach, it is important to remember that elite *skill expression* occurs most frequently within the confines of an elite body. The majority of coaches can recognize a gifted athlete rather easily, even the casual fan can identify a level of singular overt uniqueness within a group of players. But the figures and content of the above tables should best be used to assist coaches in understanding the minimal critical thresholds required to justify specialized investment from the coaching staff and or parents.

Athletic Competitive Frame Metrics					
General Athlete	Avg. Height Ranges	Weight Ranges	Pounds per Inch	Lean Mass Pounds	Fat Mass Pounds
(Male)	6.0 to 6.5 ft.	180 to 223	2.5 to 2.9	162 to 190	18 to 33
(Female)	5.5 to 6.2 ft.	120 to 166.5	1.85 to 2.25	102 to 137	18 to 29

Figure 5.5. The Ideal Structure for Sport

Sport participants who deviate from the optimal competitive frame requirements of success will have to acquire significant skill mastery and physical conditioning to compete at each progressive level of their sport (elementary, junior high school, high school, college, professional) then their naturally well-suited counterparts.

Body Height

The height of an individual is arguably the most significant quantifiable athletic variable (ahead of strength, speed, jumping ability, weight, etc.) one can measure (Santos 2014). Refer to figure 5.2 and 5.3, height is important because it allows a coach to predict a competitive advantage into the future at the high school level or next year at the collegiate upcoming season. A coach can gauge as to how "big" their recruiting class or current team could mature into; thus, height provides the most stable and significant competitive advantage or lack thereof for years into the future. A high school varsity coach can alter schemes and plays at the freshman and sophomore level to account for or take advantage of this attribute at the varsity level a year or two into the future. In a similar way, a collegiate coach may desire to redshirt an undersized (weight) freshman to allow for additional physical development.

Height values are also of increasing importance for female sport participants due to their limited ability to develop type 2 muscle fibers and substantially increase their bio-motor power expression

(Prince 1977, Springer 2001). Thus, for coaches, a special emphasis for recruiting and developing both tall male and female athletes is warranted. Height alone in many cases can predict overall future competitive sport success (Monsoon 2018). A male athlete who is below 6 ft. tall or female athlete that is below 5'4" is likely going to compete at a general disadvantage (undersized mismatch) and more than likely be unable to develop physically or express skills at a professional level for the more popular American team sports: basketball, football, hockey, etc. (Springer 2001, Monsoon, 2018).

Body Weight

As seen in figure 5.1, healthy humans have a range of lean mass adaptability when exposed to a predictive weight training stimulus, diet structure, and an aerobic conditioning program. Review the weight in pounds and the pounds per inch rows within the figure 5.1.

The Average Athletic Competitive Frame Metrics					
General Athlete	**Avg. Height Ranges**	**Weight Ranges**	**Pounds per Inch**	**Lean Mass Pounds**	**Fat Mass Pounds**
(Male)	6'.0" to 6'.5"	180 to 223	2.5 to 2.9	162 to 190	18 to 33
		LEAN MASS	**RATIO TO**	**FAT MASS**	**5.7–9 to 1**
(Female)	5'.5" to 6'.2"	120 to 166.5	1.85 to 2.25	102 to 137	18 to 29
		LEAN MASS	**RATIO TO**	**FAT MASS**	**4.7–5.6 to 1**

Figure 5.6. (D) Body Composition Ratios for Athletes

For competitive males, their ideal weight per pound range is approximately 2.5 to 2.9 pounds per inch of height, and for competitive females, the range is between 1.85 to 2.25 pounds per inch of height. Weight like height is a large component in the sport success equation. However, weight is not purely overall mass but rather ratios of tissues in the body termed body composition (muscle, fat, bone, water, organs). In athletics, the dominant ratio that portends the greatest sport success is the muscle mass to fat mass ratio. Knowing, understanding, and maximizing weight and muscle to fat ratios (ideally athletes need to be in range between 5 to 10 pounds of lean mass to 1 pound of fat) will allow players to adjust their diet and or conditioning program to enhance their ability to resist injury, improve recovery, increase bio-motor expression, optimize stamina, and maximize skill execution (Santos 2014, Monsoon 2018).

Weight can be greatly manipulated in most individuals and therefore must be effectively managed (via diet, weight training, water intake, and cardiovascular conditioning) to optimize their competitive potential. The larger, heavier athlete if more muscular in comparison to a smaller one when exposed to a similar training stimulus will get a larger muscular amplification and therefore become more dominant.

Size Matters 1.0					
General Athlete	**Avg. Height Ranges**	**Weight Ranges**	**Bench Press**	**Back Squat**	**Competitive Disadvantage**
(Male)	6'.0" to 6'.5"	180 to 223	225 to 279	315 to 390	
Smaller Males	**5'5" to 5'11"**	**162 to 206**	**203 to 258**	**284 to 360**	**22 to 30 lbs.**
(Female)	5'.5" to 6'.2"	120 to 166.5	120 to 166	150 to 208	
Smaller Females	**5'0" to 5'4"**	**111 to 144**	**111 to 144**	**139 to 180**	**9 to 28 lbs.**

Figure 5.7. Size Makes a Difference

Pounds per Inch

Pounds per inch provides the projected optimal adaptability a coach can expect with commitment to a proper eating and conditioning program. Lean mass should be approximately 85 to 90 percent of the male athlete's ideal weight and 82 to 88 percent of a female athlete's weight (Norton 2001, Santos 2014). Review the weight in pounds and the pounds per inch rows within figure 5.1. For competitive males, the approximate weight per pound range is between 2.5 lbs. to 2.9 lbs., and for competitive females, the range is between 1.85 lbs. to 2.25 lbs. A coach such be aware what their athletes' weight to effectively manage their conditioning commitments, diet requirements, and game utilization.

Size Matters 2.0					
General Athlete	Avg. Height Ranges	Pounds per Inch	Weight Ranges		Competitive Disadvantage
(Male)	6'.0" to 6'.5"	2.5 to 2.9 lbs.	180 to 223		
Smaller Males	**5'5" to 5'11"**		**162 to 206**		**17 to 18 lbs.**
(Female)	5'.5" to 6'.2"	1.85 to 2.25 lbs.	120 to 166.5		
Smaller Females	**5'0" to 5'4"**		**111 to 144**		**9 to 28 lbs.**

Figure 5.8. Size Makes a Difference 2.0

Lean Mass

Lean mass and *bone density* are two crucial pillars that provide an athlete with the foundation to build long-term strength, bio-motor expression, reduce injury risk, and master skill execution (Poliquin, 2001, Hoff 2016). The maximal development of lean mass can be accomplished for elementary up through middle school ages (10–13 years old), with a three-day-a-week calisthenic routine and adherence to proper daily behaviors (proper sleep of eight to nine hours a day and whole food intake with adequate calories) (Campbell 2011). It is recommended that once an athlete reaches high school competitive sports, they should engage in formal annual periodization resistance training program that utilize progressive loads with targeted compound exercises (Hoff 2016). If an athlete is training as previously mentioned, consuming the correct amounts of foods and living the proper lifestyle, the division one strength values can certainly be achieved within a four-year high school athletic career.

Male	8th-Grade Off-Season	9th-Grade Periodization	10th-Grade Periodization	11th-Grade Periodization	12th-Grade Periodization
Height	**5'11"**	**6'0"**	**6'1"**	**6'2"**	**6'3"**
Body Weight	156.5 2.2	162 2.25	168 2.3	174 2.35	180 2.4
Push-Up	25	50	75	100	100
Bench Press	80–115 lbs.	120–150 lbs.	155–195 lbs.	205–250 lbs.	250–280 lbs.
Back Squat	155–185 lbs.	195–245 lbs.	250–305 lbs.	315–355 lbs.	360–390 lbs.
Female	**8th-Grade Off-Season**	**9th-Grade Periodization**	**10th-Grade Periodization**	**11th-Grade Periodization**	**12th-Grade Periodization**
Height	**5'8"**	**5'10"**	**6'0"**	**6'0"**	**6'0"**
Body Weight	122	129	136	140	144
Push-Up	12	25	35	50	65
Bench Press	75–90 lbs.	95–115 lbs.	115–135 lbs.	140–160 lbs.	160–180 lbs.
Back Squat	115–135 lbs.	135–155 lbs.	155–175 lbs.	175–195 lbs.	195–215 lbs.

Figure 5.9. Division One Strength Progression

The one caveat to building peak lean mass is that prolonged high frequency aerobic conditioning sessions promote type 1 muscle conversion of the intermediate muscle fiber types, and it increases catabolic hormone levels in the body (Wilson 2012). Thus, high frequency combined with long duration aerobic sessions both degrades explosive type 2 lean mass and shifts muscular adaption to greater slow twitch muscle fiber type expression. High endurance athletes will only be able to support a limited amount of days per week (1 to 2) of intense strength training activities (Millet 2002). Review the cross country columns for male and female pounds per inch in figure 5.2. In both these athletic populations, the lean mass of these participants is significantly less than the standard athletic average.

Sport (Male)	Avg. Height Ranges	Weight Ranges	Lean Mass Pounds	Fat Mass Pounds	Peak Strength Comparative Disadvantage	
Basketball	6.3 to 7.2 ft.	185 to 250	164 to 212	19–38	**Bench** 265 to 180	**Squat** 365 to 250
Football	5.11 to 6.5 ft.	178 to 254	160 to 216	18–38	**Bench** 320 to 180	**Squat** 405 to 250
C. Country	5.0 to 5.11 ft	126 to 170	113 to 144	13–26	180	250

Figure 5.10. (E) Truncated Comparison of Peak Strength by Sport

Therefore, coaches in all sports must be aware of the impact of long duration aerobic conditioning programs or several weeks of two-a-day multi-hour practice sessions on the speed and power expression of their athlete's performance potential. These types of practice schedules will require cycling with recovery days and close monitoring of lean mass degradation. Failure to do so will place athletes at risk for considerable muscle loss (especially fast twitch) and thus reduction of in-season competitive advantage and individual athletic ability.

Fat Mass

In addition to managing overall weight and lean mass values of athletes, it is also important for coaches to be aware of their athletes' level of fat mass and overall fat percentage. For males, an athlete's fat percentage should not exceed 15 percent, and for females, no more than 20 percent (Miller 2012, Santos 2014).

Body Fat Percent Ranges						
Healthy to Wellness Ranges			Fitness to Varsity Sports		Division 1 to Pro	
Poor	**Fair**	**Average**	**Good**	**Excellent**	**Superior**	**Elite**
Males	Males	Males	Males	Males	Males	Males
>30%	**29 to 25%**	**25 to 20%**	**19 to 15%**	**14 to 11%**	**10 to 6%**	**≤5%**
Healthy to Wellness Ranges			Fitness to Varsity Sports		Division 1 to Pro	

Poor	Fair	Average	Poor	Fair	Average	Poor
Females	Females	Females	Females	Females	Females	Females
>35%	**35 to 30**	**29 to 25%**	**25 to 20%**	**19 to 15%**	**14 to 11%**	**10 to 6%**

Figure 5.11. Body Fat Values by Population

These percentages are general guidelines for body composition standards for most sports. However, there are several sports, sporting events, and positions within team sports where fat percent may need to vary substantially. Increased values can be found in football lineman, track-and-field shot put, hammer, discus, girls' softball, etc. and decreased values occur in wrestling, boxing, bodybuilding, figure skating, cheerleading, cross country, etc. In the instances of increased fat mass for enhanced sport performance, the diet of the athlete must remain nutritious and physiologically restorative. Coaches need to encourage larger athletes not to engage in poor lifestyle choices or eating practices. Athletes need to held accountable to make high-calorie healthy foods (nuts, seeds, olive oils, egg yolk, dark meat animal protein, grains, avocados, beans, dried fruit, starchy root vegetables, and fatty fish) their primary choices while maintaining their overweight or obese status. These obese or overweight athletes should still avoid excessive consumption of junk food and alcohol and follow recommended restorative practices, such as getting the required sleep hours and water intake. In sports that require extremely low levels of body fat, athletes will need to be consume low-calorie nutrient rich foods (organ meats, non-starchy vegetables, white meat, low-fat proteins, egg whites, leafy greens, citrus fruits, or berries) in abundance to avoid deficiency and maintain high levels of physiologic expression and tissue repair (Campbell 2011).

Sport Specific Physical Capacity Goals

The last component of the bigger, stronger, faster adage to be examined will be that of bio-motor expression "faster." Getting an athlete more explosive involves three areas of emphasis: (1) reaching an optimal weight, (2) creating optimal muscular strength, and (3) developing optimal neuromuscular control.

Bio-motor Optimization				
Optimize Athletic Weight Standards			**Optimize Peak Strength**	**Plyometric Progression**
Number 1			**Number 2**	**Number 3**
Male Height	Multiply by Pounds per Inch 2.4 to 2.9	= Ideal Weight **(x)**	**(B. Wt.)** Upper Body × 1.25 **(B. Wt.)** Lower Body × 1.75	Low Intensity & Volume **to** High Intensity & Volume
Female Height	Multiply by Pounds per Inch 1.85 to 2.25	= Ideal Weight **(x)**	**(B. Wt.)** Upper Body × 1.0 **(B. Wt.)** Lower Body × 1.5	Low Intensity & Volume **to** High Intensity & Volume

Figure 5.12. Increasing Bio-motor Expression

Figure 5.1 provided coaches with appropriate weight ranges for athletes based on their height and sport. Figure 5.2 provides strength goals based on their anthropometric metrics and sport demands. Figure 5.13 below illustrates how competitive collegiate level sport skills are expressed within a specific amount of muscular capability. It is important to remember that maximum height, strength, and speed are the three most significant variables that separate men from women and mediocre athletes from elite sport competitors.

Varsity Male Athletes							
Sport (Male)	**Vertical Leap**	**Broad Jump**	**40-Yard Dash**	**60-Sec. Speed Jump Rope**	**60-Sec. Double Jump Rope**	**5-10-5 Cone Drill**	**Seated (M. B.) Toss (Ft.)**
General Athlete	>25.5 (in)	>140 in	**<4.8**	>180	50	<4.5	>2 × Height
Varsity Female Athletes							
Sport (Female)	**Vertical Leap**	**Broad Jump**	**40-Yard Dash**	**60-Sec. Speed Jump Rope**	**60-Sec. Double Jump Rope**	**5-10-5 Cone Drill**	**Seated (M. B.) Toss (Ft.)**
General Athlete	>20.5 (in)	>90 in	**<5.5**	>150	25	<5	>1.5 × Height

Figure 5.13. Minimal Bio-motor Varsity Athletic Thresholds

Figure 5.13 depicts the functional expression of strength, mobility, and neurologic control of an athlete. These attributes combined are termed "athleticism" and best predict in a competitive environment were a strategic advantage or weakness can be exploited. Coaches as previously stated need to be aware that any improvement to these bio-motor skills will come through primarily increasing muscular strength, reducing weight, improving flexibility, and optimizing *neurologic control* via movement technique and plyometric training (Poliquin 2001, Hoff 2016).

Vertical Jump/Leap

Vertical leap is a test used to assess the ability to display lower body power and explosive strength. Test scores correlate strongly with vertical jumping ability and leg strength. In a competitive environment, it is easily observed by an individual leaping off the ground high above their competition.

Standing Long Jump Test (Broad Jump)

The *broad jump* is a test used to assess the ability to display lower body power, speed, and explosive strength. Test scores correlate strongly with running acceleration ability. In a competitive environment, it is easily observed by an individual being able to reach top speed in a limited number of steps.

Pro Agility Test (5-10-5 Cone Drill)

The *cone drill* is a test used to assess lateral quickness. Test scores correlate with multidirectional acceleration ability and general agility.

40-Yard Dash

The aim of the *40-yard dash* is to determine overall linear acceleration ability. This sprint distance is most associated with athletic speed maximum capability.

Jump Rope Drills

Jump rope drills are used to assess intramuscular coordination (hand-eye, foot-eye), total body power, balance, general coordination, and quickness. Test scores correlate with coordination, proprioception, and dexterity.

Medicine Ball Toss

The *medicine ball toss* is a test used to assess upper body power. Test scores correlate with maximal throwing, punching ability, and upper body strength.

When comparing these three attributes, athletic strength expression is the most modifiable through consistent participation in an athletic development program (see figure 5.9). An athlete cannot naturally enhance their height or drastically improve their top-end speed. Strength improvement by default becomes the physical variable that serves as the equalizer or gateway to athletic success when height and speed are average to suboptimal. An athlete who is stronger than their competitors will possess several competitive advantages:

1. **Injury reduction**—due to the stronger, thicker tissue being able tolerate reoccurring maximal forces
2. **Reduced fatigue**—strong athletes can produce greater repeated maximum and submaximal athletic efforts (jumps, sprints, throws, etc.), with lower total muscle contribution
3. **Improved recovery**—stronger athletes recuperate faster than their weaker counterparts and manage the intensity of their sport demands easier. The repeated practice bouts or intense game play will not require all their available muscular capacity.
4. **Increase daily performance**—bigger, thicker muscles will perform more "work" with less stress and trauma to its structure allowing for an increased average performance standard

Youth coaches and parents as previously mentioned should also note that competitive athletic strength and muscular endurance is arguably the "easiest" to develop of all the sport performance attributes (figure 5.9) if started at the appropriate age (twelve to fourteen years old). A commitment of two to four days a week beginning in middle school will allow most athletes to achieve division-one muscular strength thresholds in four to six years.

Coaches should look at figure 5.14 as a continuum of required strength development for optimum skill expression. The exercise max loads display ranges based on height. The taller the player is, the greater the shift to the lower weight range goals there initially needs to be. An example would be to take two Division I basketball players coming into a program looking to increase their upper body strength. One recruit is a center with a height of seven foot, the other a point guard with a height of six foot and four inches tall. A coach, if selecting the bench press as an example, would aim for the center to lift for a one-time repetition maximum weight load between his ideal body weight and 210 pounds. The smaller player would aim for a max load goal between his ideal body weight and 300 plus pounds.

Male Sport Strength Capacities																												
Sport (Male)	Bench Press		Seated Row		Barbell Squat		60 sec-Plank		Shoulder Press		Lat Pulldown		Prone Leg Curl		60 sec-Low Back Ext		Bicep Curl		Parrallel Dips		Seated Calf		Barbell Shrugs		60 sec-Side Plank		1 Mile Run	
Basketball	206	316	206	316	274	413	138	103	134	206	206	316	178	268	69	51	103	158	206	316	151	275	274	413	34	26	6	7:30
Volleyball	228	288	228	288	304	375	125	114	148	187	228	288	198	244	63	57	114	144	228	288	167	250	304	375	31	29	7	8:30
Swimming	210	265	210	265	280	345	115	105	137	172	210	265	182	224	58	53	105	132	210	265	154	230	280	345	29	26	7	8:30
Average Height Above Six Feet Three Inches																												
Tennis	177	278	177	278	236	363	121	89	115	181	177	278	153	236	61	44	89	139	177	278	130	242	236	363	30	22	6	7:30
Football	200	385	200	385	266	330	110	100	130	250	200	385	173	215	55	50	100	193	200	385	146	220	266	330	28	25	6	7:30
Hockey	183	290	183	290	244	363	121	92	119	189	183	290	159	236	61	46	92	145	183	290	134	242	244	363	30	23	7:00	8:00
Baseball	173	276	173	276	230	345	115	86	112	179	173	276	150	224	58	43	86	138	173	276	127	230	230	345	29	22	7:00	9:00
Track & Field	206	330	206	330	274	330	110	103	134	215	206	330	178	215	55	51	103	165	206	330	151	220	274	330	28	26	5:30	7:00
Average Height Above Six Feet and Below Six Feet Three Inches																												
Soccer	183	265	183	265	244	345	115	92	119	172	183	265	159	224	58	46	92	132	183	265	134	230	244	345	29	23	5:30	7:00
Cross Country	162	265	162	265	216	345	115	81	105	172	162	265	140	224	58	41	81	132	162	265	119	230	216	345	29	20	5:30	7:00
Golf	168	265	168	265	224	345	115	84	109	172	168	265	146	224	58	42	84	132	168	265	123	230	224	345	29	21	8:00	9:00
Bodybuilding	270	276	270	276	360	360	120	135	176	179	270	276	234	234	60	68	135	138	270	276	198	240	360	360	30	34	7:30	9:00
Wrestling	177	265	177	265	236	345	115	89	115	172	177	265	153	224	58	44	89	132	177	265	130	230	236	345	29	22	5:30	7:00
Average Height Above Five Feet and Eight Inches, Below Six Feet																												
General Athlete	206	253	206	253	274	330	110	103	134	164	206	253	178	215	55	51	103	127	206	253	151	220	274	330	28	26	6	7:15

Figure 5.14. (A) (Male Strength Goals by Sport)

Female Sport Strength Capacities																														
Sport (Female)	Bench Press		Seated Row		Barbell Squat		60 sec-Plank		Shoulder Press		Lat Pulldown		Prone Leg Curl		60 sec-Low Back Ext		Bicep Curl		Parrallel Dips		Seated Calf		Barbell Shrugs		60 sec- Side Pla		1 Mile Run	
Basketball	105	218	105	218	158	273	53	145	68	153	131	185	102	177	39	72	53	109	105	164	105	218	158	273	20	36	6:30	7:45
Volleyball	112	218	112	218	168	273	56	145	73	153	140	185	109	177	42	72	56	109	112	164	123	218	168	273	21	36	7:30	9:00
Swimming	111	187	111	187	167	234	56	124	72	131	139	159	108	152	42	62	56	94	111	140	122	187	167	234	21	31	7:30	9:00
Average Height Above Six Feet (Inches)																														
Tennis	108	224	108	224	162	280	54	149	70	157	135	190	105	182	41	74	54	112	108	168	119	224	162	280	20	37	6:45	8:30
Lacrosse	108	202	108	202	162	253	54	134	70	141	135	172	105	164	41	67	54	101	108	152	119	202	162	253	20	34	6:45	8:30
Field Hockey	108	176	108	176	162	220	54	117	70	123	135	150	105	143	41	59	54	88	108	132	119	176	162	220	20	29	7:15	8:30
Softball	108	196	108	196	162	245	54	130	70	137	135	167	105	159	41	65	54	98	108	147	119	196	162	245	20	33	8:00	9:00
Track & Field	108	177	108	177	162	221	54	118	70	124	135	150	105	144	41	59	54	89	108	133	119	177	162	221	20	29	6:30	7:30
Average Height Above Five Feet and five (inches)																														
Soccer	108	176	108	176	162	220	54	117	70	123	135	150	105	143	41	59	54	88	108	132	119	176	162	220	20	29	6:15	7:30
Cross Country	108	168	108	168	162	210	54	112	70	118	135	143	105	137	41	56	54	84	108	126	119	168	162	210	20	28	5:30	7:30
Golf	108	168	108	168	162	210	54	112	70	118	135	143	105	137	41	56	54	84	108	126	119	168	162	210	20	28	8:30	9:30
Bodybuilding	108	158	108	158	162	198	54	105	70	111	135	134	105	128	41	53	54	79	108	119	119	158	162	198	20	26	7:30	9:30
Cheerleading	95	158	95	158	143	198	48	105	62	111	119	134	93	128	36	53	48	79	95	119	105	158	143	198	18	26	6:30	7:30
Average Height Below Five Feet and five (inches)																														
General Athlete	112	196	112	196	168	245	56	130	73	137	131	185	109	159	42	65	56	98	112	147	123	196	168	245	21	33	6:45	7:15

Figure 5.15. (B) (Female Strength Goals by Sport)

Coaches can reassess their players' skill expression and bio-motor ability as they get stronger to see if greater strength levels or individual weight loss is required to increase individual or team success. This is so because smaller participants will become stronger relative to larger athletes faster. However, the smaller athlete when directly compared may not be stronger due to their size. Let me explain, take two seventh-grade kids, child one at 108 lbs. and child two at 136 lbs. Sport coaches and parents alike realize that "big" kids are less athletic than "smaller" kids. This is so because if both kids are untrained and have not developed their muscular strength, the smaller athlete has less overall mass to move and additionally has shorter arms and legs, reducing baseline inertia. The smaller kid who weighs less mass will have to overcome a smaller amount of resistance to move (run, jump, etc.) and to remain moving (i.e., stamina). Thus, smaller untrained athletes appear better conditioned and more athletic. The smaller child will have better speed, agility, and jumping capacity compared to the larger athlete. The larger kid who is significantly stronger and weighs 136 lbs. will have to either become considerably stronger or lose the excess weight if required to become equally athletic.

Attribute	***Untrained Child One***	***Untrained Child Two***	
Grade	*7th*	*7th*	
Height	*5 feet 0 inches*	*5 feet 8 inches*	
Weight	*108*	*136*	
Projected Upper Body Strength 30% of Total Body Weight	*32.4*	*40.8*	
Projected Lower Body Strength 50% of Total Body Weight	*54*	*68*	
Absolute Strength Upper Body	*X*	*+8.2 lbs.*	***One-on-One Competitive Advantage***: *Child Two*

Absolute Strength Lower Body	***X***	*+14 lbs.*	***One-on-One Competitive Advantage:*** *Child Two*
Relative Strength Upper Body (body weight required to overcome for movement)	*75.6 lbs.*	*95.2 lbs.*	***Greater Bio-motor Expression:*** *Child One (-20.4 lbs.)*
Relative Strength Lower Body (body weight required to overcome for movement)	*54 lbs.*	*68 lbs.*	***Greater Bio-motor Expression:*** *Child One (-14.4 lbs.)*

Figure 5.16. Relative to Absolute Strength Comparison

Relative strength is the amount of strength in direct comparison to individual body weight or how strong one is relative to their own weight. Thus, impacting an athlete's ability to control, transmit, and absorb force throughout their body in a competitive environment. In vision, a gymnast competing with a football player in all the individual events at a gymnastic meet. The football can probably lift more weight one time than the gymnast, but the football athlete also may outweigh the gymnast by two to three times. Thus, the football athlete will struggle considerably to manage their weight throughout space and in relation to the use of each gymnastic apparatus. The other end of the strength continuum is *absolute strength*, which is the maximum amount of force that can be generated whether against an object or another individual. Think of a strong man contest or a sumo wrestling match. Large, powerful, oversize athletes that usually lack speed endurance and frequent repetitive, successive, explosive muscular expression capability. The gymnast is no match for the lineman on the football field when paired to exchange force.

Coaches and players as a final thought need to understand that conditioning is not their actual sport and becoming better at performing conditioning exercises is not the end goal of a sport conditioning program but instead the means to improved athletic success. Chronic exercise can become detrimental and lead to injury or skill regression. Performing the requisite sport skills at an enhanced physical baseline level for the entire season is the conditioning program singular purpose.

Male Generalized Athlete Vs the General Population

Height	6 ft to 6' 5"	Height	5' 9" to 5' 11"
Weight	150 to 220	Weight	175 to 205
Muscle Mass	123 to 198	Muscle Mass	138 to 162
Fat Mass	14 to 22	Fat Mass	35 to 40
Mus./ Fat Ratio	9 to 1	Mus./ Fat Ratio	4 to 1
Neck	<18	Neck	<18
Shoulders Circ.	49 to 52 in	Shoulders Circ.	49 to 52 in
Waist Circ.	32 to 39 in	Waist Circ.	38 to 39 in
Hips Circ.	40 to 44	Hips Circ.	42 to 47
1 Mile Run Stationary Bike 10 min	5:30 to 7 min 3 to 4 Miles	1 Mile Run Stationary Bike 10 min	9:00 to 12 min 1.5 to 2.25 Miles
Bench Press	205 to 275 lbs.	Bench Press	100 to 185 lbs.
Leg Press	850 to 1250 lbs.	Leg Press	500 to 750 lbs.
60 sec. Sit-up	>55 Reps	60 sec. Sit-up	15 to 30 Reps

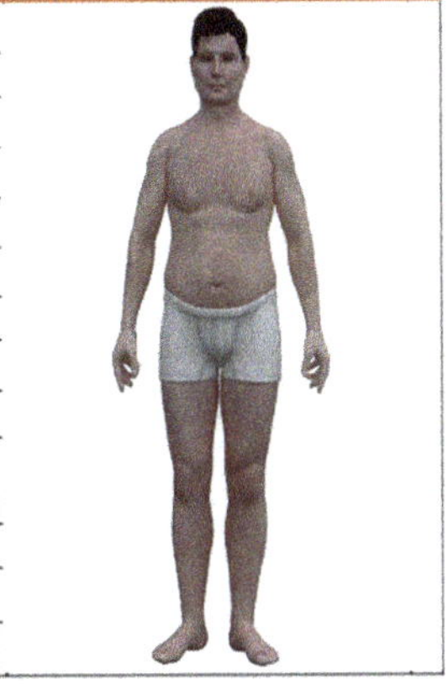

Figure 5.17. (A) Athletic to General Population Comparison (Male)

Female Generalized Athlete Vs the General Population

Height	5 ft to 6' 3"	Height	5' 2" to 5' 6"
Weight	110 to 158	Weight	125 to 150
Muscle Mass	91 to 130	Muscle Mass	87.5 to 105
Fat Mass	19 to 28	Fat Mass	37.5 to 45
Mus./ Fat Ratio	4-5 to 1	Mus./ Fat Ratio	2.5-3 to 1
Neck	<14	Neck	<14
Shoulders Circ.	37.5 to 46.5 in	Shoulders Circ.	43 to 52 in
Waist Circ.	26 to 32 in	Waist Circ.	33 to 40 in
Hips Circ.	34.5 to 42.5	Hips Circ.	39 to 48.5
1 Mile Run Stationary Bike 10 min	6:30 to 7:45 min 2.5 to 3 Miles	1 Mile Run Stationary Bike 10 min	9:00 to 12 min 1.5 to 2.25 Miles
Bench Press	90 to 165 lbs.	Bench Press	45 to 100 lbs.
Leg Press	450 to 650 lbs.	Leg Press	300 to 450 lbs.
60 sec. Sit-up	>50 Reps	60 sec. Sit-up	15 to 30 Reps

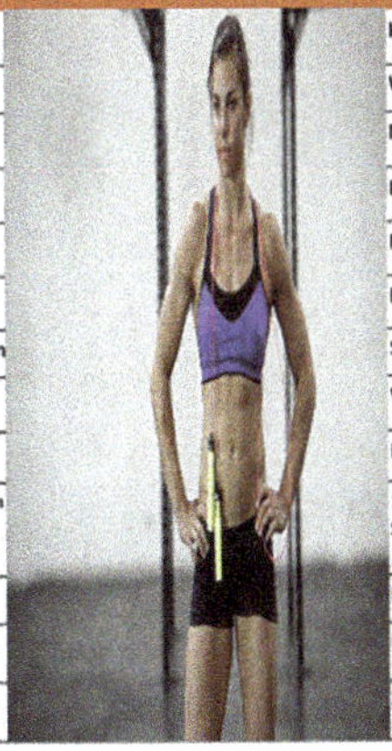

Figure 5.18 (B) Athletic to General Population Comparison (Female)

Figure 5.8 is used to illustrate to coaches and sport professionals that competitive athletes look distinct and adapt to generalized stress very differently than their nonathletic counterparts. Athletes are bigger and considerably more muscular. Their recovery and growth are regulated by anabolic and catabolic hormone production, the balance between the two, and the sensitivity of the body tissues to each (Poliquin 2001, Santos 2016, Monson 2018).

The majority of individuals in a given population are not born with the biologic design or adaptive potential to become elite professional athletes or compete robustly at the Division I level of a particular sport (Santos 2014, Monsoon 2018). As a coach, parent, or sport participant, it is critical to understand this point when performing, administering, or participating in a physical strength and conditioning program. A comprehensive, well-designed training program will raise the average individual's level of physical ability and conditioning level from above average to good or good to excellent. However, professional standards of elite speed, jumping ability, motor control, or strength cannot be produced without a significant level of inherent genetic potential (Norton 2001, Monsoon 2018). These facts can be a sobering and depressing reality for determined athletes, supportive parents, and hopeful coaches, but it does not make the truth any less factual.

Sport performance professionals with the training and coaching techniques, supplements, and even drugs available today cannot on demand manufacture an athlete with elite bio-motor capability (Norton 2001, Poliquin 2001). These individuals are stochastic in the population. Therefore, when accessing player sport potential, one should include some physical evaluation of the athlete's stature, muscular capacity, and parental sport background, as well as their willingness to earnestly work on their skills. Early and proper identification of the available pool of natural talent in the surrounding area is critical for building a year-to-year highly competitive program. Recruiting and developing the youth in the school district who possess the key physical attributes to succeed in sport will create a dominant advantage for any sporting program within a region. In addition, any varsity level coach should engage in routine (monthly) communication with physical education teachers within your school district feeder junior high and grade school levels to keep an eye out for undiscovered talent.

In summary, developing elite performance athletes is not possible. Developing highly skilled athletes who have athletic ability that is above average to excellent, however, is quite possible. Athletes who want to earn Division I scholarship will need to enhance their physical capacity to a point that does not put them at a competitive disadvantage. Sports performance programs will enhance any athlete, but it will not make them elite level. Physical size, inherent bio-motor ability, and skill level will be the three pivotal factors. The next chapters will discuss how to structure the athlete's day to include dedication to sport and education while allowing some recovery. Chapter 7 will introduce how to properly replenish and feed the athletic body for optimal growth and recovery, and lastly chapter 8 will provide an overview on how to construct an annual plan of muscular development and skill refinement for college scholarship potential.

Summary of Key Points

Major Concepts	Review Pages
Sport Specific Optimal Physiques	
Physical Development Guidelines	
Minimal Bio-Motor Thresholds for Competitive Sports	

Trainer's Corner

Professional Insights	Video Links
"Sport Specific Optimal Physiques"	
"Sport Specific Minimal Capacities"	
"Performing Team Evaluations"	

Discussion Questions:

1. *Elite athleticism* is easy to produce, it comes down to working hard in an intense annual strength program. True/False
2. The majority of the people born in society today have the mental and physical capacity to be a Division I scholarship recipient. True/False

3. The three attributes that produce the greatest competitive advantage in sport are height, strength, and speed, which of the three is most significant?
4. The three attributes that produce the greatest competitive advantage in sport are height, strength, and speed, which of the three is most modifiable?
5. When comparing male and female athletes, the ability to build muscle and enhance bio-motor ability is similar. True/False
6. When comparing young untrained athletes, the smaller athletes will appear to be more athletic and possess greater stamina. True/False
7. The majority of youth athletes can attain the Division I strength standards for scholarship candidacy in what time frame?
8. Athletes who participate in long duration, high frequency aerobic training, or skill practice sessions will induce fast twitch muscle fiber breakdown or conversion to slower twitch fiber types. True/False
9. The younger athletes (pre high school) should primarily focus on body weight exercise mastery and skill refinement opposed to entering a formal resistance annual program. True/False
10. When looking to optimize bio-motor ability in athletes, coaches should recommend what three basic practices?

CHAPTER 6

APPLIED PROGRAM DESIGN

Key Terms	Page
Postseason—the period of an athletic year following the competitive sport season used to heal injuries and restore muscular symmetry to the body	
Off-Season—the time of year when an athlete is most self-directed in their development and is not engaging in sanctioned competition or obligated by a mandated team practice regimen	

Preseason—the time frame before the start of the competitive sport season used to get the athlete into optimal physical condition through mandated physical training sessions and skill refinement practices	
In-Season—the largest time frame of the year in which an athlete actively engages in sanctioned competitive events and structured practice sessions	
Emotional Stability—the balanced recognition and expression of positive and negative feelings as one fails and succeeds at achieving goals	
Mental Stability—is the acceptance of one's current ability, talent, and role as they work to improve their capacity, value, and contribution to the individuals and or organization around them	
Periodization—the strategic implementation of distinct training phases for developing specific aspects of performance, most commonly, endurance, strength, hypertrophy, power, and recovery	
Skill Instructors—A practitioner that instills, corrects, or modifies fundamental or advanced movement patterns (mechanics) that allows an athlete to express a coordinated pattern properly in a competitive environment. Examples include throwing, shooting, catching, kicking, swinging, etc.	
Performance Trainer—A practitioner that develops the body and mind to prepare an athlete for the demands of a specific sport or achieve a specific quantifiable outcome. It differs from a personal trainer or a speed coach in that the athlete is developed with precision opposed to enhanced in a broader qualitative manner.	

Structuring the Program

Chapter 6 is about providing coaches with a framework to understand the annual planning cycle of sport development referred to as periodization and the successful relational structure between coaches, parents, players, skill instructors, and performance coaches that accompany each season. The periodization process should be followed by a competitive varsity level athlete who has at least mastered (fifty consecutive repetitions) level 4 body weight exercise. The athlete without a sufficient strength foundation should begin with the phase 1 plan presented in chapter 2. The competitive varsity athlete should start with the post- or off-season cycle when starting the periodization program for the first time.

Postseason
Primary Goal: Physical, Emotional, Social, and Psychological Recovery
Cardiovascular Training Focus: Low Intensity, Low Impact Aerobic Conditioning
Resistance Training Focus: Isometric and Unilateral Dumbbell High Repetition Training
Skill Training: None/Recreational Play
Agility Drills: None
Competitive Play: None
Duration: Four to Twelve Weeks

The post season is the immediate time frame after the competitive sport cycle. The in-season phase is the most emotionally and psychologically taxing on the athlete, which often necessitates substantial time off from active sport participation, teammate relationships, and management by coaching staff. This time is best used to reconnect with loved ones, restore social balance, address academic concerns, and restore motivation to improve skills and athletic capability. The physical energy that is allocated in this phase should be used to address the following: heal current injuries, reestablish optimal movement mechanics due to past injury or muscular overuse, and correct muscular imbalances that have occurred due to performing recurring asymmetrical sport patterns (throwing, kicking, catching, jumping, swinging, shooting, etc.). The table below depicts postseason exercise with dumbbells that can be performed either unilaterally or bilaterally. Weight loads begin modestly and progress heavier each week. The routine can be followed three or four days a week with a day apart for recovery. The postseason of the three phases is the most individualized. Athletes can enter the off-season cycle after four weeks at any point on the twelve-week continuum. As a rule, athletes that are injured, struggling academically, or in need of social reconnection should extend their postseason to minimally eight weeks up to the full twelve weeks.

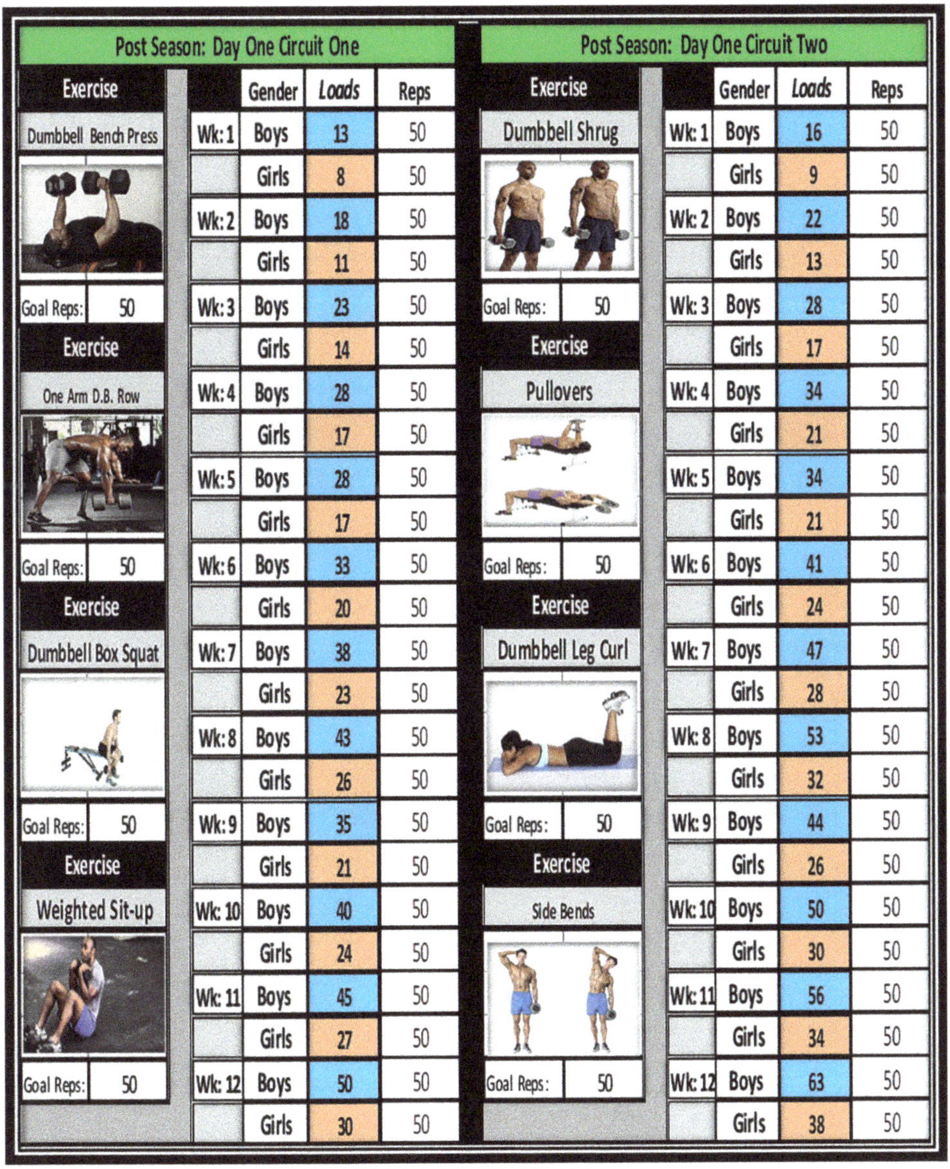

Post Season: Day One Circuit One

Exercise	Goal Reps
Dumbbell Bench Press	50
One Arm D.B. Row	50
Dumbbell Box Squat	50
Weighted Sit-up	50

	Gender	Loads	Reps
Wk: 1	Boys	13	50
	Girls	8	50
Wk: 2	Boys	18	50
	Girls	11	50
Wk: 3	Boys	23	50
	Girls	14	50
Wk: 4	Boys	28	50
	Girls	17	50
Wk: 5	Boys	28	50
	Girls	17	50
Wk: 6	Boys	33	50
	Girls	20	50
Wk: 7	Boys	38	50
	Girls	23	50
Wk: 8	Boys	43	50
	Girls	26	50
Wk: 9	Boys	35	50
	Girls	21	50
Wk: 10	Boys	40	50
	Girls	24	50
Wk: 11	Boys	45	50
	Girls	27	50
Wk: 12	Boys	50	50
	Girls	30	50

Post Season: Day One Circuit Two

Exercise	Goal Reps
Dumbbell Shrug	50
Pullovers	50
Dumbbell Leg Curl	50
Side Bends	50

	Gender	Loads	Reps
Wk: 1	Boys	16	50
	Girls	9	50
Wk: 2	Boys	22	50
	Girls	13	50
Wk: 3	Boys	28	50
	Girls	17	50
Wk: 4	Boys	34	50
	Girls	21	50
Wk: 5	Boys	34	50
	Girls	21	50
Wk: 6	Boys	41	50
	Girls	24	50
Wk: 7	Boys	47	50
	Girls	28	50
Wk: 8	Boys	53	50
	Girls	32	50
Wk: 9	Boys	44	50
	Girls	26	50
Wk: 10	Boys	50	50
	Girls	30	50
Wk: 11	Boys	56	50
	Girls	34	50
Wk: 12	Boys	63	50
	Girls	38	50

Figure 6.1. (A) Postseason Day One

Daily Commitment			Day Two Circuit One			
Physical Hours	0 to 1.5		Boys	6'3"	185	278
Skill Training ho	0 to 1		Girls	5'7"	125	156
Post Season (Divide the weight in half for the shoulder extension)						
Exercise				Gender	Loads	Reps
umbbell Shoulder Pre			Wk: 1	Boys	9	50
				Girls	5	50
			Wk: 2	Boys	12	50
				Girls	7	50
Goal Reps:	50		Wk: 3	Boys	16	50
Exercise				Girls	9	50
Shoulder Extension			Wk: 4	Boys	19	50
				Girls	12	50
			Wk: 5	Boys	19	50
				Girls	12	50
Goal Reps:	50		Wk: 6	Boys	23	50
Exercise				Girls	14	50
Cross-Over Lunges			Wk: 7	Boys	26	50
				Girls	16	50
			Wk: 8	Boys	30	50
				Girls	18	50
Goal Reps:	50		Wk: 9	Boys	25	50
Exercise				Girls	15	50
Weighted Leg lifts			Wk: 10	Boys	28	50
				Girls	17	50
			Wk: 11	Boys	32	50
				Girls	19	50
Goal Reps:	50	11	Wk: 12	Boys	35	50
Goal Reps:	50	6		Girls	21	50

Daily Commitment		Day Two Circuit Two			
Physical Hours	0 to 1.5	Boys	6'3"	185	278
Skill Training ho	0 to 1	Girls	5'7"	125	156
Post Season (Divide the weight in half for the Contralateral Tap)					
Exercise			Gender	Loads	Reps
Dumbbell Curls		Wk: 1	Boys	6	50
			Girls	4	50
		Wk: 2	Boys	9	50
			Girls	5	50
Goal Reps:	50	Wk: 3	Boys	11	50
Exercise			Girls	7	50
Dumbbell Overhead Ext.		Wk: 4	Boys	14	50
			Girls	8	50
		Wk: 5	Boys	14	50
			Girls	8	50
Goal Reps:	50	Wk: 6	Boys	16	50
Exercise			Girls	10	50
Weighted Lateral Step-up		Wk: 7	Boys	19	50
			Girls	11	50
		Wk: 8	Boys	21	50
			Girls	13	50
Goal Reps:	50	Wk: 9	Boys	18	50
Exercise			Girls	11	50
Quadraped Contralateral Ta		Wk: 10	Boys	20	50
			Girls	12	50
		Wk: 11	Boys	23	50
			Girls	14	50
Goal Reps:	50	Wk: 12	Boys	25	50
			Girls	15	50

Figure 6.2. (B) Postseason Day Two

Post Season

Exercise	
Dumbbell Wrist Curl	

Goal Reps:	50
Exercise	
Dumbbell Wrist Extension	

Goal Reps:	50
Exercise	
Standing 1 Leg Calf Raise	
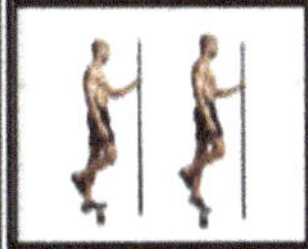	
Goal Reps:	50
Exercise	
Side Plank Taps	

Goal Reps:	50

	Gender	Loads	Reps
Wk: 1	Boys	5	50
	Girls	3	50
Wk: 2	Boys	7	50
	Girls	4	50
Wk: 3	Boys	10	50
	Girls	6	50
Wk: 4	Boys	12	50
	Girls	7	50
Wk: 5	Boys	12	50
	Girls	7	50
Wk: 6	Boys	14	50
	Girls	8	50
Wk: 7	Boys	16	50
	Girls	10	50
Wk: 8	Boys	18	50
	Girls	11	50
Wk: 9	Boys	15	50
	Girls	9	50
Wk: 10	Boys	17	50
	Girls	10	50
Wk: 11	Boys	19	50
	Girls	11	50
Wk: 12	Boys	21	50
	Girls	13	50

Post Season

Exercise	
Isometric Strengthening	

Goal Reps:	120 sec. Hold
Exercise	
Isometric Strengthening	

Goal Reps:	120 sec. Hold
Exercise	
Isometric Strengthening	

Goal Reps:	120 sec. Hold
Exercise	
Isometric Strengthening	

Goal Reps:	120 sec. Hold

	Gender	Loads	Tension Sec.
Wk: 1	Boys	Body Wt.	5
	Girls	Body Wt.	10
Wk: 2	Boys	Body Wt.	15
	Girls	Body Wt.	20
Wk: 3	Boys	Body Wt.	25
	Girls	Body Wt.	30
Wk: 4	Boys	Body Wt.	35
	Girls	Body Wt.	40
Wk: 5	Boys	Body Wt.	45
	Girls	Body Wt.	50
Wk: 6	Boys	Body Wt.	55
	Girls	Body Wt.	60
Wk: 7	Boys	Body Wt.	65
	Girls	Body Wt.	70
Wk: 8	Boys	Body Wt.	75
	Girls	Body Wt.	80
Wk: 9	Boys	Body Wt.	85
	Girls	Body Wt.	90
Wk: 10	Boys	Body Wt.	95
	Girls	Body Wt.	100
Wk: 11	Boys	Body Wt.	105
	Girls	Body Wt.	110
Wk: 12	Boys	Body Wt.	115
	Girls	Body Wt.	120

Figure 6.3. (B) Postseason Day Three

Off-Season
Primary Goal: Physical Development and Skill Improvement
Cardiovascular Training Focus: Low to Moderate Intensity, Aerobic Conditioning
Resistance Training Focus: Heavy Load, Barbell, Moderate Repetition Training
Skill Training: Self and Professionally Directed
Agility Drills: Low to Moderate Intensity
Competitive Play: Summer League, Travel Teams, AAU Participation, Camps
Duration: Four to Twenty Weeks

The off-season is the time frame most strongly associated with weight training, agility development, and individual skill practice. Athletes after the postseason phase will need to increase total body muscular strength and size before returning to maximum velocity speed, skill, and power training. Athletes are encouraged to perform two distinct training sessions divided by a least three hours to eat and recover between workouts. The resistance training session is advised to be the first workout of the two due to most athletes being better focused earlier and having the basic priority of becoming stronger. The agility session if performed should be prior to lifting weights. Agility drills will vary widely by the sport and age of the athlete, but foundational exercises will utilize cones, a ladder, and a jump rope. Athletes should schedule their skill practice several hours later after a meal and adequate recovery has occurred.

The off-season phase does allow some flexibility in scheduling and inclusion of family functions and limited social activities. Athletes must schedule these events carefully in a manner that does not impact physical or psychological recovery. Resistance routines and agility drills should be performed three days a week with a day apart for recovery. Skill training session should be scheduled at least five days a week.

Daily Commitment	
Physical Hour	1 to 3
Skill Training	2 to 4

Day One Circuit One			
Boys	6'3"	185	278
Girls	5'7"	125	156

Off Season

Exercise		Gender	*Loads*	Reps
Barbell Bench Press	Wk: 1	Boys	118	8-8-8.
		Girls	66	8-8-8.
	Wk: 2	Boys	130	6-6-6.
		Girls	73	6-6-6.
Goal Reps: 12-12-12	Wk: 3	Boys	142	4-4-4.
Exercise		Girls	80	4-4-4.
Barbell Row	Wk: 4	Boys	153	2-2-2.
		Girls	86	2-2-2.
	Wk: 5	Boys	130	12-10-8.
		Girls	73	12-10-8.
Goal Reps: 12-12-12	Wk: 6	Boys	142	10-8-6.
Exercise		Girls	80	10-8-6.
Barbell Squat	Wk: 7	Boys	153	8-6-4.
		Girls	86	8-6-4.
	Wk: 8	Boys	165	6-4-2.
		Girls	93	6-4-2.
Goal Reps: 12-12-12	Wk: 9	Boys	165	12-12-12.
Exercise		Girls	93	12-12-12.
Weighted Plank	Wk: 10	Boys	177	12-10-8.
		Girls	100	12-10-8.
	Wk: 11	Boys	189	12-6-4.
		Girls	106	12-6-4.
127.5 / Add 10 sec	Wk: 12	Boys	236	12-4-2.
65 / per week		Girls	133	12-4-2.

Daily Commitment	
Physical Hours	0 to 1.5
Skill Training ho	0 to 1

Day One Circuit Two			
Boys	6'3"	185	278
Girls	5'7"	125	156

Off Season

Exercise		Gender	*Loads*	Reps
Barbell Shrug	Wk: 1	Boys	118	8-8-8.
		Girls	66	8-8-8.
	Wk: 2	Boys	130	6-6-6.
		Girls	73	6-6-6.
Goal Reps: 12-12-12.	Wk: 3	Boys	142	4-4-4.
Exercise		Girls	80	4-4-4.
Lat Pulldown	Wk: 4	Boys	153	2-2-2.
		Girls	86	2-2-2.
	Wk: 5	Boys	130	12-10-8.
		Girls	73	12-10-8.
Goal Reps: 12-12-12.	Wk: 6	Boys	142	10-8-6.
Exercise		Girls	80	10-8-6.
Deadlift	Wk: 7	Boys	153	8-6-4.
		Girls	86	8-6-4.
	Wk: 8	Boys	165	6-4-2.
		Girls	93	6-4-2.
Goal Reps: 12-12-12.	Wk: 9	Boys	165	12-12-12.
Exercise		Girls	93	12-12-12.
Weighted Side Plank	Wk: 10	Boys	177	12-10-8.
		Girls	100	12-10-8.
	Wk: 11	Boys	189	12-6-4.
		Girls	106	12-6-4.
60 / Add 10 sec	Wk: 12	Boys	236	12-4-2.
30 / per week		Girls	133	12-4-2.

Figure 6.4. (A) Off-Season Day One

Daily Commitment	
Physical Hours	0 to 1.5
Skill Training ho	0 to 1

Day Two Circuit One			
Boys	6'3''	185	278
Girls	5'7''	125	156

Off Season

Exercise	
Barbell Curls	

Goal Reps:	12-12-12.
Exercise	
Tricep French Press	
Goal Reps:	12-12-12.
Exercise	
Smith Machine Lateral Step -up	
Goal Reps:	12-12-12.
Exercise	
Weighted Bridge	
128	Add 10 sec per week
65	

	Gender	*Loads*	Reps
Wk: 1	Boys	59	8-8-8.
	Girls	33	8-8-8.
Wk: 2	Boys	65	6-6-6.
	Girls	37	6-6-6.
Wk: 3	Boys	71	4-4-4.
	Girls	40	4-4-4.
Wk: 4	Boys	77	2-2-2.
	Girls	43	2-2-2.
Wk: 5	Boys	65	12-10-8.
	Girls	37	12-10-8.
Wk: 6	Boys	71	10-8-6.
	Girls	40	10-8-6.
Wk: 7	Boys	77	8-6-4.
	Girls	43	8-6-4.
Wk: 8	Boys	83	6-4-2.
	Girls	46	6-4-2.
Wk: 9	Boys	83	12-12-12.
	Girls	46	12-12-12.
Wk: 10	Boys	88	12-10-8.
	Girls	50	12-10-8.
Wk: 11	Boys	94	12-6-4.
	Girls	53	12-6-4.
Wk: 12	Boys	118	12-4-2.
	Girls	66	12-4-2.

Daily Commitment	
Physical Hours	0 to 1.5
Skill Training ho	0 to 1

Day Two Circuit Two			
Boys	6'3''	185	278
Girls	5'7''	125	156

Off Season (divide the weight in half for the upright row)

Exercise	
Barbell Shoulder Press	

Goal Reps:	12-12-12.
Exercise	
Upright Row Snatch	
Goal Reps:	12-12-12.
Exercise	
Smith Machine Cross-Over Lunge	
Goal Reps:	12-12-12.
Exercise	
Side Leg Raise Hold	
11	Add 10 sec per week
6.5	

	Gender	*Loads*	Reps
Wk: 1	Boys	77	8-8-8.
	Girls	43	8-8-8.
Wk: 2	Boys	84	6-6-6.
	Girls	47	6-6-6.
Wk: 3	Boys	92	4-4-4.
	Girls	52	4-4-4.
Wk: 4	Boys	100	2-2-2.
	Girls	56	2-2-2.
Wk: 5	Boys	84	12-10-8.
	Girls	47	12-10-8.
Wk: 6	Boys	92	10-8-6.
	Girls	52	10-8-6.
Wk: 7	Boys	100	8-6-4.
	Girls	56	8-6-4.
Wk: 8	Boys	107	6-4-2.
	Girls	60	6-4-2.
Wk: 9	Boys	107	12-12-12.
	Girls	60	12-12-12.
Wk: 10	Boys	115	12-10-8.
	Girls	65	12-10-8.
Wk: 11	Boys	123	12-6-4.
	Girls	69	12-6-4.
Wk: 12	Boys	153	12-4-2.
	Girls	86	12-4-2.

Figure 6.5. (B) Off-Season Day Two

Daily Commitment	
Physical Hours	0 to 1.5
Skill Training ho	0 to 1

Day Three Circuit One			
Boys	6'3"	185	278
Girls	5'7"	125	156

Off Season (divide the weight in half for the wrist ext)

Exercise	
Barbell Wrist Curl	

Goal Reps:	12-12-12.
Exercise	
Barbell Wrist Ext.	

Goal Reps:	12-12-12.
Exercise	
D.B. Standing 1 Foot Calf Raise	

Goal Reps:	12-12-12.
Exercise	
Dumbbell Tibialis Raise	

Goal Reps:	12-12-12.

	Gender	*Loads*	Reps
Wk: 1	Boys	50	8-8-8.
	Girls	28	8-8-8.
Wk: 2	Boys	55	6-6-6.
	Girls	31	6-6-6.
Wk: 3	Boys	60	4-4-4.
	Girls	34	4-4-4.
Wk: 4	Boys	65	2-2-2.
	Girls	37	2-2-2.
Wk: 5	Boys	55	12-10-8.
	Girls	31	12-10-8.
Wk: 6	Boys	60	10-8-6.
	Girls	34	10-8-6.
Wk: 7	Boys	65	8-6-4.
	Girls	37	8-6-4.
Wk: 8	Boys	70	6-4-2.
	Girls	40	6-4-2.
Wk: 9	Boys	70	12-12-12.
	Girls	40	12-12-12.
Wk: 10	Boys	75	12-10-8.
	Girls	42	12-10-8.
Wk: 11	Boys	80	12-6-4.
	Girls	45	12-6-4.
Wk: 12	Boys	100	12-4-2.
	Girls	56	12-4-2.

Daily Commitment	
Physical Hours	0 to 1.5
Skill Training ho	0 to 1

Day Three Circuit Two			
Boys	6'3"	185	278
Girls	5'7"	125	156

O. S. (1 Set: Concentric Slow -Eccentric Slow -Normal- Static Hold)

Exercise	
Dumbbell Ext. Rotation	
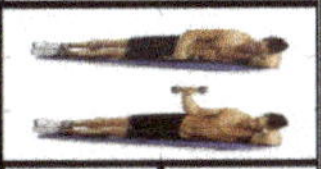	
Goal Reps:	12-12-12.
Exercise	
Horizontal Adduction	

Goal Reps:	12-12-12.
Exercise	
Lying Abduction	

Goal Reps:	12-12-12.
Exercise	
Dumbbell Internal Rotation	

Goal Reps:	12-12-12.

	Gender	*Loads*	Reps
Wk: 1	Boys	12	8-8-8-8.
	Girls	7	8-8-8-8.
Wk: 2	Boys	13	6-6-6-6.
	Girls	7	6-6-6-6.
Wk: 3	Boys	14	4-4-4-4.
	Girls	8	4-4-4-4.
Wk: 4	Boys	15	2-2-2-2.
	Girls	9	2-2-2-2.
Wk: 5	Boys	13	10-10-10-10
	Girls	7	10-10-10-10
Wk: 6	Boys	14	8-8-8-8.
	Girls	8	8-8-8-8.
Wk: 7	Boys	15	6-6-6-6.
	Girls	9	6-6-6-6.
Wk: 8	Boys	17	4-4-4-4.
	Girls	9	4-4-4-4.
Wk: 9	Boys	17	12-12-12-12.
	Girls	9	12-12-12-12.
Wk: 10	Boys	18	10-10-10-10
	Girls	10	10-10-10-10
Wk: 11	Boys	19	8-8-8-8.
	Girls	11	8-8-8-8.
Wk: 12	Boys	24	6-6-6-6.
	Girls	13	6-6-6-6.

Figure 6.6. (C) Off-Season Day Three

Preseason
Primary Goal: Physical Conditioning and Skill Improvement
Cardiovascular Training Focus: High to Moderate Intensity, Aerobic, and Anaerobic Conditioning
Resistance Training Focus: Heavy Load, Barbell, Moderate Repetition Training
Skill Training: Self, Program, and Professionally Directed
Agility Drills: High to Moderate Intensity
Competitive Play: Summer League, Travel Teams, AAU Participation, Camps
Duration: Four to Eight Weeks

The preseason strength and conditioning phase prepare an athlete for the strenuous upcoming season. The preseason of the four phases is the shortest, most intense cycle and includes all aspects of sport conditioning. Unique to the preseason is the higher volume of sport-related activities and metabolic conditioning demands. This combination places increased demands on diet, sleep, and social availability. The athlete will experience the greatest physical fatigue and reduction in social life during this phase as well. The athlete's physical and skill strengths and weaknesses will determine the frequency, duration, and intensity of their preseason program to get them ready for the season. The preseason program will usually have a team-structured cardiovascular conditioning and agility session, supervised skill practice sessions, and limited periods of intrateam competition. The athlete will have to either substitute skill training or intrateam competition time to improve their conditioning level or spend extra personal time each week outside of team-sponsored activities. Preseason strength and conditioning is very challenging, it is designed to transition athletes into peak sports condition for the season. Exercise is high repetition and explosive patterns with little rest intervals. Preseason resistance plans are to be performed three or four days a week, in combination with five to six days a week cardiovascular conditioning and skill training sessions.

Pre-season Exercise Reccomendations

Exercise	Goal Reps
Med Ball Chest Pass	50 to 100
Med Ball Swings	50 to 100
Med. Ball Leg Ext.	50 to 100
Sit-up Toss	50 to 100

	Gender	Loads	Reps
Wk: 1	Boys	M1: 14	10 to 20
	Girls	M1: 8	5 to 10
Wk: 2	Boys	M1: 14	20 to 40
	Girls	M1: 8	10 to 20
Wk: 3	Boys	M1: 14	30 to 60
	Girls	M1: 8	15 to 30
Wk: 4	Boys	M1: 14	40 to 80
	Girls	M1: 8	20 to 40
Wk: 5	Boys	M2: 20	30 to 45
	Girls	M2: 12	15 to 35
Wk: 6	Boys	M2: 20	35 to 60
	Girls	M2: 12	20 to 45
Wk: 7	Boys	M2: 20	40 to 75
	Girls	M2: 12	25 to 55
Wk: 8	Boys	M2: 20	45 to 90
	Girls	M2: 12	30 to 65
Wk: 9	Boys	M3: 30	20 to 40
	Girls	M3: 16	20 to 45
Wk: 10	Boys	M3: 30	30 to 60
	Girls	M3: 16	25 to 55
Wk: 11	Boys	M3: 30	40 to 80
	Girls	M3: 16	30 to 65
Wk: 12	Boys	M3: 30	50 to 100
	Girls	M3: 16	35 to 75

Pre-season Exercise Reccomendations

Exercise	Goal Reps
Med. Ball Halos	50 to 100
Lat Swings	50 to 100
Med. Ball Prone Curl	50 to 100
Russian Twist Slams	50 to 100

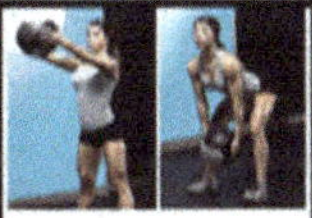

	Gender	Loads	Reps
Wk: 1	Boys	M1: 14	10 to 20
	Girls	M1: 8	5 to 10
Wk: 2	Boys	M1: 14	20 to 40
	Girls	M1: 8	10 to 20
Wk: 3	Boys	M1: 14	30 to 60
	Girls	M1: 8	15 to 30
Wk: 4	Boys	M1: 14	40 to 80
	Girls	M1: 8	20 to 40
Wk: 5	Boys	M2: 20	30 to 45
	Girls	M2: 12	15 to 35
Wk: 6	Boys	M2: 20	35 to 60
	Girls	M2: 12	20 to 45
Wk: 7	Boys	M2: 20	40 to 75
	Girls	M2: 12	25 to 55
Wk: 8	Boys	M2: 20	45 to 90
	Girls	M2: 12	30 to 65
Wk: 9	Boys	M3: 30	20 to 40
	Girls	M3: 16	20 to 45
Wk: 10	Boys	M3: 30	30 to 60
	Girls	M3: 16	25 to 55
Wk: 11	Boys	M3: 30	40 to 80
	Girls	M3: 16	30 to 65
Wk: 12	Boys	M3: 30	50 to 100
	Girls	M3: 16	35 to 75

Figure 6.7. (A) Preseason Day One

Pre-season Exercise Reccomendations				
Exercise		Gender	Loads	Reps
Bicep Curl Speed Toss	Wk: 1	Boys	M1: 14	10 to 20
		Girls	M1: 8	5 to 10
	Wk: 2	Boys	M1: 14	20 to 40
		Girls	M1: 8	10 to 20
Goal Reps: 50 to 100	Wk: 3	Boys	M1: 14	30 to 60
Exercise		Girls	M1: 8	15 to 30
Tricep Slams	Wk: 4	Boys	M1: 14	40 to 80
		Girls	M1: 8	20 to 40
	Wk: 5	Boys	M2: 20	30 to 45
		Girls	M2: 12	15 to 35
Goal Reps: 50 to 100	Wk: 6	Boys	M2: 20	35 to 60
Exercise		Girls	M2: 12	20 to 45
Lateral lunge w/Med Ball	Wk: 7	Boys	M2: 20	40 to 75
		Girls	M2: 12	25 to 55
	Wk: 8	Boys	M2: 20	45 to 90
		Girls	M2: 12	30 to 65
Goal Reps: 50 to 100	Wk: 9	Boys	M3: 30	20 to 40
Exercise		Girls	M3: 16	20 to 45
Med ball Low Back Ext.	Wk: 10	Boys	M3: 30	30 to 60
		Girls	M3: 16	25 to 55
	Wk: 11	Boys	M3: 30	40 to 80
		Girls	M3: 16	30 to 65
Goal Reps: 50 to 100	Wk: 12	Boys	M3: 30	50 to 100
		Girls	M3: 16	35 to 75

Pre-season Exercise Reccomendations				
Exercise		Gender	Loads	Reps
Shoulder Press Toss	Wk: 1	Boys	M1: 14	10 to 20
		Girls	M1: 8	5 to 10
	Wk: 2	Boys	M1: 14	20 to 40
		Girls	M1: 8	10 to 20
Goal Reps: 50 to 100	Wk: 3	Boys	M1: 14	30 to 60
Exercise		Girls	M1: 8	15 to 30
Overhead Wall Toss	Wk: 4	Boys	M1: 14	40 to 80
		Girls	M1: 8	20 to 40
	Wk: 5	Boys	M2: 20	30 to 45
		Girls	M2: 12	15 to 35
Goal Reps: 50 to 100	Wk: 6	Boys	M2: 20	35 to 60
Exercise		Girls	M2: 12	20 to 45
Med Ball Side Leg Adduction	Wk: 7	Boys	M2: 20	40 to 75
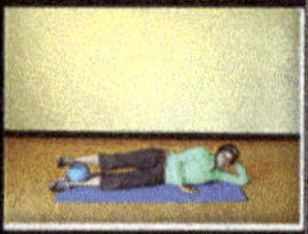		Girls	M2: 12	25 to 55
	Wk: 8	Boys	M2: 20	45 to 90
		Girls	M2: 12	30 to 65
Goal Reps: 50 to 100	Wk: 9	Boys	M3: 30	20 to 40
Exercise		Girls	M3: 16	20 to 45
Med. Ball Seated Tucks	Wk: 10	Boys	M3: 30	30 to 60
		Girls	M3: 16	25 to 55
	Wk: 11	Boys	M3: 30	40 to 80
		Girls	M3: 16	30 to 65
Goal Reps: 50 to 100	Wk: 12	Boys	M3: 30	50 to 100
		Girls	M3: 16	35 to 75

Figure 6.8. (B) Preseason Day Two

Pre-season Exercise Reccomendations

Exercise		Gender	Loads	Reps
Med Ball S. Extension	Wk: 1	Boys	M1: 14	10 to 20
		Girls	M1: 8	5 to 10
	Wk: 2	Boys	M1: 14	20 to 40
		Girls	M1: 8	10 to 20
Goal Reps: 50 to 100	Wk: 3	Boys	M1: 14	30 to 60
Exercise		Girls	M1: 8	15 to 30
Tubing External Rotation	Wk: 4	Boys	M1: 14	40 to 80
		Girls	M1: 8	20 to 40
	Wk: 5	Boys	M2: 20	30 to 45
		Girls	M2: 12	15 to 35
Goal Reps: 50 to 100	Wk: 6	Boys	M2: 20	35 to 60
Exercise		Girls	M2: 12	20 to 45
(Low box) Speed Hops	Wk: 7	Boys	M2: 20	40 to 75
		Girls	M2: 12	25 to 55
	Wk: 8	Boys	M2: 20	45 to 90
		Girls	M2: 12	30 to 65
Goal Reps: 50 to 100	Wk: 9	Boys	M3: 30	20 to 40
Exercise		Girls	M3: 16	20 to 45
Rotational M.B. Toss	Wk: 10	Boys	M3: 30	30 to 60
		Girls	M3: 16	25 to 55
	Wk: 11	Boys	M3: 30	40 to 80
		Girls	M3: 16	30 to 65
Goal Reps: 50 to 100	Wk: 12	Boys	M3: 30	50 to 100
		Girls	M3: 16	35 to 75

Pre-season Exercise Reccomendations

Exercise		Gender	Loads	Reps
Ball Partner Perturbation Drills	Wk: 1	Boys	M1: 14	10 to 20
		Girls	M1: 8	5 to 10
	Wk: 2	Boys	M1: 14	20 to 40
		Girls	M1: 8	10 to 20
Goal Slaps: 50 to 100	Wk: 3	Boys	M1: 14	30 to 60
Exercise		Girls	M1: 8	15 to 30
Ball Partner Perturbation Drills	Wk: 4	Boys	M1: 14	40 to 80
		Girls	M1: 8	20 to 40
	Wk: 5	Boys	M2: 20	30 to 45
		Girls	M2: 12	15 to 35
Goal Slaps: 50 to 100	Wk: 6	Boys	M2: 20	35 to 60
Exercise		Girls	M2: 12	20 to 45
Banded Tibialis Raise	Wk: 7	Boys	M2: 20	40 to 75
		Girls	M2: 12	25 to 55
	Wk: 8	Boys	M2: 20	45 to 90
		Girls	M2: 12	30 to 65
Goal Reps: 50 to 100	Wk: 9	Boys	M3: 30	20 to 40
Exercise		Girls	M3: 16	20 to 45
Shoulder Cuff Strengthening	Wk: 10	Boys	M3: 30	30 to 60
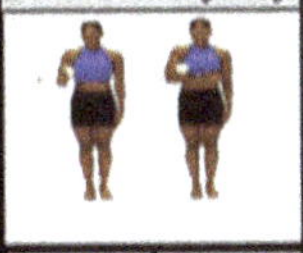		Girls	M3: 16	25 to 55
	Wk: 11	Boys	M3: 30	40 to 80
		Girls	M3: 16	30 to 65
Goal Reps: 50 to 100	Wk: 12	Boys	M3: 30	50 to 100
		Girls	M3: 16	35 to 75

Figure 6.9. (C) Preseason Day Three

In-Season
Primary Goal: Strength Maintenance/Injury Prevention
Cardiovascular Training Focus: Unique to the Demands of the Sport
Resistance Training Focus: Calisthenic High Repetition
Skill Training: Team Practice
Competitive Play: Weekly
Duration: Sixteen Weeks

The in-season program has two primary goals: maintain the strength and conditioning advances the athlete has gained (during the off-season and preseason training phases) and minimize the chance of season ending injury. The exercise selection and intensity are moderately stimulating to allow for maintenance of strength and endurance adaptations without creating drastic muscular and joint trauma. The exercise stress should not require a significant amount of recovery on the body due to the rigors of the highly competitive environment. Athletes are often competing hard in games and potentially just as hard in practice for increased playing time. Calisthenic exercise is appropriate for athletes that are normal or slightly overweight (BMI range of 20 to 28) but not obese participants. Obese athletes will have to modify their exercise positions or substitute the use of resistance bands in place of body weight exercise altogether. In-season resistance training should be performed two or three days a week with a least one day in between for recovery. If the athlete is unable to recover and complains of chronic muscular soreness or joint pain reduce frequently of program to one workout session every five calendar days.

In- Season: Day One Circuit One

Exercise	Goal Reps
Basic Push-up 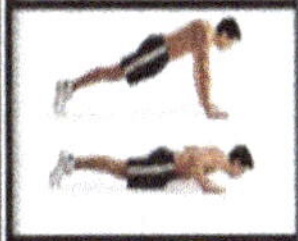	50
Table Row or use a Broom 	50
Low Squat 	50
Anchored Sit-ups 	50

	Gender	Loads	Reps
Wk: 1	Boys	Body Wt.	10 to 20
	Girls	Body Wt.	5 to 10
Wk: 2	Boys	Body Wt.	20 to 40
	Girls	Body Wt.	10 to 20
Wk: 3	Boys	Body Wt.	30 to 60
	Girls	Body Wt.	15 to 30
Wk: 4	Boys	Body Wt.	40 to 80
	Girls	Body Wt.	20 to 40
Wk: 5	Boys	Body Wt.	30 to 45
	Girls	Body Wt.	15 to 35
Wk: 6	Boys	Body Wt.	35 to 60
	Girls	Body Wt.	20 to 45
Wk: 7	Boys	Body Wt.	40 to 75
	Girls	Body Wt.	25 to 55
Wk: 8	Boys	Body Wt.	45 to 90
	Girls	Body Wt.	30 to 65
Wk: 9	Boys	Body Wt.	20 to 40
	Girls	Body Wt.	20 to 45
Wk: 10	Boys	Body Wt.	30 to 60
	Girls	Body Wt.	25 to 55
Wk: 11	Boys	Body Wt.	40 to 80
	Girls	Body Wt.	30 to 65
Wk: 12	Boys	Body Wt.	50 to 100
	Girls	Body Wt.	35 to 75

In- Season: Day One Circuit Two

Exercise	Goal Reps
Scapular Dip 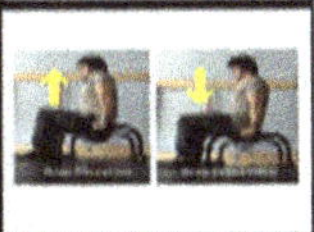	50
Prone Lat Row (Head) 	50
Bench Hip Ext. 	50
Oblique Combo Crunch 	50

	Gender	Loads	Reps
Wk: 1	Boys	Body Wt.	10 to 20
	Girls	Body Wt.	5 to 10
Wk: 2	Boys	Body Wt.	20 to 40
	Girls	Body Wt.	10 to 20
Wk: 3	Boys	Body Wt.	30 to 60
	Girls	Body Wt.	15 to 30
Wk: 4	Boys	Body Wt.	40 to 80
	Girls	Body Wt.	20 to 40
Wk: 5	Boys	Body Wt.	30 to 45
	Girls	Body Wt.	15 to 35
Wk: 6	Boys	Body Wt.	35 to 60
	Girls	Body Wt.	20 to 45
Wk: 7	Boys	Body Wt.	40 to 75
	Girls	Body Wt.	25 to 55
Wk: 8	Boys	Body Wt.	45 to 90
	Girls	Body Wt.	30 to 65
Wk: 9	Boys	Body Wt.	20 to 40
	Girls	Body Wt.	20 to 45
Wk: 10	Boys	Body Wt.	30 to 60
	Girls	Body Wt.	25 to 55
Wk: 11	Boys	Body Wt.	40 to 80
	Girls	Body Wt.	30 to 65
Wk: 12	Boys	Body Wt.	50 to 100
	Girls	Body Wt.	35 to 75

Figure 6.10. (A) In-Season Day One

In- Season: Day Two Circuit One

Exercise	Goal Reps
Standing Towel Curl	50
Bench Dip (feet- up)	50
Lateral Step -up	50
Quadraped Ipsilateral Hold	50

	Gender	Loads	Reps
Wk: 1	Boys	Body Wt.	10 to 20
	Girls	Body Wt.	5 to 10
Wk: 2	Boys	Body Wt.	20 to 40
	Girls	Body Wt.	10 to 20
Wk: 3	Boys	Body Wt.	30 to 60
	Girls	Body Wt.	15 to 30
Wk: 4	Boys	Body Wt.	40 to 80
	Girls	Body Wt.	20 to 40
Wk: 5	Boys	Body Wt.	30 to 45
	Girls	Body Wt.	15 to 35
Wk: 6	Boys	Body Wt.	35 to 60
	Girls	Body Wt.	20 to 45
Wk: 7	Boys	Body Wt.	40 to 75
	Girls	Body Wt.	25 to 55
Wk: 8	Boys	Body Wt.	45 to 90
	Girls	Body Wt.	30 to 65
Wk: 9	Boys	Body Wt.	20 to 40
	Girls	Body Wt.	20 to 45
Wk: 10	Boys	Body Wt.	30 to 60
	Girls	Body Wt.	25 to 55
Wk: 11	Boys	Body Wt.	40 to 80
	Girls	Body Wt.	30 to 65
Wk: 12	Boys	Body Wt.	50 to 100
	Girls	Body Wt.	35 to 75

In- Season: Day Two Circuit Two

Exercise	Goal Reps
Inverted Half Push-up	50
Bent-Knee Finger-Tip Pus	50
Supine V- Slides	50
Leg Lifts	50

	Gender	Loads	Reps
Wk: 1	Boys	Body Wt.	10 to 20
	Girls	Body Wt.	5 to 10
Wk: 2	Boys	Body Wt.	20 to 40
	Girls	Body Wt.	10 to 20
Wk: 3	Boys	Body Wt.	30 to 60
	Girls	Body Wt.	15 to 30
Wk: 4	Boys	Body Wt.	40 to 80
	Girls	Body Wt.	20 to 40
Wk: 5	Boys	Body Wt.	30 to 45
	Girls	Body Wt.	15 to 35
Wk: 6	Boys	Body Wt.	35 to 60
	Girls	Body Wt.	20 to 45
Wk: 7	Boys	Body Wt.	40 to 75
	Girls	Body Wt.	25 to 55
Wk: 8	Boys	Body Wt.	45 to 90
	Girls	Body Wt.	30 to 65
Wk: 9	Boys	Body Wt.	20 to 40
	Girls	Body Wt.	20 to 45
Wk: 10	Boys	Body Wt.	30 to 60
	Girls	Body Wt.	25 to 55
Wk: 11	Boys	Body Wt.	40 to 80
	Girls	Body Wt.	30 to 65
Wk: 12	Boys	Body Wt.	50 to 100
	Girls	Body Wt.	35 to 75

Figure 6.11. (B) In-Season Day Two

In- Season: Day Three Circuit One

Exercise: Shoulder Extension

Goal Reps: 50

Exercise: Internal Rotation

Goal Reps: 50

Exercise: Two Feet Standing Calf Raise

Goal Reps: 50

Exercise: Bicycles

Goal Reps: 50

	Gender	*Loads*	Reps
Wk: 1	Boys	Body Wt.	10 to 20
	Girls	Body Wt.	5 to 10
Wk: 2	Boys	Body Wt.	20 to 40
	Girls	Body Wt.	10 to 20
Wk: 3	Boys	Body Wt.	30 to 60
	Girls	Body Wt.	15 to 30
Wk: 4	Boys	Body Wt.	40 to 80
	Girls	Body Wt.	20 to 40
Wk: 5	Boys	Body Wt.	30 to 45
	Girls	Body Wt.	15 to 35
Wk: 6	Boys	Body Wt.	35 to 60
	Girls	Body Wt.	20 to 45
Wk: 7	Boys	Body Wt.	40 to 75
	Girls	Body Wt.	25 to 55
Wk: 8	Boys	Body Wt.	45 to 90
	Girls	Body Wt.	30 to 65
Wk: 9	Boys	Body Wt.	20 to 40
	Girls	Body Wt.	20 to 45
Wk: 10	Boys	Body Wt.	30 to 60
	Girls	Body Wt.	25 to 55
Wk: 11	Boys	Body Wt.	40 to 80
	Girls	Body Wt.	30 to 65
Wk: 12	Boys	Body Wt.	50 to 100
	Girls	Body Wt.	35 to 75

In- Season: Day Three Circuit Two

Exercise: Horizontal Adduction

Goal Reps: 50

Exercise: Horizontal Abduction

Goal Reps: 50

Exercise: Double Standing Toe Raise

Goal Reps: 50

Exercise: External Rotation

Goal Reps: 50

	Gender	*Loads*	Reps
Wk: 1	Boys	Body Wt.	10 to 20
	Girls	Body Wt.	5 to 10
Wk: 2	Boys	Body Wt.	20 to 40
	Girls	Body Wt.	10 to 20
Wk: 3	Boys	Body Wt.	30 to 60
	Girls	Body Wt.	15 to 30
Wk: 4	Boys	Body Wt.	40 to 80
	Girls	Body Wt.	20 to 40
Wk: 5	Boys	Body Wt.	30 to 45
	Girls	Body Wt.	15 to 35
Wk: 6	Boys	Body Wt.	35 to 60
	Girls	Body Wt.	20 to 45
Wk: 7	Boys	Body Wt.	40 to 75
	Girls	Body Wt.	25 to 55
Wk: 8	Boys	Body Wt.	45 to 90
	Girls	Body Wt.	30 to 65
Wk: 9	Boys	Body Wt.	20 to 40
	Girls	Body Wt.	20 to 45
Wk: 10	Boys	Body Wt.	30 to 60
	Girls	Body Wt.	25 to 55
Wk: 11	Boys	Body Wt.	40 to 80
	Girls	Body Wt.	30 to 65
Wk: 12	Boys	Body Wt.	50 to 100
	Girls	Body Wt.	35 to 75

Figure 6.12. (C) In-Season Day Three

Relationships for Optimal Performance

Coach Sport Instructor Performance Coach Parent

IN-SEASON			Behavior	Communication Tree	Primary Goal
Player	High Input	Coach	Directing	Coach - Youth - Parents	Team Developement
	Low Input	Performance Coach	Recusation		
	Low Input	Skill Instructor	Recusation		
	Low Input	Parent	Supportive		
POST- SEASON			**Behavior**	**Comuncation Tree**	**Primary Goal**
Player	Low Input	Coach	Recusation	Youth- Parents - Performance Coach	Individual Recovery
	High Input	Performance Coach	Directing		
	Moderate Input	Skill Instructor	Supportive		
	High Input	Parent	Directing		
OFF- SEASON			**Behavior**	**Comuncation Tree**	**Primary Goal**
Player	Moderate Input	Coach	Supportive	Skill Instructor - Performance Coach - Parents- Youth	Individual Development
	High Input	Performance Coach	Directing		
	High Input	Skill Instructor	Directing		
	Moderate Input	Parent	Supportive		
PRE- SEASON			**Behavior**	**Comuncation Tree**	**Primary Goal**
Player	High Input	Coach	Directing	Coach Skill Instructor - Performance Coach - Youth- Parents	Individual Peak Condition
	Low Input	Performance Coach	Supportive		
	Low Input	Skill Instructor	Supportive		
	Low Input	Parent	Supportive		

Figure 6.13. Relationships for Optimal Performance

Postseason
Primary Goal: Physical, Emotional, Social, and Psychological Recovery
Primary Relationships: The Athlete and Parent/Caregiver
Secondary Relationships: The Athlete and Performance Coach
Recommended Relationship Cessation: The Athlete and Head Coach
Recommended Relationship Cessation: The Athlete and Skill Instructor
Duration: Four to Twelve Weeks

The postseason is the time that is allocated to recapture social balance, facilitate emotional restoration, and allow for psychological refocus for the athlete. Immediately after the sport season, feelings can be extremely high or low. The season can entail multiple scenarios in which athletes, coaches, and their families alike can be chronically pushed to a point of eroding motivation and desire to continue participation; therefore, it is recommended to allow for a period of recalibration and alignment with a series of goals and vision for the next season.

Coaches after a postseason exit meeting with their athletes and in some cases parents need to recuse themselves for a limited period (four to twelve weeks) from strong oversight and direct player management. This helps to allow for their players to redevelop hunger for the game and restore their desire for self-improvement in their skills and physical capacity to return. The time away from athletes also allows for the relationship between coaches and their athletes to settle. The competitive process is intense, and strong feelings between players and coaches often develop.

Reestablishing boundaries of dependency and intimacy is equally important to coach and players alike. This time frame is extremely individualized for each athlete based on the player's needs and financial capacity of the family. In this phase, some of the more common professional relationships that may occur with the athlete is the involvement of a rehabilitative professional (athletic trainer, physical therapist, chiropractor), academic tutor, conditioning and strength coach, counsellor, and or sport psychologist. Socially, athletes may spend large amounts of time with their family, friends, and a romantic interest. These are all natural and as a coach should be encouraged. In fact, an argument can be made that if your athlete ends the season and moves too quickly into an intense off-season training structure, the odds for injury burnout, poor academic performance, and depression increase opposed to skill mastery and athletic ability (Breuner 2012).

Off-Season
Primary Goal: Physical Development and Skill Improvement
Primary Relationships: The Athlete and Performance Coach
Primary Relationships: The Athlete and Skill Instructor
Secondary Relationships: The Athlete and Parent/Caregiver
Secondary Relationships: The Athlete and Head Coach
Duration: Four to Twenty Weeks

The off-season phase is the time frame in which athletes develop their game and physical attributes following a volitional schedule devoid of direct competition. In this phase, athletes work hard on their skills and body, but they are also encouraged to have a managed social schedule. Friends and family activities are reduced from the postseason frequency but are still significant. The priority of this phase is now definitely sport and physical improvement, but emotional satisfaction is not completely omitted. This is important to understand because the engagement of the athlete around the workout sessions and skill training in this phase should be primarily positive.

Coaches and other developmental professionals should be friendly, supportive, honest, but in an optimistic manner to facilitate the greatest amount of growth possible in this phase. Coaches should be mindful that the athlete is not being "motivated" in manner that is going to create emotional or psychological degradation. This phase of training is used to create specific changes in the athlete's game and body, but relationships between teammates and coaching staff should also be included. Engagement by the coach and or staff members needs to be deliberate, and ideally, any negative residue lingering from the season here needs to be resolved. Coaches during this phase should expect to work with outside strength and conditioning professionals, skill instructors, AAU coaches, and restorative practitioners to optimize their athletes for the upcoming season. Developing a strong and positive relationship with these individuals will solidify a smooth transition for the athlete to return under the direct supervision of the coach and or coaching staff personnel during the preseason and in-season phases.

Preseason
Primary Goal: Physical Conditioning and Skill Improvement
Primary Relationships: The Athlete and Coach
Secondary Relationships: The Athlete and Performance Coach
Secondary Relationships: The Athlete and Skill Instructor
Secondary Relationships: The Athlete and Parent/Caregiver
Duration: Four to Eight Weeks

The preseason, in addition to beginning formal conditioning and skill practice sessions, is the time to orient players to the coaching staff, observe their personalities, and create the desired team culture of communication and management. During this phase, any disagreements from the past season between teammates, players, and coaches, or players and managers that are unresolved need to be settled and a vision for the upcoming season initially introduced.

Previous chapters discuss coaching styles and management preferences; the preseason is the phase where these theories become implemented. Trying to organize athletes ahead of the official start of the sport season poses a series of unique challenges for coaches at various levels. To begin with, players are often participating on multiple teams and in multiple sport programs (AAU team, travel team, and or school team summer league), as well as being potentially supervised by a private conditioning professional and or skill instructor. The athletes have established relationships for several weeks to months with these individuals, and if experiencing renewed success can become quickly bonded. These relationships can become hard to penetrate and difficult to manage, placing communication with the player, their parent, and other invested professionals at a premium to avoid misunderstandings.

Coaches at different levels and settings will need to set preseason participation guidelines clearly ahead of time in the off-season phase prior to potential conflict. Players need to be made aware of what portions of the programs they join are volitional and what portions are not. Lastly, during the preseason, school-team-based coaches who have budget, time, and or staffing constraints may choose to outsource a portion of the preseason program to a private club organization, conditioning coach, or skill instructor to enhance the value of the school program to the athletic programs participants.

In-Season
Primary Goal: (Strength Maintenance/ Injury Prevention)
Primary Relationships: The Athlete and Coach
Secondary Relationships: The Athlete and Parent/ Caregiver
Recommended Relationship Cessation: The Athlete and Performance Coach
Recommended Relationship Cessation: The Athlete and Skill Instructor
Duration: Sixteen Weeks

The in-season phase is the most demanding emotionally and psychologically on the athlete of all the four phases. Athletes at the competitive high school level and beyond frequently sacrifice family and friend relationships, romantic interests, and academic preparation to make team success and personal sport achievement their leading priority. Coaches in this phase need to be clear in providing their athletes with a two-sided map of how they can succeed in attaining both individual and team goals that fit into the year-end season vision. This map needs to include the athlete's current role on the team and what role potentially the athlete could fill if they maximize their ability. In addition, coaches should clearly outline how to earn and lose competitive playing time and what type of conduct is expected at school or university and out in the community.

The sport season is long and arduous and is often filled with micro cycles of team and individual vicissitudes. As a coach, one cannot completely control team personality dynamics, player injury, athletic eligibility, general health status, and the competitive viability of the surrounding schools in the league from year to year. These events all include a varying component of randomness. Therefore, coaches and their staff need to focus on their program and establish fundamentals which portend greater odds of success, the most significant being providing an open, honest, and supportive environment to develop players. The second being a willing coaching staff to adjust their system to maximize the current physical attributes and skill expression on the team's roster.

Coaches, as a final summary for this sports performance section, keep the following thoughts in mind:

1. Elementary school participants should focus on skill development and emotional maturity
    a. playing the game the correct way
    b. being a good teammate
    c. respecting officials, coaches, opponents, parents
2. Junior high school participants
    a. playing the game the correct way
    b. being a good teammate
    c. respecting officials, coaches, opponents, parents
3. High school participants
    a. playing the game the correct way
    b. being a good teammate
    c. respecting officials, coaches, opponents, parents
4. College sport participants
    a. playing the game the correct way
    b. being a good teammate
    c. respecting officials, coaches, opponents, parents

Summary of Key Points

Major Concepts	Review Pages
Introduction to Periodization	
Understanding Relationships for Optimal Performance	

Trainer's Corner

Professional Insights	Video Links
"Training Athletes on a Limited Athletic Budget"	
"Communication for Optimal Performance "	
"Understanding the Four Phases of Strength and Conditioning"	

Discussion Questions:

1. High school athletes who are committed to being their best should train with heavy weights year around to maximize their development. True/False
2. Each phase in a periodization plan is important and should be implemented to avoid injury and increase results. True/False
3. Athletes who complete a difficult sport season are encouraged to begin skill and physical development sessions as soon as possible to take advantage of the post- and off-season time frame. True/False
4. In a periodization program, which phase allows for the most time to break from skill training?
   a) Postseason b) Off-Season c) Preseason d) In-Season
5. In a periodization program, which phase requires the most intense cardiovascular conditioning?
   a) Postseason b) Off-Season c) Preseason d) In-Season

6. In a periodization program, which phase promotes the most strength development?
   a) Postseason b) Off-Season c) Preseason d) In-Season
7. In a periodization program, which phase promotes the most muscular strength and injury prevention?
   a) Postseason b) Off-Season c) Preseason d) In-Season
8. Which phase in a periodization program does a coach have the least contact with their players?
   a) Postseason b) Off-Season c) Preseason d) In-Season
9. Which phase in a periodization program does a coach have the highest contact with their players?
   a) Postseason b) Off-Season c) Preseason d) In-Season
10. Which phase in a periodization program does a player have the most involvement with outside development professionals?
   a) Postseason b) Off-Season c) Preseason d) In-Season

CHAPTER 7

ATHLETIC NUTRITION

Key Terms	Page
Recommended Daily Allowances (RDA)—the daily amounts of essential nutrients that, on basis of scientific knowledge, can be correlated to prevent deficiency syndromes or degenerative conditions. These values are most appropriate for healthy adults whom are not chronically sick or are elite athletes.	
Simple Carbohydrates—Fast-digesting, high-sugar, low-fiber foods; examples include fruit, syrup, juice, candy, etc.	
Female Athlete Triad—is an interrelationship of menstrual dysfunction, low energy availability (over activity or undereating or both) and decreased bone mineral density	

A significant component of any physical development program must be a nutrition plan that will fuel the body for peak performance, appropriate growth, and physiologic rebuilding (Dunford 2019). In athletic nutrition, a key consideration to keep in mind is that guidelines for increased performance, muscular development, and physiological repair are not the same for preventing disease or healing from a surgery or injury (Swain et al. 2014). Caloric adjustment, nutrient levels, and food choice will need to change depending on the inflammatory state of the body and reduction in daily activity level. That said, to feed an athlete, one must answer two primary questions: first, what concentration of nutrients (water, vitamins, minerals, proteins, fiber, fats, carbohydrates) are required daily to support their training schedule and recovery needs, and second, how many calories are required to maintain their ideal competitive weight?

Review figure 7.1 below as a working general guideline for most high school athletes. The table provides a guideline for the number of macronutrients (proteins, carbohydrates, fats, fiber, and water) as well as the food servings used to supply the *recommended daily allowance* (micronutrients: vitamins and minerals) that an athlete will require based on their size, gender, and sport participation.

Male Ranges												
Sport Average	Height (inches)	Pounds Per Inch	Weight Ranges	Lean Mass	Fat Mass	Total Cals	Water Cups	Protein Grams	Protein Ounces	Fat Grams	Carbs Grams	Fiber Grams
Low	72	x 2.4	173	156	17	3419	9	156	22	146	371	51
Ranges	72	x 2.9	209	177	31	4923	13	177	25	183	641	74
Medium	77	x 2.4	185	166	18	3587	10	166	24	155	382	54
Ranges	77	x 2.9	223	190	33	5126	13	190	27	194	655	77
High	83	x 2.4	199	179	20	3789	10	179	26	166	395	57
Ranges	83	x 2.9	241	205	36	5370	14	205	29	206	673	81

Male Ranges												
Sport Average	Weight Ranges	Protein Ounces	Leaves cups	Non-Starchy Veggie Cups	Starchy Veggies Cups	Fruit Cups	Bean Cups	Grain Cups	Avacado Whole	Seeds or Nuts TBSP	Allicin Veggies Cloves	Green Tea Bags
Low	173	22	5	2	2.5	3	2	2		7	3	6.2
Ranges	209	25	5	2	2.5	3.5	2	2	1	7	4	7.1
Medium	185	24	6	2.5	3	4	2.5	2.5		8	3	6.7
Ranges	223	27	6	2.5	3	4.5	2.5	2.5	1	8	4	7.6
High	199	26	7	3	3.5	5	3	3		9	4	7.2
Ranges	241	29	7	3	3.5	5.5	3	3	1	9	4	8.2

Figure 7.1. (A) Projected Athletic Dietary Guidelines (Male)

Female Ranges												
Sport Average	Height (inches)	Pounds Per Inch	Weight Ranges	Lean Mass	Fat Mass	Total Cals	Water Cups	Protein Grams	Protein Ounces	Fat Grams	Carbs Grams	Fiber Grams
Low	65	x 1.85	120	102	18	2443	7	102	15	99	286	37
Ranges	65	x 2.25	146	117	29	3755	10	117	17	129	531	56
Medium	71	x 1.85	131	112	20	2576	7	112	16	107	292	39
Ranges	71	x 2.25	160	128	32	3917	11	128	18	138	540	59
High	77	x 1.85	142	121	21	2709	8	121	17	114	299	41
Ranges	77	x 2.25	173	139	35	4079	11	139	20	147	550	61

Female Ranges												
Sport Average	Weight Ranges	Protein Ounces	Leaves cups	Non-Starchy Veggie Cups	Starchy Veggies Cups	Fruit Cups	Bean Cups	Grain Cups	Avacado Whole	Seeds or Nuts TBSP	Allicin Veggies Cloves	Green Tea
Low	120	15	4	2	2	3	1	1		1	2	4.8
Ranges	146	17	4	2	2	3	1	1	1	1	3	5.9
Medium	131	16	5	2.25	2.5	3.5	1.25	1.25		2	3	5.3
Ranges	160	18	5	2.25	2.5	3.5	1.25	1.25	1	2	3	6.4
High	142	17	6	2.5	3	4	1.5	1.5		3	3	5.7
Ranges	173	20	6	2.5	3	4	1.5	1.5	1	3	3	6.9

Figure 7.2. (B) Projected Athletic Dietary Guidelines (Female)

Athletes and coaches often underappreciate the role that nutrition can occupy as it relates to recovery, rate of progression, injury potential, and stamina. Athletes, parents, coaches, and skill instructors many times are meticulous about training regimens and practice sessions but fail to understand how to fully maximize their athlete's commitment. *Nutrition* is often the missing link in a dedicated athlete's program to solidify progress and mitigate their body breaking down.

The following sections explain some of the more significant benefits of consuming specific food groups on daily basis.

Protein Intake: .5 to .75 gram per pound of ideal weight

Importance: *Protein* builds, maintains, and repairs the bodies tissues as well as the structure for hormones and enzymes. Protein can also be utilized for energy if calories from fat and carbohydrate are insufficient (Swain et al. 2014).

Behavior Focus: Choices can vary but aim for higher quality animal options, such as organic, pasture-raised eggs; organic, grass-fed animals, wild caught seafoods, and organic organ meats. Severely restrict or avoid the following: processed meat options, such as bacon, hotdogs, sausages, canned meats, sulfite- and nitrite-prepared deli meats, and grilled charred meats. Athletes who are non-northern

European descent have a high probability of lactose intolerance and should be mindful of their dairy product intake (cheese, milk, yogurt, cottage cheese, ice cream, sour cream, custard, pudding, cream).

Athletic Significance: When athletes engage in strenuous activities (team practice, skill sessions, aerobic conditioning, or weight training), their muscles and other tissues will incur minor damage that require repair. Athletes generally will require more protein in their diets with the increasing duration, intensity, and frequency of their physical workouts, skill practice, and competitive play events (Dunford 2019).

Fat Intake: 20 to 30 percent of total calories

Importance: Dietary fat provides essential fatty acids that optimizes hormone production, promotes healthy endocrine and immune function, balances inflammation, maintains satiety, and improves body composition when substituted in place of *simple carbohydrates* (Swain et al. 2014).

Behavior Focus: Intake levels should be maintained at 20 to 30 percent of your diet depending on the sport. The recommendation for linoleic acid is 17 grams for males and 12 grams for females and for alpha linolenic acid, 1.6 grams for males and 1.1 grams for females (Swain et al. 2014). These levels can easily be met by consuming 1 to 6 tablespoons of nuts or seeds daily, consuming adequate protein from high quality dark meat protein animal sources, fatty fish, cooking vegetables with olive oil, butter, or coconut oil and or eating 1/4 to 1/2 of an avocado a day. Like protein, fat intake should be consumed with each meal except potentially a pre-workout meal within two hours of activity.

Athletic Significance: When athletes engage in strenuous activities (team practice, skill sessions, aerobic conditioning, or weight training), their bodies will become inflamed and slightly injured. Athletes therefore will require adequate intake of omega-3 fats (seafood, fish, chia seeds, walnuts, or DHA, EPA, and GLA supplementation) to manage this condition (Swain et al. 2014).The larger the athlete combined with increasing exercise commitment will further increase requirements of these essential fats (high school athletes will have a range of one to four grams a day).

Carbohydrate Intake: 2.5 to 4.5 grams of carbohydrates per pound of ideal weight or 25 to 60 percent of total calories

Importance: *Carbohydrates* from a health perspective are the only source in the diet for fiber. Athletically, it provides the body with the primary dietary option for energy or fuel during high intensity, repeated bouts of exercise. During this type of exercise after blood levels are sufficiently decreased, liver stores of carbohydrate (glycogen) provide the principal source of energy (Swain et al. 2014).

Therefore, these stores will become depleted in direct portion to the exercise design being performed and will require repletion by daily meal intake. Failure to do so will negatively impact future physical adaption and worse promote potential breakdown of lean mass in athletes.

Behavior Focus: Intake levels should be between 2.5 to 4.5 grams of carbohydrates per pound of desired body weight spread at least over two meals but ideally three or four.

Athletic Significance: When athletes engage in strenuous activities (team practice, skill sessions, aerobic conditioning, or weight training), their blood sugar levels get depleted, requiring muscles and liver stores to be released to maintain adequate levels. Athletes that workout multiple times a day or who participate in multiple sports will need to monitor their calories and carbohydrate intake closely to maintain their optimal performance expression. Aerobic-endurance-based athletes who are ideal weight, as a rule, will require their carbohydrate recommendations near the higher thresholds of the range (three or four grams per pound of ideal weight); when compared to power-, strength-, and physique-dependent athletes, they are at the lower range (one to two in half grams per pound of ideal weight) (Dunford 2019). Coaches need to also be aware of the intake of simple carbohydrate choices for obese or overweight athletes. Intake for these athletes may need to be reduced or substituted with low-sugar fruits and high-fiber vegetables or at worst restricted to once-a-day post-physical exertion.

Seaweed

Kelp, Dulse, Alaria, Wakame

Leaves

Kale, Mustard, Dandelion, Turnip Greens, Parsley, Spinach

Fruits (A-Whole) 1

Plum, Banana, Peach, Kiwi, Lemon, Lime, Apple, Pear

Fruits (B-Cups) 2)

Blackberries, Strawberries, Raspberries, Blueberries, Cranberries,

Nut Options

Hazelnuts, Cashews or Almonds

Seeds

Sesame, Pumpkin, Chia, Sunflower Seeds, Milled Flax Seeds,

Non-Starchy Vegetables (Cruciferous)

Broccoli, Cauliflower, Brussels Sprouts, Cabbage

Non-Starchy Vegetables (Allicin)

Onions, Garlic, Shallots, Scallions, Leeks

Beans

Adzucki, Garbanzo, Lima or Black-eye, Black

Starchy Vegetables

Sweet Potato, Squash, Pumpkin, Green Peas, Turnips, Rutabaga, Egg Plant, Carrots

Protein

Liver, Eggs, Crab, Calamari, Sardines, Haddock, Walleye Pike, Rib-eye, Turkey

Seed Milks

Almond, Cashew, Hemp, Soy, Oat, Pea, Coconut

Figure 7.3. High Nutrient Food List for Peak Athletic Capacity

Leaves

Key Dietary Nutrient Sources: Beta Carotene (Vit. A), Folate (B-9), Vit. K, Vit. C

High-Nutrient Food Sources: Kale, Turnip, Mustard, Dandelion Greens, Parsley

Behavior Focus: Intake levels: 2 to 6 cups daily; typical consumption strategies are fresh-tossed salads blended in a smoothie or steamed as a side dish to a meal

Athletic Significance: *Leaves* contain nutrients that aid in that body in managing inflammation (i.e., tissue trauma), reducing the impact of increased cellular oxidation (i.e., cardiovascular activity), skin protection from sun damage, maintaining bone health, and supporting growth and repair.

Special Considerations: Leaves should be consumed daily by all types of athlete; they are a critical food for physique-dependent athletes or athletes who need to reduce their fat mass.

Non-Starchy Vegetables

Key Dietary Nutrient Sources: Folate (B-9), Vit. K, Vit. C, Assorted Phytonutrients

High-Nutrient Food Sources: Broccoli, Brussel Sprouts, Cauliflower, Cabbage

Behavior Focus: Intake levels: 1/2 to 2 cups daily; typical consumption strategies are fresh-tossed salads blended in a smoothie, steamed as a side dish to a meal, or eaten raw with a dip

Athletic Significance: *Non-starchy vegetables* contain nutrients that aid in that body in reducing the impact of increased cellular oxidation (i.e., cardiovascular activity), maintaining bone health, supporting growth and repair, and improving energy production (i.e., stamina).

Special Considerations: Non-starchy vegetables should be consumed daily by all types of athlete; they are a critical food for athletes who consume large amounts of calories, especially from starches. They also assist in removing excess fat in the thighs and glute area for athletes who need to reduce their fat mass.

Starchy Vegetables

Key Dietary Nutrient Sources: Beta Carotene (Vit. A), Potassium, Assorted Phytonutrients

High-Nutrient Food Sources: Sweet Potato, Carrots, Butternut Squash

Behavior Focus: Intake levels: 1/2 to 2 cups daily; typical consumption strategies are steamed as a side dish to a meal.

Athletic Significance: *Starchy vegetables* contain nutrients that aid the body in reducing the impact of increased cellular oxidation (i.e., cardiovascular activity), protecting the skin from sun damage, increasing energy production (i.e., stamina), and reducing muscle cramping.

Special Considerations: Starchy vegetables should be cautiously consumed because they are extremely rich in carbohydrates and lower in fiber per calorie than leaves and non-starchy vegetables. Therefore, athletes who need weight loss, it is advised to restrict or omit these selections until they are weight stable. Athletes who are at their ideal weight can consume these selections with no restrictions or cause to fear that intake will lead to accumulation of unwanted body fat. Be mindful of consuming these selections with excess butter or sour cream or in fried forms.

Fruit

Key Nutrient Sources: Potassium, Vitamin C, Assorted Phytonutrients

High-Nutrient Food Sources: Berries, Citrus

Behavior Focus: Intake levels: 1/2 to 4 cups daily; typical consumption strategies are blended in a smoothie, as a snack with nuts or seeds, as a toping on a hot cereal, or yogurt

Athletic Significance: Fruits contain nutrients that aid in the body managing inflammation (i.e., tissue trauma), reducing the impact of increased cellular oxidation (i.e., cardiovascular activity), improving energy production (i.e., stamina), and reducing muscle cramping.

Special Considerations: Fruits can be consumed in an athlete's daily diet; however, some considerations must be taken. Athletes who need weight loss should consume only citrus or berries and restrict intake to one or two servings daily. Athletes who are at their ideal weight can consume a variety of fruit selections with no restrictions or cause to fear that intake will lead to accumulation of unwanted body fat. Be mindful of consuming fruit quantities greater than 4 cups daily and eating them alone without proteins, nuts, or seeds.

Bean

Key Nutrient Sources: Copper, Folate (B-9), Manganese, Molybdenum, Potassium

High-Nutrient Food Sources: Lima, Garbanzo, Adzucki

Behavior Focus: Intake levels: 1/2 to 2 cups daily; typical consumption strategies are in soups or chili, with a grain as a snack, boiled as a side dish, prepared, and blended to form a dip for vegetables

Athletic Significance: *Beans* contain minerals that aid in the body in creating strong tissues to resist injury and enhance recovery. Beans also is the primary source in the diet for potassium (helps fight muscle cramping).

Special Considerations: Beans can be consumed in any athlete's daily diet due to their relatively high level of protein, fiber, and resistant starch. Beans do contain significant amounts of carbohydrate, but it is not released quickly in the bloodstream and thus create a minimal impact on inducing weight gain. However, some considerations must be taken. Athletes who require weight loss should be mindful of consuming beans with chips, cheese, sour cream, or other high-calorie meal accompaniments.

Grain

Key Nutrient Sources: Copper, Manganese

High-Nutrient Food Sources: Steel Cut Oats, Buckwheat, Quinoa, Amaranth

Behavior Focus: Intake levels: 1/2 to 2 cups daily; typical consumption strategies are in soups or chili, with beans as a snack, boiled as a side dish, boiled as a breakfast hot cereal

Athletic Significance: *Grains* contain minerals that aid in the body in creating strong tissues to resist injury and enhance recovery. In addition, grains provide a decent source of potassium and a large economical source of dietary carbohydrate and calories.

Special Considerations: Grains provide large amounts of carbohydrate (energy) in the diet. Athletes who are ideal weight that are engaging in highly intense daily workouts will need to make grains part of their dietary staples. Athletes who require weight loss should be mindful of reducing or avoiding grain intake and when consuming them limit the use of butter, high-sugar fruits, sweeteners, and seeds or nuts as toppings.

Seeds and Nuts

Key Nutrient Sources: Vit. E, Copper, Manganese, Essential Fats (omega-6)

High-Nutrient Food Source: Almond, Hazelnut, Cashew, Sunflower, Hemp, Pumpkin, Chia

Behavior Focus: Intake levels: 2 to 6 tablespoons of raw unroasted and unsalted varieties; typical consumption strategies are blended in a smoothie, as a snack with fruit, as a topping on a hot cereal, or yogurt, or added to a salad.

Athletic Significance: *Nuts and seeds* contain nutrients that aid in the body managing inflammation, reducing the impact of increased *cellular oxidation*, improve tissue integrity, and improve hormonal balance.

Special Considerations: Seeds and nuts provide large amounts of fat (energy) in the diet. Athletes who require weight gain or struggle to maintain their weight can utilize nuts as a high calorie addition that can quickly add a surplus of mineral-rich calories. Athletes who require weight loss should reduce nut and seed intake to 1 to 3 tablespoons daily. Whether an athlete requires weight loss or not, nut or seed intake should be from only raw, plain, unroasted, unsalted varieties.

Tea

Key Nutrient Sources: Assorted Phytonutrients

High-Nutrient Food Source: Green, White, Black, Oolong (green and black tea combined)

Behavior Focus: Intake levels of tea are optional: two to eight tea bags daily; typical consumption strategies are brewed daily or blended to make a base liquid in a smoothie

Athletic Significance: *Tea* provides compounds that aid in the body managing inflammation, increase fat burning, increase circulating testosterone, improve alertness, and boost stamina.

Special Considerations: *Green tea* has by far the most scientific study of the four tea varieties, but each has unique concentrations of phytonutrients and caffeine levels that can be of benefit. Athletes that require fat loss or struggle to manage their weight could benefit from including tea daily as part of their routine.

Proposed Athletic Physical Progression				
Supplement Products	**Elementary: 4th to 5th Grade**	**Junior High School: 6th to 8th Grade**	**High School: 9th to 12 Grade**	**College**
Dietary	Multivitamin & Mineral Essential Fats	Multivitamin & Mineral Meal Replacement Essential Fats	Multivitamin & Mineral Meal Replacement Protein Powder Essential Fats	Multivitamin & Mineral Meal Replacement Protein Powder Essential Fats
Musculoskeletal Support	Minerals Vitamin D Fish Oil	Minerals Vitamin D Fish Oil	Minerals Vitamin D Fish Oil Creatine	Minerals Vitamin D Fish Oil Creatine
Inflammation	Fish Oil	Fish Oil	Fish oil Turmeric Enzymes	Fish oil Turmeric Enzymes
Recovery			Glutamine Branch Chain Amino Acids	Glutamine Branch Chain Amino Acids
Energy	B Vitamins	B Vitamins	B Vitamins Creatine Green Tea Adaptogen Herbs	B Vitamins Creatine Green Tea Adaptogen herbs

Figure 7.4. Supplement Considerations for the Developing Athlete

Supplementation

The last component of a sport development program is supplementation. Athletic achievement is determined by consistent hard, purposeful work period. One cannot expect a pill or a powder alone to transport them into the victory circle. However, supplements do have several important roles in the dedicated athletes training plan. *Supplements* when applied correctly will reduce dietary deficiency, allow for convenient lost cost quality meal replacement, increase musculoskeletal support, promote greater recovery, and reduce systematic inflammation (Dunford 2019).

Dietary Deficiency

Athletes are usually more active and considerably larger than the average individual in society (Norton 2001, Monsoon 2018). Therefore, athletic caloric and nutrient requirements are often one in half to two times greater than that of a normal individual. Daily food preparation and supplying the body with quality calories often becomes a considerable challenge for one's budget and time management. An athlete's day is dominated with school commitments, skill practice, team practice, physical conditioning, and physical, mental, and emotional recovery. Consistent high-quality fresh food preparation tends to be replaced with quick, processed, low-cost, tasty meals. The most significant macronutrient requirement for high school age athletes and beyond is protein intake per day. High quality protein is expensive and for most athletes and is often under consumed. Therefore, for most individuals to meet the daily requirement, they will need to augment their animal protein diet with sources from plant-based powder. *Plant-based proteins* tend to avoid triggering food allergies that dairy or egg proteins could stimulate and contain less hormones and antibiotics. One should increase supplemental protein slowly and work to meet the desired goal intake value over a 2- to 3-week period.

The second macronutrient to consider is fat but especially the essential fats of EPA, DHA, and GLA. Fats are critical for hormone production, inflammation management, and meeting overall energy requirements. Fats (seeds, nuts, olive oil, egg yolks, and avocado) are frequently maligned in the public lexicon but are often cheaper, higher in nutritional value, promote fat loss, and possess greater portability and satiety than non-vegetable source carbohydrates. The *essential fats* are contained in the seafood, fish, nut, and seed food groups. If athletes are not consuming these selections with high frequency and significant concentration, fat supplementation is indicated. Fish oil (EPA and DHA) will need to be consumed between a

1- to 4-gram range each while GLA is between .5 to 1.5 grams a day. Larger values are indicated based on the size of the athlete.

The third macronutrient is carbohydrate. Carbohydrate is probably the most misunderstood and confusing of the three. In part because there is no carbohydrate requirement for optimal health, yet it is by far of the three the most consumed (Dunford 2019). Athletes who exercise at high intensities physiologically prefer glucose as their primary fuel source (Dunford 2019). Carbohydrates also contain arguably the most food groupings (breads, cereals, fruit, vegetables, most snacks, most desserts, softs drinks, juices, energy drinks, etc.). Thus, when individuals state "I am 'avoiding carbs,'" it typically means they are not eating the low-nutrient, high-sugar simple varieties. Athletes who are training two hours or under at a time in a moderate temperature and consuming three to five nutrient rich meals a day will not require carbohydrate or electrolyte drink products for replenishment to maintain optimal performance (Dunford 2012). In select cases of training in high temperatures or multiple high intense training sessions a day or multi-hour endurance events, carbohydrate-rich beverages and products may be advantageous. For those specific individuals, seeking customized guidelines from a credentialed professional is recommended (Dunford 2012).

Meal replacement products and multivitamins (and minerals) are therefore critical to the foundation of an athlete's supplement program. Selecting a quality product can be difficult due to the many techniques manufactures use in their production practices and marketing campaigns. However, here is a table below to decrease your odds of selecting an inferior product.

Low Quality Forms	**High Quality Forms**	**Low Quality Forms**	**High Quality Forms**	**Low Quality Forms**	**High Quality Forms**
Vitamins	Vitamins	Minerals	Minerals	E. Fats	Essential Fats
Folic acid	Folate or 5-MTHF (L-5-Methyltetrahydrofolate	Carbonate	Glycinate	Omega-3 Fatty Acids	Eicosapentaenoic Acid (EPA)
Cyanocobalamin	Methylcobalamin	Gluconate	Citrate		Docosahexaenoic Acid (EPA)

Cholecalciferol Vitamin D2	Cholecalciferol Vitamin D3	Oxide	Malate	Omega-6 Fatty Acids	Gamma-linolenic acid (GLA)
Vitamin K 1	Vitamin K 1 and 2	Hydroxide	Lactate		
Vitamin E Alpha tocopherol	Vitamin E Mixed Tocopherols	Sulfate			

Figure 7.5. Comparing High- and Low-Quality Supplement Forms

In addition to the above table, coaches want to check if the product the athlete is taking meet any of the following criteria:

1. The product should be pharmaceutical grade or medical grade and have the GMP standard (good manufacturing practices) on the website or product label (Dunford 2019).
2. Products sold for pet use should be avoided altogether.
3. Be sure the product is third party tested for toxins or impurities; look for one of these on the label or website: NSF International, US Pharmacopeia, Underwriters Laboratory, or Consumer Lab seal (Dunford 2019).
4. Be sure the product has been researched and has shown it can support its label claims (Dunford 2019).
5. Products sold in retail or nutrition stores can be purchased with caution. Chiefly the products with a long-track record of brand quality and scientific support. Be extremely critical of products with celebrity endorsement. Keep in mind that general supplement regulations for retail products are typically extremely low and overpriced (Dunford 2019).

Behavior Focus: *Multivitamins* are usually recommended to be taken with food either once or twice a day. My recommendation would be to take them at breakfast and or dinner, depending on the product to increase compliance.

Meal Replacement

In addition to the information above, a meal replacement supplement needs to contain a macronutrient relationship that is roughly equal protein and carbohydrate and half to 25 percent fat. Protein and carbohydrate total will vary based on the requirement of the athlete. The following total are appropriate for a male athlete who is looking to maintain two hundred pounds and eats an additional three meals a day; the female totals are for an athlete who is looking to maintain one hundred and twenty pounds and eats an additional three meals a day.

Macronutrients	Females	Calories	Macronutrients	Males	Calories
Protein (grams)	20 to 30	80–120	**Protein (grams)**	40 to 50	160–200
Carbohydrate (grams)	20 to 30	80–120	**Carbohydrate (grams)**	40 to 50	160–200
Fat (grams)	5 to 15	45–135	**Fat (grams)**	10 to 25	90–225
	Total Cals	205–375		**Total Cals**	410–625

Figure 7.6. Meal Replacement Macronutrient Ratios

Musculoskeletal Support

The following primary nutrients are required to promote ideal *musculoskeletal health*: calcium, magnesium, phosphorus, vitamin D, vitamin C, and vitamin K. Secondarily, these nutrients assist in influencing the process positively: manganese, copper, iron, potassium, and vitamin A. Maintaining the structure of an athlete (bones, ligaments, tendons) is critical to avoiding injury and maximizing performance. Consuming select additional nutrients may be required if the foods that supply these nutrients are not readily consumed or are not highly concentrated in the diet. These nutrients can be consumed rather easily if an athlete eats a balance whole food diet, except for calcium, vitamin D, and, for female athletes, iron. These three nutrients may have to be taken in addition to a multivitamin if the athlete does not consume considerable concentrations of red meat (iron source), green leaves (calcium, vitamin C, vitamin A, and vitamin K source), and are outside several days a week in the sun (vitamin D source). This would be especially true if the athlete is suffering from repeated fractures or broken bones.

Athletes looking to increase lean mass should consider adding creatine to their strength program to augment their resistance training. *Creatine* is very researched, extremely safe for healthy individuals and highly effective. Coaches should not recommend its use to athletes until they reach high school age and or until they can perform at least twenty-five technique repetitions of level 4 body weight exercise. Research provides several different protocols for effective use; the following is one that is repeated very commonly in research studies:

Step One	**Step Two**	**Step Three**	**Step Four**	**Step Five**	**Step Six**
Find Athletes Ideal Weight	Divide Weight by 2.2	Multiply value by .3	Divide **23.5** by 4: Take for 6 days	Maintain 10% of Loading Dose: 23.5 × .1	Take during off-season, preseason, and in-season cycles
Males Ht. × 2.4 to 2.9	72 inches × 2.4 = **173/2.2**	78.5 × .3 = **23.5** grams	**6 grams,** 4 × a day for 6 days	23.5 × 10% = **2.35 grams**	
Females Ht. × 1.8 to 2.25	64 inches × 1.8 = **115/2.2**	52.3 × .3 = **15.7** grams	**4 grams,** 4 × a day for 6 days	15.7 × 10% = **1.57 grams**	

Figure 7.7. Creatine Supplementation for High School and Collegiate Athletes

Behavior Focus: Cardiovascular conditioning and skill practice sessions if the weather is conducive should be performed outside. Vitamin D levels should be checked via a blood test to confirm status and proper supplement dosing.

Inflammation

Inflammation is the process the body uses to communicate between its different systems to protect itself from infection, illness, injury, and poor lifestyle choices. Signals are released to rebuild the damaged tissues or defend the infected areas depending on the availability of nutrients in the body. Inflammation response is highly variable but depends heavily on the nutrient tissue reserves of the body, the quality of vitamin and mineral content in the diet, and the continuous burden of environmental stressors impacting the body at a given time. The more classic signs of an acute immune response include redness, pain, heat, a reduction in strength, and swelling. Supplementation works to address inflammation in the following ways: first, it supports the communication process of injury response (fish oil) so that resources are not overly committed to stressed areas; secondly, supplements quickly address the damage areas and upregulate the repair process (enzymes); lastly, supplements decrease the pain magnitude (curcumin) to promote a quicker return to normal physical capacity.

Behavior Focus: Inflammatory protocols generally are not required for healthy athletes who are high school age or younger who do not participate in high-contact sports. However, larger athletes may benefit from these protocols due to the stress of aggressive, explosive movement patterns against their joints, tendons, and ligaments or athlete who participate in contact sports.

Recovery

Athletes, as discussed earlier, due to their intense physical conditioning and skill practice, may for a period require additional assistance in promoting their body back into physiologic balance. The tissue in the body that is most often used to drive this process is skeletal muscle. This is not obviously a desirable situation for athletes, so therefore recovery products from time to time may be required in periods of intense training and conditioning (late off-season and preseason). These products tend to be protein and simple carbohydrate combinations or specialized protein precursors called branch chain amino acids (BCAAs). Athletes may benefit from recovery protocols if they participate in more than one sport at the same time, participate in a sport and are also engaging in a strength and conditioning program, or fail to consume at least a half a gram of bodyweight of protein from the diet daily.

Behavior Focus: Most products are either a powder or a drink that can be easily mixed into a beverage or consumed as a stand-alone product post-workout session.

Energy

The final area of supplementation is energy support. These products should generally be reserved for older high-performing senior varsity athletes or college-level sport participants. If younger athletes at the elementary and junior high level are having serious bouts of fatigue, review their lifestyle structure, sleep hygiene, and dietary intake. Recommending athletes that young to consume caffeine from green tea or utilize adaptogenic herbs that augment adrenal function is not recommended. The only supplement products at that age appropriate to address energy concerns is brewer's yeast (natural source of B vitamins), a high-quality multivitamin, and potentially a plant-based protein powder. High school varsity athletes may benefit from adding green tea, and depending on their training schedule and academic demands, some limited herbal products like Rhodiola rosea, Siberian ginseng (Eleuthero), and Schisandra.

Behavior Focus: Energy protocols should only be added if the athlete's lifestyle, dietary intake, and physical activity schedule have been properly structured and adhered too. A coach should not provide an athlete with recommendations or tools to further their dysfunction or promote poor time management practices.

Coaches who are working with female athletes need to be aware of what is termed the *female athlete triad.* A condition of endocrine dysregulation resulting from typically excessive activity levels and low caloric intake. However, not all situations include both extremes. This condition can be profoundly serious and highly personal, often requiring outside professional assistance and management. Coaches when working with female athletes should record weight, body fat percentages, and be aware of the following key symptoms: recurring stress fractures, large durations and frequency of exercise, low daily caloric intake, isolated eating, and irregular menstruation cycles (Dunford 2019).

In summary, high quality nutritional recommendations for athletes can be made basic. Junior and high school athletes require essentially one gram of protein per pound of ideal weight. Fat recommendations become satisfied when the recommended protein totals are achieved. Appropriate carbohydrate totals can be reached when athletes eat the recommended number of fruit and vegetables daily (8 to 12 servings for males, 5 to 8 servings for females) and make those selections from the critical high-nutrient categories. Additionally, athletes should include beans and grains (1/2 to 1 1/2 cups each for male, 1/4 to 1 cup for female) and nuts or seeds, 3 to 6 tablespoons combined.

Athletes now have a simple structure to gauge the nutritional status. Coaches who want a more custom solution for their athletes can review the introduction to nutrition video for the tutorial on how to use the excel worksheet that produces customized recommendations. The final chapter puts the previous information together in annual plan to systematically increase varsity athletic and college scholarship potential. The coach will need to implement the structure of management and accountability for development of the athlete, but chapter 8 will illustrate the framework.

Summary of Key Points

Major Concepts	Review Pages
Introduction to Athletic Dietary Structure	
Understanding High-Nutrient Food Groups	
Introduction to Athletic Supplementation	

Trainer's Corner

Professional Insights	Video Links
"Introduction to Athletic Nutrition"	
"Supplementation Protocols: A Closer Look"	

Discussion Questions:

1. Athletes are young, extremely healthy, and possess a robust metabolism; therefore, if they consume adequate calories, what they eat should not have a large impact on performance. True/False
2. Fresh fruits and vegetables both contain significant amounts of micronutrients. Consuming a "balanced" diet with several servings of these foods groups is the best way to ensure optimal nutrition. True/False
3. Athletic nutrition is not significantly different than eating for maximal longevity or weight loss. Calories are often reduced, protein is restricted, and fiber recommendations are high. True/False
4. Male and female nutrition is completely different and should be advised to consume different foods and concentrations of the macronutrients. True/False
5. Which of the following food groups are a good source of protein?
   a) fruit b) vegetables c) fish d) nuts and seeds
6. Which of the following food groups are a good source of fat?
   a) fruit b) beans c) fish d) nuts and seeds
7. Which of the following food groups are a good source of carbohydrate?
   a)fruit b) beef c) fish d) nuts and seeds
8. Which macronutrient contains fiber?
   a) carbohydrates b) protein c) fat d) water
9. Supplementation has proven to be better at increasing athletic performance than a fresh diet of fruit, vegetables, and high-quality protein choices because the nutrients in each pill is standardized. True/False
10. Supplement products sold in retail stores undergoes a rigorous process of testing and research before it can be sold to the public. Therefore, these products typically are highly effective for addressing or attaining most label claims. True/False

APPENDIX

Male Athletic Nutritional Intake Ranges

Sport (Male)	Avg. Height Ranges	Weight Ranges	Pounds Per Inch	Lean Mass Pounds	Fat Mass Pounds	Total Cals	Water (Cups)	Protein (G)	Protein (G	Fats (G)	Carb (cals)	Fiber (G)	Leaf Cup	Non-Starchy	Starchy Veg	Fruit Cup	Bean Cup	Grain Cup	Seeds (Tbsp)	Onion Cloves	Green Tea Bags	Total Dietary Cals	Junk cals
Basketball	6.3 to	185	2.5 to 2.9	164 to	19	3220	12	148.0	21.1	107.3	1662.0	48.3	5.0	2.5	2.5	5.1	1.1	2.8	8.4	3.7	12.3	2819	401
	7.2 ft	250		212	38	4000	16	200.0	28.6	133.3	2000.0	60.0	6.0	3.0	3.0	6.2	1.4	3.4	10.1	5.0	16.7	3485	515
Volleyball	6.4 to	185	2.4 to 2.9	166 to	19	3220	12	148.0	21.1	107.3	1662.0	48.3	5.0	2.5	2.5	5.1	1.1	2.8	8.4	3.7	12.3	2819	401
	6.10 ft	238		202	36	3856	15	190.4	27.2	128.5	1937.6	57.6	5.8	2.9	2.9	6.0	1.3	3.3	9.7	4.8	15.9	3362	494
Swimming	6.2 to	178	2.4 to 2.9	160 to	18	3136	11	142.4	20.3	104.5	1625.6	47.0	4.9	2.4	2.4	5.0	1.1	2.8	8.2	3.6	11.9	2747	389
	6.7 ft	229		194	35	3748	14	183.2	26.2	124.9	1890.8	56.2	5.7	2.8	2.8	5.8	1.3	3.2	9.5	4.6	15.3	3269	479
Average Height Above Six Feet Two Inches						Total Cals	Water (Cups)	Protein (G)	Protein (G	Fats (G)	Carb (G)	Fiber (G)	Leaf Cup	Non-Starchy	Starchy Veg	Fruit Cup	Bean Cup	Grain Cup	Seeds (Tbsp)	Onion Cloves	Green Tea Bags	Total Dietary Cals	Junk cals
Tennis	5.7 to	147	2.2 to 2.5	132 to	15	2764	9	117.6	16.8	92.1	1464.4	41.5	4.4	2.2	2.2	4.5	1.0	2.5	7.4	2.9	9.8	2430	334
	6.9 ft	202		171	31	3424	13	161.6	23.1	114.1	1750.4	51.4	5.3	2.6	2.6	5.4	1.2	3.0	8.8	4.0	13.5	2993	431
Football	5.11 to	178	2.5 to 3.3	160 to	18	3136	11	142.4	20.3	104.5	1625.6	47.0	4.9	2.4	2.4	5.0	1.1	2.8	8.2	3.6	11.9	2747	389
	6.5 ft	254		216	38	4048	16	203.2	29.0	134.9	2020.8	60.7	6.1	3.0	3.0	6.2	1.4	3.4	10.2	5.1	16.9	3525	523
Hockey	5.8 to	170	2.5 to 2.9	153 to	17	3040	11	136.0	19.4	101.3	1584.0	45.6	4.8	2.4	2.4	4.9	1.1	2.7	8.0	3.4	11.3	2665	375
	6.9 ft	235		200	35	3820	15	188.0	26.9	127.3	1922.0	57.3	5.8	2.9	2.9	5.9	1.3	3.3	9.7	4.7	15.2	3331	489
Baseball	5-6 to	190	2.6 to 3.3	171 to	19	3280	12	152.0	21.7	109.3	1688.0	49.2	5.1	2.5	2.5	5.2	1.2	2.9	8.5	3.8	12.7	2870	410
	6.11 ft	290		246	44	4480	18	232.0	33.1	149.3	2208.0	67.2	6.6	3.3	3.3	6.8	1.5	3.8	11.1	5.8	19.3	3894	586
Track &	6.0 to	172	2.4 to 2.6	155 to	17	3064	11	137.6	19.7	102.1	1594.4	46.0	4.8	2.4	2.4	4.9	1.1	2.7	8.1	3.4	11.5	2686	378
Field	6.5 ft	195		165	30	3340	12	156.0	22.3	111.3	1714.0	50.1	5.1	2.6	2.6	5.3	1.2	2.9	8.7	3.9	13.0	2921	419
Average Height Above Five Feet Eight Inches						Total Cals	Water (Cups)	Protein (G)	Protein (G	Fats (G)	Carb (G)	Fiber (G)	Leaf Cup	Non-Starchy	Starchy Veg	Fruit Cup	Bean Cup	Grain Cup	Seeds (Tbsp)	Onion Cloves	Green Tea Bags	Total Dietary Cals	Junk cals
Soccer	5.8 to	122	2.5 to 2.75	110	12	2464	8	97.6	13.9	82.1	1330.4	37.0	4.0	2.0	2.0	4.1	0.9	2.3	6.8	2.4	8.1	2174	290
	6.5 ft	210		178	32	3520	13	168.0	24.0	117.3	1792.0	52.8	5.4	2.7	2.7	5.5	1.2	3.1	9.0	4.2	14.0	3075	445
Cross	5.0 to	126	2.1 to 2.4	113	13	2512	8	100.8	14.4	83.7	1355.2	37.7	4.1	2.0	2.0	4.2	0.9	2.3	6.9	2.5	8.4	2215	297
Country	5.11	170		144	26	3040	11	136.0	19.4	101.3	1584.0	45.6	4.8	2.4	2.4	4.9	1.1	2.7	8.0	3.4	11.3	2665	375
Golf	5.5 to	162	2.5	146	12	2944	10	129.6	18.5	98.1	1542.4	44.2	4.6	2.3	2.3	4.7	1.1	2.6	7.8	3.2	10.8	2583	361
	6.2 ft	185		157	28	3220	12	148.0	21.1	107.3	1662.0	48.3	5.0	2.5	2.5	5.1	1.1	2.8	8.4	3.7	12.3	2819	401
Bodybuilders	5-5 to	208	3.2 to 3.5	197	11	3406	13	166.4	23.8	116.5	1781.6	52.4	5.3	2.7	2.7	5.5	1.2	3.0	9.0	4.2	13.8	3054	442
	6.2 ft	259		233	26	4108	16	207.2	29.6	136.9	2046.8	61.6	6.1	3.1	3.1	6.3	1.4	3.5	10.3	5.2	17.3	3577	531
Wrestling	5.0 to	132	2.2 to 2.4	125	7	2584	8	105.6	15.1	86.1	1380.4	38.8	4.2	2.1	2.1	4.3	0.9	2.4	7.1	2.6	8.8	2276	308
	5.8 ft	163		147	16	2956	10	130.4	18.6	98.5	1547.6	44.3	4.6	2.3	2.3	4.8	1.1	2.6	7.8	3.3	10.9	2594	362
Average Male Athlete Six foot and Two and half inches						Total Cals	Water (Cups)	Protein (G)	Protein (G	Fats (G)	Carb (G)	Fiber (G)	Leaf Cup	Non-Starchy	Starchy Veg	Fruit Cup	Bean Cup	Grain Cup	Seeds (Tbsp)	Onion Cloves	Green Tea Bags	Total Dietary Cals	Junk cals
General	6.0 to	180	2.5 to 2.9	162	18	3160	11	144.0	20.6	105.3	1636.0	47.4	4.9	2.5	2.5	5.0	1.1	2.8	8.3	3.6	12.0	2768	392
Athlete	6.5 ft	223		190	33	3676	14	178.4	25.5	122.5	1859.6	55.1	5.6	2.8	2.8	5.7	1.3	3.2	9.4	4.5	14.9	3208	468

INTEGRATED WELLNESS
Personal Health and Performance Consultant Group

Female Athletic Nutritional Intake Ranges

Sport (Female)	Height	Weight Ranges	Pounds Per Inch	Lean Mass	Fat Mass	Total Cals	Water (Cups)	Protein (G)	Protein (G)	Fats (G)	Carb (G)	Fiber (G)	Leaf Cup	Non-Starchy	Starchy Veg	Fruits Cup	Bean Cup	Grains Cup	Seeds (Tbsp)	Whole Grain	Green Tea Bags	Total Dietary Cals	Junk cals
Basketball	5.3	116	1.85 to 2.1	99	17	2302	7	92.8	13.5	79.7	1303.2	35.9	3.9	2.0	2.0	4.0	0.9	2.2	6.6	2.3	7.7	2112	280
	6.8 ft	184		152	32	3208	12	147.2	21.0	106.9	1656.8	48.1	5.0	2.5	2.5	5.1	1.1	2.8	8.4	3.7	12.3	2809	399
Volleyball	5.5	120	1.85 to 2.3	102	18	2440	8	96.0	13.7	81.3	1324.0	36.6	4.0	2.0	2.0	4.1	0.9	2.3	6.8	2.4	8.0	2153	287
	6.8 ft	184		152	32	3208	12	147.2	21.0	106.9	1656.8	48.1	5.0	2.5	2.5	5.1	1.1	2.8	8.4	3.7	12.3	2809	399
Average Height Above Five Feet Seven Inches						Total Cals	Water (Cups)	Protein (G)	Protein (G)	Fats (G)	Carb (G)	Fiber (G)	Leaf Cup	Non-Starchy	Starchy Veg	Fruits Cup	Bean Cup	Grains Cup	Seeds (Tbsp)	Whole Grain	Green Tea Bags	Dietary Cals	Junk cals
Softball	5.4 to	118	1.85 to 2.45	100	18	2416	7	94.4	13.5	80.5	1313.6	38.2	3.9	2.0	2.0	4.0	0.9	2.2	6.7	2.4	7.9	2133	283
	6.0 ft	176		145	31	3112	11	140.8	20.1	103.7	1615.2	46.7	4.8	2.4	2.4	5.0	1.1	2.8	8.2	3.6	11.7	2727	385
Swimming	5.3 to	116	1.85 to 2.15	99	17	2302	7	92.8	13.3	79.2	1303.2	36.0	3.8	2.0	2.0	4.0	0.9	2.2	6.6	2.2	7.7	2112	280
	6.0 ft	155		128	27	2860	10	124.0	17.7	95.3	1500.0	42.5	4.5	2.5	2.3	4.6	1.0	2.6	7.8	3.1	10.3	2512	348
Tennis	5.3 to	116	1.85 to 2.2	99	17	2392	7	92.8	13.5	79.7	1303.2	35.9	3.9	2.0	2.0	4.0	0.9	2.2	6.6	2.3	7.7	2112	280
	5.10 ft	154		127	27	2848	10	125.2	17.6	94.9	1500.8	42.7	4.5	2.5	2.5	4.6	1.0	2.8	7.8	3.1	10.3	2501	347
Average Height Above Five Feet Five Inches						Total Cals	Water (Cups)	Protein (G)	Protein (G)	Fats (G)	Carb (G)	Fiber (G)	Leaf Cup	Non-Starchy	Starchy Veg	Fruits Cup	Bean Cup	Grains Cup	Seeds (Tbsp)	Whole Grain	Green Tea Bags	Dietary Cals	Junk cals
Track & Field	5.3 to	116	1.85 to 2.1	99	17	2302	7	92.8	13.3	79.2	1303.2	36.0	3.8	2.0	2.0	4.0	0.9	2.2	6.6	2.3	7.7	2112	280
	5.10 ft	147		121	26	2764	9	117.6	16.8	92.1	1444.4	41.5	4.4	2.2	2.2	4.5	1.0	2.5	7.4	2.9	9.8	2430	334
Soccer	5.2 to	114	1.85 to 2.2	97	17	2368	7	91.2	13.0	78.5	1292.8	35.5	3.9	1.9	1.9	4.0	0.9	2.2	6.6	2.3	7.8	2092	276
	5.9 ft	152		125	27	2824	10	121.6	17.4	94.1	1490.4	42.4	4.5	2.2	2.2	4.6	1.0	2.5	7.6	3.0	10.1	2481	343
Lacrosse	5.2 to	114	1.85 to 2.3	97	17	2368	7	91.2	13.0	78.9	1292.8	35.5	3.9	1.9	1.9	4.0	0.9	2.2	6.6	2.3	7.8	2092	276
	5.8 ft	156		128	28	2872	10	124.8	17.8	96.7	1511.2	43.1	4.5	2.3	2.3	4.6	1.0	2.6	7.7	3.1	10.4	2522	350
Golf	5.2 to	114	1.85 to 2.3	97	17	2368	7	91.2	13.0	78.9	1292.8	35.5	3.8	1.9	1.9	4.0	0.9	2.2	6.6	2.3	7.6	2092	276
	5.9 ft	159		131	28	2908	10	127.2	18.2	96.8	1526.0	43.6	4.6	2.3	2.3	4.7	1.0	2.6	7.7	3.2	10.6	2553	355
Average Height Below Five Feet Five Inches						Total Cals	Water (Cups)	Protein (G)	Protein (G)	Fats (G)	Carb (G)	Fiber (G)	Leaf Cup	Non-Starchy	Starchy Veg	Fruits Cup	Bean Cup	Grains Cup	Seeds (Tbsp)	Whole Grain	Green Tea Bags	Dietary Cals	Junk cals
Bodybuilding	5.0 to	106	2.1 to 2.4	90	16	2272	7	84.8	12.1	75.2	1211.2	34.1	3.8	1.9	1.9	3.8	0.9	2.1	6.4	2.1	7.1	2010	262
	5.4 ft	154		127	27	2848	10	125.2	17.6	94.9	1500.8	42.7	4.5	2.5	2.5	4.6	1.0	2.8	7.8	3.1	10.3	2501	347
Cross Country	5.0 to	106	1.65 to 1.85	90	16	2272	7	84.8	12.1	75.7	1251.2	34.1	3.8	1.9	1.9	3.8	0.9	2.1	6.4	2.1	7.1	2010	262
	5.4 ft	118		97	21	2416	7	94.4	13.5	80.5	1313.6	36.2	3.9	2.0	2.0	4.0	0.9	2.2	6.7	2.4	7.8	2133	283
Cheerleading	4.11 to	98	1.67 to 1.85	83	15	2176	6	78.4	11.2	72.5	1209.6	32.6	3.6	1.8	1.8	3.7	0.8	2.1	6.2	2.0	6.5	1928	248
	5.4 ft	118		97	21	2416	7	94.4	13.5	80.5	1313.6	38.2	3.9	2.0	2.0	4.0	0.9	2.2	6.7	2.4	7.9	2133	283
Average Female Athlete Five Feet and seven inches						Total Cals	Water (Cups)	Protein (G)	Protein (G)	Fats (G)	Carb (G)	Fiber (G)	Leaf Cup	Non-Starchy	Starchy Veg	Fruits Cup	Bean Cup	Grains Cup	Seeds (Tbsp)	Whole Grain	Green Tea Bags	Dietary Cals	Junk cals
The General Athlete	5.5	120	1.85 to 2.21	102	18	2440	8	96.0	13.7	81.3	1324.0	36.6	4.0	2.0	2.0	4.1	0.9	2.3	6.8	2.4	8.0	2153	287
	6.2 ft	166.5		137	29	2998	10	133.2	19.0	99.9	1566.8	45.0	4.7	2.3	2.3	4.8	1.1	2.7	7.9	3.3	11.1	2629	369

CHAPTER 8

STRUCTURING THE ATHLETIC LIFESTYLE

Key Terms	Page
Mindset—the mood, inclination, intention, or area of primary focus of individual	
Lifestyle Behaviors—a set of daily practices that become habit and work to either help the body grow and rebuild or degenerate and age	
Recovery Practices—a set of daily practices that restore ideal hormonal balance that allow trauma induced by training to heal	
Physiologic Structure—the relationship of the other body systems to muscular and skeletal systems	

Chapter 6 illustrates how athletes are physically different than spectators and fans. They are usually larger, stronger, and possess far greater bio-motor ability than the typical person. Athletes are often quite different from most of their unathletic counterparts emotionally and psychologically as well (Schinke 2016, Breuner 2012). Athletes who are going to compete successfully for a Division I scholarship are required to continually stress the limits of their physical and mental limitations to optimally develop themselves. An athlete that is a Division I scholarship candidate will have to put substantial time into individual skill development, physical conditioning, and competitive play while making routine weekly sacrifice to their personal and social life (Poliquin 2001).

Chapter 6 is about how to provide an athlete with positive *lifestyle behaviors* at various levels of sport participation to avoid injury, emotional burnout, adverse academic performance, and complete social exclusion. If an individual incurs increasing obligation (physical or otherwise) on their time and energy reserves, they must reconfigure their daily behaviors to minimize stress, anxiety, and injury to meet the new responsibilities. The athletic body will be subjected to and required to heal from repetitive physical injury as well as emotional and psychological setbacks. This conditioning process combined with the proper recovery practices adapts the youth athlete to an elite level of physical and mental performance.

In this chapter, we will examine the program components and daily behaviors required to raise an average individual into the atmosphere of elite Division I scholarship candidacy. Physical adaptation, as discussed earlier, is uniquely fixed per the individual based on their genetic expression and program dedication (Monsoon 2018, Poliquin 2001). Thus, as a coach, not much can be done with your player's genetic inheritance, so their long-term success is highly determined by the management of their *mindset* and guidance of their practice schedules, weekly workouts, and adherence to daily recovery practices (Haff 2016). We begin by first examining the general level of sacrifice it will require to develop Division I physical capacity and skill mastery. Figure 8.1 illustrates a hypothetical day in the life of a committed athlete at different grade levels.

Proposed Athletic Schedule			
Daily Components	**Elementary: 4th to 5th Grade**	**Junior High School: 6th to 8th Grade**	**High School: 9th to 12 Grade**
Sleep	**10 Hours**	**9.5 Hours**	**8.5–9 Hours**
School	**7 Hours**	**7 Hours**	**7 hours**
Homework	**30 Min. to 1 Hour**	**1.5 Hours**	**2 Hours**
Team Sport Practice	**0 to 1 Hour**	**1.5 Hours**	**2.5 Hours**
Individual Skill Work	**30 Min**	**60 Min.**	**60–90 Min.**
Sport Video Study	**Recreational Game Viewing**	**Recreational & Instructional Game Viewing**	**Film Sessions 0–30 Min.**
Free Recreation	**5**	**3**	**0 to 2**
Athletic Recovery	**None**	**None**	**30 Min**
Physical Development	**15 Min.**	**30 Min.**	**30–60 Min.**

Figure 8.1. Athletic Lifestyle Design

This table depicts that athletes not only will be required to maintain a different physical commitment than their nonathletic peers, but they will also be required to make substantial social and emotional sacrifice as they pursue higher levels of competitive sport achievement (Schinke 2016, Breuner 2012). Coaching and developing competitive elementary and middle school sport athletes is quite different than coaching high school varsity level and Division I college sports (Breuner 2012). Elementary and junior high sport development require a high priority being placed on supervised skill practice, competitive play opportunities, and managing the emotional states of winning or losing.

At the earlier levels of sport, the focus on physical improvement and recovery behaviors is low. Skill mastery and the relationships between teammates and sport officials should be highlighted.

In addition to building emotional maturity and respect for competition, sport participation at these levels allow athletes a reasonable level of social exchange and family emotional normalcy. Youth athletes should not be required to forgo family events until late junior high school if elite or high school. Coaches need to be cautious about demanding premature and unnecessary sacrifice at this level will predispose an athlete to burn out and negative coping behaviors (Breuner 2012). However, athletes with a goal of competing at elite level varsity sports or playing at the college level will absolutely be required to make a significant prolonged restructuring to their days as well as compromise important family, friend, and romantic interests during the preseason and in-season cycles.

Chapter 5 covers the topic in greater detail. Coaches at the high school level will need to be cognizant of the length of the season, scheduled off days, and in-season holidays to allow for personal and player social and emotional recharging. Let us next examine the aspects of the proposed athletic lifestyle design.

Sleep

Importance: The optimal environment for growth, repair, weight maintenance, and daily learning consolidation

Behavior Focus: Getting to sleep before 10:30 p.m. and sleeping continuously for eight to nine hours

Athletic Significance: While individuals are asleep, their bodies can concentrate dietary and physiologic resources to repair and manufacture new cells. Adequate sleep creates the hormonal environment necessary for the body to reset or lower the stress (catabolic) hormones that prevent positive physical adaptation to intense exercise (Fullagar 2015).

Athletes should aim to sleep eight and a half plus hours per day, with recommendations varying between 8.5 to 10 hours depending on age (Malina 2004). Adult athletes require slightly less 8 to 9.5 hours while the recommendation for youth athletes (those < 18 years) is nine to ten hours. The recommendations are based on continuous hours of sleep, not intermittent sleep patterns of waking or multiple daily naps. If your athletes or coaching staff have a difficult time getting their recommended amount of sleep, even after significant lifestyle restructuring, refer to figure 8.2 for individualized improvement strategies that can help improve suboptimal sleep patterns. Coaches should screen for poor sleep behaviors in players aggressively. Sleep, if compromised, is extremely detrimental to the global development of the athlete. The impact will be felt in both the academic and athletic environments equally; thus, compromising player athletic eligibility, physical growth, practice recovery, and learning potential.

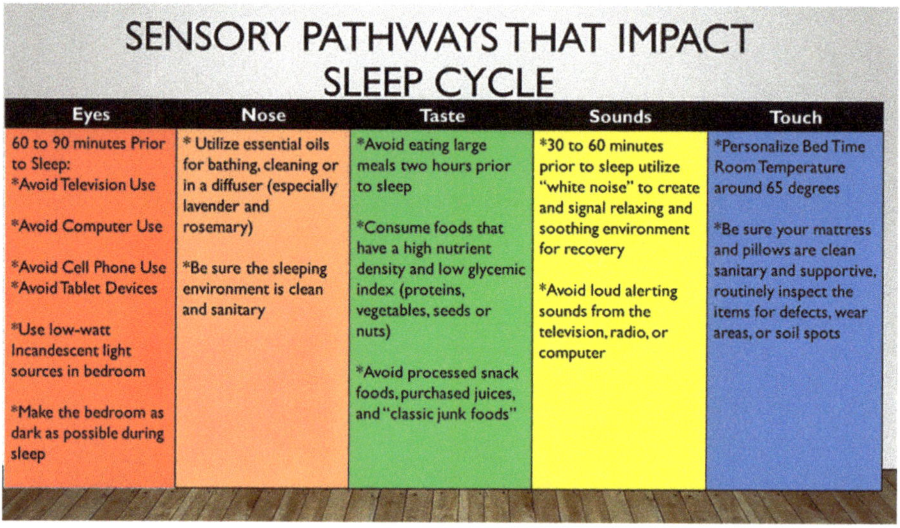

Figure 8.2. Sleep Optimization

In addition to the tips provided in figure 8.2, individuals who are struggling with restless sleep should remove electronics from the bedroom and reduce daily screen exposure from television and smart devices, especially at night. Evening blue light (phone, television, and computer light emission) screen exposure has been demonstrated to negatively alter hormone production, healthy metabolism, circadian rhythm, growth, and general recovery (Knufinke 2019).

School

Importance: School is the system that contains the rights and privileges of most sport youth amateur participation.

Behavior Focus: Attending all classes, avoiding disciplinary trouble, and remaining academically eligible

Athletic Significance: Sport participation will be severely impacted if not terminated if academic eligibility is compromised.

Homework

Importance: Homework is critical to learning time management skills and building problem-solving skills and thus critical to remaining eligible for sport participation.

Behavior Focus: Completing and turning in all assignments on time

Athletic Significance: Time management and the prioritization of daily tasks will become the most critical skills to master for athletes as they progress in their academic and athletic career. Athletes must become very proficient in designing and adhering to their daily routines to remain a good student, improve as an athlete, and have a decent social life.

Team Practice

Importance: Team practice creates the primary learning environment for sport position refinement, team growth, competitive socialization, and learning about the rules of game.

Behavior Focus: Punctuality, attendance, and opponent preparation

Athletic Significance: Team practice is the competitive environment in which athletes earn and maintain playing time, develop team skills, refine offensive and defensive sets, and refine the weekly game plan.

Individual Skill Practice

Importance: The primary environment of individual skill development and technique refinement

Behavior Focus: Athletes must constantly perfect their dominant skill and improve skill weakness in their game. Skill development can be self- or coach-directed.

Athletic Significance: Skill practice is the environment for players to become better at their position, earn more playing time, and expand their value to the team.

Individual Physical Development

Importance: The primary environment for physical improvement, bio-motor enhancement, and aesthetic changes

Behavior Focus: Athletes must design their day with the correct balance of behaviors (sleep, dietary intake, exercise routines, and recovery practices) to keep progressing while avoiding injury.

Athletic Significance: Physical change provides the necessary foundation to participate in higher levels of competitive sports.

Sport Video Study

Importance: The primary environment for understanding sport strategy and self-critique

Behavior Focus: Athletes must observe better players competing under competitive game situations to enhance their level of game mastery. Video review may have to occur under the supervision of a coach or with a more experienced player to be of significant value.

Athletic Significance: Development must occur for an athlete both physically and intellectually. Athletes must improve their skills, physical ability, and their understanding of game strategy, special situations, and opponent tendencies to properly master their sport. In addition, observing your own mistakes in a competitive situation can serve as a powerful motivator for change.

Free Recreation

Importance: A variable daily, weekly, or monthly time frame that is used to recover physically, emotionally, socially, and intellectually from ongoing obligations and dedication to the program.

Behavior Focus: Scheduled time frames of cessation from commitments must be kept but not extended as to avoid jeopardizing the progress earned in the annual development plan.

Athletic Significance: Motivation must be recycled for athletes due to their daily routine requiring extended periods of social isolation, increasing physical pain management, and prolonged mental focus. Thus, spending time with loved ones or engaging in fun activities with friends works strongly to keep individuals on an upward track.

Athletic Recovery

Athletic recovery is a set of physical, emotional, or psychological behaviors that allows the body to heal, rebuild, and increase capacity. Coaches need to be aware of some basic, low-cost, self-managed practices that an athlete can perform daily to restore themselves from the rigors and mental focus that athletic development requires at the late junior high and beyond levels of sport participation.

Athetic Recovery Practices		
Foam Roller	**Daily Reccomendations**	
	Each Muscle Group	10 to 20 rolls
Sleep	**Daily Reccomendations**	
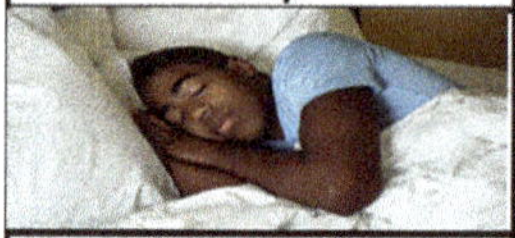	Continuous Hours	8 to 9 Hours
Supplements	**Daily Reccomendations**	
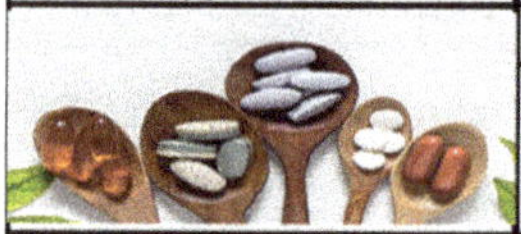	Anti-Inflammatory	Ezymes
		Fish Oil
		Tumeric
Epson Soak Bath	**Daily Reccomendations**	
	Continous Hours	Epson Salt
		Baking Soda
		Essential Oil
Stretch	**Daily Reccomendations**	
	Each Muscle	15 to 30 seconds
Dry Suana	**Daily Reccomendations**	
	Three to Six Days	174 F. 20 to 30 min
Music	**Daily Reccomendations**	
	Music	Relaxing Sounds/Lyrics
Ice Pack	**Daily Reccomendations**	
	After Actvity	15 to 30 minutes
Meditation/ Visualization	**Daily Reccomendations**	
	Daily	15 to 30 minutes

Figure 8.3 Recovery Behaviors

Foam Roller

Athletic Significance: Muscles are prone to fatigue, shortening from trauma, and strains from overuse. *Foam rolling* is an ideal activity to restore normal functioning, relieve muscular tension, decrease soreness, and enhance blood flow and decrease soft tissue density restriction.

Behavior Focus: Perform four to six days a week a series of ten to thirty rolls each muscle group prior to workout, skill proactive, or competitive play.

Supplements

Athletic Significance: Muscles and joint structures are prone to damage and trauma depending on sport characteristics, size of athlete, diet quality, and additional conditioning practices. Therefore, athletes may require extra support in returning the body to a pain-free, anabolic baseline. The combination of these products help relieve muscular soreness and decrease systemic inflammation.

Behavior Focus: Take supplements daily per individual requirements and dietary intake

Epsom Salt Soak

Athletic Significance: *Epsom salt baths* decrease musculoskeletal pain and improve joint range of motion from day-to-day. Athletes as they participate in high school and beyond are often in physical pain and will appreciate any advice that is low cost, effective, and uncomplicated to implement.

Behavior Focus: Perform Epsom baths prior to sleep. Scientific studies show that it decreases pain and improves range of motion, and anecdotal reports state that it may improve relaxation and enhance sleep.

Dry Sauna

Athletic Significance: *Dry high heat sauna* improves anabolic hormonal balance, raises total body blood perfusion, and increases aerobic conditioning levels. Safe, low cost, passive options for decreasing muscle breakdown, and enhancing physiologic repair is especially important both in developing young and mature older athletes alike. Dry sauna is most appropriate for high school athletes and beyond.

Behavior Focus: Research states that most of the benefits occur at temperature of 150 to 174 degrees Fahrenheit, at a frequency of three to six days a week for a duration of twenty to thirty minutes.

Static Stretching

Athletic Significance: Static stretching improves muscular flexibility through primary neurological inhibition.

Behavior Focus: Static stretching improves flexibility through a slight inhibition of fast twitch muscle activation. Therefore, it is advised to perform static stretching after the muscular activity is over, as a cool down, or on an off day.

Music

Athletic Significance: Music therapies has been researched in a variety of settings with a wide range of subjects, and the findings were: pain reduction and reduced perception, decreased anxiety, decreased depression, improved exercise recovery rates and stamina.

Behavior Focus: Listen to relaxing music before and after stressful situations to decrease anxiety, enhance mood, and increase healing. Immediately pre-event or during event, listen to something more stimulating to decrease pain and fatigue.

Icing

Athletic Significance: Icing has demonstrated a strong ability to decrease local inflammation to a joint or tissue when locally applied for up to twenty minutes several times a day. Ice baths have recently come into prominence for enhanced recovery for older or larger athletes who may be subject to greater trauma or inflammation.

Behavior Focus: Athletes when using ice need to remember to provide a thin layer between the ice and skin when relieving joint pain locally and for an "ice bath" soak in water temperatures that are between 50 to 59° F (10 and 15° C) for approximately twelve minutes.

Meditation/Visualization

Athletic Significance: Meditation has several benefits for athletes that include the following: lowering stress hormones, improving focus under adverse conditions, increases emotional stability, improved aerobic endurance, decreases anxiety, and increase pain tolerance.

Behavior Focus: Meditation does not have to be performed for several hours a day in some special area to be effective. The more impactful aspect of meditation is frequency and intensity opposed to duration. Most of the benefits cited in research can occur within a daily practice of twenty minutes.

Massage

Athletic Significance: Research states that massage is highly effective at assisting the damaged and fatigued muscles in upregulating the repair and recovery process.

Behavior Focus: Massage can be expensive when utilized as a weekly practice. If available seek out college programs or massage schools that will provide services at a discount in your area.

Physical Development (Resistance Training)

Chapter 5 approximates the objective measures it takes to reach the physical requirements of Division I scholarship candidacy. The major pathway to physical enhancement is dedication to a well-developed resistance and dietary program while maintaining adequate sleep patterns. Athletic nutrition is a large topic and will be presented alone in chapter 7. The following tables illustrate a general progression to elite level muscular endurance which combined with skill practice is the cornerstone of youth sport excellence. The young, developing athlete must avoid injury while increasing daily commitment to skill training and competitive play. Thus, coordinated, balanced muscular development is critical for long-term sport success (Breuner 2012).

The tables begin with the least challenging exercise in the leftmost column and progresses in exercise difficulty and intensity as one crosses the table to the right. Individuals can progress to the next column once they completed fifty continuous repetitions of the exercise. The table begins with calisthenic exercise progression, which is an appropriate starting point for athletes as young as eight years old (Shaikh 2016). Athletes who are older or more advanced in their physical development can begin with level 4 exercise. However, the athlete must be able to perform at a minimum fifteen repetitions of the exercise. Resistance training is challenging, but outcomes are not strictly determined by personal effort. Physical expression is accompanied by inherent genetic determinants in addition to commitment.

Elite level athletic ability is innate, as discussed earlier, training merely refines and optimizes it. Performing more than fifty repetitions with strict technique for athletes will have minimal impact on strength and bio-motor ability. Athletes at the point will need to seek greater loads by using dumbbells, barbells, or weight machines. Athletes and coaches need to keep in mind that hard work refines and maximizes the existing physiologic structure, it does not change it. Take for example the intrinsic differences between a bird and a fish; as a natural rule, birds do not swim effectively, and fish do not fly at all. These two animals not only struggle to perform these two "skills" effectively, it works against their natural design to force them to do so. These animals are created with fixed traits that uniquely allow them to maximize their separate and specific environments (like a track, a wrestling mat, ice rink, football or baseball field, swimming pool, basketball court, or tennis court etc.). One cannot train a fish to fly like a bird or a bird to swim like a fish regardless of dedication, desire, program design, professional instruction, or parental support. These animals have a pre-programed biologic threshold that limits their capacity to adapt irrespective of environmental stimuli or exposures (diet, sleep, training practice, supplements, coaching etc.). A fish will literally die (i.e., not be able to compete optimally) if left out of the water for too long. Therefore, for a coach, recruiting and developing an ideal physique already equipped with desirable traits is important to understand (chapter 5: figures 5.1 and 5.2).

The previous example of a fish and a bird are easy to contrast and understand in relation to sports and athletes because it depicts a strong natural dichotomy between two distinct species. The athlete will in a similar fashion share a comparable limitation to their biologic adaptability. Elite athletes are still in fact humans, they are stronger, bigger, more explosive, and more resilient than their "normal" counterparts yet still have limits. High school elite athletes can effectively dominate their competition across multiple sports but they increase in competitive challenge specialize at the collegiate level.

A limited review of sport history has shown that physical capacity is extremely fixed for even the most successful bodies of all time. Note that in all of recorded sport, there has only been a few individuals who have been born with an elite set of traits that could adapt to a professional standard in two sports—Bo Jackson, Deion Sanders, Jim Brown, Dave DeBusschere, Jim Thorpe, and a select limited number of others—and no athlete has been in Hall of Fame for two sports. The routine presented below should be thought of as phase one introduction to resistance training and performed six days a week. The young or physically underdeveloped should only perform one routine a day. The advanced (those level 4 and up) should use day one and day three together, day two and day four together, and day five and day six together. This will deliver a stimulus to the working muscle groups twice a week. Athletes upon mastery of level 4 exercise (50 to 75) continuous repetitions should then graduate to a year-around program of periodization presented in chapter 5.

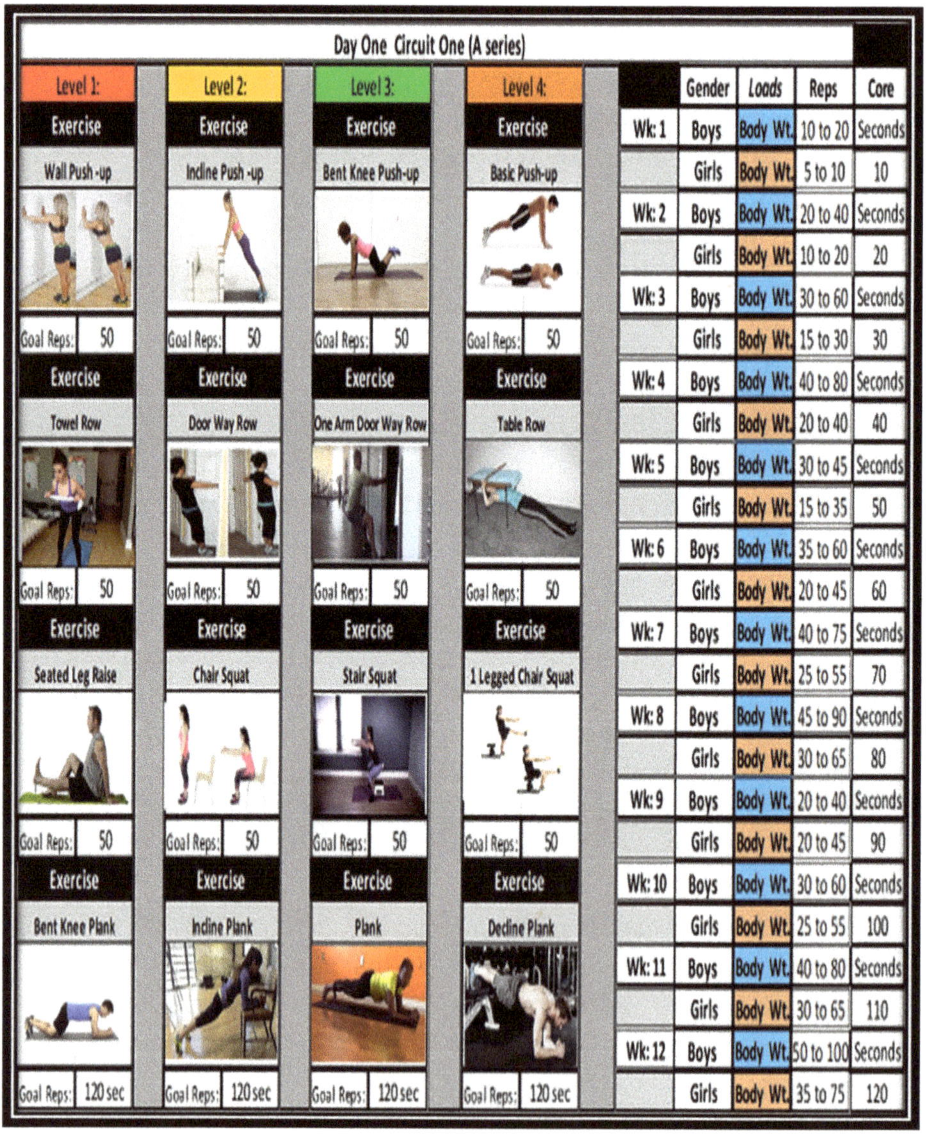

Day One Circuit One (A series)

Level 1:	Level 2:	Level 3:	Level 4:
Exercise	Exercise	Exercise	Exercise
Wall Push-up	Incline Push-up	Bent Knee Push-up	Basic Push-up
Goal Reps: 50	Goal Reps: 50	Goal Reps: 50	Goal Reps: 50
Exercise	Exercise	Exercise	Exercise
Towel Row	Door Way Row	One Arm Door Way Row	Table Row
Goal Reps: 50	Goal Reps: 50	Goal Reps: 50	Goal Reps: 50
Exercise	Exercise	Exercise	Exercise
Seated Leg Raise	Chair Squat	Stair Squat	1 Legged Chair Squat
Goal Reps: 50	Goal Reps: 50	Goal Reps: 50	Goal Reps: 50
Exercise	Exercise	Exercise	Exercise
Bent Knee Plank	Incline Plank	Plank	Decline Plank
Goal Reps: 120 sec	Goal Reps: 120 sec	Goal Reps: 120 sec	Goal Reps: 120 sec

	Gender	Loads	Reps	Core
Wk: 1	Boys	Body Wt.	10 to 20	Seconds
	Girls	Body Wt.	5 to 10	10
Wk: 2	Boys	Body Wt.	20 to 40	Seconds
	Girls	Body Wt.	10 to 20	20
Wk: 3	Boys	Body Wt.	30 to 60	Seconds
	Girls	Body Wt.	15 to 30	30
Wk: 4	Boys	Body Wt.	40 to 80	Seconds
	Girls	Body Wt.	20 to 40	40
Wk: 5	Boys	Body Wt.	30 to 45	Seconds
	Girls	Body Wt.	15 to 35	50
Wk: 6	Boys	Body Wt.	35 to 60	Seconds
	Girls	Body Wt.	20 to 45	60
Wk: 7	Boys	Body Wt.	40 to 75	Seconds
	Girls	Body Wt.	25 to 55	70
Wk: 8	Boys	Body Wt.	45 to 90	Seconds
	Girls	Body Wt.	30 to 65	80
Wk: 9	Boys	Body Wt.	20 to 40	Seconds
	Girls	Body Wt.	20 to 45	90
Wk: 10	Boys	Body Wt.	30 to 60	Seconds
	Girls	Body Wt.	25 to 55	100
Wk: 11	Boys	Body Wt.	40 to 80	Seconds
	Girls	Body Wt.	30 to 65	110
Wk: 12	Boys	Body Wt.	50 to 100	Seconds
	Girls	Body Wt.	35 to 75	120

Figure 8.4. Calisthenic Progression Series Day One—Circuit A
(Above photos from DuPage Fitness & Rehabilitation Center, Chap Earl)

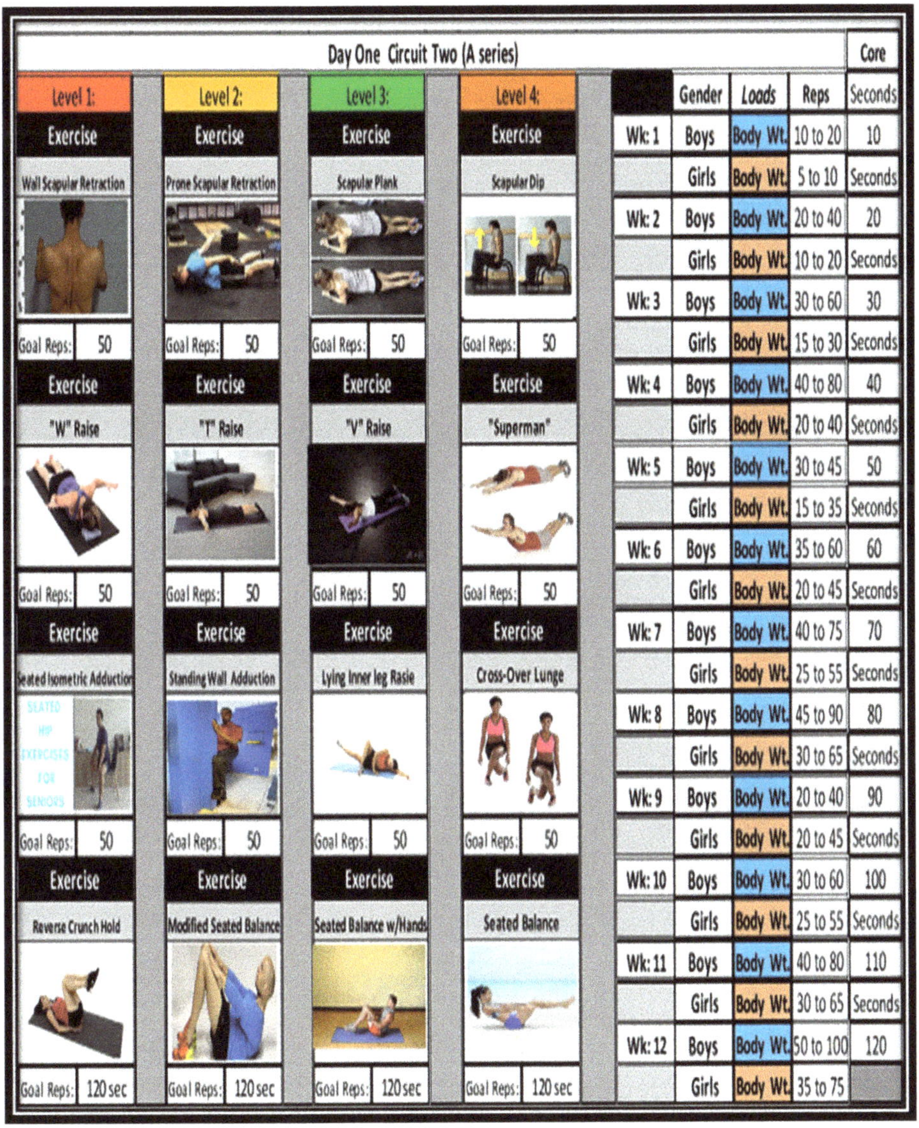

Figure 8.5. Calisthenic Progression Series Day One—Circuit B
(Photos from DuPage Fitness & Rehabilitation Center, Chad Earl)

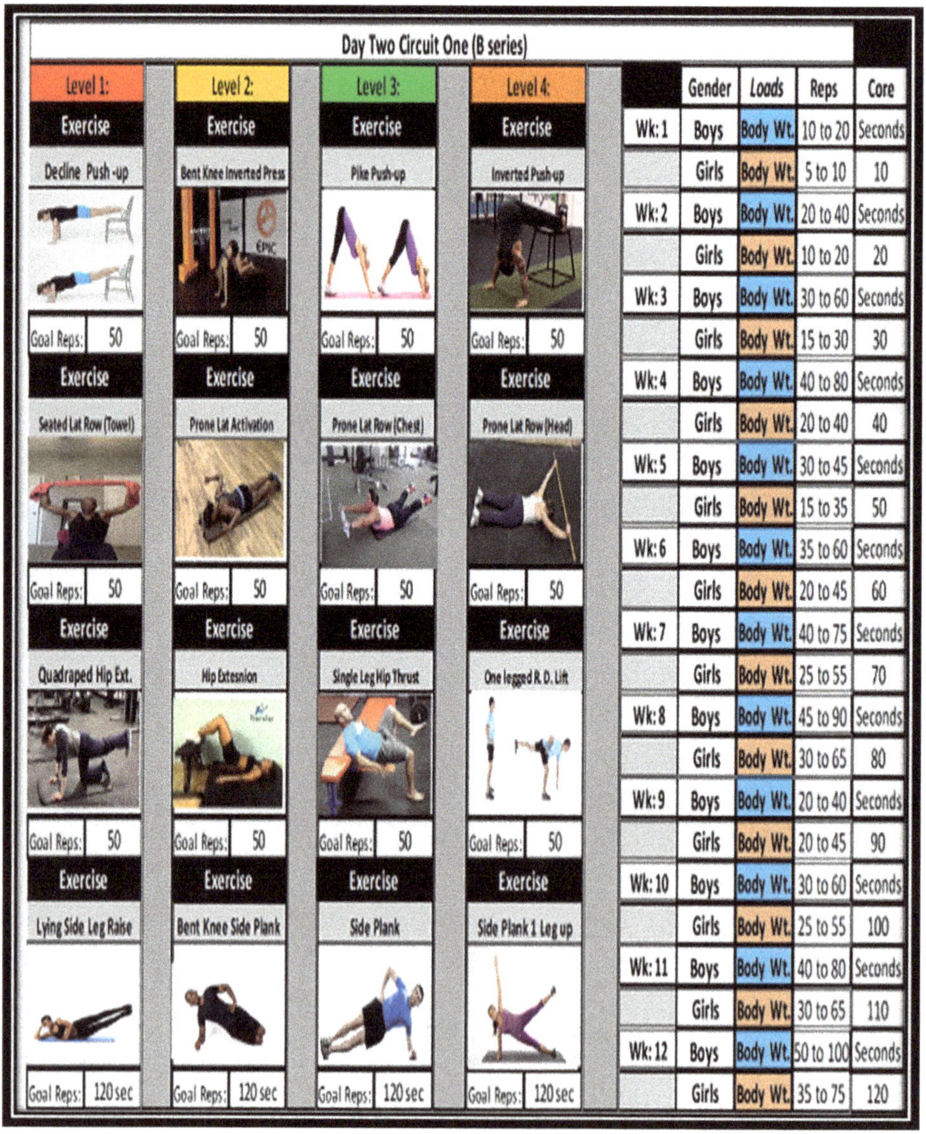

Day Two Circuit One (B series)

Level 1:	Level 2:	Level 3:	Level 4:
Exercise	Exercise	Exercise	Exercise
Decline Push-up	Bent Knee Inverted Press	Pike Push-up	Inverted Push-up
Goal Reps: 50	Goal Reps: 50	Goal Reps: 50	Goal Reps: 50
Exercise	Exercise	Exercise	Exercise
Seated Lat Row (Towel)	Prone Lat Activation	Prone Lat Row (Chest)	Prone Lat Row (Head)
Goal Reps: 50	Goal Reps: 50	Goal Reps: 50	Goal Reps: 50
Exercise	Exercise	Exercise	Exercise
Quadraped Hip Ext.	Hip Extesnion	Single Leg Hip Thrust	One legged R.D. Lift
Goal Reps: 50	Goal Reps: 50	Goal Reps: 50	Goal Reps: 50
Exercise	Exercise	Exercise	Exercise
Lying Side Leg Raise	Bent Knee Side Plank	Side Plank	Side Plank 1 Leg up
Goal Reps: 120sec	Goal Reps: 120sec	Goal Reps: 120sec	Goal Reps: 120sec

	Gender	Loads	Reps	Core
Wk: 1	Boys	Body Wt.	10 to 20	Seconds
	Girls	Body Wt.	5 to 10	10
Wk: 2	Boys	Body Wt.	20 to 40	Seconds
	Girls	Body Wt.	10 to 20	20
Wk: 3	Boys	Body Wt.	30 to 60	Seconds
	Girls	Body Wt.	15 to 30	30
Wk: 4	Boys	Body Wt.	40 to 80	Seconds
	Girls	Body Wt.	20 to 40	40
Wk: 5	Boys	Body Wt.	30 to 45	Seconds
	Girls	Body Wt.	15 to 35	50
Wk: 6	Boys	Body Wt.	35 to 60	Seconds
	Girls	Body Wt.	20 to 45	60
Wk: 7	Boys	Body Wt.	40 to 75	Seconds
	Girls	Body Wt.	25 to 55	70
Wk: 8	Boys	Body Wt.	45 to 90	Seconds
	Girls	Body Wt.	30 to 65	80
Wk: 9	Boys	Body Wt.	20 to 40	Seconds
	Girls	Body Wt.	20 to 45	90
Wk: 10	Boys	Body Wt.	30 to 60	Seconds
	Girls	Body Wt.	25 to 55	100
Wk: 11	Boys	Body Wt.	40 to 80	Seconds
	Girls	Body Wt.	30 to 65	110
Wk: 12	Boys	Body Wt.	50 to 100	Seconds
	Girls	Body Wt.	35 to 75	120

Figure 8.6. Calisthenic Progression Series Day Two—Circuit A
(Photos from DuPage Fitness & Rehabilitation Center, Chad Earl)

Day Two Circuit Two (B series)

Level 1:	Level 2:	Level 3:	Level 4:
Exercise	Exercise	Exercise	Exercise
Bicep Contraction	Standing Towel Curl	Incline Towel Curl	Horizontal Towel Curl
Goal Reps: 50	Goal Reps: 50	Goal Reps: 50	Goal Reps: 50
Exercise	Exercise	Exercise	Exercise
Bench Dip (Bent Knee)	Bench Dip (feet down)	Bench Dip (Feet up)	Parallel Bar Dip
Goal Reps: 50	Goal Reps: 50	Goal Reps: 50	Goal Reps: 50
Exercise	Exercise	Exercise	Exercise
Lying Leg Rasie	Standing Leg Rasie	Wall V-Slide	Lateral Step-up
Goal Reps: 50	Goal Reps: 50	Goal Reps: 50	Goal Reps: 50
Exercise	Exercise	Exercise	Exercise
Bridge	Single Leg Bridge	Bench Bridge	One Leg Bench Bridge
Goal Reps: 120sec	Goal Reps: 120sec	Goal Reps: 120sec	Goal Reps: 120sec

	Gender	Loads	Reps	Core Seconds
Wk: 1	Boys	Body Wt.	10 to 20	10
	Girls	Body Wt.	5 to 10	Seconds
Wk: 2	Boys	Body Wt.	20 to 40	20
	Girls	Body Wt.	10 to 20	Seconds
Wk: 3	Boys	Body Wt.	30 to 60	30
	Girls	Body Wt.	15 to 30	Seconds
Wk: 4	Boys	Body Wt.	40 to 80	40
	Girls	Body Wt.	20 to 40	Seconds
Wk: 5	Boys	Body Wt.	30 to 45	50
	Girls	Body Wt.	15 to 35	Seconds
Wk: 6	Boys	Body Wt.	35 to 60	60
	Girls	Body Wt.	20 to 45	Seconds
Wk: 7	Boys	Body Wt.	40 to 75	70
	Girls	Body Wt.	25 to 55	Seconds
Wk: 8	Boys	Body Wt.	45 to 90	80
	Girls	Body Wt.	30 to 65	Seconds
Wk: 9	Boys	Body Wt.	20 to 40	90
	Girls	Body Wt.	20 to 45	Seconds
Wk: 10	Boys	Body Wt.	30 to 60	100
	Girls	Body Wt.	25 to 55	Seconds
Wk: 11	Boys	Body Wt.	40 to 80	110
	Girls	Body Wt.	30 to 65	Seconds
Wk: 12	Boys	Body Wt.	50 to 100	120
	Girls	Body Wt.	35 to 75	

Figure 8.7. Calisthenic Progression Series Day Two—Circuit B
(Photo from DuPage Fitness & Rehabilitation Center, Chad Earl)

Day Three Circuit One (C series)

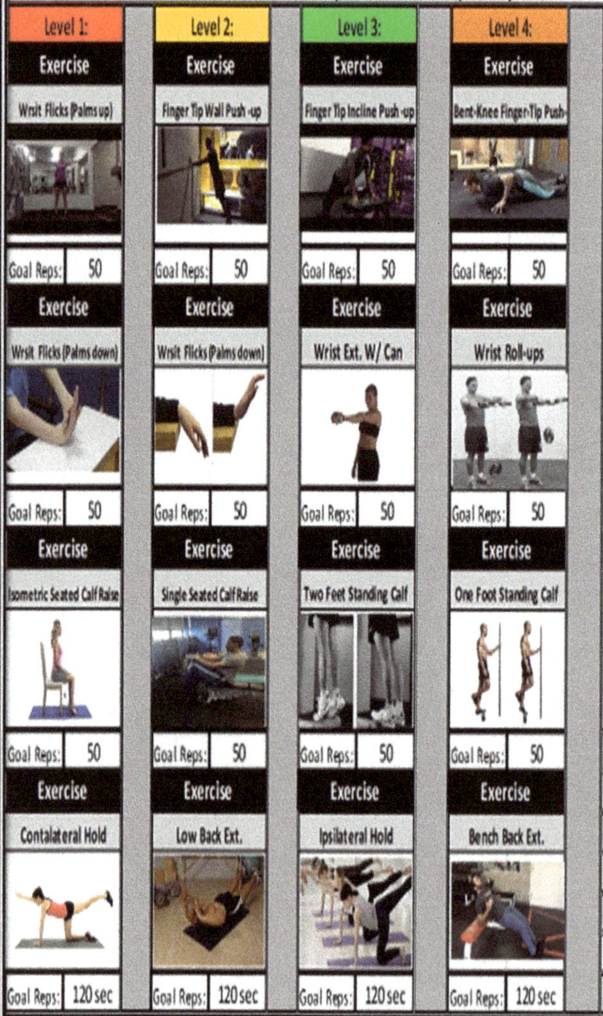

	Gender	Loads	Reps	Core
Wk: 1	Boys	Body Wt.	10 to 20	Seconds
	Girls	Body Wt.	5 to 10	10
Wk: 2	Boys	Body Wt.	20 to 40	Seconds
	Girls	Body Wt.	10 to 20	20
Wk: 3	Boys	Body Wt.	30 to 60	Seconds
	Girls	Body Wt.	15 to 30	30
Wk: 4	Boys	Body Wt.	40 to 80	Seconds
	Girls	Body Wt.	20 to 40	40
Wk: 5	Boys	Body Wt.	30 to 45	Seconds
	Girls	Body Wt.	15 to 35	50
Wk: 6	Boys	Body Wt.	35 to 60	Seconds
	Girls	Body Wt.	20 to 45	60
Wk: 7	Boys	Body Wt.	40 to 75	Seconds
	Girls	Body Wt.	25 to 55	70
Wk: 8	Boys	Body Wt.	45 to 90	Seconds
	Girls	Body Wt.	30 to 65	80
Wk: 9	Boys	Body Wt.	20 to 40	Seconds
	Girls	Body Wt.	20 to 45	90
Wk: 10	Boys	Body Wt.	30 to 60	Seconds
	Girls	Body Wt.	25 to 55	100
Wk: 11	Boys	Body Wt.	40 to 80	Seconds
	Girls	Body Wt.	30 to 65	110
Wk: 12	Boys	Body Wt.	50 to 100	Seconds
	Girls	Body Wt.	35 to 75	120

Figure 8.8. Calisthenic Progression Series Day Three—Circuit C
(Photo from DuPage Fitness & Rehabilitation Center, Chad Earl)

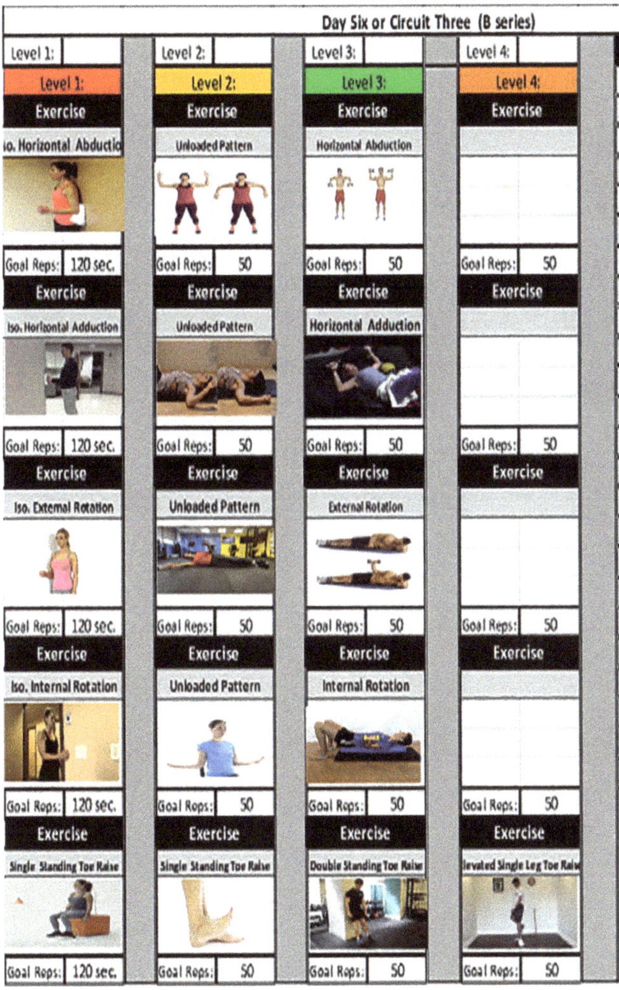

	Gender	Loads	Reps	Core Seconds
Wk: 1	Boys	Body Wt.	10 to 20	10
	Girls	Body Wt.	5 to 10	Seconds
Wk: 2	Boys	Body Wt.	20 to 40	20
	Girls	Body Wt.	10 to 20	Seconds
Wk: 3	Boys	Body Wt.	30 to 60	30
	Girls	Body Wt.	15 to 30	Seconds
Wk: 4	Boys	Body Wt.	40 to 80	40
	Girls	Body Wt.	20 to 40	Seconds
Wk: 5	Boys	Body Wt.	30 to 45	50
	Girls	Body Wt.	15 to 35	Seconds
Wk: 6	Boys	Body Wt.	35 to 60	60
	Girls	Body Wt.	20 to 45	Seconds
Wk: 7	Boys	Body Wt.	40 to 75	70
	Girls	Body Wt.	25 to 55	Seconds
Wk: 8	Boys	Body Wt.	45 to 90	80
	Girls	Body Wt.	30 to 65	Seconds
Wk: 9	Boys	Body Wt.	20 to 40	90
	Girls	Body Wt.	20 to 45	Seconds
Wk: 10	Boys	Body Wt.	30 to 60	100
	Girls	Body Wt.	25 to 55	Seconds
Wk: 11	Boys	Body Wt.	40 to 80	110
	Girls	Body Wt.	30 to 65	Seconds
Wk: 12	Boys	Body Wt.	50 to 100	120
	Girls	Body Wt.	35 to 75	

Figure 8.9. Calisthenic Progression Series Day Three—Circuit B
(Photo from DuPage Fitness & Rehabilitation Center, Chad Earl)

In summary, developing high-performing athletes is more comprehensive than playing the sport year around, lifting weights, and going to the gym or field to develop skills. Coaches need to allow for some emotional and social growth as well. Dedication is part of any meaningful achievement process, however early unbalanced or excessive restriction. The next chapter informs a coach about the differences between various levels of competition, community college, division I, II, III and NAIA. Chapter 9 introduces coaches to a structure for annual planning to optimize college athletic development and college scholarship potential. The coach will need to communicate with athletes and parents a vision for this transition, the mandatory rules of team participation, and what role or roles incoming athletes can fill.

Summary of Key Points

Major Concepts	Review Pages
Athletic Lifestyle Overview	**1–8**
Introduction to Athletic Recovery Practices	**3–7**
Introduction to Athletic Resistance Training	**3–5**

Trainer's Corner

Professional Insights	Video Links
"Athletic Conditioning with Minimal Equipment Level 1 to 4"	

Discussion Questions:

1. Young athletes should focus on developing their bodies solely when preparing themselves for competitive varsity athletics and collegiate scholarship potential. True/False
2. A junior high school or elementary-age athlete to be a standout high school varsity athlete will have to make social

and family sacrifices similar to an elite athlete to maximize their sport potential. True/False

3. A standout elementary-age athlete to maintain their sport success should focus on which of the following in the off-season: competitive play opportunities, supervised skill development sessions, structured physical strengthening, skill development?
4. Athletes that are untrained and want to get stronger should begin with a calisthenic program. True/False
5. Sleep is extremely important for growth, recovery, and educational learning, but if an athlete requires more time to work on their skills, develop physically, or study for classes, sleep hours should be reduced. True/False
6. Junior high athletes who dedicate themselves to the appropriate commitment to resistance training can expect to reach the critical thresholds for strength in high school. True/False
7. Most elite level athletes because of their supreme genetics can be conditioned to excel in any sport. True/False
8. Recovery practices to be effective must be utilized with some level of weekly consistency and quality. True/False
9. Increasing calisthenic repetitions above fifty repetitions is an appropriate and effective method to increase strength and bio-motor ability in high school and collegiate athletes. True/False
10. Coaching young athletes is about developing them to be better athletes through skill work and physical refinement, instruction around attitude, and respect is left for their parents. True/False

CHAPTER 9

DIFFERENCES BETWEEN COMMUNITY COLLEGE, DIVISION I, II, III, AND NAIA SPORT PROGRAMS

Formation of the NJCAA

The *National Junior College Athletic Association* was formed in 1937 in Fresno, California. Junior or community college representatives met to organize an association that would oversee a national program of sports and activities consistent with the educational objectives of junior or community colleges.

After the NJCAA reorganized in 1949 and divided its association into sixteen regions, California community colleges decided to separate, and although the NJCAA was founded in California, it no longer operates there and has been supplanted instead by the unaffiliated *California Community College Athletic Association* (CCCAA) with over one hundred colleges participating. The organization has grown and evolved over the years, and in 1953, the organization adopted the "Statement of Guiding Principles for Conducting Junior College Athletics." Over the years, the organization has continued to add sports programs to its scope and continued to structure divisions that allow for tournament play of many of the sports they oversee.

Today, the National Junior College Athletic Association is considered the primary governing body for community college sports nationwide. It is also the second-largest governing body of college-level athletics behind the National College Athletic Association

(NCAA). Each year, this association sees as many as 60,000 student athletes from 525 member colleges participate in twenty-eight different sports.

Division History

Each institution belonging to the NJCAA must decide to compete at the Division I, II, or III level in designated sports. Those community colleges that choose to compete on the Division I level may offer full athletic scholarships, tuition, fees, room and board, course-related books, and up to two hundred and fifty in course-required supplies and transportation cost one time per academic year to and from the college by direct route. *Division II* colleges are limited to awarding tuition, fees, course-related books, and up to $250 in course-required supplies. *Division III* institutions may provide no athletically related financial assistance. However, NJCAA colleges that do not offer athletic aid may choose to participate at the Division I or II level if they choose to do so.

Benefits of Sports at the Community College

Community colleges enroll between 11 and 12 million students annually. Over 50,000 of those students participate in intercollegiate athletics. Almost one half of the community colleges have intercollegiate sports programs. Community college are enhancing greater participation in athletic by starting new programs or expanding existing programs. These sport programs vary considerably, both in the type and number of sports available. Sport programs at the community college are not traditionally revenue generated. However, the advantages offered to the student-athlete make the cost of the programs worthwhile because it provides a full college experience.

Most community college students are adults with other professional and job responsibilities that prohibit them from spending additional time on campus. Few community colleges offer on campus housing, which further isolates students from one another. However, a basketball, volleyball, or football game is the perfect venue for bringing students, faculty, and community residents together to cheer on a common cause.

What to Play?

There are a variety of sports at community colleges, and they vary from college to college. Some community colleges are well-known for an outstanding athletic program while other may offer fewer programs due to cutbacks and budget constraints or a focus on academics. Generally speaking, the National Junior College Athletic Association lists the following sports for male athletes:

Baseball
Basketball
Bowling
Cross Country
Football
Golf
Ice Hockey
Indoor and Outdoor Track-and-Field
Lacrosse
Soccer
Tennis
Swimming
Wrestling

Women may also enjoy a wide range at the community college level, including:

Softball
Basketball
Bowling
Cross Country
Golf
Indoor and Outdoor Track-and-Field
Lacrosse
Soccer
Tennis
Swimming
Wrestling

The Representation of Women at the Community College Level

Although there are sports opportunities for women at the community college level, there is concern that women athletes may be underrepresented due to the lack of female athletes at the two-year colleges across the country (Thomas, K. 2011). There appears to be a shortage at community colleges of female athletes across the country, according to an article that points out this issue at Los Angeles Southwest College, where two-thirds of the student body is female. However, the large female population only account for one quarter of all athletes on the campus (Community College Review, 2003–2019). This report asserts that the demographic makeup at Los Angeles Southwest College is representative of many of the two-year schools across the country. Two-year colleges that face this same dilemma are failing to provide sufficient athletic opportunities for women. Many two-year colleges offer a range of athletic options for men but may only provide a few sports for women. These colleges claim that there are budget constraints or lack of interest from female students. It is hoped that there is a resurgence of athletic opportunities for female athletes at the two-year colleges that suffer from proposed budget constraints or claim that there is a lack of interest by females to participate in athletics.

How to Succeed in Community College Athletics

For student athletes who decide to begin their postsecondary athletic careers at a two-year institution, here are some strategies:

- **Develop Academically**—Sports may be your passion, and it may or may not be the occupation that supports you after college. However, establishing a thorough academic foundation is essential to the success of any student. It's important that as a student-athlete, you complete the core courses required to transfer to a four-year institution regardless if you plan on continuing to play sports or just further your education. Your coach should have an understanding of the courses required for you to transfer.

- **Develop Athletically**—Some student-athletes begin college and need to develop physically in order to compete in athletics at the four-year institutions. These athletes may find that the community college offers all the tangibles, physical development, skill enhancement, and academic preparation to increase the possibility of transferring to the next level.
- **Save Money**—Community college can offer a budget-friendly path to postsecondary education, coupled with the opportunity to participate in sports. The tuition at the community college is considerably less than four-year colleges, and you basically take the same courses for the first two years.

Athletics are an important part of many students' lives, and those who choose to begin their postsecondary academic and athletic careers at the community college will be pleased to find that they don't have to put their athletic prowess on hold during the first two years of their college experience, and parents will enjoy the reasonable cost of tuition in comparison to most four-year institutions.

Why Coach Sports at the Junior College Level

As illustrated in the preceding chapters regarding rationales to coaching sports at any level, the community college level offers coaches an opportunity to learn the various nuances of recruiting, coaching, and understanding academic requirements needed for both incoming high school and transferring student athletes.

Some community colleges offer scholarships and have housing, which allows the coach to gain experience of managing these tangibles related to coaching at the college level. Although community college sports present a competitive arena, coaches are not under great pressure to win. Providing an opportunity for student-athletes to develop their physical, psychological, social, mental, and personal being can be rewarding to individuals who aspire to coach at this level.

Another incentive for coaching at the community college level is establishing contacts and relationships with Division I, II and III colleges that offer scholarships (Division I and II), and many times, the community college is used to support the transition of a premiere student-athlete who was not a qualifier coming out of high school and could not transfer to a four-year institution that wanted to offer them a full scholarships. The relationships serve to be beneficial to both the community college and the four-year coach.

There are hundreds of professional athletes who have journeyed the two-year college route prior to becoming a professional athlete. Many of these athletes have given high praise to their community college coach for developing their skills and providing mentoring protocols that enabled them to achieve professionally in sports.

Division III Athletics

In April 2011, NCAA Division III celebrated the 190,000 student-athletes who represented about 450 DIII colleges and universities. Christina Riordan stated, "It was a time set aside to recognize the philosophy and educational values underlying this college level"(Riordan, C. M. 2017).

Division III was established in 1973, and the philosophical approach was to differentiate from the concept of big-time college athletics, which sometimes loses the concept that "athletes" are students first and should not be subjected to the undue pressure of "winning." Athletes should be part of the educational process and should be treated in a manner similar to other students. Balancing the tensions between athletics and academics in theory required no scholarships, shorter practices, and reduced time spent away from studying.

There is a power and prominence in sports that our culture has come to embrace. However, many administrators and coaches at the Division III level are fighting to ensure that the student-athlete and coaches are shielded from the excesses of a hypercompetitive environment. This has not curtailed the student-athlete experience of playing at the Divisions III level.

As part of a philosophical structure, Division III colleges cannot award athletic scholarships, but this does not diminish the competitive competition. Although the athletic department can't label the aid that is available for need-based sport participant, they leverage other types of aid that student-athletes may qualify for, such as merit-based scholarships and grants. With Division III mostly made up of small private schools, they tend to have these types of funds readily available.

Merit-based scholarships, for example, can be used for student-athletes who have excellent academic and leadership qualities. As a sport coach for a Division III college, you can target a perspective athlete for your program that has a high GPA and competitive test scores and work with the admission office at your college and come up with a favorable scholarship package made up of merit-based accolades. If the money isn't for their athletic abilities, the institution and coach are in the clear. The other possibility of the student-athlete being awarded a favorable financial aid package is if the family of the athlete qualifies for a substantial amount of need-based aid. In this case, the coach may make a scholarship offer that relies heavily on grants so that there is no requirement to pay the institution back. Even though this isn't an athletic scholarship, it can be an attractive financial offer.

Being a well-rounded athlete who can make an academic impact at the university is appealing to coaches. As a student-athlete, make sure you volunteer at your high school, participate in clubs within in the school and outside of sports, and most importantly focus on your academics. With a good GPA and test scores, you increase your opportunity to have your tuition paid for.

Parents' Note

To understand your son or daughter's scholarship opportunities at the Division III level, make sure to ask the college coach recruiting them what grants they offer and application requirements. Also be prepared to discuss how much your family needs to pay for college.

Do not be afraid to discuss your income earnings, this is a criterion to determining the financial assistant your family is eligible for. Keep in mind that sharing this information is confidential and is only used to determine you financial need.

Why Coach at the Division III Level

Dr. Thomas E. Reed was a Division III Head Men's Basketball coach, assistant women's volleyball, and men's soccer coach at Oberlin College. Although Oberlin College academic standards were very challenging and it was extremely competitive to gain admission as a student-athlete, Dr. Reed states, "The competitive teams in the conference made coaching a challenge, and as a young coach, it really challenged me to hone in on all the necessary skills to become a successful coach." Dr. Reed was fortunate to coach some outstanding student-athletes who after graduating became some of the most successful people in the country.

"It was a great experience mentoring and coaching at this level and the student-athletes I recruited were not only outstanding athletes but great human beings." Although winning was important to me personally, the institution was more concerned about the overall experience the student-athletes attained during their tenure at the college. Some of the other coaches in the conference would attest that coaching at the Division III level was gratifying, and most of them ended their coaching and teaching careers at their respected colleges.

History of Division II

In 1973, members of the NCAA voted to establish three divisions for athletic competition. This three-division structure gave NCAA members a varied menu to classify their programs. Before then, NCAA schools were classified as either "university" or "college" to distinguish between the larger and smaller athletics programs. The key distinction is that Division II institutions offer "partial scholarship" coupled with need-based financial aid, and this combination assist in covering the student-athlete college expense.

Uniqueness of Division II

Division II comprises of more than 300 NCAA colleges and universities, housed in forty-five states and enrollment throughout the various institutions range from twenty-five thousand to less than twenty-five hundred. It is the only division that has international membership (Simon Fraser University) and three other schools located in Puerto Rico. It provides thousands of student-athletes an opportunity to compete at a high level and excel in the classroom, coupled with engagement in college campus experience. The balance, in which student-athletes are recognized, also consists of academic success, athletics contributions, and campus/community involvement. Division II student-athletes are as competitive than any other athlete in the various divisions, and coaches at this level tend to do a good job recruiting perspective student-athletes despite the fact that many of the institutions that represent Division II don't have the financial resources to fully support their athletic programs or choose not to place such a heavy financial emphasis on athletics, which calls for additional strategies to generate revenue.

Division II features the best championship participant ratio among the three divisions, as well as an emphasis on regional competition in order to reduce missed class time. Division II is known for National Championship Festivals, Olympic-style events, whereas a number of national championships are held at a single site over several days. Almost all Division II championships finals are either broadcast live or live-streamed online.

Division II student-athletes generally represent a high percentage of the student body, which indicates that athletics and academics is an important component of the learning experience at these institutions. NCAA Division II currently requires fourteen core courses, three years of English, two years of mathematics (Algebra I or higher), two years of natural/physical science (one year of lab if offered by high school), two years of additional English, mathematics, or natural/physical science, two years of social science, three years of additional courses (from any area above, foreign language, or comparative religion/philosophy), and a minimum SAT score of

820 or an ACT sum score of 68. If you enroll on or after August 1, 2013, Division II will require sixteen courses. The new requirement are three years of additional English, mathematics, or natural/physical science and four years of additional courses (from any area above, foreign language, or comparative religion/philosophy).

It's Your Experience

In 2016, at the NCAA convention, Division II members created the brand "Make It Yours," where student-athletes who choose to attend these institutions should make graduating a priority, earning scholarship dollars for your athletic ability, and competing for championships. Your athletic participation should be a part of your college experience, coupled with all other experiences that are college related, making friends that will be lifelong because the campus affords a more intimate setting and your academic experience should be more personal, meaning professors, coaches, and staff care about you as a student and person. The coach should help the athlete develop their résumés as much as their athletic skills, and it should be a custom-fit approach to athletics and education.

Why Coach at the Division II Level

Coaching at the Division II level can be rewarding for coaches who are looking for a challenge, an opportunity to recruit with some scholarship finances but also respect the academic challenges that student-athletes will face while competing at this level. According to *Brady Bergeson*, Head Men's Basketball Coach at Regis University, "It's a matter of priorities, doing things really well, being driven by the game of basketball, the challenge, competition, and the relationships that are bonded through adversity, coupled with the never-ending learning processes, both professionally and personal." Having said that, I also respect that the student-athletes I have recruited placed academics as a high priority, which provides a balance for them.

Division II athletics can be a stepping-stone to professional athletics, but it is slightly more difficult than Division I. Many coaches feel that the focus on player development can actually help an athlete reach their potential faster and easier than at the Division I level.

History of Division I

Prior to splitting into various divisions in 1973, *Division I* was called the University Division of the NCAA. In 1973, it was renamed Division I while the College Division was split in two: the College Division members that offered scholarships or wanted to compete against those who did became Division II while those college who did not want to offer scholarships became Division III. There was a moratorium on any additional movement up to Division I until 2012. Colleges or universities that wanted to move to Division I must first be accepted for membership in a conference and show the NCAA that it has the financial ability to support a Division I program.

Division I Athletics

Considered by some as the major league of college athletics, Division I is heavily funded and a publicly well-known organization that is proud of having the best athletes. Among the three NCAA divisions, Division I colleges generally have the biggest student bodies, manage the largest athletic budgets, and offer the most scholarships. Colleges and universities who are members of Division I have made commitment to high academic standards that student-athletes have to maintain. Division I provides a plethora of opportunities for athletics participation.

There are close to three hundred and fifty colleges and universities in the Division I membership, and these colleges and universities field more than six thousand athletic teams, providing opportunities for more than one hundred and seventy thousand student-athletes to compete in NCAA sports each year.

Division I is subdivided based on football sponsorship. Colleges and universities that participate in bowl games belong to the Football Bowl Subdivision.

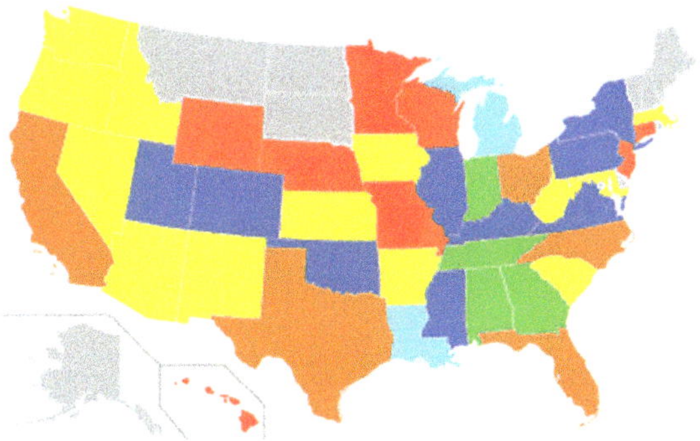

Number of FBS teams per state/territory as of 2014:[6]
Six or more FBS schools in the state
Five
Four
Three
Two
One
No FBS schools

There is another subdivision of the NCAA football championship, which is categorized as the Football Championship Subdivision. Those colleges and universities that do not have football programs are simply in Division I.

A League of Its Own

Division I athletics tend to breed Olympic hopefuls, future professional athletes, and superstars. Division I athletes focus more on the "athlete" aspect of student-athlete. However, this is not to say that Division I athletes don't take academics seriously.

High level competition best describes Division I sports because it is the pinnacle of amateur athletic competition. Almost every

To learn more:

6 https://en.wikipedia.org/wiki/NCAA_Division_I_Football_Bowl_Subdivision#cite_note-3

Division I program offers plenty of scholarships. However, it also depends on the sport. There is no doubt that Division I sports receive attention from media coverage, and sometimes a student-athletes highlight reel is featured on ESPN or everyone on campus knows who they are. Division I athletics is a place to shine and gain popularity, coupled with the level of competition provides a stepping-stone to the life of professional athletics. Many of the professional athletes in the National Basketball Association, Major League Baseball, or National Football League competed in Division I athletics, and although a small percentage make it to the professional level, Division I athletics provides an opportunity like no other NCAA Division level.

Unlike the other NCAA colleges and universities, there is so much money tied in with Division I athletics that the concept of developing the student-athlete into a well-rounded functioning adult is superseded by the pressure to win.

Why Coach at the Division I Level

Having the passion to coach at the Division I level requires commitment, a willingness to spend a lot of hours recruiting, game preparation, scouting, fundraising, player mentoring, and management, to name a few of the responsibilities. Most coaches who inspire to coach at this level have a burning desire to coach at an elite level, and some assume they will move up to the next level if they establish enough success and that is based on "winning." Some coaches just aspire to becoming a head coach at Division I college of university, others like the thrill of playing in front of big crowds and chasing the dream of winning some type of championship. The pay for coaching at a Division I college or university is substantially more than coaching at a Division II or III. However, there are expectations you must meet if you plan on retaining some type of tenure.

History of the NAIA

On March 10, 1940, the *National Association for Intercollegiate Basketball* (NAIB) was formed in Kansas City, Missouri. It was not until 1952 that NAIB changed to the National Association of Intercollegiate Athletic, and this also brought additional sponsorship for implementation of men's golf, tennis, and outdoor track-and-field. Football in the NAIA was split into two divisions in 1970 based on enrollment (Div. I and Div. II); it was consolidated back into a single division in 1997 (naiahoops.com 2011).

NAIA

The National Association of Intercollegiate Athletics (NAIA) is an association for small colleges and universities in North America. It has 251 member institutions, two are in British Columbia, one in the U.S. Virgin Islands, and the rest in the United States. The NAIA sponsors twenty-six national championships. The association announced in April 2018 that it would discontinue its Division II basketball championships for both men and women after the 2019-20 season. However, the proprietary approach that the NAIA takes is "Return on Athletics." Providing member institutions the tools and opportunities to support their institutional strategic priorities through data analytics that provides institutional level insight so members can maximize the impact athletics has on enrollment, student success and financial viability.

Benefits of Playing Sports in the NAIA

NAIA institutions take pride in providing the best for their student-athlete needs, desire, and ambitions. These member institution's philosophy is that the student-athlete are the driving force that makes "character" a core component and benefit of all intercollegiate sports. NAIA member colleges and universities give student-athletes the chance to compete and learn the benefit of teamwork and accomplishment. Administrators and coaches strive to impact the educational, athletic, and emotional development of their sport participants, and the tight-knit campus community allows for stronger relationships, personalized attention, and closer interaction both in and out of the classroom

Why Student-Athletes Choose to Play for NAIA Institutions

"The NAIA allowed me to be a competitor again. Every athlete should consider the NAIA. It was as exciting to compete in NAIA as any other level. There is nothing lesser about it."

Bryce Pierce, Cumberlands (Kentucky)

"It is being able to represent your school. Being able to see all the people you have been training with all season grow and seeing all the hard work pay off, in the end, is special."

Kassidy Boldt, Aquinas (Michigan)

"Basically, we get to compete against many other amazing teams. It's a very friendly yet competitive environment. All the teams are there working their hardest to achieve the same goal, doing the best that they can. It can be overwhelming at times, but being there with your team is a challenging yet amazing experience, and I would highly recommend it to any athlete to try and make it their goal."

Kayla Inlay, Morningside (Iowa)

"Competing in the NAIA can be so competitive, so stepping up to the next level is great."

Kelli Schrauth, Cardinal Stritch (Wisconsin)

"Growing up and playing basketball your whole life, it's cool to see all your hard work pay off by going to a national championship. It is something we have been working toward, and being able to play at this level is a blessing."

Kevin Vroegh, Cornerstone (Michigan)

"A championship event is where you see the best stars shine, and you get to see the best competition in one place. At the championship level, you normally bring you're a game and you really get to see what you have to offer as an athlete. It shows a lot about what kind of person you are whether you lose by a lot, win by a lot, or lose by a little bit. It shows how you react to circumstances, and you can see better of who you are as a person."

Logan Brettell, Baker (Kansas)

"I think most student-athletes are so competitive that they want to be the best and want to be the team that finished their season with a win. I think that playing in the national championship was that for me. We, as student-athletes, seek the games where we can play on the biggest stages. To play under the brightest lights, on the biggest stage, in front of as many people as they can play, and to play against a team that is the best in the country. The magnitude of those games was a lot more than I expected as a freshman coming into the NAIA, but I'm so glad that I chose to come to Baker and play in the NAIA because that experience is something that I will remember forever."

Makenzie Montano, Lindsey Wilson (Kentucky)

"You grow up watching championships, and I just couldn't believe that I was going to be on a team that was going to be considered one of the best in the country. I was given another shot to play while all these other teams' seasons were ending. I cried the first time we went to the national championship, I was so excited."

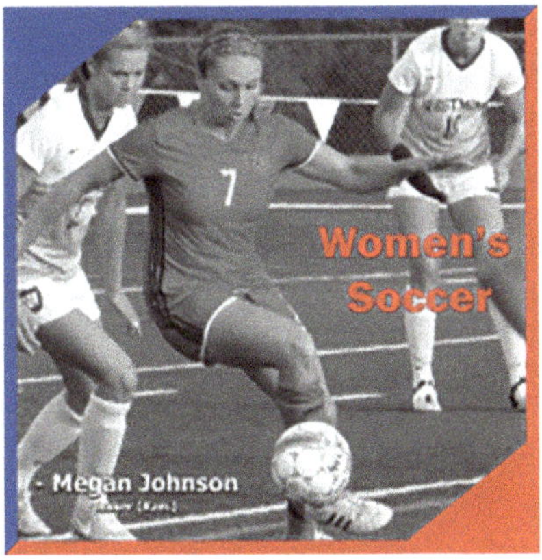

Megan Johnson, Baker (Kansas)

"The national championship was a phenomenal experience. I know that it has contributed to some of my favorite soccer memories without a doubt."

Noelle Miller, Lourdes (Ohio)

"We are in the gym every day for two or more hours, and it's not easy. We have practices where everything is great and we laugh. But there are also practices where we are tired and injured, and we have to overcome. It is wonderful though to show everyone what we have been working on at competitions."

Ruben Lopez, Wayland Baptist (Texas)

"The competitive nature. Every time we step on the court, we want to prove the people wrong who are doubters or who thought we shouldn't be there. Proving people wrong and having the motivation to compete for a national championship is surreal."

**Tamika Russell,
College of Idaho**

"Being a collegiate athlete is a good goal in general, but making it further to a national championship is something that you should strive for because it's a once-in-a-lifetime experience. It's accomplishing something that you probably thought that you would never do."

Tanner Irwin, Williams Baptist (Arkansas)

"Getting your hand raised and getting a team trophy. Being in the atmosphere and being around all the great competitors is amazing. I want to put my school and name on the map. I want to show all the hard work that we and our coaches have put in the whole year."

Tim Johnson, Grand View (Iowa)

"I was blessed to be a part of Grand View's program with guys from different places all over the world. They established a unique team culture. We have a saying 'One team, one family,' and it's something that we really believe in."

Discussion Questions:

1. When was the NJCAA formed and where?
2. When did community colleges in California form their own organization?
3. Discuss various scholarship opportunities at the community college level.
4. Discuss why there may be budget constraints and lack of interest in female sports at the community college level.
5. Discuss why attending a community college can be cost-efficient.
6. What was the philosophical approach of Division III athletics?
7. Before 1973, how were NCAA schools classified? And what did the distinction represent regarding athletics?
8. What NCAA Division has international membership?
9. Discuss why Division I is considered the "major league" of athletics.
10. Discuss the difference between coaching at the Division I, II, and III level.

CHAPTER 10

SEMIPROFESSIONAL, MINOR LEAGUE, FEEDER, AND PROFESSIONAL SPORTS: WHAT DOES IT MEAN?

Origin of Semipro

The concept or origin of the term *semipro* originated in California when the *San Francisco Olympic Club* started an American football team in the late eighteen hundred. The Olympic Club was accused by a rival club of enticing athletes to play on its team and transfer to the semipro ranks by offering players jobs. The ideal of this concept was not received very well by the Amateur Athletic Union and spearheaded an investigation that the Olympics' pay for play concept was not actually full-time professional but a "semi" form of it. This started the term "semipro." After the investigation, it was also decided that club teams could offer employment opportunities to athletes without them losing their amateur status or compromising the athlete.

What Does Semipro Mean

As we review the meaning of semipro, we want to define it for the readers. "Semi" means half or part, where the athlete participating in a particular sport may not be what is considered a full-time professional. "Professional" has been defined by Coach Acie Earl as with any profession, a person receiving income in a profession. Having said that, let's provide a little more clarity. Semiprofessionals are not amateur because in most cases, they receive payment from their team (company) but at a much lower rate than a full-time professional athlete. When a player or person is earning a living in the semipros, it is likely that the salary and or conditions are not up to the normal professional pay rate of what the full-time professionals make and experience. Coach Acie Earl has witnessed many semipro athletes being paid a very low wage and in some cases below the minimum wage. These players have to find another job in order to live respectable lives.

A semipro player could also represent his or her place of employment, meaning that the player or players play for the company sport team, and only employees of the organization are allowed to play on the team. In this case, it is considered semipro because the employer pays the employee who is the player while the player is maintaining a job within the company. In other word, you are paid for not only working in the company but also as a player of that organization's sport team. Sometimes, meals and lodging are also provided, and in some cases, the coaches and team personnel work for low wage and or no salary. For some, it is a dream to say they played or coached at a semiprofessional level despite the low pay and mediocre living expenses.

Semiprofessional Sports

Semiprofessional athletes and teams were common in the early and mid-20th century than they are today, particularly in North America (North America covers an area of about 9,540,000 square miles). Unlike the Amateur Athletic Union, the *NCAA* forbid college athletes being paid in conjunction with a scholarship, including job offers or endorsements that could be tied to their amateur status. If you are a college athlete and compete in the world Olympic games, you are required to maintain amateur status. However, some athletes (not college athletes) may be supported by government-funded money, business sponsorships, and other financial systems.

Today, sports have become such a massive and remunerative business that even many low-level teams can afford to have fully paid professional athletes.

Why Do Semiprofessional Athletes and Coaches Make the Sacrifice

Each year, there are athletes and coaches who play and coach semipro sports for the opportunity to move up to the professional level. Some have played and coached for multi seasons in the semiprofessional ranks and ultimately was given the opportunity to move up to the professional level and make more money. Some examples are *Andre Ingram* who played in the semiprofessional NBA-G league for ten years before being called up by the Los Angeles Lakers. In his debut game with the Lakers, he scored an amazing nineteen points and received great notoriety for his efforts.

Adam Smith did not make a British league full appearance but was able to apply his trade in nonleague football (soccer). Adam made over 150 first team semiprofessional appearances and later became a full-time soccer coach in the US.

Kimbo Slice became a famous name in sports in a very unpredictable semiprofessional yet totally fitting way for the 21st century. He used YouTube to catapult his boxing career. His real name was *Kevin Ferguson*, and he started doing backyard boxing or brawls in 2003. However, when YouTube became relevant in 2005, he used this media to become popular, and in 2007, he started fighting for a legit promotion company (EliteXC) and appeared on national TV in 2008 as an MMA star and champion.

These are just a few examples of individuals who were able to successfully move to a higher level of coaching or playing. Often, the players, staff, coaches, and team personnel work for low wage or no salary in the semiprofessional leagues for the chance to make it to the big leagues. For some, it is a dream come true to say they played or coached in a semiprofessional sport, with the ultimate goal to play or coach at the professional level in their sport.

The major sports that have minor leagues are many, we watch each season, such as basketball, hockey, soccer, football, baseball, pro wrestling, and even boxing. Countries, such as Canada and other foreign countries, provide leagues for athletes to compete and hone their skills. Soccer, basketball, and hockey often come to mind when we think of minor leagues. Athletes and coaches try to build up their résumés and dream to one day get to the top pro teams we see on television. Despite the many challenges of making it to the top level of playing or coaching, it is enticing for some to make the effort to be at the top level as a player or coach. With the salary caps in several pro sports today, it's hard to blame athletes or coaches for attempting to attain their dreams. At the time of this book being published, the NFL cap is 198.2 million, NBA 109.14 million, MLB and pro wrestling and boxing are unlimited with no cap. Players, agents, and coaches see the potential benefits and strive to make it to the top level of professional sports.

Canada, Europe, and United States Hockey Semiprofessional

Junior ice hockey is a semiprofessional sport that is popular in Canada, and top-level players are paid at a semiprofessional level. These teams comprise mostly of teenagers still in or just out of high school. The highest level is major junior and is governed by the Canadian Hockey League. There are three constituent leagues: Ontario Hockey League, Quebec Major Junior Hockey League, and Western Hockey League. The second tier is Junior A, governed nationally by the Canadian Junior Hockey League. In the United States, athletes who compete in college ice hockey are the same age as those that play in Canada. The junior leagues in the United States generally operate as fully amateur teams, which allows players to maintain their eligibility to play in college. The top tier in the United States is Tier I, represented by the United States Hockey League. Tier II is represented by the North American Hockey League. There are independently sanctioned leagues throughout the country, and a limited number of teams in the Canadian major junior leagues are based in the United States.

In Europe, junior teams are often sponsored by professional teams and act as development and feeder associations for professional hockey organizations.

Minor League Feeder or Farm Teams

Minor leagues are professional sports leagues which are not regarded as the premier leagues. Minor league teams tend to play in smaller, less elaborate venues, often competing in smaller cities/markets. This term is used in North America with regard to several organizations competing in various sports, which generally have lesser fan bases and smaller budgets.

The minor league concept is a manifestation of the franchise system[7] used in North American sports, whereby the group of major league teams in each sport is fixed for long periods between expansions or other adjustments, which only take place with the consent of the major league owners. In Europe, and many other parts of the world, the football leagues have many divisions below the top-flight league, which creates the football pyramid in other parts of the world. There is usually either a system of annual promotion and relegation[8], meaning that clubs have no fixed status in the hierarchy or there is only one professional league per country in each sport, rendering the major/minor distinction irrelevant.

The NBA, MLB, NHL, and NFL are affiliates of the more prominent minor league teams. They have an established yearly budget and qualified support staff. The budget is often secure and guaranteed, so it's easy to staff and sign players from year to year.

The term farm team, farm system, feeder team, or nursery club serve as teams that provide experience and training for young players, with an agreement that any successful player can move on to a higher level at a given point. Some of these athletes are compensated and have an affiliation with a major-level parent team. The distinction between an athlete that is affiliated with a minor league team is that they are not considered semiprofessional; they are professional athletes who play for a major parent farm or feeder team. Note the term feeder and farm teams is a metaphor for any organization or activity

To learn more:

7 https://en.wikipedia.org/wiki/Professional_sports_league_organization

To learn more:

8 https://en.wikipedia.org/wiki/Promotion_and_relegation

that provides a person higher level endeavors, provided they can perform to move to the higher level. Business schools can be referred as "farm clubs" in the world of business. The minor league and feeder team can be considered synonymous in concept.

Club team, not to be confused with those teams associated with a college, is a term where a local group of amateur athletes form teams among themselves and compete periodically. At its most complex term, it can be an international professional league making large amounts of money and involving dozens of teams and thousands of players.

Minor league teams like feeder or farm system programs play in smaller markets, often competing in smaller cities. The term is used in regard to several organizations competing in various sports. Generally, there is a lesser fan base and smaller budget, whereas semiprofessional athletes compete in these venues.

The minor league concept is a manifestation of the franchise system, meaning the professional sport leagues are organized in several ways, characterized by a tiered process that involves promotion and regulation in a hierarchy of leagues or divisions. Promotion and regulation are a process where teams are transferred between multiple divisions based on their performance for the completed seasons. Teams can be promoted to higher division the next season or relegated to a lower division. This process can continue through several levels of divisions, with teams being exchanged between levels one and two, three and four, and so on. Teams in the "league table" that qualify for promotion are sometimes said to be in the promotion zone, and those at the bottom are in the relegation zone. This movement has an effect on the semiprofessional pay structure, and contrary to the fact that some semiprofessional are not paid very well, there is a select group who earn a very significant salary.

An alternate system of league organization which is used primarily in the US and Canada is a closed model-based on licensing or franchises. This sport structure maintains the same teams from year to year, with occasional admission of expansion teams, relocation of existing teams, and with no team movement between the major league and minor league.

For any young aspiring coaches and people wanting to get into coaching and or working for a pro team, a minor league path is a good one. Often there is a defined salary and perks available, such as bonuses for ticket and sponsorship packages sold. It a great way to see and learn the ins and outs of a pro franchise and league. This is valuable experience that most people do not have the chance to experience at a lower level to prepare them for the big-time world of pro sports.

Professional Sports

After spending several years as a professional basketball player and coach, Acie Earl was afforded the opportunity to travel to many countries and meet athletes and coaches from various different sports. He provides a breakdown and historical perspective of some professional sports that folded and some of the more prominent ones in today's society.

The *Federal League* was an American professional baseball league that operated as a third major league[9] from 1914 to 1915. This league was in competition with the established National and American Leagues. Interference by the National and American Leagues in their operations caused the Federal League to fold after the 1915 season. There was a federal landmark lawsuit, *Federal Baseball Club vs. National League*, which ruled in favor of the National League from the standpoint of preserving a competitive marketplace to protect consumers from abuses. The Federal League had no salary cap and basically wanted to entice players to play in their league by offering high salaries.

The *Atlantic League of Professional Baseball* is an independent professional baseball league[10] located primarily in the Mid-Atlantic and Northeastern United States. The league operates in cities not served by Major League Baseball (MLB) or Minor League. Cities

---

To learn more:

[9] https://en.wikipedia.org/wiki/Major_League_Baseball

[10] https://en.wikipedia.org/wiki/Independent_baseball_league

who host these teams must have the market for a four thousand to seventy-five hundred seat ballpark, and the facility must be maintained at or above Triple-A standards. In 2019, the Atlantic League started a three-year partnership with the Major League.

The *Mexican Pacific League* is an independent professional baseball[11] league in Mexico.[12] There are ten league teams, and the season commence during the winter, followed by a playoff series to determine the league champion. The league's winner takes part in the Caribbean Series each year.

While the Mexican Pacific League is not officially recognized by Minor League Baseball, it is probably a stronger organization than a number of circuits north of the border. Almost all eight Mex-Pac teams average more than 5,000 fans per opening over their sixty-game schedules, and the level of play is comparable to Class AAA ball as team rosters feature a sixty-eight mix of Mexican League veterans and top prospects from Major League Baseball organizations although MLB teams are not sending as many young players to spend their winters in Mexico or other Caribbean leagues because of the growth of offseason programs in their spring training complexes in Florida and Arizona.

Major League Baseball (MLB) is a professional baseball organization and the oldest of the major professional sports leagues in the United States and Canada. The league consists of thirty teams, fifteen in the National league (NL) and fifteen in the American League (AL). The two leagues formed as separate legal entities in 1876 and 1901. Although the two leagues cooperated, they remained separate entities. In 2000, the leagues merged into a single organization led by the Commissioner of Baseball. Today, MLB has thirty teams, twenty-nine in the United States and one in Canada. Each team plays one hundred and sixty-two games, and five teams in each league advance to a four-round postseason tournament that culminates in the World Series, a best-of-seven championship series between the two league champions. Major League Baseball has the highest season attendance

---

11 https://en.wikipedia.org/wiki/Professional_baseball

12 https://en.wikipedia.org/wiki/Mexico

of any sport league in the world with more than sixty-nine million spectators in 2018.

The *Canadian Football League* (CFL) is a professional sport league and the highest level of competition in Canada. The league consists of nine teams, each located in a city in Canada. The league is divided into two divisions. Four teams in the East Division and five teams in the West Division. The league features a twenty-one-week regular season where each team plays eighteen games with three by weeks. The season runs from mid-June to early November.

The CFL was officially founded in 1958. The league was formed through a merger between the interprovincial Rugby Football Union (founded in 1907) and the Western Interprovincial Football Union (founded in 1936).

The women have sport leagues that represent top-level competitions of team sports in various genres. The top women leagues include Women's National Basketball Association (WNBA), National Women's Soccer League (NWSL), National Pro Fastpitch (NPF), Canadian Women's Hockey League (CWHL), National Women's Hockey League (NWHL), Women's Flat Track Derby Association (WFTDA), and the National Ringette League (NRL). There are also some individual sports featuring women including tennis (WTA Tour) and golf (LPGA). Both were founded in the United States and host events around the world.

The PGA Tour is the organizer of the main professional golf tours[13] played primarily by men in the United States and North America. Most of the events are based on an annual series of tournaments known as the PGA Tour, as well as PGA Tour Champions (for golfers age fifty and older) and the Korn Ferry Tour (for professional players who have not yet qualified to play in the PGA Tour). Other tournaments include the PGA Tour Canada, PGA Tour Latino-America, and PGA Tour China. The *Professional Golfers' Association of America* was established in December 1968 and was spun off into a separate organization for tour players as opposed to club profes-

To learn more:

[13] https://en.wikipedia.org/wiki/Professional_golf_tours

sionals. The name PGA was adopted in 1975, and the tournaments runs most of the week-to-week professionals golf events on the tournament known as the PGA tour.

The *National Football League* is a professional American football league consisting of thirty-two teams and considered the highest level of American football in the world formed in 1920 as the American Professional Football Association before renaming itself the National Football League. Following an agreement to merge the NFL with the American Football League, the Super Bowl was first in 1967 to determine a champion between the best teams from the two leagues and has remained as the final game of each NFL season since the merger was completed in 1970. The Super Bowl is considered one of the biggest club sporting events in the world.

The National Basketball Association (NBA) is the men's professional basketball league in North America comprising of thirty teams (twenty-nine in the United States and one in Canada). It is one of the four major professional sports leagues in the United States and Canada and is considered the premier men's professional basketball league in the world. The league was founded in 1946 as the Basketball Association of America (BAA). The league changed its name to the National Basketball Association in 1949 after merging with the National Basketball League. Each team plays an eighty-two-game schedule, with the playoffs extending into June. As of 2015, NBA players are the world's best paid athletes by average annual salary per player. Below is a worksheet that illustrates the contracts of 564 NBA players contracts through the year 2024.

What Does It Mean

The table below displays the amount of money an elite athlete can make in the sport of basketball participating at the highest professional level. It is this type of incentive that drives individuals to participate in sports as a player or coach, and realistically, only a select few have what it takes to make the type of money displayed below. However, the dream of becoming a top player or coach is what many sports participants chase. Sports are an essential and important aspect of American society; they are so addictive when it comes to their impact on a plethora of public arenas, including economics and the mass media. Sports segue with community values and political agencies. For the sport participant, it's a reaffirmation of societal values, sometimes good or bad, as they give meaning to their lives (Brummett 2009).

For the coach, sport participation can serve as fulfilling a purpose to shape sport participants' lives while some coaches may place value on economic gain, success, and a sense of belonging to a special club (coaching). Ultimately, the joy, amusement, and diversion from life challenges can be common denominators that entice one to undertake the challenge of coaching (Delaney 2009).

Rk	Player	Tm	Salary 2019–20	2020–21	2021–22	2022–23	2023–24	2024–25	Signed Using	Guaranteed
1	Stephen Curry	GSW	$40,231,758	$43,006,362	$45,780,966				Bird Rights	$129,019,086
2	Chris Paul	OKC	$38,506,482	$41,358,814	$44,211,146				Bird Rights	$79,865,296
3	Russell Westbrook	HOU	$38,178,000	$41,006,000	$43,848,000	$46,662,000			Bird Rights	$123,032,000
4	John Wall	WAS	$37,800,000	$40,824,000	$43,848,000	$46,872,000			Bird Rights	$122,472,000
5	James Harden	HOU	$37,800,000	$40,824,000	$43,848,000	$46,872,000			Bird Rights	$122,472,000
6	LeBron James	LAL	$37,436,858	$39,219,565	$41,002,273				Cap Space	$76,656,423
7	Kevin Durant	BRK	$37,199,000	$39,058,950	$40,918,900	$42,778,850			Sign and Trade	$117,176,850
8	Blake Griffin	DET	$34,234,964	$36,595,996	$38,957,028				Bird Rights	$70,830,960
9	Kyle Lowry	TOR	$33,296,296	$30,000,000					Bird Rights	$63,296,296
10	Paul George	LAC	$33,005,556	$35,450,412	$37,895,268				Maximum Salary	$68,455,968
11	Klay Thompson	GSW	$32,742,000	$35,361,360	$37,980,720	$40,600,080	$43,219,440		Bird Rights	$189,903,600
12	Jimmy Butler	MIA	$32,742,000	$34,379,100	$36,016,200	$37,653,300			Sign and Trade	$103,137,300
13	Kemba Walker	BOS	$32,742,000	$34,379,100	$36,016,200	$37,653,300			Sign and Trade	$103,137,300
14	Kawhi Leonard	LAC	$32,742,000	$34,379,100	$36,016,200				Cap Space	$67,121,100
15	Gordon Hayward	BOS	$32,700,690	$34,187,085					Cap space	$32,700,690
16	Mike Conley	UTA	$32,511,623	$34,504,132					Cap Space	$54,938,006
17	Kyrie Irving	BRK	$31,742,000	$33,329,100	$34,916,200	$36,503,300			Cap space	$136,490,600
18	Tobias Harris	PHI	$31,034,483	$33,517,241	$36,000,000	$38,482,759	$40,965,517		Bird Rights	$180,000,000
19	Khris Middleton	MIL	$30,603,448	$33,051,724	$35,500,000	$37,948,276	$40,396,552		Bird Rights	$137,103,448
20	Paul Millsap	DEN	$30,500,000						Cap space	$30,500,000
21	Damian Lillard	POR	$29,802,321	$31,626,953	$43,750,000	$47,250,000	$50,750,000	$54,250,000	1st Round Pick	$257,429,274
22	Kevin Love	CLE	$28,900,000	$31,300,000	$31,300,000	$28,900,000			Bird Rights	$120,400,000
23	Nikola Vučević	ORL	$28,000,000	$26,000,000	$24,000,000	$22,000,000			Bird Rights	$100,000,000
24	Al Horford	PHI	$28,000,000	$27,500,000	$27,000,000	$26,500,000			Cap Space	$97,000,000
25	DeMar DeRozan	SAS	$27,739,975	$27,739,975					Cap Space	$27,739,975
26	CJ McCollum	POR	$27,556,959	$29,354,152	$30,864,198	$33,333,333	$35,802,469		1st Round Pick	$156,911,111
27	Joel Embiid	PHI	$27,504,630	$29,542,010	$31,579,390	$33,616,770			1st Round Pick	$122,242,800

Rk	Player	Tm	Salary 2019–20	2020–21	2021–22	2022–23	2023–24	2024–25	Signed Using	Guaranteed
28	Andrew Wiggins	GSW	$27,504,630	$29,542,010	$31,579,390	$33,616,770			1st Round Pick	$122,242,800
29	Kristaps Porziņģis	DAL	$27,285,000	$29,467,800	$31,650,600	$33,833,400	$36,016,200		Bird Rights	$122,236,800
30	D'Angelo Russell	MIN	$27,285,000	$28,649,250	$30,013,500	$31,377,750			Sign and Trade	$117,325,500
31	Otto Porter	CHI	$27,250,576	$28,489,239					Bird Rights	$27,250,576
32	Devin Booker	PHO	$27,250,000	$29,430,000	$31,610,000	$33,790,000	$35,970,000		1st round pick	$158,050,000
33	Karl-Anthony Towns	MIN	$27,250,000	$29,430,000	$31,610,000	$33,790,000	$35,970,000		1st Round Pick	$155,870,000
34	Bradley Beal	WAS	$27,093,019	$28,751,775	$34,502,130	$37,262,300			Cap Space	$90,346,924
35	Anthony Davis	LAL	$27,093,019	$28,751,775					1st Round Pick	$27,093,019
36	Andre Drummond	CLE	$27,093,019	$28,751,775					Cap Space	$27,093,019
37	Hassan Whiteside	POR	$27,093,018						Cap Space	$27,093,018
38	Nikola Jokić	DEN	$26,573,595	$28,542,009	$30,510,423	$32,478,837			Bird Rights	$118,104,864
39	Jrue Holiday	NOP	$26,131,111	$26,131,111	$27,020,000				Bird Rights	$52,262,222
40	LaMarcus Aldridge	SAS	$26,000,000	$24,000,000					Cap Space	$50,000,000
41	Steven Adams	OKC	$25,842,697	$27,528,090					1st Round Pick	$53,370,787
42	Giannis Antetokounmpo	MIL	$25,842,697	$27,528,090					1st Round Pick	$53,370,787
43	Marc Gasol	TOR	$25,595,700						Bird Rights	$25,595,700
44	Nicolas Batum	CHO	$25,565,217	$27,130,434					Cap Space	$25,565,217
45	Chandler Parsons	ATL	$25,102,511							$25,102,511
46	Rudy Gobert	UTA	$25,008,427	$26,525,281					1st Round Pick	$51,533,708
47	Harrison Barnes	SAC	$24,147,727	$22,215,909	$20,284,091	$18,352,273			Bird Rights	$85,000,000
48	Serge Ibaka	TOR	$23,271,604						Cap space	$23,271,604
49	Danilo Gallinari	OKC	$22,615,559						Sign and Trade	$22,615,559
50	Victor Oladipo	IND	$21,000,000	$21,000,000					1st Round Pick	$42,000,000
51	Malcolm Brogdon	IND	$20,000,000	$20,700,000	$21,700,000	$22,600,000			Sign and Trade	$85,000,000
52	Terry Rozier	CHO	$19,894,737	$18,900,000	$17,905,263				Sign and Trade	$56,700,000
53	Aaron Gordon	ORL	$19,863,636	$18,136,364	$16,409,091				Bird Rights	$54,409,091

Rk	Player	Tm	Salary 2019–20	2020–21	2021–22	2022–23	2023–24	2024–25	Signed Using	Guaranteed
54	Zach LaVine	CHI	$19,500,000	$19,500,000	$19,500,000				Cap space	$58,500,000
55	Kent Bazemore	SAC	$19,269,662						Cap Space	$19,269,662
56	Tyler Johnson	PHO	$19,245,370							$19,245,370
57	Goran Dragić	MIA	$19,217,900						Bird Rights	$19,217,900
58	Jeff Teague	ATL	$19,000,000						Cap space	$19,000,000
59	Evan Turner	MIN	$18,606,557						Cap Space	$18,606,557
60	Draymond Green	GSW	$18,539,130	$22,246,956	$24,026,712	$25,806,469	$27,586,225		Bird Rights	$90,619,267
61	Tristan Thompson	CLE	$18,539,130						Bird Rights	$18,539,130
62	Tim Hardaway	DAL	$18,150,000	$18,975,000					Cap space	$18,150,000
63	Myles Turner	IND	$18,000,000	$18,000,000	$18,000,000	$18,000,000			1st Round pick	$72,000,000
64	Julius Randle	NYK	$18,000,000	$18,900,000	$19,800,000				Cap Space	$40,900,000
65	Gary Harris	DEN	$17,839,286	$19,160,714	$20,482,143				1st Round Pick	$57,482,143
66	Allen Crabbe	MIN	$17,818,456							$17,818,456
67	Derrick Favors	NOP	$17,650,000						Bird Rights	$17,650,000
68	Reggie Jackson	DET	$17,286,956							$17,286,956
69	Andre Iguodala	MIA	$17,185,185	$15,000,000	$15,000,000				Bird Rights	$32,185,185
70	Bojan Bogdanović	UTA	$17,000,000	$17,850,000	$18,700,000	$19,550,000			Cap Space	$73,100,000
71	Evan Fournier	ORL	$17,000,000	$17,000,000					Cap Space	$17,000,000
72	Bismack Biyombo	CHO	$17,000,000						Cap Space	$17,000,000
73	Clint Capela	ATL	$16,456,522	$17,500,000	$18,543,478	$19,586,957			Bird Rights	$72,086,957
74	Gorgui Dieng	MEM	$16,229,213	$17,287,640					1st Round Pick	$33,516,853
75	Ricky Rubio	PHO	$16,190,476	$17,000,000	$17,809,524				Cap Space	$51,000,000
76	Jonas Valančiūnas	MEM	$16,000,000	$15,000,000	$14,000,000				Bird Rights	$45,000,000
77	Brandon Knight	DET	$15,643,750						Bird Rights	$15,643,750
78	Eric Bledsoe	MIL	$15,625,000	$16,875,000	$18,125,000	$19,375,000			Bird Rights	$54,525,000
79	Kelly Oubre	PHO	$15,625,000	$14,375,000					Bird Rights	$30,000,000
80	Dennis Schröder	OKC	$15,500,000	$15,500,000					1st Round Pick	$31,000,000

Rk	Player	Tm	Salary 2019–20	2020–21	2021–22	2022–23	2023–24	2024–25	Signed Using	Guaranteed
81	Ian Mahinmi	WAS	$15,450,051						Cap Space	$15,450,051
82	James Johnson	MIN	$15,349,400	$16,047,100					Cap space	$15,349,400
83	Marvin Williams	CHO	$15,006,250							$15,006,250
84	Bobby Portis	NYK	$15,000,000	$15,750,000					Cap Space	$15,000,000
85	Marcus Morris	LAC	$15,000,000						Cap Space	$15,000,000
86	Danny Green	LAL	$14,634,146	$15,365,854					Cap Space	$30,000,000
87	Cody Zeller	CHO	$14,471,910	$15,415,730					1st Round Pick	$29,887,640
88	Eric Gordon	HOU	$14,057,730	$16,869,276	$18,218,818	$19,568,360	$20,917,902		Cap Space	$68,714,184
89	Mason Plumlee	DEN	$14,041,096						Cap space	$14,041,096
90	Rudy Gay	SAS	$14,000,000	$14,000,000					Early Bird Rights	$28,000,000
91	J.J. Redick	NOP	$13,486,300	$13,013,700					Cap Space	$26,500,000
92	Jordan Clarkson	UTA	$13,437,500						Cap Space	$13,437,500
93	Dewayne Dedmon	ATL	$13,333,334	$13,333,333	$13,333,333				Cap space	$40,000,000
94	Solomon Hill	MIA	$13,258,781						Cap Space	$13,258,781
95	Justise Winslow	MEM	$13,000,000	$13,000,000	$13,000,000				1st Round Pick	$26,000,000
96	Michael Kidd-Gilchrist	CHO	$13,000,000							$13,000,000
97	Will Barton	DEN	$12,960,000	$13,920,000	$14,880,000				Bird Rights	$26,880,000
98	Thaddeus Young	CHI	$12,900,000	$13,545,000	$14,190,000				Cap space	$32,445,000
99	Courtney Lee	DAL	$12,759,670						Cap Space	$12,759,670
100	Larry Nance	CLE	$12,727,273	$11,709,091	$10,690,909	$9,672,727			1st Round pick	$44,800,000
101	Marcus Smart	BOS	$12,553,471	$13,446,428	$14,339,285				Bird Rights	$40,339,184
102	Terrence Ross	ORL	$12,500,000	$13,500,000	$12,500,000	$11,500,000			Bird Rights	$50,000,000
103	Miles Plumlee	MEM	$12,500,000							$12,500,000
104	Patty Mills	SAS	$12,428,571	$13,285,714					Bird Rights	$25,714,285
105	Patrick Beverley	LAC	$12,345,679	$13,333,333	$14,320,988				Bird Rights	$40,000,000
106	Trevor Ariza	POR	$12,200,000	$12,800,000					Cap Space	$14,000,000

Rk	Player	Tm	Salary 2019–20	2020–21	2021–22	2022–23	2023–24	2024–25	Signed Using	Guaranteed
107	Dion Waiters	MEM	$12,100,000	$12,650,000						$24,750,000
108	Brook Lopez	MIL	$12,093,024	$12,697,675	$13,302,325	$13,906,976			Cap Space	$52,000,000
109	Jusuf Nurkić	POR	$12,000,000	$12,000,000	$12,000,000				Bird Rights	$28,000,000
110	Cory Joseph	SAC	$12,000,000	$12,600,000	$12,600,000				Cap Space	$24,600,000
111	Joe Ingles	UTA	$11,954,546	$10,863,637	$14,000,000				Bird Rights	$36,818,183
112	Kelly Olynyk	MIA	$11,667,885	$12,198,243					Cap space	$11,667,885
113	Maurice Harkless	NYK	$11,511,234						Cap Space	$11,511,234
114	Tony Snell	DET	$11,392,857	$12,178,571					Cap space	$11,392,857
115	Robert Covington	HOU	$11,301,219	$12,138,345	$12,975,471				Cap Space	$36,415,035
116	Meyers Leonard	MIA	$11,286,515						Cap Space	$11,286,515
117	T.J. Warren	IND	$10,810,000	$11,750,000	$12,690,000				1st Round Pick	$35,250,000
118	Andre Roberson	OKC	$10,740,741						Bird Rights	$10,740,741
119	Spencer Dinwiddie	BRK	$10,600,000	$11,400,000	$12,300,000				Minimum Salary	$22,000,000
120	Jeremy Lamb	IND	$10,500,000	$10,500,000	$10,500,000				Cap Space	$31,500,000
121	Dwight Powell	DAL	$10,259,375	$10,185,185	$11,000,000	$11,814,815			Cap Space	$43,259,375
122	Norman Powell	TOR	$10,116,576	$10,865,952	$11,615,328				Cap Space	$20,982,528
123	Josh Richardson	PHI	$10,100,000	$10,800,000	$11,600,000				Minimum Salary	$20,900,000
124	Tomáš Satoranský	CHI	$10,000,000	$10,000,000	$10,000,000				Sign and Trade	$25,000,000
125	DeAndre Jordan	BRK	$9,881,598	$10,375,678	$9,881,598	$9,821,842			Cap space	$39,960,716
126	Taj Gibson	NYK	$9,800,000	$10,290,000					Cap Space	$9,800,000
127	Zion Williamson	NOP	$9,757,440	$10,245,480	$10,733,400	$13,534,817			1st Round Pick	$20,002,920
128	Markelle Fultz	ORL	$9,745,200	$12,288,697					1st Round Pick	$22,033,897
129	John Henson	DET	$9,732,396						1st Round Pick	$9,732,396
130	Matthew Dellavedova	CLE	$9,607,500						Cap Space	$9,607,500
131	Dante Exum	CLE	$9,600,000	$9,600,000					Cap Space	$18,200,000
132	Deandre Ayton	PHO	$9,562,920	$10,018,200	$12,632,950				1st Round Pick	$19,581,120
133	Delon Wright	DAL	$9,473,684	$9,000,000	$8,526,316				Sign and Trade	$27,000,000

Rk	Player	Tm	Salary 2019–20	2020–21	2021–22	2022–23	2023–24	2024–25	Signed Using	Guaranteed
134	Jerami Grant	DEN	$9,346,153	$9,346,153					Bird Rights	$9,346,153
135	Al-Farouq Aminu	ORL	$9,258,000	$9,720,900	$10,183,800				MLE	$29,162,700
136	George Hill	MIL	$9,133,907	$9,590,602	$10,047,297				Cap Space	$21,000,000
137	Kyle Anderson	MEM	$9,073,050	$9,505,100	$9,937,150				MLE	$28,515,300
138	Fred VanVleet	TOR	$9,000,000						Bird Rights	$9,000,000
139	Ja Morant	MEM	$8,730,240	$9,166,800	$9,603,360	$12,119,440			1st Round Pick	$17,897,040
140	C.J. Miles	WAS	$8,730,158							$8,730,158
141	Lonzo Ball	NOP	$8,719,320	$11,003,782					1st Round Pick	$19,723,102
142	E'Twaun Moore	NOP	$8,664,928						Cap Space	$8,664,928
143	Marvin Bagley	SAC	$8,556,120	$8,963,640	$11,312,114				1st Round Pick	$17,519,760
144	Bogdan Bogdanović	SAC	$8,529,386						Cap space	$8,529,386
145	Tyus Jones	MEM	$8,408,000	$7,965,100	$7,522,200				MLE	$23,895,300
146	P.J. Tucker	HOU	$8,349,039	$7,969,537					MLE	$16,318,576
147	Cristiano Felício	CHI	$8,156,500	$7,529,020					Cap space	$15,685,520
148	Ben Simmons	PHI	$8,113,930	$29,250,000	$31,590,000	$33,930,000	$36,270,000	$38,610,000	1st Round pick	$177,763,930
149	Kentavious Caldwell-Pope	LAL	$8,089,282	$8,493,746					Cap Space	$8,089,282
150	Maxi Kleber	DAL	$8,000,000	$8,250,000	$8,750,000	$9,000,000			Early Bird Rights	$25,000,000
151	Lou Williams	LAC	$8,000,000	$8,000,000					Cap Space	$16,000,000
152	Elfrid Payton	NYK	$8,000,000	$8,000,000					Cap Space	$9,000,000
153	Thomas Bryant	WAS	$7,936,508	$8,333,333	$8,730,159				Early Bird Rights	$25,000,000
154	RJ Barrett	NYK	$7,839,960	$8,231,760	$8,623,920	$10,900,635			1st Round Pick	$16,071,720
155	Jayson Tatum	BOS	$7,830,000	$9,897,120					1st Round Pick	$17,727,120
156	Jae Crowder	MIA	$7,815,533						Bird Rights	$7,815,533
157	Wayne Ellington	NYK	$7,804,878	$8,195,122					Cap Space	$7,804,878
158	Luka Dončić	DAL	$7,683,360	$8,049,360	$10,174,391				1st Round Pick	$15,732,720
159	Joe Harris	BRK	$7,670,000						Early Bird Rights	$7,670,000

			Salary							
Rk	Player	Tm	2019–20	2020–21	2021–22	2022–23	2023–24	2024–25	Signed Using	Guaranteed
160	Seth Curry	DAL	$7,441,860	$7,813,953	$8,186,047	$8,558,140			MLE	$32,000,000
161	Doug McDermott	IND	$7,333,334	$7,333,333					Cap Space	$14,666,667
162	Langston Galloway	DET	$7,333,333						MLE	$7,333,333
163	Derrick Rose	DET	$7,317,073	$7,682,927					MLE	$15,000,000
164	Brandon Ingram	NOP	$7,265,485						1st Round pick	$7,265,485
165	D.J. Augustin	ORL	$7,250,000						Cap Space	$7,250,000
166	Darius Miller	NOP	$7,250,000	$7,000,000					Early Bird Rights	$7,250,000
167	De'Andre Hunter	ATL	$7,068,360	$7,422,000	$7,775,400	$9,835,881			1st Round Pick	$14,490,360
168	Josh Jackson	MEM	$7,059,480						1st Round Pick	$7,059,480
169	Dāvis Bertāns	WAS	$7,000,000						Early Bird Rights	$7,000,000
170	Ersan İlyasova	MIL	$7,000,000	$7,000,000					MLE	$7,000,000
171	Jaren Jackson	MEM	$6,927,480	$7,257,360	$9,180,560				1st Round Pick	$14,184,840
172	DeMarre Carroll	SAS	$6,842,307	$6,167,887	$1,252,127					$14,262,321
173	Nemanja Bjelica	SAC	$6,825,000	$7,150,000					Cap Space	$6,825,000
174	Jaylen Brown	BOS	$6,534,829	$22,991,071	$24,830,357	$26,669,643	$28,508,929		1st Round pick	$109,534,829
175	Jabari Parker	SAC	$6,500,000	$6,500,000					Cap Space	$6,500,000
176	Ivica Zubac	LAC	$6,481,482	$7,000,000	$7,518,518	$7,518,518			Bird Rights	$21,000,000
177	Joakim Noah	NYK	$6,431,666	$6,431,666	$6,431,666					$19,294,998
178	Darius Garland	CLE	$6,400,920	$6,720,720	$7,040,880	$8,920,795			1st Round Pick	$13,121,640
179	De'Aaron Fox	SAC	$6,392,760	$8,099,627					1st Round Pick	$14,492,387
180	Trae Young	ATL	$6,273,000	$6,571,800	$8,326,471				1st Round Pick	$12,844,800
181	Montrezl Harrell	LAC	$6,000,000						Bird Rights	$6,000,000
182	Ish Smith	WAS	$5,853,659	$6,146,341					MLE	$12,000,000
183	Marco Belinelli	SAS	$5,846,154						MLE	$5,846,154
184	Jarrett Culver	MIN	$5,813,640	$6,104,280	$6,395,160	$8,109,063			1st Round Pick	$11,917,920
185	Jonathan Isaac	ORL	$5,806,440	$7,362,566					1st Round Pick	$13,169,006

Rk	Player	Tm	Salary 2019–20	2020–21	2021–22	2022–23	2023–24	2024–25	Signed Using	Guaranteed
186	Rodney Hood	POR	$5,718,000	$6,003,900					MLE	$5,718,000
187	Mohamed Bamba	ORL	$5,697,600	$5,969,040	$7,568,742				1st Round Pick	$11,666,640
188	Timofey Mozgov	ORL	$5,573,333	$5,573,333	$5,573,334					$16,720,000
189	Trey Lyles	SAS	$5,500,000	$5,500,000					MLE	$5,500,000
190	Deron Williams	BRK	$5,474,787							$5,474,787
191	Aron Baynes	PHO	$5,453,280						Non-Bird Exception	$5,453,280
192	Kris Dunn	CHI	$5,348,007						1st Round pick	$5,348,007
193	Josh Smith	DET	$5,331,729							$5,331,729
194	Coby White	CHI	$5,307,120	$5,572,680	$5,837,760	$7,413,955			1st Round Pick	$10,879,800
195	Lauri Markkanen	CHI	$5,300,400	$6,731,508					1st Round Pick	$12,031,908
196	Ryan Anderson	MIA	$5,214,583	$5,214,583	$5,214,584					$15,643,750
197	Wendell Carter	CHI	$5,201,400	$5,448,840	$6,920,027				1st Round Pick	$10,650,240
198	Pau Gasol	SAS	$5,100,000							$5,100,000
199	Daniel Theis	BOS	$5,000,000	$5,000,000					Early Bird Rights	$5,000,000
200	Luol Deng	LAL	$4,990,000	$4,990,000	$4,990,000					$14,970,000
201	Jaxson Hayes	NOP	$4,862,040	$5,105,160	$5,348,280	$6,803,012			1st Round Pick	$9,967,200
202	Buddy Hield	SAC	$4,861,208	$24,431,818	$22,477,273	$20,522,727	$18,568,182		1st Round pick	$90,861,208
203	Frank Ntilikina	NYK	$4,855,800	$6,176,578					1st Round Pick	$11,032,378
204	Ed Davis	UTA	$4,767,000	$5,005,350					Room Exception	$9,772,350
205	Richaun Holmes	SAC	$4,767,000	$5,005,350					Room Exception	$9,772,350
206	Frank Kaminsky	PHO	$4,767,000	$5,005,350					Room Exception	$9,772,350
207	Mike Scott	PHI	$4,767,000	$5,005,350					Room Exception	$9,772,350
208	Avery Bradley	LAL	$4,767,000	$5,005,350					Room Exception	$9,772,350
209	Robin Lopez	MIL	$4,767,000	$5,005,350					Room Exception	$4,767,000
210	JaMychal Green	LAC	$4,767,000	$5,005,350					Room Exception	$4,767,000

Rk	Player	Tm	Salary 2019–20	2020–21	2021–22	2022–23	2023–24	2024–25	Signed Using	Guaranteed
211	Justin Holiday	IND	$4,767,000						Room Exception	$4,767,000
212	Garrett Temple	BRK	$4,767,000	$5,005,350					Room Exception	$4,767,000
213	Enes Kanter	BOS	$4,767,000	$5,005,350					Room Exception	$4,767,000
214	Collin Sexton	CLE	$4,764,960	$4,991,880	$6,349,671				1st Round Pick	$9,756,840
215	Rodney McGruder	LAC	$4,629,630	$5,000,000	$5,370,370				Cap Space	$15,000,000
216	Rui Hachimura	WAS	$4,469,160	$4,692,840	$4,916,160	$6,263,188			1st Round Pick	$9,162,000
217	Kevon Looney	GSW	$4,464,286	$4,821,429	$5,178,572				Bird Rights	$9,285,715
218	Dennis Smith	NYK	$4,463,640	$5,686,677					1st Round Pick	$10,150,317
219	Jamal Murray	DEN	$4,444,746	$29,250,000	$31,590,000	$33,930,000	$36,270,000	$38,610,000	1st Round pick	$174,094,746
220	Kevin Knox	NYK	$4,380,120	$4,588,680	$5,845,978				1st Round Pick	$8,968,800
221	Cam Reddish	ATL	$4,245,720	$4,458,000	$4,670,160	$5,954,454			1st Round Pick	$8,703,720
222	Zach Collins	POR	$4,240,200	$5,406,255					1st Round Pick	$9,646,455
223	Mikal Bridges	PHO	$4,161,000	$4,359,000	$5,557,725				1st Round Pick	$8,520,000
224	Alex Len	SAC	$4,160,000						Room Exception	$4,160,000
225	Cameron Johnson	PHO	$4,033,440	$4,235,160	$4,437,000	$5,887,899			1st Round Pick	$8,268,600
226	Malik Monk	CHO	$4,028,400	$5,345,687					1st Round Pick	$9,374,087
227	Dorian Finney-Smith	DAL	$4,000,000	$4,000,000	$4,000,000				Bird Rights	$12,000,000
228	JaVale McGee	LAL	$4,000,000	$4,200,000					Cap Space	$8,200,000
229	Patrick McCaw	TOR	$4,000,000	$4,000,000					MLE	$8,000,000
230	Reggie Bullock	NYK	$4,000,000	$4,200,000					Room Exception	$5,000,000
231	Shai Gilgeous-Alexander	OKC	$3,952,920	$4,141,320	$5,495,532				1st Round Pick	$8,094,240
232	Nicolò Melli	NOP	$3,902,439	$4,097,561					Room Exception	$8,000,000
233	P.J. Washington	CHO	$3,831,840	$4,023,600	$4,215,120	$5,808,435			1st Round Pick	$7,855,440
234	Luke Kennard	DET	$3,827,160	$5,273,826					1st Round Pick	$9,100,986
235	Miles Bridges	CHO	$3,755,400	$3,934,320	$5,421,493				1st Round Pick	$7,689,720

Rk	Player	Tm	Salary 2019–20	2020–21	2021–22	2022–23	2023–24	2024–25	Signed Using	Guaranteed
236	Jakob Poeltl	SAS	$3,754,886						1st Round pick	$3,754,886
237	Tyler Herro	MIA	$3,640,200	$3,822,240	$4,004,280	$5,722,116			1st Round Pick	$7,462,440
238	Donovan Mitchell	UTA	$3,635,760	$5,195,501					1st Round Pick	$8,831,261
239	Stanley Johnson	TOR	$3,623,000	$3,801,000					Bi-annual Exception	$3,623,000
240	Jake Layman	MIN	$3,581,986	$3,761,085	$3,940,184				Sign and Trade	$11,283,255
241	Thon Maker	DET	$3,569,643						1st Round pick	$3,569,643
242	Jerome Robinson	WAS	$3,567,720	$3,737,520	$5,340,916				1st Round Pick	$7,305,240
243	Allonzo Trier	NYK	$3,551,100							$3,551,100
244	Danuel House	HOU	$3,540,000	$3,717,000	$3,894,000				MLE	$11,151,000
245	Domantas Sabonis	IND	$3,529,555	$17,187,500	$18,562,500	$19,937,500	$21,312,500		1st Round pick	$80,529,555
246	Mirza Teletović	MIL	$3,500,000	$3,500,000						$7,000,000
247	Boban Marjanović	DAL	$3,500,000	$3,500,000					Bi-Annual Exception	$7,000,000
248	T.J. McConnell	IND	$3,500,000	$3,500,000					Cap Space	$4,500,000
249	DeMarcus Cousins	LAL	$3,500,000							$3,500,000
250	Taurean Waller-Prince	BRK	$3,481,986	$13,942,308	$15,057,692				1st Round pick	$32,481,986
251	Dario Šarić	PHO	$3,481,986						1st Round pick	$3,481,986
252	Romeo Langford	BOS	$3,458,400	$3,631,200	$3,804,360	$5,634,257			1st Round Pick	$7,089,600
253	Bam Adebayo	MIA	$3,454,080	$5,115,492					1st Round Pick	$8,569,572
254	Kyle Korver	PHO	$3,440,000							$3,440,000
255	Michael Porter	DEN	$3,389,400	$3,550,800	$5,258,735				1st Round Pick	$6,940,200
256	Denzel Valentine	CHI	$3,377,569						1st Round pick	$3,377,569
257	Juan Hernangómez	MIN	$3,321,030						1st Round pick	$3,321,030
258	Sekou Doumbouya	DET	$3,285,120	$3,449,400	$3,613,680	$5,539,771			1st Round Pick	$6,734,520
259	Justin Jackson	DAL	$3,280,920	$5,029,650					1st Round Pick	$8,310,570
260	Troy Brown	WAS	$3,219,480	$3,372,840	$5,170,564				1st Round Pick	$6,592,320

Rk	Player	Tm	Salary 2019–20	2020–21	2021–22	2022–23	2023–24	2024–25	Signed Using	Guaranteed
261	Jon Leuer	MIL	$3,169,348	$3,169,348	$3,169,347					$9,508,043
262	Yogi Ferrell	SAC	$3,150,000						Cap Space	$3,150,000
263	Guerschon Yabusele	BOS	$3,117,240							$3,117,240
264	Zhaire Smith	PHI	$3,058,800	$3,204,600	$4,915,856				1st Round Pick	$6,263,400
265	Dwight Howard	MEM	$3,039,097							$3,039,097
266	Khem Birch	ORL	$3,000,000	$3,000,000					Early Bird Rights	$6,000,000
267	Ryan Arcidiacono	CHI	$3,000,000	$3,000,000	$3,000,000				Cap space	$6,000,000
268	Quinn Cook	LAL	$3,000,000	$3,000,000					Cap Space	$4,000,000
269	Ömer Aşık	CHI	$3,000,000							$3,000,000
270	Nickeil Alexander-Walker	NOP	$2,964,840	$3,113,160	$3,261,480	$5,009,633			1st Round Pick	$6,078,000
271	D.J. Wilson	MIL	$2,961,120	$4,548,280					1st Round Pick	$7,509,400
272	Cedi Osman	CLE	$2,907,143	$8,750,000	$8,050,000	$7,350,000	$6,650,000		MLE	$27,057,143
273	Donte DiVincenzo	MIL	$2,905,800	$3,044,160	$4,675,830				1st Round Pick	$5,949,960
274	Bryn Forbes	SAS	$2,875,000						Early Bird Rights	$2,875,000
275	Andrew Nicholson	POR	$2,844,429	$2,844,429	$2,844,429	$2,844,429	$2,844,429			$14,222,145
276	Goga Bitadze	IND	$2,816,760	$2,957,520	$3,098,400	$4,765,339			1st Round Pick	$5,774,280
277	T.J. Leaf	IND	$2,813,280	$4,326,825					1st Round Pick	$7,140,105
278	Lonnie Walker	SAS	$2,760,480	$2,892,000	$4,447,896				1st Round Pick	$5,652,480
279	Alex Caruso	LAL	$2,750,000	$2,750,000					Room Exception	$5,500,000
280	Malik Beasley	MIN	$2,731,714						1st Round pick	$2,731,714
281	Luka Šamanić	SAS	$2,689,920	$2,824,320	$2,959,080	$4,556,983			1st Round Pick	$5,514,240
282	John Collins	ATL	$2,686,560	$4,137,302					1st Round Pick	$6,823,862
283	Kevin Huerter	ATL	$2,636,280	$2,761,920	$4,253,357				1st Round Pick	$5,398,200
284	Caris LeVert	BRK	$2,625,718	$16,203,704	$17,500,000	$18,796,296			1st Round pick	$55,125,718
285	Marko Guduric	MEM	$2,625,000	$2,750,000					Bi-annual Exception	$5,375,000

			Salary							
Rk	Player	Tm	2019–20	2020–21	2021–22	2022–23	2023–24	2024–25	Signed Using	Guaranteed
286	DeAndre' Bembry	ATL	$2,603,982						1st Round pick	$2,603,982
287	Matisse Thybulle	PHI	$2,582,160	$2,711,280	$2,840,160	$4,379,527			1st Round Pick	$5,293,440
288	Harry Giles	SAC	$2,578,800						1st Round Pick	$2,578,800
289	Jeff Green	UTA	$2,564,753							$2,564,753
290	Pau Gasol	POR	$2,564,753							$2,564,753
291	Wesley Matthews	MIL	$2,564,753	$2,692,991					Minimum Salary	$2,564,753
292	Kyle Korver	MIL	$2,564,753						Minimum Salary	$2,564,753
293	Udonis Haslem	MIA	$2,564,753						Minimum Salary	$2,564,753
294	Jared Dudley	LAL	$2,564,753						Minimum Salary	$2,564,753
295	Rajon Rondo	LAL	$2,564,753	$2,619,605					Minimum Salary	$2,564,753
296	Dwight Howard	LAL	$2,564,753						Minimum Salary	$2,564,753
297	Thabo Sefolosha	HOU	$2,564,753						Minimum Salary	$2,564,753
298	Tyson Chandler	HOU	$2,564,753						Minimum Salary	$2,564,753
299	Gerald Green	DEN	$2,564,753							$2,564,753
300	J.J. Barea	DAL	$2,564,753						Minimum Salary	$2,564,753
301	Wilson Chandler	BRK	$2,564,753						Minimum Salary	$2,564,753
302	Nenê Hilário	ATL	$2,564,753							$2,564,753
303	Vince Carter	ATL	$2,564,753						Minimum Salary	$2,564,753
304	Josh Okogie	MIN	$2,530,680	$2,651,040	$4,087,904				1st Round Pick	$5,181,720
305	Vincent Poirier	BOS	$2,505,793	$2,619,207					Minimum Salary	$5,125,000
306	Rondae Hollis-Jefferson	TOR	$2,500,000						MLE	$2,500,000
307	Brandon Clarke	MEM	$2,478,840	$2,602,920	$2,726,880	$4,343,920			1st Round Pick	$5,081,760
308	Terrance Ferguson	OKC	$2,475,840	$3,944,013					1st Round Pick	$6,419,853
309	Grayson Allen	MEM	$2,429,400	$2,545,320	$4,054,695				1st Round Pick	$4,974,720
310	Anthony Tolliver	SAC	$2,419,852							$2,419,852

			Salary							
Rk	Player	Tm	2019–20	2020–21	2021–22	2022–23	2023–24	2024–25	Signed Using	Guaranteed
311	Grant Williams	BOS	$2,379,840	$2,498,760	$2,617,800	$4,306,281			1st Round Pick	$4,878,600
312	Jarrett Allen	BRK	$2,376,840	$3,909,902					1st Round Pick	$6,286,742
313	Pascal Siakam	TOR	$2,351,839	$29,000,000	$31,320,000	$33,640,000	$35,960,000		1st Round pick	$132,271,839
314	Skal Labissière	ATL	$2,338,847						1st Round pick	$2,338,847
315	Chandler Hutchison	CHI	$2,332,320	$2,443,440	$4,019,459				1st Round Pick	$4,775,760
316	Patrick Patterson	LAC	$2,331,593						Minimum Salary	$2,331,593
317	Dejounte Murray	SAS	$2,321,735	$14,285,714	$15,428,571	$16,571,429	$17,714,286		1st Round pick	$66,321,735
318	Alec Burks	PHI	$2,320,044						Minimum Salary	$2,320,044
319	Isaiah Thomas	LAC	$2,320,044							$2,320,044
320	Damian Jones	ATL	$2,305,057						1st Round pick	$2,305,057
321	Darius Bazley	OKC	$2,284,800	$2,399,160	$2,513,040	$4,264,629			1st Round Pick	$4,683,960
322	OG Anunoby	TOR	$2,281,800	$3,872,215					1st Round Pick	$6,154,015
323	Ante Žižić	CLE	$2,281,800						1st Round Pick	$2,281,800
324	Monta Ellis	IND	$2,245,400	$2,245,400	$2,245,400					$6,736,200
325	Markieff Morris	DET	$2,241,808							$2,241,808
326	Aaron Holiday	IND	$2,239,200	$2,345,640	$3,980,551				1st Round Pick	$4,584,840
327	Luke Kornet	CHI	$2,195,122	$2,304,878					Room Exception	$4,500,000
328	Ty Jerome	PHO	$2,193,480	$2,303,040	$2,412,840	$4,220,057			1st Round Pick	$4,496,520
329	Willie Cauley-Stein	DAL	$2,177,483	$2,286,357					MLE	$2,177,483
330	Austin Rivers	HOU	$2,174,318	$2,369,663					Minimum Salary	$2,174,318
331	Carmelo Anthony	POR	$2,159,029						Minimum Salary	$2,159,029
332	Anfernee Simons	POR	$2,149,560	$2,252,040	$3,938,818				1st Round Pick	$4,401,600
333	Matt Barnes	SAC	$2,133,541							$2,133,541
334	Nassir Little	POR	$2,105,520	$2,210,640	$2,316,240	$4,171,548			1st Round Pick	$4,316,160
335	Torrey Craig	DEN	$2,100,000						Cap Space	$2,100,000
336	Moritz Wagner	WAS	$2,063,520	$2,161,920	$3,893,618				1st Round Pick	$4,225,440

			Salary							
Rk	Player	Tm	2019–20	2020–21	2021–22	2022–23	2023–24	2024–25	Signed Using	Guaranteed
337	Dylan Windler	CLE	$2,035,800	$2,137,440	$2,239,200	$4,037,278			1st Round Pick	$4,173,240
338	Caleb Swanigan	POR	$2,033,160						1st Round Pick	$2,033,160
339	Trey Burke	PHI	$2,028,594							$2,028,594
340	Kyle O'Quinn	PHI	$2,028,594						Minimum Salary	$2,028,594
341	Michael Carter-Williams	ORL	$2,028,594						Minimum Salary	$2,028,594
342	Mike Muscala	OKC	$2,028,594	$2,283,034					Minimum Salary	$2,028,594
343	Nerlens Noel	OKC	$2,028,594						Minimum Salary	$2,028,594
344	Troy Daniels	LAL	$2,028,594							$2,028,594
345	Ben McLemore	HOU	$2,028,594	$2,283,034					Minimum Salary	$2,028,594
346	Spencer Hawes	MIL	$2,007,058							$2,007,058
347	Edmond Sumner	IND	$2,000,000	$2,160,000	$2,320,000				Cap Space	$4,160,000
348	Avery Bradley	MEM	$2,000,000							$2,000,000
349	Noah Vonleh	DEN	$2,000,000						MLE	$2,000,000
350	Landry Shamet	LAC	$1,995,120	$2,090,040	$3,768,342				1st Round Pick	$4,085,160
351	Mfiondu Kabengele	LAC	$1,977,000	$2,075,880	$2,174,880	$3,923,484			1st Round Pick	$4,052,880
352	Kyle Kuzma	LAL	$1,974,600	$3,562,178					1st Round Pick	$5,536,778
353	Jordan Poole	GSW	$1,964,760	$2,063,280	$2,161,440	$3,901,399			1st Round Pick	$4,028,040
354	Tony Bradley	UTA	$1,962,360	$3,542,060					1st Round Pick	$5,504,420
355	Keldon Johnson	SAS	$1,950,600	$2,048,040	$2,145,720	$3,873,025			1st Round Pick	$3,998,640
356	Derrick White	SAS	$1,948,080	$3,516,284					1st Round Pick	$5,464,364
357	Robert Williams	BOS	$1,937,520	$2,029,920	$3,661,976				1st Round Pick	$3,967,440
358	Josh Hart	NOP	$1,934,160	$3,491,159					1st Round Pick	$5,425,319
359	Jacob Evans	MIN	$1,925,880	$2,017,320	$3,641,263				1st Round Pick	$3,943,200
360	Anderson Varejão	POR	$1,913,345	$1,913,345						$3,826,690
361	Džanan Musa	BRK	$1,911,600	$2,002,800	$3,615,054				1st Round Pick	$3,914,400

			Salary							
Rk	Player	Tm	2019–20	2020–21	2021–22	2022–23	2023–24	2024–25	Signed Using	Guaranteed
362	Omari Spellman	MIN	$1,897,800	$1,988,280	$3,588,845				1st Round Pick	$3,886,080
363	Shabazz Napier	WAS	$1,882,867						Cap Space	$1,882,867
364	Glenn Robinson	PHI	$1,882,867	$2,071,978					Minimum Salary	$1,882,867
365	James Ennis	ORL	$1,882,867	$2,071,978					Minimum Salary	$1,882,867
366	Tim Frazier	DET	$1,882,867							$1,882,867
367	Larry Sanders	MIL	$1,865,547	$1,865,547	$1,865,547					$5,596,641
368	Bruno Caboclo	HOU	$1,845,301						Minimum Salary	$1,845,301
369	Markieff Morris	LAL	$1,750,000						DPE	$1,750,000
370	Mario Hezonja	POR	$1,737,145	$1,882,867					Minimum Salary	$3,620,012
371	Emmanuel Mudiay	UTA	$1,737,145						Minimum Salary	$1,737,145
372	Raul Neto	PHI	$1,737,145						Minimum Salary	$1,737,145
373	JaKarr Sampson	IND	$1,737,145						Minimum Salary	$1,737,145
374	Pat Connaughton	MIL	$1,723,050						MLE	$1,723,050
375	Jahlil Okafor	NOP	$1,702,486						Minimum Salary	$1,702,486
376	Rodions Kurucs	BRK	$1,699,236	$1,780,152	$1,861,068				Cap space	$3,479,388
377	Jonah Bolden	PHI	$1,698,450							$1,698,450
378	Georges Niang	UTA	$1,678,854	$1,783,557					Non-Bird Exception	$1,678,854
379	Cheick Diallo	PHO	$1,678,854	$1,824,003					Minimum Salary	$1,678,854
380	Dragan Bender	MIL	$1,678,854							$1,678,854
381	David Nwaba	BRK	$1,678,854							$1,678,854
382	Treveon Graham	ATL	$1,678,854						Minimum Salary	$1,678,854
383	Willy Hernangómez	CHO	$1,676,735						Cap Space	$1,676,735
384	Derrick Jones	MIA	$1,645,357						Minimum Salary	$1,645,357
385	Jordan McRae	DET	$1,645,357						Minimum Salary	$1,645,357
386	Christian Wood	DET	$1,645,357						Minimum Salary	$1,645,357

Rk	Player	Tm	Salary 2019–20	2020–21	2021–22	2022–23	2023–24	2024–25	Signed Using	Guaranteed
387	Furkan Korkmaz	PHI	$1,620,564	$1,762,796					Minimum Salary	$1,620,564
388	Jordan Bell	MEM	$1,620,564							$1,620,564
389	Justin Patton	DAL	$1,620,564							$1,620,564
390	Royce O'Neale	UTA	$1,618,520	$8,035,714	$8,678,571	$9,321,429	$9,964,286		Cap space	$37,618,520
391	Dillon Brooks	MEM	$1,618,520	$11,400,000	$12,200,000	$11,400,000			MLE	$36,618,520
392	Wesley Iwundu	ORL	$1,618,520						Cap Space	$1,618,520
393	Abdel Nader	OKC	$1,618,520	$1,752,950					Cap Space	$1,618,520
394	Damyean Dotson	NYK	$1,618,520						Minimum Salary	$1,618,520
395	Frank Jackson	NOP	$1,618,520						MLE	$1,618,520
396	Sterling Brown	MIL	$1,618,520						MLE	$1,618,520
397	Dwayne Bacon	CHO	$1,618,520						MLE	$1,618,520
398	Semi Ojeleye	BOS	$1,618,520	$1,752,950					Cap space	$1,618,520
399	Chris Boucher	TOR	$1,588,231						Minimum Salary	$1,588,231
400	Malcolm Miller	TOR	$1,588,231						Minimum Salary	$1,588,231
401	Monte Morris	DEN	$1,588,231	$1,663,861					Minimum Salary	$1,588,231
402	Mitchell Robinson	NYK	$1,559,712	$1,663,861	$1,802,057				MLE	$1,559,712
403	Vlatko Čančar	DEN	$1,517,981	$898,310	$1,782,621				MLE	$2,416,291
404	Isaiah Roby	OKC	$1,500,000	$1,517,981	$1,782,621	$1,930,681			MLE	$3,017,981
405	Nigel Williams-Goss	UTA	$1,500,000	$1,517,981	$1,782,621				Cap Space	$1,500,000
406	J.R. Smith	CLE	$1,456,667	$1,456,667	$1,456,666					$4,370,000
407	Shake Milton	PHI	$1,445,697	$1,701,593	$1,846,738	$1,997,718			Cap Space	$4,994,028
408	Thanasis Antetokounmpo	MIL	$1,445,697	$1,701,593					Minimum Salary	$3,147,290
409	Amile Jefferson	ORL	$1,445,697							$1,445,697
410	Theo Pinson	NYK	$1,445,697	$1,701,593					Minimum Salary	$1,445,697
411	Brad Wanamaker	BOS	$1,445,697						Minimum Salary	$1,445,697

			Salary							
Rk	Player	Tm	2019–20	2020–21	2021–22	2022–23	2023–24	2024–25	Signed Using	Guaranteed
412	Derrick Walton	ATL	$1,445,697							$1,445,697
413	Ryan Broekhoff	DAL	$1,443,842							$1,443,842
414	Gary Trent	POR	$1,416,852	$1,663,861					MLE	$3,080,713
415	Isaac Bonga	WAS	$1,416,852	$1,663,861					Cap Space	$1,416,852
416	Chimezie Metu	SAS	$1,416,852	$1,663,861					MLE	$1,416,852
417	Jevon Carter	PHO	$1,416,852						MInimum Salary	$1,416,852
418	Elie Okobo	PHO	$1,416,852	$1,663,861	$1,802,057				Cap Space	$1,416,852
419	Melvin Frazier	ORL	$1,416,852	$1,663,861					MLE	$1,416,852
420	Deonte Burton	OKC	$1,416,852	$1,663,861					Minimum Salary	$1,416,852
421	Hamidou Diallo	OKC	$1,416,852	$1,663,861					MLE	$1,416,852
422	Kenrich Williams	NOP	$1,416,852						Minimum Salary	$1,416,852
423	Jarred Vanderbilt	MIN	$1,416,852	$1,663,861					Cap Space	$1,416,852
424	Duncan Robinson	MIA	$1,416,852	$1,663,861					MLE	$1,416,852
425	Kendrick Nunn	MIA	$1,416,852	$1,663,861					Minimum Salary	$1,416,852
426	De'Anthony Melton	MEM	$1,416,852						Cap Space	$1,416,852
427	Alize Johnson	IND	$1,416,852						Minimum Salary	$1,416,852
428	Isaiah Hartenstein	HOU	$1,416,852							$1,416,852
429	Sviatoslav Mykhailiuk	DET	$1,416,852	$1,663,861					Cap Space	$1,416,852
430	Bruce Brown	DET	$1,416,852	$1,663,861					MLE	$1,416,852
431	Keita Bates-Diop	DEN	$1,416,852	$1,663,861					MLE	$1,416,852
432	Devonte' Graham	CHO	$1,416,852	$1,663,861					MLE	$1,416,852
433	Jalen Brunson	DAL	$1,416,582	$1,663,861	$1,802,057				Cap Space	$3,080,443
434	Bruno Fernando	ATL	$1,400,000	$1,517,981	$1,782,621				Cap space	$4,700,602
435	Jaylen Nowell	MIN	$1,400,000	$1,517,981	$1,782,621	$1,930,681			MLE	$1,400,000
436	Alfonzo McKinnie	CLE	$1,361,046	$1,762,796	$1,910,860	$2,165,298			MLE	$2,253,031
437	Kevin Porter	CLE	$1,290,960	$2,033,160	$2,130,240	$3,845,083			1st Round Pick	$3,324,120

			Salary							
Rk	Player	Tm	2019–20	2020–21	2021–22	2022–23	2023–24	2024–25	Signed Using	Guaranteed
438	Carsen Edwards	BOS	$1,228,026	$1,517,981	$1,782,621	$1,930,681			Cap space	$4,528,628
439	Cody Martin	CHO	$1,173,310	$1,517,981	$1,782,621				MLE	$4,473,912
440	Gary Payton	WAS	$1,090,781						Minimum Salary	$1,090,781
441	George Hill	MIL	$1,000,000							$21,000,000
442	Terance Mann	LAC	$1,000,000	$1,517,984	$1,782,621	$1,930,681			Minimum Salary	$2,517,984
443	Jonathon Simmons	WAS	$1,000,000							$1,000,000
444	Justin Hamilton	TOR	$1,000,000							$1,000,000
445	Kyle Singler	OKC	$999,200	$999,200	$999,200	$999,200				$3,996,800
446	Marvin Williams	MIL	$956,349						Minimum Salary	$956,349
447	David Nwaba	HOU	$903,111	$1,862,250					MLE	$903,111
448	Admiral Schofield	WAS	$898,310	$1,517,981	$1,782,621				MLE	$4,198,912
449	KZ Okpala	MIA	$898,310	$1,517,981	$1,782,621				MLE	$4,198,912
450	Eric Paschall	GSW	$898,310	$1,517,981	$1,782,621				MLE	$4,198,912
451	Nicolas Claxton	BRK	$898,310	$1,517,981	$1,782,621				Minimum Salary	$4,198,912
452	Justin James	SAC	$898,310	$1,517,981	$1,782,621				Minimum Salary	$2,416,291
453	Jalen Lecque	PHO	$898,310	$1,517,981	$1,782,621	$1,930,681			Cap Space	$2,416,291
454	Ignas Brazdeikis	NYK	$898,310	$1,517,981	$1,782,621				Minimum Salary	$2,416,291
455	Talen Horton-Tucker	LAL	$898,310	$1,517,981					Minimum Salary	$2,416,291
456	Daniel Gafford	CHI	$898,310	$1,517,981	$1,782,621	$1,930,681			Minimum Salary	$2,416,291
457	Alen Smailagić	GSW	$898,310	$1,517,981	$1,782,621	$1,930,681			MLE	$2,415,891
458	Matt Thomas	TOR	$898,310	$1,517,981	$1,782,621				MLE	$1,623,310
459	Miye Oni	UTA	$898,310	$1,517,981	$1,782,621				Minimum Salary	$898,310
460	Dewan Hernandez	TOR	$898,310	$1,517,981	$1,782,621				MLE	$898,310
461	Terence Davis	TOR	$898,310	$1,517,981					Minimum Salary	$898,310
462	Wenyen Gabriel	POR	$898,310						Minimum Salary	$898,310
463	Naz Reid	MIN	$898,310	$1,517,981	$1,782,621	$1,930,681			MLE	$898,310

Rk	Player	Tm	Salary 2019–20	2020–21	2021–22	2022–23	2023–24	2024–25	Signed Using	Guaranteed
464	Jalen McDaniels	CHO	$898,310	$1,517,981	$1,782,621	$1,930,681			Minimum Salary	$898,310
465	Caleb Martin	CHO	$898,310	$1,517,981	$1,782,621				Minimum Salary	$898,310
466	Shaquille Harrison	CHI	$898,310						Minimum Salary	$898,310
467	Javonte Green	BOS	$898,310	$1,517,981					Minimum Salary	$898,310
468	Damion Lee	GSW	$842,327	$1,762,796	$1,910,860				MLE	$1,442,327
469	Khyri Thomas	DET	$838,464	$1,663,861					MLE	$838,464
470	DeMarre Carroll	HOU	$811,447						Minimum Salary	$811,447
471	Michael Kidd-Gilchrist	DAL	$810,763						Minimum Salary	$810,763
472	Marquese Chriss	GSW	$758,804							$2,213,272
473	Juwan Morgan	UTA	$746,054						Minimum Salary	$746,054
474	Patrick Patterson	OKC	$737,067	$737,067	$737,066					$2,211,200
475	Reggie Jackson	LAC	$734,025						Minimum Salary	$734,025
476	Alfonzo McKinnie	CLE	$708,871							$2,253,031
477	Gary Clark	HOU	$708,426							$708,426
478	Jeff Green	HOU	$695,526						Minimum Salary	$840,427
479	Cole Aldrich	MIN	$685,340	$685,340						$1,370,680
480	Shaun Livingston	GSW	$666,667	$666,667	$666,666					$2,666,666
481	Marquese Chriss	GSW	$654,468	$1,824,003					Minimum Salary	$2,213,272
482	Timothé Luwawu-Cabarrot	BRK	$654,468	$1,824,003					Minimum Salary	$844,170
483	Rayjon Tucker	UTA	$578,573	$1,517,981					Minimum Salary	$578,574
484	Chris Clemons	HOU	$568,422	$1,517,981	$1,782,621				MLE	$568,422
485	Gary Clark	ORL	$555,409						Minimum Salary	$718,765
486	Brandon Goodwin	ATL	$522,738	$1,701,593					Minimum Salary	$522,738
487	Dion Waiters	LAL	$503,656						Minimum Salary	$503,656
488	Ryan Anderson	HOU	$500,000							$500,000

Rk	Player	Tm	Salary 2019–20	2020–21	2021–22	2022–23	2023–24	2024–25	Signed Using	Guaranteed
489	Anžejs Pasečņiks	WAS	$482,144						Minimum Salary	$482,144
490	Troy Daniels	DEN	$481,000						Minimum Salary	$481,000
491	Chris Silva	MIA	$466,918	$1,517,981	$1,782,621				MLE	$1,984,899
492	Dakari Johnson	MEM	$459,414	$459,414						$918,828
493	Iman Shumpert	BRK	$419,443							$419,443
494	Max Strus	BOS	$415,414							$415,414
495	Justin Robinson	WAS	$395,866							$395,866
496	Dean Wade	CLE	$375,000	$1,517,981	$1,782,621	$1,930,681			MLE	$375,000
497	Ivan Rabb	MEM	$371,758							$371,758
498	Norvel Pelle	PHI	$350,189						Minimum Salary	$350,189
499	Ky Bowman	GSW	$350,189	$1,517,981	$1,782,621				MLE	$350,189
500	Juan Toscano-Anderson	GSW	$350,189	$1,517,981	$1,782,621				MLE	$350,189
501	A.J. Hammons	MIA	$350,087	$350,087						$700,174
502	Festus Ezeli	POR	$333,333							$333,333
503	C.J. Watson	ORL	$333,333							$333,333
504	Anthony Tolliver	MEM	$289,803						Minimum Salary	$434,704
505	Joakim Noah	LAC	$289,803	$1,737,274					Minimum Salary	$434,704
506	Corey Brewer	SAC	$289,803						Minimum Salary	$289,803
507	J.R. Smith	LAL	$289,803						Minimum Salary	$289,803
508	Michael Beasley	BRK	$289,803						Minimum Salary	$289,803
509	Jamal Crawford	BRK	$289,803						Minimum Salary	$289,803
510	Stanton Kidd	UTA	$250,000							$250,000
511	Jordan Bell	CLE	$250,000						MLE	$250,000
512	Tyler Zeller	SAS	$245,686	$2,436,046					Minimum Salary	$245,686
513	Trey Burke	DAL	$229,220						Minimum Salary	$229,220

			Salary							
Rk	Player	Tm	2019–20	2020–21	2021–22	2022–23	2023–24	2024–25	Signed Using	Guaranteed
514	Joe Johnson	DET	$220,000							$220,000
515	Tyler Johnson	BRK	$212,753						Minimum Salary	$212,753
516	Jemerrio Jones	WAS	$199,000							$199,000
517	Jontay Porter	MEM	$197,933	$1,517,981					Minimum Salary	$197,933
518	Jerian Grant	WAS	$196,288						Minimum Salary	$196,288
519	Cameron Payne	PHO	$196,288	$1,977,011					Minimum Salary	$196,288
520	Timothé Luwawu-Cabarrot	BRK	$189,702							$844,170
521	Dragan Bender	GSW	$189,702						Minimum Salary	$189,702
522	Mychal Mulder	GSW	$187,782	$1,517,981	$1,782,621				Minimum Salary	$238,534
523	Justin Patton	DET	$183,115	$1,762,796					Minimum Salary	$183,115
524	PJ Dozier	DEN	$183,115						MLE	$183,115
525	Alfonzo McKinnie	CLE	$183,114							$2,253,031
526	Gary Clark	ORL	$163,356							$718,765
527	Jaylen Adams	POR	$163,356						Minimum Salary	$163,356
528	Ryan Broekhoff	PHI	$163,356						Minimum Salary	$163,356
529	Joe Chealey	CHO	$163,356						Minimum Salary	$163,356
530	Luguentz Dort	OKC	$155,647	$1,517,981	$1,782,621	$1,930,681			Minimum Salary	$2,298,628
531	Cameron Payne	TOR	$150,000							$150,000
532	Jeff Green	HOU	$144,901							$840,427
533	Anthony Tolliver	MEM	$144,901							$434,704
534	Joakim Noah	LAC	$144,901							$434,704
535	Troy Williams	HOU	$122,741	$122,741	$122,741	$122,741				$490,964
536	Johnathan Williams	WAS	$106,181							$106,181
537	Tyler Cook	CLE	$101,504							$151,504
538	Donta Hall	DET	$101,504							$101,504

			Salary							
Rk	Player	Tm	2019–20	2020–21	2021–22	2022–23	2023–24	2024–25	Signed Using	Guaranteed
539	Yante Maten	MIA	$100,000							$100,000
540	Jaylen Adams	ATL	$100,000							$100,000
541	Justin Anderson	BRK	$98,144							$98,144
542	Demetrius Jackson	BOS	$92,857	$92,857	$92,857	$92,857	$92,857			$464,285
543	Jeremy Pargo	GSW	$91,557							$91,557
544	Chasson Randle	GSW	$91,557						Minimum Salary	$91,557
545	Jonah Bolden	PHO	$81,678							$81,678
546	Josh Magette	ORL	$81,678							$81,678
547	Jarrod Uthoff	MEM	$81,678							$81,678
548	Dusty Hannahs	MEM	$81,678							$81,678
549	Derrick Walton	DET	$81,678							$81,678
550	J.P. Macura	CLE	$81,678							$81,678
551	Sheldon Mac	CLE	$81,678						Minimum Salary	$81,678
552	Mychal Mulder	GSW	$50,752							$238,534
553	Eric Mika	SAC	$50,752							$50,752
554	Zach Norvell	GSW	$50,752							$50,752
555	Malik Newman	CLE	$50,752							$50,752
556	Marques Bolden	CLE	$50,752							$50,752
557	Sir'Dominic Pointer	CLE	$50,752						Minimum Salary	$50,752
558	Paul Watson	ATL	$50,752							$50,752
559	Tyler Cook	CLE	$50,000							$151,504
560	William Howard	UTA	$50,000							$50,000
561	Isaiah Taylor	TOR	$50,000							$50,000
562	Tyler Lydon	SAC	$50,000							$50,000
563	Hollis Thompson	SAC	$50,000							$50,000
564	Tyler Ulis	SAC	$50,000							$50,000

Discussion Questions:

1. Discuss what the term semiprofessional mean.
2. Why do you think the Amateur Athletic Union was not in favor of the "Olympics" paying athletes to participate in sports?
3. Do you think the semipro model could be used for Division I college athletes, where they have the opportunity to receive compensation from sponsor if they work for the sponsor in some capacity?
4. Name the four major league teams that are sponsors of minor league teams.
5. Discuss what being a professional in sports means.
6. What are the top professional women's league?
7. Name the three constituent leagues in Canada.
8. Discuss how participating in the semipro league could be beneficial to a sport participant.
9. Based on the pay model for the NBA, can you figure out what the average salary would be?
10. In Europe, what ice hockey teams are sponsored by professional team that act as a developmental and feeder association?

CHAPTER 11

RECRUITING

Introduction

The first recruiting initiative took place in the late 1890s, with the development of student-directed athletic club teams on college campuses throughout the country. During this period, players were recruited from mills, factories, and other workplaces. There were individuals who were deemed as "team managers" or (ringers) who handled the recruiting process, and although they were not affiliated with the college in any way, their main responsibility was to recruit players. However, when the abuses of their recruiting tactics were noticed, the faculty of the respected institution took control of the process.

In today's sports, it is important as a coach that you understand the various processes of recruiting. Regardless of the level you coach, you will need to familiarize yourself with this part of being a coach. The *recruiting landscape* is one littered with many different factors, and studies have analyzed social, demographics, and institutional settings as a major role in how athletes make their choices to play for or join a sports program. Other initiatives include developing a recruiting philosophy, recruiting in the 21st century, recruiting paradigm shifts, coach time investment, developing a recruiting dialogue, recruiting differentiation, commitment level of the athlete, how good is the athlete's work ethic, goal achievement, discipline, speed, quickness, competitive spirit, understanding roles, and playing with passion. These are a few examples of areas that should be considered as not only topic of recruiting conversations when you recruit but part of your recruiting philosophy to become the best recruiter at the level and sport you coach?

Recruiting Philosophy

Developing a *recruiting philosophy* is your road map to establishing a solid foundation that will give you consistency in your recruiting efforts. This philosophy will assist in guiding you when you are evaluating prospects at the middle school, high school, travel team, college, and professional level. All these levels require a different philosophy that caters to your team and the type of athlete you are pursuing.

The culture of today's recruiting is different from what it was ten years ago. Recruiting practices that were once associated with educational entities is now common in all sports programs (AAU, travel team, club). The way in which you identify prospects and communicate with them has changed drastically, causing coaches to restructure their recruiting philosophy. No exact formula will necessarily produce a great recruiting class, but the coach's philosophy should be institution- or program-specific coupled with individual consideration that are aligned to the culture of your program. Identify your program culture and make that a starting point to building your philosophy.

Recruiting in the 21st Century

The Internet has affected our daily lives from the way we communicate to the accessibility of information regarding a variety of topics. As most people know, athletics has become a big cyber industry user, and it has made a major impact on sports. Several Internet sites highlight the visibility of sports in various different ways, and prospective student-athletes from all genres use these sites to promote themselves. This philosophical change has made recruiting a little easier process for coaches because they can gather information of player achievement, statistics, and outside interests. Being able to access information without having a conversation with the player's coach, parent, or seeing them compete in person gives the coach valuable insight before they engage in a more in-depth recruiting process. Establishing some base knowledge about a perspective student athlete should create some talking points when you do engage in a conversation with the athlete, their coach, or other stakeholders.

There have been various paradigm shifts regarding recruiting over the past few years, forcing coaches to adjust their philosophy and recruiting strategies. One concept that has changed is *sport specialization* of student-athletes at a younger age. Some coaches used to be thrilled to recruit an athlete who played and excelled in multiple sports. However, due to the extended playing seasons, which led to more sport specialization, athletes in various sports, and at all levels are participating in one sport. The philosophy of recruiting a well-rounded multi-sport athlete has changed to recruiting a prospect who can play multiple positions, which has caused some coaches to adjust their ideologies to the changing recruiting culture.

Investing Time in the Recruiting Process

Whoever you choose to lead the recruiting efforts on your staff, make sure that they are the right fit. Recruiting requires a tremendous time commitment, and you want to ensure that the process is done professionally. There is plenty of truth to the saying "Your time is not your own" when referring to the number of hours dedicated to recruiting. Those coaching staff members that are delegated recruiting responsibilities need to be available when recruits can speak with them on the cell phone, after school, or during practice. Follow-ups by Internet research or communication with the high school or club coach cannot always be completed during traditional work hours, so the recruiters need to be prepared to sacrifice personal time advancing the programs recruiting. If you as the head coach are not taking the lead on the recruiting initiative, consider which coach has established rapport with AAU, club team, or high school coaches. Examine other program responsibilities to determine which coach has the ability to devote most of the day to the recruitment of prospects.

Another important piece to this process is developing a good recruiting dialogue, where a mutual respect and trust is established with the recruit, parents, club, or AAU coach and other stakeholders. As you develop a bond with the athlete based on your dialogue, it should become relational in nature, that is it is based on expectations of values, beliefs, honesty, expectations, and commitment. As the dialogue begins to "flow," you may discuss gaps that you need to fill in the program and technical and nontechnical roles needed for the program. The higher the level, the more in-depth your conversation can be about the advantages the athlete brings to the program.

Differentiate Your Recruiting Tactics

How do you differentiate your recruiting tactics from other programs? What unique approach can you use that may not be a normal practice by other coaches? These are a few strategies that you should consider when you recruit. When or if you make a visit to an athlete's home or use *social media* (video conferencing, Snapchat, Twitter, Facebook), consider including all family members in the process. If the athlete you are recruiting has a younger brother or sister, involve them in the recruiting process. Ask if you can have a conversation with the younger sibling and ask them to describe their brother or sister's personality. Ask if they help with homework or attend extracurricular activities. This tactic could also be used if you are recruiting a young athlete, ask to speak with the older brother or sister.

You may wonder what is the benefit of using this tactic, well you are involving all members of the family in the recruiting process, and usually, siblings will tell the truth about a brother or sister's character traits. This could be a unique tactic used by all coaches at every level particularly if you are not a college coach but coaching a travel team or middle school, where recruiting may not be a traditional practice for this level of coaching.

Coaches and recruiter are going to great lengths to make each prospective athlete recruitment process unique. At the higher level, schools use tactics like portraying the recruit as a "cover person" (Keeley 2014). The point is that you should develop a unique recruiting tactic or differentiate the way you will recruit.

Commitment and Buy-In

In society today, some athletes have a hard time making and staying committed to one program, be it a travel team, middle school, high school, college, or professional team. Making a commitment to join a program or attend an institution is psychologically challenging for an athlete.

During this phase of the recruiting process, discuss with the athlete the stress they will experience, making that pledge, vow, and declared intention to be a part of your program (Bennett and Pravitz 1987). Keep in mind that there may be other programs the student-athlete is considering, so clearly identify the concrete plan, purpose, and passion you as the coach will commit to regarding his or her academic growth, athletic growth, and overall well-being.

When you attain a commitment from the student-athlete, your next step is to work on establishing *buy-in*. As the coach, you create an atmosphere in which you connect with and transform your athletes. The recruiting process allows you to meet new recruits where they are and assist them in becoming part of the team. All your athletes come from different backgrounds, having them buy in to your coaching philosophy requires you to show them that you care about them as a person and not just an athlete. Below are six strategies to getting buy-in from your recruit once they have committed to your program.

1. During the recruiting process, you are gaining information on what motivates them. Ask them to think ahead to the end of their career or time in your program. What would things look like if everything went ideally for them? The answer to this question provides you with tremendous insight regarding their motivation perspective.
2. Let the recruit know that they will be involved in deciding goals, rules, and standards for the program. When you value their input, you clearly show that the entire team is in this together. By providing them co-ownership of the team could be enticing and result in buy-in.

3. Ask the recruit to plan a practice and see how creative he or she can be. Don't be concerned about it being a bad practice because you know that when you plan practice, it is of high quality. Make sure you keep their practice plan and implement it in a future practice.
4. Your recruit needs to feel like what they are doing has important value to the team. If he or she is not a starter the first year, make sure you give them praise during practice of every little feat they achieve, it's your reserve players who especially need to be acknowledged for the things they do in practice. The coach should be their biggest fan because fans and the media often overlook their important contributions.
5. Keep in mind that the speed of the leader determines the pace of the pack, and your recruit is part of the pack. Your buy-in level as a coach sends an unmistakable message to your players about the importance of your buy-in to them. To gain the recruit and team buy-in, you must prove to your athletes that you are worthy of their buy-in. Consistently show them you are willing to pay the price for success.
6. If your recruit feels like you are using them to advance yourself with a higher-paying job at another program, expect them to see through you very quickly, which could result in their buy-in to drop off significantly. As mentioned earlier, stay connected with things outside of the sport, like their families, friends, and future goals and interest.

Training Commitment Dialogue

Talk to the athlete about commitment to training regimes, explain the consistency that they will need to put out maximal effort in all their workouts, how to overcome fatigue, frustration, and failure. Most recruits do not have an idea about striving to find every possible way to develop and improve by using strength training, conditioning, video analysis, mental training, and leadership training. Discussing the importance of maintaining a healthy diet, hydrating properly, getting enough rest and sleep, stretching and rehabbing to prevent and minimize injuries, avoiding or abstaining from using alcohol and drugs are beneficial. The athlete should understand that making a commitment to training means preparing one's self in every way to consistently be at your best. These are great topics and should be implemented in your recruiting philosophy.

Teammate Commitment Dialogue

Explaining the importance of committing to teammates requires knowing about the athletes' personality. I mentioned talking to siblings and other stakeholders who may not have a bias toward the athlete but will speak the truth about their personality. The commitment to teammates could mean a variety of tangibles. Being a selfless team player, consistently giving your best effort, supporting, and challenging yourself and teammates.

Surrounding Other's Commitment

Athletes may not understand the concept of "surrounding other's commitment." How conscientious do you think the athlete may be to those who evaluate, support, and criticize individuals connected to a sport program? In the world of athletics, there is a plethora of people, such as athletic trainers, administrators, advisors, teachers, professors, family members, community members, and fans, who will develop expectations of the athlete. This can be a challenge if the athlete has not had to deal with this type of scrutiny. Discussing how the athlete behavior patterns can create a supportive culture for themselves, the program, teammates, and surrounding others, who consistently evaluate from outside the program.

Coaching Staff Commitment

The athlete will obviously need to make a commitment to the coaching staff. Becoming part of a team means agreeing to the vision, values, and standards the program has established. Ask how coachable the athlete is and can they except constructive criticism. Being honest, responsible, displaying accountability, accepting the role assigned because it benefits the team.

Having a conversation with a perspective athlete about the type of work ethic you would like to see of those coming into your program can be challenging. Think about how you will establish a deep level of conversation regarding work ethic and its importance to achieving goals. Obviously, this will take some practice if you are not experienced with this part of recruiting. You must be able to convey how establishing a great work ethic consists of perseverance through the ups and downs associated with becoming your best and maintaining your best performance in and off the court. Discuss the concept of "igniting self" that inner strength drives one to excel and commit daily to being the best version of one's self.

Work ethic is not a "light switch" concept where you turn it on and off. It is an educational process of awareness. Sport performance researchers have found that an athlete's work ethic was highest with those athletes who found pleasure in the sport they compete in and who made sport investment (sacrifice). Talk the athlete about body awareness and how it parallels with moments of enriched personal meaning or moments of total immersion in sport that provided a sense of self-fulfillment (Scanlan, Carpenter, Schmidt, Simon, and Keeler 1993).

Goal Achievement

During the recruitment dialogue, you may mention goals as a general topic of conversation and bring up subcategories like objective and subjective goals, furthering the conversation with outcome, performance, and process goals as they relate to behavior change. However, discussing how the athlete will realistically achieve goals can be as beneficial as the subcategories mentioned. Athletes may have a tendency to identify affirmations about goals they want to achieve because they think it is what the coach wants to hear, and the coach may find pleasure in hearing these affirmations even if some are not realistic. For example, many of the athletes I recruited to play on the basketball team, coupled with those registered in the various courses I facilitated and those I mentored as an academic and sport coach advisor, stated that they wanted to play professionally in the sport they participated in. Now, far be it from me to shatter anyone's dream goals, but most of those goals were not realistic based on other tangibles.

It would behoove the coach to discuss with the athlete during the recruiting process the goals they have achieved and how they managed to accomplish them. This could frame the conversation, where the athlete has a realistic view of goals they want to achieve in your program.

Discipline Dialogue

As a sport coach, you know that success is predicated on discipline, the essential foundation for the athlete's success. It builds character to help them set their mind to achieve great things, beyond sports; it is also instrumental in other areas of life. So, developing this part of your recruiting dialogue is important. If the athlete has been competing in sports from an early age, you can explain how they have already established a lifelong sense of discipline. Have the athlete give you an example of discipline that he or she has had to utilize to accomplish a challenging feat. You can further elaborate the benefits they can get from being disciplined. Express how discipline teaches the value of hard work and that the less you take shortcuts, the more successful you can become.

Most athletes are familiar with Michael Jordan, and in the documentary *The Last Dance*, it was illustrated how Michael's discipline helped him achieve many of his outstanding accomplishments. Having discipline can often be as valuable as "natural" athletic talent. Let your recruit know that talent without discipline isn't enough to be successful.

Discipline coincides with work ethic, hard work, goal achievement, and as importantly, sacrifice. You may want to use an example of assignments you gave to the team or individual and it required them to cut back on TV time, video games, and spending times with friends. Express how the team or individual felt after making the sacrifice and displaying the discipline to accomplish the task.

Most athletes have a tough time with losing, so discuss with the athlete how they handle losing and listen very critically the response they give to you. Remind the athlete that discipline will not allow them to dwell on the loss but instead learn from it. Losses are only temporary setbacks.

Having the discipline to prepare for practice each day is vital to individual and team success. Stress the importance of having the discipline to be on time consistently. You can state how you arrive to practice early to greet players and have the practice plan prepared, which demonstrates the discipline you reflect in preparing for practice.

Athletic Speed

Most coaches would agree that speed is a major component in most sports, and when you are recruiting, you look for speed, meaning the ability the athlete can move over a set distance in the shortest possible time (Kawamori, N.; Nosaka, K.; Newton, R.U. 2012). All sports, even endurance sports, rely on some type of speed for performance of selected movements or in specific situations. If the recruit possesses "speed," this could be a great segue into a conversation of this gifted ability that he or she has and how it will benefit their growth in your program.

Discuss how speed that reflects movements from point A to point B are positives in all sports and how efficient acceleration qualities can pay dividends in athletic performance. I like the notion of explaining on a small scale some concepts related to science and athletic performance during the recruiting process. You can further elaborate about training protocols, where speed in your sport coincides with explosive training, and raw power without coordination can be more taxing and sometimes results in slower and stiffer movement. Athletes in ball sports need to be fast while multitasking, so utilizing speed efficiently enables the athlete to be smooth and adds to their skill set (see chapter 5 and 6 for more specific guidelines).

This type of dialogue may be more suited for an older athlete as opposed to a younger one. In summary, maximal speed is the destination of acceleration. While most sports events may not commonly involve top speed, but the ability to accelerate becomes more efficient with coordination development (Gavat, C.; Halil, T.; Fatma, A.; Alin, L.; and George, S. 2012).

Athletic Quickness

Coaches may question discussing speed and quickness during a recruiting visit, but I have found these discussions to be very effective, and although the athletes were young and older adults, the language was presented in a way that it was engaging to both age groups. Some coaching colleagues have used the term "train the brain"; well studies have shown that quickness is involved in movements that do not require a significant strength or energy expenditure or difficult coordination. The physiological mechanism of quickness is associated with the multifunctional capacity of the motor cortex of the brain (see chapter 5 and 6 for specific guidelines).

As you recruit for your sport, having somewhat of an understanding of how an athlete's quickness can be utilized is important. Does your sport require an athlete with *Slow Twitch Fibers (STF)* or *Fast Twitch Fibers (FTF)*? These fibers have different contractile and metabolic characteristics; movement quickness depends on which of the two are primarily aroused. Studies have revealed that an athlete whose muscle fibers are predominantly FT has high parameters of speed of movement and strength. For example, if you are a track coach and was recruiting a sprinter, this person's muscle most likely contains a higher percentage of FTF, contrary to a distance runner whose muscle fibers contain more STF.

The following are specific examples of quickness movement:

- A short latent period of muscular reaction
- Quickness in performing a simple, isolated movement (no overload), with an upper limb, a lower limb, the trunk, or head
- Quickness in performing a movement with more than one joint and requiring a variation of body positions in space or the transition from one action to the other, without great external reaction
- The rate of a movement without overload

Research states that these qualities are only slightly related to one another or related to the degree of physical conditioning. Furthermore, the relative independence of these qualities of quickness can be observed early when the athlete is between nine and thirteen years of age.

Competitive Spirit

There are times as a coach you may have the feeling that you want to win more than your players do. Some athletes seem to lack the competitive fire that makes for a special athlete. Contrary to a lack of *competitive spirit* is when they do have a strong competitive fire, the energy may be out of control, which leads to sportsmanship issues, not take ownership for their mistakes when they lose, taunting others, and boasting when they win.

As the coach, it can be a challenge creating the appropriate competitive spirit in your athletes, and some coaches usually wait until preseason training or the start of the regular season to deliver those competitive spirit incentives.

If the coach can take advantage of discussing a "competitive spirit" dialogue during the recruiting process, it's possible the recruit will divulge their interpretation of competitive spirit, giving the coach some insight on how competitive spirit is interpreted by the recruit.

Legendary basketball coach John Wooden highlighted "*competitive greatness*" as one of his top pyramid of success items. He wanted players to have a passion for a hard-fought competition and understanding that it presents the opportunity for one to be at their best when the best is required.

What are some strategies coaches can use to develop that competitive spirit? Below are a couple of suggestions that could serve to be beneficial.

1. Emphasize that respect plays an important part of developing a competitive spirit. Don't focus on demoralizing or speaking poorly of an opponent in an effort to motivate your team or teammates. Yes, "trash talking" is part of many a game. However, respecting opposing teams and opponents will not diminish one's competitive spirit but in many ways enhance it.
2. After the competition, be the first to congratulate your opponent. This shows that you were able to persevere through the ups and downs during competition, and regardless of win or lose, you were able to deal with the effort you displayed good or bad. This demeanor can drive one's competitive spirit.
3. Respect your competitive spirit by being grateful. Don't blame referees, umpires, or judges of competition, thank

them along with all other personnel who help with the event. There are a lot of moving parts to making an event successful, and if you can recognize and appreciate the efforts of those stakeholders, it will drive you to be at your best when you compete.

4. As the competitive spirit is being embraced by players or the concept conveyed by the coach, reinforce the value in the process. Don't demoralize losers and glorify winners. As the coach, communicate to your players or player that sports is just a game and one's performance does not define them as a person. What matters is who you become through the process. This could be part of a mission statement in your coaching philosophy, where the participants in your program will grow as athletes and as people by using sports and competition both in practice and in games to learn and grow.
5. Create a competitive practice environment wherein nearly every aspect of the practice is competitive and recorded. Make sure you are promoting healthy competition within a practice. Competition in and of itself can drive a wedge between players and foster a fixed mindset; when it is implemented and reinforced with the right incentive, it will create a healthy competitive spirit and bring players together.

Athletes Understanding Their Role on a Sport Team

Be it a team or individual sport, it's important to discuss the role you expect the athlete to partake when they join the sport program. Sometimes, it's difficult for a sport participant to be given a role because they may view themselves as playing a more defined or different role than you as the coach has identified. Having this dialogue early in the recruiting process may curtail some confusion or issues regarding the role you want the athlete to play. The coach should have a clear vision and understanding of the skill set, demeanor, and character the athlete is bringing to the table and what impact the participant will have immediately or in the future.

Sport participant roles can have several meanings, not just the number of minutes or times the participant plays in a game or a specific athletic skill. Educating the recruit on your definition of an athletes' role based on your ideology can be beneficial.

Based on *Michelle L. Mahoney*'s study of both men and women who participated on the golf, basketball, baseball, track-and-field sport teams and their perception of their academic and *athletic roles* (2011), she states that when discussing their athletic role, sport participants described how being an athlete was "part of me." In other words, the role they played on their sport team was not something they put on and take off like a jersey, it was an essential component of who they were and something that they have been accustomed to (athletic role) since a very young age. The time, energy, and effort that student-athletes (in her study) invested in their athletic role both on and off the court was not viewed as cumbersome or onerous but rather as a part of their normal, everyday lives although some of the participants had different experiences of their prescribed athletic role including athletic role conflict on their respected sport team. However, they still viewed athletic role as a part of their daily lives. There is some credence to this philosophical view, and I would attest based on my experience of coaching and advising that hundreds of student athletes cherish their role on the sport team and feel that it is beneficial to all parties involved in the sport program.

Discussion Questions:

1. Who was responsible for recruiting in the late 1800s?
2. Discuss how the recruiting process has changed in the 21st century.
3. Why is developing a recruiting philosophy important?
4. Discuss what the concept "The speed of the leader determines the pace of the pack" means regarding recruiting.
5. Name various training topics that can be discussed with a potential recruit.
6. Explain legendary coach John Wooden interpretation of "competitive greatness."

7. Do you believe the concept that one's performance does not define them as a person?
8. Define "role" as it pertains to team sports.
9. What do you think an athlete means when they state that athletics is a "part of me"?
10. Discuss important criteria you would employ in a recruiting dialogue.

CHAPTER 12

GENERAL COACHING REQUIREMENT FOR SPECIFIC STATES

Certification Process: Illinois

To become certified to coach in the State of Illinois, you must have the appropriate certification. According to the Illinois High School Association (IHSA), schools that use *nonfaculty coaches* must be in compliance to the following:

- Persons who are certified teachers but are not members of the faculty at a school where they will be coaching (head or assistant) must have a copy of their current valid Illinois Professional Educator License (PEL) on file in the school office.
- Retired persons who were certified to teach and were teaching in Illinois at the time of retirement may continue to coach at any member school. They must also have a copy of their PEL on file within the school office.
- Persons who are not certified teachers but are at least nineteen (19) years old may be head or assistant coaches, provided they successfully complete a coaching education course approved by the IHSA Board of Directors.
- Person who are not certified teachers but are as least nineteen (19) years old may qualify to be an assistant coach, provided they have completed a bachelor's degree and obtain an Illinois Substitute Teaching License through

their local ROE. The cost for this process may be more than the IHSA Coaching Orientation package through Human Kinetics Coach Education.

- Persons who stop teaching and do not possess a valid/current PEL are not eligible to coach in Illinois without coaching certification.

These are just minimum requirements mandated by IHSA. Member schools could require additional endorsements (i.e., CPR/AED certification). Teachers' aides and ancillary staff do not meet IHSA Coaching Qualifications, they must also complete and pass an approved coaching certification course. School personnel, individuals who maintain a teaching certificate from the Illinois State Board of Education (ISBE) can coach without a coaching certification. The license issued by the Illinois State Board of Education allows a teacher to conduct a classroom without supervision during the school day.

One of the courses that is the most frequently used to attain a coaching certification is the Human Kinetics Coach Education (formally known as the American Sport Education Program, ASEP). Requirements must be completed and notification of passing grades received before a coach can have coaching interaction with any high school individual participant or team. Another option is to take Coaching Principles or Sport First Aid as a classroom course. You must register for the class through a Human Kinetics Coach Education certified instructor in your area. You can go to: www.asep.

com/courseinfo/findCal.cfm for a complete list of classroom sites in Illinois.

Clinics are taught through a network of Human Kinetics Coach Education certified instructors in Illinois. If you enroll in a clinic course, you will receive the course materials from the instructor on-site on that day in the clinic. You cannot register for a classroom course through the Human Kinetics Coach Education website; all registrations for classroom courses are through the regular process of the institution or the course instructor. You will need the IHSA Handbook with illustrations as a tool to complete the IHSA Bylaw Exam. You can find it on the IHSA website: www.ihsa.org/abouttheIHSA/ConstitutuionBylawsPolicies.aspx. Purchase it from the IHSA office or check with your school to borrow a copy while testing. Additional coaches' certification option approved by the IHSA is National Federation of High School Association (NFHS) Certification. Go to www.mfhslearn.com. Customers must add the following to the cart to purchase: Fundamentals of Coaching and First Aid for Coaches. *The Sports First Aid component* is completed at an American Red Cross location, it is not completed online.

Here are additional coaching education programs currently approved by the IHSA Board of Directors: Human Kinetics Coach Education (Formerly ASEP), Champaign, Illinois; "The Coach in Organized Sports and Athletics" offered by Illinois State University Normal, Illinois; Department of Kinesiology Coaching Endorsement in the Undergraduate Studies Program; University of Illinois Champaign, Coaching Minor offered by Northern Illinois University, DeKalb, Illinois; Coaching Minor offered by Olivet Nazarene University, Kankakee, Illinois; Program for Athletic Coaches' Education; PACE offered by Michigan State University, Institute for the Study of Youth Sports, East Lansing, Michigan; Coaching Minor offered by Southern Illinois University, Department of Physical Education, Carbondale, Illinois; Coaching Education Program offered by Ashford University, Clinton Iowa; Coaching Minor offered by Quincy University, Quincy, Illinois; Coaching Certification Program offered by the University of Wisconsin Parkside, Kenosha, Wisconsin; Iowa Coaches Authorization Board of Education Examiners Bureau, Des Moines, Iowa; Coaching Minor offered by Blackburn College, Carlinville, Illinois 62626; and Coaching Minor offered by Loras College, Dubuque, Iowa.

The age requirement for a head, assistant, or volunteer coach is nineteen years of age. All coaches must meet the nineteen-year age requirement whether the coaching position is paid or voluntary. You can take the exam before age nineteen. However, you cannot coach until you reach your nineteenth birthday. School representatives can check NFHS certification dates and exam scores (pass/fail) by going to the following website: www.nfhslearn.com/CoachSearch.aspx.

It's important that the representative have the correct city, name, and spelling used by the coach during certification application. The applicant is not eligible to coach until notified of a passing grade. When testing online, your score will be given upon completion of the exam, and a certification can be printed. Once you have completed a Human Kinetic Coach Education or NFHS course, you do not need to take the course again if you have taken time off.

If a school has a competitive cheerleading program, the coach of the program will need to become certified to meet the bylaw requirement. If the school has sideline cheerleaders only, the coach does not have to acquire certification. In this case, sideline cheerleading is classified as an activity. Activity sponsors or coaches are not currently required to acquire coaching certification. You have one year from the day the course starts to complete the course. If you need to retest, you can go to the Human Kinetics Education Center home page and select "Courses" to take a test and follow the instructions provided on your computer screen.

If you need a copy of your Human Kinetic Coach Education or NFHS certification, you can download it from the Human Kinetics Coach Education Center or NFHS websites or contact the Human Kinetics Coach Education office at (800) 747-5698 or the NFHS office at (317) 972-6900.

Certification Process: Iowa

A coaching authorization is required to coach in middle school, junior high school, and high school in the State of Iowa. There are several processes to attaining certification, one is successful completion of a fifty-five-hour course.

Kirkwood Community College offers a variety of state-approved classes, online, or face-to-face to fulfill requirement coursework.

Classroom instruction or online certification is available through Kirkwood Continuing Education. Additionally, applicants must submit transcripts to the state and pass a background check with fingerprinting before earning certification. Fingerprinting is offered during the coaching seminar, otherwise, you can contact the local law enforcement agency to find out if and when they offer fingerprinting services to the public. Applicants under twenty years old will also need to upload a copy of their high school diploma as a required transcript into the online application.

Coursework completed in the past may be used to satisfy all (or parts of) the coaching authorization requirements. If you'd like further assistance with your transcript or if you'd like to have a member of the BOEE review your coursework, please contact Kirkwood's Iowa Coaching Authorization Online Courses representative. If you have a current Iowa teaching license, you can choose to add a coaching endorsement to your license by taking courses for college credit. Kirkwood Community College offers credit courses that will satisfy the requirement for the coaching endorsement.

Within five years of obtaining your coaching authorization, you need to participate in five renewal activities. These renewal activities must be sponsored or offered by an accredited college or university, Area Education Agency, professional athletic association, the Iowa High School Athletic Association, or the Iowa Girls High School Athletic Union. Classes, clinics, and rules meetings all qualify as renewal activities. Kirkwood Coaching Recertification classes are offered online for your convenience. Below are five courses that meet the qualifications:

Coaching Recertification as Good as It Gets (online)
Coaching Recertification Coaching Teams vs. Individuals (online)
Coaching Recertification Ethics and Issues in Coaching (online)
Coaching Recertification Inside the Weight Room (online)

If you have a current Iowa teaching license, you can choose to add a coaching endorsement to your license by taking course for college credit at Kirkwood Community College. The college offers credit courses that will satisfy the requirements for the coaching endorsement.

Certification Process: California

California uses the CIF-Coaching Education Program to enhance the experience of student-athlete by assuring that their coaches meet a minimum level of professional training. The program provides strong, pragmatic, and comprehensive instruction for coaches of interscholastic athletics in California that is consistent with the highest national standards as set by legislature, state Department of Education, California Interscholastic Federation, and National Federation of State High School Associations.

The primary requirements for coaching high school sports in California is taking a General Coaching Education Course. The most commonly utilized are the Fundamentals of Coaching through the NFHS, https://nfhssleam.com/courses/61001; CIF principles course offered through HKCE; CIF Coaching Orientation course offered in a classroom setting or online through ASEP; Concussion in Sports offered through NFHS, https://nfhslearn.com/courses/38000; concussion-wise offered through HKCE, https://coacheducation.humankinetics.com/collections/28/products/ssi-concussionwise-online-courses. NFHS offers a free course titled "Sudden Cardiac Arrest (SCA) Training," and HKCE also offers the course, http://nfhslearn.com/courses/61032/sudden-cardiac-arrest.

As of January 1, 2019, state law went into effect for Heat Acclimatization Course also offered by NFHS, https://nfhslearn.com/courses/61140/heat-illness-prevention. Frist Aid and CPR certification are required, and you can consult the school district for this requirement. The Sudden Cardiac Arrest, Heat Acclimatization, and first aid and CPR certifications have to be renewed when your first aid/CPR renewal date is due.

If you are a cheer coach, the AACCA Sprit Safety Certification course is offered through HFHS https//nfhslearn.com/courses/10000/aacca-spirit-safety-certification. At the present time if you pass the course and complete the test, you do not have to take the course or test again. You will be listed on the "Coaches Registry" database.

Coaches required to pass the coaching education courses are defined as any individual that the school district is required to approve under *California education code 33190-33192, 45125.01 and 45125.1.* Simply stated, the law applies to anyone who is required to be fingerprinted and or is approved by their school board directors to have contact with students. This law applies to all CIF member schools, public and private. Specifically, the courses that meet California's standards for coaching education are the NFHS "Fundamentals of Coaching" Course, the HKCE "Coaching Principles," and the HKCE "CIF Coaching Orientation." Coaches can go online on their own to www.nfhslearn.com and take the Fundamental of Coaching course. Any representative from a school district can also go to www. nfhllearn.com and purchase license numbers in bulk for their coaches. The coaches then go online and complete the "Fundamental of Coaching" course to become certified. The CIF will also accept the "Coaching Orientation" course offered by HKCE.

If a situation occurs where a school needs to hire a coach immediately, the CIF Bylaw and the Education Code allow for this common situation. A school/district may hire a coach that is not certified but only for one season. The coach must complete the certification before they can coach another season and or a second sport. The state law allow for this one sports season exception in the case of an emergency. Keep in mind that there are online options for same-day certification; it should be a rare situation when this exception is utilized.

The CIF recommends you to consult the school district you currently work for or plan to work for before selecting or taking any certification courses as the district may have more specific or additional requirements.

Certification Process: Florida

In order to coach in the State of Florida (coaching defined as those who are paid a coaching supplement but don't hold a valid temporary or professional educator certificate or cheerleading coaches, where the sport is considered a competitive sport, and unpaid volunteers who are employees of the District School Board or Collier County and do not hold a temporary or professional certificate must have the appropriate certification to coach), the Florida Department of Education issues two types of Athletic Coaching Certificates, a three-year temporary certificate and a five-year certificate. The three-year "temporary" certificate is issued to give the coach time to complete the requirement for the five years. The three-year temporary certificate is not renewable.

An application for the Athletic Coaching Educator Certification must be made online with the Department of Education at https://ficertify.fldoe.org/datamart prior to starting coaching. You must also have fingerprint results that are no older than one year.

The five-year certificate requires nine semester in athletic coaching to include the following areas: three semester hours in care and prevention of athletic injures and the dangers of drug use, including performance enhancing drugs, three semester hours in coaching theory, a course in theory and practice of coaching a specific sport, and a valid cardiopulmonary resuscitation certificate issued by the American Heart Association or the American Red Cross. A CPR certificate or card issued by an entity approved by the Florida Department of Health is also acceptable.

The five-year Athletic Coaching certificate must be renewed every five years by submitting an application and fee. However, if the course requirement has changed since the last certificate was issued, the applicant must complete the new requirement to be eligible for a new five-year certificate.

Certification Process: New York

If you have aspirations to coach an interschool athletic team in New York State, you must meet the minimum requirements as set forth in the Regulations of the Commissioner of Education. This includes all head coaches and assistant for varsity, junior varsity, freshman, and junior high teams of public schools.

Anyone wishing to coach an interschool athletic team in New York State must meet certain minimum requirements as set forth in the Regulations of the Commissioner of Education. This includes all head coaches and assistants for varsity, junior varsity, freshman, and junior high (modified) teams of public schools.

The certification requirements vary depending on your background: Certified Physical Education Teacher, Other Certified Teacher, or Nonteaching Coaches. The person who holds a valid certificate to teach physical education in New York State may coach any sport in any school but must meet the first aid/CPR requirement prior to starting to coach.

Other Certified Teachers coaching a secondary school athletic team is considered teaching physical education. However, a person who holds a valid teaching certificate in an area other than physical education may also be appointed to coach. The person may either complete appropriate courses or meet the provisions of the "grandfather" clause. The *grandfather clause* qualifies a teacher under Section 80.2 (c) of the Regulations of the Commissioner of Education to do incidental teaching (coaching) in an area other than the one for which the person holds a certificate. In addition to the first aid/CPR requirement to starting to coach, the certified teacher must complete an approved course in Philosophy, Principles, and Organization of Athletics in Education within two years from the date of initial appointment as a coach, complete a course on Health Sciences Applied to Coaching within five years of appointment as a coach, and also within that same five years, complete a course on Theory and Techniques of Coaching the sport or sports for which he or she is appointed. A certified teacher does not need to apply for a Temporary Coaching License.

A person who does not hold a current New York State teaching certificate may be appointed as a temporary coach only if there are no certified teachers available with experience and qualification to coach the team. The nonteacher coach must obtain a Temporary Coaching license from their school districts BOCES (Board of Cooperative Educational Services) by applying online through the NYDED TEACH systems and meet all the same course requirements for coaching as does the certified classroom teacher within the same timeline and extensions.

Persons who have completed all the required coaching courses, child abuse, and violence abuse workshops, maintain fingerprint clearance, has a valid first aid and CPR certification, and has held a minimum of three Temporary Coaching License for a sport may apply for a three-year renewable Professional Coaching License.

Regardless of experience of teaching certification, anyone coaching an interschool athletic team must have valid first aid and CPR certifications. If you are not a certified physical education teacher, you must complete a series of courses unless you meet the provisions of the "grandfather" clause. The following courses to date meet course requirements: Philosophy, Principles, and Organization of Athletics in Education, Theory and Techniques of Coaching, and Health Science Applied to Coaching.

In conjunction with minimum requirements, if you do not have any type of teacher certification, you will also need to complete workshops in Child Abuse Identification, School Violence Intervention and Prevention, and Dignity for All Students. In addition, you will need fingerprint clearance and a recommendation from the school district where you will be coaching.

Certification Process: Texas

Most coaches in the State of Texas have a bachelor degree although other requirements may suffice one coaching in the state. A state teaching certification, CPR training, job training, leadership and communication skills, drug test, and background checks are usually required.

The formerly called Rules Compliance Program (RCP) consists of both University Interscholastic League (UIL) and state law requirements. The UIL has required coaches to complete prescribed components of the RCP on a yearly basis. In 2018, the RCP became the Coaches Certification Program (CCP), which recognize coaches as UIL certified. New requirement also includes a Fundamentals or Coaching course for all first year Texas coaches and also requires all football coaches to take and pass a mandatory tackling certification course once every two years.

The Texas High School Coaches Association (THSCA) offers lectures at coaching school each year that assist coaches to satisfy their CCP requirements. Lectures at coaching school have THSCA staff on hand, and our responsible for communicating the verification of completion list directly to the UIL. The UIL will then use the THSCA member number you have added to your profile to verify course completion and update your UIL portal profile in Register My Athlete website (uil.registermyathlete.com).

If you are coaching for the first time in the state of Texas, you must complete two hours of Concussion Training. The mandate is that coaches must receive two hours of Concussion Training every two years. Once a coach has fulfilled the two hours, they only need to take one-hour course each year to be current. Other course requirements include Steroid Training, Constitution and Contest Rules, Ethics and Sportsmanship, Safety Training, Fundamentals of Coaching in Texas, and rules updates on each sport you coach.

The Arizona Department of Education is the certifying body for individuals to coach in the State of Arizona by attaining the *Standard Athletic Coaching Certificate.* The certificate is valid for twelve years. However, requirements may be subject to change and are fully referenced in the Arizona revised statutes and administrative code.

The certificate entitles the holder to perform coaching duties in interscholastic and extracurricular athletic activities. It is not required for teachers who hold a valid elementary, secondary, or special education certificate. Requirements for the Standard Athletic Coaching Certificate are completed Application for Certification and a photocopy of your valid Arizona Department of Public Safety Identity Verified Prints (IVP) fingerprint card. For more information, visit http://WWW.azed.gov/educator-certification/fingerprintclearance-card-ivp/. You must have valid certification in first aid and coronary and pulmonary resuscitation, completion of courses, seminars, or modules of study which include the following: Methods of Coaching, Anatomy and Physiology, Sports Psychology, Adolescent Psychology, Prevention and Treatment of Athletic Injuries, Signs of Physical Abuse, Emotional Abuse, Neglect, Bullying, Hazing and Cyberbullying, and two hundred and fifty hours of verified coaching experience in the sport to be coached.

Coaching experience may include experience as a head coach or assistant coach in a school program or in an organized athletic league. You must submit a letter on official letterhead to Arizona Department of Education to verify clock hours of coaching experience. If you move from another state to Arizona, you can use your Athletic Coaching Certification provided it is comparable to Arizona requirements and you have to be in good standing with the state you came from. You must submit a photocopy of your valid comparable Athletic Coaching certificate to Arizona Department of Education.

Certification Process: Pennsylvania

The following continuing education courses are required if you plan on coaching at a Pennsylvania Interscholastic Athletic Association (PIAA) member school. All coaches currently employed or engaged by a PIAA member school must complete two courses: Fundamentals of Coaching and First Aid, Health, and Safety.

All coaches currently employed or engaged by a PIAA member school must complete two courses as provided above. First time coaches hired at any PIAA school after July 1, 2016, will have two years from their date of hire to complete this requirement. Addition courses are Fundamentals of Coaching, Sports First Aid, and Coaching Principles.

PIAA will also accept college level courses from Safe School Training for Coaching Education as long as your school or school district has purchased the Safe School Training for all staff.

Here are modules that satisfy the Fundamental of Coaching coursework: Athletic Liability, Conflict Management, Managing the Angry Parent, Title IX and Gender Equity in Athletics, Hazing, Steroid and PED Awareness in Athletics, Emergency Operations Planning, Emergency Operation Planning, Sensitivity Awareness, Conflict Management Student to Student, Diversity Awareness Student to Student, and Online Safety Cyberbullying.

Modules that satisfy the first aid coursework are the following: First Aid, Supervision and Safety, Heat Illness Prevention, Student Drug and Alcohol Abuse, AED, and Cardiopulmonary Resuscitation (CPR). Once completed, coaches will receive two certificates for all modules completed through Safe Schools Training One for the Fundamental of Coaching coursework and the other for the First Aid coursework. Prior to holding a practice, coaches must also complete NFHS Concussion in Sports What You Need to Know or Concussion-Wise to meet the Concussion Training Course modules and Cardiac-Wise to meet the Sudden Cardiac Arrest Training Course module.

Coaching Process: Ohio

The coaching requirements for the State of Ohio require individuals who will direct, supervise, or coach a student activity program that involves athletics, routine, or regular physical activity or activities with health and safety considerations. School districts determine which staff members need to have a permit. An individual hired to direct, supervise, or coach a pupil activity program that does not involve athletics or routine or regular physical activity or health and safety consideration is not required to hold a pupil activity permit pursuant to the Ohio Revised Code, if that individual holds a current valid educator license issued under the Revised Code.

School district e-signers will confirm that all applicants for coaching permits have valid training or certification in all required areas. There are five categories of training, and coaches should check with their school districts about preference and procedures related to each category and provide documentation to their districts that they met requirements.

The training modules are as follows: Fundamentals of Coaching, which is a one-time training requirement; Cardiopulmonary Resuscitation (CPR) training; First Aid for Coaches; Sports First Aid; First Aid Health and Safety or First Aid. Other courses that meet certification requirements is Concussion in Sports or Heads Up to Youth Sports. These courses may fall under a specific category, and you may only need to take one course within the appropriate category. Each year, coaches must review the Ohio Department of Health video and related fact sheet. After you review the material, you must take a short exam.

Discussion Questions:

1. If you are a teacher aide in the State of Illinois, can you coach without attaining a coach's certification?
2. If you are a certified teacher, do you need to attain a coaching certification to coach a sport?
3. Explain the state that allows you to coach without a teaching certification and what are the ramifications.
4. If you hold a certification to teach physical education courses in the State of New York, can you coach any sport and are there other requirements?
5. If you are coaching for the first time in the State of Texas, what other certification must you attain?
6. Name the certification that is most commonly use in most states?
7. What is the name of the sport certification organization in the State of Arizona?
8. What state has a bylaw that allows for a person to coach for one year without a certification if there is a special circumstance?
9. What two courses are required if you want to coach at a Pennsylvania Interscholastic Athletic Association member school?
10. What community college in the State of Iowa offers state-approved courses for coaching certification?

BIBLIOGRAPHY

Althof, W., and M. W. Berkowitz. 2006. "Mural Education and Character Education: Their Relationship on Youth Sport Attrition." *Sport Psychologist* 6 (2): 11–127.

Bandura. A. 1977b. "Social Learning Theory." New York: General Learning Press.

Bandura. A. 1999. "Social Cognitive Theory of Moral Thought and Action." In W. M. Kurtines and J. L Gewirtz, eds. *Handbook of Moral Behavior and Development: Vol. I. Theory* 45–103. Hillside. NJ: Lawrence Erlbaum.

Barker, T., T.B. Martins, H. R. Hill, C. R. Kjeldsberg, R. H. Trawick, L. K. Weaver, and M. G. Traber, M.G. 2011. "Low Vitamin D Impairs Strength Recovery After Anterior Cruciate Ligament Surgery." JEBCAM 16: 201-209.

Barker, T., T.B. Martins, H. R. Hill, C. R. Kjeldsberg, D. M. Dixon, E. D. Schneider, V. T. Henriksen, and L. K. Weaver, 2014. "Vitamin D Sufficiency Associates with an Increase in Anti-Inflammatory Cytokines After Intense Exercise in Humans Cytokine" 65: 134–137.

Baumeister. R.F. 2016. "Toward a General Theory of Motivation: Problems, Challenges, Opportunities, and the Big Picture, Motivation and Emotions" 40, 1. Crossref.

Belenky, G., N. J. Wesenten, and Dr. Thorn Thorne. 2003. "Patterns of Performance Degradation and Restoration During Sleep Restriction and Subsequent Recovery: A Sleep Dose Response Study." Wiley Online Library.

Bennett, J.G. and J. E. Pravitz. 1987. "Profile of a Winner: Advanced Mental Training for Athletes." Ithaca, New York: Sport Science International and Bets Ltd.

Berkowitz, M.W. and M. C. Bier. 2005. "What Works in Character Education: A Research-Driven Guide for Educators." Washington, DC: Character Education Partnership.

Bianconi, E., A. Piovesan, and F. Facchin. 2003. "An Estimation of the Number of Cells in the Human Body." *Annals of Human.* Taylor and Francis.

Bischoff – Ferrari, H. A., T. Dietrich, E. J. Orav, F. B. Hu, Y. Zhang, E. W. Karlson, and B. Dawson-Hughes. 2004b. "Higher 25-Hydroxyvitamins D Concentration Are Associated with Better Lower Extremity Functions in Both Active and Inactive Persons Aged > or =60 y." Am. J. Clin. 80: 752–758.

Brand, S., M. Gerber, Beck, and M. Hatzinger. 2010. "High Exercise Levels Are Related to Favorable Sleep Patterns and Psychological Functioning in Adolescents: A Comparison of Athletes and Control." *Journal of Adolescent.*

Brummett, B. 2009. "Sporting Rhetoric: Performance, Games, and Politics." New York: Peter Lang.

Breuner, C. 2012. *Avoidance of Burnout in the Young Athlete.*
Pediatric Annals. *41* (8).

Camire, M. and P. Trudel. 2010. High School Athletes' Perspectives on Character Development through Sports Participation." *Physical Education & Sport Pedagogy* 15 (2): 193–207.

Chudacoff, H.P. 2007. "Children at Play: An American History." New York University Press.

Clutterbuck, D. and D. Megginson. 2011. "Critical Theory: A Philosophy of Coaching." 38–39.

Coakley, J. 2011. "Youth Sports: What Counts as 'Positive Development?'" *Journal of Sport and Social Issues* 35 (3): 306–324.

Daniel, J. O'Rourke, E. R. Smith, F. L. Smoll, and S. P. Cumming. 2011. "Trait Anxiety in Young Athletes as a Function of Parental Pressure and Motivational Climates: Is Parental Pressure Always Harmful? *Journal of Applied Sport Psychology* 23: 4: 398–412. Doi: 10.1080/10413200.2011.552089.

Delaney, T. 2009. "The Sociology of Sport." *The Sociology of Sport: An Introduction* 3–21.US.

Dubois, G., K. O. Kyvik, M. Girard, F. Tatone-Tokuda, D. Perusse, J. Hjelmborg, A. Skytthe, F. Rasmussen, M. J. Wright, P. Lichtenstein, and N. G. Martin. *Genetic and Environmental Contributions to Weight, Height, and BMI from Birth to 19 Years of Age: An International Study of Over 12,000 Twin Pairs.* Published: February 8, 2012. https://doi.org/10.1371/journal.pone.0030153.

Dunford, M. and J. Doyle. 2019. *Fourth Edition Nutrition for Sport and Exercise.* Wadsworth, Cengage Learning.

Engel., S. G., C. Johnson, P.S. Powers, R. D. Crosby. *Predictors of Disordered Eating in a Sample of Elite Division I College Athletes: Eating Behaviors.* 2003. Elsevier.

Engh, Fred. 2002. *Youth League Sports: How It All Began* 30–40. Square One Publishing.

Ewing, M.E. and V. D. Seefeldt. 2002. *Sport Volunteer Coach Motivation* 128–139. Published online.

Ewing, M.E., V. D. Seefeldt and T. P. Brown. 1996. *Role of Organized Sports in the Educational and Health of American Children and Youth.* East Lansing, Michigan: Institute for the Study of Youth Sports.

Farrokhyar, F., D. R. Tabasinejad, D. Dae, D. R. Peterson, R., O. R. Ayeni, R. Hadioonzadeh, and M. Bhandari. 2015. "Prevalence of Vitamin D Inadequacy in Athletics: A Systematic Review and Meta-Analysis." *Sports Med* 45: 365–378.

French, M. 2002. "Efc Micronutrients and Genomic Stability: A New Paradigm for Recommended Dietary Allowance (RDAs)." *Food and Chemical Toxicology*, Elsevier.

Fullagar, HHK., S. Skorski, R. Duffield, D. Hammes. 2015. "Sleep and Athletic Performance: The Effects of Sleep Loss on Exercise Performance and Physiologic and Cognitive Responses to Exercise." *Sports Medicine.*

Gevat, C., T. Halil, A. Fatma, L. Alin, and S. George. 2012. *The Effects of 8-Week Speed Training Program on the Acceleration Ability and Maximum Speed Running at 11 Years Athletes.* Romania: Ovidius University of Constanta.

Gibson, A., D. Wagner, V. Heyward. 2019. *Eighth Edition Advanced Fitness Assessment and Exercise Prescription.* Human Kinetics.

Gill. D. 2000. "Psychological Dynamics of Sport and Exercise." Champaign, Illinois: Human Kinetics.

Gould, D., R. Eklund, L. Petlichchkoff, K. Peterson, and L. Bump. 1991. "Psychological Predictors of State Anxiety and Performance in Age-Group Wrestlers." *Pediatrics Exercise Science* 3: 198–208.

Gould, D. J. and R. C. Eklund. 1992. "US Olympic Wrestling Excellence: I. Mental Preparation, Precompetitive, Cognition, and Effort." *The Sport Psychologist* 6: 371–394.

Halliday, T. N., J. Peterson, T. K. Kleppinger, B. Hollis, and D. Larson-Meyer. 2011. "Vitamin D Status Relative to Diet, Lifestyle, Injury, and Illness in College Athletes." *Med. Sci. Sports Exerc.* 42: 335–343.

Haff, G., N. Triplett. 2016. *Fourth Edition Essentials of Strength Training and Conditioning.* Human Kinetics.

Halliwell, B. and JMC Gutteridge. 2015. *Free Radicals in Biology and Medicine.*

Hellstedt, J. 1987. "The Coach/Parent/Athlete Relationship." *The Sport Psychology* 1: 121–160.

Hollander, E. R. 1967. "Principles and Method of Social Psychology: Structure of Personality." New York: Holt, Rinehart & Winston.

Huitt, W. 1996. "Systems Model of Human Behavior." *Educational Psychology Interactive.* Valdosta, Georgia. Valdosta State University. Retrieved December 2003 from http: // chiron.valdosta.edu/whuitt/materials/sysmdlbb.html.

James, W. 1890. *Principles of Psychology*. New York: Holt, Rinehart & Wilson.

Kant. I., J. Schneewind, M. Baron, and S. Kagan. 2002. *Groundwork for the Metaphysics of Morals.* A. Wood A. Wood, eds. and trans. New Haven, CT: Yale University Press.

Kawamori N., K. Nosaka, RU Newton. "Relationships between Ground Reaction Impulse and Sprint Acceleration Performance in Team-Sport Athletes." J Strength Cond Res, 2012 (e-pub ahead of print).

Koba, M. 2014. "Spending Big on Kid's Sports. You're not alone." Accessed Nov. 3, 2018 www.cnbc.com/id/101326773.

Kohlberg, L. 1981. "The Philosophy of Moral Development: Moral Stages and the Idea of Justice." *Essays on Moral Development Vol. 1*. San Francisco, CA: Harper & Row.

Kohlberg, L. 1984. "The Psychology of Moral Development: The Nature and Validity of Moral Stages." *Essays on Moral Development Vol. 2*. Harper & Row.

Krista, Pritle. Oct. 2016. lubbuckonline.com.

Knufinke, M., Els L. Fittkau-Koch, I. S. Michael, M. Kompier, A. J. Kompier, and A. Nieuwenhuys. 2019. "Restricting Short-Wavelength Light in the Evening to Improve Sleep in Recreational Athletes. A Pilot Study." *European Journal of Sport Science 19 (6).*

Laver. L. and C. Paiement. 2009. "The Playing Tough and Clean Hockey Program." *The Sport Psychologist* 23: 543–561.

Lastella, M., G.P. Lovell, and C. Sargent. 2014. "Athletes' Precompetitive Sleep Behavior and Its Relationship with Subsequent Precompetitive Mood and Performance." *European Journal of Sports*. Taylor & Francis.

Lickona. T. and M. Davidson. 2005. "Smart and Good High Schools: Integrating Excellence and Ethics for Success in School, Work, and Beyond." *Courtland, NY: Center for the 4th and 5th Rs (Respected Responsibility).* Washington. DC, Character Educational Partnership.

Locke, E.A., K.N. Shaw, L. M. Saari, and G. P. Latham. 1981. "Goal Setting and Task Performance: 1969–1980." i, 125–152.

Locke, E.A. and G.P. Latham. 2002. *Building a Practical Useful Theory of Goal Setting and Motivation: A 35-Year Odyssey American Psychology* 57, 705–717. doi: 10. 1037/0003006x.57.9.705

Long, T., N. Pantaleon, G. Bruant, and F. D' Arripe-Longveville. 2006. "A Qualitative Study of Moral Reasoning of Young Athletes." *The Sport Psychologist 20*, 330–347.

Malina, R., C. Bouchard, O. Bar-Or. *Growth, Maturation, and Physical Activity (2004).* Human Kinetics.

Marks, D. F. 1977. "Imagery and Consciousness: A Theoretical Review from an Individual Differences Perspective. *Journal of Mental Imagery* 2: 275–290.

Martens, R. 2004. *Successful Coaching 4th ed.* Champaign, IL: Human Kinetics.

Martens, R. 1975. *Social Psychology of Sports.* New York: Harper & Row.

Martens. R. 2004. "Developing a Coaching Philosophy." *Successful Coaching 4th ed.* Champaign, IL: Human Kinetics.

Martens, R. 1976. *Competition: In Need of a Theory Social Problems in Athletics.* Urbana, IL: University of Illinois Press.

Mastens, A. S., K. M. Best, and N. Garmezy. 1990. Cambridge.org

Moran, A. "Sport and Exercise." *Psychology: A Critical Introduction.* London: Routledge

Monson, T. A., M. F. Brasil, and L. J. Hlusko. 2018. "Allometric Variation in Modern Humans and the Relationship between Body Proportions and Elite Athletic Success." *Journal of Anthropology of Sport* 2 (3).

Nideffer, R. M. 1976a. *The Inner Athlete.* New York: Crowell

Nideffer, R, M. and M. Segal. 2001. "Concentration and Attention Control Training." In J. M. Williams, ed., *Applied Sport Psychology: Personal Growth to Peak Performance 4th ed.* 312–332. Mountain View, CA: Mayfield.

Norton, K. and T. Olds. 2001. *Sports Medicine.*

Poliquin, C. 2001. *Modern Trends in Strength Training: Volume 1, Sets and Reps (Second Edition) Paperback Unabridged.*

Power. F. C. and K. Sheehan. 2014. "Promoting Children's Development through the Ministry of Coaching Education." University of Notre Dame, Notre Dame, IN, USA.

Power, F. C. and A.M.R. Power. 2012. *The Handbook of Pro Social Education.*

Power, F. C. and K. Sheehan. 2014. "Moral and Character Education through Sports." L. Nucci., T. Krettenauer, and D. Narv'aez, eds. *Handbook of Moral and Character Education 2nd ed.* 488–506. Routledge.

Power, F. C. and K. Sheenan. 2012b. "Effectiveness of Play Like Champion Today Workshop on Coaches Character." Notre Dame, IN: Play Like a Champion Program.

Power, F. C., A. Higgins, and L. Kohlberg. 1989. *Lawrence Kohlberg's Approach to Moral Education.* New York, NY: Columbia University Press.

Prince, F. P., R.S. Hikada, and F. C. Hagerman. 1977. *Muscle Fiber Types in Women Athletes and Nonathletes.* J. Appl. Physiol 42.

Ross, C., B. Caballero, R. Cousins., K. Tucker, and T. Ziegler. 2014. *Eleventh Edition Modern Nutrition in Health and Disease.* Lippincott Williams and Wilkins.

Santos, D. A., J. A. Dawson, C. N. Matias, and M. Paulo. 2014. "Reference Values for Body Composition and Anthropometric Measurements in Athletes." *Plus One.* https://doi.org/10.1371/journal.pone.0097846.

Scanlan, T. K., P. J. Carpenter, G. W. Schmidt, J. P. Simons, and B. Keeler. 1993. "An Introduction to the Sport Commitment Model." *Journal of Sport and Exercise Psychology* 15: 115.

Schinke, R. and D. Hackfort. 2016. 1st Edition. *Psychology in Professional Sports and the Performing Arts: Challenges and Strategies (Key Issues in Sport and Exercise Psychology).* Abe Books.

Shields, D. L., B. L. Bredemeier, N. M. LaVoi, and F. C. Power. 2005. "The Sport Behavior of Youth, Parents, and Coaches: The Good, the Bad, and the Ugly." *Journal of Research in Character Education* 3 (1): 43–59.

Shields, D. L. L. and B. J. L. Bredemeier. 1995. "Character Developmental and Physical Activity." Champaign, IL: Human Kinetics.

Short, S., E. Monsma, and M. Short. 2004. "Is What You See Really What You Get? Athletes' Perception of Imagery's Functions." *The Sport Psychologist* 18: 341–349.

Spieler, M., D. R. Czech, A. B. Joyner, and B. Munkasy. 2007. *Predicting Athletic Success: Factors Contributing to the Success of NCAA Division I AA Collegiate Football Players.* Athletic Insight. 9(2)

Stuart, M. E. 2003. "Moral Issues in Sport: The Child's Perspective." *Research Quarterly for Exercise and Sport* 74 (4): 445–454

Swain, D., C. Brawner, A. Swank, H. Chambliss, P. Nagelkirk, and M. Paternostro-Bayles. 2014. *Seventh Edition ACSM's Resource Manual for Guidelines for Exercise Testing and Prescription.* Lippincott Williams and Wilkins.

Tugade, M. M. and B. L. Fredrickson. 2011. "Resilient Individuals Use Positive Emotions to Bounce Back from Negative Emotional Experiences." *Social Psychology Manual.*

Tugade, M. M., B. L. Fredrickson, and L. F. Barrett. 2005. "Psychological Resilience and Positive Emotional Granularity: Examining the Benefits of Positive Emotions on Coping and Health. Resilience and Development: Contributions from the Study of Children Who Overcome Adversity." *Social Psychology Manual.*

Vallerand, R. J. 1997. "Toward a Hierarchical Model of Intrinsic and Extrinsic Motivation." In M. P. Zanna, ed. *Advances in Experimental Social Psychology Vol. 29.* 198–276. New York: Academic Press.

Vallarand, R. J., N. M. Briere, C. J. Blanchard, and P. Provencher. 1997. "Development and Validation of the Multidimensional Sports Person Orientation Scale." *Journal of Sport Exercise Psychology* 19: 197–206.

Weinberg, R. S., J. Butt, B. Knight, K. L. Burke, and A. Jackson. 2003. "The Relationship between the Use and Effectiveness of Imagery: An Explanatory Investigation." *Journal of Applied Sport Psychology*, 15: 26–40.

Weiss, M. R. 2008. C. H. McClay Lecture. "Fields of Dreams: Sport as Context for Youth Development." *Research Quarterly for Exercise and Sports*, 79 (4): 434–449. doi. 10. 1080/02701367. 2008. 10599510.

Welham, W. C. and A. R. Behnke. 1942. "The Specific Gravity of Healthy Men: Body Weight Volume and Other Physical Characteristics of Exceptional Athletes and of Naval Personnel." *Journal of the American Medical.*

Widmeyer. W. N., K. D. Dorsch, S. R. Bray, and E. J. McGuire. 2002. "The Nature, Prevalence, and Consequences of Aggression in Sport." In J. M. Silva and D. E. Stevens, eds. *Psychological Foundations Sport* 328–351. Boston: Allyn & Bacon.

Williams, S. and J. Cummings. 2011. "Measuring Athlete Imagery Ability: The Sport Imagery Ability Questionnaire." *Journal of Sport and Exercise Psychology*, 32, 339–358.

Wilson, J.M., J. P. Loenneke. J. O. Wilson, G. J. Zourdos, and J. Kim. 2012. *The Effects of Endurance, Strength, and Power Training on Muscle Fiber Type Shifting.*

www.Youtube.com. "Guide Imagery (Allina Health)."

PHOTO AND DIAGRAM CREDITS

Chapter 1: Getty Images, /mid majors madness photos (Tubby Smith)

Chapter 1: Form 1.1. permission granted from R. Martens's *Successful Coaching 4th edition*

Chapter 1: Four Color Temperament, www.wearbowline.com

Chapter 1: Photo by College of DuPage Sport Editor (Dr. Thomas E. Reed)

Chapter 2: Aggressive role model, nonaggressive role model, and control group no model, www.simplepsychology.org BoBo-doll

Chapter 3: Stock Images Microsoft Word (girls soccer players)

Chapter 3: 1 The goalie diagram, www.soccerpilot.com

Chapter 3: All basketball diagrams brasilbowl 2012 wordpress.com

Chapter 3: Defense diagrams created by Dr. Thomas E. Reed

Chapter 3: Football diagram brasilbowl 2012 wordpress.com

Chapter 3: Getty Images, Roberto Schmidt (tennis player 1)

Chapter 3: Getty Images, Eduardo Munoz-Alvarez (tennis player 2)

Chapter 4: Stock Images/Microsoft Word (female golfer)

Chapter 4: Stock Images/Microsoft Word (male swimmer)

Chapter 4: Getty Images/Stockbyte (little girl tennis player)

Chapter 4: Sports imagery questionnaire permission granted from R. Martens's *Successful Coaching 4th edition*

Chapter 4: Guided Imagery for relief stress, changetochill.org

Chapter 5: Figure 5.1. Training Expectations. Graph created by Chad Earl, data taken from A.C.S.M. Guidelines 2016, *Essentials of Strength Training and Conditioning 2008.*

Chapter 5: Figure 5.2. (A) Male Competitive Athletic Frame. Graph created by Chad Earl, data taken from A.C.S.M. Guidelines 2016, *Essentials of Strength Training and Conditioning 2008*

Chapter 5: Figure 5.3. (B) Female Competitive Athletic Frame. Graph created by Chad Earl, data taken from A.C.S.M. Guidelines 2016, *Essentials of Strength Training and Conditioning 2008*

Chapter 5: Figure 5.4. (C) Truncated Comparison by Competitive Frame. Graph created by Chad Earl, data taken from A.C.S.M. Guidelines 2016, *Essentials of Strength Training and Conditioning 2008.*

Chapter 5: Figure 5.5. The Ideal Structure for Sport. 1.0 Figure Three: The Ideal Structure for Sport. Graph created by Chad Earl, data taken from A.C.S.M. Guidelines 2016, *Essentials of Strength Training and Conditioning 2008.*

Chapter 5: Figure 5.6. (D): Body Composition Ratios for Athletes. Graph created by Chad Earl, data taken from A.C.S.M. Guidelines 2016, *Essentials of Strength Training and Conditioning 2008.*

Chapter 5: Figure 5.7. Size Makes a Difference. Graph created by Chad Earl, data taken from ACSM Guidelines 2016, *Essentials of Strength Training and Conditioning 2008.*

Chapter 5: Figure 5.8. Size Makes a Difference 2.0. Graph created by Chad Earl, data taken from ACSM Guidelines 2016, *Essentials of Strength Training and Conditioning 2008.*

Chapter 5: Figure 5.9. Division One Strength Progression. Graph created by Chad Earl, data taken from ACSM Guidelines 2016, *Essentials of Strength Training and Conditioning 2008.*

Chapter 5: Figure 5.10. (E) Truncated Comparison of Peak Strength by Sport. Graph created by Chad Earl, data taken from ACSM Guidelines 2016, *Essentials of Strength Training and Conditioning 2008*

Chapter 5: Figure 5.1. Body Fat Values by Population. Graph created by Chad Earl, data taken from ACSM Guidelines 2016, *Essentials of Strength Training and Conditioning 2008.*

Chapter 5: Figure 5.12. Increasing Bio-motor Expression. Graph created by Chad Earl, data taken from ACSM Guidelines 2016, *Essentials of Strength Training and Conditioning 2008*

Chapter 5: Figure 5.13. Minimal Bio-motor Varsity Athletic Thresholds. Graph created by Chad Earl, data taken from ACSM Guidelines 2016, *Essentials of Strength Training and Conditioning 2008*

Chapter 5: Shutterstock/iStockphotos; Stockfresh (Male Trainer and Athletes)

Chapter 5: Shuttlestock; Getty Images (Male Generalize Athlete Vs. General Population)

Chapter 5: Shuttlestock; Getty Images (Female Generalize Athlete Vs. General Population)

Chapter 6: Applied Program Design. Photo taken by Chad Earl. Shutterstock/iStockphotos, Stockfresh.

Chapter 6: Figure 6.4. (A) Off- Season Day One. Photos taken and graph created by Chad Earl, DuPage Fitness & Rehabilitation Center

Chapter 6: Figure 6.6. (C) Off-Season Day Three. Photos taken and graph created by Chad Earl, DuPage Fitness & Rehabilitation Center

Chapter 6: Figure 6.7. (A) Pre-Season Day One. Photos taken and graph created by Chad Earl, DuPage Fitness & Rehabilitation Center

Chapter 6: Figure 6.8. (B) Pre-Season Day Two. Photos taken and graph created by Chad Earl, DuPage Fitness & Rehabilitation Center

Chapter 6: Figure 6.9. (C) Pre-Season Day Three. Photos taken and graph created by Chad Earl, DuPage Fitness & Rehabilitation Center

Chapter 6: Figure 6.10. (A) In-Season Day One. Photos taken and graph created by Chad Earl, DuPage Fitness & Rehabilitation Center

Chapter 6: Figure 6.11. (B) In-Season Day Two. Photos taken and graph created by Chad Earl, DuPage Fitness & Rehabilitation Center

Chapter 6: Figure 6.12. (C) In-Season Day Three. Photos taken and graph created by Chad Earl, DuPage Fitness & Rehabilitation Center

Chapter 6: Figure 6.13. Relationships for Optimal Performance. Photos taken and graph created by Chad Earl, DuPage Fitness & Rehabilitation Center

Chapter 7: DuPage Fitness & Rehabilitation Center. Photographer: Chad Earl

Chapter 7: Figure 7.1. (A) Projected Athletic Dietary Guidelines (Male). Graph created by Chad Earl, data taken from *Sport Nutrition for Health and Performance 2000*

Chapter 7: Figure 7.2. (B) Projected Athletic Dietary Guidelines (Female). Graph created by Chad Earl, data taken from *Sport Nutrition for Health and Performance 2000.*

Chapter 7: Protein Intake: .5 to .75 gram per pound of ideal weight. Photo Seventh Edition ACSM's *Resource Manual for Guidelines for Exercise Testing and Prescription 2014*

Chapter 7: Fat Intake: 20 to 30 percent of total calories. Photo Seventh Edition ACSM's *Resource Manual for Guidelines for Exercise Testing and Prescription 2014*

Chapter 7: Carbohydrate Intake: 2.5 to 4.5 grams of carbohydrates per pound of ideal weight or 25 to 60 percent of total calories. Photo Seventh Edition ACSM's *Resource Manual for Guidelines for Exercise Testing and Prescription 2014.*

Chapter 7: Figure 7.3. High Nutrient Food List for Peak Athletic Capacity. Graph created by Chad Earl, data taken from DuPage Fitness & Rehabilitation Center

Chapter 7: Leaves, veggieprime.com

Chapter 7: Non-Starchy Vegetables, veggieprimer.com

Chapter 7: Starchy Vegetables, veggieprimer.com

Chapter 7: Fruit, veggieprimer.com

Chapter 7: Bean, veggieprimer.com

Chapter 7: Grain, veggieprimer.com

Chapter 7: Seeds and Nuts, veggieprimer.com

Chapter 7: Teas, veggieprimer.com

Chapter 7: Figure 7.4. Supplement Considerations for the Developing Athlete. Graph and Data created by Chad Earl DuPage Fitness & Rehabilitation Center

Chapter 7: Figure 7.6. Meal Replacement Macronutrient Ratios. Graph and data created by Chad Earl, DuPage Fitness & Rehabilitation Center

Chapter 7: Figure 7.7. Creatine Supplementation for High School and Collegiate Athletes. Graph and Data created by Chad Earl, DuPage Fitness & Rehabilitation Center

Chapter 8: Figure 8.1. Athletic Lifestyle Design. Graph created by Chad Earl, data taken from DuPage Fitness & Rehabilitation Center 2018

Chapter 8: Figure 8.2. Sleep Optimization: Graph created by Chad Earl, data taken from "Restricting Short-Wavelength Light in the Evening to Improve Sleep in Recreational Athletes." *A Pilot Study: European Journal of Sport Science* 19(6)

Chapter 8: Figure 8.3. Recovery Behaviors. Shutterstock;/iStockphotos;/Getty images; focus stock

INDEX

ABOUT THE AUTHORS

Acie Earl, Chad Earl, and Dr. Thomas E. Reed have had a long history of teaching, coaching, and administration at the professional, college, and high school level.

Acie Earl had an outstanding basketball career. He was a three-year starter at the University of Iowa, a number one draft pick by the Boston Celtics, played in the NBA for four years with the Boston Celtics, Toronto Raptors, and Milwaukee Bucks. He continued his professional career overseas for eight years playing in twelve countries and an MVP in China, Kosovo, and Turkey. Acie Earl has his degree in Bachelor of Arts in Leisure Studies (University of Iowa), degree in Master of Science in Sports and Recreation (University of Iowa), and degree in Master of Science in Higher Education (University of Purdue). Coach Earl has two training camps, Venom Sports and Junior Phenom Basketball.

Chad Earl participated in two sports in high school, basketball, and track-and-field. He played three years on the varsity basketball team and two years on the track team at Moline High School in Illinois. He was assistant director of the Shooting Stars Girl's academy for twelve years. As the assistant director, the program won several state girl's AAU championships at various levels. The program has sent a plethora of athletes to various college-level athletic programs. Chad Earl has logged over sixty thousand hours of sport performance training, and many of his clients have benefited and continued their athletic careers at the college level. He is also the owner of DuPage Fitness and Rehabilitation Performance studio located in Naperville, Illinois. He received his degrees in Bachelor of Science in Dietetics from Bradley University and Master of Science in Nutrition and Wellness from Benedictine University.

Dr. Thomas Earl Reed has expanded over thirty years of coaching at the collegiate level. He participated on the varsity basketball team at Millikan High School located in Long Beach, California. He played college basketball at Los Angeles Harbor Community College and California State University, Chico. Dr. Reed's basketball coaching career started at Yuba Community College as the assistant men's basketball coach. He later went back to his alma mater, CSU, Chico, and coached there for two years before assuming the head coaching position at Oberlin College located in Oberlin, Ohio. Dr. Reed was the assistant men's tennis coach, the head women's and men's basketball coach, and was also the Director of Athletics and Associate Dean of Physical Education throughout his tenure at College of DuPage. He has won a National Championship with the men's tennis team, two National Championships as the head coach of the women's basketball, and numerous "Coach of the Year" awards. In his four-year tenure as director of athletics, the program was awarded three consecutive National Alliance of Two-Year College Athletic Administration (NATYCAA) program of the year awards.

CPSIA information can be obtained
at www.ICGtesting.com
Printed in the USA
BVHW020035150221
599891BV00001B/1

9 781662 437137

THE INCLUSIVE CLASSROOM

STRATEGIES FOR EFFECTIVE DIFFERENTIATED INSTRUCTION

SEVENTH EDITION

THE INCLUSIVE CLASSROOM

STRATEGIES FOR EFFECTIVE DIFFERENTIATED INSTRUCTION

Margo A. Mastropieri
George Mason University

Thomas E. Scruggs
George Mason University

Kelley S. Regan
George Mason University

Pearson

Content Development: Linda Bishop
Content Management: Rebecca Fox-Gieg
Content Production: Neha Sharma
Product Management: Drew Bennett
Product Marketing: Krista Clark
Rights and Permissions: Jenell Forschler

Please contact https://support.pearson.com/getsupport/s/contactsupport with any queries on this content
Cover Image by Sorin Tudorică/500px/gettyimages

Library of Congress Cataloging-in-Publication Data

Names: Mastropieri, Margo A., 1951- author. | Scruggs, Thomas E., 1948- author. | Regan, Kelley, author.
Title: The inclusive classroom : Strategies for effective differentiated instruction / Margo A. Mastropieri, George Mason University, Thomas E. Scruggs, George Mason University, Kelley Regan, George Mason University.
Description: Seventh edition. | Hoboken, NJ: Pearson, [2023] | Includes bibliographical references and index.
Identifiers: LCCN 2022043903 | ISBN 9780137848942 (paperback) | ISBN 9780138056384 (ebook)
Subjects: LCSH: Mainstreaming in education–United States. | Classroom management–United States.
Classification: LCC LC1201 .M37 2023 | DDC 371.9/046–dc23/eng/20220915
LC record available at https://lccn.loc.gov/2022043903

15 2025

Pearson

ISBN 10: 0-13-784894-3
ISBN 13: 978-0-13-784894-2

Pearson's Commitment to Accessibility

Accessibility

We are committed to providing products that are fully accessible to all learners. As per Pearson's guidelines for accessible educational Web media, we test and retest the capabilities of our products against the highest standards for every release, following the WCAG guidelines in developing new products for copyright year 2022 and beyond.

- You can learn more about Pearson's commitment to accessibility at **https://www.pearson.com/us/accessibility.html**

Contact Us

For accessibility-related issues, such as using assistive technology with Pearson products, alternative text requests, or accessibility documentation, email the Pearson Disability Support team at **disability.support@pearson.com**

Pearson

Dedication

To the numerous students, teachers, administrators, families, and researchers who have guided us over the course of our careers

ABOUT THE AUTHORS

MARGO A. MASTROPIERI, PhD, is University Professor Emerita and past coordinator of the Special Education Program, College of Education and Human Development, George Mason University (GMU). She has served as a diagnostic remediator for the Learning Center at Mount Holyoke College and as a classroom teacher for students with disabilities, from preschool to secondary levels, in Massachusetts and Arizona. Prior to working at GMU, Margo served as Professor of Special Education at Purdue University and as Assistant Professor of Special Education at Utah State University, where she also worked as a researcher at the Early Intervention Research Institute. She earned her PhD from Arizona State University. Margo has codirected federally funded research projects in mnemonic strategy instruction, inclusive science and social studies education, and writing instruction at the elementary, middle school, and high school levels, in addition to directing undergraduate and doctoral-level training grants. She has served as coeditor of *Learning Disabilities Research & Practice*, the journal of the Division for Learning Disabilities of the Council for Exceptional Children (CEC); coeditor of the research annual *Advances in Learning and Behavioral Disabilities* (Emerald); and coeditor of the CEC journal *Exceptional Children*. Among Margo's publications are over 200 journal articles, over 60 chapters in books, and more than 30 coauthored or coedited books. She is also the recipient of the distinguished University Professor title from George Mason University, the GMU Teaching Excellence Award, and the Virginia Outstanding Faculty Award, which is the Commonwealth's highest honor for faculty at Virginia's public and private colleges and universities.

THOMAS E. SCRUGGS, PhD, is University Professor Emeritus, College of Education and Human Development, George Mason University. He served as a classroom teacher for students with a variety of mild, moderate, and severe disabilities, including gifted students, at the preschool to secondary levels in Massachusetts and Arizona. Prior to working at GMU, Tom served as Professor of Special Education at Purdue University, where he was also the director of the Purdue Achievement Center, and was a research/evaluation specialist at Utah State University. He earned his PhD from Arizona State University. He has directed or codirected externally funded research projects in peer tutoring, test-taking skills, mnemonic strategy instruction, and inclusive science and social studies education at the elementary, middle school, and high school levels. With Margo, Tom served as coeditor of *Learning Disabilities Research & Practice*, *Advances in Learning and Behavioral Disabilities*, and *Exceptional Children*. Among his publications (mostly in collaboration with Margo) are over 200 journal articles, over 60 chapters in books, and more than 30 coauthored or coedited books. Tom is also a recipient of the Scholarly Achievement Award from the College of Education and Human Development at GMU.

Tom and Margo are the recipients of the CEC Special Education Research Award and the Distinguished Research Award from the American Educational Research Association: Special Education Special Interest Group for their research efforts in working with and advocating on behalf of individuals with exceptionalities.

KELLEY S. REGAN, PhD, is Professor and former Academic Program Coordinator of the Special Education–General Curriculum program at George Mason University. She has served as a special education teacher of students with learning disabilities, emotional/behavioral disorders, attention-deficit/hyperactivity disorders, and autism at the elementary and middle school levels in public day schools or self-contained settings and as a lead mentor teacher at a Professional Development School site. Prior to working at GMU, Kelley was Assistant Professor at The George Washington University where she prepared teachers of students with emotional/behavioral disorders. She received her PhD from GMU. Dr. Regan has led or co-led state and federally funded research projects in *e*Coaching to support the clinical preparation of inservice teachers and in writing instruction with the integration of a technology-based graphic organizer for students with and without disabilities in grades 3–12. She has also managed federally funded projects related to program improvement and the preparation of leadership personnel. Kelley is the former editor of the *Teacher Educators' Journal*, published by the Virginia Association of Colleges for Teacher Educators. Her research has been published in numerous research journals, including *Exceptional Children*, *Behavioral Disorders*, *Journal of Special Education*, *Teacher Education and Special Education*, and *Learning Disability Quarterly*. Kelley teaches graduate and undergraduate courses in literacy and instructional methods and mentors and teaches doctoral students.

Diversity is one of the major features that characterize our classrooms today. Not only have classrooms become more diverse with respect to race, religion, language, and ethnicity, but significantly more students with disabilities are being included in general education classrooms. Data reported by the U.S. Department of Education indicate that over three-fourths of students with disabilities are now being served largely within the general education classroom setting. This represents an exciting advance in establishing equity in education, as well as an enormous improvement from the days in which children with disabilities were routinely denied access to free and appropriate public education.

In spite of these impressive advances, however, a number of challenges remain. Many teachers consistently report that they do not feel prepared to teach students with disabilities in their general education classrooms. Although teachers overall are supportive of the ideals of inclusion, most do not believe that they possess the skills or have received the training necessary for effective inclusive teaching. We have written this book in order to place before teachers a wide variety of effective, evidence-based practices that can be successfully applied in today's inclusive classrooms. In short, we have tried to prepare the kind of textbook that we wish had been available to us when we were beginning special education teachers.

About This Book

We wrote *The Inclusive Classroom: Strategies for Effective Differentiated Instruction* to directly support the opportunities and challenges facing teachers today. We believe that teachers certainly should be provided with the necessary information regarding legal foundations and the characteristics of students with a variety of disabilities and other special learning needs. However, we focus on and emphasize a wide variety of research-based, practical teaching and learning strategies that are directly relevant to the tasks and academic demands required of teachers in inclusive classrooms in today's schools. In this book, we describe in detail strategies to address issues that are commonly experienced by teachers. In addition, we provide strategies for meeting the special challenges that often occur in today's classrooms. We have tried to focus on the strategies that are of the greatest importance to successful inclusive teaching.

However, we do not believe that individual "inclusion strategies" can be effectively implemented in the absence of overall effective teaching skills. That is, we believe that effective overall teaching and classroom management skills are necessary prerequisites for working with students with disabilities and other special learning needs of students who attend inclusive classrooms. And indeed, research has shown that the most effective general education teachers also make the most effective teachers in inclusive settings. Therefore, we have described inclusion strategies within the overall framework of effective instruction and management of general education classrooms and have emphasized this connection throughout the text. The organization and content of this book reflects our perspective.

New to the Seventh Edition

For the seventh edition, we made a number of changes as a result of helpful suggestions from editors and reviewers that we believe have greatly improved the text. We have:

- Added a new Part 4 with **Chapter 16, Transitions**, to improve an important emphasis on facilitating transitions to new settings and situations that occur throughout the student's school experience, and culminating with transition from school to work, postsecondary, and residential environments.

- Included new information on the **Council for Exceptional Children's (CEC) high-leverage practices (HLPs)** throughout the book. These practices have always formed an important part of our approach to teaching as described in the book; however, in this edition, we highlight specifically where these CEC HLPs fit within the overall framework of our book and provide examples.
- Increased coverage of **diversity**, **cultural responsiveness**, and **equity** throughout the text, including examples, strategies, and culturally responsive teaching skills, and enhanced by our **Diversity, Equity, and Inclusion in the Classroom** feature content.
- Increased coverage of **early, secondary, and middle school** throughout the text and in the features. Many strategies can be found to be useful for different age/grade levels, depending on student skill level, but we have highlighted most appropriate grade levels throughout the text.
- Updated the ***In the Classroom*** features and ***Classroom Scenarios*** to provide the context for specific teaching strategies and offer tips, strategies, and resources that may be used directly in classroom situations to address diversity, equity, and inclusion.
- Highlighted recent research and research references throughout the text, including new and updated ***Research Highlight*** features, which describe a variety of different types of research conducted in inclusive environments.
- Updated and greatly increased our coverage of relevant technology applications, by topic area, in the ***Apps for Education*** feature.
- Added a link to the new 2020 Initial Practice-Based Professional Preparation Standards for Special Educators at the end of each chapter and identified the specific standards that align with the learning objectives for each chapter.
- Added to and revised Learning Objectives (formerly Learning Outcomes) to align with updated content and to reflect deeper and more advanced levels of learning.
- Added many **Video Examples** in each chapter to exemplify classroom practices. Some video examples are from CHIME, a fully inclusive school in Los Angeles, and some are from the Dr. William W. Henderson School in Boston, also an exemplary inclusion campus for K–12 students.
- Added a **Glossary**, which will allow digital users to link to boldface terms in each chapter.

Key Content Updates by Chapter

- **Chapter 1:** Added information about *Endrew F. v. Douglas County School District*; updated percentages in Table 1.1 according to the 43rd annual report to Congress; updated Figure 1.1 to include the expansion of acronyms; added a definition of paraprofessional; added questions for reflection following the *Classroom Scenario: Volunteerism* and updated the scenario by integrating the individualized education program (IEP).
- **Chapter 2:** Added information about HLPs at the beginning of the chapter and integrated this concept throughout; incorporated new content, including digital tools for home/school communication, roles of paraprofessionals, and communication with paraprofessionals; updated *Diversity, Equity, and Inclusion in the Classroom* and the *Apps for Education* features; added parental/caregiver perspective in Table 2.1; added new content in *Classroom Scenario: Collaborating for Aliyah* to provide a more authentic context; added definition of universal design for learning (UDL).

- **Chapter 3:** Updated prevalence statistics throughout the chapter; added new content, including the *Diversity, Equity, and Inclusion in the Classroom* feature, the distinction between language delay versus difference, examples in each of the *In the Classroom* features, and examples of strategies and instructional adaptations; expanded the description in the *Classroom Scenario: Adaptations for Maria* feature; updated the *Apps for Education* feature; added Figure 3.1 as an example of a self-monitoring checklist and Figure 3.2 as an example of an interval recording checklist.
- **Chapter 4:** Updated prevalence statistics and the *Diversity, Equity, and Inclusion in the Classroom* feature; added discussion of person-first versus identity-first language; expanded discussion of social language use for students with autism spectrum disorders; expanded on and/or added new examples of instructional strategies and techniques; added new *Research Highlight* feature; increased coverage of emergency procedures.
- **Chapter 5:** Added Table 5.1 to provide examples of enrichment activities in specific content areas; added a new section on the COVID-19 pandemic; added a new *Research Highlight* and *Diversity, Equity, and Inclusion in the Classroom* feature; revised Figure 5.1; updated Figure 5.3.
- **Chapter 6:** Updated learning objectives; expanded information on content standards; added Figure 6.1a and 6.1b to illustrate differentiation to meet different learner needs; added content about choral responding, scaffolding, and a new *Diversity, Equity, and Inclusion in the Classroom* feature; added a new section on "flexible grouping" and a new section to specifically introduce "CEC's High-Leverage Practices for Special Education."
- **Chapter 7:** Reorganized the delivery of response to intervention discussions to provide clear directives for each Tier of instruction. Added Table 7.1 to show an example of weekly progress monitoring; added examples of screening measures; expanded and reorganized progress monitoring content in the discussion of the multi-tiered systems of support to identify how progress monitoring differs to inform instruction for additional needs for intervention; added new content for the *Research Highlight* and the *Diversity, Equity, and Inclusion in the Classroom* feature; updated content in the *Apps for Education* feature.
- **Chapter 8:** Added information about HLPs at the beginning of the chapter and integrated this concept throughout; Added learning objective 8.3 and a new *Research Highlight*; added discussion and description of "check in, check out" as a Tier 2 intervention; added new content about goal setting, behavior-specific praise, bullying prevention, and social skills; expanded discussion of the ABC (antecedent, behavior, consequence) analysis example; added definition of self-determination skills; updated the *Apps for Education* feature; added description of a strategy for promoting equity in disciplinary practices.
- **Chapter 9:** Added a new *Research Highlight* and *Diversity, Equity, and Inclusion in the Classroom* feature; added new content on peer networks and peer mediation; added Table 9.2 to provide examples of UDL principles represented in peer tutoring and cooperative learning; updated the *Apps for Education* feature.
- **Chapter 10:** Added a new *Apps for Education*, *Research Highlight*, and *Diversity, Equity, and Inclusion in the Classroom* features; integrated information about the IEP, including learning goals and accommodations; integrated connection to HLPs throughout the chapter.

- **Chapter 11:** Added new content for self-management of homework and a strategy for peer revising; expanded coverage of digital tools to support study skills at home and for note taking; Added new *Research Highlight*, *Diversity, Equity, and Inclusion in the Classroom*, and *Apps for Education* features; updated Figure 11.6.
- **Chapter 12:** Integrated information about HLPs throughout; Added new *Research Highlight*, *Diversity, Equity, and Inclusion in the Classroom*, and *Apps for Education* features; added new content, including an example of an alternative state assessment and an example of a student's assessment data in Table 12.2, which integrates the individualized education program (IEP); expanded discussion of formative assessment, grading procedures, and adjusting scoring procedures; updated Figure 12.1.
- **Chapter 13:** Added new *Research Highlight*, *Diversity, Equity, and Inclusion in the Classroom*, and *Apps for Education* features; expanded example of standards for reading; updated digital tools, apps, and assistive technologies to support literacy instruction; added descriptive adaptations for secondary students including examples of tiered instruction at the secondary level.
- **Chapter 14:** Expanded discussion of math standards; incorporated new content, including strategies for fact fluency, use of the self-regulated strategy development framework for math, use of calculators, and progress monitoring; added a new *Research Highlight* feature; updated the *Diversity, Equity, and Inclusion in the Classroom* and *Apps for Education* features; updated digital tools and apps to support math instruction.
- **Chapter 15:** Added a new *Research Highlight* and *Diversity, Equity, and Inclusion in the Classroom* feature; updated the *Apps for Education* feature; incorporated new content, including science and social studies standards, differentiated curriculum enhancements for content vocabulary acquisition, and new examples of instructional adaptations and universally designed strategies to support student learning.
- **Chapter 16** (previously part of Chapter 15): Added new *Research Highlight*, *Diversity, Equity, and Inclusion in the Classroom*, and *Apps for Education* features; added new content for planning transitions to kindergarten, elementary school, middle school, secondary settings, and postsecondary environments; increased coverage of transition strategies; added new *Classroom Scenario* and *In the Classroom* features; added new content, including curriculum for enhancing self-determination skills and examples for applying these skills across grade levels.

TEXT ORGANIZATION

PART 1: THE FUNDAMENTALS The first part of this book presents the fundamentals of inclusive teaching, including the history of special education, the legislation that requires it, and the necessary and relevant practical information for developing IEPs. Chapters in Part I also provide a framework for understanding the stakes for making inclusion necessary and equitable, the characteristics of specific disabilities and abilities covered under the law, and the practices that make inclusion possible, including collaboration among caregivers and professionals. Featured coverage also includes students with special gifts and talents, students representing cultural linguistic diversity, and students living in poverty.

PART 2: DEVELOPING EFFECTIVE TEACHING SKILLS Part 2 presents effective teaching skills across grade and skill levels—those techniques teachers can do to maximize student learning in inclusive settings. This part is concerned with teaching skills that can be effective across content and subject matter and discusses how to increase teacher effectiveness in such areas as classroom organization and teacher presentations, efficient behavior management, motivating students to learn, improving attention and memory, enlisting the support of classroom peers, improving study skills and test-taking skills, and employing assessment materials and techniques to maximize overall instruction. Extensive discussion is also made of the response-to-intervention model or multi-tiered systems of support that are presently applied in many educational settings to accommodate students with disabilities. Overall, Part 2 is dedicated to developing the skills needed to become an effective teaching professional in an inclusive classroom.

PART 3: TEACHING IN THE CONTENT AREAS Part 3 is concerned with applying effective teaching strategies in specific content areas. Included in this part are strategies for maximizing teaching effectiveness in literacy skills from pre-reading to essay composition; mathematics from early number concepts to algebra; life, physical, and earth science; and social studies. Teaching techniques and strategies in these significant areas are described across grade and skill levels.

PART 4: FACILITATING TRANSITIONS The last part is devoted exclusively to facilitating transitions students make throughout their school years, including transitioning from preschool and throughout the grade levels, to graduation and transition to employment, postsecondary education, or other settings.

The Purposes of Our Pedagogical Features

Teaching Strategies and Skills That Sustain Inclusive Classrooms

In writing the seventh edition, as in previous editions, we wanted to emphasize the practical, research-based teaching and learning strategies essential in inclusive environments. For this reason, we focus on the basic tools effective educators use and directly relate this content to the academic and professional demands of teachers in inclusive settings.

STRATEGIES FOR

MAKING ADAPTATIONS FOR STUDENTS WITH SPEECH OR LANGUAGE IMPAIRMENTS

Instruction is effectively differentiated when adaptations are made in the physical environment, instructional materials, instructional procedures, and assessment methods appropriate to the needs of individual learners. Following are some adaptations that are generally appropriate for students with speech and language impairments. More specific techniques are provided in Parts 2 and 3 of this text.

Strategies for . . . features in the text in Chapters 2 through 16 provide a significant number of research-based strategies included specifically for teachers to use in their inclusive classrooms with all students. Research-based strategies link research to teaching and promote student competency.

In the Classroom

Preparing Classmates of Students with Disabilities

- ______ Some schools have disability-awareness programs for students and teachers. If not, ask a special educator or counselor to talk about disabilities and explain strengths and differences of individuals with disabilities.
- ______ Expose students in the elementary grades to books that portray characters with disabilities.
- ______ Encourage older students to ask questions and set a model of open acceptance.
- ______ Promote cooperative relationships between students with disabilities and students without disabilities.
- ______ Tell students about their roles as possible peer tutors and helpers. Provide models of how peers can assist, but make it clear that they should ask before helping and also encourage independent functioning. They should not try to do everything for students with disabilities.
- ______ Explain that all classmates, even if they are not peer tutors or helpers, can encourage students with disabilities to be active participants and members of the class.

In the Classroom features offer tips, checklists, templates, and practical strategies that serve as effective classroom applications.

Inclusion Checklist

IMPROVING ATTENTION AND MEMORY

If students are having problems with attention, have you considered the following? If not, see the pages listed here.

STRATEGIES FOR IMPROVING ATTENTION

- ☐ Address the preconditions of attention with teacher effectiveness, 252
- ☐ Provide assistance with basic skills problems, 252–253
- ☐ Use direct appeal, 253
- ☐ Use proximity, 253
- ☐ Break up activities, 254
- ☐ Allow sufficient movement to reduce restlessness, 254
- ☐ Provide student activities, 254
- ☐ Use classroom peers to promote attention, 254
- ☐ Provide direct consequences for attention, 254–255
- ☐ Teach self-recording strategies, 255

STRATEGIES FOR ADDRESSING EXTREME CASES OF ATTENTION DEFICITS

- ☐ Provide intensive teacher-led instruction, 256
- ☐ Consider strengths and weaknesses of stimulant medication, 256–258
- ☐ Provide behavioral techniques, 258
- ☐ Promote joint attention, 258

If students are having problems with memory, have you considered the following? If not, see the pages listed here.

STRATEGIES FOR IMPROVING MEMORY

- ☐ Address memory preconditions, 259
- ☐ Develop "metamemory," 259–260
- ☐ Use external memory, 260
- ☐ Enhance meaningfulness, 260
- ☐ Use concrete examples, pictures, or imagery, 260–262
- ☐ Minimize interfering information, 262
- ☐ Use enactments and manipulation, 262
- ☐ Promote active reasoning, 262–263
- ☐ Increase practice, 263
- ☐ Use clustering and organization, 263
- ☐ Promote elaboration, 263–264

STRATEGIES FOR IMPROVING MEMORY WITH MNEMONIC TECHNIQUES

- ☐ Use the keyword method for verbal associations, 265–269
- ☐ Use the pegword method for numbered or ordered information, 269–271
- ☐ Use letter strategies for lists, 271–272
- ☐ Create mnemonic pictures, 272–273
- ☐ Combine mnemonic strategies with other classroom activities, 273

Inclusion Checklists at the end of each chapter summarize the strategies described in the chapter and are helpful for finding immediate references for specific strategies, pinpointing challenges students or teachers might be having, or planning specific interventions. Teachers may wish to consider the suggestions contained in the appropriate checklists prior to referring students for special education services. For example, if a teacher is considering referring a student for special education based on observed problems with attention or memory, the teacher could first consult the Inclusion Checklist in Chapter 10 for a list of possible interventions in these areas and page references for those interventions in the text.

Learning Strategies That Support Students' Educational Progress

The end goal of education is to ensure *all* students make educational progress. Individual educational plans, written for students with disabilities, should include goals that have high expectations for the progress of students with annual goals that are both realistic and ambitious so that the annual measurable progress is meaningful. Two features of this text offer insights in planning for educational progress and ensuring that planning is equitable.

Classroom Scenarios provide context for teaching strategies featured in the text by modeling cases that illustrate how to identify students who would benefit from instruction using those specific strategies.

CLASSROOM SCENARIO

James

James is a 10-year-old fifth-grader who was having trouble succeeding academically in school. His teacher, Ms. Marshak, believed that James had the overall ability to succeed in her classroom, but he rarely completed his work. As a result, he was falling far behind the other students in the class.

Ms. Marshak began to pay more attention to how James was spending his time. She found that he was often the last student to organize materials on his desk and begin working. During this period, James also spent more time than other students setting up his Chromebook, asking to get a drink of water, daydreaming, or playing with objects from his backpack. When Ms. Marshak recorded his behavior at the end of every minute over a 30-minute period, she found that James was actually working on his assignment only 10 of the 30 times she sampled his behavior. Clearly, he needed to increase the amount of time he put into his schoolwork.

QUESTIONS FOR REFLECTION

1. Why is James off-task so often? How could you find out?
2. Why doesn't concern about poor grades motivate James to work harder?
3. What are some simple things Ms. Marshak could do to help James?

Diversity, Equity, and Inclusion in the Classroom features illustrate how classrooms are more diverse not only with respect to students with disabilities but also with respect to race, gender, religion, language, and ethnicity. Specific strategies are presented to support students, families, and caregivers representing such diverse groups. Each feature ends with a question for classroom or peer discussion.

Diversity, Equity, and Inclusion in the Classroom

Cooperative Learning Activities in Multiethnic Classrooms

Many students prefer to work with peers for some school activities. Most students who have participated in peer tutoring or cooperative learning activities have reported enjoying working with partners. Sometimes students with disabilities have reported they have felt more comfortable reading with a single partner during peer tutoring than reading aloud in front of the entire class (see Mastropieri et al., 2001), and English learners have reported gaining confidence in their abilities (Norland, 2005). Similar, related findings have been observed when students from various ethnic backgrounds have been placed in structured small-group cooperative learning situations. In some studies, students from diverse ethnic backgrounds were found to have increased popularity following multiple cooperative learning lessons. Oortwijn et al. (2008) implemented cooperative learning lessons in elementary schools that included authentic math problem assignments with multiple possible solutions in heterogeneous cooperative groups. Improved cooperativeness and friendships among students from all ethnic groups were observed over time. More recently, Van Ryzin et al. (2020) implemented cooperative learning in a project involving 15 middle schools over a 2-year period and reported that students in cooperative learning conditions overall reported positive gains in peer relatedness (acceptance from other classmates), academic support (help and support from other students), and engagement (motivation and effort to do well in school) than students who had not participated in cooperative learning. Furthermore, it was found that overall gains in peer relatedness, academic support, and engagement were even greater for students from a variety of racial-ethnic groups than they were for White students. Van Ryzin and colleagues concluded that cooperative learning helped reduce ethnic disparities because it reduced interpersonal competition and provided opportunities for students of different racial-ethnic groups to work together to achieve common goals. These findings offer promise for using small-group activities such as cooperative learning when working with diverse groups of students.

Discuss: What are the advantages for students when learning in diverse cooperative groups?

Research-Based Resources That Reinforce Inclusion

The strategies in this text are research based, which means they have the greatest probability of affecting student learning. In addition to the wealth of research-based strategies and their application described in this text, two features support the use of researched-based strategies:

Research Highlight

Using Students with Emotional/Behavioral Disorders as Peer Tutors

Teachers and researchers have frequently observed that tutoring may produce benefits beyond the increase in academic learning being targeted. Students acting as tutors have been said to improve in interpersonal skills, attitude toward school and the subject matter being tutored, personal responsibility, and overall self-esteem, although these findings have not been consistently demonstrated (Scruggs & Mastropieri, 1998). Previous research has suggested students with emotional and behavioral disorders (EBD) may serve successfully as both tutors and tutees (Spencer, 2006; Watts et al., 2019). Spencer et al. (2003), for example, employed students in a middle school for students with EBD as peer tutors and tutees within social studies classes using paragraph summary strategies and reported higher test scores and improved on-task behavior in the tutoring condition. However, it was less certain whether students with EBD can benefit socially or behaviorally from acting as cross-age tutors of younger students, a question investigated by Watts et al. (2020).

Watts and colleagues (2020) identified five fifth- and sixth-grade students who had been identified as having EBD or students with learning disabilities who also had challenging classroom behaviors and/or IEP goals directly concerned with improving social or behavioral skills. Students were also given a measure of internalizing or externalizing behavior and their scores were included if they fell within moderate- to high-risk ranges. All tutors were concurrently participating in a Check-in, Check-out (CICO) program in which their behaviors were monitored regularly on a daily progress record (DPR).

Tutees included kindergarten students nominated by their teacher as exhibiting difficulties with early numeracy knowledge and skills. These students scored an average standard score of 76.2 on a test of early mathematics skills (about the 5th percentile).

Tutors were individually trained to implement tutoring to the kindergarten students using a number line board game intended to improve early number concepts and skills. Tutors were trained in providing the materials, modeling rules and procedures, demonstrating guided practice, providing corrective feedback and positive behavioral reinforcement strategies, and keeping students on task. Participating teachers were trained in two sessions, while tutors were trained in one-to-one sessions for 45 minutes and supervised by the special education teacher while tutoring. Fidelity of implementation was assessed using a procedural checklist aligned with the training manual.

Tutees received three tutoring sessions per week for 25–30 minutes each in a separate classroom setting. Maintenance was assessed following the end of the tutoring session. The investigation employed a multiple-baseline design, in which all students were monitored for 3–6 weeks prior to the tutoring intervention in the baseline condition, followed by up to 10 weeks of tutoring and 2 weeks of maintenance testing. Tutees were tested weekly on an early mathematics inventory, and tutors were assessed daily on their DPRs for percent of DPR behavioral points earned.

Fidelity of implementation data revealed that tutors were able to implement the intervention with a high degree of fidelity. At the end of the tutoring and maintenance program, Watts et al. (2020) reported that the kindergarten tutees had demonstrated consistent progress on their weekly math inventory scores and maintained these gains over the maintenance period. Furthermore, they had progressed over the course of the intervention from a mean standard score of 76.2 (about the 5th percentile) to a mean standard score of 93 (about the 32nd percentile) on a standardized test of early mathematics ability. Tutors generally improved in their CICO daily progress report scores, and most maintained these gains. In addition, tutors' mean scores on the measure of externalizing behaviors showed a pre-post decrease of 13.2 to 9.8, and on the measure of internalizing behaviors a decrease of 9.8 to 9.4. For two students, risk status for externalizing behavior decreased from "high" to "moderate."

Watts and colleagues (2020) concluded the tutoring intervention had been highly successful for both the academic learning of the tutees and the behavioral progress of the tutors. Teachers noted some difficulty with scheduling the tutoring sessions, but all teachers and students agreed the program had been beneficial, and all tutors and tutees expressed a desire to participate in more tutoring in the future.

QUESTIONS FOR REFLECTION

1. Why do you think tutoring kindergarten students improved the social behavior of fifth- and sixth-grade students with EBD?
2. Do you think the behavioral gains made by the students with EBD justified the use of their time as tutors? Why or why not?
3. What other tutoring interventions can you think of in which students with disabilities might benefit from being tutors?

Research Highlight features explain the recent research behind certain teaching strategies developed for use with students with disabilities. They provide resources for further information and explanation and then tie chapter content to the research with questions for reflection. The descriptive nature of the *Research Highlight* allows readers to see the need to verify strategies teachers use to account for their use appropriately.

Apps for Education

Managing Time with the Time Timer™

Many students have difficulties with understanding the concept of time, especially when told they need to keep working for a specified amount of time. Other students have difficulties with transition periods and changing from one activity to the next. A technological device called the Time Timer can help students visually see the amount of time left as they work and help them comprehend in a more concrete fashion the amount of time left for work or the amount of time left for one activity before moving to the next activity. The visual timer is a clock that comes in various sizes. One standard version is approximately 8 inches square and has a 60-minute timer. A smaller, 3-inch-square version is also available that can be clipped to a student's belt. When setting a specified amount of time—say, 15 minutes—that amount of time appears in red. A red disk shows on the timer when a time is set. As the time passes, the red disk disappears bit by bit, such that when time is up, the red disk is gone. As this happens, students can visually see the red disk disappearing as time passes and obtain a better picture of the amount of time left. Such a device may help students feel more comfortable with the concept of time because it makes the concept more concrete for them.

An app version of Time Timer, the *iPad Edition* (Time Timer LLC), is available that functions similarly but is designed for use with an iPad. Again, the visual counting-down of the minutes provides students with immediate cues about remaining time. Many additional timer apps are also available, including *Timer*' (Minima Software LLC) and *Easy Stop Watch&Timer* (BND Co., Ltd.), which include similar features for counting down time; some also include stopwatch features.

Source: From Time Timer LLC. Reprinted with permission.

Other apps help teachers track student behaviors. For example, *Teacher's Assistant: Track Student Behavior* (Lesson Portal, LLC) and *TeacherKit* (ITWorx Egypt) organize students by class, enable note taking for comments, allow storage of grades, interface with e-mail for contacting parents and caregivers, and interface with Dropbox for backing up files. These and other assistive and instructional technologies can become an important component of effective instruction, as described throughout this text.

Apps for Education provide up-to-date information on new technologies and how they can be employed to improve the academic or social functioning of students with disabilities.

Pearson eTextbook, Learning Management System (LMS)–Compatible Assessment Bank, and Other Instructor Resources

Pearson eTextbook

The Pearson eTextbook is a simple-to-use, mobile-optimized, personalized reading experience. It allows you to easily highlight, take notes, and review key vocabulary all in one place–even when offline. Seamlessly integrated videos and other rich media will engage you and give you access to the help you when you need it. To gain access or to sign into your Pearson eTextbook, visit: https://www.pearson.com/pearson-etext. Features include:

- **Video Examples** Each chapter includes *Video Examples* that illustrate principles or concepts aligned pedagogically with the chapter. These video clips enable you to know what educators do when they are engaged in instruction and include captions that ask you to consider how you would respond to situations depicted in the video. They are not just for you to view and enjoy; they are for you to reflect on and take into account as part of your education. With this edition, we are excited to introduce new videos that present professionals from the Dr. William W. Henderson K–12 Inclusion School in Boston and the CHIME school in Los Angeles. Both schools practice full inclusion and are exemplars in the field. Other videos come from Pearson's own library of custom-made videos from various classrooms and teachers across the nation.
- **Interactive Glossary** All key terms in the eTextbook are bolded and provide instant access to full glossary definitions, allowing you to quickly build your professional vocabulary as you are reading.

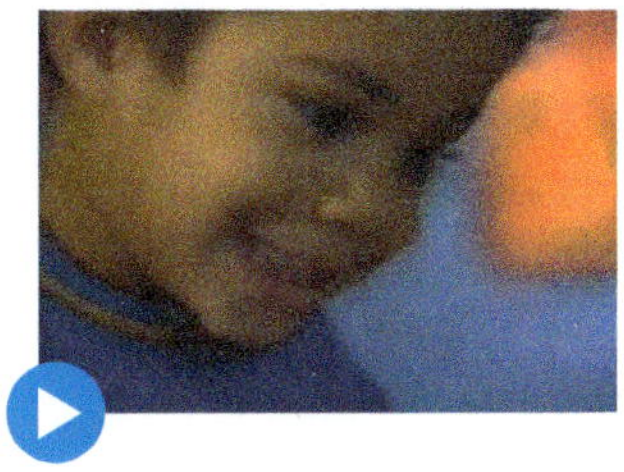

Pearson eTextbook
Video Example 3.6
In this video, the clinical director and therapists of a day treatment setting for children discuss the characteristics of ADHD and its possible causes. Notice the strategies used with this student.

Pearson eTextbook
Video Example 14.1
As a group, seventh-graders solve math problems and describe the operations that they use. How do the students benefit from being in this inclusive classroom?

LMS-Compatible Assessment Bank

With this new edition, all assessment types—quizzes, application exercises, and chapter tests—are included in LMS-compatible banks for the following learning management systems: Blackboard Canvas, D2L, and Moodle. These packaged files allow maximum flexibility to instructors when it comes to importing, assigning, and grading. Assessment types include:

- **Learning Objective Quizzes** Each chapter learning outcome is the focus of a *Learning Objective Quiz* that is available for instructors to assign through their LMS. Learning objectives identify chapter content that is most important for learners and serve as the organizational framework for each chapter and therefore each chapter quiz. The higher-order, multiple-choice questions in each quiz will measure your understanding of chapter content, guide the expectations for your learning, and inform the accountability and the applications of your new knowledge. Each multiple-choice question includes feedback for the correct answer and for each distractor.

- **Application Exercises** Each chapter provides opportunities to apply what you have learned through *Application Exercises*. These exercises are usually in a short-answer format and can be based on Pearson eTextbook Video Examples; written cases; scenarios supported by pedagogical text features, including text figures and tables. A model response written by the authors is provided to help guide your learning.
- **Chapter Tests** Suggested test items are provided for each chapter and include questions in multiple-choice and short-answer/essay formats.

Instructor's Manual

The Instructor's Manual is provided as a Word document and includes resources to assist professors in planning their course. The resources in this manual include chapter learning objectives, key terms, detailed chapter outlines that can be used as presentation guides, chapter summaries, application activities, discussion questions, and additional suggested resources.

PowerPoint® Slides

PowerPoint slides are provided for each chapter and highlight key concepts and summarize the content of the text to make it more meaningful for students. Often, these slides also include questions and problems designed to stimulate discussion and to encourage students to elaborate and deepen their understanding of chapter topics.

Note: All instructor resources—LMS-compatible assessment bank, instructor's manual, and PowerPoint slides are available for download at www.pearson.com. After searching for your title, be sure you have selected "I'm an educator", and then select "Instructor resources" tab.

Acknowledgments

We thank Rebecca Fox-Gieg for her constant support throughout this revision process. We thank Linda Bishop, our Developmental Editor, for her tireless reading and providing excellent feedback throughout the entire revision process. We thank Neha Sharma and Hemalatha Loganathan, and Prathiba Rajagopal and the entire content and production staff for their detailed editing with helpful suggestions throughout all development phases. We thank Drew Bennett, Krista Clark, and Jenell Forschler for their assistance on production and marketing areas of expertise. We thank graduate research assistant, Roba Hrisseh, for her invaluable suggestions and particular expertise in assistive and instructional technology.

The authors also would like to thank the reviewers whose input forged new ideas and whose revision guidelines improved this new seventh edition. We are indebted to Wendy Cavendish, University of Miami; Gina Conner, Arizona State University; Mary Frances Hanline, Florida State University; Mark Moody, Central Michigan University; Laura Reissner, Northern Michigan University; and Kimberly Viel-Ruma, University of Georgia. Thanks to each of you.

Kelley would like to acknowledge her husband, Chris, and son, Parker, for their smiles, encouragement, and support throughout the revision process. In addition, Kelley would like to express her gratitude to Margo and Tom for the invitation to join them for this edition. Their mentorship continues to have a profound and lasting impact. Tom and Margo also thank Lisa Mastropieri for her continuous support and encouragement.

BRIEF CONTENTS

PART 1 THE FUNDAMENTALS

1 

2 

3 

CHAPTER 3

Teaching Students with Higher-Incidence Disabilities 55

4 

CHAPTER 4

Teaching Students with Autism and Lower-Incidence Disabilities 83

7

8

11

CHAPTER 11

Teaching Study Skills 279

12

CHAPTER 12

Assessment 305

PART 3 TEACHING IN THE CONTENT AREAS

PART 1 The Fundamentals

Ruud Gompel/Shutterstock

CHAPTER 1

Introduction to Inclusive Teaching

LEARNING OBJECTIVES

After studying this chapter, you should be able to:

1.1 Understand and describe educational rights for individuals with disabilities.

1.2 Describe the concept of *least restrictive environment* and identify the general characteristics of each of the disability categories defined by the Individuals with Disabilities Education Act (IDEA).

1.3 Summarize the legal foundations, litigation, and legislation concerning students with disabilities, such as the Individuals with Disabilities Education Act, the Vocational Rehabilitation Act (Section 504), and the Americans with Disabilities Act (ADA).

1.4 Contrast the models of service delivery and the continuum of services available to students with disabilities.

In 1975, Congress passed a law that would change the face of public education in the United States. The Education for All Handicapped Children Act—now known as the **Individuals with Disabilities Education Act**, or **IDEA**—specified that all children, including those with disabilities formerly excluded from school, were entitled to a **free, appropriate public education (FAPE)**. This law went far beyond any previous legislation in specifying that, to the greatest extent possible, this "special" education was to be provided in the **least restrictive environment (LRE)**. In other words, students with disabilities were to be educated to the greatest extent possible in the general education classroom. This text is dedicated to describing the means by which this "least restrictive environment" can become a reality.

The passage of IDEA and its subsequent amendments has largely achieved its purpose. More than ever, students with disabilities now receive FAPE. Furthermore, this education is being provided more often in the general education classroom.

Before the passage of IDEA, students with disabilities were often denied access to public education (Yell, 2019). In some cases, they were placed in institutions. In other cases, the parents and caregivers were forced to pay for private schools, often in inappropriate settings. Today, all students with disabilities are legally entitled to a free, appropriate education suited to their needs. The following scenarios compare a case from many years ago with a similar case from today. As a result of IDEA and related legislation, society has an increased understanding of individuals with disabilities and is much better able to accommodate individual differences in schools, in workplaces, and in social settings.

HISTORICAL SCENARIOS

Mr. and Mrs. Patterson

In 1960, Mrs. Patterson gave birth to a beautiful baby girl whom the Pattersons named Hope. Their initial excitement about the successful pregnancy and delivery was soon shrouded by a dark cloud. The Pattersons were informed by the doctors that their infant was "retarded." Mrs. Patterson tells their story:

"When the physician informed us that our precious baby girl was 'retarded,' we were traumatized. I can still hear the doctor's words: 'You probably don't want to keep her. The state institution is the best place for infants like her. The staff at the institution will be able to take care of her better than you.'

"I immediately hated the doctor. How could he be saying this to me about my baby girl whom I already loved with all my heart? I felt as if I was having a nightmare and that at any moment I would awake and find that everything was okay.

"At first we both were so angry and couldn't help thinking thoughts like, *Why did this happen to us? We didn't do anything wrong; this is unfair!* We looked for someone to blame. We blamed the doctors and the staff at the hospital. It must be their fault—something must have happened during Hope's birth. Then we racked our brains for things that we might have done incorrectly during the pregnancy. Did I fall? Was I exposed to any harmful substances? We both felt so guilty and didn't know whom to turn to for help. We felt overwhelmed and lost. The only individuals we knew to speak with were the doctors and staff at the hospital and they had already expressed their opinions to us.

"Then we decided. We loved Hope and we took her home with us. She was very slow at developing. We were always searching for effective ways to help her. Everything was so hard. Each little thing we did seemed like an enormous journey. By the time Hope reached kindergarten age, she had passed some important developmental milestones. But we knew she wasn't developmentally the same as other children her age. We hoped, however, that being with other children her age would encourage her and she might begin to catch up once she was in school.

"Unfortunately, however, within the first week of kindergarten, we were contacted by the school and asked to remove Hope from the school. We were told that she wasn't ready for school and that she took too much time away from the other children in the class. The local school administrators further told us that Hope had too many problems to allow her to ever attend the local schools. If we wanted Hope exposed to any educational program, the only solution available to us was to place Hope in the state institution's school.

"We were again devastated with the decision we had to make. We felt as if we had no choice but to provide Hope an opportunity to develop as much as she could. We went through the same grieving process as we did when Hope was born. We were angry and felt guilty for sending Hope away, but we sincerely believed we had no other options available to us. Although we made the best decision at that time, we still feel guilty."

Mr. and Mrs. Molina

Now imagine a family in circumstances similar to those of the Pattersons, 55 years later. Mr. and Mrs. Molina have a brand-new baby girl, Carmen. Like the Pattersons, the Molinas are instantly in love with their new daughter. They are saddened, however, when they are informed by the doctors that their precious infant is severely developmentally delayed. This time, however, the Molinas have additional legal guarantees in place that will provide a free and appropriate education for Carmen beginning with early intervention services, the least restrictive environment throughout her education, and continuing supported employment options into adulthood.

Some early intervention opportunities available are close by in their own community. Some of the program options are center based, in which the intervention occurs at the school; some are home based, in which the intervention takes place in the home; and others are a combination of center- and home-based programs. This means that Carmen can participate daily in relevant educational programs in a variety of setting options.

Additionally, established networks of organizations provide support to parents, caregivers, and families of children with disabilities. Although the Molinas will still have some of the same emotional experiences that the Pattersons had, at least the federal government has mandated services for families with children with severe disabilities. Mrs. Molina tells her story:

> "We felt disappointed and guilty when the physician informed us that our beautiful baby girl was developmentally delayed. Her words still ring in my ears: 'Your baby has a serious disability.' We were stunned. We barely heard the rest of her statement: 'We have a staff of early childhood specialists and nurses who will be in contact with you later today.' We felt that the doctor must have us mixed up our child with someone else. There must be a huge mistake. How could anything be wrong with our new baby girl? I felt as if I was living in a nightmare and that at any moment I would wake up and find that everything was okay."

The Molinas, like the Pattersons, went through the same questions of "Why us?" and "What happened?" and the associated feelings of denial, anger, guilt, and aloneness. Later on the same day, however, the Molinas felt the support from an early childhood specialist and a nurse. As Mrs. Molina reported:

> "The early childhood specialist and the nurse explained the types of intervention services available for our baby and for us. At first, everything seemed like a blur, but as reality sank in, we realized that we had hope for Carmen. Specialized services were available, she would receive assistance, and we would receive educational support. Although we still felt stressed and angry—we wanted to blame someone—we began to realize there were individuals and support services that would help us do everything we could for Carmen and provide well for her individual needs."

QUESTIONS FOR REFLECTION

1. Describe the various feelings experienced by the Pattersons. In what way were they similar to the feelings expressed by the Molinas? How do you think you would feel as a caregiver facing these issues?
2. Which of the Molinas' program options do you think you would have chosen? Why?

What Are the Educational Rights for Individuals with Disabilities?

Learning Objective 1.1 Understand and describe educational rights for individuals with disabilities.

Before the passage of federal legislation mandating services for students with disabilities, these individuals were routinely and legally excluded from school. Johnson (1986, pp. 1–2) documented several instances from years past across the United States, including the following examples:

- In Massachusetts in 1893, a child with disabilities was excluded by a school committee because "he was so weak in mind as to not derive any marked benefit from instruction and further, that he is troublesome to other children . . . " (*Watson v. City of Cambridge*, 1893).
- In Wisconsin in 1919, a 13-year-old with normal intelligence but physical disabilities was excluded for the following reasons:

  His physical condition and ailment produces a depressing and nauseating effect upon the teachers and school children; . . . he takes up an undue proportion of the teacher's time and attention, distracts attention of other pupils, and interferes generally with discipline and progress of the school (*Beattie v. Board of Education of City of Antigo*, 1919).

- In 1963, Nevada excluded any student whose "physical or mental conditions or attitude is such as to prevent or render inadvisable his attendance at school or his application to study" (Nevada Revised Statutes, 1963).

- In 1971, Alaska excluded students with "bodily or mental conditions rendering attendance inadvisable" from school (Alaska Statutes, 1971).
- Virginia law in 1973 allowed school exclusion for "children physically or mentally incapacitated for school work" (Code of Virginia, 1973).

Today, these laws are no longer applicable. According to federal law, all students, regardless of disability, are entitled to a free and appropriate public education, including access to the general education curriculum. Since 1975, public education has truly become "education for all."

Pearson eTextbook

Video Example 1.1

In this video, we are provided a glimpse into our country's history to right the wrongs of the past for all, and ensure equal rights under the law. During the era of this film, students with disabilities were not granted the right to an equal education.

Along with increased rights of individuals with disabilities from legislation such as IDEA come increased responsibilities for teachers. General education teachers today have more students with disabilities in their classrooms than ever. In fact, only a small proportion of students with disabilities currently receives more than 60% of their education outside the general education classroom (see Table 1.1). Today, therefore, teachers must be especially aware of their responsibilities in providing appropriate instruction for students with disabilities.

Although more responsibilities are placed on the general education teacher, they should not be considered a burden. On the contrary, classroom diversity—whether in the form of culture, language, sexual orientation, race, ethnicity, or ability—is something to be valued in its own right. Diversity provides a more exciting, dynamic classroom and the opportunity for students to learn that all people are not the same. Diversity provides opportunities for students to understand, respect, and value others for their differences.

Finally, diversity provides the opportunity for you to use all of your imagination, skills, and resources to be the best teacher you can be. In the end, effective inclusive teaching is about being the most effective teacher possible and supporting all students to learn in the least restrictive environment.

TABLE 1.1 Percentage of Students Ages 5 Through 21 with Disabilities Receiving Services in Different Educational Environments

	Served Inside the Regular Classroom			
Disabilities	**80% or More of the Day (%)**	**40–79% of the Day (%)**	**Less Than 40% of the Day (%)**	**Separate Environments (e.g., Residential, Separate Facilities, Correctional, Home-Bound/ Hospital Environments) (%)**
Specific learning disabilities	73.5	20.4	4.2	1.8
Speech or language impairments	87.9	4.4	3.7	4.0
Intellectual disabilities	16.6	27.9	48.7	6.7
Emotional disturbance	50.2	17.1	16.9	15.8
Multiple disabilities	14.3	17.8	44.9	23.0
Hearing impairments	63.7	14.6	9.9	11.8
Orthopedic impairments	55.6	15.2	21.1	8.1
Other health impairments	68.2	19.5	8.1	4.2
Visual impairments	68.8	12.1	8.7	7.9
Autism	39.8	18.3	33.5	8.4
Deaf-blindness	26.5	13.3	34.8	25.3
Traumatic brain injury	51.5	21.2	19.4	7.9
Developmental delay	66.6	17.7	14.2	1.5
All disabilities	**64.8**	**17.4**	**12.9**	**5.0**

Source: 43rd Annual Report to Congress on the Implementation of Individuals with Disabilities Act (Section I, p. 57), 2021, Washington, DC: U.S. Department of Education.

The Least Restrictive Environment

Learning Objective 1.2 Describe the concept of *least restrictive environment* and identify the general characteristics of each of the disability categories defined by the Individuals with Disabilities Education Act (IDEA).

WHERE ARE STUDENTS WITH DISABILITIES SERVED?

Critical to IDEA legislation is the concept of least restrictive environment (LRE; Rozalski et al., 2011). This phrase means that students with disabilities must be educated in the setting least removed from the general education classroom. To the greatest extent possible, students with disabilities are not to be restricted to education in special schools or special classrooms but, rather, should have access to the same settings to which students without disabilities have access. When students with disabilities are educated, to any extent, in a different setting, there must be a compelling reason that this setting is in the student's best interest.

MAINSTREAMING AND INCLUSION Mainstreaming was the first movement devoted to the placement of students with disabilities within the general education classroom. Advocates of **mainstreaming** three or four decades ago did not necessarily want to see students with disabilities placed in special classes for the entire school day, but they argued that more exposure to the general classroom would be in everyone's best interest (e.g., Blankenship, 1981). Often, mainstreaming was thought to be something individual special education students could "earn" by demonstrating that their skills were adequate to function independently in general education settings. Since then, the term **inclusion** has been used to describe the education of students with disabilities in general education settings. Although many definitions have been used to describe *inclusion*, the term is generally taken to mean that students with disabilities are served primarily in the general education classroom, under the responsibility of the general classroom teacher. When necessary and justifiable, students with disabilities may also receive some of their instruction in another setting, such as a resource room. Additional support can also be provided within the general education classroom by paraprofessionals or special education teachers. Although this is a similar concept to mainstreaming, a critical difference of inclusion is the view of the general classroom as the primary placement for the student with disabilities, with other special services regarded as ancillary (Lipsky & Gartner, 1997).

Pearson eTextbook

Video Example 1.2

Review the descriptions of mainstreaming and the LRE identified in this video. How does the LRE benefit students with disabilities?

In addition to mainstreaming and inclusion, the term *full inclusion* is also used, referring to the practice of serving students with disabilities and other diverse learning needs entirely within the general classroom. In full-inclusion settings, all students with disabilities are served for the entire day in the general classroom, although special education teachers and other personnel may also be present in the general classroom at times (Kauffman et al., 2011; Zigmond, 2015).

WHO IS SERVED UNDER IDEA?

The Individuals with Disabilities Education Act is intended to provide necessary support services to students with disabilities. To accomplish this goal, students with disabilities are categorized in particular disability groups. It is important to remember, however, that all students served by IDEA are first human beings and individuals, capable of achievement, accomplishment, friendship, affection, and all other attributes of any other individual. Disability status may not be a permanent characteristic of all individuals; in fact, most people can expect to be considered "disabled" at one time or another in their lives. This in no way detracts from their fundamental worth as human beings. In fact, it is this principle of individual worth that has inspired much of today's special education legislation.

In short, although students served under IDEA have been given a disability "label," it is important to consider the individual first and then consider the label as a secondary factor, along with other characteristics that help identify the unique aspects of the individual. For this reason, it has been recommended that "person-first" language be adopted (Russell, 2008; for a different view, see Pulrang, 2020). For example, we speak of "students with hearing impairments," rather than "hearing-impaired students." It is also important to remember that we use these descriptions only when it is directly relevant to a situation. When it is not relevant to list hearing impairment as a characteristic, for example, we speak simply of "Chris," or "Devon," or "Ana." For example, Margo, as a high school student, was best friends with Gia, a student 1 year older. They played on the basketball team together and spent much of their after-school time together. After several years of close friendship, Margo expressed surprise that Gia had not gotten her driver's license, even a year after her 16th birthday. Furthermore, Gia went to a separate setting to take the SAT. When she asked Gia about these things, Gia revealed that she was legally blind. Margo was astonished to hear this—and this situation demonstrated clearly to her that many characteristics of individuals, such as warmth, caring, sincerity, and understanding, can be much more important than disability status. It also demonstrated that important relationships can be developed and maintained that have little or nothing to do with disability status.

GENERAL CHARACTERISTICS Students served by IDEA are distributed among 13 disability categories. Following is a brief description of each category (see Assistance to States for the Education of Children with Disabilities and Preschool Grants for Children with Disabilities, 2006; IDEA, 2004). Note that individual states may use different terminology.

- *Autism.* Autism is a developmental disability generally manifested within the first 3 years of life. Major characteristics can include impairments in communication and reciprocal social interaction, resistance to change, engagement in repetitive activities, and unusual responses to sensory stimuli.
- *Deaf-blindness.* Individuals in this category have moderate to severe impairments in both vision and hearing, causing such severe communication and educational needs that programming solely for children with deafness or children with blindness is not appropriate.
- *Deafness.* Individuals with deafness have hearing impairments so severe that processing linguistic information through hearing is severely limited, with or without amplification, and educational performance is negatively impacted.
- *Emotional disturbance (or serious emotional disturbance).* This category includes individuals with a condition in one or more of the following areas over an extended period of time: (1) inability to learn, not due to intellectual, sensory, or health problems; (2) inability to build and maintain social relationships with peers and teachers; (3) inappropriate behavior and affect; (4) general pervasive depression or unhappiness; (5) tendency to develop fears or physical symptoms associated with school and personal problems; and (6) schizophrenia (a disorder in perception of reality). According to the federal definition, emotional disturbance is not intended to apply to socially maladjusted children unless they are also characterized as having serious emotional disturbance.
- *Hearing impairments.* Hearing impairments, with or without amplification, affect educational performance and developmental progress. The impairment may be permanent or fluctuating, mild to profound, unilateral or bilateral, but this category includes impairments not included under the definition of deafness.
- *Intellectual disabilities.* Intellectual disabilities (referred to as *mental retardation* in IDEA) describes significantly below-average intellectual functioning, as well as concurrent deficits in "adaptive behavior" (age-appropriate personal independence and social responsibility). It is manifested between birth and age 18 and negatively affects educational performance.
- *Multiple disabilities.* This category includes any individuals with two or more disabling conditions. However, this category often includes intellectual disability as one of the categories and is usually used when disorders are serious and interrelated to such an extent that it is difficult to identify the primary area of disability. It does not include deaf-blindness.
- *Orthopedic impairments.* Orthopedic impairments are associated with physical conditions that seriously impair mobility or motor activity. This category includes individuals with cerebral palsy, individuals with diseases of the skeleton or muscles (such as poliomyelitis), and those who are victims of accidents.

- *Other health impairments.* This category includes chronic or acute health-related difficulties that adversely affect educational performance and are manifested by limited strength, vitality, or alertness. It can include such health problems as heart conditions, sickle-cell anemia, lead poisoning, diabetes, and epilepsy. It can also include **attention-deficit/hyperactivity disorder (ADHD)**.
- *Specific learning disabilities.* This category refers to a disorder in one or more of the basic psychological processes involved in understanding or using spoken or written language, which can result in difficulties in reading, writing, listening, speaking, thinking, spelling, or mathematics. The term *learning disabilities* does not apply to children with learning problems that are primarily the result of visual, hearing, or physical disabilities; intellectual disability; emotional disturbance; or environmental, cultural, or economic disadvantage.
- *Speech or language impairments.* This category includes disorders of articulation, fluency, voice, or language that adversely affect educational performance.
- *Traumatic brain injury.* Traumatic brain injury is an acquired injury to the brain due to external force resulting in a total or partial disability, psychosocial impairment, or both that negatively affects educational performance (does not apply to congenital or degenerative injuries or to brain injuries acquired during birth).
- *Visual impairments, including blindness.* A visual impairment is a loss of vision that, even when corrected, affects educational performance. It may be mild to moderate to severe in nature. Students who are blind are unable to read print and usually learn to read and write using braille. Students with low vision can usually read when the print is enlarged sufficiently.

In addition, children age 3–9 can be classified as experiencing developmental delay if they have developmental delays in one or more of the following areas: physical, cognitive, communication, social or emotional, or adaptive development. Such children may need special education and related services.

OTHER INSTANCES OF CLASSROOM DIVERSITY IDEA mandates services for most of the recognized disability areas. However, there are other sources of classroom diversity, not associated with disabilities, that you need to consider when planning and implementing classroom instruction. These areas include the following:

- *Culturally and linguistically diverse groups.* These students are culturally and/or linguistically different from the majority U.S. culture or different from the teacher. Teachers should plan and implement equitable instruction that is considerate of and sensitive to all students' linguistic and/or cultural differences (Gollnick & Chinn, 2017).
- *At-risk students.* Students categorized as "at risk" exhibit characteristics, live in an environment, or have experiences that make them more likely to fail in school, drop out, or experience a lack of success in future life. These factors are many and varied, but they include "slow learners" not served by IDEA categories and individuals who have sociocultural disadvantages, are at risk for suicide, or come from dysfunctional home environments (e.g., marred by drug or alcohol abuse, domestic violence, or child abuse). Such learners may require trauma-informed approaches (Craig, 2008) or any of a variety of adaptations to help them succeed in school and later in life (Frieman, 2001).
- ***Gifted, creative, and talented.*** These students exhibit skills or abilities substantially above those of their age in areas such as academic achievement in one or more subject areas, visual or performing arts, or athletics. If the abilities of such students greatly exceed classroom standards or curriculum, special adaptations or accommodations may be appropriate. Although many states have passed laws providing for the identification and education of gifted and talented students, in many cases, funding for gifted programs is not provided (Rimm et al., 2018).

Pearson eTextbook
Video Example 1.3
In this video, the administrator for CHIME, an award-winning public charter school in California, explains why the school is a model for full inclusion. Why does this institute embrace a fully inclusive approach for teaching and learning?

Legal Foundations

Learning Objective 1.3 Summarize the legal foundations, litigation, and legislation concerning students with disabilities, such as the Individuals with Disabilities Education Act, the Vocational Rehabilitation Act (Section 504), and the Americans with Disabilities Act (ADA).

In the years following World War II, political change, litigation, and resulting legislation began to emerge that increased the inclusion of all groups of people in U.S. society. Most significant was the civil rights movement, which primarily addressed the rights of African Americans in U.S. society. This movement influenced the ideas on which much litigation and legislation involving individuals with disabilities are based. In the *Brown v. Board of Education* (1954) decision, the Supreme Court ruled that it was unlawful to discriminate against any group of people. With respect to schoolchildren, the Court ruled that the concept of "separate-but-equal" educational facilities for children of different races was inherently unequal. The justification for this ruling was found in the 14th Amendment to the U.S. Constitution, which states that individuals cannot be deprived of life, liberty, or property without due process of law.

LEGAL PROCEEDINGS AND LEGISLATION

People with disabilities also began to be identified as a group whose rights had been denied. In the years following *Brown v. Board of Education*, court cases were decided that underlined the rights of individuals with disabilities to a free, appropriate education. Other cases supported nondiscriminatory special education placement of individuals from nonwhite groups in the United States. Some of the important court cases relating to individuals with disabilities demonstrate a progression of increasing rights for these individuals (see also Murdick et al., 2014; Wright & Wright, 2007; Yell, 2019; Yell & Katsiyannis, 2019):

- *1954: Brown v. Board of Education* (Kansas). The Supreme Court determined that "separate-but-equal" education is illegal.
- *1970: Diana v. State Board of Education* (California). The court ruled that children cannot be placed in special education based on culturally biased tests.
- *1972: Pennsylvania Association for Retarded Children (PARC) v. Commonwealth of Pennsylvania* and *Mills v. Board of Education* (District of Columbia). These cases established the right to education for students with disabilities and found that denial of education violates the 14th Amendment.
- *1977: Larry P. v. Riles* (California). The court ruled that the use of standardized IQ tests for placement into special education classes for students with "educable mental retardation" was discriminatory.
- *1982: Board of Education v. Rowley* (New York). The Supreme Court defined "free and appropriate education" and directed that public schools must provide appropriate special education services.
- *1988: Honig v. Doe* (California). This decision was concerned with extensive suspensions of students with emotional disturbances from school for aggressive behavior that the court determined was disability related. The court ruled that a suspension of longer than 10 days was effectively a change in placement, requiring all the necessary procedures governing a change in placement.
- *1992: Oberti v. Board of Education of the Borough of Clementon School District* (New Jersey). A federal district court ruled that a self-contained special education class was not the LRE for a student with Down syndrome. The court ruled that school districts were obligated to consider regular class placement first, with supplementary aids and services, before considering alternative placements.

Along with this litigation, laws began to be passed that provided further support for the rights of students with disabilities. Some of these laws are summarized in Figure 1.1. In the following sections, some of the most significant legislation involving individuals with disabilities is described (see also Murdick et al., 2014; Rothstein & Johnson, 2021; Yell, 2019). This legislation includes **Section 504** of the **Vocational Rehabilitation Act (Section 504)**, the

Figure 1.1 History of Relevant Legislation

1973	Section 504—Rehabilitation Act of 1973 (Section 504), U.S.C. Section 794: Recipients of federal funds cannot discriminate on the basis of disability.
1975	Education for All Handicapped Children Act (EAHCA) (PL 94–142) (IDEA), 20 U.S.C. Sections 1400–1461: This law requires, and provides support to, states to implement a plan to provide free education and appropriate related services (on an individualized basis) to students with disabilities, including due process provisions. It requires individualized education programs for each student served under this law. This law was amended in 1983, 1986, 1990, 1997, and 2004. The 1990 amendments also renamed this law the Individuals with Disabilities Education Act.
1977	Final regulations of EAHCA are passed.
1978	Gifted and Talented Children's Education Act. This act provides financial incentives for state and local educational agencies to develop programs for gifted and talented students.
1983	Amendments to the Education of the Handicapped Act (EHA) (PL 98–199) (IDEA): These amendments mandate states to collect data on students with disabilities exiting systems and to address transition needs of secondary students with disabilities. In addition, they give incentives to states to provide services to infants and preschoolers with disabilities.
1984	Developmental Disabilities Assistance and Bill of Rights Acts (DD Act) (PL 98–527): These acts provide for the development of employment-related training activities for adults with disabilities.
1984	Perkins Act, 20 U.S.C. 2301, 2332–34: This act mandates that 10% of all vocational education funding must be for students with disabilities. Vocational education should be provided in the least-restrictive environment; secondary support is provided for students with disabilities.
1986	(EHA) Amendments (PL 99–457) (IDEA): These amendments encourage states to develop comprehensive services for infants and toddlers (birth through age 2) with disabilities and to expand services for preschool children (ages 3–5). After the 1990–1991 school year, all states must provide free and appropriate education to all 3- to 5-year-olds with disabilities or forfeit federal assistance for preschool funding.
1986	Rehabilitation Acts Amendments (PL 99–506) (Section 504): These amendments provide for the development of supported employment programs for adults with disabilities.

Sources based on Murdick et al., 2014; Wright & Wright, 2007; Yell, 2019; Yell & Katsiyannis, 2019.

Americans with Disabilities Act (ADA), and the most significant law for special education, the Individuals with Disabilities Education Act (IDEA).

SECTION 504

Section 504 of the Vocational Rehabilitation Act of 1973 (reauthorized as the Carl D. Perkins Career and Technical Education Act of 2006; U.S. Department of Education [DOE], 2006) is a civil rights law that prevents discrimination against individuals with disabilities by any institution that receives federal funds and provides for a FAPE. Some private schools that do not receive federal funding may be exempt from Section 504. This law applies both to schools and to the workforce. Section 504 provides for equal opportunities in all aspects of education. Students may not be classified as disabled according to the IDEA guidelines, but they must demonstrate a significant learning problem that affects their ability to function in school. Under Section 504, disability is considered to be an impairment, physical or mental, that substantially limits a major life activity (Lazarus et al., 2009; DOE, 2006). Some students who may not be served under IDEA because they do not meet the definitional requirements of one of the IDEA disability categories can still obtain services under Section 504 (Zirkel, 2009). For example, some students with ADHD, as well as some students who require modifications for severe allergies or asthma, may be covered under this law. Other types of disabilities likely covered under Section 504, but not IDEA, might include the following (Smith, 2002):

- Students who had been placed in special education programs but have transitioned out
- Students thought to be socially maladjusted or who have a history of alcohol or drug abuse
- Students who carry infectious diseases such as **acquired immunodeficiency syndrome (AIDS)**.

Students can be referred for Section 504 services by anyone but are usually referred by teachers or parents/caregivers. If a group of knowledgeable school personnel believes the child is eligible, the school must then conduct an evaluation to determine eligibility and the nature of services needed to ensure a FAPE. The decision is based on professional judgment rather than test scores and numerical indicators. If a student is considered eligible, the law does not provide funding; however, it does require that school personnel create a written plan that will help accommodate these individual needs and provide an accessible environment. Accommodation plans can include a statement of student strengths and weaknesses, a list of accommodations to be implemented, and designation of the person(s) responsible for implementation. Accommodations are usually inexpensive, commonsense modifications intended to provide nondiscrimination and FAPE (Smith, 2002).

AMERICANS WITH DISABILITIES ACT

The **Americans with Disabilities Act (ADA)** was signed into law in 1990 and mandated that individuals with disabilities should be provided with "reasonable accommodations" in the workplace and that such individuals could not be discriminated against. ADA also included protections for individuals enrolled in colleges and universities. Adults with disabilities attending universities are also entitled to appropriate modifications in classes. These modifications, in many ways, parallel those made in public schools in compliance with IDEA. Major components of the ADA are given in Figure 1.2.

The ADA is of particular significance because of its aim to maximize the employment potential of millions of Americans with disabilities. It can be considered an important extension of IDEA because it provides for reasonable accommodations and nondiscriminatory treatment of individuals with disabilities beyond the high school years.

INDIVIDUALS WITH DISABILITIES EDUCATION ACT

IDEA is the major special education law. Originally signed in 1975 as the Education for All Handicapped Children Act, IDEA has been amended several times since then, most recently in 2004 as the Individuals with Disabilities Education Improvement Act, as summarized in Figure 1.3. The most important provision in IDEA is that all children, from 3 through 21 years of

Figure 1.2 Major Components of ADA

- Employers may not discriminate on the basis of disability.
- Employers may not ask if applicant has a disability.
- "Reasonable accommodations" must be provided in the workplace.
- New buses must be made accessible.
- Most communities must provide transportation.
- Rail service must accommodate individuals with disabilities within 20 years.
- Public locations—hotels, stores, and restaurants—must be accessible.
- State and local governments may not discriminate.
- Telephone companies must provide adapted communication options for the deaf.

Source: U.S. Department of Justice (2022).

Figure 1.3 IDEA 2004 Amendments

Content of IEPs
- Present level of performance must include the "child's academic achievement and functional performance."
- Annual goals must be measurable.
- Short-term objectives are required only for children who take alternative assessments.
- IEPs must describe how progress will be measured and when reports will be issued.

Research-based practice
- Statements supporting special education services must be based on peer-reviewed research.

Accommodations and alternative assessments
- Statements indicating the need for individual accommodations for testing and alternative statewide assessments must be provided.
- Justification for participation in alternative assessments must be provided.

IEP meetings
- The teacher's attendance may be waived (1) if the teacher's curriculum area is not addressed or (2) if a report based on the curriculum area is submitted prior to the meeting and is approved by the student's parents and the local education agency (LEA).
- Fifteen states may apply for an optional multiyear IEP pilot program. This means that, in some cases, annual IEP meetings may not be required and may be conducted no less than every 3 years.

Discipline
- If students violate a code of conduct at school, they may be suspended for up to 10 days.
- If the behavior was related to the disability, a functional behavior assessment and behavior intervention plan must be completed for the child.
- If the behavior was unrelated to the disability, students may be suspended for more than 10 days, like any other student in the school.
- If students are suspended for more than 10 days, they must be provided with a free and appropriate education, and the IEP team must identify alternative placements.

Identification of learning disabilities
- Schools can use a *response-to-intervention* (see Chapter 3) model to determine eligibility for learning disabilities.

Early intervention funding
- Local Education Agencies (LEAs) may apply some of its special education funding to develop coordinated early intervention services, which may include students not identified for special education but in need of academic or behavioral support.

Special education teacher licensure
- A highly qualified teacher is one who holds full teaching credentials required by a state in conformance with the *No Child Left Behind Act*. Special education teachers who teach in core subject areas must also hold the full teaching credentials in those subject areas.

Sources: Based on IDEA (2004), Mandlawitz (2006), and Wright and Wright (2005).

age, regardless of type or severity of disability, are entitled to a FAPE (see Yell & Crockett, 2011). Discretionary assistance is also provided to develop interagency programs for all young children with disabilities from birth to 3 years of age. This provision overrides previous legislation and decisions that limit the attendance of students with disabilities in public schools. Overall, six major principles have remained in the law throughout its amendments (Murdick et al., 2014; Yell et al., 2011). These principles are as follows:

1. *Zero reject.* This principle requires that no child with a disability can be excluded from public education.
2. *Nondiscriminatory testing.* Schools are required to use a variety of nondiscriminatory methods to determine whether a student has a disability and, if so, whether special education is required. Testing must not discriminate on the basis of race, culture, or ethnicity, and it must be administered in the student's native language. A variety

of measures is required so that placement decisions are not made on the basis of a single test score. Furthermore, the law is intended to address multicultural issues, as described in the *Diversity, Equity, and Inclusion in the Classroom* feature.

3. *Free and appropriate education.* Students who have been referred to special education must have an **individualized education program (IEP)** that details their individual learning needs and mandates appropriate services. Short- and long-term goals and objectives for students are listed explicitly in their IEPs.
4. *Least restrictive environment.* Students with disabilities are entitled to be educated with their nondisabled peers to the greatest extent possible.
5. *Due process.* Due process must be followed in all placement decisions and changes in placement. Records are to be kept confidential, and parents and caregivers are to be involved in all aspects of the planning and placement process.
6. *Parent participation.* Schools must collaborate with parents and caregivers in the design and implementation of special education services (see also Rodriguez et al., 2014; Staples & Diliberto, 2010).

Along with these six common principles, several additions have been made to the original law:

1. *Transition services.* All 16-year-old students with disabilities must be provided with a statement of transition-services needs in their IEPs. These services, which must be included in the IEP by age 16, are intended to facilitate the student's transition from school to community, vocational programs, college, or employment. The transition plan can involve professionals from other agencies, such as social or vocational services. Transition planning conferences are also specified for the transition from infant and toddler programs to preschool programs. Check with your state because many states now require transition plans at a younger age.
2. *Early childhood education.* Amendments to the Education for All Handicapped Children Act (now IDEA) in 1986 and 1990 provided for services to infants, toddlers, and preschoolers with disabilities. Very young children (younger than 3) are entitled to an **individualized family service plan (IFSP)**, which replaces the IEP and takes family needs and responsibilities into account. Necessary components of the IFSP are listed in Table 1.2. States are required to take action to locate as many young children as possible who may require special education services.
3. *Assessments.* Students with disabilities must participate in general state- and district-wide assessment programs. If students cannot participate in state- and district-wide assessments, justification must be provided, and these students must participate in alternative assessments.
4. *Early intervention services.* The 2004 amendments to IDEA specify that not more than 15% of the funding that the local education authority receives from the federal government can be allocated to programming for students (K–12, with an emphasis on K–3) not currently identified for special education but who need additional academic and behavioral support to succeed in the general education environment (U.S. Department of Education, Office of Special Education and Rehabilitative Services, 2006). These services can include those referred to as **response to intervention (RTI)** or **multi-tiered systems of support (MTTS)** services.

TABLE 1.2 Necessary Components of the Individualized Family Service Plan

1.	A current statement of the child's functioning levels
2.	A current statement of the family's needs and strengths in relation to the child with disabilities
3.	A statement of the major expected outcomes, including a timeline
4.	A statement of the specific services to be provided to meet the individual needs of the child and the family
5.	The initiation and anticipated duration dates for services
6.	Designation of a case manager
7.	A statement of the transition steps from infant early intervention services to preschool services

Diversity, Equity, and Inclusion in the Classroom

Multicultural Considerations for the Identification of Individuals with Disabilities

Legal Assistance

Federal legislation has provided protections and guidance for the equitable identification of individuals with disabilities. These assurances are to guarantee that only individuals who have been identified as having disabilities receive special education services. It is especially important that individuals from culturally and linguistically diverse backgrounds are not overrepresented in special education programs. The following protections are part of IDEA:

- *Disproportionality requirement:* States must devise plans to prevent overidentification and provide data to document whether disproportionality by race is occurring with respect to identification and placement of individuals with disabilities.
- *Development, review, and revisions of IEPs:* Consider the language needs as related to the IEP for individuals with limited English proficiency.
- *Evaluation procedures:*
  - Test materials are not to be discriminatory against races or cultures.
  - Tests must be administered in the individual's native language.
  - Test materials for individuals with limited English proficiency must be used to measure a disability and not the individual's English skills.
  - Tests must be valid and reliable and administered by trained professionals.
  - No single procedure can be used as a sole criterion for determining whether a disability exists.
- *Eligibility determination:* An individual may not be eligible if the only difficulty appears to be limited English proficiency.

The U.S. Office of Civil Rights also provides guidance and protections and is the compliance monitor for prereferral practices that may also influence overrepresentation of individuals from culturally and linguistically diverse backgrounds. These protections include the following:

- *Section 504 of the Rehabilitation Act of 1973 and Title II of the Americans with Disabilities Act:* Provide protection against discrimination for individuals with disabilities and those perceived as having disabilities or those who have been misclassified.
- *Title VI of the Civil Rights Act:* Provides protection from discrimination based on national origin, color, or race.

Although these federal legislations are to guide school policies, practices, and procedures relevant to disproportionality, they may not be interpreted or applied equitably by states and local education agencies (Sullivan & Osher, 2019). One example is how states may be inconsistent in how they use numerical, descriptive, and/or contextual data to determine significant disproportionality. Local education agencies should be proactive and monitor the fidelity of related procedures and practices, including the identification of students with disabilities and the implementation of a tiered intervention framework. When districts are out of compliance with federal laws and have an overrepresentation of individuals from culturally or linguistically diverse backgrounds, they may become involved in legal actions and asked to provide a plan to correct the problems.

Discuss: What challenges do you think you will face when teaching a diverse population?

NO CHILD LEFT BEHIND ACT AND EVERY STUDENT SUCCEEDS ACT

The **No Child Left Behind Act (NCLB)** of 2001, a reauthorization of the 1965 **Elementary and Secondary Education Act (ESEA)**, was not written specifically for students with disabilities. However, many aspects of the legislation had important implications for students with disabilities (Chrismer et al., 2006).

The law required that all children be tested in grades 3–8, in reading and math, through tests developed by the states. Schools must demonstrate **adequate yearly progress (AYP)** toward the goal of 100% proficiency in reading, math, and science for all students. Schools must demonstrate that students make progress in equal increments toward this goal, that is, that they are making steady, equivalent gains from year to year. Schools that fail to make AYP for 2 consecutive years must offer parents and caregivers of the students the option to transfer to another public school, and the districts must pay the cost of transportation (if allowed under state law). The school district must provide technical assistance to the school. If schools fail to make AYP for more than 2 consecutive years, further corrective measures can be taken (**Council for Exceptional Children [CEC]**, 2002). Other aspects of the law include compensatory education grants (Title I), bilingual and immigrant education programs, and standards and provisions for teacher training and recruitment of "highly qualified" teachers who hold full state certification or licensure (Wright et al., 2004). IDEA has aligned itself with features of the NCLB, including AYP, highly qualified personnel, and **evidence-based practices (EPBs)** (Crockett, 2011; Yell et al., 2006).

In 2015, another reauthorization of ESEA, referred to as the **Every Student Succeeds Act (ESSA)**, replaced NCLB. According to this new legislation, the highly qualified teacher requirement was eliminated and replaced with state certificate and licensure requirements. States can choose their own academic standards and can develop their own accountability systems to identify and support struggling schools, not necessarily based solely on federally mandated testing. The federal government provides support for struggling schools but may not prescribe specific interventions that schools must use (National School Boards Association, 2016). The act also places a statewide cap of 1% for students with the most significant cognitive disabilities to participate in alternate assessments, aligned to alternate academic achievement standards.

Beyond the passing of IDEA, there has been litigation surrounding the IDEA principle of FAPE. In 1982, the *Board of Education v. Rowley* decision established the standard for school districts to provide FAPE. Three decades later, legislation extended the *Rowley* decision by changing the interpretation of FAPE. In 2017, the *Endrew F. v. Douglas County School District* decision clarified the *level* of educational benefit that school districts must provide students with disabilities in order to be in compliance with FAPE. The Supreme Court ruled that a school must offer an IEP that is "reasonably calculated to enable a child to make progress appropriate in light of the child's circumstance." This significant ruling means that the IEP team should have high expectations for the progress of the student and design annual goals that are both realistic and ambitious so that the measurable progress toward those goals over a 12-month span is meaningful.

COMMON CORE STATE STANDARDS

Both NCLB and ESSA made reference to high standards for student achievement. State education standards have been employed since the early 1990s. By the early 2000s, each state had developed and adopted its own academic standards that identified specifically what students in grades 3–8 and high school should be able to do, in compliance with federal regulations. However, each state also had its own definition of proficiency, which led to disparities in standards across states. Because of this, many states joined in the effort to develop the **Common Core State Standards (CCSS)** in 2009 (National Governors Association Center for Best Practices & Council of Chief State School Officers, 2016). Over time, most states have adopted these standards, which address achievement in English language arts and mathematics from kindergarten through high school. The CCSS note that students with disabilities are expected to meet the same high standards, although with needed supports such as instructional supports based on **universal design for learning (UDL)** principles (see Chapter 6), assistive technology, and instructional accommodations, as described throughout this book. The CCSS are described with respect to specific topics in subsequent chapters; for a complete listing of the standards, see *http://corestandards.org*.

One important feature of federal legislation is that it is constantly changing. Some technological approaches for keeping abreast of federal legislation are described in the *Apps for Education* feature.

Apps for Education

Federal Government Updates

One way to keep abreast of the changes in federal legislation is to check regularly the U.S. Department of Education (DOE) website (www.ed.gov). This website contains a wealth of frequently updated information as well as links to relevant research and legislation sites. For example, a link to the Every Student Succeeds Act (formerly the No Child Left Behind Act) provides an overview of the act, which was signed in December 2015, as well as commonly asked questions and answers that are presented in an easy-to-understand format, links to specific state-level contacts, information on how states can apply for waivers in the law, links for parents and caregivers and for educators and policymakers, newsletters, and even slide presentations that emphasize key points.

Additional helpful websites linked to the DOE page are directly relevant to special education initiatives. These sites are the Office of Special Education and Rehabilitative Services and the Office of Special Education Programs. These sites contain information such as current special education initiatives, including the recent IDEA legislation; possible changes in the procedures for identification of learning disabilities; recent research findings from projects funded by the DOE; model programs and personnel preparation; and the annual reports to Congress indicating the status of special education programs across the country with respect to numbers of children served, from birth to age 21. The Library of Congress website (https://loc.gov) allows individuals to research federal legislative information such as the Congressional Record, bills, and congressional activities. Information about sponsored special education research can also be found on the websites of the Institute of Education Sciences (https://ies.ed.gov) and the What Works Clearinghouse (WWC; https://ies.ed.gov/ncee/wwc). The WWC site also contains a database of research revealing evidence-based practices, practice guides, intervention reports, single-study reviews, and other reviews.

The Council for Exceptional Children (CEC) website (www.cec.sped.org) has numerous updates and interpretations of federal legislation relevant to special education. Check the CEC website for updates to this information and the CEC's journals *Exceptional Children* and *Teaching Exceptional Children* for the most recent research and teaching articles. The CEC has numerous disability- and area-specific divisions, such as the Division for Learning Disabilities, that have their own journals (e.g., *Learning Disabilities Research and Practice*) and websites (e.g., http://teachingld.org) that contain a wealth of disability-specific information, from research to practice to advocacy.

Apps are available that describe relevant legislation or funding opportunities. The *Americans with Disabilities Act Reference* app (Connecting People Software) provides the actual bill in sections and is easy to use. The *Federal Register* (Allogy Interactive) and *Federal Register Mag* (PressPad Sp) apps provide regular listings of all federal funding opportunities and notices.

- www.ed.gov (U.S. Department of Education)
- https://loc.gov (Library of Congress)
- https://ies.ed.gov (Institute of Education Sciences)
- https://ies.ed.gov/ncee/wcc/ (What Works Clearinghouse)
- https://exceptionalchildren.org (Council for Exceptional Children)
- https://teachingld.org (Teaching LD)

Models of Service Delivery

Learning Objective 1.4 Contrast the models of service delivery and the continuum of services available to students with disabilities.

THE CONTINUUM OF SERVICES

The initial emphasis of legal actions was to provide access to educational services for students with disabilities. Once access was obtained, the focus shifted to the setting and placement of students with disabilities during education. Most placement guidelines emphasized the availability of a range of services and programs, commonly referred to as a **continuum of services**, within the LRE for students with disabilities. *LRE* is defined in IDEA as meaning that students with disabilities should be educated in a setting that resembles the general education program as closely as possible while simultaneously meeting the unique needs of each individual with disabilities (Rozalski et al., 2011; Zigmond, 2015). The basic model of a continuum of services ranges from full-time placement in the general education classroom to full-time placement in a non–public school facility, on a day or residential basis, based on student need. As the needs of the individual with a disability increase, the LRE may be further removed from the general education class on the continuum of services. Figure 1.4 presents a sample of the range of placement options.

WHERE ARE MOST STUDENTS WITH DISABILITIES SERVED?

Most students with disabilities are served in public schools with their nondisabled peers in the placement options, Levels 1–5. In other words, these students receive their education in their local public schools. Most students with mild disabilities, including those with learning disabilities, mild intellectual disabilities, speech and language disabilities, and serious emotional disturbance, are currently served in Levels 1–4. That is, these students spend some, if not all, of the day in the general education classroom along with students without disabilities. The general education teacher is responsible for their education for some, if not all, of the day, depending on the amount of time spent in that general education class. Table 1.1 provides a listing of disability categories and the corresponding proportion of students currently served outside general education classrooms.

WHAT ARE GENERAL EDUCATION CLASSROOM AND CONSULTATION SERVICES?

In some cases, students may be served in general education classes by general education teachers. Some special services may be provided by a **consultant** who works with individuals as needed. Special education teachers frequently provide consultative services to general education teachers. This consultation is intended to provide assistance and ideas for how to teach and work with the students with disabilities who are placed in general education classes. Although special education teachers may not work directly with identified students, they may meet regularly with general education teachers, review assessment and progress data, and make specific

Figure 1.4 Sample Continuum of Services: From Least Restrictive to Most Restrictive

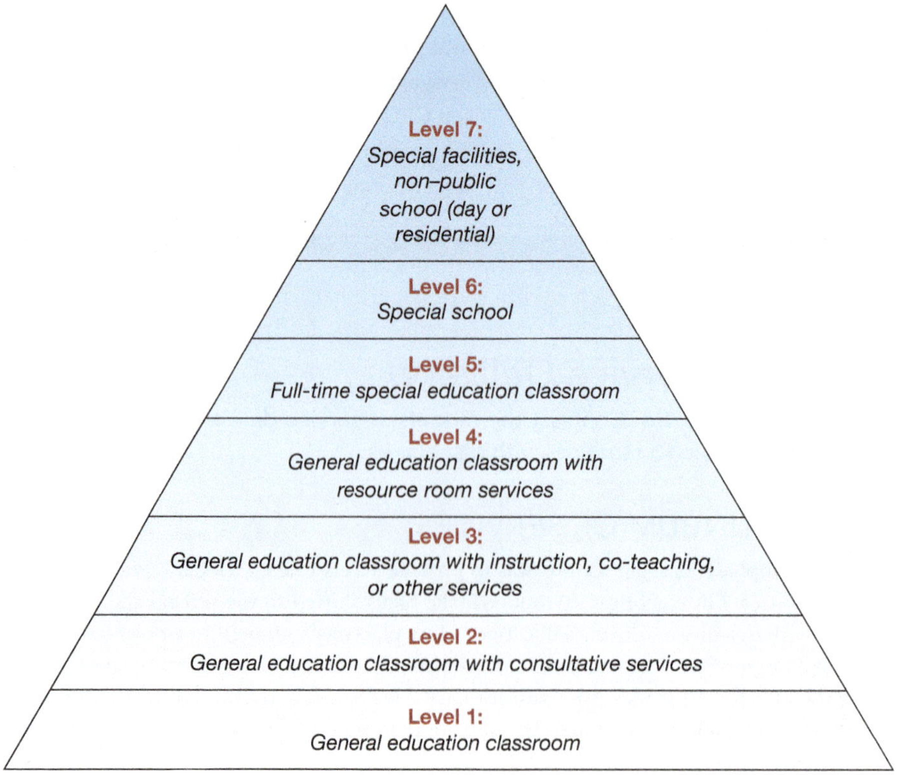

recommendations for addressing individual learning needs. These students would be receiving services at Levels 1 or 2 of the continuum-of-services model.

In other cases, special education teachers, classroom assistants, or paraprofessionals may deliver instruction to students with diverse learning needs in the general education classroom. Paraprofessionals are individuals who support the special education teacher, student(s) with disabilities, and/or other teachers in the school (see Chapter 2). Students with disabilities still receive all their instruction in the general education classroom, but it may be delivered by different teachers or supported by paraprofessionals. Teachers collaborate and share instructional responsibilities in one of several **co-teaching** models (Knackendoffel et al., 2018). For example, a special education teacher may lead instruction for small groups of elementary students with diverse learning needs during classroom reading instruction. At the secondary level, the special education teacher may co-teach with a general education teacher in a high school biology class. The two teachers share teaching responsibilities, with the special education teacher focusing on strategies for addressing individual learning needs. These students would be receiving services at Level 3 of the continuum-of-services model.

In the continuum model, teachers adapt instruction and classroom procedures to meet the learning needs of individual students. This approach to teaching is referred to as **differentiated instruction** (Tomlinson, 2017) and could be employed in any level of service delivery.

WHAT ARE RESOURCE AND SELF-CONTAINED SERVICES?

Special education teachers also provide instruction in resource and self-contained classrooms within the public schools. In a *resource room* model, students with disabilities leave the general education class for a designated time period to visit the resource room and receive specialized instruction in areas such as language, reading, and math. For example, Keira is a sixth-grader who has been classified as having learning disabilities. Keira is functioning intellectually within the average ability range, but she has reading, spelling, and written language skills at an upper-third-grade level. The multidisciplinary team recommended that Keira should receive specialized instruction in reading, written communication, and spelling with a special education teacher for 1.5 hours per day in her school's resource room. This means that Keira would be receiving services at Level 4 of the continuum-of-services model.

Most of her school day will be spent in the LRE of her general education class with Mrs. Gomez. Mrs. Gomez will be responsible for Keira's instruction for the entire time that she is in the general education class. This might even include making some adaptations in instructional procedures and assignments to accommodate Keira's individual learning needs in the general education sixth-grade classroom. For example, during content-area classes, Mrs. Gomez will need to provide adapted reading and study materials appropriate to Keira's skill levels. During her 1.5 hours in the resource room, Keira will receive instruction from Mr. Halleran, the special education teacher in the same school. This resource room arrangement represents the LRE to meet Keira's individual needs in reading, written communication, and spelling while maintaining her placement in her general education class for the majority of the school day.

The resource room model is sometimes referred to as a *pull-out* model, indicating that students with disabilities are pulled out of the general education class for special education instruction. In a *self-contained* model of instruction (Level 5 of the continuum-of-services model), students with disabilities receive all or most of their classroom instruction from special education teachers. Even in these models, however, students with disabilities often have opportunities to interact with their nondisabled peers during such activities as art, music, recess, lunch, and assemblies in elementary schools and electives such as physical education, band, and drama in secondary settings.

SPECIAL SCHOOLS AND SPECIAL FACILITIES

In some cases, the need for specialized instruction is considered so significant that a special school or other facility is considered necessary. In some cases, special public schools are established to focus specifically on the unique learning needs of the students. In other cases, students are sent to non–public schools, either as special day schools or as residential schools. These students would be receiving services at Level 6 or 7 of the continuum-of-services model. The numbers of special schools or other facilities have declined since the early years of IDEA, as traditional public schools have accommodated more students with disabilities and other diverse learning needs within their educational programs.

Charter schools receive government funding but function independently of the public school systems in which they are located. In some cases, charter schools are privately owned. In some states, charter schools are linked to **local education agencies (LEAs)** whereas in other states they may be considered separate from LEAs (National Center for Technology Innovation, 2011).

WHAT OTHER RELATED SERVICES ARE AVAILABLE?

Students with disabilities are also eligible to receive related services if it is determined that the students require these services to benefit from special education. According to IDEA, related services may include parent or caregiver counseling and training, physical therapy, occupational therapy, school health services, or special transportation. This means that in addition to receiving special services along the continuum of services for a primary disability area, some students may also be eligible to receive additional related services. Related services may be delivered to individuals with disabilities in any of the setting options. Although described as "related" services, in many cases, these services may be of critical importance in attending to the diverse learning needs of individual students (Downing, 2004). For example, Michael, a student with intellectual disabilities, receives physical therapy in addition to his educational program to meet his individual needs; Janice requires special transportation services to accommodate her wheelchair and adaptive physical education, which are provided as related services.

The continuum-of-services and related-services models have been effectively applied throughout the history of IDEA. However, over this same time period, there have been recommendations regarding how all or most students with disabilities could be more easily served entirely within the general education classroom, often referred to as the full-inclusion movement.

FULL INCLUSION

Over the past three decades, the full-inclusion movement came to the forefront (Fuchs & Fuchs, 1994). *Full inclusion* has been referred to as placing and serving all students with disabilities, regardless of severity or type of disability, entirely within the general education classroom for the entire school day.

Consider the case of Keira, our sixth-grader with learning disabilities. If Keira were placed in a full-inclusion classroom, Mrs. Gomez, her general education teacher, would have Keira in her room all day, every day with all of the other sixth-grade students. Mrs. Gomez would be primarily responsible for all of Keira's instruction and for making adaptations appropriate for addressing her learning disabilities. In some full-inclusion models, Mr. Halleran, the special education teacher, would consult with Mrs. Gomez and provide ideas for her to use in teaching Keira in her IEP need areas. In other full-inclusion models, Mr. Halleran might go into Mrs. Gomez's room and teach Keira reading, spelling, and writing in that room. In this model, instruction with Mr. Halleran and Keira may occur at a small table, perhaps with other students with individual needs, while other groups of students meet for literacy activities. In still other full-inclusion models, Mr. Halleran may co-teach with Mrs. Gomez for part or all of the school day. During co-teaching, they would work collaboratively on planning and implementing instruction for the entire class. In any of these full-inclusion models, however, Keira remains in the general education class with her nondisabled peers all day.

Pearson eTextbook

Video Example 1.4

The students in this inclusive general education setting are learning about parts of a seed. What strategies did the teacher use so the student with a visual impairment could fully participate in the lesson?

As might be expected, debate surrounds the issue of full inclusion. It is important to remember that virtually all educational professionals recommend placement in general education classes for students with disabilities and other diverse learning needs; the disagreement usually centers on the extent to which students should be placed in general education settings. Both proponents of full inclusion and proponents of a continuum of services have articulated their positions, which are summarized in Figure 1.5 (see also Fuchs & Fuchs, 1994; Huefner, 2015; Kauffman et al., 2011; Lipsky & Gartner, 1997, 2012; Zigmond, 2015; Zigmond & Kloo, 2011).

As can be seen, the issue of full inclusion versus a continuum of services is still under debate. Professional organizations and advocates do not always agree on the best service options (e.g., Andrews et al., 2011). General education students have expressed various opinions (e.g., Siperstein et al., 2007); parents or caregivers also seem to be divided between those who favor specialized placement and services and those who favor integration in the general education class (de Boer et al., 2010).

Figure 1.5 Arguments of Proponents of Full Inclusion and Proponents of a Continuum of Services

Proponents of Full Inclusion	Proponents of a Continuum of Services
1. *Full inclusion is a civil right.* Students with disabilities have a right to be educated alongside their nondisabled peers. Separate educational settings are inherently not equal. 2. *Full inclusion reduces stigma.* Harmful stigmatizing effects may be associated with students attending special schools or special classrooms. 3. *Full inclusion is beneficial.* Students in full-inclusion classrooms improve their interactions with others, learn to communicate better, develop better social skills, and increase their friendships. 4. *Full inclusion is more efficient.* Fully included students avoid the disruptive and time-consuming effects of being "pulled out" of the general education class to receive special services. Full inclusion guarantees access to the general education curriculum. 5. *Full inclusion promotes equality.* Including all students in the same classroom is simply the most fair and equitable solution to the problem of placement. Including all students in the same classroom actively promotes the idea of equality.	1. *A continuum-of-service options is necessary.* Many services needed by students with disabilities are not usually available in the general education classroom. Court decisions have usually placed more emphasis on "appropriate education" than "least-restrictive" components. 2. *The regular classrooms may also be stigmatizing.* Special services, such as speech therapy, physical therapy, or specialized reading instruction, may be stigmatizing when undertaken in the company of general education peers. 3. *General education teachers may not be prepared for full inclusion.* Many general education teachers lack the necessary time and training to make full inclusion a success. 4. *General education classrooms may lack appropriate resources.* Students with disabilities may require materials at lower reading levels, braillers, speech synthesizers, specialized computers, or specialized training materials that general education classrooms lack. 5. *Research evidence does not support the superiority of full inclusion.* Although research data are to some extent equivocal, clear evidence of the superiority of full-inclusion placements is presently lacking.

WHAT DOES THIS DEBATE MEAN FOR TEACHERS?

Teachers need to be aware of the arguments for and against full inclusion. As a teacher, you also must become familiar with your own legal responsibilities. For example, what are general education classroom teachers' legal responsibilities with respect to the IEP when all instruction is implemented in the general education classroom? Other questions, although not necessarily legal in nature, may be relevant to the spirit of the law.

Teachers should approach the issue in a practical way, with respect to their own school and district. Specific questions to ask about full inclusion include the following:

- What are the school- and district-wide policies and procedures regarding full inclusion?
- What are my obligations as a general educator with respect to the IEP, IEP meetings, case conferences, assessment procedures, annual review meetings, and meetings with parents and caregivers?
- What types of modifications are expected, and is there a "reasonableness" standard associated with the number and types of modifications expected?
- Is this the best placement option for the particular student with disabilities?
- How will we evaluate whether or not this placement and this set of accommodations are successful?

Pearson eTextbook

Video Example 1.5

The teachers in this video are part of the faculty of CHIME, a charter school in Los Angeles, California, that is fully inclusive. What advantages do these teachers see to teaching in a school with an inclusive approach to education?

- What resources are available to assist me in working with the student with disabilities?
- How can I receive necessary training for working with students in specific disability areas?
- What kinds of records and documentation should I maintain?

Answers to questions such as these can help determine the best placement options for students with disabilities.

CLASSROOM SCENARIOS

Volunteerism

In a small rural elementary school, Mrs. Ghardisi, the fourth-grade teacher, volunteered to take all of the fourth-grade students with disabilities into her classroom. Because she worked well with Mrs. Rana, the special education teacher, she went to her principal and said, "Next year, I would like to have all five of the fourth-graders who have disabilities in my room. They can still go to the resource room for part of the day, but during science class and other content classes, I would like to have all of them. Also, Mrs. Rana and I would like to team-teach during science class when all five children are included."

That summer, Mrs. Ghardisi and Mrs. Rana met and discussed curriculum and planning issues for their science class. They both had high expectations for all students. Mrs. Ghardisi was considered the "content expert," whereas Mrs. Rana was the "adaptation expert." When the school year began, they reviewed each students' IEP and then met at least once a week after school to co-plan the activities for each science class. Plans included any modifications and/or adaptations needed to the content or delivery of instruction for the students with disabilities. Three of the five students had a specific annual goal on their IEP related to improving their performance on comprehension questions after independently reading an expository passage. Knowing how new vocabulary can impede how well a student comprehends text, Mrs. Ghardisi would prioritize the essential vocabulary for each science unit. Then, when working with the students outside of the team-taught science class, Mrs. Rana would pre-teach these new vocabulary words to build students' familiarity with the terms in advance of the hands-on science lesson. Mrs. Rana would also reinforce the content by finding relevant books from the library written at the students' reading level. Mrs. Ghardisi and Mrs. Rana had a good working relationship that enabled them to solve problems as they arose. Because they planned together, they took turns presenting information and monitoring students during class. They were both enthusiastic and worked hard to design adaptations so that the five students with disabilities could be active participants. They viewed science as an opportunity to have fun, and their students appeared to really enjoy science.

Mandated Inclusion

In a suburban middle school, Ms. Irby, the special education teacher, was told by her building principal 2 days before school began that she was going to implement inclusive instruction for one period per day during the coming year. She was told she would be working with six students with learning disabilities in Mrs. Toro's sixth-period, seventh-grade history class on a daily basis.

Unfortunately, Mrs. Toro, the history teacher, had not been informed by the principal that Ms. Irby was going to be team-teaching with her. When Ms. Irby went to see Mrs. Toro and explained the situation, Mrs. Toro appeared visibly shaken. Mrs. Toro also questioned if two teachers in one classroom was an efficient use of the school's resources.

QUESTIONS FOR REFLECTION

1. What teacher attributes contribute to the positive working relationship described between Mrs. Ghardisi and Mrs. Rana?
2. Why do you think Mrs. Toro was so visibly shaken? How would you have reacted?
3. What are some ways to improve the feelings of self-confidence and self-efficacy of teachers moving to more inclusive settings?

Research Highlight

Teacher Attitudes Toward Inclusion

Teacher attitudes have been considered fundamental to successful inclusion (Cullen et al., 2010). But what are teacher attitudes, and have they changed over time? Scruggs and colleagues (2011) and Scruggs (2012) summarized the results of 61 survey, comparative, and qualitative investigations of teacher attitudes published between 1996 and 2010, and they compared these with the results of a previous investigation (Scruggs & Mastropieri, 1996) that studied attitudes from 1958 through 1995. For the survey research, it was reported that 62.8% of teachers (vs. 65.0% from the 1996 investigation) overall supported the concept of inclusion, and 61.4% (vs. 54.4%, 1996) expressed willingness to teach students with disabilities. These numbers were remarkably similar over the years. Furthermore, it was found that there was higher agreement for more generally worded items of less intensity. That is, whereas 70.8% voiced general support for inclusion, only 40.5% supported inclusion for all students with disabilities for most or all of the school day. Again, these percentages were very similar to data from earlier decades. Across all years of surveys, teachers generally expressed a wish for additional time and training, as well as personnel and administrative support for implementing inclusion in their classrooms. Analysis of comparative studies revealed that, similar to previous years, more positive attitudes were reported by elementary teachers (vs. secondary teachers), special education teachers (vs. general education teachers), female teachers (vs. male teachers), and teachers who had taken more (vs. less) coursework relevant to inclusion. Qualitative studies generally confirmed other types of research, especially with reference to both the benefits and challenges of inclusion. Reported benefits include social benefits, support from the special education teacher, and the general enrichment provided by a more diverse classroom. Reported challenges included class size, student skill levels, and making accommodations. More recent studies have reported similar findings (Majoko, 2016; Yu & Cho, 2021).

Scruggs (2012) concluded that teacher attitudes are generally positive and have changed very little over the past several decades. Teacher attitudes seemed to be less influenced by prejudice toward students with disabilities and more oriented toward practical classroom concerns, including appropriate class size, time to prepare for inclusive instruction, and training appropriate to teaching inclusive classes. Appropriately supported teachers are more likely to have positive attitudes toward including students with disabilities.

QUESTIONS FOR REFLECTION

1. Why do you think attitudes toward inclusion have changed so little over the years?
2. How might overall attitudes toward inclusion be improved?
3. Why do you think elementary-grade teachers report more positive attitudes than secondary-grade teachers?

TEACHER ATTITUDES

One of the most important determinants of inclusion success is the attitude of the general education teacher toward accommodating students with disabilities. Although most teachers are positive about inclusion, general education teachers report a need for additional planning time, additional training for inclusive teaching, and additional resources, in the form of personnel and specialized instructional materials (Cook et al., 2000; Scruggs, 2012; see also the *Research Highlight*). Teacher and administrator support for collaborative efforts in schools can also affect attitudes. The previous two scenarios help illustrate the initial implementation of inclusion in two different schools under very different circumstances.

It is clear that many aspects must be considered in order for inclusive placements to be successful. These involve careful planning and attention to the multiple perspectives of general education teachers, special education teachers, parents and caregivers of students with and without disabilities, and, of course, the students themselves. However, with careful planning and appropriate programming, inclusive instruction can prove to be a successful and rewarding experience for everyone.

1 Summary

- Before the passage of federal law, students with disabilities were routinely excluded from public school. Public Law 94-142 (IDEA) and its subsequent amendments established the rights of students with disabilities to a free, appropriate public education.
- Six important principles in IDEA are (1) zero reject, (2) nondiscriminatory testing, (3) free and appropriate education, (4) least restrictive environment, (5) due process, and (6) parent/caregiver participation.
  - Least restrictive environment refers to the environment that is least removed from the general education classroom and can meet a student's individual learning.
- Other court rulings and federal laws, such as Section 504 and the Americans with Disabilities Act, have provided for nondiscriminatory treatment of individuals with disabilities.
- Current educational practice provides for a continuum of services for students with disabilities, from full-time placement in the general education classroom to special residential schools. Currently, most students with disabilities are served in general education classrooms.
  - "Full inclusion" is the full-time placement of students with disabilities in general education classrooms. Important points have been raised by concerned individuals on both sides of this issue.
  - Most teachers favor some form of inclusion for their own classes. However, teachers report a need for sufficient time, training, and resources to teach effectively in inclusive classrooms. When these supports are provided, attitudes toward inclusive teaching improve.

PROFESSIONAL STANDARDS LINK:
Introduction to Inclusive Teaching

Information in this chapter links most directly to:

- CEC 2020 Initial Practice-Based Professional Preparation Standards for Special Educators (Initial K–12 standards) (see https://exceptionalchildren.org/standards/initial-practice-based-professional-preparation-standards-special-educators): Standards: 1 (Engaging in Professional Learning and Practice within Ethical Guidelines), 2 (Understanding and Addressing Each Individual's Developmental and Learning Needs), 7 (Collaborating with Team Members)
- **Interstate New Teacher Assessment and Support Consortium (InTASC)** Standards (see https://www.ccsso.org/sites/default/files/2017-11/InTASC_Model_Core_Teaching_Standards_2011.pdf): 2 (Learning Differences), 3 (Learning Environments), 4 (Content Knowledge)

Note: CEC is the Council for Exceptional Children, an organization dedicated to improving educational outcomes for students with disabilities and gifted students. InTASC is the Interstate New Teacher Assessment and Support Consortium, which created standards for licensing new teachers to be compatible with the National Board for Professional Teaching Standards.

Yifei Fang/Offset/Shutterstock

CHAPTER 2

Collaboration: Partnerships and Procedures

LEARNING OBJECTIVES

After studying this chapter, you should be able to:

2.1 Describe collaboration and how it can be used to meet students' needs.

2.2 Summarize the six major steps involved in effective interpersonal communication.

2.3 Explain procedures for collaboration and communication for intervention, including prereferral procedures employing response to intervention (RTI) and multi-tiered systems of support (MTSS) models.

2.4 Describe the process of collaboration for referrals and placements.

2.5 Apply strategies for establishing partnerships between general education teachers and special education teachers, paraprofessionals, and families.

The Individuals with Disabilities Education Act (IDEA, 2004) provides the legal right for individuals with disabilities to receive free, appropriate public education (FAPE). However, for the law to be effective, constructive and collaborative partnerships must be established among parents and caregivers, families, teachers, school specialists, school administrators, and community agencies. The school and parents/caregivers must accept certain basic responsibilities for the system to work effectively. (See Table 2.1.) These responsibilities involve a willingness to collaborate to achieve shared goals.

Collaboration—involving cooperation, effective communication, shared problem solving, planning, and finding solutions—is the process for ensuring that all students receive the FAPE mandated by IDEA. Collaboration is identified by the Council for Exceptional Children (CEC) as a category of **high-leverage practice**, or **HLP** (see Chapter 6). HLPs in special education are foundational skills or evidence-based practices used frequently in classrooms that have shown to increase student success. Three HLPs are relevant to collaboration (McLeskey et al., 2017):

Collaboration

HLP 1: Collaborate with professionals to increase student success.

HLP 2: Organize and facilitate meetings with professionals and families.

HLP 3: Collaborate with families to support student learning and secure needed services.

The establishment of excellent partnerships among all involved in working with students with disabilities—parents, caregivers, family members, teachers, administrators, specialists, paraprofessionals, and community leaders—is essential for constructive collaboration.

TABLE 2.1 School and Parent/Caregiver Responsibilities

School Responsibilities	Parent/Caregiver Responsibilities
Provide free and appropriate education through age 21.	Provide consent for educational evaluation and placement.
Inform parent/caregiver of the rights of participation in educational decision making for the individual with a disability.	Review your participatory rights and ask questions, as needed.
Provide an individualized education program (IEP) for each student who requires special education and related services.	Participate in the case conference committee, including development of the IEP.
Ensure testing, evaluation materials, procedures, and interpretations are nonbiased.	Advocate for your child.
Cooperatively listen to information provided by parents/caregivers.	Cooperatively listen to information provided by the school and teachers.
Educate students with disabilities in the least restrictive environment.	Attend case reviews and provide input to ensure the IEP remains appropriate.
Ensure confidentiality of records for individuals with disabilities.	Reinforce procedures and policies (e.g., help with homework routines).
Conduct searches to identify and evaluate students with disabilities from birth through age 21.	Assist with any home–school behavioral contracting efforts.
Provide procedural due-process rights for students and parents/caregivers.	Ask questions as needed and maintain open communication with the school and teachers.

CLASSROOM SCENARIO

Collaborating for Aliyah

Aliyah is a ninth-grader with physical disabilities and communication difficulties. After a month of high school, she has been challenged by the workload. Her mild traumatic brain injury causes her to tire easily and she has frequent headaches, a variety of medical needs, and anxiety. Aliyah transitioned from the middle school last year and her high school teachers are still learning how to meet her needs in the classroom. The special education teacher, Mr. Graetz, is one of the case managers for freshman with disabilities. Recently, Aliyah spoke to Mr. Graetz on multiple occasions about some challenging assignments in her content classes. He decided to coordinate a meeting among Aliyah's teachers before school. Four of her teachers could attend—her math teacher, Ms. Juarez; her English teacher, Mr. Mantizi; her science teacher, Mr. Wong; her history teacher, Ms. Banks; and her paraprofessional, Ms. Meyer. The speech–language therapist, Ms. Ramirez, was able to join as well. The meeting was held in a small conference room near the front office. The teachers are aware of Aliyah's unique learning needs in the classroom and they want to know how to help her be more successful in high school.

Mr. Graetz began the conversation by saying, "Thanks for agreeing to meet this morning. I wanted to get feedback from you all about Aliyah in class. Recently, Aliyah has expressed some anxiety with some planned assignments and she appears to be stressed and is having a hard time keeping up with all of her work."

Ms. Banks, the history teacher, says, "I know that Aliyah is interested in our first unit. She performed okay on some initial quizzes. I have her second period and she is attentive at that time of the day. But I am surprised to see that she does not use her communication device in class at all—even during small-group work with her peers. Does she use it in your classes?"

Mr. Wong shakes his head and says, "Not in science. Aliyah will talk in class but it is slow and some of her peers do not understand what she is saying. She seems tired in class and visibly frustrated at times when her peers do not understand her. I wish she would use her device." Ms. Ramirez suggests, "I will say that Aliyah has expressed some reluctance to use her device—to have it talk for her. She may be self-conscious. Have you tried allowing Aliyah to use a mobile device like an iPad to type out her responses and then have her pass the iPad to her peers to read the response when in the small group?"

Ms. Juarez, the math teacher, adds, "I have a scribe who provides her with a copy of daily notes. And sometimes I stop the discussion and allow extra time for Aliyah to type her responses. I have found that this provides additional thinking time for everyone."

Ms. Meyer responds, "I think that is helpful, but I have gotten to know Aliyah pretty well, so let me check with her about why she is reluctant to use her communication device." Mr. Graetz thanks Ms. Meyer and says, "Related to this, Aliyah did mention an oral PowerPoint presentation that was due next month in your class, Ms. Juarez. Is there any possible alternative to publicly presenting to her peers? Her IEP does include flexibility with presentations as a classroom accommodation."

And so the discussion continues. These teachers are collaborating by sharing suggestions in instructional modifications with the intention of trying something that will promote school success for Aliyah.

QUESTIONS FOR REFLECTION

1. How could any disagreements that arise be handled in this meeting?
2. If you were Mr. Graetz, how could you determine that the suggestions made in this meeting would be carried out?
3. What do you think would be some of the challenges in arranging a meeting such as this?

Collaboration to Meet Students' Needs

Learning Objective 2.1 Describe collaboration and how it can be used to meet students' needs.

Collaboration to decide how to best meet students' needs can occur among teachers and other school specialists during informal meetings, co-teaching, and formal meetings of professionals to recommend interventions or consider the appropriateness of special education services. Collaboration also takes place with parents/caregivers, siblings, guardians, and families—during parent or caregiver conferences as well as during day-to-day communication with family members regarding the progress of their children.

Table 2.1 lists shared responsibilities for schools and parents/caregivers. To meet these responsibilities, parents/caregivers and school personnel must engage in problem-solving strategies, working together to devise procedures necessary for identification, referral, assessment, and placement processes to differentiate instruction to accommodate students with exceptionalities and other at-risk students.

SHARED GOALS

Collaboration means working jointly with others, willingly cooperating with others, and sharing in goal setting, problem solving, and goal achievement. For example, a special education teacher might have Anthony, who is classified as having mild intellectual disabilities, for three periods a day, while he is in the general education seventh-grade classroom the remainder of the school day. General and special education teachers must collaborate effectively to implement the goals and objectives on Anthony's IEP. Anthony's IEP specifies that general education teachers prioritize learning objectives, use positive reinforcement, adapt learning activities to reduce the amount of reading and writing required, adapt testing situations, and provide Anthony with additional support as necessary. For these goals to be implemented consistently throughout the day for Anthony, this team of teachers must work collaboratively and share ideas for best meeting Anthony's needs. For collaboration to be productive, teachers must communicate effectively. This is best achieved when collaborators hone their interpersonal skills and interject a positive attitude into the collaboration efforts.

Effective Communication

Learning Objective 2.2 Summarize the six major steps involved in effective interpersonal communication.

Interpersonal interactions revolve around in-person communication and/or e-communication (e.g., mobile phone messaging, e-mail, video conferencing). When communication is effective, several common elements are in place: listening actively, depersonalizing situations, identifying common goals and solutions, and monitoring progress to achieve those goals (Gordon, 2003; see also Ginott, 1998; Ginott et al., 2003; Vostal et al., 2015).

STRATEGIES FOR COMMUNICATING EFFECTIVELY

USE ACTIVE LISTENING TECHNIQUES Active listening is demonstrated through both nonverbal and verbal actions. Nonverbally, you demonstrate active listening by maintaining direct eye contact, leaning toward the speaker, nodding your head in agreement or understanding, and demonstrating that you are devoting all of your attention to the speaker. Verbal components of active listening involve responding with affirmative words, such as "Yes," "Yes, I see," "I understand," and "Can you tell me more?" An active listener is able to restate or summarize the major points of the conversation and may do this during the course of the conversation with statements such as, "So, what you are telling me is . . . ." Teachers who use active listening techniques are more likely to maintain open communication and to avoid misunderstandings (review the feature, *Research Highlight*). Active listening is a way of informing speakers that their views are important to you, and it can be helpful in keeping interactions positive.

DEPERSONALIZE SITUATIONS Depersonalized conversations avoid negative comments that may be offensive and instead emphasize a goal. For example, if a fifth-grade student, Lisa, has not been turning in homework assignments, a "depersonalized" statement is, "Lisa, 7 out of the last 10 homework assignments are missing; what can we do to improve that?" A negative statement that might hinder finding a solution is, "Lisa, you obviously do not care enough about science to turn in your homework." Depersonalized conversations are beneficial when communicating with everyone, including students, other teachers, school specialists, administrators, parent(s)/caregiver(s), and professionals from community organizations. Use of objective data like the mention of 7 out of 10 assignments can also inform development of a goal to attain.

FIND COMMON GOALS It is important to restate and summarize conversations to identify common goals. Once common goals are found, conversations can be more positive and productive. Questions such as "Lisa, what do you want to learn in science?" and "Lisa, what are the barriers currently preventing you from turning in your homework?" can help direct the conversations toward the identification of common goals. A positive and productive common goal among Lisa's teachers, her caregivers, and Lisa could be the following:

> We all want Lisa to succeed, and one way to help her succeed is to find ways to assist her in turning in her homework.

Once common goals are stated positively, it is easier to turn the entire conversation into productive problem solving geared toward goal attainment.

BRAINSTORM POSSIBLE SOLUTIONS Effective communicators can use brainstorming techniques during meetings to help identify ways to achieve any common goals. During brainstorming, suggestions for solutions are compiled by participants, without passing judgment on any of them. The list of possible solutions can then be prioritized from those offering the most potential for success to the least. When all participants join in the creation of possible alternatives for helping Lisa succeed, they are more invested in reaching their goal. In Lisa's case, a brainstormed list created by her, her teachers, and her caregivers might include the following: serving detention for a month; quitting her job; keeping an assignment notebook; eliminating or restricting her television-watching time; staying after school once a week for homework assistance; and rewarding Lisa if she meets a certain criterion by the end of the quarter.

Pearson eTextbook
Video Example 2.1
Effective teacher/parent/caregiver communication is essential. What steps of effective interpersonal communication are demonstrated in the video?

Research Highlight

An Active Listening Strategy for Teachers

Effective parent/caregiver/teacher communication is critically important to effective collaboration and building cooperative relationships. McNaughton et al. (2007) developed and implemented an active-listening strategy for preservice teachers, and Vostal et al. (2015) replicated and extended the strategy. They refer to this strategy as "LAFF" and list the following components:

- L = Listen, empathize, and communicate respect.
- A = Ask questions and ask permission to take notes at the meeting.
- F = Focus on the problem, or issues, and summarize issues as described by the parent/caregiver.
- F = Find a first step by identifying and agreeing upon appropriate procedures and how they will be implemented.

Empathetic listening allows the teacher to understand clearly the problems or issues as perceived by the parent or caregiver. Asking questions and taking notes help clarify issues and provide information to be considered for future meetings. By focusing on the problem at hand, attention is directed away from ancillary issues, which helps lead to the exploration of relevant first steps to undertake for resolving the problem.

McNaughton et al. (2007) taught this strategy to a group of preservice teachers and applied it to a series of role-play scenarios with parents/caregivers, including one pretest scenario, six training scenarios, and one posttest scenario. After training, it was found that the trained preservice teachers exhibited a significantly higher number of effective communication skills compared with their pretest scores and the scores of control preservice teachers. Furthermore, a diverse panel of parents/caregivers overwhelmingly identified the trained teachers as exhibiting stronger communication skills. All trained participants agreed, or strongly agreed, that the training would be helpful to them professionally. For example, one participant said, "This strategy has helped me to communicate more effectively in situations dealing with problems" (McNaughton et al., 2007, p. 229).

Vostal et al. (2015) extended the strategy to applications with preservice special educators for use with general education teachers when addressing a student issue. In addition to the previous training, preservice students were taught to think about asking questions using the mnemonic "What When Who—4, 3, 2," which represented asking four "what" questions to define the problem, three "when" questions to pinpoint when the problem happened, and two "who" questions to identify individuals associated with the problem. Findings revealed that preservice students improved significantly following training. Participants reported that the strategy was very helpful. For example, one person said that it provided "some structure to an otherwise stressful and unpredictable situation." Another candidate wrote, "Pointing out these ways to communicate seemed obvious, but they are quite necessary!" (Vostal et al., 2015, p. 10).

McNaughton and Vostal (2010) noted some things to avoid when communicating with family members and suggested a "LAFF, don't CRY" strategy, whereby you do not:

- C = Criticize others not present at the meeting;
- R = React hastily, promising something that can't be delivered; and
- Y = "Yakety-yak-yak," or use unnecessary talk that is not related to the issues.

Considering things to avoid as well as things to implement may help solidify active-listening techniques.

QUESTIONS FOR REFLECTION

1. What mistakes do you think teachers may make when conferring with parents, caregivers, or other teachers?
2. Why do you think this particular strategy is helpful to engage parents or caregivers in discussion and dialogue?
3. What do you think is most important about active listening?
4. What does "don't CRY" add to the LAFF strategy?

SUMMARIZE GOALS AND SOLUTIONS Summarizing the statement of goals and proposed solutions verbally (and perhaps in writing), before the end of the meeting, is beneficial for all participants. This prevents any misunderstandings and provides an opportunity for clarification. In our example, the teacher uses a communication summary sheet (see the *In the Classroom* feature) and verbally summarizes the meeting by stating, "Let me summarize what we all agreed on. We all want Lisa to succeed in science. One way to have Lisa be more successful is to help her turn in all of her homework assignments. One thing Lisa will do is keep an assignment notebook in which she records her assignments and due dates, which she will show daily to her teachers

In the Classroom

Communication Summary Sheet

For: ______________________ On: ______________________

(Student's Name) (Date)

Conversation Among (list participants):

______________________ ______________________

______________________ ______________________

Goals Identified:

1.

2.

3.

Solution Steps to Be Implemented (and by whom): *Person Responsible* ______________________

Solution Steps

1.

2.

3.

Progress Toward Goals Will Be Reviewed On:

______________________ ______________________

(Date) (By Whom)

for accuracy. Teachers will then initial the assignment notebook. Another step will be for Lisa and her caregivers to find a place at home for her to complete her homework. Her caregivers will assist her by initialing her assignment notebook after verifying assignment completion. Finally, Lisa will attend after-school help sessions if she does not understand what to do to complete the assignments. We will meet and review Lisa's progress toward her goals within one month, at which time we will determine whether we need to modify any of the possible solutions."

FOLLOW UP TO MONITOR PROGRESS Summarization makes the entire conversation positive and concrete. A goal statement is made, possible solutions are listed, one is selected for implementation and evaluation, and follow-up target dates are set for monitoring progress toward goal attainment.

All steps promote communication with everyone involved in educating students with disabilities. Review the *In the Classroom* feature, which can be used to ensure decisions made by the group during problem solving are more easily executed. Whatever model of communication you use, note that practicing good communication skills enables you to be effective in the many roles associated with collaboration.

Collaboration and Communication for Intervention

Learning Objective 2.3 Explain procedures for collaboration and communication for intervention, including prereferral procedures employing response-to-intervention (RTI) and multi-tiered systems of support (MTSS) models.

Many types of collaboration occur in larger groups or "teams" within schools. One type of schoolwide team is the general education **prereferral assistance team**. Depending on the school district, these teams may also be referred to as multidisciplinary teams, student study teams, general education assistance teams, prereferral intervention teams, problem-solving teams, or teacher assistance teams and may vary in the way they are implemented (Bennett et al., 2012). Many schools today have employed teams implementing *response to intervention* or *multi-tiered systems of support* to provide for prereferral procedures. These programs employ schoolwide screening and progress monitoring to help identify students in need of supports, and they employ multiple levels, or tiers, of instructional intensity to meet student needs (Division for Learning Disabilities, 2007). No matter what the team is called, its function is to determine the need for educational interventions to assist individual students who are struggling to succeed at school. In addition, the teams' intervention strategies assist teachers who, after careful observation, are unsure whether a student needs special education services. Hence, the team's first purpose is to determine whether intervention strategies can make a difference for the student so that special education placement is averted. The team usually convenes after a formal request is made to the building principal or other designated individual within a school.

GENERAL EDUCATION PREREFERRAL REQUEST

A formal prereferral request can be made by a teacher, school specialist, parent/caregiver, school administrator, or the student at any time. For example, a request might be made by a general education teacher who has worked with a student for a period of time and finds that all her efforts have not made the differences they should have in that child's educational success. In the case of schools implementing **RTI** procedures, this request may be based on general education classroom screening and progress-monitoring measures.

Documentation of observations, student work samples, test scores, and other relevant data are often submitted with a formal intervention request. It is important to reiterate that before Omar's teacher, Mrs. Mayer, requested help from the intervention team, she had taken a number of steps to address the problem (see *Classroom Scenario: Helping Omar*). Often, these steps are sequential, in that each item checked should be undertaken before the next concern. However, referrals do not always follow this order. It is best to check with your state and/or school district for procedures and forms and for any software relevant to the process. Mrs. Mayer first reviewed Omar's records to verify that vision and hearing screenings had taken place. Conferences with Omar's family members and student interviews were conducted to discuss the problem areas and consider possible solutions. She collected, analyzed, and filed samples of Omar's recent academic classwork and evidence of disciplinary actions. She informally asked for advice from other teachers, school counselors, special education teachers, and the prereferral assistance teams. Mrs. Mayer made documentation available to the team of specific intervention strategies she had tried before asking the team for help.

CLASSROOM SCENARIO

Helping Omar

Mrs. Mayer is a second-grade general education teacher. At the beginning of the school year, she noticed that Omar seemed to be behind his classmates on schoolwide screening measures and was not progressing well academically. In spite of additional review of first-grade material, Omar continued to have problems with reading and writing tasks and had a hard time maintaining attention to tasks.

When Omar continued to struggle, Mrs. Mayer decided that she and Omar needed some assistance. She contacted her school's prereferral assistance team. The team members included a first-, third-, fourth-, and fifth-grade teacher; a school psychologist; the principal; and a special education teacher. The team scheduled a meeting to discuss the nature and severity of Omar's difficulties and designed intervention strategies that Mrs. Mayer could implement and review within a specified timeline.

QUESTIONS FOR REFLECTION

1. How would you determine whether a problem was serious enough to contact the prereferral intervention assistance team?
2. How would you determine whether your assessment of Omar's problem was objective and unbiased?

All of this information was useful to team members in deciding what other modifications, adaptations, or interventions might be tried to find the best educational program for Omar. For an illustration of all the steps in the referral process in a three-tier RTI model, see Figure 2.1.

Table 2.2 presents a comparison of the sequence of steps that might be implemented with a second-grade student who starts to experience reading challenges in schools using a prereferral assistance team approach with an **RTI** or **MTSS** approach. Notice the similarities and differences. Both systems intend to help struggling students, but they use slightly different approaches.

Figure 2.1 Steps in the Referral Process

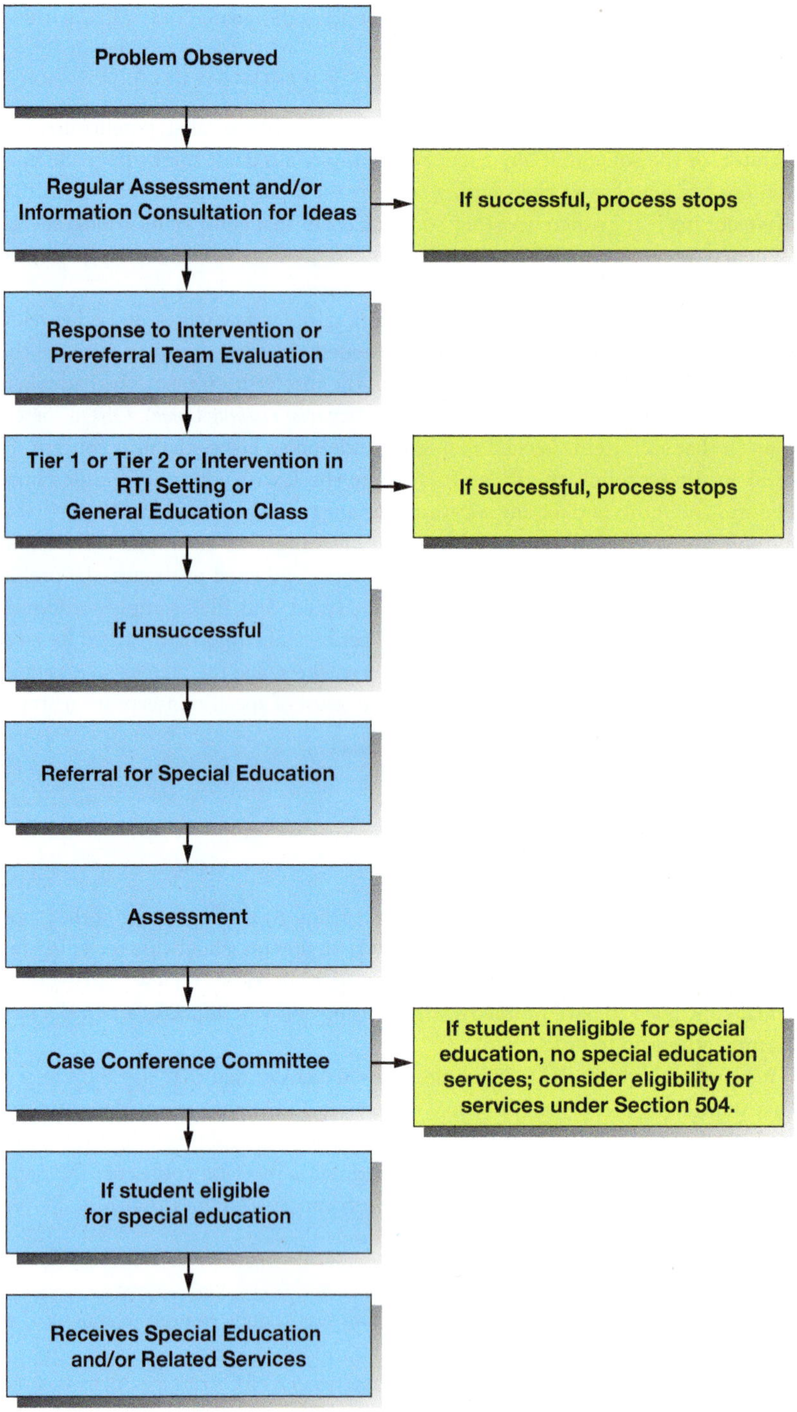

TABLE 2.2 Prereferral Assistance Team versus Multi-Tiered System of Support

	Typical Steps in Process to Referral to Special Education*	Prereferral Assistance Team	Multi-Tiered System of Support or Response to Intervention
Starts School	Child starts third grade	Teacher teaches reading using the school- and district-adopted curriculum materials and approaches	Teacher teaches reading using Tier 1 procedures, which are scientifically based instructional techniques, and collects regular performance data as part of the program (e.g., 5–10 minutes every 2–3 weeks)
Experiences Challenges	Third-grade child experiences challenges in reading and reading comprehension	Teacher talks to parent(s) or caregiver(s), checks all data on child's performance, documents additional instructional procedures that the teacher has implemented, and may talk to other teachers for suggestions and assistance	Teacher teaches using Tier 1 procedures, which are scientifically based instructional techniques, and collects regular performance data as part of the program; teacher may have noticed this child struggling and spoken with parent(s) or caregiver(s) and MTSS team members
Challenges Persist	Third-grader still experiences challenges in reading	Teacher brings all data collected on various adaptations made in reading to the prereferral assistance team, which evaluates the data and makes recommendations to be implemented	Teacher makes a decision based on student's Tier 1 performance data to have the child enter a small-group Tier 2 reading program
Special Education Referral Process Initiated	Still experiencing challenges	Referral to special education begins; possible special education placement	Teacher makes a recommendation for Tier 3, which in many districts is also a referral for special education
Special Education Placement	Still experiencing challenges	More intensive interventions	More intensive interventions, which may be Tier 3

* At any time, a parent/caregiver or teacher can make an immediate referral to special education.

THE INTERVENTION PROCESS

The strategies addressed in the intervention process are designed, implemented, and evaluated before any formal referral for special education services. These are not special education procedures but are part of the general education system required by some state special education legislation (schools implementing RTI procedures may allocate up to 15% of federal special education funds to these procedures). The *In the Classroom* feature identifies a checklist of steps in a prereferral process.

All prereferral procedures, including RTI and MTSS, are preventative in nature; they are intended to reduce inappropriate referrals and decrease the likelihood of future problems. These procedures provide general education teachers and students with immediate assistance with classroom-related problems, including disciplinary issues. To determine whether the general education intervention is appropriate, team members may observe the student before the prereferral intervention takes place. It is wise to try to involve the parent(s) or caregiver(s) whenever possible; however, before any general education intervention plan is implemented, parent(s) or caregiver(s) must be notified in writing of the team's recommendation for intervention strategies and the rationale for implementing them. Finally, the intervention is implemented.

ESTABLISHING TIMELINES Once intervention strategies are developed, timelines are set to accompany the implementation and review of those strategies. In Mrs. Mayer's case, a strategy was designed to be implemented with Omar. In some cases, the prereferral assistance team could recommend strategies Mrs. Mayer could implement in her class to help Omar.

In the Classroom

Checklist for Steps in General Education Prereferral Intervention Process

- _______ Formal request for assistance
- _______ Timelines for decisions to be made
  - _______ At referral
  - _______ For implementation of intervention
  - _______ For review of intervention
- _______ Strategies for interventions
- _______ Parent/caregiver rights, including the following:
  - _______ Notification of types of and rationales for general education prereferral interventions
  - _______ Timelines for implementation and review of general education prereferral intervention strategies, including RTI
  - _______ Right to meet with those involved
- _______ Right to begin a formal educational evaluation request
  - _______ Cannot hold up a formal educational evaluation for special education

In a schoolwide RTI system, Omar could be referred to a Tier 2 RTI program (possibly a more intensive small-group supplemental instruction several times a week) if he had not responded sufficiently to Tier 1, that is, interventions employing **evidence-based practices (EBPs)** in the general education classroom. Omar's family members will be contacted and asked to give permission for an educational evaluation for possible special education services. Omar's family members can request an educational evaluation for special education at any time during this process, and their request will be honored and not delayed due to the implementation of the general education intervention.

INTERVENTION STRATEGIES Intervention strategies vary depending on the specific needs of the student but may include adaptations in (1) the curriculum, (2) instructional procedures, (3) classroom management, or (4) the classroom environment. Curriculum adaptations involve altering the curriculum, such as using universal design for learning (UDL) materials (i.e., those that are accessible for all students and provide for multiple means of representation; Meyer et al., 2014). **UDL** allows students to change text to larger fonts and have text-to-voice features. Adaptations in instructional procedures include providing additional instruction or using different presentation formats; varying the types of practice activities; altering testing procedures, such as having tests read aloud; and regrouping students within instructional activities. Adapting classroom management procedures involves intensifying behavioral monitoring for increasing attention to task, providing individual student behavioral contracts, or increasing reinforcement. Environmental changes consist of rearranging the classroom desks, making the classroom more accessible, or changing seating positions. Finally, other resources available within the school and community may be used to assist in implementing general education interventions. Tier 2 interventions, usually consisting of intensive small-group instruction, could be employed for students who do not benefit from evidence-based general education classroom (Tier 1) instruction.

RESEARCH ON PREREFERRAL INTERVENTIONS Truscott et al. (2005) surveyed state departments of education regarding their prereferral intervention practices and found that there was considerable variability from state to state in whether prereferral interventions were required, the terminology used to describe them, and how they were carried out (see also Scott et al., 2014). Similar variability has been observed in the implementation of RTI (Berkeley et al.,2020; Prewett et al., 2012). Although prereferral intervention practices are not always successful (Barrio, 2017), they may be effective in preventing special education placement (Young & Gaughan, 2010). Some evidence suggests that RTI procedures may reduce the placement of students in special education programs (Wanzek & Vaughn, 2011).

RESPONSE-TO-INTERVENTION PROCEDURES As described previously, since the passage of the IDEA 2004, schools have been allowed to use federal funds to provide *early intervention services* for students experiencing difficulty in school but not yet referred for special education. These services may be delivered in *tiers* of increasing intensity, where, for example, Tier 1 interventions may be research-validated teaching practices, with targeted adaptations implemented in the classroom when needed. Resources from the RTI Action Network (www.rtinetwork.org) explain how Tier 2 interventions can be planned for students who fail to respond to Tier 1 interventions (Johnson, n.d.). These second-tier interventions can take place with small groups of students who have not responded well to Tier 1 interventions and may be considered an intensive and systematic type of prereferral intervention. Tier 2 interventions may include, for example, 20 or 30 minutes of intensive small-group instruction in reading. The goal is to help students acquire needed classroom skills within a specific time period (e.g., 10–15 weeks; National Center on Response to Intervention, 2010). If students still do not make acceptable progress, they may be provided with even more intensive (Tier 3) services, including referral for evaluation for special education placement (see Hoover, 2010). Research suggests that Tier 2 interventions in reading can help many students gain important skills (Burns et al., 2020; Solis et al., 2015) and may lead to a reduced rate of referral for special education services (Wanzek & Vaughn, 2011). Additional information on RTI and MTSS is provided in Chapter 7.

Collaboration for Referrals and Placements

Learning Objective 2.4 Describe the process of collaboration for referrals and placements.

The special education referral process is usually initiated by the student's teachers or parent(s)/caregiver(s) but can also be initiated by others, including the student. Each school has written referral procedures, designated staff for the various positions within the referral process, and accompanying forms.

Once the prereferral team determined that the strategies Mrs. Mayer had implemented on her own (or Tier 1 and Tier 2 interventions in schools implementing RTI) were insufficient to help Omar successfully perform in second grade, the referral process for educational evaluation began. Mrs. Mayer completed the school's "Referral Evaluation Form" (see Figure 2.2 for a sample referral form). Once the referral form was completed, Omar's family members were contacted and asked to meet with school personnel. They were told that their son had been referred for an educational evaluation. They were told why he was referred and were asked to provide written permission to proceed. Omar's family members were informed about the evaluation procedures and told that a case conference committee meeting would be scheduled within 65 school days of the family members' signing the permission for testing. They were also reminded that the school had already attempted to help Omar through the general education program (or Tier 1 and Tier 2 programs in schools implementing RTI).

All information should be presented verbally and in writing for the family member(s), in the parents'/caregivers' native language. If the caregiver(s) speak Spanish, for example, then school personnel must communicate with the parent(s)/caregiver(s) using Spanish. Figure 2.3 contains a listing of parental/caregiver rights.

THE EDUCATIONAL EVALUATION OR ASSESSMENT STEP

The educational evaluation for a referral to special education is much more comprehensive than the evaluation described for prereferrals by the general education teams. This evaluation provides extensive information on how the student learns best and the student's level of performance and it identifies strengths and potential need areas. The evaluation team includes a school psychologist and other school specialists as needed (see Figure 2.4). For example, if a child is suspected of having a problem involving speech or language, then a speech–language therapist would be a member of that evaluation team. In the case of Omar, who is suspected of having reading and writing problems that may be associated with learning disabilities, a teacher of students with learning disabilities will be a member of that team.

Figure 2.2 Sample Referral Form

Date Received ________

Student's Name ______________________________ Gender _____ Birthdate ________

School ____________________________ Grade _______ Teacher ________________

Parent/Guardian ________________________ Primary Language _________________

Address _________________________ Home Phone _________ Work Phone _________

Current Educational Program ____

Referring Person ____
(signature) (title) (date)

Principal/Designee ____
(signature) (date)

1. Please describe briefly the reason(s) for this referral.

2. Documentation of the general education intervention (attach copy of the general education intervention plan): What are the effects of the intervention?
   Comments from the remedial reading instructor, if applicable:

3. Documentation of support services such as counseling or psychological (nontesting) services provided by school or other agency.
   Comments and observations from the school counselor:

   Has a previous psychological evaluation been conducted?
   Yes _____ No _____ Date ________ Agency ____________________________

4. Documentation of conferences, or attempts to conference, with the parent and appropriate school personnel concerning the student's specific problem(s).

5. Which of the disabilities do you suspect?
   _____ Autism _____ Communication disorders _____ Emotional disability
   _____ Hearing impairment _____ Learning disability _____ Intellectual disability
   _____ Orthopedic impairment _____ Other health impairment
   _____ Traumatic brain injury _____ Visual impairment

6. In what subjects are the student's problems most apparent?

7. List schools previously attended and dates:

Figure 2.2
(Continued)

8. Comments from school nurse:

   Current general health ______________________________

   Previous medical problems ______________________________

   Is the student taking medication? ___ If yes, specify ______________________

   Vision: L ____________ R ____________ Correction ______________________

   Date of vision screening ________________ (must be done within a year)

9. Comments from speech, hearing, and language clinician:

   Hearing: L ____________ R ____________ Correction ______________________

   Date of hearing screening ________________ (must be done within a year)

   Is the student receiving speech and language therapy? In the past?

10. Copy and attach information from the student's education record:

    1. Previous achievement test results
    2. Grades earned since school entry
    3. Attendance record
    4. Summary of disciplinary actions

Complete and send all referral information to Special Services.

Figure 2.3 Parental/Caregiver Rights Under IDEA

Source: Contributed by Catherine Creighton Thompson. Reprinted with permission.

Eligibility and Evaluations

Parents can:

- Request special education evaluations.
- Provide or revoke consent for evaluations.
- Consent to or deny special education and related services.
- Have access to written records, including copies of evaluations and IEPs.

Schools must:

- Explain evaluation results to parents.

Independent Education Evaluations (IEEs)

- If parents disagree with school evaluations, then parents can request independent education evaluations (IEEs) at public expense.
- Parents can privately pay for IEEs and present them to IEP teams for nonbinding consideration.

IEP Participation

Parents:

- Have the right to participate in IEP meetings.
- Must receive written documentation stating parental legal rights.
- Can invite individuals or advocates familiar with their child to IEP meetings.

Local Education Agency:

- Must appoint a surrogate parent when a child is a ward of the state or parental identification is impossible.

Changes in Placement or Denial of Services

- Parents have rights to request prior written notice regarding any changes in placement, or refusal of services.
- After requesting prior written notice, schools must document rationale behind placement changes or service refusals.
- Parents can use this documentation in any mediation or due process proceeding.

Figure 2.4 School Personnel as Team Members and Their Roles

General Education Teachers teach any grade level, any subject area, K–12; may be responsible for implementing part or all of a student's IEP.
Special Education Teachers teach any grade level, any disability area, K–12; may teach in any of the settings described for general education teachers; usually have primary responsibility for the implementation of the IEP.
School Psychologists or Diagnosticians take the lead on the educational evaluations, have major responsibilities in administering, scoring, and interpreting tests; sometimes serve as behavioral consultants to teachers.
Counselors advise students; may conduct some social and emotional assessment; may deliver counseling sessions or advise teachers on how to deal with social-emotional needs for their students.
Speech/Language Therapists work with students who require assistance with any speech and/or language needs.
Physical Therapists provide assessment and interventions in gross motor areas.
Occupational Therapists provide assessment and interventions for students in the fine motor areas.
School Nurses often provide medical histories, distribute medications to students; provide a link between families and other school personnel.
School Administrators provide administrative assistance among all involved; may include school principals, vice principals, directors of special education, directors of special services, and special education coordinators.
Social Workers provide the link between families and schools; have similar roles to that of counselors.
Paraprofessionals provide assistance to teachers, special education teachers, and students with disabilities.
Other School Specialists provide assistance in specialized ways, including adaptive physical education; sign language interpreting; bilingual special education; mobility specialists, psychometrists (complete educational testing), probation officers, and other consultants as necessary.

Pearson eTextbook
Video Example 2.2
This video features a case conference committee. Who are the members of the committee? Pay attention to everyone's role in the process.

The education evaluation includes various activities, procedures, and tests. A physical examination, developmental history, and vision and hearing tests may be required. A battery of academic, intellectual, adaptive, and social-emotional tests will be administered, depending on the specific referral reason. Observations of the student throughout the school day may be completed. The classroom teacher is asked to evaluate the student's classroom strengths and need areas. If the school is using an RTI model, data showing inadequate progress with Tier 2 interventions are also presented.

All testing must be culturally unbiased, be completed in the student's native language, and consider cultural background and presumed disability to provide the most accurate picture of the student's current level of functioning. This means, for example, that if a student's native language is Vietnamese, then it may be important to administer tests in Vietnamese; otherwise, an inaccurate picture of the student's abilities may be obtained. Parent(s) or caregiver(s), teachers, or other school personnel can request a reevaluation whenever one is deemed necessary.

THE CASE CONFERENCE COMMITTEE

A case conference committee or multidisciplinary team is composed of all individuals concerned with a particular student. The amendments to IDEA require that general education teachers participate in the development, review, and revision of IEPs. Moreover, the amendments require that parent(s)/caregiver(s) be included as members of any group that makes educational decisions about their child. The members include the parent(s)/caregiver(s), their child, and family advocates, if desired; general and special education teachers; the school psychologist; school administrators, such as the building principal or special education director; and any other related personnel, such as the school nurse, counselor, and social worker, or specialists such as speech and language, physical, or occupational therapists.

A case conference committee meeting is convened after the educational evaluation is finished. The meeting is intended to determine whether the student is eligible for special education and related services. If so, then the IEP is developed, and appropriate educational services decisions are made. Case conference committee meetings also take place during each annual review.

EASE THE CONCERN OF PARENTS/CAREGIVERS AND STUDENTS

The CEC's second high-leverage practice in special education is to organize and facilitate effective meetings with professionals and families (McLeskey et al., 2017). During these meetings, all members of the committee should be made to feel welcome and comfortable. Parent(s)/caregiver(s) and students may feel overwhelmed, intimidated, or frightened by attending a meeting with so many school personnel. Prepare for meetings by thinking about how to present information in comprehensible ways for parent(s)/caregiver(s) and students. It may be beneficial to practice with another teacher when describing classroom routines. For example, parent(s)/caregiver(s) may be unfamiliar with terminology that is used so commonly among teachers (e.g., **decoding** is a term frequently used by teachers but not necessarily by parent(s)/caregiver(s) and children). Try to describe class activities, student performance, and behaviors using concrete, simple, direct language. Teachers frequently use abbreviations or acronyms when speaking with each other (e.g., saying "LD" instead of "learning disabilities"), but they should avoid doing so when speaking at case conference committees so that parent(s)/caregiver(s) do not become lost in the educational jargon. Secure brochures describing common disabilities in ways suitable for parent(s)/caregiver(s) and for students. Brochures, important phone numbers, e-mail addresses, and websites can be printed and shared as handouts for parent(s)/caregiver(s).

Martin et al. (2006) reported that special education teachers spoke 51% of the time at IEP meetings, whereas family members spoke only 15% of the time. These findings suggest that input from parents and/or other family members should be more actively solicited in order to gather all relevant information. Parents/caregivers are also allowed to invite a family advocate to the IEP meeting but should notify the school in writing ahead of time.

When parent(s)/caregiver(s) feel comfortable at the meeting, they will be more likely to share important information about their child. Longitudinal national studies indicate that parents/caregivers want to be more involved in making decisions at meetings (Wagner et al., 2012). Parental/caregiver input at the meeting can be invaluable. Parent(s) or caregiver(s) have insight into their child's behaviors that no one at the school may have considered. They can provide input regarding the student's study habits at home and any difficulties encountered during homework. During the case conference committee, one member records the information on the case conference summary form. A copy of this is distributed to the parent(s)/caregiver(s) at the end of the meeting. Figure 2.5 displays a sample case conference summary form. If the student does not qualify for special education, the student may still qualify for services under Section 504 of the Vocational Rehabilitation Act.

RELATED SERVICES Related services are other services that are necessary to help students with disabilities benefit from special education services. Related services may include physical therapy; occupational therapy; audiological services; counseling; rehabilitation counseling; social work services; parent/caregiver counseling; psychological services; school health services; medical services; early identification, transportation, and recreation services; adaptive physical education; or other services identified by the case conference committee. If a situation requires substantial mobility adaptations, the case conference committee might recommend bus routes with special or adapted vehicles, assign an aide as an assistant, or acquire special equipment such as oxygen, ramps, or lifts.

THE INDIVIDUALIZED EDUCATION PROGRAM

An IEP is written by the case conference committee when it is determined that a student is eligible for special education services (Bateman, 2017). The IEP has several major components, including the following:

- Student's current level of academic achievement and functional performance
- Statement of measurable annual goals, including academic and functional goals

Figure 2.5 Summary from Case Conference Committee Meeting

CASE REVIEW CONFERENCE SUMMARY

Student's Name ______________________ DOB ____________ School ______________

Parents/Guardian ______________________ Address ______________________

Phone ______________________ Surrogate Parent ______________________

Committee Meeting ____

(date) (time) (location)

The Case Review Committee was composed of the following:

____

Chairperson Administrator

____

Teacher Teacher Teacher

____

Evaluation Team Member(s)

____

Parent(s) Student

____

Others

The eligibility decision has been ______________________________

Least restrictive placement has been ______________________________

Purpose of conference ______ initial evaluation ______ re-evaluation ______ review of IEP

______ transition planning ______ new to district

Multidisciplinary report of present level of performance:

____

____

____

____

Based on the data presented, the following eligibility decision was made:
The student is

____

Placement recommendation:

____

Harmful effect considered: _________ yes

Options considered: ______________________________

Reasons options were rejected: ______________________________

Other factors relevant to the proposed placement ______________________________

____

Signatures of committee members with dissenting opinions:

____

____

____

- Statement of short-term objectives for children who take alternative assessments
- Statement of special and related services, based on peer-reviewed research and any program modifications to be provided for support for the child
- Statement of any individual modifications in state- or district-wide assessment procedures
- Statement of why a child cannot participate in state- or district-wide assessment procedures if an alternative assessment is recommended
- Initiation dates of service delivery and the duration and frequency of services
- Statement of transition services for all students 16 years of age and older, including appropriate postsecondary goals and transition services needed to meet those goals
- Statement of how annual goals will be measured, how parent(s)/caregiver(s) will be informed, and how progress will be monitored

Pearson eTextbook
Video Example 2.3
Who writes a student's IEP? What are the components of an IEP?

Moreover, when a special education student is placed in a general education setting, the IEP will contain modifications needed, including curriculum, instructional procedures, staffing, classroom organization, and special equipment, materials, or aides.

Although IEP formats used by school districts vary across the country, all must contain the required components. Some computerized IEP programs are available commercially and are used to assist in developing the basic format of the IEPs (see the *Apps for Education* feature).

School districts provide the parent(s)/caregiver(s) with a written summary of the case conference committee meeting (see Figure 2.5), a copy of the IEP, and a copy of parental/caregiver rights (see Figure 2.3), and parents/caregivers must provide written consent agreeing to the IEP before any services can begin. Parents/caregivers should be part of the development of the IEP so the copy they receive reflects their input.

WRITING GOALS AND OBJECTIVES A critical component of the IEP is the specification of the long-term annual goals and short-term objectives. Short-term objectives are required only for students who take alternative assessments. Long-term annual goals are based on the case conference committee's judgment of what the individual student should accomplish within a year. Annual goals can refer to academic functioning, such as reading grade-level textbooks at specific skill levels, or social behavior, such as exhibiting appropriate behavior in the cafeteria. In some cases, annual goals can refer to adaptive behavior or life skills, such as ordering independently in a restaurant or managing a personal bank account.

Annual goals are measurable, positive, student-oriented, and relevant (Yell et al., 2016). Goals that are measurable can be more easily evaluated. For example, "[Student] will read and comprehend grade-level reading materials" is much easier to measure at the end of the year than "[Student] will improve reading." Positively written goals (e.g., "[Student] will use appropriate language in the classroom at all times") provide better implications for instruction than negatively written goals (e.g., "[Student] will stop swearing"). Student-oriented goals describe what the student will do (as in the previous examples) rather than what others will do (e.g., "[Student] will be given spelling worksheets"). Finally, relevant goals are not always limited to academic goals but also provide for the student's current and future needs, including social-emotional functioning, communication, and career/vocational areas, when appropriate (Peterson et al., 2013).

Short-term objectives are more limited and precise, and they specify the steps to be taken to achieve long-term annual goals. For example, short-term objectives relevant to a long-term annual goal in reading should specify the subskills (e.g., letter identification, word recognition) that students will acquire on the way to meeting the long-term goal. Short-term objectives should also be measurable, positive, student oriented, and relevant. In addition, short-term objectives are usually best when they specify conditions, behavior, and criteria. As an example, consider the following objective: "In the lunchroom, [Student] will use appropriate tone of voice at all times." In this case, "lunchroom" specifies the conditions, "appropriate tone of voice" specifies the behavior, and "at all times" (i.e., 100% of the time) specifies the criteria. When objectives are specified in this way, they can be easily evaluated on the way toward meeting long-term goals.

Apps for Education

IEP Software

Special education paperwork can be reduced by using efficient systems for recording data, for maintaining records, and for communications. Advances in technology can help teachers save valuable time. For example, teachers can share information and collaborate online (e.g., Dropbox; Google Docs Editors suite) to address student needs. They can use basic templates in word-processing programs with school stationery for communications, as well as databases containing frequently used names and addresses. Such timesaving programs are common features on most computers.

Numerous apps are available to assist with understanding and developing IEPs and running and scheduling IEP meetings. *IEP Goals & Objectives with Common Core State Standards* (NASET) contains sections on annual goals, objectives, common core standards, activities, and measuring progress designed to assist in preparing IEPs. The *IEP Checklist* (Nurvee; PEATC.org) app provides a checklist in English and Spanish for parents/caregivers and teachers to consider as they develop IEPs. *IEP Facilitation* (Region 10 Education Service Center) describes the roles, responsibilities, and purpose of having a facilitator at IEP meetings. *Schedule My IEP* (CME Apps, Inc.) contains a calendar with built-in reminders for meetings and important due dates.

Each state can decide what its IEPs look like so some states and individual school systems may have their own online IEP systems. If not, there are numerous software programs commercially available to assist with writing IEPs and other aspects of special education in general. Many of these programs share common features in that they work easily on both PC and Mac computer platforms, smartphones, and tablets. Many contain general templates for information that is required by law to be included in the IEP. Some also contain banks of possible IEP objectives. Some of the available programs include the following: *GoalView* by Public Consulting Group, *Synergy Special Education* by Edupoint, *IEP Planner* by AbleData, and *EasyIEP* by PCG Education. Spectrum K12 School Solutions provides software for RTI implementation as well as IEP development. Interventioncentral.org contains a wealth of resources, including academic and behavior intervention planners, chart construction tools, and test construction ideas. TechMatrix.org allows users to search for educational and assistive technologies to support student learning. A simple search using a search engine such as Google will provide numerous commercially available programs. Commercially available programs are usually advertised as highly relevant, timesaving devices that help teachers produce high-quality IEPs. Although this may be true in many cases, teachers should use caution to ensure that students' IEP objectives are not limited simply to what is available within individual software programs.

The Common Core Standards (Mastery Connect) presents all the reading and math standards, which can be used as a reference and when preparing for IEP meetings and can be helpful for educators and parents/caregivers.

Finally, there are numerous apps available for monitoring behavior at home and school that can be linked to IEP objectives. For example, the *iRewardChart* (Gotclues) app allows parents/caregivers to monitor behaviors and implement rewards for chore completion, homework completion, or other good behaviors. Progress is charted, and rewards are awarded when prespecified standards are met. Coordination between home and school management programs is also possible.

TRANSITION SERVICES Transition services are required to be written into IEPs when students turn 16 but, in fact, may be appropriate at younger ages (Cimera et al., 2014). IDEA and its amendments also require transitioning for preschoolers.

Often, transition services can be implemented the year before students begin to accumulate credits toward high school graduation. At the annual review meeting, when the student is 16, the case conference committee determines student educational, vocational, or employment training needs. Specific interagency linkages and responsibilities must be explicated in the individualized transition plan, which is a supplement to the IEP. The committee also determines whether students may require continual adult services upon completion of high school. More information on transition services is provided in chapter 16.

MONITORING IEPs Legal safeguards are provided to ensure IEPs are monitored to reflect accurately the needs of individuals with disabilities. Regular reviews and evaluations of progress are required. Due-process procedures are always available to resolve any disputes between the parents/caregivers and the school district regarding the student's education.

Due Process Due process is how conflicts are resolved between parents/caregivers and schools regarding the student's education. Disagreements can arise in several areas: whether a student is eligible for special education, the outcome of an educational evaluation, the educational placement, the IEP, or some aspect of the FAPE guaranteed by IDEA.

Several alternatives exist for resolving these disagreements, some of which take place before a formal due-process hearing. The simplest procedure for resolving conflicts is through informal meetings with parents/caregivers and school personnel.

If conflicts remain unresolved during informal meetings, mediation can be used to try to resolve the dispute. Mediation is a voluntary process that must be requested by both parties. After a formal mediation request is signed by both parties, the state selects a mediator and schedules a hearing within 10 working days. Mediators should be trained in special education and mediation, possess excellent interpersonal skills, and serve as neutral facilitators. If mediation is successful, a written agreement is completed and forwarded to the case conference committee for its approval. Many conflicts can be resolved through mediation (Mueller, 2014).

A request for a due-process hearing is a formal request by either the parents/caregivers or the school district to have the dispute arbitrated by an independent hearing officer. This process is more formal than mediation and must take place within timelines as specified in the law. The case is presented to the independent hearing officer, who makes a decision based on the evidence presented by both parties. Parent(s)/caregiver(s) and the school district may be represented by legal counsel, present information pertaining to the case, and bring forth relevant witnesses, and both are entitled to see, at least 5 days before the hearing, any evidence the other party plans to introduce. Due-process hearings can be open or closed to the public, and the student may or may not be present. After listening to all the evidence, hearing officers produce a written decision. After the hearing decision but within a specified number of days, the decision must be either executed or appealed to the appropriate state board of special education by either party.

The appeal of the due-process-hearing decision must describe the parts of the decision that are objectionable and the associated rationale. The state board of special education is required to schedule another impartial review of the hearing and report on its decision. Its decision is considered final unless either party appeals to the civil court within 30 calendar days. Throughout this process, the students remain in their current placement unless both parties agree to something else.

Special education departments in each school district have policies and procedures outlining teachers' roles and responsibilities should they become involved in these processes. The intent of the law is to best serve the student with disabilities, and these safeguards are in place to ensure that parent(s)/caregiver(s) and school district personnel are afforded due-process rights.

Annual Reviews Annual review meetings are conducted to monitor progress. During these meetings, teachers, parents/caregivers, and other team members discuss the student's progress and make recommendations to amend, modify, or adjust the IEP as necessary. Changes in a student's educational placement to a more or less restrictive environment might be made based on the review.

Collaboration as Partnerships

Learning Objective 2.5 Apply strategies for establishing partnerships between general education teachers and special education teachers, paraprofessionals, and families.

Relationships develop among the many individuals working together to design optimal educational programs for students with disabilities. Relationships of special education and general education teachers may develop into collaborative consultation for shared decision making and planning, as well as co-teaching relationships. Collaborative partnerships can also develop with paraprofessionals and with parents, caregivers, and families. These partnerships can substantially improve the school and life functioning of students with disabilities.

Pearson eTextbook
Video Example 2.4
Collaboration among the case manager and general education teachers allow them to monitor a student's progress. Why is monitoring progress critical to ensuring IEP goals are met?

CONSULTATION BETWEEN SPECIAL AND GENERAL EDUCATORS

The CEC's first high-leverage practice in special education is to collaborate with professionals to increase student success (McLeskey et al., 2017). Consultation exists when two individuals, such as special and general educators, work together to decide on intervention strategies for a specific student. During these meetings, which can be formal or informal and verbal or in writing, effective communication procedures are critical.

For example, special education teachers may send weekly notes or e-mails to general education teachers to ask about the progress of specific students with disabilities. Teachers then describe any potentially difficult assignments for which they expect students with disabilities will require additional assistance, as in the following examples:

- A biology teacher indicates that a science fair project is being assigned next week. It will be due in a month, and students with disabilities may benefit from extra assistance.
- A history teacher indicates that an important unit test is approaching, and students with disabilities may require additional studying assistance.

This information alerts special education teachers, who can then help decide whether additional assistance is needed and work with teachers in developing appropriate interventions as needed for students with disabilities.

In other cases, teachers may ask for specific input from the special education teacher, for example, on how to deal with behavior problems. Kampwirth and Powers (2016) described how a special education teacher partnered with a general education teacher. After discussion, the general education teacher focused on two specific concerns: teasing and not turning in homework. The two teachers worked out specific plans for conferencing with the student, home–school notes with the parent/caregiver, and peer mediation in class. These interventions were monitored and found to be effective in improving the student's behavior.

Pearson eTextbook
Video Example 2.5
The teacher in this video discusses collaborative efforts in her middle school. Notice the different types of collaboration, including co-teaching, as they are explained.

CO-TEACHING

Different models of collaboration and co-teaching are used to meet the needs of diverse learners within a single classroom setting. During co-teaching, two teachers are present in the inclusive classroom during instructional periods in order for students with disabilities to receive specially designed instruction (Friend, 2016; Friend & Cook, 2017).

There are several different ways co-teaching can be carried out. In **team-teaching**, teachers take turns presenting and leading classroom activities and share responsibilities equally. In other cases, one teacher assumes more responsibility for delivering instruction, and the other teacher assists individual students, enhances instruction, or observes individual students to improve instructional decision making (**one teach, one assist**). In **station teaching**, smaller groups of students move through several independent workstations for new information, review, or practice while the teachers monitor different stations. In **parallel teaching**, the class is divided into skill or ability groups, and each teacher leads one group. In **alternative teaching**, one teacher leads the larger group while the other teacher (often, the special education teacher) provides additional practice or strategies to students who may require additional support. In practice, however, the roles of the two teachers can deviate from these (Friend & Cook, 2017).

Co-teaching at the secondary level can present some unique challenges because of such factors as increased emphasis on content knowledge, the pace of instruction, scheduling constraints, the expectation for independent study skills, and high-stakes testing (Friend et al., 2010). Murray (2004) suggested that general education teachers develop "dream lists" of what they would like most from the special education teachers with whom they would be collaborating. These teachers then meet with special education teachers to revise and discuss the lists and reflect on the outcome of the meetings. Similarly, Murawski and Dieker (2004) recommended systematically sharing hopes, preferences, attitudes, responsibilities, and expectations before proceeding with co-teaching. They provided a chart of teacher activities to help organize tasks. For example, if one teacher is lecturing, the other teacher could be modeling effective note-taking procedures or managing classroom behavior. While one teacher is passing out papers, the other teacher could be reviewing directions and demonstrating the first problem. As one teacher prepares lesson plans, the other teacher could provide suggestions for accommodations and adaptations for diverse learners. Establishing a chart such as this could help maximize efficiency during co-teaching. Murawski (2012) underlined the importance of focused and common planning (i.e., at least 20 minutes a week) for inclusive teaching, parity in teacher roles, and the use of varied instructional models.

Sufficient planning time for the two teachers to work cooperatively to develop lessons to co-teach is very important (Conderman, 2011). Co-teachers can address many of the HLPs during co-planning. Ask for assistance from school administrators to include as much co-planning time as possible. Consider using the following guidelines when establishing co-teaching:

- Decide goals and objectives for co-teaching.
- Inform parent(s)/caregiver(s) and request their support and permission, especially if co-teaching alters any IEP placement decisions that were made with parental/caregiver consent.
- Determine student and teacher attitudes toward co-teaching.
- Determine how instructional responsibilities will be shared during co-teaching, what co-teaching models will be implemented, how parity of co-teaching roles will be established, what instructional adaptations will be made for students with disabilities, and how the effectiveness of co-teaching arrangements will be evaluated.

RESEARCH SUPPORT Generally, teachers and students have reported positive attitudes toward co-teaching. Reported benefits of co-teaching include improved instruction, increased enthusiasm for teaching, more communication, and more opportunities to generalize learned skills to the general education class environment (Cook et al., 2017).

Challenges to effective co-teaching have also been described (Brown et al., 2013; Murray, 2004; Weiss & Lloyd, 2003) that include budgetary constraints, lack of sufficient planning time, lack of cooperation, personality conflicts, and increased teacher workloads. Other concerns include maintaining the full continuum of services for students, fear of losing necessary services, confronting negative attitudes, and confidentiality issues. Finally, the diminished role of the special education teacher and the frequent use of a whole-class approach to instruction has sometimes been a concern. Use of the effective communication strategies discussed earlier, and the effective teaching strategies described throughout this book, can help ensure that the co-teaching experience is pleasant and productive.

Scruggs and colleagues (2007) summarized 32 qualitative studies of co-teaching, describing over 400 co-teachers using interviews, observations, and classroom products. They found that teachers generally appreciated co-teaching and felt it was beneficial to teachers as well as students with and without disabilities. However, they also identified a number of challenges, including the need for more administrative support, more time to plan for co-teaching, and additional training. The most common model was "one teach, one assist," with the general education teacher presenting traditional, whole-class teaching and the special education teacher often assuming a subordinate role. Several observed classrooms, however, demonstrated special and general education teachers in true partnerships, actively collaborating on the best instruction for all students.

Conners (2008) observed and interviewed 30 special education middle school teachers during co-taught and self-contained classes. All teachers were previously identified as expert special education teachers by district personnel. Based on the observations and interviews, Conners concluded that these expert special education teachers demonstrated excellent co-teaching behaviors. These behaviors included those described in Table 2.3.

A considerable amount of research has described the process and characteristics of co-teaching. However, more research needs to be conducted on its overall effectiveness for students with disabilities and the relative benefits of one model of co-teaching over another (Cook et al., 2017; Friend et al., 2010). The limited efficacy research that has been conducted to date (e.g., Castro, 2007; McDuffie et al.,2009) has been effective in describing the benefits of co-teaching; however, teachers implementing co-teaching should collect evidence in their own classrooms to support the effectiveness of their practice.

TABLE 2.3 Expert Co-Teaching Characteristics and Behaviors

Collaborative Co-Teachers
• *Capitalize* on each other's strengths. • *Complement* each other's teaching styles. • *Negotiate* all practice. • *Respect* what each "brings to the table." • *Exhibit* comfort and trust with each other's teaching style. • *Make* their personalities and teaching styles complement one another and work to establish good rapport. • *Demonstrate* evidence of co-planning and personal commitment to the co-teaching relationship.
Both Teachers Viewed as a "Teacher"
• *Share and value* all students and have high expectations for everyone. • *Share* roles and all responsibilities in an equal partnership. • *Demonstrate* flexibility within roles. • *Exhibit* smooth transitions between teachers during instruction. • *Alternate* roles continuously during instruction while both teachers exhibit a teaching mode at all times.

Source: From Conners (2008). Adapted with permission from the author.

STRATEGIES FOR COLLABORATING WITH PARAPROFESSIONALS

CLARIFY ROLES AND RESPONSIBILITIES *Paraprofessionals* (also called *paraeducators*, *instructional assistants*, or *teacher assistants*) may be aides to special education teachers, specialized aides for students with disabilities, or general aides for teachers within a school. Within those roles, paraprofessionals assume a variety of responsibilities, including recordkeeping, supervising, monitoring seatwork and classroom behavior, assisting with feeding and toileting, and providing instruction. It is important that paraprofessionals are viewed as part of a team and that they receive appropriate role clarification, training, and supervision (Giangreco et al., 2010; Walker & Smith, 2015). To avoid communication problems, paraprofessionals need to be informed specifically of what their duties are (Stewart, 2019). Specify the activities that require student support from paraprofessionals (e.g., checking student notes, prompting students to stay on task). Inform paraprofessionals of any student accommodations and/or modifications identified in the IEP so that they can best meet students' needs.

Develop workday schedules for paraprofessionals that include the person responsible and the date for completion of specific tasks. Also schedule where all people will be at different times of the day or week (Stewart, 2019).

Very specialized responsibilities may be assigned to a paraprofessional. In the case of Jamal, for example, a third-grader who uses a motorized wheelchair and has difficulties communicating and using his hands, a paraprofessional accompanies him throughout the school day. The paraprofessional functions as Jamal's assistant and accompanies him before, during, and after school in any activities, including helping him eat at lunch and dress appropriately for physical education and recess. It may be a new experience for general education teachers to have another adult in their classrooms during instruction, but once teachers become familiar with the activities Jamal can accomplish independently, they will gain a better understanding of how to maximize the role of the paraprofessional. For example, activities the paraprofessional can help Jamal with include handling his class materials, reading tests out loud to him, writing down his responses, and assisting with mobility.

Paraprofessionals assist students in their tasks throughout the school day. However, it is possible for paraprofessionals to spend too much time in close proximity with their students. This can lead to a more limited sense of ownership by and less interaction with the teacher, separation from classmates and peer interaction, overdependence on adults, and a loss of personal control (Giangreco & Broer, 2007; Giangreco et al., 2011). Rather, paraprofessionals can encourage students' independence by promoting self-determination skills (see Chapter 16), such as self-management, problem solving, and self-awareness (Lane et al., 2012). Students should receive all the assistance they need but not more than they require.

COMMUNICATE EFFECTIVELY On occasion, teachers may feel overwhelmed with their responsibilities and find it difficult to know what to do with paraprofessionals. This may be especially true if paraprofessionals have strong personalities, or have worked in schools longer than the teacher. Take time regularly to plan and check in with paraprofessionals in order to consider each other's needs, share resources, and minimize burnout among paraprofessionals, especially those who serve students with emotional and behavioral disorders (Garwood et al., 2018). If a touchy situation arises, such as disagreeing on the amount of assistance necessary for a student, relations may become strained. To defuse these situations, use effective communication and problem-solving strategies to identify the problem and brainstorm potential solutions. It is important for teachers to foster an environment where productive relationships are established. If you do not think you can handle the situation alone, seek the assistance of a more established teacher within your school. Often, simply discussing the situation makes everyone feel more comfortable.

Pearson eTextbook
Video Example 2.6

Paraprofessionals can provide an important service for teachers and students with disabilities. Why might communication be key in working successfully with a paraprofessional?

STRATEGIES FOR
COLLABORATING EFFECTIVELY WITH PARENTS, CAREGIVERS, AND FAMILIES

The third high-leverage practice in special education is to collaborate with families to support student learning (McLeskey et al., 2017). Building positive partnerships with parents, caregivers, and families yields important benefits to your students' education and is a significant component of IDEA legislation (Kampwirth & Powers, 2016; Yell & Bateman, 2020). Establish positive communication early in the school year and aim toward strengthening home–school cooperation. You will learn a great deal about your students from the parent(s)'/caregiver(s)' perspective of how they learn and interact in the home and outside of school. Overall, family members can be important and powerful allies in the education of children with diverse learning needs (Singer et al., 2017; Turnbull et al., 2015).

BE SENSITIVE TO VARIABILITY IN BACKGROUNDS AND FAMILY STRUCTURES

Parents, caregivers, and families represent the continuum of educational backgrounds, as well as racial-ethnic backgrounds and socioeconomic status. Be sensitive to all individual family member needs and make all parents or caregivers welcome in your classroom (see Zhang et al., 2011). Many parents/caregivers feel intimidated by teachers or alienated from their child's school and teachers, so be sure to let families know you share their goal of wanting the best for their child (Hsiao et al., 2017).

State information in such a way that noneducators can understand what you are saying. If parents or caregivers do not read or speak English, make the communications available in formats that are comprehensible to them. This may mean providing accessible, printed information with visuals and text in the family's preferred language or offering use of interpreter services as needed for those with hearing impairments or who speak another language. Remember to have information read to parents, caregivers, or family members who may not have the prerequisite literacy skills.

Pearson eTextbook
Video Example 2.7

In this video, a teacher shares strategies she has used to establish a positive relationship with parent(s)/caregiver(s) of students in her classroom. Why is it critical to establish trust with a parent or caregiver?

Families of today represent a wide array of configurations. The chances are good that the stereotypical family, consisting of a mother who stays at home taking care of children and a father who works outside of the home, may not be representative of many of your students' families. You may be working with single-parent families, same-sex parents, or with an individual who is not a parent but rather is the legal guardian or caregiver of your student. Be sensitive to all family living situations. The *Diversity, Equity, and Inclusion in the Classroom* feature provides some culturally-responsive approaches for interacting with diverse families.

MAINTAIN POSITIVE COMMUNICATION A good way to initiate positive communication with parents or caregivers is to send introductory notes home at the beginning of the school year. For example, Ms. Susan Chung, an eighth-grade English teacher, sends home a short note introducing herself and describing her class.

A positive first communication is especially important if a problem arises later and contact with home becomes necessary. Parent(s) or caregiver(s) may be more likely to feel comfortable discussing sensitive issues concerning their child if you have contacted them earlier. If you only communicate when there is a problem, parents or caregivers get the understandable impression that you only want to see them when something bad has happened, and they may become more reluctant to maintain communication with the school.

Many teachers also request family members' assistance regularly in their classes. This happens more frequently at the elementary level but also occurs at the secondary level. For example, letters may be sent home asking if any parent/caregiver could volunteer in the class. Sometimes teachers specify what types of volunteer activity would be beneficial (e.g., making photocopies, organizing materials, or baking cookies for class parties). At other times, teachers might ask for help in obtaining specialized materials needed during specific units of instruction. But no matter what the request, it is important to emphasize that you realize it may be impossible for a family member to volunteer in class due to their other responsibilities or to contribute financially to class activities. Be sure parents/caregivers understand that neither of these limitations undermines the value of their roles in supporting the education of their children.

Sending home "happy notes" is another way to maintain positive communication with parent(s)/caregiver(s). Happy notes communicate positive things from school events that day, week, or month. ClassDojo is a free school–home communication app that many teachers use to send photos, videos, information, and positive, personal messages to families. The app can translate messages in more than 35 languages. School-to-home notebooks can also be an effective means of maintaining communication with family members. Balance affirming messages with areas of concern, ask parents or caregivers how they wish to communicate, and determine what information is most important to them by giving them opportunities to ask questions (Francis et al., 2016). E-mail and text messages are also possible avenues for ongoing communication with parents or caregivers; however, be aware that all parents, caregivers, and families might not be willing or able to communicate in this way (Turnbull et al., 2015).

COMMUNICATE ABOUT HOMEWORK Establish a "homework communication line" with parent(s), caregiver(s), or families. Some teachers have students maintain assignment notebooks in which daily homework assignments are recorded, including a listing of the materials necessary to complete assignments. When Mrs. Hesser, a fifth-grade teacher, assigned problem numbers 2 through 8 on page 27 in the math book, due Thursday, the students wrote down that information, along with the notation that they need to take home their math books to complete the assignment. If there is no assignment, students are required to write "No homework tonight" in the assignment book. The parent(s)/caregiver(s) are shown the assignment books nightly and are asked to check and initial the book. This extra supervision keeps parent(s)/caregiver(s) informed of assignments and provides opportunities for monitoring homework. In some schools, "homework hotlines" have been established, in which parent(s)/caregiver(s) can call a phone number or check a website (e.g., *ParentVUE* by Edupoint) that informs them of their child's homework assignments.

RESOLVE DISAGREEMENTS On occasion, parent(s), caregiver(s), or family members may appear hostile toward teachers. In these cases, being prepared is an important step. Be sure you understand the problem and have developed, or are prepared to collaboratively develop, a plan of action (Turnbull et al., 2015). Use the strategies for communicating effectively discussed earlier in this chapter, especially active listening and depersonalizing situations. For significant or persistent problems, it is recommended that teachers obtain school or district assistance. Some districts may recommend that specific documentation procedures be implemented; others may recommend that parent/caregiver conferences be scheduled and attended by several teachers, including the building administrators (Steedman, 2012). Understand that parent/caregiver hostility might be attributable to a number of reasons and assistance is available to help improve family relations and ensure the best possible education for the student.

PARTNER WITH PARENT/CAREGIVER ADVISORY GROUPS Set up a parent/caregiver advisory group in your school to meet every month or two. This group can function as a liaison between parents/caregivers and the school regarding class projects, special curriculum areas, or regular school functions and as a disseminator of information. Teachers can share information about special class projects with all parents/caregivers at regular parent/caregiver advisory group meetings. For example, these meetings might be a nice time for Mrs. Hesser

Diversity, Equity, and Inclusion in the Classroom

Working with Families from Diverse Backgrounds

Family involvement is a critical component of the special education process but is particularly critical for children from diverse backgrounds (Gertzel-Short et al., 2019). Families representing diverse cultural and linguistic backgrounds can provide important information on their child's culture, language spoken at home, beliefs, customs, and other relevant background information (Wilt et al., 2021). Schools need to be sensitive to all cultural values, beliefs, and needs when working with families from culturally and linguistically diverse backgrounds. A lack of cultural competence and difficulties in family-educator partnerships can result in inequitable services for students with disabilities. The following strategies can help build strong trust and collaboration with diverse families:

- Maintain open and good lines of communication with families from the start of the school year.
- Ask families how they can help participate in their child's educational program at home and school. Since research suggests that some Black parents or caregivers who have children with disabilities may feel alienated from their child's school, Brandon et al. (2021) suggests using a Parent Reflection Questionnaire at the start of the school year as a way for educators to understand barriers that may impede their school involvement.
- When families speak a language other than English, have interpreters present for parent/caregiver conferences and other school events such as open houses, school plays, concerts, and athletic events.
- Address any bias you may have toward multilingual parents or caregivers.
- For individuals who speak English as a second language, consider your rate of speaking, choice of words, and use of acronyms.
- Translate home announcements and other school-related documents that go home so that parents or caregivers can access the content.
- Advertise locations of English as a second language classes for interested families.
- Arrange for child care during family school visits when necessary.
- Take action to learn about individual parents or caregivers who may have different cultural practices and norms.
- Determine whether families require transportation assistance to attend school functions.
- Arrange tutoring programs to assist both students and family members who may require additional assistance with understanding school assignments.
- Schedule multicultural events during which individuals from different backgrounds have opportunities to share information about their respective backgrounds, food, clothing, and culture.

Discuss: When communicating with parents or caregivers who are culturally and linguistically diverse, what conversational adaptations can you use to ensure equitable dialogue and participation during an IEP meeting?

to let parents/caregivers know about the assignment notebooks. She could make sure that all the parents/caregivers knew that during the upcoming parent/caregiver advisory meeting, she would be presenting that information and that she welcomed their comments regarding how they thought the process was working.

Other suitable topics include discussing the upcoming co-teaching planned by the sixth-grade and special education teachers or discussing special education referral information. Again, these meetings afford extra opportunities for positive communication and collaboration efforts among family members and school personnel. Finally, teachers can ask the group to assist in identifying topics of interest to parents, caregivers, and families and specific presentations could be tailored to their needs.

HELP PARENTS, CAREGIVERS, AND FAMILIES COPE WITH DISABILITY CHALLENGES

It may be difficult for a parent(s)/caregiver(s) to understand and accept that their child has a disability. In these cases, request assistance from the school social worker, counselor, or special education teacher. Parent(s)/caregiver(s) may be frightened or feel overwhelmed when trying to understand why their child has a disability, what needs to be done, and how they can help. It may be beneficial for parent(s)/caregiver(s) to attend support groups for parents/caregivers of children with specific disabilities. Use the expertise of the specialists within your school district to gather as much information as possible for the parents/caregivers (Turnbull et al., 2015).

Most schools have brochures and reference lists of sources suitable for parent(s)/caregiver(s) to read concerning specific disability areas. Many parents and caregivers appreciate knowing the names of books or articles that can provide additional information on their child's disability (e.g., Conroy et al., 2010). Reference lists can identify where the materials can be located (e.g., the town library, the school library, the special library for parents and caregivers). Professional organizations also maintain reference lists for specific disability areas. For example, the Council for Exceptional Children is a major special education organization that not only maintains reference lists but also has divisions specific to disability areas, such as the Division for Learning Disabilities and the Division for Emotional and Behavioral Health. Each division provides information pertaining to specific disability areas, including journals, newsletters, and websites.

2 Summary

- Collaboration—involving cooperation, effective communication, shared problem solving, planning, and finding solutions—is the process for ensuring that all students receive the free, appropriate public education mandated by IDEA.
- Effective communication is critical for successful collaboration. Effective communication involves active listening, depersonalizing situations, finding common goals, brainstorming steps for achieving common goals, identifying possible solutions, and summarizing the conversation. These steps can be very helpful in solving problems.
- General education prereferral interventions and response to intervention are steps taken by schools to promote success in the regular classroom before deciding on referral for special education. These actions can involve general and special education teachers, specialists, administrators, parents, caregivers, family members, and students, and they are often undertaken as part of a school response-to-intervention program.
- Building effective collaborative partnerships is a high-leverage practice and one of the most significant tasks of a successful inclusive teacher. With effective teamwork, solutions can be found to any number of problems.
- Collaboration can take the form of consultation, in which teachers work together to decide on intervention strategies for a specific student. Collaboration can also take the form of co-teaching, in which a general education and special education teacher teach together in an inclusive classroom setting.
- Effective collaboration with paraprofessionals can improve communication and provide clarification of roles and responsibilities. Effective collaboration with parent(s)/caregiver(s) is a key to effective inclusive teaching. Teachers should consider variability in family backgrounds and family structures and maintain close, positive contacts with parents, caregivers, and family members.

PROFESSIONAL STANDARDS LINK:
Collaboration: Partnerships and Procedures

Information in this chapter links most directly to:

- CEC 2020 Initial Practice-Based Professional Preparation Standards for Special Educators (Initial K–12 standards) (see https://exceptionalchildren.org/standards/initial-practice-based-professional-preparation-standards-special-educators): Standards: 2 (Understanding and Addressing Each Individual's Developmental and Learning Needs), 5 (Supporting Learning Using Effective Instruction), 6 (Supporting Social, Emotional, and Behavioral Growth), 7 (Collaborating with Team Members)
- InTASC Standards (see https://www.ccsso.org/sites/default/files/2017-11/InTASC_Model_Core_Teaching_Standards_2011.pdf): 2 (Learning Differences), 3 (Learning Environments), 7 (Planning for Instruction), 8 (Instructional Strategies), 10 (Leadership and Collaboration)

COLLABORATION: PARTNERSHIPS AND PROCEDURES

If you would like to improve your communication and collaboration skills, have you employed effective communication strategies, including the following? If not, see the pages listed here.

STRATEGIES FOR COMMUNICATING EFFECTIVELY

- ☐ Use active listening techniques, 30
- ☐ Depersonalize situations, 30
- ☐ Find common goals, 30
- ☐ Brainstorm Possible Solutions, 30
- ☐ Summarize goals and solutions, 31–32
- ☐ Follow up to monitor progress, 32

STRATEGIES FOR COLLABORATING WITH PARAPROFESSIONALS

- ☐ Clarify roles and responsibilities, 48–49
- ☐ Communicate effectively, 49

STRATEGIES FOR COLLABORATING EFFECTIVELY WITH PARENTS, CAREGIVERS, AND FAMILIES

- ☐ Be sensitive to variability in backgrounds and family structures, 49
- ☐ Maintain positive communication, 49–50
- ☐ Communicate about homework, 50
- ☐ Resolve disagreements, 50
- ☐ Partner with parent/caregiver advisory groups, 50–51
- ☐ Help parents, caregivers, and families cope with disability challenges, 51–52

Catuncia/123rf

CHAPTER 3

Teaching Students with Higher-Incidence Disabilities

LEARNING OBJECTIVES

After studying this chapter, you should be able to:

3.1 Describe and discuss the prevalence and characteristics of students with speech and language impairments and explain strategies for classroom adaptations.

3.2 Describe and discuss the prevalence and characteristics of students with learning disabilities and explain strategies for classroom adaptations.

3.3 Describe and discuss the prevalence and characteristics of students with intellectual disabilities and explain strategies for classroom adaptations.

3.4 Describe and discuss the prevalence and characteristics of students with behavioral disorders and emotional disturbance and explain strategies for classroom adaptations.

3.5 Describe and discuss the prevalence and characteristics of students with attention-deficit/hyperactivity disorder (ADHD) and explain strategies for classroom adaptations.

Individuals who have higher-incidence disabilities—the disabilities that are most commonly seen in schools—include a wide range of abilities and disabilities, from mild to severe in intensity. Some higher-incidence disabilities are temporary, whereas others are lifelong conditions. Higher-incidence disability areas include speech or language impairments, learning disabilities, mild or moderate intellectual disabilities, and emotional disturbance. Together, these disability areas make up over 60% of the total population of students age 5 to 21 with disabilities served under the Individuals with Disabilities Education Act (IDEA; U.S. Department of Education, 2021) and about 6% of the school-age population. Within the population of students with disabilities, percentages of students in each high-incidence category in the United States are as follows:

Speech or language impairment—16.3%

Learning disabilities—37.1%

Intellectual disabilities—6.5%

Emotional disturbance—5.4%.

In addition, about 5.7% (girls) to 11.7% (boys) or more of all school-age children have attention-deficit/hyperactivity disorder (ADHD) (National Center for Health Statistics, 2019), and ADHD may also be associated with other conditions. Although the intellectual disability figure includes those with severe intellectual disabilities, about 85% of the individuals would be characterized as having mild or moderate intellectual disabilities, as described in this chapter.

Speech or Language Impairments

Learning Objective 3.1 Describe and discuss the prevalence and characteristics of students with speech and language impairments and explain strategies for classroom adaptations.

PREVALENCE, DEFINITIONS, AND CHARACTERISTICS OF SPEECH OR LANGUAGE IMPAIRMENTS

Individuals classified as having speech or language impairments make up 16.3% of all students age 5 to 21 served under IDEA and represent 1.6% of the school-age population. **Speech** is the system of forming and producing sounds that are the basis of language, whereas **language** is considered the system of communicating ideas. Most students receiving speech and language therapy work individually or in small groups with a specialist for brief sessions several times a week and usually spend the remainder of the day in general education classes. In some schools, speech and language teachers may conduct therapy sessions in the general education classroom (Owens et al., 2019).

Some students with speech and language disorders may have another primary disability area, such as a learning disability, cerebral palsy, traumatic brain injury, or other severe disabilities. The latter groups are more likely to be using **alternative and augmentative communication (AAC)** devices to help them communicate.

Pearson eTextbook
Video Example 3.1
In the video, the child is playing with objects and speaking with the speech–language therapist. How would you characterize the child's expressive and receptive language including her articulation of words?

EXAMPLES AND CHARACTERISTICS OF SPEECH DISORDERS Speech disorders may exist as voice, articulation, or fluency disorders. Voice disorders affect the volume, pitch, flexibility, and quality of the voice and affect about 6% of school-age children (Owens et al., 2019). Examples of voice disorders include speech that is chronically strained, hoarse, breathy, or nasal. In the most severe instances, voice is not present at all.

Articulation disorders represent the largest subgroup of communication disorders (about 75%) and include difficulty pronouncing words, including omissions (e.g., "libary" for *library*), additions (e.g., "terribubble" for *terrible*), distortions (such as lisping), and substitutions (e.g., "tram" for *clam*). A child with articulation problems might say, "Wabbits aw fuwwy animals."

Fluency disorders are interruptions in the natural flow or rhythm of speech. A common fluency disorder is **stuttering**, "a communication disorder that interferes with a person's ability to speak fluently. It involves the repetition, prolongation, or blockage of sounds, syllables, or words" (Scott, 2010, p. 1). Most people who stutter begin stuttering before age 5 but only after they have begun to speak in sentences.

EXAMPLES AND CHARACTERISTICS OF LANGUAGE DISORDERS Language disorders are problems in using or comprehending language, either expressive (using language) or receptive (understanding the language of others). Language disorders may involve difficulties with phonology, morphology, syntax, semantics, or pragmatics. **Phonology** involves the ability to blend and segment the sounds that individual letters or groups of letters make to form words. For example, it may be difficult for students to identify the final sound in the words *cap* and *cat* if they have a phonological problem. **Morphology** involves the meaningful structure of words, as expressed in **morphemes**, the smallest units of language that carry meaning or function. For example, the word *teacher* contains two morphemes: a **free morpheme** (can stand alone as a word; *teach*) and a **bound morpheme** (depends on other words; *-er*). **Syntax** is the grammatical structure of language and is concerned with such things as word order and noun–verb agreement. **Semantics** refers to the meanings of words used in language. For example, the sentence "Walk can I take?" may convey a semantic meaning but is not syntactically correct. **Pragmatics** refers to the use of language in the context of social situations. For example, students typically speak to teachers in a different manner than they would speak to classmates (Owens et al., 2019).

One of the most severe language disorders is **aphasia**, defined as difficulty speaking (expressive aphasia) or comprehending (receptive aphasia) language. Aphasia often accompanies brain injuries, and individuals may experience difficulty retrieving words that they knew before the injury (Owens et al., 2019).

In the most severe communication disorders, individuals cannot speak and must learn to rely on AAC devices (Beukelman & Light, 2020).

CAUSES OF SPEECH OR LANGUAGE IMPAIRMENTS

In most cases, specific causes of speech and language disorders are unknown. Some children have severe language delays during early childhood development, but the reasons for the delay are unknown. Voice disorders can be caused by growths, infections, or trauma to the **larynx** (structure containing the vocal cords); infections of the tonsils, adenoid glands, or sinuses; or physical disorders such as **cleft palate**, in which the upper part of the oral cavity is split. The cause of stuttering is presently unknown (Scott, 2010).

IDENTIFICATION AND ASSESSMENT OF SPEECH OR LANGUAGE IMPAIRMENTS

Caregivers are usually the first to identify a potential speech or language problem, when, for example, their 2-year-old has not begun to develop language. Sometimes a young child may exhibit a slower onset or sequence of language skills. This may be a **language delay** and not a speech or language impairment. If the delay persists, however, primary school teachers may be the first to refer a child for a speech and language evaluation when they notice problems with speech or language. Frequently administered tests include articulation tests, auditory discrimination tests, language development tests, vocabulary tests, and language samples taken from a variety of social contexts. If the student speaks a language other than English, be sure to administer tests written in the student's preferred language to determine if the difficulties presented in the second language also occur in the student's first language. If they do not, this may be a **language difference** and not a speech or language impairment.

STRATEGIES FOR

MAKING ADAPTATIONS FOR STUDENTS WITH SPEECH OR LANGUAGE IMPAIRMENTS

Instruction is effectively differentiated when adaptations are made in the physical environment, instructional materials, instructional procedures, and assessment methods appropriate to the needs of individual learners. Following are some adaptations that are generally appropriate for students with speech and language impairments. More specific techniques are provided in Parts 2 and 3 of this text.

ADAPT THE PHYSICAL ENVIRONMENT Place students with communication disorders near the front of the room for easier listening. This will also enable easier access if they need help or if you have devised a special cueing system with them for responding orally in class. The following *In the Classroom* feature provides a checklist for consideration of different types of adaptations in the physical environment.

ADAPT MATERIALS Allow students to use any technology that may help them with their disability area. Various alternative methods are available to improve classroom communication. For example, the Nearpod website (https://nearpod.com) or app allows students to type a response to a teacher's open-ended question presented on interactive slides. The teacher's view on the platform displays each student's real-time response. Teachers can also make student responses visible for sharing with peers.

Use Alternative or Augmentative Communication Adaptive communication methods are referred to as AAC techniques. AAC symbols and techniques fall into two broad categories: aided and unaided. Aided communication involves the use of some external device, such as simple handmade materials, a picture board, or more sophisticated computer-assisted devices. Unaided communication does not involve any apparatus other than the individual's own body. Examples include manual signing, making physical gestures, miming, pointing, and moving the eyes (Beukelman & Light, 2020).

Alternative communication techniques involve the use of communication boards to assist communication. Communication boards contain pictures or words of commonly asked questions and responses to questions. When asking or responding to questions, students can point to the picture that communicates what they mean. Pointing devices that attach to the head can be used for students who have difficulty pointing with their hands or fingers.

In the Classroom

Sample Environmental Adaptation Considerations

Seating Position

_______ Near teacher

_______ Near peer assistant

_______ Near paraprofessional

_______ Near board

_______ Near front of room

_______ Alone

_______ Outlined area for sitting/standing (e.g., carpet squares)

_______ Quiet space

_______ Other

Seating Planned for

_______ Lunchroom

_______ Assemblies

_______ Bus

_______ All classes

_______ Other

Rearrange Physical Space

_______ Move desks

_______ Move class displays

_______ Adjust classroom lighting

_______ Adapt furniture (e.g., slant boards, desk/chair height)

_______ Other

Reduce Distractions

_______ Visual (e.g., away from the window)

_______ Auditory

_______ Movement (e.g., away from the door)

_______ Minimize clutter/limit use of color

_______ Other

Provide Daily Structure

_______ Display a daily calendar and agenda

_______ First thing to do when entering class

_______ Second thing

_______ Third thing

_______ Being prepared

_______ Other

Provide Designated Places

_______ Inboxes

_______ Outboxes

_______ Other

Provide Orderly Models

_______ Backpack area

_______ Organized desks

_______ Organized lockers

_______ Other

Pearson eTextbook
Video Example 3.2
Observe the interaction between a teacher and a young girl with language disabilities in this video as she uses her communication board to request a specific toy. How would you describe the girl's expressive and receptive skills?

When the AAC user is unable to point, a communication partner can help identify the correct symbol. Some commercially available boards, such as the *Accent*™ *1400* available from the Prentke Romich Company, produce speech output when the corresponding symbol or picture is touched. Communication devices including text-to-speech apps are also available on tablets such as the iPad.

ADAPT INSTRUCTIONAL PROCEDURES Effective teaching practices, including clear, well-organized presentations and activities, will help meet the needs of students with speech and language disorders in your classroom. Some practices, such as providing a standard, 5-second wait time after posing a question, can benefit all students, especially students with receptive and expressive language difficulties. Appropriate pace of instruction and maximized student engagement—including frequent questioning and feedback—can help ensure academic success.

Facilitate Verbal Responding Allow sufficient time for students with communication disorders to speak when responding. Do not impose time pressures on oral responses and resist the temptation to finish words or talk for the student with a speech disorder. When a student finishes, repeat or paraphrase the response for the entire class to hear when needed. For example, Mr. Lee allowed Natalie, a fourth-grade student with a speech and language disorder, sufficient time to respond and then said, "Natalie, that was a good answer. Yes, the numbers 11 and 23 are both prime numbers." When referring to a speech disorder, talk about it like any other matter; do not treat it as something to be ashamed of.

When checking for student understanding in class, ask a student who stutters questions that can be answered in just a few words. Talk with the student about a preferred time to be called on. Some students may prefer to speak in small groups rather than in front of the entire class. If you are going to call on many students in class to answer questions, the student who stutters may prefer to be called on relatively early, to allow less time for anxiety to develop (Scott, 2010). For example, at the beginning of the school year, Mrs. Stobey, a high school history teacher, met with Marcus, a student who stuttered. Social pressures including speaking situations for high school students can be especially stressful, so Mrs. Stobey wanted to reduce any communicative tension for Marcus. Together, they decided that if Marcus raised his hand, then he felt comfortable trying to participate in the discussions, and only then would Mrs. Stobey call on him to talk. She also suggested that they meet again to talk about how Marcus could try using the strategy to self-disclose his stuttering to peers when working in a small group.

Monitor your pace of instruction, especially when introducing new vocabulary to students with receptive language disorders. Use language cards containing representational pictures and illustrations depicting the definitions. Whenever possible, use concrete examples, rather than lengthy verbal descriptions, to illustrate new concepts. For example, when introducing the concept of *sequencing* in language arts, you may ask the student to verbally describe the morning routine before going to school or to select the steps of the morning routine represented on a set of picture cards. Selecting and ordering the steps of a personal experience is a concrete example of *sequencing*. Multiple concrete examples may be needed to reinforce a concept.

Practice Oral Presentations If oral presentations are mandatory, practice alone with students first and provide feedback. Consider allowing students to present with partners or in small groups, such that each group member has a different role during oral presentations.

Enlist Peer Assistance Sometimes students who stutter are teased or bullied by their peers. Speak privately to the student about teasing and brainstorm ways to respond. Speak to peers (particularly those suspected of teasing) and enlist their support in ensuring that all students are treated fairly (Scott, 2010). Suggest to peers that they try to support a student who stutters by being patient and using a slower, more relaxed rate of speech.

ADAPT ASSESSMENT METHODS Some students may require extended time periods to complete class tests. Others may require the assistance of readers, scribes, or communication boards and communication partners while taking tests. If your testing parallels your classroom instruction, students should be able to use the same materials and procedures they normally do in class when taking tests.

Learning Disabilities

Learning Objective 3.2 Describe and discuss the prevalence and characteristics of students with learning disabilities and explain strategies for classroom adaptations.

PREVALENCE AND DEFINITIONS OF LEARNING DISABILITIES

Learning disabilities (**LD** referred to as **specific learning disabilities, or SLD**, in IDEA) is a general term describing a group of learning problems. Students with LD are highly represented in general education classes, as LD is the largest single disability area. Approximately 3.6% of all school-age children are classified as having LD, or 37.1% of the children requiring special education services in the schools (U.S. Department of Education, 2021). About twice as many males as females are identified as having LD (Pullen et al., 2017).

CLASSROOM SCENARIO

Adaptations for Maria

Maria is a 12-year-old girl of average intelligence who is shy and has a pleasant, cooperative disposition. She meets grade-level expectations for listening to directions and will occasionally ask questions to clarify ideas or extend discussions. Maria tries hard to succeed in school but has a learning disability. Specifically, she has great difficulty reading independently. She can decode one-syllable words and some two-syllable words but has a difficult time with multisyllabic words. So, she reads very slowly. Whereas Maria can understand information during her teacher's oral instruction, her lack of reading fluency negatively impacts her reading comprehension. She also writes slowly, using simple statements and words that are easy for her to spell. Her writing is labored and does not accurately reflect her thinking.

Maria participates in an intensive reading intervention class (Tier 2) and she receives assistance with her writing in the resource room 2 days a week. Mr. Bashar, Maria's social studies teacher, has prioritized her class assignments. Mr. Bashar does not require that she read or write independently to participate in class activities. For example, when the class is given an assignment to read parts of the textbook and answer comprehension questions, Maria is allowed to read together with a classmate. The classmate reads the majority of the text out loud and then reads questions from the assignments aloud, and Maria is allowed to write brief answers to the questions or dictate longer answers to her partner or into a tablet with a speech-to-text app. Mr. Bashar uses clear, structured presentations to maximize Maria's understanding of the lessons. He also provides her with a study guide that aligns with each section of the chapter (e.g., framed outline, fill-in-the-blank). Finally, Maria's performance on the class assignments is systematically monitored to ensure that she is understanding the social studies content adequately and that the need for further adaptations is examined. By the second semester, her reading skills have improved enough that she is encouraged to independently complete some reading assignments in social studies when possible. Mr. Bashar chunks the larger reading assignments into smaller sections for Maria and she may ask a classmate or teacher for specific assistance when required.

QUESTIONS FOR REFLECTION

1. What else could be done to help improve Maria's reading and writing skills?
2. What other adaptations could be provided to help Maria show what she knows?

Learning disabilities is used as an umbrella term to classify those individuals with average or above-average intelligence who nonetheless have difficulties with academic tasks. The federal definition is given as follows:

> "Specific learning disability" means a disorder in one or more of the basic psychological processes involved in understanding or using language, spoken or written, which may manifest itself in an imperfect ability to listen, think, speak, read, write, spell, or to do mathematical calculations. The term includes such conditions as perceptual handicaps, brain injury, minimal brain dysfunction, dyslexia, and developmental aphasia. The term does not include children who have learning problems that are primarily the result of visual, hearing, or motor handicaps, of mental retardation, of emotional disturbance, or of environmental, cultural, or economic disadvantage. (Assistance to States for Education of Handicapped Children, 1977)

The standard that learning problems are not the result of sensory, motor, intellectual, emotional, or sociocultural influences is sometimes referred to as an **exclusionary clause**. Over the years, many definitions of *learning disability* have been proposed by various task groups and professional organizations (Hallahan et al., 2014). Most definitions share components with the federal definition.

Most states previously required the presence of a *discrepancy* between cognitive ability and achievement to support the identification of a LD. An intelligence quotient (IQ) is a measure of an individual's cognitive ability. A score of 100 is considered the average IQ with individuals scoring below, around, or above the average. For example, Edward had a full-scale IQ (intelligence quotient) score of 101 and a standard score of 85 on a test of reading achievement (low average range for that skill). This amounts to a discrepancy of 16 standard score points between ability (the IQ test) and achievement (the reading achievement test), where the full-scale IQ is average (about the 50th percentile) and the reading achievement score is substantially lower (about the 16th percentile). Other evidence in support of the presence of LD was also usually required (Alfonso & Flanigan, 2018). According to the most recent IDEA amendments, states may no longer require schools to use discrepancy criteria for identification purposes. Instead, schools are encouraged to determine whether students respond sufficiently to research-based intervention, as described later in the chapter (go to the RTI Action Network website at rtinetwork.org; see also Wright & Wright, 2005).

CAUSES OF LEARNING DISABILITIES

The specific causes of LD remain unknown but are generally believed to be associated with brain function. Three major factors—organic, genetic, and environmental—have been hypothesized as possible causes. Organic factors include indications of brain differences in size or functioning, perhaps due to differences during the development of the brain. Medical research in detecting brain dysfunctions has yielded evidence for a neurological basis that may be linked to possible causes of LD (Pullen et al., 2017). Possible genetic factors include heredity, in that students with reading problems often have other family members with similar problems and identical twins are more likely than fraternal twins to share LD (Erbeli et al., 2018; Kirkpatrick et al., 2011). Finally, environmental factors such as poor diet and nutrition and exposure to toxins such as alcohol, smoke, and cocaine, either prenatally or postnatally, may contribute to LD for some students (Raymond, 2017).

ISSUES IN IDENTIFICATION AND ASSESSMENT OF LEARNING DISABILITIES

One controversial issue involves whether students classified as learning disabled represent a truly specific category—that is, that they are distinguishable from students who are simply low achievers (e.g., the bottom 25% in achievement). Some researchers have maintained that there are few meaningful differences between the two groups of students (Fletcher et al., 2002). However, Fuchs and colleagues (2002) conducted a **meta-analysis** (research synthesis) of 86 studies comparing students with LD and low-achieving students in reading and found that students with LD generally scored considerably lower than low-achieving students. Debate on this issue continues.

Another related issue is the use of IQ–achievement discrepancy criteria. Over 20 years ago, Lyon et al. (2001) argued that discrepancy criteria are not conceptually sound, are vulnerable to measurement error, and inhibit early identification of LD. In addition, Fletcher (2012) suggested that schools may not always apply discrepancy criteria correctly in identifying students with LD. Nevertheless, these students are generally thought to experience serious academic problems in spite of average or above-average general ability, and therefore they could be expected to demonstrate some type of discrepancy (Council for Exceptional Children, 2012; Mastropieri & Scruggs, 2002). Although discrepancy models are still used, schools are not required to use IQ–achievement discrepancy criteria for identification (Alfonso & Flanagan, 2018; Wittaker & Burns, 2019).

As an alternative to discrepancy criteria, schools are now encouraged to employ a response-to-intervention (RTI) approach (also referred to as a *multi-tiered system of supports*), where general education teachers implement scientifically-based practices and use curriculum-based measurement to document student progress on a regular basis. Students who prove to be "treatment resisters" (do not show adequate progress in spite of extra attention) may be eligible for more intensive interventions administered via different "tiers" or referral to special education (Johnson, n.d.; National Center on Intensive Intervention, 2016). Evidence of failure to respond appropriately to these interventions can be used in the referral process to identify LD. These standards are now specifically encouraged in the most recent IDEA amendments (Wright & Wright, 2005).

RTI approaches are also associated with some controversy. Consistent implementation procedures have not yet been developed, the degree to which RTI discriminates between LD and other disabilities such as intellectual disabilities is not known, and procedures for intervention and identification are less clear in areas other than early reading (Berkeley et al., 2020; Hauerwas et al., 2013). However, these issues may continue to be addressed in the future as schools implement ongoing RTI procedures.

Pearson eTextbook

Video Example 3.3

The mother in this video is an educator whose daughter Carmen has been diagnosed with a specific learning disability. What does this mother share about her experiences at the old school Carmen attended and Carmen's new school?

CHARACTERISTICS OF LEARNING DISABILITIES

Individuals with LD possess a variety of characteristics that distinguish them from other students. However, not all individuals with LD have all the characteristics described in this section.

LANGUAGE AND LITERACY Many students with LD experience difficulties with both expressive and receptive language, including the following:

- Discriminating between sounds (e.g., mistakes *cat* for *cap*)
- Misunderstanding grammar (including use of certain pronouns and prepositions)

- Understanding subtleties in language
- "Word-finding" abilities or retrieving appropriate words when needed (Schmitt et al., 2014).

Most students with LD have significant reading problems (Gunning, 2018; Raymond, 2017). Many students with LD lack **phonemic awareness**—the awareness that words are made up of individual speech sounds (Siegel & Mazabel, 2014). Reading problems result when such students are unsuccessful in learning the sound codes represented by the letters in the alphabet and in applying those codes for successful reading ("decoding"). These individuals often have slow and labored oral reading abilities, are not inclined to read for pleasure, and lack effective strategies for fluent reading. Additionally, even after repeated practice of a word pattern, students with a LD may forget the pattern the very next day (Gunning, 2018). Reading comprehension difficulties frequently accompany decoding problems (Petscher et al., 2019). Other literacy problems encountered by students with LD include handwriting, spelling, and written composition (e.g., Graham et al., 2017).

MATHEMATICS It is estimated that two-thirds of all students with LD and 6% of overall elementary school population have mathematics disabilities (Montague, 2011; Wong et a al., 2017). Students may exhibit difficulties in learning math facts, rules, procedures, or concepts and in personal math such as managing money (Geary, 2014).

ATTENTION AND MEMORY Many students with LD experience difficulties with sustaining attention to tasks. Some have more serious problems, referred to as **attention-deficit/hyperactivity disorder (ADHD)** (American Psychiatric Association, 2013). Many students who have a primary disability area such as learning disabilities, emotional disabilities, or intellectual disabilities may also have ADHD (Denckla et al., 2014).

Many students with LD have deficits in both long- and short-term memory, memory for verbal information (**semantic memory**), and working memory, which provides the ability to hold information while simultaneously processing the same or other information (Swanson & Zheng, 2014). Memory problems can impede successful school performance unless students are provided with effective strategies to help compensate for such difficulties.

THINKING AND REASONING Thinking and reasoning difficulties are apparent in many individuals with LD. Abstract reasoning may be especially problematic (Lerner & Johns, 2015; Raymond, 2017). Individuals may take longer than others to learn new tasks and information. Other problems may include difficulty in organizing thinking, difficulty in drawing conclusions, over-rigidity in thinking, and general lack of effective strategies for solving problems.

METACOGNITIVE ABILITIES **Metacognition** refers to knowledge about one's own learning and understanding. Students with well-developed metacognitive skills know how to study effectively, monitor their own understanding (**self-monitoring**), and wisely plan and budget their time. They are familiar with cognitive strategies that help them learn and remember more efficiently, and they regulate their own strategy use (**self-regulation**). In contrast, many students with LD lack the metacognitive skills necessary to become successful, self-sufficient learners (Lerner & Johns, 2015). They may appear disorganized and lack an understanding of what to do or how to proceed with academic tasks or assignments.

SOCIAL-EMOTIONAL FUNCTIONING As many as one-third to one-half of students with LD may also exhibit problems with social or emotional functioning. Social-emotional problems include social skill difficulties, low self-esteem, low self-awareness and self-perception, low self-concept, weak self-confidence, anxiety, and depression (Al-Yagon & Margalit, 2014). Individuals with LD are more susceptible to adjudication than the population as a whole (Gonzalez et al., 2015).

GENERALIZATION AND APPLICATION Most students with LD—as well as those in other high-incidence disability areas—have difficulty generalizing learned information to novel situations. Some students may master content-area material in special education settings but fail to apply that information to the general education classroom or real-life settings (Raymond, 2017).

STRATEGIES FOR

MAKING CLASSROOM ADAPTATIONS FOR STUDENTS WITH LEARNING DISABILITIES

Following are adaptations that may be of use in differentiating instruction for students with LD. Adaptations can be made in the environment, instructional materials, instructional procedures, and assessment methods. (More specific techniques are provided in Parts 2 and 3 of this text.)

ADAPT THE PHYSICAL ENVIRONMENT Rearrange seating positions near students or personnel who can help students in the classroom and during school functions and who can help them focus their attention. Arrange desks so they face away from any obvious distractions. When needed, arrange for a special quiet space within your classroom. Model organization for the physical environment by designating specific locations for books, coats, lunch boxes, and other personal materials. In addition, demonstrate how desks, lockers, and notebooks should be organized. Structure daily routines and schedules: Clearly identify the first, second, and third thing to be done when entering the class and provide clear schedules for students to follow. After modeling and demonstrating, provide opportunities for students to practice and receive feedback on their organization and adherence to daily routines and schedules.

ADAPT INSTRUCTIONAL MATERIALS For students with literacy problems, adapt materials to reduce literacy requirements whenever possible; for content-area learning, use hands-on learning activities, media presentations, computer simulations, and partner reading. **High-interest, low-reading-level** (or **"hi-lo"**) books provide exciting, age-appropriate content for elementary and high school students who read below grade level (published by, e.g., High Noon Books, Capstone Press, and High Interest Publishing). Use of a word processor has obvious advantages over writing by hand and allows for easy revision and access to additional supports such as spell checkers and speech recognition (Morphy & Graham, 2012). Additionally, assistive technology applications to reduce literacy requirements are described in the *Apps for Education* feature. Teach students to adapt their own materials as study skills for classroom learning. These adaptations could include keeping assignment notebooks, scheduling time, and developing prompts for using cognitive strategies when studying.

ADAPT INSTRUCTIONAL PROCEDURES Instructional procedures can be modified to facilitate successful inclusion of students with LD (Vaughn & Bos, 2021). The use of high-leverage practices (see Chapter 6) and teacher effectiveness variables—including maximizing student engagement, providing structured and clearly presented lessons, and monitoring student progress toward goals—can help students with LD learn more effectively. For example, provide clear organization to your presentations and make your expectations very explicit. Question students frequently (with a high probability of successful answers) and ask students to rephrase information in their own words to monitor their understanding; use their answers to monitor and adjust your instruction. In addition to increasing the number of opportunities to respond, use active response strategies. For example, have students use premade response cards (e.g., True/False; Yes/No), dry-erase boards for writing and displaying their answers, or digital modes of responding like Nearpod, mentioned earlier in the chapter. Periodically review previously learned material to promote long-term learning and use specific strategies to enhance memory. Use peer tutors when needed to support learning. Provide clear directions and frequent reminders for assignments. Use research-based literacy practices and explicit instruction of study skills.

ADAPT ASSESSMENT METHODS Adapt test formats (e.g., multiple choice, matching) so that they are easy to understand. Provide opportunities for students to practice taking tests and teach test-taking skills (e.g., elimination strategies; see Chapter 12). Read test items to students with LD when this practice does not violate test standardization and reading is not being tested. Consider alternatives such as portfolio assessment and performance assessment, rather than relying entirely on traditional test formats. Use frequent formative evaluation so that you can evaluate regular progress toward meeting objectives. These adaptations will help ensure that you are obtaining a fair and accurate picture of what students with LD know and whether they are meeting their objectives. Formative evaluation techniques can also provide evidence that students with LD are benefiting from differentiated instruction in the inclusive classroom environment (Tier 1) or whether a more intensive form of instruction (Tier 2) may be required.

Research Highlight

Inclusive Instruction for Common Core Math Standards

Teachers are experiencing not only more students with math disabilities in their inclusive classes but also expectations for all students to meet the **Common Core Math Standards (CCMS)**. The CCMS are academic benchmarks for what students should know and be able to do in math. Anchored instruction research using a problem-solving approach delivered by video obtained generally favorable results (e.g., Bottge et al., 2001, 2010); however, several unmet-need areas for students with disabilities were also identified. For example, many students required additional practice activities, and the anchored instruction did not teach or improve skills for solving fractions. In addition, supplemental instruction was required to teach sub-problem-solving skills using manipulatives, either delivered technologically or with hands-on activities. Bottge et al. (2015) designed **enhanced anchored instruction (EAI)** to test whether features added to address previous shortcomings would improve the math learning of middle school inclusive classes containing students with and without disabilities. Students with and without disabilities from 25 inclusive middle school co-taught classes were assigned to either a **business-as-usual (BAU)** condition ($N = 248$) or an EAI condition ($N = 223$). Students with disabilities ($N = 134$) included those with specific learning disabilities, emotional and behavioral disorders, intellectual disabilities, autism, and other health impairments. Experimental condition students were provided training on five areas from the CCMS covering probability, ratios, fractions, geometry, and statistics in general education math classes over 66 instructional days. EAI employed author-developed computerized instruction, videos, and hands-on activities for each major unit designed to facilitate learning. For example, one unit required application of skills learned in previous units to design, build, determine costs, and test rollover cages for hovercrafts.

In the BAU condition, teachers and students completed instruction and activities complying with their assigned district and state math curriculum. Tests administered included a researcher-developed fractions computation test and a problem-solving test along with the Computation and Problem Solving and Data Interpretation subtests of the **Iowa Tests of Basic Skills (ITBS)** (Hoover et al., 2007). Analysis of post-test scores indicated that students in the EAI condition significantly outperformed BAU condition students on researcher-developed tests but not on the standardized subtests of the ITBS. It was also found that when special education teachers provided more instructional support to students with disabilities in inclusive classes, those students significantly outperformed students in the BAU condition. An analysis of the co-teaching revealed that the most frequently observed model of co-teaching was one teach and one assist (44%), during which the special educator assumed the assistant role. Team-teaching was observed 17% of the time, no co-teaching model was observed 21% of the time, and any other co-teaching models were infrequently observed. When special educators provided explicit assistance and instruction to students with disabilities during co-taught classes, the performance of students with disabilities improved. These results suggest that the EAI approach can be effectively implemented in inclusive classrooms for the benefit of all students, but it will be more effective for students with disabilities when special educators provide more explicit instructional support (see Bottge et al., 2021, for formative evaluation strategies).

QUESTIONS FOR REFLECTION

1. Why did general education students benefit as much from this EAI as the students with disabilities?
2. Why do you think more supportive classes were able to provide more explicit instruction for students with disabilities?
3. Can you think of some other ways to enhance the implementation of EAI? How would you implement it?

Intellectual Disabilities

Learning Objective 3.3 Describe and discuss the prevalence and characteristics of students with intellectual disabilities and explain strategies for classroom adaptations.

PREVALENCE AND DEFINITIONS OF INTELLECTUAL DISABILITIES

Individuals identified as having intellectual disabilities represent 6.5% of the students age 5 to 21 served under IDEA (U.S. Department of Education, 2021) or about 0.6% of the population in general. Although this number includes all individuals with intellectual disabilities served under IDEA, 80–90% have mild or moderate intellectual disabilities, as opposed to severe disabilities (Polloway et al., 2017; Raymond, 2017).

Intellectual disability (or *intellectual disabilities*) is also referred to as one type of the more general term *developmental disability* (Polloway et al., 2017). The American Association on Mental Retardation has changed its name to the **American Association on Intellectual and Developmental Disabilities** (**AAIDD**; Schalock et al., 2021). The AAIDD's definition of intellectual disability is as follows:

> Intellectual disability is a disability characterized by significant limitations both in **intellectual functioning** and in **adaptive behavior** as expressed in conceptual, social, and practical adaptive skills. This disability originates before the age of 22. (Schalock et al., 2021, p. 1)

Five assumptions should be used in applying the definition: (1) consideration of the context of community, peers, and culture; (2) consideration of cultural and linguistic diversity; (3) consideration of strengths as well as weaknesses; (4) the necessity of developing a profile of needed supports; and (5) the expectation that the individual's functioning will improve over time with appropriate supports.

Within the general area of intellectual disability, different levels of severity are often noted. Previously, professional organizations such as the American Psychological Association described levels of functioning with corresponding IQ levels, including mild (IQ about 55–70), moderate (about 35–54), severe (about 20–34), and profound (below about 20) (Jacobson & Mulick, 1996). (In the general population, the average IQ is 100, and about two-thirds of the population score between 85 and 115.) Today, the AAIDD (2010) does not employ a classification system based on IQ level; rather, the AAIDD definition suggests that individuals can be evaluated relative to a system of services and supports. These include support areas (e.g., human development, teaching and education, home and community living), relevant support activities (e.g., individual's interest, activities, and settings for participation), and levels and intensity of supports (intermittent, limited, extensive, or pervasive). These levels were intended to replace previous classification systems of mild to severe intellectual disabilities, although these latter terms are still widely used (Polloway et al., 2017; see also American Psychiatric Association, 2013). Similarly, the American Psychological Association now emphasizes adaptive functioning in conceptual, social, and practical domains more than cutoffs in IQ scores.

Students under the age of 9 who are experiencing delay, or who are considered at risk for developing delay, may be characterized as having *developmental delay*, a classification provided by the federal government to provide early services to children without reference to the intellectual disability or mental retardation label (Batshaw et al., 2019; Polloway et al., 2017).

CAUSES OF INTELLECTUAL DISABILITIES

Although a variety of causes for intellectual disabilities have been identified, many, if not most, causes are unknown (Polloway et al., 2017; Raymond, 2017). Overall, the causes of mild intellectual disabilities are more difficult to determine than the causes for severe and profound intellectual disabilities. Known or suspected causes can be categorized as genetic factors, brain factors, and environmental influences.

GENETIC FACTORS Genetic disorders or damage to genetic matter can cause intellectual disabilities. Disorders can include chromosomal abnormalities and genetic transmission of traits through families. **Down syndrome** is an example of a genetic disorder based on a chromosomal

Apps for Education

Assistive Technology Ranges from Low Tech to High Tech

Assistive technology (AT) refers to supports that help individuals maintain, increase, or improve their capabilities. AT, a critical component of individualized education program for students with disabilities, was written into IDEA 2004. AT consists of devices and services. *AT devices* refer to any tools that range from low tech to high tech or represent the range of simple adaptations to more complex technological solutions. *AT services* refer to the supports and training an individual might require to learn and use the AT devices. The following table presents examples of low- and high-tech solutions.

Area	Low Technology	High Technology
Writing	Pencil grip; scribes take notes for individual; graphic organizers; slant board	Notebook computers, tablet PCs, mobile devices, audio recorders, apps such as *SoundNote* (David Estes) to record notes or *Dragon Dictation* (Nuance Communications, Inc.) to dictate notes, word-prediction software such as *Co:Writer Universal* (integrates across desktop, iPads, Google) (Don Johnston) or *WordQ and SpeakQ* (GoQ Software)
Reading	Picture cards to enhance meaning; audiobooks; peer assistants; annotation; highlighter	Software such as *Boardmaker* or *Boardmaker Plus* (Mayer-Johnson) or use of text-to-speech reader (TTSReader) such as *NaturalReader, Snap&Read* (Don Johnston), *Aspire Reader* (Aequus Technologies), *IntelliTalk* (Intellitools), *Victor Reader Soft Bookshare Edition* (HumanWare) for blind or low vision; programs for beginning literacy such as *WiggleWorks* (Scholastic), *Let's Go Read* (Riverdeep Interactive Learning), or the free Immersive Reader available from www.microsoft.com
Math	Lined or graph paper and pencil; calculator; manipulatives	Activities and virtual tools available on websites (e.g., learning games available at http://illuminations.nctm.org, Unifix cubes available at didax.com, and virtual manipulatives available at nlvm.usu.edu) Tools with web-based activities using interactive web-based components; software such as *Unifix Software* (Didax Inc.), *MatchTime*™ (Attainment Company Inc.), *Mighty Math Astro Algebra* (Edmark, Inc.)

anomaly. It is sometimes referred to as trisomy 21 because the 21st pair of chromosomes divides into three (trisomy) instead of a single pair of chromosomes. Down syndrome is associated with some specific characteristics, including intellectual functioning in the mild to moderate ranges, short stature, upward slanting of the eyes, and a susceptibility to heart defects or upper respiratory infections. Of course, as with any population with or without disabilities, individuals with Down syndrome also exhibit a wide variety of individual characteristics. The most common inherited cause of intellectual disabilities is **fragile X syndrome**, which is caused by a mutation on the X chromosome and affects only males (Polloway et al., 2017).

BRAIN FACTORS Brain factors refer to defects in the brain or central nervous system. These can occur during prenatal development, perinatally (during the birth process), or postnatally (after the baby is born). Brain factors may be congenital (present at birth) or may appear later in life. Prenatal factors include exposure to rubella (German measles) and syphilis. Exposure to alcohol during prenatal development can lead to fetal alcohol syndrome, which may result in intellectual disabilities (Batshaw et al., 2019). Infections such as meningitis and encephalitis, which cause inflammations to the brain, may result in brain damage. Some forms of intellectual disabilities are associated with cranial malformations that result in microcephaly or hydrocephaly. **Microcephaly** is associated with a very small skull, whereas **hydrocephaly** is often characterized by an enlarged head due to an interference in the flow of cerebral spinal fluid in the head. Finally, it is known that **anoxia**, or lack of oxygen to the brain, at any time, including during birth, causes brain damage and may result in intellectual disabilities, depending on the extent of the damage (Batshaw et al., 2019).

ENVIRONMENTAL INFLUENCES Environmental influences refer to factors such as poor nutrition during prenatal development that can influence the development of the brain and result in intellectual disabilities (Raymond, 2017). Many premature and low-birth-weight babies may have intellectual disabilities. The ingestion of lead, often through lead-based paint, can also cause intellectual disabilities. Although factors such as poverty and lack of early sensory stimulation are associated, it is more difficult to prove that such environmental factors always lead to intellectual disabilities. Future research may uncover additional important factors related to causes and prevention of intellectual disabilities.

ISSUES IN IDENTIFICATION AND ASSESSMENT OF INTELLECTUAL DISABILITIES

Both intellectual functioning and adaptive behavior are assessed in making determinations regarding intellectual disability. Individually administered intelligence tests are used in most states to assess intellectual functioning and usually contain, for example, measures of vocabulary, common knowledge, short-term memory, and ability to solve mazes and jigsaw puzzles. Adaptive behavior scales assess how well individuals are able to perform daily living skills, self-help care, communication skills, and social skills. Although there is variability across states, in most states an individual should be functioning at least two standard deviations below average (approximately the second percentile) on both measures to be classified as having an intellectual disability. The level of services and supports thought to be required for an appropriate education is also frequently considered (Schalock et al., 2021).

CHARACTERISTICS OF INTELLECTUAL DISABILITIES

The most common features associated with intellectual disabilities include slower pace of learning, lack of age-appropriate adaptive behavior and social skills, and below-average language and academic skills. Many individuals with intellectual disabilities exhibit poor motor coordination, which can be improved by working with occupational therapists, physical therapists, or adaptive physical educators (Wessendorp et al., 2011). However, most students with mild and moderate intellectual disabilities have the ability to learn to read, write, and do mathematics up to the sixth-grade level, or higher in some cases. Following is an autobiographical statement written by Kirstin Palson, an individual with intellectual disabilities who was institutionalized as a child many years ago, before IDEA legislation. Her statement was included in a book of poetry she wrote.

> **From "About the Author":**
>
> My name is Kirstin Ann Palson. I was born in Boston, Massachusetts, in 1952 with complications. My diagnosis was mental retardation plus cerebral palsy, due to brain damage at birth. It was difficult those early years. Because of my behavior problems, I was sent to the Wrentham State School when I was seven years old. Those were horrendous times. At the age of fourteen I came out of Wrentham. I have overcome my handicaps, graduated from High School at twenty-two, and worked as a volunteer library aid in two elementary schools. For two years after graduation, I had a struggle getting employment. Finally, I got a full time job in a company and worked five years. The company moved out of town and I struggled with unemployment and job search for six and a half months. I have gained employment in another company full time. I got both jobs on my own.
>
> I have a great love for words. When I was growing up, it was the reading of children's stories by Mom at bedtime which gave me the ability for reading and loving books. During the past years I have given books of my poetry to family members as gifts, especially at Christmas. My love for poetry is still with me and will remain forever more. K. A. P. (Palson, 1986)

INTELLECTUAL AND COGNITIVE FUNCTIONING Individuals with intellectual disabilities exhibit deficits in intellectual functioning. In addition, these individuals usually function substantially below their age peers in related areas, including metacognitive abilities, memory, attention, thinking, and problem-solving abilities. Like students with LD, individuals with intellectual disabilities often have difficulty generalizing learned information to novel situations (Polloway et al., 2017).

In the Classroom

Preparing Classmates of Students with Disabilities

_______ Some schools have disability-awareness programs for students and teachers. If not, ask a special educator or counselor to talk about disabilities and explain strengths and differences of individuals with disabilities.

_______ Expose students in the elementary grades to books that portray characters with disabilities.

_______ Encourage older students to ask questions and set a model of open acceptance.

_______ Promote cooperative relationships between students with disabilities and students without disabilities.

_______ Tell students about their roles as possible peer tutors and helpers. Provide models of how peers can assist, but make it clear that they should ask before helping and also encourage independent functioning. They should not try to do everything for students with disabilities.

_______ Explain that all classmates, even if they are not peer tutors or helpers, can encourage students with disabilities to be active participants and members of the class.

SOCIAL AND ADAPTIVE BEHAVIOR By most definitions, individuals with mild intellectual disabilities have less-well-developed adaptive behavior than their peer counterparts, including such behavior as using the telephone or dressing appropriately. They may appear socially immature, exhibit inappropriate social behavior, or have difficulty making and maintaining friendships. Some individuals may become easily frustrated when they experience difficulty and then may act inappropriately, drawing negative attention to themselves. On the other hand, some individuals with intellectual disabilities have particularly amiable dispositions and are well liked by others (Raymond, 2017).

Some individuals with intellectual disabilities tend to have an external "locus of control," meaning they see their lives as being controlled and influenced by factors outside of themselves (e.g., fate, chance, other people). This external locus of control may hinder their development of self-reliance. A related problem is "outerdirectedness"—that is, looking to external cues or modeling behavior of others rather than relying on their own judgments. These characteristics may sometimes contribute to a lower level of motivation (Batshaw et al., 2019).

LANGUAGE Both receptive and expressive language are problem areas for individuals with intellectual disabilities. There is usually a direct relationship between the severity of intellectual disabilities and all aspects of language development (Houwen et al., 2016). Communication skills are typically less well developed, which can result in misunderstandings of directions (Westling et al, 2021). Students may exhibit difficulties with comprehension of abstract vocabulary and concepts (Roording-Ragetlie et al., 2018).

ACADEMIC SKILLS Individuals with intellectual disabilities may have difficulty learning the basic skills of reading, writing, and mathematics. The rate of learning new information may be very slow, and students may require repetition and concrete, meaningful examples for all learning activities (Spooner & Brown, 2017).

STRATEGIES FOR

MAKING CLASSROOM ADAPTATIONS FOR STUDENTS WITH INTELLECTUAL DISABILITIES

MAKE PREPARATIONS Careful preparation can greatly enhance the successful inclusion of students with intellectual disabilities. First, have an open, accepting classroom environment so that students feel welcome as genuine class members. Provide students with the same materials—desks, lockers, mailboxes—as the other students. Involve students in daily activities. Meet with them privately and pre-teach the daily routine. Show them where materials are kept and how class activities proceed. This will help build their confidence before they come in for the first time in company with their general education peers. More information for preparing classmates is given in the *In the Classroom* feature.

Diversity, Equity, and Inclusion in the Classroom

Culturally Responsive Instruction

The student population in the United States has become increasingly diverse, and schools and individual classrooms reflect that diversity. In fall 2018, over half of all students in public elementary and secondary schools were students of color, including Hispanic or Latinx/o/a, Black, Asian, American Indian/Alaska Native, Pacific Islander, or students who identified two or more races (Hussar et al., 2020). Students with higher-incidence disabilities may also represent diversity in ethnicity, race, and cultural backgrounds (Graves, 2010) and include many students who are considered English learners (U.S Department of Education, 2020). With estimates of the numbers of children and their families who have relocated to the United States increasing, there are also growing numbers of languages spoken within a single school. For example, as many as 160 different languages have been reported within the Fairfax County, Virginia, public school system (Shapiro, 2012). Nationally, languages other than English are spoken at home by over 20% of the school-age population (Camarota & Zeigler, 2014). Fortunately, there is accumulating evidence to provide teachers with guidance for working more effectively within these diverse classrooms to meet the needs of the children and their parent(s)/caregiver(s) (Casteel & Ballantyne, 2006).

Aceves and Orosco (2014) described emerging evidence-based practices for delivering culturally responsive instruction. One important aspect is to consider the culture, language, ethnicity, and racial identity of all students when planning instruction and implement educational practices that connect to and reflect culture, race, language, values, customs, daily lives, and beliefs (see Aceves & Orosco, 2014). Another consideration is to increase multicultural awareness by teaching about the various cultures, modeling and encouraging respect for and sensitivity to others, and using child-centered and problem-solving approaches while motivating all students to become engaged, active learners (see Aceves & Orosco, 2014; Echevarria & Graves, 2011, 2015). Instructional suggestions to address diverse learning needs, including for homework, are provided by Vatterott (2018).

Whereas student diversity is increasing, teachers continue to be primarily White and female. Research has indicated that students can benefit academically from having teachers who share their racial-ethnic background (see Bettini et al., 2018). Policymakers and leaders of school districts should actively consider ways to diversify the special educator workforce.

Discuss: How can learning about a child's background, language, experiences, and culture influence instruction?

MONITOR PEER RELATIONSHIPS Although peers can be good friends and strong supporters of students with intellectual disabilities, teachers also should be aware that some students may try to take advantage of students with intellectual disabilities. For example, in one sixth-grade class, several boys bullied a boy with an intellectual disability and consistently took away part of his lunch. In another example, high school students who had been smoking cigarettes in the girls' restroom handed their cigarettes to a girl with an intellectual disability when a teacher entered the restroom. Careful monitoring can decrease the likelihood of such negative situations occurring and increase the likelihood that peer relations will be positive and productive. School districts should employ policies and practices such as bullying prevention programs to ensure a safe environment for students with disabilities (see Maag & Katsiyannis, 2012).

ADAPT INSTRUCTIONAL MATERIALS Reduce the vocabulary and complexity of reading, writing, and language requirements and use scaffolds to limit memory demands. Teachers may need to adapt or create age-appropriate texts for students to access the curriculum, especially at the high school level. Use visual supports, concrete examples (simple to more complex), relevant experiences, and hands-on materials for activities whenever possible.

Use specialized curriculum when necessary. Some students with intellectual disabilities may benefit from an alternative, more functional curriculum. Such a curriculum may include language and communication, community living, domestic skills, socialization, self-help, and vocational and leisure skills. Additionally, some students may benefit from a life-skills curriculum that emphasizes transition to adulthood. This curriculum could include education in home and family/caregiver skills, community involvement, seeking employment, emotional and physical health, and personal responsibility and relationships (see Moljord, 2018).

ADAPT INSTRUCTIONAL PROCEDURES Many of the modifications described in the LD section may also be helpful for students with intellectual disabilities. However, additional modifications probably will be required if the general education experience is to be successful, such as the following:

- *Prioritize objectives* for students with intellectual disabilities in general education classes by determining the most important things for students to learn from specific lessons and teach directly to these prioritized objectives.
- *Adapt instruction* by employing clear, organized presentations; providing concrete, meaningful examples and activities; providing frequent reviews; and encouraging independent thinking. Use frequent feedback and reinforcement for longer or more difficult tasks.
- *Communicate with families/caregivers* to further your understanding and obtain additional information on how students work and learn best. The *Diversity, Equity, and Inclusion in the Classroom* feature describes practices for culturally responsive instruction.

ADAPT ASSESSMENT METHODS Use alternative assessments for statewide assessments such as measures that are based on the grade-level content but at reduced depth, breadth, and complexity as appropriate. Individual testing, portfolio assessments, audio or video recordings, or other techniques may also be appropriate.

Emotional Disturbance

Learning Objective 3.4 Describe and discuss the prevalence and characteristics of students with behavioral disorders and emotional disturbance and explain strategies for classroom adaptations.

PREVALENCE AND DEFINITIONS OF EMOTIONAL DISTURBANCE

Individuals classified as having emotional disturbance (or behavioral disorders) represent 5.4% of all students age 5 to 21 served under IDEA, or about 0.5% of the school population (U.S. Department of Education, 2021). However, prevalence studies have suggested that the actual percentage of students requiring some type of intervention may be much higher, perhaps as high as 6–10% of the school-age population (Kauffman & Landrum, 2018). Boys outnumber girls in this category by about 2 to 1 (National Center for Health Statistics, 2019).

Although *emotional disturbance* (or emotional disability) is commonly used, other terms are used to describe this condition, including *emotional handicap*, *behavioral disorder*, *emotional/behavioral disorder*, or *social and emotional disorder* (Raymond, 2017).

Emotional disturbance refers to a number of different, but related, social-emotional disabilities. Individuals classified as emotionally disturbed meet at least one of several characteristics that persist over time and that negatively affect school performance, including the following:

- Inability to learn that cannot be explained by intellectual, sensory, or health factors.
- Inability to build or maintain satisfactory interpersonal relationships with peers and teachers.
- Inappropriate types of behavior or feelings under normal circumstances.
- General pervasive mood of unhappiness or depression.
- Tendency to develop physical symptoms or fears associated with personal or school problems (Assistance to States for the Education of Children with Disabilities, 2002).

Individuals classified as emotionally disturbed represent a range of severity, and the disability itself may be temporary or permanent. Specific emotional disturbance areas include childhood-onset **schizophrenia**; **selective mutism** (failure to speak in selected circumstances); seriously aggressive or acting-out behavior; conduct disorders; inappropriate affective disorders, such as depression, social withdrawal, psychosomatic disorders, anxiety disorders, and self-mutilating behaviors; and excessive fears (or phobias). Individuals characterized as socially maladjusted (e.g., juvenile delinquency) are not considered emotionally disturbed according to IDEA unless they also exhibit other evidence of emotional disturbance (Kauffman & Landrum, 2018).

CAUSES OF EMOTIONAL DISTURBANCE

Most behavioral disorders or emotional disturbances have no known cause. However, possible causes include biological, family, school, and cultural factors (e.g., Landrum, 2017).

Biological factors are genetic, biochemical, and neurological influences that interact and result in emotional disabilities. Schizophrenia and **Tourette syndrome**—a tic disorder characterized by involuntary muscular movements, vocalizations, and/or inappropriate verbal outbursts—appear to have biological bases that interact with other factors and may contribute to emotional disturbances. However, Tourette syndrome is not necessarily associated with emotional disturbance. Family/caregiver factors (such as domestic violence) are also considered to be strong contributing factors to emotional disturbance. School factors (such as failure to accommodate for individual needs, inappropriate expectations, or inconsistency) can also contribute to an emotional disability. Finally, certain cultural and environmental factors (including peer group, urbanization, bullying, and neighborhood factors) interact with the individual, the home, and the school and may also contribute to emotional disabilities (Kauffman & Landrum, 2018).

ISSUES IN IDENTIFICATION AND ASSESSMENT OF EMOTIONAL DISTURBANCE

Individuals with emotional disabilities are difficult to identify and classify objectively. Moreover, there appears to be reluctance on the part of school personnel to label a child "emotionally disturbed." Traditional measures to identify emotional or behavioral disabilities come from a variety of sources and include teacher checklists; parental/caregiver checklists; classroom behavioral observations; and tests of intelligence, achievement, and psychological status (Raymond, 2017). Checklists are listings of frequently observed behaviors. Behavior rating scales used for identification and assessment include the Behavioral and Emotional Rating Scale (BERS-3; Epstein et al., 2022) and the Behavior Assessment System for Children (BASC-3; Kamphaus & Reynolds, 2015). Teachers and caregivers complete checklists by indicating the types and severity of problem behaviors. Direct observations are conducted during classes, on the playground, at lunch, and in other parts of the school (Kauffman & Landrum, 2018).

CHARACTERISTICS OF EMOTIONAL DISTURBANCE

As with other categories of exceptionality, not all individuals with emotional disturbance will exhibit all the characteristics described in this section.

SOCIAL BEHAVIOR Most students with emotional disturbance have problems with their social behavior, often manifested as less mature or inappropriate social skills (Kauffman & Landrum, 2018). Some students may be particularly aggressive with peers and adults and cause harm when playing or interacting with others. These students act out in class, do not appear to respond appropriately to discipline from teachers, and may seem oblivious to class and school rules (Turtura et al., 2014). Students with behavioral disorders are at higher risk for substance abuse (Swendsen et al., 2011).

Other students may exhibit social behavior similar to that of younger children and act socially immature. Some students may withdraw from others and appear socially isolated. Although withdrawn students may not call as much attention to themselves as students with conduct disorders, they nonetheless may require intensive interventions (Stormont et al., 2015). These students may exhibit symptoms of depression. Social isolates do not interact with any peers or adults and, in the most severe cases, they may exhibit selective (or elective) mutism. Individuals with selective mutism have the physical ability to talk but nevertheless do not speak in appropriate situations (Monzo et al., 2015). All of these emotional or behavioral disorders share the characteristic of an inability to interact appropriately with others, including peers, teachers, siblings, and family/caregiver members, which negatively affects school performance (Landrum, 2017).

Students with emotional disturbance may also inappropriately attribute their behavioral or social problems to causes outside of themselves, saying such things as, "Teachers are out to get me" or "Other kids always get me into trouble." By doing this, these students are able to avoid acknowledging or evaluating their own behavior and their own role in behavior problems.

AFFECTIVE CHARACTERISTICS Some students with emotional disturbances have serious affective disorders. Affective disorders can take many forms, but the most commonly recognized forms include depression, severe anxiety disorders, phobias, and psychosomatic disorders (Kauffman & Landrum, 2018). Individuals with some of these disorders may be treated with different medications.

ACADEMIC CHARACTERISTICS Research has indicated that students with emotional disturbances may function 2 or more years below grade level in reading, math, writing, and spelling (Algozzine et al., 2011; Siperstein et al., 2011). These deficiencies may be related to the emotional disabilities. For example, if students have severe anxieties or feelings of anger, they may be unable to attend, listen, and learn in school. Some students lack social skills that are necessary for school success. Others may exhibit severe deficiencies in metacognitive skills, memory skills, and attention, which may lead to academic underachievement (e.g., Scruggs et al., 2010). Students with emotional disturbance are at risk for dropping out of school, hindering their future life possibilities. Nevertheless, some students with emotional or behavioral disabilities attain average, or even above-average, academic achievement in some areas.

STRATEGIES FOR

MAKING CLASSROOM ADAPTATIONS FOR STUDENTS WITH EMOTIONAL DISTURBANCE

General adaptations can facilitate the inclusion of students with emotional and behavioral disorders into inclusive classes. The *In the Classroom* feature lists some examples. Some specific adaptations for differentiating instruction to promote successful inclusion are presented next.

PREPARE THE CLASS Prepare your class for students with emotional disabilities by describing any relevant individual needs the students might have. Set up models for tolerance and acceptance. Establish systems to reinforce the class and/or individuals who demonstrate appropriate behavior and follow routines. Provide opportunities for students with emotional disabilities to assume class responsibilities, such as distributing papers. Give examples of ways general education peers can help these students, such as how to ignore inappropriate behaviors. Some students may be able to serve as peer tutors or assistants to help support and reinforce appropriate behaviors from students with emotional disabilities (see Watts & McKenna, 2021). However, select peers carefully; not all peers would be good choices. Remember that sometimes students with emotional disabilities will do better working alone even when the rest of the class is working in small groups.

ADAPT THE PHYSICAL ENVIRONMENT Adjust seating arrangements where needed to help prevent challenging behavior. Consider increasing the degree of proximity to good peer models and positive teacher and teacher aide attention. Conversely, arrange seating to avoid proximity to other students with whom the target student interacts negatively. Keep all potentially harmful objects or substances away from easy access.

ADAPT INSTRUCTIONAL MATERIALS When appropriate, use the suggestions listed for students with learning disabilities and intellectual disabilities. Devise self-monitoring checklists (see Figure 3.1) that students can use to check off activities as they complete them (e.g., Mastropieri et al., 2014). Self-monitoring checklists can be customized at https://www.interventioncentral.org/tools/self-check-behavior-checklist-maker. Break assignments into short segments to avoid overwhelming students. Teach students the social skills necessary for success.

ADAPT INSTRUCTIONAL PROCEDURES Use the teacher effectiveness variables and teacher presentation variables to ensure that content is covered adequately (see Chapter 6). Help students focus by teaching clearly and enthusiastically, providing additional review, and teaching self-monitoring for attention. Figure 3.2 shows an interval recording checklist for a student to self-monitor the presence or absence of target behaviors. For example, when it is time to take notes in class, the student will stop at a designated interval (a tone or timer goes off) and

Figure 3.1 Self-Monitoring Checklist for Entering the Room Appropriately

This form includes all elements of the customized self-monitoring checklist. The format is suitable for one self-rating during a session.

Checklist Item
❑ I have my homework ready to turn in.
❑ I have turned off my cell phone and put it away in my backpack.
❑ I have closed up my backpack and placed it on the floor.
❑ I have cleared my desk of unneeded materials.
❑ I am sitting quietly.
❑ I am working on the assigned start-of-class activity.

Note: Customized using the Self-Check Behavior Checklist Maker at https://www.interventioncentral.org/tools/self-check-behavior-checklist-maker.

Figure 3.2 Self-Monitoring Interval Recording Checklist for Taking Notes in Class

This form displays the self-monitoring checklist items and includes columns for 5-minute interval-recording of behaviors. For each target behavior write Y in the column if the student displays each of the 3 behaviors; N if the student does not display the behavior. The format is suitable for multiple self-ratings during a session.

	Intervals									
Target Behavior	**1**	**2**	**3**	**4**	**5**	**6**	**7**	**8**	**9**	**10**
I am listening to the teacher's presentation.										
I am looking at the board or at the teacher.										
I am not talking to other students.										

Note: Customized using the Self-Check Behavior Checklist Maker at https://www.interventioncentral.org/tools/self-check-behavior-checklist-maker.

Pearson eTextbook

Video Example 3.4

In this video, an expert explains how self-monitoring of one's own behavior can help improve a student's attention in class. What are the practical considerations to plan for if you were to use this practice in class?

self-check with a Y or N. The checklist in Figure 3.2 allows the behavior to be recorded every 5 minutes in a 50-minute class session (see Chapter 8).

You can help prevent challenging behavior through effective planning and scheduling, by implementing rules and procedures, and through effective instruction (Scheuermann & Hall, 2022). Illustrate rules with clear examples and specify rewards for following rules as well as consequences when rules are disobeyed. For very young students, the rules and consequences can be represented with a series of visual images or Picture Communication Symbols (Mayer-Johnson, 2000). The images can serve as visual reminders of the problem/positive behaviors and the negative/positive consequences that follow (see Tobin & Simpson, 2012).

Be consistent when enforcing rules, but make sure the overall classroom atmosphere is positive, not punitive. Provide models of acceptable behaviors to avoid confusion or misinterpretation on the part of students:

> "Here's one thing you can say if you think another student is sitting too close to you . . ." "Here is something you should *not* say . . ."

In the Classroom

General Accommodations for Students with Emotional Disabilities

_____ Establish an open, accepting environment.

_____ Clearly state class rules and consequences.

_____ Establish a structured routine inclusive of transitions.

_____ Emphasize positive behaviors and program for success.

_____ Reinforce positive behavior by providing behavior-specific praise.

_____ Supply extra opportunities for success.

_____ Be tolerant.

_____ Use good judgment.

_____ Teach social skills.

_____ Teach self-control, self-monitoring, and conflict resolution.

_____ Teach academic survival skills.

_____ Teach positive attributions.

_____ Carefully select partners.

_____ Have alternative activities available.

_____ Design activity checklists.

_____ Provide students with choices.

_____ Use carefully selected peers as assistants.

_____ Allow students to work alone rather than in small groups when appropriate.

_____ Use behavioral contracts.

Maintain a positive relationship with students with emotional disabilities by responding to them as human beings, rather than responding simply to their overt behavior, which may sometimes be unpleasant (see Regan, 2009). Use positive and specific comments frequently to reinforce good behavior when you see it. Say things like the following:

- "Antonio, I appreciate the way you tried hard in class today. I know that math is not your favorite subject."
- "Brianna, I am glad that you volunteered an answer in class today. Thank you for doing that."

Positive comments can be varied so that they are suitable for either elementary-, middle-, or secondary-level students.

Before reprimanding negative social behavior, say, "Stop and think about what you just did. What should you have done? Now, try to do it more appropriately."

Be tolerant and use judgment in allocating times for enforcing compliance, times for cooling off, and times for allowing divergent responding. For example, one fifth-grade teacher, Mr. Bahs, allowed a student with emotional disabilities to remain at his desk even though he had asked all students to move to the floor in the front of the room to view a new class iguana. In this way, he was able to prevent a confrontation and allow the student to participate in his own way.

Some students may have specific fears and anxieties, such as fear of the dark, water, or getting dirty; in some cases, they may not acknowledge these fears (e.g., "I'm not afraid of snakes; I just don't like them!"). Be aware of those fears by communicating with special education teachers, parent(s)/caregiver(s), and the students themselves. If class activities seem to bring out those fears in some students, have alternative activities available that they can work on independently.

Many students in your classes, especially students with emotional disturbance, can benefit from general social skills instruction. For example, review more acceptable ways of asking and answering questions and more suitable ways of resolving conflicts at appropriate times.

Teach students to monitor their own behavior and to make positive attributions. Teach students how to attribute their successes to positive strategies and effort on their part, rather than to luck or other external forces. Likewise, teach them to attribute their failures to things under their control, such as their own behavior, and not to external factors, such as "The teacher hates me." Model effective positive attributions by saying, for example, "I used the 'stop and think' strategy before acting, so I stayed out of trouble!" (see Polsgrove & Smith, 2004).

Use behavioral contracts with students with emotional disabilities. Behavioral contracts are individually negotiated contracts between the teacher and student. Specific behaviors students are expected to complete are listed, along with designated rewards for the positively accomplished goals.

ADAPT ASSESSMENT METHODS Maximize student potential on exams by providing distraction-free environments, providing extended time allocations during testing periods, and ensuring that students have the skills to take tests efficiently (Scruggs & Marsing, 1988; Shriner & Wehby, 2004). In some cases, individual testing, where this does not violate standardization, can lead to more accurate and valid test results.

SUPPORT MULTI-TIERED INTERVENTIONS Many schools now promote a schoolwide system of **positive behavior interventions and supports (PBIS)** to promote positive social behavior. Like other multi-tiered systems, PBIS can be implemented at different levels, or tiers, of increasing intensity; it is used to provide increasing behavioral support as needed and, ultimately, referral to special education where necessary (Evanovich & Scott, 2016).

Attention-Deficit/Hyperactivity Disorder

Learning Objective 3.5 Describe and discuss the prevalence and characteristics of students with attention-deficit/hyperactivity disorder (ADHD) and explain strategies for classroom adaptations.

DEFINITIONS, PREVALENCE, AND CHARACTERISTICS OF ADHD

Robert has ADHD; his family/caregiver and teacher could benefit from suggestions as to how to best work with him. Robert's disruptive behaviors and his inability to sustain attention could put him at risk for failing in school (Rooney, 2017). ADHD refers to a "neurological condition that involves problems with inattention and hyperactivity that are developmentally inconsistent with the age of the child" (U.S. Department of Education, 2008, p. 1). Observations made in the classroom will identify these students as those who often say "Huh, what?" immediately following directions; often appear to be daydreaming; act before they think; blurt out answers; interrupt; and constantly fidget, wiggle, and move around. Table 3.1 compares the sharp contrast between commonly noted behaviors on elementary school report cards and those noted for students with ADHD.

The Centers for Disease Control and Prevention reported that 8.8% of children and adolescents ages 3 to 17 have been diagnosed with ADHD (National Center for Health Statistics, 2019). Most students with the disorder are served full time in general education classrooms, with some individuals qualifying for special education services under the "Other Health Impairment" category of IDEA (Rooney, 2017).

The fifth edition of the *Diagnostic and Statistical Manual of Mental Disorders* (American Psychiatric Association, 2013) describes criteria for the classification of ADHD. The symptomatic behaviors must be maladaptive and must be present for a minimum of 6 months to warrant a classification as either inattentive ADHD or hyperactivity-impulsivity ADHD. Several symptoms should have been present before 12 years of age. Furthermore, a child must display a minimum number of identifying characteristics before ADHD is diagnosed. For example,

Pearson eTextbook

Video Example 3.5

In this video, an administrator and behavioral specialist discuss a process to reduce a targeted student behavior. How is the students' behavior monitored throughout the school day? What behavioral supports are put in place?

TABLE 3.1 Elementary School Report Cards and Commonly Observed Statements Describing Students with ADHD

	Typical Behaviors on Report Cards	Observed Statements Describing Students with ADHD
Compliance	• Follows directions • Obeys rules	• Frequently ignores directions • Talks continuously
Self-Control	• Waits turn • Tolerates frustration	• Impatient • Gives up easily
Social	• Polite, courteous	• Often interrupts
Development	• Keeps hands to self	• Touches everything
Attention	• Stays on task • Makes efficient use of time	• Rarely finishes work • Frequently fidgeting

Source: From Cherkes-Julkowski et al. (1997). Copyright 1997 by Brookline Books. Adapted with permission.

students must meet six of nine characteristics under "Inattention" (e.g., fails to give close attention, often easily distracted, is often forgetful) or six of nine characteristics under "Hyperactivity/Impulsivity" (e.g., often fidgets, often leaves seat, often interrupts or intrudes on others). There also must be evidence of impairment in social, occupational, or academic functioning and some impairment from the symptoms must be present in at least two settings.

Any inattentiveness, impulsivity, and hyperactivity must be observed across settings (American Psychiatric Association, 2013). Or, as in the case of Robert, the teacher and his caregiver(s) must observe similar behavior patterns at school and at home. Although some symptoms change over time, ADHD is now considered potentially a lifelong disorder. Males outnumber females in this disorder (Rooney, 2017). Students with ADHD are thought to be more likely to have a LD than other children (Wei et al., 2014).

CAUSES OF ADHD

Precise causes of ADHD are unknown; however, it is thought that many factors contribute to it. These factors include genetic, nongenetic, psychosocial, and neurobiological bases. Genetic evidence is based on research with families whose members have ADHD. Some researchers estimate that as many as 40% of children with ADHD have a parent(s) with the disorder, and concordance of ADHD has been seen to be much higher in identical (monozygotic) twins than in fraternal (dizygotic) twins, suggesting a genetic component (Rooney, 2017). Many children with ADHD exhibit attention and self-control difficulties at a very early age (Kauffman & Landrum, 2018). Nongenetic factors include prenatal and perinatal factors, allergies, and thyroid disorders. Although both food additives (Nigg et al., 2012) and sugar (Stevens et al., 2015) have been proposed as direct causes of ADHD, research has not substantiated these as plausible (Rooney, 2017); however, they may play a role in some individual cases. Other research has investigated the psychosocial and neurological correlates associated with ADHD, with evidence growing in support of neurological indicators. To date, however, as with many disorders, no definitive single etiological factor has been uncovered. At present, it seems that ADHD appears to be more influenced by neurological and genetic factors than by social or environmental factors (Barkley, 2014).

CLASSROOM SCENARIO

Brady

Brady Lee had so much energy that his behaviors exhausted everyone around him, including his family members; his teacher, Ms. Moore; and his classmates. When he arrived at school, everything around him appeared to get caught in a whirlwind of activity: papers flew to the floor, books were dropped, toys were broken, classmates were annoyed, and teachers threw their hands up in dismay. Brady was a nice 8-year-old boy, but he could not focus on one thing at a time. He seemed mesmerized by everything, moving from activity to activity with limitless energy. When someone spoke, he would interrupt and start talking about something that popped into his head. If he saw something that interested him, he would immediately take it in his hands. Brady's feet, hands, and eyes seemed to be moving constantly. He seemed unable to sit still. Ms. Moore was frustrated and unsure of how to handle Brady in the classroom, so she called Mr. and Mrs. Lee and asked them to come in for a conference. What became immediately evident at the conference with the family members was that Mr. and Mrs. Lee were experiencing similar problems and frustrations at home with Brady—and had been since he was 2 years old.

QUESTIONS FOR REFLECTION

1. Why do you think Mr. and Mrs. Lee were experiencing similar challenges with Brady at home?
2. What types of strategies might be helpful for Brady and his family member(s) to use at home?
3. What behavioral and instructional supports are available for working with Brady in school?

ISSUES IN IDENTIFICATION AND ASSESSMENT OF ADHD

There is no individual test to identify ADHD. Most experts recommend a multidisciplinary assessment (Rooney, 2017). A first step is to determine whether ADHD exists, and a second step could attempt to determine whether the student's educational progress is adversely affected by it. During the first step, information is collected on observations of the individual's behavior throughout the day, medical history, family/caregiver information, school information, social-emotional functioning, and cognitive-academic functioning. A medical exam, clinical interview, and rating scales of the individual's behavior completed by parent(s)/caregiver(s) and teachers can be part of this evaluation process (Kauffman & Landrum, 2018).

There is no IDEA category representing ADHD, so identified students do not necessarily qualify for services. To qualify for special education services in the "Other Health Impairment" category of IDEA, it must be documented that the ADHD has an adverse effect on educational performance. To qualify for special services under Section 504 of the Vocational Rehabilitation Act, it must be documented that the ADHD substantially limits learning. If either of these requirements is met, an intervention plan is designed and implemented as either part of the individualized education program in compliance with IDEA or the accommodation plan for compliance with Section 504. In the event that students with ADHD do not meet criteria for either IDEA or Section 504, no special accommodations are designed as part of any legally mandated system. However, these students with ADHD also frequently benefit from some of the general classroom adaptations described here and listed in the following section.

STRATEGIES FOR MAKING CLASSROOM ADAPTATIONS FOR STUDENTS WITH ATTENTION-DEFICIT/HYPERACTIVITY

Many strategies described earlier in this chapter for differentiating instruction by adapting the physical environment, materials, instruction, and assessments for students with higher-incidence disabilities are appropriate for students with ADHD. The following *In the Classroom* feature provides some suggestions for accommodations that can add to classroom success (see also Kauffman & Landrum, 2018; Wolraich et al., 2010).

ADAPT INSTRUCTION WITH BEHAVIORAL INTERVENTIONS

Behavioral interventions are strategies used to analyze and modify behavior. Students' behaviors are first analyzed with respect to **antecedent** and **consequent** events (i.e., what happened before and after the undesirable behavior occurred). Strategies are then implemented systematically based on that analysis (Lewis et al., 2017). For example, a teacher observed that every time a worksheet was distributed in class, Jasmine got out of her seat to sharpen her pencils and get a drink of water, bothering several classmates in the process. After this, the teacher would reprimand Jasmine, which would make her feel sullen and resentful. After analyzing this behavior, it seemed likely that she was reacting to the difficulty or interest level of the task and her own predisposition toward physical activity. The teacher decided to have Jasmine sharpen her pencils and get a drink of water before class every day. In addition, the teacher would praise her for remaining in her seat and leaving classmates alone after the worksheets were passed out. The teacher also monitored the content of the academic activities to make sure they were of the appropriate difficulty level and held some interest for Jasmine. He provided alternative opportunities for her to leave her seat under teacher supervision so that she could engage in some physical movement when needed. Such strategies can be effective when they are designed to meet the specific needs underlying problem behaviors.

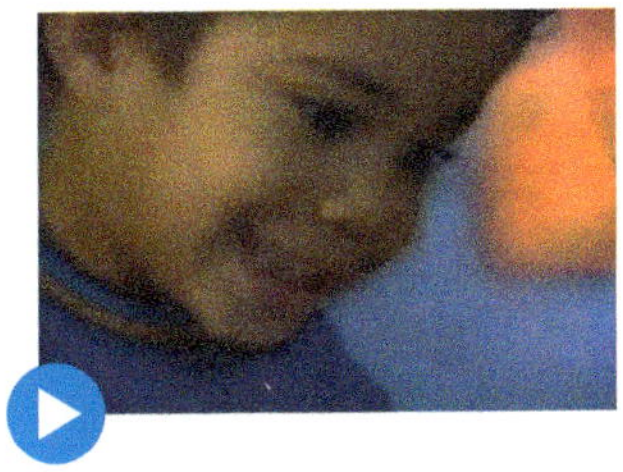

Pearson eTextbook
Video Example 3.6
In this video, the clinical director and therapists of a day treatment setting for children discuss the characteristics of ADHD and its possible causes. Notice the strategies used with this student.

ADAPT INSTRUCTION WITH COGNITIVE-BEHAVIORAL INTERVENTIONS

Cognitive-behavioral interventions use the same principles of behavior management just described but, in addition, they add a **self-instruction and self-monitoring** component to the intervention. For example, Jasmine could be taught to keep daily records of (1) how often she remembered to sharpen her pencils and get a drink of water before class and (2) whether she was able to stay in her seat once the worksheet was handed out. Specific rewards might even be paired with how well Jasmine monitored her own behavior. Other commonly used cognitive-behavioral interventions involve the use of self-monitoring for on-task behavior and task completion. The self-monitoring practice is recommended for use when students are

In the Classroom

Accommodation Suggestions for Students with ADHD

For Beginning Activities

_____ Give small amounts of work.

_____ Provide student with choices.

_____ Provide signals to begin.

_____ Use timers and encourage self-monitoring.

_____ Use verbal and written directions.

_____ Provide additional structure (e.g., classroom expectations displayed; large-lined paper).

_____ Highlight directions using larger fonts or colors.

For Keeping on Task

_____ Use behavior-specific praise.

_____ Increase the frequency of positive reinforcement.

_____ Use peer assistants.

_____ Make tasks interesting.

_____ Break tasks into smaller "manageable" units.

_____ Allow breaks.

_____ Use hands-on activities.

_____ Use varied responding techniques (e.g., verbal, gestural, written, or digital).

For Listening

_____ Teach note taking and encourage the use of notebook organizers.

_____ Use positive reinforcement.

_____ Allow doodling.

_____ Allow standing or relocating to preferred area of room.

For Excessive Activity

_____ Use activity as a reward (run errands, extra recess time, move desks, get a drink of water).

_____ Allow standing during class.

_____ Encourage active participation.

_____ Reward sitting.

For Impulsive Behavior

_____ Provide acceptable alternatives (e.g., choice for order of instructional tasks).

_____ Encourage trying to continue with another part of the assignment before interrupting the teacher.

_____ Recommend note taking during lectures.

_____ Recommend writing down questions and answers before blurting out.

_____ Teach acceptable social behavior for conversations, class behavior, and interacting with peers.

_____ Reward listening and appropriate behaviors.

For Working Independently

_____ Ensure tasks match ability levels.

_____ Provide brief directions.

_____ Assign brief tasks.

_____ Assign checklists for self-monitoring.

_____ Use positive reinforcement and behavior-specific praise.

For Following Class Rules

_____ Keep rules simple.

_____ Post and review class rules.

_____ Model and role-play following rules.

_____ Reinforce students for following class rules.

_____ Be consistent with enforcement of rules.

_____ Provide students with copies of rules.

assigned seatwork they are capable of completing independently. Strategies such as these have been particularly successful with students with ADHD.

MONITOR USE OF MEDICATIONS As many as 2 million students with ADHD take psychostimulant medications, such as Ritalin (methylphenidate) or Adderall (dextroamphetamine and amphetamine), to help control their attention and hyperactivity (Rooney, 2017). The number of children taking medications for ADHD has risen considerably over the years. If students are taking medications, teachers must keep thorough records of behavior to help monitor their effects. Reviews of research on the effects of stimulant medication generally indicate positive benefits, in that attention to task increases and hyperactivity decreases (Barkley, 2014). However, the practice of administering medications has remained controversial. Some educators and physicians argue that the side effects of medications can be harmful and that no students should be given them to control their classroom behavior. When medication is prescribed, however, concomitant behavior therapy, such as the cognitive-behavioral interventions described previously, is generally also recommended (Rooney, 2017).

3 Summary

- Students with communication disorders may exhibit problems with speech or language. Speech disorders may involve voice, articulation, or fluency; language disorders may involve difficulties with phonology, morphology, syntax, semantics, or the pragmatics of language use.
- Students with learning disabilities make up about half of students with higher-incidence disabilities. These students may exhibit specific problems in basic academic skill areas, as well as areas such as language, attention, memory, social skills, and metacognition.
- Students with intellectual disabilities exhibit deficiencies in intellectual functioning and corresponding levels of adaptive behavior. These students also may exhibit learning problems related to language, social behavior, attention, reasoning, academics, comprehension, and problem solving.
- Students with behavioral disorders or emotional disturbance may exhibit problems in classroom behavior and social relations or may exhibit disorders of affect, such as anxiety or depression.
- Students with attention-deficit/hyperactivity disorder may be served under Section 504 or IDEA. Adaptations for this group of individuals may include behavioral approaches, cognitive-behavioral training, medication, or a combination of the three.

PROFESSIONAL STANDARDS LINK:
Teaching Students with Higher-Incidence Disabilities

Information in this chapter links most directly to:

- CEC 2020 Initial Practice-Based Professional Preparation Standards for Special Educators (Initial K–12 standards) (see https://exceptionalchildren.org/standards/initial-practice-based-professional-preparation-standards-special-educators): Standards: 1 (Learner Development and Individual Learning Differences), 2 (Understanding and Addressing Each Individual's Developmental and Learning Needs), 5 (Supporting Learning Using Effective Instruction), 6 (Supporting Social, Emotional, and Behavioral Growth)
- InTASC Standards (see https://www.ccsso.org/sites/default/files/2017-11/InTASC_Model_Core_Teaching_Standards_2011.pdf): 2 (Learning Differences), 3 (Learning Environments), 7 (Planning for Instruction), 8 (Instructional Strategies)

TEACHING STUDENTS WITH HIGHER-INCIDENCE DISABILITIES

If a student with higher-incidence disabilities is having difficulties in your classroom, have you tried the following general modifications? If not, see the pages listed here.

STRATEGIES FOR MAKING ADAPTATIONS FOR STUDENTS WITH SPEECH OR LANGUAGE IMPAIRMENTS

STRATEGIES FOR MAKING CLASSROOM ADAPTATIONS FOR STUDENTS WITH LEARNING DISABILITIES

STRATEGIES FOR MAKING CLASSROOM ADAPTATIONS FOR STUDENTS WITH INTELLECTUAL DISABILITIES

STRATEGIES FOR MAKING CLASSROOM ADAPTATIONS FOR STUDENTS WITH EMOTIONAL DISTURBANCE

STRATEGIES FOR MAKING CLASSROOM ADAPTATIONS FOR STUDENTS WITH ATTENTION-DEFICIT/HYPERACTIVITY DISORDER

Bill Stevenson/Aurora Photos/Offset/Shutterstock

CHAPTER 4

Teaching Students with Autism and Lower-Incidence Disabilities

LEARNING OBJECTIVES

After studying this chapter, you should be able to:

4.1 Describe and discuss the prevalence and characteristics of students with autism and explain strategies for classroom adaptations.

4.2 Describe and discuss the prevalence and characteristics of students with physical disabilities and other health impairments and explain strategies for classroom adaptations.

4.3 Describe and discuss the prevalence and characteristics of students with severe and multiple disabilities and explain strategies for classroom adaptations.

4.4 Describe and discuss the prevalence and characteristics of students with visual impairments and explain strategies for classroom adaptations.

4.5 Describe and discuss the prevalence and characteristics of students with hearing impairments and explain strategies for classroom adaptations.

Individuals who have lower-incidence disabilities are far less commonly represented in schools than individuals with higher-incidence disabilities. Lower-incidence disabilities cover a wide range of disabilities, which can be present at birth (**congenital**) or acquired later in life (**adventitious**). Some lower-incidence disabilities are associated with very severe impairments; others involve only mild impairments. Some lower-incidence disabilities are temporary; others are permanent or even life-threatening. Lower-incidence disabilities include physical and other health impairments, severe and multiple disabilities, visual impairments, and hearing impairments. It is exciting to see some of the creative adaptations that have been developed to help students with lower-incidence disabilities become more successful in inclusive classes.

In this chapter, we also include autism spectrum disorder. Formerly a low-incidence disability, autism is as commonly identified in schools today as one of the higher-incidence disabilities. We include it with lower-incidence disabilities because of its historical connection and because many students with autism are more severely involved.

Autism

Learning Objective 4.1 Describe and discuss the prevalence and characteristics of students with autism and explain strategies for classroom adaptations.

PREVALENCE, DEFINITIONS, AND CHARACTERISTICS OF AUTISM

Autism is a disorder characterized by impairments in social, emotional, and intellectual functioning. Although the range in ability is varied, children with autism are often described as having great difficulty communicating and interacting with and responding to other people. Many individuals with autism also exhibit stereotypic behavior such as **self-stimulating behaviors** (e.g., **stimming**, rocking, hand flapping); atypical speech patterns, such as repeating the words of other people over and over again (echolalia) or using no tone inflection, a high pitch, or gibberish; and disruptive behavior, sometimes including self-injury (Hall, 2018). Children with autism are typically identified before the age of 3. Frequently, parents and caregivers are the first ones to become concerned when their infants do not respond positively to being touched and held closely and when language does not develop according to traditional developmental milestones.

The causes of autism are unknown, although genetic, neurological, and environmental factors have been proposed (Hall, 2018). Individuals with autism make up approximately 1.1% of the school-age population, or 11.0% of the students served under the Individuals with Disabilities Education Act (IDEA; U.S. Department of Education, 2021). The prevalence of autism appears to be increasing in recent years, although the reasons for this are not completely clear. For instance, in 2010, students with autism represented only 0.5% of the school-age population, more similar to the rates of other low-incidence disabilities (U.S. Department of Education, 2020). The percentage of students with autism among all students with disabilities ages 6 to 21 increased to 11% in 2019 (U.S. Department of Education, 2021). One possibility is that changes in diagnostic criteria, along with more public awareness of autism, have led to increased rates of identification (Hill et al., 2015).

Related diagnostic categories include autistic disorder, Rett syndrome, childhood disintegrative disorder, Asperger Syndrome, early infantile autism, and pervasive developmental disorder. These categories are now collected under the broader term **autism spectrum disorders (ASD)** (Stichter et al., 2017). The American Psychiatric Association (2013) no longer considers Asperger Syndrome—thought to be a milder form of autism—to be distinct from autism spectrum disorder. The current diagnoses indicate that individuals with autism may function along a continuum of severe to mild disabilities and that educational accommodations vary according to an individual's functioning level. Individuals with severe autism may have limited to no expressive and receptive language, whereas individuals with milder forms of autism may have developed more sophisticated communication. Although symptoms and severity level can vary greatly among individuals with autism, communication and social competence are typically the two greatest challenges. Many individuals with autism have cognitive deficits similar to those of individuals with intellectual disabilities. Individuals with Asperger Syndrome, however, can be highly intelligent (Stichter et al., 2017), but may need support with social competence.

It is important to acknowledge that some individuals with a diagnosis of autism prefer identity-first language, in which the disability is mentioned first (e.g., an autistic person). Others may prefer person-first language (e.g., a person with autism) (see Vivanti, 2020). Individual preferences and terminology can change over time, so it is important to represent individuals in the way they would self-identify. Confirm how an individual would self-identify or ask a family member or caregiver of the person, if possible.

STRATEGIES FOR

MAKING CLASSROOM ADAPTATIONS FOR STUDENTS WITH AUTISM

Classroom adaptations for individuals with autism can be classified into adaptations for those with severe autism and those with mild autism. Individuals with severe forms of autism may function similarly to individuals with severe disabilities, and it is recommended that you employ the suggested adaptations for those individuals. Conversely, for individuals with milder forms of autism, you may wish to consider using modifications recommended for students with mild disabilities, including learning disabilities and behavior disorders. In both cases, work closely with special education teachers, parents, and caregivers. This collaboration ensures that individualized education program (IEP) goals and objectives are being addressed and that you have assistance in interacting with students. The National Professional Development Center on Autism Spectrum Disorder (2014) at the Frank Porter Graham Center of the University of North Carolina identified 27 evidence-based practices (EBPs) demonstrated to have effectiveness with students with autism spectrum disorder (Wong et al., 2015). EBPs include social behavior, social skills, communication, applied behavior analysis, self-management, and peer-mediated interventions, among others. The following adaptations may also be generally helpful for differentiating instruction for students with autism in general education classes.

ESTABLISH EFFECTIVE COMMUNICATION Discuss optimal communication patterns and design communication strategies with special education teachers, parents, caregivers, and peers. For students with limited or no verbal language, strategies might include sign language or augmentative and alternative communication (AAC) methods. For example, in the following classroom scenario, Tuan is a young boy with autism who does not have expressive language but communicates with an AAC procedure referred to as the **Picture Exchange Communication System (PECS)**. PECS teaches students to use pictures and symbols to initiate communication and respond to communication from others (Bondy & Frost, 2011). Apps have been developed for tablets such as the iPad to assist with communication. Figure 4.1 presents examples of commonly used symbols in different communication systems. For students with mild autism or Asperger Syndrome who typically have more verbal language skills, they may need support in their use of language when communicating. For example, adolescents with Asperger Syndrome may use pedantic speech, only talk about one specific topic, misread social cues, and/or make insensitive, blunt statements. Prompting a student at lunch, for example, to use a script (e.g., visual words to use when greeting a peer) before they engage with a peer(s) and explicitly teaching social skills and practicing how to read social cues through role plays or social stories can help students with autism build and maintain friendships (Steinbrenner et al., 2020).

USE DIRECT INSTRUCTION AND APPLIED BEHAVIOR ANALYSIS Many students with autism (and many other students as well) benefit from direct instruction, including flexible small-group or one-to-one structured, teacher-directed lessons, with lots of direct questioning, student responding, teacher feedback and praise, and careful recording and monitoring of progress toward predetermined objectives. Instruction is carefully sequenced according to student needs (e.g., Wheeler et al., 2015). For example, if a student had no expressive language, teaching might begin with the teacher providing reinforcement for imitating sounds, such as "aaa," followed by imitating words (e.g., *hat*), then by responding to simple directions ("Point to the hat"), followed by word production ("What is this?" [teacher points to a hat]). Throughout this progression, the teacher would provide explicit feedback and reinforcement for attending and for correct responding. **Applied behavior analysis (ABA)** involves the use of reinforcement (e.g., praise, tokens, edible reinforcers) for displaying appropriate behaviors (e.g., sitting, attending, responding) and carefully recording student behaviors on charts that are used in decision making (Hall, 2018; Martin & Pear, 2019). These practices may also employ functional behavioral assessments and positive behavioral interventions and supports (see Chapter 8 for additional information on behavioral supports). Teachers may use an antecedent–behavior–consequence chart to document the antecedents as well as observed consequences of specific behaviors (e.g., screaming, tantrums) and then arrange the environment and environmental consequences to minimize inappropriate behaviors (see also Stichter et al., 2017).

DEVELOP SOCIAL COMPETENCE Unless you design behavior plans with the student's IEP team and implement these plans systematically, you may find it easy to become overwhelmed by the student's challenging behaviors. Teach students to wait their turn, to share materials, and to know when they need to be quiet and when they can talk. These may be new skills for students that require scaffolding or high levels of guidance. One visual strategy to provide such scaffolding is an individualized First-Then board to help a student complete specific tasks. The display on the board shows a picture of the behavior that needs to be done first (e.g., quietly listening to the teacher read a story) and then the picture to the right is an image of a preferred activity (e.g., talking with friends). Replace the images with new tasks, as needed. Use of this type of scaffold can be reduced or withdrawn as the teacher sees the student

Figure 4.1 Sample Communication Board Symbols

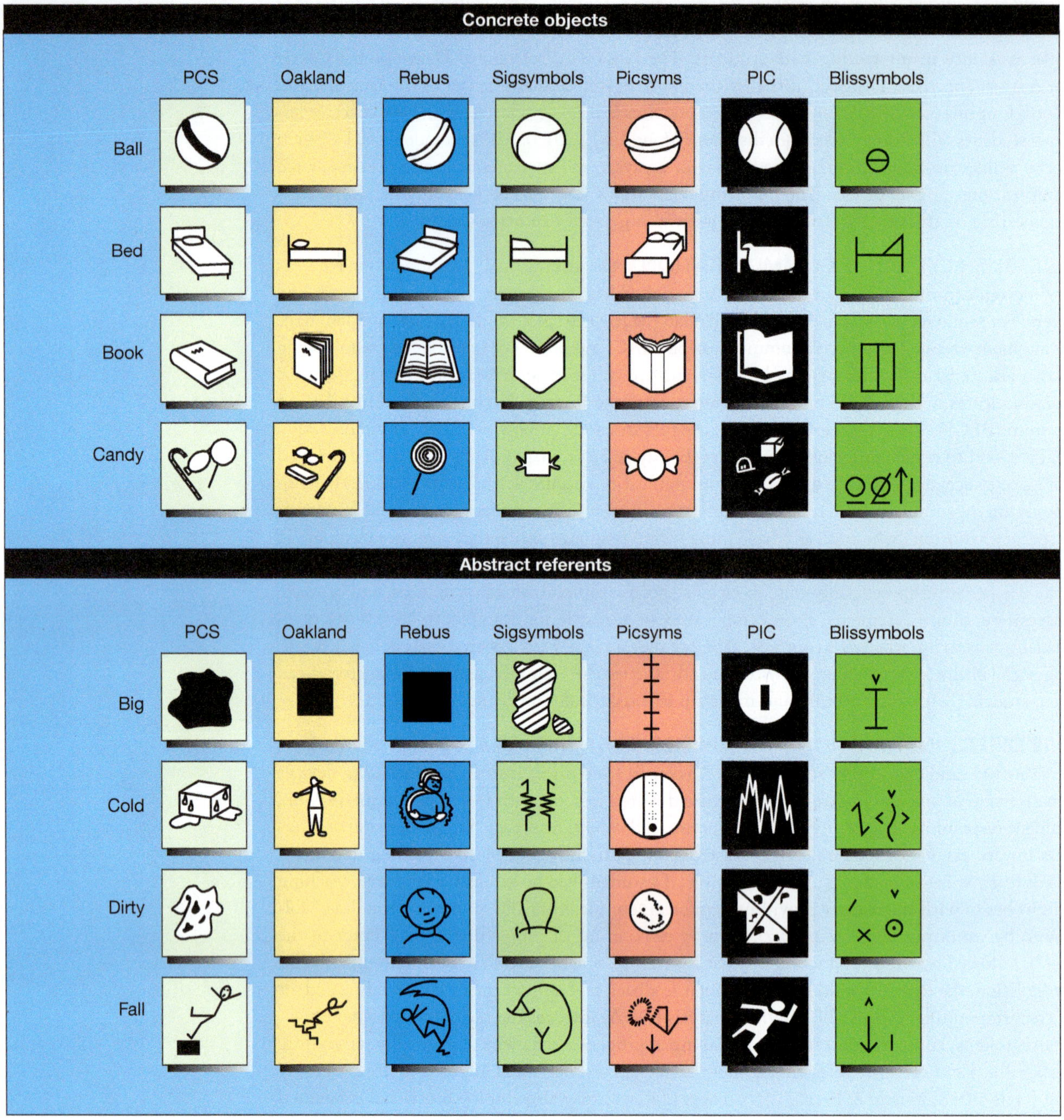

Note: PCS, Picture Communication Symbols; PIC, Pictogram Ideogram Communication.

Source: Reprinted with permission from "Non-speech modes and systems," by G. C. Vanderheiden and L. L. Lloyd, 1986, in S. W. Blackstone (Ed.), Augmentative communication (pp. 48–161), Rockville, MD: American.

CLASSROOM SCENARIO

Helping Tuan Socialize

Tuan had a difficult first day in his inclusive kindergarten. His teachers saw his crying, tantrum-throwing, and acts of aggression and, fortunately, realized that much of his behavior reflected not simply the fact that he had autism, but rather his inability to communicate in a new environment. Tuan's teachers used the Picture Exchange Communication System (PECS) to teach him to use socially appropriate ways to obtain what he wanted, using the six phases of the training program (e.g., Thiemann-Bouroque et al., 2016). In the first phases, they determined that Tuan enjoyed playing with a particular toy truck. When he reached for it, they placed the picture card of a truck in his hand, then guided him to give the picture to his teacher. The teacher immediately gave him the truck. In later phases, Tuan was encouraged to go to a touch board for the picture, then discriminate the truck from other pictures, and then build sentence structure by choosing first the "I want" card, followed by the picture of the desired object. In the fifth phase, he responds to "What do you want?" questions, and in the sixth phase, he uses the PECS cards to answer teacher questions, such as "What do you have?" or "What do you see?"

As Tuan learns the PECS program, his tantrum-throwing and inappropriate behavior diminishes, and he learns more socially appropriate ways of interacting with others. Other students use the PECS materials to interact with him. The PECS training continues to include additional language concepts, such as adjectives, verbs, and yes–no responses. Tuan is learning important lessons for communicating and socializing with teachers and classmates.

QUESTIONS FOR REFLECTION

1. Why do you think using the PECS system is easier for Tuan than using spoken language?
2. Why would a language training program help to improve Tuan's social behavior?
3. How could Tuan's classroom peers assist in developing his communication skills?

Pearson eTextbook

Video Example 4.1

In this video, the teacher uses direct instruction. Notice the carefully sequenced structure, the simple directions, and the explicit feedback and reinforcement she uses. Notice also her use of frequent direct questioning, recording, and monitoring of progress.

performing the task independently without the visual reminder. Teach students to use socially appropriate behaviors throughout the school day to help promote generalization of appropriate social behavior. Reward successive approximations (as students come closer to their goals) and work toward having students become more independent. Develop behavior management plans based on an analysis of student preferences and classroom dynamics. Direct instruction and ABA techniques can be helpful in these areas (Wheeler et al., 2015).

Create a learning environment in which the student with autism feels comfortable, including a predictable schedule of daily activities, a pattern of events, and class routines. Post a visual schedule with pictures or photos of the routine. Use pictures to list the sequence of activities if the student is a nonreader and allow the student to order the sequence, if possible. If you change the class routine, prepare the student in advance to avoid undue stress.

Goldstein and colleagues (2014) reviewed available research on social skills interventions for preschoolers with autism and concluded that these techniques had been generally effective in improving social functioning. Techniques included modeling, peer mediation, self-monitoring, and other interventions. Similarly, Carr et al. (2014) reviewed research on self-management interventions for students with autism, across age levels, and concluded that these interventions also were effective.

One promising technique for improving social behavior is the use of *social stories* (Qi et al., 2018; Wheeler et al., 2015). Social stories use simple sentences and pictures to demonstrate the anticipated sequence of desired social behaviors (e.g., when eating lunch at the school cafeteria) and the feelings and reactions of others. In this instance, the student could be shown a photo of himself returning his tray with the teacher smiling at him, with a caption such as, "When I return my tray after I have finished eating, my teacher is happy." Social stories have been seen to improve the social functioning of students with autism in a variety of school settings (e.g., Graetz et al., 2009).

Pearson eTextbook

Video Example 4.2

In this class, peers have been taught to interact with a classmate with autism. Describe the socially appropriate behaviors of the classmates observed in the video.

Technological advances, now and in the future, may prove helpful in improving social competence in students with ASD. For example, the Autism Glass Project at Stanford University has been working with a Google Glass device that has been modified to interpret facial expressions to describe how the person facing the individual wearing the Google Glass is feeling, for example, "happy" if the individual is smiling (Voss et al., 2019).

Enlist the help of peers to reinforce socially appropriate behavior. Group students with autism with higher-functioning students. Students with autism can be included successfully in cooperative learning groups when paired with partners who have been taught to communicate effectively with them (Zhang & Wheeler, 2011).

Look out for signs that the student is becoming stressed. Students with autism may react aggressively or withdraw completely under novel or stressful situations. Try to predict when the class demands might become stressful and attempt to eliminate the sources of stress. For example, individuals with autism can experience sensory input differently. So, certain sounds, lights, smells, and textures may be stressors. Try to limit background noise and audible distractions if a person with autism is hypersensitive to sounds. Limiting visual distractions and stimuli may help students with ASD focus better on the teacher when learning new information

(Martin & Wilkins, 2021). Also, physical exercise and the use of varied standing and seating options in the classroom can help reduce sensory overload for an individual with autism.

Finally, establish and maintain effective communication with all individuals who are in contact with students with autism. Communicate regularly with parents and caregivers. Send home weekly or daily notes, short, recorded messages, or a school–home communication system (e.g., journal) that travels back and forth between you and parents and caregivers.

Physical Disabilities and Other Health Impairments

Learning Objective 4.2 Describe and discuss the prevalence and characteristics of students with physical disabilities and other health impairments and explain strategies for classroom adaptations.

PREVALENCE, DEFINITIONS, AND CHARACTERISTICS OF PHYSICAL DISABILITIES AND OTHER HEALTH IMPAIRMENTS

Physical disabilities (or *orthopedic impairments*, according to IDEA) and other health impairments include many types of disabilities that range from mild to moderate to severe and from temporary to permanent or life-threatening. Approximately 1.6% of the school-age population has a physical (<0.05%) or other health-related disability (1.6%), or 17.3% of the students served under IDEA (U.S. Department of Education, 2021). Physical disabilities are often described as either orthopedic or neuromotor impairments, and IDEA considers neuromotor impairments part of the orthopedic impairments category. **Orthopedic impairments** involve damage to the skeletal system, and **neuromotor impairments** involve damage to the nervous system (Best, 2010b). Frequently, physical disabilities are referred to by the affected parts of the body. For example, a person living with **quadriplegia** means that the person has paralysis in both the arms and legs. **Paraplegia** is defined as paralysis of the legs. A person living with **hemiplegia** means that there is paralysis in either the left or right side of the body. **Diplegia** means that both legs are involved more than the arms (Best & Bigge, 2010). Common physical disabilities include cerebral palsy, epilepsy, spina bifida, muscular dystrophy, rheumatoid arthritis, scoliosis (curvature of the spine), osteogenesis imperfecta (brittle bone disease), and arthrogryposis (joint contractures) (Best, 2010b).

Other health impairments include physical or medical conditions resulting from diseases or illnesses. Great variability exists in the severity level of impairment. Some health impairments improve over time, whereas others do not. Major health conditions include cancer, **acquired immunodeficiency syndrome (AIDS)**, allergies, asthma, and fetal alcohol syndrome (Heller, Forney, et al., 2009). Other conditions are presented in Figure 4.2.

School-related difficulties due to physical disabilities and other health impairments are covered by the provision of "special education services" under IDEA 2004. Sometimes physical disabilities or other health impairments do not lead to difficulties in academic or intellectual functioning. Some students with other health impairments—including asthma, AIDS, tuberculosis, diabetes, drug or alcohol addiction, or behavioral problems—might not qualify for services under IDEA, but they may qualify for services under Section 504 of the Vocational Rehabilitation Act (Zirkel, 2020).

PHYSICAL AND HEALTH-RELATED DISABILITIES

CEREBRAL PALSY *Cerebral palsy* is the most common physical disability, with approximately 1 to 2.4 occurrences in every 1,000 births and affecting approximately 15% of premature infants. It is a neurological disorder that causes permanent disorders of movement and positions. Cerebral palsy is not progressive in nature, which means it does not worsen over time. It does, however, range in impairment levels from mild to moderate to severe. Individuals with cerebral palsy may or may not have coexisting difficulties in language, communication, vision, hearing, psychosocial, self-help, and intellectual development. Between 25 and 50% of individuals with cerebral palsy may be subject to seizure disorders (Heller & Garrett, 2009).

The most common forms of cerebral palsy are spastic (characterized by increased muscle tone), athetosis (involuntary nonpurposeful movements), ataxic (lack of coordination in balance and equilibrium), and mixed (Heller & Garrett, 2009). Many individuals with cerebral

Figure 4.2 Other Health-Related Disorders

Cystic fibrosis. Cystic fibrosis is an inherited disease in which upper respiratory and digestive problems are chronic due to the inability of the pancreas to produce digestive enzymes (Ioannu et al., 2016). Glands in the bronchial tubes also malfunction and produce thick mucus that stagnates in the bronchial tubes. Treatments include special diets and intensive respiratory therapy (Ioannu et al., 2016). Work closely with medical staff to monitor the condition.

Hemophilia. Hemophilia is an inherited sex-linked disorder in which the blood does not clot properly and excessive bleeding may occur with minor cuts or injuries (Ioannu et al., 2016). Know relevant first aid information. Internal bleeding is very serious. Watch for falls at recess or during physical education classes. Avoid dangerous situations in which cuts are possible. Follow safety guidelines when using sharp objects or cutting tools.

Rheumatic fever. Rheumatic fever usually begins with a throat infection that may lead to painful swelling in the joints that can spread to the heart or brain and result in severe damage. Consult with medical personnel and your student's family/caregiver to design optimal interventions.

Cancer. Cancer is a group of diseases in which the normal process of cell production malfunctions. Cell growth is uncontrolled, becomes malignant, and damages healthy tissues. Individuals with cancer may require special supports for both social-emotional well-being and for accommodating less energy and pain during school activities. Radiation treatments have been associated with learning disabilities, so additional instructional accommodations may be needed (Best, 2009).

Tuberculosis. Tuberculosis is a disease in which bacteria infect the lungs, and may spread to the brain, kidneys, or bones.

Nephrosis and nephritis. Nephrosis and nephritis are disorders of the kidneys. These disorders, if left untreated, can result in kidney failure.

Sickle-cell anemia. Sickle-cell anemia is an inherited disease in which an abnormal red hemoglobin is formed (Ioannu et al., 2016). This results in less oxygen in the body, and the malformed cells may move improperly through the bloodstream, resulting in additional complications. Students with sickle-cell anemia may tire more easily and may need accommodations such as reduced assignments commensurate with their energy-ability levels.

palsy use wheelchairs or other motorized vehicles to assist with mobility or use other adaptive devices to assist with fine motor control and speech and language difficulties. AAC techniques used with some individuals with cerebral palsy and other disabilities include communication boards containing pictures or words of commonly asked questions and responses to questions and computerized devices using synthesized speech. The *Apps for Education* feature describes two uses of technology, *News-2-You* and *Boardmaker*, to improve communication.

SPINA BIFIDA *Spina bifida* is caused during fetal development when the vertebrae do not properly enclose the spinal cord, causing the nerves that control muscles in the lower body to develop incorrectly. Spina bifida occurs in approximately 1 in 2,000 births. Resulting motor impairment can range from mild to severe and include loss of sensation to paralysis in the lower body. Spina bifida is often associated with hydrocephalus, a condition in which cerebrospinal fluid collects in the brain tissues. If left untreated, swelling can cause severe brain damage and result in intellectual disability and attention and learning problems (Heller, 2009). Shunts, or one-way valves, are inserted surgically to drain the fluid from the brain to reduce the risk of pressure on the brain and possible resulting brain damage. Shunts need to be replaced as children grow. Be aware of warning signs or changes in a student's behavior, as sudden changes may indicate shunt blockage or infections. Alert parents and caregivers immediately of any changes.

Individuals with spina bifida—and other physical disabilities—may lack bladder and bowel movement control due to paralysis of the lower body. Most children lacking bladder control use a catheter, attached to a bag, to collect their urine. Many children are taught to use a procedure called *clean intermittent catheterization* (CIC) or **intermittent self-catheterization (ISC)** (Heller et al., 2010). Request guidance from school nurses or other educational team members to learn how to assist a child with this procedure. Plan restroom breaks to accommodate these students' specialized toileting needs.

Many children with spina bifida walk with braces or crutches, relying on wheelchairs for longer distances. In these cases, maintain classroom space to ensure clear, wide, and open walkways for students with mobility difficulties. Arrange storage for crutches or removable braces near students for easy access.

MUSCULAR DYSTROPHY *Muscular dystrophy* refers to a group of diseases that weaken and progressively destroy muscle tissue. Muscular dystrophy occurs in approximately 1 in 3,500 births. No known cure exists. Some forms of muscular dystrophy are fatal, but other forms are not life-threatening. At birth, children appear to function normally; however, between the ages of 2 and 6 they may begin to experience motor difficulties, which increase with age. Often by age 10 to 14, children lose the ability to walk. Children with muscular dystrophy should be lifted only by those with explicit training, as their limbs are easily dislocated. Because the disease is often progressive, it is important to learn what types of muscular difficulties may be expected throughout an academic year (Heller, Mezei, et al., 2009).

TRAUMATIC BRAIN INJURY **Traumatic brain injury (TBI)**, a separate category of exceptionality under IDEA, represents a type of physical and cognitive disability. TBI is the result of an external injury that impedes learning along the continuum from mild to severe disabilities and may result in physical, cognitive, attention, memory, problem-solving, sensory, and psychosocial difficulties (Lijiness-O'Neill et al., 2017). The resulting disabilities may be temporary or permanent. Often, TBIs result from falls or motor-vehicle accidents. Child abuse also can be a cause of brain injury (Grandinette & Best, 2009).

According to the U.S. Department of Education (2021), only 0.4% of students with disabilities and approximately 0.04% of the student population are characterized as having TBI. However, this number is considered to be a substantial underestimate of the entire population because over 1 million students per year are affected by TBI. Among elementary-age students, TBI is often the result of play or bicycling accidents, falls, and motor-vehicle accidents. Adolescents most often acquire TBIs from motor-vehicle accidents, intensive sports activities, assault, and risk-taking behaviors. TBI can also result from gunshot wounds, suicide attempts, and abuse of drugs or alcohol (Grandinette & Best, 2009). Special education services are provided when the resulting difficulties have educational impact. Teachers can play an important preventative role by encouraging students to take safety precautions, such as wearing helmets when riding bicycles.

A significant role of the classroom teacher is in assisting with the reintegration and transitions the individual has to make from the hospital to rehabilitation to the classroom. Successful transition planning includes preparing peers for the changes in the behavior of the affected classmate. IEPs may need to be adjusted and modified more frequently due to changing conditions in students with TBI.

Students with TBI who recover adequate intellectual functioning but who continue to exhibit difficulties in learning may resemble students with learning disabilities in some respects. Students may continue to change neurologically, even months after their readmission to school. Achievement test scores may be misleading because they may reflect knowledge or skills acquired prior to the injury. Furthermore, psychosocial problems may emerge as a consequence of coping with the challenges associated with TBI. Unpredictable difficulty could occur even years after the injury if parts of the brain were injured that are needed for later maturation (Best, 2010b).

EPILEPSY A seizure occurs when abnormal electrical energy is released in the brain that can cause a loss of consciousness and lack of motor control. The effects can be minimal or severe, depending on the amount of energy released and the number of brain cells affected. The precise cause of epilepsy is not well understood (Heller & Cohen, 2009), but some cases are due to brain damage from physical trauma or infections.

Any child may have a seizure. Individuals may experience a single seizure associated with a head injury or high fever and never have one again. Repeated seizures are indicative of epilepsy. About half of those with seizure disorders also have intellectual disabilities. No matter what the physical condition that leads to a seizure, be aware that seizures vary in duration, frequency, onset, associated movements, and causes, and individuals with seizures may have varying associated disabilities and levels of control during seizure events.

Apps for Education

Alternative and Augmentative Communication: *News-2-You* and *Boardmaker*

Many students with low-incidence disabilities require some adaptations in literacy materials that will aid their ability to communicate. Alternative and augmentative communication devices are widely available and range from high-tech to low-tech options, including apps. This means that some use very little technology, whereas others are reliant on more complex technological systems for delivery. One alternative and augmentative version of a newspaper is *News-2-You* (AssistiveWare). *News-2-You* is published weekly during the school year and is available for a subscription fee. The newspaper features relevant, newsworthy stories printed using visual symbols that represent words. Each paper includes four to five pages of weekly current-event news stories, a recipe, a joke, a game page, a sports story, and a weekly quiz based on the paper and is available in printable, audio, and booklet formats. The paper also includes sample communication boards as downloads that can be used as part of *Boardmaker*, a software program that contains graphics that can be used to develop and design communication displays or Microsoft Word documents (for those who do not have access to *Boardmaker*). The newspaper provides an excellent vehicle for access to news for many students who might otherwise be unable to read a paper. Because the paper is available online on a weekly basis, a teacher can select to have students read it online, from a saved online version on a computer or tablet or in a printed hard-copy format. There is also a speaking version, which reads text material. The newspaper provides an excellent tool for working on reading comprehension skills with the short quizzes that accompany the weekly papers. Teachers can also decide to make their own versions of newspapers and reading materials using similar formats.

For example, teachers who like the format of *News-2-You* will most likely want to obtain the software *Boardmaker* or the online version, which can be used to develop a wide range of displays using the over 3,000 graphic picture communication symbols and over 100 templates for calendars, schedules, and other formats. Pictures can be sized to meet your needs, and *Boardmaker* for Windows comes with 19 languages, including English, Spanish, German, Portuguese, Vietnamese, Russian, and Turkish, but has space for over 150 languages. The software is available from Mayer-Johnson (http://mayer-johnson.com). *Boardmaker* can also be combined with *Speaking Dynamically Pro* to include speech capabilities. With this combination, the symbols are used as overlays with the corresponding sounds spoken aloud, which is effective for students who require hearing the symbols in addition to looking at them. *Boardmaker Plus* adds sound, voice, animation, and video capabilities to the software.

Apps are also available for assistive technology and adaptive communications. *SpeakText FREE* (BorG Technology) converts keyed-in text and web pages to speech and also translates into more than 30 languages. *Speakall!* (Speak MODalities) can be used with a Picture Exchange Communication System and developers can import custom pictures and record speech. *iCommunicate* (Grembe Apps) is costlier but allows the user to design and develop visual schedules, communication boards, storyboards, and flashcards. Developers can record their own voice or use the text-to-speech option. Finally, *My Pictures Talk—Video Modeling Tool* (Grembe Apps) enables uploading and editing of videos so that users can create their own social stories or video modeling sequences.

Seizure disorders can be treated with antiepileptic medications, special diets, vagus nerve stimulation, and surgery (Heller & Cohen, 2009). Because of the chance of body injury or brain damage, it is wise to learn about the correct handling of seizures and to educate all students about seizures and their treatment. Some suggestions are provided later in the chapter.

ARTHRITIS *Arthritis* is a disease in which the muscles and joints are affected. Juvenile rheumatoid arthritis is chronic arthritis present in an individual before the age of 16. Arthritis can be painful and can severely impede mobility. Treatments are directed toward relieving pain, increasing function, and avoiding further deterioration and include heat–cold therapy, massage, electrical stimulation, and exercise, such as aquatic movement, under the supervision of a physical or occupational therapist. However, at present, no known cause or cure exists (Heller & Avant, 2009). Because mobility may be hindered, some children with severe arthritis use canes or braces while walking. Be aware that these students will have good days and bad days and build in extra rest periods during more painful days. Students may experience great difficulty trying to grip a pencil. Writing may be extremely tedious and painful. Reduce writing demands by allowing students to use audio recorders, speech-to-text features on electronic devices, or other students as scribes. Provide extended time for written assignments.

ASTHMA AND ALLERGIES *Asthma* is associated with breathing difficulties due to sensitivity to airborne particles and can be exacerbated during exercise. Children with severe asthma often require restricted athletic activities and may need to be reminded to take appropriate medication (Best, 2010a). Physicians can provide relevant information on particular adaptations for individual cases.

Allergies are conditions in which elements in the environment cause allergic reactions in some individuals. Exposure to pollens, molds, dusts, animal dander, and carpet fibers can cause reactions such as congestion in the nose, chest, and eyes. Allergic reactions to certain foods, such as milk, fish, or peanuts, can cause skin rashes and more serious mouth and throat reactions. Still other reactions are caused by insect bites, such as honeybee stings, and can result in anaphylactic shock, a condition that can be fatal if not treated immediately (Best, 2010a). Many individuals who know they have these conditions carry emergency kits with them. Be sure to have plans in place for dealing with such medical emergencies, including the quickest ways to seek medical assistance.

Know which of your students have asthma and allergies, the associated allergens, the preventative medications, first aid, and the specific nature of the allergic reactions. In some cases, it may be necessary to maintain an environment that is free of dust and animal dander to avoid allergic reactions. In other cases, teachers or other school staff can monitor food consumption during lunchtime and class parties (Best, 2010a).

DIABETES *Diabetes* is an inherited condition in which sugar is not metabolized correctly due to insufficient production of insulin in the pancreas (Heller, 2009). Individuals with diabetes have strict diets and special schedules for administering medication that need close monitoring. Learn the warning signs of diabetic shock and be ready to administer first aid (Best, 2010a). The school nurse can usually provide relevant information for classroom teachers, who can then share the information with all students. Monitor dietary needs during the school day for students with diabetes (or create a plan for an aide to do so), especially if extra food or physical activities are added to the regular schedule. Careful planning with the family, caregivers, and health care providers is necessary to ensure safety during daily class activities, especially for special events such as field trips or overnight trips.

FETAL ALCOHOL SYNDROME *Fetal alcohol syndrome* results when pregnant mothers consume alcohol, which damages the developing fetus (Jones et al., 1973). This places a child at risk for a variety of developmental disabilities, including intellectual disability, learning disabilities, and physical disabilities, in addition to problems with attention and impulsivity (Polloway et al., 2017). Exposure to substances during the first trimester is likely to cause neurological and structural damage to the developing fetus (Briggs et al., 2021). Effective service delivery for infants born under these conditions comes from personnel in health, social services, mental health, children's services, education, and drug and alcohol programs, who must collaborate to work effectively with the family and caregivers.

ACQUIRED IMMUNODEFICIENCY SYNDROME *Acquired immunodeficiency syndrome* is caused by the human immunodeficiency virus (HIV), which destroys a type of white blood cell, weakening the immune system. HIV can be transmitted to an unborn fetus during pregnancy, during childbirth to an infant, or through infected breast milk during nursing. Other sources of transmission include sexual activity and blood exposure through, for example, shared needles in intravenous drug use or transfusions of contaminated blood (although this occurred most frequently prior to 1984, when blood screening was initiated).

HIV is not spread by casual contact. Children with AIDS may have coexisting characteristics such as developmental delay, cognitive disabilities, and any of a number of physical or health conditions, including problems with respiratory, cardiovascular, motor, or kidney functioning (Best & Heller, 2009).

Recently developed combination therapies, known as **highly active antiretroviral therapy (HAART)**, have proven very effective in reducing HIV/AIDS symptoms and have even restored the functioning of the immune system. However, HAART does not eliminate the infection. Improved preventative treatments have also significantly reduced the transmission of HIV from mother to child (Best & Heller, 2009).

STRATEGIES FOR

MAKING CLASSROOM ADAPTATIONS FOR STUDENTS WITH PHYSICAL DISABILITIES AND OTHER HEALTH IMPAIRMENTS

Although each individual and disability area may require specific adaptations, the following general guidelines can help you develop adaptations for differentiating instruction for individuals with physical and other health impairments (see also Best et al., 2010; Drasgow et al., 2017; Wehmeyer & Shogren, 2017).

Pearson eTextbook

Video Example 4.3

In this video, you will meet Oscar, a high school student with a severe physical disability. Identify the classroom modifications made for Oscar.

PREPARE THE CLASS Prepare the class for students with disabilities who are about to enter the class. Describe the students' diverse learning needs and the roles of classroom peers in supporting the inclusive classroom. One way to enhance disability awareness in students is by using classroom simulation activities and providing demonstrations of adaptive devices. Simulations allow students to perform a variety of activities under conditions that allow them to temporarily experience how it feels to have a disability. For example, students can use the assistive devices that students with disabilities use and/or participate in online disability simulations, such as using a virtual wheelchair (see Salend, 2005). Discussions with all students following simulation activities can help increase their awareness of the frustrations that may be encountered by students with disabilities. Although disability simulations are not without some controversy and may not always improve attitudes significantly (Flower et al., 2007), such activities may provide students with some insights into the challenges faced by individuals with disabilities and the need for adaptations (Ison et al., 2010).

Exposing students to literature in the classroom that represents the protagonist as an individual with a disability can also help build awareness and encourage positive perspectives of persons who are different from themselves (Prince & Hayden, 2021). Puppet shows, such as "Kids on the Block" (http://amazingkids.org), have also been used to educate younger children about different types of disabilities and to help dispel fears, myths, and misconceptions about them. Dunst (2014) reviewed research on use of such puppet shows and concluded that they had generally been effective in improving attitudes and knowledge toward individuals with disabilities.

MONITOR MEDICAL GUIDELINES Medical needs are of primary concern. Devise checklists containing reminder steps for general class and emergency procedures specific to the medical conditions of students. For example, a medical checklist could include items such as the following: check medication schedule, monitor medication effects and side effects, monitor first-aid and emergency procedures, and communicate with parents and caregivers. Maintain careful records of student behavior (such as lethargy or fatigue) and communicate clearly any changes in your students' behavior.

Be Aware of Medications An awareness of the types of medications, specific uses, and potential side effects is necessary. Careful monitoring of students' behaviors while on and off medication (e.g., with observational records) can provide valuable educational insights for teachers, parents, caregivers, and prescribing physicians.

A school nurse or other designated school official distributes medications to students from a centralized location in the school, usually the nurse's office. Be sure that students obtain their medication at the scheduled times and that they ingest the medication when administered. Some students may feign taking their medication and attempt to give or sell it to others. This is a serious problem that can become troublesome or dangerous if not monitored closely.

Plan for Fatigue Students with physical disabilities or other health impairments, such as traumatic brain injury and muscular dystrophy, may tire more easily than other students. If so, schedule frequent rest breaks throughout the day, prioritize daily schedules, and schedule break periods in the nurse's office, if needed. If students lack the strength to carry necessary materials from class to class and to and from school, obtain duplicate sets of books and materials. Some students may require a shortened school day while they recuperate from illnesses. Reduce assignments, prioritize to ensure that students receive the most critical information, and assign peers to share class notes and materials.

Establish Emergency Procedures All classes containing students with physical and other health impairments may require specialized classroom procedures for emergencies such as fire, tornadoes, a school shooter, or a lockdown. Ask school or district leaders if there are schoolwide procedures and/or emergency plans to keep students safe during school crises (Clarke et al., 2014). For example, assistance may be required to move adaptive equipment along with the student. Also, depending on the position of the individual in the class when the emergency alarm sounds, students may need assistance into their wheelchairs, braces, or other adaptive mobility devices. During fire drills, students often proceed to an athletic field adjacent to the school, and mobility across the uneven grass may be especially difficult for some students with physical disabilities. Others tire easily and cannot walk quickly enough to maintain the speed of evacuation with the rest of the class.

Pair students with and without disabilities for evacuation efforts during emergencies. It may be helpful to have more than one student assigned to assist each student with disabilities. You can add the names of peer assistants to the overall listing of procedures on your "emergency chart." Be prepared: Outline emergency procedures in advance and practice them many times so that if an actual emergency situation occurs, all students are well prepared for any evacuation procedures.

Plan for Seizures Know which of your students are likely to have seizures and what first-aid treatment is appropriate. Have an established emergency plan that includes contacting the school office immediately, implementing procedures for supporting the student with a seizure, and reassuring the rest of the class. Because seizures range in severity from very minor to very intense and severe, consult your student's family, caregivers, and physician for precise medical treatment. If a seizure does occur, stay calm. You are a model for your students; if you stay calm, so will they. Help the student to the floor. Gently tilt the head to the side so that the child does not choke. In any seizure, do not attempt to restrain the movements of the individual or place anything in between the teeth or in the mouth of the affected person. Clear all harmful objects out of the way and place a blanket or pillow under the student's head to minimize the potential for injury.

Try to remember all of the distinctive features associated with the seizure to record on monitoring sheets and share with parents, caregivers, and attending physicians later. Record the date and time of the seizure as well as the behavior exhibited before, during, and after the seizure. Note the student's and peer reactions to the seizure and any other information that seems relevant. If it is the student's first seizure, have the office or school nurse contact a physician and the parents and caregivers immediately. Moreover, if seizures persist for more than 5 minutes, immediate medical attention should be sought. Notify parents and caregivers when seizures have occurred (Best & Bigge, 2010).

Learn how to handle a student who has just recovered from a seizure. Some students may feel tired and disoriented after a seizure and may want to lie down and rest. Others may feel fine and simply want to continue with the class activity. Still others may feel embarrassed and may need time outside of the class to regain self-control and self-respect. It is also important to redirect the attention of peers away from the student who had the seizure. The individual having a seizure should not be made to feel self-conscious. Do anything necessary to make the student feel comfortable. Provide all students with relevant information about seizures and proper ways of handling situations emotionally during and after seizures (Best & Bigge, 2010).

Moving and Positioning Students Determine what special procedures are required for moving, lifting, or transferring body positions of students with disabilities. Some students—for example, those with brittle bone disease (osteogenesis imperfecta)—should be lifted only by people with specialized knowledge about how to lift and position the individual. Physical therapists, who often work directly with these students, can provide valuable information to teachers and paraprofessionals.

Find out whether students feel more comfortable in some positions than others. Periodically check their positions throughout the school day. Some types of positioning devices, such as braces and wedges, help improve personal comfort, control muscle movements, and position students to more easily communicate or complete schoolwork. Figure 4.3 shows examples of positioning devices.

ADAPT FOR CHRONIC MEDICAL CONDITIONS If students in your class have chronic medical conditions, you should know how to accommodate them. Consult with medical personnel to learn to recognize the signs and symptoms of relevant medical problems and any modifications you can make. Limiting physical activity, administering medications, providing diet and fluid supplements as needed, and providing easy access to bathrooms are common modifications, depending on the condition.

Dealing with Terminal Illness Health care and mental health professionals are good sources of information about dealing with terminally ill students, as are the students' parents and caregivers. Ask how you should interact with the terminally ill student and the student's classmates. In many cases, school may be the most "normal" component of their lives, and students may appreciate the distraction provided by educational activities. If the student dies, request assistance from the school's crisis intervention team and mental health professionals. Different individuals may react to death in different ways; teachers should share their own personal feelings and reactions with the class (Best, 2009). Mental health professionals can sometimes provide extra guidance and counseling sessions to small groups of students to address their questions about interacting with a terminally ill student.

ADAPT THE PHYSICAL ENVIRONMENT Arrange the classroom to meet the mobility requirements of students with physical disabilities. Provide sufficiently wide aisles to accommodate wheelchairs, walkers, three-wheel motorized wheelchairs, crutches, canes, braces, or other adaptive devices. Most wheelchairs require passages at least 32 inches wide for one wheelchair to pass. Keep aisles clear of debris and monitor regularly to ensure that no books, book bags, backpacks, toys, or other objects impede mobility. Verify that the heights of doorknobs, shelves, desks, water fountains, sinks, and cabinets are accessible for students with physical disabilities. If not, perhaps minor adaptations can be made to ensure equal accessibility.

Examine the type of flooring in your classroom with respect to whether carpeting or tile is used and the extent to which surfaces either facilitate or impede the mobility of individuals with physical disabilities. For example, carpeted floors can decrease slippage, but they may also impede the mobility of some adaptive devices. Conversely, tile surfaces may be dangerously slippery, especially after washing and waxing.

Figure 4.3 Alternatives to Allow Change of Position Throughout the Day: (1) Sidelyer, (2) Wedge, (3) Tricycle with Built-Up Back and Pedals (Adult Three-Wheeled Bikes Are Available for Older Children)

Source: From Best et al. (2009). Reprinted by permission.

ADAPT INSTRUCTIONAL MATERIALS Commercially available materials include communication boards; computers to assist with voice-synthesizer production; specially designed hand grippers, head pointers, keyboards, and touchscreens to assist with computer usage; and speech-reading or word-prediction software to minimize difficulty producing output for assignments. Other adaptive devices include flap switches and reaches that can be added to pencils or dowels to extend the grasp of individuals and are available from suppliers such as the Prentke Romich Company.

The pages of electronic books can be turned easily with a light touch on the edge of the page. Some teachers assist students with fine motor difficulties in turning book pages by placing double-sided foam tape or cardboard between the pages. Tongue depressors can also serve as handles for turning pages. A book stand can be designed to hold instructional materials at an appropriate height and distance for easy viewing for students with restricted mobility. Choose books that are larger and easier to manipulate. Anchor materials in place by using clipboards or magnets to help stabilize papers (see Best et al., 2010).

Enlarge the gripping area of pencils by attaching spongelike material, plastic tubing, or plastic golf balls around pencils and pens. Use felt-tip pens, which require less pressure than some other writing tools. Specialized rubber stamps with large handles that contain commonly written items, such as names, *yes*, *no*, *restroom*, and *hungry*, can also help students communicate, as can communication boards.

Larger paper with extra space between lines helps accommodate writing needs for some students. When class activities involve charting or graphing, provide larger graphs, stickers, or magnets for students to place on graphs rather than using smaller paper-and-pencil versions. Felt boards and pieces of felt are easier for some students to manipulate. Place vocabulary words or other content inside clear picture photograph cubes. Put clear plastic folders or sheet protectors on paper handouts. These are easier to grip than a single sheet of paper and can be held together with a clip. The coating also protects the papers from spills. Use calculators with large numbers that are easier to touch and read. Speech-recognition functions on tablets such as the iPad may also facilitate writing.

Stabilize instructional materials with Velcro. Slatted trays or trays with built-in dividers can be used to hold small objects that need to be manipulated during activities. Place a detachable bag or backpack onto the wheelchair for carrying books and other materials. Notes or recorded messages to parents and caregivers can be placed in the bag before students leave school. Often, simple modifications such as these can allow students with physical disabilities to participate more independently (Best et al., 2010).

Some students with physical disabilities may also have the assistance of an animal, such as a service dog, that is specially trained to perform such actions as pulling a wheelchair, retrieving small objects, or opening doors and that accompanies the students throughout the school day. Teachers need to know how they and their students in the class and throughout the school should interact with the animal. Usually, no one is allowed to pet or interact with the animal other than the individual with disabilities. The student's family and caregivers can provide detailed information on how to interact appropriately with service animals (Best et al., 2010).

ADAPT INSTRUCTION Schedule extra reading, studying, and instructional support time when needed. Students who have difficulty speaking require extra time to respond to teacher questions. When calling on an individual during class discussions, provide sufficient wait time and make students feel comfortable and not rushed while responding.

Instruction can be adapted, with respect to individual needs, in all academic areas, including literacy, math, and academic content areas, as well as vocational education. Refer to the relevant chapters throughout this text when planning instruction for students with physical disabilities and other health impairments.

Consider assigning a peer assistant to work with individuals with physical disabilities or health impairments. Peer assistants can enable the student to be a more active participant during class activities. In some cases, paraprofessionals are assigned to accompany students throughout the school day. Work closely with paraprofessionals to design effective modifications.

ADAPT ASSESSMENT METHODS Testing and assessment modifications are necessary for students with physical disabilities and other health impairments. Because many of these students have difficulty reading and writing independently, schedule their tests when a special education teacher, paraprofessional, aide, peer assistant, or tutor can read the test items and record responses. Students can use communication boards during testing situations, and helpers can record responses as students point to answers on response sheets. These individualized sessions may require more time than the regularly scheduled time slots for exams. See also Chapter 12 for additional suggestions.

Severe and Multiple Disabilities

Learning Objective 4.3 Describe and discuss the prevalence and characteristics of students with severe and multiple disabilities and explain strategies for classroom adaptations.

PREVALENCE, DEFINITIONS, AND CHARACTERISTICS OF SEVERE AND MULTIPLE DISABILITIES

Many individuals with severe disabilities have severe and profound intellectual disability. Some individuals with moderate intellectual disability may also be included in this group (Bruce & Ivy, 2017; Dymond, 2017). Individuals with severe impairments may have several coexisting disabilities (e.g., sensory or physical disabilities). Moderate intellectual disability has been classified according to an IQ test score continuum of 35 to 54, severe intellectual disability is represented by scores between 20 and 34, and profound intellectual disability is classified as any score less than 20 (Jacobson & Mulick, 1996). The American Association on Intellectual and Developmental Disabilities (2010; Schalock et al., 2010) supports a classification system for intellectual disabilities based on the level of support needed, with severe and profound intellectual disability requiring more extensive and pervasive support. The American Psychiatric Association (2013) has similarly placed less emphasis on psychometric IQ and maintained that IQ scores are less valid at these lower levels. Individuals with moderate, severe, and profound intellectual disability represent approximately 15% of all individuals with intellectual disabilities, or approximately 0.09% of the school-age population and 1.0% of the students served under IDEA, as estimated from U.S. Department of Education (2021) data. Just as with other disability categories, individuals with severe disabilities are a heterogeneous group, with much variability in strengths and weaknesses, abilities, and personal characteristics (Westling et al., 2021).

Multiple disabilities refers to the presence of two or more impairments that significantly influence an individual's ability to learn and function without adaptations and that cannot be accommodated in special education programs devoted to only one of the impairments. A major disability with minor impairments or secondary conditions is not considered multiple disabilities; at least two separate categories of impairment must be present (Best, 2010c). The only exception to this is deaf-blindness, which is a separate category of disability under IDEA. Deaf-blindness is a dual sensory impairment with diverse combinations of vision and hearing impairments. Individuals who are deaf-blind may have additional disabilities as well. Students with multiple disabilities represent approximately 0.2% of the school-age population and approximately 2% of the students served under IDEA (U.S. Department of Education, 2021).

EDUCATIONAL PLACEMENT CONSIDERATIONS The optimal educational placement and the design of effective instruction for students with severe and multiple disabilities are usually determined by the case conference team. The priorities vary depending on the age, severity level, and needs of the individual. Priorities come from family, caregiver, medical, school, leisure, transitional, vocational, and peer-support concern areas and are designed to match each student's needs and strengths.

Students with severe and multiple disabilities generally have severe cognitive and adaptive behavior difficulties and require instruction in self-help, communication, functional academic, and daily living skills and community awareness, as well as recreation, social, and vocational education skills (Spooner & Brown, 2017). These students benefit greatly from positive social interactions with their general education peers (Wehmeyer & Shogren, 2017). The creation of peer-support networks, friendship circles, and social circles and participation in after-school activities are strongly advocated for individuals with severe disabilities (Westling et al., 2021).

Some have suggested that instruction for students with severe cognitive disabilities should focus primarily on essential life skills (Ayres et al., 2011). Conversely, Browder and colleagues described reasons for providing students with severe disabilities access to the general education curriculum and the **Common Core State Standards (CCSS)** (Browder, 2015; Courtade et al., 2012). Browder and her colleagues argued that students with severe disabilities have the right to full educational opportunities, including increased expectations. Since the adoption of the CCSS, all students have a right to preparation for the real-life demands of adulthood. Browder also argued that the potential of students with severe disabilities in this area is unknown because they have historically been denied access to the general education curriculum; therefore, it is appropriate that they are included in these new standards. Finally, she pointed out that life skills and academic skills are not mutually exclusive and can be taught concurrently, and as students learn, expectations will change.

STRATEGIES FOR MAKING CLASSROOM ADAPTATIONS FOR STUDENTS WITH SEVERE AND MULTIPLE DISABILITIES

Because of the nature of severe and multiple disabilities, most students require special education and related services from many educational team members, including physical therapists, occupational therapists, speech–language therapists, adaptive physical education specialists, special educators, and paraprofessionals. Establish good working relationships with these partners and arrange the classroom for easy access by these specialists. Specialists may include their activities along with general education instruction. For example, they can assist with positioning and grasping techniques during classes involving art activities or computer applications. Arrange a special place in the classroom for specialists to work with the students with severe disabilities within the general education classroom. This should be done in a way that neither draws unnecessary attention to students with severe disabilities nor distracts the rest of the class. The *Research Highlight* describes a peer-support project in secondary classes. The *Diversity, Equity, and Inclusion in the Classroom* feature describes a comprehensive model for supporting diverse families and/or caregivers.

ESTABLISH GOOD WORKING RELATIONSHIPS WITH PARAPROFESSIONALS

Paraprofessionals (or paraeducators) are often assigned to accompany students with severe disabilities during the school day. This means general education teachers would have another adult in the classroom whenever the student with severe disabilities is present. Because many teachers are used to being alone in their classrooms, having another adult in the room while teaching may require some adjustment. However, the benefits can outweigh the disadvantages because paraprofessionals can assist in many instructional and administrative responsibilities as well as self-help care (Giangreco et al., 2014). Such assistance might include the following:

- Adapting materials under the direction of the teacher or special education teacher
- Administering tests individually to students with severe disabilities
- Reviewing and practicing materials already covered in class
- Presenting adapted materials to students
- Taking notes for students
- Assisting teachers during a class presentation
- Promoting peer cooperation during class
- Helping to arrange the classroom environment to accommodate activity needs
- Grading papers and assisting with recordkeeping
- Assisting with duplicating or laminating class materials
- Attending case conferences or team meetings as necessary
- Assisting with feeding and toileting
- Assisting with dressing before and after recess
- Supervising during recess
- Assisting with mobility during class-changing time periods, including going to lunch and before and after school

Research Highlight

Peer Support for Adolescents with Disabilities

Asmus et al. (2017) extended the research of Carter et al. (2011) examining how peers could assist a student with severe disabilities with social experiences. Carter et al. examined how peers could assist in supporting students with severe disabilities in accessing social and academic experiences in inclusive classes. They hypothesized that students with severe disabilities and their general education peer assistants might profit from a peer-assistance arrangement in their general education classes. Findings revealed that social interactions involving both academic and social topics increased between students and their peer assistants. Carter and his colleagues (Hochman et al., 2015) extended that research to include peer networks to work with high school students with both autism spectrum disorders (ASD) and intellectual disabilities in order to increase their social connections in school. Peer network interventions are intended to form a cohesive student group to meet both formally and informally during an entire semester with assistance from a school facilitator (Carter et al., 2013).

Asmus et al. (2017) extended the use of peer network interventions to improve social connections and experiences in a randomized control design in which 95 high school students with severe disabilities (ASD and intellectual disabilities) from 9th to 12th grade with a range of classes and functioning levels participated in either the peer-network-intervention condition ($N = 47$) or the business-as-usual condition ($N = 48$). In addition, 192 typically achieving peers were trained to be part of a group of three to six students in a social peer network for each focus student with disabilities. Facilitators including special and general educators, paraprofessionals and other school staff were trained by research team members to recruit and work with peer network students.

Facilitators were given orientation meetings, a peer network manual that included the purpose and goals of the intervention, recruitment and selection of peers, supporting students, fading support, and checklists to ensure consistency of meetings. Selected peers also participated in orientation meetings to (1) understand the goals of the peer networks; (2) learn about others in the program; (3) generate ways to improve social interactions and increase social involvement of target students at lunch, during other school activities, and in clubs; and (4) become familiar with the roles and responsibilities, including confidentiality and attendance at weekly meetings. More specific activities were included in weekly network meetings during which target students and peers had time to eat, play board games or engage in other shared activities, converse about upcoming school and sporting events and school vacations, and report any social interactions that occurred outside of weekly meetings.

Findings revealed that students in the social-network condition increased significantly in social contacts and friendships than students in the business-as-usual condition. Reported findings indicated more social interactions occurred during network meetings but also throughout the week in informally organized situations, such as in the school lunchroom, in between classes, in hallways, and before and after school. Students with disabilities described their network peers as their friends with whom they wanted to maintain contact. Many, but not all, friendships continued for another semester. Kunts and Carter (2019) provide a comprehensive review supporting these findings.

QUESTIONS FOR REFLECTION

1. Why do you think interactions and social engagement with students with disabilities increased?
2. Why do you think the weekly peer network meetings facilitated social interactions with the students with disabilities?
3. What implications are associated with the results of this study?
4. What other extensions of this study could be conducted?

Diversity, Equity, and Inclusion in the Classroom

Supporting Diverse Families and Caregivers: The Comprehensive Support Model

Educators who use culturally responsive pedagogy value the partnership(s) with the caregiver(s) and family members of students with disabilities from diverse cultures. Mueller (2017) provides recommendations for increasing involvement for all families and caregivers, including diverse families and caregivers. One culturally sensitive model, the Comprehensive Support Model (CSM), is intended to provide better services for students with exceptionalities and their diverse families and caregivers (Obiakor et al., 2002). CSM is based on the model educational services used in an African village, which values all parts of society. That is, the student, family, caregiver(s), school, community, and government work together to solve educational problems. Five interacting components are important for effective implementation of CSM.

First, CSM assumes students will have active roles in the planning, self-responsibility for, and implementation of their educational programs. Students are encouraged to be motivated and active participants in school. Second, CSM acknowledges that caregivers are important members who provide critical linkages between home and school. Families and caregivers are encouraged to participate in activities during and after school hours. Third, CSM recognizes that school personnel are important, as they can provide understanding and valuing of diverse cultures and help to infuse culturally responsive instruction in classes. Schools can be catalysts for organizing programs for all teachers on culturally responsive practices. Programs can provide assistance on using culturally appropriate assessments and promotion of self-concept for students from all cultures. Fourth, CSM acknowledges that the community contains numerous untapped resources to enhance the education of all students. Some of these resources of the entire community include clergy from all religions, community leaders, and members of the various neighborhoods. Community members can serve as mentors and role models for students. Finally, local, state, and federal governments play important roles in CSM. Governments provide funding for school programs and provide guidance to ensure protection of rights for all students with disabilities from diverse cultures. When all components of CSM are working together, students with disabilities from diverse cultures and their caregivers will have greater opportunities for success (see also Gay, 2018; Turnbull et al., 2015).

Discuss: How could you engage the community in the academic lives of children with disabilities?

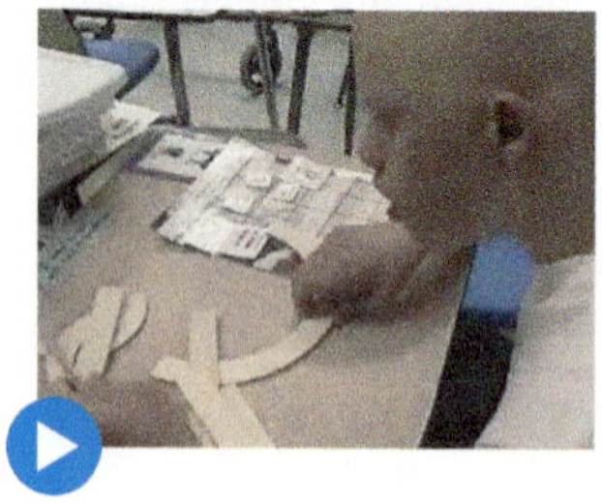

Pearson eTextbook

Video Example 4.4

In this class, paraprofessionals are shown working on a range of tasks with different students. What important role do paraprofessionals play in the classroom?

Use strategies to promote positive interactions with paraprofessionals. Also, be careful that paraprofessionals assist students with disabilities when needed without preventing their access to other students or teachers. Be certain the student is able to interact with the teacher and other students as much as possible (Giangreco et al., 2011).

INCREASE DISABILITY AWARENESS Prepare your students for the arrival of a student with severe or multiple disabilities. Information regarding the strengths and needs of the individuals can be conveyed using a variety of formats to promote students' awareness of disability-related issues. One method of presenting information is to have guest speakers present information on specific disability-related issues pertaining to the student who will be included within the class. Special education teachers, parents, and caregivers of students with disabilities, speech–language therapists, physicians, school psychologists, or local disability organizations such as the Council for Exceptional Children (CEC) or the ARC can present relevant information.

Tiana, a first-grade teacher, described how her students began to express their natural curiosity about fellow classmate Nora. Tiana used their curiosity to provide a teaching moment:

> One of the advantages of teaching first grade is that the children are totally honest. After about a week of having Nora with us and watching her communicate with sign language and using her book with symbols, the children began to ask questions about how Nora was learning. The paraprofessional and I seized the moment and began

answering questions about Nora. The children were so concerned and interested in their fellow classmate. How did she learn, can she see them (she tends to hold her head sideways and to be involved in her own world), would she ever go to college, could they help her learn, could they learn to talk with her, and where did she go when she was not with us? I listened to their questions with tears in my eyes as I realized they had a genuine interest in her and wanted to be a part of her learning experience. Aren't children wonderful with their nonjudgmental behavior!

CONCEPTUALIZE INCLUSIVE INSTRUCTION Several authors have suggested a variety of ways to begin to conceptualize the inclusion of students with severe disabilities into general education classes (Brown et al., 2020; Westling et al., 2021). These include the following:

- Focus on activities that can be engaged in by all students, without modification, such as homeroom or music class.
- Use *multilevel curriculum instruction*, or **differentiated instruction**, such as having a student in a wheelchair work on control of different muscles while the rest of the class does exercises on floor mats during physical education class. Students' learning goals are within the same subject but they differ in difficulty or specific application.
- Engage in *curriculum overlapping*, for example, having the student work on communication skills in the context of working on another academic area, such as mathematics. In curriculum overlapping, the subject area may differ but students share similar activities.

MONITOR SPECIAL HEALTH CARE NEEDS Many students with severe disabilities have coexisting medical needs and require special health care adaptations and accommodations. Some students may be medically fragile, have infectious diseases, or simply have coexisting severe medical needs.

Consider writing daily health care plans for individuals with severe medical needs. Health care plans, written with input from the student's health care provider, can detail information pertaining to the condition itself, restrictions in activities or precautions to be considered, the independence of the student in health care, medication schedules, whether students can recognize signs or symptoms of their own disorders, toileting schedules, and emergency plans for medical or other emergency situations (such as procedures for contacting medical assistance and parental/caregiver notification).

Some students need assistance from medical technology, such as respirator support, intravenous or nutritional support, alternative bowel and bladder assistance, breathing support with the use of ventilators, suctioning to remove mucus (especially for those with tracheostomies), and continuous feedings provided by pumps. With the establishment of good open lines of communication with health care professionals, parents and caregivers will enable general education teachers to better accommodate individuals requiring such assistance in their classes (Best et al., 2010).

ADAPT MATERIALS AND THE PHYSICAL ENVIRONMENT Students with severe disabilities may have coexisting physical disabilities. In these cases, adaptations to the physical environment and instructional materials—such as those detailed earlier in the section on students with physical disabilities—will be required.

In addition, many of the adaptations described for use with students with intellectual disabilities in Chapter 3 may be beneficial. Prioritize the educational and social objectives for the time spent in the general education class. Once the goals are prioritized, you will be in a better position to design and implement any necessary adaptations.

Primary adaptations for students with severe and multiple disabilities may involve devising procedures for communication systems (including ACC devices), handling instructional materials, allowing additional time to complete activities, and devising activities that are instructionally relevant and meaningful for students.

Work closely with the special education teacher to develop an appropriate and effective manner of interacting with students with severe disabilities. Because many students with severe disabilities have limited language skills, make certain that all your communications are clear and understandable.

Students with severe disabilities may be learning different things than other students in the classroom and therefore will have different learning objectives. Make certain that you are familiar with all the IEP objectives for students with severe (or any other) disabilities. All objectives should be stated in a way that progress can be directly observed and recorded. For example, if one of a student's objectives involves interacting more positively with other students, be certain you know exactly what is meant by *positive interaction* (e.g., more direct eye contact, friendly expression, positive statements or gestures), and monitor progress on this objective (Brown et al., 2020).

ADAPT ASSESSMENT METHODS Students with severe and multiple disabilities may require different assessment methods than other students. A variety of assessment methods may be appropriate to determine achievement and chart progress. Use curriculum-based assessment, monitor progress on specific personal objectives toward predetermined goals and objectives, use alternative state assessments, and utilize portfolio assessments, as described in Chapter 12.

Visual Impairments

Learning Objective 4.4 Describe and discuss the prevalence and characteristics of students with visual impairments and explain strategies for classroom adaptations.

PREVALENCE, DEFINITIONS, AND CHARACTERISTICS OF VISUAL IMPAIRMENTS

Individuals with visual impairments make up one of the smallest disability areas, approximately $<0.05\%$ of the school-age population and 0.4% of the students served under IDEA (U.S. Department of Education, 2021). Vision loss can range from mild to moderate to severe, and both legal and educational definitions exist. The legal definition includes acuity assessment information, and the educational definition is linked to learning to read. Individuals are classified as legally blind if their **visual acuity** is 20/200 or less, even with corrective lenses, and partially sighted if their visual acuity is 20/70. This means that a person who is legally blind can see something at 20 feet that a person with normal vision can see at 200 feet, and a person who is partially sighted can see something at 20 feet that a person with normal vision can see at 70 feet. Legal classification qualifies individuals for tax advantages and some other legal benefits (Zimmerman & Zebehazy, 2011).

Educational definitions are based more on the method necessary for learning to read. For example, many individuals classified as legally blind have some vision and can learn to read using enlarged print. These students are often referred to as students with low vision. Other individuals have such limited vision that they are referred to as totally blind and learn to read using the **braille** system (raised dots that are read with fingertips) or by ear using audio recordings. The federal definition is "an impairment in vision that, even with correction, adversely affects a child's educational performance. The term includes both partial sight and blindness" (Definitions; Child with a Disability; Specific Learning Disability, 2004; U.S. Department of Education, 2006).

Low or total vision loss can be present at birth or acquired later in life. Common causes of visual impairments include **glaucoma** (excessive pressure on the eyeball), **cataracts** (clouding of the lens), **diabetic retinopathy** (lack of blood to the retina), **coloboma** (parts of the retina are improperly formed), **retinitis pigmentosa** (degeneration of the retina), and **retinopathy of prematurity** (caused by excessive oxygen given to premature infants). Muscle-functioning disorders of the eye, such as strabismus (crossed eyes) and nystagmus (rapid involuntary eye movements), may also result in visual impairments.

Individuals with visual impairments can have one or more of a wide range of disabilities, from mild to severe. A common characteristic is delayed language development due to the restriction of visual experiences. Students with severe visual impairments may rely on the tactile and auditory senses rather than the visual sense (Zebehazy & Lawson, 2017). These students need to hold and feel three-dimensional objects to obtain a sense of their characteristics. Because these students may miss opportunities for learning incidentally from seeing everything in their environment, it is necessary to present this information in alternative formats (Zebehazy & Lawson, 2017).

Some students with visual impairments engage in such repetitive behavior as head weaving or body rocking. These are known as stereotypic behaviors and are not harmful, but they can attract unwanted or negative attention. Stereotypic behaviors are sometimes addressed by reinforcement, self-monitoring, or physical prompts (Zebehazy & Lawson, 2017).

Mobility skills vary among individuals with visual impairments depending on the age of onset, degree of severity, and the individual's spatial ability. Spatial ability appears to affect the mobility access of individuals with visual impairments. Some individuals with visual impairments learn to walk with canes, although the training can be lengthy and difficult. Some canes have light sensors near the tip that emit sounds when the amount of light changes, indicating shadows or objects in the path ahead. Some individuals walk with human guides and guide dogs, although the latter are not as often seen with children (Davis, 2003).

STRATEGIES FOR

MAKING CLASSROOM ADAPTATIONS FOR STUDENTS WITH VISUAL IMPAIRMENTS

First, ensure that your classroom has clear, open walkways. Devise and teach classroom procedures for responding to emergency situations, including fire and tornado drills. Assign peers to assist students with visual impairments during emergency evacuations. Develop safety guidelines for using objects that are potentially harmful to students with visual impairments.

Following are strategies you can use to differentiate instruction to make your classroom more inclusive for students with visual impairments (see also Best et al., 2010; Zebehazy & Lawson, 2017). The described adaptations align with the principles of universal design for learning (UDL) (see Chapter 6).

ADAPT THE PHYSICAL ENVIRONMENT Keep aisles clear, wide, and open. Familiarize students with the physical arrangement of the room and notify students if any changes are made. Extra space will be necessary to accommodate equipment for braille and reading enlarged-print materials. Allow the student to sit where it will maximize any residual vision.

ADAPT INSTRUCTIONAL MATERIALS If possible, consult with school library personnel and/or an assistive technology specialist to ensure that class materials use accessible formatting (Hashey & Stahl, 2014). For example, Microsoft products have an Accessibility Checker. Enlarge and enhance printed materials, including dramatically increasing the size of fonts. Increase the visibility of materials, which might include the use of bold-lined paper, special lighting, and magnification lenses. Certain technology may be used, such as projection microscopes, closed-circuit television, scanners, and equipment to convert print and other images to tactile formats (Best et al., 2010). Convert print, such as class notes, to braille formats with the Perkins brailler or specialized computer programs such as *Duxbury* (Duxbury Systems). Figure 4.4 shows examples of braille. Use oral-output devices, which produce speech, to enable students with visual

Figure 4.4 Samples of Braille

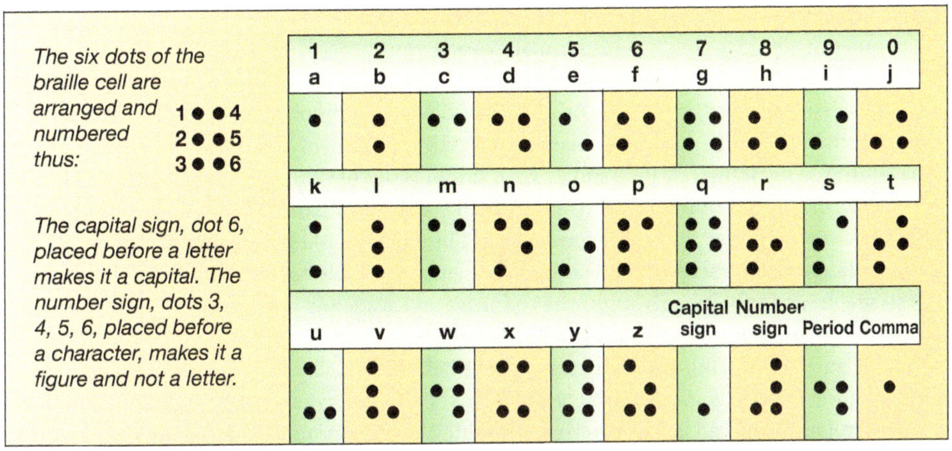

Source: Reprinted with permission from the Division for the Blind and Physically Handicapped, Library of Congress, Washington, DC.

impairments to participate in the same activities as their peers. These include the *Jaws* screen reader (Freedom Scientific) and *Kurzweil 1000* (Kurzweil Education). Use descriptive video services, provided on many public television broadcasts, to provide additional verbal descriptions of visual events. Use tactile and three-dimensional models to enhance conceptual understanding.

Pearson eTextbook
Video Example 4.5

The special education and general education teachers in this video collaborate when planning math instruction for Rudy, a male student with a visual impairment. Identify the adaptations they plan to use to meet Rudy's needs while maintaining high academic expectations.

ADAPT INSTRUCTION Be explicit when giving oral presentations. Avoid vague phrases such as *over here*, *almost*, *this*, and *that*, and use specific language such as *above your head*, *on your right*, and *the beaker in my hand*. Teach and use time orientations such as, "The model is on my desk at 2 o'clock." When walking with students, describe upcoming barriers by saying, for example, "We are approaching an uphill ramp." When addressing students with visual impairments, always state their names first so they know you are speaking to them and speak in a normal tone of voice.

In whatever way you adapt your instruction, provide sufficient time for students with visual impairments to complete class activities. For example, allow the student time to listen to an audio recording of the lecture after class. Remember that reading enlarged print and braille takes longer than reading regular print. Check with students to determine the optimal pace at which they are capable of working.

ADAPT ASSESSMENT METHODS When assessing students with visual impairments, allocate sufficient time for students to complete tests. Extra time is required to transcribe responses from braille to print formats or to use peer assistants. When standardization of the test is not violated, consider individual teacher or paraprofessional administration of tests.

Hearing Impairments Including Deafness

Learning Objective 4.5 Describe and discuss the prevalence and characteristics of students with hearing impairments and explain strategies for classroom adaptations.

PREVALENCE, DEFINITIONS, AND CHARACTERISTICS OF HEARING IMPAIRMENTS

Individuals with hearing impairments make up 0.1% of the school-age population and 1.0% of the students served under IDEA (U.S. Department of Education, 2021). Hearing impairments range in severity from mild to moderate to severe to profound, with the greatest educational distinctions occurring between those who are hard of hearing and those who are Deaf. Individuals classified as hard of hearing can hear speech tones when wearing hearing aids, whereas persons who are Deaf cannot hear even with hearing aids.

The age at which a child loses hearing affects the degree of language delay and development. Children who are born with deafness have congenital hearing losses (**prelingual**) and more difficulty with language development than those who acquire deafness after age 2 (**postlingual**).

Pure-tone audiometers are used to assess hearing ability. Tones with different pitches (or frequency, measured in **Hertz [Hz]**) and volume (measured in **decibels [dB]**) are presented via headphones, and individuals respond (by, e.g., raising their hands or pushing a button) when they hear a sound. Levels of hearing loss are classified along a continuum, with 0 dB indicating the quietest sound a person with normal hearing can detect. Individuals with slight hearing losses (27–40 dB) may not have difficulty in most school situations. Individuals with mild losses (41–55 dB) may miss up to 50% of classroom discussion if voices are faint or faces cannot be seen. Individuals with moderate losses (56–70 dB) can understand only loud speech and may have limited vocabularies. Individuals with severe losses (71–90 dB) may be able to hear loud voices within 1 foot of the ear, and speech is likely to be impaired. Individuals with profound losses (>90 dB) may hear some loud sounds but are more likely to sense vibrations, and they may rely on vision rather than hearing as a primary vehicle for communication. Specialized tests are needed to accurately assess the cognitive and academic functioning of individuals with hearing impairments (Owens & Farinella, 2018).

Causes of hearing impairments include heredity, prenatal infections such as maternal rubella, ear infections, meningitis, head trauma, prematurity, and oxygen deprivation during birth. Impairments can be **conductive**, meaning the outer or middle ear along the passageway is damaged; **sensorineural**, referring to inner-ear damage; or a combination of the two (Lomas et al., 2017).

Many children with hearing impairments have academic and cognitive deficiencies or developmental lags due to difficulties processing language. Without early intervention, children with severe to profound hearing impairment generally do not achieve skills any higher than the fourth-grade level (although many exceptions exist) (American Speech-Language-Hearing Association, 2005). In many inclusive classes, there may be less interaction between students who are Deaf and students who hear normally, perhaps increasing feelings of isolation and loneliness (Lomas et al., 2017).

Like the autistic community, some individuals of the Deaf community prefer identity-first language, in which the disability is mentioned first (e.g., a Deaf person). Others may prefer person-first language (e.g., an individual with hearing loss). How one self-identifies may also influence the educational programming and instructional practices used to teach the individual.

EDUCATIONAL PROGRAMMING

An ongoing debate exists over what should be considered the best approach for teaching individuals with severe hearing impairments. Some advocate **total communication** (Owens & Farinella, 2018), which involves using speech (lip) reading, gestures, and sign language or both oral and manual methods. Teachers using total communication rely on the structure of the English language and speak while signing during communications with students who are Deaf. Some advocate the use of only oral approaches, eliminating any manual components used in total communication. Teachers using only oral approaches rely heavily on parental, caregiver, and family involvement as well as auditory, visual, and tactile methods of presentation. Finally, others advocate using only sign language or manual approaches. These individuals advocate the exclusive use of sign language because they maintain that a unique "culture of the Deaf" exists among those who communicate with sign language. They believe that when individuals with hearing impairments are taught only to speech-read or use oral techniques, they are denied full participation in the culture of the Deaf (Hamill & Stein, 2011; Owens & Farinella, 2018). Individuals with this perspective argue that they are not disabled but are part of another cultural group composed of Deaf persons.

Cochlear implants have in some cases provided more access to sound for many students who are Deaf, and many students with cochlear implants have shown progress in oral language and reading. However, family and caregiver support, resources, maintenance, and speech therapy are needed over time for the success of the implants. Overall effectiveness varies widely among individuals (Lomas et al., 2017).

Several signing systems are in use today, including American Sign Language, Fingerspelling, and Signing Exact English. All systems use manual signs made with the hands and fingers to represent words, concepts, and ideas. However, they are based on different systems. **American Sign Language (ASL)** is a visual-spatial language and, unlike English, is not phonologically based. Each sign has three parts: hand shape, location, and movement. ASL has its own rules of semantics, syntax, and pragmatics and its own vocabulary (Owens & Farinella, 2018). Fingerspelling involves a manual alphabet of 26 distinct hand positions used to represent each letter in the English alphabet. Fingerspelling is especially appropriate for unfamiliar words such as proper names. Several apps are available to teach Fingerspelling, such as *ASL Fingerspelling* (Michael Bartmess) and *Sign Language Alphabet Trainer* (BidBox, LLC). Some teachers use Fingerspelling while speaking to students with hearing impairments. Signing Exact English is a system that employs components of ASL but attempts to use correct English usage for facilitating the learning of reading and writing skills in English for students who are Deaf. No clear research evidence exists to promote one approach over the other in teaching these students. Therefore, it is likely that this debate will continue into the future.

STRATEGIES FOR
MAKING CLASSROOM ADAPTATIONS FOR STUDENTS WITH HEARING IMPAIRMENTS

Students with hearing loss can benefit from instruction in general education classes if specific adaptations are made. Specific accommodations vary depending on the degree of hearing loss and whether students have interpreters to accompany them throughout the school day. If you have a student with hearing impairments in your class, establish classroom emergency procedures for use during fire and tornado drills. Many fire alarms can be equipped with a light that flashes while the bell rings, alerting students with hearing impairments. Consider assigning a peer assistant who can pass along information that comes from the announcement system and who can be a buddy during any emergency situations. In addition to these guidelines, consider differentiating instruction with the following strategies (see also Luckner et al., 2012; Marshark et al., 2002; Stewart & Kluwin, 2001).

ADAPT THE PHYSICAL ENVIRONMENT Seat students close enough to the front of the class to maximize their hearing and enable them to read speech. They should also be able to turn to face other students while they are speaking. Because hearing aids are especially sound-sensitive, loud or irritating noises should be avoided. Consider choosing a room with carpeting and located away from noisy school areas, such as the cafeteria and gym.

ADAPT INSTRUCTIONAL MATERIALS Use technology, including hearing aids, television captioning, adapted telephone equipment (TTY), computer-assisted instruction, and the Internet. When appropriate, use frequency-modulation (FM) sound systems, which include cordless microphones for teachers and receivers that attach to hearing aids for students. Pass your microphone to classmates who are speaking in a class discussion so that they can also be heard. Audio enhancement systems using infrared microphones have also been installed in classrooms. Some teachers report that these devices improve the volume and clarity of their speech, for the benefit of all students (Mathews, 2008). Use visuals such as illustrations, diagrams, pictures, and three-dimensional models to introduce vocabulary and concepts and enhance comprehension. Explicit instruction of vocabulary is needed. Use language cards that contain vocabulary and illustrations of concepts and definitions that can accompany verbal presentations and be used to pre-teach. Encourage students to maintain personal dictionaries of their language cards. The described adaptations align with the principles of UDL (see Chapter 6).

Pearson eTextbook
Video Example 4.6
In this class, middle school students with hearing impairments use technology during instruction. Ms. Cook uses an interactive smartboard, visual cues, signing, and oral language to support instruction.

ADAPT INSTRUCTION Create authentic experiences by connecting new language and knowledge to real-world experiences in a context relevant to the student's linguistic and experiential background. As you teach, reiterate major points, write out assignments, or write down questions on overhead transparencies or the chalkboard. Give students outlines or closing summaries as handouts. Repeat questions or answers that other students contribute to enable students with hearing impairments to participate fully in class. Sequence steps or procedures on written cards and place them in clear view.

Use hand signals or devise a signaling system to denote transitions and allow students with hearing impairments or interpreters to review questions, answers, and concepts. Alert students as to when to look or listen and position yourself so that students with hearing impairments can clearly see your face and body language, without shadowing from backlighting or the reflection of glaring light.

Use a "listen, then look, then listen" sequence of instruction so that students can focus on your face as you speak, then focus on the other aspects of the lesson separately, then focus on your face again. Say, for example, "Now, I'm going to pour the oil in with this water" (listen); then pour the oil (look), then say, "I poured the oil into the water. Who can tell me what happened?" (listen).

Repeat information from the school public address system to ensure students have understood the announcements.

Be sure to plan for interpreters. Interpreters often assist students who are Deaf by translating lecture information, tutoring, and assisting special and general education teachers (Luckner et al., 2012). Extra space, including chairs or desks, may be required for interpreters to be near students with hearing impairments. Because interpreters are typically adults and taller than your students, check to see that all children have a clear view of important classroom information. Prepare your students for the interpreter, and clearly explain the roles and functions the interpreter will have while in your classroom. Schedule time alone with the interpreter to discuss your typical classroom procedures, materials, and routines. Remember that an interpreter cannot proceed at the same pace as your verbal presentation; you need to slow your rate of presentation accordingly.

Work with family members and caregivers to maximize the educational experience of students. Parents, caregivers, and other family members have an important influence on students with hearing impairments, with respect to such activities as going out and interacting with people, joining sports and other recreational activities, and monitoring and assisting with homework (Stewart & Kluwin, 2001). Work with family members and caregivers to help them prioritize and encourage their participation in activities.

ADAPT ASSESSMENT METHODS Testing and evaluation modifications for students with hearing loss might include providing individual testing times in separate rooms and extending the time limit as necessary. Remember to allow sufficient time for interpreters during oral testing situations. Permit students to draw illustrations of concepts. Use performance-based testing measures and identification formats whenever possible.

4 Summary

- Students with autism or autism spectrum disorder function along a continuum of severe to mild disabilities but usually have pronounced challenges with social behavior. Students with more severe autism have difficulties with language, communication, cognitive tasks, attention, memory, and basic skills.
- Students with physical disabilities may have limited to no use of their arms, legs, or both the arms and the legs. Some of these students may exhibit challenges with communication. Specific adaptations for increasing mobility, assisting with fine motor control, and improving communication skills help students become more independent and successful. Students with other health impairments may have serious medical needs that require special attention and that restrict their learning in school. Coordination with medical professionals while monitoring health and educational needs helps these students with school success.
- Some students with severe disabilities have severe intellectual disabilities and exhibit difficulties in cognition and adaptive behavior as well as academic, social, self-help, problem-solving, attention, and memory skills.
- Individuals with visual impairments represent among the smallest categories of exceptionality. Students may have very low vision to no vision. These students require adaptations, such as arranging the physical environment for easy accessibility; enhancing printed materials; using braille and oral formats; and using concrete, tactile, and three-dimensional examples.
- Individuals with mild to moderate hearing impairments usually wear hearing aids, whereas individuals who are Deaf use sign language, total communication, or other aural techniques for communication. Students may require specific language, communication, and social skills instruction.

PROFESSIONAL STANDARDS LINK: Teaching Students with Autism and Lower-Incidence Disabilities

Information in this chapter links most directly to:

- CEC 2020 Initial Practice-Based Professional Preparation Standards for Special Educators (Initial K–12 standards) (see https://exceptionalchildren.org/standards/initial-practice-based-professional-preparation-standards-special-educators): 1 (Learner Development and Individual Learning Differences), 2 (Understanding and Addressing Each Individual's Developmental and Learning Needs), 4 (Using Assessment to Understand the Learner and the Learning Environment for Data-Based Decision Making), 5 (Supporting Learning Using Effective Instruction), 7 (Collaborating with Team Members)
- InTASC Standards (see https://www.ccsso.org/sites/default/files/2017-11/InTASC_Model_Core_Teaching_Standards_2011.pdf): 2 (Learning Differences), 3 (Learning Environments), 6 (Assessment), 7 (Planning for Instruction), 8 (Instructional Strategies), 10 (Leadership and Collaboration)

TEACHING STUDENTS WITH AUTISM AND LOWER-INCIDENCE DISABILITIES

If a student with autism or lower-incidence disabilities is having difficulties in your classroom, have you tried the following? If not, see the pages listed here.

STRATEGIES FOR MAKING CLASSROOM ADAPTATIONS FOR STUDENTS WITH AUTISM

STRATEGIES FOR MAKING CLASSROOM ADAPTATIONS FOR STUDENTS WITH PHYSICAL DISABILITIES AND OTHER HEALTH IMPAIRMENTS

STRATEGIES FOR MAKING CLASSROOM ADAPTATIONS FOR STUDENTS WITH SEVERE AND MULTIPLE DISABILITIES

STRATEGIES FOR MAKING CLASSROOM ADAPTATIONS FOR STUDENTS WITH VISUAL IMPAIRMENTS

STRATEGIES FOR MAKING CLASSROOM ADAPTATIONS FOR STUDENTS WITH HEARING IMPAIRMENTS

Richard Aldred/Offset/Shutterstock

CHAPTER 5

Teaching Students with Gifts and Talents and Other Diverse Learning Needs

LEARNING OBJECTIVES

After studying this chapter, you should be able to:

5.1 Describe the prevalence and characteristics of students who are gifted, creative, or talented and identify strategies for classroom adaptations.

5.2 Discuss the prevalence and characteristics of students from culturally and linguistically diverse backgrounds and explain strategies for classroom adaptations.

5.3 Summarize the prevalence and characteristics of students at risk for school failure and recognize strategies for classroom adaptations.

Not all individuals with diverse learning needs are classified as having disabilities. Students with other diverse learning needs represent a wide range of abilities and include (1) students who are gifted and talented, (2) students from diverse cultural and linguistic backgrounds, and (3) students who may be considered at risk for school failure. These students belong to an increasing population in schools and are served in general education classes.

Gifted, Creative, and Talented

Learning Objective 5.1 Describe the prevalence and characteristics of students who are gifted, creative, or talented and identify strategies for classroom adaptations.

DEFINITIONS, PREVALENCE, AND CHARACTERISTICS OF GIFTED, CREATIVE, AND TALENTED

Individuals with special gifts and talents may be extraordinary in intellectual ability, specialized academic areas, music, or the arts (Clark, 2013). Although gifted, creative, and talented individuals are not included in the Individuals with Disabilities Education Act (IDEA), these students have unique needs that require special attention and accommodations for them to succeed in school. Various definitions of *gifted*, *creative*, and *talented* exist in the literature, and there is little agreement on the best definition (Plucker & Callahan, 2017). Earlier definitions relied heavily on the use of IQ scores for identifying gifted individuals. The Javits Gifted and Talented Act, passed in 1978 (Public Law 95-561, Title IX, § 902) and reauthorized in 1994, included creative capabilities or high performance in the performing arts and has been widely adopted by states and school districts:

> Children and youth with outstanding talent perform or show the potential for performing at remarkably high levels of accomplishment when compared with others [of] their age, experience, or environment. These children and youth exhibit high performance capability in intellectual, creative, and/or artistic areas, possess an unusual leadership capacity, or excel in specific academic fields. They require services or activities not ordinarily provided in the schools. Outstanding talents are present in children and youth from all cultural groups, across all economic strata, and in all areas of human endeavor. (Definitions; Gifted, 1998; see also U.S. Department of Education, 1993, p. 5)

These federal definitions highlight the areas of giftedness, talent, and creativity and are more representative of trends in gifted education. Other conceptualizations of giftedness continue to broaden the single-intelligence notion (see Plucker & Callahan, 2014a, 2014b). The following are examples of broadened definitions for gifted, creative, and talented youth: (1) three-trait definition, including above-average ability, task commitment, and creativity (Renzulli, 2005); (2) especially high aptitude, potential, or ability (Feldhusen & Moon, 1995); (3) synthetic, analytic, and practical intelligence (Sternberg, 2005); and (4) multiple intelligences (Gardner, 2006). All proposed models include more than a single IQ score as criteria, most include talents as critical components, and many recommend advice on counseling gifted and talented youth. Although general intelligence is the most widely accepted consideration in state definitions of giftedness and talent, specific academic ability, creative thinking, talent in the visual or performing arts, and leadership are also considered by many states (Rinn et al., 2020). The National Association for Gifted Children and the Council of State Directors of Programs for the Gifted provide a periodic report titled *State of the States in Gifted Education* (https://www.nagc.org/2018-2019-state-states-gifted-education) inclusive of definitions, identification, services, and other relevant information for each of the 50 states and the District of Columbia.

Given the variety of definitions, it is not surprising that little consensus exists on the actual number of gifted and talented youth. Many reports indicate that 3–6% of the population is gifted and talented; others believe the figures are much higher. Great variability also exists in how individual states identify students with gifts and talents, with some states identifying for 2018–2019 fewer than 1.7% of students and other states identifying as many as 17% (https://nagc.org/state-of-states).

INTELLECTUALLY GIFTED Intellectually gifted students are those who have scored very high on standardized tests and usually excel in school. They are frequently very highly skilled verbally and have outstanding memories and literacy abilities—especially in reading and writing—compared with their typical same-age peers. They also tend to have outstanding critical thinking and problem-solving abilities and insatiable curiosities (Bireley, 1995). Intellectually gifted youth acquire, retain, and manipulate large amounts of information and may appear to learn in intuitive leaps (Davis et al., 2018).

CREATIVE AND TALENTED The definitions of creative and talented are widely varied, but consensus usually converges on the identification of individuals with exceptional talents in particular areas (Clark, 2013). Creatively gifted and talented youth often excel in the visual or performing arts. These individuals typically show outstanding abilities at young ages in particular areas. Davis et al. (2018) listed the following characteristics related to creativity: original, independent, takes risks, aware of creativeness, motivated, curious, sense of humor, attracted to complexity, artistic, open-minded, need for time alone, intuitive, and intelligent.

HIDDEN GIFTED, CREATIVE, AND TALENTED Many students who are gifted and talented remain unidentified or hidden (may be referred to as **hidden gifted**). This may be due to a number of factors. First, they might be underachievers and, consequently, their scores fall below the cutoff scores for classifying gifted students. Second, intelligence tests and standardized tests may underidentify some students because of cultural or linguistic diversity (Ford, 2012; Ford et al., 2022). Research also suggests that using teacher discretion or nomination for referring students of color for gifted services instead of universal screening may play a factor in their underrepresentation in gifted programs (Grissom & Redding, 2016). Third, girls who may be gifted and talented may be underidentified (Navan, 2008), although precise reasons for this are unknown. Finally, some students may not be identified because of existing disabilities in other areas (learning or physical disabilities), which then mask their advanced abilities in another area(s). Students with a learning disability who are also gifted are referred to as **twice-exceptional** (2e) (Yssel et al., 2014).

Special attention during classification and screening efforts aimed at identifying gifted and talented youth can help eliminate underidentification of giftedness. Specific suggestions for finding and nurturing potential giftedness among Hispanic/Latinx and Black students have been provided by Ford (2011), Castellano and Frazier (2021), and Gregory and colleagues (1988), including the following:

- Develop a "belief system" in school that culturally and linguistically diverse students can be and are gifted and talented.
- Develop an identification process that reflects an appreciation of the culture, language, values, and worldviews of culturally and linguistically diverse students and their families/caregivers.
- Employ a multidimensional assessment process that includes qualitative as well as quantitative measures.
- Develop professional development programs to educate teachers and the public in ways that giftedness may be manifested (and sometimes concealed) in different cultures. Collaborate with people knowledgeable in the particular culture for assistance and support.
- Ensure that insights gained in the identification and assessment process are incorporated into the instructional program.

The *Diversity, Equity, and Inclusion in the Classroom* feature describes how one school district made changes to promote equity in its gifted education program.

Pearson eTextbook

Video Example 5.1

An expert in this video describes students who are gifted and talented. How do students who are gifted and talented show similar characteristics to students who are at risk or have disabilities?

ISSUES IN IDENTIFICATION AND ASSESSMENT OF GIFTED, CREATIVE, AND TALENTED

Several approaches exist for identifying gifted and talented children and youth. Common approaches include nomination methods, standardized test scores, talent pool searches, and a multiple-measures/multiple-criteria approach. Nomination approaches consist of distributing nomination forms to teachers, parents, and caregivers. Schools often implement an approach by which parents and caregivers, teachers, peers, and students are provided nomination forms in which they detail reasons for nominating a student (or self) for the gifted and talented program.

Standardized-test-score approaches include the use of intelligence and achievement test scores. These may be individually or group-administered tests. Cutoff scores to qualify students as gifted and talented are often designated to identify high-scoring students, for example, in the top 8% (Plucker & Callahan, 2017). This approach is usually combined with some other approach, in that standardized test scores are seldom the only criteria considered.

A multiple-measures/multiple-criteria approach is implemented in many schools (Davis et al., 2018). This approach combines many of the pieces of evidence collected in the approaches discussed previously but may also include detailed family and caregiver histories, student work samples and inventories of interests, and discussion of all evidence by a gifted-and-talented screening committee.

STRATEGIES FOR

MAKING ADAPTATIONS FOR STUDENTS WHO ARE GIFTED, CREATIVE, AND TALENTED

Several educational approaches exist for programming curriculum and classes for gifted and talented youth. These include acceleration and enrichment and are provided in general education classes, resource classes, self-contained classes, and university classes and through mentoring programs (Davis et al., 2018). Careful pretesting identifies skills and information that gifted students have and can be used to place them in a more appropriate curriculum. In the inclusive classroom, differentiated instruction can include a number of appropriate adaptions.

IMPLEMENT ACCELERATION OR ENRICHMENT PROGRAMS *Acceleration* refers to moving students through the curriculum at a faster pace than that of general education students (Davis et al., 2018). Acceleration can mean admitting a child to school early, skipping grades, providing level-appropriate curriculum, or testing out of classes. Advancing students refers to placing them in programs that match their achievement levels. For example, a fourth-grader who is working at a sixth-grade level academically might be advanced to the sixth-grade general education classroom. Another example is maintaining students in the age-appropriate class but providing them with the appropriate-level curriculum (sixth-grade level, in this example), which can be described as differentiation in the general education classroom. In 2019, this type of acceleration program was reportedly the most common service delivery model for students in the elementary and middle school grades who are gifted and talented (see https://www.nagc.org/2018-2019-state-states-gifted-education).

Acceleration might also mean advancing students several grade levels but only in specific academic classes. This may be particularly relevant for a student who is 2e with a gift in one particular subject area. For example, if seventh-grade students were gifted mathematically, they might be placed with juniors in an Algebra II class but remain with their same-age peers for other subjects. This type of situation may not be possible, however, for a sixth-grade student in a K–6 elementary school who is gifted mathematically but not able to go down the hall to join a seventh-grade math classroom. In this case, vetted online math programs or virtual learning opportunities could be considered. Universities may also allow students who are gifted or talented to enroll in college-level courses when prerequisite criteria are met. Students who are gifted or talented may take an accelerated math class while in high school that has a summative Advanced Placement (AP) test for college at the end of the course. If the student passes the AP test, this will enable them to skip college-level courses. AP was reportedly the most common service delivery model for meeting the needs of U.S. high school students who are gifted and talented (Rinn et al., 2020). Finally, many students are admitted early to colleges and universities.

Acceleration is controversial, with proponents arguing strenuously for and opponents arguing strenuously against acceleration programs. Proponents claim students need acceleration to maintain interest in school and to be challenged adequately. Opponents claim that acceleration harms the social-emotional development of gifted students. Unfortunately, research results are ambiguous and yield no clear, definitive answers (Davis et al., 2018).

Numerous models of enrichment exist (Clark, 2013). The common element across enrichment programs is the expansion of the existing curriculum. Students are allowed and encouraged to study topics in depth that extend beyond the scope of the general education curriculum. The goals behind enrichment activities are to allow opportunities for critical thinking and problem solving through in-depth analyses of specific content areas. In some cases, schools might provide integrated curriculum that includes **science, technology, engineering, and mathematics (STEM)** as either regular classes or activities. See Table 5.1 for examples. This is often accomplished by having students work independently on projects within general education classes. However, enrichment may also take place in off-campus settings. For example, students may be assigned to work with mentors

TABLE 5.1 Examples of Enrichment Activities in Specific Content Areas

Content Area	Enrichment Activity
Math	Mentoring Mathematical Mind Project M^3 (grades 3–6; Kendall Hunt Publishing) aligns with math standards but is one to two grade levels above the regular curriculum. Project M^3 simulates real-life problems so students can actively solve them in the same ways that mathematicians do. Students discuss and write about mathematical concepts and they question the answers rather than simply answer the questions.
Civics/Social Studies	Primary sources such as photographs, newspapers, films, and documents are used throughout the curriculum for students to practice literacy skills. In advanced academic classes, students may use the Document Based Question Project Method™ or DBQ (dbqproject.com). Students are provided a series of primary sources. The primary sources relate to a specific question (e.g., How did the Constitution guard against tyranny?) and students synthesize the evidence to develop an argumentative essay and answer the question. The DBQ method has students engage like a natural historian.
STEM	STEM (science, technology, engineering, and mathematics) topics can be integrated throughout the curriculum and/or as extracurricular activities. School clubs may involve students in robotics, Lego, coding, app development, and programming. Schools may also have events such as cyber-defense competitions, science fairs, and engineering challenges (e.g., building a bridge, designing a propeller-powered car).

in business and industry or in university settings. In either case, general education teachers can facilitate coordination of programming for students who are gifted or talented.

ADAPT INSTRUCTIONAL MATERIALS In the case of either acceleration or enrichment, it may be necessary for general educators to adapt curriculum materials to better meet the needs of students who are gifted or talented. When students have demonstrated mastery of content, be prepared to move them ahead in the curriculum or design suitable enrichment activities that enable them to study more in depth in that area. Survey student interests to help provide directions for instructional enhancements. Seek assistance from teachers who work with students who are gifted or talented, content-area experts, guidance counselors, and the students' support system at home.

Pearson eTextbook

Video Example 5.2

In this video, a teacher assigns students who are gifted and talented with a task to problem-solve. The students will need to use critical and creative thinking skills.

ADAPT INSTRUCTIONAL AND EVALUATION PROCEDURES Be prepared to adapt your instructional procedures for students who are gifted or talented. They may not require intensive or explicit instruction on new content. You may be able to meet with them independently and briefly explain new concepts and content, thus allowing more time for either acceleration or enrichment activities. Students who are gifted or talented may also be able to provide tutorial assistance to their same-age peers. Be aware that some gifted and talented youth may also require explicit instruction in study and organizational skills when work demands increase for them. Finally, evaluation methods can be modified to allow for assessment of enrichment and acceleration activities. Johnsen et al. (2022) provide a downloadable appendix with assessments measuring outcomes for gifted students. More performance-based measures may need to be devised to obtain true indicators of students' abilities on such tasks.

Students Who Are Culturally and Linguistically Diverse

Learning Objective 5.2 Discuss the prevalence and characteristics of students from culturally and linguistically diverse backgrounds and explain strategies for classroom adaptations.

PREVALENCE, DEFINITIONS, AND CHARACTERISTICS OF CULTURALLY AND LINGUISTICALLY DIVERSE STUDENTS

Evidence exists that many students from culturally and linguistically diverse backgrounds are at a higher risk for school failure than students from European American backgrounds (Gollnick & Chinn, 2021). Furthermore, the prevalence rates for students with disabilities are different from those expected in some culturally and linguistically diverse groups. Table 5.2 presents risk ratios provided by the U.S. Department of Education (2021) for each racial-ethnic group in each category of disability.

This means, for example, that during the fall of 2018, Black or African American students were nearly twice as likely to receive services for emotional disturbance as were their same-age peers from all the other racial-ethnic groups. Asian students were 0.3 times as likely (i.e., less likely) to receive services for learning disabilities as students in other racial-ethnic groups.

Similar findings have been presented in the past (Chinn & Hughes, 1987; Harry, 1992, 1994). This indicates that little has changed with respect to over- and underrepresentation issues by racial or ethnic groups in past decades. Disproportional representation by race/ethnicity has also been reported in a number of other countries (Anastasiou et al., 2011; Harry et al., 2008; Kalyanpur, 2008).

Although exact reasons for observed overrepresentation of some racial-ethnic backgrounds are uncertain, several reasons have been hypothesized (see Ford et al., 2022; Harry & Klingner, 2014). Some have suggested that there are insufficient successful role models in schools and society for students from culturally and linguistically diverse backgrounds. Others suggest that cultural and linguistic differences often are inaccurately perceived as detriments (Cartledge et al., 2007; Gollnick & Chinn, 2021; Harry & Klingner, 2014), whereas others have suggested that students from these underrepresented groups are discriminated against because educational methods, traditional assessments, and grading procedures do not accommodate students from various cultural and linguistic groups (Artiles et al., 2010; Baca et al., 2004a). Some have proposed that percentages of some nonwhite populations in special education are relatively higher due in part to families/caregivers living below the federal poverty line and resulting in disabilities associated with poverty, such as higher rates of exposure to harmful toxins (lead, alcohol, and

TABLE 5.2 Risk Ratios for 5- to 21-Year-Old Students with Disabilities, by Race/Ethnicity and Disability Category: Fall 2019

Disability	American Indian or Alaska Native	Asian	Black or African American	Hispanic/ Latino	Native Hawaiian or Other Pacific Islander	White	Two or More Races
Specific learning disability	1.8	0.3	1.4	1.4	1.7	0.7	1.0
Speech or language impairment	1.4	0.7	0.9	1.1	1.1	1.0	1.1
Intellectual disabilities	1.5	0.5	2.2	1.1	1.8	0.6	0.8
Emotional disturbance	1.6	0.2	1.8	0.7	1.1	1.0	1.5
Multiple disabilities	1.9	0.7	1.3	0.8	2.2	1.1	1.0
Hearing impairment	1.5	1.2	0.9	1.4	2.6	0.7	0.9
Orthopedic impairment	1.1	1.0	0.9	1.2	1.8	0.9	0.9
Other health impairment	1.2	0.3	1.4	0.8	1.1	1.1	1.2
Visual impairment	1.8	0.9	1.1	0.9	1.8	1.0	0.9
Autism	0.9	1.2	1.1	1.0	1.3	0.9	1.2
Deaf-blindness	1.5	1.0	0.8	0.9	2.6	1.1	1.0
Traumatic brain injury	1.6	0.5	1.1	0.8	1.2	1.2	1.0
All disabilities	1.6	0.5	1.4	1.1	1.5	0.9	1.1

Source: Data from U.S. Department of Education (2021).

tobacco), low birth weight, poorer nutrition, and less effective schools (Donovan & Cross, 2002; Gollnick & Chinn, 2021). It has also been suggested that representation in special education reflects the larger issue of representation in other remedial or compensatory programs such as Title 1 (MacMillan & Reschly, 1998).

Whatever the theory, however, the fact of overrepresentation of students who are culturally and linguistically diverse in special education is evidence that schools must pay greater attention to issues of cultural diversity. It is of critical importance that assessment instruments and procedures be nondiscriminatory, free of bias, and administered in the student's native language (Gollnick & Chinn, 2021). The National Research Council has suggested that a student should be considered eligible for special education only when the student's performance differs markedly from typical performance in specific academic or social-emotional domains, and there is evidence that the student has not responded to high-quality interventions in these specific domains of functioning (Donovan & Cross, 2002). Although states vary their policies and practices as they relate to culturally and linguistically diverse students, these standards are compatible with response-to-intervention (RTI) initiatives (Scott et al., 2014).

Salend and Duhaney (2005) listed a number of suggestions for reducing overrepresentation of culturally and linguistically diverse students, including the following:

- Help create a diverse and culturally sensitive multidisciplinary planning team for making educational decisions.
- Provide effective prereferral and other ancillary services that can make culturally sensitive recommendations for interventions.
- Use alternatives to standardized testing, such as portfolio assessment, curriculum-based measurement, rubrics, and performance-based assessment.
- Look for any cultural factors that might contribute to learning problems and include these in intervention plans.
- Employ culturally responsive curriculum of interest to diverse learners.
- Use behavior-management strategies that are sensitive to cultural differences in social behavior and include such strategies as culturally relevant reinforcers and group-oriented behavior-management techniques.

- Employ culturally responsive teaching strategies, such as, for example, verbal interactions, cooperative learning, divergent thinking, small-group instruction, real-world tasks, and positive teacher–student interactions.
- Encourage family and caregiver involvement by using positive and respectful language, encouraging face-to-face meetings, and planning creatively to interact with family/caregiver in a manner convenient to them.

CULTURAL DIVERSITY Assimilation and cultural pluralism are two prevalent philosophical approaches toward the education of culturally diverse populations. Assimilation refers to having students from diverse ethnic and cultural groups assimilate into the dominant cultural group and essentially leave their own culture behind. Conversely, cultural pluralism refers to encouraging students from diverse ethnic and cultural groups to retain their own culture while succeeding in school (Gollnick & Chinn, 2021).

The concept of cultural pluralism becomes increasingly important as the number of individuals from diverse cultural and ethnic groups increases. This means that greater attention is needed to increase respect for all cultural and ethnic diversity in U.S. schools (Banks, 2015). Many proactive approaches can be implemented in schools to increase appreciation and awareness of cultural and ethnic differences. This approach is sometimes referred to as **multicultural education** because cultural pluralism is endorsed, which means appreciation of all cultures is taught and fostered (Gollnick & Chinn, 2021).

It is difficult to increase respect for all cultural groups without having some knowledge about cultural differences and commonalities among groups. However, it must be remembered that it is dangerous to generalize from cultural groups to individuals. As Lynch (1992) stated:

> Culture is only one of the characteristics that determines individuals' and families' attitudes, values, beliefs, and ways of behaving. . . . Assuming that culture-specific information . . . applies to all individuals from the cultural group is not only inaccurate but also dangerous—it can lead to stereotyping that diminishes rather than enhances cross-cultural competence. When applying cultural-specific information to an individual or family, it is wise to proceed with caution. (p. 44)

Just as students with a particular disability may lack all of the characteristics associated with a disability area, the same is true of someone from a particular culture. An individual representing a particular ethnic or cultural group may not be "representative" of that cultural group. However, when teaching and learning about cultures, some general characteristics can serve as guidelines for learning about the various cultural groups. Suggestions for teaching toward a more proactive, culturally pluralistic approach and away from a biased, monocultural approach are as follows:

- *Reduce teacher bias.* Increase awareness of prejudices and decrease prejudices and broad stereotypes. Record yourself teaching (video or audio) and analyze the recording for instances of language or behaviors that do not promote culturally responsive teaching.
- *Eliminate curriculum bias.* Select curriculum to reflect the diversity of all cultural groups; avoid stereotyping and overgeneralizations of cultural groups.
- *Teach about prejudice.* Discuss racism and discrimination; consider having middle school or high school students examine texts, policies, and historical events for instances of racism; invite guest speakers; eliminate stereotypes.
- *Improve group relations and help resolve conflicts.* Use case studies and teach problem-solving strategies.

RECOGNIZE THE NEEDS OF STUDENTS FROM MULTIRACIAL/ETHNIC FAMILIES

There is also an increasing number of multiracial and multicultural families or caregivers in the United States. In the 2020 census, 10.2% of the population identified themselves as being multiracial, non-Hispanic (U.S. Census Bureau, 2020a). Moreover, interracial and interethnic marriages have resulted in more than ever multiracial children being born in the United States. Many of these children cannot be classified by only one part of their race and/or ethnicity. For example, Dorothy Adams, a 36-year-old whose father is Black and mother is Japanese American, stated:

> I'm for the multiracial category. When I was a kid, the first time I paid attention to the race box was on a Social Security form. It was a problem to check one box,

so I checked Black and Japanese. The teacher said to check only one box, so I checked "Other," then wrote in "Black and Japanese." I've never gone back to see how I'm listed with Social Security. (Grossman, 1997, p. 13)

Be aware that many people represent a variety of racial-ethnic backgrounds and wish to be treated with sensitivity with respect to their particular heritage. For example, to provide a more thorough and accurate depiction of how people self-identify, the design of the 2020 census was changed to include two separate questions (as opposed to one) when asking about how individuals identify their race and ethnicity (i.e., Hispanic, Latinx, or Spanish-origin population groups). In addition, the census question on race now includes a write-in response area with examples. For instance, if selecting American Indian or Alaska Native as one's race, the individual can also write in an origin (e.g., Navajo Nation) (see Marks & Rios-Vargas, 2021).

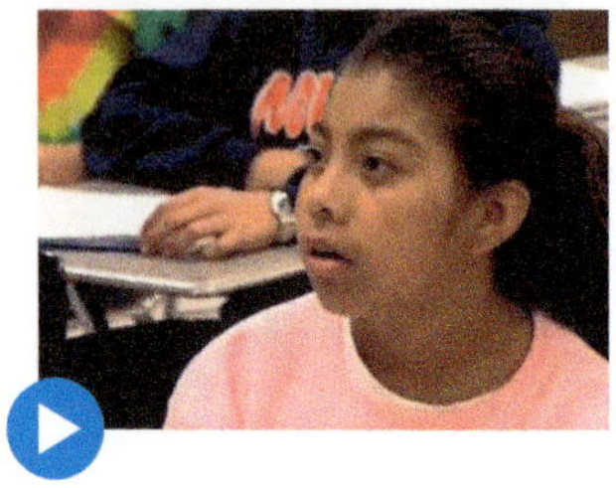

Pearson eTextbook
Video Example 5.3
The expert in this video discusses cultural considerations a teacher should expect from students who are culturally and linguistically diverse. What cultural patterns does the expert identify and what strategies does she suggest?

DEVELOP A PLAN TO ADDRESS LINGUISTIC DIVERSITY Linguistic diversity is still an increasing issue within public schools in the United States. Currently, as many as 5 million U.S. children have limited proficiency in English, or 10.2% of all students in public schools. The U.S. Census Bureau (2020b) revealed that 21% of respondents reported speaking a language different from English at home. Furthermore, this number has tripled since 1998. Spanish is currently the second most commonly spoken language in the schools (Echevarria & Graves, 2015), but the Census Bureau employs a list of 42 languages in assessing language use in the United States, including the category of "other languages" (U.S. Census Bureau, 2020c). The *Apps for Education* feature describes the use of multilingual translators.

These data indicate that difficulties with learning are likely because students may not have acquired the necessary English-language skills for success in English-speaking schools. In addition, it is more challenging to establish effective communication between caregivers/families, and the school when common languages are unknown. It is necessary to enlist the assistance of interpreters who can translate communications, schoolwork, notes, papers, and materials between school and home settings (Gollnick & Chinn, 2021).

Several approaches are available for teaching students who are **English learners (ELs)** or multilingual learners, and some controversy exists regarding the best approach. It is a matter of debate whether children should be "immersed" in English-speaking classrooms (with English instruction also provided by teachers of ELs) or whether English and non-English languages should be combined in classroom instruction. Furthermore, even if different languages are used during instruction, there is disagreement concerning how this can best be done to optimize the performance and learning of all students. It has been suggested that students may acquire practical, conversational skills in English much sooner than skills in more formal English for academic areas and that it may be useful to support students in academic learning in their native language for several years until English skills are maximized (Gollnick & Chinn, 2021; Ovando & Combs, 2018). It is important to note that virtually all concerned professionals agree that some level of support is needed for students who are not fluent in English.

Linguistic diversity is not limited to different languages. Some students may speak a dialect of English rather than a different language. A dialect is not the same as having an accent; a dialect of English refers to the use of similar English sounds and words but a different grammatical use of English. For example, a Southern dialect may use words such as "ain't" or "y'all" and Nigerian English may omit articles before nouns such as "You take paper" for "You take the paper." Using a dialect in school may present some communication difficulties, especially with respect to written language assignments (Gollnick & Chinn, 2021), if teachers are not familiar with the dialect. Teachers can encourage students with linguistic differences to use online software when the use of Standard English is expected. Students can check for correct grammar usage with programs such as Grammarly (Grammarly Inc.) (www.grammarly.com).

BILINGUAL SPECIAL EDUCATION Bilingual special education refers to services provided for students with limited English proficiency who also have a disability. Although students may speak more than two languages, *bi-* means "two": the dominant native language spoken at home and English. It is estimated that 15% of students with disabilities do not primarily use English in their homes. These students must accommodate two or more languages and two or more cultures, as well as face the challenges posed by their disabilities. Students who are

Apps for Education

Multilingual Translators

Students for whom English is not their first language may benefit from the use of a multilingual pocket translator. Multilingual translators can be small, pocket-sized electronic devices that contain a keyboard and a small screen. Students can enter text in one language, press a key, and have the text translated into another language. The devices are small enough to be carried from class to class in an unobtrusive fashion. They can provide valuable assistance and allow students to participate in class more frequently and to perform more optimally on class assignments and tests. In some schools, students are allowed to use these during the school day and even during statewide competency testing situations. Such devices would also be beneficial for teachers to have to enhance their communication with students, families, and caregivers of individuals who are multilingual learners.

The functions of the various devices range from that of a dictionary to explanations of phrases and idioms, to calculator functions, to data storage functions, to speech output. Some hand-held devices such as the Pocketalk Language Translator allow individuals to converse in 82 different languages and the camera on a device will even translate signs (pocketalk.com). The WT2 Language Translator is not a hand-held device but has two wireless ear pieces for each person communicating. The person you are speaking to can hear their translation at the same time you listen to yours. The translation is estimated to be 95% accurate. Microsoft Translator for Education (microsoft.com/en-us/translator/education/) allows the spoken language to be translated to another language and the words can be viewed on a screen during presentations, lectures, and caregiver/parent–teacher conferences. For example, a parent/caregiver can download the app in advance of an individualized education program meeting, scan or enter the conversation code when they arrive, and in real time both parties can speak and see the translation on their device. Smartphones, tablets, and computers also feature apps such as Google Translate and SpeakText Free, which includes speech-recognition features and translates over 100 languages from speech or text. Google Translate also has a Snap feature that translates pictures or photos of text into different languages.

bilingual or multilingual and are also referred to special education are in need of both types of services and may be particularly at risk for inappropriate classification because of difficulties communicating in English (Echevarria & Graves, 2015). Bilingual special education teachers or English Speakers of Other Languages (ESOL) teachers, deliver services to those students who require bilingual education and special education services (Ehlers-Zavala, 2011).

CLASSROOM SCENARIO

Daniel

Daniel Vargas came to the United States from Central America. When he arrived, he was placed by age into sixth grade at Lakeside Elementary School. Daniel's teacher, Mr. Larken, noticed that during the first week of school, Daniel did not engage with his peers and used limited English in class. He answered most questions with "I don't know" and sat back in his seat avoiding eye contact with Mr. Larken and his peers during instructional time. Daniel showed limited use of oral language, made no effort to read aloud or write in class, and seemed disinterested with class activities.

Mr. Larken knew that Daniel's family had recently relocated to the United States from Honduras and he realized that it was important to speak with his parents as soon as possible. Mr. Larken wanted to learn more about Daniel's history of development in his first language to see if there were similar patterns of difficulty. Before Mr. Larken met with Daniel's parents, they requested a translator to assist with communication since the Vargas' could understand English but did not speak English fluently. During the meeting, they shared that when living in Honduras, Daniel had repeated third grade twice and he ran away from school often. They also reported that he could not read in Spanish or English and was resistant to any help his parents offered. The family did not report any history of learning disabilities.

After meeting with the Vargas', Mr. Larken sought input with the reading specialist and the teacher of English learners (ELs) who was an expert in multicultural education. They all agreed to make their own observations of Daniel and to gather more information.

Fortunately, the EL teacher at Lakeside spoke Spanish fluently and she spent time with Daniel asking about his interests, opinions, and feelings. Daniel often responded in Spanish to the questions with "I don't know." When the reading specialist conducted an early phonological assessment in English, the results identified that he had limited knowledge of the English alphabetic principle. A comparable phonemic awareness assessment in Spanish had the same result. He identified only four phonemes to the corresponding graphemes. For the next 5 months at school, the reading specialist provided Daniel with a daily intensive reading intervention to acquire phonemic awareness and phonics skills. This reading intervention was for 25–30 minutes every school day. Mr. Larken differentiated his instruction in the general education classroom and continued to build a relationship with Daniel and his parents. The EL teacher provided Daniel with one-on-one instruction in basic math such as single-digit addition and subtraction. The team met every 2 weeks to discuss his progress.

At the end of the 5-month period, Daniel could connect 10 phonemes to the corresponding graphemes and he could identify rhyming words. He was not able to produce rhyme independently and he had difficulty manipulating phonemes, including the blending and segmenting of sounds. In math, Daniel still did not have one-on-one correspondence and made errors in single-digit addition and subtraction. Given the assessment data conducted in both English and Spanish, and the limited progress after 20 weeks of an intensive reading intervention, Mr. Larken began the process for referring Daniel for eligibility of special education services.

QUESTIONS FOR REFLECTION

1. What could Mr. Larken have done to support Daniel during the first week of school?
2. What additional questions would you have asked the Vargas' in regard to Daniel's language development and history of school behavior and academic performance?
3. Do you think adequate steps were taken prior to beginning the referral process for Daniel? Why or why not?

ISSUES IN IDENTIFICATION AND ASSESSMENT OF CULTURALLY AND LINGUISTICALLY DIVERSE STUDENTS

IDEA provides stipulations for evaluations and assessments that are free of cultural and linguistic bias. It is especially important to monitor testing and assessment procedures to ensure this right for students from culturally and linguistically diverse backgrounds. Special precautions should be taken to ensure that ethnicity or cultural differences are not misinterpreted. For example, students in some cultures may tend to avoid direct eye contact with adults, a practice that may be misinterpreted by some teachers unfamiliar with cultural norms other than their own.

Overrepresentation in many cases may be attributed to inappropriate identification, assessment design and procedures, and disciplinary consequences (Gollnick & Chinn, 2021; Harry & Klingner, 2014). For example, Black students may be mistakenly referred for classification as having emotional or behavioral disabilities because of cultural misunderstandings (Obiakor & Roratori, 2014; Taylor & Whittaker, 2009). Likewise, research has suggested that some students who are multilingual exhibit behaviors that may be interpreted as behaviors similar to those of students with learning disabilities or behavioral disabilities (Sullivan, 2011). For example, when students cannot understand the spoken language in class, they may appear uninterested or confused or they may act inappropriately. Because these are some of the distinguishing characteristics of students with higher-incidence disabilities, general education teachers may misinterpret such behaviors and overrefer these students for special education services. Baca et al. (2004b) described the use of prereferral intervention for preventing inappropriate referrals for students who are bilingual, including assessing students in their dominant language. See the *Diversity, Equity, and Inclusion in the Classroom* feature for a discussion of the RTI model as a multiculturally responsive prereferral intervention strategy. Also, the *Classroom Scenario: Daniel* feature demonstrates practical application of the prereferral process.

Evaluation procedures need to be closely monitored to ensure that appropriate tests, testing situations, and familiar examiners are provided for such individuals. For example, students who do not speak and understand English fluently should not be placed in special education classes based on their performance on tests administered in English. Because many parents/caregivers of students from diverse cultural and linguistic backgrounds speak several languages or only their native language fluently, it is important to have translators available to help facilitate communication efforts between family/caregiver members and schools when language barriers exist (Echevarria & Graves, 2015).

Teachers of multilingual learners can provide valuable information on students who are beginning to learn English. They can provide suggestions to facilitate comprehension during classes. Teachers of multilingual learners may provide academic instruction in students' native language. They may also work with special education teachers to ensure that instruction is sufficiently adapted to meet any specific disability needs. Use these specialists to help understand how to better serve students from different linguistic backgrounds. Bilingual special education teachers assume responsibility for the implementation of individualized education programs (IEPs) and provide EL and special education instruction for students with both types of needs (Echevarria & Graves, 2015). These specialists work closely with general educators in inclusive models and coordinate instruction and instructional approaches to ensure IEP goals are met. Finally, consider the following:

- Test scores are only a single indicator of performance.
- Multiple observations of students' behaviors provide insight into decision making.
- Students who are culturally and linguistically diverse may have social language but limited academic language. Teachers may observe a silent period of at least 6 months with students who have recently arrived in the United States.
- Testing by itself is insufficient for special education classification.
- Obtain assistance from bilingual and cultural diversity experts.
- Work closely with the families/caregivers of students who are culturally and linguistically diverse to obtain the most valid and relevant information (Baca & Cervantes, 2004; Obiakor & Rotatori, 2014).

STRATEGIES FOR
MAKING ADAPTATIONS FOR STUDENTS FROM CULTURALLY AND LINGUISTICALLY DIVERSE BACKGROUNDS

Many of the adaptations described for students with disabilities may be beneficial for accommodating students from diverse cultural and linguistic backgrounds.

CREATE A CULTURALLY RESPONSIVE ENVIRONMENT Create an open, accepting classroom environment to ensure that students from all cultural and linguistic backgrounds feel comfortable in classes. Make all students and their families and caregivers feel welcome in your class. Model acceptance and tolerance of individual differences. For example, build a positive and meaningful relationship with each of your students and show an interest in each student as an individual. Try connecting with students outside of the classroom, in the hallway, or at high school sporting events after school. Teach students that we are all alike and different and that individuals who have recently relocated to the United States—from all parts of the world—have historically settled in the United States and contributed to its development (Gollnick & Chinn, 2021). Keep expectations high: Expect the best from all students and be sure your students are aware of your expectations.

Complete a needs assessment to determine the ethnic, cultural, and linguistic backgrounds of the school, students, and community. Learn how school knowledge is perceived in students' cultures and the types of knowledge and skills that are valued (Gollnick & Chinn, 2021). Assess students' prior knowledge of and experience with academic content. As described in the English Learner Tool Kit (U.S. Department of Education, 2017), conduct a needs assessment that can include information about language use as well as culturally relevant information about the community, family/caregiver, school, and classroom. Information obtained can be used to plan activities that address all cultural and linguistic backgrounds.

Promoting Equity in Gifted Education

Although students from culturally/linguistically diverse backgrounds are overrepresented in several categories of disability, unfortunately in gifted education the opposite is true: Students from these same backgrounds, particularly African American and Latinx students, are underrepresented in gifted education (Young & Young, 2022). According to the U.S. Department of Education (2022), Black (15.1%) and Hispanic (27.2%) students collectively make up 42.3% of the total number of public school students, but only 26.5% of identified students in gifted programs. The reasons for this are varied and complex; however, Wells (2021) has argued that several barriers exist that hinder identification: (1) English as a second language (ESL), (2) nomination or referral processes, (3) identification procedures, (4) previous learning, (5) cultural conflict, and (6) biases.

April Wells is an educational consultant and gifted coordinator for a large, diverse school district in suburban Chicago. About 20% of students were English learners, while 51% came from impoverished backgrounds. In 2004, this district faced a discrimination lawsuit, alleging the school system (1) purposefully discriminated against race, (2) purposely discriminated against students for special education services, and (3) discriminated against Black and Latinx students with respect to gifted and advanced placement services. This lawsuit was finally resolved 9 years later. While the plaintiffs did not prevail on the first two allegations, the judge determined that the district had discriminated with respect to its gifted education program. As a result of that decision, the district decided to rethink its program of gifted services and develop a revised and expanded program for gifted students, in collaboration with a nearby university and the Illinois Association for Gifted Children. It became known as the IGNITE (Inquiry and Gifted Network for Ingenuity Talent Exploration) program (Wells, 2021).

This new program implemented several features to help promote equity in gifted education. They began with a definition of giftedness, referring to those who perform or are potentially able to perform at remarkably high levels when compared with peers of comparable age, experience, and/or environments. Considering this definition, they maintained that gifted students can be found in all socioeconomic or ethnic groups and that these students require specialized instructional services not ordinarily provided in general education. In order to provide all students an equitable opportunity to receive gifted services, the district implemented several changes. One major change was emphasizing local norms for consideration in the identification process, rather than relying exclusively on standardized test scores. Using local norms to identify outstanding students significantly increased the diversity of the gifted program. Another change was universal screening, where all students were considered potential candidates for the gifted program—rather than, for example, simply selecting students who had been referred by teachers or parents/caregivers—and are then invited to participate in testing. The screening measures include a cognitive abilities test, an academic progress measure, and a teacher observation checklist.

The district also promoted talent development in the primary grades through the AIM (Access to Inquiry and Meaning) program. In this program, district gifted specialists provide targeted thinking skills instruction, while classroom teachers are trained to observe and collect data on how students respond to the intervention. Teachers have shared how observing their students' performance during AIM has provided them with greater insight into their students' abilities.

To maintain equity in teaching, the district requires all teachers in the gifted program to also have their ESL endorsement. Once identified, students are informed they will be allowed to matriculate through the entirety of the program, and that any difficulties encountered through, for example, underachievement or lack of engagement will be met with supports and problem solving rather than termination from the program. Although an exit procedure does exist, it is employed only when other means have not succeeded, and with parents/caregivers, teachers, the principal, and the gifted coordinator participating in the decision.

Wells (2021) acknowledged that the program has only been implemented for a few years and that there has sometimes been resistance to the changes. However, she believes that the IGNITE program has addressed important issues of equity and inclusion and will continue to support these values in the future.

Discuss: Why do you believe there is disproportionate representation in gifted programs throughout the country? Why do you think a program like Wells describes would result in more equitable outcomes than traditional gifted programs?

Accommodate culturally diverse families/caregivers. Culturally diverse families may (or may not) differ in areas such as discipline practices, home–school communication, and school involvement (Echevarria et al., 2017). Learn to avoid preconceptions and to recognize and respect differences as you develop appropriate interactions with parents, caregivers, and family members (Grassi & Barker, 2010).

Include books and stories to enhance understanding of other cultures. East and Thomas (2007) have developed annotated bibliographies of over 450 titles in multicultural literature (see also Norton, 2012; Taylor & Whittaker, 2009). Some recommended books are presented in Figure 5.1 (see also National Education Association, 2021).

ADAPT MATERIALS AND INSTRUCTION Teach about sensitivity and acceptance issues. Role-play scenarios that are concrete and meaningful to students. Examine curriculum materials to ensure they eliminate stereotypes. Examine your teaching style and practices to ensure all students are treated equally and offered chances of success. Figure 5.2 provides suggestions to increase appreciation of others.

Monitor the pace of instruction to ensure students with limited English proficiency are succeeding. Use concrete and familiar examples as frequently as possible when describing new concepts. Provide hands-on activities to ensure active involvement and active learning for all students. By using many modalities when teaching, you will help clarify language and provide multiple examples for developing new vocabulary words. Help students relate any prior knowledge to new concepts you present (Grassi & Barker, 2010). Incorporate feedback from assessments and from solicited student opinions to maximize the effectiveness of your classroom and to make your classroom motivating, enjoyable, and productive. The *Research Highlight* feature presented later in this chapter describes reading instruction research with ELs.

Figure 5.1 Books to Promote Multicultural Awareness

Title	*Subject (estimated reading grade level)*
My Two Borders by David Bowles (Kokila, 2021)	A boy who lives on the U.S.–Mexico border shares his trip to the other side (K–4)
I Love My Hair by Natasha Anastasia Tarpley (Little, Brown Books for Young Readers, 1998)	A young girl discovers the beauty of her hair and pride in her heritage (K–3)
The Arabic Quilt: An Immigrant Story by Aya Khalil (Tilbury House, 2020)	The story of a little girl who experiences school after coming to America from Egypt (1–3)
Separate is Never Equal by Duncan Tonatiuh (Abrams Books for Young Readers, 2014)	The Mendez family's fight for justice and desegregation in schools (K–4)
When Lola Visits by Michelle Sterling (Katherine Tegen Books, 2021)	A young girl's grandmother visits from the Philippines (K–3)
Brown Girl Dreaming by Jacqueline Woodson (Puffin Books, 2014)	Poetry about a young girl's awareness of the civil rights movement (5–12)
Harvesting Hope: The Story of Cesar Chavez by Katherine Krull (Harcourt, 2003)	Biography of the Mexican American labor leader (6–12)
Teaching with Folk Stories of the Hmong by D. Cha & N. J. Livo (Libraries Unlimited, 2000)	Teaching resources on Hmong cultural traditions, companion to *Folk Stories of the Hmong* (9–12)
What Are You?: Voices of Mixed-Race Young People by Pearl Fuyo Gaskins (Holt, 1999)	Stories about multiracial children (8–12)
New from Here by Kelly Yang (Simon & Schuster, 2022)	An Asian American boy fights for his family and stands up to racism during the coronavirus outbreak (4–7)

Figure 5.2 Classroom Practices to Increase Appreciation for Others

For Younger Students	*For Older Students*
Share children's literature and stories about many cultures.	Complete a class, school, and community cultural and linguistic diversity profile.
Make a classroom "quilt."	Teach about inequity and individuals who have fought to combat inequitable practices.
Develop a class family/caregiver cookbook.	Teach about cultural contributions: The arts, folk art, music, dances, literature, and crafts. Traditions, holidays, festivals, myths. Distinguished individuals and their accomplishments.
Discuss foods eaten at meals by different cultural groups.	Prepare, cook, and eat ethnic foods.
Prepare, cook, and eat ethnic foods.	Dress in ethnic clothing.
Dress in ethnic clothing.	Play ethnic music.
Wear ethnic jewelry and accessories.	Teach ethnic dances.
Play ethnic music.	Teach words and phrases from different languages.
Teach ethnic dances.	Bring in international newspapers or newspapers written in a language other than English.
Teach words and phrases from different languages.	
Invite parents/caregivers in to share family traditions.	
Make illustrated family/caregiver histories and post them in the classroom.	

Students at Risk

Learning Objective 5.3 Summarize the prevalence and characteristics of students at risk for school failure and recognize strategies for classroom adaptations.

DEFINITIONS, PREVALENCE, AND CHARACTERISTICS OF STUDENTS AT RISK

Students **at risk** for school failure come from diverse environments and represent all racial-ethnic and linguistic backgrounds. They also span all socioeconomic classes, although students with backgrounds of severe poverty may tend to be at higher risk than others. There is no clear definition of what it means to be "at risk," but these are students who face circumstances that could impede their well-being and their academic success. The Centers for Disease Control and Prevention (https://www.cdc.gov/violenceprevention/aces/index.html) refers to these experiences as *adverse childhood experiences* (ACEs), or potentially traumatic events that occur in childhood (birth to age 17). Some examples of trauma include child abuse and neglect, witnessing violence in or outside of school, and community/school victimization such as bullying.

Students who have or are currently experiencing ACEs are at risk of ultimately giving up on school and will likely experience difficulties later in life because childhood trauma can have long-term effects. These students are usually found in general education classes, may require additional assistance from teachers and may benefit from classroom modifications similar to those suggested for students with higher-incidence disabilities. Many educators have identified factors associated with at-risk students (e.g., Beach, 2014; Frieman, 2001). These factors are listed in Figure 5.3 and describe a variety of situations.

CHILDREN WHO HAVE EXPERIENCED ABUSE AND NEGLECT Child abuse and neglect can have devastating emotional, physical, cognitive, social, and intellectual effects on children, and reported cases have been increasing in the United States (Crosson-Tower, 2021). Federal legislation, the Child Abuse Prevention and Treatment Act of 1974 and its subsequent amendments, defined child abuse and neglect as maltreatment, sexual abuse or exploitation, mental or physical injury, withholding medical treatment for life-threatening conditions, or negligent treatment of children younger than age 18 by persons responsible for the child

Figure 5.3 Major At-Risk Factors

- Children with poor academic performance
- Students who identify as lesbian, gay, bisexual, transgender, or questioning
- Students struggling with a sense of self, including gender or sexual identity
- Children who are born exposed to alcohol and other narcotic substances
- Children who abuse alcohol and drugs
- Children who experience abuse and/or neglect
- Children living in poverty conditions
- Children with mental health conditions such as depression and anxiety
- Children with suicidal tendencies
- Students who are pregnant or parents
- Children who are experiencing homelessness and children who move frequently
- Children with excessive absenteeism
- Students who have been suspended two times within a year
- Students who stop coming to school
- Children who find school very difficult and require a lot of academic support
- Students who have experienced traumatic events such as a school shooting, the death of someone close to them, or victimization
- Children whose parents or caregivers abuse alcohol or drugs
- Students who are older than their grade-level peers due to retention
- Children who are angry, socially alienated, or bullied
- Students who have experienced instability, separation from family, or incarceration of a family member or caregiver
- Children who did not acclimate well to the educational disruption of the global COVID-19 pandemic

(Child Welfare Information Gateway, 2011). In some cases, child abuse has been linked to be the cause of disabilities (Shaahinfar et al., 2015). For example, severe shaking of infants has been linked to brain injury (Klein & Stern, 1971), some cases of abuse have been related to cerebral palsy (Diamond & Jaudes, 1983), and other cases have been linked to intellectual and learning disabilities (Caplan & Dinardo, 1986). The best overall predictor of child abuse and neglect is poverty (Grandinette & Best, 2009; Sedlak et al., 2010). Table 5.3 presents behavioral and physical indicators of child abuse and neglect.

As mandatory reporters, schools and teachers have the responsibility to report any signs of child abuse or neglect as per state and local definitions and guidelines. Determine state definitions and local procedures for reporting any cases and adhere to those policies and procedures upon noticing any cases of child abuse or neglect (Crosson-Tower, 2021).

CHILDREN WHO ARE EXPERIENCING HOMELESSNESS Individuals who lack a nighttime home, cannot afford housing, or live in provided public or private shelters, cars, or elsewhere can be said to be experiencing homelessness (Herbers et al., 2020). The children may be living in shelters, hotels, or motels; awaiting foster care; doubling up and living with another family/caregiver; or living in unsheltered residences such as a car, park, campground, or an abandoned building. The number of individuals experiencing homelessness in the United States is rapidly growing and includes an increasing number of families and caregivers with children, from infants to teenagers (Wixom, 2016). A large portion of students experiencing homelessness are in grades K-5; and there are also many unaccompanied youth, or adolescents, not under the care of an adult who are homeless. Youth who are lesbian, gay, bisexual, transgender, or questioning tend to be overrepresented in the population experiencing homelessness. Some estimates indicate that most of the families experiencing homelessness consist of single mothers with an average of two to three children (National Coalition for the Homeless, 2007). The percentage of students

TABLE 5.3 Some Physical and Behavioral Indicators of Child Abuse and Neglect

Type of Abuse or Neglect, Definition	Physical Indicators	Behavioral Indicators
Physical abuse: Any act that, regardless of intent, results in a nonaccidental physical injury to a child	Questionable injuries, such as the following: • Bruises, welts, or other injuries • Burns • Fractures • Lacerations or abrasions	• Being uncomfortable with physical contact • Being wary of adult contacts • Showing behavioral extremes, either aggression or withdrawal • Showing symptoms of depression and/or anxiety • Not wanting to go home • Reporting an injury by a parent, caregiver, or family member • Complaining of soreness or moving uncomfortably • Wearing excessive clothing to cover the body • Chronically running away from home (adolescents) • Reluctance to change clothes for gym activities (attempt to hide physical injuries)
Neglect: A caregiver's failure to provide something that a child needs	• Undernourished appearance • Lethargic • Signs of inadequate food or sleep • Untreated injuries • Evidence of unattended illness	• Begging for or stealing food because of persistent hunger • Poor hygiene • Inappropriate dress for the weather • Accidents and injuries • Risky adolescent behavior • Promiscuity, drugs, and delinquency • Being shunned by peers • Clinging behavior • Showing symptoms of depression and/or anxiety
Sexual abuse: The misuse of adult authority by involving children in sexual activities	• Most physical indicators would be found during a physical exam by a health care provider	• Expressions of age-inappropriate knowledge of sex and sexually "pseudo-mature" behaviors • Sexually explicit drawings • Highly sexualized play • Statements of unexplained fear of a person or place • Stated desire to avoid a familiar adult • Expressions of excessive concern about gender identity (boys) • Nightmares • Sleep interruptions • Withdrawal • Child's statement of sexual abuse • Showing symptoms of depression and/or anxiety

Source: Virginia Institute for Social Services Training Activities (2016).

enrolled in schools who are homeless is 2.71% (U.S. Census Bureau, 2018). Approximately 87% school-age children experiencing homelessness are enrolled in school, and approximately 77% attend school regularly (National Coalition for the Homeless, 2007). Children experiencing homelessness are twice as likely to receive services for learning disabilities and are three times as likely to receive services for emotional disturbance (Taormina-Weiss, 2012).

It is important to realize that children experiencing homelessness have to confront many barriers and stressors to succeed in school and in life. Issues for these children include transportation problems; social barriers due to transience; lack of money for food, clothing, and shelter; appearance; acceptance by peers; legal barriers; family/caregiver problems; and excessive absenteeism. Even more important are issues surrounding their mental health, self-esteem, security, safety, and trust. Some schools with high rates of children experiencing homelessness have modeled examples of safe, comfortable environments with the following actions:

- Assessing students' abilities and strengths directly rather than assuming they will require a lot of academic support
- Arranging for toys and play time for younger children

- Adjusting expectations for homework for students who must live in homeless shelters, which typically do not provide a place to do homework
- Helping to identify funds for supplies and trips
- Maintaining an emphasis on building self-esteem (Frieman, 2001).

ALCOHOL AND SUBSTANCE ABUSE Students who use alcohol and illegal drugs are at a higher risk of failing in school and in life. In a report on drug, alcohol, and tobacco use among teens in the United States, the Centers for Disease Control and Prevention (CDC, 2020) reported that about 2/3 of all high school students have reported trying alcohol, about half have used marijuana, about 40% have tried cigarettes, and nearly 20% report misusing prescription drugs. This figure is distressing, but even more alarming are the reports that indicate that children in elementary schools are also using drugs. These students are at a greater risk of failing. Students may become more withdrawn and act irrationally. Moreover, many may become involved in stealing and other illegal activities to maintain their drug habits.

Miksic (1987; see also Kauffman & Landrum, 2018) described elements of a successful substance-abuse education program. These elements include a clear, well-defined school policy regarding how teachers and administrators will deal with drug use and possession; a basic drug education classroom curriculum; increasing teacher awareness; a supportive atmosphere for teacher training in dealing with drug-abuse problems; involving families/caregivers as well as students; teacher self-evaluation; use of peer-group approaches; and promoting understanding that emotional concerns, such as self-esteem, are often associated with substance abuse.

Drug abuse is not appropriately treated in the classroom (Frieman, 2001); however, teachers should know whom to contact if a drug-related emergency occurs. Watch for unusual behavior or sudden changes in mood or behavior. It is appropriate to make referrals when drug use has been identified, particularly when it is associated with disruptive classroom behavior or problems in academic functioning (Kauffman & Landrum, 2018).

FAMILY/CAREGIVER POVERTY It has been well documented that children living below the federal poverty line are at high risk of failing in school and life (Frieman, 2001; Tornquist et al., 2009). Poverty complicates life success and places children at risk for failure for a variety of complex reasons. First, prenatal care may be inadequate or nonexistent for those families/caregivers living below the federal poverty line. Food insecurity and malnutrition may result in low-birth-weight infants who are at higher risk for ill-health and disabilities. Second, children born of parents who misuse drugs or alcohol are at a greater risk for health-related problems. Third, children born to teenage mothers who have limited access to resources are more likely to be impoverished. And fourth, continued poor nutrition, infrequent access to health care, and the low educational achievement of parents or caregivers are factors associated with poverty that can perpetuate failure in school (Frieman, 2001; Jensen, 2009). In addition, families or caregivers living below the federal poverty line are less able to provide the educational materials, computers, or travel experiences that can enrich students' backgrounds and provide support for school learning. Children from families or with caregivers who live below the federal poverty line, especially those from single-income households, are more likely to be obligated to work to contribute to the household income; these responsibilities may detract from schoolwork and cause difficulties focusing in school. In addition to providing children with a high-quality education so that they may reach their full potential, teachers can help by developing trust and planning predictable, secure, and stable environments.

CORONAVIRUS PANDEMIC In recent years, COVID-19 has had an enormous impact on schooling, and it is possible that other similar pandemics or epidemics will occur in the future. Although the long-term effects of the global pandemic are yet to be determined, the transition to emergency remote instruction disrupted all aspects of a child's social, emotional, and schooling experience, causing stress, anxiety, and concerns of potential impact on student learning (Kuhfeld et al., 2020). The pandemic caused schools to close; suspended school-related social events, including sports; and shifted the schooling experience for all students to remote instruction. Teachers delivered lessons from home via video conferencing, assigned asynchronous activities to be completed by students and posted on a learning management system, and/or mailed or delivered educational materials to students' homes. Teachers of students with disabilities had to think about accessibility for remote learning and plan for student accommodations in a virtual

Research Highlight

Reading Interventions for English Learners

The number of students who are English learners (ELs) or multilingual learners has been increasing dramatically in America's schools (U.S. Department of Education, 2020). Teaching reading to ELs can be challenging for teachers because students may be below their grade and age levels in understanding spoken English and reading and speaking English, and they may have lower English vocabulary levels than in their native languages. The need for improved reading instruction for ELs is even more important with emphasis that the Common Core State Standards place on academic vocabulary and language. The Institute of Education Sciences recommended EL reading teaching guidelines that included building academic language and vocabulary and using explicit instruction with small groups of students (Baker et al., 2014). Explicit instruction provides clear learning objectives with multiple opportunities for practice and feedback, and learning in supported small groups provides teachers with more opportunities to interact with and address individual students' needs.

Ludwig et al. (2019) reviewed and synthesized the findings from 26 studies that examined the effects of reading interventions on at-risk and not-at-risk ELs' reading skills and the factors influencing their effectiveness. The majority of the studies were conducted with students in kindergarten and first grade; five studies were conducted with students in grades 2 and higher. Three studies covered reading accuracy (i.e., decoding/phonics), reading fluency, and reading comprehension), five reported on a combination of those three areas of reading, and 17 reported results on only one reading outcome. Although the interventions were different in each study, estimated effect sizes suggest that instruction inclusive of the essential reading elements in combination or in isolation (i.e., phonemic awareness, phonics, fluency, vocabulary, and comprehension) work well for ELs. For example, Vadasy and Sanders (2016) provided additional attention to orthographic and phonological word features during reading instruction for kindergarten ELs and reported gains in vocabulary, word reading, and spelling. Across all studies, large effects were shown for ELs' reading accuracy and reading fluency and a moderate effect was shown on reading comprehension. The size of the effects did not vary according to the type of intervention. The interventions in 17 of the studies were conducted in kindergarten or first grade and emphasized the beginning reading skills, such as decoding and phonics, whereas the studies involving older students included interventions to address more vocabulary, fluency, and reading comprehension skills. Intervention sessions ranged from two to five sessions a week, with each session lasting between 32 and 42 minutes. Overall, findings from this meta-analysis suggest that reading interventions that have been effective for other populations are also effective for ELs.

QUESTIONS FOR REFLECTION

1. Why might ELs require intensive reading instruction?
2. What are the educational implications of these findings?
3. How might you adapt these intervention findings to EL reading instruction in your school?

setting. For example, could a parent/caregiver or someone in the household of a child with severe disabilities use a hand-over-hand technique to support the student? Initial projections suggest that learning loss will disproportionately affect students with disabilities and those who were out of school the most (Lane et al., 2021).

Upon returning to in-person learning, schools implemented a variety of measures for mitigating the spread of the virus, including social distancing (e.g., at least 3–6 feet apart), requiring that individuals quarantine if exposed, mask wearing, and frequent cleaning of surfaces. Research findings suggest that school closings and remote instruction can have a negative effect on student learning (Skar et al., 2021) and heighten the stress of family members or caregivers who act as proxy educators under these conditions (Brown et al., 2020).

Remote learning can be difficult for students without a stable home environment, access to reliable Internet, and/or sufficient skill with technology. Throughout the country, school responses varied, but some schools provided electronic devices and hot spots to support access. Furthermore, if students with disabilities contract a disease and miss more than 10 days of schooling, it is considered a change in educational placement and must be addressed by the students' IEP team. The Office of Special Education Programs of the U.S. Department of

Education (2021) has provided a resource for students with disabilities experiencing "long COVID," that is, the continuation of symptoms for more than 4 weeks after the onset of their illness. In order to mitigate lost instructional time during the pandemic, states and school districts should plan for learning recovery programming ("9 Recommendations for Inclusive Learning Recovery," 2021).

YOUNG, PREGNANT, AND PARENTS Teenagers who are pregnant or become parents need additional assistance in school and present a high at-risk factor for their unborn children. Teenage pregnancy is found across all racial-ethnic and socioeconomic strata. Teenagers who are pregnant or parenting can find themselves in a challenging environment to continue and maintain their learning. They may have interrupted schooling, have poor prenatal care, and/or have babies that are also at very high risk for needing additional assistance in school and in life. Educational programs are needed on a widespread basis to inform youth about teenage pregnancy. Some school districts may offer programs that can provide flexibility when schooling is interrupted and/or even provide daycare within the school building for students who are parenting. However, more programs are needed to provide child care for teenagers with babies to help them complete their high school requirements and pursue advanced-degree training (Hoffman & Maynard, 2008).

WARNING SIGNS FOR SUICIDE OR VIOLENCE Many students in today's schools are at risk for suicide or violence, so it is important to be alert for warning signs. On average, eight children or teens commit suicide every day, and nine children or teens are killed by firearms each day (Children's Defense Fund, 2020). According to the Suicide Prevention Lifeline (2021), suicide warning signs include (1) talking or writing about death or suicide, (2) feelings of hopelessness or uncontrolled anger, (3) engaging in risky behavior without thinking, (4) using drugs or drinking alcohol more frequently, (5) withdrawing from friends and family/caregiver, and (6) feeling anxious or displaying extreme mood changes. In the classroom, teachers may also observe a decline in the students' quality of schoolwork or frequent complaining of a stomachache, headaches, or fatigue. In addition, students may give away prized personal possessions or make overt threats of suicide.

If you encounter a student who is threatening suicide, stay with the student and speak directly in a calm and nonthreatening manner. Try to get the student to talk; listen to and acknowledge the student's feelings. Do not judge; reassure the student that there is help and that feeling like this is not forever. Provide continuous supervision and remove means for self-harm. Call for immediate assistance if needed. Remind the student that others care and would like to help. Peers should be encouraged not to keep suicidal thoughts secret (National Association of School Psychologists, 2021). Teachers should take all threats of violence, to self or others, seriously and report them promptly to parents or caregivers, co-teachers, counselors, and building administrators. Learn your school's policies regarding suicide prevention.

COORDINATING INSTRUCTION WITH COMPENSATORY EDUCATION PROGRAMS

Schools may qualify for federal funding for compensatory education under Title I of the Every Student Succeeds Act if they have concentrations of students from families/caregivers who live below the federal poverty line and/or those who have recently relocated to the United States. Funds may be provided for additional teachers, paraprofessionals, and supplies so that additional remedial instruction can be applied. If students are receiving additional assistance in basic skills under Title I, it is important that these programs are well coordinated with other types of instruction the student may be receiving.

STRATEGIES FOR
MAKING ADAPTATIONS FOR STUDENTS AT RISK

Students at risk for failure represent a wide and varied range of problems and potential difficulties. Most important is to maintain an open, accepting classroom environment and let your students know they are welcome in your room. Seek assistance from other school support personnel and students' families or caregivers. Be considerate of students' needs, maintain realistic but high expectations, and encourage them to succeed in class. Provide additional opportunities for them to be successful in school. For instance, implement adaptations for computer use for students with sensory, physical, or learning disabilities, as described throughout this text, particularly in the *Apps for Education* features. Model enthusiasm toward learning, encourage active participation, make students feel comfortable, and be ready to provide for additional supports and adapt instruction, as described next.

PROVIDE FOR ADDITIONAL SUPPORTS Help to coordinate services among community social services agencies, school, and parents/caregivers to maximize the effectiveness of service delivery. Find out about and inform parents and caregivers of all available services, including free meals, education, health care services, special education, and mental health services. Keep in contact with parents, caregivers, or guardians because they may be unaware of all the services available to them. For example, there may be remote sites set up in school parking lots for students without reliable Internet access. Provide assistance in obtaining support services such as counseling and social services, when needed. Help arrange before- and after-school care and activities for students who may need additional assistance outside of school hours. Arrange for awareness training for personnel in your school so that they can better identify children at risk and at-risk factors (Mizerek & Hinz, 2004).

ADAPT INSTRUCTION Remediate basic skills when needed by providing for additional instruction with paraprofessionals or tutors so that students can apply themselves on higher-order academic tasks. To support remote learning of students with diverse learning needs, consider providing training for siblings, family members, or caregivers. Consider using the instructional adaptations suggested for students with higher- and lower-incidence disabilities with students considered at risk for school failure. These include adapting the physical environment, instructional materials, instructional procedures, and evaluation procedures with respect to specific individual needs. When in-person schooling is disrupted, adaptations could include mailing or delivering individualized educational packets and/or holding FaceTime meetings. Many students at risk may have a more limited experiential background, so be sure that the necessary prerequisite knowledge is understood by all students. Make sure that your classroom environment is seen as welcoming and supportive to all students and that they feel safe in your classroom. Do not hesitate to seek assistance from school administrators or other personnel when uncertain.

Students at risk for school failure present some unique and special challenges for educators. Nevertheless, successfully differentiating instructional practices to help a student succeed, who might otherwise have given up, can be one of the most rewarding experiences you can have as a teacher.

5 Summary

- Students who are gifted, talented, or creative may be identified by a variety of methods, including test scores, behavioral descriptions, and qualitative/descriptive methods. Students who are gifted, talented, or creative may be served by acceleration programs, enrichment programs, or a combination of approaches.
- Students who are culturally or linguistically diverse may also present some individual learning needs. Teachers should adopt a culturally sensitive, pluralistic approach that incorporates an awareness of cultural differences and their implications for learning.
- Because students who are culturally or linguistically diverse are often overrepresented in special education placements, teachers should be particularly careful when considering referral for special education. Unbiased testing, culturally sensitive behavioral expectations, and prereferral intervention strategies can help address this important issue.
- Factors that may place students at risk for school failure include families/caregivers who live below the federal poverty line, drug use, homelessness, teenagers who are pregnant or parents, and child abuse and neglect. Contact and communication with students in question, their families, caregivers, relevant school personnel, and community agencies can help address risk factors.

PROFESSIONAL STANDARDS LINK:
Teaching Students with Gifts and Talents and Other Diverse Learning Needs

Information in this chapter links most directly to:

- CEC 2020 Initial Practice-Based Professional Preparation Standards for Special Educators (Initial K–12 standards) (see https://exceptionalchildren.org/standards/initial-practice-based-professional-preparation-standards-special-educators): Standards: 1 (Engaging in Professional Learning and Practice within Ethical Guidelines), 2 (Understanding and Addressing Each Individual's Developmental and Learning Needs), 4 (Using Assessment to Understand the Learner and the Learning Environment for Data-Based Decision Making), 5 (Supporting Learning Using Effective Instruction), 7 (Collaborating with Team Members)
- InTASC Standards (see https://www.ccsso.org/sites/default/files/2017-11/InTASC_Model_Core_Teaching_Standards_2011.pdf): 2 (Learning Differences), 3 (Learning Environments), 6 (Assessment), 7 (Planning for Instruction), 8 (Instructional Strategies), 10 (Leadership and Collaboration)

TEACHING STUDENTS WITH GIFTS AND TALENTS AND OTHER DIVERSE LEARNING NEEDS

If a student with other diverse learning needs is having difficulties in your classroom, have you tried the following? If not, see the pages listed here.

STRATEGIES FOR MAKING ADAPTATIONS FOR STUDENTS WHO ARE GIFTED, CREATIVE, AND TALENTED

- ☐ Implement acceleration or enrichment programs, 114
- ☐ Adapt instructional materials, 115
- ☐ Adapt instructional and evaluation procedures, 115

STRATEGIES FOR MAKING ADAPTATIONS FOR STUDENTS FROM CULTURALLY AND LINGUISTICALLY DIVERSE BACKGROUNDS

- ☐ Create a culturally responsive environment, 121–123
- ☐ Adapt materials and instruction, 123–124

STRATEGIES FOR MAKING ADAPTATIONS FOR STUDENTS AT RISK

- ☐ Provide for additional supports, 130
- ☐ Adapt instruction, 130

PART 2 Developing Effective Teaching Skills

CHAPTER 6

Effective Differentiated Instruction for All Students

CHAPTER 7

Response to Intervention and Multi-Tiered Systems of Support

CHAPTER 8

Improving Motivation and Social Behavior

CHAPTER 9

Promoting Inclusion with Classroom Peers

CHAPTER 10

Improving Attention and Memory

CHAPTER 11

Teaching Study Skills

CHAPTER 12

Assessment

Sue Barr/Image Source/Offset/Shutterstock

CHAPTER 6

Effective Differentiated Instruction for All Students

LEARNING OBJECTIVES

After studying this chapter, you should be able to:

6.1 Define differentiated instruction and describe the purpose of the PASS variables in applying differentiated instruction in inclusive settings.

6.2 Discuss how to prioritize instruction.

6.3 Describe how to adapt instruction.

6.4 Explain how to systematically teach in inclusive settings using the SCREAM variables.

6.5 Give examples of how to systematically evaluate the outcomes of inclusive instruction.

6.6 Define high-leverage practices and how they relate to the PASS variables.

To be an effective inclusive classroom teacher, you must first be an effective teacher. You must employ the skills that enable you to expect, and receive, the very best in learning and achievement from your students. This chapter describes the variables most important for maximizing student learning and ways you can implement these variables in your classroom. As you learn to apply these strategies consistently and systematically, you will see the learning, achievement, and attitudes of all of your students, including those with diverse learning needs, increase dramatically.

Research over the past several decades, known as *teacher effectiveness research*, has identified the variables most strongly associated with student achievement (e.g., Archer & Hughes, 2011; Danielson, 2010; Good & Brophy, 2007; Mastropieri & Scruggs, 2004; McLeskey et al., 2019; Rosenshine & Stevens, 1986). Some of this research has also shown that teachers who are most effective at including students with disabilities and other diverse learning needs are also effective classroom teachers in general (Larrivee, 1985; Scruggs & Mastropieri, 1994b). Overall, this research has been critically important in identifying the things teachers should do and not do to maximize learning for all students. In this chapter, we summarize much of what has been learned from this research and its implications for effective differentiated instruction.

What Is Differentiated Instruction?

Learning Objective 6.1 Define differentiated instruction and describe the purpose of the PASS variables in applying differentiated instruction in inclusive settings.

As described in previous chapters, differentiated instruction means making adjustments in the delivery of instruction to meet the individual needs of all learners in inclusive classrooms. According to Tomlinson (2014a):

> Teachers who differentiate instruction provide specific alternatives for individuals to learn as deeply as possible and as quickly as possible, without assuming one student's road map for learning is identical to anyone else's. (p. 4)

Throughout this text, we identify and discuss methods for adjusting general education classrooms to meet a variety of individual needs, and these methods can be fairly characterized as differentiated instruction.

Years ago, "mainstreaming" often referred to students with individual needs "earning" their right to placement in the general education classroom for some or all of the school day by demonstrating that they could function independently in that setting. The inclusion movement established the appropriateness of general education placement whenever students could succeed with appropriate supports—that is, when the students' learning experience could be appropriately "differentiated" to meet their individual needs.

In previous chapters, we have discussed how instruction can be differentiated to meet the learning needs of students with specific disabilities and diverse learning needs areas. We refer to differentiating instruction by adapting the environment, instructional materials, instructional methods, and evaluation of instruction that are similar to the elements of learning environment, content, process, and product described by Tomlinson (2014a, 2014b).

DIFFERENTIATING THE LEARNING ENVIRONMENT In many cases, environments must be modified to meet the needs of students with physical disabilities—for example, wider aisles for students using crutches or wheelchairs or appropriate seating options for science lab. But environments can also be modified to provide for other differential learning needs, such as the need for a quiet space in the classroom or adaptations to address the need of some students for movement. Moving a student away from a window or away from the pencil sharpener is also an example of differentiating the environment. Also, environments can be altered to reflect a variety of different cultures or different home environments to make the classroom more inviting for all learners. For example, include objects, images, and books in the classroom that represent the children's community and consider arranging desks for collaboration to build relationships and engagement.

DIFFERENTIATING INSTRUCTIONAL MATERIALS Instructional materials can be differentiated in a number of ways to address the needs of individual learners. For example, differentiation could include the use of textbooks and reading materials with different fonts or differing difficulty levels, a text-to-speech reader, vocabulary guides, or physical manipulative materials. Likewise, worksheets or other student activities can be differentiated to meet different learner needs. For examples, Figure 6.1a and 6.1b show worksheets for middle-schoolers to complete after watching a video on coal mining during the Industrial Age. The worksheet in Figure 6.1b has been modified.

DIFFERENTIATING INSTRUCTIONAL METHODS *Process* and instructional methods refer to the activities students participate in to learn the content. When process is differentiated, this means that students may be given different means by which they can meet learning objectives. Some students may learn better when paired with a partner, in small groups, or in a peer-tutoring arrangement. Another example is the use of tiered activities, where some students may receive more support, more challenge, or more complexity in order to meet the same objectives. Teachers may find opportunities to reteach essential concepts for particular learners in need of additional instruction. Additionally, some students may be given more time to complete a task they are having difficulty with or more time for a task because of a special interest or a desire to explore the topic in more depth.

Figure 6.1a Coal Mining Worksheet

Choose at least three of the four questions below to answer.

1. Explain reasons for coal mining during the Industrial Age.
2. Who were most of the coal miners during the Industrial Age?
3. What kinds of hardships did miners experience?
4. What brought the decline of the coal mining industry?

Figure 6.1b Differentiated Coal Mining Worksheet

Choose three of the four questions below to answer.

1. What was the primary reason for coal mining during the Industrial Age?
   a. To find gold and buy land with the money
   b. To provide cheap fuel for the locomotives and to heat homes
   c. To clear the land for growing crops
2. Who were many of the coal miners during the Industrial Age?
   a. People born in Montana
   b. Farmers
   c. Immigrants
3. Use as many of these words as possible in a sentence to summarize coal mining in the 1880s:
   Coal, danger, blasting, control, disease
4. Circle the two TRUE statements in this list.
   a. Coal was needed to run the locomotives.
   b. Coal was a cheap fuel found out West during the Industrial Age.
   c. Coal replaced oil and electricity as a source of domestic fuel.

Pearson eTextbook

Video Example 6.1

In this video, a principal describes students in her school. How does she encourage teachers to differentiate learning for students?

DIFFERENTIATING EVALUATION Evaluation of instruction can also be differentiated to address individual needs, for example, by allowing verbal instead of written responses to test questions, allowing additional time to complete the test, reading questions aloud to individual students, or allowing the use of calculators when mastery of math facts is not a requirement. Remember that changes in evaluation procedures in standardized tests may limit the interpretability of test results; nevertheless, in many cases, differentiating evaluation methods can lead to more beneficial outcomes.

PROMOTING EFFECTIVE DIFFERENTIATED INSTRUCTION: THE PASS VARIABLES

To maximize the success of students with diverse learning needs in inclusive settings, we recommend using the **PASS** variables (Mastropieri & Scruggs, 2002; Scruggs & Mastropieri, 1995). PASS represents a way of thinking and approaching differentiated, inclusive instruction. PASS stands for the following variables:

1. Prioritize instruction.
2. Adapt instructional methods, instructional materials, or the learning environment.
3. Systematically teach with the **SCREAM** variables.
4. Systematically evaluate the outcomes of your instruction.

The PASS variables can be used as a guideline for planning, delivering, and evaluating effective inclusive instruction for specific students with individual needs. Using these variables and other information from this chapter, you can deliver effective instruction to all of your students. The following sections detail the PASS variables.

P: Prioritize Instruction

Learning Objective 6.2 Discuss how to prioritize instruction.

The first PASS variable describes how to prioritize instruction. When planning instruction, it is very important that you determine the relative importance of what you will teach. There are elements of your instruction that are very important for every student to learn; others are of less importance. For example, a teacher found that some students spent a lot of time staining slides of onion cells; there was a lot of mess to clean up, and poorly stained slides could not be viewed easily. She determined that understanding cell structure was the most important element of this unit and that staining slides was less important, and she adjusted her instruction accordingly to spend the most time on the content with the highest priority. Teachers should prioritize both long-term instructional goals and objectives.

Prioritizing instruction should not be thought of as something teachers can only apply to individual lessons; you should prioritize all of your instruction by planning for content coverage, basing your instruction on prioritized objectives, considering scope and sequence, selecting appropriate curriculum, and pacing instruction to maximize coverage of your prioritized objectives.

STRATEGIES FOR PLANNING CONTENT COVERAGE

The importance of content coverage is obvious, in that students almost certainly will not learn content that has not been covered. However, the amount of content covered must be appropriate to the skills and abilities of the students learning the content and must reflect your instructional priorities. Careful planning of content coverage can help ensure that learning will be maximized for all students. Several important considerations to make when planning content coverage include objectives, scope and sequence, curriculum, and pacing.

BASE INSTRUCTION ON SPECIFIC PRIORITIZED OBJECTIVES All content to be covered should be based on specific instructional objectives designed to address specific learning goals. Objectives state the outcomes of instruction in ways that allow you to find out whether your instruction was successful. Objectives specify (1) the content of the objective (what is being taught), (2) the conditions under which a student's performance will be assessed (e.g., in writing, oral responding), and (3) the criteria for acceptable performance (level of achievement). For example, consider the following objective: "The student will write five precipitating causes of the Civil War with 100% accuracy." The content of the objective is the causes of the Civil War, the conditions specify that students will write, and the criterion for acceptable performance is five causes written with 100% accuracy. Another example of an objective is as follows: "The student will read three pages from the grade-level reading materials at a rate of 120 words per minute with 95% of words read correctly." This objective also specifies the content, the conditions, and the criteria to be achieved. Another objective could state, "After silent reading of a grade-level narrative reading assignment, the student will verbally restate the setting, main characters, problem, and resolution with 100% accuracy."

Because the content of instruction is based on objectives, it is important to include as many objectives as necessary to maximize content coverage. This is particularly important for students who receive special education services because their individualized education programs (IEPs) are based on objectives. An effective inclusive teacher specifies objectives and translates IEP objectives into relevant methods and materials, with the assistance of the special education teacher.

In order to ensure that all students are learning and engaged with the curriculum, teachers may need to select and prioritize objectives for some students with disabilities. This means examining all instructional objectives, determining which are the most important for students with disabilities who are included in general education classes, and eliminating objectives that are unnecessary for those students. For example, Cliff has severe arthritis and has a great deal of difficulty using a pencil and completing tasks that require much fine motor control. He uses canes to assist with mobility. His fifth-grade teacher, Mr. Masoodi, employs a hands-on approach to science instruction. To accommodate Cliff's needs, Mr. Masoodi prioritized his class objectives. He examined the content and selected the most important objectives for Cliff. He determined that understanding of critical scientific concepts and a positive attitude toward science had the highest priority as objectives. Handwriting and physical manipulation of instructional materials had a lower priority and were not always required in Cliff's case. By first examining all the class objectives and then reviewing Cliff's instructional needs, Mr. Masoodi was able to prioritize objectives for Cliff.

PLAN INSTRUCTION BASED ON SCOPE AND SEQUENCE Scope and sequence refer to the breadth and depth of content that will be presented in school (scope) and the order in which the content will be presented (sequence). All areas of instruction should be presented with

In the Classroom

Checklist for Curriculum Materials for Inclusive Environments

_____ Do the materials provide sufficient opportunity for active student involvement, or do they simply provide verbal information to be recalled?

_____ Are the materials written on a level that is most comprehensible to all students, or do they include unnecessary complexity or an overabundance of unnecessary vocabulary?

_____ Do the materials lend themselves to use by cooperative learning groups or other peer-interactive activities?

_____ Do the materials allow for sufficient practice of key concepts before moving on to other content?

_____ Do the materials provide simple means for frequent evaluation of learner progress toward prespecified goals and objectives?

_____ Do the materials include examples of individuals from culturally diverse backgrounds and people of diverse learning abilities?

_____ Do the materials provide recommendations for modifications for students with disabilities or other learning needs?

_____ Do the materials provide evidence-based practice data that demonstrate that positive learning gains can be realized from use of the materials?

respect to an overriding scope and sequence of prioritized instructional objectives. Scope and sequence allow for long-term planning and evaluation of instruction, provide implications for time allocations, and set the overall pace of instruction. Most states have published curriculum guidelines that contain scope and sequence for all subject areas across grade levels. Prioritized content should receive substantial attention within the scope and sequence of instruction.

The **Common Core State Standards (CCSS)** Initiative introduced in 2011 is a state-led effort to provide a clear and consistent framework in order to prepare students for college and the workforce by the time they graduate from high school. The Common Core Standards were written for mathematics and English language arts/literacy. Review these standards documents at www.corestandards.org. Many states are participating in this initiative, whereas other states are employing their own standards. Teachers in participating states should determine what these standards are and how they will be implemented in inclusive classrooms in their own schools (Scruggs et al., 2013). The national associations for science and social studies have their own standards.

The Next Generation Science Standards (NGSS) can be found at https://www.nextgenscience.org. The National Council for Social Studies (NCSS) post their standards at https://www.socialstudies.org/standards.

SELECT AN APPROPRIATE CURRICULUM The curriculum not only includes the instructional materials used for learning but also refers to the course of study for each discipline and the scope and sequence within each grade level necessary to build conceptual understanding. The curriculum serves as an interface between the student and the learning objectives and has been described as the overall experience provided to a student by the school (Gartin et al., 2002; Moore, 2011).

Curriculum decisions can play an important role in inclusive schooling. The accompanying *In the Classroom* feature shows a checklist of curriculum materials being considered to maximize learning for all students. When serving on curriculum adoption committees or making a choice from existing school materials, be certain to consider the points noted to maximize learning for all students. Curriculum materials that feature many of these characteristics should be given a higher priority than those with fewer of these characteristics.

The curriculum need not be the same for every student. In fact, the curriculum can be carefully selected to address specific learner needs, and individual curriculum decisions are an important component of differentiated instruction.

PACE INSTRUCTION EFFECTIVELY Pacing refers to the rate at which teachers and students proceed through the curriculum and is another way of prioritizing instruction. For example, Mr. Isaac teaches American history but has only gotten to World War II by the end of the school year. He has determined (intentionally or not) that events in American history from 1945 to the present have a lower priority, as he did not cover this content. Unless the content at the beginning of the text has a higher priority, and content at the end of the text is judged to be of less value, however, more efficient planning would have produced a pace of instruction that better reflected instructional priorities.

One of the most significant problems teachers encounter in inclusive settings is adjusting the pace of instruction to diverse learning needs. Whereas some students appear to master new content almost as soon as they are exposed to it, other students require substantially more instructional time to learn the same content. Students who have learned certain concepts should not be held back and instead could be engaged in learning more in-depth knowledge about a concept or learning about related concepts while other students receive additional practice.

Once objectives have been prioritized, instruction has been planned based on scope and sequence of prioritized objectives, and curriculum has been selected and paced appropriately, it is necessary to implement appropriate adaptations.

A: Adapt Instructional Methods, Instructional Materials, or the Learning Environment

Learning Objective 6.3 Describe how to adapt instruction.

Pearson eTextbook

Video Example 6.2

The teacher in this video describes how she plans for differentiation of her lessons, including differentiation of methods and materials. How does she differentiate her instruction to benefit students with disabilities?

The second PASS variable identifies how to make adaptions to methods, materials, and the learning environment. So, once instructional objectives have been prioritized, the instructional methods, materials, and/or the environment can be adapted to accommodate more completely the needs of the students with disabilities. These adaptations carefully link the characteristics of the curriculum with the characteristics of the learner and are at the heart of differentiated instruction. For example, students in Cliff's group often recorded Cliff's notes for him or carried out experiments according to Cliff's directions when needed. Mr. Masoodi provided extra time for Cliff to work on the science activities, if necessary. He also adapted materials, for example, by acquiring hand-held lenses that were larger and easier to handle. Mr. Masoodi also adapted the environment by rearranging desks to create more aisle space for Cliff and his two canes. Similar adaptations for differentiated instruction, for a wide variety of objectives, are described throughout this text.

According to the Individuals with Disabilities Education Improvement Act (IDEA; 2004), special education is "specially designed instruction," and IDEA defines specially designed instruction as follows:

> (3) *Specially designed instruction* means adapting, as appropriate to the needs of an eligible child under this part, the content, methodology, or delivery of instruction—
> (i) To address the unique needs of the child that result from the child's disability; and
> (ii) To ensure access of the child to the general curriculum, so that the child can meet the educational standards within the jurisdiction of the public agency that apply to all children. [§300.39(b)(3)]

IDEA does not specifically define adaptations with respect to "accommodations" and "modifications." However, accommodations are generally understood to mean those adaptations that do not involve changing the goals and objectives of instruction. For example, a student who is given a specially designed study guide to organize study skills may still take the same test, with the same evaluative criteria, as all other students. Modifications, on the other hand, generally refer to those adaptations that change to some degree the expectations or standards of instruction. For example, taking a specially designed spelling test for a student's individual target spelling words might constitute a modification. In practice, the terms *accommodations* and *modifications* have been used interchangeably (Center for Parent Information and Resources, 2016). However, it is important to know whether a particular adaptation is intended to help a student meet an instructional objective or whether the level of expectation has been changed.

Appropriately developed adaptations allow students of different abilities to succeed within the same curriculum and constitute the core of differentiated instruction. When planning adaptations to improve student learning, consider specifically *what* will be taught and to *what level of proficiency*. These considerations have been referred to as **types and levels of learning** (Mastropieri & Scruggs, 2002). Knowing what types and levels of learning are desired provides guidelines for planning instructional adaptations for differentiated instruction.

STRATEGIES FOR

MAKING ADAPTATIONS

BASE ADAPTATIONS ON STUDENT CHARACTERISTICS All instruction is concerned with the interaction of characteristics of the learner with the characteristics of the instructional methods, materials, and environment. Appropriately adapted methods or materials take this interaction into account. Specific adaptations in a variety of academic and behavioral skills and content areas are described in detail throughout this text. Table 6.1 lists some examples of possible adaptations based on specific learning characteristics.

BASE INSTRUCTIONAL ADAPTATIONS ON TYPES OF LEARNING Different types of learning occur in school, across all different subject areas. These types include learning of discriminations, facts, rules, procedures, and concepts, as well as problem solving/critical thinking (Mastropieri & Scruggs, 2002). Although there can be much overlap on school tasks, it is helpful to examine some of the distinctions among the categories. Teachers who understand the different types of learning required of students are more able to plan effective instruction. They are also more able to plan effective instructional adaptations, focused specifically on the nature of the learning task. That is, when a student is demonstrating difficulty with a learning task,

TABLE 6.1 Adaptations Based on Student Characteristics

Learner Characteristics	Possible Adaptations
Physical	• Optimal location of student in classroom (preferential seating) • Rearrangement of classroom layout to promote mobility and accessibility for wheelchairs or braces • Adaptations to promote grasping (e.g., pencil grips, alligator clips, Velcro) • Peer assistance to support physical manipulation • Assistive Technology for computer use
Sensory	• Environmental adaptations to accommodate low vision (e.g., clear routes through the classroom) or hearing ability (e.g., carpets to reduce extraneous noise) • Adaptations to promote access to text (e.g., braille, Kurzweil readers) • Peer assistance to support access to visual or auditory stimuli (e.g., repeat information, describe images, provide notes) • Sign language or frequency-modulation systems to provide support for hearing impairments
Language	• Language cards for specific vocabulary • Boardmaker or teacher-made communication boards • Targeted language instruction • Peer mediation/peer assistance • Sign language instruction
Literacy	• Direct teaching of literacy skills and strategies • Digital texts • Text-to-speech systems (e.g., Kurzweil readers) • Peer reading/writing assistance • Hands-on/activity-oriented instruction
Emotional/Behavioral	• Safe areas of classroom for target student to use when needed • Reduced interaction with peers, if needed • Recording chart for monitoring target behaviors with token systems • Peer support • Class rewards for target student behavior • Parent or caregiver involvement for social behavior

it is helpful to determine the type of learning the task represents (e.g., factual learning rather than math or social studies or English) when planning adaptations. Table 6.2 summarizes types of learning and example adaptations.

Discrimination Learning Discrimination often occurs early in learning and involves determining how one stimulus is either the same as or different from another stimulus. Making discriminations is important in early learning of such things as the alphabet, numbers, colors, shapes, and math concepts. For example, learning to discriminate between a triangle and a square may be difficult at first for students with disabilities. Careful attention to the relevant and irrelevant distinctions between various stimuli can help improve **discrimination learning**. For example, the critical feature that distinguishes *p* from *q* is the relative placement of the round part of the letter. The critical feature that distinguishes squares from triangles is the number of sides (and not, for example, size). For students exhibiting difficulty in discrimination learning tasks, additional repeated practice that emphasizes comprehension of the critical distinctions can provide a beneficial adaptation.

Factual Learning *Factual learning* is a common aspect of school learning and includes vocabulary words and their definitions, names of famous people and their accomplishments, dates and causes of historical events, addition facts, and names of rivers and other geographical features.

TABLE 6.2 Adaptations Based on Types of Learning

Type of Learning	Possible Adaptations
Discrimination	• Present examples and nonexamples (e.g., "This is purple; this is not purple. Is this purple?"). • Use models, prompts, and feedback. • Teach relevant dimensions (e.g., "Everybody raise your right hand").
Factual	• Use repetition, rehearsal, and practice (e.g., "Cheyenne is the capital of Wyoming. What city is the capital of Wyoming? Cheyenne, yes, good."). • Present information in clusters or chunks. • Use overlearning (teaching beyond a criterion) and distributed practice with frequent review. • Use verbal elaboration and mnemonics ("A 'buoy' can help you remember the meaning of *buoyant*").
Rule	• Practice using rules and provide feedback. • Use "sayings" for rules (e.g., "*i* before *e*, except after *c*"). • Model applications for rules. • Remind students of rules (e.g., "What is the rule for recess?").
Procedure	• Model use of procedures. • Write out steps of procedures as reminders. • Use drill and practice. • Practice applications of the procedure and recognizing, retrieving, and executing steps in the procedure. • Use acronyms for procedure steps (e.g., "What is the first step in answering an essay question using the SNOW strategy? 'S = Study the question,' good.") (see Chapter 12).
Concept	• Directly teach relevant rules and discriminations. • Use examples and nonexamples (e.g., "Is this an example of radial symmetry?"). • Enhance meaningfulness with multiple concrete examples.
Problem solving	• Use modeling and think-alouds ("Here's how I would try to solve this problem"), coaching, and prompting. • Reteach any relevant procedures; practice with similar, simpler problems. • Activate prior knowledge; help students learn more about the problem to be solved.

Some factual learning is in the form of **paired associates**, where one thing is paired with another (e.g., Austin = Capital of Texas; the French word *petit* = "small"). Other factual learning is in the form of a **serial list** (e.g., "a–b–c–d–e–f–g ..."; "2–4–6–8–10 ..."), where information is learned with respect to a specific sequence. Appropriate strategies include redundancy, drill and practice, enhancing meaningfulness, and use of elaborations or other memory-enhancing techniques. All of these strategies can be useful in adapting instruction for individual learning needs.

Rule Learning Rules are also pervasive in school, and many students with disabilities and other needs have difficulties learning these rules. Examples of **rule learning** include social behavior rules (e.g., "Always raise your hand before speaking in class") and math rules (e.g., "When dividing fractions, invert the divisor and multiply"). Rules often include discriminations, facts, and appropriate circumstances for the use of those rules. For example, students might need to know that the rules for speaking in class are different in Mr. Halleran's class than they are in Ms. Butcher's class and that they need to learn to apply the rules appropriately in each class. Some individual students may have more difficulty assimilating these differences and may require additional practice as an adaptation.

Procedural Learning *Procedural learning* involves the sequential execution of multiple steps and is frequently found in both elementary and secondary school tasks. Remembering and executing the steps involved in going through the cafeteria lunch line (e.g., take your place at the end of the line, take your tray, pick up your silverware) is an example of procedural learning. Cognitive and meta-cognitive strategies are also important examples of procedural learning. Academic examples include reading-comprehension strategies (e.g., determine the purpose, survey the material, read, recite, review), math algorithms (e.g., learning to execute the steps in solving long-division problems), and study strategies. This can involve describing or listing the steps in the procedure, modeling or demonstrating the application of the procedure, or prompting students to execute the steps of the procedure. Procedural learning requires that students (1) *recognize* when a specific procedure is called for (e.g., a strategy for learning a list of spelling words), (2) *retrieve* the steps in the procedure (e.g., C–C–C, or cover, copy, and compare), and (3) correctly *execute* the procedure (e.g., use the strategy correctly to learn the list). When students exhibit difficulty with procedural learning tasks, consider which of these three steps they have not mastered.

Conceptual Learning Most tasks involve some *conceptual learning*, which can be taught using procedures similar to those for discrimination-, factual-, and rule-learning paradigms. **Concepts** are completely learned only when they can be applied to a new instance. For example, students do not know the concept of "dog" if they can only identify their own household pet as a dog—they must be able to identify dogs they have never seen before.

Concepts can range from simple ("red") to more complex ("radial symmetry," "nonpolar covalent bonding"). Conceptual learning can be enhanced by the use of examples (e.g., of radial symmetry or of the color red), provision of noninstances ("This is *not* an example of a carnivore"), and statement and application of rules ("Insects have six legs; how many legs does this specimen have?"). These enhancements can be helpful adaptations for any students who do not immediately master relevant concepts.

Problem Solving/Critical Thinking *Problem solving* refers to determining solutions when no specific strategy for solving the problem is known. Similarly, **critical thinking** refers to the use of active reasoning to acquire novel concepts, ideas, or solutions or to evaluate or analyze information to reach a justifiable conclusion. These types of learning are commonly found in science and mathematics curricula (e.g., geometric proofs) but could also be found in any other area (e.g., understanding or solving a social problem in social studies). Problem solving and critical thinking are important goals in education, but they also present some of the greatest challenges for students with disabilities. They can be enhanced by the use of teacher modeling and **think-alouds** ("Here's how I think as I try to solve this problem ...") and careful questioning or coaching techniques, as described elsewhere in this chapter.

BASE INSTRUCTIONAL ADAPTATIONS ON THE APPROPRIATE LEVEL OF LEARNING Another important consideration for teachers when planning instructional adaptations is the level of proficiency to be attained by the student for any of the previously described types of learning. Levels of learning address *how well* something will be learned, and it may be possible to isolate learning problems within these parameters (Mastropieri & Scruggs, 2002; Scheuermann et al., 2022). For example, if we say that a student "has not learned" something, it may be that the student *has* learned at one level (e.g., initial acquisition) but not at the level necessary for success (e.g., fluency or application). These levels include—in order of complexity—initial acquisition, fluency, application, and generalization. Consideration of the appropriate level of learning can help when planning adaptations.

Acquisition and Fluency **Acquisition** refers to simple accuracy-level criteria, such as 9 out of 10 correct responses to listing 10 letters of the alphabet. Accuracy criteria are important in the initial stages of learning. **Fluency** combines the accuracy criteria with specified amounts of time—for example, 90% accuracy within 2 minutes, or 90 out of 100 letters correct in 5 minutes. Fluency is particularly important when tasks need to become automatic, such as in basic literacy, math, and letter-formation skills. Many students, for example, have acquired the skills needed to read individual words but are not sufficiently fluent to comprehend what they are reading. Such students would benefit from fluency instruction.

Application and Generalization **Application** refers to applying learned skills or content to relevant contexts, and **generalization** is the ability to transfer previous learning to novel situations. For example, applying a social skill learned in a lesson in the special education setting to a role-play activity is an example of the application level. An example of generalization is employing appropriately, in an inclusive classroom setting, a social skill previously learned in the special education classroom.

Application and generalization levels of learning can be difficult for some students with disabilities to attain (Sabornie & deBettencourt, 2009). Simply because a student has learned a particular skill (e.g., telling time or a social skill for greeting new people) in one situation, you should not assume the student will now apply or generalize that skill to every appropriate situation. In many cases, specific strategies to promote application and generalization are needed.

Application and generalization levels of learning can be promoted by training "loosely" and allowing flexibility in responding; by using "indiscriminable contingencies" (rewarding students when they do not know they are being observed); by using modeling and role play; by employing classroom peers; by encouraging self-monitoring, where students evaluate their own performance; and by retraining the desired behavior in a variety of different circumstances (see also Alberto et al., 2022; Scruggs & Mastropieri, 1994a).

Identification versus Production For any of the levels of learning, students can be asked to identify or produce relevant responses. **Identification** includes such responses as pointing to the correct answer (e.g., on a communication board) and responding to matching, multiple-choice, or true/false test formats and is usually learned more readily. **Production** is more difficult and includes such responses as writing, saying, computing, orally spelling, and exhibiting appropriate behavior. When planning instruction, consider whether students will be required to identify or produce correct responses. For example, if students are required to produce correct responses (such as spelling words), it is important that they practice producing, rather than simply identifying, correctly spelled words during instruction.

Consider Types and Levels of Learning to Address Specific Learning Problems To best address diverse learning needs, first determine where the problems lie. For example, Janine cannot remember the correct sequence of steps in multiplying an algebraic expression. Mario can identify but not produce correctly spelled words from his weekly list. Shawna can control her impulsivity in the classroom but not in the cafeteria. Once these are identified as problems of procedural learning, identification/production, and generalization, respectively, they can be specifically addressed. As such, your instruction can be much more precise (and much more effective) than if these problems are simply considered to be problems with math, spelling, or social behavior. Tables 6.2 and 6.3 present some examples of adaptations to address problems in specific levels and types of learning. Remember that many different strategies may be successful and that identification and production formats can be considered with any of the other levels and types of learning.

TABLE 6.3 Instructional Strategies for Specific Levels of Learning

Levels of Learning	Instructional Strategies
Acquisition	• Slow the pace of instruction and provide for additional practice. • Use modeling and demonstrations. • Provide frequent reinforcement for accurate responding.
Fluency	• Provide a faster pace of instruction. • Practice with timed responding (e.g., "How many words can you read in a minute this time?"). • Provide reinforcement for rapid, accurate responding.
Application	• Provide several instances of different application problems. • Model procedures and directions in different cases. • Provide meaningful demonstrations and examples. • Use active coaching with questioning to prompt correct responding (e.g., "Remember how we did . . .; this is just like it, only now . . .").
Generalization	• Ensure students have mastered relevant skills. • Train and retrain "loosely" in real-world settings. • Use multiple examples of stimuli. • Use peer assistance and indiscriminable contingencies. • Train students to use self-monitoring; use modeling and role play. • Reinforce appropriate generalization. • Practice skills to be generalized (e.g., "When we go to the store, we are going to use the *polite behaviors* that we practiced before. Now, if you need help, how will you ask?").

USE PRINCIPLES OF UNIVERSAL DESIGN FOR LEARNING Universal design for learning (UDL) principles involve developing materials or structuring the environment to improve accessibility for all learners (CAST, 2018; Hall et al., 2012); thus, it is very compatible with the principles of differentiated instruction. For many years, the CAST organization has been developing software intended to address a diversity of learner needs. For example, in reading text, students with physical disabilities may benefit from page-turning technology, students with limited vision or reading disabilities may benefit from text-to-speech technology, and students with limited vocabulary may benefit from links to definitions. These and other options could potentially be embedded within a single digital book (Meyer et al., 2014). Whenever possible, UDL seeks to present highly similar curricula to all students that can be accessed by all in ways that address individual learning needs.

Pearson eTextbook
Video Example 6.3
In this video, a school leader describes UDL as a core element of an inclusive classroom. How can UDL principles be represented in a lesson plan?

Three guiding principles for UDL proposed by CAST and its National Center for UDL are (1) multiple means of engagement (e.g., recruiting interest, sustaining effort and persistence), (2) multiple means of representation (e.g., perception, language, expressions, and symbols), and (3) multiple means of action and expression (e.g., physical action, expression, and communication) in order to design curricula that address the needs of all types of learners (see also https://www.cast.org). These are each described as follows.

Multiple Means of Engagement Providing *multiple means of engagement* is intended to develop purposeful, motivated learners. This is accomplished by providing options for self-regulation, which include promoting positive expectations and beliefs, facilitating coping skills, and teaching self-assessment and reflection. Additionally, multiple means are needed for sustaining persistence of effort, for example, by encouraging collaboration with others, varying demands and resources, and increasing feedback toward personal mastery. Finally, it is important to promote interest on the part of individual learners by providing personal choice, enhancing task relevance and value, and minimizing interfering or distracting stimuli. In supplying and promoting multiple means of engagement, UDL seeks to address the affective component of learning.

Multiple Means of Representation Providing *multiple means of representation* is intended to develop resourceful, knowledgeable learners. In order to achieve this, a variety of options should be provided for comprehension, including activating background knowledge, highlighting significant features and ideas, guiding the multiple ways the information can be processed, and directly focusing on generalization and transfer of learned information and skills. In addition, options should be provided for different uses of language as well as mathematical and symbolic communication, by clarifying vocabulary and syntax, and by use of a variety of means for enhancing comprehension. It is also of significant importance to provide options for how information is perceived, including alternatives for auditory or visual information, and customizing how information is displayed. These multiple means of representation provide options for all learners to access information.

Multiple Means for Action and Expression Providing *multiple means for action and expression* is intended to develop strategic, goal-directed learners. These means are concerned with how students respond to instructional stimuli. They include options for executive functioning, including goal setting, planning, strategy development, and progress monitoring. Options are also provided for expression and communication, including the use of multimedia, multiple tools for composition, and fluency-building activities. Physical activity is also considered, including providing various methods to respond to instructional materials and navigate the curricula and providing optimal access to tools and assistive technologies. In planning instruction, it is important to consider how students will respond to instructional curriculum and to ensure that multiple options are available for different learning needs.

CAST provides specific guidelines for the development of new materials to promote accessibility for diverse learners, rather than adapting existing materials. One example of a curriculum material designed with UDL principles is *WiggleWorks* (produced and distributed by Scholastic), which provides a blend of technology, literature, and teacher support to help students develop reading and writing skills. However, because many materials were developed without the principles of UDL, those existing materials may be adapted or differentiated more successfully by using the UDL guidelines.

Rao and colleagues (2014) summarized research studies evaluating UDL principles and reported that research generally supported the effectiveness of these applications. However, the number of studies identified was limited, terminology was used in widely varying ways, and many of these studies were qualitative or descriptive, rather than experimental. Rao et al. recommended that researchers should (1) use terminology related to UDL consistently, (2) identify specifically the relations between their own intervention components and UDL principles, and (3) conduct more empirically based research that directly examines the efficacy of applications of UDL principles.

As can be seen, many of the strategies recommended in this chapter are consistent with the principles of UDL. Essentially, when instruction considers the needs of all learners and provides multiple alternative means for engagement with curricula, representation of information, and action and expression in response to the curriculum, principles of UDL are being employed.

S: Systematically Teach with the SCREAM Variables

Learning Objective 6.4 Explain how to systematically teach in inclusive settings using the SCREAM variables.

Systematic teaching is the third component of the PASS variables and builds on the previous ones; indeed, in order to systematically teach, you need to incorporate planning for content and prioritizing objectives as well as adapting instruction, materials, and/or the environment. Systematic teaching refers to the use of effective teaching techniques for content coverage and teacher presentations, known as the SCREAM variables: *structure*, *clarity*, *redundancy*, *enthusiasm*, *appropriate rate*, and *maximized engagement* through questioning and feedback (Mastropieri & Scruggs, 2002, 2004; Scruggs & Mastropieri, 1995). If you implement differentiated instruction using these techniques and consider the specific needs of students with disabilities, all students may be more successfully included and overall classroom achievement will improve. The *Research Highlight* later in the chapter describes investigations of teachers' understandings of evidence-based practice.

STRATEGIES FOR

IMPLEMENTING THE SCREAM VARIABLES

STRUCTURE YOUR LESSONS *Structure* refers to the organization of the components of the lesson. Structure does not necessarily mean that the content of your lesson will be teacher driven or that your students sit in rows doing worksheets. Rather, lessons are structured when you (1) communicate to students the overall organization and purpose of the lesson, (2) display outlines of the lesson and indicate transition points, (3) emphasize the critical points of the lesson, and (4) summarize and review throughout the lesson. Following is an example of structure in teacher dialogue, taken from a fourth-grade science lesson on ecosystems:

> The first thing—and Mrs. [name of special education teacher], (if you would like to write this on the board) the first thing you're going to do is get your supplies and aquarium.... The second thing that I want you to do is put your gravel in, which is step number 2 ... [repeats].... The third thing that's going to happen is that you are going to fill out parts of your activity sheet.... (Mastropieri et al., 1998, p. 18)

Structure is particularly helpful for students who have difficulty sustaining attention or who exhibit difficulties in language comprehension. Structure refers not only to providing an overall organizational framework for the lesson but also to ensuring that students understand this organization.

Communicate Lesson Structure to Your Students Carefully design your lessons with a clear idea of the structure, including stating the purpose, reviewing the main ideas, and making clear transitions between lesson elements (Good & Brophy, 2007). You will communicate structure best to your students if you yourself are very familiar with the structure and organization of your lessons.

Tell students the structure of the lesson. This can be done by announcing the components of the lesson directly, by writing the agenda on the board or on a whiteboard, and by using illustrations or handouts to indicate the lesson's sequence.

Remind students about the structure throughout the lesson. Say, for example, "Remember, when you finish your group work, we are going to meet again as a class to review what we have learned about bird migration."

PROMOTE CLARITY IN YOUR PRESENTATIONS A teacher exhibits clarity by speaking clearly and directly to the point of the objective; avoiding unclear or vague language or terminology; and providing concrete, explicit examples of the content being covered. Clear presentations address only one objective at a time and are directed explicitly to the lesson objective.

Select Vocabulary and Syntax That Are Familiar to All Students in the Class If you use a word that is unfamiliar to some or all students, take a minute to explain the word's meaning. If English learners are included in the class, use illustrations, physical modeling, or hand gestures to support verbally provided directions. These procedures are also beneficial for communicating with students with hearing impairments who have language difficulties and students with learning disabilities who have language comprehension difficulties. When employing co-teaching, the special education teacher can assume the role of promoting clarity and understanding where needed.

Eliminate Vague Language in Your Presentations Smith and Land (1981) reported that vague terms added to teacher presentations consistently lowered achievement. Vague terms are in italics in the following teacher presentation:

> This mathematics lesson *might* enable you to understand *a little more* about *some things* we *usually call* number patterns. *Maybe* before we get to *probably* the main idea of the lesson, you should review *a few* prerequisite concepts. *Actually,* the first concept you need to review is positive integers. *As you know,* a positive integer is any whole number greater than zero. (p. 38)

Clarity is also impeded by *mazes*, which include confusing word patterns ("We don't know it can't be done without ..."), false starts ("Facilit ... I mean, make it better to ..."), and unnecessary or irrelevant repetition ("This is, this is ... it's true that this is the most important ..."). Smith (1977) reported that lower student achievement was found in classrooms where teachers said "uh" frequently. Also avoid vague language such as "kind of," "you know," "sort of," and "pretty much." Avoid *negated intensifiers* ("not a lot," "not much," "not very"), *indeterminate quantification* ("a number," "a few of," "several"), and *ambiguous designation* ("some kind of," "somewhere"). Instead, use clear, direct, and precise language (Good & Brophy, 2007; Smith & Land, 1981). Clarity can be particularly important when restating comments made by individual students so that they will be more understandable to all students.

EMPLOY REDUNDANCY EFFECTIVELY Redundancy increases learning by emphasizing and reinforcing the most important aspects of lessons. Unlike unnecessary and irrelevant repetition of words, continued emphasis on key concepts, procedures, and rules is critical to the success of the lesson. Many students with disabilities require additional opportunities to review and practice lessons before mastering the objectives. It is unnecessary for components of the lesson to be identical to provide redundancy for students (Archer & Hughes, 2011).

Embed redundancy in your presentations. Discuss the main points of the lesson, and then be sure to refer to the key concepts throughout the lesson. Question students directly on these key concepts to reinforce their learning.

Create opportunities for extra practice to help provide redundancy for selected students. For example, supplemental practice times can be arranged for students either before or after school or during lunch and study hall periods. Peers who have mastered the topics can be asked to provide assistance during these additional practice periods. Focus on the most important content and provide many opportunities for responding.

Create opportunities to apply and generalize learned information to novel situations. For example, prompt students to use newly learned arithmetic to compute the cost of a single slice of a whole pizza or to use a reading-comprehension strategy to study a social studies book.

TEACH WITH ENTHUSIASM! Students consistently learn more and appreciate the content more when teachers display enthusiasm in their teaching. Enthusiasm also creates higher levels of student engagement with the lesson, increasing academic learning time. Enthusiastic teachers create exciting learning environments, in which students perceive that learning is fun, challenges are great, curiosity is enhanced, and thinking is encouraged (Good & Brophy, 2007). Enthusiastic teaching can be especially helpful for students who have histories of academic failure and are poorly motivated to succeed in school. For example, some students with disabilities are used to performing poorly in classes and have little motivation to attempt to succeed; however, an enthusiastic teaching style can provide the necessary excitement and encouragement to motivate such students to be successful (Wentzel & Brophy, 2014).

Teaching with enthusiasm can be used to stimulate student interest and attention, and it involves the use of several techniques that have been described by researchers, including the following:

- Varying speaking rates and using an upbeat tone of voice
- Using physical gestures to emphasize important points
- Using facial expressions and eye movements that convey positive interest
- Choosing a variety of expressive words
- Exhibiting a high overall energy level (e.g., Brigham et al., 1992; Kunter et al., 2010).

These techniques demonstrate that enthusiasm is something that teachers *do*, not something that teachers *are*. It is clear that teachers can change the amount of enthusiasm they display and improve student motivation and affect when they do so.

Enthusiasm is an attribute that you can vary within your own teaching (Brigham et al., 1992). And although it may make you a little self-conscious at first, you can practice being enthusiastic simply by raising and lowering the intonation of your voice and by using your hands and arms when you talk to students to explain or elaborate on a point. Statements made enthusiastically can gain students' attention. For example, one fourth-grade teacher used the following statement to gain attention and to manage transitions within her classroom during an ecosystems science activity: "Class, when I say 'ecosystems are a *blast*,' everyone go to your science groups!"

Enthusiastic teaching also involves open acceptance of student contributions. This is of critical importance for students with individual needs, who may believe their contributions are not welcome. In the case of disabilities such as communication disorders or hearing impairments, it may take longer for students to communicate ideas to the class. In other cases, the ideas, answers, or suggestions offered may seem less sophisticated than those of some other students. In these instances, it is particularly important for teachers to demonstrate enthusiastically that ideas and input from all students are welcome.

Can enthusiasm be overdone? Possibly. But one essential element of enthusiasm is that it must be (or appear to be) sincere. If students regard teachers' enthusiasm as genuine, they will probably welcome and appreciate very high levels of enthusiasm. On the other hand, if the enthusiasm seems forced or insincere, students will be less likely to appreciate it. Overall, however, our experiences (and research evidence) have convinced us that teacher enthusiasm promotes motivation and positive affect and that enthusiasm is often underused but rarely overused.

USE AN APPROPRIATE RATE OF PRESENTATION Effective teachers deliver instruction at the optimal rate. Generally, a brisk rate of presentation throughout the lesson and a brisk rate of interacting with students work well with enthusiasm variables and help keep lessons interesting and motivating. During basic skills instruction, a fast pace may be important in increasing learning (Carnine, 1976; Gleason et al., 1991). However, an excessively rapid rate of presentation may not be related to increased learning. When learning outcomes are not being met, changing the overall rate of presentation may allow information to be better understood by all students.

Begin with a brisk presentation rate, and frequently question students. Students' answers to your questions will tell you whether you are proceeding too rapidly. Record yourself and evaluate your rate of presentation. Perhaps your rate of presentation is good, but other presentation elements (speaking directly and clearly and with sufficient volume) are inhibiting understanding and need to be modified.

Some teachers begin lessons with a brisk rate of presentation, but they later slow down and lose student attention by overly focusing on minor issues or by questioning some students repetitively while the rest of the class waits. If some individual students, but not others, need additional practice, provide differentiated instruction by working with them individually, in small groups, or with peer tutors (Good & Brophy, 2007).

CLASSROOM SCENARIO

James

James is a 10-year-old fifth-grader who was having trouble succeeding academically in school. His teacher, Ms. Marshak, believed that James had the overall ability to succeed in her classroom, but he rarely completed his work. As a result, he was falling far behind the other students in the class.

Ms. Marshak began to pay more attention to how James was spending his time. She found that he was often the last student to organize materials on his desk and begin working. During this period, James also spent more time than other students setting up his Chromebook, asking to get a drink of water, daydreaming, or playing with objects from his backpack. When Ms. Marshak recorded his behavior at the end of every minute over a 30-minute period, she found that James was actually working on his assignment only 10 of the 30 times she sampled his behavior. Clearly, he needed to increase the amount of time he put into his schoolwork.

QUESTIONS FOR REFLECTION

1. Why is James off-task so often? How could you find out?
2. Why doesn't concern about poor grades motivate James to work harder?
3. What are some simple things Ms. Marshak could do to help James?

MAXIMIZE ACADEMIC ENGAGEMENT Research has consistently supported the idea that the more time students devote to a particular subject or skill, the more likely they are to master it. This is true whether the area is reading, science, creative writing, archery, music, or debate: More time effectively engaged in learning leads to more (and better) learning outcomes. Maximizing student engagement and time on-task is the single best way of increasing your students' learning.

In the previous scenario, it seems clear that James's learning will not improve until he can increase the amount of time spent on his work. Although most teachers **allocate** appropriate time for learning a certain subject (by, for example, scheduling a specific amount of time per day to reading instruction), a far smaller number of teachers will ensure that students are actually **engaged** in learning, to the greatest extent possible, during this allocated time. This distinction between allocated and engaged academic time is critical for student learning. In some cases, teachers may be able to greatly increase classroom learning simply by increasing student engagement rates (Seo et al., 2008).

But what are the specific techniques you can use to maximize academic engaged time? In a broad sense, teachers need to maximize student learning by maximizing student engagement with instruction and instructional materials. Selecting materials that are at the correct level of difficulty and that are motivating and interesting for students will help with this. Additionally, teachers need to carefully plan, monitor, and reward high rates of engagement, such as in the scenario about James, and carefully implement questioning, praise, and feedback. However, the first step is to understand what is meant by academic engaged time, or "on-task" behavior.

On-task behaviors of students vary depending on the grade level of the students, the curriculum, the type of lesson, the learning activities, and the behavior of the teacher. However, in general, students are considered on-task when they are doing such things as actively looking at or otherwise attending to the teacher, instructional materials, or other students who are actively engaged. Giving direct answers to relevant teacher questions or asking relevant questions are also considered on-task behaviors. During teacher presentations, examples of on-task student behavior include actively listening, taking notes, outlining, and asking for clarification. Likewise, being appropriately engaged in science experiments or math manipulatives and engaging in relevant debate in social studies can also be considered on-task behaviors. Overall, student behavior is usually considered on-task if it is logically related to instructional activities.

Some students with disabilities may be engaged in different ways. For example, some students, including students with visual impairments, with emotional disabilities, or with autism, may not be actively watching the teacher but may nonetheless provide other signs that they are attending. Students with physical disabilities may interact differently with educational materials, but they nonetheless can be observed to be interacting. Students with hearing impairments may need to watch the interpreter rather than the teacher. Some students with learning disabilities are unable to listen and take notes simultaneously, but they may be on-task. Careful consideration of the individual needs and abilities of different learners will reveal how different students may display appropriate on-task behavior.

On the other hand, off-task behavior is not logically related to academic learning. Off-task behavior can include tardiness, daydreaming, attending to inappropriate material, asking irrelevant questions or making irrelevant statements, or interacting inappropriately with peers or instructional materials. These activities are negatively related to learning; in other words, the more off-task behavior that occurs in a classroom, the less learning takes place.

STRATEGIES FOR MAXIMIZING ON-TASK BEHAVIOR

Your on-task behaviors as a teacher influence how much students learn. These include statements directly relevant to the lesson, questioning and feedback directly relevant to the lesson, and demonstrations and modeling directly relevant to the lesson.

USE EFFECTIVE QUESTIONING TECHNIQUES Teachers must be effective at questioning students. Generally, the more questions asked that are directly relevant to the lesson, the more students learn from the lesson. Questioning has several purposes. First, questioning allows teachers to monitor students' understanding of the content being presented. In inclusive classrooms, questioning can be particularly helpful in determining whether all students understand the content being presented and whether instruction should be differentiated further. When breakdowns in understanding are revealed through questioning, teachers can modify and adjust

Research Highlight

Beliefs versus Knowledge of Effective Teachers

Urbach et al. (2015) studied the beliefs of more and less accomplished special education teachers regarding teacher roles and responsibilities and how those beliefs influenced their practice. Beliefs versus knowledge can impact teachers' practice and determine whether practice is evidence based or not. Beliefs can be conscious or unconscious expectations about teaching and students but may be derived from experiences, whereas knowledge is based on truths agreed upon by experts (e.g., Richardson, 2003). Use of evidence-based practices is based on knowledge, whereas the generation of idiosyncratic teaching practices is more likely derived from personal experiences. Guckert et al. (2016) reported that highly competent teachers reported more knowledge about and use of evidence-based practices, whereas less qualified teachers relied on personalized experiences to guide their teaching practices. Ruiz et al. (1995) reported that teacher beliefs can be modified through effective training.

Urbach et al. (2015) used the Reading in Special Education (RISE) rating scale to identify more and less accomplished teachers. The RISE instrument consisted of 22 items addressing reading instruction, classroom management, and instructional practice and was intended to evaluate effective reading instruction. Teachers were observed, and those with higher versus lower scores were classified as more or less accomplished. All teachers were then interviewed on such topics as teacher efficacy, teaching influences, teacher roles and responsibilities, and effective teaching. Interviews were recorded, coded, and analyzed using methodologies for qualitative data analysis.

Urbach et al. (2015) identified themes related to beliefs that were shared and that differentiated these more versus less accomplished teachers: (1) providing instruction; (2) being resourceful; (3) communicating and collaborating with general educators, parents, caregivers; and (4) building relationships. The more accomplished teachers were relatively consistent in addressing these themes; however, less accomplished teachers were not. For example, more accomplished teachers linked their responses to student learning outcomes, identified the need for intensity of instruction, and determined what they could do to improve instruction, including adapting instruction to improve outcomes. More accomplished teachers also reported better self-efficacy and use of problem-solving techniques focusing on what they could implement to improve academic performance. In addition, more accomplished teachers adopted an attitude of teaching all students regardless of barriers. Relationship building with students was reported differently across groups. More accomplished teachers viewed relationship building as part of the academic learning process and never lost sight of the academic outcomes. In contrast, less accomplished teachers focused more on building relationships with their students at the expense of academic outcomes. This suggests that teachers who are more accomplished have beliefs related to knowledge, have higher self-efficacy, and are more likely to improve learning outcomes in their students.

QUESTIONS FOR REFLECTION

1. Why do you think a teacher's beliefs can play such an important role in instruction?
2. What could teachers do to become more knowledgeable and alter their beliefs?
3. Would strategies for changing teacher beliefs differ between elementary and secondary grade levels?

their instruction (considering such things as rate of presentation, choice of vocabulary, and use of examples) to address students' learning needs more effectively.

Second, questioning allows students to actively practice the information being covered. In this way, repeated questioning related to the same concept can provide the redundancy necessary for information to be learned and remembered. For example, consider the following dialogue:

TEACHER: In Boston in 1770, what was one of the major concerns of the colonists, Marcia?

MARCIA: Taxation without representation.

TEACHER: Taxation without representation. What's another way of saying that, Dan?

DAN: That, uh, you have to pay taxes, but you don't have someone to represent you in the government.

TEACHER: You pay taxes, but don't have a representative, good!

Questioning can be delivered to individuals or groups. When addressing questions to individuals, state the question first before calling on a particular student. If you give a student's name first, other students may be less likely to carefully consider an answer. For example, ask, "Why do you think Germany would strengthen its relations with Mexico during the first years of World War I? Frederick, why do you think this happened?" Rather than, "Frederick, why do you think Germany ...?" (Archer & Hughes, 2011).

Be certain the question is clearly stated so that students will know what type of response is expected and so that instructional time will not be lost in subsequent clarification. For example, referring to a passage in a text, a teacher might ask, "What problem do you see with this statement?" Although the teacher may be expecting an answer regarding verb tense, students might not know what the teacher means by "problem." Instead, she might ask, "Is there a problem with verb tense in this statement?" or, more generally, "Is there a grammatical problem in this sentence?" (Good & Brophy, 2007).

When addressing the question to groups, in which the answer is short and there is only one answer, **choral responding** may be appropriate (Archer & Hughes, 2011). Choral responding can promote active engagement for all students. Prompt students to respond to questions together when a specific signal is given (e.g., a raised finger or dropped hand). When using this technique, monitor whether all students are responding promptly and accurately. It may also be possible to promote "covert" responding on the part of all students, which will maximize student engagement. For example, "Now I want everyone to think about this problem and make a prediction: If I add weight to this pendulum, will it swing more rapidly? Everyone think [pause], now, thumbs up for yes, thumbs down for no." Alternatively, ask students to write down answers to questions individually to be read back later. For example, "Everybody, write down a definition of *metonymy*, and give an example. When you're done, we'll compare answers." These answers can provide insights into how your instruction can be further differentiated.

There are also different types of questioning, including lower-level questioning and higher-level questioning. Lower-level questioning usually involves repetition or restatement of previously covered information and is often used in basic skills instruction or in early stages of learning. For basic skills and basic facts, questioning should be fast paced and require simple, direct answers (e.g., "What is the silent-*e* rule?"; "What is the Pythagorean theorem?"; "What are the three branches of government?"). For this type of questioning, teachers should aim for 80–100% correct responding. This type of questioning is frequently used when building fluency with responding, such as when practicing math facts or vocabulary definitions using flashcards.

Higher-Level Questioning Higher-level questioning requires more in-depth thinking. For higher-level responses requiring thinking and reflection, questioning should proceed at a slower rate and may not require simple, direct answers. For example, "Why do you think a type of moss is often found on the north side of trees? Would this be true all over the world?" In this example, students could consider the general position of the sun in the Northern Hemisphere and conclude that the south side of trees may often be drier. Considering the characteristics of moss, students may conclude that it may more frequently—but not always—grow on the north side of trees. This, of course, would not generally be true in the Southern Hemisphere. With such questioning, you should consider that students will need more time for reflection and may need additional questioning to direct their thinking (e.g., "What conditions are favorable for moss growth? When would moss not grow on the north side of a tree in the Northern Hemisphere? Is there a rule that would better predict where moss would grow on a tree?").

Research has documented that when students with mild disabilities have been "coached" to answer higher-level questions, they can be successful (Scruggs et al., 1994; Sullivan et al., 1995). For example, consider the coaching dialogue in Figure 6.2 used with students with learning disabilities and mild intellectual disabilities to promote thinking about animals. This type of explicit coaching provides the structure and support students need to promote reasoning, but it still allows them to come up with their own answers.

Some questions—some may say the most important questions—do not have simple answers with which everyone would agree. These include such questions as "Who was the United States' most important president?"; "Should the Ten Commandments be displayed in schools?"; and "Does life exist on other planets?" Some students may have difficulty answering questions like these. When presenting these types of questions, inform students that a specific answer is not required and that, instead, the answer should reflect both knowledge of the

Figure 6.2 Coaching Dialogue

Experimenter: Anteaters have long claws on their front feet. Why does this make sense?

Student: I don't know.

Experimenter: Well, let's think. What do you know about anteaters? For example, what do they eat?

Student: Anteaters eat ants.

Experimenter: Good. And where do ants live?

Student: They live in holes in the ground.

Experimenter: Now, if anteaters eat ants, and ants live in holes in the ground, why do you think that anteaters have long claws on their front feet?

Student: To dig for ants.

Experimenter: Good. To dig for ants.

Source: From Mastropieri (1995). Copyright 1995 by Juvenilia. Reprinted with permission.

subject and careful thought about the answer. Give students models of good possible answers. Ask students to consider subquestions, such as "What qualities are considered important in a president?"; "What is the relevance of the 'establishment of religion' clause in the First Amendment?"; or "What conditions appear necessary for life to develop? What is the likelihood that these conditions exist elsewhere in the universe?"

Good and Brophy (2007) suggested that teachers generally should avoid four types of questions:

1. Questions that require yes-or-no answers
2. "Tugging" questions ("What else?"; "Tell me more ...")
3. "Guessing" questions, that is, asking students to guess when they do not have relevant information
4. Leading questions ("Isn't that so?").

Overall, the best questions are clear, purposeful, brief, phrased in simple language, sequenced, and thought provoking. This is true for all students but particularly for those with diverse learning needs.

PROVIDE HELPFUL FEEDBACK How teachers respond to student answers is as important as how the questions are asked. Appropriate feedback can be helpful in informing students of their level of understanding, providing redundancy, and encouraging students to continue to learn (Burnett, 2003). Feedback should be clear and overt so that there is no ambiguity about the teacher's evaluation of the answer. When appropriate, it should provide the entire class with information on the correctness of the response of an individual student.

During rapid questioning, drill and practice of skills, or review of previously learned material, feedback may be simple and brief. In some cases, the fact that the teacher has continued with the lesson imparts the information that the previous answer was correct (e.g., multiplication facts prompted by flashcards). At other times, feedback may be more substantive.

The type of feedback delivered depends to some extent on the response that has been given. If a student does not respond right away, you should try to elicit some type of response to determine the level of student understanding. It is important to consider whether the question is a lower-level question that should require only a short "wait time" (the amount of time the teacher waits for a response) or a higher-level question that may require a longer wait time for the student to develop a more thoughtful answer. Research has shown that longer wait times (when appropriate to the question) are associated with better and longer student responses and an increase in voluntary student contributions (Good & Brophy, 2007).

When students do not respond correctly, it is important to determine whether the answer is unknown, whether the question was unclear, or whether the student simply did not hear the question. You should also determine whether students can answer the question with additional coaching or prompting. Teachers should not appear to "badger" students who clearly do not know how to respond. However, it is important to retest students later in the lesson.

For completely incorrect responses, a simple, tactful statement that the answer was incorrect may be sufficient. Simply state the correct answer, provide the student with a prompt or additional information and restate the question, or call on another student for the answer.

If an answer is partially correct, first acknowledge the part of the answer that is correct, and then provide additional prompts or restate the question to elicit the rest of the answer, or call on another student. For any question that was incorrectly answered, partially or completely, teachers should make an effort to return to the question with individual students later in the lesson to ensure that the material was learned.

If the question was correctly answered, acknowledge the correctness of the answer and move on in the lesson, as in the following example:

TEACHER: Now, which astronomer first determined that the planets travel in an elliptical pattern? Juanita?

JUANITA: Kepler.

TEACHER: Kepler, correct. Good remembering.

Pearson eTextbook

Video Example 6.4

In this video, the co-teachers engage their students' attention in a lesson about shapes. Notice their use of the SCREAM variables throughout the video.

PRAISE STUDENTS FREQUENTLY Praise can be an important motivator for students. When the situation warrants it, actively praise your students for paying attention to the lesson, carefully considering teacher questions, and providing answers that are correct, or at least reasonable and thoughtful. Effusive or overly elaborate praise may not be helpful in many instances because it may interrupt the flow of the lesson or embarrass students (particularly students at the secondary level). However, most teachers deliver too little praise to students. Praise may be particularly important to help students with disabilities or diverse learning needs persist in their efforts to learn.

STRATEGIES FOR

MAXIMIZING TIME FOR LEARNING

MAXIMIZE ON-TASK TEACHER BEHAVIOR Teachers also may be off-task, and this behavior can impede student achievement. One example of off-task behavior is making unnecessary digressions, such as talking about personal experiences or current events that are irrelevant to the lesson. Students with diverse learning needs may find it especially difficult to follow teachers when they are making irrelevant digressions. During practice activities, teachers can be off-task by being unprepared with student materials or by speaking loudly to an individual student and disrupting other students. Teachers can also be off-task by not returning promptly after breaks, allowing longer-than-necessary transition times, and being unprepared for teacher presentations. The *Apps for Education* feature describes a helpful timer for class use.

Cultural diversity may also influence classroom interactions. The *Diversity, Equity, and Inclusion in the Classroom* feature describes culturally responsive teaching for English learners.

Research suggests that much **academic engaged time** is lost for a number of reasons, including inefficient transition activities, inappropriate verbalizations, and inappropriate social behavior.

STREAMLINE TRANSITION ACTIVITIES **Transition activities** involve students moving from one location, subject, or group to another. Academic engaged time can be lost during transitions through such activities as going to the restroom, sharpening pencils, and unnecessary socializing. Students with disabilities can lose time going between the regular classroom and the resource room.

One way to maximize transition efficiency is to set time limits and reinforce adherence to those limits. For example, if classes begin at the sound of a bell, let students know exactly what is expected of them when the bell rings. Typically, students should be in their places and prepared with their materials at this time. Any time lost after the bell—for example, searching through papers or finding workbooks or other materials—takes away from instructional time. Likewise, at the end of the class, if materials are not put away before students leave, time may

Apps for Education

Managing Time with the Time Timer™

Many students have difficulties with understanding the concept of time, especially when told they need to keep working for a specified amount of time. Other students have difficulties with transition periods and changing from one activity to the next. A technological device called the Time Timer can help students visually see the amount of time left as they work and help them comprehend in a more concrete fashion the amount of time left for work or the amount of time left for one activity before moving to the next activity. The visual timer is a clock that comes in various sizes. One standard version is approximately 8 inches square and has a 60-minute timer. A smaller, 3-inch-square version is also available that can be clipped to a student's belt. When setting a specified amount of time—say, 15 minutes—that amount of time appears in red. A red disk shows on the timer when a time is set. As the time passes, the red disk disappears bit by bit, such that when time is up, the red disk is gone. As this happens, students can visually see the red disk disappearing as time passes and obtain a better picture of the amount of time left. Such a device may help students feel more comfortable with the concept of time because it makes the concept more concrete for them.

An app version of Time Timer, the *iPad Edition* (Time Timer LLC), is available that functions similarly but is designed for use with an iPad. Again, the visual counting-down of the minutes provides students with immediate cues about remaining time. Many additional timer apps are also available, including *Timer*⁺ (Minima Software LLC) and *Easy Stop Watch&Timer* (BND Co., Ltd.), which include similar features for counting down time; some also include stopwatch features.

Source: From Time Timer LLC. Reprinted with permission.

Other apps help teachers track student behaviors. For example, *Teacher's Assistant: Track Student Behavior* (Lesson Portal, LLC) and *TeacherKit* (ITWorx Egypt) organize students by class, enable note taking for comments, allow storage of grades, interface with e-mail for contacting parents and caregivers, and interface with Dropbox for backing up files. These and other assistive and instructional technologies can become an important component of effective instruction, as described throughout this text.

be lost at some other point in the day. If your students are transitioning to a resource room, you should document the time they left the classroom and report the time to the resource teacher. Similarly, the resource teacher should inform you when students have left the resource room to return to your class.

One obvious way to promote efficient transitions is to inform students that time lost in transition will be made up during free time or during other preferred student activities. However, teachers can also reinforce prompt transitioning more positively by awarding points, stickers, or tokens or simply by responding positively to students when they make smooth transitions.

As the teacher, you can facilitate efficient transitions by being prepared ahead of time with materials for the next activity and not losing time looking for instructional materials, organizing supplies, or inefficiently passing out student materials. By setting a good model for transitions, you can promote good transitions in your students.

REDUCE INAPPROPRIATE VERBALIZATIONS Academic engaged time is lost when class discussions drift away from the point of the lesson. Teachers may find themselves wandering off-topic, and students may also wander by raising irrelevant issues. Some students deliberately attempt to keep teachers off-task to avoid getting to homework, tests, or other undesired activities. Monitor inappropriate verbalizations with video or audio recordings of individual lessons, and review them in reference to the purpose of the lesson and the appropriateness of teacher and student verbalizations.

At times, however, digressions may reflect genuine curiosity or interest on the part of students or a developing understanding of the concepts. When this happens, acknowledge that the lesson objective has changed, and evaluate it with respect to the changes that were made. Alternatively, you can inform students that the class can talk about those other important ideas after finishing the present activity.

REDUCE INAPPROPRIATE SOCIAL BEHAVIOR Inappropriate social behavior—including passing notes or electronic messages, teasing, arguing, and fighting—is one of the greatest threats to academic engaged time. Handle inappropriate social behavior quickly and efficiently so that as little instructional time as possible is lost. Punitive classroom environments that include long-winded lectures on social behavior are not as effective (or as time efficient) as positive learning environments where good behavior is expected and rewarded and misbehavior is dealt with efficiently (Scheuermann et al., 2022). More information on reducing inappropriate social behavior is provided in Chapter 8.

USE FLEXIBLE GROUPING On-task behavior can be maximized when teaching students with similar skill levels in small groups. This is particularly true when most students in the classroom have already mastered relevant objectives. Large-group instruction can be efficient when all students are on similar skill levels or when teachers wish to promote grade-level, content-oriented conversations (McLeskey et al., 2017). During whole-class instruction, co-teachers or paraprofessionals may be able to assist individual students when needed. In inclusive classrooms, co-teachers or paraprofessionals may be able to lead small-group instruction where needed.

USE STRATEGIES FOR INDIVIDUAL CASES Many inclusive classrooms contain one or more students who seem to spend far less time on schoolwork than other students. Frequently, these are the very students who need to spend more time on their schoolwork, such as James in the earlier scenario. In such cases, try to increase the students' amount of engaged time on-task. Following are some procedures that may be helpful:

1. *Be certain the student can do the work.* Many students become off-task if they cannot (or believe they cannot) do the assigned work. If you find that the work is too difficult, assign more appropriate work or modify assignments. Also, consider enlisting support from special education teachers, paraprofessionals, or classroom peers.
2. *Try simple strategies, such as direct appeal and proximity.* Tell individual students that you would like to see them working better on schoolwork. Tell them that you will send a signal when they are getting off-task by approaching their desks. When students return to work, walk away.
3. *Provide simple rewards or consequences.* Students can be offered stickers, free time for a preferred activity, or other rewards for completing all work in a specified time period. Alternately, students can be required to make up work they have not completed.
4. *Notify parents or caregivers.* Contact parents or caregivers to elicit their suggestions or support for increasing on-task behavior. Perhaps arrangements can be made to link home privileges or rewards to assignment completion in school. In some cases, simply communicating the idea that parents, caregivers, and teachers are interested in the student's academic progress can make an important difference.

S: Systematically Evaluate the Outcomes of Your Instruction

Learning Objective 6.5 Give examples of how to systematically evaluate the outcomes of inclusive instruction.

The last *S* in PASS stands for *systematic evaluation*. Systematic evaluation means frequently measuring students' progress toward meeting the instructional objectives of the class, as well as IEP objectives, using formative evaluation procedures. Teachers should continuously monitor and adjust instruction based on student progress as documented by formative evaluation measures. Formative evaluation measures can help identify which students may need differentiated instruction.

Diversity, Equity, and Inclusion in the Classroom

Culturally Responsive Teaching for English Learners

Diversity in schools has increased significantly as more students and their parents and caregivers from various cultural and linguistic backgrounds move to the United States and enroll their children in local schools (Banks, 2015). With these increasing numbers, there is a need for educators to gain more information and skills for creating culturally inclusive classes and schools. Many of these students and their parents/caregivers lack facility with English and have not yet mastered speaking, understanding, reading, or writing English (Echevarria & Graves, 2015). In addition, some of these English learners (ELs) may be at risk for learning disabilities or have disabilities that may compound any difficulties encountered in school. By examining each student's, parent's, and caregiver's unique background, culture, ethnicity, and language, educators can begin to understand students' and their parents' and caregivers' needs. Improper placement of students in schools may result in deleterious effects on student academic and social-emotional well-being (e.g., Agirdag, 2009).

A promising approach for addressing these unique needs is the Sheltered Instruction Observation Protocol (SIOP) model used for assessing, planning, implementing, and monitoring instruction for ELs (e.g., Echevarria et al., 2011). The SIOP model starts by evaluating and designing instruction with content-area and language objectives. Content objectives can be linked to the Common Core standards in English, math, science, or social studies. The lesson plan includes linking students' prior knowledge and learning experiences, developing meaningful activities and ordering them in a logical sequence, and planning for lesson review and informal assessment of objectives. Student activities are embedded within lessons with meaningfully designed content and language and vocabulary practice that students demonstrate at the end of lessons. Teachers are encouraged to use modeling and demonstrations and to provide corrective feedback as necessary throughout lessons. By combining language with content objectives, ELs are provided more opportunities to learn and practice the new vocabulary typically encountered in their content-area classes. Echevarria and Graves (2015) provide numerous illustrations of how teachers of ELs can incorporate the SIOP model within their instruction to accommodate students from various language and cultural backgrounds.

Discuss: How can students who are ELs show their understanding of new vocabulary during a science lesson?

FORMATIVE EVALUATION *Formative evaluation* refers to the frequent and systematic monitoring of learner progress toward prespecified goals and objectives. It is different from summative evaluation, in which, for example, tests are given at the end of a school year to determine how much was learned during the year. Teachers who use formative evaluation monitor student progress continuously throughout the school year and do not wait until the end of the year to determine whether learning took place.

Research has suggested that formative evaluation works best when it is used at least twice a week. In some cases, student learning (e.g., words read correctly per minute) can be recorded on a chart or graph so that rate of learning can be assessed. In other cases, student progress may be more difficult to place on a chart, but progress can still be monitored. For example, for evaluation of handwriting, weekly or monthly samples can be collected in student folders.

Systematic evaluation of student performance or products over time can provide teachers with important information regarding the adequacy of students' progress. This information is used, in turn, to make further adaptations in instruction to ensure learning is maximized for all students. When progress for one or more students is not acceptable, teachers can consider how to differentiate instruction to help students meet learning goals. For example, using the information from this chapter, a teacher could decide to increase academic engagement, increase review activities, improve teacher presentations, or make further adaptations in instructional materials. The Inclusion Checklist at the end of this chapter provides suggestions for improving instruction in specific areas in response to the outcomes of systematic evaluation of student performance.

Formative evaluation can be conducted on a variety of student outcomes, including regular "probes" of student skills and knowledge, evaluations of regularly implemented practice activities, and evaluation of homework products, as described in the following section.

STRATEGIES FOR
PROMOTING SYSTEMATIC EVALUATION OF INSTRUCTION

IMPLEMENT CURRICULUM-BASED MEASUREMENT *Curriculum-based measurement (CBM)* refers to regular assessment of student progress toward prespecified goals and objectives using frequently administered "probes" of student performance. For example, in reading instruction, Ms. Sánchez assigned Billy regular 1-minute timed readings of grade-appropriate text. For each timed reading, Ms. Sánchez calculated correct and incorrect words read per minute and placed the results on a chart that demonstrated Billy's progress over time. Teachers can evaluate progress on these measures to determine whether instructional modifications are necessary for the student to meet long-term goals. Curriculum-based measurement can also be used with a variety of student activities, as described next.

MONITOR AND EVALUATE PRACTICE ACTIVITIES Practice activities are intended to reinforce memory and comprehension of information that was gained in the lesson. If the lesson involves the teaching of skills, such as how to write the letters *p*, *d*, and *q* in cursive, practice activities are used to promote application and skill development and to ensure that the skills learned will be remembered. If the lesson involves the acquisition of content information, such as the causes of the War of 1812, practice activities promote recall, comprehension, and application objectives. The products of practice activities can provide teachers with formative evaluation of student understandings of and progress within the curriculum.

Practice activities are particularly helpful for students with disabilities because they provide more engaged time to ensure relevant concepts are fully understood. Often, practice activities are taken from worksheets or workbooks, but they can take other forms as well, such as practice with tutors or classroom peers, flashcards, computer programs or apps, group problem solving, or application tasks using relevant materials. Table 6.4 provides examples of appropriate practice activities.

Practice activities can be divided into *guided* and *independent* practice (Archer & Hughes, 2011; Rosenshine & Stevens, 1986). Guided practice takes place under teacher supervision and is most appropriate immediately after presentation of the initial concept. Students' rates of correct responding may be lower in this type of practice, and more teacher supervision is needed than when students practice independently. Guided practice is an example of **scaffolding** or **scaffolded supports**, that is, the practice of teachers providing more supports for students as they are introduced to a new skill, and then gradually removing supports as they master the skill. For example, students may have learned the purpose and steps of a cognitive strategy but still need teacher support as they learn to apply the strategy independently. Modeling, think-alouds, prompting, and immediate feedback are components of scaffolded supports that can be used in guided practice (IRIS Center, 2021). Independent practice uses indirect teacher supervision (some activities can be done as homework) and is undertaken when students' rates of correct responding are very high and when students can correct themselves by proofreading and checking their work.

Both types of practice are necessary to ensure that concepts are mastered and remembered and that learning is complete for all students. Request assistance from special educators for devising supplemental practice activities and determine when and where the extra practice can

TABLE 6.4 Appropriate Practice Activities

Lesson	Practice Activity
Writing words in cursive for handwriting practice	*Guided:* Teacher provides dictation; work is checked after every sentence. *Independent:* Students write from manuscript models, then check each other's work at the end of the period.
Solving quadratic equations from a formula	*Guided:* Students solve problems one at a time while the teacher monitors their execution of each step. *Independent:* Students solve problems independently, which are corrected by the teacher at the end of the activity.

occur—for example, study hall, other school periods, or homeroom. Any successful practice activity must meet several criteria. First, it must be directly relevant to the objective of the lesson. Second, practice activities must be used to enhance learning that occurred during the earlier part of the lesson; practice activities are usually not intended to introduce new information or skills. Students with disabilities or other diverse learning needs are particularly unlikely to learn new information from worksheet-type activities. Therefore, select practice activities that enhance and augment learning that has already occurred.

Practice activities also must be at an appropriate level of difficulty. If they are too difficult, students will not be able to work on them independently. If they are too easy, student learning will not be enhanced. Finally, it must be remembered that students soon tire of repetitive, worksheet-type activities. Keep the pace and enthusiasm level as high as possible during guided practice (e.g., "Everyone who thinks they have the answer, put your thumbs up!"). During independent practice, teachers should reinforce prompt, accurate, and neat responding and should keep the activity moving at an efficient pace.

Homework can often be considered a type of independent practice activity, undertaken outside the classroom. Because teachers are less likely to be available to answer questions when homework assignments are being completed, it is necessary that students completely understand assignments before taking them home. It may be helpful to complete the first part of the homework assignment in class, as a guided practice activity, to be certain every student knows how to complete the assignment. Homework completion can be facilitated by having students meet in groups at the beginning of class, under the direction of rotating group leaders, to record and provide peer feedback on homework assignments (Jakulski & Mastropieri, 2004; Sheridan, 2009).

When using guided and independent practice activities in the form of classroom and homework activities, evaluate student products carefully, and use this information as a formative evaluation to determine whether students are making adequate progress and, if not, how instruction will be modified and adjusted to meet student goals and objectives. For example, satisfactory performance on independent practice and homework activities indicates that students have learned the material and are functioning satisfactorily. Difficulties in independent practice and homework activities suggest that students need further examples, explanation, and guided practice.

FREQUENTLY REVIEW IMPORTANT MATERIAL AND EVALUATE STUDENT PERFORMANCE Near the end of a lesson, it is important to summarize what has been learned and review this information with students. It is also important to review information weekly and monthly to ensure that previously learned information is not forgotten and that students understand the relation between previous and current learning. Information gained from regular review can provide formative data on student learning and retention over time, as well as important information for possible instructional modifications.

Although frequent review is helpful for all students, it is particularly so for students with disabilities, who may be more likely to forget or not understand the relevance of previously learned material. This extra review and evaluation may be especially helpful before exams. As discussed in the section on redundancy, students with disabilities not only benefit from review, but they may require more review to be successful. Additional review of successfully learned content can be helpful in "**overlearning**" information, which can help promote long-term retention, application, and generalization.

Pearson eTextbook

Video Example 6.5

At the end of class, the teacher summarizes the lesson for her students. How does she address the *S* of the PASS variables?

Special education teachers can assist in providing additional review for students with disabilities and in brainstorming ideas for review. For example, you could make video recordings of the class engaged in activities during the instructional unit and then show them to students who may benefit from extra review of the information. Students can make "descriptive video scripts" (narrations describing everything in the video) to accompany the videos, either on paper or using an audio recorder. Students with visual impairments may benefit from these descriptions. Photographs, student journals (including photo and vocabulary journals), and daily logs can also provide material for review.

Using a digital camera and scanner, you and your students can create websites that contain their journals and portfolios. Web Workshop, SchoolMessenger, and WordPress, for example, contain many easy-to-use templates to help students create websites. Student performance on these activities can also provide the basis for formative evaluation.

Putting the PASS Variables to Work: Including Model Lesson Components in Instruction

Learning Objective 6.6 Define high-leverage practices and how they relate to the PASS variables.

The teacher effectiveness variables most closely related to high achievement have been described. But how do these variables appear in a real lesson? As you review the structure of a model lesson, observe how teacher effectiveness variables fit into a lesson sequence, as indicated in Figure 6.3.

CEC'S HIGH-LEVERAGE PRACTICES FOR SPECIAL EDUCATION

Over the past several years, education professionals and professional organizations across disciplines, such as reading, math, and science, have begun to identify a specific number of important teaching practices, referred to as "high-leverage" practices, that all teachers should employ in

Figure 6.3 Putting the PASS Components into a Model Lesson

Daily Review

- Begins with a review of previous learning.
- Provides teacher with information on how much was learned and retained from previous lessons.
- An example of daily review:
  "We have been studying ecosystems. Hold up your hand if you can tell me what an ecosystem is [calls on individual students]. Yesterday, we said that ecosystems have nonliving and living parts. We listed several nonliving parts of ecosystems. Write down on your paper three nonliving parts of an ecosystem. [The teacher waits for a minute or two, walking around the classroom to encourage students to think and write answers.] Now, who can tell me what you wrote . . ."

Statement of Purpose

- State the main objective of the current lesson in language meaningful to students.
- An example stated clearly and simply is the following:
  "Today we are going to learn about the living parts of ecosystems, and how they may interact with the nonliving parts."

Presentation of Information

- Present the content of the lesson using a variety of instructional materials, depending on the purpose and objectives of the lesson.
- Use the teacher presentation or SCREAM variables. That is, deliver content or procedures with structure, clarity, redundancy, enthusiasm, appropriate rate, and maximized engagement using questioning, feedback, and praise.

Guided Practice

1. Practice newly acquired content, skills, or concepts with teacher guidance.
2. Carefully monitor students and provide corrective feedback, as necessary.

Independent Practice

- Provide opportunities for students to repeat, apply, and extend information from the lesson more independently.

Formative Evaluation

- Evaluate students' independent performance.
- An example could take the form of a brief quiz: "See if you can solve the following problems independently."
- Results provide the basis for decisions about the adequacy of student progress and can be considered in planning future lessons.

their teaching. The Council for Exceptional Children (CEC), special education's major professional organization, approved in 2016 a set of these high-leverage practices (HLPs) for special education teachers (McLeskey et al., 2019). Included were important, research-based, high-frequency instructional practices that are broadly applicable and fundamental to effective teaching and intended for inclusion in K–12 teacher preparation programs (Billingsley et al., 2019; McLeskey et al., 2017). These practices can be considered appropriate for any teacher of students with disabilities, including all teachers in inclusive classes.

The CEC HLPs are grouped into four "practice types," including (1) collaboration, (2) assessment, (3) social/emotional/behavioral, and (4) instruction. The collaboration HLPs have already been discussed in Chapter 2. Assessment and social/emotional/behavioral HLPs are discussed in Chapter 12 and Chapter 8, respectively. The 12 instruction HLPs (using their assigned numbers) include the following:

Instruction

HLP 11: Identify and prioritize long- and short-term learning goals.

HLP 12: Systematically design instruction toward a specific learning goal.

HLP 13: Adapt curriculum tasks and materials for specific learning goals.

HLP 14: Teach cognitive and metacognitive strategies to support independence.

HLP 15: Provide scaffolded supports.

HLP 16: Use explicit instruction.

HLP 17: Use flexible grouping.

HLP 18: Use strategies to promote active student engagement.

HLP 19: Use assistive and instructional technologies.

HLP 20: Provide intensive instruction.

HLP 21: Teach students to maintain and generalize new learning across time and settings.

HLP 22: Teachers provide positive and constructive feedback to guide students' learning and behavior (learning focus) (McLeskey et al., 2019, p. 333; as summarized from McLeskey et al., 2017).

As can be seen, these HLPs for instruction are entirely consistent with the information provided in this chapter and throughout the text, and as such, seek to provide an important foundation for effective teaching practices that should be employed frequently by all special education teachers.

McLeskey et al. (2019) also described four important considerations to provide context for employing these essential HLPs in teacher preparation programs. First, these practices do not represent all that needs to be known about effective teacher practice. Additional knowledge about practice as well as knowledge of the content being taught, and how these practices are delivered in this context, is of critical importance. Additionally, teacher judgment, experience, and decision making based on ongoing data collection is important in dealing with unexpected events. Also of critical importance is ensuring that these practices are based on teacher knowledge of culturally responsive practice (Gay, 2018) and that effective special education teachers "value diverse perspectives and incorporate knowledge about students' backgrounds, culture, and language in their instructional decisions" (McLeskey et al., 2017, p. 17). Finally, this set of HLPs should be considered an important beginning and should be subjected to continual evaluation and refinement over time.

At present, the 22 high-leverage practices for special education approved by the Council for Exceptional Children provide an important foundation for special education teachers and a basis for continued efforts to improve teacher practice. Further discussion of HLPs is provided in Chapters 8 and 12.

Pearson eTextbook
Video Example 6.6
In this video, a science teacher supports student learning during independent practice. Notice how she provides scaffolded supports and adapts curriculum materials to support individuals in the classroom.

6 Summary

- Differentiated instruction means making adjustments to meet the needs of all learners in an inclusive classroom.
- The PASS variables stand for prioritize instruction; adapt instruction, materials, or the environment; systematically teach; and systematically evaluate the outcomes of instruction. The PASS variables provide a model for planning and delivering effective differentiated instruction in inclusive settings.
- *Prioritize* instruction to ensure that students are working on the most important objectives and that individual objectives reflect individual student needs.
  - — Planning for content coverage involves prioritizing instruction and is a critical component of teacher effectiveness. Teachers must carefully consider the role of prioritized objectives, scope and sequence, curriculum, and pacing of instruction over time.
- *Adapt* instruction, materials, and/or the environment to meet the specific characteristics of the student. Appropriately adapted instruction is a significant component of *differentiated instruction.*
  - — Types of learning include discrimination, factual, procedural, rule, conceptual, and problem solving/critical thinking.
  - — Levels of learning include acquisition, fluency, application, and generalization. Students can provide either identification or production responses.

  Consideration of types and levels of learning can be beneficial when planning appropriate differentiated instructional strategies.
- *Systematic teaching* refers to maximizing the effectiveness of your instruction and includes effective teacher presentations using the SCREAM variables.
  - — Effective teaching strategies include maximizing academic time on-task, developing effective teacher presentations, monitoring practice activities, providing opportunities for review, and completing formative evaluations. All are critical components of effective teaching for all students.
  - — Effective teacher presentations use the SCREAM variables: structure, clarity, redundancy, enthusiasm, appropriate rate, and maximized engagement. Additionally, effectively used questioning, feedback, and praise are all important contributors to student learning.
- *Systematic evaluation* refers to the continuous measurement of student progress toward meeting the specific objectives. Teachers should continuously monitor and adjust instruction based on their students' progress on formative evaluation measures.
  - — Curriculum-based measurement provides the basis for evaluating student progress in learning and determining whether student goals and objectives are being met.
  - — Practice activities provide opportunities for students to solidify and apply their learning and provide more opportunities for formative evaluation of student progress over time. Practice activities can include guided practice, in which teachers closely monitor student responding, and independent practice, in which students work more independently. Homework can be considered a type of independent practice activity.
  - — Frequent review promotes retention and long-term learning and provides teachers with opportunities to evaluate student learning. Students with disabilities may especially require frequent review of previously learned material.
- The PASS variables align with high-leverage practices and provide an important foundation for effective teaching.

PROFESSIONAL STANDARDS LINK:
Effective Differentiated Instruction for all Students

Information in this chapter links most directly to:

- CEC 2020 Initial Practice-Based Professional Preparation Standards for Special Educators (Initial K–12 standards) (see https://exceptionalchildren.org/standards/initial-practice-based-professional-preparation-standards-special-educators): 1 (Learner Development and Individual Learning Differences), 2 (Understanding and Addressing Each Individual's Developmental and Learning Needs), 5 (Supporting Learning Using Effective Instruction), and 6 (Supporting Social, Emotional, and Behavioral Growth)
- InTASC Standards (see https://www.ccsso.org/sites/default/files/2017-11/InTASC_Model_Core_Teaching_Standards_2011.pdf): 2 (Learning Differences), 3 (Learning Environments), 6 (Assessment), 7 (Planning for Instruction), 8 (Instructional Strategies)

EFFECTIVE DIFFERENTIATED INSTRUCTION FOR ALL STUDENTS

If you are having problems with classroom or individual academic achievement, have you examined the following? If not, see the pages listed here.

STRATEGIES FOR PLANNING CONTENT COVERAGE

- ☐ Base instruction on specific prioritized objectives, 138
- ☐ Plan instruction based on scope and sequence, 138–139
- ☐ Select an appropriate curriculum, 139
- ☐ Pace instruction effectively, 139–140

STRATEGIES FOR MAKING ADAPTATIONS

- ☐ Base adaptations on student characteristics, 141
- ☐ Base instructional adaptations on types of learning, 141–143
- ☐ Base instructional adaptations on the appropriate level of learning, 143–144
- ☐ Use principles of universal design for learning, 145–146

STRATEGIES FOR IMPLEMENTING THE SCREAM VARIABLES

- ☐ Structure your lessons, 147
- ☐ Promote clarity in your presentations, 147–148
- ☐ Employ redundancy effectively, 148
- ☐ Teach with enthusiasm!, 148–149
- ☐ Use an appropriate rate of presentation, 149
- ☐ Maximize academic engagement, 150

STRATEGIES FOR MAXIMIZING ON-TASK BEHAVIOR

- ☐ Use effective questioning techniques, 150–153
- ☐ Provide helpful feedback, 153–154
- ☐ Praise students frequently, 154

STRATEGIES FOR MAXIMIZING TIME FOR LEARNING

- ☐ Maximize on-task teacher behavior, 154
- ☐ Streamline transition activities, 154–155
- ☐ Reduce inappropriate verbalizations, 155–156
- ☐ Reduce inappropriate social behavior, 156
- ☐ Use flexible grouping, 156
- ☐ Use strategies for individual cases, 156

STRATEGIES FOR PROMOTING SYSTEMATIC EVALUATION OF INSTRUCTION

- ☐ Implement curriculum-based measurement, 158
- ☐ Monitor and evaluate practice activities, 158–159
- ☐ Frequently review important material and evaluate student performance, 159

Staci Kleinmaier/Offset/Shutterstock

CHAPTER 7

Response to Intervention and Multi-Tiered Systems of Support

LEARNING OBJECTIVES

After studying this chapter, you should be able to:

7.1 Identify the purpose and background of response to intervention (RTI) and multi-tiered systems of support (MTSS) and define schoolwide screening, progress monitoring and data-based decision making.

7.2 Describe Tier 1 instruction in general education and characterize progress monitoring.

7.3 Describe Tier 2 interventions, remediation, and collecting data for decision making.

7.4 Describe Tier 3 and individualized, intensive instruction and standards for evaluating academic progress.

7.5 Discuss fidelity of implementation and challenges with executing RTI strategies.

The Individuals with Disabilities Education Improvement Act (IDEA; 2004) regulations specified that states must not require discrepancy between ability and academic achievement as the means for determining learning disabilities (although individual schools may choose to use discrepancy). The regulations further specified that schools may use response to instructional intervention as part of the identification process. This means that schools may consider, as part of an evaluation process, the fact that students have not responded well to research-based instructional procedures. These regulations resulted in response-to-intervention (RTI) procedures that have been implemented throughout the country (O'Connor & Sanchez, 2011; O'Connor et al., 2017). Schools are now allowed to allocate up to 15% of their federal special education funding to implement RTI (IDEA, 2004).

In this chapter, we discuss the overall characteristics of RTI, followed by its components, including screening and progress monitoring, implementing the multiple tiers of intervention, and fidelity of implementation; we also present issues involving RTI. Although most attention on RTI to date has focused on early reading, RTI can be implemented in any academic or behavioral area at any grade level.

Some states prefer to use the term multi-tiered systems of support (MTSS) rather than RTI because they regard this term as more inclusive in addressing the needs of all students, including social/behavioral areas in addition to academic issues. In this text, we use RTI and MTSS interchangeably to refer to all multi-tiered systems of support, keeping in mind that the language and practices used in tiered systems across the nation vary among different state and local education authorities and even within individual schools (Berkeley et al., 2020; Vaughn & Bos, 2020).

What Is RTI?

Learning Objective 7.1 Identify the purpose and background of response to intervention (RTI) and multi-tiered systems of support (MTSS) and define schoolwide screening, progress monitoring and data-based decision making.

Response to Intervention (RTI) is a multilevel system of intervention designed to address different learning needs, reduce disability identification, and provide evidence for the appropriate identification of learning disabilities. It is intended to improve the overall quality of instructional offerings in schools and to integrate general education more completely with special education (Mellard & Johnson, 2008). It is also intended to provide appropriate services to students as soon as they are needed and prior to a formal referral to special education.

RTI is conceptually related to the Every Student Succeeds Act (ESSA) and the previous Elementary and Secondary Act (ESEA) and the No Child Left Behind Act, particularly its Reading First component, as well as IDEA. Common components include use of evidence-based practices (EBPs) (instructional practices that have been validated by research evidence, as described by Stoiber and Gettinger (2016), early intervention, and careful monitoring of progress. These common components are intended to integrate early identification and remediation with special education and to develop a more integrated framework to serve the interests of students with diverse learning needs (Mellard & Johnson, 2008).

STRATEGIES FOR IMPLEMENTING RESPONSE TO INTERVENTION

Response to Intervention (RTI) or multi-tiered systems of support provide multiple tiers of instruction based on the needs of students. The multilevel system of intervention is designed to address different learning needs, reduce disability identification, and provide evidence for the appropriate identification of learning disabilities. These tiers or levels occur in the general education classroom initially and may be delivered in different settings as the level of student need increases to require more intensive and possibly individualized instruction. For example, Tier 1 occurs in the general education classroom, Tier 2 occurs in small groups, and Tier 3 occurs in very small groups and possibly individualized. Tier 3 may also involve special education services. Some school districts have implemented standard protocol approaches to treatment while other districts use a problem-solving approach. The goal of the tiers is to meet the educational needs for all students by increasing the intensity of instruction.

MEETING STUDENTS' INSTRUCTIONAL NEEDS RTI attempts to integrate special education with general education more effectively by providing a series of instructional interventions of increasing intensity, as needed, to deliver the most effective instruction based on students' individual needs. Although many different models have been proposed and implemented, we discuss the three-tiered model most commonly employed in schools today (Berkeley et al., 2020). In this model, Tier 1 represents scientifically based instruction implemented in general education classrooms. Tier 2 is intended for those students for whom Tier 1 instruction is found to be insufficient, and it typically includes more intensive instruction delivered to smaller groups of students. Tier 3 is intended for those students for whom Tier 2 instruction is found to be insufficient, and it is often represented by a referral for placement in special education. Across all tiers, specific features may be represented differentially, such as (1) instructional group size, (2) duration and frequency of the intervention, (3) instructor training and focus of content or skills being taught, and (4) performance standards and frequency of progress monitoring (Mellard & Johnson, 2008). Although the focus of RTI to date has been primarily on reading (and to a lesser extent, math and writing), effective Tier 1 instruction can include all relevant content and skill areas. According to Mellard and Johnson (2008, p. 64), interventions at the different tiers are distinguished by specific features at each, including the following:

1. Size of instructional group (e.g., whole class, small group, individualized)
2. Performance standards, including mastery requirements
3. Frequency of delivery of the intervention

4. Overall duration of the specific intervention
5. Frequency of progress monitoring, using screening measures
6. Training of the teacher or other specialist in the target content area
7. Focus of the content or skills.

DOCUMENTING STUDENTS' PROGRESS As an alternative or supplement to discrepancy criteria for identifying learning disabilities, schools have been encouraged to employ an RTI approach in which general education teachers implement scientifically based practices and use curriculum-based measurement (see Chapter 12) to document student progress on a regular basis. Students who prove to be "treatment-resisters" (those who do not show adequate progress in spite of extra attention) or nonresponders may be eligible for more intensive interventions or referral to special education (Division for Learning Disabilities, 2007; Gresham, 2002; Scruggs & Mastropieri, 2002). These criteria are now specifically encouraged in the most recent IDEA amendments (Wright & Wright, 2005). Current multi-tiered approaches address learning and behavioral needs more generally (Jimerson, Burns, et al., 2016).

PREVENTING SCHOOL FAILURE RTI is intended to prevent school failure through early intervention, frequent progress monitoring, and a system of increasingly intensive evidence-based interventions (implemented in multiple levels, or *tiers*) for children who fail to respond sufficiently. In three-tiered systems, the differences in the level of instruction have been referred to as Tier 1, Tier 2, and Tier 3, or the universal, targeted, and tertiary levels of intervention. Increasing intensity is usually associated with (1) more systematic and explicit instruction, (2) increasing the number of instructional sessions and/or the length of the sessions (dosage), (3) incorporating behavioral and motivational supports, (4) working with students in smaller and more homogeneous groups, and (5) using instructors with greater expertise (Fuchs et al., 2017). As noted, students who are nonresponders to multiple tiers of intervention are referred to an individualized education program team for special eligibility consideration.

Pearson eTextbook
Video Example 7.1
The teacher in this video describes how RTI is used in her school. What factors do you think influence successful RTI implementation at her school?

TIERS OF INTERVENTION

Different versions of RTI include a varying number of tiers of intervention, although three is the most common (Berkeley et al., 2020; Fuchs et al., 2012). In addition, RTI varies with respect to the approach employed. Most present RTI models employ either a **problem-solving approach** or a **standard-treatment-protocol approach**. For example, in the problem-solving approach, at Tier 1, the teacher may confer with the student's parents/caregivers to help resolve the learning or behavioral problem. If the problem is not resolved, at Tier 2, the teacher may meet with the school-identified assistance team to identify the problem and plan an intervention. If the student does not succeed at this level, the agency staff may be called in to redesign and coordinate the implementation of Tier 3, which in many cases may include special education (Ervin, n.d.; Fuchs & Fuchs, 2006). However, because some schools employ more than three tiers of intervention, check with your own district regarding the specific number of tiers and how each is defined.

In the standard-treatment-protocol approach, Tier 1 could include some specific, evidence-based reading practice in the general education classroom, perhaps including classwide peer tutoring in reading, explicit instruction in reading skills and subskills where needed, and monitoring of student progress. For students who do not succeed in this program, Tier 2 might include standard small-group (four or five students) instruction in reading, perhaps for 30 minutes per day, 4 days per week, for 10–12 weeks. For students who do not succeed on this level, Tier 3 might include highly intensive, individualized instruction based on the student's individual needs, for example, 50 minutes of instruction 5 days per week with daily progress monitoring. In many cases, Tier 3 may include special education identification and placement (Berkeley et al., 2020). Special education referral can also be initiated by parents/caregivers or school personnel at any time. As with the problem-solving approach, there are presently many different versions of the standard-treatment-protocol approach (King & Coughlin, 2016). The *Diversity, Equity, and Inclusion in the Classroom* feature describes the importance of culturally appropriate teaching practices throughout the implementation of RTI.

Diversity, Equity, and Inclusion in the Classroom

Cultural Considerations for RTI/MTSS

The RTI/MTSS model holds promise for the achievement of all students by providing early attention and intervention programs to students from a diversity of backgrounds. The model also provides a vehicle for K–12 schools to foster racial and ethnic equity by employing culturally relevant pedagogy, culturally sensitive discipline strategies, and empowering students and caregivers/families who have been marginalized (Wells, 2020). For example, Klingner and Edwards (2006) proposed a model of culturally responsive literacy instruction employing RTI with four tiers of intervention (rather than the three tiers described in most of this chapter), as follows.

Tier 1: Culturally Responsive Instruction in the General Education Classroom

This tier should be characterized not only by evidence-based interventions but also interventions that are implemented by teachers who are familiar with models of culturally responsive teaching and aware of methods for promoting academic growth for the particular groups of students in their classrooms (e.g., Gay, 2018; Harry & Klingner, 2014). Gaining cultural competence, knowledge, and familiarity with teaching students of other races or ethnicities is first influenced by the varied professional and educational field experiences offered during preservice teacher training (Moore et al., 2021). Thereafter, teachers should engage in professional development, critical reflection, and activities that promote an understanding of the students and their families/caregivers in their school communities. Teachers with students who are English learners (ELs) should also be aware of evidence-based methods that are effective with these populations.

Tier 2: Intensive Supports

When students receiving culturally appropriate instruction are nevertheless still struggling to meet achievement expectations, culturally relevant Tier 2 instruction can provide intensive support to help promote student achievement. Culturally and linguistically responsive Tier 2 instruction should include content materials with varied perspectives and practices that demonstrate a teacher's knowledge of students' cultural, ethnic, and social identities (see Linan-Thompson et al., 2018). Because research support for culturally responsive Tier 2 interventions is less widely available, progress monitoring is of particular importance. Ongoing progress monitoring can be especially helpful in validating interventions when sufficient evidence-based practices are not available.

Tiers 2–3: Teacher Assistance Teams

This step, which can overlap as an additional component of Tier 2 interventions, involves the creation of a teacher assistance team or child study team. This team, which includes experts in the appropriate intervention area as well as experts in culturally responsive teaching, carefully considers the situation from the perspective of the individual student's academic, behavioral, and cultural needs; recommends specifically designed instruction; and follows up on the effectiveness of these interventions. For example, a team member with knowledge of the second language acquisition process and the role of native and English language proficiency in reading could support planning of Tier 2 reading interventions for ELs.

Tiers 3–4: Special Education

This tier (which is 3 in some districts or 4 in other districts) is tailored to the individual needs of the student, does not have a specific ending date, consists of intensive interventions, and is for students with persistent below-grade-level performance. Given the problem of overrepresentation of some nonwhite groups in special education (Harry & Klingner, 2014; U.S. Department of Education, 2020), it is of particular importance to determine that the evaluation for special education has been culturally fair and that all other possibilities for instructional supports have been implemented prior to referral.

Orosco and Klingner (2010) described the implementation of a three-tiered RTI model in one elementary school with a large proportion of enrolled ELs. The results of their investigation suggested the need for teachers to implement culturally appropriate instruction and revealed the challenges that occur when teachers are not appropriately trained in these practices. Over the last decade, research has provided guidelines toward a more equitable assessment of the language and literacy skills for ELs (e.g., Ortiz et al., 2018) as well as guidance for teachers when engaging in culturally responsive data-based decisions within an RTI framework (e.g., Kressler et al., 2020).

Discuss: How would you characterize a culturally relevant RTI framework?

MTSS may also focus on social behavior. Schoolwide behavior systems, such as **positive behavioral interventions and supports (PBIS)**, have been employed in multi-tiered prevention systems, or RTI for behavior management (Scheuermann & Hall, 2022). In this model, universal intervention (or Tier 1) for social skills might include schoolwide instruction of all students in positive social behaviors, targeted intervention (Tier 2) could be small-group instruction on specific social skills, and intensive (Tier 3) intervention could include individualized and comprehensive instruction in social skills.

Although not required by law, most states today are implementing some form of RTI, adopting MTSS models, or designing their own multitiered approach (Berkeley et al., 2020). The RTI process employs multiple components, including screening and progress monitoring, data-based decision making, implementation of multiple tiers of intervention, and fidelity of implementation. Where appropriate, RTI procedures can facilitate meeting Common Core State Standards (Jimerson, Stein, et al., 2016).

SCHOOLWIDE SCREENING, PROGRESS MONITORING, AND DATA-BASED DECISION MAKING

In order to implement RTI efficiently, schools must identify and apply measures to identify students who may be at risk for academic failure. It is hoped that schools will be able to identify potential learning problems early, so they can be treated before more serious academic consequences emerge. It is also important that student progress is monitored over time in order to evaluate the rate of progress or lack thereof. Both schoolwide screening and progress monitoring use student performance data to make programming decisions (Deno, 2016). Before engaging in RTI, educators begin with screening.

STRATEGIES FOR ADMINISTERING SCHOOLWIDE SCREENING

Schoolwide screening measures are intended to be easy to implement and score yet still provide a general picture of academic achievement in a particular area, such as reading. Screening measures may be brief and may be administered to all students at all grade levels. These screening measures should be used to indicate which students may require additional evaluation to determine if further assistance is needed. In addition to the screening held at least three times per year (fall, winter, and spring), multiconfirming data from formative assessments is recommended. These may be administered approximately three times per year and may utilize district benchmark assessments or measures such as the Dynamic Indicators of Basic Early Literacy Skills (DIBELS; University of Oregon, 2021), Gray Oral Reading Tests (GORT-5; Wiederholt & Bryant, 2011), the Oral Reading Fluency Test (Kaminski & Good, 1998), or the Gates-MacGinitie Reading Tests (MacGinitie et al., 2000), which may also be reviewed.

Pearson eTextbook

Video Example 7.2

In this video, a student from the University of Oregon talks about using the Dynamic Indicators of Basic Early Literacy Skills 8 system. Notice the varied subtest measures and how they are administered.
https://www.youtube.com/watch?v=unKMetSEFe4

SCREENING MEASURES For a screening measure to be effective, it must possess both *sensitivity* and *specificity*. Sensitivity means that it identifies students who are at risk for academic difficulties in the area being measured (i.e., "true positives"), and specificity means that students who perform acceptably on the measure are unlikely to have academic problems in that area ("true negatives"). Screening measures are constructed to minimize both "false positives" (students inaccurately identified as having academic problems) and "false negatives" (students inaccurately identified as not having academic problems). These measures also must be implemented with fidelity, meaning they should be implemented exactly as intended.

It is important that schools identify the greatest number of students who truly are having learning difficulties so that they can receive appropriate services; however, if too many students are incorrectly identified, school resources can be misdirected to unnecessary treatments. Therefore, it is important for schools to determine optimal "cut scores" or "cut points" (which represent the line between adequate and inadequate performance) that reliably identify students in need of assistance but nevertheless do not overidentify. Some schools employ more than one instance of the same measure, for example, repeated administrations of the DIBELS for students who did not score adequately on the first administration, or use of multiple measures such as aimsweb or the Phonological Awareness Literacy Screening (PALS) (Mellard & Johnson, 2008).

Pearson eTextbook

Video Example 7.3

In this video, a teacher describes the value of collecting and using data to enhance instruction for students with disabilities.
https://www.youtube.com/watch?v=bYurgW20Juw&list=UUQ2-KgUHhixii64uOQFEZUQ

PROGRESS MONITORING AND DATA-BASED DECISION MAKING Screening measures are appropriate for identifying which students may be in need of additional attention, whereas *progress monitoring* is appropriate for assessing how individual students are progressing. The ongoing process of collecting and analyzing student-level data to guide instructional decisions—like who needs intensive interventions—has been referred to as **data-based decision making (DBDM)** or **data-based individualization (DBI)** (Jung et al., 2018; National Center on Intensive Intervention, 2013). This process relies on progress monitoring. **Progress monitoring** involves collecting multiple performance measures over time, in order to (1) determine whether progress is appropriate and, if progress is not appropriate, (2) help identify more effective programs. Progress monitoring also can help determine whether individual students are not responding appropriately to different levels of instruction and may need to be evaluated for learning disabilities.

According to Mellard and Johnson (2008), progress monitoring must employ the following eight features to be effective within the context of RTI:

1. Progress monitoring is conducted in all tiers of instruction.
2. Progress-monitoring measures are based on and directly relevant to the curriculum, as well as the grade level and tier level of RTI.
3. In order to facilitate data collection, measures must be easy to administer and effective.
4. Results should be displayed in a manner that makes interpretation simple and efficient, for example, in charts or line graphs.
5. Rules for decision making must be determined for all aspects of progress-monitoring data, including cut scores for level (performance score), slope (change in performance over time), and percentage of mastery.
6. Cut scores and decision rules must have a clear rationale.
7. Progress-monitoring measures must be collected frequently enough to inform instructional and placement decisions. Frequency of administration may differ across different tiers, and guidelines for these should be specified.
8. Results of progress monitoring, although important, should be considered only one of several sources that inform instructional decision making.

Within the model of RTI, progress monitoring is undertaken at all tiers but in somewhat different ways. Consider how progress monitoring differs in the descriptions of Tier 1, Tier 2, and Tier 3.

Tier 1: Effective Instruction in General Education

Learning Objective 7.2 Describe Tier 1 instruction in general education and characterize progress monitoring.

Tier 1 instruction, often referred to as core instruction, occurs in general education classrooms and is delivered by general education teachers. The important principle regarding Tier 1 instruction is that it employs scientifically based instructional programs, as addressed in the ESSA and previously ESEA and its Reading First component. The terms **scientifically-based research**, or evidence-based research, refers to research that employs rigorous and systematic procedures; that employs experimental or quasi-experimental research designs and reliable, valid measures; and that has been subjected to review by experts, for example, in peer-reviewed journals (Sugai et al., 2010). This research forms the foundation for evidence-based practice—instructional methods proven to be effective by such scientific methods. Evidence-based practice can be in the area of social behavior as well as academic skills (Ihlo & Nantais, 2010).

Although RTI could address any content or skill area, much of the emphasis in RTI treatments has been placed on reading. In that area, the National Reading Panel's report (National Institute of Child Health and Human Development, 2000) focused on explicit and systematic instruction of five components of reading: phonemic awareness, phonics development, reading fluency, reading comprehension, and vocabulary development. In middle and high school classrooms, reading and writing are in all content areas, so core Tier 1 literacy instruction should incorporate vocabulary and comprehension strategies into daily instruction (Reed et al., 2012). In all content and skill areas, however, instruction should be scientifically based. This means that states, districts, and schools must identify evidence-based programs and instructional practices that can be implemented effectively in general education classrooms.

Differentiation of instruction can be employed as needed to address individual needs within the general education classroom. This can take many forms but could include physical placement and arrangement of the classroom; classwide peer tutoring; collaborative grouping based on student needs; individual assistance from teachers, paraprofessionals, or volunteers; modified instructional materials; or assistive technology such as accessible keyboards or text-to-speech (TTS) software. These instructional features can include universal design for learning (UDL) characteristics for assisting all students. Text with embedded text-to-speech capacity is a good UDL example because students can access the speech component when needed. Other examples involving UDL include visual presentations, Internet links to definitions, enlarged print, and multimedia presentations (Hall et al., 2012). The overall feature of Tier 1 instruction is that the teacher is leading the general education classroom, and all students are proceeding through a specified curriculum, using scientifically based practices.

In this text, we present instructional strategies and materials that are appropriate for addressing diverse needs in the general education classroom and that are supported by scientific research. To this extent, the entire book is devoted to effective instruction in general education classrooms, or Tier 1 instruction; however, many of the strategies are also appropriate for Tier 2 or Tier 3 instruction if employed in a different context.

Pearson eTextbook
Video Example 7.4
In this video, a teacher is engaging students in word study. Why is this lesson an example of Tier 1 instruction?

FEATURES OF TIER 1 INSTRUCTION

In the case of Tier 1 instruction, then, the instructional group size would be the entire classroom. Performance standards would be those benchmarks determined by the states and school districts to be appropriate indicators of grade-level performance. These indicators are screened frequently throughout instruction, and teachers make instructional modifications to accommodate individual students. Screening measures are implemented at least every week or two, with students at risk being monitored more frequently. Students remain in Tier 1, of course, throughout the school year, unless more intensive procedures are indicated; instruction is provided by general education teachers according to school schedules (e.g., daily). Instruction reflects the school's content standards for the full instructional program (Mellard & Johnson, 2008).

Pearson eTextbook
Video Example 7.5
In this video, an educator gives an overview of Tier 1. What are the responsibilities of a teacher at this tier?

STRATEGIES FOR IMPLEMENTATION OF TIER 1 INSTRUCTION

Tier 1 implementation is not simply "general education as usual." Although Tier 1 instruction does involve general educators teaching the school's content standards in general education classrooms, it also requires substantial changes in school structure and staff roles. Instruction must include universal screening and progress monitoring, based on common standards and program coherence. In this case, all elements, including curriculum, instruction, intervention, and assessment, are aligned both horizontally (across curriculum) and vertically (across grade levels) throughout the schools. Schools, in turn, must work collaboratively to integrate all elements of this system coherently and to address the needs of both students and teaching staff (in terms of professional development). Reed et al. (2012) suggest having a five- to eight-member RTI leadership team at the secondary level and assigning each member a primary responsibility towards RTI implementation. The team could include the principal, special education coordinator, counselor, math/science teacher, English learner teacher, and so on.

PROGRESS MONITORING Progress monitoring is a component of each level of tiered instruction. Its purpose is to ensure whether or not individual students are making adequate progress in the general education classroom. In some cases, students have been returned to the general education classroom from a higher-tier placement, and progress monitoring can help determine whether the general classroom is effectively meeting the student's needs.

TABLE 7.1 Second-Grade Descriptive Statistics for Oral Reading Fluency Scores by Season

Season	Fall	Winter	Spring
10th percentile	23	35	43
25th percentile	36	59	72
50th percentile	50	84	100
75th percentile	84	109	124
90th percentile	111	131	148

Source: Hasbrouck and Tindal (2017), p. 10.

Progress monitoring at Tier 1 differs from screening in its overall purpose and the frequency of administration. An entire classroom may be given a general screening measure three times per year. After these measures are given, individual students may be determined to be in need of further evaluation. For example, Hasbrouck and Tindal (2017) have determined that students accurately read at an average rate of 84 words per minute by the middle of second grade (see Table 7.1). A screening measure may identify some students who read below 59 words per minute, which is the 25th percentile according to Hasbrouck and Tindal's norms (updated norms from Hasbrouck & Tindal, 2006). Students scoring below the 25th percentile may then be provided with more frequent progress monitoring (e.g., weekly, three times per week) in order to determine whether their lowered *level* of performance is also accompanied by a reduced *slope* of performance.

Consider an example in which screening identified that three students in a class (Tanya, Phil, and Jamal) scored below the 25th percentile (a lower level of performance) on oral reading fluency. These students were then provided with weekly progress monitoring. Figure 7.1 shows individual progress in the fall for words correct per minute. The data points were charted using easycbm.com. The orange line indicates the level of performance at the 25th percentile and the gray line represents the 50th percentile. Performance data demonstrated that Tanya was responding well to instruction and making good progress (a positive performance slope), so current instruction was continued along with further progress monitoring. However, Phil's and Jamal's reduced levels of performance were also found to be associated over time with a reduced rate of progress (slope), so placement in a Tier 2 program was considered.

CURRICULUM-BASED MEASUREMENT Performance monitoring can be conducted using curriculum-based measurement (CBM). Using CBM, skills from the entire year's curriculum are sampled in alternate forms. Web-based versions of CBM in reading and math include DIBELS (2006). Other CBM materials are shown in Table 7.2.

The Intervention Central website (interventioncentral.org) provides a system for generating CBM in reading, writing, and math. An area is identified (e.g., early reading measures such as letter and word reading; early math, math calculations and concepts; written expression), the parameters are set (e.g., grade level, number of items), and the calculators in the website generate CBM measures for individualized purposes. These calculators can be used for progress monitoring for individual school purposes. This site also contains links to many CBM manuals, training materials, assessments, and scoring guides.

THE DYNAMIC INDICATORS OF BASIC EARLY LITERACY SKILLS DATA SYSTEM DIBELS keeps track of progress on measures for students, classes, schools, and school districts. Reports can be created as soon as scores are recorded, which can facilitate prompt decision making. The DIBELS Data System is operated by the Center on Teaching and Learning at the University of Oregon in Eugene.

Apps are available to assist teachers with recording data. *BehaviorSnapLENS* (SuperPsyched, LLC) provides options for recording interval, frequency, duration, and ABC (antecedent, behavior, consequence) data. *iBAA* (Future Help Designs) enables recording of qualitative and

Figure 7.1 Weekly Progress Monitoring for Tanya, Phil, and Jamal

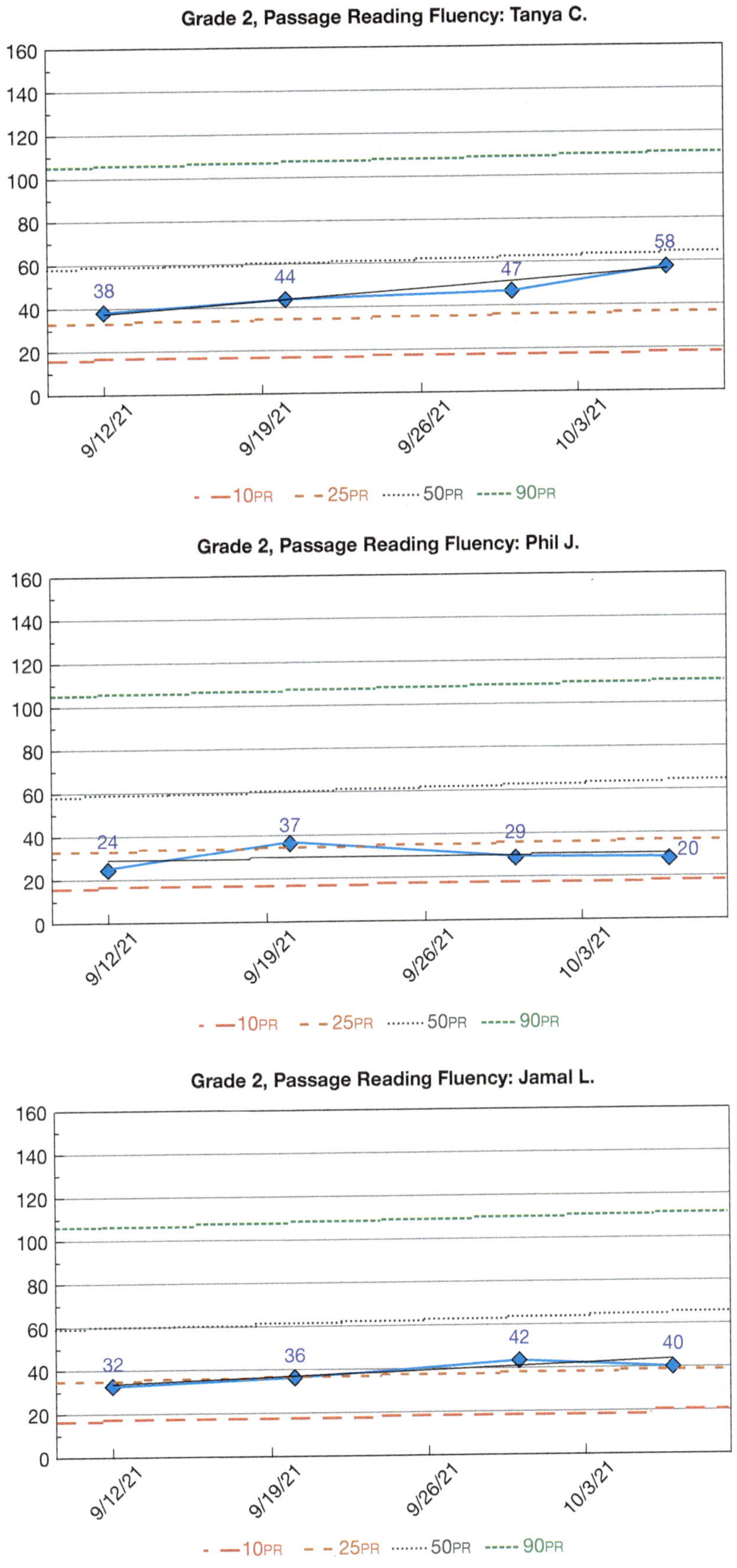

TABLE 7.2 CBM Measures for Progress Monitoring

Measure	Areas	Publisher
DIBELS Data System	Early reading skills	University of Oregon dibels.uoregon.edu
Reading Fluency Progress Monitor (RFPM)	Reading fluency	Read Naturally readnaturally.com
aimsweb	Reading, writing, math, social behavior	Pearson aimsweb.com
EdCheckup	Reading, writing, math	EdCheckup edcheckup.com
Vanderbilt CBM Materials	Reading, math	Vanderbilt University Peabody #328 230 Appleton Place Nashville, TN 37203-5721
STAR Assessments	Reading, writing, math	Renaissance Learning renlearn.com
Test of Silent Word Reading Fluency (TOSWRF)	Word reading	ProEd proedinc.com
Test of Word Reading Efficiency (2nd ed.) (TOWRE-2)	Sight-word reading, phonetic decoding	Western Psychological Services wpspublish.com
Yearly ProgressPro	Reading, language arts, math	McGraw-Hill ctb.com

cumulative observations, interval and functional behavior, and environmental assessments, as well as summarizing of data in reports. The *Apps for Education* feature provides additional relevant resources.

TEACHER RESPONSIBILITIES Teachers must be more oriented to scientifically based practices, must work to actively conduct screening and progress monitoring, and must systematically attend to the needs of individual students who may not be making adequate progress. Teachers will need to work collaboratively with others to ensure a seamless system of instructional delivery across tiers and, ultimately, with special educators when the need arises. Teacher responsibilities include timely administration of screening measures, charting and evaluating results over time, identifying students in need of additional assessments or accommodations, and providing information to parents/caregivers when appropriate. Support staff and specialist responsibilities include assisting the general education teachers in implementation efforts, data collection, and identification of students in need of additional attention. Administrators will be responsible for leading the effort across the school; providing needed resources, including professional development activities; ensuring the program is being implemented faithfully; working with committees to identify screening tools; monitoring the performance of entire classrooms; reviewing data to inform decision making; and integrating this system with multiple requirements, such as those of the ESSA (Mellard & Johnson, 2008; Reed et al., 2012).

In some ways, Tier 1 is the most important tier—it is the most cost-effective, addresses all students, covers all relevant school content, and represents the first gate for more intensive levels of service, when needed (Denton & Vaughn, 2010; Mellard & Johnson, 2008). Tier 1 provides the broad foundation for all further educational interventions.

Computer-Based CBM for Progress-Monitoring Tools

Software has been developed to facilitate progress monitoring using curriculum-based measurement (CBM). Such software can increase accuracy and save time in implementing CBM, scoring and recording data, identifying trends, and making instructional decisions. Descriptions of some available programs follow.

The *EcoBehavioral Assessment Systems Software* was designed based on research at the Juniper Gardens Children's Project of the University of Kansas to assess the quality of core instruction. For example, student behaviors and academic instruction during Tier 1 classroom observations are analyzed to provide an overall assessment of core instruction relating to specific students.

The National Center on Intensive Intervention (NCII; 2021) has published charts with information about evidence-based academic and behavior progress-monitoring tools for consumers to select that best meet their individual needs. NCII's charts include ratings on performance level standards (e.g., validity, reliability), growth standards, and usability (see https://intensiveintervention.org/sites/default/files/pdf/APM_Updates_2021_508.pdf).

The user can filter the results by grade level and subject area and compare the monitoring tools. Below is a sample of the academic progress-monitoring tools.

The *DIBELS Data System* is a web-based database that can be used by schools and districts to enter the results of student assessments. The data system can also create reports based on these scores. Measures include the following:

- DIBELS® (*Dynamic Indicators of Basic Early Literacy Skills*) 8th edition
- IDEL (*Indicadores Dinámicos del Éxito en la Lectura*) for native Spanish speakers
- DIBELS® Next, a new version of reading assessments
- The easyCBM Math program
- One local or state outcome measure.

Kearns (2016) developed an Excel template that allows users to collect all of the academic progress-monitoring data for multiple students across multiple measures and then easily graph student progress. School personnel can access this tool on the NCII site and set individualized instructional goals for students.

	Elementary (K–5)	Middle School (6–8)	High School (9–12)
Reading			
easyCBM Passage Reading Fluency	X	X	
easyCBM Proficient Reading (comprehension)	X	X	
easyCBM Vocabulary	X	X	
Star Reading		X	X
Acadience Reading K–6 (DIBELS Next®)	X	X	
Mathematics			
Acadience Math Computation	X	X	
aimswebPlus Math Number Sense Fluency	X	X	
FAST CBMmath (automaticity)	X		
STAR Math	X	X	X
Spelling/Written Expression			
Istation's Indicators of Progress	X	X	

Pearson eTextbook

Video Example 7.6

The educator in this video provides an overview of Tier 2 interventions. Why is collaboration a key component of effective RTI implementation?

Tier 2: Intervention to Remediate

Learning Objective 7.3 Describe Tier 2 interventions, remediation, and collecting data for decision making.

Tier 1 instruction is intended to ensure that students are receiving high-quality instruction in general education classrooms. If progress monitoring reveals that individual students are not making adequate progress over time in the general education classroom, it may be appropriate to consider a more intensive level of instruction, represented by Tier 2. This instruction should be implemented as soon as it is determined that individual students are not progressing adequately. Tier 2 instruction includes several features parallel to those of Tier 1 instruction (Powell & Fuchs, 2015; see also Vaughn & Bos, 2020).

FEATURES OF TIER 2 INSTRUCTION

Tier 2 instruction may be delivered to small groups of students (e.g., two to five) who have demonstrated similar areas of difficulty. This instruction may take place in a separate area in the general education classroom or in a separate setting, and it is generally delivered by specialized instructional personnel (e.g., reading specialist, speech–language specialist). Like Tier 1 instruction, Tier 2 instruction employs scientifically based instructional programs oriented specifically to the students' areas of difficulty. Typically, specialized curriculum materials are used, instruction is more intensive and focused, and progress monitoring is conducted more frequently (e.g., one to three times per week).

Tier 2 instruction may be provided over an extended time period (e.g., 9 to 12 weeks in length), from three to four times a week, in 30- to 60-minute sessions. Longer time periods may be expected to help promote greater learning gains. Although Tier 2 instruction can take many forms, it is generally considered that it will include direct, systematic teaching to specific targeted objectives, including explicit presentation of information, modeling, provision of multiple examples, and direct, immediate feedback; multiple opportunities for student responding; relevant practice activities; appropriate pacing of instruction; and continuous monitoring of student performance.

It is generally considered that students in Tier 2 instruction will continue to receive Tier 1 instruction in the same content or skill area in general education classrooms. Therefore, Tier 2 instructors must ensure that their instruction is directly relevant to Tier 1 instruction and that continuous monitoring of Tier 1 performance is implemented to provide evidence of educational benefit. The *Research Highlight* provides an example.

STRATEGIES FOR
IMPLEMENTATION OF TIER 2 INSTRUCTION

Overall, two different approaches have been developed to implement Tier 2 instruction: the problem-solving and the standard-protocol approaches (Fuchs et al., 2003, 2010). Although the differences between these two approaches are substantial, both aim to provide high-quality, specialized instruction intended to facilitate adequate achievement in general education classrooms.

PROBLEM-SOLVING APPROACHES Most schools have teams of teachers and specialists referred to by various terms, such as *multidisciplinary teams*, *student instructional teams*, or *student study teams*. In problem-solving approaches, these teams meet, consider evidence regarding student academic progress, and, when needed, outline a plan to address learning challenges. When members of the RTI team are problem solving, general and special education teachers can address the following questions, as described by Hunt and Little (2014):

- What do we know about the problem or concern?
- Why is the student having this problem?
- What can be done to address the problem or improve performance?
- Has the intervention plan been effective and how do I know?

States such as Nebraska and North Carolina have implemented problem-solving approaches (Berkeley et al., 2009). In Tilly's (2003) Heartland Early Literacy Project (Project

Research Highlight

A Tier 2 Reading Intervention for Fourth-Grade Students

Stevens and colleagues (2020) examined the efficacy of a Tier 2 intervention in content-area reading (social studies) for fourth-grade students identified as struggling readers and/or those who were receiving special education services in the general education classroom. Almost 200 students across 12 schools participated and each school was assigned to one of three conditions in a multi-tiered system of support. Condition A included alignment between Tier 2 intervention and Tier 1 instruction. In condition B, Tier 2 intervention did not align with Tier 1 instruction. In the third condition, both tiers were not specified by the researchers. In sum:

Condition A: Tier 2 intervention (intensified STRIVE) aligned with Tier 1 instruction (STRIVE)
Condition B: Tier 2 intervention (intensified STRIVE) not aligned with Tier 1 instruction (BAU); and
Condition C: Tier 2 and Tier 1 instruction was social studies instruction with business as usual (BAU).

The quasi-experimental design sought to compare student performance across these three conditions on measures of reading comprehension, vocabulary, and content knowledge using content-area text. Apart from the BAU condition, Tier 1 instruction was Strategies for Reading Information and Vocabulary Effectively or STRIVE which encompassed teaching vocabulary with semantic maps and context clues for word learning, activating background knowledge prior to reading, identifying main ideas of text during reading, combining main ideas for a summary paragraph, discussing text and answering varying question types (i.e., who, what, where, when, why, how), and learning how to identify evidence in text to support answers. Following professional development, fourth-grade teachers taught STRIVE in three units of twelve, 45-minute lessons (total of 36 lessons) taught two times a week with grade-level informational text.

Tier 2 intervention was an intensified version of STRIVE in which trained tutors provided 30 minutes of instruction using content-area text in groups of five to six students, three times a week, for a total of 54 lessons. The goal of Tier 2 intervention was to supplement STRIVE instruction and intensify the intervention by providing students with ample practice, high-quality feedback, and a repeated reading routine to support students with accessing grade-level text.

Students in Condition A in which Tier 2 intervention was highly aligned with Tier 1 instruction outperformed students in the nonaligned intervention condition and those in the BAU condition on proximal measures of reading comprehension, content knowledge, and vocabulary outcomes. However, there were no differences in scores from pretest to posttest on the standardized measures of reading comprehension and vocabulary.

Cohesion or overlap between Tier 1 and Tier 2 is not currently typical practice in multi-tiered systems of support and may present some practical challenges for implementation; however, alignment among tiers may maximize the intensity that is needed for students with disabilities. Although this study and Fien et al. (2015) provide preliminary support for the benefits of aligning Tier 1 and Tier 2 instruction for elementary students, there is a need for additional research regarding the efficacy and fidelity for aligning tiers of instruction in both elementary and secondary schools.

QUESTIONS FOR REFLECTION

1. Why do you think students in the aligned condition in this study improved performance on reading comprehension, vocabulary, and content knowledge in comparison to the other conditions?
2. What may a school need to consider if Tier 1 instruction and Tier 2 intervention are to be closely and intentionally aligned?

HELP), which was successful with reducing the number of children who were placed in special education, some of the scientifically based strategies include CBM and evaluation, functional analysis of behavior and positive behavioral supports, direct instruction, peer-assisted learning strategies, and learning strategy instruction. Overall, the distinguishing feature of Tier 2 problem-solving approaches is in the individualized evaluation and planning for each student's specific needs. The approach is most likely to be effective if it combines scientifically based interventions, continuous progress monitoring with information from a variety of sources, effective collaborative relationships in the schools, and direct connection to regular classroom instruction (Mellard & Johnson, 2008). The *Research Highlight* describes the implementation of a Tier 2 intervention with fourth-grade students at risk for reading failure.

STANDARD-PROTOCOL APPROACHES Using the standard-protocol approach, students are grouped according to instructional need and provided with interventions that have been validated through experimental research, for example, specific strategies for improving reading fluency (Steinle et al., 2022) and reading comprehension at the elementary and secondary levels (e.g., Berkeley et al., 2010; Filderman et al., 2022). These are intensive instructional interventions intended to remediate specific skill deficits. Schools implementing such approaches must choose an effective program or intervention and indicate that their interventions replicate the intensity, duration, frequency, and procedures of interventions validated in previous research. They should also describe the skills addressed, the place of instruction, appropriate instructional materials, and means for assessing progress (Fuchs et al., 2003; Mellard & Johnson, 2008).

Most efforts to date to develop standard protocols of instruction have addressed reading, whereas other areas such as writing and math are continuing to be developed (Fuchs et al., 2016). In the absence of specific standardized protocols, schools can implement practices that have been demonstrated to enhance performance in different areas. These practices include self-monitoring and questioning, direct instruction, strategy instruction, and appropriate feedback and are described in more detail throughout this text.

CONSIDERATIONS IN IMPLEMENTATION OF TIER 2 INSTRUCTION

Given the small group size and intensive procedures of Tier 2 instruction, appropriate allocation of resources such as funding for professional development may prove to be an important consideration. For example, selected interventions for Tier 2 should be delivered by interventionists who are knowledgeable about ways to individualize and intensify instruction. Additionally, challenges may be faced in the areas of implementation across the various grade and content areas represented in the schools. Although much progress has been made in the area of early reading, additional work needs to be done in other skill and content areas at other grade levels. In addition, appropriate implementation of Tier 2 instruction will require substantial efforts in professional development; recruiting and funding new staff; effective scheduling of Tier 2 instruction; implementing skill-monitoring procedures throughout Tiers 1 and 2; and coordinating all aspects of RTI across grade levels and teaching staff into a single, coherent program (Mellard & Johnson, 2008). Although the challenges of implementation are great, the results could bring increased achievement for all students throughout the grade levels.

PROGRESS MONITORING When placed in Tier 2 programs, all students may be provided with frequent progress monitoring. Here, the purpose is a little different. Progress monitoring at this level can help determine whether the student has made adequate progress to resume placement in the Tier 1 setting (the general education classroom). If progress is not adequate, the information may be used to adapt the intervention. Using the earlier example, progress monitoring at Tier 2 indicated that Phil was making adequate progress, so no instructional changes were made. Jamal, however, was making less progress, so it was decided to adapt his reading materials and provide more time for instruction. If progress monitoring reveals that Tier 2 instruction, after instructional modifications, is not resulting in adequate progress, evaluation for referral to Tier 3 (special education) may be appropriate. Figure 7.2 shows how progress-monitoring data can be calculated to indicate whether adequate progress is being made in Tier 2 interventions. After a period of ineffective Tier 1 instruction (slope $= 0.125$), a Tier 2 intervention was implemented; after this 9-week Tier 2 intervention, much greater progress was evident (slope $= 2.0$). These data can be compared with longer-term expectations to determine whether individual students should be returned to Tier 1, continued in Tier 2 interventions, or considered for special education placement in Tier 3.

CALCULATING SLOPES How are slopes calculated for purposes of progress monitoring? One approach is Tukey's (1977) method of "tri-split slopes," as shown in Figure 7.3 (see also Fuchs & Deshler, 2007; Hosp et al., 2016). Using this method, the number of total data points is divided into thirds (or the closest approximation when the number is not an exact multiple of 3). Examining the first third of the data points, the median value of the three is placed at the

Figure 7.2 Calculating Slopes Across Interventions

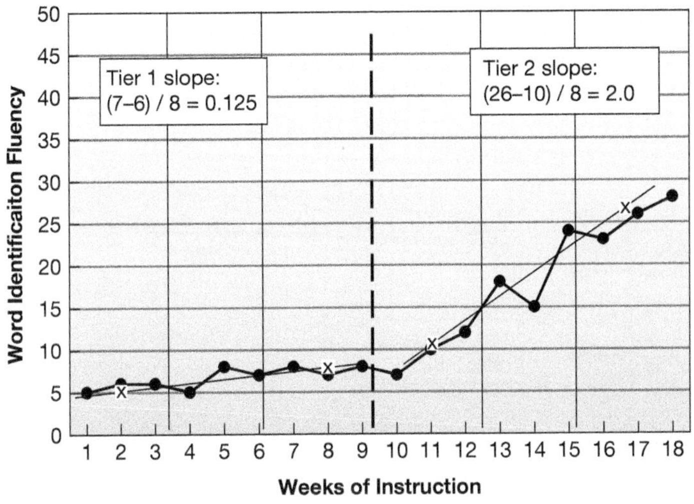

1. The slope for Tier 1 was calculated by dividing the first 9 data values into thirds, and identifying the median value and median week for the first and third, in this case 6 and 7. Subtract 6 from 7, and divide the difference by (9–1), or 8, to obtain (7–6)/8 = 1/8 = 0.125.

2. For the second set of 9 weeks (Tier 2 intervention), the median value/week of the third section is 26 and the median value/week of the first section is 10. Therefore, the slope is (26–10)/8 = 16/8 = 2.0.

Figure 7.3 Calculating Slopes: An Example

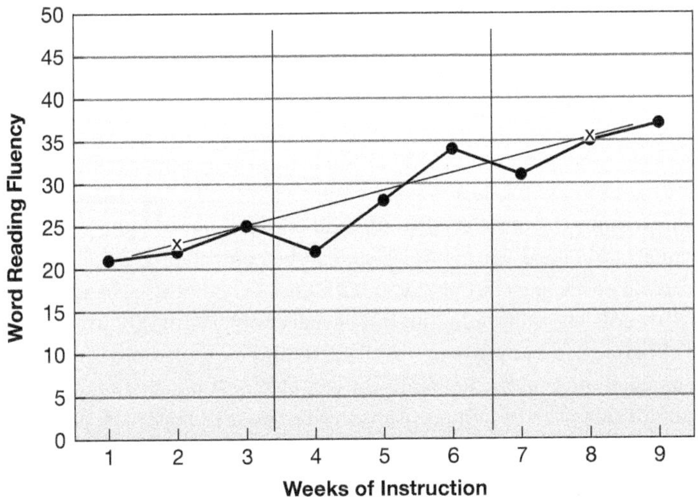

Steps in Calculating Slope According to the Tukey (1977) Method:

1. Divide graphed data points into three equal (or roughly equal) sections.
2. For each of the first and last sections, identify the median (middle) data value (in this case, 22 and 35), and the median time value (in this case, weeks 2 and 8). Draw an "x" at the median value at the median time.
3. Draw a line connecting the two "x"s, and extend the line through the data values.
4. Slope can then be calculated by subtracting the median data point of the first section from the median data point from the third section, and dividing the difference by one less than the total number of data points. In this case, subtract 22 from 35 (= 13), and divide 13 by 9 – 1, or 8, so 13/8 = 1.625. Therefore, slope equals:

$$\frac{\text{Median value from 3}^{\text{rd}}\text{ section} - \text{Median value from 1}^{\text{st}}\text{ section}}{\text{Total number of data points} - 1}$$

Figure 7.4 Growth Rate and Long-Term Goals

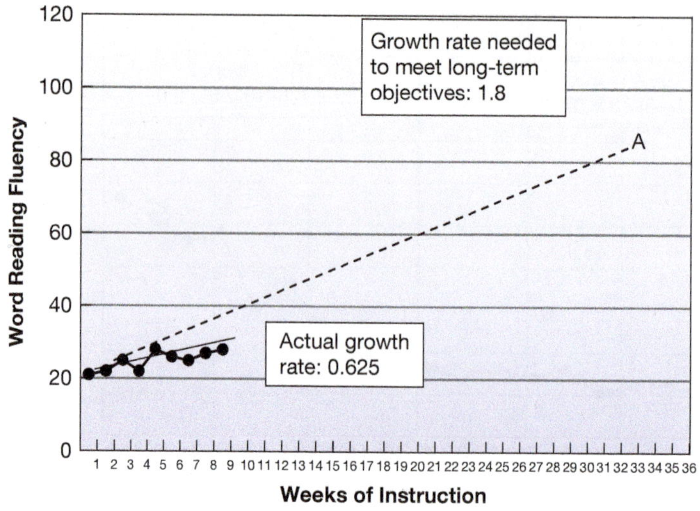

In the first 9 weeks of instruction, Darcy's reading fluency has grown from 22 to only 27 words per minute, a growth rate (slope) of 0.625. If Darcy's long-term goal (A) is to read grade-level materials at 80 words per minute (wpm) by the end of the year, she will need to have a growth rate of 1.8.

Actual growth rate: 27 wpm – 22 wpm = 5 wpm, divided by 8 (9 weeks – 1) = 0.625

Projected growth rate (goal line): 85 wpm – 22 wpm = 63 wpm, divided by 35 weeks = 1.80

median (in this case, the second) observation point, where the *x* is placed (in the case of an even number of data points, the point halfway between the two "middle" values). In examining the final third of the data points, an *x* is also placed at the median value, at the median (in this case, eighth) observation point. Then a line is drawn between the two *x*'s to indicate the slope. The numeric value of the slope can be calculated by subtracting the first median value from the third median value (in this case, 35–22) and dividing the difference by 1 less than the total number of data points (in this case, 9 – 1), to give a slope of 13/8, or 1.625. In the present case, it means that this student is increasing the number of words read correctly per minute by 1.625 words per week. Slope estimates obtained in this way then can be compared with published norms of progress in reading. They can also be compared with established goals. For example, Darcy is expected to read 80 words per minute by the end of the school year, as shown in Figure 7.4. The obtained slope of her actual reading progress (0.625) can be compared with the slope that would be necessary to reach the goal by the end of the year (1.80). If the obtained slope does not appear to be adequate for this purpose, a modification of methods or materials, or placement in a Tier 2 program, can be planned.

ASSESSING PROGRESS Stecker et al. (2005) reviewed literature on the effectiveness of curriculum-based measurement and concluded that progress should be assessed twice per week during Tier 2 interventions. Research literature suggests that teachers select progress-monitoring schedules that are accurate and timely for making individualized instructional decisions (Gesel & Lemons, 2020; Jenkins et al., 2017). These data should be charted and reviewed regularly. These reviews should employ preexisting criteria to determine whether the intervention is adequate or whether further modifications are necessary.

Mellard and Johnson (2008, p. 50) described one use of the DIBELS (2006) and Read Naturally (readnaturally.com) reading and comprehension probes for a Tier 2 elementary-grade program. For first grade, the DIBELS weekly assessments included fluency measures of letter naming, phoneme segmentation, nonsense-word reading, and oral reading. For second grade, nonsense-word reading and oral reading fluency were assessed. In third through fifth grades, oral reading fluency was assessed. These progress data were compared with an "aim line" or "goal line" for each student, drawn on a chart from present performance to the student's longer-term aims. If the student had three consecutive weekly data points that were above this aim line, the goal was increased until the student was able to perform at the grade-level benchmarks. Conversely, if three consecutive weekly data points were below this line, instructional modifications were undertaken. If three additional weekly data points continued below the aim line, even after modifications, the student was considered for a Tier 3 placement.

DECISION MAKING Tier 2 instruction can be implemented over a period of 9 to 12 weeks during which student progress is monitored in both the Tier 2 setting and in the general education classroom. Near the end of the implementation period, a determination must be made regarding the effectiveness of the Tier 2 instruction. If the student's progress in the Tier 1 setting is now regarded as adequate, the student resumes being served in the general education classroom, and Tier 2 services are discontinued. If, however, progress is not regarded as adequate at the end of the instructional period, one of two decisions must be made. If the student is making progress but has not yet achieved at the level of the student's peers, additional Tier 2 instruction may be implemented. If, however, the level of functioning and progress is markedly different from that of the student's peers, Tier 3 services are considered and a referral for special education may be warranted.

Tier 3: Individualized, Intensive Instruction

Learning Objective 7.4 Describe Tier 3 and individualized, intensive instruction and standards for evaluating academic progress.

If progress of students in Tier 2 is not satisfactory and additional Tier 2 instruction is not considered appropriate, students may be moved into an even more intensive level of instruction. Tier 3 involves intensive, individualized (or very small-group) instruction that is implemented more frequently and over a longer period of time than Tier 2 interventions and is focused directly on precise learning objectives (Powell & Fuchs, 2015; Vaughn et al., 2010; Vaughn & Wanzek, 2014). Tier 3 may or may not involve referral to special education, depending on state and local guidelines. In some cases, referral to special education may be a component of Tier 3 in a three-tiered system; in others, referral may be part of a fourth or higher tier in schools where more than three tiers are employed.

Pearson eTextbook
Video Example 7.7
This researcher provides an overview of Tier 3 interventions. Tier 3 is considered special education in many RTI models.
https://www.youtube.com/watch?v=wpkbAIh0e1I

STRATEGIES FOR IMPLEMENTATION OF TIER 3 INSTRUCTION

Whereas Tier 1 instruction occurs in the general education class and Tier 2 instruction occurs in small groups (in addition to core instruction), Tier 3 instruction is implemented individually or in very small groups (or in inclusive classrooms) to meet specific goals and objectives. If students are placed in special education, instruction may address any number of skills and content areas, as well as social behavior (as identified on IEPs), and is usually associated with intensive instruction using specialized materials.

USE INTENSIVE, INDIVIDUALIZED INSTRUCTION Special education for students with disabilities is typically associated with intensive, systematic, and explicit instruction (Archer & Hughes, 2011). "Use intensive instruction," (high-leverage practice [HLP] 20) is intended to refer generally to the type of instruction found in Tier 3 settings (see Chapter 6) (McLeskey et al., 2017). This can include task analysis (breaking the task or skill down into teachable, sequential steps), direct instruction (explicit modeling and guided practice with direct drill and practice of target objectives), and strategy instruction (explicit provision of cognitive routines needed to execute a task) (Hughes et al., 2017; Powell & Fuchs, 2015). Special education can also include teacher modeling, frequent feedback, overlearning, generalization training, explicit reinforcement of appropriate behavior and/or skill mastery, and frequent monitoring of learner progress toward prespecified goals and objectives. Effective special education teachers monitor progress continuously and are prepared to modify and adjust instruction as needed when progress is insufficient.

REFERRAL TO SPECIAL EDUCATION Special education, which may include placement in general education classes for much or all of the school day with appropriate supports, may be part or all of the final tier in a three-tiered RTI system. Although there are usually no other placement options (special schools or other facilities may be appropriate in some limited cases), it is believed that many students placed in special education may make sufficient progress to be reintegrated into the general education class as regular education students. If that is not possible, students referred to special education should have as much access to general education classrooms and the general education curriculum as feasible (Fuchs et al., 2012).

PROGRESS MONITORING Progress monitoring at Tier 3 involves frequent measurement of learning outcomes and immediate and dynamic instructional decision making. In many cases, progress monitoring is undertaken after an individual student has been evaluated and found eligible for placement in special education, based on state and district standards. In this placement, progress monitoring is implemented in part to meet the requirements of IDEA, which mandates that progress toward students' short-term and annual goals must be assessed. In addition, progress monitoring continues to provide information about the adequacy of instruction and the possible need for modifications or adjustments in instructional programming. Progress-monitoring data may also be useful if student progress is considered sufficiently strong over time to justify consideration for placement in a less restrictive setting.

STANDARDS FOR EVALUATING PROGRESS MONITORING Measures and procedures for progress monitoring must reflect specific requirements and therefore vary among states, districts, and schools. Nevertheless, it is important that progress monitoring be conducted efficiently and effectively. Review Table 7.3 (from Mellard & McKnight, 2006) and the standards for evaluating progress monitoring. These criteria should be employed whenever progress monitoring is undertaken to maximize its effectiveness.

TABLE 7.3 Standards for Evaluating Progress Monitoring

Directions: If the practice is implemented, indicate this with a checkmark (√); if the practice is being developed, rank by priority: 1 = highest priority; 2 = medium priority; 3 = lowest priority.

Practice	Priority
Progress monitoring occurs in all tiers (including general education).	
Scientifically based instruction includes the continuous progress monitoring of student performance across tiers.	
Teachers follow a designated procedure and schedule for progress monitoring and for regrouping students as needed.	
Measures are administered frequently to inform instruction and curricular placement decisions (in Tier 1, at least once every 3 weeks; in Tier 2 and beyond, one to two times per week; in special education, three to five times per week).	
Progress-monitoring measures are appropriate to the curriculum, grade level, and tier level.	
Data resulting from classroom-level progress monitoring are documented and analyzed.	
Teachers use progress-monitoring data to evaluate instructional effectiveness.	
An established data management system allows ready access to students' progress-monitoring data.	
Progress-monitoring data are graphed to indicate percentages of students at varying levels of achievement.	
A graph is completed to display data for analysis and decision making to indicate percentages of students at risk, at some risk, and at low risk.	
Staff members receive training in the administration and interpretation of progress-monitoring measures.	
The school has designated reasonable *a priori* cut points and decision rules for the level, slope, or percentage of mastery to help determine responsiveness and distinguish adequate responsiveness from inadequate responsiveness.	
The efficacy of cut points is reviewed frequently; cut points are adjusted as necessary.	
A rationale is provided for the cut points and decision rules (e.g., normative or specific criteria reference).	

Source: Mellard & McKnight (2006), p. 6.

Fidelity of Implementation

Learning Objective 7.5 Discuss fidelity of implementation and challenges with executing RTI strategies.

Although RTI models can be planned and developed skillfully, they cannot be effective unless they are implemented faithfully. **Fidelity of implementation** refers to the degree to which instruction is delivered in the way it was intended (Gresham et al., 2000, 2017) and is important because treatments, however effective on paper, will not be successful unless they are implemented correctly. It is important to ensure that both the school's procedures for RTI and instruction across the different tiers are implemented with fidelity.

The concept of treatment fidelity is predicated on the fact that instructional methods and interventions must use *evidence-based practices*, or practices that are supported by scientific evidence for effectiveness when implemented as intended. That is, it is of little use to effectively implement a treatment or intervention that is not known to be effective in the first place. Criteria for evidence-based practices (EBPs) are explored in detail in Volume 71, Issue 2, of *Exceptional Children* (2005).

Mellard and Johnson (2008; see also Johnson et al., 2006) have suggested that three elements, or "dimensions," are important to fidelity of implementation: (1) the *method* of evaluating fidelity, (2) the *frequency* of fidelity evaluations, and (3) the *support systems* needed to implement the program with fidelity. Each is discussed separately here.

STRATEGIES FOR
DETERMINING FIDELITY OF IMPLEMENTATION

Gresham et al. (2000, 2017) described three types of fidelity assessments. The first is **direct assessment measures**, indirect methods of fidelity assessment

For example, for a particular type of reading instruction, the checklist may include items such as the following:

- The classroom is well organized, including accessible materials, appropriate seating, and efficient transitions between activities.
- All parts of the lesson are covered.
- Appropriate pace and engagement of all students are maintained throughout the lesson.
- Teacher demonstrates enthusiasm and provides appropriate praise and feedback.
- Effective error correction is employed, according to the procedures outlined in the method.
- Both group and individual responses are solicited.
- Teacher ensures accurate responding before introducing new skills.
- Classroom behavior is effectively managed (students are motivated, expectations are clear, misbehavior is efficiently redirected).
- Reading checkouts (e.g., 1-minute reading timings) and evaluations are conducted efficiently and appropriately.

In most cases, items would also be specifically referenced to details of the method and curriculum being employed. Using a checklist prepared or approved by the district or school, a percent mastery score may be calculated by dividing the steps met adequately by the total number of steps in the checklist. For example, if the checklist contained 15 steps and the teacher was observed meeting 12 steps appropriately, the percent mastery could be calculated by dividing 12 by 15, for a total of 80%. Schools that employ standards for mastery also determine specifically what standard (e.g., 90%, 85%) constitutes fidelity. Many treatment-fidelity checklists can be found on the Internet; however, each school should determine that obtained checklists are appropriate for their own purposes.

INDIRECT ASSESSMENT **Indirect methods of fidelity assessment** include teacher self-reports of implementation, more general rating scales, teacher interviews, and permanent products of teacher and student work. Of these, permanent products are thought to be the most reliable (Mellard & Johnson, 2008) and may include, for example, products such as relevant completed student assignments or written teacher feedback that corresponds to components of the intervention. Other indirect assessments can also contribute to the overall picture of fidelity. Using rating scales, teachers can evaluate the extent to which they believe (e.g., 5 = *strongly disagree* to 1 = *strongly agree*) that they implement components of the intervention. Similarly, observers could rate the observed lesson as a whole using such measures. Also, when direct measures of fidelity are not high, interviews and rating scales can help provide important information for improving fidelity.

TREATMENT MANUALS Some interventions have accompanying manuals detailing the components of their effective implementation. Some benefit may be obtained by providing teachers with manuals to accompany their treatments. However, unless these manuals are consulted frequently and supplemented with more direct measures, they are unlikely to ensure faithful implementation (Gresham et al., 2000).

FREQUENCY Schools must determine how frequently they will conduct fidelity evaluations, based on such considerations as the need for specific types of information and the availability of resources. Mellard and Johnson (2008) suggested that fidelity checks may depend in part on (1) the experience of the teacher, (2) teacher requests for support in implementation, (3) the performance of individual classes on screening and progress-monitoring measures, and (4) the number of special education referrals coming from individual classes.

Schools should determine how frequently (e.g., weekly, monthly, annually, as needed) they will check the fidelity of implementation for a number of tasks, and they should keep records of this information. Relevant tasks for which frequency should be established can include the following:

- Review of state and school district assessment results
- Implementation of screening measures
- Implementation and review of progress monitoring
- Completion of teacher fidelity evaluations
- Collection of input from teachers and staff
- Evaluation of new staff for treatment fidelity.

Although frequency guidelines have been suggested for some measures (e.g., screening conducted three times yearly), schools should determine for themselves how frequently evaluations and fidelity checks should be conducted.

SUPPORT SYSTEMS Schools can always use fidelity-of-implementation data to help determine areas in need of remediation, as well as relative areas of strength. For example, fidelity-of-implementation data can be employed to identify teachers who are implementing their treatments with a high degree of fidelity. Newly hired teachers, as well as teachers who need additional support in implementing specific interventions, may need professional development and training. This may, in some cases, require reallocation of school resources. Overall, the purpose of fidelity-of-implementation evaluation should be to determine where additional supports are needed and then provide the necessary resources and training. Information from a variety of sources, including indirect and direct measures, teacher self-referral, and progress monitoring, can be employed to determine where to provide additional supports to assure optimal implementation of RTI.

Establishing fidelity of implementation involves several different steps. A task list for establishing fidelity-of-implementation procedures includes development of a timeline and assignment of individual responsibility for tasks. Staff professional development and schedules for continuous professional development are important. The data-collection system needs to include clear measures for data collection (e.g., observation checklists and products), the criteria for acceptable performance, and implementation schedules.

Reed et al. (2012) described how a high school RTI leadership team led a monthly meeting to review direct observational fidelity data for providing ongoing professional development support as needed. At the meeting, the assistant principal at Lincoln High School reported observing more English and social studies teachers implementing the targeted vocabulary strategy instruction with fidelity than science or math teachers. The English language teacher agreed, recalling that faculty were overwhelmed at the initial professional development last year. She said that faculty needed support with how to integrate the vocabulary strategies better into their content-area classes. The principal and assistant principal decided to meet to plan how to increase implementation of the literacy strategies into the content-area classes.

INTERVENTIONS FOR SECONDARY SKILLS AND CONTENT

RTI in secondary schools may address various skills and content domains, as needed. Tier 1 would include evidence-based differentiated instruction in the content areas in the general education classroom, whereas Tier 2 interventions might include intensive instruction in reading, especially emphasizing reading fluency, word study, vocabulary, and passage comprehension (e.g., Vaughn et al., 2011). For example, if a ninth-grade student is especially behind in reading, they may need to be directly placed in a class that is small with an intensive reading intervention (Reed et al., 2012). So, the student may have English 9 during second period, and during fifth period, the student would attend the tiered reading intervention class as a course elective. These Tier 2 interventions also may emphasize basic math, fundamental skills students are missing, reading in the content areas, or supplemental subject-area instruction (Johnson et al., 2009). For example, Vaughn et al. (2015) taught content reading skills to high school students in small groups over a period of 2 years. Skills taught addressed word study, vocabulary in content-area text, comprehension of content-area text, and engagement. Because the Common Core State Standards require students to read increasingly difficult texts to build content-specific knowledge in reading, it is important that supports for students are provided throughout the curriculum (National Governors Association Center for Best Practices & Council of Chief State School Officers, 2010).

Another intervention that has been implemented at the secondary level is "double-dose" instruction, in which an elective class is replaced by a second, supporting class in the target area. For example, Cortes and colleagues (2013) described a program in which target students enrolled in two periods of ninth-grade algebra per day, with the second class providing support and additional practice. These courses were well coordinated, with 90% or more overlapping content. Cortes et al. concluded that the program had a facilitative effect on test scores and graduation rates. As with all RTI programs, formative evaluation is necessary to ensure that programs are leading to desired outcomes.

A system of positive behavioral supports may be implemented for problems with social behavior (Ihlo & Nantais, 2010). RTI procedures at the secondary level in these various areas are addressed in relevant chapters in this book.

STRATEGIES FOR IMPLEMENTING RTI AT THE SECONDARY LEVEL

The challenges of implementing RTI at the secondary level may in some ways be greater than those for RTI at the elementary level. Scheduling can be more complicated and students are completing classes for credits, a much greater and more varied number of subject areas are involved, and areas such as reading and basic math are in most cases no longer individual subjects of instruction. In addition, much less research has been conducted on RTI at the secondary level (Vaughn & Bos, 2020).

Shinn and colleagues (2016) suggested that a confused or poorly articulated purpose is the major barrier to secondary RTI implementation. Clearly, RTI at the secondary level is no longer focused on early intervention as an important objective, as is RTI at the elementary level; however, at secondary levels, important goals include dropout prevention and development of skills and content knowledge sufficient to promote success and, ultimately, graduation from high school.

Like their elementary counterparts, screening, progress monitoring, and data-based decision making are key components of RTI implementation at the secondary level as well. For example, at Lincoln High School, Reed et al. (2012) described how the RTI leadership team members reviewed screening measures and student progress-monitoring data. Lincoln had formerly determined that the state reading assessment would be used as a screening measure for all incoming freshmen and a cut score was used to identify students in need of a Tier 2 reading intervention course. At the meeting, the leadership team also reviewed recent schoolwide benchmark results and identified 15 freshmen who did not meet grade-level expectations. The RTI team members sought additional data as they discussed if those freshmen should now move into the Tier 2 class. The team members also discussed the biweekly progress-monitoring data for those students currently attending the reading intervention course. The reading interventionist reported that apart from one or two students, those in the Tier 2 intervention mastered literal comprehension with main ideas and details. But since they were not applying their skills to grade-level text yet, her instruction would now focus on inferences and vocabulary (Reed et al., 2012).

Components of RTI that remain very similar between elementary and secondary levels include screening and progress monitoring, data-based decision making, fidelity of implementation, continuous improvement, and multi-tiered implementation. Although less attention has been paid to RTI at the secondary level, it nevertheless remains a very important component of a comprehensive program.

CHALLENGES WITH IMPLEMENTING RTI

Although research and practice have developed greatly concerning RTI and its implementation, a number of challenges remain for the field. The role of RTI in evaluating students for placement in special education programs is not generally agreed upon, and the degree to which evaluations based on RTI discriminate between learning disabilities and other disabilities such as intellectual disabilities is not known. Presently, there are many different versions of RTI, and procedures for determining "success" in a given tier also vary widely. Furthermore, general and special educators report having a better understanding of RTI then preparedness to implement (Al Otaiba et al., 2019; Regan et al., 2015). Many voices have called for more specific characterizations of each of the mechanisms of RTI in the future (Berkeley et al., 2020; Fuchs et al., 2010; Hudson & McKenzie, 2016).

When conducted by researchers using systematic protocols, Tier 2 instruction has resulted in substantial gains. Wanzek et al. (2016) conducted meta-analyses of 72 Tier 2 reading interventions with students from kindergarten through third grade and reported that, overall, students had benefited substantially from the intervention, in reading skills as well as comprehension. However, in a large-scale study of 146 schools in 13 states in which RTI was implemented by the schools themselves, Balu et al. (2015) reported that Tier 2 and Tier 3 instruction had no overall effect on reading outcomes in grades 1 through 3, although the effects varied significantly across schools. These findings help underscore the need for schools to implement treatments systematically and to collect and evaluate outcome data systematically, to ensure that the interventions are achieving their intended purpose.

A substantial amount of research has been conducted on RTI for early reading; however, effective and appropriate Tier 2 strategies for math, writing, and other content areas such as science and social studies await further development, particularly at the secondary level (Mastropieri & Scruggs, 2005; Vaughn & Bos, 2020). Some programs are under way in a number of different areas (e.g., Johnson et al., 2009), but more information is needed on optimal RTI programs in these areas. Many of these issues may be addressed more satisfactorily in the future as schools develop more experience with RTI.

Although RTI was intended to implement needed services promptly, in some cases, extended exposure to RTI programs may delay the evaluation process for special education. Dr. Melody Musgrove, former director of the Office of Special Education Programs, communicated the following to the State Directors of Special Education:

> It has come to the attention of the Office of Special Education Programs (OSEP) that, in some instances, local education authorities (LEAs) may be using RTI strategies to delay or deny a timely initial evaluation of children suspected of having a disability. States and LEAs have an obligation to ensure that evaluation of children expected of having a disability are not delayed or denied because of implementation of an RTI strategy. (2011, p. 1)

Fuchs et al. (2012) suggested future procedures for implementation of RTI, referred to as *Smart RTI*. These procedures include (1) collecting screening measures in multiple stages (e.g., two levels of assessment) to reduce the number of false positives referred to Tier 2 unnecessarily; (2) "fast tracking" those students whose failure to respond can be predicted (i.e., without implementing Tier 2) to special education; and (3) providing Tier 3 as intensive special education that features data-based individualized instruction, access to the general education curriculum, and movement across the different tiers of RTI as needed (see also Fuchs et al., 2015).

7 Summary

- Response to intervention is a multi-tiered system of support designed to address different learning needs and intended to improve instruction.
  - Much progress has been made to date in conceptualizing, implementing, and evaluating RTI (Glover, 2010), and additional progress continues to be made.
- Schoolwide screening, progress monitoring, and data-based decision making assist in identifying students at risk for academic failure, monitoring their progress, and making instructional decisions based on students' performance data.
  - At present, RTI holds considerable promise for identifying academic and behavioral problems in schools, providing appropriate intervention, and creating an integrated system of service delivery in general education and special education.
- Tier 1 instruction is scientifically based and delivered in the general education setting.
  - Teachers will benefit greatly by becoming well informed regarding their local school and district procedures for implementing RTI, and children with diverse learning needs will benefit from the implementation of a systematic, multi-tiered process for identifying and correcting learning and behavioral problems, beginning in the inclusive classroom.
- Tier 2 instruction provides more intensive interventions to identified smaller groups of students who continue to receive Tier 1 instruction.
- Tier 3 is more intensive and includes special education in many RTI models.
- Fidelity of implementation means that instruction is delivered as intended.
- Challenges exist with implementing RTI, but schools, teachers, and researchers are attempting to address these challenges.

PROFESSIONAL STANDARDS LINK: Response to Intervention and Multi-Tiered Systems of Support

Information in this chapter links most directly to:

- CEC 2020 Initial Practice-Based Professional Preparation Standards for Special Educators (Initial K–12 standards) (see https://exceptionalchildren.org/standards/initial-practice-based-professional-preparation-standards-special-educators): 2 (Understanding and Addressing Each Individual's Developmental and Learning Needs), 4 (Using Assessment to Understand the Learner and the Learning Environment for Data-Based Decision Making), 5 (Supporting Learning Using Effective Instruction), 6 (Supporting Social, Emotional, and Behavioral Growth), 7 (Collaborating with Team Members)
- InTASC Standards (see https://www.ccsso.org/sites/default/files/2017-11/InTASC_Model_Core_Teaching_Standards_2011.pdf): 2 (Learning Differences), 3 (Learning Environments), 6 (Assessment), 7 (Planning for Instruction), 10 (Leadership and Collaboration)

In considering implementing RTI, have you tried the following? If not, see the pages listed here.

Mint Images/Offset/Shutterstock

CHAPTER 8

Improving Motivation and Social Behavior

LEARNING OBJECTIVES

After studying this chapter, you should be able to:

8.1 Identify preconditions and techniques for improving and enhancing student motivation and affect.

8.2 Describe how to manage classroom behaviors.

8.3 Explain schoolwide behavior management systems and strategies that support schoolwide positive behavior.

8.4 Describe techniques for teaching social skills.

Teachers often report that management of classroom behavior is of significant importance and is a great influence on student learning (Tauber, 2007). Disciplined, well-managed classrooms are much more likely to promote learning for all students. However, classroom behavior is much more easily managed when students are motivated to learn and succeed in school (Wentzel, 2021). When students feel sufficiently motivated and empowered, they work their hardest and take control of their own learning. Teachers who learn evidence-based motivational techniques and implement them are more likely to manage their classroom successfully. In addition to using motivational techniques, handling social/emotional behavior by exercising high-leverage practices can also make a difference in classroom management.

Four high-leverage practices (HLPs) recommended by the Council for Exceptional Children are concerned with social/emotional/behavioral practices and support successful classroom management. These important practices are among those described in this chapter and include the following:

Social/Emotional/Behavioral Practices

HLP 7: Establish a consistent, organized, and respectful learning environment.
HLP 8: Provide positive and constructive feedback to guide students' learning and behavior.
HLP 9: Teach social behaviors.
HLP 10: Conduct functional behavioral assessments to develop individual student behavior support plans (McLeskey et al., 2017).

Setting the Stage for Academic Success

Learning Objective 8.1 Identify preconditions and techniques for improving and enhancing student motivation and affect.

Because of their combined effect on student learning, motivation and affect are among the most important topics in this book. Although motivation and affect overlap to some extent, they represent important, separate aspects of school functioning. **Motivation** refers to the degree to which students desire to succeed in school, whereas **affect** refers to the students' emotional mood and personal feelings. **Intrinsic motivation** refers to participation in an activity purely out of curiosity, desire to succeed, or desire to contribute. **Extrinsic motivation**, on the other hand, refers to participation in an activity in anticipation of an external reward (Wentzel, 2021).

Given that instruction is adequate, high levels of motivation and positive affect provide students opportunities to master the learning tasks set before them. However, at one time or other, students—particularly those with disabilities and other diverse learning needs—can lack motivation and positive affect (e.g., Carlson et al., 2002; Wolters et al., 2014). Students who lack a life history of success may be more likely to quit working on a task because they believe they have little chance of succeeding (Nelson & Manset-Williamson, 2006).

Some students with disabilities may be more likely to fail at academic tasks and to attribute such failure to personal inadequacies rather than to lack of effort. Finally, students with disabilities and other diverse learning needs may be more at risk for affective problems such as anxiety (Nelson & Harwood, 2011), depression (Mazzone et al., 2013), and low self-esteem (Sideridis, 2007). The following scenario describes Cameron's struggle with motivation in school.

CLASSROOM SCENARIO

Cameron

Cameron is enrolled in a ninth-grade mathematics class. In fifth grade, he was classified as having a learning disability in reading, and he attends the resource room for four 50-minute periods per week for help with his reading. He is interested in basketball and has many friends. In math class (pre-algebra), however, Cameron's manner is anything but cheerful. He received a failing grade the first semester, and he seems to be headed for another at the end of the next grading period. During lecture or class discussion, Cameron seems to simply stare off into space. When given classroom assignments, he makes a modest effort to complete them, but it is clear from his manner that he is just waiting for the bell to ring. He turns in only about half of his homework assignments—and most of these are either incomplete or incorrect. Clearly, mathematics is neither an academic strength nor an interest area for Cameron; nevertheless, it seems likely that he could produce more work and work of a much higher quality if he applied himself more and developed a more positive attitude toward math. However, when his math teacher, Mr. Hamilton, spoke with him about his classroom behavior, Cameron seemed to believe that changing his behavior and attitude was hopeless. "What's the use?" he said. "You know I'll just fail anyway."

QUESTIONS FOR REFLECTION

1. Why do you think Cameron feels this way about math?
2. When do you think simple statements of encouragement by his teacher would be likely to help? What kinds of statements would be best?
3. What are some ways Cameron's friends or peers could help?

The best way to handle the motivational and affective problems of all students, including those with disabilities, is to start by making the classroom a positive and motivating experience for all students.

STRATEGIES FOR IMPROVING MOTIVATION AND AFFECT

Making decisions to create the most ideal conditions for motivating students and increasing positive affect is within your control as a teacher, and it can make an enormous difference in the classroom atmosphere and in student achievement.

PRECONDITIONS Before any attempt to improve motivation and affect will succeed in inclusive classrooms, several preconditions must exist (Wentzel, 2021). These are not motivational strategies in themselves, but they set the stage for the development of motivation and positive classroom affect. These preconditions include (1) a supportive, organized classroom environment; (2) instructional materials that are at an appropriate difficulty level; (3) meaningful and relevant instructional tasks; and (4) task-oriented classrooms. Students are much more likely to become motivated in classrooms in which they feel welcome and important, for example, when teachers make supportive statements or enlist peer support. Allday and Pakurar (2007) reported that greeting middle school students at the door at the beginning of class considerably improved on-task behavior of students with problem behaviors during the class period. Another important consideration for creating a supportive atmosphere is ensuring your classroom is culturally responsive. The *Diversity, Equity, and Inclusion in the Classroom* feature provides some suggestions. Students are more likely to maintain their motivation when tasks are relevant and meaningful to them and are neither too difficult nor too easy (Lavoie, 2008). Finally, students are more likely to feel motivated in what Nicholls (1989) referred to as "task-oriented" rather than "ego-oriented" classrooms. In task-oriented classrooms, students are rewarded and encouraged for what they do (e.g., work hard, pay attention), with respect to particular tasks. In contrast, in ego-oriented classrooms, students are more likely to be evaluated with respect to "who they are" (e.g., the "brightest", the "best"), as compared with other students. And while anyone is free to work harder, or apply study skills (task-orientation), few students feel they can be the "best" student in the class (ego-orientation). Therefore, higher overall levels of motivation are more likely to be found in task-oriented classrooms (see Anderman & Patrick, 2012). Table 8.1 provides some examples of teacher comments representative of task-oriented and ego-oriented classrooms.

Once the important preconditions have been met to create a positive classroom atmosphere, you can turn to several general categories of techniques to enhance motivation and affect both in individual students and in your class as a whole: improving self-esteem and self-efficacy, increasing personal investment in learning, making learning fun and enjoyable, and using praise and rewards (Scruggs & Mastropieri, 1994).

RAISE STUDENTS' SELF-ESTEEM **Self-esteem** is a general term for the regard in which individuals hold themselves. Generally, students who feel good about who they are and what they can do are more successful than students who do not feel good about themselves (Zheng et al., 2014). Self-esteem has been found to differ among boys and girls, students from different racial-ethnic groups, and students with and without disabilities. However, self-esteem has also been seen to be quite variable within all of these groups. That is, some students with disabilities exhibit very high self-esteem, and some high-achieving students exhibit low self-esteem. Some evidence suggests that students with milder disabilities may in some cases exhibit lower self-esteem than students with more significant disabilities (Harter, 2012).

Students with disabilities may be particularly vulnerable to beliefs that they do not compare favorably with their classmates (Ferro & Boyle, 2013). This suggests that students with disabilities should be carefully monitored for such affective characteristics as self-esteem and that the student's sense of worth and efficacy should be promoted wherever possible. This can be accomplished by providing students with tasks at which they can succeed and direct positive feedback and rewards for their success. Ensure that students with disabilities know that they have an important role to play in the classroom by assigning roles in which they can assume responsibility and ownership, such as taking care of classroom pets, distributing materials, or collecting papers. Such assignments, as well as public statements of support, can convince students with diverse learning needs that their presence is valued. Classroom peers can also assist in helping other students feel better about themselves.

TABLE 8.1 Ego-Oriented versus Task-Oriented Classrooms

Classroom Orientation	Representative Teacher Comments	Explanation
Ego-oriented	"Imani, you're the smartest student in the class!"	Praises student for being "smart"
	"Class, look at how smart Fredrica is, to have figured this out!"	Attributes success to being "smart"
	"Richard, why can't you be more like Jordan?"	Compares one student negatively to another
Task-oriented	"Imani, this is your best work yet!"	Describes work product as personal "best"
	"Fredrica must have worked very hard to have figured this out!"	References success to effort
	"Richard, I know you can do much better on this assignment if you use the strategies we practiced and put more effort into it."	Relates improvement to effort and strategy use

Diversity, Equity, and Inclusion in the Classroom

Creating a Culturally Responsive Classroom

Culture influences all aspects of life and school. Students' cultures shape their language, behavior, emotions, customs, and traditions. Because of the importance of culture, students feel more motivated to learn if the classroom is responsive to their cultures. Gollnick and Chinn (2021) referred to students' cultures as microcultures consisting of interactions of race, ethnicity, language, gender, class, religion, age, geography, and disability. All of these characteristics merge to form an individual's culture, which in turn interacts with the dominant culture (see also Banks, 2015).

Gaining an understanding and an appreciation of these cultural influences will assist in developing culturally responsive education, which, in turn, should increase student motivation and investment in learning. For example, learn how education is viewed from the perspectives of your students and their families or caregivers. Find out how students and families perceive school visits, homework, school authority figures, and school activities. Learn about the cultural identities and strengths of your students and their families and caregivers. Design instruction and strategies to encourage involvement for members of all cultures in relevant school activities. Emphasize cooperation and motivation while relating educational goals to students and their families or caregivers in culturally meaningful ways.

Set up or expand a literacy center at your school that emphasizes literacy for all and represents all cultural and linguistic groups. For example, King Middle School's literacy center began providing literacy assistance to adults and families in the evenings while supporting students during the school day (Ginsberg & Wlodkowski, 2009). Attendance at the center was encouraged for anyone requiring assistance with English. Community members from similar linguistic backgrounds might be available to help individuals feel more comfortable. The literacy center became a motivating focal point for the community and held events such as book discussions and folk art festivals sponsored by the local parent organization. The events were inclusive, relevant, and educational experiences.

Demonstrate a sincere, caring, accepting attitude toward all individuals. Help students and families know that everyone, regardless of cultural or linguistic background, is an important member of your school's community.

Discuss: What school activities, community events, or classroom practices can promote equity and inclusivity?

PROMOTE SELF-EFFICACY Students are motivated to persist on tasks at which they believe they will succeed. They are more apt to think they will succeed on future tasks if they have succeeded on similar previous tasks. In this situation, students believe they have the knowledge and the skills to ensure their attainment of the goal. This confidence in one's own abilities has been referred to as self-efficacy (Zimmerman & Kitsantas, 2007). You can improve self-efficacy by structuring academic tasks that can be accomplished with a reasonable effort and high rate of success and providing direct feedback when students are successful. Classroom activities benefit all students—especially students with disabilities—when they provide additional practice, continually assess understanding, make connections to prior learning, organize learning in advance of instruction, recognize good social models, and offer support for learning.

Other strategies that may improve self-efficacy include the following:

- **Provide additional practice to reinforce prior knowledge.** Initiate regular reviews and **overlearning** (additional practice after goals have been achieved) to reinforce any knowledge previously presented and increase student confidence. Additional practice could be provided by the special education teacher or by a parent, caregiver, volunteer, or aide.
- **Use ongoing assessment strategies.** Monitor students' comprehension by providing frequent opportunities to respond (OTR) such as use of response cards and unison responding. OTRs can provide in the moment assessment data for teachers to adjust the pace, content, or method of instruction (Van Camp et al., 2020). Ask frequent questions and provide independent practice only after you are certain students can be successful independently so that they will learn to expect success in the classroom.

- **Point out appropriate social models.** Students may believe they can be successful—even if they have no experience with a task—if they observe students like themselves succeeding at the task. Say, for example, "Hey, last week, Jamal couldn't do this either. Jamal worked hard and learned to do this, so I'm sure you can learn to do it, too!"
- **Provide positive support.** Direct encouragement from teachers can help students' self-efficacy. Saying, "I really believe you will be able to do this if you give it a try!" provides positive support for effort, rather than criticism for failure, and can demonstrate your confidence in individual students.

Demonstration of genuine teacher interest at appropriate times can also improve student motivation and attitude toward schoolwork, as shown in the continuation of Cameron's scenario.

Avoid Counterproductive Statements One well-meaning strategy that is often counterproductive is characterizing a particular task as "easy" by saying, for example:

- "You can do this. It's easy!"
- "Anybody should be able to do this!"

Such statements are often intended to convince students that a task is doable and within their reach, but the effects of such statements can be very different. Because teachers rarely need to encourage a student to accomplish truly "easy" tasks, this strategy has often been used with tasks that the student considers difficult. However, the strategy can undermine motivation: Little satisfaction is gained from accomplishing an "easy" task; shame and embarrassment result from failing at a task that is considered "easy."

Also, remember that if students express satisfaction in their performance by stating that a particular task was easy, use prudence in agreeing completely with such students. You could say something like, "It may have been easy for you because you worked hard to learn it, but I don't think it was really that easy!"

CLASSROOM SCENARIO

Cameron

Mr. Hamilton arranged for a meeting with Cameron. During this meeting, Mr. Hamilton expressed his concern about his progress in math and his hope that he could improve. Cameron seemed pleased with the extra attention from Mr. Hamilton but indicated his overall pessimistic attitude: "I appreciate you trying to help me, Mr. Hamilton, but it's no use. I'll never learn this math." Mr. Hamilton replied, "Cameron, I know pre-algebraic concepts are challenging. I think there are some strategies you can try and they may make a difference in your learning. But it is up to you to try them." Cameron agreed to try.

Mr. Hamilton arranged to edit Cameron's homework assignments so that he could spend more time on a smaller number of problems within his current skill level. Mr. Hamilton would discuss the math problems briefly with Cameron in the few minutes before the class started; he would also arrange for a peer to help him during class exercises. Mr. Hamilton also began to privately praise Cameron when he made an effort and completed his assignments: "You see? I think your effort to connect with me before class and to work with your classmate is making a difference—I see you focusing in class and your homework assignments are now showing what you can do!" When Cameron's assignments were not completed, Mr. Hamilton displayed disappointment but expressed hope that the next assignment would be done correctly: "Cameron, we have seen your best work and know from before that you can do better—I hope to see something really impressive on your next assignment!"

By the end of the second quarter, Cameron's grade had improved from an F to a D+. On the last test of the semester, he earned a C+. Mr. Hamilton emailed Cameron's parents stating that he was the most improved student in his class. With additional prompting, Cameron continued to perform successfully throughout the second semester. Cameron concluded, "At first, I thought I could never do it. But pre-algebra is really not that bad if you put your mind to it!"

QUESTIONS FOR REFLECTION

1. Why do you think Mr. Hamilton was frustrated with Cameron's performance in math?
2. What types of additional strategies might be helpful for Cameron to use at home?
3. How can a monitoring system be established to determine whether the instructional interventions are working effectively?

TEACH STUDENTS TO SET GOALS Once students believe they are capable of accomplishing a task, involving them in goal setting can increase their motivation to complete that task. Research has found that students often increase their achievement when they help set their own goals (Konrad et al., 2007; Wentzel, 2021). Estrapala and Reed (2020) provide a step-by-step guide for explicitly teaching high school students how to self-set goals that are SMART (specific, measurable, achievable, relevant, and time-bound). Students involved in setting their own goals and in monitoring their own progress will be more likely to see learning goals as meaningful and personal—more so than if they are simply imposed by the teacher. Motivation can be maximized when the goal is difficult for the student to attain but can be achieved with vigorous or persistent effort.

Establish realistic but challenging goals and monitor progress on graphs or charts. For example, students can select goals for solving a certain number of math problems, reading a specific number of pages in a book daily, or getting 90% correct on weekly spelling tests. When progress is made, the goal can be adjusted gradually to improve performance over time (e.g., completing and checking at least 50%/75%/100% of the homework problems with accuracy). A sample goal sheet is depicted in Figure 8.1.

Parents or caregivers are usually the primary advocates for their children and can be an invaluable source for promoting self-efficacy and supporting the continued efforts of students. Communicate frequently with parents, family members, or caregivers to share your expectations for the student and ask for their help in meeting these goals. Families often will agree to participate in a reinforcement system, through which the student is rewarded at home for positive efforts made during school (e.g., phone or TV time after homework is completed).

TEACH STUDENTS TO USE POSITIVE ATTRIBUTIONS With **attribution training**, students are taught to attribute success to their own efforts and academic strategies and to attribute failure to their lack of effort or failure to use appropriate strategies. Students who learn to attribute success and failure to things they control are more likely to try hard and succeed in the future than those who do not (Berkeley et al., 2011).

Figure 8.1 Sample Goal-Setting Sheet

GOAL SHEET
Student name ____________________
Dates ____________________
Class ____________________

# of daily math problems	Monday	Tuesday	Wednesday	Thursday	Friday
Daily Goal	20	20	20	25	25
Accuracy Goal	18	19	20	20	22
Number Completed	16	19			
Number Correct	16	19			
Teacher Comment	Good work; try working faster	Super job!			

TABLE 8.2 Student Attributions for Success and Failure

Positive Attributions	Negative Attributions
Success	**Success**
"I succeeded on the spelling test because I used the spelling strategy I learned."	"I succeeded on the spelling test because I got lucky."
"I got an A on my science project because I started early and used my time effectively."	"I got an A on my science project because my teacher likes me."
Failure	**Failure**
"I failed the math test because I put off studying until the last minute, and then I fell asleep. Next time, I'll start earlier."	"I failed the math test because I'm stupid at math."
"I didn't do as well as I could have on the test because I didn't study for an essay test. Next time, I'll practice writing essay answers when I study."	"I didn't do well on the test because the teacher doesn't grade fairly."

Attributions that correctly attribute success or failure to student behavior—things a student does or could do—are called *positive attributions*. *Negative attributions*, on the other hand, attribute success or failure to such things as inherent ability or teacher prejudices. Examples of positive and negative attributions are given in Table 8.2.

As a teacher, you should be alert to the development of negative attributions, particularly for students with disabilities. To counter these kinds of attributions, first, make certain that all assignments and/or the set goals are achievable. Then simply do not accept negative statements such as "I'm stupid" or "I never get it right." These declarations should not be allowed to justify failure. You can reply to such attributions with statements such as, "No, the reason you were not successful is that you gave up too soon" or "No, the reason you did not meet your goal is that you didn't use the strategies you practiced for that test."

When students succeed, be sure to reinforce the value of strategy use. For example, say, "The reason you did so well is that you used the strategy we have been learning" (Berkeley et al., 2011). Showing evidence such as graphed data of the improved outcomes, along with these types of statements, can improve students' academic success (Koenig et al., 2016).

ARRANGE COUNSELING INTERVENTIONS WHEN NEEDED Students with disabilities may experience problems of affect such as anxiety, depression, and low self-esteem. Counseling interventions have been designed to address affective problems of students and may involve a number of techniques (Campbell et al., 2015; Perihan et al., 2020). School counselors frequently use both individual and group counseling to work with students with disabilities and may provide self-esteem activities, social skills training, and college readiness training; in addition, they can provide valuable feedback for multidisciplinary teams. Counseling interventions for students with disabilities have been found to increase relaxation, decrease school truancy, and increase self-esteem and general well-being (Leichtentritt & Shechtman, 2009). Although the training and activities of counselors may vary from school to school (Milsom & Akos, 2003), counselors should be considered potentially important participants in the lives of students with disabilities, and they should be consulted as appropriate in individual situations.

EXERCISE CARE WHEN HANDLING SERIOUS AFFECTIVE DISORDERS Some disorders of affect are very serious and may not be substantially improved with the application of the strategies described in this chapter. If you encounter students with very serious affective problems, obtain professional assistance and contact the parents/caregivers. Special education teachers, counselors, or school psychologists may help or refer you to other professionals if you have a student who appears to exhibit signs of severe depression, anxiety, or suicidal behavior.

Pearson eTextbook

Video Example 8.1

The teacher in this video is eliciting ideas from her elementary students when creating the class rules. Notice how the students participate and think about how this exercise would contribute to a positive classroom community.

INCREASE STUDENTS' PERSONAL INVESTMENT IN THE CLASSROOM

Students who believe they have some ownership in what is happening in your classroom are also more likely to make an effort to help the classroom be successful. If they have had some input in classroom decision making, students are also more likely to identify positively with classroom activities. Conversely, students who think they have no influence in how classroom business is conducted are more likely to lose motivation and interest.

Allow students to participate in decision making when possible, for example, in determining seating assignments or the sequence in which lessons and activities will be presented. Offering choices to students provides them with a sense of independence and control, which may encourage intrinsic motivation. Find out about your students' opinions with surveys and questionnaires and implement suggestions when appropriate. If you are able to adapt the way you manage the classroom in response to student opinion, students are likely to feel that they are an important part of the classroom.

MAKE LEARNING MORE FUN AND ENJOYABLE

Motivation and positive affect will improve when students have enjoyable activities to look forward to each morning, rather than routine procedures that have become dull and stale.

Make Tasks More Interesting

Numerous strategies are at your disposal to make learning more interesting and fun (Wentzel, 2021), such as the following.

1. *Prepare more concrete, meaningful lessons.* To increase motivation for learning, use personal examples, classroom exhibits and demonstrations, hands-on curriculum materials, and concrete models and illustrations.
2. *Create cognitive conflict.* Interest in learning can be aroused by discussion or demonstration of situations that promote **cognitive conflict**, situations that are not easily predictable or explainable at first. The presentation of discrepant events can create cognitive conflict in students. A discrepant event is an event (often in science) whereby things behave differently than expected (Gable, 2003; Kaya & Lundeen, 2010). An example of a discrepant event is "dancing" raisins, where raisins appear to move up and down independently in a soft drink. Further observation and deduction reveal that the raisins move because of the carbon dioxide in the soft drink. Discrepant events can enhance curiosity and interest and increase motivation to learn (Gonsalez-Spada et al., 2010).
3. *Use novel ways to engage students.* Sometimes students begin to lose motivation simply because instruction has become stale and predictable. In this case, interest may be restored by incorporating novel ways of doing things. Changing the order of classroom routines, reallocating classroom responsibilities, and rearranging classroom seating are all ways to increase novelty.

   You can also provide variety in the way instruction is delivered by using different media, inviting guest speakers or student presenters, and using different applications of technology. Keep in mind that some students—for example, those with autism—may respond negatively to changes in classroom routines (Anckarsäter et al., 2010). However, in many cases, novelty can be useful in improving motivation and affect, especially when combined with other techniques described in this chapter.
4. *Develop competitive and gamelike activities.* Competition that pits students against one another and for which students may not perceive an equal chance of winning may be detrimental to motivation; such competition is more characteristic of ego-oriented classrooms. However, when students believe they have a fair chance of winning, and when the same small group of students does not always win, competition and gamelike activities can provide a high degree of motivation and interest in the class.

   The following is an example of small-group competition in a practice activity. First, divide students randomly into several small groups. Then direct one individual student from each group to take turns answering questions about the topic being studied. Allow the selected students to accept suggestions from other students in their groups, but let them know that they must decide on the answer individually.

When an answer is correct, the group receives a point. At the end of the activity, the group with the most points is the "winner." In some cases, the winning group may be given a reward or privileges of some kind, but students may find it sufficiently rewarding simply to be on the winning team. Each time the game is played, assign students to different groups. Students with diverse learning needs can be included in activities such as this one because they are able to contribute.

5. *Make use of cooperative learning.* Cooperative learning strategies can also be used to enhance student interest, affect, and motivation. Group projects, group participation in science activities, group studying, guided-practice activities, and group competition in gamelike activities as described in the previous section are helpful in enhancing student interest. Chapter 9 provides additional examples for implementing cooperative learning. However, monitor group activities carefully to ensure that all students are being treated fairly and that all students are participating equally and learning adequately from the activities (McMaster & Fuchs, 2002).
6. *Be enthusiastic!* Enthusiasm is one of the teacher presentation variables that helps to develop student interest and make learning more fun. Enthusiastic teachers enhance motivation by modeling interest in the subject being learned and the amount of enjoyment that can be attained when learning occurs. Enthusiastic teachers are also more interesting presenters, so students are more likely to pay attention to what is being presented.

PRAISE STUDENTS AND REWARD THEIR EFFORTS Praise and concrete rewards are often the first things people think of when considering ways to increase motivation and affect. Naturally, most people (including teachers) feel more valued and more motivated when they are praised and positively rewarded for their achievements.

Praise Student Effort The effective use of praise is of paramount importance to enhancing motivation and affect and, when appropriately employed, use of praise closely conforms to the idea of a task-oriented classroom. Praise is highly motivating to students because it provides encouraging feedback for student efforts and demonstrates that their work is being appreciated. Unfortunately, teachers may sometimes provide the most praise to the highest-achieving students and withhold praise from lower-achieving students.

Praise should be linked to specific student actions and behaviors while specifying the criteria being met, such as "Good work on your math problems—you had no errors!" rather than vague statements such as "Good work." This behavior-specific praise has been seen to reduce disruptive behavior and increase student engagement in classrooms (Mrachko et al., 2017). Praise must be genuine and sincere and not sound like repetitive, insincere statements ("Good job," "Good job," "Good job") and should be given for especially noteworthy accomplishments. Indicate the relationship between student effort and achievement to promote personal satisfaction, such as, "You should be very proud of the well-organized writing you did on this project!" Finally, suggest that similar efforts will result in the same future successes with statements such as, "If you keep planning your writing in advance so that it is organized, you will earn A's on all your future assignments this quarter!" (Wentzel et al., 2021).

Research suggests that providing behavior-specific praise is better than general praise (Jenkins et al., 2015). Overall, praise that is vague or that describes general traits of students (e.g., "You are very bright") is not successful in promoting motivation and positive affect. Praise such as this—comments that give students the message that they are praiseworthy without making any particular effort—often does not motivate students. Conversely, praise that links accomplishment with effort, persistence, and effective study strategies is much more likely to be effective.

Table 8.3 presents sample praise statements with corresponding explanations for both elementary- and secondary-level students. Keep in mind that while younger students may not mind being praised out loud in front of their peers, secondary-level students may prefer receiving praise discreetly, so walking over to the student and/or sharing written statements of praise is recommended. The *In the Classroom* feature provides some adjectives that can be used for praising students and corresponding behaviors that can be combined with them to create many alternatives to "Good job!"

Pearson eTextbook
Video Example 8.2
This video shows a teacher using a point-based reward system in an inclusive classroom. Notice the teacher's use of verbal praise and how the students respond to the point system.

Apps for Education

Technology to Assist with Self-Monitoring of Attention and Apps for Recording and Praising Behavior

Self-monitoring of attention can be successfully implemented with students of various ages with attention difficulties. Several types of self-monitoring procedures have proven effective. Key elements in the self-monitoring system include (1) precisely defined behaviors to be monitored, (2) a recording sheet or system that is easy to use, and (3) a predetermined system for knowing when to monitor the behaviors. Once these elements are established, many students can greatly improve their attention to school-related tasks.

Work closely with the student to describe exactly what is meant by "paying attention" or by "staying on-task during class." Specific examples of the behaviors using instances and noninstances are usually helpful at first. A simple recording sheet that contains two columns, one for on-task and one for off-task, on which students are taught to place a check mark if they are on- or off-task is also a good starting place.

Technology can be employed to help students monitor their behaviors. The MoBeGo (Lizzy B. Good Behavior Consulting LLC), or "Monitoring Behavior on the Go," is an app that allows students to self-monitor behavior in real time and includes a goal-setting feature as well. The Juniper Gardens Children's Project at the University of Kansas has developed the I-Connect application with features to monitor, record, and store responses. The I-Connect allows for a variety of customizable prompt phrases and has unique notifications such as flashing lights and auditory chimes.

Smartphones have timer applications that can produce a ringtone or vibration at specified intervals. Smart wristwatches, such as *WatchMinder* (WatchMinder, Inc.), provide a vibrating sensation on the wrist and can be used to self-monitor behaviors on set time intervals. *VibraLITE* (Global Assistive Devices) makes several types of vibrating watches. Teachers can also use these devices to prompt their personal use of proactive classroom management strategies such as the delivery of behavior-specific praise. For example, the *Periodic Timer* app can be downloaded on an Apple Watch and initiated to have a looping alarm to vibrate every 90 seconds as a cue to provide praise.

Additional types of vibrating devices have also been developed. The *MotivAider* is a small, pager-size device that can be programmed to vibrate at various intervals and at different duration and intensity levels (see habitchange.com). Similar devices that can be worn on a belt or in a pocket to produce vibrations or audible sounds include *Polder Digital Timer with Vibrating, Audible, and Illuminated Alarm* (Polder), the *Invisible Clock II Vibrating Reminder* (Time Now Corporation), and the *Multifunction Vibrating Timer* (TN Corporation).

Apps are also available to assist with recording and teaching student social behavior. *ABC Behavior Assessment* (Reticent Arts) allows recording of antecedents, behaviors, and consequences. Three additional apps are *Intervals*, an *ABA Interval Recording App*; *Duration*, an *ABA Duration Recording App*; and *Frequency*, an *ABA Frequency Recording App* (Christopher Mays); these provide the capacities to use duration, frequency, or interval recording of behavior. The *Social Skills Sampler* (Conover Company) teaches varied workplace and school-based social skills via video models. The *Social Skill Builder* (Social Skill Builder) also presents videos of many different problem-solving social situations to engage students in selecting correct social responses.

TABLE 8.3 Praise Statements and Explanations for Praise

Elementary-Level Examples	Secondary-Level Examples
• "That's wonderful! You showed me how to write your name!" • "Super! I can tell you are trying your very best!" • "I like the way you are working!" • "Exactly right! You completed all the problems!"	• "That's a great observation! You understand how a pendulum works!" • "Terrific paper! Your writing has really improved." • "Keep up the hard work! Your compositions are really improving!" • "Great sentences! Will you share your paper with the class?"

Note: Many statements could be used with either elementary or secondary students.

In the Classroom

Example Alternative Statements for Praise

Use any of the following praise adjectives and match them with a variety of behavior words:

Adjectives:
Amazing, astonishing, fantastic, super, beautiful, lovely, fine, gorgeous, splendid, wonderful, terrific, I like the way you are . . ., fabulous, incredible, remarkable, marvelous, neat, very impressive

Behaviors:
work, job, performance, thinking, reflection, judgment, paper, assignment, reading, homework, exercise, lesson, practice activity, sitting, problem solving, paying attention

Combinations of Adjectives and Behaviors:
amazing work, amazing job, amazing performance, astonishing thinking, astonishing reflection, fantastic judgment, fantastic paper, super assignment, super reading, beautiful homework, lovely exercise, fine lesson, terrific practice activity, splendid worksheet, wonderful sitting, wonderful problem solving, terrific paying attention

USE REWARDS TO REINFORCE STUDENT SUCCESS Rewards, when appropriately employed, can be very effective in promoting motivation to succeed. For example, Matson and Boisjoli (2009) described the powerful effect of extrinsic reward systems for individuals with autism and intellectual disabilities. Rewards can be intangible (e.g., verbal praise, privileges, free time) or tangible (e.g., stickers, pencils, snacks) and are discussed further in the classroom management section of this chapter. When employing rewards to increase motivation, apply them when intrinsic motivation is low and be sure to link rewards to specific expectations, such as achieving a specific goal.

Improving Classroom Behavior and Social Skills

Learning Objective 8.2 Describe how to manage classroom behaviors.

All students must know how to interact with others appropriately in group learning experiences, how to engage in classroom discussion, and how to distinguish between classroom behavior that promotes learning and classroom behavior that disrupts learning. Classrooms are well managed when students stay on-task academically but also feel free to participate actively in classroom activities, take risks, and interact positively with others. By attending to two important components of the classroom social environment—classroom behavior and social skills—you can dramatically improve the success of your students.

MANAGING CLASSROOM BEHAVIOR

Student behavior is in many ways a response to the environment, which includes the teacher, peers, other school personnel, and even the physical environment (Kerr & Nelson, 2010). In all cases, an important key to effectively managing classroom behavior—and controlling the negative behaviors of some individual students—lies in establishing positive and caring relationships with all students in your class, implementing and consistently enforcing effective rules for classroom behavior, and helping students learn to make positive choices that increase their level of success in school (Sullivan et al., 2014).

One problem teachers frequently have is precisely describing the problem behavior that they would like the student to change. Although it may be true from the teacher's point of view that a student "misbehaves" or "has a bad attitude," such terms do not specify the behavior problem so that strategies for changing the behavior can be easily implemented and evaluated. Before effective interventions can be implemented, you must first carefully define classroom behavior so that it can be easily observed and recorded.

STRATEGIES FOR
OBSERVING AND RECORDING CLASSROOM BEHAVIOR

DEFINE BEHAVIOR Before interventions on classroom behavior can be carried out, you must carefully observe and document the targeted behaviors. This process allows you to determine precisely what behaviors need to be changed and to evaluate whether progress is occurring after interventions. Several observation systems can be employed to accomplish this.

The first step in observing and recording behavior is to *operationally define* the behavior in question. This means that you describe the behavior so that another person knows exactly what is meant. For example, if you describe a student as "has a negative attitude," it may be difficult to know exactly what you mean. However, if you use specific behavioral descriptions, such as "late to class 70% of the time" or "takes at least 10 minutes after the assignment has been given to become actively engaged, 50% of the time," it is much easier to know what is meant. It is also much easier to specify how the behavior is to change and to know whether it has changed. For example, if "late to class less than 20% of the time" is specified as a behavioral objective, it will not be difficult to determine whether this objective has been met. Many students with disabilities have behavioral objectives such as these included on their individualized education program.

Following is an example of an **operational definition** of "on-task" behavior (other definitions are possible and may be more appropriate in particular situations):

- *On-task.* The student's eyes are directed toward the teacher (or classmate, if making a relevant contribution) or instructional materials (e.g., books, pencil, paper, laboratory materials), and the student is manually engaged with instructional materials in an appropriate way.

When you use operationalized behaviors, it is easier to create a behavioral objective specifying (1) the content of the objective, (2) the conditions under which a student's performance will be assessed, and (3) the criteria for acceptable performance. For example, an objective for on-task behavior could be: "The student will exhibit on-task behavior in social studies class, to a criterion of 85%, on 4 out of 5 consecutive days." This behavior can then be recorded, in baseline (preintervention) or intervention conditions, to determine whether it has improved.

USE OBSERVATION AND RECORDING SYSTEMS Table 8.4 provides some examples of observation and recording systems. These can be used to record specific behaviors, depending on the type of target behavior and the circumstances under which it is exhibited (Alberto et al., 2022; Martin & Pear, 2019).

TABLE 8.4 Observation and Recording Systems

Name	Description
Event recording	Observer tallies the number of times a particular behavior occurs. This procedure is best when documenting behaviors that are discrete, such as talk-outs, tardiness, or tantruming. If the duration of these behaviors is always similar, or irrelevant, the observer simply records the number of events.
Duration recording	Observer records (e.g., with a stopwatch) the cumulative amount of time during which the behavior occurs. This system is appropriate when the length, or duration, is of concern. For example, a teacher may wish to record the total amount of time a socially withdrawn student engages in solitary play activities during recess. The observer starts the stopwatch when the socially isolated play begins and stops it when the child begins interacting with others. The recording resumes when the child returns to isolated play.
Interval recording	The observer sets an interval—say, 1 minute—and documents whether a particular behavior has occurred at any time during that interval. For example, if talking to classmates is the target behavior, the observer records for each 1-minute interval whether the behavior has occurred. At the end of the period in question (e.g., a 50-minute class period), the number of intervals in which the behavior has occurred is divided by the total number of intervals (e.g., 50). Therefore, if talking to classmates was recorded for 10 intervals, then the amount of talking for the time period could be recorded as $50 \div 10 = 20\%$.
Time sampling	At a specific point of time, the observer records whether a behavior is occurring. For example, a "beep" goes off in an observer's headphones every 5-minute segment and, at that instant, the observer records whether the behavior (e.g., on-task) is being exhibited. At the end of the period, as with interval recording, the observer can divide the number of times a target behavior occurred by the total number of times sampled.

Observing and recording behaviors are much more difficult with large numbers of students. Some strategies for observing with large classes include enlisting the assistance of an aide or paraprofessional, enlisting peer assistance, observing a small number of students at a time, and video-recording the entire class and recording observations later. When observing the whole class, try using seating charts and time sampling at longer intervals. For example, at the end of every 10-minute interval, make a check mark on the square representing the desk of every student who is off-task.

DETERMINE THE CONTEXT OF BEHAVIOR One good strategy for determining the dynamics of classroom behavior is to use an "ABC" chart (Bijou et al., 1968; Kerr & Nelson, 2010). The teacher creates a chart with three columns: *A*ntecedent, *B*ehavior, and *C*onsequence (see Figure 8.2 for an example). The target behavior to be observed is noted in the middle column (e.g., pushing, hitting), and the events that occurred immediately before the behavior (antecedent) are also noted, as well as the consequence, or what happened following the behavior.

In examining the ABC chart, you can ask, for example, when and where does the target behavior occur, who is present when it occurs, and what activities or events precede the target behavior. It is also important to note what happens after the target behavior occurs, what changes after the target behavior is exhibited, and what the student receives (or avoids) after the target behavior occurs (McDaniel & Flower, 2015). For example, you may find that peer attention was almost always a consequence of the behavior (verbal aggression toward teacher) or that independent work assignments usually were the antecedent. Such analysis can lead to a better understanding of where, when, and why the behavior is occurring (Crone et al., 2015). The example in Figure 8.2 shows that Shawna gains peer attention by provoking Marcie three times in the cafeteria. The ABC analysis helps to define the problem behavior that Shawna is using negative words and gestures toward Marcie at lunch. More information is needed to determine if this is an isolated incident between two friends who are not getting along or if this is a reoccurring event that occurs in many settings during the school day. Strategies to address bullying are provided later in this chapter.

Insights from an ABC chart are helpful in planning interventions. Consider a case in which Vinh, a 10th-grade student, typically acts out in socially immature ways when given written assignments in English class. This gains the attention of some students, which appears to reinforce Vinh. You may decide to examine the assignments to determine whether they are (or Vinh perceives them to be) too difficult or uninteresting. If so, you could reduce the difficulty level of the assignments, increase the interest level, and provide some specific positive support for Vinh's assignment completion. Furthermore, you could arrange an intervention in which you support other students for ignoring Vinh when he acts out. Although these strategies are likely to work, they may not. To be more certain of their effectiveness, graphically present data on Vinh's behavior both before and after the intervention.

Figure 8.2 Example Record Form for an ABC Analysis

Student's name: Marcie   Observer: Mrs. Wilson

Setting: Cafeteria   Date: April 3, 2023

Observation time period: Lunch, 12:15 – 12:45

Antecedent Events	Behaviors Observed	Consequent Events
12:22: Marcie approaches a table in the lunchroom where several students are seated.	Shawna told Marcie, "You can't sit here!"	Marcie sits at another table.
12:28: Students seated at lunch table.	Shawna calls out to Marcie, "Marcie, you stay over there."	Marcie makes a face at Shawna.
12:45: Students are leaving the lunch area.	Shawna steps in front of Marcie, ostentatiously.	Marcie pushes Shawna, and says, "You get away from me!"

MAKE GRAPHIC PRESENTATIONS OF STUDENT BEHAVIOR Behavior is much easier to evaluate over time if it is presented in some type of chart or other graphic display (Martin & Pear, 2019). For example, suppose the percent of time on-task during math class is recorded for that week. Usually, the amount of behavior exhibited is recorded on the vertical axis and the time (e.g., days) is recorded on the horizontal axis, as shown in Figure 8.3.

In Figure 8.3, the vertical axis records the percentage of on-task behavior for each day, and the horizontal axis records the days when the behavior was measured. In this example, on-task behavior is *stable* (does not appear to be going up or down over time) but is lower than desirable. If an intervention is planned, such as praise for on-task behavior and task completion, the effectiveness of this intervention can be evaluated, as illustrated in Figure 8.4. The vertical line represents the initiation of the intervention.

From the data in Figure 8.4, it appears that the intervention is having a positive effect on the behavior, at least initially (for more complex designs for establishing the validity of an intervention, such as the multiple baseline or reversal design, see Martin & Pear, 2019). For the most positive behavioral effects, use effective classroom management strategies.

Pearson eTextbook
Video Example 8.3
A teacher and the assistant principal in this video describe how the school community teaches behavioral expectations and consequences to middle and high school students. How is the student involved in this process?

STRATEGIES FOR USING EFFECTIVE CLASSROOM MANAGEMENT METHODS

ESTABLISH A POSITIVE CLASSROOM ATMOSPHERE The first and most important step in effective classroom management is establishing and maintaining a positive, supportive classroom atmosphere. Students are more likely to follow directions, work hard, and exhibit positive classroom behavior when they feel wanted and appreciated by the teacher. This may be especially true of particularly difficult students, who may not trust adults and may feel that most teachers are "out to get them."

Project a feeling, caring persona. Convince students that you like them (even though you might not always appreciate their behaviors) and value them as individuals. Address students by name and express an interest in their preferred activities. Build up a store of positive comments to individual students so that if you must deliver negative feedback later, it is not the first evaluation you have made of the student. As described earlier in this chapter, teach with sincerity and enthusiasm, using interesting and motivational activities. If students enjoy your class and are interested in the subject, they will be less likely to misbehave. To build student confidence, try to maintain a very high rate of correct student responses to your questions.

If a student in your class exhibits hostile or aggressive behaviors, it is particularly important that you have established relations that are as positive as possible. This is true even if the student is rarely or never positive with you. You must enforce rules fairly and consistently, and you must not give in to student attempts to control the classroom agenda; nevertheless, you should always remain calm and polite, reminding difficult students that you simply wish to see them make good decisions.

Figure 8.3 Recording On-Task Behavior

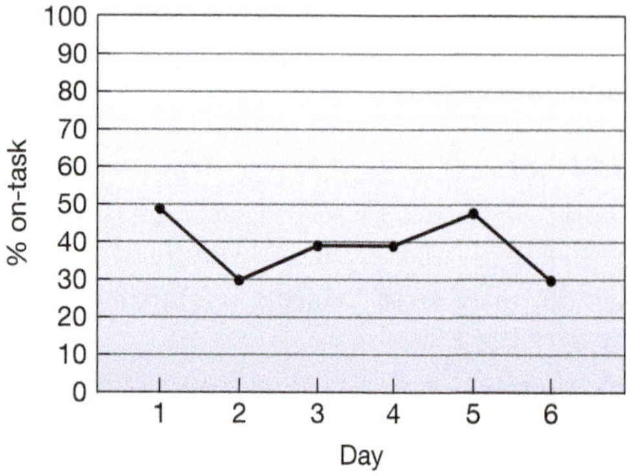

Figure 8.4 Recording an Intervention on On-Task Behavior

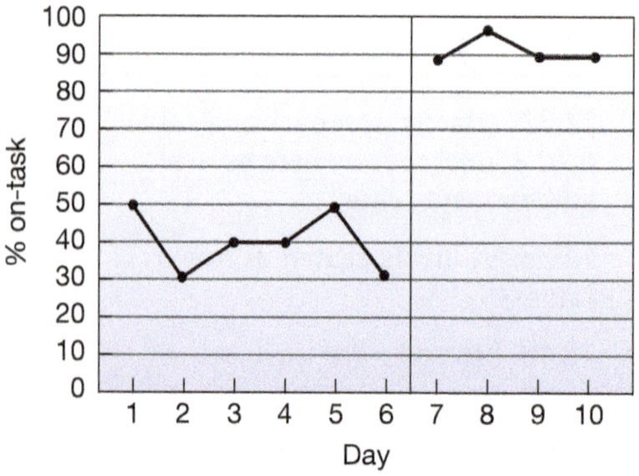

STRATEGIES FOR
LESS-INTENSIVE CLASSROOM MANAGEMENT METHODS

As much as possible, keep your management strategies simple, low-key, direct, and practical. Low-intensity behavior management can be more effective for you in the long run and can reduce the danger of behavior escalating in the face of more intensive interventions. Such strategies include rules, praise and ignoring, proximity, direct appeals, and the judicious use of reprimands.

POST AND DISCUSS CLASSROOM RULES An important early consideration for effective classroom management is familiarizing all students with your classroom rules. For younger students, post the classroom rules in a place where all students can observe them. Write them as positively as possible. When rules are first posted, describe them carefully to the class, model the behaviors covered by the rules, and ask students to give their own examples. Discuss instances and noninstances of following the rule. For example, a third-grade teacher might say about a rule, "If a student takes another student's eraser without asking to borrow it, is that respecting other people?" Refer to these rules often when discussing classroom behavior.

Providing rules is an important first step in classroom behavior management, but rules that are not enforced will soon lose their effectiveness. Several low-intensity strategies can help enforce your classroom rules.

PRAISE POSITIVE BEHAVIORS AND IGNORE INAPPROPRIATE BEHAVIORS Although potentially dangerous disruptive behavior must be attended to immediately, many inappropriate behaviors can be effectively managed by ignoring and pointing out positive models (Jones et al., 2016). For example, Sandra's fifth-grade teacher noticed that she was not getting her materials ready for a new lesson, so she acknowledged a positive example of a student seated near Sandra and said, "I like the way Marketa has put away her notebook and taken out her reading book. She has all her materials at hand and is ready to start class. Thank you, Marketa." Such comments show well-behaved students that their efforts are appreciated and they provide a model for other students.

CONTROL BEHAVIOR WITH PROXIMITY Moving closer to students who are beginning to demonstrate off-task or disruptive behavior can, in many instances, help to minimize classroom behavior problems. Conroy and colleagues (2004) found that teacher **proximity** generally increased appropriate behaviors of students with autism in general education settings (although a smaller number of students with autism did not respond positively to adult proximity). Additionally, be careful that your proximity does not become a reinforcer. Carey and Bourbon (2004) reported that a student with attention-deficit/hyperactivity disorder (ADHD) began to act out more frequently so that he could receive the reward (for him) of more teacher proximity.

MAKE DIRECT APPEALS Although they are often overlooked as a behavior management strategy, **direct appeals** can be effective. Students can simply be asked personally to follow class rules more carefully; alternately, a more systematic procedure can be used (Beck et al., 1982). Mary, an eighth-grader in Ms. Simms's math class, frequently whispered and giggled with her neighboring classmate during whole-class activities. During an independent seatwork activity, Ms. Simms asked to speak to Mary privately. She asked Mary directly not to talk to her neighbor during class time. Ms. Simms also related that if she saw Mary talking again, she would prompt her to stop by moving toward Mary's desk (proximity). After this conversation, Mary's talking decreased substantially and, after a few prompts, it remained in control throughout the school year.

USE REPRIMANDS JUDICIOUSLY Although positive responses to positive behavior are among the best overall methods of classroom management, negative feedback in the form of reprimands is sometimes necessary to help students succeed in your class (Simonsen et al., 2008). Overall, reprimands are best viewed as direct feedback that the student's behavior is inappropriate. If they are provided in a way that indicates concern for the student's well-being, they can be effective in improving behavior. Reprimands are less effective when viewed as punishment—that is, when criticism and scorn or a negative, aggressive, or hostile tone of voice is expected to prevent the student from repeating the inappropriate behavior.

In the Classroom

A Summary of Research on Reprimands

____ Reprimand students privately, not publicly, to avoid humiliating or embarrassing students.

____ Stand near the student you are reprimanding. This allows you to use a more confidential tone of voice. However, remaining one-leg-length away respects the student's personal space.

____ Use a normal tone of voice. Students can become desensitized over time to raised voices and may be less inclined to respond defensively to a calm tone.

____ Look at the student while you are speaking, but do not insist that the student must return your eye contact. Forced eye contact can be viewed as hostile and aggressive and, in some cases, it can violate cultural norms.

____ Do not point your finger at the student you are reprimanding because this conveys aggression and hostility.

____ Do not insist on having the last word. This may be particularly true when dealing with adolescents. The final goal of your reprimand is increased student compliance with class rules, and if this goal is achieved in the long run (e.g., the student ultimately returns to work or stops bothering a classmate), a little face-saving posturing may be allowable.

Source: From Kerr & Nelson (2010), p. 233. Adapted and reprinted with permission from Merrill/Prentice Hall.

The *In the Classroom* feature offers a list of recommended guidelines for using reprimands (Kerr & Nelson, 2010). It is also important that teachers link reprimands directly to class rules and avoid warnings, threats, sarcasm, or ridicule that may further alienate the student. In addition, if students respond with sentences like the following examples, do not engage them by arguing further.

- "For what? What'd I do?"
- "I didn't do anything!"
- "You let Fredericka do it!"
- "James started it!"

In some instances, excessive warnings have been known to increase the amount of inappropriate behavior (e.g., Twyman et al., 1994). If your reprimand is ineffective and the behavior persists, avoid making additional reprimands. Instead, a more intensive, prearranged contingency should be enforced (e.g., the student loses a privilege or a call is made to the student's home). If a student repeatedly argues with you, it may be helpful to set "arguing" as a personal target for that student to work on.

STRATEGIES FOR MORE FORMAL CLASSROOM MANAGEMENT METHODS

Informal management systems can be helpful; however, when problems continue, more formal management systems may be necessary as a supplement to your ongoing informal management strategies.

SYSTEMATICALLY REINFORCE POSITIVE BEHAVIOR Intangible rewards such as written or verbal praise can be an effective method of promoting a positive classroom atmosphere and positive social behavior. However, sometimes more tangible reinforcement is required. Tangible reinforcement includes such things as stickers, stars, and **primary reinforcers** such as snacks or drinks. Positive reinforcement can be very effective with students with a variety of disabilities in a variety of circumstances (Scheuermann et al., 2022; Watling & Schwartz, 2004). Some teachers disapprove of tangible reinforcers because they believe students should learn to work for the satisfaction of doing well in school. However, for some students, more tangible rewards may be necessary to help them succeed in the general education classroom. Survey students or keep personal records to determine what sort of reinforcers appeal to your students. Check-out teacher stores that carry posters, stickers, pencils, or other supplies that could be used as rewards. Reinforcers for middle or high school students may include free choice, specific activities, or social reinforcers. Rewards should be *applied consistently* for following specific rules or meeting specific academic or behavioral objectives.

Sometimes a student with disabilities may require rewards for doing things for which other students in the classroom do not require rewards. For example, Larry is a student with intellectual disabilities who is newly enrolled in a general education sixth-grade classroom, and he exhibits a great deal of difficulty in sustaining attention on academic tasks. Larry does not respond well to reprimands, but he loves animal crackers. With the approval of Larry's mother, Ms. Irby made an arrangement with Larry that if he continued working on his assignments for 5 minutes, he would receive 1 point. After he collected 25 points, he could receive an animal cracker to eat at lunch. She made a point sheet and let Larry know after every 5-minute period whether he had earned a point.

Sometimes individual rewards can be combined with group rewards. If students feel "left out" because students with diverse learning needs are receiving rewards while they do not, allow the class to have some group reward if the students with disabilities meet their goals. Emphasize that students have different needs to succeed in school and that fairness has more to do with meeting people's needs than with everyone being treated exactly the same.

REWARD STUDENTS WITH TOKEN SYSTEMS **Token systems**, or token economies, can be used with individual students, small groups of students, or entire classrooms (Scheuermann et al., 2022). In a token system, students who follow class rules are awarded points at the end of specified time periods, such as class periods. The points are symbolic representations that can later be exchanged for a reinforcer of value. The positive benefits of token systems have long been observed (Jenkins & Gorrafa, 1974; McLaughlin & Malaby, 1976). Remember Larry and how points to be exchanged for animal crackers were used as a reward for increased on-task behavior? His points were offered in shorter increments of time because this met his individual learning need. For other situations, however, you may want to award bonus points for unusually diligent work or cooperative behavior. A sample chart that can be used to record tokens or points awarded to individual students is presented in Figure 8.5.

Figure 8.5 Sample Recording Chart for Token System

Class Rules

1. Always respect other people.
2. Raise your hand before speaking.
3. Remain in your seat.
4. Ask for help when you need it.
5. Complete all assignments.

	Rule				
Student	**1**	**2**	**3**	**4**	**5**
Marybeth	*	*	*	*	*
Bill	*	*	*	*	
Shawna		*	*		*
Michelle	*	*	*	*	*
Arnold	*	*	*	*	
James	*	*	*	*	*
Dustin	*	*	*	*	*
Chico		*	*	*	*
Kelly	*			*	*
Pam	*	*	*	*	*

In the token system corresponding to the recording chart, students receive a star if they follow a classroom rule throughout a particular time period. In some cases, the period can be the entire school day. For younger students or students with disabilities, it may be more appropriate to evaluate behavior after each period. Students can accumulate stars or points and exchange these later for small prizes (such as stickers or school supplies) or privileges (such as line leader or a homework pass). Entire classrooms can be awarded points after each period, depending on the behavior of all students, and thus accumulate points toward group rewards, such as a popcorn party or a longer recess break. Teachers can also post a "menu" of prizes or privileges that can be exchanged for tokens and the corresponding "price" of each. For older students, try holding an "auction" of possible prizes that students can bid on. Students can be surveyed ahead of time on their preferences for prizes.

Like all behavior management systems, token systems are most effective when they are used primarily to reward positive behavior. In many cases, not earning positive points can motivate students to exhibit appropriate behavior. However, when necessary, token systems can also be used as punishment for individual students who exhibit seriously inappropriate behavior. In a procedure also known as **response cost** (Buchard & Barrera, 1972; Simonsen et al., 2008), previously earned points are withdrawn for serious misbehavior. If using response cost, be certain that students have been informed of this possible consequence ahead of time and that the procedure produces the desired results. For example, you would never want to publicly humiliate or shame a student when using a classwide response cost procedure.

TEACH POSITIVE ATTRIBUTIONS FOR SOCIAL BEHAVIOR Attribution training can be effective as a motivational strategy, as described previously, but it is also important in linking social behavior to things under students' control. For example, students with problem behaviors often make **negative attributions**—that is, they attribute things that happen to them to forces outside of their own control, for example, that they were picked on or treated unfairly, which caused them to misbehave.

The teacher's job is to help students learn to attribute social consequences to behavior that they control (Maag, 2006). Guiding students toward more appropriate attributions usually takes time and may require frequent review of appropriate attributions for positive outcomes:

The reason you got to come with us to the zoo today was that you tried very hard to control your talk-outs this week. Good job!

And negative outcomes:

The reason you got detention today is that you chose not to do your work, and you argued with your teacher. Let's talk about some ways to keep out of detention in the future.

POST POSITIVE BEHAVIOR Public posting of students' behaviors has also been shown to reduce behavior problems (Troup et al., 2014). In one instance, public posting of daily quiz scores where behavior had been a problem improved both behavior and quiz scores (Jones & Van Houten, 1985). The daily quiz scores were displayed on laminated pieces of poster board and were recorded for 5-day periods. In other variations, students' behavior can be evaluated and recorded on a publicly posted chart. Students who follow all class rules can be given a star next to their names for each class period, day, or other appropriate length of time.

USE NEGATIVE CONSEQUENCES JUDICIOUSLY Punishment, in the form of negative consequences for inappropriate behavior, is less effective in the long run than positive reinforcement, and punishment should not be used when more positive alternatives are available (Maag, 2001; Wheeler & Richey, 2014). However, punishment is sometimes necessary to maintain order and provide a safe environment for all students. Canter and Canter (2010) recommended posting a "discipline hierarchy" so that students are informed about the consequences for violating a rule. Another advantage of posting rules and consequences is that the teacher can assume the role of enforcer or arbiter of class rules, rather than the role of a dictator who administers rewards and punishments at whim. If rules are consistently enforced, the teacher can merely state, "I'm sorry you broke the rules, too, but you were aware of the consequences. I will try to help you follow the rules better in the future." Punishment is not appropriate for students who developmentally may not understand the rules or in instances when the consequences give unintended attention to the child.

A sample discipline hierarchy for grades 4 through 6, recommended by Canter and Canter (2010), lists consequences for rule infractions that progress as follows: "warning" (first time), sending a completed "think sheet" (described in the following paragraph) to parents or caregivers (second time), brief amount of time away from the group (third time), calling parents or caregivers (fourth time), and sending to the principal (fifth time). A "severe" clause refers to any severe breach of class rules, such as vandalism or fighting, and it replaces the routine sequence of the discipline hierarchy. That is, if a student disrupts the entire class or endangers the safety of other students, the student is sent directly to the principal, regardless of whether it is the first, second, or third violation of a rule.

A "think sheet" documents that the student understands the rule that was broken, why the rule was broken, and the consequences of breaking the rule and has a strategy for dealing with the same situation more appropriately in the future.

Other, more substantial types of punishment are also sometimes used. **Suspension** involves not allowing the student to return to school for a specified time period. Some schools use **in-school suspension**, in which the student must attend a specific suspension room in the school and is not allowed in the regularly assigned classroom. Removing the student from school usually involves a group decision of teachers and administrators. Many states limit the number of days a student with disabilities may be suspended (e.g., 10 days) until it is considered a change of placement, which will then require a formal placement decision of the multidisciplinary team. It is also important to consider whether the behavior for which the student is being suspended is a consequence of the disability. If so, suspension may be considered a type of denial of school services because of the student's disability—which, of course, is inappropriate (Jones et al., 2016).

Some states also allow teachers or administrators to administer **corporal punishment**, such as paddling or some other method of inflicting physical pain. Professional organizations and others have long advocated against the use of corporal punishment because it is almost never more effective than alternatives and is almost certain to promote resentment and anger in the student (Council for Children with Behavioral Disorders, 1990; Scheuermann et al., 2022; U.S. Department of Education, 2017).

USE TIMEOUT FOR SPECIFIC BEHAVIOR PROBLEMS **Timeout** refers to some type of separation of the student from the routine classroom environment, usually for a violation of class rules. It can include **contingent observation timeout**, where the student is seated nearby and can still observe group activities; **exclusionary timeout**, where the student is removed from the instructional activity; and **seclusionary timeout**, where the student is removed from the instructional setting to another setting, such as a timeout room.

Timeout can be useful to protect the safety of the student and other students and staff, help students cool down after a volatile situation, or provide them time to reflect quietly on their behavior. In other cases, timeout may serve as tangible feedback about their classroom behavior. Overall, timeout is most effective when the classroom activities the students are excluded from are enjoyable and rewarding (so they will not view timeout as an avoidance of undesirable schoolwork), and the students do not feel reinforced for the attention they receive when placed in timeout. It is also important that timeout periods be brief (e.g., 1–5 minutes) and that timeout is part of a larger behavior management plan that is mostly positive. Timeout should not be used if there is a possibility of self-injury. Student behavior should be monitored while in timeout, and it should never be considered a type of incarceration (Scheuermann et al., 2022). That is, students should not be isolated and if there is a door to the timeout area, it should be unlocked. Additionally, school personnel who monitor timeout should be trained with performance feedback, as needed. Behaviors that would result in timeout, such as specific disruptive events, should be posted and discussed with the class before implementation of the procedure. Many states have specific policies regarding the use of timeout, so be certain to check with state as well as local policies when implementing this procedure.

Use Debriefing Procedures After Timeout Regardless of the type of timeout, students need to be debriefed before returning to full status in the classroom. This is a form of attribution training and serves to ensure that students are aware of the behavior that resulted in the timeout and how they could handle a similar situation better in the future. Before returning to the classroom, students should be able to state clearly why they were placed in timeout (i.e., for which specific behaviors) and how such events can be avoided in the future. If, for example, a student's misbehavior was the apparent response to the perceived actions of another student ("Billy was teasing me"), the student should discuss how to respond appropriately to such behavior in the future.

PLAY THE GOOD-BEHAVIOR GAME Researchers (e.g., Harris & Sherman, 1973; Leflot et al., 2010) have described a behavior management technique referred to as the Good-Behavior Game (GBG). The GBG is an evidenced-based strategy that has been effective at increasing pro-social behaviors and reducing disruptive and off-task behaviors of students in K–12 (Bowman-Perrott et al., 2016; Flower et al., 2014). In one variation of the GBG procedure, the teacher divides the class into two or more groups, alternating group members frequently. During an instructional period, each disruptive or noncompliant behavior counts as a point for the team of the offending student. Rules such as the following are set: "(a) raise your hand before talking; (b) sit in your seat properly; (c) pay attention; (d) keep your hands to yourself; and (e) stay in your seat" (Brigham et al., 1992, p. 7). At the end of a designated time period, the team with the fewest points is declared the winner and may be provided with a group reward.

SET UP STUDENT CONTRACTING Behavioral **contracting** involves the establishment of a written agreement that formalizes the behaviors a student agrees to exhibit and the positive consequences that will result from the fulfillment of the contract (Simonsen et al., 2008). Contracts should identify the reinforcer, the behavior, the time frame, and the criterion. Often, the negative consequences of not fulfilling the contract are also specified. Contracts can be a positive way to provide a role for families and caregivers in improving classroom behavior. For example, Morris has been erratic in turning in his homework for math class. Sometimes he completes his homework assignments and turns them in promptly; other times, he does not turn in his homework and acts defensive and belligerent when questioned about it.

In a written, dated, and signed contract, Morris's parents agreed to take him to a popular amusement park for 2 days (the reinforcer) if he turns in all of his homework assignments in math (the behavior) for the next 2 months (the time frame), with no more than two lapses (the criterion). Conversely, if Morris misses more than two homework assignments in the next 2 months, he will lose some of his television privileges, according to the severity of his lapses.

Pearson eTextbook

Classroom Management Simulation 8.1: Creating Classroom Behavioral Expectations

This simulation provides an interactive review of methods for ensuring that students will understand, accept, and consistently follow agreed-upon classroom behavior expectations.

STRATEGIES FOR HANDLING CLASSROOM CONFRONTATIONS

One of the things that frightens teachers most is being directly confronted by students. Confrontations can constitute direct challenges to the authority of the teacher and can, depending on how they are handled, have a profound effect on the classroom environment.

The problems of confrontations can be seen in the dialogue in the following *Classroom Scenario* (see also Canter & Canter, 1993).

CLASSROOM SCENARIO

Marcus

Ms. Amani, the English teacher, has practiced brainstorming and organizing ideas with the class, and she has just directed them to start working on the first draft of their persuasive essays. Several minutes after giving the direction, she notices that Marcus has still not begun to write.

MS. AMANI: Marcus, time to get started.

MARCUS: I don't feel like it. Leave me alone, okay?

MS. AMANI: Do you need some help getting started?

MARCUS: I said I don't feel like it. Get out of my face.

MS. AMANI: I don't appreciate your tone, young man. I gave you a direction, and I expect you to follow it.

MARCUS: (*raising his voice*) Back off. I told you I don't feel like it!

MS. AMANI: (*raising her voice*) Now you listen to me! I've had enough of your attitude. Now get started on your assignment or else!

MARCUS: (*mumbling*) I'll tell you where you can put your assignment . . .

(*students laugh*)

MS. AMANI: That's it, Marcus. I've had enough of your backtalk. Apologize right now, or you'll be in detention for the rest of the year.

MARCUS: Yeah? Well, I don't care what you think. I'm out of here. (*overturns desk and storms out of the classroom*)

Marcus has placed himself in a situation where his anger and anxiety can only escalate. By also being confrontational, the teacher has helped place Marcus in this position. The teacher has reacted emotionally, and this emotional reaction has fed into Marcus's desire to control the situation. A difficult situation has become more difficult, the teacher's relationship with Marcus has deteriorated, and now the entire class is off-task. Some students, such as Marcus, may not believe that teachers can be trusted to act in the students' best interest and may feel compelled to fight teachers in these situations.

QUESTIONS FOR REFLECTION

1. What factors could have prompted Marcus's strong response to such a reasonable teacher direction?
2. What contributions are made by both Marcus and the teacher that escalate this conflict?
3. What are some alternative responses by the teacher and by Marcus that could have improved this situation?

DIFFUSE CONFRONTATIONS WITH A CALM, MEASURED RESPONSE Canter and Canter (1993) recommended several steps for dealing with this type of confrontation. The most important thing to remember is to *remain calm.* Count to 3, 4, 5, or 10 if necessary. Control your breathing by taking long, slow breaths. Take yourself out of the situation by depersonalizing it. In Marcus's case, if you have been doing your job as a teacher, he is probably responding to his own past experiences, lack of trust, and his own needs at the moment. *Don't take it personally.* Remind yourself, "This is not about me!" If you are able to remain calm, you will have more control of the situation. Your calmness and task orientation in the face of hostility can go far toward resolving the situation.

The most effective approach would be not to escalate the situation in the first place by making loud reprimands and threats. Remain calm, restate your desire privately to Marcus that he return to work, and restate your personal interest in his success in your classroom:

MS. AMANI: *(quietly and calmly)* I understand you're upset, Marcus, but I really need you to go back to work now. If you need my help, let me know. I know you have great ideas about this writing topic.

If necessary, move Marcus away from his peers and speak to him privately—preferably with Marcus seated with his back to the class. Then, if Marcus is still upset, give him a little time and space to make a positive choice.

Speak to the student later if this seems a better solution. Ultimately, of course, your rules must be enforced. However, keep in mind the bigger picture of establishing trust and helping Marcus fit into the classroom environment. Do not behave in such a way that Marcus feels heroic by standing up to your raised voice and threatening manner. Make Marcus believe that you wish him to get started on his work simply because you want him to succeed in school and do not want to see him get a failing grade on the assignment. Do not feel that you must have the last word in the dialogue. As one principal said, "Teenagers need the last word a lot more than I do!" (Kerr & Nelson, 2010, p. 262). If Marcus returns to work, even while grumbling and rolling his eyes, you have achieved your purpose for the moment and you have prevented an unpleasant situation from escalating.

If a student's behavior seems very much out of character, it may be wise to ignore the behavior for the moment and discuss the problem later when the student has calmed down somewhat. It may also be necessary to back off for a certain period of time if the student's behavior appears particularly volatile or threatening or if a student refuses to leave the peer group. If you believe that situations such as these are possible in your classroom, find out ahead of time how to call for support (Canter & Canter, 1993).

Kerr and Nelson (2010) provided several additional suggestions for de-escalating verbal confrontations, including the following:

- "Pick your battles" by declining to fight over inconsequential issues.
- Listen to what the student is saying to reduce hostility and help find a good solution.
- Avoid sarcasm, which often escalates tension.
- Allow students to save face by avoiding humiliating or embarrassing a student.
- Stay in control of your own emotions.

Kerr and Nelson emphasized that you should get to know your students, including their personal and cultural backgrounds and beliefs. Better awareness of your students can lead to better communication and better overall classroom management.

Implementing Schoolwide Behavior Management Systems

Learning Objective 8.3 Explain schoolwide behavior management systems and strategies that support schoolwide positive behavior.

An obvious advantage of schoolwide discipline systems is that the same rules are enforced in the same way throughout the school and the structured consistency can be beneficial to limit-seeking students, as well as to students who have difficulty adjusting to different standards or rules being enforced in different classrooms (Kerr & Nelson, 2010). Some disadvantages of schoolwide discipline systems are that, unless specifically programmed, they may not effectively address the needs of all individual students and that, if misunderstood or misapplied, they can promote an overall punitive atmosphere throughout the school. Any behavior management system must be as positive toward and supportive of the needs of students as possible because systems that are perceived as punitive or oppressive will be resented and may actually encourage noncompliance and vandalism (Mayer et al., 1987; Rosenberg & Jackman, 2003). These concerns have led to the development and application of positive behavioral interventions and supports (PBIS).

POSITIVE BEHAVIORAL INTERVENTIONS AND SUPPORTS

Previously, schoolwide discipline emphasized reacting to specific student misbehavior with the use of punishment-based strategies (e.g., expulsion, suspension). However, teaching the behavioral expectations and rewarding students for following them is a much more positive approach than simply waiting for misbehavior to occur before responding. The overall purpose of schoolwide PBIS is to establish a positive climate in which appropriate behavior is the expectation for all students (OSEP Technical Assistance Center on PBIS, 2012). As such, PBIS employs, on a schoolwide level, principles very similar to those discussed previously in this chapter.

Positive behavioral interventions and supports rely on behavioral principles to produce socially important outcomes with procedures that are socially appropriate and culturally responsive (Crone et al., 2015; Kerr & Nelson, 2010; Leverson et al., 2021). Behavioral support is not viewed simply as a way of reducing or eliminating inappropriate social behavior through punishment or extinction; rather, it is a multi-tiered behavioral framework for assisting students in being successful within a social or educational context (Horner et al., 2010; see https://www.pbis.org). When needed, PBIS involves a functional behavioral assessment (FBA) to determine the nature of problem behavior and how it is maintained within a social system (typically including ABC charts, such as the one shown in Figure 8.2). Based on the FBA, a behavioral support plan can be developed that focuses on (1) altering the environment so that problem behaviors become irrelevant, (2) teaching new skills to students to supplant previous counterproductive behaviors, and (3) establishing consequences that make inappropriate behaviors less effective and, ultimately, irrelevant (Crone et al., 2015; Lewis et al., 2010).

Nelson and Sugai (1999; see also Crone et al., 2015) described the schoolwide application of PBIS as a four-stage process that is undertaken by a rotating committee of eight (or fewer) members representative of the entire school staff (behavior support team).

Stage 1 During Stage 1, the committee defines and identifies the problems to be addressed by the schoolwide PBIS program. This can be accomplished with the use of surveys and interviews, direct observations, and archival school data.

Stage 2 During Stage 2, the committee undertakes a site analysis to determine that the necessary aspects of PBIS are in place.

Stage 3 In Stage 3, the committee works to develop and implement the PBIS programs in four systems: schoolwide, for all staff, students, and settings; specific settings or nonclassroom settings (e.g., restrooms, cafeterias); classroom systems; and systems for support of individual students, usually those with serious and chronic problem behavior. The program is developed and revised through a multistep consensus-building process.

Stage 4 As the programs are implemented, progress is monitored in Stage 4 with respect to baseline data collected during a needs assessment. Findings of the evaluation are shared with all staff members on a regular basis and the programs are adjusted as needed, based on the results of the evaluation.

For example, office referral data could indicate that inappropriate behavior often occurs outside the music room during transitions. These instances could be further investigated with interviews of the relevant teachers and direct observations of the hallways at this time. It could be determined, for example, that much of the inappropriate behavior is involved with the unstructured milling about of many students in a relatively small area. Potential solutions could include announcing that students are to stay to the right when exiting the music room, ensuring that one class has exited the room before others enter, or having students exit by a different door. The selected interventions are then monitored to determine whether they have addressed the problem (Kerr & Nelson, 2010).

PBIS programs have produced positive results (Coffey & Horner, 2012; Sugai & Horner, 2020). PBIS programs try to solve significant behavior problems by examining behavior in the context of the entire social system and by devising overall positive alternatives to inappropriate behavior (Robbie et al., 2021; Safran & Oswald, 2003). Because teachers and schools in many instances choose reactive, negative consequences to disruptive or noncompliant behavior (Hawken et al., 2021), PBIS provides significant positive alternatives for achieving success.

Pearson eTextbook
Video Example 8.4
School personnel in this video describe a schoolwide positive behavioral support strategy in which all students can earn "Hawk Wings." Pay particular attention to how students are positively reinforced for demonstrating appropriate behavior.

STRATEGIES FOR IMPLEMENTING MULTI-TIERED SYSTEMS OF SUPPORT WITHIN A PBIS FRAMEWORK

Multi-tiered systems of support are designed to address different needs, reduce special education placement, and provide evidence for the appropriate identification of disabilities. They are intended to better integrate general education with special education and to provide appropriate services as soon as they are needed, prior to a formal referral to special education.

Scheuermann et al. (2022) described appropriate procedures for Tier 1 (universal), Tier 2 (targeted), and Tier 3 (tertiary) levels of support. Universal levels of support include optimal classroom management strategies, such as those described in this chapter, that are provided in every classroom. These can include consistent enforcement of rules and explanation of the procedures for following these rules, classroom organization and management, and effective instructional planning and delivery with frequent opportunities to respond (OTR). Also included are procedures for observing and recording behavior in order to determine whether the interventions and supports are effective for all students. This level of support is expected to be successful with 80–90% of students (Scheuermann et al., 2022).

PROMOTE SELF-MONITORING **Self-monitoring strategies** involve teaching students to monitor and evaluate their own classroom behavior (Jones et al., 2016; Maag, 2018). In some cases, students may be asked to monitor their general on-task behavior. In other cases, students may monitor themselves for the occurrence/nonoccurrence of a specific behavior, such as teasing. Before implementing self-monitoring interventions, meet individually and discuss with the students the purpose and importance of good classroom behavior and how they will benefit personally from it. Also, explain why the intervention is in their best interest.

To implement a self-monitoring system for a target behavior, such as teasing, provide the student with a self-monitoring sheet for the target behavior. The behavior should be operationalized so that it is very clear what constitutes teasing and what does not. These definitions will depend on the particular student's behavior. For example, teasing could in some cases include making statements such as, "Cornelius is a stupid jerk." Teasing in other cases could involve making faces at another student, staring at another student, or scratching the head with the middle finger while looking at another student. Familiarize the student with the self-monitoring sheet and how to use it. After each specified time interval (e.g., 5 or 10 minutes), prompt the student, play a timed and audio-recorded "beep" (or, e.g., timer function on a smartphone), or ask the student to take responsibility for monitoring the clock. The student then checks the appropriate column for "teasing" or "not teasing" over the time interval. At the end of a class period or the end of a day, compare their results with your own observations. Although paper-based self-monitoring is common, see the *Apps for Education* feature for some technology-based suggestions for self-recording. Students may not only receive rewards or consequences for behavior but also receive rewards for matching your recording of the behavior. The purpose is to foster independence and to encourage students to be conscious of their behavior so that they have more control of their actions. Although learners may initially need adult support, this assistance is faded over time. Self-monitoring strategies could be used across grade levels, settings, and content areas and with multiple students at a time to record several different target behaviors.

TEACH STUDENTS SELF-INSTRUCTION STRATEGIES **Self-instruction** or **self-regulation** training involves teaching students to employ self-directed statements or questions that guide social problem solving and may be particularly useful at the upper-elementary or secondary level. Questions can involve defining the situation, thinking through possible solutions, and choosing the best option (see also Glago et al., 2009; Isbell & Jolivette, 2011). Following is a possible example for social problem solving:

Check each step and think before you act!

1. What happened?
2. What are all possible solutions?
3. What is my goal for right now?
4. What is the best thing for me to do?
5. Did I make the best choice?

Teachers should model and role-play these thought processes. For example, the teacher should provide an example by saying:

> **What happened** is that Kimberly is making faces at me. The **possible solutions** are that I could make faces back at her, I could tell the teacher, or I could try to ignore her and finish my work. **My goal for right now** is just to finish this assignment, so I think the **best thing to do** is try to ignore her and see if she stops. If she doesn't, I tell the teacher. Well, she stopped making faces at me (or if she didn't, I didn't notice), so I think I made the **best choice**.

Self-instruction and self-regulation are components of **self-determination skills,** a construct associated with personal values and characteristics, such as autonomy, independence, intrinsic motivation, self-advocacy, and self-efficacy. **Self-determination instruction** refers to teaching people how to increase control of their own lives and destinies (Agran & Wehmeyer, 2003, see Chapter 16).

TEACH FOR GENERALIZATION Most positive social behaviors are of limited use unless they can be shown to generalize to appropriate situations outside the training context (Maag, 2018). It is particularly important that students in inclusive settings are able to generalize all the positive social behaviors they have learned in other settings; however, students with disabilities often demonstrate problems in generalizing learned behavior (Kerr & Nelson, 2010). As important social behaviors are learned, make a list of all the settings and situations for which the behavior must generalize and all the individuals who will observe the generalized behavior. Then, create a plan to promote generalization across all of these settings and individuals.

Several strategies are available for promoting generalization, some of which have already been described. Self-monitoring and self-instruction are very relevant in promoting generalization through the use of cognitive routines. Students can use self-monitoring techniques to evaluate and modify their behavior in different contexts, as in the teasing example described previously. In addition, strive to teach behaviors that will be reinforced in natural settings, such as positive social responding. On other occasions, be sure that all relevant teachers and staff are aware of the behavior and reinforce it whenever it occurs. Classroom peers can also be very helpful in ensuring that target behavior is maintained over time and generalized by, for example, providing positive attention when students exhibit target behaviors. Teach "loosely" so that students are provided with a variety of situations and a number of possible responses. Be ready to reinforce any unprompted generalization of a learned behavior. Finally, when needed, reteach positive behaviors in several appropriate contexts; for example, reteach appropriate sitting in all relevant contexts, such as in the classroom, in the resource room, in homeroom, during assemblies, and on the school bus. By using a variety of possible strategies and monitoring their effectiveness, students will be much more likely to generalize their positive behaviors.

PROMOTE EQUITY IN DISCIPLINARY PRACTICES Exclusionary disciplinary practices such as suspensions and office referrals have been seen to negatively impact achievement and school climate (Reynolds et al. 2008). Additionally, students of color, particularly Black students, receive more exclusionary disciplinary referrals than White students (Girvan et al., 2017). Cook et al. (2018) developed a strategy for teacher interactions referred to as GREET-STOP-PROMPT (GSP). This strategy employed many of the procedures recommended in this chapter and was based around three overall components.

The GREET component was designed to increase proactive classroom management practices. Teachers were encouraged to greet students at the door (G); reinforce students frequently for specific behaviors (R); establish, review, and cue expectations for behavior (E); engage students with multiple opportunities to respond (E), to improve learning and on-task behavior; and take time to deliver wise feedback (T), to promote engagement and help students understand their own behavior.

The STOP component was designed to increase teachers' awareness of their own decision making and potential biases through self-regulation. Teachers were taught about implicit biases and how they occur in specific situations. When confronting problem behavior, teachers were encouraged to first stop (S) and not do anything while they bring their attention to the present moment and to take (T) a deep breath and attend to their own reactions (e.g., unproductive thoughts, anger, or frustration). Teachers then were encouraged to observe (O) what is happening in the environment and then to proceed (P) in the most positive manner to address the issue.

The PROMPT component was intended to promote teachers' use of effective and positive reactive strategies for correcting problem behavior, maintain the student in the learning environment, and preserve the teacher–student relationship. The PROMPT strategy included proximity control (P), moving closer to the student as a reminder, and redirection strategies (R) to correct problem behavior by making a request with a low probability of student resistance, such as asking the student to collect or hand out papers, get a drink of water, sharpen a pencil, or deliver a message next door. Teachers were taught to practice ongoing monitoring of behavior (OM) by reinforcing peers exhibiting the desired behavior or by praising successive approximations of the desired behavior in the target student. Prompting the desired behavior (P) is accomplished by privately directing the student toward desired behaviors in a calm, nonthreatening, and positive manner (e.g., "Do this" rather than "Don't do that"). The teaching interaction (T) is intended to maintain positive communication with the student through expressing empathy, clearly defining appropriate and inappropriate behavior and providing the rationale, warning of the natural classroom-based consequence and allowing the student time to think. Finally, the teacher must reinforce the student for making a good decision or provide the behavioral consequence.

The GSP strategy was implemented in three elementary schools in an urban school district that was employing a schoolwide disciplinary system over a period of 5 months. In these schools, Black male students were receiving office disciplinary referrals at a rate 2.5 times as high as other students. After the implementation of the intervention, Cook et al. (2018) reported that the schools had reduced overall disciplinary referrals by more than 50%. They also reported that students reported being more "connected" to the school experience and that overall risk ratios (Black male students being more likely to receive a disciplinary referral) had declined very considerably as a result of the intervention. Many of the techniques employed in the GSP strategy can be helpful in dealing with direct confrontations by students, as described in the following section.

CHECK-IN, CHECK-OUT INTERVENTION If it is determined that individual students are not succeeding with the universal level of support, a PBIS leadership team (usually including administrators, general and special education teachers, and support staff) can help evaluate problem behaviors and recommend interventions and supports at the second tier. These interventions can include targeted social skills training (see the Social Skills section of this chapter), often through small-group instruction, or "check-in, check-out" interventions (Hawken et al., 2021).

Check-in, check-out (CICO) is a standardized behavioral intervention that is used for students whose behaviors have not been responsive to Tier 1 practices, are observed across settings or situations, and do not require more immediate intervention (Hawken et al., 2021). CICO is commonly used as a Tier 2 intervention (Van Camp et al., 2020). It is a group-based intervention that is cost-effective and can be applied to a number of students with similar needs for behavioral support.

In order for CICO to be successfully implemented, several components must be successfully accessed:

1. **CHECK-IN.** CICO student participants check-in with a school-designated CICO facilitator each morning before class begins. The facilitator provides each student with a Daily Progress Report (DPR) and provides guidance about behavioral expectations and point goals for the day (see Figure 8.6). The DPR is similar to the recording chart for token systems described previously and provides expectations for each period. For example, "Respect others" and "Work on task" may be appropriate expectations for the intervention. In some cases, a "target" expectation, which may vary for each individual student, may be added.
2. **REGULAR TEACHER FEEDBACK.** The regular classroom teacher provides feedback on student behavioral performance based on the expectations provided in the DPR. This feedback normally occurs at the end of class periods or other natural transitions occurring throughout the day. The interval for feedback may vary with the intensity of the behavioral support needed. The teacher provides praise for meeting expectations, corrective feedback when appropriate, and then provides a rating of student demonstration of expectations using a predetermined point system (e.g., 1–3, based on number of reminders needed; see Figure 8.6).
3. **CHECK-OUT.** The student meets with the CICO facilitator who then provides the "check-out" at the end of each day. During this time, the facilitator totals the points earned for the day and provides feedback. If daily or weekly goals are met, the facilitator may provide additional praise and may provide a token for meeting daily or weekly goals, associated with the schoolwide behavior recognition system. When point goals are not met, facilitators may re-teach expectations and provide encouragement for meeting goals in the future.
4. **DATA RECORDING AND PROGRESS MONITORING.** CICO facilitators record the percent of DPR points earned periodically into a data recording system. These points are graphed and used in progress review by the Tier 2 team. Results of these graphs can be used to evaluate the effectiveness of the intervention and to support intervention decisions.
5. **FAMILY PARTICIPATION.** At the end of each school day, students are expected to take their DPR home for review by their parent or caregiver, who is asked to review the information and provide additional feedback and a signature. The student is encouraged to return the DPR to school the following day (Hawken et al., 2021; Missouri Schoolwide Positive Behavior Support, 2018, Ch. 5).

Research has consistently supported the efficacy of the CICO as a Tier 2 intervention (e.g., Park & Blair, 2020; Todd et al., 2008; Van Camp et al., 2020). Miller et al. (2015) demonstrated that, in some cases, the intervention can be faded over time and replaced with self-monitoring of behavior ratings and feedback. Majeika et al. (2019) reviewed literature and

Figure 8.6 Sample Daily Progress Report for Check-In Check-Out (for more examples, see Hawken et al., 2021; Missouri Schoolwide Positive Support, 2018).

Daily Progress Report

Washington Elementary School

Student Name________________________ Date____________

Points: 3 = 0 – 1 Reminders; 2 = 2 Reminders; 1 = 3+ Reminders

Allotted Time Period*	Respect Others *Teachers + Peers*	Work On Task *Follows* *directions*	Ask for Help *When* *needed*	Target Behavior ______	Teacher Initials	Success Notes
Early Morning	3 2 1	3 2 1	3 2 1	3 2 1		
Late Morning	3 2 1	3 2 1	3 2 1	3 2 1		
Early Afternoon	3 2 1	3 2 1	3 2 1	3 2 1		
Late Afternoon	3 2 1	3 2 1	3 2 1	3 2 1		

Today's Goal ________%

Today's Points ________/48 Possible Points = Today's Percent ____________

Family/Caregiver Signature ____________________ *I'm pleased because*

____

* This column could represent class periods, specific times, or transitions between activities.

reported that in 71% of studies using CICO, adaptations had been made to the procedures to address individual contexts. These included adaptations of the DPR, inclusion of targeted social skills training, and use of peer mentors, for example to conduct CICO sessions. Some studies included a homework check, or time for students to complete homework. Other adaptations included caregiver training, or adapted expectations based on initial nonresponsiveness to the standard CICO protocol. Since these investigations were generally successful, it can be concluded that CICO is an effective Tier 2 intervention for standard use in schools that is nevertheless versatile for adaptation to address specific circumstances. For additional information on implementing CICO, see Hawken et al. (2021) and Missouri Schoolwide Positive Behavior Support (2018).

If individual interventions and supports are needed beyond the targeted level, students can receive Tier 3, or the tertiary level of support, which may or may not include placement in special education. Tertiary-level interventions can include individualized, formal systems of behavior monitoring and systems of positive reinforcement or negative consequences when necessary that are intended to promote positive growth in social behavior, as planned and monitored by a PBIS leadership team. For an application of a schoolwide behavior management program based on the response-to-intervention model, see the *Research Highlight* feature.

STRATEGIES FOR CONFRONTING BULLYING

IMPLEMENT A BULLYING-PREVENTION PROGRAM Bullying is a fact of life in all schools across the nation, and students with disabilities are frequently the targets of bullying (Council for Exceptional Children [CEC], n.d.; Rose et al., 2011), although in some cases they also may act as the aggressors. Students with autism may be particularly at risk for involvement as a victim or an aggressor (Matthias et al., 2020). Sustained bullying can become a significant problem for schools and can contribute to an anxious and fearful environment (Davis & Davis, 2007). **Cyberbullying**, in which harassing messages or malicious rumors are sent through computers or cell phones, has been widely reported (Kowalski et al., 2012).

Heinrichs (2003) described characteristics of successful bullying-prevention programs and Raskauskas and Modell (2011) suggested some modifications to such programs when including students with disabilities. These include the following:

- Increase the awareness and involvement of adults.
- Provide a clear definition about bullying when surveying students and consider alternative methods of response, as needed.
- Supervise high-risk areas during breaks.
- Form teacher discussion groups and coordinating groups to build awareness.
- Practice identifying instances of bullying behavior and strategies for responding to bullying behavior.
- Display class rules about bullying.
- Have class meetings on bullying with students.
- Provide strategies for students with communication difficulties to report instances of bullying.
- Provide support and education for bullies and targets of bullying.
- Communicate schoolwide bullying policies and procedures to parents/caregivers.

Pearson eTextbook
Video Example 8.5
A teacher of students with emotional and behavioral disabilities explains an incident of bullying. What strategies did she use to address the bullying behavior?

Targets of bullying can be provided with specific strategies, for example, to recognize the signs of bullying, to not display behaviors that may invite bullying, and to avoid high-risk areas. Bullies can be provided with appropriate social skills training and consequences for aggressive acts toward others. Communicate with parents, caregivers, or other family members of bullies and targets of bullying. Bystanders (almost always present when bullying occurs) can be encouraged not to support or reinforce such behavior. Finally, all parties can be encouraged to contact responsible adults when they see bullying occurring. Richard and colleagues (2011) identified school security and positive teacher–student relations to be very important factors in bullying prevention. Effective schoolwide bullying prevention programs have reduced bullying problems by more than 50% and have also been integrated within schoolwide PBIS programs (Good et al., 2011). The integration of schoolwide PBIS and bullying prevention programs is a necessary step toward reducing school-based bullying (Gage et al., 2019).

Teaching Social Skills

Learning Objective 8.4 Describe techniques for teaching social skills.

Appropriate behavior from students is often limited because some students lack adequate knowledge of certain **social skills**. Social skills are the behaviors we use to work and socialize with other people. Good, or at least adequate, social skills are necessary for successful functioning in school, in society, and on the job.

Many different types of behaviors or responses can qualify as social skills. In fact, it could be argued that specific social skills are required for any social act a person engages in throughout life. Some of the social skills described and studied by researchers are listed in Table 8.5.

It may be useful to distinguish among the factors that seem to control particular social skills deficits. For example, Rohan is an affectionate boy with intellectual disabilities who is disposed to hug nearly anyone he encounters. Rohan's behavior is apparently controlled by the social satisfaction he gains from hugging, as well as his seeming inability to distinguish when his hugging is welcome and when it is not. Kyle, conversely, is a student with emotional/behavioral disorders who is often verbally abusive to other students and teachers. Kyle is aware that his behavior is not appreciated by others; his behavior is apparently controlled by the attention and reinforcement he seems to receive from upsetting others with his speech.

In both cases, students exhibit inappropriate social skills and seem unaware that it is in their own long-term interest to improve their social behavior. However, Rohan does not seem to be fully aware of the effects of his social behavior, whereas Kyle does appear to be aware of the social consequences of his behavior. For both Rohan and Kyle, intervention is necessary; for Rohan, training of specific social skills may be helpful, whereas for Kyle, rearranging the environmental contingencies that control his behavior may be appropriate.

Research Highlight

Equity in Multi-Tiered Systems of Support for Academic and Problem Behaviors

Multi-tiered systems of support seek to identify and treat behavior and learning problems within a multiple-tier system or response-to-intervention framework. For example, all students are provided with evidence-based instruction in reading (Tier 1). For students who exhibit learning problems, a second tier of small-group, higher-intensity instruction is delivered (Tier 2). For students who fail to show adequate progress in this second tier, a third tier of services that are even more intensive (perhaps including assessment for special education services) is implemented.

Fairbanks et al. (2007) extended this multiple-tier system of support (MTSS) to classroom behavior problems. That is, the Tier 1 intervention could include a universal schoolwide behavior management system, where behavioral expectations are explicitly stated, consequences are consistently applied, and progress toward meeting schoolwide goals is regularly monitored. The Tier 2 intervention is targeted toward students who do not succeed in the Tier 1 program, and it could include "check-in, check-out" interventions that include additional structure and feedback, as well as daily behavior report cards in some cases. If students still exhibit problem behaviors, a Tier 3 individualized intervention, such as a functional behavior assessment (see the Positive Behavioral Interventions and Supports section in this chapter) and appropriate, intensive individual interventions may be necessary.

Algozzine et al. (2012) examined the combined effects of a multi-tier system of support for academic and behavior interventions for children who were difficult to teach in kindergarten through grade 3. Students identified as difficult to teach (sample = 768) from five schools participated in one of three cohorts. Findings revealed that students significantly improved nonsense-word fluency and phonemic segmentation skills in reading and had significantly fewer discipline referrals. These results, taken together, demonstrate the potential of implementing MTSS to improve classroom behavior in inclusive classes. See also Sugai and Horner (2020) for a description of the sustainability of positive behavioral interventions and supports (PBIS).

Although positive PBIS findings have been reported, culturally diverse students remain more at risk than their peers for not achieving an equivalent amount of success (Girvan et al., 2017). The Michigan Equity PBIS Pilot Project was intended to assess methods for reducing the school discipline issues for students representing culturally diverse populations. Michigan's Technical Assistance Center (MTAC) partnered with the Office of Special Education's PBIS Center to develop a program in a middle school (McIntosh et al., 2018; Payno-Simmons, 2021). Over a 3-year period, MTAC worked extensively with a suburban middle school consisting of 864 students (73% White, 12% African American, and 10% Latino). Prior to the pilot study's implementation, the middle school participated in district-wide intensive PBIS coaching and training led by MTAC, who also provided technical assistance.

The pilot school's leadership team consisted of a district-level coach, the building administrator, and five classrooms. The school used district and school resources to obtain more coaches and to use the School Wide Information System (SWIS; www.swis.org). SWIS was a data collection system enabling schools to collect and use students' behavior data disaggregated by race and ethnicity to identify successes, problems, and decision making. During Year 1 the school improved their disciplinary system and clarified their disaggregated data. For example, the school corrected errors on race and ethnicity coding. Staff observed that office discipline referrals (ODRs) and motivation for ODRs were coded for African American students 40% of the time with "unknown" motivation. Projected staff then removed "unknown" as a possible response. It was also observed that since school personnel defined "defiance" and "disrespect" differently, project staff, including the MTAC equity specialist, worked with school personnel to further operationalize these terms. Vulnerable decision points (VDPs) identified from SWIS data revealed that students who were African American were often referred in classes for "disrespect" and "defiance," which increased during the second and third period and after the lunch period. Moreover, teachers referred students for "disrespect" as motivation to avoid tasks but also frequently listed "unknown" as a motivation. School staff developed action plans for addressing unconscious or implicit bias by providing strategies for teachers to stop and think before acting during VDPs.

Professional development activities including readings, lectures, and discussions led by MTAC's equity specialist and the school's leadership team were implemented to improve culturally responsive procedures within their PBIS program. In addition, improved communications and Town Hall meetings were conducted with school personnel and with families and community members to gather input and share their progress.

Research Highlight

Equity in Multi-Tiered Systems of Support for Academic and Problem Behaviors—*continued*

The school staff gradually began to focus on changing its system to be more responsive to students from diverse backgrounds.

Office discipline referrals (ODRs) were the main project outcome. Initially, students who were African American received 3.67 more monthly ODRs compared with students who were White. The ODR gap decreased from 3.95 to 0.43 over the course of the project. Moreover, ODRs decreased for all students during the same period. These findings provide promising preliminary data suggesting that these steps concentrating on equity address discipline gaps but are also good for all students.

QUESTIONS FOR REFLECTION

1. Could this model be effective at all age and grade levels?
2. What other behavior and academic outcome measures would be helpful to convince your school administrators to implement this intervention?
3. What would you need to do prior to implementing this on a schoolwide basis?

TABLE 8.5 Specific Social Skills

Content Area	Example Component Skills
Conversation skills	Starting a conversation Maintaining a conversation Use of appropriate distance and eye contact
Assertiveness skills	Making requests Denying requests Negotiating requests
"Play" interaction skills (e.g., making friends)	Sharing with others Inviting others to play Encouraging others
Problem-solving and coping skills	Staying calm and relaxed Listing possible solutions Choosing the best solution
Self-help skills	Good grooming (clean, neat) Good dressing (wearing clothes that fit well) Good table manners
Classroom task-related behaviors	On-task behavior Following directions Trying your best
Job interview skills	Being prepared (dress, attitude, etc.) Being attentive Asking for clarification

Note: From Mastropieri & Scruggs (2002), p. 252. Copyright 2002 by Pro-Ed. Reprinted with permission.

STRATEGIES FOR
TEACHING STUDENTS SOCIAL SKILLS

Several methods are available for assessing the social skills and social acceptance of students in your classroom, such as student surveys and teacher rating scales (e.g., Gresham & Elliot, 2008b). Probably the best overall method of assessing social skills is by direct observation of social behavior in naturalistic settings, using observational procedures such as event recording, described previously. These observations, based on operationalized behaviors, can determine the specific levels of the behavior being exhibited. For example, you could observe a particular student and record the number of positive versus negative comments made to others during a cooperative learning activity. Further observations could determine whether a chosen intervention was effective.

Many different interventions to improve social skills have been undertaken. These include commercially available curriculum materials, such as the *Social Skills Intervention Guide* (Gresham & Elliott, 2008a) and *Social Skills Solutions: A Hands-On Manual for Teaching Social Skills to Children with Autism* (Krempa & McKinnon, 2002). However, most social skills training procedures are classified into four categories: (1) modeling, (2) shaping, (3) coaching, and (4) modeling/reinforcement (Mastropieri & Scruggs, 2002; Matson et al., 2007). Modeling involves demonstrating the appropriate social behavior and allowing students to observe. Shaping involves the use of positive reinforcement to gradually promote the use of a social skill. Coaching requires the use of verbal cues to improve target behaviors, and modeling/reinforcement employs a combination of demonstration and reinforcement techniques. Peers have also been enlisted to help train social skills, such as social initiations and turn-taking, for students with autism (e.g., Hochman et al., 2015).

INSTRUCT STUDENTS WITH SPECIFIC SOCIAL SKILLS Social skills training often begins with a definition and discussion of the target social skill. The teacher models positive and negative examples of the social skill (e.g., inviting others to play; using polite words in appropriate circumstances) and asks students to identify these examples. Then the teacher may describe some scenarios for role-playing guided practice activities, and students offer suggestions or demonstrate examples of appropriate behavior. Students may be given independent practice activities, in which they are asked to record their own social behavior in relevant social situations outside of class. Formative evaluation is used to determine whether the purposes of the lessons have been accomplished. In this way, social skills instruction parallels the components of academic instruction, including review, statement of objective, presentation of information, guided practice, independent practice, and formative evaluation.

Similar types of instruction have been employed with students with autism through the use of social stories that are developed for individual students to work on specific target behaviors, such as appropriate cafeteria behavior. Social stories are simple, short individual narratives that describe a behavior(s) from the student's perspective and incorporate visuals such as pictures, cartoons, or photographs. For example, the teacher reviews photographs of the student exhibiting appropriate behavior and shows others being pleased by this behavior (Graetz et al., 2009). Hanrahan and colleagues (2020) used iPads to show social stories about turn-taking, sitting appropriately, and respecting personal space for elementary-level students with autism. Video modeling has also been used in conjunction with social stories to teach a wide range of skills to individuals with autism of all ages. For example, Stauch and Plavnick (2020) used video modeling to provide a step-by-step guide of how to perform vocational skills such as accepting a compliment, accepting criticism, and maintaining small talk for adolescents with autism. When using curriculum materials, be sure the objectives of the materials parallel the objectives for your students and include suggestions for evaluating the effectiveness of the training.

CONDUCT ON-THE-SPOT TRAINING It is also important to monitor appropriate social skills outside of your training situations. If specific social skills have been targeted and practiced with particular students, prompt and reinforce those skills throughout the day. For example, Colin has a habit of taking things that he needs from classmates and teachers without asking permission. Even though he has learned and practiced more appropriate ways of interacting with others, he may still benefit from additional practice whenever this behavior reoccurs. If Colin takes a pencil without asking during math class, you could correct his behavior by reminding him to "ask politely," as covered in social skills training.

COACH FOR GENERALIZATION In most cases, trained social skills are of limited use if these skills do not generalize to other social situations. Generalization of social skills, as with the other behaviors described previously, must be specifically programmed (Alberto et al., 2022) and may include the following strategies (see also Bellini et al., 2007; Whalon et al., 2015):

- Make sure that students have mastered the skills they are to generalize. For example, a conversation skill that is not completely learned is not likely to generalize to other settings.
- Make the training as meaningful and realistic as possible so that students can recognize situations for which generalization is appropriate. For example, when training for job interview skills, make the situation as much like a real job interview as possible.
- Teach behaviors that will maximize students' social success and minimize their failures. This will make students want to generalize and maintain their behavior.
- Promote the application of learned social skills in other settings. For example, have students apply their skills in maintaining a conversation outside of class and report on their success the next day.
- Enlist the help of peers, parents, caregivers, and school personnel with prompting and reinforcing the social skills. Teach others what social skills to prompt or watch for and how they can be appropriately rewarded.
- When appropriate, initially accompany the student into the generalization setting or situation and prompt and reinforce the student in that setting.
- Teach self-management skills so that students learn to recognize appropriate situations for generalizing a social skill and monitor their success.
- Use periodic re-teaching and reminders of social skills (e.g., "Remember how we practiced accepting feedback?").

VALIDATE TREATMENTS Comprehensive reviews of research on social skills training have concluded that although social skills training generally produces positive effects, these effects are often relatively modest (Bellini et al., 2007; Kauffman & Landrum, 2018; Whalon et al., 2015). Nevertheless, there is no doubt that many students lack important social skills and that many students benefit from social skills training. Kerr and Nelson (2010) suggested that teachers implementing social skills training (1) directly assess and systematically treat specific behaviors for chosen environments, (2) determine that the student lacks the specific skill ("can't") rather than simply refusing to demonstrate the skill ("won't") when planning interventions, and (3) be certain the social skill being trained will achieve the desired social outcome. Carefully document the effectiveness of your training to ensure that social skills instruction is having a maximum impact in improving the social skills of your students.

8 Summary

- Motivation and affect can be improved by meeting preconditions and by engaging in specific practices, including raising students' self-esteem; promoting goal-setting behaviors; training positive attributions; promoting ownership in the classroom; making learning fun and interesting; and using positive feedback, praise, and rewards whenever possible to acknowledge and promote student accomplishment.
- Classroom behavior can be managed effectively by several techniques.
  - Operationalize and monitor behavior with formal observation and recording systems, such as event recording, duration recording, time sampling, and interval recording.
  - Less-intensive strategies, such as establishing rules, praise and ignoring, proximity, direct appeals, and reprimands, are helpful in maintaining appropriate classroom behavior.
  - Formal management systems for effective behavior management include positive reinforcement, punishment, token systems, attribution training, public posting, timeout and level systems, the Good-Behavior Game, and contracting.
  - Self-monitoring and self-instruction training is helpful in allowing students to become more aware and take more control of their own behavior.
  - A variety of strategies can be used to deal with confrontations effectively and to prevent them from escalating.
- Schoolwide behavior management systems, such as positive behavioral interventions and supports, have been effective in managing classroom behavior across entire school environments.
  - In a multi-tiered system of support, check-in, check-out is a common Tier 2 intervention.
  - Integrating bullying prevention programs and schoolwide PBIS can help to reduce school-based bullying.
- Social skills are usually taught by modeling, reinforcement, shaping, and modeling/reinforcement. Several strategies can be effective in promoting generalization of social skills.

PROFESSIONAL STANDARDS LINK: Improving Motivation and Social Behavior

Information in this chapter links most directly to:

- CEC 2020 Initial Practice-Based Professional Preparation Standards for Special Educators (Initial K–12 standards) (see https://exceptionalchildren.org/standards/initial-practice-based-professional-preparation-standards-special-educators): 2 (Understanding and Addressing Each Individual's Developmental and Learning Needs), 4 (Using Assessment to Understand the Learner and the Learning Environment for Data-Based Decision Making), 5 (Supporting Learning Using Effective Instruction), 6 (Supporting Social, Emotional, and Behavioral Growth), 7 (Collaborating with Team Members)
- InTASC Standards (see https://www.ccsso.org/sites/default/files/2017-11/InTASC_Model_Core_Teaching_Standards_2011.pdf): 2 (Learning Differences), 3 (Learning Environments), 7 (Planning for Instruction), 8 (Instructional Strategies)

IMPROVING MOTIVATION AND SOCIAL BEHAVIOR

If you are having problems with student motivation or social behavior, have you considered the following? If not, see the pages listed here.

STRATEGIES FOR IMPROVING MOTIVATION AND AFFECT

- ☐ Preconditions, 192–193
- ☐ Raise students' self-esteem, 193
- ☐ Promote self-efficacy, 194–195
- ☐ Teach students to set goals, 196
- ☐ Train students to use positive attributions, 196–197
- ☐ Arrange counseling interventions when needed, 197
- ☐ Exercise care when handling serious affective disorders, 197

STRATEGIES FOR OBSERVING AND RECORDING CLASSROOM BEHAVIOR

- ☐ Define behavior, 202
- ☐ Use observation and recording systems, 202–203
- ☐ Determine the context of behavior, 203
- ☐ Make graphic presentations of student behavior, 204

STRATEGIES FOR USING EFFECTIVE CLASSROOM MANAGEMENT METHODS

- ☐ Establish a positive classroom atmosphere, 204

STRATEGIES FOR LESS-INTENSIVE CLASSROOM MANAGEMENT METHODS

- ☐ Post and discuss classroom rules, 205
- ☐ Praise positive behaviors and ignore inappropriate behaviors, 205
- ☐ Control behavior with proximity, 205
- ☐ Make direct appeals, 205
- ☐ Use reprimands judiciously, 205–206

STRATEGIES FOR MORE FORMAL CLASSROOM MANAGEMENT METHODS

- ☐ Systematically reinforce positive behavior, 206–207
- ☐ Reward students with token systems, 207–208
- ☐ Teach positive attributions for social behavior, 208
- ☐ Post positive behavior, 208
- ☐ Use negative consequences judiciously, 208–209
- ☐ Use timeout for specific behavior problems, 209–210
- ☐ Play the Good-Behavior Game, 210
- ☐ Set up student contracting, 210

STRATEGIES FOR HANDLING CLASSROOM CONFRONTATIONS

- ☐ Diffuse confrontations with a calm, measured response, 211–212

STRATEGIES FOR IMPLEMENTING MULTI-TIERED SYSTEMS OF SUPPORT WITHIN A PBIS FRAMEWORK

- ☐ Promote self-monitoring, 213–214
- ☐ Teach students self-instruction strategies, 214
- ☐ Train for generalization, 214–215
- ☐ Promote equity in disciplinary practices, 215–216
- ☐ Check-in, check-out intervention, 216–217

STRATEGIES FOR CONFRONTING BULLYING

- ☐ Implement a bullying-prevention program, 217–218

STRATEGIES FOR TEACHING STUDENTS SOCIAL SKILLS

- ☐ Instruct students with specific social skills, 221
- ☐ Conduct on-the-spot training, 221–222
- ☐ Coach for generalization, 222
- ☐ Validate treatments, 222

Cary Kalscheuer/Shutterstock

CHAPTER 9

Promoting Inclusion with Classroom Peers

LEARNING OBJECTIVES

After studying this chapter, you should be able to:

9.1 Describe how to implement peer-supported social acceptance.

9.2 Explain how students can be employed as peer assistants and identify different uses of peer assistance.

9.3 Describe peer tutoring and discuss how peer tutoring programs can be implemented.

9.4 Explain cooperative learning and summarize how it can be implemented to benefit diverse learners.

Your general education classroom students can play a critically important role in the successful inclusion of students with diverse learning needs. You and your students can set the stage for celebrating diversity in your class by openly accepting all students as equal members of the class and building a true community of learners. Within this community, an accepting atmosphere is established in which all students help and encourage one another to reach their own potential. You can assist your students by teaching them several strategies for working more effectively with classmates who have disabilities. These strategies help promote acceptance of all students and teach them how to support one another using peer assistance, peer tutoring, and cooperative learning. All of these strategies can be implemented during academic and nonacademic situations and will help you and your students maintain a helpful, positive class environment.

Peer-Supported Social Acceptance

Learning Objective 9.1 Describe how to implement peer-supported social acceptance.

STRATEGIES FOR PROMOTING SOCIAL ACCEPTANCE

Classroom peers can become involved in accepting students with disabilities from their first placement in a general education classroom. As you would with every new student who transitions to your classroom, describe the new student before arrival to class, remind the class what it feels like to enter a new classroom environment, and ask them to brainstorm strategies to help the new student feel more accepted. Then select one or more of these strategies that seem promising and ask for volunteers to implement them. For example, some younger students may volunteer to create a poster welcoming the new student into the classroom. Older students may volunteer to offer personal words of encouragement and support. Still other students may offer to help the new student orient to the new classroom or offer contact via telephone or email.

At the same time, introduce the new student to the materials, expectations, and tasks of the general education classroom, a procedure known as "priming" (Myles, 2007). Cihak et al. (2010) have used "video priming" for students with autism spectrum disorders (ASD) in order to review expectations for transitioning between classroom activities.

When you help students with diverse learning needs become valued members of your class and school community, you will help prevent them from being ostracized or rejected by classroom peers (McLeskey et al., 2014). In many ways, classroom peers are the key to social acceptance and, under the right circumstances, they can provide necessary assistance for helping students with disabilities be more accepted in the classroom (Carter et al., 2015).

BUILD COMMUNITY WITH THE CIRCLE OF FRIENDS In the **Circle of Friends** activity (Frederickson & Turner, 2003; Frederickson et al., 2005; Hassani et al., 2021), you distribute papers showing four concentric circles, with a stick figure in the middle. Students are told to write in the first circle the most important people in their lives, such as family members. In the second circle, they are to put their best friends, and in the third circle, they are to put other people they enjoy playing with or interacting with. In the fourth circle are people who are paid to be in their lives, such as doctors and dentists. When students have filled out the circles, ask the class how they would feel if they only had one parent or caregiver in the first circle and no one in the second and third circles. After students share their feelings (e.g., "I would be unhappy all the time"), inform the class that some students might not have very many people in the second and third circles. The point of the activity is to demonstrate that everyone needs "circles" of friends, with people in every circle. Not everyone needs to be a best friend, but all can be friendly and interact well with each other.

Pearson eTextbook
Video Example 9.1
This video illustrates how teachers can capitalize on the use of informal peer buddies to help bring out the potential of a student with a disability. Notice how Abby provides peer assistance to Jacob during math.

The Circle of Friends strategy has been used to build a network of social support within an inclusive classroom community for a "focus student" with a disability and/or those students without a disability who may feel isolated or excluded (Hassani et al., 2021). Six to eight students are selected to form the Circle of Friends, and weekly meetings led by an outside facilitator (e.g., the classroom teacher) are held for 6–10 weeks. In these meetings, mutual support is emphasized, and target goals and strategies are developed and discussed (e.g., listening to others, playing games fairly). Previous successes are celebrated and problem-solving strategies for the future are discussed. Role play can be used to practice particular behaviors (e.g., a particular social skill target and students' suggested responses). Circle of Friends activities have been found to increase social acceptance and peer interactions at the primary and elementary grades (Frederickson et al., 2005; O'Conner, 2016).

PROMOTE ACCEPTANCE WITH SPECIAL FRIENDS Meyer and Ostrosky (2016) described a **Special Friends** program in which kindergarten students in inclusive classrooms were exposed to disability-related themes and given frequent opportunities to interact with students with mild to severe disabilities. The program involved teachers reading a story about a child with a disability followed by discussion and 15 minutes of cooperative learning groups. The students interacted with their Special Friends in these mixed-ability learning groups three times per week, 15 minutes per session, for 6 weeks. Students enrolled in this program enjoyed the interactions with their Special Friends and maintained their contact with them after the sessions ended (see also Favazza et al., 2016).

Another positive classroom activity to promote social acceptance among young adolescents involves dividing all students into pairs based on shared interest areas and asking them to complete a joint project on a subject in which they are both interested. Or, divide students into pairs and ask each student to complete a list of positive attributes of the other student (Mastropieri et al., 1994). These lists can then be read to the class.

Peer Assistance

Learning Objective 9.2 Explain how students can be employed as peer assistants and identify different uses of peer assistance.

Peer assistance, or *peer support*, refers to pairing students for the purpose of having one student available to assist another student when necessary (Carter et al., 2011; Ziegler et al., 2020). Peer assistance from a peer partner or peer buddy can be helpful in promoting success in inclusive classrooms. However, peers should lend assistance only when help is required. For example, some students may need directions read to them, others may need assistance getting materials to their desks, and others may require help transcribing lecture notes. Peers can support students who might need a door opened or furniture moved to accommodate a wheelchair. But when help is unnecessary or not appropriate (dressing, personal care), students with disabilities should be encouraged to perform tasks as independently as possible (Ziegler et al., 2020).

Peer assistance need not be arduous or time-consuming for the helpers. Many of the activities are tasks the peer assistants would be performing anyway and helping their peers usually does not take much extra time. Peers can share responsibilities with peer assistants. Carter and colleagues (Carter et al., 2009, 2011, 2016) described peer-support strategies for assisting students with disabilities and reported increases in peer interactions for all students. Overall, however, it is important to consider that peer assistance can be beneficial for the student helper, promoting such positive attributes as awareness of the needs of others and social responsibility.

STRATEGIES FOR ENLISTING PEER ASSISTANCE

TRAIN STUDENTS IN PEER ASSISTANCE Peer assistance programs should be set up in a systematic manner. The following *In the Classroom* feature offers a checklist for implementing peer assistance programs. The first consideration is to determine the precise nature of the situation that requires peer assistance. It is insufficient, for example, to think, "Mario has a visual impairment. I must assign a peer assistant to help Mario." Rather, consider the specific need that you believe peer assistance can address and how it can be addressed. For example, you may think, "Mario has a visual impairment and sometimes needs someone to read information to him that is written on the blackboard."

Next, identify the student or students who can serve as peer assistants. In selecting peer assistants, teachers must exercise their best judgment based on their knowledge of the students in their class. In the past, teachers usually considered only the most responsible students, those who exhibited qualities of academic responsibility and conscientiousness as peer assistants. However, it may be as beneficial to consider less obvious students, such as those who are shy or who at times have minor difficulties themselves with classroom assignments. These students are usually not only very capable of assuming the responsibilities but also may flourish when given the opportunity to be a peer assistant.

Provide advanced training to both the peer assistant and peer before starting the peer assistance. Inform students exactly what the relationship will entail. For example, to motivate and engage an adolescent student with ASD to participate in conversational turn-taking, peers can use three strategies: (1) show interest in what is being said, (2) keep the conversation going, and (3) help your friend to repair the conversation if distracted (see Bambara et al., 2018). When the procedures are clear to both participants, role-play a few practice sessions and then implement the peer assistance program. Finally, monitor the program to determine that it is meeting its objective.

TRAIN PEERS TO ASSIST STUDENTS WITH DIFFERENT TYPES OF DISABILITIES

Peers can assume the role of assistant with any student. Table 9.1 provides some tasks and strategies that peer assistants can engage in with students with disabilities. Although some tasks appear very disability specific, others are more general and extend across disability areas. For example, during emergency situations, it is essential that specific students have been designated to assist students with disabilities who may require special assistance. Closely monitor all emergency-related procedures.

Peer assistants can also help address safety issues by assisting with the handling of potentially dangerous materials—such as those that are breakable, sharp, or hot—that may be used in laboratory activities. Peers can describe or assist with the proper handling of materials that may be dangerous for someone with vision or fine motor difficulties.

When classroom activities are to be undertaken, peer assistants can provide concrete visual models to demonstrate what students are to do. When extensive listening is required, such as during teacher presentations, peer assistants can make copies of their notes so that students with hearing impairments or writing difficulties can focus their attention on the speaker or interpreter. Peers can also assist with speaking tasks if students with communication difficulties lack the stamina to complete a classroom presentation. For any kind of oral assignment, a peer assistant could share some of the speaking responsibilities.

In the Classroom

Checklist for Peer Assistance Programs

_____ Identify situations and students who may require assistance.

_____ Target students who may be able to serve as peer assistants.

_____ Pair each peer assistant with one student with disabilities.

_____ Teach important general procedures, such as social interactions and corrective feedback, for working with students with disabilities. Ensure both students have been trained in social interaction skills.

_____ When appropriate, provide occasions for peer assistants to observe the student and discuss how assistance can be provided.

_____ Teach peer assistants any specialized need areas for particular students (e.g., specific needs for students with physical or sensory disabilities).

_____ Arrange for a meeting time between peers to explain the process.

_____ Observe the first few interactions carefully and compare observations with the objectives of the peer assistance program. Monitor progress and make adjustments, if needed.

TABLE 9.1 Suggestions for Use of Peer Assistants by Specific Disability and Task/Situation Area

Disability Area	Tasks/Situations	Strategies for Peer Assistants
All disabilities	Classroom activities	Answer questions and provide examples.
All disabilities	Emergencies (fire or tornado drills)	Provide assistance in exiting rapidly and safely.
Visual impairments	Mobility in unfamiliar places or rearranged rooms	Verbally describe the layouts of the rooms; guide students around new places.
Visual impairments	Written materials that are not enlarged print or braille	Read orally; provide assistance in utilizing common accessibility features (e.g., text-to-speech, magnification features) on mobile devices (e.g., tablets, Chromebooks, laptops).
Visual impairments	Videos that are not in descriptive video format	Provide additional verbal descriptions.
Hearing impairments	Lectures or videos without closed-captioning	Provide supplemental verbal or written information.
Hearing impairments	Abstract materials or concepts	Provide concrete models or descriptions.
Physical disabilities	Mobility	Provide assistance as necessary.
Physical disabilities	Fine motor tasks such as writing	Turn book pages, hold objects, take notes, act as scribe, provide copies of own notes; provide assistance with accessibility features (e.g., text-to-speech) on mobile devices.
Attention-deficit/ hyperactivity disabilities	Attending	Reward student for on-task behavior and prompt student to get back to task.
Behavioral disabilities	Social skills	Provide appropriate social model; sit next to the student; help the student organize assignments and materials.
Learning and cognitive disabilities	Writing	Act as scribe, take notes, share copies of notes; provide encouragement and assistance in using common accessibility features on devices or relevant applications (e.g., Grammarly).
Learning and cognitive disabilities	Reading	Read orally and provide summaries of materials; highlight the important information on a worksheet; explain assignments

Peers can assist with physical mobility by moving obstructions or collecting classroom materials. Peers can also assist students with classroom organization skills, including locker organization, keeping track of homework assignments, and keeping notebooks organized. In some cases, peers can promote appropriate social behavior by providing explicit models of positive classroom behavior and subtle prompts when appropriate.

PROMOTE PEER SOCIAL INITIATION **Peer social initiation** refers to procedures intended to enlist peer assistance in promoting social interaction with withdrawn students, including children with autism (Bene et al., 2014; Kerr & Nelson, 2010). Peer social initiation may also be referred to as *peer-mediated instruction*, or PMI, in which the peer receives training and coaching from an adult to support the learning goal(s) of a student(s) with autism (Steinbrenner et al., 2020). This is done by such acts as asking the student to play, giving or sharing a desired toy, or assisting the student in using a particular material. This technique has also been used successfully with students (often, preschool or primary-grade students) from a variety of disability areas, including nondisabled students who exhibit some social withdrawal (e.g., Tsao et al., 2008). These procedures can also be used with any shy child. Very young peer assistants, and even assistants with autism, have been successfully trained in initiating social interactions (Barber et al., 2016).

According to Kerr and Nelson (2002), teachers should choose peer assistants who (1) attend school regularly, (2) consistently exhibit appropriate social skills with peers, (3) follow instructions reliably, and (4) can maintain concentration on the task for at least 10 minutes per session.

The first step in training is to explain to the peer assistant what will be expected (e.g., "Try to get Chris to play a game with you"). Assistants should be prepared for rejection, and teachers can role-play ignoring a positive social gesture from the peer assistant. Tell the student not to give up and to keep trying. If toys are being used to initiate social interaction, point out the target student's favorite toys or provide cue cards to prompt the peer assistant. Continue to role-play until the student becomes skilled at persisting to prompt appropriate interaction; this may require at least four 20-minute sessions. Be sure the peer assistant is reinforced and supported for efforts and understands the importance of this intervention. Kerr and Nelson (2002) suggest setting aside at least 6 minutes per day, in the same setting, for reviewing with the peer assistant the activities that are most likely to succeed. Reward the peer assistant for persistence in initiating interaction with the withdrawn student.

Peer networks can also be beneficial in providing support for greater integration in inclusive social environments for students with significant social deficits, including ASD. This may be particularly relevant for adolescents with disabilities during noninstructional times of the school day like before or after school and lunch time. For example, in Hochman et al.'s (2015) investigation of a peer network intervention for high school students with ASD, students without a disability were trained to participate in peer network meetings. At least once a week, the student with ASD and a few of the peers in the network sat together during lunch. The 30-minute lunch meetings included eating lunch, participating in a shared activity (e.g., board game), talking about a topic, discussing upcoming school events, and reflecting on how the meetings were going. These interventions involve adult facilitation and direct teaching with repeated exposure to social learning opportunities. Peer networks have been found to improve skills such as initiating, responding, and maintaining social interactions (Kamps et al., 2015). Students without disabilities in Hochman et al.'s (2015) study reported understanding their classmates with disabilities more and the participating students with ASD identified the members of the peer network as their friends.

Overall, classroom peers can be used in many ways to promote social acceptance. By considering the great potential of peer assistance in promoting social acceptance, assisting with academic tasks, and planning strategies, you and your students can create positive and accepting social environments.

Peers can also be employed to increase socialization skills, such as sharing ideas, correcting and praising others, and helping others, in students with autism.

Peer Tutoring

Learning Objective 9.3 Describe peer tutoring and discuss how peer tutoring programs can be implemented.

Peer tutoring is one of the most widely studied interventions in education. Many positive effects of tutoring have been noted, indicating that tutoring can be a powerful tool in improving performance in the inclusive classroom (Harris & Meltzer, 2015; Moeyaert et al., 2021; Okilwa & Shelby, 2010). The following scenario discusses an application of peer tutoring.

CLASSROOM SCENARIO

Peer Tutoring in Seventh-Grade History

This year Ms. Conners, the seventh-grade history teacher, found the overall performance of her students with learning disabilities on weekly quizzes to be well below the class average, and she was beginning to wonder whether some of the students belonged in her class.

"Why should they be in my class if they cannot keep up with the work?" she asked Ms. Cuenca-Sanchez, the seventh-grade special education teacher. Ms. Cuenca-Sanchez knew something had to be done soon. She believed that with additional practice, the students with learning disabilities could master the class content.

After meeting with Ms. Conners and examining the students' schedules, she decided that she could set up a 25-minute peer tutoring program 3 days a week during seventh-period study hall so that most of the students could practice studying and reviewing history with one another. The steps in the program are described as follows:

Step 1: *Determine the Content for Tutoring Material*

Ms. Cuenca-Sanchez met with Ms. Conners weekly and generated a list of the most important information from each social studies chapter. For example, some of the information on the World War I chapter included the following:

- Woodrow Wilson was the president of the United States.
- William Jennings Bryan, a pacifist, was secretary of state.
- Definition of alliance system, and how military alliances contributed to the start of World War I.
- Names of countries in the Central Powers and in the Allied Powers.
- Initial U.S. position was neutrality.
- Incidents leading up to the U.S. involvement in World War I, including the Zimmermann Note and the sinking of the *Lusitania*.
- Famous individuals of the era and their accomplishments, including civil rights activist and writer W. E. B. Dubois and musician Louis Armstrong.

Step 2: *Devise a Tutoring Plan*

Ms. Cuenca-Sanchez designed a plan for tutoring that included specific procedures for students to use while tutoring each other and rules for appropriate behavior during tutoring sessions. In her program, students would serve as both tutors and tutees during sessions because they all needed review and practice in history. She put the questions and answers on index cards, to be used as the tutoring materials. For example, one card read on one side: "Who was Louis Armstrong, and what was he famous for?" The other side held the answer: "Louis Armstrong was a famous musician and was one of the most influential figures in jazz. "

Ms. Cuenca-Sanchez established guidelines for the tutoring session, which she posted on the wall:

1. Be nice to your partner and sit facing each other.
2. Decide who will be the tutor first. The first tutor will go through the cards, asking each question in order. When the tutee responds, the tutor will verify the answer. If it was answered correctly, the tutor will place it in the "correct" pile. If answered incorrectly, the tutor will correct the tutee, ask the question again, and after it is answered correctly, will place it in the "incorrect" pile. The cards in the "incorrect" pile are asked again after the set of cards is completed. After 10 minutes, a timer rings, and students reverse roles.

3. Speak in a pleasant tone when asking questions and when responding.
4. Encourage your partner by using statements like, "Great job, good answer" or "Can you think of anything else?" For incorrect answers, the tutor can state, "No, the answer is ____. What (who) is ____?"
5. At the end of the two tutoring periods, students should quiz each other on the entire list and record the number of correct answers.

Step 3: *Tutor Roles and Behaviors*

Next, Ms. Cuenca-Sanchez planned a couple of sessions to review the tutoring roles and behaviors. She presented the guidelines and modeled both the tutor and tutee roles for the students. She then provided them with opportunities to practice both roles and provided feedback. When students had mastered the tutoring behaviors and understood their roles, she began the tutoring sessions.

Step 4: *Monitor Performance*

During the tutoring sessions, Ms. Cuenca-Sanchez collected systematic data on the efficacy of the tutoring. She wanted to know whether tutoring improved students' scores on their weekly quizzes in Ms. Conners's history class and if students enjoyed the tutoring. She began to collect students' weekly quiz scores and charted them. She also devised a questionnaire for students to answer periodically regarding their opinions of tutoring.

After a month of tutoring and collecting data, Ms. Cuenca-Sanchez found that students' quiz scores had increased an average of 30 points and that nearly all students reported enjoying being both tutors and tutees. Nearly all students reported that they did better on the weekly quizzes as a result of the tutoring sessions.

Step 5: *Collaborate with the History Teacher*

Ms. Conners also observed that many of the students were doing much better on the weekly quizzes. She considered the tutoring program successful and believed that there were many other students in her class who could benefit from tutoring sessions. With Ms. Cuenca-Sanchez's help, she began implementing 15-minute sessions in her own class 3 days per week. Under this new tutoring program, all students in her class benefited. Ms. Cuenca-Sanchez was able to reduce the students' tutoring sessions to 1 day per week, arranging for additional tutoring sessions only before major tests.

QUESTIONS FOR REFLECTION

1. Why do you think Ms. Cuenca-Sanchez felt she needed to include directions such as "be nice" and "speak in a pleasant tone"?
2. If tutoring has been found to be effective by research, why did Ms. Cuenca-Sanchez add Step 4?
3. In what other areas do you think tutoring would be helpful?

BENEFITS OF PEER TUTORING Tutoring can be helpful in addressing diverse learning needs in inclusive classrooms, and it can be applied to a number of content and skill areas (Maheady & Gard, 2010). However, tutoring, just like any educational strategy, should not be considered a panacea. When using peer tutoring, monitor the effectiveness of the intervention and be prepared to adjust the program as needed.

Reviews of research have emphasized the benefits of tutoring for elementary and secondary students (Harris & Meltzer, 2015; Moeyaert et al., 2021; Regan et al., 2015) and described the circumstances in which it is most effective. Overall, peer tutoring has been effective in improving academic skills in the subject tutored, particularly when compared with nonpeer tutoring instructional arrangements or traditional, whole-class instruction (Bowman-Perrott et al., 2013). However, it may not always be more effective than other alternatives; for example, a well-implemented independent study strategy or high-intensity small-group, teacher-led instruction may be as effective as—or even more effective than—peer tutoring (Higgins, 1982; Sindelar, 1982). However, tutoring is likely to be very useful when individual teacher assistance is not available and when students lack effective independent study skills. Figure 9.1 highlights some student and teacher reactions to tutoring programs.

Figure 9.1 Comments About Tutoring Programs

I enjoy tutoring a lot. I really look forward to it. It's my favorite part of the day. Some mornings I'll wake up and not want to go to school. Then I'll remember, David gets to start a new book today, or something like that, and I'll be excited all day!

— KM, sixth-grade tutor, Franklin School.

Kara, a sixth-grader, tutored Michael, a third-grader, in reading. Kara's parents reported that she commented daily on Michael and his reading lesson. "She talks about her job all the time." Michael must also talk about Kara, for at Christmas, Michael made "candy sundaes" for Kara and his resource room teacher. Expressions of caring such as these are not uncommon.

— LMJ, special education resource teacher.

My children like working with their tutors more than anything else! P.E., music, and other activities that are usually favorites with children don't have as much appeal for them as the one-to-one companionship with their tutors.

— MD, second-grade teacher, Audubon School, Redmond, Washington.

Scott, a fourth-grade youngster 2½ years behind in reading, was being tutored by the special education resource room teacher. Due to scheduling problems he had to be tutored during his lunch recess two times a week. Scott was not terribly enthusiastic about missing lunch recess and his teacher had to "find" him on those days. Later, as part of a cross-age tutoring program, Scott was assigned a fifth-grade girl, Kelly. With Kelly as his tutor, Scott always came to the resource room voluntarily. Scott and Kelly formed a good relationship and both gave up more recess time to make a "sticker poster for good work," which was hung in the resource room. In fact, Scott enjoyed being tutored by Kelly more than by the teacher. His own involvement in planning his lesson, and his perception of Kelly's commitment toward his learning to read, made noon recess an acceptable sacrifice.

— LMJ.

Note: From Cross age and peer tutoring: Help for students with learning problems, by J. R. Jenkins & L. M. Jenkins, 1981, Reston, VA: Council for Exceptional Children. Copyright 1981 by CEC. Reprinted with permission.

Pearson eTextbook

Video Example 9.2

This video shows classwide peer tutoring in science content. What rules and procedures likely are followed by the tutor and tutee?

Students serving as tutors also usually benefit from tutoring, where tutors serve as "experts" in the content being tutored. However, the benefits are not as reliable as those for tutees. Tutors usually benefit academically from tutoring in areas in which they have gained some initial competence but still need some fluency building and comprehension development. Although it is often maintained that students can improve in general, overall self-esteem from tutoring, these benefits are less reliable. Nevertheless, appropriately trained tutors frequently benefit in terms of a positive attitude toward their tutoring partners, a positive attitude toward the content being tutored, and, in some cases, a positive attitude toward school (Scruggs & Mastropieri, 1998; Watts et al., 2019). Tutoring may increase self-concept in the more specific areas being tutored, such as verbal self-concept or interpersonal skills self-concept (Leung et al., 2013). Students with and without disabilities in tutoring programs often report making new friends and may enjoy higher levels of social acceptance (Travers & Carter, 2021). The *Research Highlight* feature describes an investigation in which students with emotional and behavioral disorders served as cross-age tutors.

STRATEGIES FOR IMPLEMENTING A TUTORING PROGRAM

Tutoring programs must be carefully planned and systematically implemented. The following *In the Classroom* feature presents some suggestions for planning and implementing tutoring programs. Remember also that students serving as tutors often model their teacher's behavior—so be sure that your own teaching style is a good model of positivity and enthusiasm for your classroom tutors.

Research Highlight

Using Students with Emotional/Behavioral Disorders as Peer Tutors

Teachers and researchers have frequently observed that tutoring may produce benefits beyond the increase in academic learning being targeted. Students acting as tutors have been said to improve in interpersonal skills, attitude toward school and the subject matter being tutored, personal responsibility, and overall self-esteem, although these findings have not been consistently demonstrated (Scruggs & Mastropieri, 1998). Previous research has suggested students with emotional and behavioral disorders (EBD) may serve successfully as both tutors and tutees (Spencer, 2006; Watts et al., 2019). Spencer et al. (2003), for example, employed students in a middle school for students with EBD as peer tutors and tutees within social studies classes using paragraph summary strategies and reported higher test scores and improved on-task behavior in the tutoring condition. However, it was less certain whether students with EBD can benefit socially or behaviorally from acting as cross-age tutors of younger students, a question investigated by Watts et al. (2020).

Watts and colleagues (2020) identified five fifth- and sixth-grade students who had been identified as having EBD or students with learning disabilities who also had challenging classroom behaviors and/or IEP goals directly concerned with improving social or behavioral skills. Students were also given a measure of internalizing or externalizing behavior and their scores were included if they fell within moderate- to high-risk ranges. All tutors were concurrently participating in a Check-in, Check-out (CICO) program in which their behaviors were monitored regularly on a daily progress record (DPR).

Tutees included kindergarten students nominated by their teacher as exhibiting difficulties with early numeracy knowledge and skills. These students scored an average standard score of 76.2 on a test of early mathematics skills (about the 5th percentile).

Tutors were individually trained to implement tutoring to the kindergarten students using a number line board game intended to improve early number concepts and skills. Tutors were trained in providing the materials, modeling rules and procedures, demonstrating guided practice, providing corrective feedback and positive behavioral reinforcement strategies, and keeping students on task. Participating teachers were trained in two sessions, while tutors were trained in one-to-one sessions for 45 minutes and supervised by the special education teacher while tutoring. Fidelity of implementation was assessed using a procedural checklist aligned with the training manual.

Tutees received three tutoring sessions per week for 25–30 minutes each in a separate classroom setting. Maintenance was assessed following the end of the tutoring session. The investigation employed a multiple-baseline design, in which all students were monitored for 3–6 weeks prior to the tutoring intervention in the baseline condition, followed by up to 10 weeks of tutoring and 2 weeks of maintenance testing. Tutees were tested weekly on an early mathematics inventory, and tutors were assessed daily on their DPRs for percent of DPR behavioral points earned.

Fidelity of implementation data revealed that tutors were able to implement the intervention with a high degree of fidelity. At the end of the tutoring and maintenance program, Watts et al. (2020) reported that the kindergarten tutees had demonstrated consistent progress on their weekly math inventory scores and maintained these gains over the maintenance period. Furthermore, they had progressed over the course of the intervention from a mean standard score of 76.2 (about the 5th percentile) to a mean standard score of 93 (about the 32nd percentile) on a standardized test of early mathematics ability. Tutors generally improved in their CICO daily progress report scores, and most maintained these gains. In addition, tutors' mean scores on the measure of externalizing behaviors showed a pre-post decrease of 13.2 to 9.8, and on the measure of internalizing behaviors a decrease of 9.8 to 9.4. For two students, risk status for externalizing behavior decreased from "high" to "moderate."

Watts and colleagues (2020) concluded the tutoring intervention had been highly successful for both the academic learning of the tutees and the behavioral progress of the tutors. Teachers noted some difficulty with scheduling the tutoring sessions, but all teachers and students agreed the program had been beneficial, and all tutors and tutees expressed a desire to participate in more tutoring in the future.

QUESTIONS FOR REFLECTION

1. Why do you think tutoring kindergarten students improved the social behavior of fifth- and sixth-grade students with EBD?
2. Do you think the behavioral gains made by the students with EBD justified the use of their time as tutors? Why or why not?
3. What other tutoring interventions can you think of in which students with disabilities might benefit from being tutors?

WORK ACROSS GRADE LEVELS TO IMPLEMENT CROSS-AGE TUTORING In **cross-age tutoring**, older students serve as tutors for younger students in need of supplemental instruction or practice. The roles of tutor and tutee are clearly established and do not alternate. An example of cross-age tutoring would be students from a nearby high school volunteering to tutor elementary school students who are having difficulty in school. The volunteers can schedule their time with the classroom teacher, be assigned a tutee, and be given explicit directions on their roles and responsibilities. The teacher may need to model the procedures and/or play the roles of tutor and tutee. It is also a good idea to have the tutors keep a notebook that details the dates and times of each session, the material tutored, and a report of the student's progress. Tutees can learn much from such partnerships, and volunteer tutors can gain valuable experiences, especially if they are considering a career in education or child care.

IMPLEMENT SAME-AGE TUTORING WITHIN YOUR CLASS Students can also tutor students of the same age. In some cases of **same-age tutoring**, students who are more skilled in a particular area can tutor less-skilled students. In other cases, pairs of students can alternate roles. This alternating-role tutoring can work particularly well when students drill one another with flashcards. In this way, the tutor does not need to know the correct answer because it is printed on the back of the card, as in the scenario with Ms. Cuenca-Sanchez.

STRATEGIES FOR PROMOTING LEARNING WITH CLASSWIDE PEER TUTORING

One of the most highly recommended strategies for promoting achievement among diverse groups of learners is **classwide peer tutoring** (Kamps et al., 2008, 2015). All students in the class are divided into pairs of students, who then alternate roles of tutor and tutee to master basic academic skills. The most significant feature of classwide peer tutoring is the dramatic increase in engaged time on-task and opportunities to respond. For example, consider a 45-minute fifth-grade reading class of 30 students, in which one student is called on to read aloud at a time. In this class, each student will read aloud for an average of no more than 1.5 minutes per class. In a classwide peer tutoring program, however, students in this same class could read aloud for an average of as much as 22.5 minutes per class, an increase of 1,500%! As described in Chapter 6, increasing engaged time on-task—or "maximizing engagement"—is closely linked to academic success, and the Council for Exceptional Children's high-leverage practice 18 in special education is to use strategies to promote active student engagement (McLeskey et al., 2017).

Although it is not successful in every case, research has documented the overall positive benefits of classwide peer tutoring in elementary and secondary settings (McMaster et al., 2006; Wexler et al., 2015). Successful classwide peer tutoring programs have been established in reading (Kearns et al., 2015; McMaster et al., 2006), elementary and secondary math (Powell & Fuchs, 2015), and spelling (Maheady et al., 2006), as well as secondary content areas such as social studies (Marshak et al., 2011; Scruggs et al., 2012). It has also been found to be successful as a strategy for English learners with learning disabilities (Bowman-Perrott et al., 2016; Richards-Tutor et al., 2015) and for students with emotional and behavioral disorders (Dunn et al., 2017) and has been recommended as a Tier 1 response-to-intervention approach (McMaster et al., 2008). Following are procedures for implementing classwide peer tutoring in reading (see Fuchs & Fuchs, 2005; Kearns et al., 2015).

IMPLEMENT CLASSWIDE PEER TUTORING IN READING The Peer-Assisted Learning Strategies (PALS) program (Hughes & Solari, 2020; McMaster et al., 2006) is a classwide peer tutoring program that supplements the reading curriculum and addresses the different learning needs of every student. To use the program, first pair each student with a partner. After the teacher announces the reading selection and tells the class to start, the stronger reader reads the passage aloud to the partner for 5 minutes. The roles are then reversed, and the weaker reader reads for 5 minutes. During oral reading, the partner follows along and corrects reading errors. After the 10-minute total reading session is a 2-minute "Retell" session, in which the weaker reader is prompted to answer the following questions:

- What did you learn first?
- What did you learn next?

In the Classroom

Planning and Implementing a Tutoring Program

1. Clarify the specific objectives of the tutoring program, including both academic and social objectives when appropriate.
2. List objectives in a form that can be easily measured. For example:
   "Students serving as tutees will improve reading fluency by 30% on classroom reading materials in the next 12 weeks."
   "Performance of all students on weekly spelling tests will improve to an average of 85%; no student will score lower than 60%."
   "Within 8 weeks, students involved in tutoring will report that math is at least their third-favorite class."
3. Choose tutoring partners carefully. No firm conclusions can be drawn to direct tutoring choices; nevertheless, several considerations should be taken into account. Some teachers have recommended choosing students as tutors who are conscientious in class and try hard to earn good grades. These teachers believed that the brightest students may have less empathy for students who do not learn easily, although exceptions to this are commonly found. Other considerations include the willingness to participate and the compatibility of the tutoring pair. Teachers should find pairs who will work together well; however, they should also encourage pairing of students who are different in gender, race, ethnicity, or socioeconomic status whenever possible, rather than exclusively supporting established social groupings.
4. Establish rules and procedures for the tutoring program. These rules should cover how students are to interact with each other and specify the type of interactions that are not acceptable. Procedures should specify the times and dates of tutoring, the materials to be used, and the specific activities to be undertaken.
5. Implement the tutoring program, monitor it carefully, and be consistent in enforcing the rules and procedures. Modify rules and procedures as necessary. Modifications may include the use of reward contingencies, especially for motivating older students.
6. Evaluate the program frequently, and do not wait for the end of the program to determine whether it was effective. Collect information throughout the program, and determine whether it is progressing satisfactorily. If progress is not being made, modify the program. Developing a fidelity checklist can assist in identifying the skills and procedures required for training and/or re-teaching students how to be tutors and tutees.

The partner provides feedback on the answers. In the third segment, "Paragraph Shrinking," the weaker student is asked by the partner to provide the following information for each paragraph:

- Name the "who" or "what."
- State the most important thing about the "who" or "what."
- Say the main idea in 10 words or less.

When an error is made, tell partners to say, "No, that's not quite correct," and encourage the student to skim the passage for the answer. The last segment is the "Prediction Relay" and is composed of four segments:

Predict	______	What do you predict will happen next?
Read	______	Read half a page.
Check	______	Did the prediction come true?
Summarize	______	Name the who or what.
	______	Tell the most important thing about the who or what.
	______	Say the main idea in 10 words or less. (Mathes et al., 1994, p. 46)

Give students prompt cards that contain this information to assist them in questioning their partners.

Every 4 weeks, rearrange the tutoring pairs and divide the entire class into two teams (e.g., a "Red" team and a "Blue" team). During classwide peer tutoring sessions, give students a scorecard, on which points are tallied for good reading and good tutoring skills. At the end of a 4-week session, tally all individual scorecards and encourage the entire class to congratulate the winning team. The second team is also congratulated. Then, two new teams are formed, and students again begin earning and accumulating points.

IMPLEMENT THE ELEMENTS OF CLASSWIDE PEER TUTORING SYSTEMATICALLY

Researchers have made recommendations for implementing classwide peer tutoring, based on several years' experience in research and practice (Abbott et al., 2011; Kearns et al., 2015; Maheady & Gard, 2010; McMaster et al., 2006). These recommendations include the following.

Tutoring Materials You can use a variety of reading materials in classwide peer tutoring programs, including basal readers, novels, library books, and content-area textbooks. It is not necessary for all pairs to read from the same book; both members of a tutoring pair are encouraged to read from the less-fluent reader's book to ensure that both students receive practice in reading. If a reader is compelled to read from a text that is too difficult, the tutoring experience may become ineffective and frustrating.

Other helpful materials include a timer or stopwatch for timing sessions and a calculator for adding up team points. Student materials include, in addition to the reading materials, a prompt card, a scorecard, and pencils.

Scheduling Schedule regular tutoring sessions, for example, 3 days per week, 35 minutes per day, for 15 weeks. Be sure to schedule the reading tutoring session when all members of the class are present (i.e., none, or as few as possible, are attending resource programs or other special services). Monitor tutoring sessions by collecting data to ensure students are on-task and progressing to ensure the 15-week tutoring sessions are successful.

Training Devote one 45-minute session to teach students how to use the materials correctly and how to be a helpful partner. Furthermore, spend about two sessions for teaching each of the three reading activities, and teach only one activity at a time. That is, you could train and practice Retelling for the first week. The second week, train Paragraph Shrinking, and the third week, practice Retelling and Paragraph Shrinking together. The fourth week, add Prediction Relay, and then begin to practice all three activities together.

Students need time and practice to acquire the skills of sequencing, skimming, summarizing, stating the main idea, and predicting. Stating the main idea and summarizing may be the most difficult concepts to teach; it may be helpful to use pictures to promote the idea of the most important "who or what" before transferring the concept to reading.

Interpersonal Skills Along with other researchers, Mathes et al. (1994) found that "many students left to their own devices may become bossy, impatient, or disrespectful toward their tutoring partner. . . . Giving positive feedback and rewards is not a natural behavior for most children" (p. 47). Teach students specific words and gestures for reinforcing partners and emphasize good sportsmanship and cooperative behavior. Close monitoring of interpersonal skills is recommended in order to keep students positive toward one another.

USE CLASSWIDE PEER TUTORING ON THE SECONDARY LEVEL Classwide peer tutoring has also been successfully implemented in middle school and high school settings in areas such as reading (Abbott et al., 2011; Fuchs et al., 2002), social studies (Marshak et al., 2011), English (Mastropieri et al., 2001), and science (Mastropieri et al., 2005; McDuffie et al., 2009). In these investigations, students with a number of different types of disabilities were able to function effectively as tutors and tutees and they improved in academic skills and classroom behavior when they did so. In addition, the tutoring content selected can be linked to Common Core State Standards.

Mastropieri and colleagues (2003) employed classwide peer tutoring in inclusive high school world history classes with students with learning disabilities, emotional disturbance, or mild intellectual disabilities. Students were divided into tutoring pairs, each including a stronger and a weaker reader. At the beginning of tutoring, "admirals" read one paragraph of the history text while "generals" listened, and then students reversed roles, reading the same paragraph a second time. Immediately after oral reading, students employed summarization strategies to promote reading comprehension. Students asked each other after reading each paragraph, "What is the most important what or who in the text?"; followed by, "What is the most important thing about the what or who in the text?" and "What is the summary sentence?"—similar to the process explained for previous applications (e.g., Fuchs & Fuchs, 2005). After the tutoring session, the teacher provided whole-class review. Compared with students receiving more traditional instruction, students who participated in classwide peer tutoring scored much higher on chapter tests, unit tests, and an end-of-year cumulative exam.

Peer tutoring has also been employed in inclusive high school chemistry classes (Mastropieri et al., 2005). Student tutoring pairs used materials with which they questioned each other on important target content (e.g., "What is nonpolar covalent bonding?") as well as broader elaborations of that content (e.g., "What else is important to know about nonpolar covalent bonding?"). Tutoring was used as a supplement to regular instruction (about 15–20 minutes of a 90-minute class) to help ensure that students mastered basic facts and concepts in chemistry. Materials also included mnemonic (memory-enhancing) strategies (see Chapter 10) to be used when needed. Students who participated in classwide peer tutoring in chemistry outperformed students who did not, and the learning gains were particularly strong for students with learning disabilities. In seventh-grade history classes, teachers divided students into tutoring pairs and had them question each other using teacher-made "fact sheets," which consisted of the most important content from the unit. Students—particularly those with disabilities—scored higher on unit tests when classwide peer tutoring was implemented (Mastropieri et al., 2008).

Similarly, McDuffie et al. (2009) employed classwide peer tutoring using "fact sheets" of important target content to improve student learning of genetics content in middle school science classes (e.g., "List the four nitrogenous bases," "What are proteins used for?"). Students in tutoring conditions enjoyed tutoring each other and scored higher on content tests than students taught by more traditional methods.

CLASSWIDE PEER TUTORING, DIFFERENTIATED INSTRUCTION, AND UNIVERSAL DESIGN FOR LEARNING Classwide peer tutoring is an ideal strategy for inclusive classrooms because it meets many of the criteria for differentiated instruction and universal design for learning (UDL). Tutoring is differentiated to the extent that learners receive instruction individually at the appropriate pace and level of redundancy and with the feedback that they need; classwide peer tutoring provides differentiation in the process of learning and in the learning environment and the products (e.g., verbal vs. written responses) of learning (Tomlinson, 2014). UDL principles are addressed by classwide peer tutoring to the extent that peer tutoring can provide for multiple means of engagement, representation, action, and expression, especially as compared with traditional, whole-class instruction (Meyer et al., 2014). See Table 9.2 for how UDL principles are represented in classwide peer tutoring and cooperative learning techniques.

TABLE 9.2 UDL Principles Represented in Peer Tutoring and Cooperative Learning

UDL Principles	Classwide Peer Tutoring and Cooperative Learning Techniques
Provide Multiple Means of Engagement	• Create an accepting and supportive learning environment (e.g., student with a physical disability can participate in a role that involves limited handwriting or typing demands) if needed. • Foster collaboration and community between peers by assigning individual responsibilities that require active participation. • Provide peers with feedback that is informative rather than competitive or comparative. • Allow for choice of peer partners.
Provide Multiple Means of Representation	• Offer repeated practice of concepts using varied, well-organized, clear materials to enhance comprehension. • Offer alternative modes of communication (verbal, written, action). • Provide an opportunity for peers to share perspectives and refine their understanding of material. • Provide flexible options for how learning can be demonstrated (e.g., poster, diagram).
Provide Multiple Means of Action and Expression	• Provide an opportunity for peer models to assist in the use of alternatives for physically interacting with materials (e.g., adapted keyboards, voice, or other digital tools). • Provide an opportunity for peers to think aloud, modeling their thinking processes. • Offer differentiated models for evaluating the collaborative process and the individual contributions.

Cooperative Learning

Learning Objective 9.4 Explain cooperative learning and summarize how it can be implemented to benefit diverse learners.

Cooperative learning has been widely recommended as a technique to promote the inclusive education of diverse learners (Johnson & Johnson, 2009, 2017; Slavin, 2015). It has been found to result in increased achievement, improved attitude toward the subject matter, and increased cooperation among students from different ethnic backgrounds (Hurley et al., 2009; Oortwijn et al., 2008). In cooperative learning, students are assigned to small groups and work collaboratively to complete group activities. To this extent, cooperative learning addresses elements of differentiated instruction in a manner similar to classwide peer tutoring—for example, in providing different roles to different group members—and addresses elements of UDL in providing multiple means of engagement, representation, and action and expression (see Chapter 6). Cooperative learning programs can be configured in many ways. Johnson and Johnson (1986, 2009) have described some important overall elements in implementing cooperative learning programs, as described next.

STRATEGIES FOR IMPLEMENTING COOPERATIVE LEARNING

CREATE OBJECTIVES Carefully specify the academic objectives to be accomplished, as well as the collaborative skills objective, which includes the interpersonal skills and small-group skills that will be addressed. Whenever you implement a cooperative learning activity, you should specify the collaborative skills that will be necessary to complete the activity successfully and teach them as purposefully as the relevant academic skills.

DETERMINE GROUP PARAMETERS Cooperative learning groups usually range from two to six students. The groups should be larger when materials are scarce or when limited time is available to complete the activities. If students are younger or inexperienced with cooperative learning activities, the group size should be smaller. Students should not work in groups of four or more if they have not mastered the preskills of group work.

It is also important to plan carefully whether students should be in homogeneous or heterogeneous groupings. Although it is helpful to have groups that work well together, it is also important to mix groups by gender, race/ethnicity, and ability level. Sometimes random assignment to groups is effective. Teachers should also consider how long they want groups to operate together. For example, for a longer project on plant growth and development, it may be necessary for groups to remain intact throughout the activity. For other projects, groups can be changed more frequently. When absenteeism is a problem in the school, group assignments may need to be made daily.

Also consider the physical arrangement of the groups. Ideally, groups sit around a circular table that is small enough to provide close proximity and large enough to accommodate relevant materials. However, teachers usually must cope with the best furniture available. Just be sure that groups are arranged so that you can easily move from one group to another. When distributing materials, try to arrange for cooperation. One way to do this is to provide only one set of materials that must be shared efficiently for the task to be completed.

It is also important to consider the roles that students will assume during the cooperative learning activity (Mastropieri & Scruggs, 1993). A cooperative learning role is an assigned action or task for a student to fulfill. Usually, it is helpful to assign specific duties to individual students to promote teamwork and cooperation. These roles vary based on the grade span and activity. For example, when completing a task that involves building or constructing an object, the cooperative roles may be a cutter, designer, gluer, or colorist. When creating a PowerPoint of key elements for a book report, roles might include a summarizer (who restates the conclusions, consensus, or plans of the group), a checker (who ensures that all students understand the activity objectives), an accuracy coach (who corrects or verifies the final products and other students' responses), and an encourager (who motivates reluctant participants and compliments team member contributions) (Kagan & Kagan, 2009). Of course, individual students are also responsible for all other aspects of the assigned tasks. Another, more procedural set of roles that involves groups of four students is recommended in the *Full Option Science System* materials (available through Delta Education) and is described in Table 9.3.

Working with Peers on Computers, Tablets, and Mobile Devices

Computers, tablets, and mobile devices provide ideal opportunities for peers to work collaboratively. Students enjoy the motivating aspects of working with digital devices, and working collaboratively on projects involving technology can be a rewarding experience for all students. For example, students who are working on developing multimedia projects can assist one another in activities such as finding appropriate sources from the Internet, downloading multimedia files, sequencing materials, developing podcasts, taking and editing pictures, and finding other multimedia items to include in their projects. Many states have adopted computer science and computational thinking standards as a required part of the curriculum (e.g., computer literacy, digital citizenship, educational technology). When two or more individuals work together on a computer or tablet, it is called *pair programming* (Campe et al., 2020). One student can be designated as the official computer or mobile device operator and the other as a co-navigator. Roles can be reversed during the project after specified amounts of time. Before assigning partners, students can be ranked according to their computer expertise along a continuum of expert to novice. This information can be used to pair students so that computer experts are paired with novices. Once students gain more proficiency with the digital devices, different searching tasks can be assigned to everyone in the group. The models suggested for implementing peer tutoring and cooperative learning in other subject areas can be applied to the use of computers, tablets, and mobile devices during either peer tutoring or cooperative learning scenarios.

Several researchers have successfully implemented collaborative group work using technologies in various ways. In an investigation by Foss et al. (2013), 10 middle school students with autism spectrum disorders, learning disabilities, and/or attention-deficit/hyperactivity disorder worked collaboratively to design a sports game that involved technology. Three researchers were design partners who used the cooperative inquiry method of instruction and facilitated the design process to smaller groups of three to four students. The design project required students to create large-scale game sketches, use arts and crafts to develop low-tech prototypes, merge their design ideas (e.g., how to log in; upgrades; sound effects), and eventually create a storyboard. One of the adults was a team programmer and created a prototype of the browser-based computer game for the students to play and then provide feedback. Although students were challenged at times to accept design ideas other than their own, they were empowered by the positive experience.

Consider pairing students to prepare presentations made on the computer. For example, some common tools that teachers can encourage students to use when developing multimedia presentations include Microsoft PowerPoint, Google Slides, Canva, and Prezi. Some of the presentations can be simple, using only text, whereas more complex presentations can involve pictures, graphs, animation, video, and sound. Pairing students to develop these projects can help all students gain computer literacy skills necessary to function independently. See Ok and Rao (2019) for free and low-cost apps and extensions ("add-ons" that extend the functionality of the browser) in Google Chrome browsers.

Apps that help organize information can be useful for project-based learning activities. Examples include Trello (Trello, Inc.), Evernote, Google Keep (Google LLC), Microsoft OneNote (Microsoft Corporation), and Notability (Ginger Labs). Many of these programs can be applications for computers and tablets, web based, or a combination. In addition, students can share, back up, export, and access files using common online tools such as Dropbox, Google Drive (Google LLC), Microsoft OneNote (Microsoft Corporation), and Box (Box, Inc.). Consulting with a school's technology department for which platforms are best supported in a school district is a good place to start when choosing these programs for students.

Programs like Zoom, Microsoft Teams, and Google Meet are all software that can allow for peer collaboration through virtual video conferencing in the instances of remote learning. In addition, class management applications such as Class Dojo, Google Classroom, Nearpod, Canvas, Blackboard, and Edmodo offer ways for students to collaborate with their peers in a digital format in real time.

The following table lists more common technologies that can be used for collaborative learning at all grade spans.

Apps for Education

Working with Peers on Computers, Tablets, and Mobile Devices—*continued*

App Name	Description
G Suite for Education	Allows students to work in the same file at the same time from multiple devices and files are automatically saved and updated. Programs include Google Docs, Google Slides, Google Sheets, Google Drive, Google Calendar, and more. Learn more at https://edu.google.com/intl/ALL_us/products/workspace-for-education/education-fundamentals/.
Padlet	Allows students to work on a "pinboard" to brainstorm topics, pin ideas, comment, add images and videos, etc. Teachers can follow up on progress immediately.
Lucidchart	Allows students to create flow charts, mind maps, and wireframes and collaborate with other students in real time.
Miro	An endless virtual whiteboard for brainstorming and writing projects visually. Students can collaborate in real time from different devices.
Flipgrid	Allows students to create videos for discussion, share ideas, and engage with options to respond to other students.

Pearson eTextbook
Video Example 9.3
This video provides an example of how to use cooperative learning in a middle school science classroom. How could the observed procedures be used in other content areas?

TABLE 9.3 Student Cooperative Learning Roles in the Full Option Science System

Role	Responsibility
Reader	Responsible for reading all instructions, for checking that everyone understands the activity, and for summarizing the activity when everything is completed.
Recorder	Record observations, predictions, and comparisons using such media as iPads, computers, audio recorders, camcorders, pens, and chart and graph paper. These observations can all be compiled in the final report.
Getter	Retrieve and return all materials at the beginning and end of activities, including iPads, cameras, microscopes, and trays. Getters can also keep track of materials during the course of the activity.
Starter	Initiate and supervise the interactions with materials, including assembling materials and providing all group members similar access to hands-on materials. Starters can also help monitor student engagement throughout the activity.

Pearson eTextbook
Video Example 9.4
This video provides a description of cooperative learning and an illustration that includes examples of differentiation of instruction.

Peers can also work cooperatively on digital activities, as described in the *Apps for Education* feature. Use of peers in these activities is particularly useful when there are more students than computers or devices in a classroom, but the use of peers can also serve important learning objectives.

EXPLAIN GOALS, RULES, AND PROCEDURES Before group activities begin, be sure that all students understand both the assignment and the purpose of the activity. Group goals and rewards should be carefully explained to all group members, for example, bonus points for completing the task within a certain time period. Overall, students should be aware that they are responsible for (1) their own learning, (2) the learning of the group, and (3) the learning of the entire class, in that order. The criteria for success should be explained to the students. Individual accountability within the group structure is necessary and should be clearly specified. Also, when appropriate, students could be informed that they can assist other groups if they have finished their own assignments first. Students trained appropriately in cooperative learning behaviors generally outperform students in less-structured cooperative learning activities (Johnson & Johnson, 2009, 2017).

Because cooperative learning activities are different from many other classroom activities, particularly independent seatwork, students need to be informed of what is and is not appropriate in cooperative learning exercises. One method of conveying expectations is by use of a **T-Chart** (Johnson et al., 2008), which employs two columns in the shape of a *T*. The T-Chart specifies what the room will look like (e.g., "All students participating") and sound like (e.g., "Low voices from students in groups") if the rule is being followed. Other classroom rules for cooperative learning that could be displayed on a T-Chart include "Everyone shares with others" and "Students encourage each other."

MONITOR GROUP ACTIVITIES When cooperative groups begin working, your role differs dramatically from that in more traditional instruction. Many teachers begin by presenting information to the class as a whole and then break students into their groups. Instead of directly presenting information or demonstrating procedures to the whole class for the entire period, the teacher's role involves moving around and monitoring group activities. Ensure that students remain on-task and interact appropriately. When necessary, you may assist with the task or demonstrate procedures. When students are interacting inappropriately, intervene to model, demonstrate, and teach the collaborative skills necessary for the task to be accomplished. Finally, when the activities are completed (or allocated time expires), you must provide closure to the lesson by restating the objectives, summarizing the major points, having students provide ideas or examples, and answering any final questions. Because cooperative learning activities are less formally structured than more traditional methods, summarizing and providing closure are critically important. Group activities can easily overrun the allotted time, so plan carefully to ensure that enough time remains for closure and summaries at the end of the activity.

EVALUATE INDIVIDUAL AND GROUP EFFORTS Evaluation needs to occur throughout the cooperative learning process and include any individual and group products. You can evaluate the process for students with individual learning needs by observing them while they are working in their groups. The *In the Classroom* feature lists some ideas for evaluating the cooperative learning process. Group efforts should be considered, and students should be individually evaluated for their own learning and their contributions to the group process. Finally, teachers and students should both evaluate how well the groups functioned and consider how the group could function better in the future.

INTEGRATE STUDENTS WITH DISABILITIES INTO COOPERATIVE LEARNING GROUPS Students with disabilities can benefit academically and socially from participating in cooperative learning. However, these benefits are not automatic. Take steps to ensure that students with diverse learning needs benefit as much as possible as well as interact positively and effectively with peers.

Prepare Students with disabilities Cooperative learning is frequently described as an important inclusion strategy because it enables students with disabilities to receive additional attention and assistance from peers while making their own contributions to the group (Johnson & Johnson, 2009). Nevertheless, students with disabilities may be fearful or anxious about joining a cooperative learning group, and some may actually prefer to work independently (O'Connor & Jenkins, 2014). Also, those students from some eastern countries of the world who are new to the United States may be uncomfortable with student-led methods of learning (Thanh et al., 2008). Therefore, it is important to explain procedures and roles carefully so that students will understand the expectations. It may be helpful to role-play the roles the students will assume before the activity. Present them with roles in the group that are appropriate for their skill levels. For example, if a student does not read at the appropriate grade level, provide a role of organizing, summarizing, or restating what others have reported. If the student lacks some specific social or academic skill that is important for group functioning, see if the special education teacher can teach some of these skills before the student joins the group.

Prepare Students Without Disabilities As stated earlier, classroom peers play an integral role in the integration of students with disabilities and other diverse learning needs into the general education classroom. However, students must be taught how to interact appropriately and how to accept individual differences in learning (O'Connor & Jenkins, 2014). Positive peer

In the Classroom

Evaluation Checklist for Cooperative Learning

Process Evaluation Component

_______ Is the student working with the group members?

_______ Does the student appear to understand what to do?

_______ Is the student capable of doing the assigned tasks?

_______ Do the group members encourage independent work when appropriate?

_______ Are all group members actively engaged in the activity?

_______ Do the group members appear to be getting along?

_______ Do the students exhibit appropriate social behavior?

_______ Do the group members share materials appropriately?

_______ Do the group members speak in a pleasant, quiet tone of voice?

_______ Does the group start and finish activities on time?

Product Evaluation Component

_______ Did each student complete the activity?

_______ Does it appear that the work completed meets the objective for the learning component of cooperative learning?

_______ When given a performance-based assessment covering the objectives, do students demonstrate mastery of their prioritized objectives?

_______ When questioned, can students with disabilities explain what they did or show you what they learned?

interactions should be prompted and carefully monitored. As an example of unproductive interactions on a group learning task, O'Connor and Jenkins (1996) provided the following observation:

> Toby, a fifth-grade boy with [learning disabilities], rarely received productive help from his partners, although he frequently requested it. By this point in our observation, Toby's partner had long since ceased to follow Toby's reading or correct his errors. Toby stopped reading and announced, "I need help." The partner supplied a word, but it was not the word in the text. Toby used it anyway, and they both laughed. This game escalated until each time Toby needed decoding help, his partner said, "I'm a dumbo," which Toby inserted into the sentence: [Toby said "I'm a dumbo" instead of the correct word because his partner did not provide the correct word for Toby] . . . Eventually, Toby tired of the game. "I need help," he said again, but from this partner he would not receive it. (p. 36)

Some students may need particular types of assistance in cooperative group situations, such as help turning pages or understanding directions. The special education teacher may be able to meet with relevant cooperative groups and explain how best to interact with the student with disabilities.

When students are working to earn group points or rewards, sometimes they are concerned that having a student with disabilities will impair the group's chances to succeed. In these cases, consider varying the group criteria for different members or the amount of material each student is expected to master. Use the students' individualized education program to determine specific instructional goals. For example, in a group spelling activity, an individual with learning disabilities may be expected to learn only certain targeted spelling words from the list. These students can also be evaluated with respect to how much they improved over the previous time period, rather than how much they learned in a particular activity. Individual students can be assigned roles that highlight their strengths (e.g., group leader) or they can be given different assignments, lists, or problems appropriate to their abilities and can be evaluated on the percentage correctly completed. Embedding these types of scaffolds for students with disabilities may make group members more receptive to including students with diverse learning needs.

CREATE DIFFERENT TYPES OF COOPERATIVE GROUP ARRANGEMENTS

Cooperative learning activities can be arranged in many ways, and many types of tasks can be adapted for cooperative learning. Johnson et al. (2008) listed several ideas, including the following, intended to help teachers get started with cooperative group activities:

1. Students discuss a lesson with their neighbors for 3–5 minutes, asking questions and clarifying.
2. Students form reading groups, in which three students serve as reader, recorder, and checker, in reading material and answering questions.
3. Students meet in small groups and check homework assignments, discussing and resolving any questions that were answered differently.
4. Students meet in groups to proofread and critique each other's papers and meet again to respond to revisions.
5. Students work in small groups to prepare for specific tests.

Slavin (1991) described several types of more formal cooperative learning arrangements and activities:

1. *Student Teams-Achievement Divisions (STAD):* After the teacher has presented a lesson, students meet in heterogeneous groups to study the material. After the study session, students take a quiz and are graded with respect to how much improvement was made over the previous test. The winning group is recognized in a class newsletter.
2. *Team-Assisted Individualization (TAI):* In this procedure, students are given pretests in an academic area and are placed in a structured curriculum based on their scores. Students are then placed in heterogeneous groups and help each other complete their assignments. Rewards are based on the number of activities completed and on percentage correct.
3. *Cooperative Integrated Reading and Composition (CIRC):* Students work in cooperative groups on reading and writing assignments. For part of the instruction, teachers lead the instruction. Then students work cooperatively on decoding, vocabulary, writing, spelling, and comprehension activities and prepare each other for tests.
4. *Jigsaw:* This is a popular cooperative learning strategy in which each student learns a particular piece of information and then contributes it to the group. Students are tested individually on their learning of all the material. In another version of jigsaw, each student contributes a particular component of a larger task, and then the larger task is presented to the entire class. For instance, one group could be preparing a presentation on Dr. Martin Luther King. One student could prepare information on King's early life, another could prepare information on King and the civil rights movement, another could gather material from King's speeches, and a fourth could collect information about King's assassination. The group then meets and cooperatively compiles the entire presentation, with each student sharing what has been learned with the group. Souvignier and Kronenberger (2007) reported successful applications of jigsaw activities in math and science with students as young as third grade; however, overall learning was not always more effective than that for teacher-directed instruction.
5. *Group investigation:* Group investigation requires the most independence on the part of cooperative groups. In this method, students decide how they will learn the material, how they will go about organizing the group to best facilitate learning, and how they will communicate their results to the other students in the class.

Whereas some activities are intended to be undertaken throughout the year, for example, in science or mathematics, other cooperative group activities can be designed for a single lesson. Teachers should consider their own classroom needs to design the best arrangement for cooperative group learning.

USE PEER-MEDIATION STRATEGIES TO RESOLVE CONFLICTS In some cases, peer-mediation strategies have been used to manage conflict situations that occur among peers. Johnson et al. (1995) trained students in how to identify conflicts, how to negotiate, and how to mediate to better resolve peer conflicts. The negotiation procedure had five parts:

1. Jointly define the conflict (i.e., both parties agree on the nature of the conflict).
2. Exchange positions and interests (each party describes their own position on the conflict).
3. Reverse perspectives (each party states the other party's point of view).
4. Invent at least three optional agreements for mutual gain (i.e., solutions that benefit all parties).
5. Reach an integrative agreement (the optional agreement that seems best to all parties).

Johnson et al. (1995) reported that after 12 training sessions of 45 minutes each, the training had a significant effect on the strategies students used and the resulting resolutions of conflicts (see also Stevahn et al., 2002).

Peers have also successfully served as interventionists to address a variety of problem behaviors in schools (see Dart et al., 2014). For example, in Collins et al. (2016), peer mentors managed the Check-in, Check-out (CICO) system (see Chapter 8) to improve their peers' social skills. In this adaptation of CICO, a peer mentor rather than a teacher collected the Daily Progress Report (DPR) from the student at check-in, reminded the student of the targeted behavior, stated the students' behavioral goal of the day, and provided an encouraging statement. The peer also successfully facilitated the check-out procedure at the end of the day.

ADVANTAGES AND CHALLENGES OF COOPERATIVE LEARNING

ADVANTAGES It has been reported that cooperative learning is an effective strategy for improving achievement, group interactions, social learning, and the learning of students with disabilities and other diverse learning needs (Johnson et al., 2008; Slavin, 1991). With cooperative learning, students with disabilities can be included in—and contribute to—activities that they otherwise may not be able to participate in individually (Mastropieri et al., 1998). Johnson and Johnson (1986) concluded the following:

> In both competitive and individualistic learning situations teachers try to keep students away from each other. "Do not copy," "Move your desks apart," and "I want to see how well you can do, not your neighbor" are all phrases that teachers commonly use in their classrooms. Students are repeatedly told, "Do not care about how other students in this class are doing. Take care of yourself!" Cooperative learning, however, should be used whenever teachers want students to learn more, like school better, like each other better, have higher self-esteem, and learn more effective social skills. (p. 554)

CHALLENGES In spite of the benefits of cooperative learning, some potential limitations also exist that teachers should consider. Tateyama-Sniezek (1990) reviewed the literature on cooperative learning in research in which students with disabilities were participants and in which their achievement was examined separately from that of students without disabilities. She concluded that students with disabilities often did not learn significantly more than if they participated in alternative learning conditions. Stevens and Slavin (1991) responded that the effects for students with disabilities were generally positive, even if they were not always statistically significant. McMaster and Fuchs (2002) conducted a review of research and concluded that outcomes were variable for students with learning disabilities and, overall, not stronger than those of other types of peer mediation. However, cooperative learning programs appeared to be more successful when they combined individual accountability and group rewards. Jenkins and O'Connor (2003) concluded that teacher classroom behavior and student social skills were important to the success of cooperative learning. It should be noted that positive effects for students with disabilities are often, but not always, realized in cooperative learning interventions, and teachers should plan and monitor the interventions carefully to ensure they are having the desired effect (see also McMaster & Fuchs, 2005).

Diversity, Equity, and Inclusion in the Classroom

Cooperative Learning Activities in Multiethnic Classrooms

Many students prefer to work with peers for some school activities. Most students who have participated in peer tutoring or cooperative learning activities have reported enjoying working with partners. Sometimes students with disabilities have reported they have felt more comfortable reading with a single partner during peer tutoring than reading aloud in front of the entire class (see Mastropieri et al., 2001), and English learners have reported gaining confidence in their abilities (Norland, 2005). Similar, related findings have been observed when students from various ethnic backgrounds have been placed in structured small-group cooperative learning situations. In some studies, students from diverse ethnic backgrounds were found to have increased popularity following multiple cooperative learning lessons. Oortwijn et al. (2008) implemented cooperative learning lessons in elementary schools that included authentic math problem assignments with multiple possible solutions in heterogeneous cooperative groups. Improved cooperativeness and friendships among students from all ethnic groups were observed over time. More recently, Van Ryzin et al. (2020) implemented cooperative learning in a project involving 15 middle schools over a 2-year period and reported that students in cooperative learning conditions overall reported positive gains in peer relatedness (acceptance from other classmates), academic support (help and support from other students), and engagement (motivation and effort to do well in school) than students who had not participated in cooperative learning. Furthermore, it was found that overall gains in peer relatedness, academic support, and engagement were even greater for students from a variety of racial-ethnic groups than they were for White students. Van Ryzin and colleagues concluded that cooperative learning helped reduce ethnic disparities because it reduced interpersonal competition and provided opportunities for students of different racial-ethnic groups to work together to achieve common goals. These findings offer promise for using small-group activities such as cooperative learning when working with diverse groups of students.

Discuss: What are the advantages for students when learning in diverse cooperative groups?

Overall, cooperative learning has been popular with participating teachers. Nevertheless, teachers have made several suggestions regarding cooperative learning, including the following:

- Plan for increased teacher preparation and transition time.
- Increase allocated time for lessons.
- Work to reduce any student anxieties about working together and teaching one another.
- Safeguard that all students are working appropriately (and collaboratively) on the activities.
- Confirm that assignments are at the appropriate level for all students.
- Enforce individual accountability systems and be prepared for higher noise levels (Jenkins & O'Connor, 2003).

Many of these potential concerns, however, may occur with other instructional arrangements, and strategies for dealing with several of these challenges have been presented earlier in the chapter. As with any educational intervention, teachers must ensure that they have maximized the positive benefits while addressing possible limitations. Gillies (2016) has described the concerns of some teachers in a time of high-stakes testing and has suggested that cooperative learning, when systematically employed and carefully monitored, can be successfully implemented to promote academic learning, especially when these procedures are employed over time.

Overall, cooperative learning can be an effective strategy for promoting inclusive instruction. For example, Mastropieri et al. (1998) employed cooperative learning to promote learning in a hands-on elementary science class that included five students with disabilities, including learning disabilities, emotional disturbance, mild intellectual disabilities, and physical disabilities. Not only did students in this class greatly outperform students in comparison classes, which employed traditional textbook-based instruction, but the students with disabilities overall achieved at about the middle level of their own class! Similarly, students with moderate intellectual disabilities successfully acquired science vocabulary following structured cooperative learning in an inclusive classroom (Jimenez et al., 2012). Cooperative small-group work has also been found to be promising with English learners and learners from other ethnic backgrounds, as described in the *Diversity, Equity, and Inclusion in the Classroom* feature (Norland, 2005; Oortwijn et al., 2008; Van Ryzin et al., 2020). When appropriately employed, cooperative learning can be an important strategy for many classroom situations.

9 Summary

- Peers can be employed to support social acceptance.
  - Circle of Friends and Special Friends are training programs that can promote classroom acceptance of students with disabilities or other diverse learning needs.
- Students can be employed as peer assistants by pairing students for the purpose of having one student available to assist another student when necessary.
  - It is important to identify the situations that require peer assistance, appropriately train students, match peer assistants and buddies carefully, and monitor progress and adapt as necessary.
- Peer tutoring can be a powerful tool in improving classroom performance, and it can also be very helpful in addressing diverse learning needs in inclusive classrooms.
  - Both tutors and tutees can gain academically and socially from tutoring interventions, although the procedures and outcomes should be carefully monitored.
  - Classwide peer tutoring, in which all students in a class are involved in peer tutoring, is one of the most highly recommended strategies for promoting achievement among diverse groups of learners.
- Cooperative learning involves the creation of cooperative learning groups of students and can improve achievement and social integration of diverse learners.
  - Cooperative learning interventions require specifying objectives, making placement decisions, explaining the task, monitoring effectiveness, and evaluating individual and group achievement.
  - A variety of formal and informal procedures for cooperative learning can be employed to address a variety of classroom situations.

PROFESSIONAL STANDARDS LINK: Promoting Inclusion with Classroom Peers

Information in this chapter links most directly to:

- CEC 2020 Initial Practice-Based Professional Preparation Standards for Special Educators (Initial K–12 standards) (see https://exceptionalchildren.org/standards/initial-practice-based-professional-preparation-standards-special-educators): Standards 2 (Understanding and Addressing Each Individual's Developmental and Learning Needs), 3 (Demonstrating Subject Matter Content and Specialized Curriculum Knowledge), 4 (Using Assessment to Understand the Learner and the Learning Environment for Data-Based Decision Making), 5 (Supporting Learning Using Effective Instruction), 6 (Supporting Social, Emotional, and Behavioral Growth)
- InTASC Standards (see https://www.ccsso.org/sites/default/files/2017-11/InTASC_Model_Core_Teaching_Standards_2011.pdf): 2 (Learning Differences), 3 (Learning Environments), 7 (Planning for Instruction), 8 (Instructional Strategies)

PROMOTING INCLUSION WITH CLASSROOM PEERS

If you wish to increase cooperation and collaboration in your inclusive classroom and increase learning, have you considered the following? If not, see the pages listed here.

STRATEGIES FOR PROMOTING SOCIAL ACCEPTANCE

- ☐ Build community with the Circle of Friends, 228
- ☐ Promote acceptance with Special Friends, 228

STRATEGIES FOR ENLISTING PEER ASSISTANCE

- ☐ Train students in peer assistance, 229
- ☐ Train peers to assist students with different types of disabilities, 229–231
- ☐ Promote peer social initiation, 231

STRATEGIES FOR IMPLEMENTING A TUTORING PROGRAM

- ☐ Work across grade levels to implement cross-age tutoring, 236
- ☐ Implement same-age tutoring within your class, 236

STRATEGIES FOR PROMOTING LEARNING WITH CLASSWIDE PEER TUTORING

- ☐ Implement classwide peer tutoring in reading, 236–238
- ☐ Implement the elements of classwide peer tutoring systematically, 238
- ☐ Use classwide peer tutoring on the secondary level, 238–239
- ☐ Classwide peer tutoring, differentiated instruction, and universal design for learning, 239

STRATEGIES FOR IMPLEMENTING COOPERATIVE LEARNING

- ☐ Create objectives, 240
- ☐ Determine group parameters, 240–242
- ☐ Explain goals, rules, and procedures, 242–243
- ☐ Monitor group activities, 243
- ☐ Evaluate individual and group efforts, 243
- ☐ Integrate students with disabilities into cooperative learning groups, 243–244
- ☐ Create different types of cooperative group arrangements, 245
- ☐ Use peer-mediation strategies to resolve conflicts, 246

Wavebreak Media/Offset/Shutterstock

CHAPTER 10

Improving Attention and Memory

LEARNING OBJECTIVES

After studying this chapter, you should be able to:

10.1 Define attention difficulties and explain preconditions and strategies for improving the school success of students with diverse learning needs.

10.2 Describe memory difficulties and identify preconditions and strategies for improving the school success of students with diverse learning needs.

Attention and memory are two fundamental psychological processes necessary for learning to occur. It is easy to understand that instruction, however well presented, is of little value if it is not remembered. Conversely, it is possible to remember only those things to which we have paid attention in the first place!

In this chapter, we describe the problems students may have with attention and memory, and we describe a number of strategies you can use to improve the attention and memory of your students. Given the significance of these important psychological processes to classroom learning, it is likely that careful application of the principles and strategies described in this chapter can make an important difference in the school success of all students, including those with diverse learning needs.

Attention

Learning Objective 10.1 Define attention difficulties and explain preconditions and strategies for improving the school success of students with diverse learning needs.

ATTENTION AND STUDENTS WITH DIVERSE LEARNING NEEDS

All students exhibit occasional lapses in attention, either because of a lack of interest in a subject, boredom, fatigue, or being distracted by temporary anxieties or concerns. However, many students with diverse learning needs frequently exhibit difficulties with attention. For example, poor attention and concentration are commonly reported characteristics of students with learning disabilities (Lerner & Johns, 2015). Students with intellectual disabilities may fail to sustain attention in class and may exhibit difficulties attending to the appropriate stimulus in a lesson, such as focusing on the shape or color of the hands of a clock rather than the position of the hands in a lesson on telling time (Beirne-Smith et al., 2005).

Some students with physical or sensory impairments also have difficulty sustaining attention when attending to particular tasks that interact with disability areas. For example, some students with cerebral palsy have difficulty keeping their heads aligned and eyes focused on a class demonstration; some students with hearing impairments may tire from lengthy intervals of speech reading (Heward et al., 2022). For some students with attention-deficit/hyperactivity disorder (ADHD), attending is a significant problem. Some students with ADHD may qualify for services under the Individuals with Disabilities Education Act (IDEA) or Section 504.

Pearson eTextbook

Video Example 10.1

This video shows a child with attention problems in the classroom. Notice the various strategies the teacher uses to redirect the student.

Serious problems with attention can severely impede learning (Barkley, 2015; Fried et al., 2016). Fortunately, many strategies are available for improving student attention, as described in the following section.

CLASSROOM SCENARIO

Sachi

Sachi is a fifth-grader with average academic abilities and a positive disposition. However, she has difficulty sustaining her attention to school tasks for more than about 3 minutes at a time. When prompted, Sachi returns to task, but within a few minutes, she is again off-task, looking out the window, playing with her pencils, or doodling on her paper. This happens during teacher presentations, seatwork activities, and sometimes during group activities. As a consequence, Sachi does not complete her assignments and misses verbal directions and her grades have been falling, especially in math.

QUESTIONS FOR REFLECTION

1. Why do you think Sachi is having problems sustaining attention?
2. What adaptations to the classroom environment might help Sachi?
3. How could peers help Sachi pay better attention?

STRATEGIES FOR IMPROVING ATTENTION

ADDRESS THE PRECONDITIONS OF ATTENTION WITH TEACHER EFFECTIVENESS

It is inappropriate for teachers to implement special interventions to improve attention without first making sure their classrooms are as interesting and engaging as possible. For example, if you lecture day after day using the same presentation style or rely extensively on individual student worksheets, it would not be surprising if the attention of many of your students begins to wander.

If getting and holding students' attention is a problem, first consider whether you are using effective teacher planning and presentation variables consistently. If each lesson does not contain elements such as structure, clarity, redundancy, and enthusiasm, it is unlikely to sustain student attention (see the SCREAM variables in Chapter 6). Determine, for example, whether you have done as much as you can to teach enthusiastically (Reid & Johnson, 2012).

A huge part of teaching effectively—and thus maintaining student attention—is using interesting and motivating examples to enhance lessons. These examples allow teachers to personalize instruction and make the subject more meaningful and useful to students.

Finally, consider whether you are using attention-getting demonstrations. Demonstrations can include the use of "real" objects in teaching mathematical operations; showing artifacts in lessons on the Civil War; demonstrating, rather than describing, the effects of certain chemical interactions; or dressing in historical clothing and acting out scenes of life from different geographic regions and time periods. Pictures and illustrations can also be helpful when actual demonstrations are not possible.

However, if some students continue to have difficulty sustaining attention, try the following strategies.

PROVIDE ASSISTANCE WITH BASIC SKILLS PROBLEMS Many students with disabilities do not read or write as well as other students in the class. These students may appear less attentive because paying attention requires reading from a text or writing notes that are beyond their skill level. For these students, find other means for them to acquire relevant information.

Some students do not complete assignments appropriately because they were not paying attention to directions. When giving directions, prompt student attending ("Listen carefully to what I'm going to say"), speak in a clear voice, and limit classroom distractions. Write the steps of the assignment so students can read as well as listen. Directions should include information about the content and format of the assignment, the reason it is being assigned, how students may receive assistance from others (e.g., adults, peers, and technology), how much time it should take to complete, and how it will be evaluated. Clear and specific directions can improve the performance of poor attenders (Smith et al., 2016).

In other cases, students may lose focus because they do not process oral language as fast as it is spoken. When this happens, try to find ways to reduce the rate of speaking, increase redundancy, provide "advance organizers," or find other means to present information. Mr. Davis, an eighth-grade social studies teacher, displayed charts containing the organizational framework of units during the entire month-long unit. Students said the charts helped them refer back to major points during classes and helped promote a better understanding of everything in the unit. Mrs. Fluke, a fourth-grade teacher, placed language cards containing pictures illustrating the concepts of new vocabulary on a bulletin board. She encouraged her students to make versions of the cards for their personal picture dictionaries.

USE DIRECT APPEAL Direct appeal is a simple, sometimes overlooked strategy for improving attention and behavior problems (Gable et al., 2009; Redl, 1965; see also Chapter 8). To use direct appeal, find a quiet time and place to speak to students individually. Explain the problem as explicitly as possible, including the effect of the problem on you and other students as well as the target students. Then make a direct request to the students to improve their behavior. This strategy is likely to be effective when students recognize they are not paying attention and would like to succeed in school. An example of direct appeal is given in Figure 10.1.

USE PROXIMITY Proximity is another simple strategy that can be effective in promoting attention (Levin & Nolan, 2022). Simply move physically toward or stand near a student who is beginning to lose attention. This can prompt the student to refocus attention. Once this strategy has been established, it may be possible to fade it over time to a direct glance or a gesture that the student can easily interpret as a prompt to refocus attention. It also may be helpful to move the student or rearrange the classroom to accommodate teacher proximity.

Figure 10.1 Example of Direct Appeal

Teacher: Christine, may I speak with you privately for a minute?

Christine: OK.

Teacher: I think you're having a problem in my class. Do you know what I think it is?

Christine: No.

Teacher: Sometimes in class, I think you are having problems paying attention.

Christine: Oh.

Teacher: I think that because sometimes I see you just looking out the window, or doodling with your pencil, or wearing a blank expression on your face, as if you're daydreaming. Do you think that happens sometimes?

Christine: Yeah, I guess so. I guess I'm just not that interested in history.

Teacher: Well, I'm afraid that when that happens, it makes class harder for me, because I think I'm not getting through to you. Also, I think other students notice you and it makes them more likely to not pay attention.

Christine: Oh.

Teacher: But here's what I'd like to suggest. You daydream in class because you aren't interested in history. But if you think about what we're discussing a little more, and you raise your hand in class more often, I guarantee that you will begin to find class more interesting. You will also find that the time passes much more quickly. And most important—and this is what I want—you will find that you will get a much better grade in my class. So what do you say? Will you give it a try?

Christine: OK, I'll try.

Pearson eTextbook

Video Example 10.2

This video shows student teachers discussing their observations about teachers working with students with ADHD. Listen for strategies identified as effective.

BREAK UP ACTIVITIES Some students may be able to sit still and concentrate on a task for a certain number of minutes. Attention spans vary with the age and maturity of students. In general, however, rather than giving a younger student the full length of time to complete a relatively large assignment, divide the task into 10 subtasks of, for example, 3 minutes each. At the end of each subtask, the student's progress could be checked, recorded, and praised by you or an assigned classroom peer. Dividing tasks into smaller segments is a great strategy for helping students with limited abilities to stay focused. This strategy works well to meet accommodations that may be identified on a students' individualized educational program (IEP). Common examples include frequent breaks, extended time to complete a task, or chunking of information or tasks.

ALLOW SUFFICIENT MOVEMENT TO REDUCE RESTLESSNESS In some cases, especially in the elementary grades, students begin to lose concentration if they have been made to sit still for a long time. Recording when student attention begins to fade is a way to determine when periods of student inactivity are too long. If students regularly begin to lose attention after extended periods of sitting, consider rearranging the classroom schedule (e.g., recess periods) to allow for more movement (Kerr & Nelson, 2010). Adjust the amount of content or time spent on each discipline and consider alternating between quiet sit-down activities and more actively involved learning activities such as peer tutoring and cooperative group learning. If your schedule cannot be easily changed, try giving students a minute to "stand, stretch, reach up to the ceiling, take a deep breath and let it out slowly, and march in place." If a student with ADHD appears to be especially restless, you may ask the student to hand-deliver a message from you to another teacher in the school building. Brief movement intervals are helpful in promoting student attention. Also, including student movement in lessons can be helpful.

PROVIDE STUDENT ACTIVITIES Students are much more likely to pay attention when they are asked to engage in activities than when they are asked to listen to someone talk. Providing relevant activities can be an excellent way of promoting attention. For example, instead of asking students to listen to a verbal presentation on how a telegraph works, students could work in small groups to construct their own telegraphs and then send and decode messages to and from one another. Such activities help to focus student attention and make relevant concepts more meaningful. Record any student's success at paying attention over a period of time and reinforce that behavior with positive recognition or rewards.

USE CLASSROOM PEERS TO PROMOTE ATTENTION Classroom peers can also be effective in working with students who have attention problems (Evans et al., 2014). Adamson and Lewis (2017) demonstrated that classwide peer tutoring (see Chapter 9) increased the percentage of academic engaged time and reduced disruptive behaviors for secondary-age students with ADHD. Peers can be trained to prompt and reinforce attending behavior. Peer interventions can be set up through group activities or working one-on-one. Peers could be asked to work in pairs with students who have some difficulty sustaining attention. Such collaborative sharing of activities can help students with attention problems by providing ongoing prompts for them to attend only to relevant tasks.

Peers seated near target students can also prompt attention. Peers can be trained to provide subtle cues to students (e.g., lightly touching the student's back) when lapses in attention are observed; they can be asked to report inattention to you only when these more subtle prompts are disregarded. Before you use this kind of strategy, be sure everyone involved is amenable to trying to use peer-intervention strategies. Inattentive or impulsive behavior of students with ADHD can impact friendships and may cause peer conflicts in the classroom. Be sensitive to the needs of the students you are trying to help. Choose peer assistants wisely, using those students who may not become overwhelmed by the students' behaviors and appear to have strong interpersonal skills.

PROVIDE DIRECT CONSEQUENCES FOR ATTENTION You can increase attention in individual students by measuring and reinforcing it (Crossairt et al., 1973; Pfiffner & DuPaul, 2015). Set a timer, such as a wristwatch alarm, vibrating watch, audio recorder, iPod, iPad, tablet, or smartphone (with, for example, built-in alarm apps found on most everyday technology devices) to sound or vibrate at random intervals (the length of the interval depends on the frequency of prompts the students need). Whenever the alarm sounds, determine whether the target students were paying attention at that instant. If so, they can be rewarded with verbal praise, points on a check sheet, or tokens that can be accumulated and exchanged at a later date for desired objects, privileges, or activities. For example, a student who earns 90% of possible tokens over a 2-week period might be entitled to take an extra recess with another class, go out for ice cream, take a homework pass, or have a special break with you. If other students appear to resent this arrangement, consider including the rest of the class in some reward scheme for good behavior, such as a pizza party or game time. Allow the target student to work for a class reward or privilege, such as bonus free time or a favored activity. In this way, the class can share responsibility for the target student's success or failure, as in the continuation of Sachi's scenario.

Pearson eTextbook
Video Example 10.3

In this video, a teacher is having a conference with a child's parent. The teacher describes and shows the parent the individualized visual schedule used in the classroom to break up activities and increase the child's time on-task. What other strategies does the teacher use to manage student attention and learning?

CLASSROOM SCENARIO

Sachi

Sachi's teacher, Mrs. Lawson, asked a responsible student to sit behind Sachi and prompt Sachi when her attention wandered for more than a few seconds. This seemed to help, but Sachi still seemed to need frequent reminders to maintain her concentration. Mrs. Lawson determined from talking to Sachi and other students that Sachi liked to please her classmates. Mrs. Lawson told her that she could help do something nice for the class. The peer who was monitoring Sachi's inattention would tally each time Sachi was prompted. If the number of prompts declined by half by the end of the week, Mrs. Lawson would allow her to distribute animal crackers to everyone in the class. Almost immediately, Sachi began to pay more attention. After 3 weeks, she only required minimal prompting to stay attentive.

QUESTIONS FOR REFLECTION

1. Why do you think these strategies were successful for Sachi?
2. What might be another way to use peers to assist?
3. How could a caregiver adapt these strategies for home use?

Mild corrections or reprimands have also been found effective for students with attention problems. Generally, short reprimands have been found to be more effective than long reprimands, and immediate reprimands have been found to be more effective than delayed reprimands (Gable et al., 2009). Saying something like, "When you pay attention in class, the teacher is very happy with you. When you don't pay attention, your grades will suffer," reminds students of the rule, their responsibilities, and the consequences without placing too much emphasis on the reprimand component. Remember that reprimands lose their effectiveness if they are used too often (see Chapter 8) and that praise for appropriate behavior should be used far more frequently.

TEACH SELF-RECORDING STRATEGIES **Self-recording** and self-regulation strategies are useful in teaching students how to monitor and evaluate their own attention (Joseph & Eveleigh, 2011; Schulze, 2016). Special educators often teach self-monitoring strategies in their classrooms as this aligns with high-leverage practice (HLP) 14: Teach cognitive and metacognitive strategies to support learning and independence (McLeskey et al., 2017). Therefore, many students with diverse learning needs may have already learned how to use self-recording strategies. Self-monitoring skills learned in a resource setting have been observed to improve student attention in the regular classroom (Reid et al., 2005; Slattery et al., 2016). With systematic communication between the regular and special education teachers, problems with attention can be improved.

To start a self-recording system, set up a procedure for delivering randomly spaced beeps, as described previously (see the *Apps for Education* feature in Chapter 8 for other suggestions). The cueing interval can be set at random between 10 and 90 seconds (average of about 45 seconds) at first and expanded as attention improves. This procedure could be used with several students at a time. If students have difficulty hearing an auditory cue, pair the sound with a vibrating or light stimulus or provide the signal to a peer who then provides a visual or tactile cue to the target student.

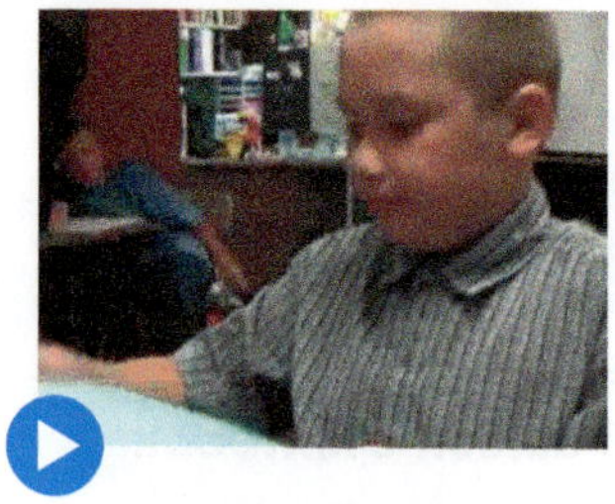

Pearson eTextbook

Video Example 10.4

A self-recording system is used in this classroom to manage student attention. What other strategies does the teacher use in this classroom to reinforce students who work independently and stay on task?

When the cue sounds, the target students should indicate whether they were paying attention by placing a checkmark on a self-monitoring sheet. The self-monitoring sheet should have two columns. At the head of the first column is, "Was I paying attention?" including examples such as "Looking at teacher" and "Reading textbook." At the head of the second column is, "Was I *not* paying attention?" including examples such as "Looking out the window" and "Daydreaming." Under each column is a numbered underline (or box) where students can record their level of attending ("yes" or "no") after each cue.

At first, you should also make your own record of student attending and compare the two records at the end of the period. Students can be reinforced for recording at all appropriate times and for approximating the results obtained by you. For example, if you record 70% paying attention, the student should be rewarded for recording a similar level between 60 and 80%. As the recording becomes reliable, create a graph of student attending and look for progress over time. Some investigators have demonstrated that it may not be necessary for teachers to verify the accuracy of attending for the procedure to be effective.

Before beginning a self-recording intervention, meet individually with the students and discuss why paying attention in class is important and how they will benefit from attending better. The students need to understand that the self-recording is in their best interest and that they will benefit as a result. It might be helpful to involve parents or caregivers to support this intervention.

As students improve in monitoring their attention, you can set timers so that they sound less frequently. However, serious attending problems are unlikely to disappear in a short time. Consistency on your part is helpful in effecting long-term improvements in attention. Continue to give frequent and regular feedback to students on their ability to attend and on their consistent self-monitoring of their own attention. The *Research Highlight* feature describes a self-monitoring for attention intervention for students with autism.

As an alternative, students can be trained to record their performance—for example, the number of times a weekly spelling list was practiced correctly (Reid & Johnson, 2012). This method has also been shown to be effective, although not always more effective than self-recording of attention, and students may prefer this method.

STRATEGIES FOR
ADDRESSING EXTREME CASES OF ATTENTION DEFICITS

Some extreme cases of attention problems are challenging to address in a general education classroom even after providing setting accommodations on the IEP (e.g., preferential seating, study carrels to block visual distractions, noise-reducing headphones). Intensive assistance from special educators may be warranted. Students with extreme attention problems may appear so distractible that they cannot reasonably be expected to attend appropriately for more than a few minutes at a time. In these cases, some special techniques may be helpful.

PROVIDE INTENSIVE TEACHER-LED INSTRUCTION For students with extreme attention problems, brief, intensive teacher-led instructional sessions may be the most realistic teaching strategy consistent with HLP 20: Provide intensive instruction (McLeskey et al., 2017). These sessions can be delivered either one-to-one or in small groups with a great deal of teacher–student interaction; novel, interesting, age-appropriate tasks; and frequent reinforcement, including preferred activities (Kerr & Nelson, 2010). Because your time for one-to-one instruction may be limited, this kind of intensive instruction may have to be accomplished by a closely supervised paraprofessional, an appropriate tier in a response-to-intervention program, or the special education teacher.

CONSIDER STRENGTHS AND WEAKNESSES OF STIMULANT MEDICATION

Another alternative is the administration (under medical supervision) of stimulant drugs to help students focus attention more appropriately. Although medication has certainly been helpful in many cases, often reducing the symptoms of ADHD, concern has been expressed that it has been overprescribed (Massuti et al., 2021; Torres-Acosta et al., 2020). Stimulant medication generally affects behavior and attention more than higher-order skills, learning, or achievement. Side effects can include insomnia, decreased appetite, irritability, mood changes,

Research Highlight

An App-Based Self-Monitoring Intervention for Students with Autism

Attending to task is an important prerequisite for school success. Unfortunately, many students with autism exhibit difficulty sustaining attention in school, especially on independent seatwork. Previous research has investigated the effects of self-monitoring (SM) interventions on attention to task of students with autism and has generally been successful (Holifield et al., 2010).

Beckman et al. (2019) investigated the effects of an app-based self-monitoring intervention for two elementary students, "Cody," and "Brian." Cody was a sixth-grade student who had been diagnosed with fragile X syndrome, pervasive developmental disorder, and autism spectrum disorder (ASD). In addition to difficulties in math and literacy skills, Cody had deficits in language and social skills. He was working on math at a second-grade level and was working to improve his calculator skills. However, he exhibited difficulty with attending to task on math assignments. Brian was a fifth-grade student of average intelligence who had also been given a diagnosis of ASD. Although functioning within grade level, he was referred to a special education setting because of high rates of challenging behavior. Brian demonstrated sufficient skills for completing writing assignments but exhibited a high level of off-task behavior during writing time, frequently refusing to complete his writing assignments.

Beckman and colleagues (2019) implemented a self-monitoring intervention for Cody and Brian intended to improve their academic engagement. For this project, Beckman et al. used the web-based application I-Connect (Wills & Mason, 2014; see iconnect.ku.edu). The application was downloaded to a Samsung Galaxy 5.0 tablet and was set to display the SM prompt "Am I on task?" that appeared at 20-second intervals for Cody and for 15-second intervals for Brian, who had initially demonstrated lower levels of on-task behavior (Beckman et al., 2019). The on-task prompt was accompanied by a brief ring tone. The students were asked to reply by touching the word "yes" or "no" within 7 seconds, which both students did on every occasion. Cody and Brian were individually trained to identify on-task and off-task behavior, and to record it on their tablet in response to the prompt, over three training sessions.

Both students were administered the treatment using an A-B-A-B design in which no treatment (baseline) and treatments were alternated across 21 sessions. These sessions lasted 20 minutes and required completion of math word problem-solving items for Cody ("Matt's school has 21 plants in their outdoor classroom. If they add 7 more this year, how many will they have in total?") or writing prompts for Brian ("Do you think a monkey would make a good pet?") (Beckman et al., 2019). Cody's responses were scored for percent accuracy, and Brian's responses were scored for percent of points earned on a writing scoring sheet. On-task behavior was also monitored by the teacher, who provided reinforcement (soda or time on an iPad) when Cody or Brian achieved 80% of on-task behavior and when the student and teacher agreement was at least 80%.

Results of the investigation indicated that Cody's on-task behavior improved from 45.7% for the baseline and treatment withdrawal (second baseline) phases, to 95.9% during the two treatment sessions. His accuracy on the word problems improved from 22.7% for baseline and second baseline to 68.6% for the two treatment phases. Brian's on-task behavior increased from 13.6% during the baseline/withdrawal phases to 95.9% during the intervention phases. On his writing assignments, he improved from 21.4% during the baseline/withdrawal phases to 61.6% during the treatment phases. Beckman et al. (2019) concluded that the app-based self-monitoring intervention had been successful in improving the academic and behavioral outcomes of students with ASD.

QUESTIONS FOR REFLECTION

1. Do you think this intervention could be implemented by paraprofessionals or classroom peers? Would any changes be needed?
2. What other areas could be addressed with self-monitoring techniques?
3. Do you think self-monitoring of academic performance (rather than attending to task) would also be effective? Why or why not?

weight loss, abdominal pain, and headaches; less common but more serious side effects include depression, agitation, and aggressive behavior (Reid & Johnson, 2012). If relevant and qualified medical professionals agree that stimulant medication is indicated for a specific student, your job as a teacher should be to collect formative data that identify how the medication affects the student's behavior both positively and negatively. It is also important for all participants to be aware that the long-term effects of stimulant medication have yet to be fully determined (Chang et al., 2019).

In some cases, stimulant medication used in conjunction with cognitive-behavioral training can be effective (Ryan et al., 2014), particularly for adolescents (e.g., Sprich et al., 2016). In addition, parent/caregiver training in cognitive-behavioral interventions and communication strategies has sometimes been effective in managing noncompliant behavior, reducing stress, and improving the quality of family/caregiver relationships. Families and caregivers can also be enlisted to provide consistency and support for school-based interventions (Mautone et al., 2012).

PROVIDE BEHAVIORAL TECHNIQUES Some students with autism have severe attention problems. These students may attend little or not at all to teachers, even though they have demonstrated adequate hearing (Stichter et al., 2017). Students with such severe attention deficits may benefit from one-to-one instruction, specialized behavioral techniques, direct provision of tangible or edible reinforcers for attending and responding appropriately, and ongoing supervision. Caregivers and special educators may be able to provide more specific information on the needs of individual students. Educational placement in the general education classroom is possible if special educators or highly trained aides are available to provide individual attention for students with severe problems.

PROMOTE JOINT ATTENTION White et al. (2011) reviewed the problems of children with autism in the area of **joint attention**, which is the ability of an individual to coordinate attention between a desired object and a person in a social context; for example, the ability to follow an adult's eye gaze directed to a specific object. Students with autism improved joint attention with intensive trial-based instruction, prompting, and reinforcement. Parents or caregivers directed their gaze to a particular object (a desired toy); if the child followed the gaze, a reinforcement (time to play with the toy) was given. If not, the child was prompted and then reinforced for a shorter period.

Developmentally appropriate interventions may also increase the attending of students with autism. For younger children, child-directed play, reinforcement, prompting, and imitation have improved attending. Other approaches that focus instruction on the student's own specific interests may also improve attending (Ninci et al., 2018). Older children have been seen to benefit from self-monitoring instruction (Rosenbloom et al., 2019).

Memory

Learning Objective 10.2 Describe memory difficulties and identify preconditions and strategies for improving the school success of students with diverse learning needs.

Memory is a psychological process that is critically important for school learning. The great majority of items on classroom tests as well as statewide high-stakes tests require students to remember specific facts and concepts relevant to the content area (Overton, 2016). Even when teachers devote more of their test questions to such higher-order tasks as analysis, synthesis, and evaluation, students must first *remember* relevant information before they can reason effectively with this information. Effective memory therefore is a necessary requirement for school success.

Many different types of memory have been described (Radvansky, 2021). These include **semantic memory** (for facts and concepts about the world), **episodic memory** (of previous personal experience), and **everyday memory** (for information encountered in everyday experience). Memory researchers distinguish between relatively limitless **long-term memory** and **short-term memory**, which holds information only briefly (e.g., a telephone number) while it is used, until it is placed in long-term memory (e.g., by rehearsal) or until it is forgotten. Information actively processed in short-term memory (e.g., in solving a two-part math problem) is referred to as **working memory** (Baddeley et al., 2020). Many students with diverse learning needs exhibit difficulties in one or more of these areas of memory (Sheng et al., 2015; Stefanelli & Alloway, 2020). However, specific strategies have been found to be effective in enhancing memory for all students, and these are described in the remainder of this chapter.

CLASSROOM SCENARIO

Jerome

Jerome was classified as having learning disabilities. With extra practice and resource room assistance, he showed progress on his IEP learning objective to accurately identify the main idea of a paragraph found in the fifth-grade materials; however, he continued to have difficulty remembering information for tests. A major concern of Jerome's was a test of states and capitals that was coming up in 4 weeks and was considered a test that all fifth-graders must pass. He had studied on his own and even with classmates, but he was still having a difficult time remembering more than a few states and capitals at a time. Jerome asked his resource teacher, Mr. Patel, for help.

QUESTIONS FOR REFLECTION

1. What are some reasons Jerome may be having trouble remembering states and capitals?
2. What are some other common facts that students may have difficulty remembering?
3. What would you recommend that Mr. Patel do to help Jerome?

STRATEGIES FOR IMPROVING MEMORY

ADDRESS MEMORY PRECONDITIONS Before implementing memory strategies, consider the preconditions that must be in place for learning and memory to occur. One critical precondition is ensuring that all students are attending appropriately to instruction—students are unlikely to remember information they did not attend to in the first place. Increase attention by maintaining a well-organized and distraction-free classroom and by using the strategies discussed in the first part of this chapter.

Next, keep students motivated to learn. Even if they are paying attention, students will learn and recall little if they are not interested in or do not see the value of the content or do not believe they can succeed. Similarly, students are unlikely to remember information if they do not have a positive affective response to the content presented—that is, if they have indifferent or negative feelings toward the subject or if their morale is low (Ormrod et al., 2019). Finally, learning will be minimized if lessons seem boring and monotonous. Once the preconditions for good memory have been met, the following suggestions should improve students' memory.

DEVELOP "METAMEMORY" **Metamemory** is the metacognitive process of knowing about memory. Specifically, metamemory is the process of knowing when, where, and how to remember (Dunlosky & Bjork, 2008). Many students, especially in the elementary grades, are unaware of the nature of memory and how they can learn to remember better. Activities and class discussions on memory and how it functions could help many students learn how to remember more efficiently; for example, help students understand some of the reasons we may forget, including the following:

- Fatigue when studying or when trying to remember
- Interference from such things as music, television, or distracting conversation
- Passing of time since the information was first learned
- Lack of effort when studying
- Unfamiliarity or difficulty of the content
- Failure to use an appropriate memory strategy.

Likewise, memory improves with age, experience, prior knowledge, and use of memory strategies. For example, using stories and scenarios, discuss with students why children may remember, or forget, certain types of information. Discuss how memory could be improved. Training aspects of metamemory, through stories, examples, and activities, can help improve students' ability to remember (Ghetti et al., 2011; Lucangeli et al., 1995). For example, share a memorable story with your students from childhood and model how aspects of the story help you to recall specific information. A personal short story about getting caught outside in a huge thunderstorm during a camping trip can provide memorable facts related to weather, temperature, and humidity.

USE EXTERNAL MEMORY External memory refers to the use of devices to increase memory (Hamilton & Yao, 2018). In schools, external memory can be used to remember homework assignments, locker numbers, and important school dates and as a reminder to bring relevant materials home (or back to school). External memory examples include writing things down in notebooks, appointment books, smartphones, or language cards; placing things to be remembered in places where they will be seen (e.g., putting homework by the outside door); and physical prompts (e.g., attaching a note to clothing or backpack). Although external memory is not permissible in all situations (e.g., most written tests), students can be informed about appropriate times to use external memory to improve school functioning. The *Apps for Education* feature provides examples of devices for enhancing external memory.

Pearson eTextbook
Video Example 10.5
This video shows an adolescent girl discussing her memory processes. Listen to the successful strategies she uses in school.

ENHANCE MEANINGFULNESS We remember meaningful information better than nonmeaningful information (Baddeley et al., 2020). You can make learning more meaningful by providing specific examples that are directly relevant to your students' experiences. For example, in a presentation about how each of the three branches of government—legislative, executive, and judiciary—functions, use examples that are directly relevant to schools and show how these examples affect students. That is, legislative bodies mandate specific laws for the establishment and operation of schools, the executive branch is responsible for enforcing these laws, and the judicial branch adjudicates and interprets these laws. Students can study and discuss how the actions of each of these branches affect their own lives personally with respect to school policy. Adapt what is taught to students appropriate to their age.

USE CONCRETE EXAMPLES, PICTURES, OR IMAGERY Concrete information is easier to remember than abstract information (Weinstein et al., 2018). You can enhance the concreteness of relevant content by bringing in examples of the topics being studied. For example, the study of trilobites (ancient marine animals) can be made more concrete by bringing in fossil specimens of trilobites, which can be used in discussions of their characteristics. Such enriched thought, activity, and discussion can greatly improve memorization of the content.

Multimedia Presentations When specific examples cannot be brought to class—for example, because of their size, cost, or limited availability—consider enhancing visual imagery through the use of CDs, movies, or pictures. For example, DVDs and YouTube presentations provide excellent recordings of things students might not ordinarily have an opportunity to see, such as tornadoes, and can provide interesting visual coverage of such varied topics as Mayan architecture, insect life, and microorganisms. When selecting multimedia presentations, be certain that they assist directly in enhancing the concreteness of specific information to be remembered. View the presentation selectively to focus specifically on instructional objectives (e.g., focusing on architecture—an instructional objective—in a media presentation on ancient Greece). Finally, do not be afraid to provide redundancy in viewing to help enhance the specific facts or concepts to be remembered. For students with visual impairments, descriptive video may be available or can be created.

Illustrations Using pictures, illustrations, or graphics enhances the concreteness and memorability of information and can promote memory more than animations when these images are more directly focused (Mayer et al., 2005). Pictures are frequently provided in student textbooks or in PowerPoint presentations included in instructors' materials. Try to locate pictures that are directly relevant to instructional objectives—for example, illustrations that document clearly the physical characteristics of insects or the living conditions of American pioneers. Some websites such as https://pixabay.com are excellent resources for finding free pictures. Always be sure any use of images from a source is compliant with copyright guidelines. Ask your students to pay attention to specific aspects of the picture that are directly relevant to your instructional objectives (e.g., "Can you point out the thorax of the insect in the picture, Ishaan?" or "Show

Mobile Devices Improve Independence

Students must remember many things to be successful in school, such as dates when projects are due and tests will be given, communications to be brought home for parents or caregivers to read and sign, dates for field trips or special events, and class schedules. Remembering all these things may be particularly difficult for students who have challenges with memory or organizational skills. To help these and other students, technology may be useful.

Mobile devices include small handheld devices—iPads, tablets, Kindle Fire, iPods, e-readers, cell phones, and smartphones—that can perform a multitude of tasks, from calendar functions, to-do lists, address books, and gaming to word processing, spreadsheets, and more. Devices can range in size from very small handheld devices to larger sizes. Memory storage on the devices may vary as well. Most mobile devices contain cameras and have the capacity to send pictures and movies via text and email.

In a study by Van Laarhoven et al. (2018), researchers evaluated the effectiveness of a universally designed prompting system on a mobile device used by adolescents with autism spectrum disorder and/or intellectual disabilities to perform vocational tasks at a school-based employment setting. Specifically, four students were responsible for configuring a conference room within their high school in preparation for different meetings. The task was not one made up of linear steps. Rather, students needed to make varied decisions based on the condition of the room and the next meeting's configuration as indicated on the calendar (e.g., erase the whiteboard or save it; put papers in the garbage or in the lost and found). The prompting system on the device provided the students with a decision tree and there were video prompts, auditory prompts, and picture/text prompts as options to assist the decision. Results indicated that the participants relied more so on video prompts initially, but the decision points built into the system enabled them to effectively problem-solve on the job. They also relied on less-intrusive prompts or no device at all after becoming more independent with the task.

Mobile devices can be utilized by students with disabilities in many other ways to promote independence. For example, a variety of applications for note taking are available for students to use on common technology devices such as tablets, iPads, smartphones, laptops, and Chromebooks. These include *Notes* (Apple), *Evernote, OneNote* (Microsoft Corporation), *Google Keep* (Google LLC), *Notability* (Ginger Labs), *GoodNotes* (Time Base Technology Ltd.), and others. Features on many of these apps can include multiple ways of taking notes, such as recording audio, typing text, or using a stylus pen compatible with a particular device. For example, some students may enjoy or prefer writing notes on a note-taking app using an Apple iPad and an Apple Pencil.

Apps that allow note taking can also be written to include important content from the Common Core State Standards associated with specific memory strategies to help facilitate learning and memory for all students. As such, this type of note is an example of universal design for learning (UDL), allowing students to access the notes with strategies when needed. Many apps suitable for assisting with attention and memory have also been developed. Consider the following:

- *First Then Visual Schedule HD* (Good Karma Applications) is an application available on the iOS store for the self-management of students that promotes independently following a visual schedule and follow-through on tasks. This can help students with focusing their attention and remembering tasks they have to do. (age 4 and above)
- *I-Connect Self-Monitoring* (University of Kansas) is a research-based application available on the iOS store for the self-management of students that can help them with focusing their attention and remembering tasks they have to do. (elementary age to adult)
- *BFT Bear Focus Timer* (IDEAMP Co. Ltd.) is an application for time management that also has animation for engagement, provides praise for students staying on-task, and has a white noise feature that can help students stay on-task and remember tasks. (age 5 and above)
- *Choiceworks Calendar* (Bee Visual, LLC) is a visual-based schedule application that helps students remember their schedules and what they need to do while also allowing students to check off their to-do items as they go along. (age 4 and above)

Pearson eTextbook

Video Example 10.6

Before reading informational text, the teacher in this video prompts fifth-graders to look at images in the text. How can the illustrations in the text support student learning?

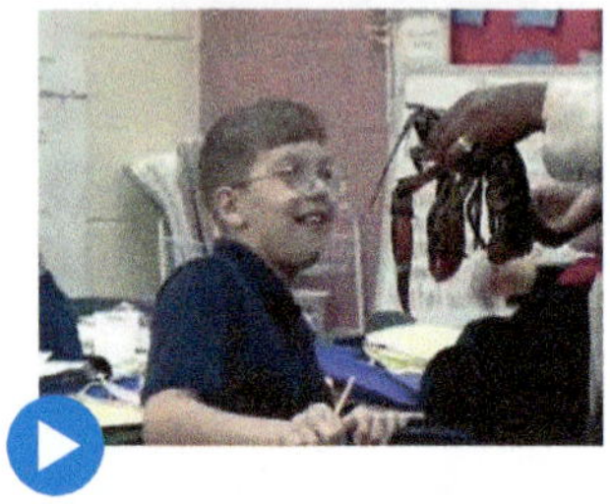

Pearson eTextbook

Video Example 10.7

In this video, fifth-grade students demonstrate using enactment in a science lesson. Notice what the students do in the lesson and how this experience can enhance students' attention, memory, and learning.

me on the picture the body parts that make you know that this is a beetle, William"). Reading through diagrams carefully with students, and questioning them frequently, helps ensure that diagrams are understood (e.g., "Where is the switch in this electrical diagram, Nia?"). After pictures and diagrams have been studied, question your students about the illustrations with their books closed, or the media turned off, so that they continue to practice studying the mental image of the illustration. Peers may assist students with visual impairments with the careful description of pictures, diagrams, or illustrations. Additionally, tactile representations of pictures can be created, as described in Chapter 4. Remember, however, that pictures may not promote learning if they are not directly relevant or if they distract students from the specific content to be learned (Uberti et al., 2003).

Imagery If you cannot locate relevant pictures and you feel unable to draw pictures yourself, you can encourage students to use their mental imagery to create pictures. For example, to help understand that whales are the largest animals on Earth, encourage students to imagine an enormous whale next to a much smaller elephant. Students should be encouraged to create details of the image and discuss them with the class for accuracy. For example, you could suggest that students imagine a very large whale and an elephant standing next to the whale that is only about as large as the whale is from its eye to the tip of its mouth. Students could then be asked other questions (e.g., "Which way is the elephant facing?") to make the image more permanent. Later, when students are asked this information ("Which animal is larger?"), they can be asked to describe the image used to compare the size of elephants and whales. With practice, students can improve their range of visual literacy skills and benefit from imagery (Rice & Dunn, 2020).

Another way to improve the concreteness of a subject is through field trips to relevant zoos, museums, or nature areas. As with media presentations, focus your students' attention on the specific objectives to be met during field trips, and monitor that students are meeting these objectives. When appropriate, call ahead so that necessary preparations for specific students with disabilities can be made.

MINIMIZE INTERFERING INFORMATION Interference, in the form of competing or distracting stimuli, can inhibit memory (Kennedy & Romig, 2021; Re et al., 2010). Sometimes students forget information because interference was present or because the emphasis on the targeted content was insufficient to promote good memory. For example, a student may not attend to a key image on a slide if they have to process the large amount of text next to the image and listen to the teacher providing oral information at the same time. Be sure your presentation focuses directly on the content to be remembered, and avoid interfering or distracting information that is not directly relevant.

Teachers can inadvertently provide interfering information if they digress from the presentation, provide unnecessary elaboration or examples that are not directly relevant, or frequently interrupt presentations and lectures to address behavior management issues. In general, consider that information is more likely to be remembered when it is presented clearly, directly, and without unnecessary embellishment.

USE ENACTMENTS AND MANIPULATION We remember things that we do better than things we hear and recite (Peterson & Mulligan, 2010). This may explain some of the positive effects typically found for hands-on science activities (Scruggs et al., 2017). For example, students who have studied firsthand the effects of weak acid on the mineral calcite are more likely to remember these effects (the calcite begins to deteriorate) than if they simply read about the subject. Similarly, students are more likely to remember series and parallel electrical circuits they have constructed than electric circuits they have read about. The *Diversity, Equity, and Inclusion in the Classroom* feature describes how to improve learning and memory with culturally responsive teaching.

PROMOTE ACTIVE REASONING Information is better remembered if students actively participate in the learning process, particularly by actively reasoning through the content (Brigham et al., 2011; Craik & Lockhart, 1972). Answering any type of relevant question usually promotes better memory than passive listening to teacher lectures. Answering factual questions helps focus attention on the significant components of the content (e.g., "Who were the major U.S. novelists of the first half of the 19th century—Joseph?"). Answering questions that require reasoning can also help improve memory (e.g., "What do you think Hawthorne is trying to say about medical science in *Rappaccini's Daughter*—Maria?").

Provide additional coaching to assist students with disabilities when support is needed in thinking through information systematically and arriving at their own conclusions. Coach students to provide their own explanations about factual information, as in the following example:

TEACHER: The camel has a double row of eyelashes for each eye. Why does this make sense?

STUDENT: I don't know.

TEACHER: Well, let's think. What do you know about camels? For example, where do they live?

STUDENT: In the desert.

TEACHER: In the desert, good. And what is it like in the desert?

STUDENT: Hot and dry.

TEACHER: Good, what else can you think of about deserts?

STUDENT: Um, it's sandy. And windy.

TEACHER: Good, sandy and windy. So why would it make sense that camels would have two rows of eyelashes?

STUDENT: Oh! To keep the sand from blowing in their eyes.

TEACHER: To keep the sand out of their eyes, good!

Sullivan et al. (1995) demonstrated that students taught with these questioning strategies remembered and understood more information than students who had been directly provided with the same information (e.g., "The camel has a double row of eyelashes for each eye to keep out the blowing sand").

INCREASE PRACTICE Information is better remembered if it is practiced or rehearsed (Baddeley et al., 2020). Rehearsal or repetition has frequently been demonstrated to improve recall among students of all ages and ability groups. To increase the effects of practice, you should first target the information that is most important to be remembered. Then provide as much practice as possible in individual lessons by questioning. Questioning and practice after learning has been achieved is referred to as **overlearning**, and it can be an effective strategy for promoting long-term memory. Independent study skills can also promote recall and retention after content has been introduced and practiced. Review at home with family members and caregivers is also an excellent way to increase recall of academic content.

Increased practice can also be given as a classwide peer tutoring activity (Bowman-Perrott, 2013; Maheady & Gard, 2010). You might be surprised to discover how much information your students can learn in brief (e.g., 10–15 minutes), fast-paced daily sessions in which pairs of students question each other on the significant parts of lessons to be remembered, such as multiplication facts, spelling words, key facts and concepts in a geography unit, or parts of speech. You can feel even more confident about student success if you pair students with disabilities with students who have demonstrated that they can be effective partners.

USE CLUSTERING AND ORGANIZATION Information is better remembered if it is organized in some meaningful way (Baddeley et al., 2020). For example, products produced and exported by a country could be grouped as agricultural, industrial, and mining products before students practice remembering the list.

Another strategy is to incorporate content within paper-based or computer-based graphic organizers, such as organizational charts, visual displays, **semantic maps**, and **relationship charts** (Ciullo & Reutebuch, 2013; Dexter et al., 2011). These displays present a spatially organized, as well as semantically organized, representation of the topic. For example, in a unit on Argentina, a visual display can be created that organizes the different areas of study in the unit, such as land features, natural resources, climate, history, and culture (see Figure 10.2).

PROMOTE ELABORATION Information is better remembered if it is elaborated (Bjorklund & Causey, 2017). You can provide simple elaborations to help students remember

Diversity, Equity, and Inclusion in the Classroom

Improving Learning and Memory with Culturally Responsive Teaching

Janice is a sixth-grade science teacher who was having difficulty reaching the students in her class in a school where 95% of the students were students of color and English learners. She expressed her concerns in a workshop led by Zaretta Hammond (2015a), a nationally recognized leader in culturally responsive teaching. Janice needed help breaking through to her students, who didn't seem to be applying themselves to learning. However, as she put it, "I won't be rapping about the periodic table."

"No problem," replied Hammond. We need not view culturally responsive teaching as an engagement strategy to inspire students to take learning seriously. Rather, culturally responsive teaching employs strategies that parents, grandparents, caregivers, and community members use to teach life skills and basic concepts outside of school situations, strategies more relevant to students' cultural and family backgrounds.

Janice said she was having particular difficulty getting students to learn and remember their weekly science vocabulary words. When Hammond asked how she was teaching them now, Janice replied that every Monday, she wrote the list of the words on the board and asked the students to copy them. Then, they were asked to look the words up in a dictionary, and finally use each word in a sentence. Janice gave a vocabulary test every Wednesday and was not satisfied with the results. Students did not seem to be very engaged in their own learning.

Hammond suggested three tips for transforming her lessons into something that would appear more culturally responsive to her students. These three tips included the following.

1. *"Gamify" it.* Games are a powerful strategy for gaining students' attention and promoting active processing. Most games involve tools relevant to culturally responsive learning, including repetition, puzzle solving, and building connections among things that appear unrelated.
2. *Make it social.* Organizing learning so that students rely on each other to build upon diverse students' communal orientation and to increase attention and engagement.
3. *"Storify" it.* Culturally responsive teaching relies on oral traditions of diverse cultures to make sense of the world and to teach important life skills. Diverse students learn content better if they can create a coherent narrative about the information presented. All students, in fact, may benefit from creating engaging narratives.

Using these tips, Janice created some activities to make learning science vocabulary more engaging. She created several sorting and matching games for students. She developed some simple card games based on principles of Go Fish or Old Maid; she also created some group activities for different teams to play, so that each week students engaged with different active ways to learn the science vocabulary. Students participated in these activities 10–15 minutes at a time, several times a week, rather than looking words up in a dictionary. Janice also provided suggestions for making similar games at home.

After several weeks, Janice reported that the difference in levels of student engagement and learning and memory were like "night and day." All students were now participating, and they were learning the new vocabulary at a deeper level. Hammond (2015a) concluded that culturally responsive teaching does not need to be some kind of performance the teacher makes in order to entertain students. Rather, a culturally responsive practice is one that better reflects the students' own cultural learning tools. These practices can be of benefit to all students and not simply targeted to culturally diverse students (see also Hammond, 2015b, 2020).

Discuss: How could Janice also incorporate Hammond's tip to "storify" it?

new words. For example, "To remember the meaning of *precipitation*, think of the 'sip' sound in 'precipitation': Animals can 'sip' from puddles left from precipitation." To promote elaboration, ask students to think of everything they can about a topic (e.g., "What else does buoyancy remind you of?" "How does a *buoy* remind you of *buoyancy*?"). Asking students simply to think about what a new word sounds like and how that links to its meaning can improve recall of the information. More formal forms of elaboration are known as *mnemonics*, as described in the following strategies.

Figure 10.2 Organizational Display

STRATEGIES FOR
IMPROVING MEMORY WITH MNEMONIC TECHNIQUES

Everyone remembers using specific mnemonic techniques to remember information. For example, most people remember using the acronym *HOMES* to remember the names of the Great Lakes. Many also remember the traditional rhyme "In fourteen hundred ninety-two, Columbus sailed the ocean blue" to remember the year that Columbus first sailed to America. What many people do not know is that mnemonic strategies are versatile and can be used in hundreds, even thousands, of situations to improve memory.

Another interesting research finding is that mnemonic strategies are powerful. Learning gains of as much as 2-to-1, or even 3-to-1, are common in mnemonic strategy research with a variety of students, including those with intellectual disabilities, learning disabilities, emotional or behavioral disorders, and even gifted and normally achieving students, and these gains have been found for students in the primary grades through high school (Mastropieri, Scruggs, Evmenova, et al., 2018; Scruggs & Mastropieri, 2013; Vaughn & Swanson, 2015).

Nevertheless, mnemonic strategies, like any other teaching or learning strategies, have their limitations. Mnemonic techniques are most effective when they are:

- Used to reinforce objectives to remember specific content
- Directly taught and practiced
- Combined with comprehension instruction
- Included with application activities.

Three specific types of mnemonic strategies—the **keyword method**, the **pegword method**, and **letter strategies**—have been successful in enhancing memory for students with memory difficulties (Scruggs et al., 2010).

USE THE KEYWORD METHOD FOR VERBAL ASSOCIATIONS The keyword method is used to strengthen the connection between a new word and its associated information. For example, *oxalis* is a clover-like plant (Figure 10.3). To strengthen this association, the learner is first provided a "keyword" for the new word, *oxalis*. A keyword is a word that is familiar to the learner but that sounds like the new word and is easily pictured. In the case of *oxalis*, a good keyword is *ox* because it sounds like the first part of *oxalis* and is easy to picture. Next, a

Figure 10.3 Keyword Mnemonic Strategy for *Oxalis* = Clover-Like Plant

picture (or image) is created of the associates interacting together. Again in the case of *oxalis*, the interactive picture could be a picture of an ox chewing on clover-like plants, as in Figure 10.3. This picture then is shown to the student while the teacher describes the picture and strategy.

Sample teacher dialogue: "*Oxalis* is a clover-like plant. The keyword for *oxalis* is *ox* [show picture]. Remember this picture of an ox chewing clover-like plants. Remember this picture of what? Good, an ox chewing clover-like plants. Now, when I ask you for the meaning of *oxalis*, think first of the keyword, *ox*. Then think back to the picture with the ox in it, remember that the ox was chewing clover-like plants, and then retrieve the answer that *oxalis* is a clover-like plant. Now, what is *oxalis*? Good, *oxalis* is a clover-like plant. And how did you remember that? Good, you thought of the keyword, *ox*, and remembered the picture of the ox chewing clover-like plants."

Keyword strategies have been successfully used to teach the following:

- Foreign-language vocabulary (e.g., to remember the Spanish word *pato* = duck, provide a picture of a duck with a pot—keyword for *pato*—on his head)
- Scientific terms such as *ranidae* (Figure 10.4)
- English vocabulary (e.g., for *barrister* = lawyer, provide a picture of a bear—keyword for *barrister*—pleading a case in a courtroom)
- People and their accomplishments, such as Zimmerman, the German foreign minister who sent the coded "Zimmerman Note" to Mexico that precipitated U.S. entry into World War I (e.g., show a swimmer—keyword for *Zimmerman*—carrying a note from Germany to Mexico)
- Map locations for Revolutionary War battles (e.g., a picture of a tiger—keyword for *Ticonderoga*—on a map showing where Fort Ticonderoga is located)
- States and capitals (see the *In the Classroom* feature and Figure 10.5)

Figure 10.4 Keyword Mnemonic Strategy for *Ranidae* = Common Frogs

Figure 10.5 Illustration of Mnemonic Strategy to Remember That Tallahassee (*Television*) Is the Capital of Florida (*Flower*). These strategies can be helpful for students who need assistance remembering long lists of information for school (see the *In the Classroom* feature).

Uberti et al. (2003) used mnemonic keyword strategies to improve learning and to recall new vocabulary words (e.g., *ionosphere, fjords, jettison*) prior to a story-reading activity in inclusive third-grade classes. Although the keyword strategies improved all students' recall of word meanings, students with learning disabilities benefited the most from the keyword method.

The keyword method can also support the vocabulary knowledge of secondary-age students (Kuder et al., 2017). Terrill et al. (2004) created keyword mnemonic strategies to help their high school students with learning disabilities learn important vocabulary words in preparation for the SAT. For example, for the vocabulary word palatable, the keyword was *table*, and a picture was shown of people sitting at a table enjoying a meal. A sentence under the picture stated, "All the food on the *table* tasted very good." Students learned and remembered 92% of the words they learned mnemonically and only 49% of the words they learned using more traditional activities, such as drill and worksheet activities.

Marshak and colleagues (2011) employed mnemonic strategies with classwide peer tutoring in inclusive middle school history classes. For example, when students needed to remember that John D. Rockefeller controlled the oil industry in the 1920s, they were shown a picture of a rock (keyword for *Rockefeller*) with oil coming out of the rock. All students learned and remembered more information in the mnemonic tutoring condition; students with disabilities in the mnemonic condition remembered nearly twice as much information taught mnemonically, and overall performance was similar to that of normally achieving students.

Haydon et al. (2017) used keyword mnemonic strategies with choral responding to assist middle school students with intellectual disabilities to identify states on a map of the United States. During instruction, the students were taught to select one of five keyword images put on a desk and place the keyword on the corresponding state on the map. The map did not have any state names labeled on it. For example, if a picture of a hamster (keyword for *New Hampshire*) was selected, the student would place it in the center of the appropriate outlined state on a whiteboard. Over an 8-week period, the students identified the state names for the geographically correct area of the map with an overall mean of 80% accuracy across all four students. Students also remembered the mnemonically instructed state names on a 1-week delayed recall test.

CLASSROOM SCENARIO

Jerome

Mr. Patel, Jerome's resource teacher, told him that he thought he had the solution to his problem. He constructed keywords and simple pictures for all the states and capitals information, such as those in the *In the Classroom* feature. Mr. Patel spent one period with Jerome in which he explained the keyword method and how it could be used to remember states and capitals. He demonstrated by teaching Jerome capitals for six states. First, they practiced state names and their keywords (e.g., Arkansas—*ark*). Next, they practiced capital names and their keywords (e.g., Little Rock—*a little rock*). Then they went over the six pictures of states and capitals and practiced the strategies, as follows:

MR. PATEL: The capital of Arkansas is Little Rock. The keyword for Arkansas is . . . ?

JEROME: Ark.

MR. PATEL: Good, and the keyword for Little Rock is . . . ?

JEROME: A little rock.

MR. PATEL: Good! Now, remember this picture [*shows picture*] of Noah's ark landing on a little rock. Remember this picture of what?

JEROME: Noah's ark landing on a little rock.

MR. PATEL: [*turns over the picture*] And the capital of Arkansas is . . . ?

JEROME: Little Rock.

MR. PATEL: Little Rock, good.

When Jerome was certain he knew how the strategies worked, Mr. Patel told him to study no more than six pictures at a time and to test himself frequently on the information he had accumulated. Mr. Patel tested him periodically and encouraged him to keep studying.

When the time for the states and capitals test came, Jerome received one of the highest scores in the class! The fifth-grade teacher, Mrs. Sullivan, was so impressed that she asked Jerome how he was able to do so well. He showed her the mnemonic pictures, and Mrs. Sullivan asked Mr. Patel if she could use the strategy with her entire class the following year.

Combine Mnemonic Strategies with Reconstructive Elaborations The term **reconstructive elaborations** refers to procedures for reconstructing information into more meaningful and memorable forms. Three types of reconstructions are acoustic (or keyword) reconstructions, symbolic reconstructions, and mimetic reconstructions (Hall et al., 2013; Scruggs et al., 2010).

The keyword method (or **acoustic reconstructions**) is best used when the information to be learned is unfamiliar. Such terms as *nepenthe* and *carnelian* are excellent candidates for the keyword method because they are unfamiliar, and similar-sounding keywords (acoustic reconstructions) can be created, such as *Neptune* or *carnation*. Unfamiliar proper names (e.g., *Modigliani, Volga*) also fit into this category.

Some information is familiar to students but is more *abstract* and difficult to picture. In such cases, teachers can use **symbolic reconstructions**, in which the information is reconstructed into a symbolic picture, rather than a keyword (acoustic) picture. For example, to demonstrate the U.S. policy of neutrality at the beginning of World War I, a picture could be shown of Uncle Sam (symbol for U.S. policy) watching the war in Europe and exclaiming, "It's not my fight!"

Some information is both familiar and concrete and does not need to be transformed into familiar forms. In these cases, **pictorial or mimetic reconstructions** work best. For example, a U.S. history text states that World War I soldiers stationed in unhealthy trenches were more likely to die from disease than from battle wounds. Because students are probably already familiar with *trench* and *disease*, it is not necessary to create keywords; rather, simply picture *sick soldiers* in *trenches* to demonstrate the relation. Students can simply think back to the picture and retrieve the answer (Mastropieri, Scruggs, Regan, et al., 2018; Scruggs et al., 2010). Similarly, to help students remember that sponges grow on the ocean floor, simply show a picture of it.

Figure 10.6 Pegwords

Number	*Pegword*	*Number*	*Pegword*
one	bun, sun, or gun	fourteen	forking
two	shoe	fifteen	fixing
three	tree	sixteen	sitting
four	door or floor	seventeen	severing
five	hive	eighteen	aiding
six	sticks	nineteen	knighting
seven	heaven	twenty	twin
eight	gate	thirty	dirty or thirsty
nine	vine or lion	forty	party
ten	hen	fifty	gifty
eleven	lever	sixty	witchy
twelve	elf	seventy	heavenly
thirteen	thirsting		

Reconstructive elaborations are procedures for classifying important information in terms of familiarity and concreteness and developing appropriate strategies. This method can be useful in planning and developing mnemonic strategies across larger units of content.

USE THE PEGWORD METHOD FOR NUMBERED OR ORDERED INFORMATION

Pegwords are rhyming words for numbers, and they are useful in learning numbered or ordered information. Commonly used pegwords are provided in Figure 10.6 (see also Higbee, 2008). For example, to remember that insects have six legs, picture an insect crawling on sticks (pegword for *six*). To remember that spiders have eight legs, picture a spider spinning a web on a gate (pegword for *eight*).

Pegwords can be helpful in remembering the three classes of levers (based on the arrangement of fulcrum, load, and force). For example, a broom is an example of a third-class lever (with the fulcrum at one end and the force at the middle), so you can provide a picture of a broom leaning against a tree (pegword for *three*). Examples of each of the three classes of levers are shown in Figure 10.7.

Figure 10.7 Pegword Mnemonic Strategy for Classes of Levers: Seesaw = First Class, Wheelbarrow = Second Class, Broom = Third Class

In the Classroom

Mnemonic Strategies for Remembering the States and Their Capitals

Other strategies are possible; test these to see if they work well with your own students. Use your own artwork, student art, or clip art to create mnemonic pictures. Practice with students (or have students practice with partners) until recall is fluent and automatic. Practice recalling capitals ("What is the capital of Maryland?") as well as states ("Of what state is Bismarck the capital?").

State (Keyword)	Capital (Keyword)	Mnemonic Picture
Alabama (*band*)	Montgomery (*monkey*)	*Monkeys* playing in a *band*.
Alaska (*"I'll ask her"*)	Juneau (*"Do you know?"*)	Students talking: "*Do you know* the capital of Alaska?" "*I'll ask her!*"
Arizona (*arid zone*)	Phoenix (*phone-x*)	*Phone-x* (telephone) in an *arid zone* (desert).
Arkansas (*ark*)	Little Rock (*little rock*)	Noah's *ark* landing on a *little rock*.
California (*calf horn*)	Sacramento (*sack of mint*)	A *sack of mint* on a *calf's horn*.
Colorado (*coloring*)	Denver (*den*)	A child's "*coloring den.*"
Connecticut (*convict*)	Hartford (*heart*)	A *convict* in prison with a broken *heart*.
Delaware (*devil*)	Dover (*dove*)	A *dove* on a *devil's* pitchfork.
Florida (*flower*)	Tallahassee (*television*)	A *flower* on a *television* set.
Georgia (*George Washington*)	Atlanta (*Atlantic Ocean*)	*George* Washington wading in the *Atlantic* Ocean.
Hawaii (*"How are ya?"*)	Honolulu (*"Honey, I'm Lou!"*)	A dialogue between two people: "*How are ya?*" "*Honey, I'm Lou!*"
Idaho (*"I don't know"*)	Boise (*boys*)	Teacher and students: "What's the answer, *boys*?" "*I don't know!*"
Illinois (*ill*)	Springfield (*spring*)	A man who drank from a *spring* is feeling *ill*.
Indiana (*Indiana Jones*)	Indianapolis (*Indianapolis 500*)	*Indiana Jones* driving a race car in the *Indianapolis* 500.
Iowa (*"I owe ya!"*)	Des Moines (*the mines*)	A boss of the *mines* telling a worker, "*I owe ya!*" (his paycheck).
Kansas (*can*)	Topeka (*top*)	A *top* spinning on a *can*.
Kentucky (*kennel*)	Frankfort (*frankfurter*)	Dogs in a *kennel* eating *frankfurters*.
Louisiana (*Louise and Anna*)	Baton Rouge (*batons and rouge*)	*Louise and Anna* wearing *rouge* and twirling *batons*.
Maine (*horse's mane*)	Augusta (*a gust of wind*)	*A gust of* wind blowing a horse's *mane*.
Maryland (*marry*)	Annapolis (*apple*)	A couple getting *married* eating *apples*.
Massachusetts (*mast*)	Boston (*boxer*)	A *boxer* boxing in front of a ship's *mast*.
Michigan (*pitch again*)	Lansing (*lamb*)	A *lamb* at bat telling the pitcher, "*Pitch again!*"
Minnesota (*mini-soda*)	St. Paul (*St. Paul*)	*St. Paul* drinking a *mini-soda*.
Mississippi (*misses*)	Jackson (*jacks*)	Two girls (*misses*) playing with *jacks*.
Missouri (*misery*)	Jefferson City (*chef*)	A *chef* in *misery* because his cake fell.
Montana (*mountain*)	Helena (*Helen of Troy*)	*Helen of Troy* standing on a *mountain*.
Nebraska (*new brass*)	Lincoln (*Abe Lincoln*)	Abe *Lincoln* polishing *new brass*.
Nevada (*new ladder*)	Carson City (*car city*)	A man climbing a *new ladder* to get to "*Car City.*"
New Hampshire (*hamster*)	Concord (*conquer*)	A *hamster* as a *conqueror*.
New Jersey (*jersey*)	Trenton (*tent*)	A *tent* with a *jersey* on it.
New Mexico (*Mexico*)	Santa Fe (*Santa Claus*)	*Santa Claus* going to *Mexico*.
New York (*new pork*)	Albany (*all baloney*)	Man at deli counter: "Is this *new pork*?" Butcher: "It's *all baloney!*"
North Carolina (*carolers*)	Raleigh (*trolley*)	*Carolers* singing in a *trolley*.
North Dakota (*northern coat*)	Bismarck (*businessman*)	A *businessman* dressed in a *northern* (cold weather) *coat*.
Ohio (*"Oh, hi!"*)	Columbus (*Christopher Columbus*)	A person saying, "*Oh, hi, Columbus!*"
Oklahoma (*oak home*)	Oklahoma City (*Oak Home City*)	Building an *oak home* in "*Oak Home*" *City*.

In the Classroom

Mnemonic Strategies for Remembering the States and Their Capitals—*continued*

State (Keyword)	Capital (Keyword)	Mnemonic Picture
Oregon (*ore*)	Salem (*sailboat*)	A *sailboat* carrying *ore*.
Pennsylvania (*pen*)	Harrisburg (*hairy*)	A *hairy* (furry) *pen*.
Rhode Island (*road to an island*)	Providence (*provide*)	A builder says he will *provide a road to the island*.
South Carolina (*southern carolers*)	Columbia (*column*)	*Carolers* singing in front of a *southern* mansion with *columns*.
South Dakota (*southern coat*)	Pierre (*pier*)	A man wearing a *southern* (warm weather) *coat* standing at a *pier*.
Tennessee (*tennis*)	Nashville (*cash*)	Playing *tennis* for *cash*.
Texas (*taxes*)	Austin (*ostrich*)	An *ostrich* says, "I'll never be able to pay these *taxes*!"
Utah (*you saw*)	Salt Lake City (*salt lake*)	Dialogue: "What was it *you saw*?" "*Salt* in the *lake*!"
Vermont (*Worm Mountain*)	Montpelier (*mountain pliers*)	Removing worms from "*Worm Mountain*" with *mountain pliers*.
Virginia (*fur*)	Richmond (*rich man*)	A *rich man* buying a *fur* jacket.
Washington (*wash a ton*)	Olympia (*Olympic*)	An *Olympic* event: *Wash a ton* of laundry.
West Virginia (*vest fur*)	Charleston (*King Charles*)	King *Charles* wearing a *vest* made of *fur*.
Wisconsin (*whisk broom*)	Madison (*maid*)	A *maid* using a *whisk broom*.
Wyoming (*Y-home*)	Cheyenne (*shy Anne*)	*Shy Anne* lives in the *Y-home* (home shaped like a "Y").

Pegwords can also be used to remember lists of information, such as the following:

- The hardness levels of minerals (pegwords can also be combined with keywords for this; Scruggs et al., 1987). For example, for *sulphur* (keyword "sofa") is hardness level 2 (pegword "shoe"), show a picture of a shoe resting on a sofa.
- The order of U.S. presidents (Mastropieri et al., 1997). For Van Buren (keyword "van") is U.S. President #8 (gate), show a picture of a van parking at a gate.
- Multiplication tables (Greene, 1999; Zisimopoulos, 2010). For example, for $4(\text{door}) \times 3(\text{tree}) = 12(\textit{elf})$, show a picture corresponding to, "Behind the door in the tree is an elf" (see Chapter 14).

USE LETTER STRATEGIES FOR LISTS Letter strategies can be useful for remembering lists of things (Reid et al., 2013). For example, the HOMES strategy prompts recall of the names of the Great Lakes (H—Huron, O—Ontario, etc.). However, this strategy will only be effective if students are familiar enough with the names of the Great Lakes that thinking of a single letter will prompt the entire name. That is, if students are not familiar with the name *Ontario*, the letter *O* will not be enough to help them remember it. To ensure letter strategies are effective, ask students to rehearse the names represented by the letters.

The HOMES strategy is an example of an **acronym**. An acronym is a word formed from the first letters of the words to be remembered. Another example of an acronym is "FARM-B," which is used to remember the names of the classes of vertebrate animals (F—fish, A—amphibian, R—reptile, M—mammal, B—bird). A picture showing vertebrate animals on a farm can help enforce this concept. In this strategy, the *B* serves no particular purpose—it is just left over after "farm" is spelled. Students need to practice this to remember it is FARM-B and not some other letter.

Acronyms are also widely used to indicate the steps in cognitive strategies, such as the SNOW strategy for taking essay tests. Each letter in the acronym stands for a step in the cognitive procedure (S = Study the question; N = Note important points; O = Organize notes;

W = Write your essay), as described in Chapter 12. Presentation of these strategies to students is usually accompanied with instruction in how to execute each of the steps indicated in the specific strategy.

In spite of their success and popularity, acronyms are not as versatile as other mnemonics. The reason for this is that many lists of things to be remembered do not contain first letters that can easily be combined into words. For example, the first letters of the planets in the solar system (M, V, E, M, J, S, U, N) cannot be easily combined into an acronym, mostly because the list contains six consonants and only two vowels. Also, it seems important to create a mnemonic that preserves the order of the planets in terms of their distance from the sun. To accomplish this, an **acrostic** can be used instead. To form an acrostic, a word is created from each first letter, and the words are arranged to make a sentence. To remember the planets, a good acrostic is, "My Very Educated Mother Just Served Us Noodles." The first letter of each of the words in this sentence represents the planets in order of their distance from the sun. Another example of an acrostic is "My Dear Aunt Sally," which reminds students to *m*ultiply and *d*ivide before they *a*dd and *s*ubtract in a math sentence (see Chapter 15). Another version is "Please Excuse My Dear Aunt Sally," which includes *p*arenthetical expressions and *e*xponents, prior to the previously described sequence of operations. The elaborated sentence "King Philip's Class Ordered a Family of Gentile Spaniels" can promote memory of taxonomic ranks: kingdom, phylum, class, order, family, genus, and species. Both acronyms and acrostics must be practiced to ensure all aspects of the mnemonic have been mastered.

Finally, letter strategies can be combined with keywords or pegwords. For example, to promote recall of three countries in the Central Powers during World War I, provide a picture of children playing tag in Central Park. *Central Park* is a keyword for *Central Powers*, and *TAG* is an acronym for Turkey (Ottoman Empire), Austria-Hungary, and Germany (Figure 10.8). To help students remember the freedoms guaranteed by the First Amendment to the Constitution, provide a picture of a rap singer who raps about buns. *Buns* is a pegword for *one*, or first, amendment, and *RAPS* is an acronym for the freedoms of religion, assembly, press, and speech.

CREATE MNEMONIC PICTURES Although some mnemonic pictures are available commercially (e.g., see Burchers & Burchers, 2007, or Harmon, 2020, for vocabulary materials), in most cases, teachers will have to develop their own materials. Some teachers feel that they cannot use mnemonic strategies because they are not artistically inclined and feel unable to draw good mnemonic pictures. However, it is not necessary that the pictures be "artistic"; rather, it is only important that they are recognizable. You can use stick figures or cutouts from magazines to create pictures. Some teachers have enlisted the assistance of an artistic student to help. However, clip art is probably the easiest way to create excellent mnemonic pictures. Software containing literally hundreds of thousands of clip-art pictures is available

Figure 10.8 Mnemonic Strategy for Central Powers

commercially, and clip art is sometimes included in word-processing and office software. As an alternative, a great deal of clip art is available on the Internet and can be located by typing in "clip art" followed by the picture being sought (e.g., "clip-art frog") on a search engine. Mnemonic pictures are not difficult to create, and once created, they can be used again and again to improve students' memory of important content. In some cases, as noted, materials have already been created.

COMBINE MNEMONIC STRATEGIES WITH OTHER CLASSROOM ACTIVITIES

Mnemonic strategies are not only powerful tools for improving memory, but they are also very versatile and can be incorporated with other means of instruction (Therrien et al., 2011). For example, the keyword method was used to improve recall of important vocabulary (e.g., predator–prey; parasite–host) for hands-on science learning. Students used the keyword method to help remember important vocabulary while they engaged in hands-on activities to enhance their understanding of important scientific concepts relevant to ecosystems (Mastropieri et al., 1998).

Mnemonic strategies have also been employed in peer-tutoring configurations in high school chemistry classes. Mastropieri et al. (2005) combined mnemonic strategies with peer tutoring to develop recall and comprehension of important science content. For example, to learn about *core* and *valence* electrons, students were shown a picture of an atom with apple cores (keyword for *core electrons*) closer to the nucleus and bridal veils (keyword for *valence*) farther away from the nucleus. Because students only used the mnemonic strategies when they were needed to enhance memory, the materials were relevant to UDL principles (Meyer et al., 2014). Students tutored each other on their recall of the fact and strategy. However, students also questioned each other on additional information about core and valence electrons, for instance, that valence electrons have higher energy levels than core electrons (see Figure 10.9; see also Marshak et al., 2011, for a social studies example).

Although mnemonic strategies have provided very powerful effects in experimental research in special and inclusive settings, they should not be considered a panacea for learning. Attend to all the strategies for improving memory, be sure to provide lots of practice, and monitor comprehension and application of learning to other domains. By using all of these strategies and evaluating progress, you can maximize each student's memory to aid in school success.

Figure 10.9 What Are Core and Valence Electrons?

What are core and valence electrons?

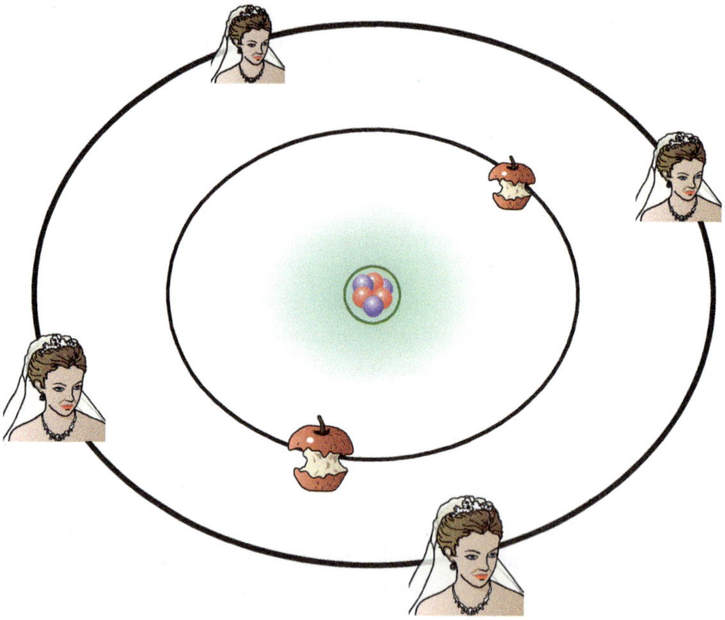

Core electrons are more stable, and closer to nucleus. Valence electrons are less stable, and farther from the nucleus.

If your partner is correct, go to ⇒
If not, review the strategy:

Strategy: *Think of the word "apple core" for core and "bridal veil" for valence. Then think of this picture of (apple) core electrons orbiting around the nucleus with the "veil" ence electrons orbiting farther out from the nucleus around the core electrons. This will help you remember that core electrons are closer to the nucleus, and are more stable than valence electrons.*

Then ask: *What is the strategy to remember core and valence electrons?*

Then ask again: *What are core and valence electrons?*

⇒ Then ask: *What else is important about core and valence electrons?*
[Answers include: Core electrons have higher energy levels than valence electrons]

10 Summary

- Attention is important for success in school, and students with learning challenges often struggle with attention difficulties. Many strategies have helped students improve their attention.
  - Preconditions for improving attention in the classroom can be implemented.
  - Teach specific strategies for improving attention.
    - Simple strategies for increasing attention include asking students directly to try to pay attention better and moving closer to the student who struggles to attend.
    - Breaking activities into smaller segments, alternating among various types of class activities, allowing opportunities for movement, using reinforcement, and teaching self-recording may also help improve attention.
    - Peer assistance can be used to promote attention of students with a variety of diverse learning needs. Reinforcement of attention and instruction in self-recording strategies can also be effective.
  - Extreme cases of attention deficits and the effects of stimulant medications can be addressed.
  - Effective teaching, including the use of teacher planning and presentation variables, can help all students pay more attention in class.
- Memory is critical for success in school-related tasks. Strategies for improving the school success of students with diverse learning needs have been identified.
  - Meeting the preconditions for improving memory may help many students remember better. These preconditions include promoting attention, motivation, and positive attitudes.
  - Teaching students metacognitive awareness strategies ("metamemory") helps promote better memory strategies for all students.
  - Using pictures, enhancing meaningfulness, using activities, providing sufficient practice, and promoting active learning all help promote better memory for students with disabilities.
  - Use of mnemonic strategies such as the keyword method, the pegword method, and letter strategies helps promote learning of unfamiliar content.

PROFESSIONAL STANDARDS LINK
Improving Attention and Memory

Information in this chapter links most directly to:

- CEC 2020 Initial Practice-Based Professional Preparation Standards for Special Educators (Initial K–12 standards) (see https://exceptionalchildren.org/standards/initial-practice-based-professional-preparation-standards-special-educators): 2 (Understanding and Addressing Each Individual's Developmental and Learning Needs), 3 (Demonstrating Subject Matter Content and Specialized Curricular Knowledge), 5 (Supporting Learning Using Effective Instruction)
- InTASC Standards (see https://www.ccsso.org/sites/default/files/2017-11/InTASC_Model_Core_Teaching_Standards_2011.pdf): 2 (Learning Differences), 3 (Learning Environments), 7 (Planning for Instruction), 8 (Instructional Strategies)

IMPROVING ATTENTION AND MEMORY

If students are having problems with attention and memory, have you considered the following? If not, see the pages listed here.

STRATEGIES FOR IMPROVING ATTENTION

- ☐ Address the preconditions of attention with teacher effectiveness, 252
- ☐ Provide assistance with basic skills problems, 252–253
- ☐ Use direct appeal, 253
- ☐ Use proximity, 253
- ☐ Break up activities, 254
- ☐ Allow sufficient movement to reduce restlessness, 254
- ☐ Provide student activities, 254
- ☐ Use classroom peers to promote attention, 254
- ☐ Provide direct consequences for attention, 254–255
- ☐ Teach self-recording strategies, 255

STRATEGIES FOR ADDRESSING EXTREME CASES OF ATTENTION DEFICITS

- ☐ Provide intensive teacher-led instruction, 256
- ☐ Consider strengths and weaknesses of stimulant medication, 256–258
- ☐ Provide behavioral techniques, 258
- ☐ Promote joint attention, 258

If students are having problems with memory, have you considered the following? If not, see the pages listed here.

STRATEGIES FOR IMPROVING MEMORY

- ☐ Address memory preconditions, 259
- ☐ Develop "metamemory," 259–260
- ☐ Use external memory, 260
- ☐ Enhance meaningfulness, 260
- ☐ Use concrete examples, pictures, or imagery, 260–262
- ☐ Minimize interfering information, 262
- ☐ Use enactments and manipulation, 262
- ☐ Promote active reasoning, 262–263
- ☐ Increase practice, 263
- ☐ Use clustering and organization, 263
- ☐ Promote elaboration, 263–264

STRATEGIES FOR IMPROVING MEMORY WITH MNEMONIC TECHNIQUES

- ☐ Use the keyword method for verbal associations, 265–269
- ☐ Use the pegword method for numbered or ordered information, 269–271
- ☐ Use letter strategies for lists, 271–272
- ☐ Create mnemonic pictures, 272–273
- ☐ Combine mnemonic strategies with other classroom activities, 273

Erni/Shutterstock

CHAPTER 11

Teaching Study Skills

LEARNING OBJECTIVES

After studying this chapter, you should be able to:

11.1 Demonstrate an understanding of tools to develop independent learners, using personal organizational skills and strategies for completing homework, for effective listening and for note taking.

11.2 Demonstrate familiarity with various research and reference skills necessary for successfully completing reports or projects.

Good study skills are necessary for success in school. Although some general education students appear to develop excellent organization and study skills independently, most students with disabilities and students at risk for failure in school can benefit from explicit instruction in organizing themselves for studying and completing assignments in a timely fashion. Research has demonstrated that individuals who are trained to use efficient study and organizational strategies perform better and are more likely to succeed in school (Dorminy et al., 2009).

CLASSROOM SCENARIO

Ravi

When Ravi, a ninth-grader with learning disabilities, entered Mr. Ford's room, he was holding a stack of books with papers sticking out from all angles. Some of the papers were bent, some were folded, and some were slightly torn, but all books had been covered with brightly colored paper. As he approached the desks, his glasses were sliding down toward the end of his nose, and he bumped the edge of one of the tables slightly. Before you could blink your eyes, everything that had been in his arms was strewn all over the floor. Ravi smiled sheepishly as he began to pick up his belongings.

Somewhere in that pile of books and papers there was evidence of Ravi's attempts at completing his homework. When Mr. Ford asked him about it, Ravi said, "I've done some of the homework, but I can't seem to find it at the moment. …" This was a typical day for Ravi. Although he usually attempted his assignments, he either could not find them or he would forget about his homework and appear confused when asked about it—almost as if it were the first time he had heard of the assignment.

QUESTIONS FOR REFLECTION

1. Why is Ravi not able to improve his organizational skills?
2. Do you think external rewards would help Ravi? Why or why not?
3. What interventions might help Ravi?

Learning strategies help all students study more effectively, but they especially benefit students with disabilities such as those with autism, learning disabilities, and emotional disabilities. This chapter describes how to help your students become more personally organized and efficient at planning for homework, developing effective listening and note-taking skills, and learning to use outlining and guided notes. In addition, strategies are presented for using libraries, writing reports, completing long-term assignments and projects, and studying for later retrieval.

Tools for Developing Independent Learners

Learning Objective 11.1 Demonstrate an understanding of tools to develop independent learners, using personal organizational skills and strategies for completing homework, for effective listening and for note taking.

Study skills are tools for learning. Several study skills books are available (e.g., Carter et al., 2011; Vorderman et al., 2016); many of these books present a number of study skills and strategies with the expectation that students will master all strategies with minimal instruction. Many students with disabilities, however, do not have good study and learning strategies and experience difficulties when trying to use these strategies independently. These students may require extensive explicit instruction in learning strategies, controlled practice, and feedback before they are able to execute them successfully and independently. Teaching students to become independent learners and thinkers includes providing "tools for learners" in self-instruction, self-monitoring, self-questioning, and self-reinforcement (Deshler & Schumaker, 2006; Reid et al., 2013).

Pearson eTextbook

Video Example 11.1

In this video, student expectations are clearly stated for students reviewing the Monday routine for reading instruction. The teacher has prepared for differentiated small reading groups and independent seatwork.

STRATEGIES FOR DEVELOPING PERSONAL ORGANIZATIONAL SKILLS

Personal organizational skills include using time schedules; understanding class and school schedules; using a daily, weekly, and monthly planner; and being organized for completing homework assignments. These skills are what some experts call good self-management skills. Other organizational skills include knowing how to analyze tasks required for assignments and optimizing performance and studying time (MacArthur, 2012). Provide general information about study skills to your entire class and arrange small groups of students who need additional instruction in study skills. Special education teachers can work with you and provide instruction in these strategies for those who need it. Finally, you may decide to team-teach groups of students who need to learn these strategies. However you present them, study and organizational skills will reap huge benefits in student performance.

POST AND REVIEW CLASS AND TIME SCHEDULES All grade levels follow systematic schedules. Present the schedules to students with disabilities in clear, comprehensible language to ensure they are prepared for each segment of the school day.

Many elementary teachers write daily agendas or schedules on the board that contain all daily class activities, such as the one shown in Figure 11.1. The list can include reminders to bring specific materials for various classes and brief descriptions of homework assignments. Future events can also be highlighted. For example, highlighting special classes such as art, music, and physical education can help students remember to bring sneakers and shorts for gym class or instruments for music class. Although many students may not require these reminders, students who do need them will not feel singled out when you make the information available to all.

Secondary schools require students to see many teachers throughout the school day. Some schools have a constant number of daily periods throughout the week, whereas other schools have rotating schedules—referred to as block scheduling—that alternate weekly. Although they allow longer class periods, block systems can be confusing. You may need to re-review schedules with some students. Figure 11.2 shows an example of a block schedule containing eight periods, including black days (periods 1–4) and red days (periods 5–8).

How to Start At the beginning of a new year or semester, you may need to describe for students how to locate rooms within the school. This is especially important in very large buildings, where one floor looks similar to another. One idea might be to make yourself, a peer, or an

Figure 11.1 Sample Elementary School Daily Agenda

8:00–8:10	Get ready for the school day (sharpen pencils, use restrooms)
8:10–8:15	Complete scrambled sentence activity
8:15–9:15	Reading
9:15–9:40	Recess and restroom breaks
9:40–10:40	Mathematics
10:40–11:15	Writing and Language Arts
11:15–12:15	Lunch and Recess
12:15–1:15	Science
1:15–2:15	Social Studies
2:15–2:45	Physical Education (Tues–Thurs)

BRING SHORTS and SNEAKERS for GYM Tomorrow!!!

Music (Mon)

Art (Wed–Fri)

Figure 11.2 Sample Secondary School Schedule

Black Day Schedule

Daily Order	Period
1. First	1. English, room 204
2. Second	2. Phys. Ed., gym
3. Third	3. Algebra I, room 105
4. Fourth	4. Study Hall, cafeteria

Red Day Schedule

Daily Order	Period
1. First	5. Biology, room 209
2. Second	6. U.S. Government, room 115
3. Third	7. Band, music room
4. Fourth	8. Spanish, room 215

aide available to meet students before or after school to go over their class schedules and walk the routes with them. Follow up by meeting students after each class when needed and walk with them to the next class until students demonstrate confidence about where they are and where they need to be at what time. All students wish to appear as competent as their peers seem to be, and although they might be confused about building layouts and schedules, they may not want to risk embarrassing themselves by asking for help. Your awareness and subtle ways of keying into students' needs can enhance students' self-perceptions.

Don't Forget Lockers As students move from class to class, they may need to visit their lockers for books or materials. This can be particularly challenging for some students with disabilities because the use of lockers requires extra time and mental and physical challenges. If students have trouble remembering the combination, practice with the students or suggest

they write the combination (secretly) on a wallet-size card they can carry with them or on a mobile device for easy access until they master the information.

Provide extra time and instructions for opening lockers. Some students have been known to carry everything (all books, notebooks, lunch, and coats) around all day simply because they could not open their lockers. Another student pretended she hated physical education and refused to participate in gym, when she actually did not know how to open her locker that contained her gym clothing. Finally, note the accessibility of lockers. Lockers or locks that are placed too high or low can cause unnecessary frustrations, especially for some students with physical limitations.

Clearly Post and Review Schedule Changes Some students, such as those with autism, do not handle changes well, but if they are prepared ahead of time, they will be more likely to adjust to the changes (refer also to the IRIS Center module titled "Autism Spectrum Disorder: An Overview for Educators" at http://iris.peabody.vanderbilt.edu). For example, explain what will happen if you are absent from school and a substitute teacher is assigned to take over the class. Believe it or not, some students with emotional disabilities may be very upset when you are absent! These changes may be particularly difficult for some students if you are gone for a long period of time, such as for an extended medical leave. When students are informed ahead of time, these transitions can be handled more smoothly.

At the middle and secondary levels, it is common for students to have different teachers for each subject. Each teacher may establish different class routines and expectations. For example, some teachers may choose to use a web-based learning platform such as Google Classroom or Canvas to share files with students and to assign homework. Many students with disabilities require extra help learning the routines that are used in each teacher's classroom (Mastropieri & Scruggs, 2002). For example, some teachers may require students to be seated when the class bell rings, whereas others may require that students only be inside the room when the bell rings. Encourage students to write down any specific expectations and routines for each class and teacher. Take care to show students your own class expectations, schedules, and routines and provide support for them while they are learning all of the new routines simultaneously. A little role-playing or memory game might help. For example, say the name of a teacher to a group of students and ask them to quickly tell you the unique expectations that teacher has.

USE STRATEGIES FOR DAILY, WEEKLY, AND MONTHLY PLANNING Many adults use paper or digital daily planner calendars that contain space for weekly and monthly entries. These planners are ideally suited to keeping track of both long- and short-term school assignments. For students who have a Google Chrome browser installed and Internet access, there are various ways to track classwork and homework assignments, including *Google Calendar*, *myHomework Student Planner*, and *Wunderlist* (Ok & Rao, 2019; refer to the feature *Apps for Education*). Show students a variety of planner formats and have them select one that meets their needs. Show them how most effective people in all disciplines use some type of planner to help keep organized. Ask other teachers, the principal, parents, caregivers, and businesspeople from the community to visit your class and share the way they plan and schedule events.

Explain the differences between long- and short-term planning. Provide examples of how studying time needs to be divided among subject areas and across types of assignments (Paulsen & Sayeski, 2013). Provide examples of "to-do" lists and show students how to prioritize them. Some people like to do the easiest thing on the list first; others prefer to get the hardest item out of the way first. Figure 11.3 shows a sample planner and to-do list that might work for individual content areas. Encourage students to discuss optimal ways of proceeding for themselves. Students with disabilities may need specific examples of each step spelled out for them. For example, general education students with good study habits:

1. Review their assignment notebooks.
2. Prioritize what needs to get accomplished.
3. Set goals of finishing tasks for themselves.
4. Work hard to accomplish those goals.

Conversely, students with disabilities may be forgetful and may not deliberately plan their activities. Some may need teachers to complete sample planners for them and take them step by step through the thinking involved in figuring out what to do.

Figure 11.3 Sample Planner and To-Do List

Student ___________ ________ Quarter

Subject	To do	Assigned on	Due date	Turned in on	Parent initials

USE TASK ANALYSIS TO ORGANIZE ASSIGNMENTS **Task analysis** is the process of taking a large task or assignment, breaking it into subcomponent smaller tasks, and estimating task completion time for each subcomponent. Teach students to write out the assignment, decide what must be done, sequence the steps of what must be done, and estimate the amount of time necessary to complete each step. For example, a biology teacher may make an assignment that students read pages 264–277 in the textbook, write a summary paragraph, and answer questions 13–21 at the end of the chapter. A task analysis may reveal that this requires the student to complete the following steps:

- Locate the textbook and a quiet area to work.
- Find the relevant text pages and read them carefully, while highlighting or taking notes.
- Write a summary paragraph based on the reading and notes.
- Locate the relevant questions at the end of the chapter.
- Answer all questions, referring to the text and notes.
- Check all work and be certain all components of the assignment are completed.

Figure 11.4 shows a planning task sequence for preparing a book report.

TEACH STRATEGIES FOR HOMEWORK COMPLETION Homework is assigned at virtually all grade levels but increases in regularity and complexity with each grade level (Langberg et al., 2011; Reid et al., 2013). Homework provides opportunities for students to develop fluency with the information being taught and to develop organizational and self-study skills.

Some homework assignments may need to be reduced in size and scope for students with disabilities, who may need more time to process and complete the same activities. Wiener and Daniels (2016) interviewed adolescents with disabilities who identified the following challenges with homework completion and study preparation: (1) disorganization of notes, (2) avoidance or procrastination, and (3) limited stamina for completing homework.

Because performance on homework is often included in computing semester grades, consider modifying the amount and type of homework (e.g., individualized education program (IEP) accommodation to shorten homework assignments by 50%) or the grading procedures for students with disabilities (Bryan & Burstein, 2004). Figure 11.5 lists some assignments and possible adaptations that are consistent with HLP 13: Adapt Curriculum Tasks and Materials for Specific Learning Goals (McLeskey et al., 2017).

Most students with disabilities find it helpful to record their assignments in an assignment notebook or homework folder. Include spaces for teachers' and parents'/caregivers' signatures to help ensure that your students asked someone to verify whether assignments were completed accurately. This also keeps parents or caregivers informed so that they can monitor homework progress daily. Most parents and caregivers likely would appreciate a letter requesting their assistance in establishing homework procedures and arranging an environment conducive to studying at home (see Figure 11.6). Hampshire et al. (2016) reported that when parents

Figure 11.4 Task Planning for a Book Report

Sun	Mon	Tues	Wed	Thurs	Fri	Sat
Week 1						
Week 2						
Week 3						
Week 4						

Assigned Date _____ Due Date _____ Time Available _____ days

1. Go to library and select book. (1 day)
2. Count chapters or pages in book and determine the number of chapters or pages that should be read daily (e.g., 13 chapters or 208 pages). Adjust according to your reading rate and the number of days available. For example, if you can read one chapter per day you will need 13 days. If you can read 16 pages a day, you will need 13 days to read the book.
3. Brainstorm book report outline. (1 day)
4. Organize outline from brainstorming activity. (1 day)
5. Fill in details on outline. (1 day)
6. Write draft book report using outline. (2 days)
7. Proof and revise first and final draft of book report. (2 days)
8. Write final version and proof carefully. (2 days)

Total number of days necessary to complete assignment—20

Sun	Mon	Tues	Wed	Thurs	Fri	Sat
Week 1	Go to library and select book	Count pages and chapters and figure out how much to read daily	Read	Read	Read	Read
Week 2	Read	Read	Read	Read	Read	Read
Week 3	Read	Read	Read	Brainstorm book report outline	Organize outline from brainstorming	Fill in outline details
Week 4	Write first draft	Write first draft	Proof and revise first draft	Proof and revise final draft	Write, edit, and proof final version	Write and proof final version

helped to design and individualize their child's self-management system during homework time, middle school students with autism spectrum disorders improved their task independence and homework accuracy. Following training, the self-management system involved parents providing a brief review of homework rules and procedures followed by students working through a daily self-monitoring checklist and gaining access to a preselected reinforcer when all tasks were completed.

When assigning homework, provide clear instructions and always explain the purpose of the assignment. Write assignments in the same location daily so that students can find them easily and copy them accurately into their assignment notebooks or digital devices. Such predictable, consistent practices can help students establish patterns that promote success.

Figure 11.5 Homework Assignments and Possible Adaptations

Subject	Assignment	Adapted Assignment
Spelling	Study 20 words.	Study 10 prioritized words.
Math	Complete 30 word problems.	Complete 15 prioritized word problems.
Reading	Read two chapters and write a summary.	Read one chapter and record a summary of the information; or listen to an audio recording of the two chapters and record a summary of both chapters.
Social Studies	Read section 3 in Chapter 4 and answer the 10 questions at the end of the section.	Read section 3 in Chapter 4 and answer the even-numbered questions at the end of the section (half the questions).
Science	Write a summary of the experiment completed during today's lab.	Record a summary of the experiment completed in today's lab (or use voice-to-text app).

Figure 11.6 Homework Procedures: Request for Home-School Cooperation

Date __________

Dear Parent/Caregiver,

As we begin this school year I want you to know how delighted I am to have your child, ____________, in my class. I am looking forward to meeting you at our first Open House. Please try to come and bring any questions you may have about this school year with you.

I would like to explain to you some of the procedures and requirements of my class so you will have a better understanding of what is expected of your child. I usually assign homework nightly. Most nights the assignments are rather short and can be completed within 20 minutes. A few times throughout the year, however, I assign longer-term projects that will require your child to work a little bit each night over a period of about a month to complete the project. Examples of the longer-term projects include the following:

- Book reports
- Library research projects
- Models of inventions
- Science fair projects
- Interviews with business people from the community

I would like to request some assistance from you to ensure that your child successfully completes his or her assignments. Every afternoon or evening, **please ask your son or daughter to show you the assignment notebook.** Ideally your child should take the initiative and bring the notebook to you. Please initial and date that day's assignments. That will let me know that you have seen the assignment and ensure that it has been successfully completed or that an honest attempt was made to complete it. Some of you may want to see the assignment book and completed assignment, while others of you may wish to see only the assignment notebook.

Second, it would be most helpful if you could establish a **regular space** for your child to complete his or her assignments. That way, when he or she arrives home from school, all necessary school materials can be placed in a specific location and kept all together. Establishing a regular place also helps ensure that the materials are together and will not be forgotten when leaving for school the next morning.

Third, it would be beneficial to **establish a regular time for your child to do his or her homework.** I realize that this can be difficult because of extra-curricular activities. However, establishing regular homework times on Mondays, Tuesdays, Wednesdays, Thursdays, and Saturdays or Sundays can help illustrate the importance of maintaining responsibility for completing homework.

Finally, please feel free to add notes to the assignment notebook if you wish to communicate any information to me. If you have questions concerning your child's performance or understanding of the assignments, I will do my best to help.

If students don't complete or turn in assignments, they will lose points from their grade and be given after-school detention after missing three assignments.

Thanks so much for your help with this important matter. Please feel free to contact me by telephone or e-mail.

Regards,

Several teaching practices can help students complete their homework successfully (see also Jakulski & Mastropieri, 2004; Vaughn & Bos, 2019):

- Give clear, concise directions for completing assignments; establish due dates that are reasonable and clearly communicated. Assignment boards and student recorders also may be helpful (see Ness et al., 2011).
- Describe any materials necessary to complete each assignment. For example, will students need to take any textbooks home with them? Will they need to go to the library and sign out materials before they can complete the work? Will they need to bring materials to class?
- If you provide a sample of the homework assignment, complete it together as a class, be specific, and ensure that students understand what they are to do by asking two or three students to repeat or explain the directions.
- Anticipate any areas of difficulty with an assignment and attempt to provide extra clarification. King-Sears et al. (2017) supported students with their chemistry homework by providing interactive PDFs on curriculum topics that allowed students to see and hear handwritten notes that were recorded with audio by the teacher using a Livescribe Smartpen (see *Research Highlight*). Providing students with additional access to the content allowed them to decide what to review at home and increased their retention of learned content.
- Explain how students can get help if they confront problems. Perhaps there is time before, during, or after the school day to meet with the teacher. Also, some students could be trained as "homework assistants" who could be contacted in the evenings by phone or text message until 8:00. With permission, distribute a list of names and phone numbers of these homework assistants.
- Establish a regular time for collecting and distributing assignments. Establish special locations for dropping off and picking up completed and corrected assignments.
- Consistently collect, grade, and return assigned work. When teachers neglect to collect or return graded assignments, some students take away the message that homework is unimportant to them.
- Coordinate assignments with other teachers. Your students with disabilities will benefit greatly from any shared planning you do with your co-teachers to avoid scheduling several exams on a single day or overlapping longer-term assignments.
- Arrange classroom incentives for completing and turning in homework. Some teachers establish either individual or class rewards to encourage timely completion of homework. For example, Zibreg Hargis et al. (2016) reported substantial improvement in the homework completion of students with and without disabilities when group rewards (e.g., free time coupons, school supplies, a movie party) were provided for homework completion.
- Remember to assign projects that are within the capability levels of all students. Homework is an opportunity to practice previously acquired skills, develop fluency, and practice applying these skills to new contexts.

Pearson eTextbook
Video Example 11.2

Clear and explicit instruction is needed to support students with organizing material for classwork and homework. In this video, the teacher leads a discussion with students about their use of an agenda book or planner.

Clearly State Class Expectations Provide students with specific expectations for completed work. Explain how you intend to evaluate work and provide examples of what you consider to be "model" assignments and insufficiently completed assignments. Is it acceptable, for example, to turn in a page torn from a spiral notebook? Can homework assignments be turned in electronically? Will you accept incomplete assignments?

Creating a checklist for students to keep in their notebooks would be helpful. Some students may need the expectations for completing homework to be scaffolded. For example, a student may need to first work toward independently showing homework initiation (an attempt is made), then build toward homework completion, and then homework accuracy (Hampshire et al., 2014). Progress toward these types of short-term goals could inform a students' annual IEP goal to increase independence and student responsibility.

Cooperative Homework Teams O'Melia and Rosenberg (1994) created cooperative homework teams (CHTs) to help middle school students with learning and behavioral disabilities complete their mathematics homework more frequently and more accurately. Students in CHT classes were assigned to three- and four-member heterogeneous CHTs. During the first period of class, immediately after the opening activity, the teams met, and a "checker" (or the teacher as in Houser et al., 2015) who had been assigned to each team on a rotating basis graded the assignments for the day, using teacher-made answer sheets. The grades were recorded and the assignments were returned to the students with corrections. Checkers then turned in all of the corrected homework. After 8 weeks of this intervention, results indicated that students who had participated in CHTs had a 74% rate of homework completion, compared with a 55% rate in comparison classes. Furthermore, CHT students were 30% more accurate in the assignments they did complete.

Similarly, Houser et al. (2015) described a "Radical Raceway" intervention using cooperative homework teams. Teams of five students matched overall for ability were created, which then met at the end of class to review and discuss homework. Teams with the highest completion or accuracy averages were allowed to advance their race cars two spaces ahead on the racetrack, whereas second-place teams advanced their cars ahead one space. The first team across the finish line was allowed to select a group reward. Houser et al. reported that when the intervention was in effect, students completed 86% of homework assignments, with an average of 78% correct. When the intervention was not in effect, student completion was just 57%, with 51% correct.

Assignment Completion Strategy Hughes et al. (2002) successfully taught middle school students with learning disabilities an assignment completion strategy that was successfully used in their inclusive general education classes. The strategy was referred to as "PROJECT" and focused on the sequence of skills necessary for assignment completion. As students worked on the strategy, they completed three forms—a monthly planner, a weekly study schedule, and an assignment sheet—all of which were included in an assignment notebook. PROJECT was employed as a first-letter mnemonic device to represent the following steps:

- Prepare your forms (fill in monthly planners and weekly study sheets).
- Record and ask (record the assignment on the assignment sheet, using abbreviations and circling appropriate words [e.g., "write"], and ask questions for clarification).
- Organize (break assignment into parts, estimate number of study sessions, schedule sessions, and take materials home).
- Jump to it (overcome task avoidance; obtain needed materials).
- Engage in the work (complete assignment and consult parents/caregivers).
- Check your work (evaluate quality of work and circle a "quality grade" (e.g., A, B, C) on the assignment sheet).
- Turn in your work.

Students were trained in 30-minute sessions, four times per week, for 4 weeks. At the end of the training, it was observed that eight of the nine students mastered the strategy and improved significantly in homework completion rates, quality of completed assignments, and quarterly grades (see also Hampshire et al., 2014).

Family involvement can also improve homework completion and improve study skills, but practices must support the diverse needs of all students. The *Diversity, Equity, and Inclusion in the Classroom* feature provides additional information for how to make homework tasks more equitable for all students.

STRATEGIES FOR PROMOTING LISTENING SKILLS

Listening skills are critical for school success (Wong, 2015). Because teachers provide oral directions and instructions continually throughout the school day, students who have good listening skills can follow along, understand what is expected of them, and be successful in school.

Many students, however, especially younger elementary-age children and students with disabilities and attention deficit disorders, lack good listening skills. This hinders their ability to succeed in classes (Deshler & Schumaker, 2006).

ADDRESS REQUISITE LISTENING SKILLS Verify whether students have the appropriate skills for listening by using the teacher checklist in the *In the Classroom* feature. First, determine if students can hear the speaker adequately. Judge whether a student's position in the classroom interferes with hearing abilities. For example, does the problem exist when information is presented over the loudspeaker or during multimedia presentations? Does it exist during teacher presentations in the classroom, in large-group sessions in auditoriums, or outdoors at recess? Difficulties in hearing in any of these environments may indicate that a referral is needed for a hearing test. Specific plans can be devised to assist students, providing them with various seating positions to meet their needs. Have students sit near audiovisual equipment or near the front of large auditoriums or ask peer assistants to help by repeating directions given outdoors.

Second, determine whether an attention problem exists. To help students come to attention and to encourage active listening from the start, try call-and-response routines (teacher calls "1, 2, 3, eyes on me" ... students respond, "1, 2, eyes on you") or pairing a visual cue with the beginning of the listening activity. For example, flip a light switch in the room to alert students that the presentation is about to begin. Pair a teacher movement, such as walking and standing still in the front of the room for a few seconds, with the beginning of new lectures. Remember that attending may be a function of the degree to which you make your presentations interesting. Be sure to use interesting and engaging materials. Miller (2003), for example, explained how the listening skills of English learners can be addressed by using culturally relevant, authentic materials.

Third, determine if students understand the speaker. It may take some time for students to get used to speakers with unfamiliar accents or dialects and/or the vocabulary and sentence structure may be beyond the lexicon level of students with disabilities. Ask students to repeat what was just said in their own words. You may need to pre-teach difficult vocabulary and concepts before students can benefit from lecture activities.

Fourth, judge whether students can recognize and select important points from lectures or presentations. Can they follow the sequence of ideas? Do they understand organizational cues used during a lecture, such as *first*, *second*, *third*, *next*, and *then*? Teach students that important points are often introduced at the beginning of lectures and then explained and elaborated on separately after organizational cue statements.

TEACH LISTENING SKILLS Some students require extra practice in learning how to listen. Design some fun lessons in which students are motivated to learn to listen (see also Spooner & Woodcock, 2010). Keep the activities short, and try the following:

- Explain the purpose of a listening activity, present information, and then have older students repeat what was presented in their own words. Have younger students act out the sequence of events or play Simon Says.
- Model and demonstrate the use of key words and phrases, such as *first*, *second*, *third*, and *next*. Give students cards containing cue words and direct them to raise the appropriate cards when they hear them.
- Have students identify important phrases and ask them to tell you when they hear relevant sequences or specific details in the presentations.
- Demonstrate how certain verbal (e.g., "I want you to remember ...") and nonverbal (e.g., extra-long pauses) cues can highlight important information. Have students act out or tell their neighbors the listening cues they hear during a presentation.
- Use topics that are interesting and motivating and include favorite characters from shows, musicians, words from songs, or interviews with famous athletes.
- Give students advance organizers of talks and have them generate questions they would like answered about the upcoming talk.
- Give students several questions before a presentation and have them try to figure out answers to the questions during the talk.

Diversity, Equity, and Inclusion in the Classroom

Homework Practices to Support Diverse Needs

Homework represents a significant extension of school into home and family life. Dr. Cathy Vatterott, an expert on the subject of K–12 homework, argues that the traditional practices of homework might be out of step with the needs of today's families (Vatterott, 2018). Several generations ago, she argues, connections between school and home were stronger, and school was more likely to have been considered the final authority on academic matters. Today, economic and cultural diversity, as well as different parenting styles, have created differing views on the parent–school relationship and homework. These realities and differing views need to be respected when assigning homework.

Vatterott describes the case of Emma, who almost always completes her homework. Her parents have the time, resources, and willingness to support her school achievement. Her parents frequently discuss with Emma the subjects she is studying. They have a home library, Internet access, and resources to hire tutors and buy school materials when needed. Emma has her own computer and a quiet room of her own for studying and schoolwork.

In contrast, Sofia, rarely completes her homework. Three days a week she comes home immediately after school to supervise her younger siblings while her mother goes out to work. Two days a week she goes after school to her part-time job to help support the family. When she does have some time, she does not have a quiet place in the house to work. There is no computer, and her mother, who does not speak English, cannot help with her homework. There is little money to support homework projects and only limited transportation. It is unsafe to walk to the library.

These two very different cases are described to demonstrate that, while in school, students have similar amounts of time, resources, and support for their schoolwork; however, after school, these conditions can vary dramatically. Vatterott (2018) recommends that, when assigning homework, teachers make the following considerations:

- Do not assume the student has a quiet place for homework.
- Do not assume the student has a parent/caregiver at home in the evening.
- Do not assume the student's parents/caregivers can speak or can read English.
- Do not assume the student's family has resources for school supplies.
- Do not assume the student has access to needed materials, such as pencils, pencil sharpener, tape, scissors, magazines, or a calculator, in the home.
- Do not assume the student has access to either a computer or the Internet.

When designing homework tasks, Vatterott recommends that teachers should first ensure the homework has a clear academic purpose that is meaningful to the student. The task should be efficient, not taking an inordinate amount of time or requiring nonacademic skills like gluing, cutting, or drawing. It should support classroom learning but also instill a sense of competence in the student's mind. Finally, it should support a sense of ownership in the student, perhaps by giving them input or choices in what they undertake.

Vatterott (2018) also suggests that teachers consider using homework as providing feedback to the student, and continuous measurement of student progress, rather than as simply a grade. Furthermore, she suggests that homework tasks be differentiated to address different students' skills and resources. Tasks can be differentiated by difficulty or amount of work (or setting a time limit), by amount of structuring or scaffolding (e.g., requiring less writing for some students), or differentiating by student preference (e.g., allowing student choice in how to study vocabulary or facts).

Finally, teachers can try to find time during the school day for students to complete homework. Although using lunch time or recess may seem punitive to the student, perhaps some time can be found during the day in the elementary classroom or during homeroom or advisory time in the higher grade levels. Overall, teachers should continue to investigate ways to make homework tasks more equitable for all students. For more information on homework considerations for diverse learners, including teacher, parent/caregiver, student surveys, and planning materials, see Vatterott (2018).

Discuss: What are some ways to make the effects of homework more equitable for diverse populations?

In the Classroom

Checklist for Effective Listening Skills

Student must be able to:

- ____ Hear the speaker
  - ____ Teacher's voice
  - ____ Loudspeaker
  - ____ Multimedia presentations
  - ____ Auditorium presentations
  - ____ Outdoors at recess or field trips
- ____ Attend to the speaker
  - ____ Come to attention
  - ____ Sustain attention
- ____ Understand the speaker
  - ____ Understand the vocabulary
  - ____ Recognize and select important points
  - ____ Follow a sequence of ideas
  - ____ Understand organizational cues (*first, then*)
- ____ Attend to transitional statements ("Next, I will")
  - ____ Understand verbal emphasis cues ("This is important")
  - ____ Understand nonverbal cues (teacher moves to the front of the room)

- Ask students to relate a presentation to their own knowledge by asking them what else this talk reminded them of or what else they know about the topic.
- Give outlines or partially completed outlines and study guides to students before listening activities.
- Have students follow along and instruct them to try to listen for "missing" information.
- Segment your presentation into three or four smaller parts. Stop after each segment, and have students summarize the major points from each segment and summarize the entire presentation at the conclusion.

When practicing listening skills, emphasize how it is necessary to try to remember the most important information and the sequence of events. Have students generate questions to use as listening guides. For example, "What is the purpose of this lecture?" or "What should I remember from this presentation?" These activities will prepare students for taking notes during lectures. There are, however, some ways you can adjust any lecture or use direct instruction for lower grade levels to effect better listening, as discussed next.

Adjust Lectures You can include simple techniques during lectures to help facilitate listening and note taking for students (Carter et al., 2011):

- Begin presentations by stating the overall objectives, such as, "Today I will be talking about a, b, and c."
- Include key words and emphasize their use during the presentations by saying in a louder voice, "This is *very* important," "Here are the three major points," "Listen to this and see if you can ____," or "There are five explanations for this event, and they are . . ."
- Write key points on a PowerPoint slide, chalkboard, or dry-erase board while presenting.
- Adjust the pace of the presentation to accommodate students who are taking notes.
- Present schematic diagrams that explain complex concepts or use concrete manipulatives whenever possible to accompany verbal information. The use of visual representations can be especially helpful for English learners who may have the conceptual knowledge but not the linguistic knowledge (Goldenberg, 2013).
- Stop frequently and encourage students to ask questions about the presented information and have them summarize the content to peers.
- Ask students to predict what a test on the material might include.
- Include "errors" in your talk and ask students to try to find the errors.

Finally, check with any students you suspect might need assistance to see if they obtained the necessary content or if they have any questions. Schedule extra help sessions, office hours, or study sessions when needed.

PLAN FOR SPECIAL LISTENING PROBLEMS Sometimes there are special problems encountered by students with disabilities during oral presentations. Some of these include the following:

- The pace of the presenter is too rapid.
- The amount of information given is too great.
- Students lack prior knowledge on the presentation topic.
- The language is too difficult.
- Students have difficulties processing and organizing information.

Some presenters speak too rapidly for students with disabilities or students learning English as a second language to comprehend. When this occurs, ask lecturers to slow down and write major points on a PowerPoint slide or dry-erase board while speaking. The act of writing while speaking may slow the rate of presentation sufficiently for students. It is appropriate to ask presenters to repeat information to provide an additional opportunity for students to hear the same information. Record important presentations that are presented rapidly, place recordings on reserve or at a listening center, and encourage students to listen to the recordings again for review. If variable-speed audio recorders are available, students can play recordings at a comfortable speed for themselves.

The following scenario describes what Mrs. Goodwin does to help her students with disabilities become more familiar with new vocabulary in their general education classes.

CLASSROOM SCENARIO

Mrs. Goodwin

Mrs. Goodwin, a special education teacher, provides all her elementary students with lists of vocabulary words that will be covered in future units. She passes the lists out a couple of weeks before the unit is introduced to pre-teach the vocabulary. All students read the words to her and to their parents/caregivers daily. This familiarizes them with upcoming vocabulary so that when they hear the words in general education classes, they are already familiar with them. For her students who are learning English, Mrs. Goodwin also encourages cross-linguistic connections by pointing out cognates in certain words, when relevant (e.g., *genetic* in English, *genetico* in Spanish). Knowing the vocabulary often puts students with disabilities one jump ahead of general education students and thus builds self-esteem. The general education teachers tell Mrs. Goodwin that because of this extra practice, students with disabilities are better able to keep up with classwork in the new units. Students also seem to enjoy using the vocabulary lists.

QUESTIONS FOR REFLECTION

1. How would you decide which words should be targeted for practice?
2. What would be the best ways to communicate with parents or caregivers about the vocabulary-learning task?
3. Could you employ a similar technique for material other than vocabulary?

Finally, some students have severe processing and organizing difficulties during listening activities. These students may require oral information to be repeated slowly before they are able to comprehend it. Handouts containing major points as well as assistance from special education teachers and speech and language specialists can provide students extra review and practice on the information covered. Also, enlist the help of peer assistants, siblings, and parents/caregivers to provide additional review and practice at home. Don't forget to use the PASS variables to determine whether all information presented is essential for all students and that it is appropriately adapted, instructed, and evaluated.

Pearson eTextbook

Video Example 11.3

This video shows how students record notes after completing a science investigation. Notice how the students' notes are organized to record observations and reflections about those observations.

STRATEGIES FOR TEACHING NOTE-TAKING SKILLS

Note taking provides students with a greater depth of processing of information and can be used to review information presented orally (Carter et al., 2011). Note-taking skills become increasingly important as grade levels increase (Deshler & Schumaker, 2006), and secondary teachers expect students to have good note-taking skills. However, many students, particularly those with disabilities, are not skilled in taking good notes and can benefit from instruction on effective note taking (Boyle, 2010; Boyle & Forchelli, 2014; see also the *Research Highlight*). Several important skills are critical for successful note taking and are listed in the teacher checklist in Figure 11.7 (see also Boyle, 2007). Determine which skills students need help with and ensure that they acquire these skills.

TEACH NOTE-TAKING SKILLS AND STRATEGIES Teach students that the purpose of notes is to facilitate recall and comprehension of information presented during lectures. Reviewing notes regularly, and particularly just before an exam, can increase a student's chances for success (Carter et al., 2011).

Be Prepared Helping students learn how they can be prepared to take notes will promote more self-sufficiency. Be sure they have the right type of paper and pencils or pens, or technology, to take notes. Encourage students to select the device or type of paper or pen that is best for them. Allowing students to select their own note-taking materials may help motivate them during note-taking activities. Tell students to write the date and topic of the lecture at the top of their papers (Boyle, 2007).

Teach How to Write Short Summaries Showing students how to write summary ideas rather than entire sentences assists them in becoming better at taking notes. Demonstrate with examples of good notes and poor notes. Good notes contain major ideas in students' own words and can be used for studying. Poor notes contain lots of unnecessary words, such as *the*, *if*, *and*, or *but*, or entire verbatim sentences. These practices may make it much more difficult to take notes efficiently, as well as result in notes that are difficult to study.

Figure 11.7 Checklist for Prerequisite Skills for Note Taking

Does the student have:

- _____ Listening skills?
- _____ Handwriting skills?
  - _____ Is the student's handwriting legible?
  - _____ Can the student write rapidly enough?
- _____ Keyboarding skills?
  - _____ Can the student type fast enough?
  - _____ Are computers and power sources readily available?

Can the student:

- _____ Determine the purpose of lectures?
- _____ Determine a plan of organization for notes?
- _____ Summarize and relate main ideas?
- _____ Write down main points?
- _____ Use abbreviations?

Does the student:

- _____ Read and revise notes?
- _____ Study notes?

Research Highlight

Note-Taking Skills of Secondary Students Using Smartpens*

*Smartpens– Livescribe Inc. (US)**

Success in content-area classes requires listening to lectures and recalling important content from those lectures. Teachers may emphasize important vocabulary, note critical points (e.g., Common Core content), and summarize content during lectures. Note taking can help organize and maintain permanent products from lectures while students process lecture content. Note taking, however, is not always an easy task for all students. Note taking requires metacognitive skills, attention, memory, and expressive writing skills. Boyle and Forchelli (2014) compared the note-taking skills of middle school students with learning disabilities, average achievers, and high achievers. Findings revealed that students with learning disabilities struggled to complete notes containing key points and vocabulary compared with higher-achieving peers. Effective note-taking strategies involve multiple skills including understanding teachers' important verbal cues, selecting important vocabulary and their definitions, and proofing notes for clarifications and elaborations. Boyle and Joyce (2019) and Joyce and Boyle (2020) extended their note-taking research with high school students with and without disabilities who were taught to use Smartpens. Smartpens, which resemble a regular pen, allow students to record the audio lecture and write notes simultaneously using special dot-designed paper.

- In the first study, Boyle and Joyce (2019) taught students the TARGET strategy in which:

  T was Tap the pen's record button,
  A was Activate by writing the topic and names and date on the page,
  R was Record or write the main points,
  G was Grab all vocabulary words and their definitions,
  E was end and stop the record button and changing from black to red color ink, and
  T was touch up or amend notes as necessary. After using the Smartpen strategy, findings indicated that students recorded more main points, more words, and modified notes with more additional information compared with students who used their typical note-taking methods.

- Joyce and Boyle (2020) extended the work by refining the Smartpen strategy to include more specificity with additional steps (JIGSAW).

  J for Jump to recording with pen;
  I for Initiate note taking;
  G for Grab cues, content, vocabulary, and definitions;
  S for Scan for missing content;
  A for Amend, correct, or elaborate notes; and
  W for Write a three-sentence summary. JIG was intended to be the note-taking strategy while SAW was to be completed within 5 minutes after the lecture ended. Results revealed significant effects favoring students with and without disabilities in the experimental group for total words, vocabulary, and amended notes.

These are promising findings for teaching note-taking skills with the use of Smartpens. Additional research is needed to extend the research across content areas for longer durations of intervention.

*Other companies have also marketed similar versions of Smartpens.

QUESTIONS FOR REFLECTION

1. How do students normally learn how to take effective notes?
2. What can be done to improve note-taking skills for students who struggle?
3. What would be good ways to support students while they learn note-taking skills?
4. How could you implement the use of Smartpens or other technologies to improve note taking?

Ask Questions for Clarification Encouraging students to ask you to repeat information or clarify the major purpose of lessons helps you monitor whether they know what to write in their notes. A good way to start is to have students ask what the purpose of the lecture is. You can help students with this process by explicitly stating the purpose of the lecture and describing an overall plan of organization before beginning a lecture.

Teach Abbreviations Using abbreviations reduces the amount of writing and increases the speed of note taking. Teach commonly used abbreviations and have students generate a list of words and possible abbreviations. For example, "w/" for *with*, "MD" for *doctor*, "<" for *less than*, and "ave." for *average* can easily be taught and are fairly easy to decipher later. Design practice activities containing common abbreviations and have students practice using and interpreting the abbreviations.

Use Specific Formats for Note Taking Different note-taking formats may be helpful in many cases (Boyle & Rivera, 2012). Depending on the subject areas in which you teach, you may choose a particular format and encourage students to use it consistently. For example, notes can be written in one column, with key words, questions, or comments in another column. Summaries are sometimes included in a space at the bottom of the page. Distribute blank template sheets containing a specific format, explain how it works, and discuss why you consider it an effective note-taking format. Figure 11.8 displays a note-taking format that you might consider. Show students the importance of leaving spaces in their notes for additions or changes after the lecture or writing on every other line.

Supplying guided notes to students helps decrease the amount of writing and increase the focus on major ideas. Guided notes are similar to partial outlines, but they usually contain more spaces for students to fill in important details during the lectures (Konrad et al., 2011). Some teachers have students complete guided notes or partial outlines together as a class activity to ensure that students are obtaining critical information from lectures. Guided notes may be especially beneficial for topics that contain a great deal of new vocabulary and concepts and that are directly linked to Common Core content. Figures 11.9 and 11.10 contain examples of partial outlines and guided notes.

Teach Speed and Accuracy Techniques Start by demonstrating what good note-takers do. Have students share the ways they take notes. For example, some students never take extra time to erase mistakes in their notes; they simply draw a single line through errors. Encouraging students to develop methods and strategies with which they feel comfortable will help them be more effective.

Teach Students How to Study Using Notes Don't forget to show students what to do with their notes. Many students take notes, close their notebooks after class, and never look at them again. Direct students to review notes after each class and make any corrections or clarifications (Boyle, 2007; Boyle et al., 2014). They should also jot down questions they may need to clarify later. Show students how they can attach "sticky notes" to various pages in their notes to remind them of places with questions.

Finally, teach students how to study using their notes by helping them identify the most important information to study. Then show them how to generate study strategies to facilitate recall and understanding of that important information (e.g., Wong, 2015). Demonstrate strategies to help them remember information in their notes. Explain how they can use their notes to supplement their textbooks when studying for exams.

Figure 11.8 Sample Note-Taking Format

Class | Date

New Information	Questions or Comments

Figure 11.9 Guided Notes

Class: Social Studies   Topic: Products of Indiana   Date: 4/1

Major Ideas	Details	Questions
Agriculture	**Major Crops:** Corn ________ ________	**Where within the state are the various crops grown?** **What are the products of the major industries?**
Industry	**Major Industries** Steel ________ ________	**Where are the major industrial areas located and why?**

Figure 11.10 Partial Outline

Initially, provide many of the elements of the partial outline for your students. As students learn the format you can leave more elements blank.

ARTHROPODS

I. What is an arthropod?
   A. Largest phylum of animals
   B. More than 3/4 of all animals
II. Characteristics of arthropods.
   A. Jointed legs
   B. Exoskeleton
   C. Special heart and blood
III. Types of arthropods
   A. Crustaceans
      1. Crabs
      2. Lobsters
   B. Insects
      1. Beetles
      2.
      3.
   C. Centipedes
   D. Millipedes

The AWARE Strategy The **AWARE strategy** was developed for college students with learning disabilities, but it can be adapted for students in secondary settings (Boyle et al., 2015; Suritsky & Hughes, 1996). The five steps in AWARE are the following:

1. **A**rrange to take notes.
2. **W**rite quickly.
3. **A**pply cues.
4. **R**eview notes as soon as possible.
5. **E**dit notes. (Suritsky & Hughes, 1996, p. 308).

Each major strategy step can remind students of additional steps to implement. For example, "Arrange to take notes" refers to getting to class with all required materials, such as a notebook, writing materials, a laptop, a Chromebook, or a tablet such as an iPad. Even if students are audio-recording the lecture, it is a good idea to take some notes on verbal cues or highlighted content. The AWARE strategy can easily be adapted for students in secondary schools. You might try this strategy in your own college courses so you can teach it to students. Provide opportunities to review and offer feedback during the initial phases of instruction.

Strategic Note Taking Boyle and Weishaar (2001) provided students with mild disabilities a note-taking form to guide their note taking during class. The form prompted students, before the lecture began, to provide the name of the topic and their prior knowledge about the topic. During the lecture, they were prompted to write, on each page, three to seven points, including details and summaries. At the end of the lecture, they were directed to write and explain five summary points. Students who had used the note-taking form scored higher on immediate and long-term recall, comprehension, and the number of notes taken.

Note-Taking Apps Apps for note-taking assistance are available for personal tablets. Digital note taking is a great way of ensuring students have access to their notes through their devices. Students with a note-taking accommodation indicated on their IEP may be able to acquire access of a pen that records as they write. Please refer to the *Apps for Education* feature in Chapter 10 for technology related to note taking. These applications can be very helpful for all students, particularly those who exhibit difficulty with note taking. However, many students with disabilities will need assistance in implementing systematic use of the app. Practice applying the app in real classroom situations, and demonstrate to students how information collected in this way can be used to maximize learning and later test performance.

ADDRESS SPECIAL NOTE-TAKING PROBLEMS Some students may experience great difficulties with note taking, in spite of attempts to teach skills to make all students successful. Table 11.1 lists some special problems that may be encountered by students when trying to take notes, as well as possible solutions that may help students overcome some of those problems.

TABLE 11.1 Special Problems with Note Taking and Possible Adaptations

Note-Taking Problem	Possible Solutions
Speed of note taking	• Provide basic outline as a handout. • Model outlining on the blackboard. • Use PowerPoint presentations during lectures. • Print slides for students.
Legibility	• Show how illegibility can affect the value of notes. • Use manuscript when needed. • Model "shorthand" and abbreviations. • Provide a variety of paper and pens, or tablets. • Use of technology, such as Chromebook for typing notes or an iPad and apple pencil. • Use recording devices and demonstrate their use.
Deciding what to write	• Organize lectures logically. • Present key points on board or slides as you lecture. • Provide guided notes as handouts or templates for students.
Deciding how to organize	• Provide a note-taking format, outlines, or guided notes. • Teach a particular note-taking strategy that suits your class.
Learning how to use notes	• Show how to review, correct, and elaborate on notes. • Model how to use notes for studying. • Schedule time for reviewing notes during class.

Research and Reference Skills

Learning Objective 11.2 Demonstrate familiarity with various research and reference skills necessary for successfully completing reports or projects.

Although many general education students possess adequate knowledge of library and researching skills, students with diverse learning needs benefit from explicit instruction, practice, and feedback when learning and using the process (Hoover & Patton, 2006). Students need to know how to use reference materials such as reference books, indexes (e.g., periodical guides), computer-assisted literature and encyclopedia searches, and Internet search engines. You can increase your students' motivation for these activities by always encouraging students to ask questions and to search for the answers. Statements like "That's an excellent question!", "What is a question we'd like to find the answer for?", and "How can we find the answer?" will show your students you value lifelong learning and library and research skills.

STRATEGIES FOR TEACHING LIBRARY SKILLS

To get students started, provide maps of the interior of libraries that indicate where various sources are located, including computer stations and the reference librarians. Arrange meetings with reference librarians so that students become familiar with them and feel comfortable asking for assistance. Librarians can schedule special instructional sessions for classes and often will meet with smaller groups of students with disabilities to provide extra guidance and practice in searching the library. Instructional sessions may initially involve a general overview of how the library functions and what is maintained in the library in both physical and electronic formats. Students will also need to become familiar with library terminology such as *library catalog*, *database*, and *call number*. Arrange to have special educators work with librarians to devise specialized training sessions for students with disabilities.

TEACH USE OF REFERENCE MATERIALS Familiarizing your students with the reference materials available in the school and public libraries can be made into a motivating activity by challenging teams of students to locate topics within all available sources. Typical materials include electronic and print versions of dictionaries, encyclopedias, biographical sources, almanacs, and various specific guidebooks, such as medical guides or natural history guides. Most reference materials are located together in libraries and usually cannot be checked out. Because print materials are often shelved in alphabetical order, provide practice or reference sheets containing the alphabet for younger students who have difficulty recalling alphabetical order. Summary guides listing reference books, types of information, and locations can serve as library guides for students. Many libraries provide their own guided tours and assistance with online reference sources. Setting up practice activities during which students are required to find and identify different pieces of information benefits all students. These activities can be made more exciting by arranging practice as part of a scavenger hunt game, conducted in the library or online. Grouping students into scavenger hunt teams may help inspire them, perhaps demonstrating how much fun it is to discover new information.

TEACH STUDENTS HOW TO USE DATABASES Many students will benefit from instruction on reference databases. Available databases may vary depending on whether the library is housed at an elementary, middle, or secondary school. High schools may have many more databases available than elementary schools. Subject areas may be identified, for example, biography, business, English/language arts, lifestyle, or science. By clicking on the appropriate subject, students can search for relevant references in a variety of areas. For example, consider a search for information about U.S. president Zachary Taylor. Clicking on a "biography" reveals a source such as the Gale Biography in Context™ database. This source provides a general entry on Taylor's life, followed by a featured article from the *Encyclopedia of World Biography*. Following these are a number of other sources, including news services, academic journals, websites, references, and magazines. Tools are also provided that allow students to bookmark, share, or e-mail entries. Dictionary access is also included for unfamiliar vocabulary. Basic facts about Taylor, images, and related people are also included. An accompanying text-reading device allows students to have the text read to them, at varying speeds, and highlights text as it is read. This may be particularly helpful for students with reading difficulties. Such databases are not difficult to

Apps for Education

Technology to Help with Time Management and Organization

Many types of technologies exist to help students with time management and organization. Some timer applications, for example, are available for desktop use and others for tablet use such as on Apple or Android devices. Users can search on Google, on the Apple App Store, or on the Google Play Store for timers by using keywords such as *timer*, *Pomodoro*, and *focus*. One example is *Forest* (Seekrtech), which uses gamification techniques to help users stay on task. The app grows virtual "trees" that continue to grow as the user stays focused, and the trees wither away if the user leaves the app. With every focus session a user completes, trees are planted in a virtual forest, which grows over days and weeks that a user utilizes the app.

Additionally, digital calendars are everyday common tools that can be essential for supporting time management and organization in and outside of school. Balint-Langel et al. (2020) successfully taught postsecondary students with intellectual and developmental disabilities to use the eight mnemonic steps of the Calendar app.

C = Calendar app
A = Add event
L = Log title
E = Enter location
N = Note the start
D = Date and time
A = Alert
R = Remind and save.

Students can use digital calendars to create one-time, recurring, or duplicate events and they also can be used to set alarms (e.g., sound, vibration, buzz) and reminders. The events can include classes, afterschool activities, field trips, tutoring sessions, homework, or project due dates. Additionally, students can sync their digital calendars across multiple devices such as their laptops or Chromebooks, tablets, iPads, smartphones, and smartwatches. Notes within the calendar events can include location, URLs, specific to-do lists, or items to bring to the event. Students can also color-code their digital calendars to denote different settings and/or components of their lives, such as having a school calendar and a personal calendar. Common digital calendars that can be used include *Google Calendar*, *Apple Calendar*, and *Microsoft Outlook Calendar*.

Checklist apps can be a fun, motivating, and organized way for students to keep track of what homework or assignment items they need to complete while allowing them to check it off as they complete the tasks. Examples include *Google Keep*, *Wunderlist*, *Apple Notes*, *Trello*, and *Evernote*.

The organization of digital materials such as notes, presentations, homework assignments, projects, reports, and other files is critical for the success of students in today's world. Several tools can be utilized for digital organization, where students can group items together in folders, label folders, color-code, and more. Some examples include *Google Drive*, *Microsoft OneDrive*, and *Dropbox*. These tools are all cloud based and can also be synced with e-mail systems and digital calendars.

School district–sponsored systems such as learning management systems (LMS) are also a way for students, teachers, parents, and caregivers to stay organized with class assignments, tests, and grades and to maintain communication. Examples of common LMS include *Blackboard*, *Canvas*, *Edmodo*, *Class Dojo*, and *Google Classroom*. LMS permit parents/caregivers, teachers, and students to access information about the student's instruction, assignments, grades, and due dates, along with a way to communicate via e-mail, messages, and alerts.

use, although basic familiarity with computer screens, electronic devices, and use of the mouse, touchscreen, or voice-command device may be necessary for students to use them unassisted. It is also important to consider that any one individual database may not provide access to all relevant materials. The school librarian can provide specific information on the availability of various databases and how they can be used. Provide explicit practice for students with disabilities, when necessary. Students should be able to locate relevant articles, copy down (or print out) identifying information, and know how to use this information to locate the articles. You can create library search activities in which you assign pairs or small groups of students to locate specific articles and identify where they can be found. If students learn to function independently with these skills, they will be able to write more thorough and informative research papers.

TEACH USE OF LIBRARY CATALOGS Library searches can also be conducted to identify print materials and e-books that are located in the library, although familiarity with particular computer systems is necessary. Searches can be completed by author, title, and subject area, and searches can be completed on books, multimedia materials, and various databases of journals by topical area. Resulting search information is displayed and can be printed out or copied by hand.

Search results contain several important pieces of information. First, the Library of Congress or the Dewey Decimal System call numbers of books are identified, along with author and publication information such as publisher, year, and city of publication. Longer formats are usually available and display abstracts of the materials. Model how reading abstracts and other displayed information helps students decide whether those materials should be included in their search. If materials appear relevant, students can print the screen information, copy it, or save it electronically, and then locate the book in the library using the call number. Give your students self-monitoring sheets containing reminders about what information they should keep for looking up materials and for their reference lists.

Searching by author or title can be simpler than searching by topic. A title or author's name will yield all sources containing that title or name. Searching by subject topic is a little more complex, and guidance may be necessary to help narrow the descriptors. For example, if students select a broad descriptor like "pollution," several thousand entries might appear. Guide students in narrowing descriptors to focus their search efforts on a more restricted topic that yields a more realistic number of books or articles for them to scan. Divide the topic into smaller subtopics, such as air pollution, groundwater pollution, waste disposal, and agricultural pollution for the previous example. The resulting search will then be narrower and more focused on the student's interest area.

Making informed decisions about which entries should be examined more closely can be difficult. The selection process requires critical thinking, and students may need assistance to focus their thinking. Teach students to group potential sources into three categories: "Yes, definitely keep," "Maybe, look further and decide," and "No, do not keep." Be sure to review what they do to verify that they understand the process.

The next step is to obtain the "yes" and "maybe" materials and determine if they should be included. If students do not do this component of the task well, they may experience great difficulties completing the remaining steps of the project. Some of your students with disabilities may have difficulty with this component because it relies on reading and thinking skills. Model some samples for the class by speaking aloud the "thinking" you use for inclusion and exclusion of sources. Say, for example, "I will keep this abstract on the hazards of using too much fertilizer because it sounds as if it fits with my topic of agricultural pollution. But I will discard this article on toxic dumps because it doesn't seem to be related closely enough to agricultural pollution." You can divide students into small groups for practicing this task and require students to defend verbally their reasons for including or excluding abstracts.

TEACH USE OF INTERNET SEARCH ENGINES So much information can be accessed via the Internet that students should have practice in these search procedures as well. Most libraries have online access and numerous search engines to help students locate information on the Internet. Because some information from the Internet may be less reliable than information from printed sources, teach students to identify the source of the information and the reliability of that source and teach them to verify information by comparing it with other source materials. Internet search engines on computers and tablets such as iPads have embedded universal design for learning (UDL) features such as voice-to-text capability, which can be used to eliminate writing and spelling difficulties while searching for relevant sources.

STRATEGIES FOR PREPARING REPORTS AND PROJECTS

Assignments that involve writing papers are usually very challenging for students with disabilities as well as for other students in your classroom (Deshler & Schumaker, 2006; Graham et al., 2017). This writing process can be taught directly by practicing some of the subskills involved in writing a report. Ability to use the different skills of planning, reading, thinking, organizing, and writing is required for successful report writing (Muchnick, 2011).

DEFINE THE WRITING TASK SYSTEMATICALLY In defining the writing task, it is important to explain the following assignment details:

- Purpose of the writing assignment (e.g., inform, persuade, demonstrate)
- Audience for the assignment (e.g., teacher, classmates, general public)

Pearson eTextbook

Video Example 11.4

A teacher discusses how she uses technology to model for her students how to take notes when reading and how to follow the writing process.

- Format for the paper, in terms of both substance (book report, newspaper article, research report, other) and style (type, handwritten, font size and style)
- Required length in pages (or word count) and required scope and detail
- Date the assignment is due

This is also the time for students to estimate how long each step in the process will take and begin to plan a schedule for completing each step. Some of the steps may require additional subdividing. Have students record steps and due dates in their calendars. Finally, students can begin to work on the project according to their time schedules (Muchnick, 2011).

PROMOTE TOPIC SELECTION, DEVELOP A WRITING PLAN, AND BRAINSTORM IDEAS Many students have difficulties selecting topics for their papers. Provide examples of topics that appear motivating and interesting to students and also are manageable in scope.

Provide sample papers that address each purpose as models for students to see how the papers are constructed to answer the intended purpose. Maintain model papers from previous classes and, with the author's permission, provide students with access. Seeing completed models helps students visualize the final product.

The development of a writing plan is crucial for students. This component requires additional subdividing: Will books, magazines, or copies of newspaper articles be needed from the library? Will reading and taking notes from those resources be required? Will students need to interview experts on the topic? Will visits to museums be necessary? This plan will vary depending on the topic and purpose of the assignment.

Show students sample writing plans from different types of written projects. Again, model the development of plans during instruction. Have students complete partially developed plans before attempting to complete plans independently. During the actual writing of assignments, have students bring in their plans so that you can provide guidance and corrective feedback.

Once the writing topic has been selected, students need to brainstorm ideas for details. Model how, during the brainstorming process, all ideas are written down and allow students opportunities to practice the brainstorming component. Then demonstrate how the brainstormed ideas are evaluated later for relevancy and how determinations are made as to whether to include them within the paper. After that, the relevant ideas are listed in order of importance for the project.

COLLECT AND ORGANIZE IDEAS AND INFORMATION Lead students to collect and find the necessary information for writing their papers. As described previously, students may use the library, the Internet, other reference materials, or interviews depending on the paper topic and format required. Demonstrate how to find and collect information.

At this stage, students may write a more detailed outline for their papers. Notes from the obtained information can be included in the outline. Traditional outlines may or may not be used but be sure to model how the use of an organizational framework facilitates the organization of the paper and assists students in completing the written product. A format may consist of titles, main ideas, supporting details under each main idea, and summary and conclusion sections. One key factor is to show students how to use the major purpose of the paper to guide the major subheadings for the paper.

WRITE FIRST DRAFT OF PAPER AND OBTAIN FEEDBACK After completing the organizational outline or format, have students write the first draft of the paper. It should be relatively easy to write a first draft if note cards containing major points and outlines are used. Each organizational heading becomes a major section of the draft, and students put that information into sentences in their own words. Then, elaborations are added to those main ideas and details to complete the rough draft. At this point or earlier, you may need to explain why copying articles is not allowed and that it is called plagiarism. Explain how you want your students to cite the information they are using for their papers. This may be especially important if students are downloading complete documents from the Internet.

Encourage students to obtain feedback from someone on their first drafts. The feedback provides them with information about what needs to be revised before completing their final versions. Teachers, parents, caregivers, siblings, and peers can all be asked for feedback on draft versions.

When possible, have students meet in pairs or small groups to provide constructive feedback on one another's draft reports. This should be done in a systematic way with practice opportunities so that both peers clearly understand the evaluation criteria. One example is the Peer Revising Strategy (MacArthur, 2016). Part of the strategy includes a checklist of steps that prompts the reviewer to (1) Listen and read, (2) Tell what the paper is about, (3) Tell what you liked best, (4) Read and make notes; Is everything clear? Can any details be added?, and (5) Discuss your suggestions with the writer.

REVISE AND REWRITE, PROOF, AND EDIT FINAL VERSION Students should then incorporate the feedback into the revision of their drafts. Explain to students how a revision process may involve several changes to the draft. Most revisions employ grammatical, syntactical, semantic, and punctuation changes to improve the paper.

Even though you will probably notice reluctant students, explain to them how important it is to edit the paper one final time. It is during this final editing and proofing stage that additional errors are often detected.

Writing papers or completing independent projects is difficult for many students, but it is critical for success in secondary schools and higher education (Englert et al., 2009). Without instruction in the entire process of writing papers and completing independent projects, many students may fail to achieve in this important area. However, by providing extra instruction in the process of writing, students may be better prepared to write papers and they will be more likely to be successful in school.

11 Summary

- Students with disabilities and those at risk for failure in school benefit from explicit instruction and practice with tools to develop as independent learners, using personal organizational skills and strategies for completing homework, for effective listening, note-taking, and study skills.
  - Personal organization skills, such as knowing about class times and schedules, using assignment notebooks and monthly planners, and organizing homework, are important for success in school and can be effectively taught to students with disabilities.
  - All students benefit from clearly stated expectations, such as those for the completion of homework.
  - Direct teaching of listening skills helps students with disabilities be prepared to learn information presented orally in school.
  - Teaching students ways to take notes—including writing short summaries, using abbreviations, using specific note-taking formats and strategies, and applying appropriate technology—facilitates learning from lectures and presentations.
- Practice and instruction in using the library, including the use of reference materials and indices, online literature searches, and Internet search engines, assists students with disabilities in learning how to search for and locate resources for schoolwork.
  - Direct instruction on how to write a research paper, including selecting topics, searching for information, organizing information, writing and editing first drafts, and preparing final versions, is essential for most students with disabilities.

PROFESSIONAL STANDARDS LINK: Teaching Study Skills

Information in this chapter links most directly to:

- CEC 2020 Initial Practice-Based Professional Preparation Standards for Special Educators (Initial K–12 standards) (see https://exceptionalchildren.org/standards/initial-practice-based-professional-preparation-standards-special-educators): 2 (Understanding and Addressing Each Individual's Developmental Learning Needs), 3 (Demonstrating Subject Matter Content and Specialized Curricular Knowledge, 5 (Supporting Learning Using Effective Instruction)
- InTASC Standards (see https://www.ccsso.org/sites/default/files/2017-11/InTASC_Model_Core_Teaching_Standards_2011.pdf): 2 (Learning Differences), 7 (Planning for Instruction), 8 (Instructional Strategies)

TEACHING STUDY SKILLS

If a student is having difficulty with study skills—including organizational skills, listening skills, note-taking skills, and library skills—have you tried specific strategies for teaching? If not, see the pages listed here

STRATEGIES FOR DEVELOPING PERSONAL ORGANIZATIONAL SKILLS

- ☐ Post and review class and time schedules, 280–282
- ☐ Use strategies for daily, weekly, and monthly planning, 282
- ☐ Use task analysis to organize assignments, 283
- ☐ Teach strategies for homework completion, 283–287

STRATEGIES FOR PROMOTING LISTENING SKILLS

- ☐ Address requisite listening skills, 288
- ☐ Teach listening skills, 288–291
- ☐ Plan for special listening problems, 291

STRATEGIES FOR TEACHING NOTE-TAKING SKILLS

- ☐ Teach note-taking skills and strategies, 292–296
- ☐ Address special note-taking problems, 296

STRATEGIES FOR TEACHING LIBRARY SKILLS

- ☐ Teach use of reference materials, 297
- ☐ Teach students how to use databases, 297–298
- ☐ Teach use of library catalogs, 298–299
- ☐ Teach use of Internet search engines, 299

STRATEGIES FOR PREPARING REPORTS AND PROJECTS

- ☐ Define the writing task systematically, 299–300
- ☐ Promote topic selection, develop a writing plan, and brainstorm ideas, 300
- ☐ Collect and organize ideas and information, 300
- ☐ Write first draft of paper and obtain feedback, 300–301
- ☐ Revise and rewrite, proof, and edit final version, 301

Stefanschurr/123rf

CHAPTER 12

Assessment

LEARNING OBJECTIVES

After studying this chapter, you should be able to:

12.1 Identify and compare norm-referenced tests, criterion-referenced tests, and curriculum-based assessments.

12.2 Describe how to adapt different types of tests for students with disabilities.

12.3 Explain specific test-taking strategies for taking standardized tests and teacher-made tests, such as multiple-choice, true–false, matching, and essay tests.

12.4 Identify procedures and rationales for adjusting grading and scoring of tests for students with disabilities.

Tests are a significant component of education because they provide information relevant to school placement, instructional needs, and future career decisions for students. Tests are also commonly used to evaluate the academic performance of schools and their ability to help all students succeed. For example, curriculum-based measurement is highly recommended to assess the use of response-to-intervention (RTI) programming and multi-tiered systems of support (Deno, 2016; Fuchs et al., 2012). Tests, however, must be administered appropriately and interpreted correctly because they are used to inform educational decisions related to students' instruction, course placement, and high school graduation.

Teachers use a variety of assessment measures to check student progress. Teachers should be aware of different types of tests, the purposes they serve, how they can be used, and how their results can be interpreted. It is especially important for teachers, or other educators who are working with parents and caregivers, to be able to correctly interpret and share the information test results provide.

Skills for maximizing students' test performance and accommodating students with disabilities can be taught. Three high-leverage practices (HLPs) recommended by the Council for Exceptional Children (see Chapter 6) are concerned with assessment. These include the following:

Assessment

HLP 4: Use multiple sources of information to develop a comprehensive understanding of a student's strengths and needs.

HLP 5: Interpret and communicate assessment information with stakeholders to collaboratively design and implement educational programs.

HLP 6: Use student assessment data, analyze instructional practices, and make necessary adjustments that improve student outcomes (McLeskey et al., 2017).

These important practices are among those described in this chapter.

Types of Tests

Learning Objective 12.1 Identify and compare norm-referenced tests, criterion-referenced tests, and curriculum-based assessments.

In education, many different tests address many different, specific needs. One general type of test is no "better" than another because different tests serve different purposes. As a teacher, it is critical to understand what information specific tests provide and what information they do not provide.

Tests commonly used in special education are listed in Figure 12.1. School districts typically have their own policies for the selection and use of tests.

NORM-REFERENCED VERSUS CRITERION-REFERENCED TESTS

One major distinction made in testing is between **norm-referenced** and **criterion-referenced** testing. In norm-referenced testing, student performance is compared with the performance of other students who are the same age or grade level. Students receive scores such as "85th percentile," which means that the student scored higher than 85% of other students who are the same age or grade level on that particular test. Some achievement tests are norm-referenced tests.

In criterion-referenced testing, student performance is compared with predetermined specified criteria, usually considered as meeting minimal competency. A written test for a driver's license, in which individuals either pass or fail to meet a certain criterion, is a good example of a criterion-referenced test. State achievement tests are also criterion-referenced tests.

CLASSROOM SCENARIO

Nate

Mr. Montoya saw Nate in his middle school resource room for 45 minutes per day. Although much of the time was devoted to basic skills development, Mr. Montoya also allocated time to helping Nate prepare for upcoming tests. Nate had particular difficulty taking tests in his U.S. Constitution and government class, and Mr. Montoya also was having difficulty helping him. For 2 days before the test, he would work with Nate by reviewing the content and creating practice questions for him to answer. However, it seemed that no matter how well prepared Nate appeared to be, he did poorly on the test. When Mr. Montoya asked Nate why this was, he just shrugged his shoulders and said the test did not make any sense to him.

QUESTION FOR REFLECTION

1. Why didn't increasing instruction improve Nate's test scores?

Figure 12.1 Common Examples of Intelligence and Achievement Tests

Intelligence Tests

Kauffman Assessment Battery for Children–Second Edition Normative Update (KABC-II NU) (Kaufman & Kaufman, 2018; Pearson/American Guidance Service)
Stanford-Binet Intelligence Scale, 5th ed. (SB-5) (Roid, 2003; Riverside Publishing)
Wechsler Intelligence Scale for Children–V, 5th ed. (Wechsler, 2014; Pearson)

Achievement Tests

Kauffman Test of Educational Achievement, 3rd ed. (KTEA-3) (Kaufman & Kaufman, 2014; Pearson/American Guidance Service)
KeyMath-3: Diagnostic Assessment (Connolly, 2007; Pearson/American Guidance Service)
Test of Written Language–3 (TOWL) (Hammill & Larsen, 1996; Pro-Ed)
Wide Range Achievement Test–5 (WRAT5) (Wilkenson & Robertson, 2017; Pearson)
Woodcock-Johnson IV: Tests of Achievement (WJ IV ACH) (Woodcock et al., 2015; Riverside)
Woodcock Reading Mastery Tests–3rd ed. (WRMT-III) (Woodcock, 2011; Pearson/American Guidance Service)

Both norm-referenced and criterion-referenced testing can be **standardized**, which means that all students take the test under the same, or standard, conditions. The information that comes from the test results, then, assumes standardized testing conditions were applied (Salvia et al., 2016). Standardized administration procedures are published in test manuals and are expected to be closely followed for the test scores to be meaningful.

Pearson eTextbook

Video Example 12.1

This video provides an overview of norm-referenced and criterion-referenced tests. What is the difference between norm-referenced tests and criterion-referenced tests?

SUMMATIVE OR FORMATIVE ASSESSMENTS

Another important distinction to know is whether a test is **summative** or **formative** in nature. Summative testing usually refers to tests given at the end of a particular educational period following instruction. Achievement tests given at the end of a school year are good examples of summative evaluation. The purpose of summative testing is to fully identify the range of knowledge and skills learned and how much has been accomplished throughout the educational period. The results may provide implications for placement in the next educational period. Many norm-referenced tests are summative in nature, but criterion-referenced tests can also be summative if they are administered at the end of a particular educational experience. Since results of some summative assessments, such as statewide achievement tests, are received several months after the assessment is completed, teachers should also employ formative assessments.

Formative assessments are used at frequent intervals prior to or during instruction so that student progress can be evaluated and teachers can make instructional decisions (e.g., provide feedback, reteach concepts, group students based on knowledge) (Graham-Day et al., 2014). The purpose of formative assessment is to continuously check for student understanding and adjust or retain instruction, as needed (i.e., HLP 6). For example, students who are attempting to learn and remember 100 multiplication facts may take a weekly test on these facts so that the rate of growth can be evaluated and instructional modifications can be made (e.g., more time on-task) when growth is unsatisfactory. Teachers can also use these weekly results to monitor progress toward an annual individualized education program (IEP) goal and identify students' common misunderstandings or errors. Formative evaluation is most frequently used in basic-skills areas (e.g., decoding words with a long vowel–consonant–silent-*e* pattern; identifying place value of each digit).

Pearson eTextbook

Video Example 12.2

In this video, a second-grade teacher describes how she monitors students' math learning. What kind of data does she use to monitor student learning of the math curriculum and how often does she gather this type of data?

CURRICULUM-BASED ASSESSMENT

Evaluation can also be curriculum based. This means that the tests are derived directly from the curriculum being taught (Hosp et al., 2016). Most teacher-made tests are intended to evaluate student learning of the curriculum, and therefore they are types of curriculum-based tests. Distinctions have been made between **curriculum-based assessment**—which could include any procedure that evaluates student performance in relation to the school curriculum, such as weekly spelling tests—and **curriculum-based measurement**—characterized by frequent, direct measurements of critical school behaviors, which could include timed (e.g., 1- to 5-minute) tests of performance on reading, math, and writing skills (Salvia et al., 2016). Curriculum-based measurement is formative in nature, and it allows teachers to make instructional decisions about teaching and curriculum while learning is taking place.

PERFORMANCE ASSESSMENTS AND PORTFOLIO ASSESSMENTS

Other types of tests include **performance assessments** and **portfolio assessments**. Performance assessments are usually curriculum based, and they require students to engage in a process or construct some product, often on real-world tasks. Performance assessments can include such diverse outcomes as playing a piece on a piano, writing a persuasive essay, or conducting a science experiment (Johnson et al., 2009). Portfolio assessment is also usually curriculum based, and it consists of student products and other relevant information collected over time and displayed in a portfolio. All of these types of tests have relevance to students with disabilities. Table 12.1 provides examples of these types of tests applied in the context of reading.

TABLE 12.1 Examples of Reading Tests

Type of Test	Example Reading Test
Standardized, norm-referenced	Published reading achievement test administered under standardized conditions. Students may answer test questions on computerized answer sheets or give answers to an examiner in an individual administration. Student's score is compared with scores of a normative sample of students.
Criterion-referenced	Students' test scores are compared with a certain predetermined criterion level to be considered competent in reading at their grade level.
Curriculum-based assessment	The test is based on the reading curriculum materials being used in class.
Curriculum-based measurement	Students take brief tests of reading speed, accuracy, and comprehension. These scores are monitored over time to determine whether progress is adequate.
Performance assessment	Students could be asked to "perform" on a variety of reading-related tasks, such as summarizing a newspaper article, looking up a reference, or identifying a certain printed label in a store.
Portfolio assessment	Various student products relevant to reading are collected, for example, list of books read, book reports written, or audio recordings of reading selections.

Regardless of the type of test, it must be demonstrated to have **reliability** and **validity** to be of value. All measures of reliability seek to determine that the test is consistent in what it measures. No less important, validity refers to the extent to which a particular test measures what it is intended to measure. Validity is often evaluated by comparing different tests of the same skills or abilities (Salvia et al., 2016). For example, students should receive similar scores on different standardized tests of reading achievement if both tests are valid.

Adapting Tests for Students with Disabilities

Learning Objective 12.2 Describe how to adapt different types of tests for students with disabilities.

STRATEGIES FOR ADMINISTERING NORM-REFERENCED TESTS

Some students with disabilities exhibit difficulties with norm-referenced tests that may limit the reliability and validity of their test scores. Challenges may include language or communication styles (e.g., the need for a sign language interpreter or communication board), the length of the testing, attentional difficulties, or reading difficulties when reading competence is not being tested. Another threat to the validity of the individual scores of students with disabilities is that in some cases individuals with disabilities are not included in the test's standardization sample (Shapiro, 2010). Furthermore, some tests may not be fair for students from culturally diverse backgrounds (Aston & Brown, 2021; Harry & Klingner, 2014). The *Diversity, Equity, and Inclusion in the Classroom* feature describes a culturally responsive approach to designing formative and summative assessments. Special considerations, including adjustments in the testing procedure, may be helpful and necessary (see also Gollnick & Chinn, 2021; Hoover & Klingner, 2011).

Unfortunately, substantive deviations from standardized administration procedures typically limit the usefulness of the test. If, for example, an individual student is provided with a calculator as an accommodation to assist with math computation on a problem-solving subtest, the resulting score cannot be fairly compared with the scores of students who did not have access to calculators. Even though it can be argued that problem solving, and not

Diversity, Equity, and Inclusion in the Classroom

Culturally Responsive Assessments

The Individuals with Disabilities Education Act (IDEA) mandates nondiscriminatory testing in the identification of individuals with disabilities. This means testing must not discriminate on the basis of race, culture, or ethnicity and must be administered in the student's native language (see Chapter 1). But how can teachers and schools design and evaluate culturally responsive classroom assessment? Dr. Carly Evans, from the National Center for the Improvement of Educational Assessment, has developed a conceptual framework based on Stembridge's (2020) six themes of culturally responsive education (Evans, 2021). This framework is intended to assist in the design and evaluation of classroom formative and summative assessments that follow culturally responsive teaching and includes the following:

1. **Engagement.** Engagement is of critical importance in learning and assessment. Students who are not engaged in learning, or in the assessment process, cannot be expected to perform well. Students should feel some personal ownership in their assessment and should be allowed more ownership over what learning they demonstrate and the circumstances under which they do so. Assessment processes and products are more meaningful when students have more agency over their learning. Such assessments could engage students behaviorally through active participation in data collection or group work, affectively through some emotional connection to the content or participation in the assessment design, or cognitively because of the rigor or challenging nature of the assessment.
2. **Rigor.** Rigor refers to the processes going on in the mind of the student in an assessment task, for example simple recall versus strategic thinking. To be cognitively rigorous, students need to be actively engaged in demonstrating, producing, or performing; to that extent, rigor and engagement are connected. Assessment design should encourage students to use higher-order thinking skills, as well as to construct their own meanings and interpretations from content as they engage in assessment.
3. **Cultural identity.** Evans argues that culture is fluid and dynamic and that we, in our own ways, are all cultural beings. Assessment can be culturally relevant when it makes reference to culture, when it allows for students to draw upon their own cultural identities and experiences, and when it supports students in bridging their cultural and social identities with their academic identities.
4. **Relationships.** Relationships are a significant part of school learning and can affirm that their school identity can coexist with their other identities and that relationships formed in school can extend into relationships with academic content. Relationships can also be integrated into assessments through collaboration, requiring students to work together to achieve a common goal. Assessment can integrate collaboration into the experience to deepen or enhance learning.
5. **Vulnerability.** Students can feel vulnerable if they have not been sufficiently prepared to succeed on rigorous assessments. In order to support appropriate student risk taking on assessments, teachers must support sufficient formative evaluation experience on relevant measures, modeling, and feedback prior to the assessment. When collaboration is an important component of some assessment experiences, how students treat and interact with each other is of importance. Students must be able to trust their peers and should expect a supportive learning and testing environment.
6. **Assets.** Assets refers to resources that students can turn to when faced with a challenging problem or task. Assets can include habits of mind—persistence, for example—controlling impulsivity, thinking flexibly, or applying previous knowledge to new situations. Students should also be aware of how to apply their cultural capital when undertaking rigorous assessments. Teachers should be aware of, and learn to actively promote, the extent to which students can draw upon their assets during assessments.

Evans (2021) recommends that all teachers should attend to issues of engagement, rigor, cultural identity, relationships, vulnerability, and assets when designing and evaluating their classroom assessments in order to promote an overall effective, successful, and culturally responsive classroom.

Discuss: Which of the six themes of Evans's framework is easier for you to attend to when designing a classroom assessment? Which theme is more challenging?

computation, is being evaluated, and the student in question has difficulty remembering math facts, it is unknown how the students in the standardization sample would have performed if they also had access to calculators. Therefore, the student's score cannot be easily interpreted with respect to the performance of the norm group (Salvia et al., 2016). Generally, it has been suggested that accommodations are appropriate when the benefit for students with disabilities is greater than that for students without disabilities (Fuchs et al., 2000; Laitusis et al., 2012). There are instances when standardized test accommodations are considered appropriate, and several states have published state-approved test accommodations (Lazarus et al., 2009; State of New York, 2019).

USE TEST ACCOMMODATIONS Many tests allow a variety of accommodations to be made, depending on individual needs and the testing situation (paper-and-pencil, computer based). For example, students with visual impairments cannot be expected to perform appropriately on tests without accommodations such as larger print, Braille versions of the test, or accommodations such as reading the test aloud. Where text-reading skill or reading of standard fonts is not being tested, accommodations seem appropriate, and even necessary, for obtaining a valid score. These accommodations include assistance before the test is administered, setting and time accommodations, assistance with directions or other assistance during test administration, use of assistive technology, revisions of test formats, and different response formats (Feldman et al., 2011; Fuchs et al., 2006; Laitusis et al., 2012; Salvia et al., 2016), such as the following:

- Preparing the student with practice tests or teaching test-taking skills
- Altering the timing or scheduling of the test
- Extending time limits
- Spreading the test over several shorter time sessions
- Administering the test over several days
- Changing the setting, such as a smaller or distraction-free room
- Simplifying or reading directions; using sign language for directions
- Testing individually
- Altering the presentation of the test
- Simplifying the language of the test
- Providing prompts and feedback (including reinforcement)
- Allowing teachers to read the test and turn the test pages
- Providing assistive technology, such as a text-to-talk converter or visual magnification device
- Providing audio, large-print, or Braille versions
- Changing the response formats
- Allowing verbal versus written responses or responses in a test booklet rather than answer sheet
- Allowing circling of answers versus filling in answer bubbles

Pearson eTextbook

Video Example 12.3

This special education teacher describes how she applies testing accommodations for her students in the classroom. Which testing accommodations can you identify from her description?

If students perform very differently under one or more reasonable accommodations, the standardized test may not have provided an accurate depiction of the student's ability. Research is somewhat equivocal regarding some of these accommodations; for example, extended time sometimes, but not always, has a differential benefit for students with disabilities (Gregg & Nelson, 2012; Lovett, 2010). Similarly, oral accommodations, such as reading tests aloud, sometimes, but not always, appears to benefit students with disabilities (Gandhi et al., 2017; Meyer & Bouck, 2017). The variability observed in research findings on test accommodations suggests that schools and classrooms should ensure that accommodations as implemented are facilitating desired outcomes. Other research has suggested that some accommodations may benefit all students, but students with disabilities may benefit more in some cases, particularly in the areas of self-efficacy and motivation (Feldman et al., 2011).

USE UNIVERSAL DESIGN FOR LEARNING Some features of universal design for learning (UDL) may have important implications for test design and development, ultimately limiting the need for separate accommodations (Meyer et al., 2014). For example, the State of

Massachusetts (2021) mandated that state tests be administered without time limits. Other considerations might include developing tests so that directions and content are edited for maximum engagement, readability, and comprehensibility (Jones et al., 2018; Thompson et al., 2002). On computer-based assessments, UDL features could include text-to-speech technology; electronic reading supports, such as navigation assistance, spoken voice, or visual highlighting; a variety of font and lighting choices and response formats; or a special mouse, trackball, or other alternate means of keyboard access. The 2021 guidelines for Massachusetts identify universal accessibility features for all students on computer-based tests such as the highlighter tool, alternative background and font color, and the magnifier or zoom tool. More of these features may be available on tests in the future.

USE INDIVIDUALLY ADMINISTERED TESTS In addition to providing more detailed information about student performance in a particular area, individually administered tests avoid some potential problems associated with group administration, such as reading directions, working independently, and using machine-scored answer sheets. For example, in group-administered tests of reading, students may respond to more complicated formats to assess reading skills, whereas on an individually administered test, a student's individual reading can be directly assessed through interaction with the examiner. Therefore, it may be appropriate to rely more on individually administered tests for students who have difficulty taking group tests independently.

TEACH TEST-TAKING SKILLS Some students may know much of the content being tested but do not understand how to apply that knowledge on the test. In these cases, students can be given specific training in **test-taking skills** appropriate to relevant tests, or they can be administered published practice tests and given feedback on their understanding of test formats (Banks & Eaton, 2014; Salend, 2009; Scruggs & Mastropieri, 1992). Practice should include exposure to the functionality of the computer, as needed, so that skills may generalize to the testing environment. Training in test-taking skills, which is appropriate for many different types of tests, is discussed later in this chapter.

INCREASE MOTIVATION In other cases, students may have relevant skills but not be sufficiently motivated to work their hardest during the test. Teachers may be able to find a way to motivate students to take norm-referenced as well as other types of tests. Although direct rewarding of test performance may violate standardization, other motivational strategies—such as goal setting and attribution training, praising students' efforts, promoting self-efficacy and self-esteem, making the classroom atmosphere fun and enjoyable, and increasing students' personal investment. Being motivated to take a test may be helpful in increasing the validity of the test performance of less-motivated test-takers.

IMPROVE EXAMINER FAMILIARITY Some students score better on standardized tests if they are familiar with the examiner than if they are responding to an examiner they have not met before. This may be particularly true of Black and Latinx students (Fuchs & Fuchs, 1989), students with learning disabilities (Fuchs et al., 1987), students with autism (Szarko et al., 2013), and students who speak English as a second language (Carey et al., 2011). Try to arrange for an administrator who is well known by, or acquainted with, the student. If an outside examiner is used, the person should first establish rapport with the student by introducing themselves, engaging the student in personal conversation, explaining the purpose of the testing, describing test activities, and encouraging student questions (Salvia et al., 2016). Such established familiarity may improve the validity of test responses.

REQUEST ACCOMMODATIONS FOR COLLEGE ENTRANCE EXAMS Some colleges and universities may or may not require the SAT or the ACT for college entrance, and others may indicate that they are optional for students. These tests are usually administered in a student's junior or senior year of high school. Both of these tests allow special accommodations to be made for students with disabilities and/or for English learners (e.g., College Board, 2015).

Students with disabilities need to make a request for accommodations. The College Board Services for Students with Disabilities may offer accommodations if the student meets eligibility requirements. Accommodations that can be requested include extended time, small-group or private room setting, large print, alternative test form with accommodations required as noted on the student's IEP, a reader or recorder, audio recording with written form, dictated responding, a magnification device, or a four-function calculator. Similarly, the GRE General Test for entrance to a graduate or professional school provides accommodations for students with disabilities (Educational Testing Service, 2018).

STRATEGIES FOR

ADAPTING COMPETENCY-BASED LOCAL AND STATEWIDE ASSESSMENT

Many school districts employ "benchmarks" to determine standards for student achievement. The implementation of statewide competency testing, sometimes known as Common Core assessments, has helped develop common standards for educational attainment and establish educational accountability. In some states, performance on competency tests has become a requirement for graduation and other issues of school operation, and it has been referred to as "high-stakes" testing. Because of federal legislation, states today have statewide competency tests, although waivers of some of the federal requirements have been awarded to individual states (U.S. Department of Education, 2012). For example, these waivers were extended to some states recently due to the impact of the COVID-19 pandemic.

Minimum competency tests share many characteristics with norm-referenced achievement tests. Although competency tests are oriented toward competencies students are expected to attain for promotion or graduation, they are also developed for comparative purposes. Therefore, allowing adaptations for diverse learning needs while still maintaining standardization is a concern of competency tests, and this can be determined through consultation with test developers or appropriate educational agencies (e.g., school district or state department of education).

IMPLEMENT TEST ACCOMMODATIONS In many cases, testing accommodations are considered appropriate because they better allow some students to demonstrate what they know. Because many students with disabilities may need accommodations, the IDEA requires that individual student IEPs provide testing accommodations for state tests as well as district and teacher-made tests (Center for Parent Information & Resources, 2020). Most states provide standard accommodations that are permissible on statewide competency tests (e.g., State of Georgia, 2021). It is important that these accommodations do not change the nature of the test, for example, by reading passages to students on a test of reading comprehension (Salend, 2008).

Lazarus et al. (2009) studied state accommodation policies over time to determine how changes had occurred. They found that earlier reports focused on "leveling the playing field" (p. 67) for students with disabilities, whereas more recent reports focused on the test validity of the accommodations (Albus et al., 2020; Kettler, 2015). More recent policies have generally supported the use of technology and extended time limits in appropriate cases; however, other accommodations, such as using calculators, reading questions aloud, and using spell checkers, have less consensus across states. For future assessments, states may need to consider policies regarding the delivery of the read-aloud accommodation (in-person read aloud, voice recordings, text-to-speech) and the use of online calculators for computerized high-stakes testing (Gelbart, 2018; Rogers et al., 2019). Teachers should check with state policy when implementing accommodations for statewide assessments.

Salend (2008, p. 17) also described *linguistically based* accommodations, including using familiar language, repeating directions, teaching the language of testing, translating tests, allowing responses in different languages or dialects, providing translators, and using multilingual materials. Cawthon (2008) surveyed professionals working with students who are Deaf or hard of hearing and reported that accommodations for statewide testing most commonly reported included extra time, small-group administration, and test items and directions read or interpreted.

Some research has been conducted on the effectiveness of accommodations in statewide assessments. To date, the results of this research are somewhat inconsistent and equivocal (Lindstrom, 2017). Lai and Berkeley (2012) suggested that the effects of accommodations should be evaluated for individual students during classroom-testing situations before determining if the accommodations are needed to support the performance of students on statewide assessments.

USE ALTERNATE ASSESSMENTS Standard statewide assessments may not be appropriate for some students with disabilities even with accommodations, including those with significant cognitive disabilities or nonverbal students with autism. A students' IEP team can decide that it may be appropriate to deliver *alternate assessment procedures based on alternate achievement standards* (AA-AAS) in order to effectively participate within large-scale assessments (Clark & Karvonen, 2020). All states have developed these alternative assessments. In the state of Virginia, for example, students for whom the state competency tests are not considered appropriate may participate in the Virginia Alternate Assessment Program (VAAP). The summative assessments were created to evaluate the performance of students with significant cognitive disabilities in third to eighth grades and in high school across the content areas of reading, mathematics, and science (Training and Technical Assistance Center at the George Mason University, 2021). The VAAP are based on Virginia Essentialized Standards of Learning (VESOL). The VESOL have been reduced in depth, breadth, and difficulty as related to the Virginia Standards of Learning. For example, in grade 5 for science, the standards include a category on living systems. Students are expected to investigate and understand organisms including their physical characteristics, cell structures, and behaviors and how their traits help them to survive. A multiple-choice practice test item on the VAAP for a fifth-grade student with significant cognitive disabilities includes an image of a mouse and a question underneath asking, *Which does a mouse need to survive?* The practice test item presents three pictures with the words beneath as answer choices, A. rocks, B. water, and C. car. In most cases, the test question and answer choices would be read aloud to the student.

Prior to the reauthorization of the Elementary and Secondary Education Act as the Every Student Succeeds Act, other alternative test formats included *assessments based upon modified achievement standards* (AA-MAS) or the *alternate assessments based upon grade-level assessments* (AA-GLAS) (Quenemoen & Thurlow, 2017). The purpose of providing modifications is to improve the accessibility of state tests for students with profound intellectual disabilities. For the AA-AAS, IEP teams can consider allowable state accommodations to support the inclusion of these students in educational assessments (Jamgochian & Ketterlin-Geller, 2015).

REQUEST ACCOMMODATIONS ON GED TESTS Competency tests also include the General Educational Development (GED) Test. GED tests evaluate the knowledge and skills that are intended to have been acquired from a 4-year high school program but that may have been acquired in a different manner, such as through independent study or tutoring. Students with disabilities who have not graduated from high school but believe they have met high school graduation criteria can take the GED tests. Individuals wishing to take the GED tests must be a resident of the state in which the test is administered, and they usually must be older than 18 years of age. Also, students must not be enrolled in a public school; so, as a teacher, you may have little direct interaction with students taking the GED tests. However, you may be able to provide information about the GED tests to students who are about to leave school without graduating or to former students who may ask you for assistance in taking the GED tests.

Individuals with disabilities may apply for special testing accommodations by creating an online account at https://GED.com and submitting a request. Guidelines on the GED tests website identify different accommodations available for students with learning and cognitive disabilities, attention-deficit/hyperactivity disorder (ADHD), physical disabilities, and other disabilities. Accommodations are made on a case-by-case basis once an individual has submitted a request online.

Another state-authorized exam in addition to the GED tests is the High School Equivalency Test (HiSET) (see https://hiset.ets.org). Like the GED tests, a pass or failing score is used to determine if a state will issue the high school equivalency certificate to the student. The HiSET also provides accommodations for individuals with disabilities.

STRATEGIES FOR ADAPTING TEACHER-MADE AND CRITERION-REFERENCED TESTS

Classroom test scores represent a significant component of student grades (Boyle, 2013). In addition, the use of state high-stakes testing places added demands on students with disabilities. Clearly, helping students be successful in dealing with the challenges of testing is critical to promoting school success. The *Apps for Education* feature provides suggestions for collecting records and monitoring progress more efficiently.

Technology Tools to Collect and Manage Student Assessment Data

The need to collect ongoing data and maintain clear, accurate records of student performance and progress is important in education, especially when monitoring the progress of students with disabilities who are included in general education classes. Organized systems for gathering, creating, and maintaining recordkeeping for students' assignments, homework, grades, attendance, portfolio assessment products, and progress monitoring will greatly reduce the amount of noninstructional time that teachers spend on these tasks. Current technologies facilitate ways to collect and manage student assessment data.

Collecting Assessment Data

Formative Assessment Data. Whereas formal formative assessments are typically conducted at prespecified times (i.e., benchmarks, short cycles), informal formative assessments are a part of everyday student learning (Graham-Day et al., 2014). In order to check for student understanding and shift instruction in the moment, teachers ask questions, lead discussions, and assign classroom and homework assignments to evaluate what students know. Technology tools such as *Flipgrid, Nearpod, ClassFlow, Kahoot!,* and *Pear Deck* offer interactive and engaging ways to quickly assess students' understanding of learning objectives throughout instruction. On these multimodal platforms, students insert individual responses to a question type on their device or they may add content to an interactive whiteboard. Another type of informal formative evaluation is poll questions (e.g., Poll Everywhere) to assess student learning. Students use a hand-held device or laptop to provide responses and teachers instantly receive individual responses from students. Educators can also collect data through online surveying or testing students with common data analysis software such as *Google Forms, Survey Monkey,* and *Qualtrics.*

Portfolio Assessments. Software enabling the use of multimedia is available that can assist with the maintenance of portfolio assessment materials. Teachers can manage their own as well as their students' portfolios using available software. Teachers can show their students how to compile their own portfolios using the available technology. Some examples of digital portfolio software include *SeeSaw* and *DIGIcation.* Common multimedia software can also be used to create digital portfolios, including *Microsoft PowerPoint, Apple Keynote, Prezi,* and *Google Slides.* With these tools, students can directly link assignments, projects, and other digital artifacts they have created from their Google Drive or other online platforms they regularly use. Digital portfolios can thus be created and stored online through a single link that can be shared with educators, parents/caregivers, and stored for future reference within a student's school career.

Curriculum-based measurement (CBM). CBM is one way to monitor student progress in academic areas. See Table 7.1 in Chapter 7 for a list of CBM measures for academic progress monitoring. As described in this chapter, teachers can develop their own CBM measures; however, software programs and websites are available to design probes, graph student performance, and facilitate the process of using CBM in basic skills such as reading, math, and spelling. For example, after registering and creating a login, easyCBM (easyCBM.com) is an accessible assessment system to be used at both the elementary and secondary levels. Teachers can select targeted measures related to reading fluency, reading comprehension, and/or math under a selected grade level. Students can take the CBM directly on the computer and the program will automatically score and report results.

The website Numberfly (https://numberfly.net) also allows teachers to create CBMs for early math fluency. For example, teachers can customize a CBM probe for quantity discrimination by selecting the lowest and highest numbers to be included, the number of problems in each row, and how many rows to include on the probe. A paper-based probe for the student is then generated, along with an answer key. In addition, directions for applying the CBM to the implementation of RTI and a time-series graph to chart student progress are provided.

Some software programs not only generate and administer online screening and progress monitoring curriculum-based measures, but also score, store, graph, and automatically analyze and aggregate the data with other sources related to behavior and social-emotional needs. Examples include RTI & MTSS Program Management (formerly *RTIm Direct*) (Frontline) and *aimsweb Plus*™ (Pearson).

Managing Assessment Data

Software that can assist with managing students' assignments, homework, attendance, behavior, and grades, as well as both student and caregiver reports, include learning management systems (LMS). Some common examples of LMS include *Blackboard, Canvas, Edmodo, Class*

Technology Tools to Collect and Manage Student Assessment Data—*continued*

Dojo, and *Google Classroom*. LMS permit caregivers, teachers, and students to remain constantly updated about students' instruction, assignments, behavior, grades, due dates, and much more. Teachers can also choose to manage data and create visual graphs of student data using spreadsheets such as *Microsoft Excel*, *Google Sheets*, and *Apple Numbers*.

A program to help special education teams develop and monitor progress of IEP goals for K–12 students is the *Goalbook Toolkit* application (https://goalbookapp.com). Goalbook takes college and career readiness standards and helps teachers to create specific and measurable learning goals that are aligned to the standard and/or modified as needed for varying student levels. The program also provides teachers with a selection of instructional strategies based on subject and grade level to consider when creating lesson plans.

Apps that manage data collection are also available. For example, *CentralReach* (CentralReach LLC) is a HIPAA-compliant data management system that allows practitioners and educators to organize, streamline, and manage data related to students with autism, including information about their IEPs and behavior plans. Some features include inputting and storing behavioral and educational data, analyzing data, and creating visuals to represent data.

Teachers can adapt their own tests in much the same way that other tests are adapted. However, be careful to ensure that your adaptations are having the desired effect of accommodating the student's disability. For example, Lewandowski et al. (2007) reported that students with ADHD gained less than the students without ADHD from extended time limits on a math computation assessment. Lai and Berkeley's (2012) review of the effectiveness of testing accommodations also noted that extended time provided no differential boost for students with learning disabilities.

REVISE TESTS In the earlier scenario, Nate performed well on answering questions on the chapter posed by the resource teacher, but he performed poorly on the actual test covering the U.S. Constitution and government. Because he apparently knew much of the required information, it is possible that Nate did not fully understand the format of the teacher-made test. Although training in test-taking skills may be important for Nate in this case, it is also possible that the social studies teacher could be encouraged to make some changes to the format of the test so that students will better understand what is required of them, as shown in the continuation of the scenario.

Most teachers view reasonable testing accommodations favorably, particularly if they are easy to make (Jayanthi et al., 1996; Stufft et al., 2009). Salend (1995) surveyed the literature on test design and concluded that poorly or carelessly designed tests can negatively impact student performance. Well-designed tests, on the other hand, can be useful for all students.

CLASSROOM SCENARIO

Nate

Mr. Montoya made an appointment to speak to Nate's social studies teacher, Ms. Leet. She acknowledged that Nate was not doing well on the tests and expressed a willingness to help solve the problem. Mr. Montoya and Ms. Leet examined the tests together, and Mr. Montoya noted that he believed Nate did know the answer to several of the questions that he had answered incorrectly. It appeared that he was more likely to answer questions incorrectly when the items contained double negatives, when items contained potentially confusing options such as "(e) all of the above except (b)," and when the test called for matching two columns of information. Mr. Montoya agreed to provide Nate with practice on test-taking skills and to provide practice tests that more closely resembled Ms. Leet's tests, and Ms. Leet agreed to make adjustments in her tests to make the individual items more understandable. She also asked her class to provide her with some sample items that they thought should be on the test.

With his training in test-taking skills and Ms. Leet's test revisions, Nate's scores increased from an average of D– to an average of C–. In addition, Ms. Leet found that the average score of her entire class seemed to improve.

QUESTIONS FOR REFLECTION

1. If test scores improve, how could you know if your revised tests are more easily understandable or simply easier?
2. What kind of students would you expect to benefit most from test revisions?
3. How could you determine what aspects of your tests need revision?

Adjust Test Formats Format adjustments that can be generally employed on teacher-made tests include the following (Gajria et al., 1994, p. 238; Salend, 1995, 2009):

- Prepare typed rather than handwritten tests.
- Space items sufficiently to reduce interference.
- Provide space for students to respond on the test itself.
- Provide items in a predictable hierarchy.
- Administer more tests with fewer items, rather than fewer, longer tests.
- When not testing reading, adjust the reading level of the items or provide assistance with reading when needed.
- Define unfamiliar or abstract words if their meanings are not directly being tested.
- Provide models of correctly answered items.
- Change the test setting for students with disabilities (e.g., a quiet space where the student can work privately).
- Allow more time for test completion so that students can read, write, or process test requirements.
- Allow students to dictate responses or use communication boards to indicate their responses.

Specific Formats Recommendations have also been made for specific types of tests (see Salend, 1995, 2009, 2011):

- For true–false items, write out the words *true* and *false* for clarity, and avoid double negatives or emphasize negatives with bold or underlining. Students may become confused when asked to choose "false" as the correct answer to a negative statement, such as, "The office of president is *not* described in the Constitution."
- For multiple-choice tests, reduce the number of options and limit the number of confusing options, such as "(a) and (b) but not (c)." If possible, have students answer on the test itself rather than a separate answer sheet, particularly in the elementary grades.
- For matching items, reduce the overall number of items. Provide an example of a correctly answered item, and place the entire list on one page.
- For short-answer questions, consider providing a choice of answers for the student to circle, rather than filling in a blank.
- For essay questions, describe what you would like to see included in the essay (without providing too much information) and recommend how the answer should be organized.

ADJUST SCORING PROCEDURES In addition to adjusting the format of tests, you can also adjust the way you score the tests. If some students have particular difficulty in areas such as spelling and grammar, it probably is unnecessary to penalize these students in science, for example, when an eighth-grade academic standard is to differentiate between physical and chemical changes. Grades for students with and without disabilities should be meaningful and based on specific skills outlined by the academic standards (Munoz & Gusky, 2015).

For some students, the special educator and general education teacher can work together to deconstruct a standard and focus on scoring a student's assignment one skill at a time. For students with disabilities who require modifications to the curriculum per the IEP, teachers can select a vertically aligned foundational skill that is closely related to the grade-level skill (Wakeman et al., 2021). If it seems important to grade on spelling, grammar, and neatness, consider grading these areas separately from actual mastery of the content. It may also be helpful to consider giving partial credit for answers that are incorrect but nonetheless demonstrate some knowledge of the content covered. This type of credit could be represented in a teacher-developed 4- to 5-point rubric that gives clear criteria for mastery. It seems reasonable that answers demonstrating even a little knowledge may be given more credit than answers reflecting no knowledge.

Pearson eTextbook
Video Example 12.4
In this video, two teachers discuss the development and design of a teacher-made fifth-grade social studies summative assessment so that items are closely aligned to the curriculum standards. What other aspects, specifically for students with disabilities, should be considered next in the conversation?

STRATEGIES FOR USING CURRICULUM-BASED MEASUREMENT

CBM was developed to document student progress through the class curriculum and to assist teachers in creating more effective instructional environments for students. When teachers actively monitor instruction and make adjustments based on CBM, learning outcomes improve (Berkeley & Riccomini, 2017). Fuchs et al. (1994) described two major distinguishing features of CBM.

First, CBM entails a standardized (but probably not norm-referenced) set of procedures for administration. These standardized procedures include sampling test items from classroom curricula, administering the test under the same or similar conditions, summarizing the test information, and using the test information in instructional decision making.

The second distinguishing feature of CBM is its focus on a long-term curricular goal—for example, the goal that you wish students will achieve by the end of the year and/or the measurable annual goal(s) on a students' IEP. To this extent, CBM differs from other types of continuous measurement (or formative evaluation), in which student progress is assessed directly through changing objectives and standards throughout the year. With CBM, the test domain remains constant from the beginning of the school year until the end.

APPLY CBM TO MONITOR LEARNING PROGRESS For an example of CBM, consider the case of Li, a 9-year-old student with a learning disability who has just entered the fourth grade. During the first few weeks of school, Li's teacher, Mr. Johnson, gathered and reviewed curriculum and assessment information around Li's spelling skills in order to determine next instructional steps as identified in Table 12.2.

As shared in Table 12.2, Mr. Johnson had reviewed Li's IEP goals, documented his observations from some formative work samples, and administered a benchmark spelling assessment. Results from the DSA aligned with Li's IEP goal. Most of Mr. Johnson's fourth-graders are independently and accurately writing words with the within-word patterns developmental spelling stage. Based on this data, Mr. Johnson knows where to target his spelling instruction for Li and decides to use CBM to monitor Li's progress in the curriculum area of spelling. He examines the level of the curriculum for an entire domain of words that fourth-grade students are expected to be able to spell by the end of the year. Then Mr. Johnson samples from this list, creating, for example, 50 versions of a 20-item spelling test that include words that students will study throughout the year. Mr. Johnson is sure to include at least 10 words on the list that target the within-word spelling pattern. He administers one of these lists about twice a week under standardized administration procedures (e.g., words are read once every 7 seconds, and students write the words on lined, numbered paper). Student performance can be scored by means of measures that may be more sensitive than the number of words spelled correctly, such as the number of correct letter sequences (Berkeley & Riccomini, 2017). See Hosp et al. (2016) for how to score correct letter sequence (CLS) and to determine the recommended CLS for students in early elementary versus upper grades.

Letter sequence scores can then be plotted over time, either for individual students or for the class as a whole (see Figure 12.2). Student progress can be plotted over time, and the teacher can estimate whether students will attain end-of-year goals if they continue to progress at the current rate. If progress seems inadequate, teachers can implement modifications, such as increased time on-task, computer-assisted instruction for spelling practice,

TABLE 12.2 Li's Curriculum and Assessment Information

Associated Curriculum Goals: (Fourth grade; Common Core State Standards)	CCSS.ELA-LITERACY.W.4.5. With guidance and support from peers and adults, develop and strengthen writing as needed by planning, revising, and editing. CCSS.ELA-LITERACY.W.4.6. With some guidance and support from adults, use technology, including the Internet, to produce and publish writing as to interact and collaborate with others; demonstrate sufficient command of keyboarding skills to type a minimum of one page in a single sitting.		
Associated IEP annual goal:	Given a dictated list of 20 grade-level words that include the within-word patterns (i.e., common long vowels, complex consonants, abstract vowels), Li will spell the words with 90% accuracy on three consecutive trials. Instructional accommodations on IEP: • Use of a word processor (and for testing) • Computer-assisted instruction for practice • Word banks provided during writing activities		
Observations: (Examples of correct and incorrect spelling of words)	Work Samples	+*couch* +*farmer* +*pretty* +*might*	–*skrim* for scream –*pach* for patch –*cowch* for couch –*yan* for yawn
	Journal	+*drive* +*sister* +*going* +*forever*	–*babys* for babies –*gril* for girl –*brige* for bridge –*kwite* for quite
	Classwork/homework observations	+*to and too* +*mother* +*gather*	–*smock* for smoke –*ulgly* for ugly –*speach* for speech –*slipt* for slipped
Formative/Benchmark Assessment: (Fall, Winter, Spring)	Developmental Spelling Assessment (DSA)	September DSA placed Li at the lower range of the instructional level for the Within Word Stage of the DSA. She spelled 13/25 words correctly. Problematic spelling features: • Common long vowels (e.g., *oa, ai, ee*) • Complex consonants (e.g., *scr, qu, ck, tch*) • Abstract vowels (digraphs/diphthongs) • (e.g., *oi/oy, au/aw, ou/ow*)	

Note: A Developmental Spelling Assessment is a type of informal spelling inventory to determine a child's stage of spelling development. The dictated screening tool identifies students' orthographic knowledge of key spelling features that relate to different spelling stages: Early Letter Name, Letter Name, Within Word, and Syllable Juncture (see Ganske, 2014; Tortorelli & Bruner, 2022).

Figure 12.2 Curriculum-Based Measurement in Spelling Chart

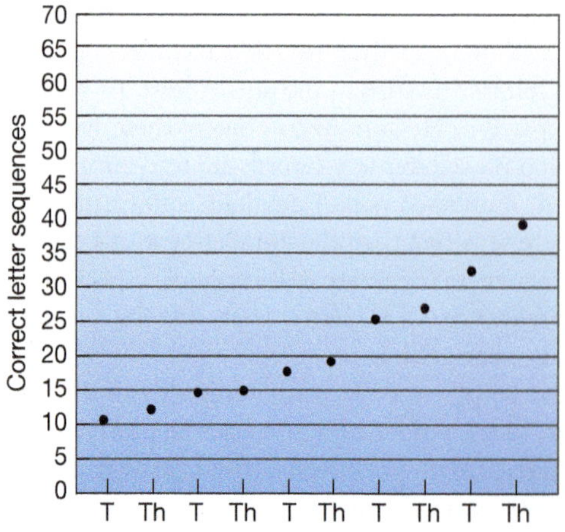

or individual work with specific difficult letter patterns. Similarly, progress can be plotted on measures of reading (e.g., word reading fluency) or math (e.g., problem-solving fluency), and estimates can then be made of whether students are making adequate progress toward end-of-year goals. When progress is not adequate, instructional modifications are made (McMaster et al., 2022).

CBM has also been recommended for use in RTI programs (see Chapter 7; Fuchs & Fuchs, 2008). Students' responses to instruction can be measured formatively, based on the curriculum being used, as a guide to evaluation. Using CBM, adequate progress toward long-term objectives can be assessed to aid in placement decisions, for example, to determine placement eligibility for Tier 2 or Tier 3 RTI programs. CBM is also employed to inform instructional modifications in RTI programs.

Pearson eTextbook

Video Example 12.5

This video describes student outcomes from a spelling inventory used with middle school students. What long-term goal is identified for the students and what short-term instructional spelling goal is identified for Dahlia?

STRATEGIES FOR USING PERFORMANCE ASSESSMENT

Performance assessment addresses students' ability to interact (perform) appropriately with relevant instructional materials and the content of instruction. As such, this type of assessment relies much less on direct recall of verbal information than do more typical classroom tests, and it relies more on students' demonstration of understanding. Elements of performance assessment include (1) defined purpose, (2) performance tasks, (3) a direction for the student's performance, and (4) methods for assessment (Johnson et al., 2009). Performance assessment is also helpful when testing students who may have word-finding (retrieval) problems, communication disorders, or other skills that limit verbal communication. The state of California, for example, has established performance standards for alternate assessments in several content and skill areas (California Department of Education, 2015).

In an investigation by Scruggs et al. (1993), students with learning disabilities performed relatively poorly on a more traditional test of their recall of vocabulary words after hands-on science instruction. However, they were much more able to demonstrate their knowledge in performance-based tests that required them to determine, for example, which of two minerals is harder or whether a mineral contains calcite. Performance assessment is an effective way of measuring all students' comprehension of academic content in at least part of virtually all school subjects, including science, math, social studies, music, art, vocational education, and physical education.

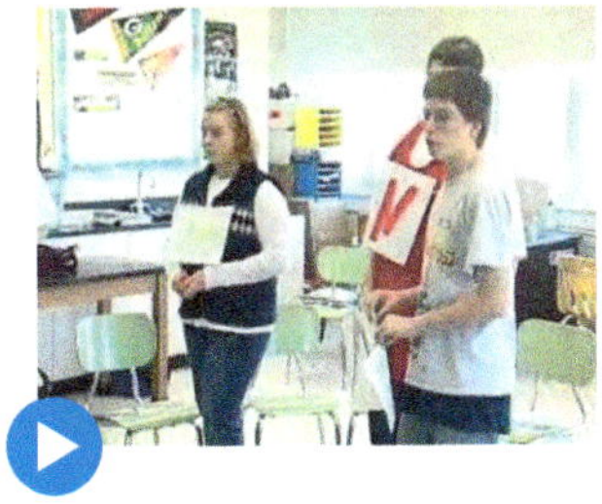

Pearson eTextbook

Video Example 12.6

This video provides an overview of performance assessment used in a high school science class. How does this type of assessment make considerations for students with disabilities?

Although performance assessments may vary widely, they often have three key elements in common:

1. Students construct their own responses, rather than selecting or identifying correct responses.
2. Teachers can observe student performance on tasks reflecting real-world or authentic requirements.
3. Student responses can reveal patterns in students' thinking and learning, as well as whether the question was correctly answered. (Fuchs, 1994)

IMPLEMENT AND ADAPT PERFORMANCE ASSESSMENT To set up performance assessment measures, first determine exactly what you want students to be able to do after the instructional unit is completed and state it as a behavioral objective. The next step is to set up the materials and provide the opportunity for the student to perform on the test. Specific tasks can be placed at several stations around the classroom and students can move from station to station individually without observing another student's performance on the test.

Scoring is typically done by using a rubric that lists test items and scoring criteria. Performance assessments can be holistic (for the entire task) or analytic (for specific task components; Brookhart, 2013).

For example, consider a performance assessment for a science unit on ecosystems (students had built their own "ecocolumns" using plants, animals, soil, water, and 2-liter bottles), which used the following test item:

- Draw a picture of an ecosystem. Label all parts.

To score this item objectively, a holistic scoring rubric was constructed by which responses could be evaluated. For this item, the scoring criteria included the following:

Scoring Rubric

Score	Scoring Criteria
3	Picture with living and nonliving things appearing to interact in some general way; living and nonliving things labeled.
2	Picture of living and nonliving things not labeled, labeled living, or labeled nonliving.
1	One of above or general relevant comment.
0	Nothing of relevance.

Using this key, then, a picture drawn by a student that included both living and nonliving things but did not have the items in the picture labeled would earn a score of 2 points. An example of a response to this particular item on a performance assessment is given in Figure 12.3.

Figure 12.3 Student Response on Ecosystem Item of Performance-Based Assessment

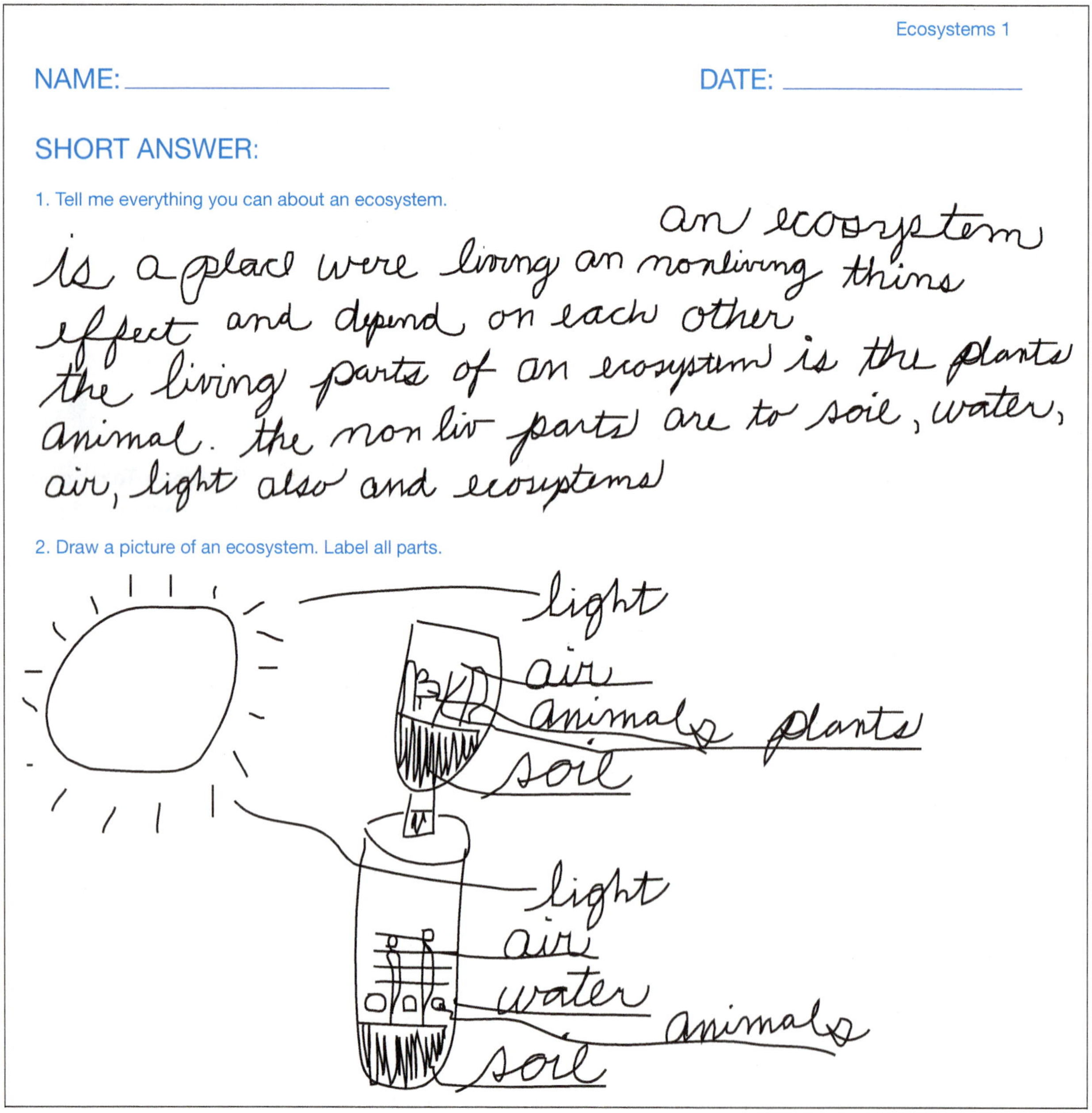

Schirmer and Bailey (2000) described the development of a rubric for writing assessment that was employed successfully with middle school students who were Deaf. They emphasized that the rubric should be a dynamic tool, capable of accommodating individual differences in student needs, content, assignments, and curriculum. That is, some students may benefit from a rubric that emphasizes word choice as a means for expanding vocabulary, whereas other students may benefit from a rubric that emphasizes organization of ideas. In creating a writing assessment rubric, teachers should:

- Identify the qualities of writing.
- Create a scale.
- Define each quality by listing the characteristics that describe performance at each point on the scale. (Schirmer & Bailey, 2000, p. 55)

For example, Regan et al. (2021) created an analytic rubric for persuasive writing assessment, that listed qualities across three areas of writing: planning, writing, and reviewing. Qualities under reviewing included word selection, grammar, spelling, punctuation, and capitalization. Specific characteristics were provided for each quality of writing at each point on a five-point scale. The *In the Classroom* feature includes a math scoring rubric.

Accommodations in performance assessments may also be helpful for students with disabilities. Crawford et al. (2004) reported some relative benefit from longer time limits on a performance assessment in writing, and Johnson et al. (2001) reported that reading math items to students with learning disabilities provided some benefit to test-takers.

STRATEGIES FOR USING PORTFOLIO ASSESSMENT

DEVELOP PORTFOLIOS A *portfolio* has been defined as a "systematic and organized collection of evidence used by the teacher and student to monitor the growth of the student's knowledge, skills, and attitudes" (Vavrus, 1990, p. 48). Portfolios can be printed documents or digital artifacts (e.g., photos, videos) that are collected together to represent a student's academic and behavioral performance and progress over time (Cleveland, 2018). Printed documents can be collected in accordion folders or in three-ring notebooks with pocketed dividers. Portfolios can be a great way for students to present their work, demonstrate progress, self-reflect, and share their accomplishments with teachers and parents/caregivers (Rao et al., 2021). Portfolios can be created in any area of student performance, including literacy, math, and science. Portfolios may also be useful in situations where more traditional standardized tests may not be appropriate to the developmental and learning needs of individual students (e.g., some students with autism). Participation in traditional testing typically requires a certain degree of engagement and attention to visual materials or auditory prompts. See the *Apps for Education* feature within this chapter for further information about how portfolio assessments can be made and stored digitally.

Because student portfolios can be tailored to the specific needs of the classroom, the student, or the curriculum, they can be considered quite versatile. However, for these same reasons, portfolios may lack standardization and objectivity, and therefore teachers must ensure that judgments based on portfolio products are both reliable and valid (Salvia et al., 2016). Helpful strategies consistent with HLP 4 include using multiple measures of the same skills or products, calculating interrater reliability (where different "experts" independently assess portfolio products), and making comparisons with more traditional measures (e.g., standardized tests or criterion-referenced measurement). Nevertheless, portfolios can provide authentic evidence of actual classroom performance or real-world, adaptive and functional skills that may be difficult to document by other methods. You can also use student portfolios to reflect on your own teaching.

Figure 12.4 provides a list of items that could be included in a literacy portfolio, and Figure 12.5 provides a list of items that could be included in a science portfolio.

ADAPT PORTFOLIO ASSESSMENT In addition to the "traditional" uses of portfolio assessment in education, portfolio assessment can also be used to document the performance of students who have been referred to special education. Portfolios are commonly used in developing alternate assessments (Salvia et al., 2016). Salend (2009) pointed out that portfolios could

Figure 12.4 Potential Items to Include in a Literacy Portfolio

- Informal assessment samples
- Audio and video recordings of oral reading, comprehension think-alouds (e.g., Voice Memo), descriptions, and story retells; interviews about performance and progress in reading over time and periodically throughout school year
- Students' notebooks, logs of read books, written paragraphs, essays, and reports
- Checklists
- Charts of curriculum-based measurement performance
- Teachers' notes, including error analysis
- Formal assessment samples
- Tests, such as teacher-made, criterion referenced, and standardized

Figure 12.5 Sample Portfolio Items for Science

- Authentic and performance assessment items
- Audio and video recordings of debates on climate change, science fair presentations, and projects in the community such as recycling education programs
- Picture updates of longer-term projects such as building an ecosystem and conducting experiments on the ecosystem, including documentation of predictions and observations and a comparison of predictions with observations
- Samples of both formal and informal tests
- Teacher anecdotal records

Pearson eTextbook
Video Example 12.7
This video clip reviews the process one teacher uses for portfolio assessment. Think about how you may need to adjust this process for students with disabilities.

be linked with individual student IEPs by including work products that show growth on IEP objectives and by periodically completing summary sheets that link IEP objectives to documentation in the portfolio.

Wesson and King (1996) provided two case studies of the use of portfolios with students with disabilities. In the first study, a sixth-grade general education teacher used a portfolio to chronicle the progress of a student, Tom, classified as seriously emotionally/behaviorally disturbed. Tom was described as having difficulties getting along with peers and frequently fighting with them, being argumentative and noncompliant with teachers, being socially isolated, and making limited academic progress. Tom's portfolio included a video (updated regularly) of his performance during cooperative group lessons, a description of his outside-school social activities, and a list of narrative observations the teacher (or teacher's aide) had made as she watched Tom in social situations, including behavioral observations of his problem behaviors.

In the second case study, a portfolio was created for the vocational experiences of Chris, a 16-year-old student with severe disabilities. This portfolio included a video showing Chris working in academic and vocational settings, a transcript of an interview the teacher conducted with her, a vocational skills checklist, and a list of her circle of friends and their roles in her life. Chris's teacher hoped the portfolio would be useful when she began applying for jobs and working in the community (Wesson & King, 1996). Kearns et al. (2006) described the use of enhanced portfolio and performance assessments to document adapted grade-level content standards for statewide testing for students with significant cognitive disabilities. Teachers should consult individual state procedures for incorporating portfolio assessments within alternate state assessments.

Teach Test-Taking Skills

Learning Objective 12.3 Explain specific test-taking strategies for taking standardized tests and teacher-made tests, such as multiple-choice, true–false, matching, and essay tests.

Tests are intended to measure knowledge and skill in specific areas; however, tests can also measure student "test-taking" skills. Many students with disabilities and at risk for failure in school perform poorly on tests in part because of poor test-taking skills (Deshler & Schumaker, 2006; Scruggs & Mastropieri, 1988, 1992).

Test-taking strategies help students with disabilities improve their performance on both standardized and teacher-made tests. Several researchers have described a number of test-taking strategies that have been helpful for all types of learners (Hughes, 1996; Hughes et al., 1988; Kesselman-Turkel & Peterson, 2004; Salend, 2009, 2016; Scruggs & Mastropieri, 1992). This section describes test-taking strategies that are successful in increasing the test performance of students with disabilities.

Anxiety reduction can also help. You can help students reduce anxieties during testing situations by encouraging their use of positive attributions—that is, by helping them focus on effort and strategies, rather than thinking about what their score will be or how others will do. Teach students to recognize signs of tension in themselves—such as grinding teeth, biting fingernails, and picking at hair or face—and to respond by consciously relaxing their muscles and controlling their breathing. Teaching test-taking and study skills can also help relieve anxiety (Lucangeli & Scruggs, 2003; von der Embse et al., 2013). The *Research Highlight* describes a recent review of investigations about test anxiety.

STRATEGIES FOR

TEACHING TEST-TAKING SKILLS

TEACH GENERAL TEST-PREPARATION STRATEGIES General preparation strategies refer to what students can do to help when preparing for any exam. Many students, but especially those with disabilities, will benefit from explicit instruction in each of these areas.

The first and most important general test strategy is academic preparation. The next general strategy is physical preparation, which includes getting enough rest and nourishment, particularly before studying and before taking the test. A positive attitude toward tests is also important. Improve test attitudes by helping students set realistic goals, providing practice tests, explaining the purpose of the particular test, rewarding effort, and providing training in test-taking skills.

TEACH GENERAL STRATEGIES FOR STANDARDIZED TESTS You can teach students general strategies that they can apply across a number of standardized tests and testing situations (Salend, 2009, 2016; Scruggs & Mastropieri, 1992). These strategies include using separate answer sheets, using elimination strategies, guessing effectively, and using time wisely.

Separate Answer Sheets Most paper-and-pencil standardized tests require students to record their responses by filling a circle or "bubble" on separate answer sheets. Provide students with practice filling in the appropriate answer bubble "quick, dark, and inside the line." If practice tests are provided by the test publisher, provide instruction on the use of separate answer sheets (if not, make simulated answer sheets and test booklets when appropriate).

Use Elimination Strategies Teach students to eliminate response options they know are incorrect. For example, if there are four answer options and a test-taker can eliminate three of them, then the remaining option must be the correct response.

Guess When Appropriate Encourage guessing where appropriate, as many students with disabilities and at risk for school failure do not realize that guessing is better than leaving an item blank on most standardized tests (when there is not a penalty for guessing).

Use Time Wisely On timed tests, monitoring time while taking the test is important. Teach students to use time efficiently on familiar items and not to waste time on items they are unlikely to answer correctly. Teach students to monitor their time as they take the test. That is,

Research Highlight

Test Anxiety

Imagine yourself entering a testing situation, perhaps an important one for which you do not feel entirely prepared. As you take your seat and begin taking the test, you begin to think about the consequences of performing poorly on this test. You imagine how other students will do and wonder how many will do better than you. You begin to experience an increased heart rate, a dry mouth, stomach discomfort, and perhaps a headache. You tap your pencil and shuffle your feet, wishing you could be anywhere else but this testing situation. You begin to sense yourself forgetting the very information you need to succeed on this test.

All of these things are symptoms of test anxiety, a condition many of us have experienced. In more extreme cases, it may cause students to perform significantly worse than they otherwise might. Test anxiety has been considered by researchers to have multiple manifestations, and measures of test anxiety address different aspects of the condition. The Children's Test Anxiety Scale, for example, includes items from domains of *thoughts* ("I think I am going to get a bad grade"), *behaviors* ("I look at other people"), and *autonomic reactions* ("My heart beats fast") (Wren & Benson, 2004, p. 234).

Test anxiety has been the subject of numerous investigations by researchers interested in understanding more about this condition. Von der Embse et al. (2018) collected all relevant research investigations of the effects, predictors, and correlates of test anxiety. They identified 238 relevant studies and combined them quantitatively using meta-analysis procedures. They were able to identify a number of variables that were associated with test anxiety, including the following:

1. **Self-concept.** Self-concept and related variables were found to have a consistent inverse relation to text anxiety, in that students with lower self-concept reported higher levels of anxiety. Related variables combined with self-concept included self-regulation (use of strategies, monitoring of learning outcomes); self-efficacy (e.g., personal belief in one's ability to perform successful task behaviors); and academic confidence (belief in one's ability to successfully meet various academic demands).
2. **Motivation.** Measures of motivation were found to be related to test anxiety. However, different results were found for intrinsic motivation (internal desire to succeed) than for extrinsic motivation (motivation based on anticipated external rewards). That is, while intrinsic motivation was negatively associated with test anxiety (i.e., higher intrinsic motivation was associated with lower anxiety), the opposite was true for extrinsic motivation (higher extrinsic motivation was associated with higher anxiety).
3. **Coping skills.** Two types of coping skills were identified: *problem-focused* or *avoidance* coping. Problem-solving coping is an active strategy designed to solve a given problem by removing or circumventing the source of stress. Avoidance coping refers to engaging in non-relevant thoughts or behaviors intended to avoid a stressful situation. These two types of coping were also found to be differently related to test anxiety. While problem-focused coping was negatively associated with test anxiety (more problem-focused coping associated with lower test anxiety), avoidance coping was positively associated (higher levels of avoidance coping was associated with higher levels of test anxiety).
4. **Gender.** There was a significant relationship between test anxiety and gender, with females overall reporting higher levels of test anxiety than males. This difference was true across all grade levels and seemed to increase from primary to secondary grades. It was seen to moderate somewhat in postsecondary environments.
5. **Race and ethnicity.** When test anxiety was compared between African American and White students, African American students reported somewhat higher levels of test anxiety.
6. **Achievement.** When achievement level was examined in relation to test anxiety, it was found that high-achieving students reported lower levels of test anxiety than lower-achieving students.
7. **Disability status.** Some investigations in this data set compared students with and without ADHD, and students with and without learning disabilities. It was found that students with diagnoses of ADHD showed higher levels of test anxiety than students without ADHD, as did students with diagnoses of learning disabilities.

Research Highlight

Test Anxiety—*continued*

8. **Other variables.** Von der Embse et al. (2018) identified some additional variables that were found to be associated with test anxiety. They reported that the most negative association between test performance and test anxiety occurred in the middle grades, while the association was the lowest in high school. It was also reported that higher levels of anxiety were more strongly associated with high-stakes tests than with typical classroom tests (Segool et al., 2013).

These results taken together paint a more detailed and nuanced conception of the nature of test anxiety and its correlates. Overall, they suggest that enhancing such variables as test familiarity, self-efficacy, self-monitoring, and test-taking skills can significantly reduce anxiety when undertaking tests. And in fact, this has been found to be the case. Von der Embse et al. (2013) reviewed intervention literature and reported that techniques such as breathing control exercises, relaxation techniques, cognitive awareness training, strategy training, and test-taking skills training were effective in reducing test anxiety. For further information on strategies for reducing test anxiety, see Bernstein (2018) and Cizek and Burg (2006). For strategies to improve intrinsic motivation, see Chapter 8.

QUESTIONS FOR REFLECTION

1. Have you ever experienced test anxiety? Do you believe it affected your test score?
2. How do you account for the differences in test anxiety between those who are intrinsically motivated versus those who are extrinsically motivated? Do you think these findings are related to the findings concerning coping skills?
3. Why do you think students with ADHD and learning disabilities are more likely to be affected by test anxiety?
4. How could you help students control their test anxiety?

when the testing period is half over, they should be finished with about half of the test. If they plan to have time at the end to review their answers, they should be finished with more than half of the test when the time period is half over.

TEACH SPECIFIC STRATEGIES FOR STANDARDIZED TESTS Strategies can be employed for specific subtests of standardized tests.

Reading-Comprehension Subtests Most standardized reading-comprehension subtests require students to read a specific passage and then answer questions about the passage. Teach students to read as much of the passage as possible because they can still answer many of the questions even if they have skipped some unfamiliar words. Encourage students to read the entire question and every stem option before selecting responses. Teach students to check back in the passage when possible to verify that their answer choice was correct. When reading selections contain information in tables, such as basketball schedules, teach students to quickly skim the information and then look to the questions and refer back to the table to identify answers.

Decoding Subtests Because students do not respond orally and decode words, decoding subtests on group-administered standardized tests may have unusual formats. For example, students may be asked to match a word that contains the same sound as that underlined in the stem:

1. Which word contains the underlined sound?
   pl<u>ay</u>
   a. plan
   b. yard
   c. afraid
   d. drag

Teach students to say the underlined sound of the word to themselves and be certain they have found an answer that matches this sound (c. "afraid"), not the appearance of the stem word (a. "plan").

In the Classroom

Sample Mathematics Scoring Rubric

4 Exemplary Response
- 4.1 Complete, with clear, coherent, unambiguous, and insightful explanation
- 4.2 Shows understanding of underlying mathematical concepts, procedures, and structures
- 4.3 Examines and satisfies all essential conditions of the problem
- 4.4 Presents strong supporting arguments with examples and counterexamples as appropriate
- 4.5 Solution and work is efficient and shows evidence of reflection and checking of work
- 4.6 Appropriately applies mathematics to the situation

3 Competent Response
- 3.1 Gives a fairly complete response with reasonably clear explanations
- 3.2 Shows understanding of underlying mathematical concepts, procedures, and structures
- 3.3 Examines and satisfies most essential conditions of the problem
- 3.4 Presents adequate supporting arguments with examples and counterexamples as appropriate
- 3.5 Solution and work show some evidence of reflection and checking of work
- 3.6 Appropriately applies mathematics to the situation

2 Minimal Response
- 2.1 Gives response, but explanations may be unclear or lack detail
- 2.2 Exhibits minor flaws in underlying mathematical concepts, procedures, and structures
- 2.3 Examines and satisfies some essential conditions of the problem
- 2.4 Draws some accurate conclusions, but reasoning may be faulty or incomplete
- 2.5 Shows little evidence of reflection and checking of work
- 2.6 Some attempt to apply mathematics to the situation

1 Inadequate Response
- 1.1 Response is incomplete, and explanation is insufficient or not understandable
- 1.2 Exhibits major flaws in underlying mathematical concepts, procedures, and structures
- 1.3 Fails to address essential conditions of the problem
- 1.4 Uses faulty reasoning and draws incorrect conclusions
- 1.5 Shows no evidence of reflection and checking of work
- 1.6 Fails to apply mathematics to the situation

0 No attempt
- 0.1 Provides irrelevant or no response
- 0.2 Copies part of the problem but does not attempt a solution
- 0.3 Illegible response

Note: To receive a particular score, a significant number of the associated criteria must be met.

Source: From Fuchs (1994), p. 24.

Mathematics Computation Subtests Mathematics computation subtests require students to look at test items, compute answers on scratch paper, and select the correct answer from the options provided. Provide students with practice in using scratch paper and identifying the correct answer from an array of choices. Teach students to rewrite the problem in the format that they are most comfortable with. Be sure students have sufficient practice with mathematics vocabulary that will be used in word problems. Review words such as *sum, product, difference, quotient*, and other words that may appear on the test.

Mathematics Concepts Subtests Mathematics concepts subtests cover a range of skills in math and are presented in a variety of formats on standardized tests. Model examples in which you read the question, rephrase it, and then think aloud through to the solution. Some math problems may contain boxes to indicate missing values, as in the following example:

2. What number should be in the □?
   $524 - \square = 425 + 75$
   a. 500
   b. 75
   c. 24
   d. 425

Practice solving problems before the test using the types of boxes or other symbols that may be used on standardized tests. If specific formats that will be used are not known (and this is likely), practice solving problems throughout the year using different answering formats. Be sure students are aware of any specialized vocabulary (e.g., *quotient, subtrahend*) that is likely to be included on the test.

Math Problem-Solving Subtests Tests of math problem solving require reading the problem, determining what is known, figuring out what operation is called for, generating a plan for a solution, computing the solution, selecting the correct answer from the options, and marking the selected response appropriately on the answer sheet. Provide students with practice using the scratch paper, which involves carefully matching the number of the problem on the scratch paper with the number in the test booklet, along with practice in executing all the other necessary steps in the procedure for solving word problems.

Tell students to practice requesting help with reading directions or word problems if they need it. If test administrators are not allowed to provide assistance in an area, they will simply say, "I cannot help you with that."

Some math problems do not contain all the necessary information to answer the question, and students are asked to furnish the missing, but necessary, information. For example:

3. Tyler is 66 inches tall. What else do you need to know to figure out how much he grew this year?

    a. How old he is this year

    b. How tall he was last year

    c. How tall his friend is

    d. How much his brother grew last year

Practice with this type of format, and others, may be necessary for students with disabilities to ensure successful performance. Model and demonstrate by thinking through the solution aloud. Have students practice using similar procedures.

Science and Social Studies Subtests Formats for science and social studies exams typically parallel the formats employed in reading-comprehension and mathematics subtests. Many items require students to read expository passages and then answer questions about the passages. Other items require students to examine charts, diagrams, reference materials, or maps and interpret them before selecting correct answers. Provide practice using these various formats with students when teaching throughout the year.

TEACH STRATEGIES FOR TEACHER-MADE TESTS Teachers sometimes use tests developed by textbook publishers to accompany adopted text materials. At other times, they develop their own tests. Some websites may be helpful to create materials for evaluating student learning of a specific skill. SuperKids (https://www.superkids.com/aweb/tools/) is a free tool that allows you to select a topic (e.g., math, vocabulary) and quickly create your own worksheet with a selected number of problems. An answer sheet can be created as well for grading. Both teacher-made and publisher-developed tests may include objective test formats such as multiple-choice, matching, and true–false items, as well as written formats that contain short-answer, fill-in-the-blank, essay, and performance-based items. The general preparation strategies, and many of the general strategies described for standardized tests, are also applicable to teacher-made tests. In addition, some specific strategies for teacher-made tests should be learned.

Objective Tests Objective tests contain multiple-choice, true–false, and/or matching items. All strategies described so far may be applicable for helping students prepare for objective tests. However, students should be familiar with the content on teacher-made tests, and they can use this knowledge, or partial knowledge, to improve their test scores.

Written Tests Written tests may contain sentence-completion, short-answer, or essay items. The following strategies can help students become better test-takers on these types of tests.

1. *Sentence-Completion Items and Short-Answer Items.* Sentence-completion items are usually short sentences containing blanks that must be filled in correctly ("The longest river in South America is __________"), whereas short-answer items ask questions requiring a brief response ("What were the causes of the War of 1812?").

Encourage students to provide some answer, even if it is only partially correct. Many teachers give partial credit for some answers, but they cannot provide any credit if the items are left blank. Have students guess if they are not completely sure, encourage them to use partial knowledge, and teach them to make the sentence sound logical in sentence-completion items. Sometimes lists of items are considered acceptable responses for short-answer items. Determine whether sentence fragments or lists will result in the same credit as complete sentences.

2. *Essay Questions.* Essay tests are difficult for students with disabilities, but strategies exist to facilitate essay test performance. One strategy is referred to as SNOW, which stands for the following:

   Study the question

   Note important points

   Organize the information

   Write directly to the point of the question. (Scruggs & Mastropieri, 1992, p. 89)

Teach students how to implement each step of this strategy and provide corrective feedback on their performance. Have them *study* the questions by underlining the specific words that tell them what to do, such as *describe, define, explain, compare, contrast, list, justify*, or *critique* (see Figure 12.6).

Next, students should *note* important points that come to mind. Then they should *organize* their notes by numbering the main and supporting points in logical order for discussion. Finally, they should *write* concisely and directly to the point of the question.

Performance Tests Performance tests are designed to parallel the exact format of what has been taught and practiced, and they are designed to provide better information about instruction (Baron, 1990). A practice test may be helpful for some students in preparing for the test. Teach students to read directions carefully and not to answer too quickly if something looks familiar. Show them how to talk through the steps of answers before responding. For older students, consider pairing a rubric with a performance test that involves a writing task or creating a product so that students may use the rubric as a guide to self-assess. Teach students to review the rubric criteria carefully so that they can self-monitor and self-evaluate their work.

TEACH OTHER TEST-TAKING STRATEGIES Other test-taking strategies may be helpful in preparing students to take tests. One strategy is called SCORER (Carman & Adams, 1991). Each letter in SCORER represents clue words to help students perform better during testing situations: Schedule time; Clue words (see Figure 12.6); Omit hard items; Read

Figure 12.6 Command Words and Their Explanations

Command Words on Test Items and Their Implications

Word	*Possible Implications*
Discuss	Provide reasoning behind; give different points of view.
Describe	Give an overall impression; give examples.
Compare	Show how two or more things are similar; provide examples of common characteristics.
Contrast	Show how two or more things are different; provide examples of differing characteristics.
Explain	Clarify or simplify; describe the rationale behind.
Justify	Argue in favor of; defend.
Critique	Argue in opposition of; find fault with.
List	Give a simple list of elements.
Outline	Give a list of elements organized into a system.

Source: From Scruggs & Mastropieri (1992), p. 90. Copyright 1992 by Brookline. Reprinted with permission.

carefully; Estimate answers; and Review work. This strategy has been successfully used with middle school students (Ritter & Idol-Maestas, 1986).

Another strategy, PIRATES, is a seven-step strategy designed to help students perform better on teacher-made tests (Hughes et al., 1993). Each letter in PIRATES represents a step of the strategy: Prepare to succeed; Inspect the instructions; Read, remember, reduce; Answer or abandon; Turn back; Estimate; Survey. Although it is often used with students with learning disabilities and emotional/behavioral disorders (e.g., Banks & Eaton, 2014; Haynes, 2011), this strategy has also been employed successfully with high-functioning students with autism (Songlee, 2007).

Another test-taking strategy is called ANSWER (Hughes, 1996). Whereas PIRATES was originally designed for improving performance on objective tests, ANSWER is designed to assist students with essay-type exams, including students with developmental disabilities (Woods-Groves et al., 2012). The steps in ANSWER can be summarized as follows:

- Analyze the situation, by reading the item carefully, underlining important words, and estimating time needed.
- Notice requirements, by marking different parts of the question and committing to a quality answer.
- Set up an outline, including main ideas, and check outline ideas with the question.
- Work in details, remembering previous learning and applying it in appropriate order, using abbreviations.
- Engineer your answer, by writing an introductory paragraph, referring back to your outline, using topic sentences and additional details, and providing examples.
- Review your work, by checking the entire answer with all components of the question. (Hughes, 1996)

Remember that any learning strategy requires students to (1) identify when the strategy should be used, (2) retrieve the steps in the strategy, and (3) correctly apply the strategy steps to the task (Mastropieri & Scruggs, 2002). Students will need repeated exposure to, and practice with, each strategy in order to learn to use it effectively.

Grading

Learning Objective 12.4 Identify procedures and rationales for adjusting grading and scoring of tests for students with disabilities.

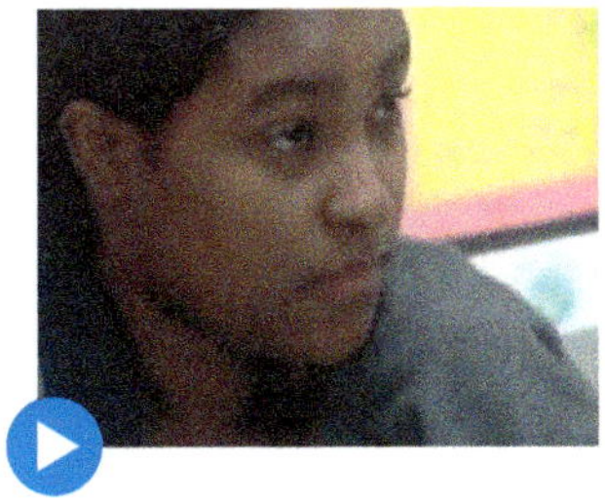

Pearson eTextbook

Video Example 12.8

The high school special education teacher in this video demonstrates how she grades her students who have varying abilities. How does the teacher determine what they know and what does she do with that information?

STRATEGIES FOR ADAPTING REPORT CARD GRADING

Report card grading is an essential component of the U.S. educational system (Brookhart, 2009), and the importance of grades in our society cannot be denied. However, across the country, standards for grading appear to be somewhat variable. Polloway et al. (1994) reported that about 39% of the districts surveyed had a specific policy for adaptations in grading for students with disabilities (see also Munk & Bursuck, 2003). The most common responses involved adaptations reflected in the students' IEPs, decisions made by a committee, and notations of accommodations noted on the report card.

ADJUST GRADING PROCEDURES There appears to be no one "right" way to proceed when issuing report card grades to students with disabilities. However, following are some considerations that could be helpful in planning grading procedures (Brookhart, 2009; Christiansen & Vogel, 1998; Jung & Guskey, 2010; Munk & Bursuck, 1998):

1. *Consult school and district policy.* Some schools have established official policies on issuing report card grades to students with disabilities. Find out whether your school has such a policy and, if so, follow its guidelines. Make recommendations when needed to appropriate school personnel.
2. *Follow recommendations on the IEP.* IEPs typically state explicit goals and objectives for the academic year. For example, an objective on an IEP may state that the

student will score at least 70% correct on tests given in a general education science class. This goal can be taken into consideration when determining the student's grade in the class.

3. *Make no grading adjustments at all.* This approach is adopted by many regular classroom teachers, and there are some advantages to this approach. Many students with disabilities can meet grade-level expectations when provided with high-quality instruction and support. The most commonly used grading method in schools are letter grades followed by percentage grades that convert to letter grades (William & Mary Training and Technical Assistance Center, 2015). The grades the students earn directly reflect their success at performing in the regular classroom and can be a source of pride. However, many students may simply not be able to compete successfully in such an environment without supports, and grading without adjustments may result in students not passing. Carefully consider the effect of adopting such a policy. Anxiety about promotion, graduation, and college can be especially pronounced for secondary students (Segool et al., 2013).
4. *Use a pass–fail system.* Consider carefully what the minimum standard for a passing grade would be, considering attendance, effort, and performance. Using the PASS variables, prioritize class objectives so that students with disabilities or other diverse learning needs receive as much appropriately adapted instruction on critical objectives as possible. At the end of the grading period, record performance with "pass" or "fail" (or "no pass").
5. *Use a double-standard approach.* With this approach, students with disabilities can be graded using different standards for letter grades. It may not be necessary simply to lower the standards, such that, for example, an "A" on the special education standard is equivalent to a "C" on the general education standard. It is also possible to consider the grade itself differently. For example, a grade using a special education standard could weigh effort, persistence, attitude, and progress more heavily (see Bursuck et al., 1996). Since assigning weights to a grade can be complicated, consider representing the grade as one of the following: an evaluation of the product (reports, projects, writings), the processes that enable the student to produce (effort, behavior, work, habits), or the progress (improvement, growth) (Jung & Gusky, 2010). Placing more importance on process or progress also demonstrates to students that the grade they receive is more in their control than one that sets unrealistic academic standards and that may lead to resignation or quitting. A special education grading standard could also more carefully consider goals and objectives for the student documented on the student's IEP.

   Often when different grading standards are applied, some notation is included that acknowledges that the standard is different. This could be done by including a discreet note on the report card (e.g., "Special grading standard") or by circling the letter awarded. Use of different grading standards can make goals more realistic and achievable for students. However, it is important to first determine that the usual grading standards are not appropriate for particular students and that another standard is more appropriate (Jung & Guskey, 2010). If it seems that students may be able, with sufficient effort and support, to meet the same standards as the rest of the class, it may be best not to use a different standard.
6. *Contracting.* In some cases, it may be helpful to establish a formal contract with a student regarding report card grades. The contract can specify what the student will do to earn a particular grade in the class, with respect to, for example, attendance, punctuality, homework completion, participation, and test scores. Grades are then allocated according to the terms of the contract.
7. *Personal grading plans.* Munk and Bursuck (2001, 2003) described the development of personal grading plans (PGPs) created by teams of general and special education teachers to provide more appropriate grading for individual students. For example, it was determined that the science grades of one eighth-grade student with learning disabilities were lower than expected because of the heavy weighting of tests and quiz scores. A PGP was developed that included specific objectives within each

thematic unit, with specified criteria and an adjusted grading scale for each objective. With thoughtful adjustments and effective communication such as this, grading can be a useful and productive experience for everyone.

COMMUNICATE GRADING PROCEDURES When planning the grading procedure for a student with a disability in an inclusive setting, general and special education teachers should collaborate to determine how to best represent a grade so that it is meaningful for that individual. Conderman and Hedin (2012) suggest sharing a spreadsheet that lists all student names and tracks their standardized testing scores, progress monitoring scores, and any accommodations or modifications to be used when developing classroom assessments. Results of Kurth et al.'s (2012) survey revealed that over 100 general and special education teachers had different preferences for grading students with disabilities and although they lacked a shared knowledge of how to assign grades for students with disabilities, teachers were reportedly open to opportunities to learn more about how grades are assigned and how the grades can contribute to student promotion.

When an individualized grading procedure that follows school district policies is determined, communicate the procedure to parents/caregivers and the student. It is important that all stakeholders have a clear and common understanding as to what grades represent when seen on a report card. When referencing assessments, teachers should help stakeholders to understand the fair grading practice, the purpose of assessments, and how any accommodations and modifications are used in the students' programming (HLP 5; McLeskey et al., 2017). When applicable, communicate with elementary and secondary students about the grading system by frequently referring to their learning targets during instruction, teaching them how to monitor and graph their own progress, and showing them how to keep a record of their formative and summative grades. Given a rubric with clear expectations, students with portfolio assessments can select their own artifacts to document evidence of their learning skills. By including students in the assessment process, grades could potentially serve as a motivational tool as well as an evaluation tool.

12 Summary

- Many types of tests are used in education, including norm-referenced, criterion-referenced, teacher-made, performance, portfolio, and curriculum-based tests. All tests must be reliable and valid to be useful.
- General strategies for adapting tests include using test accommodations, implementing individualized administration, teaching test-taking skills, and improving examiner familiarity. Other adaptation strategies can be applied to specific types of tests such as competency-based assessments and test formats.
- Many students benefit from being taught test-taking skills, including general strategies such as elimination strategies, guessing, and efficient use of time; strategies for specific test formats; and strategies that can be applied to different types of tests.
- Adjustments can be made in grading and scoring the work of students with disabilities. These adjustments can be applied to report card grades, homework, and seatwork. Be sure to communicate the grading procedures with students, teachers, and parents/caregivers.

PROFESSIONAL STANDARDS LINK: Assessment

Information in this chapter links most directly to:

- CEC 2020 Initial Practice-Based Professional Preparation Standards for Special Educators (Initial K–12 standards) (see https://exceptionalchildren.org/standards/initial-practice-based-professional-preparation-standards-special-educators): 2 (Understanding and Addressing Each Individual's Developmental and Learning Needs), 3 (Demonstrating Subject Matter Content and Specialized Curricular Knowledge), 4 (Using Assessment to Understand the Learner and the Learning Environment for Data-Based Decision Making), 5 (Supporting Learning Using Effective Instruction)
- InTASC Standards (see https://www.ccsso.org/sites/default/files/2017-11/InTASC_Model_Core_Teaching_Standards_2011.pdf): 2 (Learning Differences), 6 (Assessment), 7 (Planning for Instruction), 8 (Instructional Strategies)

ASSESSMENT

When assessing students with disabilities and other diverse learning needs, have you considered the following? If not, see the pages listed here.

STRATEGIES FOR ADMINISTERING NORM-REFERENCED TESTS

- ☐ Use test accommodations, 310
- ☐ Use universal design for learning, 310–311
- ☐ Use individually administered tests, 311
- ☐ Teach test-taking skills, 311
- ☐ Increase motivation, 311
- ☐ Improve examiner familiarity, 311
- ☐ Request accommodations for college entrance exams, 311–312

STRATEGIES FOR ADAPTING COMPETENCY-BASED LOCAL AND STATEWIDE ASSESSMENT

- ☐ Implement test accommodations, 312
- ☐ Use alternate assessments, 312–313
- ☐ Request accommodations on GED tests, 313

STRATEGIES FOR ADAPTING TEACHER-MADE AND CRITERION-REFERENCED TESTS

- ☐ Revise tests, 315–316
- ☐ Adjust scoring procedures, 316–317

STRATEGIES FOR USING CURRICULUM-BASED MEASUREMENT

- ☐ Apply CBM to monitor learning progress, 317–319

STRATEGIES FOR USING PERFORMANCE ASSESSMENT

- ☐ Implement and adapt performance assessment, 319–321

STRATEGIES FOR USING PORTFOLIO ASSESSMENT

- ☐ Develop portfolios, 321
- ☐ Adapt portfolio assessment, 321–322

STRATEGIES FOR TEACHING TEST-TAKING SKILLS

- ☐ Teach general test-preparation strategies, 323
- ☐ Teach general strategies for standardized tests, 323–325
- ☐ Teach specific strategies for standardized tests, 325–327
- ☐ Teach strategies for teacher-made tests, 327–328
- ☐ Teach other test-taking strategies, 328–329

STRATEGIES FOR ADAPTING REPORT CARD GRADING

- ☐ Adjust grading procedures, 329–331
- ☐ Communicate grading procedures, 331

PART 3

Teaching in the Content Areas

Mark Wiens/Offset/Shutterstock

Note: Some text in this chapter discussing the Common Core State Standards are reprinted with permission.

CHAPTER 13

Literacy

LEARNING OBJECTIVES

After studying this chapter, you should be able to:

13.1 Understand considerations relevant to basal textbook, whole-language, direct-instruction, and code-emphasis approaches to reading.

13.2 Describe the Common Core State Standards for reading.

13.3 Explain strategies and adaptations for teaching basic reading skills in phonemic awareness, phonics, and basic sight words; reading fluency; vocabulary and reading comprehension; and multi-tiered reading instruction with response to intervention.

13.4 Identify strategies and adaptations for teaching written expression including handwriting, spelling, and written communication.

Reading is probably the most important academic skill students will learn in school. Most students acquire this skill with little apparent difficulty; however, for a smaller number, reading can represent a major stumbling block to school success (Pullen & Cash, 2017). The process of learning to read begins very early in life and extends well into adulthood.

Skills and understandings important for learning to read begin to develop in early infancy. These include recognizing books by the cover, pretending to read, listening to stories, attending to letters, and scribbling. Between the ages of 3 and 4, children begin to understand that it is print that is read in stories and that letters can be individually named. Pre-literate children learn to name some alphabet letters, attend to repeating (e.g., rhyming) sounds in language, and can connect information from a story to life experiences. Clearly, parents and other caregivers can play a key role in promoting this important skill development (Paratore & Dougherty, 2011).

In school, children go through a sequence of levels of reading development, beginning with prereading skills such as sound segmentation, building to letter and word recognition, and continuing through expert reading (Pressley, 2006; Pullen & Cash, 2017). After the early literacy or prereading stage, learners develop decoding skills (typically, grades K–2), fluency and automaticity (grades 2–3), uses of reading for learning (grades 4–8), appreciation of multiple viewpoints and levels of comprehension (including literal, inferential, critical; grades 9–12), and construction and reconstruction of reading for one's own purposes (including personal, professional, and civic purposes; college and beyond). Common Core State Standards (CCSS) in English language arts provide grade-appropriate reading standards in foundational skills, informational text, and literature across grades K–12 (National Governors Association (NGA) Center for Best Practices & Council of Chief State School Officers (CCSSO), 2010).

Students with disabilities or other diverse learning needs may exhibit difficulties at any, or all, of these levels of learning to read. Some may have specific disabilities in reading, sometimes referred to as **dyslexia** (Lerner & Johns, 2015). Dyslexia is a type of specific learning disability and is characterized as a severe difficulty learning to read and spell despite adequate opportunity and instruction (Catts & Petscher, 2022). In other cases, reading problems are a function of more general developmental or language delays or physical disabilities (Best et al., 2010). Students with hearing impairments often acquire reading skills at a slower rate (Stewart & Kluwin, 2001), and students with visual impairments may require specialized materials. Students with emotional or behavioral disorders often read below grade level (Reid et al., 2004; Wanzek et al., 2014) and students with autism spectrum disorder also may read below grade level (Spector & Cavanaugh, 2015). However, in all cases, specific methods for teaching reading and providing interventions can significantly improve reading ability.

Approaches to Reading

Learning Objective 13.1 Understand considerations relevant to basal textbook, whole-language, direct-instruction, and code-emphasis approaches to reading.

There are several approaches to beginning reading instruction. It is important to understand these different approaches because they carry different implications for students who are having difficulty learning to read.

CLASSROOM SCENARIO

Markeisha

Markeisha is a sincere, well-liked seventh grader. However, she has struggled with reading since first grade. She marvels at how easily some of her peers are able to read. Markeisha can't figure out why it seems so easy for them and yet is so difficult for her. Sometimes when she looks at the printed page, the words make no sense at all. They don't look a bit familiar to her, even when her teacher has her repeat the words over and over. Markeisha does her best to get by in school by listening to other students read, by listening to her teachers, and by studying the illustrations in her books. She never raises her hand in class and sits quietly, hoping she will not be noticed. Markeisha really wants to learn to read better, but no one seems to be able to help her do so.

QUESTIONS FOR REFLECTION

1. Why does Markeisha not speak with her teacher about her reading problem?
2. What do you think might be the cause of this problem?
3. What could the teacher do to become more aware of reading problems in her classroom?

STRATEGIES FOR IMPLEMENTING APPROACHES TO READING

IMPLEMENT AND ADAPT BASAL TEXTBOOK APPROACHES The most traditional approach to reading instruction involves the use of **basal textbooks**, with a different text assigned for each grade level from kindergarten through middle school (Temple et al., 2018). These textbooks contain short stories and comprehension questions designed to meet certain grade-level criteria. Some basal textbooks emphasize phonics; others highlight literature-based stories.

Most basal reading series include workbooks and worksheets that provide supplemental practice on comprehension and specific word study skills. In addition, the development of literacy is often supported by language arts classes, typically distinct from reading classes, whereby students are provided separate spelling and grammar instruction.

Most students with reading difficulties have problems attending to the sounds in words and learning to decode (Pullen & Cash, 2017). If you have students with reading difficulties who are not making adequate progress in a particular basal series, determine whether your basal series offers a clear sequence of skills and sufficient review of these skills as they are learned. Consult with the special education teacher to determine whether a more structured phonetic approach might be more helpful, as a supplement or an alternative to the classroom materials. Some basal series do provide a more balanced approach to literature and phonics instruction (e.g., Carnine et al., 2017; Engelmann et al., 2008) and you might be able to use one that does.

IMPLEMENT AND ADAPT WHOLE-LANGUAGE APPROACHES The **whole-language** approach to reading emphasizes meaning and integrates all literacy tasks within reading instruction (Routman, 1991; Temple et al., 2018). A basic tenet of this approach is that the immersion of children in a literature-enriched environment promotes literacy. Many traditional skills, such as phonics, sounding out words, spelling, grammar, and comprehension strategies, are not directly taught but are often addressed within the reading context. There is an increased emphasis on meaning construction and the use of context clues to figure out unknown words.

During whole-language instruction, students engage in reading **authentic literature** (e.g., trade books that include picture books, informational books, and chapter books) independently and maintain journals documenting their progress and comprehension of reading materials. Overall, the emphasis is placed on engaging students in literacy acts and promoting meaning (Goodman, 2014).

Unfortunately, through this approach, as many as 25% of students do not discover sound–symbol relationships independently and without explicit instruction (Pullen & Cash, 2017). Students with serious reading difficulties frequently have deficits in **phonemic awareness** and need special training to learn that words are composed of smaller, individual speech sounds (phonemes). For example, the word *pin* has three phonemes, /p/, /i/, and /n/. Phonemes can be added, subtracted, or rearranged to make new words (Pressley & Allington, 2015). In fact, foundational skills for reading, including phonemic awareness, phonics, word recognition, and fluency, are important components of early reading in the CCSS for English language arts.

Most students with reading problems benefit from explicit training in phonological awareness, letter recognition and formation, sound–symbol relationships, decoding practice using controlled texts, comprehension strategies, and motivational techniques (Pressley & Allington, 2015; Pullen & Cash, 2017). Because whole-language approaches typically do not explicitly include such components, they may be less beneficial for students with serious reading difficulties unless additional instructional support is provided (Gersten & Dimino, 1993; Pressley & Rankin, 1994).

If you are using a whole-language approach to reading, collect reading performance data using curriculum-based measurement and audio recording of students' oral reading to ensure students are progressing satisfactorily. Fountas and Pinnell (2013) provide listings of thousands of trade books by graded reading level that can be used to support whole-language approaches to reading instruction (see also Wooten et al., 2018). Some students with severe reading deficits may benefit from whole-language instruction if they are also receiving specialized reading instruction from special educators (Rudenga, 1992). Finally, if you have the opportunity as a teacher to examine literature programs to make recommendations for adoption, review what considerations have been made to meet the reading needs of all students.

IMPLEMENT AND ADAPT DIRECT-INSTRUCTION AND CODE-EMPHASIS APPROACHES **Direct instruction** is an instructional method that has proved successful with students with disabilities and those at risk for school failure (Carnine et al., 2017). Direct instruction involves a systematic, teacher-led approach using materials that contain a controlled vocabulary and emphasizing a **code-emphasis approach** to reading instruction. For example, students are taught the sound–symbol relationships among letters and are provided sufficient practice in decoding specific word patterns in reading passages before being presented with reading selections containing unfamiliar words. Individual sounds and words are introduced systematically and practiced in isolation and in word lists, sentences, paragraphs, short stories, and accompanying workbook activities. Frequently, students with serious reading difficulties benefit greatly from structured code-emphasis approaches (Blachman et al., 2014; Shaywitz, 2003).

Curriculum materials are available that contain a code-emphasis approach to reading instruction. These materials include, for example, *Reading Mastery* (SRA/McGraw-Hill), a basal series intended for the entire general education classroom, and *Corrective Reading: Decoding Series* (SRA/McGraw-Hill), a series intended especially for students with reading problems up to the seventh-grade level. Both of these reading series promote an effective instruction model of delivery, including teacher modeling and demonstration, frequent student responding and feedback, and practice using controlled vocabulary materials to teach reading. Because students with reading disabilities frequently rely too much on context cues (Johnson, 1992; Pressley & Allington, 2015), the materials encourage use of word-attack skills by, for example, not providing pictures or by providing pictures that can be seen only after reading and turning

Pearson eTextbook

Video Example 13.1

In this video, an elementary school principal discusses the use of a "holistic" language-instruction approach (whole language) compared with a direct-instruction approach at a school with a large number of students for whom English is not their first language. Think about how their instructional needs may be similar to some students with reading disabilities.

the page. In the *Corrective Reading Series*, students are given high-interest reading passages with controlled vocabulary that are introduced in a systematic sequence, with review following in subsequent passages.

Other commercially available structured reading programs include The *Reading Mastery Signature Edition* (RMSE; SRA/McGraw-Hill) for grades K–5 and *Read Well* (Voyager Sopris Learning) for early reading (K–2). These code-emphasis programs address all or nearly all of the CCSS relevant to reading (e.g., National Institute for Direct Instruction, 2015). The *Edmark Reading Program* (ProEd) is a sight-word program designed for students with few or no reading skills and those who have not benefited from an explicit phonics approach or other reading approaches. *Edmark* has a printed/tabletop or a computerized version. As with all programs, monitor progress carefully to be sure the methods and materials are having the desired effect.

Considerations and Adaptations Three commonly asked questions are whether students who are taught using a code-emphasis approach can transfer these reading skills to other, less-structured reading materials; whether they will lose motivation from all the structure; and whether they will learn comprehension skills. In fact, students with reading disabilities can transfer skills acquired from code-emphasis instruction to more literature-based programs (Snider, 1997). Neither approach totally excludes the other as code-emphasis instruction should be linked to vocabulary development and language comprehension by way of teacher read-alouds, shared writing, and picture books, for example. In addition, students can maintain their motivation if teachers use enthusiasm. Finally, teachers should ensure that any reading program is balanced and includes engaging text and sufficient comprehension instruction once students learn the necessary decoding skills (Adams, 1990; Klingner et al., 2007; Pressley & Allington, 2015). Ensure that your reading program provides all the elements necessary for students to become skilled and motivated readers.

MAKE ADAPTATIONS TO PROMOTE ACCESS TO TEXT For some students, physical and motor constraints can inhibit learning to read (Coleman & Heller, 2009). Regardless of the approach to reading, students must be able to stabilize reading materials and position themselves to facilitate efficient attending to the text. Ensure that students are positioned properly, with proper posture, in midline position, using supports when needed. Check to be sure the table and chair are at the right height and that the table is slanted when needed. Provide color contrasts—for example, placing colored construction paper under a page when reading to reduce brightness—for students with visual impairments.

For students who have difficulty turning pages, provide rubber fingertips (Swingline) or a pencil with an eraser end. Separate pages with notebook tabs, paperclips, or pieces of material such as sponges or weather stripping. Pages in electronic tablets can be easily turned with a touch of a finger.

For students who lose their place on the line, prepare a clear transparency with multicolored lines, composed of 1-inch strips of different colors. Place this transparency over pages as the student reads and fade the use of the colored lines over time. Some students may become fatigued while reading, and the length of reading sessions may have to be adjusted (Heller & Alberto, 2010).

Some additional adaptations to promote access include modification of printed materials with braille or large print; use of magnifying devices; and use of optical character-recognition systems, such as *Kurzweil 1000* and *Kurzweil 3000* (Kurzweil Education), that convert text to speech or Braille. Other adaptations involve the use of audio-recording formats such as audio-recorded text . Apps such as *Voice Recorder* (TapMedia) or built-in audio recording apps allow for longer recordings on phones or tablets. Effective use of technology for Deaf students or students who have limited hearing include the use of personal amplification systems, captioning, and phones and tablets with texting, which can be helpful when receiving reading instruction. Apps for translating text to American Sign Language for phones and tablets include *ASL Translator* (Software Studios) and *Mimix Sign Language Translator* (Mind Rockets, Inc.).

Employ Principles of Universal Design for Learning Universal design for learning (UDL) is a framework for designing instruction and learning activities to accommodate all learners (see *cast.org*; Hall et al., 2012; Meyer et al., 2014) that is similar in many ways to differentiated instruction. Many new technological advances are available to accommodate students with diverse learning needs in literacy instruction. For example, text-to-speech and speech-to-text software programs are widely available and even embedded into many existing programs, such as the Microsoft Office programs Word, Excel, and Outlook and the search engine Google Chrome. *Audible* is a program used to read aloud books that have been linked with Kindles, which are hand-held devices containing downloaded electronic books. Students can begin reading a book and convert to listening to the book using Audible and revert back to reading or listening whenever desired. When starting up again, the program automatically syncs to the most recent stopping place, regardless of whether students were reading or listening. These applications, as well as the many other strategies described in this chapter, are consistent with UDL principles.

Common Core State Standards for Reading

Learning Objective 13.2 Describe the Common Core State Standards for reading.

Common Core State Standards for Reading (K–12) are found within the English Language Arts Standards and contain standards for reading in literature, informational text, and foundational skills. The grade-specific standards reflect end-of-year expectations and form, over all grade levels, a cumulative progression toward meeting college and career readiness in reading by the end of high school (NGA & CCSSO, 2010). Foundational skills for reading (K–5 only) at the fifth-grade level, for example, include the following (NGA & CCSSO, 2010):

Phonics and Word Recognition

- Know and apply grade-level phonics and word analysis skills in decoding words.
- Use combined knowledge of all letter–sound correspondences, syllabication patterns, and morphology (e.g., roots and affixes) to read accurately unfamiliar multisyllabic words in context and out of context.

Fluency

- Read with sufficient accuracy and fluency to support comprehension.
- Read grade-level text with purpose and understanding.
- Read grade-level prose and poetry orally with accuracy, appropriate rate, and expression on successive readings.
- Use context to confirm or self-correct word recognition and understanding, rereading as necessary.

Informational text standards for reading (K–12) refer to understanding expository text, for example, science or history texts. Relevant skills include understanding relevant vocabulary, determining main ideas, making inferences, summarizing text, identifying text structure, understanding how reasons and evidence are used to support points in a text, analyzing multiple accounts of the same topic, and integrating knowledge and ideas from multiple sources to write or speak knowledgeably about a given topic. For example, below is a comparison of informational text standards at the fourth- and eighth-grade levels (NGA & CCSSO, 2010).

Fourth grade:

- Refer to details and examples in a text when explaining what the text says explicitly and when drawing inferences from the text.
- Determine the main idea of a text and explain how it is supported by key details; summarize the text.

Eighth grade:

- Cite the textual evidence that most strongly supports an analysis of what the text says explicitly as well as inferences drawn from the text.
- Determine a central idea of a text and analyze its development over the course of the text, including its relationship to supporting ideas; provide an objective summary of the text.

Literature standards for reading (K–12) include quoting accurately from a text in explaining text content and drawing inferences, determining themes from details in the text, describing the role of a speaker's or narrator's point of view, and describing how different texts on the same topic address similar themes or topics (http://www.corestandards.org/ELA-Literacy/RF/5/; http://www.corestandards.org/ELA-Literacy/RI/4/; http://www.corestandards.org/ELA-Literacy/RI/8/).

Teaching Reading Skills

Learning Objective 13.3 Explain strategies and adaptations for teaching basic reading skills in phonemic awareness, phonics, and basic sight words; reading fluency; vocabulary and reading comprehension; and multi-tiered reading instruction with response to intervention.

Beyond the application of particular methods and materials reflecting different approaches to reading instruction, it is important for teachers to carefully attend to all aspects of the reading process to ensure that all students are receiving the instruction they need. It is also important that reading instruction is of high quality and based on research because, in many cases, it will represent the first tier of a school's multi-tiered support system (MTSS) or response-to-intervention (RTI) approach to reading, as described later in this chapter.

STRATEGIES FOR PROMOTING WORD IDENTIFICATION

Most students with reading difficulties require additional instruction and practice in identifying words. Readers need to become automatic and fluent at word reading so that they will be able to devote sufficient cognitive effort to comprehending what they read. However, before readers can acquire this automaticity, they must be able to read individual words. In order to do this, they must learn that words are composed of individual sounds, or phonemes.

DEVELOP PHONEMIC AWARENESS SKILLS **Phonemes** are the smallest sound units, such as /t/ and /l/. Some students do not develop an understanding that words are composed of individual sounds as quickly as others, and therefore these students may find phonics instruction confusing. Phonemic awareness includes instruction and practice in listening and using sounds in isolation initially, then sound blending and sound segmentation. The purpose of phonemic (or phonological) awareness is for students to learn that words are composed of individual sounds that can be combined and separated to create new words. Later, when students study phonics, they learn how these individual phonemes are represented by letters and letter combinations (Bursuck & Damer, 2015). Phonemic awareness is included prominently in foundational skills for grades K–1 in the CCSS for reading. Sample phonemic awareness activities include the following:

- Discriminating sounds, for example: "Tell me if these two words have the same, or different, first sound: *cap–cat*."
- Sound blending or making individual sounds into words, for example: "What word am I saying: /k/–/a/–/t/?"
- Segmenting words into individual phonemes, for example: "How many sounds are in the word *fan*? What are the sounds?"
- Rhyming sounds, for example: "Tell me some words that rhyme with *fall*. Now, tell me some 'make-believe' words that rhyme with *fall*."

Gamelike activities are available that emphasize developing phonological awareness. For example, *Phonological Awareness Training for Reading* (Pro-Ed) includes a board game for skill development. In one game, Rocky the Robot "speaks" only in phonemes or **onset-rime** constructions, that is, the sounds that precede the first vowel in a syllable (onset), followed by the remaining sounds, which are common patterns or word families (rime) (see Figure 13.1). Students must create the words Rocky is trying to say. For example, a teacher could say, "Rocky says, 't-op.' What is he trying to say?" These materials provide instruction and practice with phonemic awareness skills over a 12- to 14-week period. Apps for literacy have the potential to provide students with supplemental practice in reading. Apps such as *Phonemic Awareness Bubbles* (Preschool University), *What's Changed?* (Accessible Publishing Systems), and *Phoneme Farm* (Colvard Learning) provide phonemic awareness training. Also, *Starfall* (Starfall Education)

Figure 13.1 Examples of Onset-Rime constructions

Onset	Rime	What word?
c-	-op	cop
	-ow	cow
	-ar	car
	-an	can
br-	-ing	bring
	-ain	brain
	-oke	broke
	-ave	brave
sk-	-y	sky
	-in	skin
	-unk	skunk
	-ill	skill
sh-	-ine	shine
	-ip	ship
	-ow	show
	-ave	shave
n-	-at	nat
	-ap	nap
	-un	nun
	-ot	not

Pearson eTextbook

Video Example 13.2

In this video, a teacher works with several children on phonemic awareness activities, letter identification, and matching letters with sounds. Characterize the teaching observed, including the instructional materials and the practice opportunities.

offers pre-K to third-graders gamelike activities to practice varied skills including phoneme segmentation, phoneme substitution, and onset-rime blending, *Starfall* includes visual and audio cues and reinforcement.

Phonemic awareness skill development may benefit your entire primary-grade classroom (Ehri et al., 2001; Suggate, 2016). For other grade levels, consult with special education teachers and speech–language therapists. These specialists can recommend specific practice activities to promote better phonemic awareness. For English learners (ELs), consult with teachers of ELs to better understand the English phonemes that exist or do not exist in the child's native language.

PROVIDE PHONICS INSTRUCTION Training in *phonics* follows phonemic awareness and refers to providing instruction in the sound–symbol associations among letters and symbols. Phonics skills are important components of CCSS in reading for grades K–5 (NGA & CCSSO, 2010). Children who learn to read without any difficulties—and many do—may figure out this system independently. However, students without good phonics skills have to rely on visual memory, context clues, or picture clues to guess what the unfamiliar word is. Unfortunately, reliance on such clues is not always effective, especially when many letter–sound relationships are unknown (Pressley & Allington, 2015). These students can benefit from explicit phonics instruction. The National Reading Panel (2000) concluded that synthetic phonics—in which students are taught to convert letters into sounds or phonemes, then blend the sounds to form words—was associated with the largest overall positive effects in decoding, comprehension, and collateral skills such as spelling (Pullen & Lloyd, 2008).

According to Stahl (1992; see also Stahl et al., 2006), an exemplary phonics program has the following characteristics:

- Builds on students' knowledge about how print works
- Builds on a phonemic awareness foundation
- Is explicit, clear, and direct
- Is integrated within a reading and language arts program
- Emphasizes reading words rather than memorizing rules

- Includes learning onsets and rimes
- Emphasizes development of independent word-recognition strategies
- Emphasizes development of fluency-building word-recognition skills

Instruction in phonics proceeds systematically; practice is provided using familiar words before new words are introduced. Usually, regular words are introduced before irregular words, and sufficient practice in reading and spelling is provided before introducing new vocabulary. In phonics-based programs, instruction follows a specific sequence of skills. Although variation exists, a possible sequence could include the following components (see, e.g., Bursuck & Damer, 2015; Mercer et al., 2011):

1. Individual consonant and short vowel sounds (e.g., /s/, /a/)
2. Simple patterns such as *vc* (vowel–consonant; e.g., *at, it*) and *cvc* (consonant–vowel–consonant; e.g., *bat, hit*)
3. Consonant digraphs (e.g., *ch, sh, th*) and consonant blends (e.g., *bl, st, br*)
4. Long vowels, including final *e* (such as in *hope, tape*), and double vowels or vowel digraphs (such as in *keep, tail*)
5. *R*- and *l*-controlled vowels, such as in *car* and *call*
6. Diphthongs, such as *ow, oi, aw*

Once these skills and related skills are mastered, students can learn higher-level word-analysis skills, such as compound words, prefixes and suffixes, contractions, and syllabication. These skills should be integrated into the context of reading as they are acquired. As Stahl et al. (2006) emphasized, "Good phonics instruction should not teach rules, need not use worksheets, should not dominate instruction, and does not have to be boring" (p. 132).

Students with severe to profound hearing loss are typically far less proficient than other students in phonological skills. The reading skills of students with hearing impairments appear to be associated with language and vocabulary development (Marschark, 2010). During the elementary years, they appear to rely more on visual than acoustic cues for letters and words. In secondary school, and later in college, they may rely more on phonological information, particularly for words with regular spellings. Strategies recommended for teaching reading to students with severe hearing impairments include early access to language by means of signing and simultaneous exposure to written texts. Unfortunately, there is little research to demonstrate the effectiveness (or lack of effectiveness) of such techniques as phonemic awareness or phonics instruction, guided oral reading, and comprehension-monitoring strategies (see Hirshorn et al., 2015). Instead, amount of time spent reading, greater background knowledge, language and vocabulary development, and word-recognition activities are associated with reading achievement (Schirmer & McGough, 2005). Most programs employ basal readers; however, consideration of a variety of alternatives is recommended (Stewart & Kluwin, 2001).

Software phonics programs are also available commercially. For example, *Lexia Reading Core5* (Lexia Learning) and *Fast ForWord* (Scientific Learning Corporation) are approaches that emphasize phonemic awareness, phonics, and auditory discrimination. Lexia® provides a suite of literacy options to reinforce decoding skills at the elementary and secondary level (www.lexialearning.com). Regan et al. (2014) implemented the Lexia program (Lexia Strategies for Older Students™) with upper elementary students with learning disabilities and attention-deficit/hyperactivity disorder in order to build their consistency and automaticity with foundational phonics skills. Following a Lexia Quick Reading Test®, the software program advanced each student once the skills were demonstrated with automaticity and accuracy. Although some students also required one-to-one basic decoding instruction to reinforce skills, all students improved basic word reading skills and maintained the learned skills when they stopped using Lexia. In addition, Troia (2004) reported that a program called Fast ForWord provided gains in sight-word reading, decoding, and expressive language for a sample of migrant students with limited English proficiency. A review of several interventions using Fast ForWord, however, suggested that the program may not always be effective (Strong et al., 2011); therefore, teachers should monitor student progress to ensure objectives are being met. Also, software programs should be used as a supplement to teacher-directed instruction and not a replacement. For more information on software for promoting reading, see the *Apps for Education* feature.

Technology for Enhancing Literacy Instruction

Technological advances have provided numerous opportunities to assist with teaching literacy for K–12 students with disabilities. Hardware and software devices are available that can be used to enhance reading and writing skills for students with disabilities. *Read&Write* (Texthelp), for example, offers both reading and writing supports with the following features: text-to-speech, translation of text, proofreading, integration with web browsers and online word processors, highlighting, typing echo, word banks, and more. The tables below highlight technologies that incorporate UDL features, enabling struggling readers and writers to have more access to literacy tasks. There are a large variety of tools beyond those included here, so it is critical to examine the tools to determine whether it meets the needs of your students.

Technology	Benefits	Examples
Reading with technology		
Books	• Facilitates auditory reading • Provides vocabulary supports • Provides highlighting feature	Audio books Digital books
Text-to-Speech	• Can be used to orally read any computerized text from the Internet, a word processing program, a computer program, scanned-in materials from class, or e-text • Allows for altering volume, speed, pitch, fonts, text color • Readily available on word processor programs (e.g., Microsoft Word), tablets, phones, laptops, computers	*NaturalReader* *Snap&Read* *TextSpeechPro*
Reader Pens	• Portable • Can read-aloud textbooks • Can translate, if needed • Can define terms, as needed	*Scanmarker Air*
Other low-tech tools to support writing		Colored transparency sheets Sticky notes Line guides Highlighters
Writing with technology		
Alternative keyboards	• USB enabled (wired) • Bluetooth compatible (wireless)	Ergonomic keyboards Split keyboards High-contrast keyboards On-screen keyboards (built in within operating systems)
Speech-to-text	• Built-in to word processor programs (i.e., Microsoft Word, Google Docs), tablets, phones, laptops, computers	*Dragon Naturally Speaking* *Voice Note II* *Google Voice Typing* *iDictate*
Word processing	• Provides word prediction (i.e., students select the desired word from the word choices that are supplied) • Typing echo • Provides speech-to-text • Provides vocabulary help • Provides translations • Inserts pictures into writing • Provides spell-check • Provides visual support for organizing ideas	*Co:Writer (Don Johnston)* *Clicker8*

Apps for Education

Technology for Enhancing Literacy Instruction—*continued*

Technology	Benefits	Examples
Other low-tech tools to support writing		Graphic organizers Sticky notes Pencil grips Slant boards Dry-erase boards with markers

TEACH STRUCTURAL ANALYSIS AS STUDENTS ACQUIRE PHONICS SKILLS Older students begin to confront more complex words. **Structural analysis** refers to the ability to examine the structures of such words and break them into pronounceable syllables. Structural analysis involves examining a word by familiar word parts, such as the prefix, suffix, syllables, or smaller word parts. Teach morphemic units (e.g., *-ment*) and basic syllabication rules to help students. The *REWARDS*® reading program (Voyager Sopris) provides an approach to teaching multisyllabic-word decoding that may be useful for students in grades 4–12.

Teaching students the **DISSECT strategy** also provides them with tools they can use independently when they encounter unfamiliar words The DISSECT strategy uses structural analysis as well as some other steps and provides a multiple-step procedure for figuring out unfamiliar words (Joseph & Schisler, 2009; Lenz & Hughes, 1990). Each letter in DISSECT stands for one of the steps in the procedure. The steps of the strategy are as follows:

Pearson eTextbook

Video Example 13.3

It is important to maximize decoding practice during instructional time. How can you be sure students are provided reading practice?

- Discover the context of the word.
- Isolate the word's prefix.
- Separate the word's suffix.
- Say the word's stem.
- Examine the word's stem using the following 3s and 2s rules, then segment into pronounceable parts:

  3s rule: underline 3 letters if stem begins with a consonant (example: renewal).

  2s rule: underline 2 letters if stem begins with a vowel (example: unopened).

  Repeat for all letters in the stem.
- Check with another person to see if you are correct.
- Try finding the word in the dictionary.

Teach students other problem-solving strategies so that they will become more independent readers. For example, show them how to use context clues to guess what the word might be, based on the rest of the sentence or paragraph, title, subheadings, charts, graphs, and accompanying illustrations (Deshler & Schumaker, 2006).

USE STRATEGIES FOR PROMOTING BASIC SIGHT VOCABULARY Many words are used frequently at various grade levels; these words are often referred to as basic **sight words**. Some of these irregular words cannot be easily decoded using phonics skills, including such words as *the, a, is, to*, and *once*. Many word lists are available that contain graded sight-word lists (e.g., Dolch word lists). Students with reading difficulties may require repeated exposure and additional practice in identifying and saying these words automatically.

One suggestion for providing practice in developing basic sight-word vocabulary is to have students make and use flashcards containing their sight words. Some time each day can be devoted to saying the sight words with a partner. Cards containing words pronounced correctly and quickly can be stacked together, cards containing words said correctly but slowly in another stack, and cards containing words unknown in a third stack. Maintain records of the number of words in each stack. Gradually add new words as sight words are mastered. Using technology such as a computer, video, smartboard, or app (e.g., *See, Read, Say* HD; 28PM Software) can provide sustainable sight-word instruction in busy classrooms. A word can be shown visually with the technology, the student reads the word out loud, and then clicks on the word to have it spoken aloud.

Some teachers prepare checklists that contain new words or difficult words for students to learn, both at school and at home with their parents or caregivers. The checklists are practiced daily at school and at home, and teachers and caregivers simply put a check mark next to words read correctly under the date.

Finally, some teachers prepare large wall charts and prominently display listings of words they want students to master. Figure 13.2 has an example of a word wall chart displaying many sight words. Charts can be changed as students master words.

Students with moderate and severe disabilities may benefit from being taught specific sight words (using, e.g., the *Edmark* program) to enhance their classroom experience, daily living skills, and job skills (Browder et al., 2006). These could include words for shopping, cooking, reading warning labels, and reading signs for community recreation and could be enhanced with pictures from *Boardmaker* (Mayer-Johnson) to create a readable text (Fossett et al., 2003). Fletcher and Abood (1988) found that students with mild intellectual disabilities who could read at nearly the fourth-grade level could not read the words on many warning labels, such as *inhale, flammable*, and *inaccessible*.

Sight words have been taught to elementary students and adolescents with significant cognitive disabilities using a variety of methods, including modeling, prompting, error correction, and feedback (Browder et al., 2006; Roberts et al., 2013). Students' comprehension can be promoted by having them find the words in pictures or real settings or by having them give definitions. Try using classroom peers and sight-word cards to help promote sight-word recognition.

Figure 13.2 Wall Chart Containing Sight Words

a	came	her	look	people	too
after	can	here	looked	play	two
all	come	him	long	put	up
am	could	his	make	ran	us
an	day	house	man	run	very
and	did	how	me	said	was
are	do	I	mother	saw	we
as	don't	I'm	my	see	went
asked	down	if	no	she	were
at	for	in	not	so	what
away	from	into	now	some	when
back	get	is	of	that	where
be	go	it	old	the	will
because	going	just	on	then	with
before	good	keep	one	there	would
big	had	kind	or	they	you
boy	has	know	our	this	your
but	have	like	out	three	
by	he	little	over	to	

Pearson eTextbook

Video Example 13.4

This video discusses the importance of fluency. Why is teacher modeling important?

STRATEGIES FOR PROMOTING READING FLUENCY

Reading fluency reflects not just accuracy but also rate. The Life Span Institute (2002) at the University of Kansas estimated that students should reach the following levels of fluency at each grade level, measured in correct words per minute on grade-level passages: first grade—60, second—70, third—90, fourth—120, fifth—150. Behavioral Research and Teaching (2005), housed at the University of Oregon, updated and published similar norms in 2017: first—60, second—100, third—112, fourth—133, fifth—146, sixth—146. Norms for later grades were drawn from 2005 data: seventh—150, eighth—151 (see Hasbrouck & Tindal, 2017). The norm tables can be used to set long-term reading fluency goals for students.

Most students with reading difficulties require additional practice activities designed to help them read more fluently, even after they have mastered decoding skills. For example, in practice with recognizing high-frequency sight words such as *does, who, for*, and *said*, reading fluency improves. Several procedures are available to promote fluency (Allor & Chard, 2011; Chard et al., 2002; Kubina & Hughes, 2007).

USE REPEATED READINGS No one would expect students to learn to play the piano by continuously sight-reading new passages. Rather, students are expected to practice new pieces until they have become skilled and automatic before they move on to new and more difficult pieces (Anderson et al., 1985). Similarly, students who have struggled to learn to read a new passage should have the opportunity to reread the passage until fluent, effortless reading is achieved (Mercer et al., 2011). As their familiarity with the passage increases, their fluency and comprehension should also increase. Record reading rates on a graph and indicate which passages are "repeated readings" and which are first-time readings. Set target rates (e.g., 140 words per minute), and reward students for reaching these targets. Provide extra practice on difficult words or phrases that slow students' rate. Research has suggested that repeated readings can improve fluency for individual passages as well as overall fluency and comprehension (Lee & Yoon, 2017; Staubitz et al., 2005; Stevens et al., 2017; Therrien, 2004; Young et al., 2014). However, research is equivocal regarding the effects of repeated reading. O'Connor et al. (2007) implemented **repeated reading** and continuous reading with struggling readers in 15-minute sessions, three times per week for 14 weeks. They reported that repeated reading did not produce greater gains than continuous reading; however, each was effective compared with a control condition. At least in this case, what was most important was that students spent extra time in connected reading in order to develop their fluency skills.

USE CURRICULUM-BASED MEASUREMENT Time students' oral reading rates on assigned texts several days a week, then chart their performance. Graphed reading rates will demonstrate to students the rate at which they are improving in reading fluency. For example, identify 100-word segments and graph the amount of time taken to read the segment. Some teachers prefer to time students for a designated amount of time. For example, 1- or 2-minute time segments can be used, and teachers can graph the number of words read correctly (and incorrectly) in this time segment. To evaluate long-term progress, select several end-of-year passages and evaluate the reading rate throughout the year. Curriculum-based measurement (CBM) can help you keep track of student progress and let you know when students are falling behind in their skill development (Clemens et al., 2018; Espin et al., 2018).

USE CLASSWIDE PEER TUTORING More time spent in oral reading can help develop fluency over time. Classwide peer tutoring, in which pairs of students take turns reading to each other, is one good way of dramatically increasing the amount of time students spend actively engaged in reading (Kearns et al., 2015). In classwide peer-tutoring configurations, students can develop fluency using such other components as sustained or repeated readings, 1- or 2-minute timings, extra practice with difficult parts, and CBM.

USE SOFTWARE PROGRAMS Software designed for computers can provide an alternative means of practicing reading, decoding, and fluency-building activities. Students are usually highly motivated to use computers, and many programs contain gamelike formats to entice students to put forth extra effort. Furthermore, computer-assisted instruction can provide the individualization and flexibility needed to address gaps in decoding skills observed in the performance of students in the upper elementary and secondary grades. Computer software—for example, *Mindplay Reading Fluency* (Mindplay)—is available to help promote reading fluency and reading comprehension.

READING COMPREHENSION

Reading comprehension is the process of extracting meaning from text, and it is a major consideration in the CCSS for reading (NGA & CCSSO, 2010). Reading comprehension is the ultimate goal of reading; yet for many students, comprehension is a major problem. Fortunately, reading-comprehension research has uncovered some effective strategies for improving reading comprehension for students with disabilities and other diverse learning needs (Berkeley et al., 2010; Mastropieri & Scruggs, 1997; Pressley & Allington, 2015). Students with reading-comprehension difficulties often benefit from explicit instruction and practice using strategies that promote reading comprehension.

CLASSROOM SCENARIO

Carmen

Carmen can read the words in the stories, but when someone asks him what the story is about, he can't remember. Ms. Simpson, his third-grade teacher, always has him read orally during class and consistently gives him praise for his word reading. However, whenever Ms. Simpson says, "Now tell me what the story is about in your own words," Carmen is lost. He is beginning to dislike reading class because more and more time is being devoted to questioning about the stories rather than just reading out loud.

QUESTIONS FOR REFLECTION

1. If a student can read the words, why might that student have difficulty comprehending what was read?
2. When is a good time to begin comprehension activities?
3. How can comprehension be encouraged across subject areas?

STRATEGIES FOR TEACHING READING COMPREHENSION

Specific reading-comprehension strategies can be taught for use before, during, and after reading passages. These include basic skills approaches, text enhancements, and self-questioning strategies.

USE BASIC SKILLS AND REINFORCEMENT STRATEGIES **Reinforcement** refers to providing rewards or positive comments to students to encourage and motivate them as they work and answer comprehension questions successfully. **Vocabulary instruction** refers to providing students with practice in learning specific vocabulary words that will be encountered in the readings (e.g., Coyne et al., 2004). For students whose first language is not English, consider the students' primary language and make connections to vocabulary and cognates they may already know. **Corrective feedback** refers to providing students with immediate feedback when oral reading errors occur. The idea is that students' comprehension will improve when they are given immediate feedback on decoding errors. These strategies are often helpful; however, they may be more effective when combined with text enhancement or self-questioning strategies.

Repeated reading may also help increase comprehension of the material (Bursuck & Damer, 2015; O'Shea et al.,1987; Stevens et al., 2017). However, use caution when assigning more than several repeated readings of the same passage because as the number of readings increases, students' motivation may decrease.

Direct instruction can refer to the use of published curriculum materials such as *Corrective Reading* and *Reading Mastery* (SRA/McGraw Hill). Research has indicated that this structured phonetic approach is effective in increasing comprehension as students become more skilled and fluent readers (Carnine et al., 2017; Shippen et al., 2005).

Figure 13.3 Semantic Feature Analysis Chart: Features of Different Genres

	Science Fiction	Fiction	Biography	Informational
Includes characters	X	X	X	
A true story			X	
Includes a setting	X	X	X	
Not real; Futuristic	X			
Factual			X	X
Imaginary events	X	X		

CREATE TEXT ENHANCEMENTS **Text enhancements** can include illustrations, maps, diagrams, visual-spatial displays, semantic feature analysis charts (see Figure 13.3), mnemonic pictures, and other adjunct aids developed to accompany text materials to increase comprehension. Although publishers of curriculum materials frequently use text enhancements, they also may be developed by teachers or students, using drawings or materials found through Internet search engines.

Illustrations drawn to represent characters, events, places, and action in texts reinforce the sequence of events in the stories. Information can be organized into **concept maps** or spatially organized maps that show relationships among all events, people, and places. Mnemonic text enhancements can also be designed to promote memory of important concepts and features from reading materials.

Browder (2015) described the use of text illustrations to promote comprehension for students with moderate and severe cognitive disabilities. In one case, the student listened to the teacher read the book *Toy Story* and was able to point to symbols on her communication board to answer comprehension questions such as the following: "Who was the favorite toy first?", "Who was the new toy?", "When did the boy get the new toy?" (Browder, 2015, p. 56).

Imagery, the process of visualizing content from readings, may be a useful substitute when illustrations are unavailable. To assist students in using this strategy, model and demonstrate the imagery process. Break the strategy into three steps. First, tell students to read a passage. Second, have them think of a picture in their minds that represents important content in the story. Third, have students describe their "mental pictures" to you or a peer. Provide feedback on the quality of the images by adding any important features that may have been missing from their images. Although imagery has not yielded as powerful comprehension effects as some self-questioning strategies, actively picturing text content may be beneficial for some of your students.

Adjunct aids, including study guides, outlines, guided notes, partial outlines, and highlighting and underlining, are also examples of useful text enhancements.

TEACH SPECIFIC QUESTIONING STRATEGIES Asking students questions and teaching them to ask themselves questions about readings, helps promote reading comprehension (Berkeley et al., 2011). For example, before reading, ask students to look at the title of a passage, cover of a book, images, or figures and make predictions. Ask students, "What do you think this will be about?" During reading, ask students to revisit those earlier predictions and ask, "What do you think will happen next?" Overall guidelines for teaching reading-comprehension strategies are given in Figure 13.4. Several questioning and self-questioning strategies that are particularly effective are listed in Figure 13.5. Most of these self-questioning strategies have demonstrated positive effects on reading comprehension for elementary and secondary students with learning disabilities (Daniel & Williams, 2021). However, they have also been shown to be effective for other students with reading-comprehension difficulties (Joseph et al., 2016). When teaching specific strategies to support students' reading comprehension, use the SCREAM variables (Chapter 6) and ask yourself three questions:

- Did I model *when* to use the strategy and *why*?
- Did I explicitly model *how* to use all of the strategy steps?
- Did I model *how* to be flexible in strategy selection and application? (Regan & Berkeley, 2012)

Figure 13.4 Guidelines for Teaching Reading Comprehension

- Set clear objectives that are logically related to the use of each strategy for reading comprehension.
- Follow a specific instructional sequence:
  1. State the purpose of instruction.
  2. Provide instruction.
  3. Model use of the strategy.
  4. Prompt students to use the strategy following your model.
  5. Give corrective feedback.
  6. Provide guided practice of the strategy.
  7. Provide independent practice of the strategy.
- Inform students about the importance of the strategy.
- Monitor student performance.
- Encourage questioning that requires students to think about the strategies in relationship to the text.
- Encourage positive attributions.
- Teach for generalized use of the strategy.

Figure 13.5 Features of Self-Questioning Research

Activating Prior Knowledge Features:

- Teacher asks questions relevant to forthcoming readings
- Teacher teaches relevant vocabulary
- Teacher teaches using graphic organizers containing main ideas of forthcoming topic
- Students are taught to ask questions related to forthcoming topics
- Students complete activities containing relevant questions before reading

Summarization, Main Idea, Self-Monitoring, and Attribution Features:

- Students taught to ask questions about the reading material, such as "Who or what is the passage about?" "What is happening?"
- Students answer the questions they are asked and summarize or paraphrase readings in their own words
- Students state what the whole passage is about in their own words
- Students initially use self-monitoring cards while learning strategy steps
- Teacher encourages independent monitoring of strategy use
- Teacher encourages appropriate strategy attributions
- Teacher encourages independent use of strategy

Text Structure Based:

- Teaches passage-specific strategies for different types of text structures, including main idea, list, order, compare–contrast, problem-solving passages, as well as narrative story grammar passages

Multicomponent Packages:*

- Incorporate all or many of the above features; students are taught to ask and answer questions about the reading materials
- Questioning typically includes summarizing, predicting, and clarifying
- Teacher has direct role in instruction first and students assume more independence gradually in most models

*In some models, students assume a more active role during initial phases of instruction

Activate Prior Knowledge Several strategies can help students activate their prior knowledge on topics before they begin reading. If students have limited prior knowledge, it may be beneficial to provide them with opportunities to see images, books, videos, and artifacts related to the topic before they begin reading. When provided with text, one strategy for **activating prior knowledge** is the **TELLS strategy** fact-or-fiction strategy (Idol-Maestas, 1985; Ridge & Skinner, 2011). TELLS fact or fiction is an acronym for the following steps:

- Studying story Titles
- Examining pages for clue words
- Looking for important words
- Looking for hard words
- Describing the Setting of the story
- Answering whether the story was fact or fiction

Before starting to read, students attempt to follow the steps in TELLS and decide whether the passage is fact or fiction, and then they check their answer after reading the passage.

Pearson eTextbook
Video Example 13.5
This video illustrates a teacher using K-W-L with her students. Pay attention as she follows the steps and think about her evaluation of the strategy.

Promote Self-Generated Questions Many reading-comprehension strategies require students to self-question before, during, and after reading. As such, these strategies promote **metacognition**, the awareness of one's own cognitive processes and how they can be enhanced (Montague, 1998). Although good readers may develop these skills independently, students with disabilities (and many other students) can benefit from metacognitive training. Asking questions about reading material (e.g., "Why am I studying this passage?", "What is the main idea?", "What is a question about the main idea?") helps promote thinking about the information, which in turn facilitates recall and comprehension (Berkeley et al., 2010).

Brainstorming **Brainstorming** with students is another strategy for activating prior knowledge. Before a lesson, present students with the major topic that will be introduced, and ask them to generate as many ideas as possible that are related or similar to that topic. Students can record these ideas on individual concept maps or teachers can make a visual map of the shared ideas as a class. Asking questions about the topic can guide students to make connections to their own cultural and personal experiences. Encourage participation from all students. Brainstorming can be a component of most questioning strategies, including those intended to activate prior knowledge.

K-W-L is another strategy used to access prior knowledge before reading expository text (Ogle, 1986). KWL has been used with units of instruction as well as indivdual passages. During implementation of this strategy, students ask and answer three questions:

- "What do I Know about this topic?"
- "What do I Want to know?"
- "What did I Learn?"

For the first question, teachers and students brainstorm ideas of related topics of which they have prior knowledge and categorize their ideas. For the second question, teachers and students discuss what they want to know from reading the information. For the final step, students write down information they learned after a unit study or reading specific passages. It may be best to start with single passages and slowly increase text length for some students. You can create worksheets containing columns for answering each of the K-W-L steps. If a concept map was used prior to reading, students can add to or revise their ideas after reading.

Summarize and Paraphrase Several researchers have developed procedural steps for teaching students to summarize and paraphrase reading materials (see Stevens et al., 2018, for a review). Although each approach varied somewhat, similar components included the following:

1. Read a passage or short segment from a book.
2. Ask yourself who or what the passage is about.
3. Ask yourself what was happening in the passage.
4. Make up a summary sentence in your own words using the answers to the questions asked.

For example, Ellis (1996) described the **RAP strategy** for paraphrasing reading passages. The letters of the acronym stand for the following steps:

- **R**ead a paragraph.
- **A**sk yourself what the paragraph was about.
- **P**ut the main idea and two details in your own words. (p. 73)

Teach students that the main idea tells what the whole story (or paragraph) is about in a short summary sentence (Berkeley et al., 2010).

Similarly, reading-comprehension strategies used in classwide peer-tutoring interventions at the elementary and secondary levels (e.g., Kearns et al., 2015; McMaster & Fuchs, 2016) include the following questioning steps:

- What is the most important who or what in the text?
- What is the most important thing about the who or what?
- Write a summary sentence. (e.g., Mastropieri et al., 2001, p. 21)

Teach students to create concise summary sentences and to use their own words. Include self-monitoring instructions that list the selected procedures on cards or charts and display them prominently during reading to help students master the strategy steps. In the early phases of instruction, ask students to answer the questions either verbally or in writing to verify whether all strategy steps have been implemented correctly.

Pearson eTextbook
Video Example 13.6
Teaching text structure can help students to improve reading comprehension. How can students monitor their comprehension during reading?

Teach students to examine text structure as they study textbooks, including theme and main-idea identification (Hebert et al., 2016). In expository text, some paragraphs contain a main idea—such as wind erosion—with supporting statements or examples. Some paragraphs present a list of information, such as chief exports of Guatemala. Others contain information presented as an ordered series, such as steps in the digestive process. Still others present cause–effect relations. Students trained to identify the text structure and create appropriate outlines have significantly outperformed other students on tests of recall and comprehension (Bakken & Whedon, 2002; Bursuck & Damer, 2015).

Story Maps Story-mapping strategies demonstrate for students that most stories follow a particular pattern, or story grammar, including setting, problem, goals, action, and outcomes, as shown in Figure 13.6. Teaching students to use that pattern can promote comprehension (Browder et al., 2017). For example, Alves et al. (2014) taught students to complete story-mapping worksheets while reading and found that these worksheets improved recall and comprehension.

Helping students identify story grammar can be accomplished by using worksheets similar to those provided in Figure 13.6. Teachers can design these for student use. Provide instruction and practice using the worksheets during reading activities. Encourage students to complete similar worksheets during independent reading.

Reciprocal Teaching **Reciprocal teaching** is a reading-comprehension strategy that contains four comprehension-fostering strategies: (1) summarizing, (2) predicting, (3) questioning, and (4) clarifying (Palincsar & Brown, 1984). In addition, during reciprocal teaching, students assume the role of teacher during instruction and take the lead on asking questions. Teachers can prompt students to create good comprehension questions, as in the following dialogue:

TEACHER: What do you think, Nell?

NELL: How can a doctor know that a person is dreaming?

TEACHER: Excellent question, Nell! That is perfect; that is an amazing, great question. What do you think, Andy?

ANDY: Why did the doctors need to learn about dreaming?

TEACHER: That is another excellent question! (Speece et al., 1997, p. 183)

Reciprocal teaching incorporates the following elements:

- The teacher and the students silently read the reading selection.
- The teacher explains and demonstrates the four strategies using "talk-alouds," or talking aloud about thought processes used. For example, a teacher might say,

"To *summarize*, I might think to myself, 'What is this entire passage about? What is the overall topic, and what is being said about it?'" The talk-aloud may then describe a summary of the passage being considered and why it is a good summary.

- Students then read another passage and demonstrate out loud their strategy use for other students, while the teacher provides guidance and support (also known as *scaffolding*). Students construct their own comprehension questions.
- After practice, each student is expected to exhibit competence in the four strategies: summarizing, predicting, questioning, and clarifying (Palincsar & Brown, 1984; see also Bursuck & Damer, 2015).

Rosenshine and Meister (1994) concluded that reciprocal teaching is more effective when direct skills-based teaching (on, e.g., summarizing or predicting) occurs before the model is implemented. As with all reading-comprehension instruction, provide students with sufficient

Figure 13.6 Story Grammar Worksheet

The setting: The characters: The time: The place:
The problem in the story:
The goals in the story:
The action in the story:
The outcomes of the story:

In the Classroom

Alternative Teaching Suggestions

- Supplement texts with advance organizers:
  - Illustrations
  - Graphic organizers
  - Visual-spatial displays
  - Concrete manipulatives
  - Summary charts
  - Multimedia aids
  - Computer programs/apps
  - Descriptive video
  - Study guides
  - Guided notes
- Pre-teach:
  - Difficult vocabulary
  - New concepts
  - Organizational structure of text
  - Reading-comprehension strategies
- Provide sufficient practice activities
- Use teacher-effectiveness variables
- Use peers and cooperative groups
- Adapt assignments:
  - Reduce reading or writing requirements
  - Permit oral formats (e.g., audio-recorded answers)
  - Supply alternative materials such as digital formats

modeling, support, and guidance during the early learning phases. Later, students can be more independent in their use of the strategies (Klingner et al., 2012).

Boardman et al. (2016) implemented the Collaborative Strategic Reading (CSR) model, which incorporates elements of reciprocal teaching, in inclusive fourth- and fifth-grade classrooms that also contained a substantial proportion of students limited in English proficiency. Students were taught strategies for brainstorming and predicting, monitoring understanding (i.e., "click" {I get it} or "clunk" {I don't get it}, generating questions, and reviewing key ideas (i.e., "getting the gist"), and they then implemented these strategies in small student-led groups as part of their literacy routine. After implementation, two times a week for 14 weeks, Boardman et al. concluded that CSR had resulted in a positive impact on students' reading skills (see Klingner et al., 2012).

ADAPT FORMATS OF READING-COMPREHENSION INSTRUCTION When needed, adapt the format of instructional materials. These adaptations may be required if students cannot read the materials, have limited writing abilities, or need more time to complete assignments. Possible adaptations are listed in Figure 13.7 and *In the Classroom: Alternative Teaching Suggestions* feature.

In addition, promote culturally responsive literacy instruction to enhance the reading experience for all students. Suggestions are provided in the *Diversity, Equity, and Inclusion in the Classroom* feature.

Figure 13.7 Adapting Text Formats

- Highlight text
- Alter font, spacing, and colors of text
- Magnify text
- Record text
- Use language masters for practice with difficult words
- Use talking computerized programs (scan texts)
- Use braille formats
- Rewrite text supplements using more familiar vocabulary
- Rewrite text supplements at a lower reading level
- Supplement with high-interest, low-vocabulary texts

Diversity, Equity, and Inclusion in the Classroom

Culturally Responsive Literacy Instruction

Literacy instruction is of great importance to all students, but it is of particular importance for teachers to create and implement highly effective literacy instruction that is responsive to students from different cultures (see Echevarria & Graves, 2015). Also, additional considerations must be made when planning and delivering instruction for students from different culturally and lingually diverse (CLD) backgrounds who also have learning disabilities. Kourea et al. (2018) argue that, even when evidence-based practices are being implemented, such as RTI practices, these practices must be matched to the cultural styles of the students. According to reading researchers (e.g., Orosco & O'Connor, 2014), the reading success of students from CLD backgrounds is dependent upon how well teachers are able to integrate evidence-based reading instruction with the cultural and linguistic needs of students. To be culturally competent, teachers must reflect on their own cultural backgrounds and must work to understand the culture of their students. They must show interest in understanding students' family structure, customs, traditions, strengths, and challenges. Kourea et al. identified three elements of culturally responsive reading instruction for students with learning disabilities that are needed to maximize reading instruction for all students. These elements include culturally responsive curriculum, culturally responsive instructional delivery, and culturally responsive environmental supports. Each is described separately.

Culturally responsive curriculum. Core classroom instruction should be made as effective as possible, not only to reduce the number of students needing additional instructional assistance but also to help reduce the number of students referred for special education. Effective core reading instruction emphasizes reading components such as phonological awareness, phonics, reading fluency, reading comprehension, and vocabulary instruction. Reading subskills can be particularly important in the earlier grades, whereas direct vocabulary instruction, metacognitive strategies such as morphological awareness, team-based learning, and comprehension strategies may be more important in the upper grades.

Also important is selecting multicultural literature to increase relevance to students from diverse cultures and to promote and articulate the benefits of diversity in classrooms. Kourea et al. (2018) suggest using multicultural literature in a thematic approach in the following steps: (1) identify storybooks with common themes (e.g., family traditions, folktales, holiday celebrations), (2) select one theme that can be of interest to all or most students regardless of background, and (3) carefully choose materials and activities to present the story and the relevant themes.

Culturally responsive instructional delivery. Diverse learners with learning disabilities benefit from direct, explicit instruction in reading, as described throughout this chapter. Kourea et al. (2018) emphasize such elements as teacher modeling; instructional intensity; providing relevant examples, definitions, and guided practice; and providing immediate feedback. They recommend as one strategy a model, lead, test approach, in which teachers directly model or demonstrate the target information or skill, lead the student to respond, and test and provide immediate feedback to the student response. Students with CLD as well as those with learning disabilities require clear demonstration and guided practice with the new content until they can demonstrate competence independently. Kourea et al. also recommend small-group instruction, cooperative learning groups, and peer tutoring as potentially very beneficial for students from CLD backgrounds and those with learning disabilities.

Culturally responsive environmental supports. Kourea et al. (2018) emphasize the importance of a classroomwide or schoolwide system for providing recognition of the academic and social performance of students from CLD backgrounds. This is beneficial because it helps teachers emphasize specific academic and behavioral objectives throughout the year, it allows teachers to be more systematic in acknowledging student efforts, and because students are pleased and encouraged by receiving positive feedback from teachers. This is particularly true for those with learning disabilities, who may have a history of academic struggles leading to problems with motivation and self-esteem.

Kourea et al. (2018) recommend, as an example of environmental support, a token system (see Chapter 8) in which students identify activities, tangibles, or social events they prefer for meeting specific academic or social behavior. Teachers monitor student progress toward meeting these objectives, award tokens (e.g., a check mark or a star) when appropriate, and provide frequent immediate feedback along the way. As goals are achieved, students are allowed to spend their accumulated tokens for preferred items on the list. Such tangible environmental support can provide learners with important encouragement and feedback as they progress.

Diversity, Equity, and Inclusion in the Classroom

Culturally Responsive Literacy Instruction—*continued*

Instructional supports are also important components of environmental supports. Teachers need to ensure sufficient opportunities for student responding, maintaining attention, and providing ongoing assessment and frequent feedback. Supports should enhance active student responding and ensure that students participate equally in group activities. Kourea et al. (2018) recommend response cards, where students show their answers simultaneously to teacher questions on cards (marked, e.g., yes/no, or multiple-choice answers). Also recommended are guided notes (see Chapter 15) in which students are given partially completed worksheets to help them actively participate in teacher-led instruction. Guided notes have been seen to improve note-taking accuracy and achievement of students from CLD backgrounds (e.g., Larwin et al., 2012).

Culturally responsive curriculum, culturally responsive instructional delivery, and culturally responsive environmental supports are all important elements of culturally responsive reading instruction for students with learning disabilities. Students from diverse backgrounds can benefit greatly from teachers who carefully consider these elements in planning and implementing reading instruction.

Discuss: What other strategies can make your literacy classroom more inclusive and culturally responsive?

ADAPT INSTRUCTION FOR SECONDARY STUDENTS Many students with disabilities advance to secondary grade levels without completely mastering important reading skills. This is a particular problem because formal reading instruction ceases to be a part of the general education curriculum at secondary levels (Mastropieri et al., 2003). When difficulties with word identification, vocabulary, fluency, and reading comprehension persist beyond third grade, remediation is especially challenging. Solis et al. (2014) identified the following consistencies learned from reading research studies inclusive of secondary students with reading difficulties:

a. adolescents benefit from intensive intervention,

b. interventions associated with multiple reading comprehension strategies result in positive effects,

c. adolescents benefit from explicit instruction designed to support understanding of text, frequent modeling, feedback, and opportunities to respond, and

d. interventions for adolescents are likely to require multiple years of implementation to adequately meet student needs. (p. 220)

For example, Vaughn et al. (2015, 2019) implemented 2-year-long interventions for ninth and tenth graders with phases of multifaceted interventions supporting reading comprehension. Vaughn et al. (2015) taught important reading skills to high school students with learning disabilities and behavior disorders with low comprehension scores. Over the 2-year period, they taught word-analysis skills (identifying affixes, vowels, and vowel combinations for segmenting multisyllabic words into decodable chunks) in combination with peer mediation through collaborative strategic reading, described previously, to enhance their comprehension skills. Students received modeling, support, and practice time for a number of reading-comprehension strategies. These students made significant improvements over control students on a standardized reading-comprehension test.

There are specific actions that secondary-level teachers can take to promote reading skill development in their classes. First, ensure that the materials suit the ability levels and interests of the students when designing instruction toward a specific learning goal (i.e., HLP 12, HLP 20). For adolescents, focusing on texts related to students' content-area classes may be helpful, given text complexity, the focus of the CCSS, and graduation requirements. When choosing supplementary text written at a student's instructional level, align the selection with the content being taught so that students can become familiar with the vocabulary and readily apply learned comprehension strategies. Reed et al. (2012) found that supporting high school content-area teachers to focus on key vocabulary or concepts by using two or three word-learning strategies (see Chapter 15) is an effective entry point to addressing secondary students' learning goals.

Also, secondary teachers can support more intensive reading instruction with Tier 2 RTI (see Chapter 7) programs by working with the special education teacher and emphasizing newly learned skills in the general education classroom. Secondary teachers can also teach and promote use of word-recognition strategies, such as the DISSECT strategy described previously (Ellis, 1996), to assist with independent reading skills, understanding of the text structure, and other strategies described previously to assist with text comprehension (Bakken & Whedon, 2002; Vaughn & Roberts, 2007). Additionally, secondary teachers can provide opportunities to practice reading skills in content-area instruction through classwide peer-tutoring interventions.

For example, Mastropieri et al. (2001) implemented classwide peer tutoring in middle school English classes that contained students with learning and behavior problems. Students worked in pairs, with the stronger reader reading first for 5 minutes, followed by the second reader reading the same passage for 5 minutes. At the end of each reading turn, the tutoring partner would ask the reader to provide story restatements or encourage summarization strategies. Prompts for story restatements included, "What is the first thing you learned?"; followed by, "What was the next thing you learned?", with questions asked as often as needed to restate the story. Summarization strategies included, "What is the most important who or what in the text?", followed by "What is the most important thing about the who or what in the text?", then "What is the summary sentence?" After 5 weeks of the program, students who had participated in tutoring scored much higher than control students on a reading-comprehension test. Similar tutoring programs have helped improve reading skills as well as achievement in secondary content areas such as history, civics, and chemistry (Bowman-Perrott et al., 2013; Mastropieri et al., 2003; Spencer et al., 2003). These programs may be useful because they provide all students with additional practice on academic content and provide additional supervised reading practice for students with disabilities.

USE ASSISTIVE TECHNOLOGY TO SUPPORT SECONDARY-LEVEL READERS

Many of the features of the *Kurzweil 3000* program may be of particular benefit to secondary-level struggling readers. This program provides text-to-speech capabilities in 18 languages and includes highlighters, sticky notes, voice notes, customizable reading rate, magnification, keyboard shortcuts, background color changes, vocabulary study guides, graphic organizers, and writing templates, as well as direct access to over 1,000 texts and other content materials. It also offers support for writing, comprehension, and test-taking and study skills. *Kurzweil 300* is available as a web-based platform, as a program on a computer, or as an app on tablets and phones.

Digital highlighters such as the C-Pen (C-Pen™) are pen-sized devices that allow students to scan sentences in text to transfer them into word-recognition software programs with translation, dictionary, and text-to-speech capabilities. Some employ Bluetooth technology for wireless connections. Livescribe creates smartpens, such as the *Echo 2* and *Symphony*, that pair audio recording with note taking so that written notes are paired with audio and converted to text. Audio can be played wherever written notes are unclear or incomplete.

STRATEGIES FOR IMPLEMENTING MULTI-TIERED READING INSTRUCTION WITH RTI

RTI programs have been designed to prevent and treat academic failure, particularly in the area of reading (Division for Learning Disabilities, 2007). An RTI program employs multiple "tiers" of intervention—usually three or four—to monitor and adjust instruction to the specific needs of students, although a three-tier structure has been recommended (Fuchs et al., 2012).

IMPLEMENT PRIMARY (TIER 1) INTERVENTIONS Tier 1 programs are usually considered evidence-based (or research-supported) instruction in the general education classroom (Foorman, 2007). Evidence-based approaches would include systematic instruction in reading skills and subskills such as phonemic awareness and phonics, spelling, lots of practice in building reading fluency, instruction in relevant reading vocabulary, use of a variety of texts, and effective comprehension-enhancing activities (Al Otaiba et al., 2016). Students with disabilities would access core reading instruction at Tier 1 with accommodations as needed and differentiated instruction would be provided in large- and small-group formats. Academic engagement could be increased through the use of peer mediation, such as classwide peer tutoring.

In addition, screening measures would be implemented to identify any students demonstrating problems in reading skills acquisition.

IMPLEMENT SECONDARY (TIER 2) INTERVENTIONS Secondary (Tier 2) interventions are "directed at students who are at risk for academic problems and for whom additional, more targeted instruction is provided to close the gap between their current performance and expected performance" (Vaughn & Roberts, 2007, p. 41). Fuchs et al. (2014) further distinguish Tier 2 interventions as being not only research based but empirically validated with specific procedures for implementation, duration (amount of time each day), and frequency (how often) as typically communicated in a manual or professional development training. These interventions can take place with small groups of students who have not responded well to Tier 1 interventions. Tier 2 interventions should be more intensive and focused than those provided in Tier 1 and may include, for example, 20–30 minutes of homogeneous small-group (four or six students) instruction in addition to Tier 1 activities (Bursuck & Damer, 2015). During Tier 2 reading instruction, additional intensive instruction can be focused on phonemic awareness, phonics, spelling and writing, fluency development, vocabulary instruction, and comprehension enhancement, using many of the strategies described in this chapter. This can be implemented as a "standard protocol" approach (in which most students receive the same intervention) or a "problem-solving" approach (in which school personnel decide upon appropriate individualized interventions; Fuchs & Fuchs, 2007). Either way, the goal is to help students "catch up" with their classmates in a directed period of time (e.g., 10–20 weeks; Vaughn & Denton, 2008); however, continued interventions for adolescents with persistent reading difficulties are recommended (Vaughn et al., 2012). If, after a specified time period, students still do not make acceptable progress (according to, for example, school benchmarks or failure to demonstrate adequate progress on curriculum-based measures), these data may be used, according to the Individuals with Disabilities Education Act, in support of special education identification and placement decisions.

Finding time for Tier 2 reading instruction in high school may be challenging. Student schedules are individualized and school staffing resources are typically more limited. In Roberts et al.'s (2015) investigation to improve students' reading achievement, middle school students with persistent reading difficulties received tiered instruction during an elective period. General characteristics of Tier 2 instruction for sixth-graders in the study's treatment group included:

- Student to teacher ratio of 10:1
- 50 minutes of instruction, daily
- 160 sessions for a school year
- Phase 1 of the research-based intervention *REWARDS®* (Archer et al., 2005):
  - Word study (segmentation strategies, advanced strategies for decoding multisyllabic words)
  - Fluency (repeated reading instruction for 10–15 minutes)
  - Vocabulary (student-friendly definitions with examples and nonexamples)
  - Reading comprehension (literal and inferential questioning)
- Phase II of intervention:
  - Vocabulary and comprehension focus
  - Word relatives and parts of speech
  - Writing activities to summarize
- Phase III of intervention:
  - Apply word study and comprehension practices with expository texts

IMPLEMENT TERTIARY (TIER 3 OR INTENSIVE) INTERVENTIONS If students are still responding poorly to instruction after Tier 1 and Tier 2 interventions, they may be referred to Tier 3, which in many models includes special education referrals and treatments and may also be referred to as *intensive interventions*. Tier 3 intervention "is considered to be the most intensive and is focused on individual student need" (Stecker, 2007, p. 51), and it employs many of the strategies described in this chapter. In some models, special education referral is undertaken as a Tier 4 intervention when students do not respond positively to a separate

Tier 3 intervention (Bursuck & Damer, 2015). The National Center on Intensive Intervention (St. Martin et al., 2020) and Powell and Fuchs (2015) have provided intensive instruction activity guidelines that begin with explicit instruction and include modeling, guided practice, and feedback. Vaughn and Wanzek (2014) described longer-term (75–100 sessions) daily intensive instruction in reading for students with disabilities that included individualized or small-group instruction and direct teaching of a variety of specific reading skills. In addition to individualized instruction, these services could include (1) developing measurable shorter-term and annual goals, (2) using formative data to monitor progress and inform instruction, and (3) having special educators who have been trained to work effectively with students with disabilities serve as intervention agents (Fuchs et al., 2012; Stecker, 2007). Mastropieri and Scruggs (2014) described the importance of intensive instruction over longer periods of time to successfully promote essay writing achievement in a population of students with significant behavioral and learning disabilities.

The sixth-graders in the Roberts et al. (2015) study who did not respond to the Tier 2 intervention moved to Tier 3 as seventh-graders. General characteristics of Tier 3 instruction for the seventh-graders in the study's treatment group included:

- Student to teacher ratio of 5:1
- 50 minutes of instruction, daily
- 160 sessions for a school year
- Primary research-based intervention *REWARDS*® (Archer et al., 2005):
    - Adaptations made to the Tier 2 intervention
    - Individualized reading instruction with time allocated to an instructional focus
    - Used weekly CBM for progress monitoring
- Secondary intervention: Motivational plan built around students' interests with goal setting

Written Expression

Learning Objective 13.4 Identify strategies and adaptations for teaching written expression, including handwriting, spelling, and written communication.

Written language refers to handwriting, spelling, and composition. One or all of these may be especially problematic for students at risk for school failure. However, adaptations can be made in each area to promote success in inclusive classrooms. Although handwriting instruction has received less attention in recent years, evidence suggests that systematic handwriting instruction is an important component in preventing writing difficulties in the primary grades (Graham et al., 2000, 2012).

STRATEGIES FOR IMPROVING HANDWRITING

Competent handwriting is important for students at all grade levels in school; unfortunately, many students exhibit considerable difficulty with handwriting tasks. Students with physical disabilities can exhibit difficulty with the mechanical aspects of writing (Heller, 2010); other students have problems with fine motor skills. Some students with learning disabilities may exhibit what has been referred to as **dysgraphia**, or extreme difficulty with writing. Other students experience difficulty copying from the chalkboard or overhead projector, or what is referred to as "far-point copying." Still others have difficulty copying from models on or near their desks, or "near-point copying." Finally, forming letters from memory can present handwriting problems for some students (Lerner & Johns, 2015).

No matter what the difficulty, students need to acquire fluency with the mechanical aspects of handwriting or they will experience difficulties composing written work. Illegible, dysfluent, and laborious handwriting interferes with students' abilities to complete written assignments in a timely fashion, take notes in classes, read and study materials they have written, and undertake writing tasks such as essay writing (Berninger & Amtmann, 2003; Gregg et al., 2007). Some have suggested that illegibly written assignments receive lower grades and less careful consideration by teachers. Santangelo and Graham (2016) concluded that handwriting instruction is associated with higher quality, greater length, and increased fluency in students' writing.

For generations, students were taught to use manuscript and cursive writing. Today some states require cursive writing instruction, while others do not. However, cursive writing may be useful for several aspects of literacy; for example, to be able to read cursive writing of others, to provide a signature, and to use cursive fonts in word processing programs.

Graham and Weintraub (1996) provided a thorough analysis of research on handwriting and concluded the following:

1. Handwriting problems are greatest among students who have academic difficulties.
2. Students develop their own style of writing regardless of script style taught.
3. Successful handwriting instruction for students with handwriting difficulties emphasizes the following:
   - Use paper with more space between the lines.
   - Provide models of the order, number, and direction of strokes.
   - Provide sufficient practice in tracing, copying, and writing from memory.
   - Use behavioral techniques such as cueing, shaping, and positive practice.
   - Teach self-regulation behaviors such as self-verbalizations during activities involving tracing, copying, and writing from memory.
   - Use self-assessment as part of the handwriting instruction. (e.g., "Circle the very best *m* you wrote").
   - Use self-instruction and self-correction as part of the handwriting instruction (see also Datchuk, 2015; Graham, 2010; Santangelo & Graham, 2016).

Berninger and Amtmann (2003) reported that studying visual cues (numbered arrow cues that show students the sequence of writing individual letters) and writing from memory improved both quality of handwriting and the amount written.

INCORPORATE SELF-REGULATION AND SELF-INSTRUCTIONAL STRATEGIES It is important to model all the steps of the procedures and to provide practice opportunities for students to use self-regulation and self-instructional procedures. For example, a teacher might say the following while demonstrating the technique for writing *q*:

> I place my pen on a line of the paper and move up to the top of the *q*. Without taking my pen off the paper, I make a *circle* around to the top again. Then, I go *down* below the line, then *loop* back to the top again. Finally, I *finish* on an upswing. Remember [repeats model], "Up, circle, down, loop, finish."

Some basic self-instructions include defining tasks to be undertaken (e.g., "I must write this sentence"), focusing attention on tasks, reviewing necessary strategic steps (e.g., "For a *t*, I go up and then down the same way, and later I come back to cross the *t*"), self-evaluating and self-correcting (e.g., "Did I write a *t* correctly?"), self-control, and self-reinforcement ("My writing was correct and legible"). See Graham and Harris (2005) for some examples.

USE MATERIALS TO DEVELOP MANUSCRIPT AND CURSIVE WRITING Debate exists over whether manuscript (printing) or cursive (handwriting) both need to be taught, as well as which system for teaching each should be used (Graham, 2010; Graves, 2003). Some claim that manuscript resembles print more closely, that it is easier to learn, and that students with learning difficulties need to learn only one system. Others assert that children can write faster and are more motivated to learn to write when using a cursive system. Unfortunately, little convincing evidence supports one side over the other. You will need to decide what works best for your own individual students, within the context of district and state guidelines.

Some handwriting programs have been developed to teach handwriting skills efficiently and systematically. The *D'Nealian Handwriting* system (Savvas) teaches students a manuscript style that is said to lead more naturally into cursive writing. The *Cursive Writing Program* (SRA/McGraw Hill) provides a systematic introduction to handwriting letters, words, and then sentences. *Zaner-Bloser's Handwriting* series provides materials for handwriting instruction from kindergarten through sixth grade. *Handwriting Without Tears* (Learning Without Tears) is a program that teaches students print and cursive handwriting with paper-based and digital components.

Although many script styles exist, the quality of handwriting can be evaluated according to legibility, shape, size, spacing, alignment, line quality, speed and ease of writing, slant, uppercase and lowercase letter formations, and manuscript and cursive script styles (Berninger & Amtmann, 2003). Set criteria for what your students should focus on first, and find an instructional system that will support students' efforts. The majority of reviewed handwriting interventions follow the model-lead-test format (Datchuk & Kubina, 2013). That is, a teacher provides numerous models of letter formations, leads students to practice each letter while gradually fading visual supports, and then provides immediate correction of errors and praise. Finally, the teacher allows students to practice independently without teacher assistance.

MAKE TECHNOLOGICAL ADAPTATIONS Digital pens, described previously, can convert handwritten text to digital text. Computers are effective alternatives for students who have persistent difficulties with handwriting. Keyboarding and typing skills need to be mastered and can be taught using a variety of available programs, including *Type to Learn* (Sunburst Digital Learning), Typing.com (Teaching.com), *EduTyping, Keyboarding Without Tears* (Learning Without Tears), and *TapTyping* (Flairify LLC).

Advantages of using word processing programs include neatness, ease, increased fluency, availability of spelling and grammar checks, increased motivation, and speech-to-text features. In addition, use of the accessibility features on computers, tablets, and mobile devices can make it easier to use the mouse or keyboard, set up alternative input devices, optimize the visual display, or read text as it is typed. However, because students may not always have access to computers or related devices, supplement these programs with at least some basic handwriting skills for those with sufficient fine motor ability. For students who lack fine motor skills, speech-to-text features found in common devices such as computers, smartphones, and tablets enable students to enter information orally and receive typed output. If technological adaptations are unavailable, assign scribes for students who cannot write independently.

CLASSROOM SCENARIO

Ming

Ming, a fourth-grader with learning disabilities, is included in Ms. Wills's general education class for all subjects. Ms. Wills has weekly spelling tests every Friday. On Mondays, new spelling lists containing 20 words are distributed, and time is allocated throughout the week to study independently to prepare for Friday's test. But Ming is failing spelling. His recent weekly test scores were 50%, 45%, 30%, 40%, and 35% correct. He tries hard to learn the words, but he can't pronounce some of the words on the list. Both Ming and Ms. Wills are becoming frustrated with his spelling difficulties.

QUESTIONS FOR REFLECTION

1. What might be the cause of Ming's spelling problems?
2. What is happening in the classroom that may contribute to Ming's problem?
3. What changes can be made in the classroom routine to help Ming spell better?

STRATEGIES FOR TEACHING SPELLING

Spelling can be a complex and difficult task for students with reading and writing difficulties. Efficient spellers rely on good memory, phonological awareness, phonemic awareness, orthographic skills, phonics skills, and self-checking skills, all of which are often challenging areas for many students with disabilities. Research has identified a number of effective spelling strategies that can be implemented in inclusive settings (Graham, 1999; Graham & Santangelo, 2014; McLaughlin et al., 2013; Williams et al., 2017, 2018).

First, ensure that all students can read all the words on their spelling lists. If students are unable to read spelling words, they will surely encounter difficulties in learning how to spell them. Systematic instruction in phonemic analysis and synthesis, as well as phonics, will prove helpful in promoting good spelling skills. Other general suggestions include the following:

- Teach common irregular spellings from the beginning of spelling instruction.
- Teach useful spelling rules (e.g., vowel–consonant–silent *e* pattern: a silent *e* at the end of a word changes the vowel sound to a long vowel).
- Teach students to use their prior knowledge about root words and the relationships among words to help them spell new words (e.g., *swim* is one syllable and ends in a single consonant that follows a single vowel, so double the consonant before adding a vowel suffix = *swimming*)
- Increase independent reading to increase exposure to words in print.
- Encourage students to use the spell-checking features on their computers and other electronic devices (Spear-Swerling, 2005).

You may also improve spelling performance by shortening the list length for students with spelling problems (Harris et al., 2017). This means asking students to learn, for example, 10 rather than 20 words, or 5 rather than 10, in a week. Introduce a small number of words daily rather than providing a large list all at once. Introduce and practice three or four words on Monday; on Tuesday, review those words and introduce a few more words. However, simply shortening the list will be of little help if the words themselves are beyond the current abilities of the students.

Pearson eTextbook
Video Example 13.7
The teacher in this video uses a word wall and repetition to reinforce spelling words with her students. Notice the elements of direct instruction used in her lesson as well.

SELECT WORDS FROM READING AND WRITING ACTIVITIES Spelling words that are relevant to students' reading and writing activities can be easier to learn, and students may be more likely to see the importance of learning to spell these words. Additionally, students can apply their reading decoding skills to the spelling lists.

PROVIDE DISTRIBUTED PRACTICE SESSIONS Distributed practice—providing shorter, more frequent periods for practicing handwriting and spelling, rather than fewer, longer periods—is recommended for students with disabilities (Graham et al., 2012). For example, several 15-minute spelling activity sessions scheduled throughout the school day could reinforce learning better than one 45-minute block. Also, writing one well-constructed sentence rather than a paragraph can reinforce sentence structure development. Elementary students can practice handwriting and spelling in an authentic way by responding to picture-word prompts, for example. Sentence frames (e.g., I want . . . ; I see . . .) can be added as a scaffold (e.g., Pennington et al., 2018).

USE PEER TUTORING Peer-tutoring sessions can also help students with disabilities (Bowman-Perrott et al., 2014). Provide students with extra opportunities to practice spelling their new words (Maheady & Gard, 2010) after they have been trained in peer-tutoring procedures. Peer spelling sessions can be scheduled regularly. Flashcards can be used, and students can record their daily performance by stacking cards spelled correctly together. Keeping the stack of misspelled words to review several times within a single tutoring session or in multiple sessions can help students be more successful on tests. Alternatively, simple word lists can also be used as tutoring materials. Tutors can check off words spelled correctly. Students can be matched in almost any way for spelling tutoring sessions because the tutors can view the correct spellings on the word lists. Using tutoring for spelling can increase time on-task, including increasing opportunities for responding and increasing feedback on spelling performance. Burks (2004) implemented classwide peer tutoring in spelling and reported that spelling performance improved for three fifth-grade students with disabilities, from an average of 73% to 91% correct, over scores after more traditional methods, such as independent seatwork.

MODIFY INSTRUCTION BASED ON ANALYSIS OF SPELLING ERRORS Analyze the type of mistakes students are making in order to make instructional decisions. For example, if letters representing phonemes are deleted (e.g., *pince* rather than *prince*) or inserted (e.g., *subptract* rather than *subtract*), students may need phonics or phonemic awareness instruction. If spellings do not reflect conventional orthography (e.g., *wich* instead of *wish* or *hidn* instead of *hiding*), teach appropriate sound–spelling correspondences. Instruction may include word practice routines mentioned earlier in the chapter or word sorts and word-building routines.

In a study by Graham et al. (2002), pairs of second-grade poor spellers were tutored for three 20-minute sessions per week for 12 weeks. Students were presented with word categories, each represented by a master word card; for example, "**made**," "**maid**," and "**may**" represented three patterns for the long /*A*/ sound. Students sorted word cards into the categories, and the tutor corrected and explained as needed. The tutor also helped students state relevant rules and generate words of their own. Students then studied new spelling words they had previously misspelled that matched the word patterns. They also practiced sound–letter associations with flashcards and engaged in word-building spelling activities based on word patterns and spelling rules for consonants, blends, and digraphs. Students who participated in the training dramatically increased their spelling skills and transferred these skills to reading and writing.

If spelling errors reflect a lack of knowledge of spelling rules (e.g., doubling a consonant before adding a suffix), teach these rules. Directing instruction to individual error patterns is an efficient way of promoting good spelling (Squires et al., 2016). For errors in parts of words that are not governed by conventional rules, teach mnemonic strategies.

TEACH MNEMONIC STRATEGIES FOR SPELLING Show students mnemonic strategies to remember the difficult or unpredictable parts of words, for example, the *s* in *island* or the *d* in *Wednesday*. Create a sentence that contains the difficult word and another smaller word that includes the most difficult part of the word (Mastropieri & Scruggs, 1991). Focus on those parts and create strategies to promote learning the correct way to spell them. Shefter (1989) identified mnemonic strategies for some difficult words, for example:

- It is **VILE** to allow special pri**VILE**ge.
- Don't **MAR** your writing with bad gram**MAR**.
- You **GAIN** when you buy a bar**GAIN**.
- Draw **ALL** the lines par**ALL**el. (p. 19)

Notice that in each of these cases, there is no particular rule that governs the spelling of the word, so spelling mnemonics are appropriate. Similarly, teach distinctions between homonyms by making up sentences using the same procedures. For example:

- A princi**PAL** is your **PAL**; a princip**LE** is a ru**LE**.
- A lett**ER** is written on station**ER**y; the j**AR** is station**AR**y.

Sometimes an interactive illustration can be shown to help students remember the correct spelling, as in the mnemonic "She screamed **E-E-E** as she walked by the cemetery," to help remember the three *e*'s in *cemetery* (Figure 13.8). Dowling (1995) and Suid (1981) provide books of mnemonic spellings for difficult words. Additionally, a number of mnemonic spelling strategies

Figure 13.8 Mnemonic Spelling Strategy: Cemetery

Source: From Mastropieri & Scruggs (1991), p. 84. Reprinted with permission.

can be found on the Internet. Generally, targeted elaborations of the type described here are more useful than acrostics that represent sentences, the first letters of which spell words (e.g., for *arithmetic*: "A rat in the house may eat the ice cream"; Wordplay, 2012).

TEACH SELF-INSTRUCTIONAL AND SELF-MONITORING STRATEGIES Strategies are often taught so that students can use them independently. Self-monitoring strategies teach students to self-monitor their attention to a task, their use of particular studying strategies, and their spelling performance. A review of spelling research concluded that explicit instruction and self-correction were particularly effective for students with learning disabilities (Williams et al., 2017). The strategies are listed on a "self-monitoring" card and teach students the following steps:

- Say the spelling word.
- Write and say the spelling word.
- Check the spelling.
- Trace and say the word.
- Write the word without looking.
- Check the spelling.

Students repeat these steps as necessary (see Harris et al., 2017).

TEACH THE COVER–COPY–COMPARE STRATEGY Teach students to say the word, look at the model, and study the spelling. Students then *cover* the model and try to *copy* the word from memory. Finally, students look at the model and *compare* their spelling with the model. Students repeat the steps until the spelling of the word is mastered. Intervention Central provides student materials for the CCC strategy and a teacher log for monitoring student mastery of words (https://www.interventioncentral.org/academic-interventions/writing/how-master-spelling-or-sight-words-cover-copy-compare). This strategy has been shown to be effective for secondary students with learning and behavioral disabilities (Williams et al., 2018) as well as students without learning difficulties (Joseph et al., 2012).

USE SPECIALIZED SOFTWARE AND CURRICULUM MATERIALS Technology can help improve spelling performance (Wissick & Gardner, 2011) and is commonly used to intervene at the secondary level for students with autism, orthopedic impairment, and intellectual disabilities (Williams et al., 2018). Some software contains drill-and-practice formats in which students practice spelling new words. Numerous apps for tablets or smartphones are also available to support spelling objectives. Be sure to evaluate progress when using the following apps: *Osmo Words* (Tangible Play), *Word Wizard for Kids* (L'Escapadou), and *Word Wagon* (Duck Duck Moose LLC). Online programs are also available to teach elementary and secondary students spelling skills as well. *Spelling Stars* uses gamification to teach spelling online through spelling games, tests, and drills. The *At-Home Online Spelling Program* (Scholar Within) focuses on spelling and phonics learning with interactive videos, step-by-step instruction, spelling worksheets, and drills.

Many curriculum materials are also available commercially to teach spelling, including SRA/McGraw-Hill's *Spelling Mastery* and *Spelling Through Morphographs* for older students. These programs emphasize systematic approaches using a direct-instruction format and spelling patterns. Both programs recommend daily lessons of 15–20 minutes and have supplemental activities to provide practice with the new words. *Spell It-Write* (Zaner-Bloser) is intended to teach spelling words in a way that will promote transition and application to student writing.

The *Directed Spelling List* (first through third grade) and the *Spelling for Writing List* (including word listings for students with disabilities; Graham et al., 1994, 1996) are word lists based on analyses of commonly used words that are problematic for students. Using the *Directed Spelling Thinking Activity* (Graham et al., 1996), students actively compare and contrast words that fit different, but related, patterns.

ADAPT SPELLING OBJECTIVES Spelling may not be as important during some written activities as it is during other activities, so consider prioritizing spelling objectives for your class. For example, during written essay exams, knowledge of the content, rather than spelling, is probably the major objective, so consider focusing the weight of the evaluation on content knowledge in this case. Likewise, if students are developing sentence-structure writing skills with sentence expanding exercises (i.e., expand the sentence using different parts of speech), the primary objective should be on use of correct writing sequences rather than spelling.

Teach students compensation skills for spelling in their written work. Model how to use dictionaries to look up unknown words and how to use spell checkers on word-processing programs or apps on tablets or smartphones. The *Speaking Merriam-Webster's School Dictionary* (Franklin Electronics) can correct spellings of words and also includes a number of spelling-related word games.

APPLY SPELLING IN RTI PROGRAMS Spelling can be included as a component of literacy interventions in Tier 2 programs. Spelling can be included within the teaching of reading skills such as phonemic analysis and phonics instruction. Direct teaching and practice, systematic skill development, and CBM can help enhance instruction in spelling skills in RTI programs (Gerber & Richards-Tutor, 2011).

STRATEGIES FOR TEACHING WRITTEN COMMUNICATION

Pearson eTextbook

Video Example 13.8

The teacher in this video describes the prewriting planning that goes into a biography-writing assignment. Notice the writing-process poster and how she addresses the purpose of the assignment and makes it clear to the students what criteria to follow.

Written expression is a high level of communication that involves the integration of language, spelling, and reading skills. Students with disabilities frequently experience problems with writing assignments due to the challenges they have in reading, spelling, or language. The CCSS include a sequence of standards for grades K–12 across multiple domains of writing. For example, for grade 6, standards are provided for writing persuasive, informative/explanatory, and narrative texts. Some standards for persuasive writing include the following: introduce claim(s) and organize the reasons and evidence clearly; support claim(s) with clear reasons and relevant evidence, using credible sources and demonstrating an understanding of the topic or text; and provide a concluding statement or section that follows from the argument presented (NGA & CCSSO, 2010).

Research has demonstrated the effectiveness of planning, revising, and rewriting strategies designed to promote better writing (Gillespie & Graham, 2014; Graham et al., 2012). Involve students more actively in the writing process by having them write daily, choose their own topics, and revise their papers—often in collaboration with peers. Have students share their stories with classmates and answer questions from them. Such activities can help enforce the idea that writing is communication aimed at an audience and show students that peers can be helpful in expanding and improving that communication (Englert & Mariage, 1996). Collaborations of peer groups can also be used in planning, drafting, editing, and revising activities (Graham et al., 2015). Ask students to review and provide positive feedback on and suggestions for one another's written work and to collaborate in the revision process.

TEACH STUDENTS TO PLAN FOR WRITING According to Graham and Harris (2007), planning is an important component of skilled writing. However, students with writing difficulties often plan infrequently or ineffectively, writing the first thoughts that come to mind in order to finish the task. Efforts to enhance planning for writing, particularly for struggling writers, can have a positive impact. Before students undertake any writing task, be sure they understand the purpose of the writing assignment. They should then develop a plan that reflects careful thinking about the purpose, including the topic; how it will be developed; what information will be employed; and how the written product will be structured (Hauth et al., 2013). Discuss student plans and provide feedback before they begin writing.

PROMOTE THINKING ABOUT WRITING Students can be taught to use action words (verbs: *ran, drove, slept*), action helper words (adverbs: ran *fast*, drove *slowly*, slept *soundly*), and descriptive words (adjectives: *beautiful* scene, *delicious* meal, *enthusiastic* teacher) as they move from building simple sentences to more compound, complex, or compound–complex sentence structures (Datchuk & Kubina, 2013). You can use pictures and have students describe the action they see taking place in the pictures. For example, brainstorm lists of words relevant to students' age and backgrounds and post them in the room.

IMPLEMENT SELF-REGULATION AND SELF-INSTRUCTIONAL WRITING STRATEGIES The importance of teaching students effective strategies combined with self-regulation and self-instruction is emphasized generally in this chapter and extends to teaching writing skills. As with all strategic instruction, model the self-instruction strategy before asking students to implement it.

Figure 13.9 The Six Basic Types of Self-Instruction

Problem Definition
Sizing up the nature and demands of the task:
"What is it I have to do here?"
"What am I up to?"
"What is my first step?"
"I want to write a convincing essay."

Focusing of Attention and Planning
Focusing on the task at hand and generating a plan:
"I have to concentrate, be careful . . . think of the steps."
"To do this right I have to make a plan."
"First I need to . . . then . . ."

Strategy
Engaging and implementing writing or self-regulating strategies:
"First I will write down my essay writing reminder."
"The first step in writing an essay is . . ."
"My goals for this essay are . . .; I will self-record on . . ."

Self-Evaluating and Error Correcting
Evaluating performance, catching and correcting errors:
"Have I used all of my story parts—let me check."
"Oops, I missed one; that's okay, I can revise."
"Am I following my plan?"

Coping and Self-Control
Subsuming difficulties or failures and dealing with forms of arousal:
"Don't worry, worry doesn't help."
"It's okay to feel a little anxious; a little anxiety can help."
"I'm not going to get mad; mad makes me do bad."
"I can handle this."
"I need to go slow and take my time."

Self-Reinforcement
Providing reward:
"I'm getting better at this."
"I like this ending."
"Wait 'til my teacher reads this!"
"Hurray—I'm done!"

Source: From Harris & Graham (1992), p. 85. Reprinted with permission.

Six basic types of self-instruction exist, which are presented with examples in Figure 13.9 (see also Harris et al., 2008). Provide students with explanations of these types of self-instruction and discuss how they can be helpful in completing writing tasks. With this background understanding, they may be more able to appreciate the value and purpose of more specific strategy instruction.

CHOOSE EFFECTIVE COMPOSITION STRATEGIES Several strategies have been developed to help organize writing procedures. Story-grammar strategies were described in the reading-comprehension section of this chapter (see Figure 13.4), but they can also be applied effectively as composition strategies (Graham et al., 2012; Graham & Harris, 2005). Model all steps of the story-grammar strategy, and create smaller individual charts containing steps for students. For example, Graham and Harris (2005) described the **3-W, 2-What, 2-How strategy** for story writing:

- Who is in the story?
- When does the story take place?
- Where does the story take place?
- What happens in the story?
- What do the characters in the story do?

- **How** do the characters feel?
- **How** does the story end?

Discuss when the strategy is useful and how to use all the steps involved and provide examples of how the strategy will benefit students in a variety of situations. By doing so, students as young as first grade can improve their knowledge of story components and problem-solve when they encounter difficulty with story writing (Zumbrunn & Bruning, 2013).

After modeling all the steps for self-regulation, have students practice the steps in the strategy with partners. Facilitate practice sessions during which students complete the self-talk of the regulation and self-instruction phases while completing the story grammar. Such practice sessions enable students to master both the strategy and the self-regulatory components.

The **SPACE strategy** (or C-SPACE; Harris et al., 2008) is designed to help students think about more details that need to be included in their narrative stories and involves the following steps:

(Characters)

- Note **S**etting.
- Note **P**urpose.
- Note **A**ction.
- Note **C**onclusion.
- Note **E**motions. (Harris & Graham, 1992, p. 49)

For secondary students, the STACS **strategy** is designed to be applied to varied narrative structures including personal narrative, biography, and stories. STACS includes the following story grammar elements:

Setting (where/when the narrative takes place)

Tension (what happens to begin the plot or conflict in the narrative)

Rising **A**ction (the events leading up to the most exciting part of the narrative)

Climax (the most exciting or highest point in the narrative)

Solution (how the problem is solved) (Foxworth et al., 2017, p. 223)

Graham and Harris (2005) described the three-step strategy **THINK–STOP–DARE** for writing persuasive essays (De La Paz, 2007; Ennis et al., 2013):

1. THINK—Who will read this? Why am I writing this?
2. STOP—**S**uspend judgment, **T**ake a side or position, **O**rganize ideas, and **P**lan more as you write.
3. DARE—**D**evelop your topic sentence, **A**dd supporting ideas, **R**eject opposing arguments, and **E**nd with a conclusion.

When teaching students these strategies, use effective instruction and include models, demonstrations, and guided practice to promote independent and fluent strategy usage.

TEACH SELF-REGULATED STRATEGY DEVELOPMENT **Self-regulated strategy development (SRSD)** is a model for promoting higher-level cognitive skills and self-regulated use of cognitive strategies (Graham & Harris, 2005) for writing and has provided some of the most positive effects of all writing interventions (Gillespie & Graham, 2014; Graham & Perin, 2007). The framework of SRSD consists of several instructional stages (also see *srsdonline.org*). The seven stages are described in Figure 13.10.

Graham and Harris (2011) summarized SRSD research and concluded that it led to improved writing performance across a variety of strategic writing tasks.

One strategy for persuasive writing that also has received much research attention is the **POW + TREE strategy** (Gillespie & Graham, 2014; Harris et al., 2008; Mastropieri et al., 2009, 2014). The strategy acronym represents the following steps:

Pick my idea

Organize my notes

Write and say more

+

Figure 13.10 The Seven Stages of Self-Regulated Strategy Development

Stage 1: Activate and Develop Background Knowledge. Pre-assess student's genre knowledge. Then, get students motivated about the writing they will do, executing any pre-skills needed to acquire genre knowledge and mastery of it so students can write about it. Help students choose a writing strategy to fit students' writing level and introduce self-regulations, self-talk, and goal setting.

Stage 2: Discuss It. Focus on developing mastery of writing skills for strategy use. Use graphic organizers to compare good writing and poor writing and elements of strategy use.

Stage 3: Model It. Model planning, writing, and self-regulation through a series of steps. Use think-alouds.

- Problem definition (e.g., "I need to write a compare–contrast essay.")
- Planning ("How will I plan out the steps?")
- Strategy use ("Which strategies shall I use?")
- Self-evaluation ("How am I doing?")
- Error correction ("This part doesn't fit.")
- Self-reinforcement ("I did a good job on this!")

Stage 4: Memorize It. Expect students to learn and use mnemonics to remember and practice the steps of writing strategies such as THINK-STOP-DARE.

Stage 5: Support It. Teachers and students collaborate to use strategies and self-instructions to complete writing assignments.

Stage 6: Establish Independent Performance. Fade scaffolds and reteach, as needed.

Topic sentence

Reasons (three or more, with explanations)

Ending (wrap it up)

Examine (Do I have all the parts?)

Graham et al. (2012) suggest modifying the strategy slightly for older students by replacing the final **E** with **E**xplain reasons (Say more about each reason). When these strategies were implemented over time, combined with the general SRSD strategies, students with learning disabilities (Graham & Perin, 2007), English learners (Cuenca-Carlino et al., 2018), and students with emotional or behavioral disabilities were found to greatly improve their persuasive writing skills (Losinski et al., 2014; Mastropieri et al., 2009, 2010, 2013, 2014). The *Research Highlight* describes a technology-based writing strategy influenced by the SRSD model.

PROVIDE SUPPORT FOR WRITTEN RESEARCH REPORTS Teachers frequently assign research reports as longer-term homework assignments. Such projects are often overwhelming for students with disabilities, but teaching students specific strategies can help students to complete such assignments successfully. Several important skills are required for writing a research report, including the following:

- Brainstorming topics
- Selecting a topic
- Finding relevant sources
- Reading and note taking
- Organizing the paper's outline
- Filling in details in the outline
- Writing a rough draft
- Proofing and correcting the draft version
- Completing a final version

Research Highlight

Technology-Based Graphic Organizers for Writing

Researchers have identified that graphic organizers and word processing can positively influence students' planning and writing development (Graham & Hebert, 2011). Furthermore, the CCSS (NGA & CCSSO, 2010) require teachers to prepare students to use digital tools for reading and writing across the content areas. One digital tool that shows promise to support writing across the curriculum is the computer-based graphic organizer (Ciullo & Reutebuch, 2013). Over the past decade, researchers and teachers have collaboratively developed a series of technology-based graphic organizers (TBGOs) to support the persuasive, argumentative, and/or narrative writing of upper elementary and secondary students with and without disabilities. The series, supported by the Office of Special Education Programs in the U.S. Department of Education includes: (1) a computer-based version that can be used in *Microsoft Word*, (2) a mobile-based TBGO application, (3) a web-based TBGO for *Google Chrome*, and (4) a TBGO + enhanced version with a teacher dashboard (Evmenova & Regan, 2012; Evmenova et al., 2018).

The TBGO assists students through the entire writing process from setting a goal and brainstorming to editing and evaluating one's work. The following research-based strategies to support writing for students with disabilities are included in the TBGO: embedded self-regulated learning (SRL) strategies including goal setting, self-monitoring, and self-evaluation; a mnemonic; and UDL supports. The mnemonic IDEAS is used across all genres (e.g., persuasive:

I = Identify your opinion;
D = Determine three reasons;
E = Explain or say more;
A = *Add* transition words as you go; and
S = Summarize).

The UDL features include a graphic organizer, text-to-speech, text hints, drop-down menus, audio comments, color coding, and video models. The drop-down menus provide a list of transition words to choose from when beginning a sentence. See Evmenova et al. (2020) for a full explanation as to how to navigate the TBGO.

The TBGO has demonstrated improvement in the quantity and quality of writing among students with learning and behavioral disabilities (Evmenova et al., 2016, 2020), English learners (Regan et al., 2019), and students with and without disabilities across grades 3–12 and across instructional settings (Regan et al., 2017, 2018). For example, in a multiple-baseline design study, Regan et al. (2017) investigated student use of a TBGO among sixth- and seventh-graders without disabilities and those with learning disabilities or emotional and behavioral disabilities in self-contained, inclusive, or co-taught settings within one urban middle school. Following teacher instruction, students used laptops to produce persuasive essays in response to provided prompts. Students demonstrated an increase in the number of words, sentences, and transition words from baseline (without the TBGO) to intervention (writing with the TBGO) and an improvement in overall writing quality during intervention was observed as well. Student outcomes decreased slightly but remained above baseline levels when the TBGO was removed in maintenance testing.

Boykin et al. (2019) extended the use of the TBGO with argumentative writing by slightly altering the IDEAS mnemonic:

I = Identify your claim,
D = Determine three facts,
E = Elaborate with evidence,
A = *Add* transition words, and
S = Summarize your claim.

Boykin et al. investigated how the TBGO with embedded self-regulated learning strategies would impact fourth- and sixth-graders' quantity and quality of writing. After stratification by grade level, disability, and writing achievement, the study involved students randomly assigned to either the experimental group in which students wrote arguments about science and social studies topics with the support of the TBGO or the control group in which students wrote arguments about science and social studies topics with strategy instruction around the writing process and editing/revising. In both conditions, students were given a brief social studies passage from their text, modified for readability levels, and then asked to respond to an argumentative writing prompt related to the passage, as needed. For example, for one passage, fourth-graders read about the Powhatan Native Americans and sixth-graders read about the Inuit Native Americans. Student pre- and posttest writing responses were evaluated in both conditions for number of words, sentences, and transition words and writing quality. In the 6-point rubric for writing quality, students were scored for accuracy of content, consistency, capitalization, number of facts, and elaborations. Students in the control and experimental conditions used Microsoft Word on the computer without supports at pretest. At posttest, students in the experimental condition only used the TBGO. Students in both conditions did not use the TBGO at maintenance testing. After

Research Highlight

Technology-Based Graphic Organizers for Writing—*continued*

four instructional lessons and five practice sessions for both conditions, posttests were administered followed by a maintenance test.

Results of the investigation indicated that written arguments were significantly better for students in the experimental condition on measures of number of sentences, transition words, and writing quality at post-test. No difference was observed between groups for the measure of number of words. Since students are not permitted to access tools such as the TBGO on standardized testing, students in both conditions were asked to respond to a prompt without using the TBGO. Results showed that students in the experimental condition were able to significantly maintain gains on measures of writing quality and transition words, suggesting that regardless of abilities and needs, students were able to internalize learned strategies and maintain their gains when writing without the support of the TBGO with embedded SRL strategies.

QUESTIONS FOR REFLECTION

1. Why do you think students with and without disabilities perform well when writing with the TBGO?
2. Why do you think students in Regan et al. were able to maintain writing outcomes when the TBGO was removed?
3. What reasons do you think that there were no statistically significant differences in the number of words written for students in Boykin et al.'s experimental and control group?
4. What other extensions of the TBGO could be conducted?

Determine which of these skills need to be taught to your students. For example, you may have covered brainstorming in previous classes and can simply review the procedures with students. Once you determine which skill areas need instruction, prepare explicit instruction and provide plenty of opportunities for practice. For example, many students with disabilities require extensive instruction on how to find relevant sources. Determine the types of search procedures students need to learn, design appropriate instructional strategies to promote the acquisition of the procedures, and provide ample practice opportunities. Encourage students to meet in pairs or small groups and proofread each other's work.

USE TECHNOLOGY TO HELP WITH WRITING Computer technology is available to support writers on a number of writing tasks. Word processing and related software programs have been helpful in improving the writing of students with disabilities (Evmenova & Regan, 2019; Morphy & Graham, 2012). Keyboarding, speech-to-text, and word-prediction programs can accommodate students with slow or labored handwriting and those with physical disabilities. Spell checkers and grammar checkers can assist with proofreading if students are provided with instruction in their use. Applications for smartphones and tablets are also available to assist with writing tasks.

ADAPT INSTRUCTION TO OVERCOME MECHANICAL OBSTACLES TO WRITING Many students become frustrated with writing assignments because they are overwhelmed with the mechanical obstacles of handwriting, spelling, and punctuation. Isaacson and Gleason (1997) proposed eight methods for helping students overcome those obstacles:

1. *Allow dictation instead of writing.* Provide students the flexibility of thinking without any writing impediments; however, a scribe or a speech-to-text program or app must be provided.
2. *Pre-cue spelling of difficult words.* Write difficult words on the board or prominently displayed chart cards.
3. *Teach a word-book strategy.* Have students maintain word books containing their own dictionaries of hard words, which they can refer to at any time to check their spelling.
4. *Ask for help.* Encourage students to ask others (teachers, aides, other students) for assistance and ensure that someone is available to help them.
5. *Encourage invented spelling.* Sometimes students are reluctant to use interesting words simply because they do not know how to spell them. Encourage students to write their best guess of a word's spelling to encourage creativity and writing fluency.

However, at some point, students must learn to identify and correct any misspellings. Invented spelling can facilitate writing by helping students focus on their ideas, but it is unlikely to improve their spelling.

6. *Encourage peer collaboration*. Peer collaboration establishes a cooperative approach to writing and may be beneficial during the brainstorming, preplanning, and revising stages.
7. *Encourage self-checking*. Teach students specific self-checking strategies. Some strategies include rereading to make sure sentences make logical sense, capital letters are used appropriately, and punctuation and spelling are accurate.
8. *Use technology*. Computers have become more available and more versatile for classroom use. Computer-assisted writing and dictation may prove to be a positive alternative for students with writing difficulties.

USE SPECIALIZED CURRICULUM MATERIALS AND SOFTWARE Some materials are commercially available to promote writing competencies for students with disabilities. *Reasoning and Writing* (SRA/McGraw-Hill) uses a direct-instruction format to provide practice in learning how to think through topics and write from beginning levels to more advanced levels. *Expressive Writing* (SRA/McGraw-Hill) is another resource using a direct-instruction approach that contains approximately 50 lessons for students who can read at the third-grade level or above; it teaches writing and editing skills. Grammarly (*Grammarly, Inc.*) is a free application or browser extension that supports writers with spelling, word choice, grammar, style, and punctuation. The software can be used with e-mails, documents, and social media.

Many computerized programs to improve student writing are also commercially available. *WordQ Writing Software* (Boundless Assistive Technology) offers word-prediction, spoken feedback, and proofreading assistance. *Storybird* (https://storybird.com) is a digital online tool for all ages where students are given a library of illustrations and prompts to create a variety of written options including stories, picture books, comics, and poetry. *Inspiration* (Diagramming Apps) is software that allows users to create mind maps, diagrams, graphic organizers, outlines, and presentations for organizing their writing. Also, *Kurzweil 3000-firefly* (Cambium Learning Group) contains many features to facilitate the reading and writing process.

Carefully examine whether the programs' features are appropriate and determine whether your students have the necessary skills to benefit from the software. Some programs also teach keyboarding skills so that students can make optimal use of computerized programs designed to improve written composition.

13 Summary

- Many approaches exist for teaching students to read. Many students with reading disabilities lack phonemic awareness and phonics skills and overuse context cues when trying to read. Teachers should select reading programs that consider these areas of need.
- Common Core State Standards for reading address competencies in foundational skills, informational text, and literature and cover grades K–12.
- Teaching phonemic awareness, phonics, structural analysis, sight words, vocabulary, and reading fluency provides important basic skills for literacy. Reading-comprehension strategies can be employed before, during, or after reading. These strategies include basic skills instruction and text enhancements. Self-monitoring and self-questioning strategies are among the most effective reading-comprehension strategies.
- Written expression includes handwriting, spelling, and written communication. Problems in handwriting and spelling can be addressed by providing models and sufficient practice, using behavioral techniques, and teaching self-regulation and self-instructional strategies. Written communication problems can be addressed by using collaborative peer groups, teaching self-regulation and self-instructional strategies, and using story-grammar techniques and specific composition strategies.

PROFESSIONAL STANDARDS LINK: Literacy

Information in this chapter links most directly to:

- CEC 2020 Initial Practice-Based Professional Preparation Standards for Special Educators (Initial K–12 standards) (see https://exceptionalchildren.org/standards/initial-practice-based-professional-preparation-standards-special-educators): Standards 2 (Understanding and Addressing Each Individual's Developmental and Learning Needs), 3 (Demonstrating Subject Matter Content and Specialized Curriculum Knowledge), 4 (Using Assessment to Understand the Learner and the Learning Environment for Data-Based Decision Making), 5 (Supporting Learning Using Effective Instruction), 6 (Supporting Social, Emotional, and Behavioral Growth)
- InTASC Standards (see https://www.ccsso.org/sites/default/files/2017-11/InTASC_Model_Core_Teaching_Standards_2011.pdf): 2 (Learning Differences), 3 (Learning Environments), 4 (Content Knowledge), 7 (Planning for Instruction), 8 (Instructional Strategies)

LITERACY

If any of your students are having difficulty in literacy, have you done the following? If not, see the pages listed here.

STRATEGIES FOR IMPLEMENTING APPROACHES TO READING

- ☐ Implement and adapt basal textbook approaches, 336
- ☐ Implement and adapt whole-language approaches, 337
- ☐ Implement and adapt direct-instruction and code-emphasis approaches, 337–338
- ☐ Make adaptations to promote access to text, 338–339

STRATEGIES FOR PROMOTING WORD IDENTIFICATION

- ☐ Develop phonemic awareness skills, 340–341
- ☐ Provide phonics instruction, 341–343
- ☐ Teach structural analysis as students acquire phonics skills, 344
- ☐ Use strategies for promoting basic sight vocabulary, 344–345

STRATEGIES FOR PROMOTING READING FLUENCY

- ☐ Use repeated readings, 346
- ☐ Use curriculum-based measurement, 346
- ☐ Use classwide peer tutoring, 346
- ☐ Use software programs, 346–347

STRATEGIES FOR TEACHING READING COMPREHENSION

- ☐ Use basic skills and reinforcement strategies, 347
- ☐ Create text enhancements, 348
- ☐ Teach specific questioning strategies, 348–353
- ☐ Adapt formats of reading-comprehension instruction, 353
- ☐ Adapt instruction for secondary students, 355–356
- ☐ Use assistive technology to support secondary-level readers, 356

STRATEGIES FOR IMPLEMENTING MULTI-TIERED READING INSTRUCTION WITH RTI

- ☐ Implement primary (Tier 1) interventions, 356–357
- ☐ Implement secondary (Tier 2) interventions, 357
- ☐ Implement tertiary (Tier 3 or intensive) interventions, 357–358

STRATEGIES FOR IMPROVING HANDWRITING

- ☐ Incorporate self-regulation and self-instructional strategies, 359
- ☐ Use materials to develop manuscript and cursive writing, 359–360
- ☐ Make technological adaptations, 360

STRATEGIES FOR TEACHING SPELLING

- ☐ Select words from reading and writing activities, 361
- ☐ Provide distributed practice sessions, 361
- ☐ Use peer tutoring, 361
- ☐ Modify instruction based on analysis of spelling errors, 361–362
- ☐ Teach mnemonic strategies for spelling, 362–363
- ☐ Teach self-instructional and self-monitoring strategies, 363
- ☐ Teach the cover–copy–compare strategy, 363
- ☐ Use specialized software and curriculum materials, 363
- ☐ Adapt spelling objectives, 363–364
- ☐ Apply spelling in RTI programs, 364

STRATEGIES FOR TEACHING WRITTEN COMMUNICATION

- ☐ Teach students to plan for writing, 364
- ☐ Promote thinking about writing, 364
- ☐ Implement self-regulation and self-instructional writing strategies, 364–365
- ☐ Choose effective composition strategies, 365–366
- ☐ Teach self-regulated strategy development, 366–367
- ☐ Provide support for written research reports, 367–369
- ☐ Use technology to help with writing, 369
- ☐ Adapt instruction to overcome mechanical obstacles to writing, 369–370
- ☐ Use specialized curriculum materials and software, 370

Cristian Ravagnati/EyeEm/Getty Images

CHAPTER 14

Mathematics

LEARNING OBJECTIVES

After studying this chapter, you should be able to:

14.1 Identify current standards in mathematics education, including the NCTM standards and the Common Core State Standards for Mathematics; describe difficulties in mathematics that may be experienced by students with disabilities and interventions that can assist in developing mathematical concepts.

14.2 Discuss strategies for teaching mathematics in inclusive settings, including beginning math, addition and subtraction, multiplication and division, response-to-intervention strategies, problem solving, money and time, fractions and decimals, area and volume concepts, algebra, and functional math.

Mathematics is the academic discipline concerned with the solution of problems that involve quantity or number. Mathematics includes such branches as arithmetic, algebra, geometry, trigonometry, and calculus. Always an important field of study in education, mathematics has taken on increasing importance in contemporary society (Martin, 2007; National Council of Teachers of Mathematics [NCTM], 2000; National Mathematics Advisory Panel, 2008).

Students with disabilities need to gain proficiency in mathematics to fully participate in society (Sayeski & Paulsen, 2010). For this to occur, teachers must be fluent in a variety of instructional techniques that will allow students with diverse learning needs to meet their greatest potential in math.

Mathematics and Students with Disabilities

Learning Objective 14.1. Identify current standards in mathematics education, including the NCTM standards and the Common Core State Standards for Mathematics; describe difficulties in mathematics that may be experienced by students with disabilities and interventions that can assist in developing mathematical concepts.

STANDARDS FOR MATHEMATICS EDUCATION

Through much of U.S. history, mathematics was taught as a set of facts, rules, and procedures for dealing with numbers and quantitative concepts. Reform in mathematics education initiated by the National Council of Teachers of Mathematics resulted in the *Principles and Standards for School Mathematics* (Martin, 2007; NCTM, 2000). In this publication, six overarching principles are provided to describe features of high-quality mathematics education: equity, curriculum, teaching, learning, assessment, and technology. The Common Core State Standards (CCSS; National Governors Association [NGA] Center for Best Practices & Council of Chief State School Officers [CCSSO], 2010) Initiative provides standards in mathematics for kindergarten through high school levels in multiple areas. Standards for K–8 include 11 domains:

Counting and Cardinality (K)

Operations and Algebraic Thinking (K–5)

Number and Operations in Base Ten (K–5)

Measurement and Data (K–5)

Geometry (K–8)

Number and Operations—Fractions (3–5)

Ratios and Proportional Relationships (6–7)

The Number System (6–8)

Expressions and Equations (6–8)

Statistics and Probability (6–8)

Functions (8)

For example, at the third-grade level, under number and operations in base 10, standards include the following: "Fluently add and subtract within 1000 using strategies and algorithms based on place value, properties of operations, and/or the relationship between addition and subtraction" (NGA & CCSSO, 2010). Standards for students beyond grade 8 are separated into six domains: Number and Quantity, Algebra, Functions, Modeling, Geometry, and Statistics & Probability.

The Common Core State Standards for Mathematics (CCSSM) have generally paralleled NCTM principles, balancing an emphasis between mathematical concepts and procedural skills and mathematical process skills, referred to as Standards for Mathematical Practice in CCSS (NCTM, 2011). Furthermore, the NCTM (2000) suggests that students with disabilities and other diverse learning needs may need accommodations in the form of language support, extra time to complete assignments, oral rather than written assignments, peer mentoring, and cross-age tutoring. Teachers can use a number of strategies that may be useful in teaching mathematics to students with disabilities in inclusive settings, including the high-leverage practices (HLPs) (see Chapter 6). The *Diversity, Equity, and Inclusion in the Classroom* feature presents information on the study of mathematics in other cultures.

DIFFICULTIES AND INTERVENTIONS FOR STUDENTS WITH DISABILITIES

Some students with disabilities exhibit little difficulty in learning mathematics. For many others, however, math is an extremely challenging subject area. Many students with learning disabilities may exhibit difficulties in the areas of memory and general strategy use, literacy and communication, specific processes and strategies associated with solving math problems, and low motivation and affect (Mastropieri et al., 2012; Montague & Jitendra, 2006).

Students with intellectual disabilities may exhibit many of these difficulties, as well as problems with acquiring math concepts, remembering and executing math facts and procedures, and mathematical reasoning (Butler et al., 2001). Students with emotional or behavioral disorders often score below grade level on tests of mathematics achievement (Reid et al., 2004), and students with attention problems may exhibit difficulties in organizing information in problem-solving tasks (Marzocchi et al., 2002).

For students with hearing impairments and communication disorders (as well as for students who are English learners), math may be an area of relative strength. Nevertheless, those students may have difficulty with the English-language and communication aspects of mathematics (Lang & Pagliaro, 2007). Like many students with disabilities, students with hearing impairments may benefit from authentic mathematic experiences, integration of vocabulary development, and classroom discourse about mathematics (Stewart & Kluwin, 2001). Students with visual impairments may also generally perform well on mathematics tasks if appropriate adaptations are made (Rosenblum & Amato, 2004). Finally, some students with physical disabilities may need specific assistance if concrete manipulative materials are used (Heller, 2010).

All students can benefit from self-regulation strategies to improve math proficiency. When taught to regulate one's strategy use and performance by self-questioning or self-monitoring with a checklist, students can internalize the processes and hopefully work with

Diversity, Equity, and Inclusion in the Classroom

Multicultural Mathematics

Many people assume that mathematics, as a subject area and a discipline, is universal and constant throughout the world. However, this is not the case. The study of the multicultural contributions to mathematics can help students understand the way different cultures throughout history have viewed mathematics and can lead to a deeper understanding of mathematics as a subject area.

For example, some African cultures use base-20 systems for counting. Learning these systems could contribute to a greater depth of understanding of Western base-10 systems. The Babylonians created tables of reciprocals and used these tables to divide by multiplying by the reciprocals. Mathematics and music of different cultures can be combined in the study of polyrhythms, dividing beats in a measure in two or more ways at the same time. This is relevant to the study of fractions and least-common multiples.

Other examples of multicultural math include other African numeration and counting systems, the Arabic contribution to mathematics, Mayan calendars and numbering systems, ancient Chinese mathematics, and Egyptian and Babylonian mathematics. All of these topics are likely to be of interest to students and can help broaden their understanding of how different cultures have used mathematics (Joseph, 2011).

Several relevant books on multicultural math are available and may be useful in including multicultural considerations in math class. These books include *Math Is a Verb: Activities and Lessons from Cultures Around the World* (Barth et al., 2014); *Mathematics Lessons Learned from Across the World—PreK–8* (Lott & Lott, 2014); *Improving Access to Mathematics: Diversity and Equity in the Classroom* (Nasir & Cobb, 2007); *Africa Counts: Number and Pattern in African Cultures* (Zaslavsky, 1999); *The Crest of the Peacock: Non-European Roots of Mathematics* (Joseph, 2011); *Introduction to Cultural Mathematics: With Case Studies in the Otomies and Inca* (Gilsdorf, 2012); *The Multicultural Math Classroom: Bringing in the World* (Zaslavsky, 1995); and *Oral Storytelling and Teaching Mathematics: Pedagogical and Multicultural Perspectives* (Schiro, 2004).

Exposing students to the diversity among mathematicians may be useful, as well. Brief biographies of mathematicians from around the world and their contributions to mathematics can inspire young students. Here are a few examples:

- David Blackwell (1919–2010): African American statistician
- Shiing-Shen Chern (1911–2004): Chinese mathematician of differential geometry
- Jama Musse Jama (1967–): Somalian ethnomathematician (one who studies the relationship between mathematics and culture)
- Katherine Johnson (1918–2020): African American female mathematician for NASA who calculated trajectories of America's first manned mission to the Moon
- Diego Rodriguez (1596–1668): Spanish mathematician and astronomer who predicted measurements of eclipses.

less assistance from the teacher. This level of independence is even more important beginning with the upper elementary grades and beyond. The *Research Highlight* describes how emergency remote teaching of math impacted students' level of independence.

Teaching Math in Inclusive Settings

Learning Objective 14.2. Discuss strategies for teaching mathematics in inclusive settings, including beginning math, addition and subtraction, multiplication and division, response-to-intervention strategies, problem solving, money and time, fractions and decimals, area and volume concepts, algebra, and functional math.

Fuchs et al. (2017) described seven research-based principles for effective remediation in mathematics:

- *Explicit instruction*, in which the teacher directly provides important information and systematically supports student mastery
- *Instructional design* to minimize the learning challenge, including precise explanations and carefully sequenced instruction

Emergency Remote Teaching During the COVID-19 Pandemic

The COVID-19 pandemic swept over the world and necessitated major changes in society, including schools. Many schools had to close and move toward some version of remote learning in order to maintain schooling for their students. This has involved, in many cases, some degree of online learning. However, many experts in instructional technology have made a distinction between online learning, which includes experiences that are planned out from the beginning of the instructional period and designed to be delivered online, and what they refer to as emergency remote teaching (ERT) (Hodges et al., 2020). ERT is a necessary change of instructional delivery to alternative systems because of crisis circumstances. ERT involves implementation of fully remote teaching approaches that would ordinarily be delivered as face-to-face or hybrid instruction, and that are expected to return to the original format when the crisis or emergency has abated. These crisis situations could include natural calamities, such as damage or destruction to schools from fires, hurricanes, or tornadoes, or the spread of infectious diseases such as COVID-19.

ERT approaches to schooling arise out of necessity and involve schools and communities maintaining schooling to the greatest extent possible with the resources available. But what are the academic and behavioral consequences for students, particularly those with disabilities, who may be less able to adjust to the more limited teacher support and higher expectations for independent learning and self-regulation? Lambert and Schuck (2021) examined these issues in a qualitative (descriptive/interpretive) investigation of a special educator teaching standards-based mathematics to her elementary students during ERT. Lambert and Schuck examined the following research questions: (1) What issues were associated with ERT conducted by an experienced special educator? (2) What changes did the teacher observe in student engagement and math problem solving? and (3) How did the teacher respond to address these issues?

The teacher, referred to as Ms. Montes, taught a grade 3–5 class at a mostly Hispanic (>90%) and disadvantaged (>70%) school, which contained 18% English learners and 13% students with disabilities. Ms. Montes's 13 students (3 girls, 10 boys) had been primarily diagnosed with learning disabilities and included a few with autism. She identified as Latina and was named by district personnel as an outstanding teacher, especially in mathematics. Ms. Montes employed cognitively guided instruction (Carpenter et al., 2014) in her mathematics teaching, which focuses on encouraging students to solve problems independently using manipulatives or drawing. Lambert and Schuck interviewed the teacher during the implementation of ERT in mathematics, focusing on topics of student engagement, family/caregiver engagement, and changes in mathematics instruction. An inductive approach to data analysis resulted in the emergence of four themes: (1) Inequitable Access, (2) Socio-Emotional Focused Teaching, (3) Supporting Self-Regulation, and (4) Tensions in Planning Instruction.

Ms. Montes attempted to make contact with all her students immediately after school closing. However, many family members and caregivers were obligated to work during school hours, resulting in inequitable access to learning opportunities. One caregiver/family member placed her child with an aunt because she was not fluent in English and felt she could not provide appropriate support for at-home learning, even though Ms. Montes was bilingual. Some children had adult support throughout the day, others did not receive any individual assistance. Because of lack of support, some students did not engage in online learning, while others engaged without adult support. A few students were particularly engaged in distance learning, and one consistently requested advanced problems.

Ms. Montes started holding synchronous Zoom meetings, focused at first on social-emotional learning, and allowing her students to dictate the content of the early meetings. Shortly after, she recounted:

> *"By the end of the week, it was more academic. And I lost two students because of that; they have not returned to Zoom, once they realized it wasn't just chatting time. . . . It's concerning, because I can't get hold of those families." (Lambert & Schuck, 2021, p. 293)*

Ms. Montes also lamented the lack of her students' social-emotional connections to each other during ERT. She reported,

> *"All of a sudden, for mathematics there's no one to turn and say, 'Are you doing this today? Are you getting this? What are you going to do?'"* (p. 293)

Ms. Montes believed peer discussion, support for finding the correct answer, and instilling a sense of community were critical components of student engagement. Also, an important component of Ms. Montes's teaching was on what she referred to as "independence," including self-monitoring and self-regulation. However, she found that this type of

Research Highlight

Emergency Remote Teaching During the COVID-19 Pandemic—*continued*

independence did not always transfer from classroom to home:

> *"In school, I feel like they have this certain sense of autonomy, like there's an expected autonomy and expected, 'I can do this for myself.' And right now, at home, I'm seeing a lot of, 'Well, no, at home, I can't do stuff by myself. At home, there's people that will either do things for me or tell me when I do it wrong.'"* (p. 293)

One family member attended all their child's Zoom sessions. Another's work changed significantly, Ms. Montes believed because of overzealous adult supervision. The teacher had emphasized self-regulation in terms of deciding when they needed breaks and found that families/caregivers were not always supportive. She reported:

> *"The wall right now between us is: I can't provide that structure he needs. . . . He needs constant emotional check-in. And mom called me one day in tears because she's like, 'He's really hard to work with.'"* (p. 293)

Communicating to families/caregivers the importance of independent skills became an important issue for Ms. Montes. She also actively attempted to avoid the emotional reactions that were possible during her mathematics instruction:

> *"It's like, I don't want them to be crying at home. Like at school, they get really frustrated, but I'm there, and I can catch it right before it gets to that point."* (p. 293)

During the academic year, the school district emphasized consolidating prior knowledge for students with disabilities rather than undertaking new content. Ms. Montes struggled with this guidance, wondering if she should follow the district's expectations or attempt to teach some additional content. This created some tension in planning instruction. Additionally, some students seemed to be regressing, using less-sophisticated mathematical strategies, even when the work was very similar to what they had already done in class. For example, students were provided with a picture of 84 items and were asked to count them and document their strategies:

> *"One of my kids, his equation was literally one plus one. And he had all 84 ones in there. And I was just like, that is not what we have been doing in school. It should have at least been 10 plus 10 plus 10. . . . Like I've seen you do it in class. But he's one who needs a lot of reassurance. So, I think the ones who need reassurance always go back to the ones if there's nobody to tell them, 'You are a mathematician. You're fine.'"* (p. 294)

Lambert and Schuck (2021) concluded that their investigation had identified several challenges concerning teaching mathematics to students with disabilities during the COVID-19 school closures. These challenges included limitations on student engagement (e.g., access to technology, appropriate adult supports) and the difficulties motivating students in an online environment undertaking mathematics. The teacher underlined the importance of social-emotional connections and self-regulation in mathematics, as she began to find ways to present mathematics in a way that mirrored her classroom instruction. She acknowledged the difficulties in expecting families/caregivers to work on self-regulation skills but felt this was an opportunity to build stronger future home–school relationships.

QUESTIONS FOR REFLECTION

1. Why do you think students had problems with motivation in their online environment?
2. What other strategies might Ms. Montes have tried to increase student engagement?
3. Do you agree that schools should focus on consolidating prior knowledge during ERT, or should they try to develop new skills?

- *A strong conceptual basis* for mathematical procedures to promote understanding, reduce confusion, and maintain and integrate previously mastered content
- *Practice* to promote automaticity and overlearning
- *Cumulative review* to promote integration and retention of learning
- *Motivators* to promote effort, regulate attention, and address previous learning failures
- Systematic, ongoing *progress monitoring*

For all students, and particularly for those with cognitive or intellectual disabilities, development of mathematical understandings can be facilitated by progressing from concrete

Pearson eTextbook

Video Example 14.1

As a group, seventh-graders solve math problems and describe the operations that they use. How do the students benefit from being in this inclusive classroom?

representations of quantity (e.g., beads or blocks) to semi-concrete (e.g., pictorial) representations, then finally to abstract (graphic) representations (Fuchs et al., 2021; Mercer et al., 2011). Concrete representations as well as "virtual" manipulatives have also been helpful for autistic students (Barnett & Cleary, 2015). Mathematics functioning and fluency have been improved by direct instruction, reinforcement, mnemonics, cognitive strategy training, and timed activities (Fuchs et al., 2021; Jimenez & Staples, 2015; Mastropieri et al., 2012; Stein et al., 2018). Effective teaching strategies for different subject and skill areas are discussed in the upcoming sections.

David Rose and his colleagues at the Center for Universal Design for Learning (UDL) describe UDL as an approach to thinking about teaching and learning for all students, similar to differentiated instruction (see cast.org; Hall et al., 2012; Meyer et al., 2014). By applying UDL principles to mathematics, teachers make math instruction accessible to everyone. Examples include the use of manipulatives during instruction, provision of both verbal and written instructions, and use of technology with features such as font enlargement or text-to-voice and voice-to-text options that facilitate access to the material for all students. Other examples include allowing differentiated response formats for students based on their abilities, such as allowing the use of switch response formats for students with physical disabilities or severe disabilities and allowing oral or written responses. Most of the strategies in this chapter are consistent with UDL principles.

STRATEGIES FOR TEACHING BEGINNING MATH

TEACH EARLY NUMBER CONCEPTS Early number concepts are critically important for the development of later mathematical skills (Powell & Fuchs, 2012). These concepts include recognition of numbers, simple matching and naming simple shapes, and one-to-one correspondence. Most children are already familiar with many elementary number concepts when they begin school (Berteletti et al., 2010). These concepts are represented by words such as *more*, *less*, *any*, *none*, *none left*, *together*, *how many*, and *each*. Concepts such as these are necessary for the development of more complex understandings. It may become clear, however, from student responses to teacher questions (e.g., "Do you want more?" "Which container holds fewer pencils?") or by a student's statements that such concepts have not been mastered. Understanding of these concepts can be promoted by applying strategies for teaching language concepts. For example, during snack period, after a student eats one cracker, the teacher could say, "Do you want more?" When the student begins to reply correctly, the teacher could ask, "What do you want?" prompting the student to reply, "More crackers." Later, the teacher could hold two crackers in one hand and three in the other and ask, "Which hand has more crackers?"

TEACH STRATEGIES FOR COUNTING Learning to count is a type of factual (serial list) learning and is best acquired with practice. Counting seems to be a very simple skill, but it can appear very complicated to those who have not yet mastered it. Be sure to address all the components of counting in early numeracy. *Acoustic counting* refers to saying numbers in sequence ("Everybody say with me, 'one, two, three . . . '"). *Point counting* refers to pointing to objects as each number name is said ("Let's count all the desks in the classroom. Point and count together . . . "); when done correctly, pointing and counting are *synchronized. Resultative counting* refers to the understanding that the order in which items are counted is irrelevant to obtaining the correct total ("Now let's count them in the other direction . . . '"). *Counting on* is the ability to begin counting with a number other than 1 (and is a good way to introduce adding: "I've got five pencils in my left hand; let's count how many there are altogether: "*Five* . . . six, seven . . . '"). *Skip counting* or "count by" is counting by groups of numbers, such as 2s and 5s. Finally, *subitizing* means totaling small numbers of objects (e.g., four pennies) without directly counting (Van Luit & Schopman, 2000).

Begin with just a few numbers, such as "one, two, three," and have students clap their hands each time they count. Students who are having more difficulty may benefit from practicing with a larger group of students. As number sequences are mastered, add a few numbers at a time. For additional time on-task, ask peers to count with students who are still learning. Use of rhythms or regular emphasis may also help develop counting skills. Although group practice is helpful, it is also important to determine if individual students have mastered counting skills by asking them to count independently.

As the series of names of numbers is mastered, students should be introduced to the concept of counting *things*. Counting the students in the class or the pencils in a jar, for example, is an early means of demonstrating how similar objects can be counted. Again, practice, additional time on-task, and use of peer assistance can help enforce the concept of numeration.

Jimenez and Staples (2015) taught early numeracy skills to students with significant intellectual disabilities, in alignment with CCSSM. These skills included number identification, making sets of up to five items, and doing simple addition and used math stories, theme-based lessons, systematic prompting and feedback, and manipulatives and graphic organizers from the *Early Numeracy* materials developed by Jimenez et al. (2012). The students made substantial progress toward meeting the standards on alternative assessments.

REINFORCE ONE-TO-ONE CORRESPONDENCE *One-to-one correspondence* is the concept that sets of different objects (beads, blocks, etc.) can be matched according to quantity (Tucker et al., 2006). That is, even though blocks are not the same as beads, a set of three blocks is equivalent to a set of three beads with respect to quantity. You can reinforce this correspondence by exhibiting two sets of objects and asking students to match them item for item, as shown in Figure 14.1. Before later concepts can be mastered effectively, it is important that students understand the concept of numerical equivalence. Counting with correspondence should be a critical component of any early numeracy intervention (Nelson & McMaster, 2018).

INTRODUCE GEOMETRY CONCEPTS IN THE EARLY YEARS It may be helpful to introduce the concept of shapes during the acquisition of early math concepts. Although precise rules that define particular geometric shapes can be provided later, you can teach students to identify simple shapes such as circles, squares, and triangles by the presentation of many examples and the use of teacher questioning.

Use different types of circles to enforce the relevant attributes of a circle—that shape is what matters, not other attributes such as color and size. Presenting noninstances also enforces the concept of *circle* ("Is this a circle?" [pointing to a square]). Also, give students different shapes, then ask them to hold up the shape that matches the teacher's shape.

Pearson eTextbook

Video Example 14.2

Describe the practice routine the teacher uses in the video to promote automaticity and overlearning during a counting activity. What instructional adaptations does the teacher make for this small group of students with disabilities?

Figure 14.1 Understanding the Concept of Numerical Equivalence

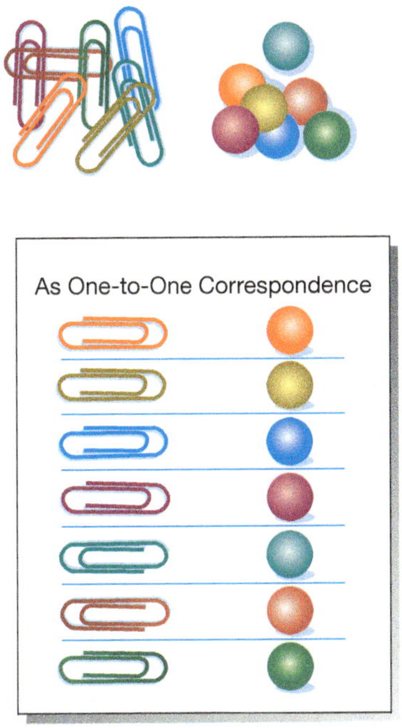

STRATEGIES FOR

TEACHING ADDITION AND SUBTRACTION

USE MANIPULATIVES FOR TEACHING ADDITION AND SUBTRACTION CONCEPTS

Manipulatives have been seen to be effective in promoting learning of a variety of concepts and skills in mathematics (Lafay et al., 2019). Using such materials as beads, buttons, dried beans, or commercially available base-10 manipulatives (distributed by companies such as Delta Education), you can help students learn the concepts of addition and subtraction by counting. For example, show students 5 beans, and ask them to add 4 more. Demonstrate how to select 4 beans to add and employ a "counting-on" strategy, where they start at 5 and add the 4 beans, counting up to 9. You can also teach students to "take away" by starting with 9 beans and taking away 4, to leave the difference of 5. (Remember that small manipulatives can represent a choking hazard for very young children.)

USE NUMBER LINES TO PROMOTE OPERATIONS A helpful intermediate step between counting actual objects and operating with numbers is the use of a **number line.** Number lines are lines with marks to represent quantity, including real and whole numbers, rational numbers, as well as positive and negative numbers (Fuchs et al., 2021). Here is an example:

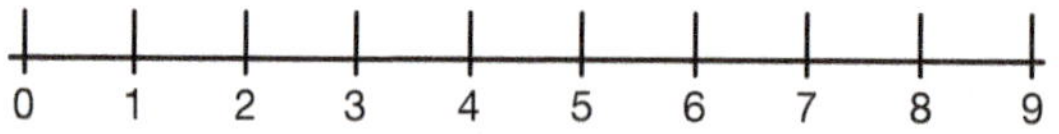

To add, have students place their pencils on the first addend on the number line and count forward using the second addend. For example, to add 2 + 3, students place their pencils on the 2 and then count forward: 1(3), 2(4), 3(5). Conversely, the subtraction problem 5 − 2 is solved by placing the pencil on the 5; counting two steps to the left, 1(4), 2(3); and noting the difference, 3. The relationship between operations with number lines and adding and subtracting beans and buttons should be made explicit. Also, number lines are useful when practicing "count-ons" and "count-backs" as precursors of learning addition and subtraction facts.

Provide physical assistance, enlarge or darken the number line, or use three-dimensional number lines to provide for individual needs. Later, number lines that include negative numbers can be substituted to help students understand the concept of negative numbers:

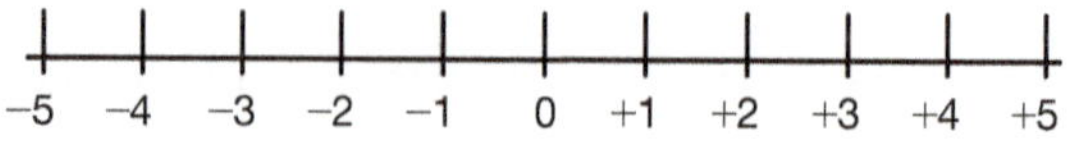

USE STRATEGIES FOR NUMBER WRITING Some students have difficulty learning to write numbers and may benefit from the use of models or stencils, from copying over dashed-line numbers, or from additional practice. Some students may reverse numbers when they write. Although many reversals may be obvious (e.g., 3), other reversals may not. A reversed 2, for example, may look like a 6 and suggest a problem with number facts when the true problem is writing, as shown in the following illustration:

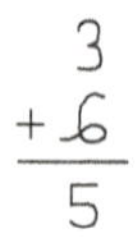

Bley (2019) suggested a strategy for remembering the spatial orientation of 3, 5, 7, and 9. That is, the curved part of 3 and 5 can be represented with the right hand; the 7 and 9 can be represented with the right hand and right forearm. That is, if 3, 5, 7, and 9 are written correctly, they can be imitated with the right hand.

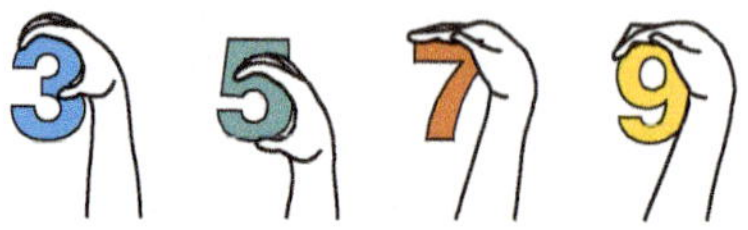

Some number-writing reversals involve two digits. For example, 18 can be written as 81. Reversals such as this may arise because the names of both numbers begin with the same word sound (*eight*). Again, practice, feedback, and self-correction can be helpful in eliminating these reversals.

Pearson eTextbook

Video Example 14.3

A CCSS for kindergarten is to count to 100 and to write numbers from 0 to 20. Why do you think the teacher in this video uses Touch Math materials and this explicit instructional routine with this kindergartener?

USE QUESTIONING TO PROMOTE UNDERSTANDING OF SYMBOLS Ginsburg (1998a, 1998b) described the case of a first-grader who could answer problems such as $3 + 4 = ?$ but could not explain what was meant by the "plus" and "equal" symbols:

TOBY: . . . it tells you three plus four, three plus four, so it's telling you, that, um, I think, the, um, the end is coming up—the end.

INTERVIEWER: The end is coming up—what do you mean, the end is coming up?

TOBY: Like, if you have equals, and so you have seven, then. [*She is gesturing to the problem on the table.*] So if you do three plus four equals seven, that would be right. (Ginsburg, 1998a, p. 42)

Other children may state that = means "makes," as in "6 + 3 *makes* 9" (Ginsburg, 1998a). As students acquire skill in mathematics, question them to determine that they also understand concepts represented by mathematical symbols. If not, reemphasize previous concept-building activities, such as equivalence.

USE TOUCH MATH TO PROMOTE ADDITION AND SUBTRACTION COMPUTATION Even when students have mastered the relevant concepts of addition and subtraction, they may not necessarily be able to calculate problems quickly and accurately. A method for assisting with calculating arithmetic problems is **Touch Math** materials (TouchMath Acquisition, LLC). These materials represent quantity by dots on each of the numbers 1–9, as shown in Figure 14.2. Touch Math materials have been found to be effective with students with a variety of disabilities, including physical disabilities, intellectual or learning disabilities, hearing impairments, and autism spectrum disorder (ASD) (e.g., Avant & Heller, 2011; Aydemir, 2015; Cox & Jimenez, 2020; Khalifa & Saad, 2021; Kit et al., 2018; Simon & Hanrahan, 2004).

Students learn that each number is associated with a certain number of dots ("touch points"), which can be counted forward or backward to compute sums and differences. Note that the numbers 1–5 have solid dots, the total representing the quantity of the number. After 5, Touch Math uses circled dots, or "double touch points," each of which represents the quantity 2. Students learn to touch each of the touch points once and to touch each double touch point twice with their pencil when counting. For example, to compute the quantity

students are taught to start with the larger number, 7, and count forward, touching each of the double touch points in the 6 twice. Students start with 7 and count "8–9, 10–11, 12–13" to arrive at the answer. To subtract, students are taught to start with the minuend and count backward on the subtrahend, using the touch points. A complete set of Touch Math materials has been developed, along with worksheets and teacher materials (see https://www.touchmath.com).

Individual students can be taught to use Touch Math methods if they are having particular difficulty remembering addition and subtraction facts and you want them to engage in computation problems with the rest of the class. As mentioned, Touch Math has been found

Figure 14.2 Touch Math Numbers

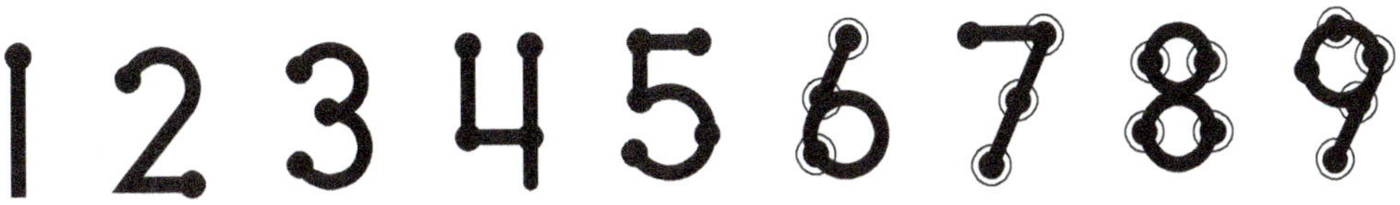

Note: Reprinted with permission of TouchMath Acquisition, LLC, formerly Innovative Learning Concepts.

to be effective with students with ASD (Barnett & Cleary, 2015). In some cases, particularly in the primary grades, teachers use Touch Math with the whole class. However, if remembering math facts is a classroom standard, it may be important to continue to teach these facts in later grades.

USE PRACTICE AND SPECIFIC STRATEGIES FOR ADDITION AND SUBTRACTION FACTS Many students, including those without disabilities, have difficulty remembering addition and subtraction facts (Geary, 2013). One way to ensure that math facts are learned is to spend enough time teaching them. Students can respond orally as a class to teacher questions ("Class, what is 4 plus 7?") or hold up numbers at their desks ("Class, hold up the answer to 6 plus 3"). Introduced in Chapter 13, the cover-copy-compare strategy can also be used for incremental rehearsal of math facts (Riccomini et al., 2017). Additionally, pairs of students can practice with each other using flashcards. Assigning facts to be mastered at home with the help of caregivers or other family members can also provide additional time on-task.

Students who appear to be learning at a slower rate may be able to practice difficult facts with a partner. You can provide opportunities for students to practice using flashcards independently. Additionally, students can also use calculators and computer software, such as *Math Blaster* (Knowledge Adventure), to practice math facts.

When teaching facts, it is important to stress commutativity, that is, $2 + 3 = 3 + 2$. Students who understand commutativity must master only half as many facts. Bley (2019) suggested that reversible cards be used to demonstrate the equivalence of, for example, $2 + 3$ and $3 + 2$. Use a card similar to the following, embedded with tags or paperclips:

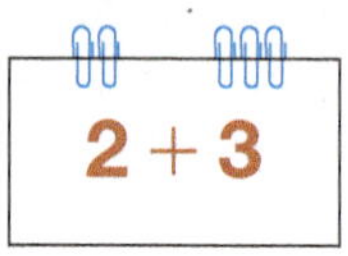

Teachers can reverse the card ($3 + 2$) to show that both sides represent the same fact. Bley (2019) described several strategies to assist students with math facts. Looking at the matrix of 100 addition facts, she was able to demonstrate that most can be mastered with the following specific strategies:

1. Nineteen facts involve addition with zero (e.g., $3 + 0 = 3$) and are easy to master.
2. Forty-five facts involve "count-ons," that is, addition with 1, 2, or 3 that can be "counted on" verbally to the other addend, for example, $8 + 2$ or $6 + 3$. Altogether, 64 of the 100 addition facts involve "zero facts" or "count-ons."
3. Of the remaining 36 facts (not covered by zero or count-ons), six facts involve "doubles" and can be represented by images or pictures of doubles. That is, $4 + 4$ is the "spider" fact, where the spider has four legs on each side; $5 + 5$ is the "fingers" fact (5 fingers on each hand); $6 + 6$ is the "egg carton" fact (6 eggs in each half dozen); $7 + 7$ is the "2-week" fact (7 days in each of 2 weeks on a calendar); $8 + 8$ is the "crayon" fact (8 in each row); and $9 + 9$ is the "double 9 domino" fact (9 dots on each side of a domino). Double facts also exist for $2 + 2$ and $3 + 3$, but these are also covered by "count-ons."
4. In addition to the zero, count-on, and doubles facts, eight additional facts represent "doubles plus one," which means their sum is one more than the double. For example, $4 + 5$ is the same as the doubles fact (spider) $4 + 4 = 8$ plus one, or 9. The doubles and doubles-plus-one facts, together with the previously described facts, account for 78 facts in all.
5. Of the remaining 22 facts, 10 are referred to as "pattern 9" facts and can be learned by the following rule: The sum of a +9 fact can be obtained by subtracting one from the other addend and adding 10. For example, to add $9 + 5$, subtract 1 from the 5 (= 4) and add 10 to make 14.
6. Two additional facts ($6 + 4$ and $4 + 6$) are "other-10 sums," or other sums to 10, and two others ($7 + 4$ and $4 + 7$) are "10-plus-1" sums. Altogether, zero,

count-ons, doubles, doubles plus one, pattern 9, other-10 sums, and 10-plus-1 sums account for 92 facts of the 100 addition facts, leaving only eight.

7. There is no specific rule for learning the remaining eight facts; however, commutativity reveals that these are actually only four facts, each of which can be expressed two ways: $5 + 7$ or $7 + 5$; $8 + 4$ or $4 + 8$; $8 + 5$ or $5 + 8$; and $8 + 6$ or $6 + 8$.

Use of the Bley strategies is likely to prove helpful in assisting students who have difficulty recalling math facts. To provide further practice with fact fluency and develop problem-solving skills and reasoning, *magic squares* can be introduced, moving from simple (3×3 array) to more complex. A magic square is a grid of numbers where the values in each of the rows, columns, and diagonals add up to the same sum, known as the "magic number."

Subtraction Facts Most students find it more difficult to learn subtraction facts than addition facts. One advantage, however, is that all subtraction facts are the inverse of particular addition facts and can be easily checked. That is, $9 - 5 = 4$ is the inverse fact of $4 + 5 = 9$. Use of base-10 blocks or other manipulatives can help enforce this concept. Some instructional materials (e.g., *Connecting Math Concepts*, published by SRA/McGraw-Hill) teach these facts together as number families. In this case, the number family would include $4 + 5 = 9$; $5 + 4 = 9$; $9 - 5 = 4$; and $9 - 4 = 5$.

Bley (2019) provided several strategies to assist with subtraction facts. Of the 100 total subtraction facts, these include 27 "count-backs" when subtracting 1, 2, or 3 (e.g., for $11 - 2$, "10, 9").

There are also 19 "zero" facts, which involve subtracting zero from a number (e.g., $9 - 0$) or subtracting two identical numbers whose difference equals zero (e.g., $4 - 4$). An additional 15 facts are referred to as "count-ups," when the difference can be counted up by 1, 2, or 3. For example, for $12 - 9$, start at the subtrahend, 9, and count up to the minuend, 12, holding up fingers as you count, if needed: "9 – 10, 11, *12*" (counting 3).

Bley (2019) also list seven "10-frame" facts, where the student imagines a "frame" of two rows of five and calculates from these.

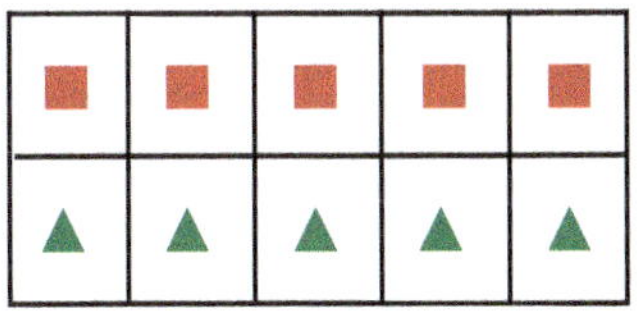

For example, for the fact $10 - 7$, subtracting 7 from the 10-frame removes all of the top row and two of the bottom rows, leaving 3. Bley (2019) also includes $9 - 5$ and $9 - 4$ in this series, beginning with a frame of 9 (5 on top, 4 on the bottom).

Finally, Bley (2019) lists six facts as "new doubles," which means that when subtracted, doubles are revealed in the difference and subtrahend (e.g., $8 - 4 = 4$). Altogether, these strategies account for 74 subtraction facts, leaving 26 "harder facts" that must be learned through drill and practice and application of addition rules. These harder facts include the following:

- (17, 16, 15, 14, 13) – 9;
- (17, 15, 14, 13, 12) – 8;
- (16, 15, 13, 12, 11) – 7;
- (15, 14, 13, 11) – 6;
- (14, 13, 12, 11) – 5; and
- (13, 12, 11) – 4.

Use of tutoring pairs, computer software, apps such as *Math Fact Master* (TipTapTech), and homework can help promote mastery of these facts. Charts, such as the following, that demonstrate students' progress toward completion can help promote motivation and persistence of effort.

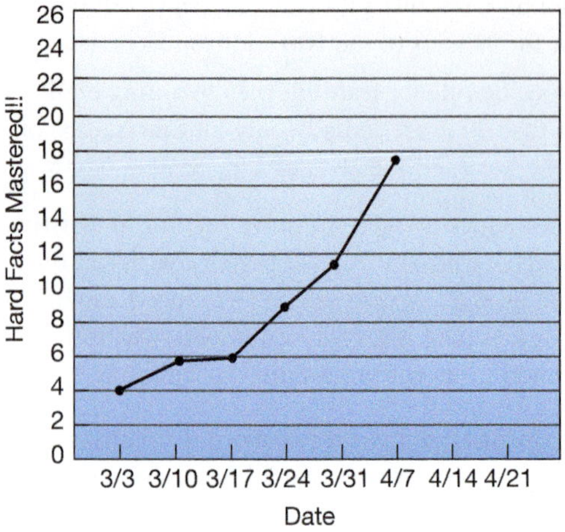

USE STRATEGIES FOR PLACE VALUE AND REGROUPING Place value is a concept that is linked to our base-10 system, and students must learn this concept as they use numbers of more than one digit. Use of **base-10 blocks,** including base-10 place value charts (Delta Education), can be helpful in establishing this concept. First, students learn to count individual base-10 units. They next learn that units are combined as groups of 10, and then they learn that groups of 10 are combined as groups of 100. Therefore, the quantity 111 can be represented as follows:

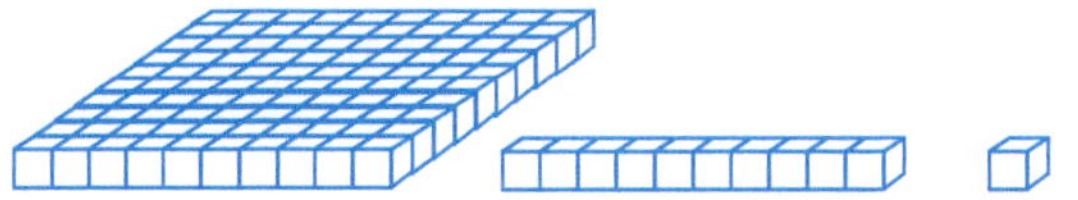

When students understand the concept of place value, they will be able to explain that the 1 in the quantity 123 represents 1 hundred, the 2 represents 2 tens, or 20, and the 3 represents 3 ones. You can practice place value by having students build, count, and record numbers from different values of ones, tens, and hundreds. Consider also virtual manipulatives, described later in the chapter.

Students can also learn to add and subtract with base-10 blocks. Making certain the appropriate values are lined up, students add or subtract within each column. Create a place value board with columns for hundreds, tens, and ones, with a picture of the appropriate base-10 block at the head of each column. Place the appropriate blocks on the place value board to represent the problem to be solved. For example, for 35 + 22, place 3 tens and 5 ones on the board in groups in the appropriate columns, and below these, place 2 tens and 2 ones. Addition is done by combining these quantities to 5 tens and 7 ones, or 57. Subtraction is done by removing the value of the base-10 blocks in the subtrahend from the minuend. In this same case, 2 tens and 2 ones are removed from 3 tens and 5 ones, leaving 1 ten and 3 ones, or 35 − 22 = 13.

Regrouping in addition occurs when the unit values of any column exceed 10. These units must then be combined and placed in the next higher value. For example, to add 35 + 18, first, represent the problem on the place value board with 3 tens and 5 ones above 1 ten and 8 ones. When these quantities are combined within their columns, the 5 ones added to the 8 ones result in 13 ones. Because this quantity exceeds 10, trade 10 ones for 1 ten, and place it in the tens column. The result is 5 tens and 3 ones, or 53. It is also important for students to see how numbers are used to represent these concepts by recording number values when the building and counting have been completed.

For regrouping in subtraction, students must learn to "trade up" for 10 of a particular value in the higher column. For example, for the problem 14 − 6, students learn that the 1 ten must be traded for 10 ones and added to the 4 ones in the ones column. Subtracting 6 from the 14 ones, then, leaves 8, the difference.

Uberti et al. (2004) described the use of a self-monitoring checklist to improve performance on regrouping algorithms. The teacher developed self-monitoring checklists for third-grade students with learning disabilities and English learners who were having difficulties with regrouping. The checklists, based on an error analysis for each student, included steps for problem solution, including writing down the unit value in the sum and carrying the tens value above the tens columns. Students checked off each step when they completed it. After several practice tests, students with disabilities performed the calculation at the level of the mean of the whole class. This type of cognitive strategy can help students become more self-directed and independent (HLP 14; McLeskey et al., 2017).

USE STRATEGIES FOR TEACHING EARLY PROBLEM SOLVING WITH ADDITION AND SUBTRACTION You can help promote the idea that mathematical operations have meaning by using manipulatives at the early stages of learning number concepts. As students move into the area of problem solving, these concepts can be enforced. Miller and Mercer (1993; see also Mercer et al., 2011) demonstrated the effectiveness of a graduated word-problem sequence strategy for teaching math problem solving, using concrete, semi-concrete, and abstract problem representations.

The word used in the word problems matched the manipulative objects in the concrete and semi-concrete levels. For example, if students were learning to subtract using cubes (concrete level), the word *cubes* was used in the problem (semi-concrete level):

4 cubes
−2 cubes
———
cubes

During the abstract level of instruction, the difficulty of word problems is increased gradually from simple words, phrases, and sentences such as:

8 pieces of candy
−8 pieces of candy sold
———
___ are left.

to more elaborate sentences:

Jennie had 4 pens.
She lost 2 of them.
———
She has _____ pens left.

Finally, students created their own word problems. This investigation demonstrated how students with learning problems in mathematics could learn to solve word problems by introducing increasing levels of complexity. This graduated sequence of instruction is commonly referred to as the concrete-representational-abstract (CRA) strategy.

Students who have difficulty determining the operation for solving problems (e.g., addition, subtraction) can construct problems like this on their own. Bley (2019) suggested several steps, summarized as follows:

1. Present a short problem that gives only the essential information (e.g., 3 apples, bought 2 more apples).
2. Tell what is missing. What is missing should be the solution of the problem (together, there are ____ apples).
3. Use numerals (3) to write number words (three).
4. Compute two-step problems separately. Color-code each step.
5. Use picture choices; for example, show two picture representations of the problem—such as 3 apples being added to 3 more, or 2 apples being removed from a group of 3—and ask the student to choose the correct one.

USE RESPONSE-TO-INTERVENTION STRATEGIES FOR EARLY PREVENTION AND IDENTIFICATION Response to intervention (RTI) is a system of increasingly intensive interventions intended to prevent academic failure and provide evidence for identification for special education when necessary. To date, instructional interventions in RTI frameworks have largely prioritized literacy with arguably more resources to support teachers' reading instruction. However, teachers can effectively implement RTI for mathematics (see The IRIS Center, 2018). In mathematics, Tier 1, or primary, interventions include high-quality instructional procedures for the general education class with adaptations as needed, as described in this chapter. Students who do not demonstrate adequate progress in Tier 1 can be considered for Tier 2 interventions, which could include intensive small-group tutoring (while still receiving Tier 1 instruction), and then Tier 3 interventions, which may include more intensive individual interventions or possible referral to special education (Fuchs et al., 2012). Numerous procedures have been recommended for implementing RTI in mathematics (Riccomini & Witzel, 2010).

Dennis (2015) implemented Tier 2 instruction with second-grade students who were experiencing difficulties in learning mathematics. Students were taught in groups of three for 20 minutes, four times a week for a 10-week period. Topics included numerical order, quantity comparison, addition and subtraction facts, place value, and multiple-digit addition and subtraction and were aligned with the CCSS for grade 2 mathematics, Number and Operations in Base Ten (NGA & CCSSO, 2010). Instructional procedures included direct modeling and teaching using scripted lessons; employing a CRA strategy when appropriate; using base-10 blocks, drawings, and numerals; and offering guided and independent practice. Overall, students improved substantially in their math scores. For three students who did not make adequate progress according to curriculum-based measurement (CBM), a Tier 3 intervention was implemented that included one-to-one instruction, additional practice and feedback, and 35-minute sessions rather than 20-minute sessions. This Tier 3 intervention was successful in promoting adequate progress in math.

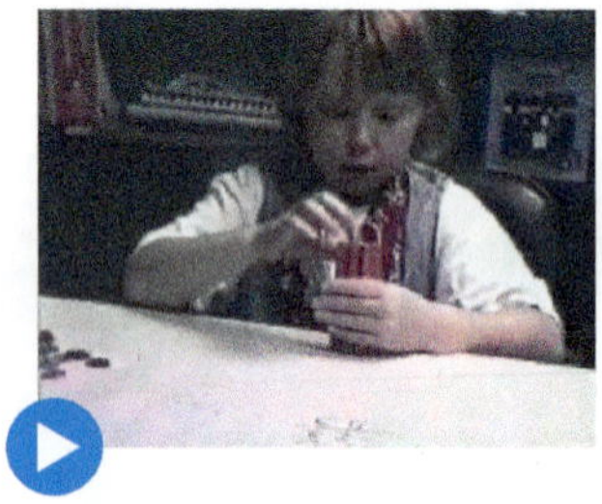

Pearson eTextbook
Video Example 14.4
In this math interview, Gretchen, a second-grader, is convinced her paper-and-pencil response is correct even as she gets a different correct answer when using manipulatives and a hundreds chart. Why might it be important to monitor student understanding in mathematics? How might a teacher work with Gretchen to address her misconceptions?

Progress Monitoring and Diagnostic Interviews As described in Chapter 13 for reading, universal screening and progress monitoring are used to make decisions about students' responsiveness to intervention and movement among tiers. Progress monitoring using CBM in math could include probes with computational problems that measure procedural knowledge, such as 20, two-digit addition problems. Probes can be scored on the number of digits correct or the number of problems answered correctly. Probes can also be used to measure conceptual knowledge with a sample of problems drawn from the semester's curriculum. When individualizing an intervention plan, Hunt and Little (2014) suggest use of a diagnostic interview to further determine students' conceptual understanding of a targeted content area. The questions asked during the diagnostic student interview are informed by the progress-monitoring data and may include "How can you make sure you are really right about that?" and "Say out loud how you figured it out" (Hunt & Little, 2014, p. 192). The interview data is used to identify students' current knowledge and what skills the student still needs.

Use Small-Group Tutoring as a Tier 2 Intervention Fuchs et al. (2007) described a model of intervention to identify students at risk for development of mathematics difficulty and a tier system for providing intervention. First-grade students who scored poorly during the third through fifth weeks of the school year (i.e., correctly answering an average of 11 or fewer of 25 problems on weekly tests) were provided with Tier 2 remedial help in the form of small-group tutoring using concrete, pictorial, and graphic materials, as well as practice on math facts with a software program. After 16 weeks of instruction, two or three times per week, 30 minutes per session, the proportion of students at risk for math difficulties was sharply reduced (e.g., from 9.75% to 5.14%). Students who failed to respond positively to the Tier 2 instruction could be considered for special education.

Fuchs et al. (2009) introduced "Pirate Math" with small-group tutoring to third-grade students having math difficulties in the general education class. They taught a strategy for developing number combination skills using number lines and finger counting (add = start with the bigger number and count up to the smaller number on your fingers, and the answer is the last number; subtract = start with the minus number—subtrahend—and count up to the number you started with, and the answer is the number of fingers you used to count up). When this approach was combined with other procedures, such as the RUN strategy for word problems (Read the problem, Underline the question, Name the problem type—total, difference, or change), students made considerable gains in important math skills (see also Powell et al., 2015).

Bryant et al. (2011) implemented a Tier 2 math intervention with first-grade students who had exhibited difficulty in early math learning. They incorporated systematic small-group tutoring instruction along with visual representations of mathematical concepts, meaningful practice opportunities, and frequent progress monitoring to develop understanding in early numeracy skills and math concepts. These students made significant gains in curriculum-based measures and number computation.

Use Intensive Interventions as a Tier 3 Intervention Students may be referred to special education for Tier 3 interventions in some districts. Tier 3 consists of very intensive interventions intended to help students who have not benefited from Tier 1 or 2 interventions and continue to perform well below grade level due to persistent difficulties. The National Center for Intensive Interventions (NCII; http://www.intensiveintervention.org) developed sample activities for providing intensive interventions in math. These include general strategies for designing math interventions (NCII, 2016b); considerations for teaching specific skills, for example, fractions; and lessons and activities to use for providing intensive interventions (NCII, 2016a, 2016c). Powell and Fuchs (2015) provided a framework for designing intensive interventions that included focusing on critical content and skills; using explicit instruction, manipulatives, modeling, feedback, multiple opportunities for practice, and motivational strategies; developing fluency skills; connecting mathematical concepts with mathematical procedures; and monitoring and adjusting based on student performance data. This framework is represented in a series of 8 online modules provided by the NCII and the University of Connecticut (i.e., Intensive Intervention in Mathematics Course; https://intensiveintervention.org/training/course-content/intensive-intervention-mathematics).

STRATEGIES FOR TEACHING MULTIPLICATION AND DIVISION

USE MANIPULATIVES FOR TEACHING MULTIPLICATION AND DIVISION CONCEPTS

Multiplication and division concepts can be enforced through the use of manipulatives, such as base-10 blocks. Show students, for example, a set of 3 units, and ask them to put together four such sets. After this has been done, inform students that they have a set of 3, four *times.* By counting total units, it can be seen that 3 taken four times, or 4 times 3, is 12.

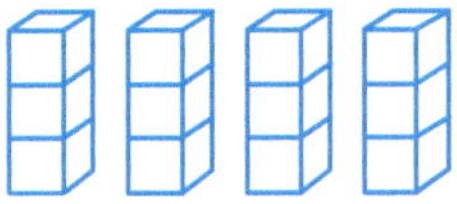

Students should come to understand that division is "the separation of a quantity into equal sized parts" (Tucker et al., 2006, p. 167). To enforce division concepts, show students a set of 12 units, and ask them how many separate groups of 3 they can make. It can then be shown that they can *divide* 12 units into 4 sets of 3. Therefore, 12 divided by 4 is 3. These concepts may not be acquired rapidly by all students, but repeated practice activities, such as those found in the *Building Understanding* series utilizing base-10 blocks (Activity Resources), can be helpful. It may also be important to extend the activities beyond base-10 blocks to enhance generalization of the concept, to, for example, beans, beads, or buttons.

TEACH "COUNT-BYS" A useful bridge between learning multiplication concepts and learning multiplication facts is the use of count-bys. Students who have learned to count by 2 (2, 4, 6, 8, etc.) can use their fingers or pencil tallies to count up to 2 × 6 (2, 4, 6, 8, 10, *12*). Students also easily learn to count by 5s because all products end in 5 or 0.

It may be helpful to learn to count by other numbers as an introduction to fact learning with those numbers. Touch Math, described earlier, uses strategies involving count-bys to compute multiplication and division facts. In multiplication, students count by one number while touching the points on the other number. For example, for 5 × 4, students count by 5s while touching the four points on the 4: 5, 10, 15, *20.* Show students that it works the

Pearson eTextbook

Video Example 14.5

A teacher asks questions to facilitate mathematical reasoning in an upper elementary class. What type of adaptations would you consider for students with disabilities during this discussion?

same if they count by 4s while touching the five points on the 5: 4, 8, 12, 16, *20*. Such procedures also enforce the concept of multiplication (e.g., 5,4 times $=$ *4*,5 times). For division, students make tally marks (/) while counting up to the divisor by units of the dividend. The number of tallies is the quotient. For example, for $12 \div 4$, students count up by 4s while tallying, 4, 8, *12* (marking, / / /, or 3).

USE SPECIFIC STRATEGIES FOR TEACHING MULTIPLICATION AND DIVISION FACTS Remember that the learning of multiplication and division facts is more of a verbal learning task than a mathematical reasoning task. That is, whereas understanding concepts relevant to multiplication and division (e.g., 6 groups of 4) involves mathematical reasoning, immediate recall of the fact ("What is 6 times 4?") requires verbal memory. Because that is the case, strategies for increasing verbal memory are appropriate. Use drill and practice with flashcards, computer or tablet activities such as *Math Blaster* (Knowledge Adventure), peer tutoring, and homework assignments.

Target the Essential Facts First, identify exactly how many multiplication facts students actually need to learn so that students will not feel overwhelmed—they may already know more than they think they do. That is, students who understand relevant concepts already know the $\times 0$ and $\times 1$ facts (i.e., any number multiplied by 0 is 0; any number multiplied by 1 is that same number). Students who know addition facts and understand relevant concepts already know the remaining $\times 2$ facts ($3 \times 2 = 3 + 3$). (Some students may also benefit from a $\times 4$ strategy; that is, a number times 4 is that number doubled, twice: $3 \times 4 = [3 \times 2]+[3 \times 2] = 12$.) Students who know how to count by 5s know or can easily determine the $\times 5$ facts.

Finally, students can use the **bent-finger strategy** for calculating the $\times 9$ facts. Using this strategy, students hold their two hands, palms down, in front of them. They then count from left to right on their fingers by the number of the fact and bend down the relevant finger. That is, for 9×5, students count to 5 starting with the left little finger to the left thumb, then bend down that thumb. Then, the fingers to the left of the bent finger represent the tens and the fingers to the right of the bent finger represent the ones of the product. In the case of 9×5, there are 4 fingers to the left and 5 fingers to the right of the bent finger, so the answer is 45.

So, if students already know, or can cope with, the $\times 0$, $\times 1$, $\times 2$, $\times 5$, and $\times 9$ facts, and if they understand the principle of commutativity (e.g., $6 \times 4 = 4 \times 6$), you can show them that they only have 15 facts left to learn (and only 10 if they can use the $\times 4$ strategy)! Use charts, games, and software formats to monitor their progress toward remembering all 100 facts.

Division facts can be taught using similar versions of the same strategies used for teaching math facts. Division by 0 is impossible (or "undefined"), but the $\div 1$, $\div 2$, and $\div 5$ facts may be similarly derived using relevant concepts. A version of the bent-finger strategy can also be applied to $\div 9$ facts: for example, for $45 \div 9 = ?$, students must first recognize that it is a $\div 9$ fact, then make the 45 with both palms down, 4 fingers on the left side, a bent finger (left thumb), and 5 fingers on the right side. The numbered finger bent down is the quotient, in this case, the fifth finger from the left (the left thumb), or 5. For $27 \div 9 = ?$, students make the 27 with their fingers; the bent finger is the third (or 3), the quotient.

Introduce students to three-number "fact families" to reinforce similarity with acquired multiplication facts (e.g., Stein et al., 2018). For example, consider the three-number fact family 3, 4, and 12. Within this family are the multiplication facts $3 \times 4 = 12$ and $4 \times 3 = 12$, as well the division facts $12 \div 4 = 3$ and $12 \div 3 = 4$. Students should refer to relevant fact families and relevant facts they already know when mastering division facts.

Use Mnemonic Strategies The remaining 15 multiplication facts still may not be easy for all students to learn, and many students may not automatically recognize the reverse (commutativity) of each fact. However, there is a mnemonic strategy that might be helpful in some cases. With the pegword strategy, rhyming words are developed for all numbers (e.g., *1* is *bun*, 2 is *shoe*, *3* is *tree*, *4* is *door*, *5* is *hive*, *6* is *sticks*, *7* is *heaven*, *8* is *gate*, *9* is *line* or *vine*). Pegwords for relevant numbers higher than 10 include the following: *12* is *elf*, *16* is *sitting*, and *18* is *aiding*; *20* is represented as *twin-ty*, so *21* is *twin buns*; *30* is *dirty* or *thirsty*; *40* is *party*; *50* is *gifty* (i.e., *gift-wrapped*); and *60* is *witchy*. Using these pegwords, sentences can be developed for each of the 15 remaining facts (see Mastropieri & Scruggs, 1991):

Fact	Pegword strategy
Three times three is nine.	**Tree**-to-**tree vine**.
Three times four is twelve.	**Tree** in **door** is **elf**.
Three times six is eighteen.	**Tree** losing **sticks** needs **aiding**.
Three times seven is twenty-one.	**Tree** in **heaven** has **twin buns**.
Three times eight is twenty-four.	**Tree** at a **gate** has **twin doors**.
Four times four is sixteen.	**Door**-by-**door sitting**.
Four times six is twenty-four.	**Door** with **sticks** has **twin doors**.
Four times seven is twenty-eight.	**Door** in **heaven** has **twin gates**.
Four times eight is thirty-two.	**Door** in **gate** has **dirty shoe**.
Six times six is thirty-six.	**Sticks**, **sticks**, and **dirty sticks**.
Six times seven is forty-two.	**Sticks** in **heaven** for **party shoe**.
Six times eight is forty-eight.	**Sticks** in **gate** is a **party gate**.
Seven times seven is forty-nine.	**Heaven** to **heaven** has **party line**.
Seven times eight is fifty-six.	**Heaven's gate** has **gifty sticks**.
Eight times eight is sixty-four.	**Gate** to **gate** is **witchy door**.

Some of these facts are easy to imagine; for example, *tree-to-tree vine* is simply a vine between two different (not twin) trees. Others, however, may be more difficult for students to imagine automatically. In these cases, a picture of the mnemonic may be helpful, such as the pictures for $4 \times 4 = 16$ and $6 \times 6 = 36$, shown in Figure 14.3.

Figure 14.3 Mnemonic Pictures of $6 \times 6 = 36$ and $4 \times 4 = 16$

Source: From Mastropieri and Scruggs (2014). Reprinted with permission.

Guide students to learn to say the paired mnemonics together, such as "Heaven's gate has gifty sticks—seven times eight is fifty-six." Reserve these strategies for the facts students appear to be having the most difficulty with, rather than teaching all 15. These mnemonic pegword strategies have been shown to improve fact learning for students with learning disabilities (Greene, 1999), and a modified version of this strategy (students were shown the pegword for the answer only) was effective for students with intellectual disabilities (Zisimopoulos, 2010).

USE CALCULATORS WHEN APPROPRIATE Although most schools remain committed to mastery of facts and computation procedures as important mathematics objectives, it is sometimes recommended that computers and calculators be used to replace memorization of math facts and computation exercises. Most tools, including phones, tablets, laptops, and computers, have built-in calculators that students can easily access. *Google Calculator* allows students to conduct calculations quickly and easily within a browser. Additionally, 37 states currently include student use of the Desmos calculator for end of the year, online testing primarily among secondary grade levels (see https://www.desmos.com/testing). Desmos, available as an app or browser-based version, offers a free digital graphic calculator, scientific calculator, and a four-function calculator. The CCSSM make reference to the use of calculators, although generally in the Standards for Mathematical Practice at the high school level when students are dealing with larger or more complicated data sets (NGA & CCSSO, 2010).

When students are required to memorize math facts, it may become evident over time that some students are simply not succeeding and are beginning to lose valuable instructional time in other areas of math because of this problem. In such cases, it may be prudent to allow individual students to use calculators for help with computation while proceeding to other math objectives. If such a decision is made, however, make sure that those students have a documented lack of progress to learn facts over time and that all known strategies and procedures have been attempted, before allowing calculator use. For those states permitting use of the Desmos calculator, the site provides free practice tests and activities for students to build familiarity.

Students should be retested periodically for their capacity to learn facts. It could be that with increasing age and cognitive development, or more familiarity with other aspects of math, fact learning can be attained at a future date.

REINFORCE ARITHMETIC VOCABULARY In addition to number concepts, algorithms, and procedures, students in math classes are generally required to learn and apply many vocabulary words, such as *addend*, *sum*, *minuend*, *subtrahend*, *difference*, *product*, and *divisor.* For some students, this vocabulary can be confusing and difficult to learn. This is especially relevant for English learners who may have a general understanding of vocabulary terms such as *table* and *factor* but less understanding when used in the context of math. Prioritize your objectives so that you spend time teaching the most important vocabulary words.

To teach math vocabulary, provide additional time on-task, use flashcards and peer tutors, and monitor progress toward mastery. Use clear, concise, and correct mathematical language to help students integrate the language into their own explanations when problem solving (Fuchs et al., 2021). Also consider using verbal elaboration strategies—for example, demonstrate to students how 3 is really the *difference* between 8 and 5; therefore, the term *difference* has some meaning. To help students remember that the *multiplier* is the number on the bottom of a multiplication problem, next to the multiplication sign (when presented vertically), draw the multiplication sign to represent an open pair of *pliers.* The *pliers* show which number is the multi*plier.* For another example, on a division problem, place *quotation marks* on the *quotient*:

$$8\overline{)\,24}^{\text{“3”}}$$

USE SPECIFIC STRATEGIES FOR TEACHING MULTIPLICATION AND DIVISION ALGORITHMS Students must learn the order or sequence of arithmetic operations in more complex problems.

$$5 + 4 \times 3 - 2 =$$

To successfully solve this problem, students must know that the multiplication of 4 and 3 must be done first, followed by the addition of 5 and subtraction of 2. A commonly used mnemonic to remember the order for math operations is as follows: *M*y *D*ear *A*unt *S*ally, who says, "*M*ultiply and *d*ivide before you *a*dd and *s*ubtract." In this case,

$$5 + (4 \times 3) - 2 =$$

where (4×3) is calculated first, followed by the addition and subtraction. An alternative strategy is "*P*lease *e*xcuse *m*y *d*ear *A*unt *S*ally," where *p* and *e* stand for *p*arenthetical expression and *e*xponents, respectively, and are completed first. In this case,

$$5 + (4 + 3)^2 + 12 \times 6$$

where the parenthetical expression $(4 + 3)$ is calculated first, followed by the exponent $(7)^2$, which is followed by multiplication, 12×6, followed by addition, $5 + 49 + 72$.

Another math procedure students need to learn is the sequence to follow when multiplying numbers of two or more digits. Learning how to do this kind of problem is often complicated because handwritten figures are not placed in proper relationship to one another. Try having students use graph paper, as shown in the illustration. Pro-Ed publishes *Guideline Math Paper*, specifically designed to assist students who have difficulty completing basic mathematics algorithms.

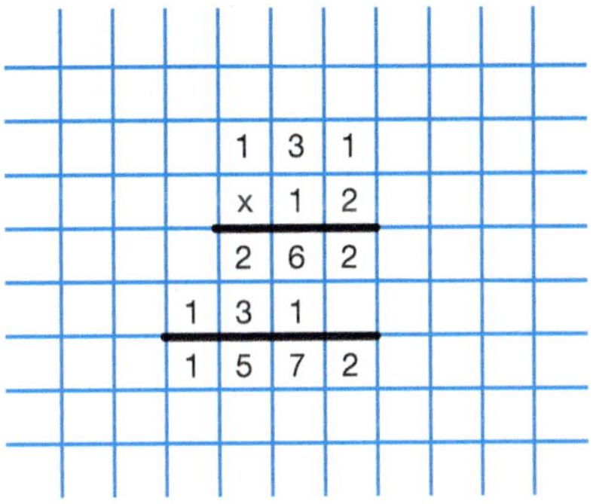

Demonstration Plus Permanent Model For addressing problems in computational arithmetic skills, use the **Demonstration Plus Permanent Model** (Mercer & Miller, 1992; Rivera & Smith, 1987); demonstrate how to complete a particular type of problem, for example, subtraction with regrouping or long division, and provide a model, with steps, written on the student's page or somewhere easily accessible for future reference. The model can be written on a 3×5-inch index card for use when needed.

Long-Division Strategies Long division involves dividing beyond the 100 division facts. Some students exhibit difficulty learning the steps in long division. To facilitate memory of these steps, teach students to use the acrostic "**D**racula **M**ust **S**uck **B**lood" to remember the steps: **d**ivide, **m**ultiply, **s**ubtract, and **b**ring down (Quintessential Education, 2016). For example:

$$\begin{array}{r} 1 \\ 13\overline{)143} \end{array} \quad \text{Divide}$$

then,

$$\begin{array}{r} 1 \\ 13\overline{)143} \\ \underline{13} \end{array} \quad \text{Multiply } (1 \times 13)$$

then,

$$\begin{array}{r} 1 \\ 13\overline{)143} \\ \underline{-13} \\ 1 \end{array} \quad \text{Subtract } (14 - 13)$$

then,

```
       1
13)143      Bring down (3 to make 13)
  -13
    13
```

Following the steps again provides 13 ÷ 13 (divide), 1 × 13 (multiply), and 13 − 13 = 0 (subtract), with no remaining numbers to bring down; therefore, 143 ÷ 13 = 11.

Modified Long Division Some students exhibit extreme difficulty with long division (Montague & Warger, 2015). If other attempts have not been successful, it may be helpful to employ a simpler procedure for long division. This procedure lacks some of the precision of traditional long division, but it employs a simpler format that some students may find beneficial (see Pushparajan, 2011).

To use modified long division, construct the problem as usual but draw a line straight down vertically from the end of the problem:

```
23)4859|
       |
       |
```

Now, ask students to guess the solution to the entire problem, "How many 23s are there in 4,859?" Even if students have difficulty estimating the answer closely, a good first guess might be 100. So, tell students to write the 100 to the right of the vertical line and multiply 23 by 100 and subtract from the dividend, like this:

```
23)4859 | 100
   2300 |
   2559 |
```

Then, ask students the same question again, with respect to the difference, "How many 23s are there in 2,559?" Because 100 times 23 is 2,300, it makes sense to try 100 again. So, you write 100 again below the first 100, multiply 23 again by 100, and subtract from 2,559:

```
23)4859 | 100
   2300 | 100
   2559 |
  -2300 |
    259
```

The remainder is now 259, so a good next guess would be 10:

```
23)4859 | 100
  -2300 | 100
   2559 |  10
   2300 |
    259 |
   -230 |
     29
```

Subtracting 230 from 259 leaves 29, so we subtract one more 23, then compute a remainder of 6. This number is smaller than the divisor, 23, so we cannot go any farther. Adding all estimates yields a sum of 211 with a remainder of 6 (or 6/23), the correct solution.

```
23)4859 | 100
  -2300 | 100
   2559 |  10
  -2300 | + 1
    259 | 211, r. 6
   -230 |
     29
     23
      6
```

Figure 14.4 Sample Error-Analysis Procedures

Error Examples	Possible Explanations	Suggested Interventions
2 + 2 = 8	1. Inadequate fact mastery. 2. Failure to apply learned strategies (e.g., "count-ons"). 3. Reversal (2 = 6).	1. Reteach facts. 2. Reteach strategies. 3. Teach strategies for writing orientation.
22 − 9 = 27	1. Inadequate fact mastery. 2. Regrouping error. 3. Reversed subtraction (9 − 2 = 7).	1. Reteach facts. 2. Reteach regrouping. 3. Reteach procedures.
22 × 12 = 66	1. Place value error: 22 (1 × 22) + 44 (2 × 22) = 66 2. Algorithmic error (incorrect alignment of addends in problem solution): $\begin{array}{r} 22 \\ \times 12 \\ \hline 44 \\ 22 \\ \hline 66 \end{array}$	1. Reteach place value concepts. 2. Reteach algorithms, using Demonstration plus Permanent Model, graph paper.

One advantage of modified long division is that it allows students to view the entire problem at once. Because of this, they may be more able to focus on the problem and less likely to become entangled in a maze of algorithmic procedures. Nevertheless, students may still need much practice in learning and applying the steps of the modified long-division procedure.

Use Error Analysis to Inform Instruction When correcting student products, it is important to determine the *type* of error students consistently make and the type of remedial instruction that is indicated by these error patterns. Figure 14.4 lists common error types in arithmetic computation and possible explanations for them. Remember, before a firm conclusion can be drawn about a particular error type, it is best to obtain evidence that such errors occur repeatedly in a given student's work.

STRATEGIES FOR TEACHING PROBLEM SOLVING

PROMOTE USE OF WORD MEANINGS Implied mathematical operations (e.g., add, multiply) are represented by the language of word problems. Some students have difficulty understanding how words are used in word problems and what specific operations are implied by these words. Some mathematics educators have criticized a strategy known as the *clue-word* or *key word* approach (not the same as the mnemonic keyword method) to solving word problems. In this approach, students are provided with key operation words and relevant operations, such as the following:

in all, *together*, *total* = add or multiply

left, *remaining* = subtract

each = divide

Students are encouraged to look in the problem for one of these words, then apply the associated operation. The concern is that students may use the method mindlessly, without carefully reasoning through problems, and answer incorrectly (Cathcart et al., 2015; Kilpatrick, 1985; Powell & Fuchs, 2018).

However, words convey meanings, and to the extent that these meanings aid in problem solution, a careful analysis of words is appropriate. *In all* does, in fact, convey the idea of combining quantities (and thus, perhaps, addition or multiplication); *remaining* does suggest diminishing quantity (and thus, perhaps, subtraction). For students who have learning disabilities that involve language or language delays, it may be important to enforce the understanding of word meanings to solve word problems.

It is true that the mindless substitution of *each* for *divide*, for example, may not be an appropriate strategy in most cases (it may be appropriate for a last-ditch effort during a timed math test). However, a problem that states a particular overall quantity and requests unstated information regarding *each* or *for one* certainly seems to be implying some type of division operation, and students should attend to the relevance of such cues.

In fact, the *"ask for one, tell for one"* strategy may be useful in helping students determine implied operations. That is, if a larger quantity and another quantity are given (10 cookies, 5 children), and the problem "asks for one (or each)" (e.g., "How many cookies does 1 child get?"), the operation is probably division. If a quantity associated with an individual unit ("tells for one") is given (e.g., 2 cookies for one or each child), and a larger number is requested ("How many cookies do 5 children get?"), the operation is probably multiplication. Encourage students to consider such linguistic information in addition to information gained from visualizing, using manipulatives, or drawing pictures of the problem. Some math interventions, such as Pirate Math introduced earlier in the chapter, embed explicit language comprehension instruction in the context of math word problems (see Fuchs et al., 2020).

TEACH COGNITIVE STRATEGIES FOR PROBLEM SOLVING A number of strategies have been found to be effective in developing problem-solving skills in students with disabilities (Kong et al., 2021). Montague (2008; Montague et al., 2011) successfully taught students to use *Solve It!*, a seven-step strategy to solve word problems:

1. *Read* the problem.
2. *Paraphrase* the problem.
3. *Visualize* (picture or diagram).
4. *Hypothesize* (a plan to solve the problem).
5. *Estimate* the answer.
6. *Compute.*
7. *Check* your answer.

Students were also given self-instructional training in implementing these cognitive processes, using SAY, ASK, and CHECK for each step. For example, for the *paraphrase* step, SAY indicates: "Underline the important information. Put the problem in my own words." ASK indicates: "Have I underlined the important information? What is the question?" CHECK indicates: Check "that the information goes with the question" (Montague, 2008, p. 41; see also Montague & Warger, 2015). Teachers provide think-alouds where they model the thinking process in solving problems as they employ the seven steps. Whitby (2013) used the *Solve It!* strategy to increase the problem-solving abilities of a sample of middle school students with ASD.

Similarly, Xin et al. (2005) taught students to identify the key problem and problem features and to map the information onto the diagram during instruction in problem schema analysis. Similar strategies have also been helpful for students with ASD (Barnett & Cleary, 2015). Shiah et al. (1994–1995) taught students with mathematics learning disabilities to use a computer program that included steps similar to *Solve It!*:

1. *Read* about the problem.
2. *Think* about the problem.
3. *Decide* the operation.
4. *Write* the math sentence.
5. *Do* the problem.
6. *Label* the answer.
7. *Check* every step.

Use of steps like these can help students solve word problems of the following type:

> There are 8 bookshelves in a library. Each bookshelf holds 26 books. How many books are in the library altogether?

Begin by providing students with a list of steps similar to that in Shiah et al. (1994–1995) so that they can check off the steps as they are completed. Be sure to teach students how to undertake each of the steps. For example, for step 2, "Think about the problem," students should be told to use visualization (Montague, 2008) and draw pictures and identify and circle cue words or phrases (Case et al., 1992). For the current example, students could visualize or draw a library with 8 bookshelves; each one of the bookshelves holds 26 books. Alternately, to guide thinking, cue words such as *each* ("tells for one"), *bookshelf*, *books*, and *altogether* could be circled. Thinking about the problem should lead to making the operation decision and writing the math sentence (i.e., $8 \times 26 =$ ______). After this step, students compute the answer, label the answer, and check every step. To enforce use of the systematic procedures, you could supply students with a self-monitoring sheet on which they can check off each step as they complete it.

USE ENHANCED ANCHORED INSTRUCTION Brian Bottge and colleagues (e.g., 2010, 2015) have implemented interventions they refer to as enhanced anchored instruction (EAI). EAI employs a problem-based learning approach, but it provides the problem in a video format; these researchers argue that the video provides for a more immediate experience than text. Students consider the "real-life" types of problems designed to motivate them, are engaged in learning through a variety of activities, and meet in groups to plan and execute problem solution, often involving fractions. The EAI strategy includes additional components to improve visualization of problems and help with calculation skills. In a number of investigations, students in inclusive classes taught problem solving with EAI outperformed control-condition students in business-as-usual conditions based on state standards in mathematics (Bottge et al., 2015).

USE TIER 2 PROBLEM-SOLVING INTERVENTIONS Problem-solving strategies can also be provided in Tier 2 RTI interventions. Many Tier 2 interventions include teaching students the schema or mathematical structure of a word problem. See Powell and Fuchs (2018) for the types of word problem schemas. Hot Math tutoring teaches students four word-problem types. Fuchs et al. (2007) implemented Hot Math for primary-grade students through small-group tutoring in specific problem-solving learning strategies combined with training in recognizing different problem types and transferring their skills to novel problem formats. During the first 3-week unit, students were taught basic problem-solving information, such as making sure answers make sense, aligning numbers correctly to perform math operations, and labeling work correctly with words and mathematics symbols. Each of the following units focused on one problem type, with solution processes, "buying bags" problems (e.g., "10 lemon drops to a bag, how many bags"), "shopping list" problems, "half" problems, and "pictograph" problems. After 16 weeks of tutoring sessions, two to three times per week, the proportion of nonresponsiveness to instruction (below the 16th percentile) dropped substantially.

STRATEGIES FOR TEACHING ABOUT MONEY AND TIME

PRACTICE COIN RECOGNITION AND COUNTING MONEY WITH APPROPRIATE MATERIALS One of the primary uses of mathematics in adult life is calculations involving money, and it is important to begin instruction in this area as soon as possible after students have mastered basic counting skills. An early concept students could learn is to identify coins of different values. This can be done through providing drill and practice and demonstrating instances and noninstances of coin values (simulated coins and bills and worksheets are available from Delta Education). *Break the Bank*, *Dolphin Dash Counting Money*, and *Learn to Count Money* (abcya.com) provide exercises on identifying coins and counting money.

Once students have learned to name coins, they need to learn the value of each coin. Again, direct teaching and drill and practice, perhaps using flashcards with the coin on one side and the value on the other, will help enforce these values. When values are mastered, students will be ready to learn to count change, as shown in the following *In the Classroom* feature. Additionally, apps such as *Dollars & Cents* (Attainment Company) and Splash Math (StudyPd Inc.) can provide useful practice. Touch Autism provides social stories with *Using and Saving Money* for iPad and other devices. *Money* (Delta Education) and *Lakeshore* (Lakeshore Learning Materials) both provide a wide variety of materials for teaching about money.

In the Classroom

Sequence of Coin-Counting Skills

1. *Count numbers of the same coins.* Start with different numbers of pennies, and have students count by 1s (e.g., 7 pennies = 7 cents). Then move to higher values and count by the relevant numbers. For example, count by 5s to calculate the value of 4 nickels = 20 cents, count by 10s to calculate the value of 6 dimes = 60 cents, and count by 25s to calculate the value of 3 quarters = 75 cents.
2. *Teach count-on strategies with same-coin values plus pennies.* That is, for 3 dimes and 3 pennies, count: "10, 20, 30 cents, 31, 32, 33 cents." For two quarters and four pennies, count: "25, 50 cents, 51, 52, 53, 54 cents."
3. *For more complex combinations of coins, teach students to first sort coins into groups containing multiples of 10.* That is, two dimes is one group, and one quarter and one nickel is one group. So, for these groups, count: "10, 20 cents: [on fingers] 30, 40, 50 cents."
4. *For making change, teach students to count up from the given value, counting first to a 10s or 25s value, then counting up to the dollar value.* For example, for making change for one dollar for a 27-cent purchase, count up: "[in pennies] 28, 29, 30; [in dimes] 40, 50; [in quarters] 75, 1 dollar."

Pearson eTextbook

Video Example 14.6

In this video, pairs of students work with coin manipulatives to identify the characteristics and the value of each coin. How does working with their own set of manipulatives benefit the students in this inclusive classroom?

USE APPROPRIATE METHODS AND MATERIALS FOR TEACHING ABOUT TIME Another important skill for all students is telling time. Materials such as student clocks that can be set to specific times and time worksheets are available from suppliers such as Delta Education. Generally, students are best taught by employing a specific set of subskills, as shown in the *In the Classroom* feature.

Teachers can model times or specific features of a clock on their own models and ask students to repeat the time on their own clock models. For example, for the subskill "Recognize the hour hand," teachers can demonstrate 4 o'clock on their own clocks, then prompt students to set the hour hands on their own clocks to 4 o'clock.

Peer partners who are fluent in telling time can be assigned to students who need more practice. Use of the time-telling checklist provided in the *In the Classroom* feature may be helpful in targeting the exact skills students need to practice. Peers can also be helpful in promoting other students' knowledge of time throughout the day. Applications are also available on smartphones or tablets to promote telling time.Finally, students who can recognize numbers but have difficulty learning to tell time may benefit from digital clocks and watches that display time in numerical formats that may be more easily recognizable. Use of digital timepieces can help improve students' knowledge of time while they are learning to tell time. *Tell Time!* (Horizon Business), *Telling Time – 8 Games to Tell Time* (Innovative Mobile Apps), and *Tic Toc Time* (Edoki Academy) are all apps that provide practice in telling time on iPads, iPhones, and other devices.

STRATEGIES FOR TEACHING FRACTIONS AND DECIMALS

USE APPROPRIATE METHODS AND MATERIALS FOR TEACHING FRACTIONS

As much as possible, the initial teaching of fractions should involve the students' own experiences. Most children know about sharing things, such as cookies, by breaking them into halves or other parts. Children are also usually aware that pizzas and pies are sliced into pieces. Use this knowledge to develop more advanced concepts of fractions. *Fraction Concepts* (Delta Education) provides many manipulative materials to promote understanding of fractions. One example is the *Fraction Burger* (Delta Education), in which the equally proportioned layers of a hamburger (e.g., meat, tomato, cheese, bun) are each made of different fractions (e.g., 3/3, 5/5) that total a circle of the same size. Demonstrate the different ways of creating a circle with different fraction pieces and have students demonstrate their conceptual knowledge by posing simple problems, such as, "Show the whole burger in two halves" or "Show me a whole circle made of one-half (burger) and two-fourths (cheese)."

When students have learned relevant concepts, they must also learn how to represent fraction concepts in writing and to perform computations on fractions. These follow specific rules (e.g., for division, invert the divisor and multiply). One problem many students have with fractions is in reducing them to their lowest values. For students who have less of a mathematical "sense," fractions that need to be reduced may not appear as obvious as they may for other students. To help students determine whether a fraction can be reduced, a self-monitoring sheet may be helpful. For example, one teacher asked students who were having difficulty to ask themselves questions such as the following:

- Can the denominator be divided by the numerator?
- Do both numbers end in 5 or 0? (If so, divide by 5 or 10.)
- Can both numbers be divided by 2?
- Can both numbers be divided by 3?

If the answer is "yes" to any of the questions, students should execute the procedure. When they have gone through the whole list and reduced the fraction, they should go through it again to see if it can be reduced further. Although this routine will not effectively address all cases it does address most cases and can serve as a foundation for later understandings.

The self-regulated strategy development (SRSD) framework (see Chapter 13) has been used to support students' conceptual and procedural learning of fractions (Ennis & Losinski, 2020). For example, fifth-graders with or at risk for emotional or behavioral disabilities were taught to add and subtract fractions with unlike denominators using the SRSD model of instruction. The mnemonic FILMS (Find the denominators, Identify the multiples, Locate the least common multiple, Multiply to make new fractions, and Solve the problem) was used as a Tier 2 intervention to support the process (Losinski et al., 2021). The special education teacher modeled the strategy one-to-one with students using think-alouds and self-instruction, checking off each step when completed, graphing daily performance, and using manipulatives and drawings of fractions as needed. Following strategy instruction, inclusive of FILMS, the students showed marked gains on fraction probes.

Shin and Bryant (2015) reviewed literature on fractions instruction for students with math difficulties and reported that the most effective techniques included concrete and visual representations; explicit, systematic instruction; a range and sequence of examples; cognitive strategies providing steps to problem solution; and the use of real-world problems. A review of research on fractions instruction for students with or at risk for disabilities also identified explicit instruction and strategy instruction to be most effective (Ennis & Losinski, 2019).

USE APPROPRIATE METHODS AND MATERIALS FOR TEACHING DECIMALS If students have exhibited proficiency in aspects of arithmetic, procedures for using decimals should not be an overwhelming challenge. Procedures for adding and subtracting numbers with decimals involve keeping the decimal points aligned; again, graph paper may be useful for this purpose. For multiplication and division of decimals, additional practice and permanent models may be helpful.

Even if students learn to calculate with decimals, they may be less certain what decimal numbers mean. To enforce decimal concepts, Decimal Squares (ETA hand2mind) may be helpful. Decimal Squares represent decimal values on cards that have been divided into 100 or 1,000 smaller components. For example, to demonstrate a decimal value of 0.36, a card can be shown that represents a square divided into 100 equal parts, for which 36 squares are shaded. Students can also be shown that this proportion is equivalent to a square divided into 1,000 parts, for which 360 squares are shaded; therefore, $0.360 = 0.36$. When 36 of 1,000 squares are shaded, this represents not 0.36 but 0.036 (see also Figure 14.5 for an illustration using base-10 blocks).

STRATEGIES FOR
TEACHING AREA AND VOLUME CONCEPTS

PROVIDE VISUAL AND THREE-DIMENSIONAL REPRESENTATIONS Concepts of area and volume can be enhanced with visual and physical depictions. *Geometry* and *Measurement* (Delta Education) may be helpful in promoting understanding of area and volume. Three-dimensional representations of solids are also available from Delta Education. These figures are matched for height so that comparisons can be more easily made. Additionally, they can be

In the Classroom

Checklist of Subskills for Telling Time

_____1. Identify the numbers on the clock face.

_____ 2. Recognize the hour hand.

_____ 3. Identify the hour indicated by the hour-hand position.

_____ 4. Identify the minute hand.

_____ 5. Identify the "o'clock" position with the minute hand on the 12 and the hour hand pointing to a specific hour.

_____ 6. Identify the position of the minute hand on quarter-hours as 15-minute segments (e.g., 15, 30).

_____ 7. Identify the position of 5-minute intervals on the clock face (e.g., 5, 10, 15, 20).

_____ 8. Recognize the minute hand and identify the minute indicated by the minute-hand position, by counting by 1s past the previous 5-minute interval (e.g., for 23: "5, 10, 15, 20, 21, 22, 23").

_____ 9. Identify the minute indicated by the minute-hand position, by counting by 15s, then 5s, then 1s (e.g., for 43: "15, 30, 35, 40, 41, 42, 43").

_____ 10. Tell a specific time of day given the positions of the hour and minute hands, by first identifying the hour, then the minute.

_____ 11. Identify time of day as a.m. or p.m.

filled with water to demonstrate relative volume measures. ETA hand2mind publishes physical models to support geometry concepts, including geoboards, geometric solids, and folding shapes. Experience with these models can provide important background for solving area and volume problems with formulas.

Browder (2015) described providing access to general education curriculum in a variety of areas, including math, for students with moderate and severe disabilities. With respect to area concepts, students were given a rectangle divided into 1-inch squares and asked to count the squares to determine the surface area of the rectangle.

TEACH "BIG IDEAS" Stein et al. (2018) emphasized the importance of teaching "big ideas" in mathematics so that students will have a more general idea of themes, rather than knowledge of a large number of unrelated formulas and problem solutions. For example, volume formulas could all proceed from the "big idea" that all represent the product of the area of the base and a multiple of the height. Then, rather than teaching separate formulas for rectangular prism, rectangular wedge, rectangular cylinder, triangular pyramid, rectangular pyramid, and conic

Figure 14.5 Base-10 Blocks Demonstrate Decimal Values (.36 and .360)

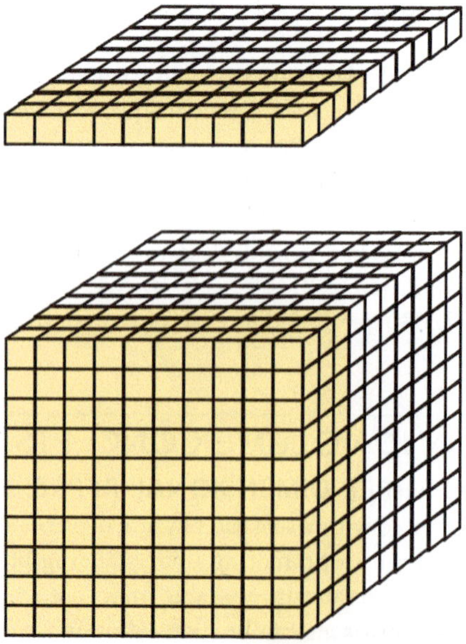

pyramid, they can all be demonstrated to be functions of the products of base area and height. That is, for figures in which the sides go straight up, such as a rectangular prism (box) or cylinder, the volume is the area of the base times the height ($b \times h$). For figures that come to a point, such as pyramids and cones, the formula is the area of the base times 1/3 of the height ($b \times 1 / 3h$). Teaching students that different procedures can stem from a common principle can help enforce understanding of the relevant concept, as well as memory for a specific formula.

CLASSROOM SCENARIO

Bashira

Ever since Bashira started in algebra, she has exhibited attitude problems. Previously a hardworking, sincere student, she becomes angry and frustrated whenever she is confronted with an algebra problem. "This is stupid!" Bashira exclaims. "Why should I have to learn this? What difference does it make? I hate algebra!" Although other subjects also provide challenges, she doesn't seem to want to make an attempt to learn algebra. Her ninth-grade teacher, Ms. Moon, is considering placing her in a remedial math class.

QUESTIONS FOR REFLECTION

1. Why does Bashira single out algebra when other subjects also pose difficulties?
2. Do you think improving Bashira's skills or improving her attitude is of greater importance?
3. Based on your answer to question 2, what strategies would you recommend to Ms. Moon?

STRATEGIES FOR TEACHING ALGEBRA

Algebra is required for more advanced problem solving, has been considered a gateway to expanded opportunities for the future, and is increasingly required for high school graduation (Impecoven-Lind & Foegen, 2010). It is well represented in the CCSSM, especially at the high school level. Algebra involves the use of letters, such as x and y, to represent unknown quantities in the solution of problems. Many students with disabilities and other diverse learning needs have problems with algebra, in part because of basic skill deficits, students' perception of self-efficacy, and the abstract nature of the content (Montague & Jitendra, 2006). General strategies for addressing achievement problems in secondary-level mathematics include organized, explicit teaching of important concepts; providing many examples of new concepts that address the overall range of the concept; direct teaching of relevant cognitive routines; and systematically teaching to prioritized, general objectives (Strickland & Maccini, 2010).

USE MANIPULATIVES TO TEACH NEGATIVE NUMBERS Many students with disabilities or other diverse learning needs have difficulty acquiring the concept of negative numbers, as in $-3 + 4 = 1$. One way of enhancing this concept is through the use of number lines, as described previously. In this instance, the student would be shown how to start at the -3, then count forward four numbers, through the 0, to 1. Another way of promoting the concept of negative numbers is by using the example of financial debt. One who owes $5, for example, must earn $5 before having $0 (no surplus but no debt).

A third way of teaching about negative numbers is through the use of **algebra tiles** (ETA hand2mind). These manipulatives use dark-colored pieces to represent positive integers and lighter-colored pieces to represent negative numbers. The positive and negative tiles can be placed together to represent an equation, such as the following:

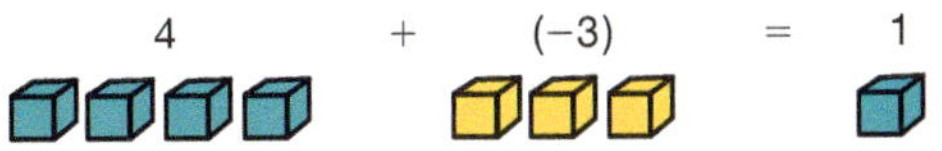

Technology for Mathematics

Numerous mathematics tools are widely available and provide supplemental practice and assistance to students in learning math facts, skills, and problem solving. Many of the tools also provide resources for teachers to enhance their math instruction. The *Khan Academy*, which is available as both an app and browser-based tool, includes over 2,700 video lessons and practice exercises in multiple content areas, including the K–12 math content of basic arithmetic, algebra, geometry, probability, and calculus. *IXL Math*, also available as both an app and browser-based tool, offers online practice for students, as well as printable resources for different types of math content such as algebra, geometry, precalculus, and calculus. *Dreambox* (Dreambox Learning) is an online adaptive math program for K–8. Dreambox has math lessons and animated adventures, games, and challenges. *GeoGebra* (https://www.geogebra.org) is a free interactive tool for teaching K–12 algebra content. The tool offers 2D and 3D calculators, lessons, simulations, exercises, and games. Teachers can see student progress as well. Finally, *Tech Matrix* (techmatrix.org) enables searching a database for assistive technology, tools, products, and resources, including research reports, across disability areas, age levels, and content areas, including math.

Many mathematics skills and concepts are more concrete for students when manipulatives are used during instruction. Manipulatives give students experience with concrete representations of underlying concepts, which helps comprehension and understanding. Teachers, however, may have a limited supply of manipulatives. An inexpensive alternative to concrete manipulatives and a more socially appropriate option for older students is the use of virtual manipulatives available on the Internet. The National Library of Virtual Manipulatives (NLVM) (http://nlvm.usu.edu) provides interactive online math lessons using virtual manipulatives in the areas of numbers and operations, algebra, geometry, measurement, data analysis, and probability (also available as an NLVM app). Within each general math category, the site contains multiple activities and problems using the virtual manipulatives. Problems can be reset to be computed again and again using different variations to provide additional practice of a general concept as necessary. In addition, all math areas are linked to grade-level standards and benchmarks with teacher, family member, and caregiver information on how to teach the concepts. For example, in the activity "Fractions—Parts of a Whole" for grades 3–5, practice with parts of a whole unit, using a written description and numeric fraction, is provided. In this activity, a picture is provided that can be divided into any number of parts. Students are taught that any whole can be divided into an equal number of parts and are asked to divide the whole picture into parts. They are then asked to highlight parts of the whole. When various fractions (parts) of the picture are highlighted, a corresponding fraction changes to reflect new values. Questions such as "How many ways can you describe parts of a unit?" are presented, and students are asked to discuss their answers with partners.

Mathematics activities are available on many other websites as well. The National Council of Teachers of Mathematics (NCTM) provides math activities, math standards, and web links on the site http://illuminations.nctm.org, which includes a virtual manipulatives link and online, interactive math activities designed to match NCTM principles and math standards. In addition, several indices of available virtual manipulatives provide links to a wealth of websites. A quick Google search using key words such as *virtual geoboards*, *virtual tangrams*, *virtual base blocks*, and *virtual number racks* can display a number of current websites that provide these types of manipulatives.

Both drill-and-practice as well as gamelike digital formats have been found to be effective in improving math skills of students with disabilities (Benavides-Varella et al., 2021). There are many apps available with varying features, but it is best to select apps that are able to track student progress to mastery and provide student corrective feedback as needed. Several apps are available that provide flashcard practice for basic math facts, including *My Math App* and *My Math Flash Cards* (Power Math Apps). *Time, Money & Fractions On-Track* (School Zone Publishing) is a beginning-level math app that provides examples and practice in some basic math. Many apps, such as *Cyberchase Shape Quest* (PBS Kids), *FETCH! Lunch Rush* (PBS Kids), and *DragonBox* (Kahoot!), are designed in gamelike formats that provide supplemental practice. The Osmo apps (Tangible Play), including *Osmo Numbers Education*, *Osmo Pizza Co.*, and *Osmo Tangram Education*, are free and offer students the opportunity to practice math skills using augmented reality for an engaging, interactive, and gamelike way to practice math skills.

The three lighter-colored pieces "cancel out" three of the darker pieces, leaving only one positive integer, or 1. An alternative is to go to the website of the National Library of Virtual Manipulatives (www.nlvm.usu.edu), where you can find virtual representations of algebra tiles that can be manipulated online, as well as virtual manipulatives for numbers and operations, algebra, geometry, and measurement. See the *Apps for Education* feature for more ideas; for additional tools for help with algebra, consider *Algebrator* (Softmath), *Kahoot! Algebra* (DragonBox), and *Algebra Touch* (Sean Berry).

TEACH ALGEBRAIC REPRESENTATIONS EARLY Consistent with the Standards for Mathematical Practice, you can begin to teach algebraic representations at an early level of problem solving. For example, students can learn to solve a problem represented as $2 + 3 =$ ______; or, $2 + 3 = ?$; or, $2 + 3 = x$. When students learn that x stands for an unknown quantity, they can also begin to solve equations such as $2 + x = 5$. Again, the concept of equivalence should be helpful in targeting the idea that both sides of the equation must represent the same quantity (Ginsburg, 1997). Using algebra tiles, a rectangular-shaped piece is used for the x value, so $2 + 3 = x$ is represented as follows:

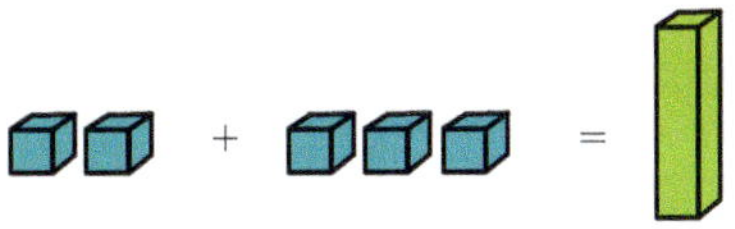

The sets of two and three pieces can easily be combined to reveal the answer, $5 = x$ or $x = 5$.

For older learners, Strickland (2021) suggests presenting concrete manipulatives, drawings, and algebraic symbols at the same time. Only when students demonstrate mastery with those representations do they move on to the abstract notation only. This type of integration (i.e., CRA) may build a stronger conceptual understanding of algebraic concepts. Additionally, use of virtual manipulatives rather than concrete manipulatives may be more socially desirable for older students (Bouck et al. 2019).

TEACH STRATEGIES FOR COMPUTATION Some algebraic notation and conventions must be learned in order to compute algebraic equations. For example, the rule that like quantities, such as $2x + 3x$, can be summed to equal $5x$ can be practiced and conceptualized using algebra tiles. Manipulatives can also be employed to demonstrate that unlike quantities, such as $2a + 3b$, cannot be added.

Mnemonic strategies may be helpful for learning and remembering some of these algorithms. For example, consider the problem involving the multiplication of binomials:

$$(x + 4)(x + 2)$$
$$= x^2 + 6x + 8$$

Students should recognize that each "symbol and digit" in parentheses must be multiplied by one another. To expand the left side of the equation into the values of the right side, it is necessary to multiply in a specific order. The first step is to multiply the *first* terms, $(x)(x) = x^2$. The second steps are to sum the products of the *outer* $(x)(2)$ and the *inner* $(x)(4)$ terms, $2x + 4x = 6x$. The final step is to multiply the *last* terms, $(2)(4) = 8$. Combined, they provide the answer, $x^2 + 6x + 8$. To remember the sequence of this operation, it may be helpful to remember the mnemonic acronym **FOIL**, which stands for first terms, outer terms + inner terms, and last terms (Kilpatrick, 1985).

TEACH STRATEGIES FOR SOLVING QUADRATIC EQUATIONS In a quadratic equation, the unknown variable is squared, and the equation can be written in the form:

$$ax^2 + bx + c = 0$$

There are several ways to solve quadratic equations, including completing the square and factoring the equation. Algebra tiles can be helpful in developing understanding of these concepts by using the square version of the x variable to represent x^2. To factor the equation, Strickland and Maccini (2010) recommended using a graphic organizer to represent steps in the solution. For example, for the equation

$$x^2 + 5x + 6 = 0$$

Strickland and Maccini presented a graphic organizer with the equation in a box at the top, two boxes in the middle, and one box on the bottom, with arrows connecting them. An arrow connects the top equation to the two middle boxes, and an arrow connects each middle box to the bottom box, where the answer will be placed. Follow the arrows from the top equation to the two middle boxes, and factor the equation in those two boxes. You can use the FOIL strategy in reverse to help arrive at these two equations: $x^2 = (x)(x)$, so x is the first element; $6 = 3 \times 2$, or 2×3, so these are the last elements; and the outer ($2x$) and inner ($3x$) terms sum to $5x$. The two factors ($x + 2 = 0$ and $x + 3 = 0$) then go in each of the middle boxes below the equation. These two smaller equations can be solved by subtracting 2 and 3 from each side, respectively: $(x + 2) - 2 = 0 - 2$, so $x = -2$. The answer is written in the bottom box:

$$x = -2$$
$$x = -3$$

A third method for solving quadratic equations involves the use of an equation developed by mathematicians:

$$x = \frac{-b \pm \sqrt{b^2 - 4ac}}{2a}$$

If the numbers in the quadratic equation are used to replace a, b, and c (from the model $ax^2 + bx + c = 0$), the equation is relatively simple to solve. For example, if the quadratic equation is $x^2 + 8x + 15 = 0$, then $a = 1, b = 8$, and $c = 15$. Replacing these values in the formula results in the value

$$\frac{-8 \pm \sqrt{8^2 - 4(1 \bullet 15)}}{2 \bullet 1}$$

When calculated, then, x is shown to equal $\{-3, -5\}$. A problem with using this method is remembering the equation. One way to promote memory is to use a mnemonic strategy, using a bee with a minus sign for a stinger for $-b$, a "square" bee for b^2, four aces for $4ac$, and an American Airlines (AA) airplane for $2a$:

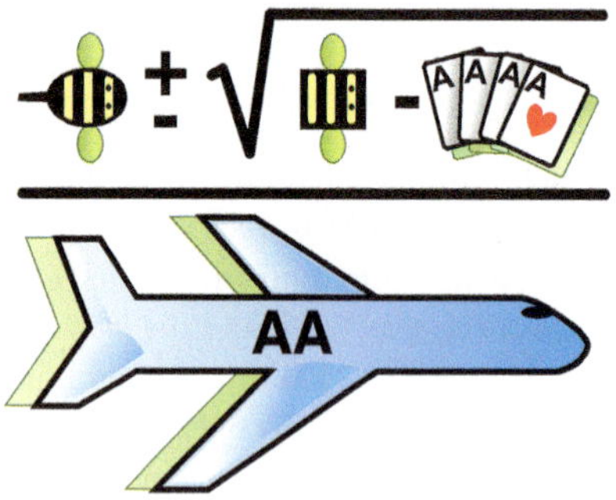

Such a strategy, of course, should be practiced many times, and particular attention must be paid to the elements that are *not* represented mnemonically (+ / −; square root). Finally, students should have many opportunities to practice the application of this equation in the solution of problems. Remember, as with any academic strategy, students must be taught to *identify* the situation in which a particular strategy is called for, *remember* the steps of the strategy, and then correctly *apply* the strategy in the appropriate context.

TEACH PROBLEM-SOLVING STRATEGIES Students can benefit from self-questioning strategies for solving algebra word problems (Impecoven-Lind & Foegen, 2010). Maccini and Hughes (2000) taught introductory algebra (e.g., operations with negative numbers) to secondary students with learning disabilities using concrete, semi-concrete, and abstract presentations, as discussed earlier. Again, the strategy considered problem representation and problem solution and employed the **STAR** strategy:

1. **S**earch the word problem (read carefully, ask questions, look for facts).
2. **T**ranslate the problem into a pictured equation (choose a variable, identify the operation, and represent the problem in a concrete [manipulative, such as algebra tiles], semi-concrete [picture], or abstract [equation] application). (Students began with concrete representations and progressed to abstract representations.)
3. **A**nswer the problem, attending to relevant signs.
4. **R**eview the solution by reading the problem again and checking whether the answer is reasonable.

All students trained using this strategy improved in introductory algebra problem solving.

Hutchinson (1993) developed a strategy-based model that considered two separate phases: problem representation and problem solution (Janvier, 1987). Problem representation refers to an internal representation of the words of the problem. Problem solution refers to solution planning and solution execution to obtain the answer. Hutchinson employed different problem types: relational problems, proportion problems, problems that employed two variables, and problems that employed two equations. For example, for relational problems, students were required to identify the relational statement that provided information about one unknown quantity in terms of its relationship to another unknown quantity. Then, the solution focused on procedures and order of operations. One relational problem was as follows:

> A man walks 6 km farther than his son. If the total distance walked by both is 32 km, how far did each walk? (Hutchinson, 1993, p. 38)

Students were then directed to use self-questioning for solving algebra problems by using a structured worksheet where they answer questions about the problem goal, known and unknown information, problem type, equation, solution, and checking the answer with the goal.

In this instance, you would prompt students to think through the fact that the man's son walked x km, and the man, who walked 6 km farther, walked $x + 6$ km. Using the worksheet questions, then, students could identify the goal, the unknowns, the knowns, the type of problem, and the equation. These two distances, x km and $x + 6$ km, totaled 32 km. Using the problem-solution strategy, students were able to obtain the correct answer, 13 km.

$$x + (x + 6) = 32$$

or

$$\begin{aligned} 2x + 6 &= 32 \\ (2x + 6) - 6 &= 32 - 6 \\ 2x &= 26 \\ x &= 13 \end{aligned}$$

so,

$$\begin{aligned} \textit{man}\text{ walked } x + 6 &= 19\,\textit{km} \\ \textit{son}\text{ walked } x &= 13\,\textit{km} \end{aligned}$$

Students then compare their solution to the stated goal and check by replacing the obtained values in the original problem.

Similarly, Lang et al. (2004) taught an algebra problem-solving strategy to students considered at risk for math failure. The following strategy steps were used in each example problem:

a. If I use this strategy, I will be successful.
b. What do we know?
c. What don't we know?
d. How can we represent the unknowns?
e. How can we represent the knowns?
f. Do we need more than one equation?
g. What is (are) the equation(s)?

h. Substitute the knowns into the equation(s).

i. Solve the equation(s).

j. Have I checked my answer?

Students went through each step of the strategy as they solved algebra problems and greatly improved their strategy use as they went through the training.

STRATEGIES FOR TEACHING FUNCTIONAL MATH

USE APPROPRIATE METHODS AND MATERIALS FOR TEACHING FUNCTIONAL MATH Many students do not take advanced math classes and instead take classes in which more emphasis is placed on basic skills and what is called **functional math** (Heller, 2010). Functional math includes aspects of mathematics that serve individuals in their daily living. These topics include using the calendar, writing checks and keeping checking and savings bank accounts, calculating household expenses, filling out income tax forms, and paying bills. These skills are important for all students to acquire, regardless of the program they are in (it is often assumed—perhaps incorrectly—that students already have these skills; Patton et al., 1998). Some strategies presented in this chapter may be helpful when teaching functional-based math. For example, in Bouck et al. (2017), students with intellectual disabilities were able to accurately make change after receiving the graduated CRA instructional sequence. Students were taught to solve problems using concrete manipulatives (i.e., plastic coins, paper bills) and then moved to problems in which they drew images to represent money (e.g., circle with numbers inside to represent coins). Finally, the students were able to demonstrate change making with coin problems when presented with the abstract representation of the problem.

A useful textbook reference on functional math skills is *The Pacemaker Curriculum: Practical Mathematics for Consumers* (Globe Fearon; reading level 3–4; Staudacher & Turner, 1998). Some materials from the *Essential Mathematics for Life* series (McGraw-Hill) also provide activities for functional math. Pro-Ed publishes the consumer math program *Real Life Math: Living on a Paycheck.* Because many of these topics may not be within the curriculum for other students, you many need to arrange some time for small-group teaching of these topics.

14 Summary

- Reform movements in mathematics have included the *Principles and Standards for School Mathematics* by the National Council of Teachers of Mathematics (2000) and the Common Core State Standards for Mathematics (NGA & CCSSO, 2010).
- Many students with disabilities encounter particular problems in learning mathematics, including acquiring math concepts, remembering and executing math facts and procedures, and mathematical reasoning. Students with sensory or physical disabilities may have problems with math in specific areas. Appropriate curriculum, effective teaching, and specific strategy instruction can help alleviate many of these problems.
- Math can be taught to students with disabilities in inclusive settings with the use of such principles as explicit instruction, appropriate instructional design, strong conceptual basis for mathematical procedures, drill and intensive practice, cumulative review, motivators, and ongoing progress monitoring. Many strategies are appropriate to the level and type of mathematics being taught.
  - — Basic number and operation concepts (e.g., addition, subtraction) can be enforced by direct teaching, number lines, and manipulatives such as base-10 blocks. Learning of vocabulary concepts can be promoted by direct teaching, manipulatives, and verbal elaboration, including mnemonic strategies.
  - — Learning of basic math facts can become a significant obstacle to many students with disabilities and other diverse learning needs. When possible, promote memory of basic facts through direct teaching, increased learning time, peer tutoring, specialized software, and independent study strategies. Additionally, use specific strategies for promoting recall of specific facts. If basic fact learning seems unproductive and frustrating for some students, consider allowing the use of calculators so that students can continue progressing in other areas of mathematics functioning. Return to fact learning when it appears it may be profitable.
  - — Word problem solving can be facilitated by using a sequence of instruction that progresses from concrete to semi-concrete to abstract. In addition, use specific problem-solving strategies, such as the seven-step self-monitoring strategy, judicious use of clue words, highlighting, imagery, pictures, and others.
  - — Important money and time concepts can be enforced by direct teaching, increased practice, use of manipulatives, and use of models and by providing a careful sequence of skills.
  - — Specific manipulative materials (commercially available or teacher made) can be helpful in promoting learning of fractions and decimals. Specific self-monitoring and other strategies can also be useful in promoting these concepts.
  - — Promote concepts in algebra by providing early concept development, computation strategies, manipulatives such as algebra tiles, mnemonics, and self-monitoring strategies.
  - — Ensure that students are acquiring sufficient "practical" mathematics skills for use in transition to community life and future employment. Curriculum materials are available that provide for instruction in these practical areas.

PROFESSIONAL STANDARDS LINK: MATHEMATICS

Information in this chapter links most directly to:

- CEC 2020 Initial Practice-Based Professional Preparation Standards for Special Educators (Initial K–12 standards) (see https://exceptionalchildren.org/standards/initial-practice-based-professional-preparation-standards-special-educators): Standards 2 (Understanding and Addressing Each Individual's Developmental and Learning Needs), 3 (Demonstrating Subject Matter Content and Specialized Curriculum Knowledge), 4 (Using Assessment to Understand the Learner and the Learning Environment for Data-Based Decision Making), 5 (Supporting Learning Using Effective Instruction)
- InTASC Standards (see https://www.ccsso.org/sites/default/files/2017-11/InTASC_Model_Core_Teaching_Standards_2011.pdf): 2 (Learning Differences), 3 (Learning Environments), 4 (Content Knowledge), 5 (Application of Content), 7 (Planning for Instruction), 8 (Instructional Strategies)

MATHEMATICS

If the student is having difficulty in mathematics, have you tried the following strategies? If not, see the pages listed here.

STRATEGIES FOR TEACHING BEGINNING MATH

- ☐ Teach early number concepts, 380
- ☐ Teach strategies for counting, 380–381
- ☐ Reinforce one-to-one correspondence, 381
- ☐ Introduce geometry concepts in the early years, 381

STRATEGIES FOR TEACHING ADDITION AND SUBTRACTION

- ☐ Use manipulatives for teaching addition and subtraction concepts, 382
- ☐ Use number lines to promote operations, 382
- ☐ Use strategies for number writing, 382–383
- ☐ Use questioning to promote understanding of symbols, 383
- ☐ Use Touch Math to promote addition and subtraction computation, 383–384
- ☐ Use practice and specific strategies for addition and subtraction facts, 384–385
- ☐ Use strategies for place value and regrouping, 386–387
- ☐ Use strategies for teaching early problem solving with addition and subtraction, 387
- ☐ Use response-to-intervention strategies for early prevention and identification, 388–389

STRATEGIES FOR TEACHING MULTIPLICATION AND DIVISION

- ☐ Use manipulatives for teaching multiplication and division concepts, 389
- ☐ Teach "count-bys," 389–390
- ☐ Use specific strategies for teaching multiplication and division facts, 390–392
- ☐ Use calculators when appropriate, 392
- ☐ Reinforce arithmetic vocabulary, 392
- ☐ Use specific strategies for teaching multiplication and division algorithms, 392–395

STRATEGIES FOR TEACHING PROBLEM SOLVING

- ☐ Promote use of word meanings, 395–396
- ☐ Teach cognitive strategies for problem solving, 396–397
- ☐ Use enhanced anchored instruction, 397
- ☐ Use Tier 2 problem-solving interventions, 397

STRATEGIES FOR TEACHING ABOUT MONEY AND TIME

- ☐ Practice coin recognition and counting money with appropriate materials, 397
- ☐ Use appropriate methods and materials for teaching about time, 398

STRATEGIES FOR TEACHING FRACTIONS AND DECIMALS

- ☐ Use appropriate methods and materials for teaching fractions, 398–399
- ☐ Use appropriate methods and materials for teaching decimals, 399

STRATEGIES FOR TEACHING AREA AND VOLUME CONCEPTS

- ☐ Provide visual and three-dimensional representations, 399–400
- ☐ Teach "big ideas," 400–401

STRATEGIES FOR TEACHING ALGEBRA

- ☐ Use manipulatives to teach negative numbers, 401–403
- ☐ Teach algebraic representations early, 403
- ☐ Teach strategies for computation, 403
- ☐ Teach strategies for solving quadratic equations, 403–404
- ☐ Teach problem-solving strategies, 404–406

STRATEGIES FOR TEACHING FUNCTIONAL MATH

- ☐ Use appropriate methods and materials for teaching functional math, 406

Angela N Perryman/Shutterstock

CHAPTER 15

Science and Social Studies

LEARNING OBJECTIVES

After studying this chapter, you should be able to:

15.1 Describe and apply strategies for adapting textbook-oriented approaches for teaching science and social studies and for selecting and adapting textbook materials to accommodate diverse learners in the classroom.

15.2 Discuss considerations and appropriate adaptations for teaching life science, earth science, and physical science activities and ways to adapt social studies activities for diverse learners.

15.3 Identify ways to use and adapt inquiry-oriented instruction for teaching science and social studies.

Science and social studies are academic disciplines concerned with concepts and knowledge of the physical and social world around us (Contant et al., 2018; Parker & Beck, 2021) and, as such, they are important subject areas for all students. Both subjects, however, present unique challenges to teachers who must adapt their instruction, materials, and procedures to accommodate students with disabilities.

Adaptations for students with disabilities must reflect the approach to instruction being used in the classroom (Scruggs & Mastropieri, 2007). That is, many schools employ a **textbook-oriented (or content-oriented) approach** in which students are taught and learn content information from science and social studies textbooks. With this approach, adaptations may focus on teacher presentations and students' independent learning from textbooks. Other schools may embrace an **activities-oriented approach** to learning in which students undertake specific projects, experiments, or other activities to enhance their understanding of the subject. With this approach, adaptations may focus on physical activities as well as reading and writing requirements. In many schools, teachers may use features of both approaches.

Using either approach, teachers may emphasize an **inquiry-based model** of learning, in which students use their knowledge or experiences to invent, discover, or construct new knowledge. Adaptations for inquiry-based learning may focus on supports or enhancements to promote the thinking and reasoning process in students with disabilities.

Adapting Textbook-Oriented Approaches in Science and Social Studies

Learning Objective 15.1 Describe and apply strategies for adapting textbook-oriented approaches for teaching science and social studies and for selecting and adapting textbook materials to accommodate diverse learners in the classroom.

CLASSROOM SCENARIO

Jeffrey

As Mr. Norland's sixth-grade science class enters the room on Monday of the second week of school, he booms, "Pick up your science lab materials on your way to your seat. Open up your textbooks to Activity 2–1 in Chapter 2 on page 26 and follow the instructions. If you have any problems with the steps, see me." After most of the class appears to have begun working, Mr. Norland notices that Jeffrey hasn't even started the activity. He speaks with Jeffrey and realizes he can't follow through with the activity because he can't read what to do. Although embarrassed, Jeffrey agrees to work through the activity with one of his peers. At the end of the day, Mr. Norland approaches Jeffrey's special education teacher. "I know Jeffrey has a learning disability but doing well in science this year is partly dependent on him being able to read. We will do many of the activities in cooperative groups, but how will Jeffrey get the content background he needs unless he can read the text?"

QUESTIONS FOR REFLECTION

1. How do Mr. Norland's classroom routines affect Jeffrey's achievement in science?
2. Why doesn't Jeffrey ask for help?
3. What strategies might Mr. Norland use to help Jeffrey succeed?

Much instruction in science and social studies involves teaching and learning of content based on relevant textbook materials. Effective teacher presentations and specific strategies for studying textbooks can address a variety of learning needs and enhance learning for all students.

COMMON CORE STATE STANDARDS RELEVANT TO SCIENCE AND SOCIAL STUDIES

The Common Core State Standards (CCSS) do not provide separate standards for science and social studies. However, beginning at the sixth-grade level, standards relevant to history/social studies, science, and technical subjects are provided within the English language arts (ELA) standards. Standards for K–5 reading and writing in subjects, including history/social studies, science, and technical subjects, are integrated into the K–5 standards (National Governors Association [NGA] Center for Best Practices & Council of Chief State School Officers [CCSSO], 2010).

Specifically, however, the reading standards for grades 6–12 in content-area subjects focus on four areas:

- *Identify key ideas and details* (e.g., cite textual evidence, determine central ideas, and analyze causal events from primary and secondary sources)
- *Analyze craft and structure* (e.g., determine meanings of words/phrases; compare points of view; and describe informational text structures such as sequential, descriptive, comparative, cause and effect, or problem/solution)
- *Integrate knowledge and ideas* (e.g., do quantitative and qualitative analysis, determine the degree to which the author's claims are supported by reasoning and evidence in a text; compare and contrast treatments of same text)
- *Engage in a range of reading levels and text complexity* (e.g., to create independent and proficient readers)

By the end of 12th grade, the Common Core Anchor Standards—written to advance college and career readiness—set expectations for students to be able to read and comprehend texts that generate knowledge around a variety of topics and themes and allow for in-depth study.

Similarly, the CCSS for writing sets the following expectations for students when writing about what they learn from a range of texts in history/social studies, science, and technology.

- *Write arguments focused on discipline-specific content* (e.g., support claims, counterclaims, reasoning, and evidence)
- *Write informative and explanatory text* (e.g., narrate historical events, write about scientific processes/experiments and technical processes, organize ideas and concepts, use precise language)
- *Produce and distribute writing* (e.g., use clear and coherent writing and engage in revising, editing, rewriting, producing, and publishing)
- *Research to build and present knowledge* (e.g., conduct short, sustained research projects; gather relevant information from multiple, authoritative sources; and draw evidence to support, analyze, and reflect)
- *Write routinely* (e.g., over extended and shorter time periods for a range of disciplines, specific tasks, purposes, and audiences)

Pearson eTextbook

Video Example 15.1

Careful instructional planning can ensure specific standards-based teaching goals are met. How do the teachers in this video identify instructional adaptations needed in their lessons?

For a complete listing of ELA standards relevant to history/social studies, science, and technical subjects, see http://www.corestandards.org/ELA-Literacy/.

Apart from the Common Core, there are other standards that states can decide whether or not to adopt. For instance, the National Council for the Social Studies (2013) provides curriculum standards for social studies (https://www.socialstudies.org/standards) and the National Research Council (2013) published a framework for the K–12 Next Generation Science Standards or NGSS (https://www.nextgenscience.org). Also, many states have adopted the K–12 Computer Science (CS) Standards (see k12cs.org). The CS framework focuses on the following core concepts: computing systems, networks and the Internet, data and analysis, algorithms and programming, and the impacts of computing. These CS concepts are integrated into the ELA and mathematics standards of the CCSS, and some high schools have added computer science classes as part of the curriculum (K–12 Computer Science Framework; https://www.k12cs.org). Many of the strategies described in the next section are appropriate for addressing these standards and the CCSS.

STRATEGIES FOR EFFECTIVE TEACHING IN SCIENCE AND SOCIAL STUDIES

You can enhance learning of science and social studies in inclusive classrooms by using the instructional high-leverage practices (see Chapter 6) and the teacher-effectiveness variables (Good & Lavigne, 2017; McLeskey et al., 2017), including the PASS and SCREAM variables.

USE EFFECTIVE TEACHING STRATEGIES Organize your science or social studies content around "big ideas" that will make subordinate concepts easier to understand (Slocum, 2004). For example, the model of convection, once clearly understood, can explain the behavior of water in a boiling pot, the movement of material in Earth's mantle, and the movement of air masses, including atmospheric convection (Grossen & Burke, 1998; see also Okolo & Ferretti, 2014). Emphasize the organization of your presentations with outlines and important information highlighted on the board or slides and refer frequently to this outline. Speak in a clear, direct manner, and avoid ambiguous language. Actively model excitement and enthusiasm about the content being covered. Repeat new or unfamiliar vocabulary or concepts and provide multiple instances of new concepts (e.g., *saprophytic*, *nullification*, *hegemony*) to strengthen comprehension. Use mnemonics or other elaborations to promote recall of new vocabulary. Question students frequently and adjust your instruction as needed. Promote the use of systematic note taking (see Chapter 11). At the end of presentations, be sure to summarize important lesson content and monitor student understanding.

PROVIDE CONTENT-ENHANCEMENT STRATEGIES Teachers can use **content-enhancement** strategies to further increase science and social studies learning. Content enhancements incorporate effective instructional design and make use of graphic organizers—including study guides, charts, diagrams, outlines, visual-spatial displays, mnemonics, and imagery—to promote learning and comprehension (Bulgren, 2004). Research has indicated that students with disabilities in inclusive classrooms have improved their performance when science and social studies teachers apply content-enhancement strategies in their teaching (Schumaker & Fisher, 2021).

SMARTER Strategy Teachers can plan for instruction using the strategy cued by the acronym **SMARTER**. This includes **S**electing important content, **M**apping the organization of the content, **A**nalyzing learning problems, **R**eaching decisions about enhancement, **T**eaching according to decisions, **E**valuating, and **R**eteaching based on the evaluation (Lenz, Bulgren, et al., 2004). When selecting important content or the "big ideas" of an instructional unit, consider developing overarching questions, or what Capin and Vaughn (2017) call "canopy" questions, to refer to throughout instruction (e.g., How did the colonists win the Revolutionary War?).

Lesson Organizer and Concept Mastery Routines Two helpful content-enhancement strategies are the lesson organizer routine and the concept mastery routine. Both are part of the work conducted at the University of Kansas Center for Research on Learning (KU-CRL) (Hock et al., 2017; see https://sim.ku.edu/sim-content-enhancement-routines). The *lesson organizer routine* is a visual advanced organizer frame to organize a lesson so students can see the main ideas, as well as how the main ideas relate to each other and to prior knowledge (Albert & Ammer, 2004; Lenz & Adams, 2006). The organizer does the following:

- Introduces the topic.
- Changes difficult vocabulary to familiar vocabulary.
- Teaches students relationships among concepts.
- Identifies appropriate strategies for learning.
- Graphically demonstrates relationships of lessons to an entire unit.
- Graphically displays organization of the content.
- Provides self-testing questions.

As teachers present the visual displays and share information with students, they help show how the information is related to previously learned content. The organizer also functions as a teacher-planning device in that the sequences of content, concepts, and vocabulary are identified before instruction to ensure a developmentally appropriate lesson.

The *concept mastery routine* addresses the teaching of difficult concepts (King-Sears & Mooney, 2004; see also Bulgren et al., 2013). This content enhancement is designed around a concept diagram, a visual device that includes the following components:

- Concept name
- Class or category of the concept
- Important information associated with the concept
- Instances and noninstances of the concept
- Blank space for additions to the diagram
- Concept definition (Bulgren et al., 1993)

Specific instructional steps are provided for teachers to use when implementing the concept mastery routine. Figure 15.1 contains a sample concept diagram.

Bulgren (2004) emphasized that the graphic itself is not presented to students in its completed form; rather, the teacher may develop a graphic organizer before instruction begins, but the actual graphic organizer is developed interactively with students as they share their own ideas, knowledge, and questions.

USE MNEMONIC STRATEGIES Keyword, pegword, and letter strategies can be extremely useful for helping students remember vocabulary, terminology, and factual information involving science and social studies (Lubin & Polloway, 2016). Much information in science (e.g., *deciduous*, *thermic*, *trichina*) and social studies (e.g., *longitude*, *anarchy*,

Figure 15.1 Sample Concept Diagram

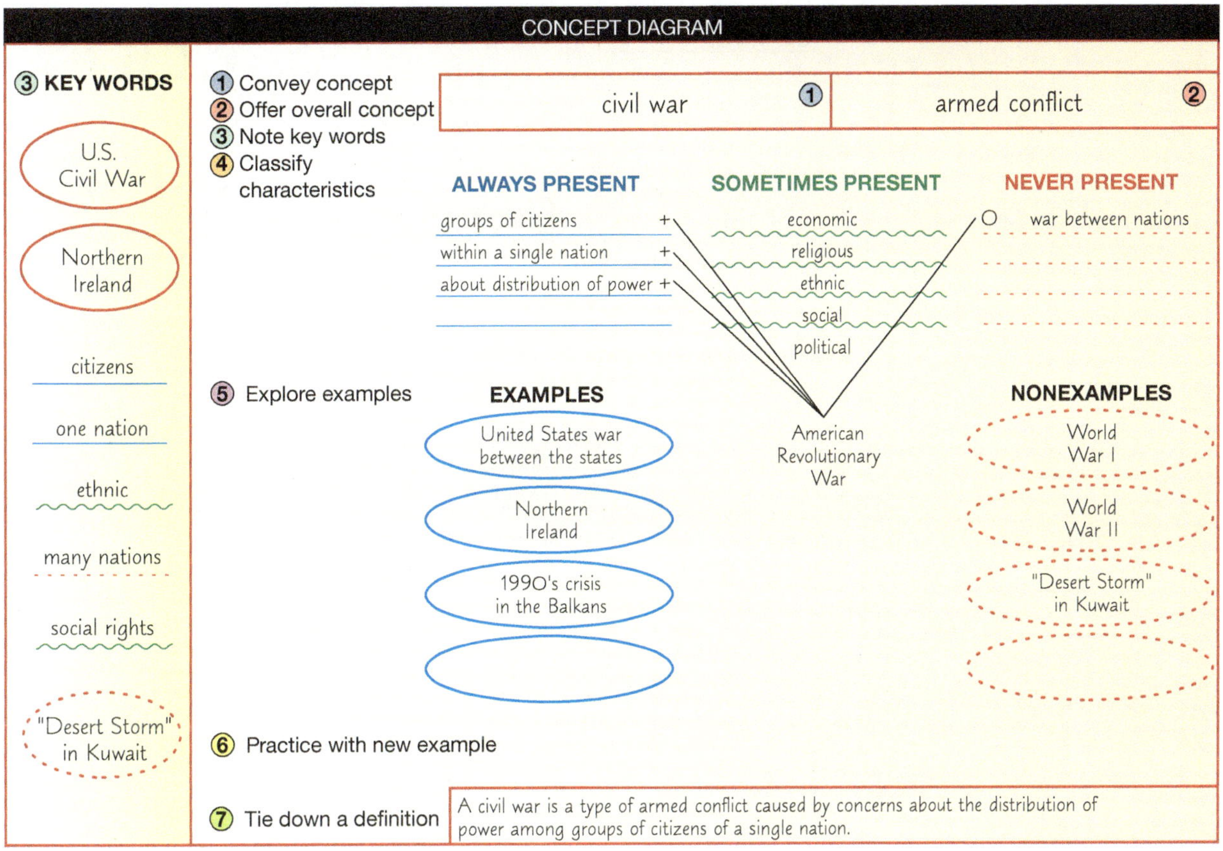

Source: From Deshler et al. (1996), p. 453. Reprinted with permission.

Potawatomi) is appropriate for mnemonic elaboration. These mnemonic strategies can be used whenever students exhibit difficulty remembering important content. For example, Mastropieri et al. (2000) developed mnemonics to help fourth-grade students remember important information in a social studies unit (e.g., *Europe*, *charter*). Although the strategies helped the entire class, students with disabilities benefited the most. Marshak et al. (2011) employed classroom peer tutoring with mnemonic strategies in middle school social studies classes and found that students significantly outperformed students in a traditional instruction condition.

Identify the most important content in science and social studies units that students have the most difficulty remembering. Create strategies for this information for class presentations and ask students to develop their own strategies in group activities. For example, after information has been organized in a graphic organizer or relationship chart, ask students which important information seems most difficult to remember and help them create effective mnemonic strategies.

ADAPT WORKSHEET ACTIVITIES Some students with disabilities are able to address the content required in worksheet activities, but they may have difficulty with the mechanical aspects of writing necessary to complete the activity in the allotted time. Figure 15.2 includes a modified version of a science assignment for students with disabilities. The modified assignment reduces the amount of reading and writing but covers the same major concepts (Mastropieri et al., 1998). This is an example of the concept of differentiated instruction (Tomlinson & Imbeau, 2010) applied to worksheet activities.

In addition to effective instruction and use of content enhancements to promote comprehension, another important area to consider is teaching students to learn independently from content-area textbooks.

Figure 15.2 Modified Worksheet Assignment

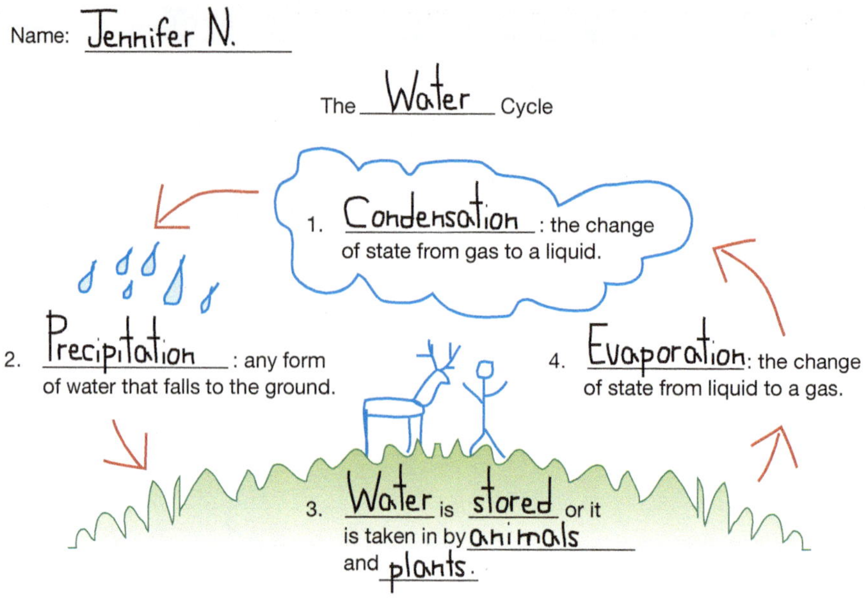

STRATEGIES FOR PROMOTING INDEPENDENT LEARNING FROM TEXTBOOKS

Pearson eTextbook

Video Example 15.2

This video shows a teacher providing small-group instruction for fifth-graders. She uses alternative texts to supplement content-area learning. How does the teacher guide student learning before they even begin reading?

A large proportion of learning that takes place in science and social studies comes from independent studying of textbooks. For assignments, students are often required to read chapters and answer questions. Teachers often move rapidly from chapter to chapter because of pressures to cover a great deal of content. Science and social studies textbooks are often complex, contain high readability levels and many formats, and introduce a significant number of new vocabulary words and concepts (Best et al., 2005; Scruggs & Mastropieri, 2015). Berkeley et al. (2014) investigated secondary history textbooks and found them to be frequently inconsiderate of less fluent readers and dense with factual information.

Given these analyses, it is not surprising that studying from textbooks can be frustrating for many students with disabilities and those at risk for school failure. When possible, use alternative texts and select textbooks that effectively promote comprehension. Volunteer to be a member of your school district's textbook adoption committee. Carefully consider such features as readability, language, vocabulary, organization, and use of illustrations and diagrams. Your input on the selection of appropriate textbooks will benefit all students but especially those with diverse learning needs. One readability measure is provided in Figure 15.3. Microsoft Word also calculates readability estimates for Word documents, using slightly different formulas.

TEACH STUDY SKILLS STRATEGIES FOR CONTENT-AREA TEXTBOOKS Successful students develop their own effective study skills and strategies to use when studying textbooks independently. However, students with disabilities may require explicit instruction in the use of these strategies. Learning how to predict text structures, how to highlight or outline essential information, and how to use text enhancements such as lesson organizers, graphic organizers, illustrations, charts, graphs, and diagrams are strategies for effectively using textbooks. Many of these strategies are appropriate for all expository text materials and therefore would be helpful for many other secondary-level classes, such as business education, foreign languages, family and consumer sciences, and physical education.

TEACH STUDENTS TO IDENTIFY TEXT ORGANIZATION Textbooks contain organizational features intended to help students learn academic content. Unfortunately, however, many students with disabilities may not figure out text organization independently. Taking time to systematically teach students how the features of their textbooks are organized can help

Figure 15.3 Fry's Readability Graph and Formula

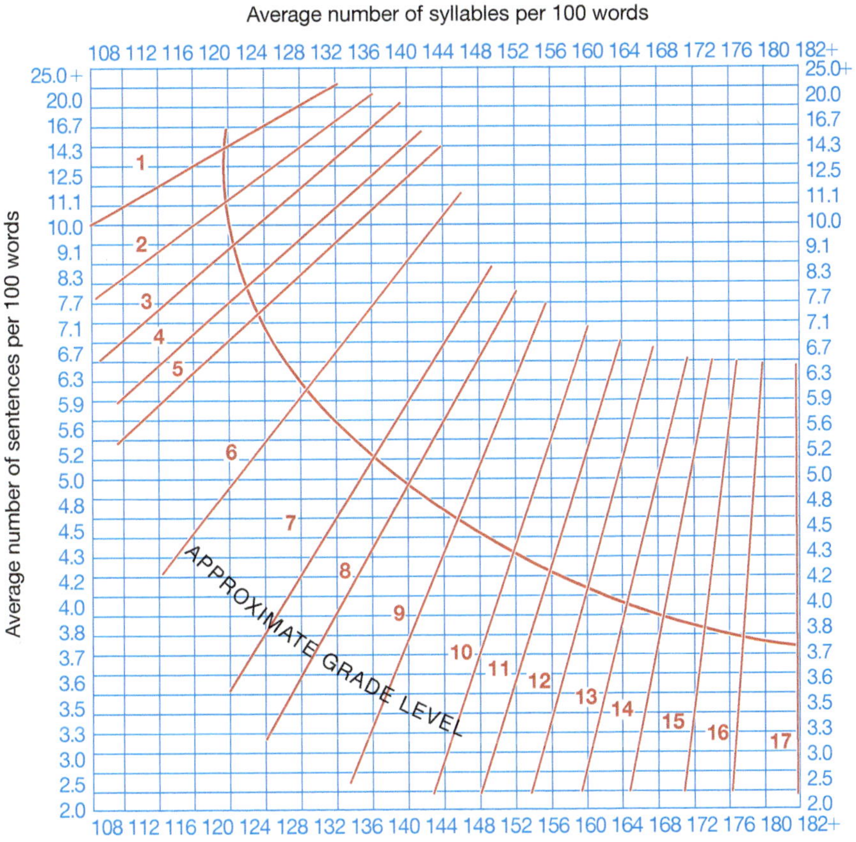

1. Randomly select three text samples of exactly 100 words, beginning with the beginning of a sentence. Count proper nouns, numerals, and initializations as words.

2. Count the number of sentences in each 100-word sample, estimating the length of the last sentence to the nearest one-tenth.

3. Count the total number of syllables in each 100-word sample. Count one syllable for each numeral or initial or symbol; for example, 1990 is one word and four syllables, LD is one word and two syllables, and "&" is one word and one syllable.

4. Average the number of sentences and number of syllables across the three samples.

5. Enter the average sentence length and average number of syllables on the graph. Put a dot where the two lines intersect. The area in which the dot is plotted will give you an approximate estimated readability.

6. If there is a great deal of variability in the syllable or sentence count across the three samples, more samples can be added.

Source: From Fry (1977). Reprinted with permission.

students learn more easily and make the use of textbooks more valuable. Point out to students how to use design features such as the following:

- The overall parts of the text (e.g., table of contents, index)
- The organizational system (sections, chapters)
- Specific features within chapters (objectives, outlines, boldface, vocabulary, illustrations, charts)
- Features associated with supplemental materials (workbooks, lab books, activity sheets)

Understanding the organization of a textbook can enhance students' comprehension of the content-area information presented. Use effective instruction principles when designing lessons to teach students about text features.

Prepare Students to Identify Text Structures Expository science and social studies textbooks use several distinct types of structures (Williams & Pau, 2013). These text structures include, for example, main idea, time–order, cause–effect, enumeration, and sequence.

All types of text structures may appear throughout a single science or social studies textbook. Therefore, students are likely to encounter many structures not only within a single textbook but also within a single chapter. Students should be taught to identify and understand these structures as a way to improve their comprehension of expository text (Hebert et al., 2016; Pyle et al., 2017).

Once passage structures are identified, structure-specific reading-comprehension strategies can be used to improve understanding and recall. Bakken et al. (1997) taught students with learning disabilities to recognize *main idea*, *list*, and *order* passage types and to apply structure-specific reading-comprehension strategies. For example, when studying main idea passages, students were taught to write down the main idea of the passage (e.g., in photosynthesis, plants convert light energy to carbohydrates) and then write supporting statements. For list passages (e.g., of a country's natural resources), students were taught to note items in the list. For order passages (e.g., the ordered steps in the digestive process), they were taught to write down the items in the appropriate sequence presented. These students greatly outperformed students who were given more general training, either to paraphrase information or to answer questions about the passages.

TEACH HIGHLIGHTING AND OUTLINING STRATEGIES Highlighting and outlining are used to increase learning and memory of text by identifying the critical information in text or notes. Both of these techniques have been adapted to increase the learning of students with disabilities (e.g., Horton et al., 1990; Reid et al., 2013). Information highlighted with bright colors, such as fluorescent yellow, stands out dramatically from the text, and such highlighting can be used to quickly find important information. Underlining is usually done in pencil or pen, but different-colored highlighting pens can also be used. Brightly colored sticky notes can be used when students are not allowed to write in their textbooks. Digital books have highlight features that allow the user to underline and add notes.

The most difficult aspect of highlighting or underlining for students is choosing which information is most important. Without modeling and practice, many students may be unable to discern what is important to highlight or underline and may highlight or underline everything on a page. Obviously, this defeats the purpose of highlighting.

When using actual science or social studies text materials, proceed through a highlighting activity in which you describe to students why you are selecting certain sections to highlight, using a think-aloud protocol. Say, for example:

- "This looks like a new science concept, so I will highlight it. This next section just provides more information on the same concept, so I won't highlight it."
- "This looks like an important person in this history chapter, so I will highlight her name, but this next paragraph just describes her background, so I won't highlight that."
- "This looks like an important vocabulary word, so I'll highlight it, but I already know what the next word means, so I won't highlight that."

Show students how to examine the features associated with their textbook. For example, organizational subheadings sometimes provide clues as to whether something is essential, and valuable information is often presented in maps, figures, charts, and diagrams within the text.

Finally, provide guided practice in which students work with partners or in small groups and practice identifying important information for highlighting. Stop occasionally and ask students whether they think some of the points meet the criteria for highlighting. Have students share with each other their rationale for the selections they highlighted.

Teach Outlining Outlining is another study strategy that students can use while studying science and social studies textbooks independently. Before expecting students to outline, be sure they can identify different text structures. Point out how textbooks are organized under various levels of subheadings, which often can be used as levels in outlines. Then be sure to teach or review how to develop outlines. Demonstrate to students how determining the main idea is a first step, followed by selecting supporting ideas and details for each major idea. Before requiring students to create outlines independently, provide them with partially completed outlines in which they complete missing information as they study independently. Outlines set up like this are called **framed outlines**, and they have been used to promote the textbook learning of students with and without disabilities (Brigham et al., 2012). Figure 15.4 displays an example of a framed outline.

INTRODUCE STUDY GUIDES Study guides take on a variety of forms and can be developed by teachers, students, or by both teachers and students using partially completed study guides similar to partially completed outlines. Lovitt and colleagues studied the effects of various study guides on the textbook comprehension of students with and without disabilities (e.g., Horton et al., 1990). Students used information in the science and social studies textbooks to complete short-answer questions on study guide forms. Students who used the study guides consistently outperformed students who did not have instruction using study guides. To create a study guide for your students, include critical features such as the formulation of questions, the use of vocabulary, the amount of content coverage, a predictable format for the guide, and time to review the study guide (Swanson et al., 2014). Consider such features as the amount of content covered, the type of study guide (question–answer, framed outline, schematic graph, graphic organizer), the difficulty level of the language, and the format of the questions (e.g., fill-in-the-blank, open-ended, or multiple-choice questions). Conderman and Hedin (2017) suggest the following ways to further differentiate study guides:

- Provide alternative response approaches for completing the study guide such as writing answers, dictating answers, drawing answers, or highlighting answers electronically.
- Use digital texts, ebooks, or audiobooks so that students have access to text-to-speech, vocabulary supports, and options to change text format and adjust readability.
- Include scaffolds such as page numbers to find the information, word banks, the first letter for fill-in-the-blank questions, and bolded words on the study guide.
- Allow for the study guide to be completed individually, in pairs, or in small groups and then discuss responses as a whole group. (pp. 23–24)

Pearson eTextbook

Video Example 15.3

In this video, the teacher has students work in cooperative groups during social studies to organize facts from non-fiction text. How could the visual displays created and shared by the groups be used as a study guide for the students?

Figure 15.4 Sample Framed Outline

Title: Types of Mountains

I. Folded Mountains
   A. Formed by the "folding"of rock layers
      1. Most occurred when ______________________.
      2. When this (1) happened, the rocks ______________.
   B. Many important mountain ranges are folded mountains.
      1. The world's highest mountains, including ______________ and ______________, are folded mountains.
      2. In the United States, ______________ are folded mountains.
II. ______________ Mountains
   A. Formed when molten rock rises through the Earth's crust.
      1. Molten rock is known as ______________.
      2. Pools of __________ get bigger, and ______________.
   B. ______________ mountains are found in the United States.
      1. The Black Hills of South Dakota.
      2. The ______________ Mountains.
III. Fault-Block Mountains
   A. Formed when____________________.
   B. Found in the Western United States.
      1. The Sierra Nevadas are fault-block mountains.
      2. The ____________ are fault-block mountains.

Try developing a few study guides annually to accompany your text. Save them or share them with another teacher who may also develop a few to share with you. Do not pressure yourself to complete the entire text at one time or you may become overwhelmed. Over time, you will have accompanying study guides developed for entire textbooks in science and social studies.

TEACH LEARNING STRATEGIES Deshler and Schumaker and their colleagues at the University of Kansas Center for Research on Learning (formerly the Institute for Research in Learning Disabilities) developed some excellent learning strategies, including an instructional model for optimal delivery of these strategies (see Deshler & Schumaker, 2006; Gildroy & Deshler, 2008; Lenz, Deshler, et al., 2004; Schumaker & Fisher, 2021). Learning strategies should be implemented slowly over time to ensure that all students master all steps involved in learning and generalizing strategies. Key elements in the learning strategies model are listed in the *In the Classroom* feature. The intent of instruction in learning strategies is for students to become independent at implementing the strategies in their own studying.

MultiPass A useful learning strategy for reading science and social studies textbooks is **MultiPass** (Schumaker et al., 1982). The steps in MultiPass are similar to those in the SQ3R strategy—Survey, Question, Read, Recite, and Review (Marchand-Martella et al., 2013; McCormick & Cooper, 1991). With MultiPass, students are taught to review textbook reading materials three times, first to "survey," second to "size up," and third to "sort out" (O'Connor & Goodwin, 2011).

During the *survey* pass, students familiarize themselves with the organization of the text chapter, including the title, beginning paragraphs, subheadings, summary paragraphs, and major ideas. Teach students to make associations with the information in this chapter and previously read chapters. Finally, teach students to summarize the information in the chapter in their own words.

For the *size-up* pass, teach students more study techniques to use when reviewing the chapter:

- Identify highlighted information.
- Read the questions at the end of the chapter.
- Make up questions from statements.
- Skim text to find answers to questions.
- Paraphrase answers without looking back at the chapter.

Finally, for the *sort-out* phase, teach students to test themselves on the information in the chapter. In addition, throughout all three phases of instruction, students can use self-monitoring procedures to ensure they have completed all necessary steps, including appropriate attribution. An example attribution statement to teach students is: "Using MultiPass should help me learn and do better on the next test."

IT FITS The IT FITS strategy was developed to help students with learning difficulties remember important information from science textbooks (King-Sears et al., 1992). IT FITS is an acronym for the steps in creating mnemonic keyword strategies. King-Sears et al. (1992; see also King-Sears & Mooney, 2004) taught students with learning disabilities to use the IT FITS strategy as follows:

Identify the term (e.g., *ptero-*, as in *pterosaur* or *pteranodon*).

Tell the definition of the term ("winged").

Find a keyword (*tire*).

Imagine the definition doing something with the keyword ("a tire with wings attached").

Think about the definition doing something with the keyword ("the attached wings lifting a tire into the air").

Study what you imagined until you know the definition (*ptero-* → tire → tire with wings → "winged").

In the Classroom

Steps in Learning a Strategy Model

Step 1: Pretest learners, and have students make a commitment to learning.
Step 2: Present purpose and describe the learning strategy.
Step 3: Model strategy usage using think-alouds, and provide initial student practice with the strategy.
Step 4: Provide additional rehearsal and verbal elaboration practice with the strategy.
Step 5: Provide controlled practice and feedback with the strategy (guided practice).
Step 6: Provide advanced practice and feedback with the strategy (independent practice).
Step 7: Provide positive feedback for the learning strategy, and enlist support for generalization of self-use of the strategy.
Step 8: Provide generalization and maintenance training, support, and feedback.

Source: From Deshler and Schumaker (1988). (See also Gildroy & Deshler, 2008.)

One student reported using the strategy to learn the meaning of *acoustic*. After *identifying* the term, he *told* the definition of the term ("having to do with hearing"), then *found* a keyword ("stick"). Next, he *imagined* the definition doing something with the keyword by considering the stick (baton) that his bandleader used, which made a noise when it was tapped. He then *thought* about this definition and *studied* what he imagined until he remembered the keyword and the definition. Results indicated that students learned more science vocabulary when they used and implemented the IT FITS strategy.

TRAVEL Boyle and Weishaar (1997) taught students with learning disabilities to use the TRAVEL strategy for developing their own cognitive organizers to improve their comprehension and recall of text content:

Topic: Write down the topic and circle it.

Read: Read a paragraph.

Ask: Ask what the main idea and three details are and write them down.

Verify: Verify the main idea by circling it and linking its details.

Examine: Examine the next paragraph and ask and verify again.

Link: When finished with the story, link all circles. (p. 230)

Students who used the TRAVEL strategy outperformed control-condition students—as well as students who had studied an expert-generated cognitive organizer—on tests of literal and inferential recall.

Self-Monitoring Strategies You can also teach students to use a self-monitoring strategy as they encounter headings and subheadings in content textbooks. For example, teach students to turn the heading, "The Election of 1976," into a question, such as, "Who won the election of 1976?" After reading the section, students should ask themselves, "Can I answer the question?" and then circle "yes" or "no" on a self-monitoring worksheet. If they circled "no," teach students to find the answer by, for example, (1) rereading the text; (2) checking their vocabulary understanding; (3) examining illustrations, tables, or figures; or (4) writing down questions to ask the teacher. Berkeley et al. (2011) taught middle school students to use this strategy in inclusive history classes and reported that those taught to use this self-monitoring strategy scored much higher on content tests than students who were simply told to read the passages and remember as much as possible (see also O'Connor et al., 2015).

STRATEGIES FOR ADAPTING TEXTBOOK MATERIALS

Because textbooks are adopted for entire school districts, it is inevitable that the reading level of some books may be too difficult, and thus inaccessible, for some students. Some suggestions to help promote learning by adapting the use of textbooks are presented in Figure 15.5.

Figure 15.5 Suggestions for Adapting and Using Textbooks

Provide alternative text formats.
- Use published recordings of texts or develop your own.
- Use digital text with audio components.
- Acquire enlarged-type versions of materials.
- As appropriate, use Braille versions of materials.
- Assign peers to read text.

Develop or plan for use of alternative curricular materials.
- Revise or rewrite text, adapting higher-level concepts and vocabulary; insert guided questions to use with simplified text.
- Prepare and distribute study guides, outlines, or guided notes.
- Prepare and distribute mnemonic illustrations.
- Supplement with software or apps focused on simpler presentation of concepts.
- Use high-interest, low-vocabulary materials.
- Use activities-based materials (see next section).
- Shorten reading and writing assignments.
- Develop pictorial versions of text materials.

Modify teaching presentations.
- Preteach difficult concepts and vocabulary.
- Provide concrete examples.
- Activate prior knowledge.
- Reduce amount of new information.
- Provide illustrative aids and spatial organizers.
- Use study guides.
- Encourage active participation.
- Schedule regular meetings with students with disabilities.
- Require frequent verbal responses to check for understanding.
- Provide additional review sessions.
- Use trade books as supplements.
- Use multimedia supplements.
- Use flashcards for studying.
- Have students maintain journals containing new concepts and vocabulary.

Use peers (or parent/caregiver volunteers) as assistants.
- To read or listen to reading.
- As study partners.
- To assist with writing tasks.

Other students may have difficulties because they are simultaneously learning to speak English and learning academic content. Students from culturally diverse backgrounds, including English learners (ELs), require additional supports in the content-area classroom. Some culturally responsive teaching approaches have been recommended, including collaborative teaching, problem solving, child-centered learning, use of appropriate assessments and materials, feedback-responsive teaching, modeling, and instructional scaffolding (Aceves & Orosco, 2014). Similarly, Linan-Thompson et al. (2018) reported that focused vocabulary development, explicit strategy instruction, and use of predictable routines can help improve culturally responsive teaching. Using multiple examples, including authentic culturally diverse examples, and connecting content-area learning to students' lives can help students make connections and relate the new content to their personal lives. However, it is also important to consider language objectives in addition to the content-area objectives when students are ELs (Aceves & Orosco, 2014). Echevarria and Graves (2015) described a model of **sheltered content instruction** to support the content learning of ELs with diverse abilities. Sheltered content instruction has many of the same components as effective instruction in general; in addition, it adds the following:

- Identifying language proficiency levels
- Adapting speech, language, and vocabulary to proficiency levels
- Adapting content to students' language proficiency

- Providing sufficient response wait time
- Providing supplemental materials
- Providing examples relevant to students' cultural and linguistic backgrounds

Other features shared with those of effective instruction include using clear language, providing consistent review, and using concrete, meaningful lessons with practice and multiple interaction opportunities.

PROMOTE PREREADING AND POSTREADING STRATEGIES Before assigning independent textbook reading, explain the purpose of the assignment. For example, you could say, "When you finish reading the section of your U.S. history text tonight, you will all be able to tell me the causes of the Civil War tomorrow at the beginning of class."

Provide organizers as overviews of the text structures and the content students will be studying. Figure 15.6 provides an example of a spatially organized template from Inspiration Software (now Diagramming Apps, LLC) that allows you or your students to create visual displays of historical events. Information from the visual display can be converted to and printed in an outline format.

Timelines can be constructed to demonstrate graphically the sequence of important events, for example, the events leading up to the Civil War. Timelines may or may not include pictures or symbols but always contain a chronological sequence in a graphic format. Design, develop, and show timelines that present detailed events that will be covered in the next social studies chapter.

Present difficult concepts or vocabulary words to students with disabilities in class before having them read about the information independently. Use some of the suggestions described in the MultiPass or mnemonic strategies sections to introduce and teach these concepts first. Demonstrate how students can use context clues, glossaries, and dictionaries to figure out new words they will encounter in the text. Have students practice these words at home and school to become familiar with the new words before hearing them for the first time in class. Figure 15.7 contains a partial vocabulary checklist.

When textbook reading assignments have been completed, provide additional assistance to ensure content mastery, including reviewing major points in class, providing additional practice with peer tutors, providing extra help sessions, reviewing study guides, directing students to tell or write summaries, and providing practice tests. This additional review on the most important content can lead to greater academic success.

MAKE ADAPTATIONS FOR STUDENTS WITH VISUAL IMPAIRMENTS OR SEVERE READING PROBLEMS As Mr. Norland discovered of Jeffrey in the scenario at the beginning of this chapter, reading problems can significantly inhibit science learning. Students with visual impairments or severe reading problems will need to have written text available to them in alternative formats. Alternative formats include audio versions, computerized versions containing audio components, larger-print versions, or Braille formats for students with very

Figure 15.6 Template for Creating Visual Display for Historical Event

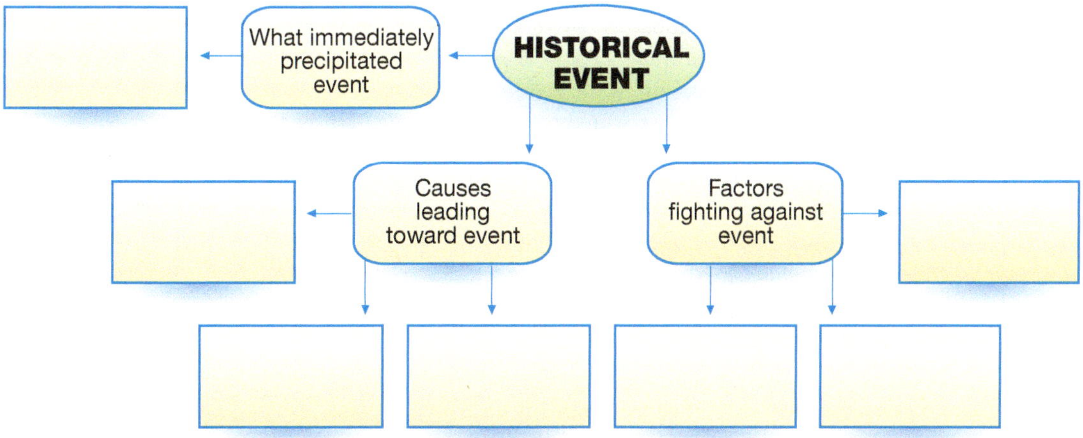

Source: Reprinted with permission from Inspiration Software, Portland, OR.

Figure 15.7 Sample Vocabulary Checklist

Vocabulary and Phrases

Directions: Place a check mark in the box if the student reads and defines the word correctly.

Chapter 4: Ecosystems S = At School H = At Home

	S	H	S	H	S	H	S	H	S	H
Vocabulary Words & Phrases	Mon	Mon	Tues	Tues	Wed	Wed	Thur	Thur	Fri	Fri
ecosystem										
producer										
consumer										
decomposer										
community										
predator										
prey										
parasite										
host										

Source: From unpublished materials by Mastropieri and Scruggs (1996), Graduate School of Education, George Mason University. Reprinted with permission.

limited vision. The *Kurzweil Reader* (Kurzweil Educational Systems) is also useful for reading and interacting with text; the *Kurzweil 3000* is intended to help students who have difficulties with textbooks keep up with reading assignments, learn study skills, complete written assignments, and test independently. The *Kurzweil 3000* is intended to facilitate text access for students with visual impairments. Services are also available to assist with completing Braille versions of materials. Tactile graphics to improve understanding of figures and diagrams in science textbooks are available from American Printing House for the Blind. Some special educators or resource centers can help create class materials accessible in Braille and raised formats.

PROMOTE LEARNING WITH CLASSWIDE PEER TUTORING Classwide peer tutoring can be an excellent way for all students to gain extra practice on the most important content of science and social studies units. For example, Maheady et al. (1988) employed classwide peer tutoring in inclusive 10th-grade social studies classrooms. Maheady et al. developed 30-item weekly study guides for the most important content of each chapter. Students tutored each other in pairs for about 30 minutes per day, 2 days per week, using items from the study guides (e.g., What is the meaning of imperialism? What is the governmental structure of the Communist Party?). When participating in the peer-tutoring condition, students scored over 21 percentage points higher than they scored before the intervention began. Mastropieri et al. (2003) implemented classwide peer tutoring using reading-comprehension strategies (Who or what is the section about? What is happening to the who or what? Write a summary sentence.) and summary sheets in 10th-grade world history classes in units on the world wars. Students who had participated in tutoring performed better on chapter tests, unit tests, and end-of-year tests than students who had studied with guided notes.

Spencer et al. (2003) implemented a similar reading-comprehension strategy using classwide peer tutoring with middle school students with emotional or behavioral disabilities studying social studies content (history and civics). Students read textbooks to each other in pairs and questioned each other about factual content (e.g., What was the Teapot Dome scandal?). Results revealed that students scored about 15 percentage points higher on weekly quizzes and chapter tests in the tutoring condition, and they were observed to have higher rates of academic, on-task behavior. One teacher expressed surprise that the tutoring pairs generally interacted well but noted the value of careful student pairings.

Mastropieri et al. (2008) implemented classwide peer tutoring in inclusive seventh-grade U.S. history classes. Teachers developed "fact sheets" of the most important textbook content to be remembered. On the fact sheets, questions (e.g., What was the position of the United States at the beginning of World War I? What was the *Lusitania*, and why was it important?) were printed in boxes on the left side of the page, with the corresponding answers on the right. Partners questioned each other on critical information using materials aligned with the high-stakes testing content and took practice tests covering the information. All families/caregivers were prepared to use the web-based *Blackboard* learning management system to access and use the same tutoring materials at home. Findings indicated that students scored higher in the peer-tutoring conditions than in the control conditions, and the families/caregivers learned to use *Blackboard* and the tutoring materials effectively. Although the materials were the same for all students, instruction can be differentiated in that all students can practice until they reach mastery. All students in this and a related investigation (Scruggs et al., 2012) benefited substantially from the tutoring intervention.

Peer tutoring has also been employed in secondary science with students with intellectual disabilities and more typically achieving peers (Jimenez et al., 2012). When matched with individual students with intellectual disabilities, peers taught important concepts in physical and earth science using a constant time-delay procedure, where intervals between questions and prompted responses were presented at a constant interval (initially, 0 seconds, then 5 seconds) systematically as students learned. In this case, also, students made use of a KWHL chart (What do you Know? What do you Want to know? How will you find out? and What did you Learn?). Use of graphic organizers like the KWHL chart can help both teachers and students with intellectual disabilities complete the steps of a science investigation (Knight et al., 2020).

Classwide peer tutoring has also been used in inclusive high school chemistry classes with the use of mnemonic techniques (Mastropieri et al., 2005). Students were assigned to tutoring pairs and provided with materials containing relevant information (e.g., exothermic and endothermic reactions, enthalpy, the periodic table of elements, alkali metals, halogens, molarity, Avogadro's number). Students questioned each other on the information (e.g., What is molarity?). If the question was answered correctly, the tutor asked for further elaborations on the content to promote comprehension (e.g., What else is important about molarity?). If the question was incorrectly answered, strategies such as the keyword method were provided, as shown in Figure 15.8. When the item was answered correctly, further elaboration was prompted. Results indicated that students in the tutoring condition outperformed comparison students in both recall and comprehension of chemistry content. In this case, instruction was differentiated in that students used elaborative strategies only when they were needed, although materials overall were the same for all students. For a similar example of cooperative learning with science content (Sormunen et al., 2020), see the *Research Highlight*.

Differentiated Curriculum Enhancements Peer-mediated interventions such as those just described, where all students proceed through the same classroom materials, which can be implemented differently depending on learner need (time to practice specific information, use of mnemonics), have been referred to as "differentiated curriculum enhancements" (Mastropieri et al., 2006; Regan et al., 2015). One advantage of this model is that it allows for differentiation without providing qualitatively different materials for different students. Similarly, you can implement it through the creation of activities of different difficulty levels, which are then completed by tutoring pairs. Mastropieri et al. (2006) developed materials for the "Scientific Method" unit for inclusive middle school science classes. For example, for the "Experimental Design" activity, students in small groups of two or three read research scenarios (e.g., an experiment involving plant growth) and matched independent (e.g., fertilizer) with dependent (e.g., plant height) variables for Level 1 activities. For Level 2, students independently produced the variables and hypotheses, with prompting when needed. Finally, students produced the names of variables and hypotheses without any prompting (Level 3). Various gamelike activities were employed for all levels. Because all students moved through all levels of all activities, there was no stigma associated with the lower-level materials. Students in classes employing these differentiated curriculum enhancements enjoyed learning scientific methods and significantly outperformed students in comparison conditions. Simpkins et al. (2009) found that similar

Research Highlight

Project-Based Cooperative Learning Using Integrated Science, Engineering, Math and the Arts

Inclusive classroom teachers face many challenges engaging while promoting learning with all students. Instructional strategies are required that accommodate all learners, including those with disabilities. Some classwide strategies have been shown to benefit students with and without disabilities. Hands-on activities (Lee & So, 2015; Scruggs et al., 2017), cooperative learning activities (Gillies, 2015; see Chapter 9, this volume), peer tutoring (see Chapter 9), and differentiated instruction (see Chapter 6) have all shown to have positive benefits for students with and without disabilities. Sormunen et al. (2020) combined elements of these strategies along with daily teacher-directed reflected discussions in a long-term learning unit. These researchers implemented a project-based learning (PBL) intervention designed to deliver appropriate instruction to all middle school students in inclusive science classes to maximize student learning and engagement. This qualitative study focused on 11 students age 12–13 (7 males, 4 females) who were assigned to one team, although 44 students, of whom one out of six were identified as having learning disabilities, took part in the overall class project. The teacher-developed content integrated science, engineering, math, and the arts in a project resulting in the construction of a scale model house. One vocational assistant, one special education teacher, and two general education teachers were assigned to the participating class. Pairs of students who had differentiated assignments were assigned to work together within each larger group.

There were multiple sessions scheduled for the PBL project starting with an introduction, which included students completing questions about who they might like to be or not be grouped with, technology to be employed, overview of electricity, and future involvement with reflection and reporting components. The second session introduced student groups, followed by pairs within those groups. In the next session, teams observed and categorized observations and knowledge about electricity, followed by teacher and student questioning. In the next session, students focused on acquiring information based on pairs' assigned subprojects and drafted their reports. In the next few sessions, students received teacher feedback and finalized their reports. Partners presented reports to their team who then compared all plans and uploaded them to a prespecified digital space. Then teachers provided additional feedback while partners drafted plans and made sketches for their respective assignments. The next several sessions always started with teacher feedback on student reports and progress. In addition, pairs worked on their subtopics by researching and then creating, for example, the building construction, the electricity plans, the landscaping, or the interior designs. Throughout the project, teachers led students in reflective discussion near the end of each session with questions such as: Were you able to do the task? Was the task challenging and fun? Did you use technology? Did you work well with your partner and all team members? Teachers guided students during the reflective discussions.

Data sources include students' digital notes and videos of reflective discussions. Qualitative data analyses revealed two major themes supporting both the process and social interactions. Process support was required at the beginning of the project and each session to assist students to decide what activities to undertake next. Content guidance was also implemented as needed such as "You [electricians] should plan how to do wiring to the house so that the interior designers can continue their work" (Sormunen et al., 2020, p. 703). Positive feedback was also consistently implemented. Teachers provided social interaction support with guidance on cooperation, leadership, and negotiation skills. When required, teachers spoke directly to individuals, for example, "Can you [student name] take guidance from [student name], or do you need my help, or do you want me to give you some other work during this project?" (Sormunen et al., 2020, p. 703). Some groups required little cooperation support after the first couple of sessions. Those groups succeeded because the pairs cooperated with one person leading or partners successfully sharing leadership roles. One group, however, required more ongoing teacher support because no true leader assumed that role. Findings indicated this PBL unit successfully included students with disabilities into building a model house. Students with and without disabilities appeared to gain from the integrated content unit. Finally, the teacher-directed reflective discussions appeared to benefit both students with and without disabilities.

QUESTIONS FOR REFLECTION

1. Why do you think daily teacher-directed reflective discussion benefited students with and without disabilities in learning cooperation skills and content?

Research Highlight

Project-Based Cooperative Learning Using Integrated Science, Engineering, Math and the Arts—*continued*

2. Do you think the idea of providing students a survey to obtain their ideas of who they would and would not like to work with was a good idea as a first step in organizing student groupings? How would you form cooperative groups with learning partners in your class?
3. What type of content or integrated content areas would you like to design a similar unit for students with and without disabilities?

Figure 15.8 What Is Molarity?

What is molarity?

Concentration of a solute in a solution; moles per liter.

If your partner is correct, go to⇒
If your partner doesn't know the answer, review the strategy.

Strategy: Think of the word "moles" for mole, and remember the picture of a number of moles in solution, to remember molarity is the concentration of a solute in a solution, in moles per liter.

Then ask: *What is the strategy to remember molarity?*

Then ask again: *What does molarity mean?*

⇒ Then ask:
What else is important about molarity?

[Answers include: molarity is a ratio, moles of solute divided by liters of solution]

Source: From Scruggs and Mastropieri (2002), p. 19. Copyright 2002 by the Division for Learning Disabilities. Reprinted with permission.

materials using gamelike formats (e.g., similar to Jeopardy, Concentration, Sorry) on two levels (Level 1: identification; Level 2: production) significantly increased learning of the content in the "Earth/Space" and "Light and Sound" units in an inclusive fifth-grade class. See Regan et al. (2015) for the game directions of these differentiated materials.

Content acquisition podcasts (CAPs) (Kennedy et al., 2014) are another means of differentiating student learning of concepts and vocabulary across the curriculum. CAPs are 10- to 15-minute, multimedia-based instructional modules designed with principles of universal design for learning and Mayer's (2009) cognitive theory of multimedia learning (see a sample at https://vimeo.com/143387419). Each module is focused on at least one, but up to three, related vocabulary terms or concepts at a time. The sequence of slides in each module aligns with explicit teaching practices and the SCREAM variables (see Chapter 6). Teacher-led vocabulary instruction includes (1) reviewing key background knowledge, (2) providing a student-friendly definition, (3) teaching relevant examples or nonexamples, (4) highlighting and teaching morphological features of the term, (5) comparing and contrasting the term with semantically related terms, and (6) repeating the definition (Kennedy et al., 2018). Since the content is in a module, students can access the CAPs and repeatedly review material as needed. When high school students with learning disabilities used CAPs, they learned information quickly and acquired vocabulary knowledge in social studies and in science (e.g., VanUitert et al., 2020).

Adapting Activities-Oriented Approaches in Science and Social Studies

Learning Objective 15.2 Discuss considerations and appropriate adaptations for teaching life science, earth science, and physical science activities and ways to adapt social studies activities for diverse learners.

Rather than relying primarily on textbooks, you can develop conceptual understanding of science and social studies with an activities-oriented approach to teaching. Research has indicated that activities-oriented approaches frequently produce superior learning in general education science and social studies classes (Chiappetta & Koballa, 2014; Parker & Beck, 2021). Some research indicates that activities-oriented approaches may be very beneficial for students with disabilities when sufficient support is provided (Brigham et al., 2011; Scruggs et al., 1993). Some of the advantages of activities-oriented approaches to science and social studies education are that they deemphasize vocabulary learning and dependence on learning from the reading of textbooks (areas of relative difficulty for many students with disabilities). In addition, activities provide direct interaction with concrete, meaningful materials (areas of relative strength for many students with disabilities) (Mastropieri et al., 1998). See the *Diversity, Equity, and Inclusion in the Classroom* feature for how an activities-oriented approach may also encourage girls of racial-ethnic groups to engage more in science. Two potential disadvantages to an activities approach are difficulty adjusting to the less-structured atmosphere of activities-oriented instruction and the fact that some students may exhibit difficulty with the inductive thinking often associated with such instruction (Scruggs & Mastropieri, 2013a).

Students who take alternate assessments based on alternate achievement standards have also participated in science activities. Knight et al. (2012) described how primary-grade students with autism spectrum disorder were taught relevant science content (e.g., *living*, *wet*, *rock*) using hands-on materials and direct teaching of instances and noninstances and were later able to generalize to novel objects. Browder (2015) described teaching students with moderate and severe disabilities early concepts in earth science (e.g., causes of earthquakes, properties of soil) using pictures and direct teaching and prompting (see also Jimenez et al., 2014, for a science study with students with autism and intellectual disabilities).

Students with disabilities may require adaptations and support when undertaking activities-oriented approaches to science and social studies learning (Courtade et al., 2021; Melber & Heller, 2010). However, there are many different types of activities, and these activities may require different adaptations. The following sections describe adaptations that may help you more effectively include your students with disabilities in science and social studies activities.

Diversity, Equity, and Inclusion in the Classroom

Girls in Science

In spite of the fact that females often earn equal or better grades than males throughout the school years (O'Dea et al., 2018), women, particularly those from diverse racial-ethnic groups, remain underrepresented in science, technology, engineering, and mathematical (STEM) fields. If achievement in STEM is not the source of this underrepresentation, another possibility is that underrepresentation can be understood better through the perspective of *identity* (Kang et al., 2019). That is, some students, even when successful in STEM-based subjects, still do not identify with STEM fields, nor do they see themselves in these professional roles.

To better understand the role of identity in girls across racial-ethnic groups, Kang et al. (2019) surveyed a large sample of middle school students in low-income communities in four midwestern states. They asked girls about their science experiences in home settings, school science settings, and out-of-school settings (such as after-school activities, summer programs, and field trips) and their self-perception in relation to science. They found that girls' self-perception in relation to science was the best predictor of the degree to which they identified with STEM-related careers. In turn, their self-perception in science was most greatly influenced by science experiences in multiple settings. Although levels of participation in science experiences differed across racial-ethnic groups, these experiences had similar influences on girls' self-perceptions in science. Kang et al. concluded that expanding girls' experiences in science at home, in school, and out of school during middle school could help improve their positive self-perception in and with STEM.

In a related investigation, Stevenson et al. (2021) studied the effects of an outdoor science education (OSE) program on science achievement of fifth-grade girls and boys. OSE experiences are thought to promote science learning by providing, for example, authentic experiences in natural settings, group learning activities, and opportunities to connect science concepts across disciplines. In this study, 21 fifth-grade teachers and 403 students from a southeastern state participated in "Muddy Sneakers," a standards-based OSE program that incorporated experiential learning, environmental literacy, and making connections to the natural world. Activities took place in the schoolyard and nearby natural areas such as state parks and were provided about once per month during full school days. Topics addressed included life science such as ecosystems, inheritance and adaptation, and living systems; earth science such as weather and landforms; and physical science including force and motion and matter and energy. These lessons typically included an outdoor hike, a relevant hands-on science investigation, writing in science journals, exploring nature, and reflecting on the day's activities. Students were divided into small groups of about 12 students and taught by special OSE educators and supervised by classroom teachers.

At the end of the school year, results were compared with a matched group of control students. Although all students reported gains in science knowledge, it was found that the girls who had participated in the OSE program improved in their science grades throughout the year, while girls in the control condition declined over the same period. This finding was true for girls of all racial-ethnic groups. These results were thought to be of particular interest because this is the age at which girls' interest in science may begin to decline. Stevenson et al. (2021) concluded that OSE activities may be effective in helping engage girls in science.

Discuss: Can you identify additional teaching approaches that may effectively engage girls across racial-ethnic groups in science?

STRATEGIES FOR ADAPTING SCIENCE ACTIVITIES

Students with disabilities can benefit greatly from the authentic learning experiences afforded by science activities, and many of these activities can be adapted to accommodate diverse learning needs (Scruggs & Mastropieri, 2013a, 2013b). When planning activities-oriented instruction in science, consider both general accommodations as well as adaptations targeted to the specific disability area and the specific science activity. Both general and specific adaptations are described in the sections that follow. Many of these suggestions are described in more detail by the American Printing House for the Blind (2006); Dion et al. (2000); Mastropieri and

Scruggs (1993); Melber and Heller (2010); Pence et al. (2003); Rule et al. (2011); Scruggs and Mastropieri (1994, 1995a, 1995b, 2013a); and Scruggs et al. (2017).

EMPLOY PRINCIPLES OF UNIVERSAL DESIGN FOR LEARNING Burgstahler (2012) describes the application of universal design for learning (UDL) principles for making science labs accessible to students with disabilities. Arguing that UDL should be proactive when possible, she argues for science labs that already contain adjustable-height workstations, for example, so accommodations will not be needed for future students who use wheelchairs. Other UDL suggestions include providing both written and verbal instructions, demonstrations, and visual aids; using large-print, high-contrast materials for laboratory signs and equipment labels; maintaining wide aisles and uncluttered work areas; and acquiring lab products that can be used by students with a variety of abilities, such as nonslip mats, support stands, tactile models, and plastic rather than glass lab products.

King-Sears and Johnson (2020) described the application of UDL instruction and materials for high school students with and without learning disabilities in chemistry. Students were learning how to calculate molar conversions. For students who received the UDL intervention, the researchers provided explicit instruction and used materials and technologies that align with the UDL framework. The UDL features that provided students with multiple means of representation and expression included visual diagrams, six interactive videos for explicit demonstration of problems, a student workbook with slides from each video clip, and a mnemonic strategy. Students with and without learning disabilities who received the UDL intervention showed significant improvement from pretest to posttest and they outperformed those students who did not receive the UDL intervention. In addition to instructional video models, technologies such as video games have also enhanced teaching and student learning in chemistry (see Marino et al., 2013).

Most of the methods and materials described in this section meet criteria for UDL because they provide assistance for a variety of student needs and abilities yet, in most cases, can be used by all students.

DEVELOP GENERAL LABORATORY PROCEDURES AND PRECAUTIONS Many adaptations can be implemented that enable students with all types of disabilities to be more active participants in science. As you think through the activity process, review the PASS variables: **P**rioritize all objectives and determine whether all objectives are necessary (e.g., Are lab activities such as slide-staining important objectives, or is observing cellular structure the most important objective?). Then, **A**dapt materials, the environment, instructional procedures, or assessment methods as needed to ensure success for all students. Next, use the SCREAM variables (e.g., **Structure, Clarity, Redundancy**) to maximize the effectiveness of your teaching. Finally, **S**ystematically evaluate whether your instruction has been successful. After considering these PASS variables (see Chapter 6), consider a number of general procedures to address diverse learning needs.

List Rules Explain, post, and strictly enforce laboratory rules. Speak privately with students when necessary. Have a "cooling-off" place in the room designated for any students who are unable to manage their behavior. Generously use praise to reinforce following of the science lab rules.

Ensure Safety Because safety is a major concern when using scientific equipment and materials, stabilize all scientific equipment and materials to avoid unnecessary spills. Velcro can be used to attach lighter objects to tables or trays, and string and trays can be used to hold larger and heavier objects. Use large, clear labels on all equipment and materials, including Braille labels when needed for students with visual impairments. Be sure there is sufficient space for easy mobility and access to materials around the room and lab tables for all students, including those with physical and visual disabilities.

Give Clear Directions Be sure directions are clearly communicated, are parallel in construction, and follow a step-by-step process. List directions on the board or slides so students can refer to them easily. Color-code tasks by order of importance. For instance, tasks written in red must be completed by all students, whereas tasks written in other colors may be less important. Provide adapted lab booklets that contain extra lines or spaces for writing or drawing examples of specimens. Make Braille and textured versions of lab booklets or use text-enhancement or text-to-speech software when necessary. Furnish checklists of what needs to be accomplished in lab to assist students who have difficulties in completing longer tasks. Frequently check on student progress during lab activities. If students are working in cooperative groups, verify that students with disabilities are active participants rather than observers while their peers complete all activities.

Enhance Stimulus Value Implement closed-circuit television (CCTV) to ensure that students with vision problems can see all phenomena being observed in labs. CCTV can show enlarged versions of anything being studied. Acquire extra lighting and magnifying lenses to help visibility when needed during lab activities. For example, a "Big Eye Lamp" (Mattingly Low Vision) is available that consists of a high-intensity light with a large magnifying lens attached. Use of such a device can enhance viewing of small objects for all students but may be especially beneficial for students with low vision. It may also be helpful for students with less well-developed fine motor skills, for example, when removing small animal bones from an owl pellet. Use video recordings to reinforce relevant concepts and provide redundancy; use or create descriptive video presentations that include audio descriptions of what's happening in the video for students who cannot see a television monitor clearly. Acquire extra microphones, stethoscopes, or tuning forks that can help students with hearing impairments hear or feel vibrations during various activities.

Prepare for Spills Prepare areas for spills by having plenty of cleanup materials handy. Place tarps on the floor before engaging in activities that may result in spills. This will save the floor or carpets and help keep custodians on your side. Have students bring in extra-large shirts that can be worn as "lab coats" that will protect their clothing in case of spills. Put felt on desk surfaces that are particularly slippery to help stabilize materials. Use trays, slatted trays, or small tubs to hold smaller items on students' desks. Anchor these trays or receptacles with bags of sand or marbles to reinforce and stabilize their positions. The trays and tubs will reduce the area of any potential spills.

MAKE ADAPTATIONS FOR TEACHING LAB SKILLS All students, including those with disabilities, benefit greatly from participating in lab activities. To ensure successful participation, prepare activity-specific adaptations, as discussed next.

Measuring and Pouring Obtain adaptive equipment for measuring and pouring activities. The Lawrence Hall of Science at the University of California at Berkeley developed many materials to help students with visual and physical disabilities. Some of these materials were included in the curriculum materials Science Activities for the Visually Impaired/Science Enrichment for the Learners with Physical Handicaps (SAVI/SELPH), which were later incorporated into the Full Option Science System for all students (FOSS Next Generation, available through Delta Education). All of their adapted materials include enlarged labels in print and Braille formats. Some specific adapted materials include enlarged type and Braille on enlarged rulers and number lines, enlarged syringe-like devices for measuring, enlarged graduated cylinders for measuring and pouring activities, and larger balance scales containing a plastic guide that students with visual or cognitive impairments can touch to determine whether the sides of the scale are equivalent.

Balancing and Weighing Obtain simpler and larger scales and balances for weighing materials. The Vox-2 Talking Scale (Assistech Special Needs) weighs objects up to 11 lbs (about 5 kg) in one of four languages. Devise your own measuring adaptations to suit the activities in your class. For example, a spring scale with raised markers can be made suitable for students with visual impairments. When repeatedly using a specific measure on rulers, place a piece of tape or a rubber band on the exact measure required to help students with motor or cognitive difficulties be more precise with measuring. Substitute three-dimensional articles made of different textures so that students with visual impairments can feel objects that others are able to see to explore weight, texture, and simple measurements.

Charting/Graphing and Recording Data Most activities in science and social studies require students to record their observations on some type of chart, graph, or pictorial or in narrative format. Students with disabilities may require some pre-instruction with the specific charting or recording procedures for your class. Pre-familiarize students with various types of charts and graphs, such as graph paper, bar charts, frequency charts, and histograms, using very concrete examples. Some of the materials in the Science and Technology for Children (STC; available from Carolina Biological Supply Company) and the Activities for Integrating Math and Science (AIMS; Education Foundation) curricula contain excellent lessons for use in teaching pre-skills in graphing, charting, and recording data. Try using some familiar topics to construct class graphs, such as students' favorite television programs.

Use larger graph paper for students with motor or visual difficulties. Label charts and graphs or use paper that has guidelines for students with reading and writing difficulties. Replace pencil or pen markings on charts or graphs with felt circles or squares or some other textured materials, such as Velcro, stickers, guide strips from computer paper, Braille dots, or tactile dots, so students with visual and cognitive disabilities can feel the differences in the types of items charted and the quantities associated with each item. Make three-dimensional graphs using clay, tiles, golf tees, pushpins, yarn, chicken wire, and other materials to help students' comprehension. Three-dimensional graphs in larger formats can be more easily made by students with fine motor difficulties. Students with visual impairments may record observations by drawing on a screen board (crayon on paper over a screen), using clay models, or using Braille numbers and raised lines.

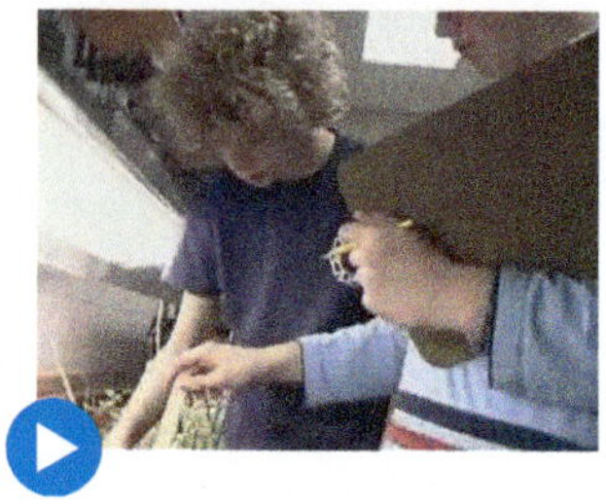

Pearson eTextbook
Video Example 15.4
In this video, middle school students with and without disabilities engage in hands-on activities during life science. What are the benefits to using this activities-oriented approach in science?

Some computer software programs, such as Microsoft Word, have charting and graphing tools and may be especially helpful for students with disabilities. In addition, many computer programs collect, record, and graph data, as do graphing calculators and smartphone and tablet applications. Finally, consider grouping students with and without disabilities to record and graph data cooperatively (see Mastropieri et al., 2006). Peers may be able to assist with some of the more difficult components of the task. However, verify that all students are completing their share of the recording activities and comprehend the relevant concepts.

STRATEGIES FOR
ADAPTING LIFE SCIENCE ACTIVITIES

Life science strands include living things, ecology, cells, genetics, and evolution. Learning for all students, especially those with disabilities, can be greatly enhanced with hands-on activities (Scruggs & Mastropieri, 2013a, 2013b). When teachers consider the following adaptations, students with disabilities may become more actively involved during science activities.

ADAPT PLANT GROWTH AND DEVELOPMENT ACTIVITIES

- Because most household plants die from overwatering and small fish are frequently overfed, set up a strict schedule for watering and feeding classroom plants and pets, using specific amounts of water or fish food. Water syringes may help students deliver the precise amount of water needed by the plant, and food portions can be prepared ahead of time.
- After planting seeds, plan other science activities to do while plants are growing. Because some students may have difficulty sustaining interest or attention over longer time periods, consider using plants that grow and develop quickly. For example, beans normally grow faster and flower sooner than peas. Furthermore, consider acquiring Wisconsin Fast Plants (available from Carolina Biological Supply), which develop much faster than most plants.
- To help students plant seeds at a standard depth, wrap a rubber band around a dowel or pencil for use as a depth gauge.
- To help students directly observe root structure, grow plants in clear plastic baggies or in hydroponic (all-water) containers. Students with visual impairments can also be encouraged to feel the sunlight in relation to a plant and feel the effect of the sunlight on the development of the plant.

ADAPT ACTIVITIES INVOLVING ANIMALS

- Carefully consider the purpose of acquiring classroom animals. Many schools have specific restrictions regarding animals, so it is important to first check out these policies before acquiring any animals.
- Any animals' characteristics or peculiarities need to be noted. For example, hamsters are largely nocturnal and may be less active during school hours. Reptiles must

be kept warm (e.g., with special heaters), or they will not eat, and they may catch "colds" and die. Newts' water must be kept clean or they may not be able to detect the presence of food placed in their tank. Crayfish are prone to diseases that may spread rapidly to other crayfish. Isolate crayfish for 5 days, check for any sign of red tinge to the underside, and quarantine affected crayfish.

- When ordering animals from supply houses, make sure the outdoor climate is appropriate for the animal being shipped, and be certain it will arrive at a time when it can be immediately attended to by an adult and at a time appropriate for the animals. For example, ordering a butterfly kit in the winter may mean releasing them when the weather is too cold for survival.
- Some animals (e.g., reptiles) require live food, so consider the effect this may have on students in your class. Some students with emotional disabilities or other diverse learning needs may react strongly to some animals or to their behaviors. Finally, some students may be disposed to abuse animals in captivity, so be certain to promote an attitude of respect toward living things and ensure that captive animals will be kept safe.

Pearson eTextbook

Video Example 15.5

Students are gathering materials and making observations to determine the behaviors of live worms. How would you prepare students in this science class to ensure that the worms are not harmed?

ADAPT ANATOMY ACTIVITIES

- Various three-dimensional models are available from supply companies, such as the Carolina Biological Supply Company. The *Visible Man/Visible Woman* (Craft House Corporation) also provides concrete information on anatomy. However, as with all models, be careful that too much valuable instructional time is not lost on assembling models versus learning relevant concepts. Anatomical models are also available from the American Printing House for the Blind.
- Students with hearing impairments who cannot use a stethoscope may be able to feel a pulse at the carotid or brachial arteries. Students with physical disabilities who cannot run in place can substitute another activity (such as raising or lowering the body from the arms of a wheelchair) to increase heartbeat.
- For students who do not have a good sense of their own bodies (e.g., younger students, students with cognitive or intellectual disabilities, or some students with emotional disturbance), use photographs, videos, and mirrors to reinforce body image.

ADAPT MICROSCOPE ACTIVITIES Microscope activities can be interesting and accessible to a wide variety of learners. Browder (2015) described how students with moderate and severe disabilities were able to view microscopic images of a living leaf and a silk leaf, then make comparisons. When acquiring microscopes, consider the Brock Magiscope® (Brock Optical). This sturdy microscope is simple to use and maintains sufficient light even when it is moved around (see also the Wolfe® Wonderscope™, available from Carolina Biological Supply). Digital microscope images can also be displayed on large monitors for students with visual or physical impairments or can be printed from the screen and made into three-dimensional images. Projection microscopes (e.g., from Cosmo Laboratory Equipment) can project a large image from a slide onto a screen where they can be viewed by the whole class. Projected images can be copied on paper with a raised-line writing tool such as the Hi-Mark pen so that images can be experienced tactually. When microscopes are not available, or their use is not practical, acquire large color pictures or three-dimensional models of the microscopic objects being studied. For example, Carolina Biological Supply Company supplies three-dimensional plant and animal cells that present cross-sectional layers of cell structure. A quick Internet search can yield relevant photographs and video presentations of microscopic organisms, and many relevant science apps are available for smartphones and tablets. YouTube provides many videos of microscopic specimens that may be useful in enforcing relevant concepts.

CONSIDER HEALTH ISSUES Students who have asthma or serious allergies may react negatively to dander in animal fur or to molds or pollens in plants. Consider the health needs of all students before including specific animals or plants in the classroom.

STRATEGIES FOR
ADAPTING EARTH SCIENCE ACTIVITIES

Earth science covers meteorology, astronomy, geology, and oceanography. Many relevant activities can be conducted in the classroom to enhance comprehension in these areas. Unlike in life sciences, students may be unfamiliar with many of the concepts and terms used, so be sure that relevant vocabulary is being learned.

ADAPT WEATHER ACTIVITIES

- Some concepts, such as humidity or air pressure, may be more difficult for younger students or students with intellectual impairments. Use students' prior knowledge of, for example, hot showers versus dry oven heat and traveling in an airplane or a fast elevator, to make the concepts more meaningful.
- Place a barometer in a glass container with a rubber top to demonstrate changes as a function of pressure generated by pushing or pulling on the rubber top.
- The American Printing House for the Blind offers adapted and talking thermometers and tactile rulers and yardsticks to assist students with visual impairments.

ADAPT ROCKS AND MINERALS ACTIVITIES

- Some versions of the FOSS materials noted earlier feature an activity titled "Mock Rocks." The teacher creates "rocks" composed of such ingredients as water, flour, aquarium gravel, crushed oyster shells, and food coloring. These are mixed, formed into rock shapes, and allowed to dry; teachers could also acquire these or similar materials and create their own "rocks." In class, students physically disassemble these rocks into component parts, enforcing the concept that rocks are composed of many other components. Activities such as this may be particularly helpful for students with cognitive or intellectual impairments.
- Models of sedimentary rock can be created from different-colored layers of sand or gravel, in white glue and water or plaster of Paris. Use of alternate layers can represent the layers of rock built up over time.
- Many specimens and models of rocks and minerals are available from supply companies. Generally, larger, loose specimens are preferable to smaller examples glued on a card. Students with visual impairments should be able to feel many properties of minerals, including heft, cleavage (see, especially, mica), fracture, and crystal faces. If students feel a specific place on a mineral before a scratch test, it may be possible to feel the scratch. It may be more difficult for students with visual impairments to detect color, luster, and streak, but students with some vision may detect these properties with enhanced illumination or magnification.

STRATEGIES FOR
ADAPTING PHYSICAL SCIENCE ACTIVITIES

Physical science activities can include sound, magnetism and electricity, force and motion, light, and powders, mixtures, and solutions.

ADAPT PHYSICS OF SOUND ACTIVITIES

- Students can observe and compare sounds made by different objects and conduct experiments on variations in the tension, thickness, and length of strings, cords, and rubber bands. Students may also examine the effect of sound-producing devices in vacuum chambers.
- Students with hearing impairments may have specific difficulties with this content area. For students with some hearing, amplification may be helpful. It may also be helpful to ensure that no other sound is detectable in the classroom other than the one being observed.
- In many cases, students with severe hearing loss may be able to feel the vibrations in different sound-producing objects. Carefully place tuning forks in water after being struck to demonstrate the vibrations in water. When using "waterphone bottle" (bottles filled with different levels of water) activities, indicate the level of the water with rubber bands placed around the bottles for students with visual impairments.

ADAPT MAGNETISM AND ELECTRICITY ACTIVITIES

- Students can make simple connections from batteries to small motors and light bulbs, identify conductors and insulators, and create series and parallel circuits, electromagnets, and telegraphs. Some science activities encourage students to find insulators and conductors by connecting circuits. Monitor these activities carefully and be certain that classroom wiring and outlets are inaccessible.
- Adapt electricity boards with alligator clips and battery holders to make them easier to work with. These adapted boards may be beneficial for students with visual and physical disabilities, as well as any students who lack well-developed fine motor skills. For students with more severe physical disabilities, wires can be permanently attached to most connections.
- For students who cannot see whether light bulbs are lighted, substitute small electric motors, which can be heard when they are connected to a battery. When using electric motors with students with hearing impairments, attach a small paper flag to the rotor so that the movement can be observed when the power is connected.
- When constructing telegraphs, connect a light bulb to flash, so that the message can be observed by students with hearing impairments.
- Students with intellectual disabilities and younger students may have less well-developed preconceptions about electricity—for example, the battery as a power source, the current that travels through a conductor, and the concept of a "circuit." Pre-teaching some of these concepts may be helpful.

ADAPT FORCE AND MOTION ACTIVITIES

- Force and motion activities include investigations with simple machines (such as levers and pulleys), pendulum motion, and rubber band–propelled airplanes. The concepts presented in force and motion activities are more abstract than they are in some other subjects; therefore, some concept-enhancement activities may be helpful for students with lower cognitive or intellectual functioning. Provide and practice many examples from students' experiences of new concepts as they are investigated.
- See-saws, hammers, rakes, and crowbars are good examples of levers; ramps and slides are good examples of inclined planes; playground swings and pendulum clocks are good examples of pendulums. Demonstrate how the principles learned in class generally apply to these more familiar objects.

ADAPT POWDERS, MIXTURES, AND SOLUTIONS ACTIVITIES

- An important first consideration for creating mixtures and solutions—and examining chemical properties and observing chemical changes such as saturation, concentration, and separation—is safety. Make certain that all students, including students with disabilities or other diverse learning needs, are familiar with specific rules about handling relevant materials. Such rules may include the following: never taste anything, clean up spilled substances immediately, avoid direct contact with the substances unless supervised, avoid blowing (or sneezing) into the powders, and use heat sources only with teacher supervision.
- Mixing substances together often produces some sound, such as fizzing. Encourage students to employ their hearing when making observations. Stethoscopes or microphones can be used to amplify the sound.
- Students with visual impairments can be encouraged to feel powders and substances that are not harmful to touch. Additionally, students can feel paper or other filters before and after mixtures and solutions have passed through them.
- For students with physical disabilities and fine or gross motor difficulties, determine whether measuring and pouring are essential parts of that particular activity. If not, perhaps these students can concentrate more on the more central aspects of the activity and rely on peers for measuring and pouring liquids. If measuring and pouring liquids are important and spilling is a concern, have students pour inside a sink or in a larger container, and practice with smaller quantities first.

STRATEGIES FOR
ADAPTING SOCIAL STUDIES ACTIVITIES

Social studies activities can address motivational problems and negative reactions to independent textbook-based assignments for students who have problems with reading or writing. These activities might include producing plays, reenacting historical events, creating maps, preparing foods from other cultures and historical periods, making historical or cultural dioramas, and interacting with experts on cultural events or historical periods. Students can also engage in discussion or debate about current issues or historical events and interact with virtual museums. Finally, students can participate in field trips to museums or historical sites. Overall, social studies activities ordinarily may not involve such a wide range of different materials and equipment as activities in science, and therefore fewer overall specific adaptations may be considered. General recommendations are noted in the following section and are also found in Okolo, Bouck, et al. (2011); Okolo, Englert, et al. (2011); Okolo and Ferretti (2014); Parker and Beck (2021); Scruggs & Mastropieri, 2011.

SUPPLEMENT TEXTBOOK-BASED INSTRUCTION As suggested throughout this book, whole-class teaching devoted solely to textbooks and worksheets is not an optimal way of addressing the diverse needs of students. Instead, use concrete activities, multimedia presentations, student projects, and technological applications whenever possible. As an example, elearningindustry.com provides 29 free U.S. history iPad apps. For additional descriptions of technology that can supplement textbooks in science and social studies, see the *Apps for Education* feature.

Because disability awareness is very much a social issue, plan lesson content in this area as a component of the social studies curriculum. Many significant historical characters either had disabilities themselves or were very concerned with promoting the rights of individuals with disabilities—for example, Alexander Graham Bell, Franklin Roosevelt, Dorothy Dix, Harriet Tubman, and Sylvia Walker (see, e.g., the website of the Disability Social History Project at disabilityhistory.org).

MAKE ADAPTATIONS FOR SPECIFIC SOCIAL STUDIES ACTIVITIES

- When planning meals from other cultures or historical periods, consider whether any of your students have specific food allergies.
- Role-play and reenactment activities can be supplemented with video recordings of the events being role-played to enhance understanding. Keep in mind students' disabilities when assigning roles; for example, in reenactments, plan or adapt appropriate roles for students with mobility impairments.
- In geography, relief maps may be helpful not only for students with low vision but also for other students who may need assistance in understanding the representative function of maps. Braille maps, raised globes, and illuminated globes are also available to assist students with visual impairments.
- Prepare students for visitors who come into the classroom to demonstrate, for example, instruments, clothing, lifestyles, and habits from different countries. Some students may need additional preparation in appropriate attending skills and suitable questions to ask.

MAKE ADAPTATIONS FOR DIVERSE LEARNING NEEDS FOR FIELD TRIPS Field trips can often allow students to obtain firsthand exposure to people and things that they may not be able to experience in the classroom. In addition to museums and zoos, field trips can include visits to historical sites, living farms, archeological sites, weather stations, observatories, and public parks, to name only a few possibilities. Many students with disabilities may benefit at least as much as other students, particularly if they have had fewer relevant background experiences or when they can benefit particularly from the enhanced stimulus value and added concreteness of the experience. Planning and supervision can ensure the field trip is a positive experience.

- Call the facility in advance and inform the staff that you will be attending and any diverse learning needs your students may have. Advance visitation and planning will help you provide the necessary supports for students' needs.
- Students with visual impairments may require modifications or adaptations in lighting, printed materials, video presentations, seating arrangements, and any visually presented information.

Science and Social Studies Apps

Spatial organizers help make content more concrete and more familiar to students when studying science and social studies. Graphic organizers can be used in almost any content area. They can also be used to teach sequences of events and cause-and-effect relationships, to compare and contrast ideas or concepts, or to illustrate hierarchies. Organizers can be used as story webs during the brainstorming phase of writing papers. Graphic organizers can be developed as story maps that include specific details to facilitate comprehension and learning about historical figures, major events, and historical themes. They can be used to develop hierarchies of important to least-important content in science and social studies. Graphic organizers can also be used to design study guides to accompany content-area textbooks.

Organizers can take many forms. Diagramming Apps, LLC provides assistance in developing graphic organizers, webs, brainstorming, diagramming, outlining, and prewriting strategies. These apps include *Inspiration® Maps* for age 10 to adult and *Kidspiration® Maps* for grades 1–5. The applications allow users to build diagrams, concept maps, outlines, flow charts, and graphic organizers. Built-in templates can be adapted to suit needs and also offer the flexibility to allow users to create custom-made templates and designs. Directions for developing organizers are fairly clear, and students who have some facility with common everyday technology use and various software programs typically experience little difficulty in developing organizers independently.

Both *Inspiration Maps* and *Kidspiration Maps* have extensive libraries of graphics and built-in symbols that can be integrated within diagrams to help make the information even more concrete and meaningful to students. Libraries of content areas—such as animals, foods, shapes, or plants—organize colored graphics. Users can also import graphics of their own from personal photos or from the Internet. The technology also offers a wide range of fonts and colors that can be changed during production of an organizer. Various fonts and colors can be used to highlight specific organized details within a single graphic organizer. Both programs have features that enable users to switch from diagrams to outlines and vice versa very easily and are printable in either format. Users can share files with other apps and with other iPads through AirDrop, Dropbox, or iCloud. Visit diagrammingapps.com for additional information.

Below are some other apps and online resources to assist student learning of both science and social studies content.

Resource	Description	Content Area
Owl Pellet Activities (Owl Brand Discovery Kits; Carolina Biological Supply) *Virtual Owl Pellet* (https://kidwings.com/virtual-pellet/)	Explore dissection of owl pellets	Life science, biology
PhET Interactive Simulation (University of Colorado Boulder) (https://phet.colorado.edu)	Virtual simulations of science concepts	Physics, chemistry, earth science, biology
Gizmos (ExploreLearning) (https://gizmos.explorelearning.com)	Interactive virtual labs and online simulations	All sciences
Slooh Online Telescope (https://www.education.slooh.com)	Online telescopes all around the world	Earth science, astronomy
Observing with NASA (https://mo-www.cfa.harvard.edu/OWN/index.html)	Control space probes and orbiting telescopes	Astronomy, astrophysics
Solar Walk-3D Solar System model (Vito Technology) (https://vitotechnology.com/apps/solar-walk)	An app with a 3-D model of the solar system	Earth science, astronomy
Scratch (ages 8–16) (https://scratch.mit.edu) *ScratchJr* (Scratch Foundation, Inc.) (ages 5–7)	Online or an app for coding block language	Computer science
U.S History Timeline (DaolSoft Co., Ltd.) (https://play.google.com/store/apps/details?id=com.daolsoft.AmericaHistoryTimeline&hl=en_US&gl=US)	An app of historic events	U.S. history
Google Earth (https://earth.google.com)	A 3-D representation of cities, countries, landscapes, and more	Earth science, geography, civics
ICONS Project (University of Maryland) (https://www.icons.umd.edu)	Virtual simulations including role play of various world topics and events	Government, civics

Figure 15.9 Teacher Guidelines for Field Trips

- Set learning objectives before the trip and discuss them with your students.
- Preview the field trip with students, including the procedures that will be involved and the behaviors they will be expected to exhibit. Obtain handouts of the facility, and preview them with the class.
- Practice any difficult or unusual vocabulary that students will encounter on the field trip to maximize comprehension.
- Discuss the behavioral objectives for the trip, and describe your behavior management plan.
- Assign peer partners, buddies, or helpers when appropriate.
- During the trip, encourage active participation of all students.
- Use familiar and descriptive language whenever possible. Summarize information from the field trip to the students as they participate, and ask them to summarize what they have done.
- When it is not possible to touch or manipulate exhibits, describe sounds, odors, shapes, colors, and textures as much as possible.
- Emphasize multisensory presentations or examples whenever possible.
- Record the field trip using photographs, video, or audio recorders. Edit the recordings and review them with the students after the field trip emphasizing important objectives.
- Make a book of the field trip for the class, or create a book as a class activity, and review it with students.

- Considerations for students with hearing impairments may include the amount of background noise, seating, distance from speaker, interpreters, rate of speaker presentation, effective visual aids, and multisensory experiences, depending on the level of the hearing ability.
- Students with cognitive or intellectual impairments may need preparation or on-site support of teachers, aides, or peers to promote understanding of the information being presented.
- Students with attentional disorders may need assistance focusing attention on relevant exhibits and efficiently sequencing their visit.

Additional guidelines for teachers to consider for field trips are given in Figure 15.9.

When certain field trips seem impractical, consider "virtual field trips" (e.g., virtualfieldtrips .org). These may be useful when the particular location is inaccessible to the class overall, such as visiting different countries or cities. *Google Expeditions* is a virtual reality application that allows users to take trips across the world virtually and explore social studies and science subjects. Users can travel virtually to Mars, visit the oceans, visit different countries, and more by downloading the app and purchasing inexpensive cardboard-based virtual reality sets. Virtual reality or (VR) is an example of immersive learning that allows learners to feel like they are experiencing and interacting in that environment (Carreon et al., 2022). Other video presentations can help provide the class with a realistic experience and help enforce concepts learned in class. The *Khan Academy* (Khan Academy), for example, contains video lessons and exercises in both science and social studies content.

Inquiry Learning in Science and Social Studies

Learning Objective 15.3 Identify ways to use and adapt inquiry-oriented instruction for teaching science and social studies.

Many advocates of science and social studies instruction strongly endorse inquiry and problem-solving approaches to teaching. Inquiry approaches involve the presentation of questions and problems to students with less direct guidance during the problem–solution stages, and such approaches can be a significant component of both activities-oriented and textbook-based learning. Inquiry approaches promote critical thinking skills in addition to increasing content knowledge. In reviews of inquiry-based science teaching (Furtak et al., 2012; Rizzo & Taylor, 2016), researchers have found that inquiry learning was effective in promoting science learning but more effective when teacher directed rather than student directed. For many students with disabilities, teacher-led inquiry could be particularly helpful (Scruggs & Mastropieri, 2011).

STRATEGIES FOR ADAPTING INQUIRY LEARNING ACTIVITIES

PROMOTE ACTIVE THINKING WITH INQUIRY AND DEBATE Ferretti et al. (2001) directed an 8-week, project-based unit in American westward expansion. Fifth-grade students were formed into groups of learners with diverse skills and prior knowledge. In these groups, students collected information and analyzed primary and secondary sources to create multimedia presentations. All of the group activities involved oral reading of the evidence and group discussion. Students were taught about perspectives and asked to provide supported answers for questions such as, What is bias in evidence? How do you know a piece of evidence is biased? and Why do historians have different opinions about things that happened in the past? All students gained in content knowledge as well as in their understanding of historical inquiry. These types of critical questions can encourage students to think about alternative perspectives, understand the inquiry process, and develop argumentative writings (De La Paz, 2005; Ferretti & Fan, 2016).

MacArthur et al. (2002) formed cooperative groups of students in inclusive sixth-grade social studies classes and asked them to represent the historical views of immigrant groups versus nativists (anti-immigration groups) in class debates. Students collected information on these topics and used this information in debates. Results revealed that students with and without disabilities and boys and girls participated equally in the debates, and all students gained similarly in tests of content knowledge. However, MacArthur et al. reported that at times debates seemed more like arguments, and guidance and modeling were necessary to shape the level of debate (see also De La Paz & Wissinger, 2017; Okolo & Ferretti, 2014).

Pearson eTextbook

Video Example 15.6

In this video, the teacher describes how she used an inquiry and problem-solving approach in her second-grade science classroom. What other natural phenomenon could be used to peak students' curiosity and promote critical thinking skills in the content-area classroom?

PROMOTE REASONING WITH GUIDED QUESTIONING Students with disabilities comprehend more and understand better when they actively reason through new information (e.g., Sullivan et al., 1995). For example, in a lesson about penguins, ask students to explain—rather than simply tell them—the fact that some penguins carry their eggs on top of their feet. If they cannot explain immediately, prompt them with directed questions, such as Where do penguins live? What is it like there? and Why would that explain why penguins carry their eggs on top of their feet?

In this case, students can be prompted to use information from their prior knowledge. In other cases (Why do stars twinkle?), additional relevant information may need to be provided.

Guided questioning can promote thinking in science classes containing students with cognitive or intellectual disabilities, as seen in this example of a discussion of the effects of capillary action when white flowers were placed in colored water:

TEACHER: What do you think happened? I have a flower in blue water and a flower in green water, a white flower, right? How did I get the colors there?

KEN: . . . Oh, you watered it with food coloring.

TEACHER: But I didn't put any up here [the flower], did I?

KEN: You put it in the dirt.

TEACHER: But there's no dirt.

KEN: Oh.

TEACHER: How did it get from there to here?

JIMMY: It went all the way up to here.

TEACHER: Went all the way through water? The what, Mary?

MARY: A stem.

TEACHER: The stem. It went all the way through the stem—you're right. (Scruggs & Mastropieri, 1995b, p. 264)

Pearson eTextbook

Video Example 15.7

After the corn stalk inquiry described in Video Example 15.7, the second-grade teacher now promotes student reasoning with guided questioning. What other techniques could she use to develop student thinking?

In social studies subjects, teachers can describe the nature and characteristics of harbors and ask students why it makes sense that many cities are located on or near natural harbors. Or, describe the "fall line" where rivers near the coast are still navigable but move swiftly enough to power industry. Then, show students a physical map and ask them to predict where major cities probably would be located. They can then test their predictions on a political map. (See Scruggs et al., 2011, for other suggestions.)

ADAPT INSTRUCTION FOR DEVELOPMENTAL DIFFERENCES Some students, especially those with intellectual disabilities, may have more difficulty with inductive reasoning tasks (Batshaw et al., 2019). For example, when a fourth-grader with intellectual disabilities was questioned about the nature of air, he said it is cold, windy, and found outdoors (Scruggs et al., 1995, p. 228), a view commonly held by preschoolers (Driver et al., 1994). Consider these possible differences in "preconceptions" or prior understandings when planning inquiry-oriented instruction, and provide additional instruction when needed.

Whereas many normally achieving students can answer higher-level questions with only subtle coaching, students with disabilities may require extensive levels of coaching to draw the same inference or to construct or discover scientific principles (e.g., buoyancy or pendulum movement; Scruggs & Mastropieri, 2007). However, more structured coaching can lead students to draw relevant inferences. For example, show students a number of pendulums with different weights attached, and ask them if they swing at different rates (they do not). Then show students a number of pendulums of different lengths and ask them the same question (the longer pendulums swing more slowly). Then ask them to construct a general rule. Be sure all students have enough time to construct answers for themselves.

In Lee and So's (2015) investigation, teachers used guided-inquiry learning for fifth-grade students with intellectual disabilities to learn science concepts. Adaptations to instruction included using a familiar scenario and sensory stimuli, eliminating extraneous tasks or steps, and prioritizing the number of science concepts. For example, when teaching *permeability*, students were provided an inquiry scenario (avoiding getting wet in the rain), engaged in evidence to respond to the inquiry (students tried out the permeability of different materials), provided explanations from the evidence (plastic blocks water), made connections from new to previous knowledge (rain makes me wet), and communicated the explanation (students chose to use plastic to avoid getting wet from the rain) (Lee & So, 2015, p. 162).

Promote deductive reasoning as well as inductive reasoning in students with disabilities (see Mastropieri et al., 2001). For example, rather than asking students to draw inductive conclusions about pendulum motion, directly provide the "rule" about pendulum motion (e.g., The longer the string, the slower the swing). Next, demonstrate different pendulums and ask students to make predictions (Which one do you think will swing faster, the short one or the long one?). Finally, provide more divergent examples to further promote generalized knowledge of the concept (What can I do to the bob of the pendulum [point to the bob] to make it run faster?).

Although inductive thinking activities have been widely promoted in education for many years, deductive thinking activities are also important and, in some cases, they may provide more realistic thinking activities for some students with disabilities.

15 Summary

- Much learning in science and social studies takes place in the context of textbook learning. Specific strategies can be employed to differentiate instruction for all in these content areas.
  - — Content-enhancement devices are means for increasing recall and comprehension of content information and include the use of graphic organizers, study guides, diagrams, visual-spatial displays, and mnemonics.
  - — Familiarization with text organization and structure can help students understand text content. Students can be taught to incorporate analysis of text structure into their study strategies. Highlighting, outlining, and study guides are also helpful.
  - — Textbooks can be adapted for students with reading problems with such methods as audio-recorded texts, Braille or enlarged-print versions, simplified texts, or modified presentations.
  - — Before assigned readings, students can be familiarized with new vocabulary and provided with advance organizers such as visual-spatial displays, timelines, or concept maps. After assigned readings, students can be provided with reviews and summaries of the readings, practice with peers, and extra help sessions.
- Activities-oriented instruction can be helpful for students who do not learn as well from reading textbooks or who benefit from the enhanced concreteness and meaningfulness afforded by such instruction.
  - — Many adaptations are available for accommodating diverse learning needs in such science activity areas as balancing and weighing, activities with plants and animals, anatomy, microscope activities, weather, rocks and minerals, and activities involving sound and light. These adaptations address specific need areas and can also enhance comprehension of the associated concepts.
  - — Adaptations can also be incorporated into social studies areas, including role play, simulation activities, and field trips.
- Inquiry-oriented approaches to science and social studies, found in both textbook and activities approaches, can also be adapted for students with disabilities. These adaptations include using hands-on materials, implementing carefully structured questioning, redirecting attention, and reinforcing divergent, independent thinking.

PROFESSIONAL STANDARDS LINK: Science and Social Studies

Information in this chapter links most directly to:

- CEC 2020 Initial Practice-Based Professional Preparation Standards for Special Educators (Initial K–12 standards) (see https://exceptionalchildren.org/standards/initial-practice-based-professional-preparation-standards-special-educators): Standards 2 (Understanding and Addressing Each Individual's Developmental and Learning Needs), 3 (Demonstrating Subject Matter Content and Specialized Curriculum Knowledge), 4 (Using Assessment to Understand the Learner and the Learning Environment for Data-Based Decision Making), 5 (Supporting Learning Using Effective Instruction)
- InTASC Standards (see https://www.ccsso.org/sites/default/files/2017-11/InTASC_Model_Core_Teaching_Standards_2011.pdf): 2 (Learning Differences), 3 (Learning Environments), 4 (Content Knowledge), 5 (Application of Content), 7 (Planning for Instruction), 8 (Instructional Strategies)

SCIENCE AND SOCIAL STUDIES

If students are having difficulty learning science and social studies, have you tried the following? If not, see the pages listed here.

STRATEGIES FOR EFFECTIVE TEACHING IN SCIENCE AND SOCIAL STUDIES

- ☐ Use effective teaching strategies, 413
- ☐ Provide content-enhancement strategies, 413–414
- ☐ Use mnemonic strategies, 414–415
- ☐ Adapt worksheet activities, 415

STRATEGIES FOR PROMOTING INDEPENDENT LEARNING FROM TEXTBOOKS

- ☐ Teach study skills strategies for content-area textbooks, 416
- ☐ Teach students to identify text organization, 416–418
- ☐ Teach highlighting and outlining strategies, 418–419
- ☐ Introduce study guides, 419–420
- ☐ Teach learning strategies, 420–421

STRATEGIES FOR ADAPTING TEXTBOOK MATERIALS

- ☐ Promote prereading and postreading strategies, 423
- ☐ Make adaptations for students with visual impairments or severe reading problems, 423–424
- ☐ Promote learning with classwide peer tutoring, 424–428

STRATEGIES FOR ADAPTING SCIENCE ACTIVITIES

- ☐ Employ principles of universal design for learning, 430
- ☐ Develop general laboratory procedures and precautions, 430–431
- ☐ Make adaptations for teaching lab skills, 431–432

STRATEGIES FOR ADAPTING LIFE SCIENCE ACTIVITIES

- ☐ Adapt plant growth and development activities, 432
- ☐ Adapt activities involving animals, 432–433
- ☐ Adapt anatomy activities, 433
- ☐ Adapt microscope activities, 433
- ☐ Consider health issues, 433

STRATEGIES FOR ADAPTING EARTH SCIENCE ACTIVITIES

- ☐ Adapt weather activities, 434
- ☐ Adapt rocks and minerals activities, 434

STRATEGIES FOR ADAPTING PHYSICAL SCIENCE ACTIVITIES

- ☐ Adapt physics of sound activities, 434
- ☐ Adapt magnetism and electricity activities, 435
- ☐ Adapt force and motion activities, 435
- ☐ Adapt powders, mixtures, and solutions activities, 435

STRATEGIES FOR ADAPTING SOCIAL STUDIES ACTIVITIES

- ☐ Supplement textbook-based instruction, 436
- ☐ Make adaptations for specific social studies activities, 436
- ☐ Make adaptations for diverse learning needs for field trips, 436–438

STRATEGIES FOR ADAPTING INQUIRY LEARNING ACTIVITIES

- ☐ Promote active thinking with inquiry and debate, 439
- ☐ Promote reasoning with guided questioning, 439–440
- ☐ Adapt instruction for developmental differences, 440

CHAPTER

16

Transitions

Cavan Images/Offset/Shutterstock

CHAPTER 16

Transitions

LEARNING OBJECTIVES

After studying this chapter, you should be able to:

16.1 Describe the meaning of educational transition and the purpose of planning and designing transition programs for students with disabilities.

16.2 Compare and contrast issues involving transition planning across age levels, including transition to elementary, middle school, high school, and postsecondary environments.

16.3 Discuss the importance of self-advocacy and self-determination skills in transition planning and provide strategies for promoting these skills.

16.4 List and compare strategies for promoting transitions for graduation, future education, job opportunities, and independent living.

Transitions are natural passages in life that happen continually as we move to new schools and new jobs and join new social communities. Students with disabilities typically have more difficulties than do students without disabilities in adjusting to new transitions (Bakken, 2020). Planning for those transitions by making instructional accommodations can promote smoother and more successful transitions for students with disabilities (Weiss & Fagella-Luby, 2020). Planning, designing, and adapting appropriate programs for students with disabilities will allow many individuals to have successful careers and become self-sufficient.

Planning for Transition

Learning Objective 16.1 Describe the meaning of educational transition and the purpose of planning and designing transition programs for students with disabilities.

WHAT DOES TRANSITION MEAN?

Transition is the process of planning for changes throughout a student's life. Most frequently, transition is referred to as the planning for a student's life after high school; however, planning for changes throughout life is a more accurate definition (Strnadová & Cumming, 2016). **Transition programs** help prepare students for changes they will undertake throughout their school years and beyond. Examples of transitions can include changing grade levels or moving from kindergarten to elementary school to middle school to high school to college or vocational training; changing placement from special education to general education settings; obtaining a job; joining recreational activities; or moving to new living arrangements or to a new community (Bouck & Park, 2020).

Preparing students for transitions after high school may include preparation for career and technical education and directions for managing employment, supported living, or independent living arrangements.

Transitions, although exciting and challenging, can be traumatic events. Planning for transitions and preparing students with disabilities for those transitions can eliminate some of the difficult aspects of adjustment.

Diversity, Equity, and Inclusion in the Classroom

Transition Service for Diverse Learners

Students and families/caregivers from culturally diverse backgrounds, including English learners, require additional supports in planning for and implementing transition services. Some families/caregivers may require assistance with English and/or require that interpreters be available while learning new information about potential transition services. In addition, implementing culturally responsive transition practices and planning will require knowledge of each family's and caregiver's cultural background and goals and student preferences, goals, and achievement levels. Unfortunately, family/caregiver involvement in transition planning has too often meant attendance at meetings rather than involvement in them (Wilt et al., 2021). Many transition outcomes associated with dominant cultural beliefs often focus on students gaining supportive or competitive employment or enrolling in postsecondary education followed by successful employment (Suk et al., 2020). However, some cultures value staying with the family/caregiver unit and helping with family/caregiver responsibilities (Chiu & Chow, 2015). Moreover, some students, caregivers, and families facing poverty or low socioeconomic status would never consider postsecondary school options including technical or community colleges due to the expenses involved. In those cases, the transition planning team should offer examples of and assist with obtaining financial resources such as scholarships and grants to cover costs of technical and career education and college (Trainor et al., 2019). Sensitivity toward each student's, caregivers', and family's unique cultural background will help ensure a transition plan will represent not only cultural backgrounds but also academic achievements, transition assessments, and family/caregiver along with personal goals. Using culturally responsive teaching working with students from diverse backgrounds will help familiarize teachers with student and family/caregiver needs.

Systematically approaching these issues can facilitate better communication and understanding with the student, caregiver, and family. Preplanning using the following list will help foster more school, family, caregiver, and child planning for transition services. Always use comprehensible language rather than education jargon when speaking with families and their children.

- *Family/caregiver cultural background.* Do we need to learn more about this caregiver's/family's cultural background?
- *Primary language at home and school.* Do we need to arrange for an interpreter for meetings? Do we need to translate all the transition planning and services information?
- *Student and family/caregiver postsecondary preferences.* Have we provided the family and student with the range of postsecondary options to consider prior to the individualized education program (IEP) transition planning meeting?
- *Student and family/caregiver postsecondary goals.* Have we provided sufficient sample postsecondary goals to facilitate family/caregiver and student understanding?
- *Student academic achievement.* Have we explained the student's academic achievement sufficiently for student and family/caregiver understanding?
- *Financial resources/needs.* Have we provided sufficient information about financial resources that might be available in scholarships, grants, and other forms of financial aid?

Consider, for example, when Su-Sung and her teacher met to discuss her postsecondary options. Su-Sung had strong academic achievement and expressed a desire to pursue some type of higher education. Her teacher presented financial options including scholarships, grants, and financial aid that might be available for Su-Sung to assist in financing college.

However, when the teacher met with Su-Sung's parents and Su-Sung together, her parents had different postsecondary goals in mind for Su-Sung. They envisioned their daughter staying home, helping with family responsibilities, and working in the family's store.

QUESTIONS FOR REFLECTION

1. How do you address this issue with Su-Sung and her family?
2. How could that type of misunderstanding be avoided?
3. How could various options be presented that might satisfy the family and Su-Sung?

The Individuals with Disabilities Education Act (IDEA) defines transition services as coordinating services for students that promote the change from school to postschool. This means IDEA emphasizes only planning for transitions from high school to vocational education, postsecondary education, adult services, independent living, and community participation (Madaus et al., 2011). Transition plans must begin by age 16 (some states require transition planning earlier). The coordination of transition services is based on student preferences, interests, and abilities and includes instruction, experiences in the community, and development of employment, postsecondary, daily living, and vocational objectives. However, it has been found that planning for transitions at all ages promotes the social and emotional well-being of students with disabilities (Bakken & Obiokor, 2020).

Planning for transitions helps prepare students for the expected changes that take place in their lives. The amount of planning for transitions and necessary adaptations varies depending on the type of transition and the severity level of disability. Planning includes involving all individuals who will be affected by the transition, including the student, parents, caregivers, all teachers, transition coordinators, specialists, community representatives, employers, and support personnel (Griffin et al., 2014). It is important to consider cultural, linguistic, and ethnic and racial backgrounds and the important role of the family in planning for transitions. In the *Diversity, Equity, and Inclusion in the Classroom* feature is an example of the important role of family/caregiver in transition planning.

The Office of Special Education and Rehabilitative Services (2020) published a resource guide for postsecondary transition planning that may be beneficial for students, teachers, schools, and parents/caregivers.

Important transitions occur throughout the lifespan (Strnadová & Cumming, 2016), and effective planning for these transitions can significantly improve chances for school success. Qualified infants and toddlers as young as birth to age 3 receive an individual family services plan that includes a plan for promoting transition to preschool settings. These plans and practices begin a process that will continue throughout the elementary and secondary grades.

Promoting Transitions

Learning Objective 16.2 Compare and contrast issues involving transition planning across age levels, including transition to elementary, middle school, high school, and postsecondary environments.

PLAN FOR TRANSITIONS TO KINDERGARTEN AND ELEMENTARY SCHOOL

Many students have a difficult time going to school for the first time. Many young children with disabilities may not have been exposed to many different situations and people. It can also be frightening to move to a new school, teachers, and peers. The new school may be farther from home, which means leaving home earlier in the morning, riding a new school bus, and having a longer school day. Students may become more tired, frightened, and anxious until they feel accepted in the new environment. Preparatory actions can be undertaken to ease transitions where everything is so different; otherwise, students with disabilities may experience difficulties transitioning to the new environment.

From preschool, children with IEPs receive plans for transition to kindergarten or first-grade settings. These plans may include school visits, in which the child is introduced to new teachers and students and provided with activities to promote familiarity with the new setting, such as physically locating entrance and exit ways, restrooms, cafeteria, and location of the new classroom. When needed, accommodations for mobility or sensory needs may need to be implemented such as desk placement and seating arrangements. Familiarity with the new setting can also be promoted with construction of social stories or picture books to help familiarize the child with the new setting. These books can include images of the new teachers the student will meet and the different environments the student will encounter (Bodine, 2020). Meetings may take place between preschool teachers, administrators, caregiver/family members, and teachers in the new setting to facilitate the transition. These meetings can identify school expectations and skills students may need to succeed in the new setting (e.g., standing in line and turn taking) and can allow time for these skills to be practiced prior to

Pearson eTextbook

Video Example 16.1

In this video, two teachers discuss strategies for supporting students' successful transition between grades. What strategies do they share for making the transition as seamless as possible for the students and the teachers who are involved?

transition (Center for Autism Research and The Children's Hospital of Philadelphia, 2020). Preschool teachers can also communicate to teachers in the kindergarten or elementary setting the incoming student's preferred activities, favorite rewards, and/or any behavioral issues the new teachers should be aware of. With careful planning and execution, transition activities can greatly benefit students and school personnel alike.

CLASSROOM SCENARIO

Gabriel

Gabriel was a bright and cheerful fifth-grader. He was making acceptable progress in school in spite of his learning disabilities for which he required additional help from the special education teacher in reading and writing skills. He was a thoughtful and responsible boy who made friends easily. Six months ago, Gabriel transitioned into his local middle school. Since that time, he has experienced difficulties. His assignments are often turned in late or not at all. When they are turned in, they are often incorrectly done. Gabriel seems inattentive in class and often answers "I don't know" when called on. He seems far less cheerful than he did the previous year, and he has generally failed to make new friends in his new setting.

QUESTIONS FOR REFLECTION

1. Why do you think Gabriel is having difficulties in school this year compared to the previous year?
2. What additional information would you need to have in order to help Gabriel?
3. What strategies can you think of now that may be helpful to Gabriel in his new environment?

PLAN FOR TRANSITIONS TO SECONDARY SETTINGS

Transitioning to middle school can be an exciting new prospect for students. However, it can also be a time of great anxiety, particularly for students with disabilities (Chen et al., 2020). Typically, such transitions involve moving from a smaller, simpler, more personal environment to one that is larger, more complicated, and more demanding. Students used to spending much of their day in the same classroom with the same teacher may now find themselves facing several different classrooms, teachers, and students. In addition to moving between different classes and teachers, they may find expectations and rules can vary among classes. The classes themselves are likely to be more demanding, with more homework and a greater emphasis on grades and an expectation of increased responsibility for students' academic and social behavior. Finally, as peer relations become more important for all adolescents concerned with fitting in with peer groups, they may become less inclined to develop friendships or other connections with students with disabilities.

Carter et al. (2005) provided a number of suggestions for smoothing transitions from elementary to middle school for students with disabilities, particularly severe disabilities, which are summarized as follows:

- **Plan early for transition.** As early as fourth grade, consider the requirements for middle school and determine whether individual students are acquiring the skills they will need to successfully make this transition. This may involve collaboration across the elementary and middle school to help determine requirements, programs, and expectations. It is also important to determine what types of supports will be needed in the new setting and communicate these needs to relevant school personnel.
- **Provide students with orientation activities** prior to entering the new setting, for example, attending a school breakfast or basketball game and speaking with school personnel about the new activities they will encounter. Teaching and administrative staff can visit the elementary school and discuss middle school life. Students should also have opportunities to visit the middle school, perhaps shadowing a volunteer to visit classrooms, meet teaching staff, and eat in the cafeteria.

- **Involve family/caregiver members in transition planning** by encouraging them to discuss expectations of the new setting. Older siblings may be particularly helpful in this regard. Families/caregivers can also address upcoming changes in school routine such as earlier starting times and additional time for homework. In order to be most effective, be sure families/caregivers are provided with all relevant information about the new school and can share pictures of the new school and other information with the student.
- **Address organizational issues** that the student will encounter in the new setting, such as lockers, books, schedules, restrooms, and tracking assignments (see Chapter 11). Teachers can discuss these issues prior to the transition, provide instruction or role-play when needed, and develop relevant accommodations, such as a checklist for assignments or a calendar for schedules. Students with physical or sensory disabilities may need specific accommodations in place for the transition to be successful.
- **Develop programs of peer support** within the new setting in which peer assistants sit next to classmates with disabilities and lend support when needed for organization, classroom procedures, and social interaction. For students with more severe disabilities, peer support can include assisting with adapting materials and facilitating interaction with teachers and peers (see Chapter 9). Peer support should also extend to unstructured times such as lunch and changing classrooms.
- **Support school involvement** for students with disabilities in the form of school clubs or other organizations and athletic teams. These activities, when appropriate, could also be included in the student's IEP, along with supports when needed, such as enlisting peer assistance and arranging individual meetings with the faculty club advisor.
- **Promote student independence with self-management** (e.g., Weiss & Fagella-Luby, 2020). Students with disabilities often overrely on others for assistance and need to develop greater self-reliance in order to help themselves meet the challenges of transitioning to middle school. Self-management strategies can help students take more responsibility for their own social and academic behavior, for example managing their time, checking school work against a rubric, using checklists to measure progress on assignments, and initiating interactions with others. Self-advocacy addresses students expressing their needs for accommodations, supports, and other educational rights. These strategies can be taught through practice, role play, and prompting in appropriate situations (for further discussion, see the section "Promote Self-Advocacy and Self-Determination").

Transition from middle school to high school can be a challenging experience for all students (Felmlee et al., 2018), and particularly so for students with disabilities. The high school setting may be larger, coursework becomes more challenging, and additional social, academic, and athletic activities are available. The social environment may have significantly changed from the previous school, and peer relationships may change. Problems with social adjustment, organizational change, and increasing academic rigor can lead to school failure and dropout, which is a higher risk during the first year of high school (Erickson et al., 2013).

Many of the suggestions for transition to middle school may be appropriate for students transitioning to high school. These include orientation activities, transition planning, peer assistance and supports, family and school involvement, and self-management training.

Students making the transition from middle school to high school may face challenges similar to those encountered transitioning to middle school, particularly with respect to new teachers, different peer environments, and more challenging academic standards. Many strategies appropriate for transitioning to middle school are also appropriate for transitioning to high school, including providing orientation activities, enlisting peer support, developing self-management skills, visiting the new setting, and collaboration between middle and high school personnel (Aldosiry et al., 2021). Emphasis on academic achievement and alignment of standards between the two settings is also associated with successful transitions (Erickson et al., 2013).

Of particular importance in making the transition to high school is course scheduling. Many students entering high school are still unaware of their postschool goals and objectives, so it is important for students, family and caregiver members, teachers, and counselors to work together to identify a schedule that will leave options open as the student's postschool objectives become clearer.

Students entering high school may also find that the strategies and accommodations that were effective in middle school have become less so in the high school setting. Teachers should be aware of strategies and accommodations they are currently implementing to meet students' individual learning needs in the transition setting and monitor their effectiveness. Students having difficulties should employ self-advocacy skills to discuss with teachers and counselors additional adjustments that may be helpful in promoting academic achievement. For example, perhaps digital textbooks or other types of assistive technology would be helpful. Likewise, additional work in study skills and self-monitoring of progress on course assignments could help facilitate a smooth transition to high school, as could additional peer support. Overall, maintaining open communication with school personnel, students, and caregivers/families is key to succeeding in the new environment (Erickson et al., 2013).

PLAN FOR TRANSITIONS TO POSTSECONDARY ENVIRONMENTS

Planning systematic transitions to adulthood is vitally important for students with disabilities. All students with disabilities who have IEPs are required to have individual transition plans (ITPs) when they reach the age of 16; many states require the process to begin by age 14. Planning and instruction include teaching students self-advocacy and self-determination skills; planning for future education, such as college or other postsecondary training; planning for future employment opportunities; and preparing students for independent living situations (Weiss & Fagella-Luby, 2020). Planning for transition typically involves the IEP transition team, which includes the student, the parents/caregivers, the special education teacher, at least one general education teacher, other relevant school personnel, and representatives of other service agencies whose services can link school experiences with postsecondary opportunities, such as employment, independent living, or vocational rehabilitation services. Special education teachers take a primary role in developing and implementing transition services. Many schools also include a **transition coordinator**, who is responsible for facilitating transition planning, ensuring all relevant school personnel are informed of transition objectives and methods, and working with interested parties to connect postsecondary goals with appropriate curriculum decisions. General education teachers may help to ensure transition goals are being addressed when appropriate in the general education classroom (Morningstar & Clavenna-Deane, 2018).

Unfortunately, some students are largely unaware of their transition plan and are unsure of how to go about planning for their future. The *Research Highlight* describes the results of interviews of students with learning disabilities regarding their perceptions of their own transition experiences.

PROMOTE TRANSITIONS WITH ASSESSMENT

Assessment for transition consists of collecting information on students from all available sources (Sitlington et al., 2010). This includes the current IEPs, school permanent records, school guidance counselors, formal and informal interviews with students and their caregivers/families, and the answers to formal and informal transition-planning and **occupational surveys**. The collected information is compiled and evaluated by members of the transition team, who then make recommendations for the ITP.

One transition planning inventory addresses the critical transition planning areas required by IDEA. The *Transition Planning Inventory–3rd Edition* (TPI-3; Pro-Ed) contains 57 transition planning statements organized around the IDEA domains on several basic forms: student preferences and interest forms, the home form for parents/caregivers, the profile and further assessment recommendations form, and the summary of performance exit form. Raters indicate their level of agreement on a 5-point scale from strongly disagree to strongly agree with statements relevant to transition, such as knowing how to get a job, manage money, and set goals.

Occupational surveys are also commercially available. For example, the *Occupational Aptitude Survey and Interest Schedule* (OASIS-3; Pro-Ed) assesses whether students like, dislike, or have neutral feelings toward occupations and job activities using a pool of 240 items ranging across 12 vocational domains: artistic, scientific, nature, protective, mechanical, industrial, business detail, selling, accommodating, humanitarian, leading-influencing, and physical performing. Findings from this survey may help develop a more comprehensive transition plan in the postsecondary vocational and educational areas.

Students with Learning Disabilities' Perspectives about Transition Planning

Federal legislation requires that students with all disabilities, including those with learning disabilities, have transition plans as components of their IEPs starting at age 16 or even younger in some states. Students with LD represent the largest group of students served under IDEA but have a reported high school graduation rate of 67.4% in the 2009–2010 year and 77.4% during the 2018–2019 year (U.S. Department of Education, 2021). Students with LD attend college at a rate of 20% compared with 40% of their nondisabled peers (National Center for Education Statistics, 2018). Students and their families should be active participants in transition planning and meetings, which should help increase graduation and college rates. Despite the legal requirements, transition plan outcomes have been less than positive overall in improving students' lives postgraduation (Lipscomb et al., 2017).

To examine this issue, Cavendish et al. (2020) interviewed high school students with learning disabilities about their own school transition experiences to gain an understanding of what students see as effective transition supports. Forty high school students with learning disabilities (52% girls, 48% boys) participated in individual semi-structured interviews. Grade levels represented were 12th (38%), 11th (31%), and 10th (31%). Students were enrolled in general education content-area classes and received special education services during co-taught classes or resource room assistance.

Students represented a range of backgrounds including 2% Asian, 14% White, 30% Black, and 55% Latinx. The interview consisted of four major sections including (1) student choice, (2) supports and testing, (3) planning and transition, and (4) supports, graduation, and future. Interviews were transcribed and analyzed.

Three common themes emerged, including course choice and diploma options, IEP and transition plan involvement, and opportunities to explore college and career transition options. The course choice and diploma options theme revealed students perceived little choice of courses and some expressed limited knowledge about diploma options and how that might impact career choices. For example, some students understood passing the Regents exams in content-area classes meant receiving a Regents diploma, which meant you received the highest-level diploma. Many students, however, indicated passing the Regents exams was difficult. Furthermore, if students failed an exam, they were required to retake the course, which limited their course options. In this sample, students from different schools expressed different levels of knowledge concerning differences in diploma options. All students generally indicated there was little course selection available and would prefer having additional course options.

Many students indicated they did not actively participate in their IEP or transition plan meetings and most seemed unaware of the existence of transition plans. Some students reported the existence of transition goals in transition plans but reported there was no mention of how to attain these goals. A smaller number of students reported a greater awareness of going to college as transition goals and hoping college would provide better learning opportunities. Prospects for visiting colleges for juniors and seniors and investigating career options were possible but as part of general school activities and not specific to transition plans. Internship programs were offered at three schools that exposed students to a particular career for a designated period. Most students reported the internship experiences provided valuable information, regardless of whether they liked or disliked the experience. Although internships experiences were valuable, some students could not afford to have lengthy unpaid internships. In addition, students had to pay for the college visits, which some could not afford. Some schools tried to bring college representatives to their schools, which made interacting with college personnel available to more students. A smaller number of students reported receiving assistance with college applications and financial aid information. Some general courses (e.g., economics) were identified by students as providing content related to jobs, salaries, and finances.

Cavendish et al. (2020) concluded that this study provides evidence that some form of transition planning may take place, but the majority of students in this study did not perceive they were actively involved in transition planning or in their IEP meetings. Moreover, most of the identified transition activities were designed for the entire school, which is good news overall but disappointing news for creating ITPs for students with learning disabilities. Most students indicated more choice in courses is preferable. Schools and teachers need an increased awareness of how family/caregiver financial situations may hinder student participation in transition planning activities and be prepared to make accommodations for such situations.

QUESTIONS FOR REFLECTION

1. Why do you think student perceptions toward transition seem incomplete?
2. How might overall students' perceptions about transition planning and activities be improved?
3. How would you design a process for implementing a transition plan?

Promote Self-Advocacy and Self Determination

Learning Objective 16.3 Discuss the importance of self-advocacy and self-determination skills in transition planning and provide strategies for promoting these skills.

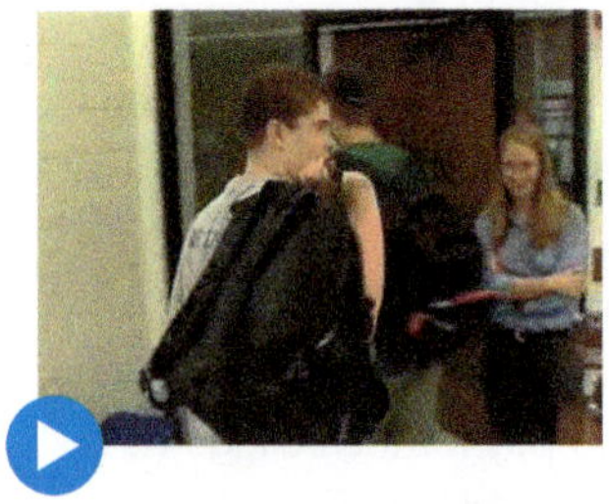

Pearson eTextbook

Video Example 16.2

In this video, the speakers explain the importance of self-advocacy. Why should this critical skill be taught to students with disabilities?

Many students with disabilities are overly dependent on others and are passive with respect to decision making. Although making decisions is difficult, students with disabilities will eventually be required to participate more actively in that process for themselves. Therefore, it is vital that opportunities, instruction, and practice in becoming more independent and in decision making are a part of a student's curriculum. Thus, training in **self-determination skills** and **self-advocacy** is a must (Shogren, 2013; Shogren et al., 2019; Wehmeyer, 2020). This means that students may need assistance, instruction, and practice in learning how to become an advocate for themselves and how to become knowledgeable about themselves with respect to learning strengths, needs, preferences, interests, and rights and responsibilities. This knowledge can be used to request accommodations that promote more success in jobs, independent living, and postsecondary education and other opportunities. Sample self-advocacy skills relevant to transition include being aware of legal rights, requesting accommodations, requesting assistance from doctors and Social Security offices, using job-related social skills, planning for the future and making informed choices, and seeking assistance whenever needed. Research has indicated that self-determination interventions improve postschool outcomes for students with disabilities (Shogren et al., 2015).

Although self-determination and self-advocacy skills are particularly important on the secondary level, students should be given practice on these skills throughout their school experience. The *In the Classroom* feature provides the application of these skills in elementary and secondary settings.

Students with strong self-determination skills generally have better postschool outcomes. Nevertheless, self-determination skills are not always taught to students with disabilities and, in fact, overprotection in some cases by teachers, advocates, and parents/caregivers may negatively affect the autonomy of students with disabilities. To be successful and independent in their lives after formal schooling, students need to have knowledge about their learning strengths and needs, to articulate those abilities and needs, and to participate actively in the IEP process. Diegelmann and Test (2018) successfully taught students with intellectual disabilities how to use a checklist to participate in their IEP meetings. Test et al. (2005) developed a conceptual framework for self-advocacy, which included four components:

1. Knowledge of self (e.g., strengths, support needs, goals)
2. Knowledge of rights (e.g., personal rights, educational rights, steps to advocate for change)
3. Communication (e.g., assertiveness, negotiation, compromise)
4. Leadership (e.g., knowledge of group's rights, political action)

All these components contribute to an overall sense of self-determination and self-advocacy.

Curriculum materials for enhancing self-determination skills include the *Self-Determined Learning Model of Instruction* (Wehmeyer et al., 2012). Using this model, teachers and students work together to learn how to solve problems, set goals, and learn what they need to do to meet these goals. Four components are used throughout this problem-solving process. The *goal* involves identifying what the student wants to achieve or make happen, for example, working as a student manager for a sports team. The *problem* is the thing or things that stand in the way of achieving the goal, for example, not knowing how to succeed in science class. The *plan* involves developing a set of steps that identify how to go about solving the problem, for example, meeting with a counselor to identify career steps toward becoming an emergency medical technician. Finally, students *evaluate* how they carried out their plan and determined whether it was successful (Shogren et al., 2019). As these skills develop, their use can be prompted and implemented across different classroom settings.

In the Classroom

Strategies for Teaching Self-Advocacy and Self Determination

Students at the elementary and secondary levels can be taught self-determination and self-advocacy skills. This includes the student's ability to request assistance, know and describe their strengths and weaknesses, problem-solve, be aware of accommodations, and know their individual rights. The specific strategies for teaching using high-leverage practices (see Chapter 6) can be used to implement modeling, role playing, practice, and feedback. At the elementary level, content used can emphasize the communication skills of requesting assistance, understanding strengths and differences, and basic problem solving. Problem solving for elementary students with disabilities has been successful using five steps:

1. Identify the problem.
2. Brainstorm solutions
3. Select the best one.
4. Test it.
5. Check for accuracy (Glago et al., 2009).

At the secondary level more about accommodations, and individual rights are introduced (Morningstar & Clavenna-Deane, 2018). McGahee et al. (2021) taught secondary students to request IEP accommodations. These strategies can be taught using think-alouds, role playing, and directed practice. Saying aloud the thinking process while modeling followed by role playing will reinforce these skills. Repeated practice will reinforce the learning. Examples of elementary and secondary levels are provided below.

Self-Determination Skill	Practice for Elementary Students	Practice for Secondary Students
Ask for assistance	• Please help me, I do not understand what to do. • Can you please tell me what that means?	• Can you please give me an example of what you mean? • Can you repeat those directions? • Can you tell me about the steps in the assignment again?
Identify strengths and differences	• I am good when I can see and hear the teacher's directions. • I am better when I can see the written directions on the board or on paper. • I do better when pictures are included in the directions. I feel badly when I cannot read all the words in our book. • I do best when I can sit near the teacher.	• Knowing students have a learning disability that hinders their ability to read is important. • I read better when I have more time and a quiet place. • I can do math problems when the room is quiet. • I get nervous when I must read aloud in front of the class.

Engage in problem solving	Break problem solving into steps by modeling, think aloud, and role playing.
	• With this math problem, first I need to read the entire problem.
	• Second, I need to decide what I am being asked to do.
	• Third, I need to put those words into numbers for either an addition problem or subtraction problem.
	• Then I need to compute the answer.
	• I need to check everything.
		Teach students to break large assignments and problems into smaller steps.
		• A report on climate change is due in 1 month. To complete this task, I must:
		  • Research the topic
		  • Find relevant sources
		  • Take notes in my own words
		  • Make an outline
		  • Introduce the topic, define and provide examples of the topic, list and define causes of the problem, list and describe solutions, and summarize overall findings
		  • I must fill in my outline with the information from my notes.
		  • I must write a draft paper using the notes and outline.
		  • I must proof my paper.

Learn knowledge of rights	• Provide students with opportunities to make personal choices. • Build disability awareness and knowledge of their disability.	Have students become aware of their IEP accommodations. • Use a checklist to monitor when in use. • Later this can be used to help facilitate discussions with college personnel about accommodations.

CLASSROOM SCENARIO

William

William, an 18-year-old with learning disabilities, is preparing to move to the local university when the next fall semester begins. He has received special education services for his learning disabilities since third grade. The local university does have an office of disability services that coordinates student accommodations. William has particular difficulties with basic literacy tasks, especially reading and writing activities, which usually require a great deal of time for him to complete. He has never lived away from home, and his parents have always been very supportive of anything he has tried to do. However, William's parents have also had a tendency to help him with everything, including organizing his schoolwork and his homework schedule.

QUESTIONS FOR REFLECTION

1. How can you help prepare William for the transition to college, in all the areas of anticipated changes?
2. How can you help William develop self-advocacy and self-determination skills?
3. How can you prepare him for the changes from IDEA to the Americans with Disabilities Act and describe what those changes will mean in terms of the responsibilities that he will have to assume?
4. What is a reasonable timeline for meeting William's transition needs?

Teach Strategies for Transitions

Learning Objective 16.4 List and compare strategies for promoting transitions for graduation, future education, job opportunities, and independent living.

Pearson eTextbook

Video Example 16.3

In this video, a parent explains how she helped her daughter find a job after high school. Identify the parent's priorities and the strategies she used to support her daughter.

The **Self-Advocacy Strategy** (SAS) includes several steps to assist students in acquiring self-advocacy skills for transition (Cease-Cook et al., 2013; Van Reusen et al., 1994). In SAS, students evaluate and plan for transition to areas such as independent living, consumer skills, citizenship skills, employment skills, family-living skills, and recreational and leisure skills. Students describe their strengths, areas to improve, and preferred accommodations; share; actively listen and discuss; and identify goals.

The analysis also includes identifying strengths, such as math computation and social skills, and needs, such as skills in reading, reading comprehension, and written expression. Specific goals are identified, such as independent living and career employment goals. Choices for student learning preferences are also included on the inventory. For example, student preferences for certain activities and listings of helpful materials and testing procedures are identified. Finally, accommodations that are necessary to help students succeed are listed. After the inventory is completed, students are taught to use communication skills more effectively, particularly in educational and transition meetings, by using the **IPLAN** and **SHARE** strategy prompts (Test & Neale, 2004):

IPLAN

Inventory of strengths, needs, goals, and accommodations is completed.

Provide the inventory to teachers.

Listen and respond to the comments.

Ask relevant questions.

Name your goals.

SHARE

Sit up straight.

Have a nice tone of voice.

Activate your thinking.

Relax and remain calm.

Engage in eye contact (Van Reusen et al., 1994).

Research reviewed and presented by Langel (2018) has indicated that training in the SAS strategy has improved the communication and social behaviors of students with disabilities and that this behavior has generalized to other settings, including IEP meetings.

TEACH ASSERTIVENESS SKILLS

Many students require explicit social skills instruction in assertiveness, such as requesting assistance, asking for clarification, and negotiating changes. Provide instruction and role-play situations during which students can practice developing and refining these skills in a safe environment. Finally, provide opportunities to practice generalizing the skills in a variety of situations with a number of different adults.

During high school, teachers assume major responsibilities for ensuring that students with disabilities are given free, appropriate public education as required by IDEA. Remember that teachers are part of the IEP team and are legally bound to implement IEP objectives and classroom modifications. However, once students leave high school and enroll in college, they are no longer covered by IDEA. They do have rights and responsibilities as identified in the Americans with Disabilities Act (ADA) and Section 504 of the Rehabilitation Act. Students, however, must meet any new classification criteria established at their respective institutions. Once student services are identified, usually with the assistance of personnel at a Dean of Students Office or Office for Students with Disabilities, accommodations such as extended testing times, test administrations in a distraction-free environment, and provision of notes or copies of PowerPoint materials may be made available. However, according to ADA, students need to be more assertive and identify themselves as having disabilities to their professors before they are guaranteed modifications to their educational programs (Madaus et al., 2011). Then they need to notify professors of their learning needs. One method devised by some college students with disabilities is to compose a brief statement containing learning strengths and needs. Figure 16.1 contains a sample letter written by a college student, Toni, who has learning disabilities. Toni distributes the letter to all of her professors each semester during the first week of classes and then meets individually with them during the next week to discuss any follow-up questions or concerns.

Consider assisting students with disabilities while they are enrolled in middle and high school in developing statements similar to the one used by Toni. This activity familiarizes students with their learning needs, helps them communicate these needs whenever necessary, and provides them with practice for doing this when they no longer have the protective services of IDEA and must be independent. The ability to describe how they learn best will be beneficial to future employers.

Pearson eTextbook
Video Example 16.4
In the video, Colin is using technology to help him successfully make a latte. Notice his level of independence.

IMPLEMENT TRANSITION CURRICULUM

Commercially prepared curriculum resources are available that provide examples of life skills and **life-centered career objectives** and materials. Most curricula are designed around basic competencies that are subdivided according to the needs of targeted students. One curriculum, *Life Centered Career Education* (Council for Exceptional Children), for example, contains the following major areas: Daily Living Skills, Personal-Social Skills, and Occupational Guidance and Preparation. Each area is then subdivided into more specific level competencies and objectives that also contain teaching suggestions to develop skills for successful living in maintaining a home and accepting responsibility for community living.

A number of apps and websites can be helpful in preparing students for transitions. The *Apps for Education* feature provides several examples of these resources.

Pearson eTextbook
Video Example 16.5
In this video, Colin describes how he uses technology to learn additional daily living skills. How may this type of video prompting assist students when transitioning to a job?

STRATEGIES FOR TRANSITIONING FOR THE FUTURE

PLAN FOR GRADUATION In many states, more demanding coursework (e.g., algebra, geometry, or foreign languages) and competency exams such as those to meet the common core state standards are being required for graduation. At the same time, some of the more basic and career-oriented courses are being phased out in favor of more academically demanding courses. Some students with disabilities may find it extremely difficult to pass one or more of these classes, even if modifications are made (Lindstrom et al., 2011). If a student's apparent inability to pass one or more particularly demanding courses appears to stand in the way of graduation,

Figure 16.1 Self-Advocacy Letter to a College Professor from Toni, a Student with Learning Disabilities

Dear Professor:

I am Toni, a student enrolled in your class this semester. I have a learning disability. I learn best by seeing and hearing information rather than by reading. I can sit through lectures and not take any notes and do fairly well on exams. When I sit in lectures and try to take notes at the same time I usually do poorly on exams. I do not seem to be able to take notes and listen at the same time very well at all. When I have had the opportunity to have my textbooks provided on audio recordings I can perform even better.

I have also noticed that I have a very keen sense of hearing but have the inability to filter out unwanted noises. This causes a problem for me in some lectures. To cope with this I usually sit near the front of the room so I can see the lecturer's face and try to lip read. Lecture outlines are also very helpful for me to be able to keep up with the information being presented in class. I record all of my lectures so that I am able to listen more carefully later on when studying for exams. I use the recordings and the lecture outlines as review. At that time I usually insert additional important points into the outline to help with studying and remembering important information.

I also do better on exams if I can take them in a private, very quiet room. I know that the Dean of Students Office has testing facilities that can be used to take my exams, and I would prefer to be able to take all of my exams for this class there.

I work very hard in school and am willing to try to work as hard as possible in your class. I am looking forward to learning in your class this semester. I can be reached by phone or by e-mail, if you would like to communicate further on this issue.

Sincerely,

Toni Sanchez

Phone: 797-555-7346
E-mail: *toni@gmu.edu*

determine whether a substitute course could be included on the student's IEP that would be accepted toward the diploma.

States have variable policies toward awarding diplomas. Some states award what is known as differentiated or tiered diplomas, which may include certificates of attendance, standard diplomas, or advanced diplomas (Johnson et al., 2009; Office of Special Education and Rehabilitative Services, 2015). For example, students meeting all requirements and who pass the state high-stakes tests or Common Core exams can be awarded an appropriate diploma; students who meet all requirements except passing the state high-stakes test could be awarded a general diploma. For individuals who have not been able to meet all the requirements for a standard diploma, an attendance certificate can be awarded for those who nonetheless have stayed in school and satisfactorily met attendance requirements throughout their school career. For students who have gone significantly beyond graduation requirements, advanced diplomas can be awarded to acknowledge this level of achievement. Any differentiated or tiered diploma may be associated with specific course and competency requirements. In your own school, find out what factors determine the type of diploma individual students will receive and how students' postsecondary futures (employment, vocational training, college entrance) will be affected by the type of diploma received.

In the attempt to ensure uniformly high standards, other states have begun to eliminate differentiated diplomas in favor of a single, more advanced diploma. Consultation with career counselors, vocational schools, parents/caregivers, and community resources can help provide relevant information on how to best meet the needs of students with disabilities under these

Transition Apps

Apps are available to help prepare students for transitions, including for students requiring some life skills, graduating with an IEP diploma, or heading to college. Some life skills applications can help students of all ages. *Quick Cues* (Fraser) presents listening skills activities, talking on the phone, and conversation tips. *Chore Pad HD* (Nannek LLC) presents chores that can be customized for school, home, or transitions, which can be viewed in daily or weekly lists. *Checkbook HD* (iBear LLC) is an e-checkbook that tracks expenses and calculates balances. *Google Maps* (Google, Inc.) displays maps, directions, points of interest, transit routes, and real-time traffic updates that can assist in navigating unfamiliar areas.

FVTC Career Explorer (FVTC Learning Innovations) assists middle school students to learn about career choices at Fox Valley Technical College. Image recognition and augmented reality is used to enhance the motivation of learning about the various career options.

Career Explorer 4-H (Move Creative, LLC) uses a gamelike format to explore career options, including potential salaries, education, and positive and negative attributes of jobs. The 4-H Career Options website (https://4-h.org/parents/curriculum/careers/) provides numerous curriculum options for exploring life skills, various careers, and provides useful links to additional occupation information.

Transition planning during high school helps students think about future career options. The U.S. Department of Labor's *Occupational Outlook Handbook* provides profiles of occupations and enables searching for qualifications, job responsibilities, and median salary (https://www.bls.gov/ooh/). For example, Nande selected Personal Care and Service Occupations. She was interested in learning additional information about Animal Care and Service Workers. From that link she learned primary work environments included kennels, zoos, pet stores, pet shelters, stables, veterinary clinics, and aquariums. Qualifications included a high school diploma or equivalent with individuals learning the required skills on the job, although experience with animals was helpful. Nande decided she might try to volunteer while still in high school at a local pet shelter, which would provide her not only with relevant experience but also let her know if she would like this type of job. Additionally, the job outlook was good, expected to grow, and provided a median salary of $28,000 annually. Another example is Leonardo, who was always interested in food preparation and cooking and researched both careers. He learned that food preparation positions worked under the directions of cooks and chefs in restaurants, schools, hospitals, and private facilities. Leonardo also learned that cooks prepare and cook a wide range of foods in the same types of environments and that many learn their skills on the job initially. Ideally, he thought he would prefer a cook position, but he also considered a food preparation career that would eventually lead to a cook or chef position. Leonardo decided to seek out a volunteer food preparation position at the local hospital while still in high school where he would gain experience, learn about food preparation skills, and decide if this type of career suited him.

For those students interested in transition to colleges, trade schools, or universities, several apps appear helpful. *The College Fair* (The Strada Education Network) assists with searching colleges and universities. Users enter their grade point average and standardized test scores to obtain a probability of acceptance. The app includes graduation rates, diversity figures, available scholarships, and how differing majors fare postgraduation. *The College Search Guide* (Dorm Mom) includes over 7,000 searchable colleges, universities, community colleges, and trade schools. Degrees offered, estimated student expenses, financial aid information, and freshman retention rates are available, among many other critical variables to consider when selecting a postsecondary program.

In addition to the *Occupational Outlook Handbook*, other apps are also beneficial when searching for jobs. Monster has several apps that assist with searching for jobs. Monster.com Job Search and Monster.com Interviews (Monster Worldwide) provide comprehensive job-searching techniques and interviewing suggestions. Career Builder (CareerBuilder, LLC) assists with creating resumés, job searching, and getting hired. Glassdoor.com and Indeed.com also assist with finding job openings and provide specific information about companies including past and current employees' reviews and ratings.

circumstances. Because IDEA allows students with disabilities to continue to attend school until age 22, some students may be able to meet the higher requirements with additional years of schooling.

PLAN FOR FUTURE EDUCATION Applying for college is an arduous task for all students but may be particularly overwhelming for students with disabilities. Provide additional assistance to those students to encourage them to pursue further education. Many resources are available commercially to help students learn more about college and university programs and their services for students with disabilities. The Learning Disabilities Association of America provides one such listing. Another helpful resource is *The Complete Learning Disabilities Directory* (Grey House Publishing) and its online database, which contains information on products, resources, books, and services that are available to help individuals with learning disabilities. For example, names, addresses, and phone numbers are provided for government agencies and professional organizations, as well as listings of books and other materials for individuals with disabilities and their parents or caregivers. Interested students and parents/caregivers should contact their state chapter of the Council for Exceptional Children for additional information on services provided within their region at the higher education level. These and other resource guides may also be available at your local library or bookstore or electronically.

Pearson eTextbook
Video Example 16.6
In this video, a coordinator for a vocational training program demonstrates the work skills that students with a range of disabilities are learning.

Provide information on the standards necessary for admission to the college that students wish to attend. For example, some colleges require courses in foreign languages; others require specific units (high school credits) in math, science, and English; and most require submission of Scholastic Assessment Test (SAT) or American College Testing (ACT) scores with the completed applications by prespecified dates. This information can help students select appropriate courses in high school. Additionally, they can prepare for taking the SAT or ACT by studying with pamphlets, commercially available books, and computer programs or by enrolling in classes designed to improve performance on the tests. SAT (*collegeboard.org*) and ACT (*act.org*) both offer practice materials on their websites. Some students may qualify for adapted testing procedures on the SAT or ACT, such as extended time or a large-print format. Seek assistance from your local high school counselor to determine whether or not students qualify for testing adaptations and help them obtain and submit the appropriate application forms.

Colleges have websites and application forms that can be submitted electronically. Provide opportunities for students to access this information so that they will be able to peruse the information independently. They can also practice completing their application forms prior to submission. Some universities offer postsecondary experiences for students with intellectual disabilities (e.g., the Mason LIFE program at George Mason University, *masonlife.gmu.edu*).

PLAN FOR FUTURE EMPLOYMENT OPPORTUNITIES Planning for future employment can include internships, adult education, trade and technical schools, competitive employment, supported employment, sheltered workshops, and methods for searching for employment (Rojewski & Gregg, 2011). Provide opportunities to discuss future job options. Relate your class content to employment options and opportunities and arrange for career and technical education when appropriate (Schloss & Gunter, 2011). Invite professionals from the community to discuss how their educational backgrounds assisted them in their vocations. Discuss what types of educational backgrounds are required for various professions. Plan field trips to community-based organizations so students can see firsthand the types of employment opportunities that are available. Use the expertise of your school guidance counselors to assist in disseminating job-related information. Whenever possible, integrate relevant job-related information within your regular curriculum. Use published curriculum materials for assessing and teaching employment-related skills. The *In the Classroom* feature describes steps to prepare students for job interviews.

PLAN FOR INDEPENDENT LIVING SITUATIONS Many students require information on preparing for future independent living situations. One important issue is selecting, managing, and maintaining a home. Questions to consider include residential options—where to live, with whom, and with what degree of support (e.g., independent, residential group home, supported living situation, semi-independent living).

Provide information on the types of resources that will be required to go with each type of living arrangement (Scanlon et al., 2011). For example, if students select an independent living arrangement as their first choice, then they need to realize what financial resources will be necessary to accomplish this goal. Many teachers have included units on planning

In the Classroom

Steps to Prepare Students for Job Interviews

Plan several sessions to prepare students for job interviews. The introduction session stresses the importance of good advance preparation for any job interview. Preparation includes (1) physical appearance; (2) reviewing the job description, roles, and responsibilities; (3) comparing your background experiences and skills with the job description; (4) practicing good communication skills, and (5) role-playing the job interview, self-evaluating performance, and listening to feedback. Participate in a presentation and discussion about job interviews whenever possible.

Physical appearance. The day of the interview students must show up clean, well groomed, and wearing professional clothing. A discussion on suitable clothing for the interview and for the job might be beneficial for students.

Job description, roles, and responsibilities. A job description provides the overall roles and responsibilities for the employee. For example, food and beverage serving involves one or more of the following: taking orders, delivering food, clearing, and cleaning tables and floors in restaurants, fast-food outlets, hospitals, and other facilities. Working in a grocery store initially as a bagger involves: placing groceries in bags and moving them to a cart and perhaps assisting the person with placing the filled bags in a vehicle. Both jobs also involve good interaction skills with customers. Both jobs also identified some high school education is required and that on-the-job training will be offered.

Comparing background experiences and skills with job description. Complete a self-examination and self-evaluation of students' background experiences and skills compared with those identified in the job description. A chart listing all job description, roles, and responsibilities in one column compared with each student's background experiences and skills in a second column can be used to identify strengths, weaknesses, and the appropriateness of a match between the student and a particular job. Any identified limitations can be practiced for improving the employability of students.

Good communication skills. Good communication skills include nonverbal communication, active listening, asking and answering questions, and speaking clearly. Nonverbal communication refers to eye contact with the speaker, looking interested, and showing respect. Active listening means paying attention to the speaker's dialogue while demonstrating nonverbal communication skills by being polite and interested. Employers will ask the interviewee questions during the interview such as "Have you ever done anything similar to this in the past?" Students should be prepared to answer the question by thinking back to their self-evaluation of background experiences compared with the job roles and responsibilities. Students might respond with "I haven't done exactly that . . . , however, I have done . . . , which shares similarities with the job's responsibilities." Employers may also ask, "Do you have any questions?" Students may have prepared a list of questions they might ask. For example, they might want to know more about the work schedule times and days.

Role-playing job interviews. Role-playing with students is a great way to practice for the interview. Students can role-play with a peer or a teacher. Recording the role-play interviews provides a vehicle for students to self-evaluate their performance after the mock interview. Self-evaluation and peer/teacher evaluation feedback helps improve the interview and likely chances of a job offer.

It is also beneficial if a prospective employer can come to the school and discuss important features for job interviews. Students can practice asking and answering questions with a potential employer.

Finally, the U.S. Department of Labor, Bureau of Statistics website at https://www.bls.gov/ooh/ provides a searchable listing of occupations with job descriptions, workplace environment, background requirements, salaries, and future growth, which could be shared with students.

for independent living within their regular curriculum and have reported that students have enjoyed the opportunities to gain familiarity with what is required to own a car and live in an apartment. Preparing budgets allows students to examine expenses they will incur and help them examine employment opportunities that will enable them to realize their goals. Efforts to increase awareness of future needs helps students to be better planners and thus more successful later in life.

Other important living skills include caring for personal needs, getting around in the community, buying and preparing food, buying and maintaining clothing, engaging in community and civic activities, and selecting meaningful recreation and leisure activities (Miltenberger et al., 2017). Individuals preparing for independent living also need to know about managing finances and credit, and how it can be used effectively.

Finally, vocational, personal, and social skills are important in independent living. Information and activities provided by Renaud (2018) can be helpful in planning and implementing programs to facilitate independent living. It is important to note that supports for students with disabilities and other diverse learning needs do not need to stop at the end of schooling; all individuals should receive the needed preparation and necessary support to ensure quality and fulfillment in all of life's activities.

TRANSITION IN THE GENERAL EDUCATION CURRICULUM

Although much of transition planning and instruction is undertaken by special education teachers, there are many ways general education teachers can include transition information in the general classroom curriculum. Such information can reinforce prior transition learning and can be beneficial to many students in the general education classroom.

First, participate in transition plan meetings for students with disabilities included in your classroom. You can meet prior to the meeting with the special education teacher or transition coordinator to determine how you may best participate. During the meeting, you can discuss the student's transition objectives, including measurable postschool outcomes, and how you might be able to support these objectives in the general education classroom. Familiarity with methods and materials used to promote transition learning can also provide implications for how this learning can be supported in your classroom.

Of course, using inclusion strategies of the type described in this text can be helpful generally in promoting student academic success, therefore meeting the transition goals of acquiring important skills and graduating from high school. Test et al. (2009) reviewed transition literature and reported that inclusion in general education classrooms was predictive of positive postschool outcomes. Important transition goals can be met simply by promoting success of all students in your classroom.

Career awareness can be implemented at any age throughout the school experience but is particularly important in high school. Consider including careers relevant to your class (e.g., government, geometry) in classroom discussions. These discussions could also include discussion of postsecondary settings most appropriate for pursuing different aspects of these careers. When possible, guest speakers can provide personal information about relevant career choices.

In some cases, transition goals can be included in general class assignments. For example, a writing assignment can require students to identify and read published information about two postsecondary institutions, identifying which one would be a more appropriate choice and providing evidence and reasons. Such an assignment may address Common Core State Standards and also address transition goals (Kellems, 2018). Other relevant assignments could focus on identifying and describing requirements for particular career goals of interest. Awareness of the content of ITPs can provide ideas for relevant course activities.

Finally, self-determination skills can be embedded in the general education curriculum (Kellems, 2018). Goal setting, problem solving, and self-advocacy are important skills for all students in all contexts and could be enforced in inclusive classrooms in the context of class content. Class assignments are appropriate opportunities to review goal setting and problem solving. Students having a problem meeting a goal can be encouraged to identify possible steps to address this problem and afterward evaluate whether these steps were successful. Self-advocacy should also be promoted whenever students encounter problems that may require teacher assistance.

Successful transitions to postschool environments are of great importance to all students, and students with disabilities may have particular difficulty succeeding in these environments (Test et al., 2009). However, with systematic planning, service coordination, and effective inclusive instruction, students with disabilities can successfully make the transition to postsecondary environments and adult life.

16 Summary

- Transition planning is critical for students with disabilities. Prepare students of all ages for transitions, including transitions to new schools, to new teachers, and, most important, to life after high school. Involve students, families/caregivers, teachers, counselors, transition coordinators, and community-based personnel as members of the transition team. Be sensitive to any ethnic, cultural, or specific language needs of families/caregivers. All students with IEPs must have individual transition plans by the age of 16.
- Promote transitions of students with disabilities to elementary and secondary settings. Provide opportunities for school visits, meetings with families/caregivers and school personnel, plan accommodations for specific disability areas, and engage peer support.
- Students with disabilities may require instruction in self-advocacy and self-determination to provide them with skills to be more successful during and after high school. Provide ample practice in safe environments for the development of these skills.
- Help prepare students for the appropriate high school graduation requirements necessary for their transition plans. Prepare students for life after high school by using appropriate transition assessment measures, carefully evaluating the results, and designing and implementing life skills programs.
- Provide educational opportunities that prepare students with disabilities for future education, jobs, and independent or supported living arrangements.

PROFESSIONAL STANDARDS LINK:
Transitions

Information in this chapter links most directly to:

- CEC 2020 Initial Practice-Based Professional Preparation Standards for Special Educators (Initial K–12 standards) (see https://exceptionalchildren.org/standards/initial-practice-based-professional-preparation-standards-special-educators): 1 (Engaging in Professional Learning and Practice with Ethical Guidelines), 2 (Understanding and Addressing Each Individual's Developmental and Learning Needs), 3 (Demonstrating Subject Matter Content and Specialized Curricular Knowledge), 4 (Using Assessment to Understand the Learner and the Learning Environment for Data-Based Decision Making), 5 (Supporting Learning Using Effective Instruction), 6 (Supporting Social, Emotional, and Behavioral Growth), 7 (Collaborating with Team Members)
- InTASC Standards (see https://www.ccsso.org/sites/default/files/2017-11/InTASC_Model_Core_Teaching_Standards_2011.pdf): 2 (Learning Differences), 3 (Learning Environments), 4 (Content Knowledge), 5 (Application of Content), 7 (Planning for Instruction), 8 (Instructional Strategies)

If you are promoting transitions, have you considered the following? If not, see the pages listed here.

STRATEGIES FOR PROMOTING TRANSITIONS

- ☐ Plan for transitions to kindergarten and elementary school, 449–450
- ☐ Plan for transitions to secondary settings, 450–452
- ☐ Plan for transitions to postsecondary environments, 452
- ☐ Promote transitions with assessment, 452
- ☐ Promote self-advocacy and self-determination, 454–456
- ☐ Teach strategies for transitions, 456–457
- ☐ Teach assertiveness skills, 457
- ☐ Implement transition curriculum, 457

STRATEGIES FOR TRANSITIONING FOR THE FUTURE

- ☐ Plan for graduation, 457–460
- ☐ Plan for future education, 460
- ☐ Plan for future employment opportunities, 460
- ☐ Plan for independent living situations, 460–462

REFERENCES

Chapter 1

Alaska Statutes, Title 14, Chapter 30 (1971).

Andrews, J. F., Shaw, P. C., & Lomas, G. (2011). Deaf and hard of hearing students. In J. M. Kauffman & D. P. Hallahan (Eds.), *Handbook of special education* (pp. 233–246). Routledge.

Assistance to States for the Education of Children with Disabilities and Preschool Grants for Children with Disabilities; Final Rule, 34 C.F.R., § 300–301 (2006).

Beattie v. Board of Education of City of Antigo, 172 N.W. 153, 154 (1919).

Blankenship, C. (1981). *Mainstreaming students with learning and behavior problems.* Harcourt School.

Board of Education v. Rowley, 458 U.S. 176 (1982).

Brown v. Board of Education, 347 U.S. 483 (1954).

Chrismer, S., Hodge, S., & Saintil, D. (Eds.). (2006). Assessing NCLB: Perspectives and prescriptions. *Harvard Educational Review, 76*, 457–460.

Code of Virginia, § 22.275.3 (1973).

Cook, B. G., Tankersley, M., Cook, L., & Landrum, T. J. (2000). Teachers' attitudes toward their included students with disabilities. *Exceptional Children*, *67*, 115–135.

Council for Exceptional Children (2002). No Child Left Behind has major implications for special education. *CEC Today*, *9*(4), 4.

Craig, S. E. (2008). *Reaching and teaching children who hurt: Strategies for your classroom.* Brookes.

Crockett, J. (2011). Conceptual models for leading and administrating special education. In J. M. Kauffman & D. P. Hallahan (Eds.), *Handbook of special education* (pp. 351–362). Routledge.

Cullen, J. P., Gregory, J. P., & Noto, L. A. (2010, February). *The Teacher Attitudes Toward Inclusion Scale (TATIS): Technical report.* Paper presented at the annual meeting of the Eastern Educational Research Association, Savannah, GA. (ERIC Document Reproduction Service No. ED509930)

De Boer, A., Pijl, S. J., & Minnaert, A. (2010). Attitudes of parents towards inclusive education: A review of the literature. *European Journal of Special Needs Education*, *25*, 165–181.

Diana v. State Board of Education, Civ. No. C-70-37 RFP (N.D. Cal. 1970, 1973).

Downing, J. A. (2004). Related services for students with disabilities: Introduction to the special issue. *Intervention in School and Clinic*, *39*, 195–208.

Endrew F. v. Douglas County School District, RE-1, 580 U.S. (2017).

Frieman, B. B. (2001). *What teachers need to know about children at-risk.* Allyn & Bacon.

Fuchs, D., & Fuchs, L. S. (1994). Inclusive schools movement and the radicalization of special education reform. *Exceptional Children*, *60*, 294–309.

Gollnick, D. M., & Chinn, P. C. (2017). *Multicultural education in a pluralistic society* (10th ed.). Allyn & Bacon.

Honig v. Doe, 484 U.S. 305 S.Ct. 592, 98 L.Ed.2d 686, 43 Ed. Law Rep. 857 (1988).

Huefner, D. S. (2015). Placements for special education students: The promise and the peril. In B. Bateman, J. W. Lloyd, & M. Tankersley (Eds.), *Enduring issues in special education: Personal perspectives* (pp. 215–230). Routledge.

Individuals with Disabilities Education Improvement Act of 2004, Pub. L. No. 108-446, 20 U.S.C. §1400 *et seq*. (2004).

Johnson, T. P. (1986). *The principal's guide to the educational rights of handicapped students.* National Association of Secondary School Principals.

Kauffman, J. M., Nelson, C. M., Simpson, R. L., & Mock, D. R. (2011). Contemporary issues. In J. M. Kauffman & D. P. Hallahan (Eds.), *Handbook of special education* (pp. 15–26). Routledge.

Knackendoffel, A. P., Dettmer, P., & Thurston, L. P. (2018). *Collaborating, consulting, and working in teams for students with special needs* (8th ed.). Allyn & Bacon.

Larry P. v. Riles, 343 F. Supp. 1306 (N. D. Cal. 1972), *aff'd* 502 F.2d 963 (9th Cir. 1974), *further action* 495 F. Supp. 926 (N. D. Cal. 1979), *aff'd* 793 F. 2d 969 (9th Cir. 1984).

Lazarus, D., Thurlow, M., Lail, K., & Christensen, L. (2009). A longitudinal analysis of state accommodation policies. *Journal of Special Education*, *43*, 67–80.

Lipsky, D. K., & Gartner, A. (1997). *Inclusion and school reform: Transforming America's classrooms.* Brookes.

Lipsky, D. K., & Gartner, A. (2012). *Inclusion: A service, not a place.* Dude.

Majoko, T. (2016). Inclusion of children with autism spectrum disorders: Listening to and hearing voices from the grassroots. *Journal of Autism and Developmental Disorders*, *46*, 1429–1440.

Mandlawitz, M. (2006). *What every teacher should know about IDEA 2004.* Pearson.

Mills v. Board of Education, 348 F. Supp. 866 (D.D.C. 1972).

Murdick, N. L., Gartin, B. C., & Crabtree, T. L. (2014). *Special education law* (3rd ed.). Pearson.

National Center for Technology Innovation. (2011). *Students with disabilities in charter schools.* LD OnLine. http://www.ldonline.org/article/43436?theme=print

National Governors Association Center for Best Practices & Council of Chief State School Officers. (2016). *Common Core State Standards initiative.* http://www.corestandards.org

National School Boards Association. (2016). *Every Student Succeeds Act (ESSA).* https://www.nsba.org/News/2016/ESSA-Anniversary

Nevada Revised Statutes, § 39.050 (1963).

Oberti v. Board of Education of the Borough of Clementon School District, 995 F. 2d 1204 (3rd Cir. 1993).

Pennsylvania Association for Retarded Children v. Commonwealth of Pennsylvania (PARC), 334 F. Supp. 1257 (E.D. Pa. 1972).

Rimm, S. B., Siegle, D., & Davis, G. A. (2018). *Education of the gifted and talented* (7th ed.). Pearson.

Rodriguez, R. J., Blatz, E. T., & Elbaum, B. (2014). Parents' views of schools' involvement efforts. *Exceptional Children*, *81*, 79–95.

Rothstein, L. F., & Johnson, S. F. (2021). *Special education law* (6th ed.). Sage.

Rozalski, M., Miller, J., & Stewart, A. (2011). Least restrictive environment. In J. M. Kauffman & D. P. Hallahan (Eds.), *Handbook of special education* (pp. 107–120). Routledge.

Russell, C. L. (2008). How are your person-first skills?: A self-assessment. *Teaching Exceptional Children*, *40*(5), 40–43.

Scruggs, T. E. (2012). Differential facilitation of learning outcomes: What does it tell us about learning disabilities and instructional programming? *International Journal for Research in Learning Disabilities, 1*, 4–20.

Scruggs, T. E., Leins, P., & Mastropieri, M. A. (2011, April). *Teacher attitudes towards inclusion: A synthesis of survey, comparative, and qualitative research, 1958–2010*. Paper presented at the annual meeting of the Council for Exceptional Children, Washington, DC.

Scruggs, T. E., & Mastropieri, M. A. (1996). Teacher perceptions of mainstreaming/inclusion, 1958–1995: A research synthesis. *Exceptional Children, 63*, 59–74.

Siperstein, G., Parker, R., Norns Bardon, J., & Widerman, K. (2007). A national study of youth attitudes toward the inclusion of students with intellectual disabilities. *Exceptional Children, 73*, 435–455.

Smith, T. E. C. (2002). Section 504: What teachers need to know. *Intervention in School and Clinic, 37*, 259–266.

Staples, K., & Diliberto, J. (2010). Guidelines for successful parental involvement. *Teaching Exceptional Children, 42*(6), 58–63.

Sullivan, A. L. & Osher, D. (2019). IDEA's double blind: A synthesis of disproportionality policy interpretations. *Exceptional Children, 85*, 395–412.

Tomlinson, C. A. (2014). *The differentiated classroom: Responding to the needs of all learners* (2nd ed.). ASCD.

U.S. Department of Education. (2006). *Carl D. Perkins Career and Technical Education Act of 2006: Reauthorization of Perkins.* http://www.ed.gov/policy/sectech/leg/perkins/index.html

U.S. Department of Education, Office of Special Education and Rehabilitative Services. (2006). *Assistance to states for the education of children with disabilities and preschool grants for children with disabilities*. Final Regulations, 71 Fed. Reg. 46540 (30 C.F.R. Parts 300 and 301). Author.

U.S. Department of Education. (2020). *42nd Annual Report to Congress on the Implementation of Individuals with Disabilities Act*. Author.

U.S. Department of Education. (2021). *43rd Annual Report to Congress on the Implementation of the Individuals with Disabilities Education Act*. Washington, DC: Author. Retrieved from https://sites.ed.gov/idea/2020-annual-report-congress-idea/.

U.S. Department of Justice (2022). *Information and technical assistance on the Americans with Disabilities Act*. Retrieved from ADA.gov

Watson v. City of Cambridge, 32 N.E. 864 (1893).

Will, M. (1986). Educating students with learning problems: A shared responsibility. *Exceptional Children, 52*, 411–415.

Wright, P. W. D., & Wright, P. D. (2005). *Wright's law IDEA 2004: Parts A & B*. Harbor House Law Press.

Wright, P. W. D., & Wright, P. D. (2007). *Wrightslaw: Special education law* (2nd ed.). Harbor House Law Press.

Wright, P. W. D., Wright, P. D., & Heath, S. W. (2004). *Wright's law: No child left behind.* Harbor House Law Press.

Yell, M. (2019). *The law and special education* (5th ed.). Pearson.

Yell, M. L., & Crockett, J. B. (2011). Free appropriate public education. In J. M. Kauffman & D. P. Hallahan (Eds.), *Handbook of special education* (pp. 77–90). Routledge.

Yell, M. L., & Katsiyannis, A. (2019). The supreme court and special educators. *Intervention in School and Clinic, 54*, 311–318.

Yell, M. L., Katsiyannis, A., & Bradley, R. (2011). The Individuals with Disabilities Education Act: The evolution of special education law. In J. M. Kauffman & D. P. Hallahan (Eds.), *The handbook of special education* (pp. 61–76). Routledge.

Yell, M. L., Shriner, J. G., & Katsiyannis, A. (2006). Individuals with Disabilities Education Improvement Act of 2004 and IDEA Regulations of 2006: Implications for educators, administrators, and teacher trainers. *Focus on Exceptional Children, 39*, 1–24.

Zigmond, N. (2015). Where should students with disabilities receive their education? In B. Bateman, J. W. Lloyd, & M. Tankersley (Eds.), *Enduring issues in special education: Personal perspectives* (pp. 198–214). Routledge.

Zigmond, N., & Kloo, A. (2011). General and special education are (and should be) different. In J. M. Kauffman & D. P. Hallahan (Eds.), *Handbook of special education* (pp. 160–172). Routledge.

Zirkel, P. A. (2009). What does the law say? New section 504 student eligibility standards. *Teaching Exceptional Children, 41*, 68–77.

Yu, S., & Cho, E. (2021). Preservice teachers' attitudes toward inclusion in early childhood classrooms: A review of the literature. *Early Childhood Education Journal.* [Epub ahead of print]

Chapter 2

Barrio, B. L. (2017). Special education policy change: Addressing the disproportionality of English language learners in special education programs in rural communities. *Rural Special Education Quarterly, 36*(2), 64–72.

Bateman, B. D. (2017). Individual education programs for children with disabilities. In J. M. Kauffman, D. P. Hallahan, & P. C. Pullen (Eds.), *Handbook of special education* (2nd ed., pp. 87–104). Routledge.

Bennett, M. S., Erchul, W. P., Young, H. L., & Bartel, C. M. (2012). Exploring relational communication patterns in prereferral intervention teams. *Journal of Educational and Psychological Consultation, 22*, 187–207.

Berkeley, S., Scanlon, D., Bailey, T. R., Sutton, J. C., & Sacco, D. M. (2020). A snapshot of RTI implementation a decade later: New picture, same story. *Journal of Learning Disabilities, 53*(5), 332–342.

Brandon, R. R., Higgins, K., Jones, V. L., & Dobbins, N. (2021). African American parents with children with disabilities: Gathering home-school reflections. *Intervention in School and Clinic*, 57(2), 119–125.

Brown, N. B., Howerter, C. S., & Morgan, J. J. (2013). Tools and strategies for making co-teaching work. *Intervention in School and Clinic, 49*(2), 84–89.

Burns, M. K., Maki, K. E., Brann, K. L., McComas, J. J., & Helman, L. A. (2020). Comparison of reading growth among students with severe reading deficits who received intervention to typically achieving students and students receiving special education. *Journal of Learning Disabilities, 53*(6), 444–453.

Castro, V. E. (2007). *The effect of co-teaching on academic achievement of K–2 students with and without disabilities in inclusive and noninclusive classrooms*. Unpublished doctoral dissertation, Fordham University.

Cimera, R. E., Burgess, S., & Bedesem, P. L. (2014). Does providing transition services by age 14 produce better vocational outcomes for students with intellectual disability? *Research and Practice for Persons with Severe Disabilities, 39*(1), 47–54.

Conderman, G. (2011). Middle school co-teaching: Effective practices and student reflections. *Middle School Journal, 42*, 24–31.

Conners, N. A. (2008). *An in-depth study of expert middle school special educators*. Unpublished doctoral dissertation, George Mason University.

Conroy, T., Yell, M., Katsiyannis, A., & Collins, T. (2010). The U.S. Supreme Court and parental rights under the Individuals with Disabilities Education Act. *Focus on Exceptional Children, 43*(2), 1–16.

Cook, S. C., Mcduffie-Landrum, K. A., Oshita, L., & Cook, B. G. (2017). Co-teaching for students with disabilities: A critical and updated analysis on the empirical literature. In J. M. Kauffman, D. P. Hallahan, & P. C. Pullen (Eds.), H*andbook of special education* (2nd ed., pp. 233–248). Routledge.

Division for Learning Disabilities. (2007). *Thinking about response to instruction and learning disabilities: A teacher's guide.* Author.

Francis, G. L., Blue-Banning, M., Haines, S. J., Turnbull, A. P., & Gross, J. S. (2016). Building our school: Parental perspectives for building trusting family–professional partnerships. *Preventing School Failure, 60*, 329–336.

Friend, M. (2016). Welcome to Co-Teaching 2.0. *Educational Leadership*, *73*, 16–22.

Friend, M., & Cook, L. (2016). *Interactions: Collaboration skills for school professionals* (8th ed.). Allyn & Bacon.

Friend, M., Cook, L., Hurley-Chamberlain, D., & Shamberger, C. (2010). Co-teaching: An illustration of the complexity of collaboration in special education. *Journal of Educational and Psychological Consultation*, *20*, 9–27.

Garwood, J. D., VanLoan, L. L., & Werts, M. G. (2018). Mindset of paraprofessionals serving students with emotional and behavioral disorders. *Intervention in School and Clinic*, *53*(4), 206–211.

Gertzel-Short, L., Kiru, E. W., Hsiao, Y. J., Hovey, K. A., Wei, Y., & Miller, R. D. (2019) Engaging culturally and linguistically diverse families of children with disabilities. *Intervention in School and Clinic*, 55, 120–126.

Giangreco, M. F., & Broer, S. M. (2007). School-based screening to determine overreliance on paraprofessionals. *Focus on Autism and Other Developmental Disabilities*, *22*, 149–158.

Giangreco, M. F., Broer, S. M., & Suter, S. M. (2011). Guidelines for selecting alternatives to overreliance on paraprofessionals: Field-testing in inclusion-oriented schools. *Remedial and Special Education*, *32*, 22–38.

Giangreco, M. F., Suter, S. M., & Doyle, M. (2010). Paraprofessionals in inclusive schools: A review of recent research. *Journal of Educational and Psychological Consultation*, *20*, 41–57.

Ginott, H. (1998). *Teacher and child.* Touchstone.

Ginott, H. G., Ginott, A., & Goddard, H. W. (2003). *Between parent and child.* Three Rivers.

Gordon, T. (2003). *T.E.T.: Teacher effectiveness training.* Three Rivers.

Hoover, J. (2010). Special education eligibility decision making in response to intervention models. *Theory Into Practice*, *49*, 289–296.

Hsiao, Y. J., Higgins, K., Pierce, T., Whitby, P., & Tandy, R. (2017). Parental stress, family quality of life, and family teacher partnerships: Families of children with autism spectrum disorder. *Research in Developmental Disabilities*, *70*, 152–162.

Individuals with Disabilities Education Improvement Act of 2004, Pub. L. No. 108-446, 20 U.S.C. §1400 et seq. (2004).

Johnson, E. (n.d.). *How to develop an effective Tier 2 system.* RTI Network. www.rtinetwork.org/essential/tieredinstruction/tier2/how-to-develop-an-effective-tier-2-system

Kampwirth, T. J., & Powers, K. M. (2016). *Collaborative consultation in the schools: Effective practices for students with learning and behavior problems* (5th ed.). Pearson.

Lane, K. L., Carter, E. W., & Sisco, L. (2012). Paraprofessional involvement in self-determination instruction for students with high-incidence disabilities. *Exceptional Children*, *78*(2), 237–251.

Martin, J. E., Van Dyke, J. L., Greene, B. A., Gardner, J. E., Christensen, W. R., Woods, L. L., & Lovett, D. L. (2006). Direct observation of teacher-directed IEP meetings: Establishing the need for student IEP meeting instruction. *Exceptional Children*, *72*, 187–200.

McDuffie, M. A., Mastropieri, M. A., & Scruggs, T. E. (2009). Differential effects of co-teaching and peer-mediated instruction: Results for content learning and student–teacher interactions. *Exceptional Children*, *75*, 493–510.

McLeskey, J., Barringer, M-D., Billinglsey, B., Brownell, M., Jackson, D., Kennedy, M., . . . Ziegler, D. (2017, January). *High-leverage practices in special education.* Council for Exceptional Children & CEEDAR Center.

McNaughton, D., Hamlin, D., McCarthy, J., Head-Reeves, D., & Schreiner, M. (2007). Learning to listen: An active listening strategy for preservice special education professionals. *Topics in Early Childhood Special Education*, *27*, 223–231.

McNaughton, D., & Vostal, B. (2010). Using active listening to improve collaboration with parents: The LAFF don't CRY strategy. *Intervention in School and Clinic*, *45*, 251–256.

Meyer, A., Rose, D. H., & Gordon, D. (2014). *Universal design for learning: Theory and practice.* CAST Professional Publishing.

Mueller, T. G. (2014). Litigation and special education: The past, present, and future directions for resolving conflicts between parents and school districts. *Journal of Disability Policy Studies*, *26*(3), 135–143.

Murawski, W. M. (2012). 10 tips for using co-planning time more efficiently. *Teaching Exceptional Children*, *44*(4), 8–15.

Murawski, W. W., & Dieker, L. (2004). Tips and strategies for co-teaching at the secondary level. *Teaching Exceptional Children*, *36*, 52–58.

Murray, C. (2004). Clarifying collaborative roles in urban high schools: General educators' perspectives. *Teaching Exceptional Children*, *36*(5), 44–51.

National Center on Response to Intervention. (2010). *Essential components of RTI: A closer look at response to intervention.* U.S. Department of Education, Office of Special Education Programs. https://rti4success.org/sites/default/files/rtiessentialcomponents_042710.pdf

Peterson, L. V., Burden, J. P., Sedaghat, J. M., Gothberg, J. E., Kohler, P. D., & Coyle, J. L. (2013). Triangulated IEP transition goals: Developing relevant and genuine annual goals. *Teaching Exceptional Children*, *45*(6), 46–57.

Prewett, S., Mellard, D. F., Deshler, D. D., Allen, J., Alexander, R., & Stern, A. (2012). Response to intervention in middle schools: Practices and outcomes. *Learning Disabilities Research & Practice*, *27*, 136–147.

Scott, A. N., Hauerwas, L. B., & Brown, R. D. (2014). State policy and guidance for identifying learning disabilities in culturally and linguistically diverse students. *Learning Disability Quarterly*, *37*(3), 172–185.

Scruggs, T. E., Mastropieri, M. A., & McDuffie, K. A. (2007). Co-teaching in inclusive classrooms: A meta-synthesis of qualitative research. *Exceptional Children*, *73*, 392–416.

Singer, G. H. S., Maul, C., Wang, M., & Ethridge, B. L. (2017). Resilience in families of children with disabilities: Risk and protective factors. In J. M. Kauffman, D. P. Hallahan, & P. C. Pullen (Eds.), *Handbook of special education* (pp. 793–810). Routledge.

Solis, M., Vaughn, S., & Scammacca, N. (2015). The effects of an intensive reading intervention for ninth graders with very low reading comprehension. *Learning Disabilities Research & Practice*, *30*, 104–113.

Steedman, W. (2012). *Independent educational evaluations.* Wrightslaw. http://www.wrightslaw.com/info/eval.iee.steedman.htm

Stewart, E. M. (2019). Reducing ambiguity: Tools to define and communicate paraprofessional roles and responsibilities. *Intervention in School and Clinic*, *55*(1), 52–57.

Truscott, S., Celinae, E., Sams, D., Sanborn, K., & Frank, A. (2005). The current state(s) of pre-referral intervention teams: A report from two national surveys. *Remedial and Special Education*, *26*, 130–140.

Turnbull, A., Turnbull, H. R., Erwin, E. J., Soodak, L. C., & Shogren, K. A. (2015). *Families, professionals, and exceptionality: Positive outcomes through partnerships and trust.* Pearson.

Vostal, B. R., McNaughton, D. M., Benedik-Wood, E., & Hoffman, K. (2015). Preparing teachers for collaborative communication: Evaluation of instruction in an active listening strategy. *National Teacher Education Journal*, *8*, 5–14.

Wagner, M., Newman, L., Cameto, R., Javitz, H., & Valdes, K. (2012). A national picture of parent and youth participation in IEP and transition planning meetings. *Journal of Disability Policy Studies*, *23*, 140–155.

Walker, V. L., & Smith, C. G. (2015). Training paraprofessionals to support students with disabilities: A literature review. *Exceptionality*, *23*, 170–191.

Wanzek, J., & Vaughn, S. (2011). Is a three-tier intervention model associated with reduced placement in special education? *Remedial and Special Education*, *32*, 167–175.

Weiss, M. P., & Lloyd, J. W. (2003). Conditions for co-teaching: Lessons from a case study. *Teacher Education and Special Education*, *26*, 27–41.

Wilt, C. L., Hirano, K., & Morningstar, M. E. (2021). Diverse perspectives on transition to adulthood among families: A qualitative exploration. *Journal of Disability Policy Studies*, *32*, 24–35.

Yell, M. L., & Bateman, D. (2020). Defining educational benefits: An update on the U.S. supreme court's ruling in *Endrew F. v. Douglas County School District* (2017). *Teaching Exceptional Children*, *52*(5), 283–290.

Yell, M. L., Katsiyannis, A., Ennis, R. P., Losinski, M., & Christle, C. A. (2016). Avoiding substantive errors in individualized education program development. *Teaching Exceptional Children*, *49*(1), 31–40.

Young, H. L., & Gaughan, E. (2010). A multiple method longitudinal investigation of pre-referral intervention team functioning: Four years in rural schools. *Journal of Educational & Psychological Consultation*, *20*, 106–138.

Zhang, D., Hsu, H., Kwok, O., Benz, M., & Bowman-Perrott, L. (2011). The impact of basic-level parent engagements on student achievement: Patterns associated with race/ethnicity and socioeconomic status. *Journal of Disability Policy Studies*, *22*, 28–39.

Chapter 3

Aceves, T. C., & Orosco, M. J. (2014). *Culturally responsive teaching* (Document No. IC-2). University of Florida, Collaboration for Effective Educator, Development, Accountability, and Reform Center. http://ceedar.education.ufl.edu/tools/innovation-configurations/

Alfonso, V. C., & Flanagan, D. P. (2018). *Essentials of specific learning disability identification* (2nd ed.). Wiley.

Algozzine, B., Wang, C., & Violette, V. S. (2011). Reexamining the relationship between academic achievement and social behavior. *Journal of Positive Behavior Interventions*, *13*, 3–16.

Al-Yagon, M., & Margalit, M. (2014). Social cognition of children and adolescents with learning disabilities: Intrapersonal and interpersonal perspectives. In H. L. Swanson, K. R. Harris, & S. Graham (Eds.), *Handbook of learning disabilities* (2nd ed., pp. 278–292). Guilford Press.

American Association on Intellectual and Developmental Disabilities (AAIDD). (2010). *Intellectual disability: Definition, classification, and systems of support* (11th ed.). Author.

American Psychiatric Association. (2013). *Diagnostic and statistical manual of mental disorders* (5th ed.). Author.

Assistance to States for the Education of Children with Disabilities: A Child with a Disability, 34 C.F.R. § 300.7 (2002).

Assistance to States for Education of Handicapped Children: Procedures for Evaluating Specific Learning Disabilities, 42 C.F.R., § 121A (1977).

Barkley, R. A. (2014). History of ADHD. In R. A. Barkley (Ed.), *Attention-deficit hyperactivity disorder: A handbook for diagnosis and treatment* (4th ed., pp. 3–50). Guilford Press.

Batshaw, M. L., Roizen, N. J., & Lotrecchiano, G. R. (2019). *Children with disabilities* (8th ed.). Brookes.

Berkeley, S., Scanlon, D., Bailey, T. R., Sutton, J. C., & Sacco, D. M. (2020). A snapshot of RTI implementation a decade later: New picture, same story. *Journal of Learning Disabilities*, *53*(5), 332–342.

Bettini, E. A., Billingsley, B., Walraven, C., & Williams, T. O. (2018). Special educators of color are underrepresented across states: A challenge for leaders. *Journal of Special Education Leadership*, *31*, 3–15.

Beukelman, D. R., & Light, J. C. (2020). *Augmentative and alternative communication: Supporting children and adults with complex communication needs* (5th ed.). Brookes.

Bottge, B. A., Heinrichs, M., Chan, S., & Serlin, R. (2001). Anchoring adolescents' understanding of math concepts in rich problem solving environments. *Remedial and Special Education*, *22*, 299–314.

Bottge, B. A., Rueda, E., Grant, T. S., Stephens, A. C., & LaRoque, P. T. (2010). Anchoring problem-solving and computation instruction in context-rich learning environments. *Exceptional Children*, *76*, 417–437.

Bottge, B. A., Toland, M. D., Gassaway, L., Butler, M., Choo, S., Griffen, A. K., & Ma, X. (2015). Impact of anchored enhanced instruction in inclusive math classrooms. *Exceptional Children*, *81*, 158–175.

Bottge, B., Xin, M., Gassaway, L., Jones, M., & Gravil, M. (2021). Effects of formal assessment strategies on the fractions computation skills of students with disabilities. *Remedial and Special Education*, *42*, 279–289.

Camarota, S. A., & Zeigler, K. (2014). *One in five U.S. residents speaks foreign language at home, record 61.8 million*. Center for Immigration Studies. http://cis.org//sites/cis.org/files/camarota-language.pdf

Casteel, C.J., & Ballantyne, K.G. (Eds.) (2006). *Professional development in action: Improving teaching for English learners*. National Clearinghouse for English Language Acquisition and Language Instruction Educational Programs. http://www.ncela.us/

Cherkes-Julkowski, M., Sharp, S., & Stolzenberg, J. (1997). *Rethinking attention deficit disorders*. Brookline Books.

Council for Exceptional Children (CEC). (2012). *Current special education topics: Identifying learning disabilities*. http://www.cec.sped.org

Denckla, M. B., Barquero, L. A., Lindstrom, E. R., Benedict, S. L., Wilson, L. M., & Cutting, L. E., (2014). Attention-deficit/hyperactivity disorder, executive function, and reading comprehension: Different but related. In H. L. Swanson, K. R. Harris, & S. Graham (Eds.), *Handbook of learning disabilities* (2nd ed., pp. 155–168). Guilford Press.

Echevarria, J., & Graves, A. (2011). *Sheltered content instruction: Teaching English language learners with diverse abilities* (4th ed.). Pearson.

Echevarria, J., & Graves, A. (2015). *Sheltered content instruction: Teaching English language learners with diverse abilities* (5th ed.). Pearson.

Epstein, M. H., Peirce, C., & Lambert, M. C. (2021). *The Behavior and Emotional Rating Scale: A strength, based approach to assessment* (3rd ed.). PRO-ED.

Erbeli, F., Hart, S. A., & Taylor, J. (2018). Genetic and environmental influences on achievement outcomes based on family history of learning disability status. *Journal of Learning Disabilities*, *52*, 135–145.

Evanovich, L. L., & Scott, T. M. (2016). Facilitating PBIS implementation: An administrator's guide to present the logic and steps to faculty and staff. *Beyond Behavior*, *25*, 4–8.

Fletcher, J. M. (2012). Classification and identification of learning disabilities. In B. Wong & D. L. Butler (Eds.), *Learning about learning disabilities* (4th ed., pp. 1–25). Academic Press.

Fletcher, J. M., Lyon, G. R., Barnes, M., Stuebing, K. K., Francis, D. J., Olson, R. K., . . . Shaywitz, B. A. (2002). Classification of learning disabilities: An evidence-based evaluation. In R. Bradley, L. Danielson, & D. P. Hallahan (Eds.), *Identification of learning disabilities: Research to practice* (pp. 185–250). Erlbaum.

Fuchs, D., Fuchs, L. S., Mathes, P. G., Lipsey, M. L., & Roberts, P. H. (2002). Is "learning disabilities" just a fancy term for low achievement?: A meta-analysis of reading differences between low achievers with and without the label. In R. Bradley, L. Danielson, & D. Hallahan (Eds.), *Identification of learning disabilities: Research to practice* (pp. 737–762). Erlbaum.

Geary, D. C. (2014). Learning disabilities in mathematics: Recent advances. In H. L. Swanson, K. R. Harris, & S. Graham (Eds.), *Handbook of learning disabilities* (pp. 239–255). Guilford Press.

Gonzalez, J. M., Cannell, M. B., Jetelina, K. K., & Froehlich-Grobe, K. (2015). Disproportionate prevalence rate of prisoners with disabilities: Evidence from a nationally representative sample. *Journal of Disability Policy Studies*, *27*, 106–115.

Graham, S., Collins, A. A., & Rigby-Wills, H. (2017). Writing characteristics of students with learning disabilities and typically achieving peers: A meta-analysis. *Exceptional Children*, *83*, 199–218.

Graves, A. W. (2010). A longitudinal study of the impact of effective beginning reading instruction for English learners: Literacy, language, and learning disabilities. In T. E. Scruggs & M. A. Mastropieri (Eds.), *Literacy and learning: Advances in learning and behavioral disabilities* (Vol. 23, pp. 155–174). Emerald.

Gunning, T. G. (2018). *Assessing and correcting: Reading and writing difficulties* (6th ed.). Pearson.

Hallahan, D. P., Pullen, P. C., & Ward, D. (2014). A brief history of the field of learning disabilities. In H. L. Swanson, K. R. Harris, & S. Graham (Eds.), *Handbook of learning disabilities* (2nd ed., pp. 15–32). Guilford Press.

Hauerwas, L. B., Brown, R., & Scott, A. N. (2013). Specific learning disability and response to intervention: State level guidance. *Exceptional Children*, *80*, 101–120.

Hoover, H. D., Dunbar, S. B., & Frisbie, D. A. (2007). *Iowa Tests of Basic Skills: Form C*. Houghton Mifflin Harcourt.

Houwen, S., Visser, L., Van der Putten, A., & Vlaskamp, C. (2016). The interrelationships between motor, cognitive, and language development in children with and without intellectual and developmental disabilities. *Research in Developmental Disabilities*, *53*, 19–31.

Hussar, B., Zhang, J., Hein, S., Wang, K., Roberts, A., Cui, J., . . . Dilig, R. (2020). *The Condition of Education 2020* (NCES 2020-144). U.S. Department of Education, National Center for Education Statistics. https://nces.ed.gov/pubs2020/2020144.pdf

Jacobson, J. W., & Mulick, J. A. (1996). *Manual on diagnosis and professional practice in mental retardation.* American Psychological Association.

Johnson, E. (n.d.). *How to develop an effective Tier 2 system.* RTI Network. www.rtinetwork.org/essential/tieredinstruction/tier2/how-to-develop-an-effective-tier-2-system

Kamphaus, R. W., & Reynolds, C. R. (2015). *Behavior Assessment System for Children* – Third Edition (BASC-3). Pearson.

Kauffman, J. M., & Landrum, T. (2018). *Characteristics of emotional and behavioral disorders of children and youth* (11th ed.). Merrill/Pearson.

Kirkpatrick, R., Legrand, L., Iacono, W., & McGue, M. (2011). A twin and adoption study of reading achievement: Exploration of shared-environmental and gene-environment interaction effects. *Learning and Individual Differences*, *21*, 368–375.

Landrum, T. (2017). Emotional and behavioral disorders. In J. M. Kauffman, D. P. Hallahan, & P. C. Pullen (Eds.), *Handbook of special education* (2nd ed., pp. 312–324). Routledge.

Lerner, J. W., & Johns, B. H. (2015). *Learning disabilities and related disabilities: Strategies for success* (13th ed.). Cengage Learning.

Lewis, T. J., Hatton, H. L., Jorgenson, C., & Maynard, D. (2017). What beginning special educators need to know about conducting functional behavioral assessments. *Teaching Exceptional Children*, *49*, 231–238.

Lyon, G. R., Fletcher, J. M., Shaywitz, S. E., Shaywitz, B. A., Torgesen, J. K., Wood, F. B., . . . Olson, R. (2001). Rethinking learning disabilities. In C. E. Finn Jr., A. J. Rotherham, & C. R. Hokanson, Jr. (Eds.), *Rethinking special education for a new century* (pp. 259–287). Thomas B. Fordham Foundation.

Maag, J. W., & Katsiyannis, A. (2012). Bullying and students with disabilities: Legal and practice considerations. *Behavioral Disorders*, *37*, 78–86.

Mastropieri, M. A., & Scruggs, T. E. (2002). Discrepancy models in the identification of learning disabilities. In R. Bradley, L. Danielson, & D. P. Hallahan (Eds.), *Identification of learning disabilities: Research to practice* (pp. 449–466). Erlbaum.

Mastropieri, M. A., Scruggs, T. E., Cerar, N. I., Allen-Bronaugh, D., Thompson, C., Guckert, M., . . . Cuenca-Sanchez, Y. (2014). Fluent persuasive writing with counterarguments for students with emotional disturbance. *Journal of Special Education*, *48*(1).

Mayer-Johnson, R. (2000). *The Picture Communication Symbols guide.* Author.

Moljord, G. (2018). Curriculum research for students with intellectual disabilities: A content analytic review. *European Journal of Special Needs Education*, *33*, 646–659.

Montague, M. (2011). Effective instruction in mathematics for students with learning disabilities. In C. Wyatt-Smith, J. Elkins, & S. Gunn (Eds.), *Multiple perspectives on difficulties in learning literacy and numeracy* (pp. 295–314). Springer.

Monzo, M. P., Micotti, S., & Rashid, S. (2015). The mutism of the mind: Child and family therapists at work with children and families suffering with selective mutism. *Journal of Child Psychotherapy*, *41*, 22–40.

Morphy, P. & Graham, S. (2012). Word processing programs and weaker writers/readers: A meta-analysis of research findings. *Reading and Writing Quarterly*, *25*, 641–678.

National Center for Health Statistics. (2021). *Health, United States, 2019: Table 012*. https://www.cdc.gov/nchs/hus/contents2019.htm.

National Center on Intensive Intervention at American Institutes for Research. (2016). http://www.intensiveintervention.org/special-topics/mtss

Nigg, J. T., Lewis, K., Edinger, T., & Falk, M. (2012). Meta-analysis of attention-deficit/hyperactivity disorder or attention-deficit/hyperactivity disorder symptoms, restriction diet, and synthetic food color additives. *Journal of the American Academy of Child and Adolescent Psychiatry*, *51*, 86–97.

Oswald, D. P., Best, A. M., Coutinho, M. J., & Nagle, H. A. L. (2003). Trends in the special education identification rates of boys and girls: A call for research and change. *Exceptionality*, *11*, 223–237.

Owens, R. E., Farinella, K. A., & Metz, D. E. (2019). *Introduction to communication disorders: A life span evidence-based perspective* (6th ed.). Pearson.

Palson, K. (1986). *Essence of Kirstin.* Author.

Petscher, Y., Solari, E. J., & Catts, H. W. (2019). Conditional longitudinal relations of elementary literacy skills to high school reading comprehension. *Journal of Learning Disabilities*, *52*, 324–336.

Polloway, E. A., Bouck, E. C., Patton, J. R., & Lubin, J. (2017). Intellectual and developmental disabilities. In J. M. Kauffman, D. P. Hallahan, & P. C. Pullen (Eds.), *Handbook of special education* (2nd ed., pp. 271–285). Routledge.

Polsgrove, L., & Smith, S. W. (2004). Informed practice in teaching self-control to children with emotional and behavioral disorders. In R. B. Rutherford, M. M. Quinn, & S. R. Mathur (Eds.), *Handbook of research in emotional and behavioral disorders* (pp. 399–425). Guilford Press.

Pullen, P. C., Lane, H. B., Ashworth, K. E., & Lovelace, S. P. (2017). Specific learning disabilities. In J. M. Kauffman, D. P. Hallahan, & P. C. Pullen (Eds.), *Handbook of special education* (2nd ed., pp. 286–299). Routledge.

Raymond, E. B. (2017). *Students with mild disabilities: A characteristics approach* (5th ed.). Pearson.

Regan, K. (2009). Improving the way we think about students with EBD in our classroom. *Teaching Exceptional Children, 41*(5), 60–65.

Rooney, K. J. (2017). Attention deficit hyperactivity disorder. In J. M. Kauffman, D. P. Hallahan, & P. C. Pullen (Eds.), *Handbook of special education* (2nd ed., pp. 300–311). Routledge.

Roording-Ragetlie, S., Slaats-Willemse, D., Buitelaar, J., & Molen, M. (2018). Working memory in children with mild to borderline intellectual disabilities: A systematic review of strengths and weaknesses. *Journal of Child Psychology, 2*, 16–22.

Schalock, R. L., Luckasson, R. A., & Tasse, M. J. (2021). *Intellectual disability: Definition, classification, and systems of support* (12th ed.). American Association on Intellectual and Developmental Disabilities.

Scheuermann, B. K., Billingsley, G. M., & Hall, J. A. (2022). *Positive behavioral supports for the classroom* (4th ed.). Pearson.

Schmitt, M. B., Justice, L. M., & Pentimonti, J. M. (2014). Language processes: Characterization and prevention of language-learning disabilities. In H. L. Swanson, K. R. Harris, & S. Graham (Eds.), *Handbook of learning disabilities* (2nd ed., pp. 256–277). Guilford Press.

Scott, L. (2010). *Stuttering: Straight talk for teachers* (3rd ed.). Stuttering Foundation of America.

Scruggs, T. E., & Marsing, L. (1988). Teaching test-taking skills to behaviorally disordered students. *Behavioral Disorders, 13*, 240–244.

Scruggs, T. E., Mastropieri, M. A., Berkeley, S., & Marshak, L. (2010). Mnemonic strategies: Evidence-based practice and practice-based evidence. *Intervention in School and Clinic, 46*, 79–86.

Shapiro, T. R. (2012, September 8). Number of Fairfax students who speak a foreign language at home to surpass 50 percent. *Washington Post*. https://www.washingtonpost.com/local/education/number-of-fairfax-students-who-speak-a-foreign-language-at-home-to-surpass-50-percent/2012/09/08/de47a92a-f84d-11e1-8253-3f495ae70650_story.html

Shriner, J. G., & Wehby, J. H. (2004). Accountability and assessment for students with emotional and behavioral disorders. In R. B. Rutherford, M. M. Quinn, & S. R. Mathur (Eds.), *Handbook of research in emotional and behavioral disorders* (pp. 216–234). Guilford Press.

Siegel, L. S., & Mazabel, S. (2014). Basic cognitive processes and learning disabilities. In H. L. Swanson, K. R. Harris, & S. Graham (Eds.), *Handbook of learning disabilities* (2nd ed., pp. 186–213). Guilford Press.

Siperstein, G. N., Wiley, A. L., & Forness, S. R. (2011). School context and the academic and behavioral progress of students with emotional disturbance. *Behavioral Disorders, 36*, 172–184.

Spooner, F., & Brown, F. (2017). Educating students with significant cognitive disabilities. In J. M. Kauffman, D. P. Hallahan, & P. C. Pullen (Eds.), *Handbook of special education* (2nd ed., pp. 617–631). Routledge.

Stevens, L. J., Burgess, J. R., Stochelski, M. A., & Kuczek, T. (2015). Amounts of artificial food dyes and added sugars in foods and sweets commonly consumed by children. *Clinical Pediatrics, 54*, 309–321.

Stormont, M., Herman, K. C., & Reinke, W. M. (2015). The overlooked children: How teachers can support children with internalizing behaviors. *Beyond Behavior, 24*, 39–45.

Swanson, H. L., & Zheng, X. (2014). Memory and learning disabilities. In H. L. Swanson, K. R. Harris, & S. Graham (Eds.), *Handbook of learning disabilities* (2nd ed., pp. 214–238). Guilford Press.

Swendsen, J., Conway, K. P., Degenhardt, L., Glantz, M., Jin, R., Merikangas, K. R., . . . Kessler, R. C. (2011). Mental disorders as risk factors for substance use, abuse and dependence: Results from the 10-year follow-up of the National Comorbidity Survey. *Addiction, 105*, 1117–1128.

Tobin, C. E., & Simpson, R. (2012). Consequence maps: A novel behavior management tool for educators. *Teaching Exceptional Children, 44*, 68–75.

Turtura, J. E., Anderson, C. M., & Boyd, R. J., (2014). Addressing task avoidance in middle school students: Academic behavior check-in/check-out. *Journal of Positive Behavior Interventions, 16*, 159–167.

U.S. Department of Education, Office of Special Education and Rehabilitative Services, Office of Special Education Programs. (2008). *Identifying and treating attention deficit hyperactivity disorder: A resource for school and home*. https://www2.ed.gov/rschstat/research/pubs/adhd/adhd-identifying-2008.pdf

U.S. Department of Education. (2020). *42nd annual report to Congress on the implementation of the Individuals with Disabilities Education Act*. Author.

U.S. Department of Education. (2021). *43rd annual report to Congress on the Implementation of the Individuals with Disabilities Education Act*. Washington, DC: Author. Retrieved from https://sites.ed.gov/idea/2020-annual-report-congress-idea/

Vatterott, C. (2018). *Rethinking homework: Best practices that support diverse learning needs* (2nd ed.). Association for Supervision and Curriculum Development.

Vaughn, S. R., & Bos, C. S. (2021). *Strategies for teaching students with learning and behavior problems* (10th ed). Pearson Education.

Watts, G. W. & McKenna, J. W. (2021). Training, supervising, and supporting students with emotional-behavioral disorders as cross-age tutors. *Intervention in School and Clinic*. [Epub ahead of print]

Wei, X., Yu, J. W., & Shaver, D. (2014). Longitudinal effects of ADHD in children with learning disabilities or emotional disturbances. *Exceptional Children, 80*, 205–219.

Wessendorp, M., Houwen, S., Hartman, E., & Visscher, C. (2011). Are gross motor skills and sports participation related in children with intellectual disabilities? *Research in Developmental Disabilities, 32*, 1147–1153.

Westling, D. L., Fox, L., Carter, E. W., Da Fonte, A. M., & Kurth, J. A. (2021). *Teaching students with severe disabilities* (6th ed.). Pearson.

Wittaker, M., & Burns, M. K. (2019). *Evaluation for specific learning disabilities: Allowable methods of identification and their implications*. National Center for Learning Disabilities. https://www.ncld.org/wp-content/uploads/2019/11/NCLD-White-Paper-Evaluation-for-Specific-Learning-Disabilities-Allowable-Methods-of-Identification-Their-Implications.Final_.pdf

Wolraich, M. L., DuPaul, G. J., & Stevens, S. W. (2010). *ADHD diagnosis and management: A practical guide for the clinic and the classroom*. Brookes.

Wong, T. T. Y., Ho, C. S. H., & Tang, J. (2017). Defective number sense or impaired access?: Differential impairment in different subgroups of children with mathematics difficulties. *Journal of Learning Disabilities, 50*, 49–61.

Wright, P. W. D., & Wright, P. D. (2005). *Wrightslaw: IDEA 2004*. Harbor House Law Press.

Chapter 4

American Association on Intellectual and Developmental Disabilities (AAIDD). (2010). *User's guide to intellectual disability: Definition, classification, and systems of support* (11th ed.). Author.

American Psychiatric Association. (2013). *Diagnostic and statistical manual of mental disorders* (5th ed.). Author.

American Speech-Language-Hearing Association (ASHA). (2005). *Effects of hearing loss on development*. Reading Rockets. https://www.readingrockets.org/article/effects-hearing-loss-development

Asmus, J. M., Carter, E. W., Moss, C. K., Biggs, E. E., Bolt, D. M., Born, T. L., . . . Weir, K. (2017). Efficacy and social validity of peer network interventions for high school students with severe disabilities. *American Journal of Intellectual and Developmental Disabilities*, *122*, 118–137.

Ayres, K. M., Lowrey, K. A., Douglas, K. H., & Sievers, C. (2011). I can identify Saturn but I can't brush my teeth: What happens when the curricular focus for students with severe disability shifts? *Education and Training in Autism and Developmental Disabilities*, *46*, 28–35.

Best, S. J. (2009). Coping with degenerative and terminal illness. In K. W. Heller, P. E. Forney, P. A. Alberto, S. J. Best, & M. N. Schwartzman (Eds.), *Understanding physical, health, and multiple disabilities* (pp. 281–292). Merrill/Prentice Hall.

Best, S. J. (2010a). Health impairments and congenital infections. In S. J. Best, K. W. Heller, & J. L. Bigge (Eds.), *Teaching individuals with physical or multiple disabilities* (5th ed., pp. 59–85). Merrill/Prentice Hall.

Best, S. J. (2010b). Physical disabilities. In S. J. Best, K. W. Heller, & J. L. Bigge (Eds.), *Teaching individuals with physical or multiple disabilities* (6th ed., pp. 32–58). Merrill/Prentice Hall.

Best, S. J. (2010c). Understanding individuals with physical, health, and multiple disabilities. In S. J. Best, K. W. Heller, & J. L. Bigge (Eds.), *Teaching individuals with physical or multiple disabilities* (6th ed., pp. 3–31). Merrill/Prentice Hall.

Best, S. J., & Bigge, J. L. (2010). Cerebral palsy. In S. J. Best, K. W. Heller, & J. L. Bigge (Eds.), *Teaching individuals with physical or multiple disabilities* (6th ed., pp. 59–81). Merrill/Prentice Hall.

Best, S. J., & Heller, K. W. (2009). Acquired infections and AIDS. In K. W. Heller, P. E. Forney, P. A. Alberto, S. J. Best, & M. N. Schwartzman (Eds.), *Understanding physical, health, and multiple disabilities* (pp. 368–386). Merrill/Prentice Hall.

Best, S. J., Heller, K. W., & Bigge, J. L. (Eds.). (2009). *Teaching individuals with physical or multiple disabilities* (5th ed.). Merrill/Prentice Hall.

Best, S. J., Heller, K. W., & Bigge, J. L. (Eds.). (2010). *Teaching individuals with physical or multiple disabilities* (6th ed.). Merrill/Prentice Hall.

Best, S. J., Reed, P., & Bigge, J. L. (2010). Assistive technology. In S. J. Best, K. W. Heller, & J. L. Bigge (Eds.), *Teaching individuals with physical or multiple disabilities* (6th ed., pp. 175–220). Merrill/Prentice Hall.

Bondy, A., & Frost, L. (2011). *A picture's worth: PECS and other visual communication strategies in autism* (2nd ed.). Woodbine House.

Briggs, G., Freeman, R. R., Towers, C. V., & Forinash, A. B. (2021). *Drugs in pregnancy and lactation* (12th ed.). Williams & Wilkins.

Browder, D. M. (2015). What should we teach students with moderate and severe developmental disabilities? In B. Bateman, J. Lloyd, & M. Tankersley (Eds.), *Enduring issues in special education: Personal perspectives* (pp. 52–72). Routledge.

Brown, F., McDonnell, J., & Snell, M. E. (2020). *Instruction of students with severe disabilities* (9th ed.). Pearson.

Bruce, S. M., & Ivy, S. E. (2017). Severe and multiple disabilities. In J. M. Kauffman, D. P. Hallahan, & P. C. Pullen (Eds.), *Handbook of special education* (2nd ed., pp. 411–427). Routledge.

Carr, M. E., Moore, D. W., & Anderson, A. (2014). Self-management interventions on students with autism: A meta-analysis of single subject research. *Exceptional Children*, *81*, 28–44.

Carter, E. W., Asmus, J. M., Moss, C. K., Cooney, M., Weir, K., Vincent, L., . . . Fesperman, E. (2013). Peer network strategies to foster social connections among adolescents with and without severe disabilities. *Teaching Exceptional Children*, *46*(2), 51–59.

Carter, E. W., Moss, C. K., Hoffman, A., Chung, Y., & Sisco, L. (2011). Efficacy and social validity of peer support arrangements for adolescents with disabilities. *Exceptional Children*, *78*, 107–125.

Clarke, L. S., Embury, D. C., Jones, R. E., & Yssel, N. (2014). Supporting students with disabilities during school crises: A teacher's guide. *Teaching Exceptional Children*, *46*, 169–178.

Courtade, G., Spooner, F., Browder, D. M., & Jimenez, B. (2012). Seven reasons to promote standards-based instruction for students with severe disabilities. *Education and Training in Autism and Developmental Disabilities*, *47*, 3–13.

Davis, P. (2003). *Including children with visual impairment in mainstream schools: A practical guide.* David Fulton.

Definition; Child with a Disability; Specific Learning Disability, 20 U.S.C., § 1401(3); 1401(30) (2004).

Drasgow, E., Wolery, M., Chezan, L. C., Halle, J., & Hajiaghamohseni, Z. (2017). Systematic instruction of students with significant disabilities. In J. Kauffman, D. P. Hallahan, & P. C. Pullen (Eds.), *Handbook of special education* (2nd ed., pp. 632–648). Routledge.

Dunst, C. (2014). Meta-analysis of the effects of puppet shows on attitudes toward and knowledge of individuals with disabilities. *Exceptional Children*, *80*, 136–148.

Dymond, S. K. (2017). Functional curriculum for students with significant disabilities. In J. M. Kauffman, D. P. Hallahan, & P. C. Pullen (Eds.), *Handbook of special education* (2nd ed., pp. 675–686). Routledge.

Flower, A., Burns, M. K., & Bottesford-Miller, N. A. (2007). Meta-analysis of disability simulation research. *Remedial and Special Education*, *28*, 72–79.

Gay, G. (2018). *Culturally responsive teaching* (3rd ed). Teachers College Press.

Giangreco, M. F., Broer, S. M., & Suter, J. C. (2011). Guidelines for selecting alternatives to overreliance on paraprofessionals: Field-testing in inclusion-oriented schools. *Remedial and Special Education*, *32*, 22–28.

Giangreco, M. F., Doyle, S. M., & Suter, J. C. (2014). Teacher assistants in inclusive classes. In L. Florian (Ed.), *Sage handbook of special education* (Vol. 2, pp. 691–702). Sage.

Goldstein, H., Lackey, K. C., & Schneider, N. J. (2014). A new framework for systematic reviews: Application to social skills interventions for preschoolers with autism. *Exceptional Children*, *80*, 262–286.

Graetz, J. S., Mastropieri, M. A., & Scruggs, T. E. (2009). Promoting social behavior for adolescents with autism with social stories. *Education and Training in Developmental Disabilities*, *44*, 91–104.

Grandinette, S., & Best, S. J. (2009). Traumatic brain injury. In K. W. Heller, P. E. Forney, P. A. Alberto, S. J. Best, & M. N. Schwartzman (Eds.), *Understanding physical, health, and multiple disabilities* (pp. 118–138). Merrill/Prentice Hall.

Hall, L. J. (2018). *Autism spectrum disorders: From theory to practice* (3rd ed.). Merrill/Pearson.

Hamill, A. C., & Stein, C. H. (2011). Culture and empowerment in the deaf community: An analysis of Internet weblogs. *Journal of Community and Applied Social Psychology*, *21*, 388–406.

Hashey, A. L., & Stall, S. (2014). Making online learning accessible for students with disabilities. *Teaching Exceptional Children*, *46*, 70–78.

Heller, K. W. (2009). Traumatic spinal cord injury and spina bifida. In K. W. Heller, P. E. Forney, P. A. Alberto, S. J. Best, & M. N. Schwartzman (Eds.), *Understanding physical, health, and multiple disabilities* (pp. 94–117). Merrill/Prentice Hall.

Heller, K. W., & Avant, M. J. T. (2009). Juvenile rheumatoid arthritis, arthrogryposis, and osteogenesis imperfecta. In K. W. Heller, P. E. Forney, P. A. Alberto, S. J. Best, & M. N. Schwartzman (Eds.), *Understanding physical, health, and multiple disabilities* (pp. 172–191). Merrill/Prentice Hall.

Heller, K. W., Bigge, J. L., & Allgood, P. (2010). Adaptations for personal independence. In S. J. Best, K. W. Heller, & J. L. Bigge (Eds.), *Teaching individuals with physical or multiple disabilities* (6th ed., pp. 289–310). Merrill/Prentice Hall.

Heller, K. W., & Cohen, E. T. (2009). Seizures and epilepsy. In K. W. Heller, P. E. Forney, P. A. Alberto, S. J. Best, & M. N. Schwartzman (Eds.), *Understanding physical, health, and multiple disabilities* (pp. 294–315). Merrill/Prentice Hall.

Heller, K. W., Forney, P. E., Alberto, P. A., Best, S. J., & Schwartzman, M. N. (Eds.). (2009). *Understanding physical, health, and multiple disabilities* (2nd ed). Merrill/Prentice Hall.

Heller, K. W., & Garrett, J. T. (2009). Cerebral palsy. In K. W. Heller, P. E. Forney, P. A. Alberto, S. J. Best, & M. N. Schwartzman (Eds.), *Understanding physical, health, and multiple disabilities* (pp. 72–93). Merrill/Prentice Hall.

Heller, K. W., Mezei, P., & Schwartzman, M. (2009). Muscular dystrophies. In K. W. Heller, P. E. Forney, P. A. Alberto, S. J. Best, & M. N. Schwartzman (Eds.), *Understanding physical, health, and multiple disabilities* (pp. 232–249). Merrill/Prentice Hall.

Hill, A. P., Zuckerman, K., & Fombonne, E. (2015). Epidemiology of autism spectrum disorders. In M. Robinson-Agramonte (Ed.), *Translational approaches to autism spectrum disorders* (pp. 13–38). Springer.

Hochman, J. M., Carter, E. W., Bottema-Beutel, K., Harvey, M. N., & Gustafson, J. R. (2015). Efficacy of peer networks to increase social connections among high school students with autism spectrum disorder. *Exceptional Children*, *82*, 96–116.

Ioannou, D., Kelly, T. E., & Tempest, H. G. (2016). The role of genetic mechanisms in childhood disabilities. In R. H. A. Haslam & P. J. Valletutti (Eds.), *Medical problems in the classroom: The teacher's role in diagnosis and management* (5th ed., pp. 31–67). Pro-Ed.

Ison, N., McIntyre, S., Rothery, S., Smithers-Sheedy, H., Goldsmith, S., Parsonage, S., & Foy, L. (2010). "Just like you": A disability awareness programme for children that enhanced knowledge, attitudes and acceptance: Pilot study findings. *Developmental Neurorehabilitation*, *13*, 360–368.

Jacobson, J. W., & Mulick, J. A. (1996). *Manual of diagnosis and professional practice in mental retardation.* American Psychological Association.

Jones, K. L., Smith, D. W., Ulleland, C. N., & Streissguth, A. P. (1973). Patterns of malformation in offspring of chronic alcoholic mothers. *The Lancet*, *1*(1267), 1271.

Kunts, E., & Carter, E. W. (2019). Review of interventions supporting secondary students with intellectual disability in general education classes. *Research and Practice for Persons with Severe Disabilities*, *44*, 101–121.

Lijiness-O'Neill, R., Erdodo, L. A., & Lichtenstein, J. D. (2017). Traumatic brain injury. In J. M. Kauffman, D. P. Hallahan, & P. C. Pullen (Eds.), *Handbook of special education* (2nd ed., pp. 377–393). Routledge.

Lomas, G. L., Andrews, J. F., & Shaw, P. C. (2017). Deaf and hard of hearing students. In J. M. Kauffman, D. P. Hallahan, & P. C. Pullen (Eds.), *Handbook of special education* (2nd ed., pp. 338–357). Routledge.

Luckner, J. L., Slike, S. B., & Johnson, H. (2012). Helping students who are deaf or hard of hearing succeed. *Teaching Exceptional Children*, *44*, 58–67.

Marshark, M., Lang, H. G., & Albertini, G. A. (2002). *Educating deaf students: From research to practice.* Oxford University Press.

Martin, G., & Pear, J. (2019). *Behavior modification: What it is and how to do it* (11th ed.). Routledge.

Martin, R., & Wilkins, J. (2021). Creating visually appropriate classroom environments for students with autism spectrum disorder. *Intervention in School and Clinic*, *57*(4). [Epub ahead of print]

Mathews, J. (2008, March 31). New microphones are bringing crystal-clear changes. *Washington Post*, p. B2.

Mueller, T. G. (2017). Promoting collaborative partnerships with families. In J. M. Kauffman, D. P. Hallahan, & P. C. Pullen (Eds.), *Handbook of special education* (2nd ed., pp. 773–792). Routledge.

National Professional Development Center on Autism Spectrum Disorder. (2014). *Evidence-based practices.* Frank Porter Graham Center, University of North Carolina. http://autismpdc.fpg.unc.edu/evidence-based-practices?utm_source=Copy+of+Ready%2C+Set%2C+Go+%7C+April++2016&utm_campaign=Ready+Set+Go+April+2016&utm_medium=email

Obiakor, F. E., Utley, C. A., Smith, R., & Harris-Obiakor, P. (2002). The Comprehensive Support Model for culturally diverse exceptional learners: Intervention in an age of change. *Intervention in School and Clinic*, *38*, 14–27.

Owens, R. E. & Farinella, K. A. (2018). *Introduction to communication disorders: A life span perspective* (6th ed.). Allyn & Bacon.

Polloway, E. A., Bouk, E. C., Patton, J. R., & Lubin, J. (2017). Intellectual and developmental disabilities. In J. M. Kauffman, D. P. Hallahan, & P. C. Pullen (Eds.), *Handbook of special education* (2nd ed., pp. 265–285). Routledge.

Prince, A. M. T. & Hayden, H. E. (2021). Repositioning disability in children's picture books through classroom read-alouds. *Teaching Exceptional Children.* [Epub ahead of print]

Qi, C. H., Barton, E. E., Collier, M., Lin, Y. L., & Montoya, C. (2018). A systematic review of effects of social stories interventions for individuals with autism spectrum disorder. *Focus on Autism and Other Developmental Disabilities*, *33*, 25–34.

Salend, S, J. (2005). Using technology to teach about individual differences related to disability. *Teaching Exceptional Children*, *38*, 32–38.

Schalock, R. L., Borthwick-Duffie, S., Bradley, V., Buntinx, W. H. E., Coulter, D. L., Craig, E. M., . . . Yeager, M. H. (2010). *Intellectual disability: Definition, classification, and systems of support.* American Association on Intellectual and Developmental Disabilities.

Spooner, F., & Brown, F. (2017). Educating students with severe cognitive disabilities: Historical overview and future projections. In J. M. Kauffman, D. P. Hallahan, & P. C. Pullen (Eds.), *Handbook of special education* (2nd ed., pp. 617–631). Routledge.

Steinbrenner, J. R., Hume, K., Odom, S. L., Morin, K. L., Nowell, S. W., Tomaszewski, B., . . . Savage, M. N. (2020). *Evidence-based practices for children, youth, and young adults with autism.* University of North Carolina at Chapel Hill, Frank Porter Graham Child Development Institute, National Clearinghouse on Autism Evidence and Practice Review Team. https://ncaep.fpg.unc.edu/sites/ncaep.fpg.unc.edu/files/imce/documents/EBP%20Report%202020.pdf

Stewart, D. A., & Kluwin, T. N. (2001). *Teaching deaf and hard of hearing students: Content, strategies, and curriculum.* Allyn & Bacon.

Stichter, J. P., Conroy, M. O'Donnell, R., & Reichow, B. (2017). Current issues and trends in the education of children and youth with autism spectrum disorders. In J. M. Kauffman, D. P. Hallahan, & P. C. Pullen (Eds.), *Handbook of special education* (2nd ed., pp. 394–410). Routledge.

Thiemann-Bourque, K., Brady, N., McGuff, S., Stump, K., & Naylor, A. (2016). Picture exchange communication system and Pals: A peer-mediated augmentative and alternative communication intervention for minimally verbal preschoolers with autism. *Journal of Speech, Language, and Hearing Research*, *59*, 1133–1145.

Turnbull, A. P., Turnbull, H. R., Erwin, E., Soodak, L., & Shogren, K. (2015). *Families, professionals, and exceptionality: Positive outcomes through partnerships and trust* (7th ed.). Pearson.

U.S. Department of Education. (2006). *The Individuals with Disabilities Act Amendments of 2004. Final regulations.* http://idea.ed.gov/explore/view/p/,root,regs,300,A,300%252E8

U.S. Department of Education (2020). *42nd annual report to Congress on the implementation of the Individuals with Disabilities Education Act.* https://sites.ed.gov/idea/2020-annual-report-congress-idea/

U.S. Department of Education (2021). *43rd annual report to Congress on the Implementation of the Individuals with Disabilities Education Act.* Washington, DC: Author. Retrieved from https://sites.ed.gov/idea/2020-annual-report-congress-idea/

Vanderheiden, G. C., & Lloyd, L. L. (1986). Non-speech modes and systems. In S. W. Blackstone (Ed.), *Augmentative communication* (pp. 148–161). American Speech-Language-Hearing Association.

Vivanti, G. (2020). Ask the editor: What is the most appropriate way to talk about individuals with a diagnosis of autism? *Journal of Autism and Developmental Disabilities*, *50*, 691–669.

Voss, C., Schwartz, J., Daniels, J., Kline, A., Haber, N., Washington, P., . . . Wall, D. P. (2019). Effect of wearable digital interventions for improving socialization in children with autism spectrum disorder: A randomized clinical trial. *JAMA Pediatrics*, *173*, 446–454.

Wehmeyer, M. L., & Shogren, K. A. (2017). Access to general education curriculum for students with significant disabilities. In J. M. Kauffman, D. P. Hallahan, & P. C. Pullen (Eds.), *Handbook of special education* (2nd ed., pp. 662–674). Routledge.

Westling, D. L., Carter, E. W., Da Fonte, A., & Kurth, J. A. (2021). *Teaching students with severe disabilities* (6th ed.). Pearson.

Wheeler, J. J., Mayton, M. R., & Carter, S. L. (2015). *Methods for teaching students with autism spectrum disorders: Evidence-based practices.* Pearson.

Wong, C., Odom, S. L., Hume, K. A., Cox, C. W., Fettig, A., Kurcharczyk, S., . . . Schultz, T. R. (2015). Evidence-based practices for children, youth, and young adults with autism spectrum disorder: A comprehensive review. *Journal of Autism and Developmental Disorders*, *45*, 1951–1966.

Zebehazy, K. T., & Lawson, H. (2017). Blindness and low vision. In J. M. Kauffman, D. P. Hallahan, & P. C. Pullen (Eds.), *Handbook of special education* (2nd ed., pp. 358–376). Routledge.

Zhang, J., & Wheeler, J. J. (2011). A meta-analysis of peer-mediated interventions for young children with autism spectrum disorders. *Education and Training in Autism and Developmental Disabilities*, *46*, 62–77.

Zimmerman, G. J., & Zebehazy, K. T. (2011). Blindness and low vision. In J. M. Kaufman & D. P. Hallahan (Eds.), *Handbook of special education* (pp. 247–261). Routledge.

Zirkel, P. A. (2020). An updated primer of special education law. *Teaching Exceptional Children*, *52*, 261–265.

Chapter 5

9 recommendations for inclusive learning recovery for students with disabilities. (2021, March 18). National Center for Learning Disabilities. https://www.ncld.org/wp-content/uploads/2021/03/9-Recommendations-for-Inclusive-Learning-Recovery-for-Students-with-Disabilities-Final-1.pdf

Anastasiou, D., Gardner, R., & Michail, D. (2011). Ethnicity and exceptionality. In J. M. Kauffman & D. P. Hallahan (Eds.), *Handbook of special education* (pp. 745–758). Routledge.

Artiles, A. J., Kozleski, E. B., Trent, S. C., Osher, D., & Ortiz, A. (2010). Justifying and explaining disproportionality, 1968–2008: A critique of underlying views. *Exceptional Children*, *76*, 279–299.

Baca, L. M., Baca, E., & de Valenzuela, J. S. (2004a). Background and rationale for bilingual special education. In L. M. Baca & H. T. Cervantes (Eds.), *The bilingual special education interface* (4th ed., pp. 1–23). Merrill/Prentice Hall.

Baca, L. M., Baca, E., & de Valenzuela, J. S. (2004b). Development of the bilingual special education interface. In L. M. Baca & H. T. Cervantes (Eds.), *The bilingual special education interface* (4th ed., pp. 101–123). Merrill/Prentice Hall.

Baca, L. M., & Cervantes, H. T. (Eds.). (2004). *The bilingual special education interface* (4th ed.). Merrill/Prentice Hall.

Baker, D. L., Al Otaiba, S., Ortiz, M., Correa, V., & Cole, R. (2014). Vocabulary development and intervention for English learners in the early grades. *Advances Child Development and Behavior*, *46*, 281–338.

Banks, J. A. (2015). *Cultural diversity and education: Foundations, curriculum, and teaching* (6th ed.). Pearson.

Beach, C. (2014). *At-risk students: Transforming student behavior.* Rowman & Littlefield Education.

Bireley, M. (1995). Identifying high ability/high achievement giftedness. In J. L. Genshaft, M. Bireley, & C. L. Hollinger (Eds.), *Serving gifted and talented students: A resource for school personnel* (pp. 49–65). Pro-Ed.

Brown, S. M., Doom, J. R., Lechuga-Pena, S., Watamura, S. E., & Koppels, T. (2020). Stress and parenting during the global COVID-19 pandemic. *Child Abuse and Neglect*, *110*(Pt. 2), 104699.

Caplan, P., & Dinardo, L. (1986). Is there a relationship between child abuse and learning disability? *Canadian Journal of Behavioral Science*, *18*, 367–380.

Cartledge, G., Gardner, R., & Ford, D. Y. (2007). *Diverse learners with exceptionalities: Culturally responsive teaching in the inclusive classroom.* Merrill Education.

Castellano, J. A., & Frazier, A. D. (Eds.). (2021). *Special populations in gifted education.* Routledge.

Centers for Disease Control and Prevention (2020). *Teen substance use & risks.* https://www.cdc.gov/ncbddd/fasd/features/teen-substance-use.html

Child Welfare Information Gateway. (2011). *About CAPTA: A legislative history.* U.S. Department of Health and Human Services, Children's Bureau.

Children's Defense Fund. (2020). *Each day in America.* https://www.childrensdefense.org/policy/resources/soac-2020-each-day/

Chinn, P. C., & Hughes, S. (1987). Representation of minority students in special education classes. *Remedial and Special Education*, *8*(4), 41–46.

Clark, B. (2013). *Growing up gifted* (8th ed.). Pearson.

Crosson-Tower, C. (2021). *Understanding child abuse and neglect* (10th ed.). Pearson.

Davis, G. A., Siegle, D. B., & Rimm, S. B., (2018). *Education of the gifted and talented* (7th ed.). Pearson.

Definitions; Gifted, Pub. L. No. 100-297, § 4103 (1998).

Diamond, L. J., & Jaudes, P. K. (1983). Child abuse in a cerebral-palsied population. *Developmental Medicine and Child Neurology*, *25*, 169–174.

Donovan, S., & Cross, C. (Eds.). (2002). *Minority students in special and gifted education.* National Research Council.

East, K., & Thomas, R. L. (2007). *Across cultures: A guide to multicultural literature for children.* Libraries Unlimited.

Echevarria, J. J., & Graves, A. (2015). *Sheltered content instruction: Teaching English learners with diverse abilities* (5th ed.). Pearson.

Echevarria, J. J., Vogt, M., & Short, D. (2017). *Making content comprehensible for English learners: The SIOP model* (5th ed.). Pearson.

Ehlers-Zavala, F. P. (2011). History of bilingual special education. In A. F. Rotatori, F. E. Obiakor, & J. P. Bakken (Eds.), *History of special education* (pp. 343–362). Emerald.

Feldhusen, J. F., & Moon, S. (1995). The educational continuum and delivery of services. In J. L. Genshaft, M. Bireley, & C. L. Hollinger (Eds.), *Serving gifted and talented students: A resource for school personnel* (pp. 103–121). Pro-Ed.

Ford, D. Y. (2011). *Reversing underachievement among gifted Black students.* Prufrock.

Ford, D. Y. (2012). Culturally different students in special education: Looking backward to move forward. *Exceptional Children, 78,* 391–405.

Ford, D.Y., Collins, K.C., & Grantham, T.C. (2022). Addressing gifts and talents, racial identity, and social-emotional learning regarding students of color: Challenges and recommendations. In Johnsen, S.K., Dailey, D., & Cotabish, A. (Eds.) *NACG Pre-K-Grade 12 Gifted education programming standards: A guide to planning and implementation.* (2nd ed., pp. 58–93), Routledge.

Frieman, B. B. (2001). *What teachers need to know about children at risk.* Allyn & Bacon.

Gardner, H. (2006). *Multiple intelligences: New horizons in theory and practice.* Basic Books.

Gollnick, D. M., & Chinn, P. C. (2021). *Multicultural education in a pluralistic society* (11th ed.). Pearson.

Grandinette, S., & Best, S. J. (2009). Traumatic brain injury. In K. W. Heller, P. E. Forney, P. A. Alberto, S. J. Best, & M. N. Schwartzman (Eds.), *Understanding physical, health, and multiple disabilities* (pp. 118–138). Merrill/Prentice Hall.

Grassi, E. A., & Barker, H. B. (2010). *Culturally and linguistically diverse exceptional students: Strategies for teaching and assessment.* Sage.

Gregory, D. A., Starnes, W. T., & Blaylock, A. W. (1988). Finding and nurturing potential giftedness among Black and Hispanic students. In A. A. Ortiz & B. A. Ramirez (Eds.), *Schools and the culturally diverse exceptional student: Promising practices and future directions* (pp. 76–85). Council for Exceptional Children.

Grissom, J. A., & Redding, C. (2016). Discretion and disproportionality: Explaining the underrepresentation of high-achieving students of color in gifted programs. *American Educational Research Association Open, 2.*

Grossman, R. (1997, July 6). What is an American? *Chicago Tribune Magazine,* pp. 11–16, 21.

Harry, B. (1992). *Cultural diversity, families, and the special education system.* Teachers College Press.

Harry, B. (1994). *The disproportionate representation of minority students in special education.* National Association of State Directors of Special Education.

Harry, B., Arnaiz, P., Klingner, J., & Sturges, K. (2008). Schooling and the construction of identity in Spain and the United States. *Journal of Special Education, 42,* 15–25.

Harry, B., & Klingner, J. (2014). *Why are so many minority students in special education? Understanding race and disability in schools* (2nd ed.). Teachers College Press.

Herbers, J. E., Cutuli, J. J., Keanu, J. N., & Leonard, J. A. (2020). Childhood homelessness, resilience, and adolescent mental health: A prospective, person-centered approach. *Psychology in the Schools, 57,* 1830–1844.

Hoffman, S. D., & Maynard, R. A. (2008). *Kids having kids: Economic costs and social consequences of teen pregnancy.* Urban Institute Press.

Jensen, E. (2009). *Teaching with poverty in mind: What being poor does to kids' brains and what schools can do about it.* Association for Supervision and Curriculum Development.

Johnsen, S. K., Dailey, D., & Cotabish, A. (Eds., 2022). *NACG Pre-K-Grade 12 Gifted education programming standards: A guide to planning and implementation* (2n ed.), Routledge.

Kalyanpur, M. (2008). The paradox of majority underrepresentation in special education in India: Constructions of difference in a developing country. *Journal of Special Education, 42,* 55–64.

Kauffman, J. M., & Landrum, T. (2018). *Characteristics of emotional and behavioral disorders of children and youth* (11th ed.). Pearson.

Klein, M., & Stern, L. (1971). Low birth weight and the battered child syndrome. *American Journal of Disabled Children, 122,* 15–18.

Kuhfeld, M., Soland, J., Tarasawa, B., Johnson, A., Ruzek, E., & Liu, J. (2020). Projecting the potential impact of COVID-19 school closures on academic achievement. *Educational Researcher, 49*(8), 549–565.

Lane, K. L., Cabell, S. Q., & Drew, S. V. (2021). A productive scholar's guide to respectful, responsible inquiry during the COVID-19 pandemic: Moving forward. *Journal of Learning Disabilities, 54*(5), 388–399.

Ludwig, C., Guo, K., & Georgiou, G. K. (2019). Are reading interventions for English language learners effective? A meta-analysis. *Journal of Learning Disabilities,52*(3), 220–231.

Lynch, E. W. (1992). Developing cross-cultural competence. In E. W. Lynch & M. J. Hanson (Eds.), *Developing cross-cultural competence* (pp. 35–59). Brookes.

MacMillan, D. L., & Reschly, D. J. (1998). Overrepresentation of minority students: The case for greater specificity or reconsideration of the variables examined. *Journal of Special Education, 32,* 15–24.

Marks, R. & Rios-Vargas, M. (2021, August, 3). *Improvements to the 2020 census race and Hispanic origin question designs, data processing, and coding procedures.* U.S. Census Bureau. https://www.census.gov/newsroom/blogs/random-samplings/2021/08/improvements-to-2020-census-race-hispanic-origin-question-designs.html

Miksic, S. (1987). Drug abuse management in adolescent special education. In M. M. Kerr, C. M. Nelson, & D. L. Lambert (Eds.), *Helping adolescents with learning and behavior problems* (pp. 226–253). Merrill/Prentice Hall.

Mizerek, E. A., & Hinz, E. E. (2004). Helping homeless students. *Principal Leadership Magazine, 4*(8). http://www.naspcenter.org/principals/nassp_homeless.html

National Association of School Psychologists. (2021). *Preventing youth suicide–tips for parents and educators.* https://www.nasponline.org/resources-and-publications/resources-and-podcasts/school-climate-safety-and-crisis/mental-health-resources/preventing-youth-suicide/preventing-youth-suicide-tips-for-parents-and-educators

National Coalition for the Homeless. (2007). *Education of homeless children and youth.* http://www.nationalhomeless.org/publications/facts/education.pdf

National Education Association. (2021). *Books by theme.* https://www.nea.org/professional-excellence/student-engagement/read-across-america/support-your-readers/books-by-theme

Navan, J. (2008). *Nurturing the gifted female: A guide for educators and parents.* Corwin Press.

Norton, D. E. (2012). *Multicultural children's literature: Through the eyes of many children* (4th ed.). Pearson.

Obiakor, F. E., & Roratori, A. (2014). *Multicultural education for learners with special needs in the twenty-first century.* Information Age.

Ovando, C. J., & Combs, M. C. (2018). *Bilingual and ESL classroom: Teaching in multicultural contexts* (7th ed.). McGraw-Hill.

Plucker, J., & Callahan, C. M. (Eds.). (2014a). *Critical issues and practices in gifted education: What the research says* (2nd ed.). Prufrock Press.

Plucker, J., & Callahan, C. M. (2014b). Research on giftedness and gifted education: Status of the field and considerations for the future. *Exceptional Children, 80,* 390–406.

Plucker, J., & Callahan, C. M. (2017). Special gifts and talents. In J. M. Kauffman, D. P. Hallahan, & P. Pullen (Eds.), *Handbook of special education* (2nd ed., pp. 428–444). Routledge.

Renzulli, J. S. (2005). The three-ring conception of giftedness: A developmental model for promoting creative productivity. In R. J. Sternberg & J. E. Davidson (Eds.), *Conceptions of giftedness* (pp. 246–279). Cambridge University Press.

Rinn, A. N., Mun, R. U., & Hodges, J. (2020). *2018–2019 State of the States in Gifted Education.* National Association for Gifted Children and the Council of State Directors of Programs for the Gifted. https://www.nagc.org/2018-2019-state-states-gifted-education

Salend, S. J., & Duhaney, L. M. G. (2005). Understanding and addressing the disproportionate representation of students of color in special education. *Intervention in School and Clinic*, *40*, 213–221.

Scott, A. N., Hauerwas, L. B., & Brown, R. D. (2014). State policy and guidance for identifying learning disabilities in culturally and linguistically diverse students. *Learning Disability Quarterly*, *37*(3), 172–185.

Sedlak, A. J., Mettenburg, J., Basena, M., Petta, I., McPherson, K., Greene, A., & Li, S. (2010). *Fourth National Incidence Study of Child Abuse and Neglect (NIS–4): Report to Congress.* U.S. Department of Health and Human Services, Administration for Children and Families.

Shaahinfar, A., Whitelaw, K. D., & Mansour, K. M. (2015). Update on abusive head trauma. *Current Opinion in Pediatrics*, *27*, 308–314.

Skar, G. B., Graham, S., & Huebner, A. (2021). Learning loss during the COVID-19 pandemic and the impact of emergency remote instruction on first grade students' writing: A natural experiment. *Journal of Educational Psychology*. [Epub ahead of print]

Sternberg, R. J. (2005). The triarchic theory of successful intelligence. In D. P. Flanagan & P. L. Harrison (Eds.), *Contemporary intellectual assessment: Theories, tests, and issues* (pp. 103–119). Guilford Press.

Suicide Prevention Lifeline. (2021). *Know the warning signs.* Substance Abuse and Mental Health Services Administration. https://suicidepreventionlifeline.org/how-we-can-all-prevent-suicide/

Sullivan, A. L. (2011). Disproportionality in special education identification and placement of English Language Learners. *Exceptional Children*, *77*, 317–334.

Taormina-Weiss, W. (2012). Homeless children with disabilities in America. *Disabled World.* http://www.disabled-world.com/disability/children/homeless-kids.php

Taylor, L. S., & Whittaker, C. R. (2009). *Bridging multiple worlds: Case studies of diverse educational communities* (2nd ed.). Pearson.

Tornquist, E. H., Mastropieri, M. A., Scruggs, T. E., Berry, H. G., & Halloran, W. D. (2009). The impact of poverty on special education. In T. E. Scruggs & M. A. Mastropieri (Eds.), *Policy and practice: Advances in learning and behavioral disabilities* (Vol. 22, pp. 169–188). Emerald.

U.S. Census Bureau. (2018). *Current Population Survey, 2018 Annual Social and Economic Supplement.* http://profiles.nche.seiservices.com/ConsolidatedStateProfile.aspx

U.S. Census Bureau. (2020a). *2020 census illuminates racial and ethnic composition of the country.* https://www.census.gov/library/stories/2021/08/improved-race-ethnicity-measures-reveal-united-states-population-much-more-multiracial.html

U.S. Census Bureau. (2020b). *About language use in the U.S. population.* https://www.census.gov/topics/population/language-use/about.html

U.S. Census Bureau. (2020c). *American Community Survey: Language spoken at home.* https://www.census.gov/acs/www/about/why-we-ask-each-question/language/

U.S. Department of Education. (1993). *National excellence: A case for developing America's talent.* https://www.ocps.net/cs/ese/programs/gifted/Documents/National%20Excellence_%20A%20Case%20for%20Developing%20America%27s%20Talent_%20Introduction.pdf

U.S. Department of Education, Office of English Language Acquisition. (2017). English Learner Tool Kit (2nd Rev. ed.). Author.

U.S. Department of Education. (2020). *42nd annual report to Congress on the implementation of the Individuals with Disabilities Education Act.* https://sites.ed.gov/idea/2020-annual-report-congress-idea/

U.S. Department of Education. (2021). *Long COVID under Section 504 and the IDEA: A resource to support children, students, educators, schools, service providers, and families.* https://www2.ed.gov/about/offices/list/ocr/docs/ocr-factsheet 504-20210726.pdf

U.S. Department of Education. (2021). *43rd annual report to Congress on the Implementation of the Individuals with Disabilities Education Act.* Washington, DC: Author. Retrieved from https://sites.ed.gov/idea/2020-annual-report-congress-idea/

U.S. Department of Education, Office of Civil Rights. (2022). *Civil rights data collection: 2017–2018 state and national estimations.* https://ocrdata.ed.gov/estimations/2017-2018

Vadasy, P. F., & Sanders, E. A. (2016). Attention to orthographic and phonological word forms in vocabulary instruction for kindergarten English learners. *Reading Psychology*, *37*, 833–866.

Virginia Institute for Social Services Training Activities. (2016). *Child abuse and neglect: Recognition, reporting, and responding.* http://www.dss.virginia.gov/family/cps/mandated_reporters/cwse5691/story.html

Wells, A. (2021). *Achieving equity in gifted programming: Dismantling barriers and tapping potential.* Routledge.

Wixom, M. A. (2016). *State and federal policy: Homeless youth.* Education Commission of the States. https://www.ecs.org/wp-content/uploads/State-and-Federal-Policy-for-Homeless-Youth.pdf

Young, J. L., & Young, J. (2022). Under representation in gifted education revisited: The promise of single-group summaries and meta-analytic quantcrit. *Gifted Child Quarterly*, *66*, 136–138.

Yssel, N., Adams, C., Clarke, L. S., & Jones, R. (2014). Applying an RTI model for students with learning disabilities who are gifted. *Teaching Exceptional Children*, *46*, 42–52.

Chapter 6

Agirdag, O. (2009). All languages welcomed here. *Educational Leadership*, *66*(7), 8–13.

Alberto, P. A., & Troutman, A. C., & Axe, J. (2022). *Applied behavior analysis for teachers* (10th ed.). Pearson.

Archer, A., & Hughes, C. A. (2011). *Explicit instruction: Effective and efficient teaching.* Guilford Press.

Banks, J. A. (2015). *Cultural diversity and education: Foundations, curriculum, and teaching* (6th ed.). Pearson.

Billingsley, B., Bettini, E., & Jones, N.D. (2019). Supporting special education teacher induction through high-leverage practices. *Remedial and Special Education*, *40*, 365–379.

Brigham, F. J., Scruggs, T. E., & Mastropieri, M. A. (1992). The effect of teacher enthusiasm on the learning and behavior of learning disabled students. *Learning Disabilities Research & Practice*, *7*, 68–73.

Burnett, P. C. (2003). The impact of teacher feedback on student self-talk and self-concept in reading and mathematics. *Journal of Classroom Interaction*, *38*, 11–16.

Carnine, D. (1976). Effects of two teacher presentation rates on off-task behavior, answering correctly, and participation. *Journal of Applied Behavior Analysis*, *9*, 199–206.

CAST. (2018). *Universal design for learning guidelines, version 2.2.* http://udlguidelines.cast.org

Center for Parent Information and Resources. (2016). *Supports, modifications, and accommodations for students.* http://www.parentcenterhub.org/repository/accommodations/

Danielson, C. (2010). *Implementing the framework for teaching in enhancing professional practice.* ASCD.

Echevarria, J., & Graves, A. (2015). *Sheltered content instruction: Teaching English language learners with diverse abilities* (5th ed.). Pearson.

Echevarria, J., Richards-Tutor, C., Canges, R., & Francis, D. (2011). Using the SIOP model to promote the acquisition of language and science concepts. *Bilingual Research Journal*, *43*, 334–351.

Gartin, B. C., Murdick, N. L., Imbeau, M., & Perner, D. E. (2002). *How to use differentiated instruction with students with developmental disabilities in the general education classroom.* Council for Exceptional Children.

Gay, G. (2018). *Culturally responsive teaching: Theory, research, and practice* (3rd ed.). New York: Teachers College Press.

Gleason, M., Carnine, D., & Vala, N. (1991). Cumulative versus rapid introduction of new information. *Exceptional Children*, *57*, 353–358.

Good, T. L., & Brophy, J. E. (2007). *Looking in classrooms* (10th ed.). Allyn & Bacon.

Guckert, M., Mastropieri, M. A., & Scruggs, T. E. (2016). Personalizing research: Special educators' awareness of evidence-based practice. *Exceptionality*, *24*, 63–78.

Hall, T. E., Meyer, A., & Rose, D. H. (Eds.). (2012). *Universal design for learning in the classroom: Practical applications.* Guilford Press.

Individuals with Disabilities Education Improvement Act of 2004, Pub. L. No. 108-446, 20 U.S.C. §1400 *et seq.* (2004).

IRIS Center. (2021). *What is instructional scaffolding?* Peabody College, Vanderbilt University. https://iris.peabody.vanderbilt.edu/module//sca/cresource/q1/p01

Jakulski, J., & Mastropieri, M. A. (2004). Homework for students with disabilities. In T. E. Scruggs & M. A. Mastropieri (Eds.), *Advances in learning and behavioral disabilities: Research in secondary settings* (Vol. 18, pp. 77–122). Elsevier.

Kunter, M., Frenzel, A., Nagy, G., Baumert, J., & Pekrun, R. (2010). Teacher enthusiasm: Dimensionality and context specificity. *Contemporary Educational Psychology*, *36*, 289–301.

Larrivee, B. (1985). *Effective teaching for successful mainstreaming.* Longman.

Mastropieri, M. A. (1995). L'instruzione mnemonica e l'interrogazione elaborativa: Strategie per ricordarsie per pensare. In C. Cornoldi & R. Vianello (Eds.), *Handicap e apprendimento: Ricerche e proposte di intervento* (pp. 117–124). Juvenilia.

Mastropieri, M. A., & Scruggs, T. E. (2002). *Effective instruction for special education* (3rd ed.). Merrill.

Mastropieri, M. A., & Scruggs, T. E. (2004). Effective classroom instruction. In C. Spielberger (Ed.), *Encyclopedia of applied psychology* (pp. 687–691). Elsevier.

Mastropieri, M. A., Scruggs, T. E., Mantzicopoulos, P. Y., Sturgeon, A., Goodwin, L., & Chung, S. (1998). "A place where living things affect and depend on each other": Qualitative and quantitative outcomes associated with inclusive science teaching. *Science Education*, *82*, 163–179.

Meyer, A., Rose, D. M., & Gordon, D. (2014). *Universal design for learning: Theory and practice.* CAST.

McLeskey, J., Barringer, M-D., Billingsley, B., Brownell, M., Jackson, D., Kennedy, M., . . . Ziegler, D. (2017, January). *High-leverage practices in special education.* Council for Exceptional Children & CEEDAR Center.

McLeskey, J., Billingsley, B., Brownell, M. T., Maheady, L., & Lewis, T. (2019). What are high-leverage practices for special education teachers and why are they important? *Remedial and Special Education*, *40*, 331–337.

Moore, K. D. (2011). *Effective instructional strategies: From theory to practice.* Sage.

Rao, K., Ok, M. W., & Bryant, B. R. (2014). A review of research on universal design educational models. *Remedial and Special Education*, *35*, 153–166.

Richardson, V. (2003). Preservice teachers' beliefs. In J. Raths & A. C. McAninch (Eds.), *Teacher beliefs and classroom performance: The impact of teacher education.* Information Age.

Rosenshine, B., & Stevens, R. (1986). Teaching functions. In M. C. Wittrock (Ed.), *Handbook of research on teaching* (3rd ed., pp. 376–391). Macmillan.

Ruiz, N. T., Rueda, R., Figueroa, R. A., & Boothroyd, M. (1995). Bilingual special education teacher's shifting paradigms: Complex responses to educational reform. *Journal of Learning Disabilities*, *28*, 622–635.

Sabornie, E. J., & deBettencourt, L. U. (2009). *Teaching students with mild and high-incidence disabilities at the secondary level* (3rd ed.). Merrill/Prentice Hall.

Scheuermann, B. K., Billingsley, G. M., & Hall, J. A. (2022). *Positive behavioral supports for the classroom* (4th ed.). Pearson.

Scruggs, T. E., & Mastropieri, M. A. (1994a). The effectiveness of generalization training: A quantitative synthesis of single subject research. In T. E. Scruggs & M. A. Mastropieri (Eds.), *Advances in learning and behavioral disabilities* (Vol. 8, pp. 259–280). JAI Press.

Scruggs, T. E., & Mastropieri, M. A. (1994b). Successful mainstreaming in elementary science classes: A qualitative investigation of three reputational cases. *American Educational Research Journal*, *31*, 785–811.

Scruggs, T. E., & Mastropieri, M. A. (1995). What makes special education special?: An analysis of the PASS variables in inclusion settings. *Journal of Special Education*, *29*, 224–233.

Scruggs, T. E., Mastropieri, M. A., & Brigham, F. J. (2013). Common core science standards: Implications for students with LD. *Learning Disabilities Research & Practice*, *28*, 49–57.

Scruggs, T. E., Mastropieri, M. A., & Sullivan, G. S. (1994). Promoting relational thinking skills: Elaborative interrogation for mildly handicapped students. *Exceptional Children*, *60*, 450–457.

Seo, S., Brownell, M. T., Bishop, A. G., & Dingle, M. (2008). An examination of beginning special education teachers' classroom practices that engage elementary students with learning disabilities in reading instruction. *Exceptional Children*, *75*, 97–122.

Sheridan, S. M. (2009). Homework interventions for children with attention and learning problems: Where is the "home" in "homework"? *School Psychology Review*, *38*, 334–337.

Smith, L. (1977). Aspects of teacher discourse and student achievement in mathematics. *Journal for Research in Mathematics Education*, *8*, 195–204.

Smith, L., & Land, M. (1981). Low-inference verbal behaviors related to teacher clarity. *Journal of Classroom Interaction*, *17*, 37–42.

Sullivan, G. S., Mastropieri, M. A., & Scruggs, T. E. (1995). Reasoning and remembering: Coaching thinking with students with learning disabilities. *Journal of Special Education*, *29*, 310–322.

Tomlinson, C. A. (2014a). *The differentiated classroom: Responding to the needs of all learners* (2nd ed.). ASCD.

Tomlinson, C. A. (2014b). *Differentiation of instruction in the elementary grades.* (ERIC Document Reproduction Service No. ED 443 572)

Urbach, J., Moore, B. A., Klingner, J. K., Galman, S., Haager, D., Brownell, M. T., & Dingle, M. (2015). "That's my job": Comparing the beliefs of more and less accomplished special educators related to their roles and responsibilities. *Teacher Education and Special Education*, *38*, 323–336.

Wentzel, K. R., & Brophy, J. (2014). *Motivating students to learn* (4th ed.). Routledge.

Chapter 7

Al Otaiba, S., Lan, P., Allor, J., Rivas, B., Yovanoff, P., & Kamata, A. (2019). Elementary teachers' knowledge of response to intervention implementation: A preliminary factor analysis. *Annals of Dyslexia*, *69*, 34–53.

Archer, A., & Hughes, C. A. (2011). *Explicit instruction: Effective and explicit teaching.* Guilford Press.

Balu, R., Zhu, P., Doolittle, F., Schiller, E., Jenkins, J., & Gersten, R. (2015). *Evaluation of response to intervention practices for elementary school reading.* U.S. Department of Education, Institute of Education Sciences.

Berkeley, S., Bender, W. N., Peaster, L. G. & Suanders, L. (2009). Implementation of response to intervention: A snapshot of progress, *Journal of Learning Disabilities 42(1),* 85–95.

Berkeley, S., Scanlon, D., Bailey, T. R., Sutton, J. C., & Sacco, D. M. (2020). A snapshot of RTI implementation a decade later: New picture, same story. *Journal of Learning Disabilities*, *53(5),* 332–342.

Berkeley, S., Scruggs, T. E., & Mastropieri, M. A. (2010). Reading comprehension instruction for students with learning disabilities, 1995–2006: A meta-analysis. *Remedial and Special Education, 31*, 423–436.

Cortes, K., Goodman, J., & Nomi, T. (2013, Winter). A double dose of algebra. *Education Next*, pp. 71–76. http://educationnext.org/files/ednext_20131_cortes.pdf

Deno, S. L. (2016). Data-based decision-making. In S. R. Jimerson, M. K. Burns, & A. M. VanDerHayden (Eds.), *Handbook of response to intervention: The science and practice of multi-tiered systems of support* (2nd ed., pp. 9–28). Springer.

Denton, C. A., & Vaughn, S. (2010). Preventing and remediating reading difficulties: Perspectives from research. In T. A. Glover & S. Vaughn (Eds.), *The promise of response to intervention: Evaluating current science and practice* (pp. 78–112). Guilford Press.

Division for Learning Disabilities. (2007). *Thinking about response to instruction and learning disabilities: A teacher's guide.* Author.

Dynamic Indicators of Basic Early Literacy Skills (DIBELS). (2006). University of Oregon, College of Education. http://dibels.uoregon.edu

Ervin, R. A. (n.d). *Considering Tier 3 within a response-to-intervention model.* RTI Network. http://www.rtinetwork.org/essential/tieredinstruction/tier3/consideringtier3

Fien, H., Smith, J. L. M., Smolkowski, K., & Chaparro, E. (2015). An examination of the efficacy of a multitiered intervention on early reading outcomes for first grade students at risk for reading difficulties. *Journal of Learning Disabilities, 48(6),* 602–621.

Filderman, M. J., Austin, C. R., & Boucher, A. N. (2022). A meta-analysis of the effects of reading comprehension interventions on the reading comprehension outcomes of struggling readers in third through 12th grades. *Exceptional Children, 88*(2). [Epub ahead of print] https://doi.org/10.1177/00144029211050860

Fuchs, D., & Deshler, D. (2007). What we need to know about responsiveness to intervention (and shouldn't be afraid to ask). *Learning Disabilities Research and Practice, 22*, 129–136.

Fuchs, D., & Fuchs, L. S. (2006). Introduction to response to intervention: What, why, and how valid is it? *Reading Research Quarterly, 41*, 93–99.

Fuchs, D., Fuchs, L. S., & Compton, D. C. (2012). Smart RTI: A next-generation approach to multi-level prevention. *Exceptional Children, 78*, 263–279.

Fuchs, D., Fuchs, L. S., Compton, D. C., Wehby, J., Schumacher, R. F., . . . Jordan, N. C. (2015). Inclusion versus specialized intervention for very-low-performing students: What does *access* mean in an era of academic challenge? *Exceptional Children, 81*, 134–157.

Fuchs, L. S., Fuchs, D., & Malone, A. S. (2016). Multilevel response-to-intervention prevention systems: Mathematics intervention at Tier 2. In S. R. Jimerson, M. K. Burns, & A. M. VanDerHayden (Eds.), *Handbook of response to intervention: The science and practice of multi-tiered systems of support* (2nd ed., pp. 309–328). Springer.

Fuchs, L. S., Fuchs, D., & Malone, A. S. (2017). The taxonomy of intervention intensity. *Teaching Exceptional Children, 50*, 35–43.

Fuchs, D., Fuchs, L. S., & Stecker, P. M. (2010). The "blurring" of special education in a new continuum of placements and services. *Exceptional Children, 76*, 301–323.

Fuchs, D., Mock, D., Morgan, P. L., & Young, C. L. (2003). Responsiveness-to-intervention: Definitions, evidence, and implications for the learning disabilities construct. *Learning Disabilities Research and Practice, 18*, 157–171.

Gay, G. (2018). *Culturally responsive teaching: Theory, research, and practice* (3rd ed.). Teachers College Press.

Gesel, S. A., & Lemons, C. (2020). Comparing schedules of progress monitoring using curriculum-based measurement in reading: A replication study. *Exceptional Children, 87*, 92–112.

Glover, T. A. (2010). Supporting all students: The promise of response to intervention. In T. A. Glover & S. Vaughn (Eds.), *The promise of response to intervention: Evaluating current science and practice* (pp. 1–6). Guilford Press.

Gresham, F. M. (2002). Responsiveness to intervention: An alternative approach to the identification of learning disabilities. In R. Bradley, L. Danielson, & D. P. Hallahan (Eds.), *Identification of learning disabilities* (pp. 467–519). Erlbaum.

Gresham, F. M., Dart, E. H., & Collins, T. A. (2017). Generalizability of multiple measures of treatment integrity: Comparisons among direct observation, permanent products, and self-report. *School Psychology Review, 46*, 108–121.

Gresham, F. M., MacMillan, D. L., Beebe-Frankenberger, M. E., & Bocian, K. M. (2000). Treatment integrity in learning disabilities intervention research: Do we really know how treatments are implemented? *Learning Disabilities Research and Practice, 15*, 198–205.

Hall, T. E., Meyer, A., & Rose, D. H. (Eds.). (2012). *Universal design for learning in the classroom: Practical applications.* Guilford Press.

Harry, B., & Klingner, J. K. (2014). *Why are so many minority students in special education? Understanding race and disability in schools* (2nd ed.). Teachers College Press.

Hasbrouck, J., & Tindal, G. (2006). Oral reading fluency norms: A valuable assessment tool for reading teachers. *The Reading Teacher, 59*, 636–664.

Hasbrouck, J. & Tindal, G. (2017). *An update to compiled ORF norms* (Technical Report No. 1702). Behavioral Research and Teaching, University of Oregon. https://intensiveintervention.org/resource/update-compiled-orf-norms

Hosp, M. K., Hosp, J. L., & Howell, K. W. (2016). *The ABCs of CBM: A practical guide to curriculum-based measurement* (2nd ed.). Guilford Press.

Hudson, T. M., & McKenzie, R. G. (2016). Evaluating the use of RTI to identify SLD: A survey of state policy, procedures, data collection, and administrator perceptions. *Contemporary School Psychology, 20*, 31–35.

Hughes, C. A., Morris, J. R., Therrien, W. J., & Benson, S. (2017). Explicit instruction: Historical and contemporary contexts. *Learning Disabilities Research & Practice, 32*, 140–148.

Hunt, J. H. & Little, M. E. (2014). Intensifying interventions for students by identifying and remediating conceptual understandings in mathematics. *Teaching Exceptional Children, 46*, 187–196.

Ihlo, T., & Nantais, M. (2010). Evidence-based interventions within a multi-tier framework for positive behavioral supports. In T. A. Glover & S. Vaughn (Eds.), *The promise of response to intervention: Evaluating current science and practice* (pp. 239–266). Guilford Press.

Individuals with Disabilities Education Improvement Act of 2004, Pub. L. No. 108-446, 20 U.S.C. §1400 *et seq.* (2004).

Jenkins, J., Schulze, M., Marti, A., Harbaugh, A. G. (2017). Curriculum-based measurement of reading growth: Weekly versus intermittent progress monitoring. *Exceptional Children, 84*(1), 42–54. https://doi.org/10.1177/0014402917708216

Jimerson, S. R., Burns, M. K., & VanDerHayden A. M. (2016). From response to intervention to multi-tiered systems of support: Advances in the science and practice of assessment and intervention. In S. R. Jimerson, M. K. Burns, & A. M. VanDerHayden (Eds.), *Handbook of response to intervention: The science and practice of multi-tiered systems of support* (2nd ed., pp. 1–6). Springer.

Jimerson, S. R., Stein, R., Haddock, A., & Shahroozi, R. (2016). Common Core State Standards and response to intervention: The importance of assessment, intervention, and progress monitoring. In S. R. Jimerson, M. K. Burns, & A. M. VanDerHayden (Eds.), *Handbook of response to intervention: The science and practice of multi-tiered systems of support* (2nd ed., pp. 165–184). Springer.

Johnson, E., Mellard, D. F., Fuchs, D., & McKnight, M. A. (2006). *Responsiveness to intervention (RTI): How to do it.* National Research Center on Learning Disabilities. https://eric.ed.gov/?id=ED496979

Johnson, E. S., Smith, L. A., & Harris, M. L. (2009). *How RTI works in secondary schools.* Corwin Press.

Jung, P. G., McMaster, K. L., Kunkel, A. K., Shin, J., & Stecker, P. M. (2018). Effects of data-based individualization for students with intensive learning needs: A meta-analysis. *Learning Disabilities Research & Practice*, *33*(3), 144–155.

Kaminski, R. A., & Good, R. A. (1998). Use of curriculum-based measurement to assess early literacy: Dynamic indicators of basic early literacy skills. In M.R Shinn (Ed.), *Advances in curriculum-based measurements and its use in a problem-solving model* (pp. 113–142). Guilford.

Kearns, D. M., (August, 2016). Student progress monitoring tool for data collection and graphing [Computer software]. U.S. Department of Education, Office of Special Education Programs, National Center on Intensive Intervention.

King, D., & Coughlin, P. K. (2016). Looking beyond RtI standard treatment approach: It's not too late to embrace the problem-solving approach. *Preventing School Failure: Alternative Education for Children and Youth*, *60*, 244–251.

Klingner, J. K., & Edwards, P. A. (2006). Cultural considerations with response to intervention models. *Reading Research Quarterly*, *41*, 108–117.

Kressler, B., Chapman, L. A., Kunkel, A., & Hover, K. A. (2020). Culturally responsive data-based decision making in high school settings. *Intervention in School and Clinic*, *55*, 214–220.

Linan-Thompson, S., Lara-Martinez, J. A., & Cavazos, L. O. (2018). Exploring the intersection of evidence-based practices and culturally and linguistically responsive practices. *Intervention in School and Clinic*, *54*, 6–13.

MacGinitie, W. H., MacGinitie, R. K., Maria, K., Dreyer, L. G., & Hughes, K. E. (2000). *Gates MacGinitie reading tests* (4th ed.). Riverside.

Mastropieri, M. A., & Scruggs, T. E. (2005). Feasibility and consequences of response to intervention (RTI): Examination of the issues and scientific evidence as a model for the identification of individuals with learning disabilities. *Journal of Learning Disabilities*, *38*, 525–531.

McLeskey, J., Barringer, M-D., Billingsley, B., Brownell, M., Jackson, D., Kennedy, M., . . . Ziegler, D. (2017, January). *High-leverage practices in special education.* Council for Exceptional Children & CEEDAR Center.

Mellard, D., & Johnson, E. (2008). *RTI: A practitioner's guide to implementing response to intervention.* Corwin Press.

Mellard, D. F., & McKnight, M. A. (2006). *RTI implementation tool for reading: Best practices.* [Brochure]. National Research Center on Learning Disabilities. https://www.researchgate.net/profile/Daryl_Mellard/publication/265279115_RTI_Implementation_Tool_for_Reading_Best_Practices/links/5707e14908ae2eb9421bdbd9.pdf

Moore, A. L., Giles, R. M., & Paige, V. (2021). Prepared to respond?: Investigating preservice teachers' perceptions of their readiness for culturally responsive teaching. *Journal for the Scholarship of Teaching and Learning*, *15*(1), Article 10.

Musgrove, M. (2011). *A response to instruction (RTI) process cannot be used to delay-deny an evaluation for disability under the Individuals with Disabilities Education Act (IDEA).* Memo sent to State Directors of Special Education. Department of Education, Office of Special Education Programs.

National Center on Intensive Intervention. (2013). *Data-based individualization: A framework for intensive intervention.* Office of Special Education, U.S. Department of Education.

National Governors Association Center for Best Practices & Council of Chief State School Officers. (2010). *Common Core State Standards for English language arts and literacy in history/social studies, science, and technical subjects.* Authors.

National Institute of Child Health and Human Development (NICHD). (2000). *Report to the National Reading Panel. Teaching children to read: An evidence-based assessment of the scientific research literature on reading and its implications for reading instruction* (NIH Publication No. 00-4769). U.S. Government Printing Office.

O'Connor, R. E., & Sanchez, V. (2011). Issues in assessment for intervention in implementation of responsiveness to intervention models. In T. E. Scruggs & M. A. Mastropieri (Eds.), *Assessment and intervention: Advances in learning and behavioral disabilities* (Vol. 24, pp. 149–170). Emerald.

O'Connor, R. E., Sanchez, V., & Kim, J. (2017). Responsiveness to intervention models for reducing reading difficulties and identifying learning disability. In J. Kauffman, D. P. Hallahan, & J. Lloyd (Eds.), *Handbook of special education* (pp. 189–202). Routledge.

Orosco, M. J., & Klingner, J. (2010). One school's implementation of RTI with English language learners: "Referring into RTI." *Journal of Learning Disabilities*, *43*, 269–288.

Ortiz, A. A., Robertson, P. M., & Wilkinson, C. Y. (2018). Language and literacy assessment record for English Learners in bilingual education: A. framework for instructional planning and decision-making. *Preventing School Failure: Alternative Education for Children and Youth*, *62*, 250–265.

Powell, S. R., & Fuchs, L. S. (2015). Intensive interventions in mathematics. *Learning Disabilities Research and Practice*, *30*, 182–192.

Reed, D. K., Wexler, J., & Vaughn, S. (2012). *RTI for reading at the secondary level: Recommended literacy practices and remaining questions.* Guilford Press.

Regan, K., Berkeley, S., Hughes, M., & Brady, K. (2015). Understanding practitioner perceptions of responsiveness to intervention. *Learning Disability Quarterly*, *38*, 234–247.

Scheuermann, B. K., Billingsley, G., & Hall, J. A. (2022). *Positive behavioral supports for the classroom* (4th ed.). Pearson.

Scruggs, T. E., & Mastropieri, M. A. (2002). On babies and bathwater: Addressing the problems of assessment and identification of learning disabilities. *Learning Disability Quarterly*, *25*, 155–168.

Shinn, M., Windram, H. S., & Bollman, K. A. (2016). Implementing response to intervention in secondary schools. In S. R. Jimerson, M. K. Burns, & A. M. VanDerHayden (Eds.), *Handbook of response to intervention: The science and practice of multi-tiered systems of support* (2nd ed., pp. 563–586). Springer.

Stecker, P. M., Fuchs, L. S., & Fuchs, D. (2005). Using curriculum-based measurement to improve student achievement: A review of research. *Psychology in the Schools*, *42*, 795–819.

Steinle, P. K., Stevens, E., & Vaughn, S. (2022). Fluency Interventions for struggling readers in grades 6 to 12: A research synthesis. *Journal of Learning Disabilities*, *55*(1). [Epub ahead of print]

Stevens, E. A., Vaughn, S., Swanson, E., & Scammacca, N. (2020). Examining the effect of a tier 2 reading comprehension intervention aligned to tier 1 instruction for fourth grade struggling readers. *Exceptional Children, 86(4),* 430–448.

Stoiber, K. C., & Gettinger, M. (2016). Multi-tiered systems in evidence-based practices. In S. R. Jimerson, M. K. Burns, & A. M. VanDerHayden (Eds.), *Handbook of response to intervention: The science and practice of multi-tiered systems of support* (2nd ed., pp. 121–141). Springer.

Sugai, G., Horner, R. H., Fixen, D., & Blase, K. (2010). Developing systems-level capacity for RTI implementation: Current efforts and future directions. In T. A. Glover & S. Vaughn (Eds.), *The promise of response to intervention: Evaluating current science and practice* (pp. 286–309). Guilford Press.

Tilly, W. D. (2003, December). *How many tiers are needed for successful prevention and early intervention?: Heartland Area Education Agency's evolution from four to three tiers*. Paper presented at the NRCLD Responsiveness to Intervention Symposium, Kansas City, MO. http://citeseerx.ist.psu.edu/viewdoc/download?doi=10.1.1.520.4453&rep=rep1&type=pdf

Tukey, J. W. (1977). *Exploratory data analysis*. Addison-Wesley-Longman.

University of Oregon (2021). *8th edition of Dynamic Indicators of Basic Early Literacy Skills (DIBELS®): Administration and scoring guide, 2021 edition*. https://dibels.uoregon.edu

U.S. Department of Education. (2020). *42nd annual report to Congress on the implementation of the Individuals with Disabilities Education Act*. Author.

Vaughn, S., & Bos, C. (2020). *Strategies for teaching students with learning and behavior problems* (10th ed.). Pearson.

Vaughn, S., Denton, C. A., & Fletcher, J. M. (2010). Why intensive interventions are necessary for students with severe reading difficulties. *Psychology in the Schools*, *47*, 432–444.

Vaughn, S., Roberts, G., Schnakenberg, J. B., Fall, A. M., Vaughn, M. G., & Wexler, J. (2015). Improving reading comprehension for high school students with disabilities: Effects for comprehension and school retention. *Exceptional Children*, *82*, 117–137.

Vaughn, S., & Wanzek, J. (2014). Intensive intervention in reading for students with reading disabilities: Meaningful impacts. *Learning Disabilities Research and Practice*, *29*, 46–53.

Vaughn, S., Wexler, J., Roberts, G., Barth, A. A., Cirino, P. T., Romain, M. A., . . . Denton, C. A. (2011). Effects of individualized and standardized interventions on middle school students with reading disabilities. *Exceptional Children*, *77*, 391–407.

Wanzek, J., Vaughn, S., Scammacca, N., Gatlin, B., Walker, M. A., & Capin, P. (2016). Meta-analyses of the effects of Tier 2 type reading interventions in grades K–3. *Educational Psychology Review*, *28*(3), 551–576.

Wells, A. S. (2020). Racial, ethnic, and cultural diversity across K–12 schools and higher education sectors: Challenges and opportunities for cross-sector learning. *Change: The Magazine of Higher Learning*, *52*, 56–61.

Wiederholt, J. L., & Bryant, B. R. (2011). *Gray Oral Reading Test (GORT-5)* (5th ed.). Pearson.

Wright, P. W. D., & Wright, P. D. (2005). *Wrightslaw: IDEA 2004*. Harbor House Law Press.

Chapter 8

Agran, M., & Wehmeyer, M. (2003). Promoting the self-determination of students with severe disabilities. In D. L. Ryndak & S. Alper (Eds.), *Curriculum and instruction for students with significant disabilities in inclusive settings* (pp. 259–275). Allyn & Bacon.

Alberto, P. A., Troutman, A. C., & Axe, J. (2022). *Applied behavior analysis for teachers* (10th ed.). Merrill/Pearson.

Algozzine, B., Wang, C., White, R., Cooke, N., Marr, M. B., & Algozzine, K. (2012). Effects of multi-tiered academic and behavior instruction on difficult-to-teach students. *Exceptional Children*, *79*, 45–64.

Allday, R. A., & Pakurar, K. (2007). Effects of teacher greetings on student on-task behavior. *Journal of Applied Behavior Analysis*, *40*, 317–320.

Anckarsäter, H., Stahlberg, O., Larson, T., Hakansson, C., Jutblad, S., Niklasson, L., . . . Rastam, M. (2010). The impact of ADHD and autism spectrum disorders on temperament, character, and personality development. *Focus*, *8*, 269–275.

Anderman, E. M., & Patrick, H. (2012). Achievement goal theory, conceptualization of ability/intelligence, and classroom climate. In S. L. Christenson, A. L. Reschly, & C. Wylie (Eds.), *Handbook of research on student engagement* (pp. 173–191). Springer.

Banks, J. A. (2015). *Cultural diversity and education: Foundations, curriculum, and teaching* (6th ed.). Pearson.

Beck, M. A., Roblee, K., & Johns, C. (1982). The psychoeducational management of disturbed children. *Education*, *102*, 232–235.

Bellini, S., Peters, J. K., Benner, L., & Hopf, A. (2007). A meta-analysis of school-based social skills interventions for children with autism spectrum disorders. *Remedial and Special Education*, *28*, 153–162.

Berkeley, S., Mastropieri, M. A., & Scruggs, T. E. (2011). Reading comprehension strategy instruction and attribution retraining for secondary students with learning and other mild disabilities. *Journal of Learning Disabilities*, *44*, 18–32.

Bijou, S. W., Peterson, R. F., & Ault, M. H. (1968). A method to integrate descriptive and experimental field studies at the level of data and empirical concepts. *Journal of Applied Behavior Analysis*, *1*, 175–191.

Bowman-Perrott, L., Burke, M. D., Zaini, S., Zhang, N., & Vannest, K. (2016). Promoting positive behavior using the good behavior game: A meta-analysis of single-case research. *Journal of Positive Behavior Interventions*, *18*(3), 180–190.

Brigham, F. J., Bakken, J., Scruggs, T. E., & Mastropieri, M. A. (1992). Cooperative behavior management: A technique for improving classroom behavior. *Education and Training of the Mentally Retarded*, *27*, 3–12.

Buchard, J. D., & Barrera, F. (1972). An analysis of time out and response cost in a programmed environment. *Journal of Applied Behavior Analysis*, *5*, 271–282.

Campbell, J. M., Ruble, L. A., & Hammond, R. K. (2015). Children and Adolescents with Disabilities: Implications for Interventions. In H. T. Prout & A. L. Fedewa (Eds.), *Counseling and psychotherapy with children and adolescents: Theory and practice for school and clinical settings* (4th ed., pp. 357–389). Wiley.

Canter, L., & Canter, M. (1993). *Succeeding with difficult students: New strategies for reaching your most challenging students*. Solution Tree Press.

Canter, L., & Canter, M. (2010). *Assertive discipline: Positive behavior management for today's classroom* (4th ed.). Solution Tree Press.

Carey, T. A., & Bourbon, W. T. (2004). Countercontrol: A new look at some old problems. *Intervention in School and Clinic*, *40*, 3–9.

Carlson, C. L., Booth, J. E., Shin, M., & Canu, W. H. (2002). Parent-, teacher-, and self-rated motivational styles in ADHD subtypes. *Journal of Learning Disabilities*, *35*, 104–113.

Coffey, J. H., & Horner, R. H. (2012). The sustainability of schoolwide positive behavior interventions and supports. *Exceptional Children*, *78*, 407–422.

Conroy, M. A., Asmus, J. M., Ladwig, C. N., Sellers, J. A., & Valcante, G. (2004). The effects of proximity on the classroom behaviors of students with autism in general education settings. *Behavioral Disorders*, *29*, 119–129.

Cook, C. R., Duong, M. T., McIntosh, K., Fiat, A.E., Pullman, M. D., & McGinnis, J. (2018). Addressing discipline disparities for Black male students: Linking malleable root causes to feasible and effective practices. *School Psychology Review*, *47*, 135–152.

Council for Children with Behavioral Disorders. (1990). Position paper on behavior reduction strategies with children with behavioral disorders. *Behavioral Disorders*, *15*, 243–260.

Council for Exceptional Children (CEC). (n.d.). *Maltreatment/bullying*. https://exceptionalchildren.org/topics/maltreatmentbullying

Crone, C. A., Hawken, L. S., & Horner, R. (2015). *Building positive behavior support systems in schools: Functional behavioral assessment* (2nd ed). Guilford Press.

Davis, S., & Davis, J. (2007). *Schools where everyone belongs: Practical strategies for reducing bullying* (2nd ed.). Research Press.

Estrapala, S., & Reed, D. K. (2020). Goal-setting instruction: A step by step guide for high school students. *Intervention in School and Clinic, 55(5),* 286–293.

Fairbanks, S., Sugai, G., Guardino, D., & Lathrop, M. (2007). Response to intervention: Examining classroom behavior support in second grade. *Exceptional Children, 73,* 288–310.

Ferro, M. A., & Boyle, M. H. (2013). Testing measurement invariance and differences in self-concept between adolescents with and without physical illness or developmental disability. *Journal of Adolescence, 36,* 947–951.

Flower, A., McKenna, J. W., Bunuan, R. L., Muething, C. S., & Vega, R., Jr. (2014). Effects of the good behavior game on challenging behaviors in school settings. *Review of Educational Research, 84*(4), 546–571.

Gable, D. (2003). Enhancing the conceptual understanding of science. *Educational Horizons, 81,* 70–76.

Gage, N. A., Rose, C. A., & Kramer, D. A. (2019). When prevention is not enough: Students' perceptions of bullying and school-wide positive behavior interventions and supports. *Behavioral Disorders, 45,* 29–40.

Ginsberg, M. B., & Wlodkowski, R. J. (2009). Diversity and motivation: Culturally responsive teaching in college (2nd ed.). Jossey-Bass.

Girvan, E. J., Gion, C., McIntosh, K., & Smolkowski, K. (2017). The relative contribution of subjective office referrals to racial disproportionality in school discipline. *School Psychology Quarterly 28,* 77–100.

Glago, K., Mastropieri, M. A., & Scruggs, T. E. (2009). Improving problem solving of elementary students with mild disabilities. *Remedial and Special Education, 30,* 372–380.

Gollnick, D. M., & Chinn, P. C. (2021). *Multicultural education in a pluralistic society* (11th ed.). Merrill/Prentice Hall.

Gonsalez-Spada, W. J., Bieeiel, J., & Birriel, I. (2010). Discrepant events: A challenge to students' intuition. *Physics Teacher, 48,* 508–511.

Good, C. P., McIntosh, K., & Gietz, C. (2011). Integration bullying prevention into schoolwide positive behavior support. *Teaching Exceptional Children, 44,* 48–56.

Graetz, J. S., Mastropieri, M. A., & Scruggs, T. E. (2009). Promoting social behavior for adolescents with autism with social stories. *Education and Training in Developmental Disabilities, 44,* 91–104.

Gresham, F. M., & Elliott, S. N. (2008a). *Social Skills Improvement System (SSIS) intervention guide.* Pearson.

Gresham, F. M., & Elliott, S. N. (2008b). *Social Skills Improvement System (SSIS) rating scales.* Pearson.

Hanrahan, R., Smith, E., Johnson, H., Constantin, A., & Brosnan, M. (2020). A pilot randomized control trial of digitally-mediated social stories for children on the autism spectrum. *Journal of Autism and Developmental Disorders, 50,* 4243–4257.

Harris, V. W., & Sherman, J. A. (1973). Use and analysis of the "Good Behavior Game" to reduce disruptive classroom behavior. *Journal of Applied Behavior Analysis, 6,* 405–417.

Harter, S. (2012). *The construction of the self: A developmental perspective* (2nd ed.). Guilford Press.

Hawken, L. H., Crone, D. A., Bundock, K., & Horner, R. H. (2021). *Responding to problem behavior in schools : The check-in, check-out intervention* (3rd ed.). Guilford Press.

Heinrichs, R. R. (2003). A whole-school approach to bullying: Special considerations for children with exceptionalities. *Intervention in School and Clinic, 38,* 195–204.

Hochman, J. M., Carter, E. W., Bottema-Beutel, K., Harvey, M. N., & Gustafson, J. R. (2015). Efficacy of peer networks to increase social connections among high school students with and without autism spectrum disorders. *Exceptional Children, 82,* 96–116.

Horner, R. H., Sugai, G., & Anderson, C. M. (2010). Examining the evidence base for school-wide positive behavior support. *Focus on Exceptional Children, 42,* 1–14.

Isbell, J. S., & Jolivette, K. (2011). Stop, Think, Proceed: Solving problems in the real world. *Intervention in School and Clinic, 47,* 31–38.

Jenkins, J. R., & Gorrafa, S. (1974). Academic performance of mentally handicapped children as a function of token economies and contingency contracts. *Education and Training of the Mentally Retarded, 9,* 183–186.

Jenkins, L. N., Floress, M. T., & Reinke, W. (2015). Rates and types of teacher praise: A review and future directions. *Psychology in the Schools, 52,* 463–476.

Jones, D. B., & Van Houten, R. (1985). The use of daily quizzes and public posting to decrease the disruptive behavior of secondary school students. *Education and Treatment of Children, 8,* 91–106.

Jones, V., Greenwood, A., & Dunn, C. (2016). *Effective supports for students with emotional and behavioral disorders.* Pearson.

Kauffman, J., & Landrum, T. (2018). *Characteristics of emotional and behavioral disorders of children and youth* (11th ed.). Pearson.

Kaya, S., & Lundeen, C. (2010). Capturing parents' individual and instructional interest toward involvement in science education. *Journal of Science Teacher Education, 21,* 825–841.

Kerr, M. M., & Nelson, C. M. (2010). *Strategies for managing behavior problems in the classroom* (6th ed.). Prentice Hall.

Koenig, A., Eckert, T., & Hier, B. O. (2016). Using performance feedback and goal setting to improve elementary students' writing fluency: A randomized controlled trial. *School Psychology Review, 45,* 275–295.

Konrad, M., Fowler, C., & Walker, A. R. (2007). Effects of self-determination interventions on the academic skills of students with learning disabilities. *Learning Disability Quarterly, 30,* 89–113.

Kowalski, R. M., Limber, S. P., & Agatston, P. W. (2012). *Cyberbullying: Bullying in the digital age* (2nd ed.). Blackwell.

Krempa, J., & McKinnon, K. (2002). *Social skills solutions: A hands-on manual for teaching social skills to students with autism.* DRL Books.

Lavoie, R. (2008). *The motivation breakthrough: Six secrets to turning on the tuned-out child.* Simon and Schuster.

Leflot, G., van Lier, P., Onghena, P., & Colpin, H. (2010). The role of teacher behavior management in the development of disruptive behaviors: An intervention study with the Good Behavior Game. *Journal of Abnormal Child Psychology, 38,* 869–882.

Leichtentritt, J., & Shechtman, Z. (2009). Children with and without learning disabilities: A comparison of processes and outcomes following group counseling. *Journal of Learning Disabilities, 43,* 169–179

Leverson, M., Smith, K., McIntosh, K., Rose, J., & Pinkelman, S. (2021, March). *PBIS cultural responsiveness field guide: Resources for trainers and coaches.* Center on PBIS, University of Oregon.

Lewis, T. J., Jones, S. E. L., Horner, R. H., & Sugai, G. (2010). School-wide positive behavior support and students with emotional/behavioral disorders: Implications for prevention, identification, and intervention. *Exceptionality, 18,* 82–93.

Maag, J. W. (2001). Rewarded by punishment: Reflections on the disuse of positive reinforcement in schools. *Exceptional Children, 67,* 173–186.

Maag, J. W. (2006). Social skills training for students with emotional and behavioral disorders: A review of reviews. *Behavioral Disorders, 32,* 5–17.

Maag, J. W. (2018). *Behavior management: From theoretical implications to practical applications* (3rd ed.). Cengage Learning.

Majeika, C. E., Van Camp, A. M., Wehby, J. H., Kern, L., Commisso, C. E., & Gaier, K. (2019). An evaluation of adaptations made to Check-In Check-Out. *Journal of Positive Behavior Interventions, 22*, 25–37.

Martin, G., & Pear, J. (2019). *Behavior modification: What it is and how to do it* (11th ed.). Routledge.

Mastropieri, M. A., & Scruggs, T. E. (2002). *Effective instruction for special education* (3rd ed.). Pro-Ed.

Matson, J. L., & Boisjoli, J. A. (2009). The token economy for children with intellectual disability and/or autism: A review. *Research in Developmental Disabilities, 30*, 240–248.

Matson, J. L., Matson, M. L., & Rivet, T. T. (2007). Social-skills treatments for children with autism spectrum disorders: An overview. *Behavior Modification, 31*, 682–707.

Matthias, C., Lavelle, J. M., Johnson, D. R., Wu, Y. C., & Thurlow, M. L. (2021). Exploring predictors of bullying and victimization of students with autism spectrum disorder (ASD): Findings from NLTS 2012. *Journal of Autism and Developmental Disorder, 51*, 4632–4643.

Mayer, G. R., Nafpaktitis, M., Butterworth, T., & Hollingsworth, P. (1987). A search for the elusive setting events of school vandalism: A correlational study. *Education and Treatment of Children, 10*, 259–270.

Mazzone, L., Postorino, V., De Peppo, L., Fatta, L., Lucarelli, V., Reale, L., . . . Vicari, S. (2013). Mood symptoms in children and adolescents with autism spectrum disorders. *Research in Developmental Disabilities, 34*, 3099–3708.

McIntosh, K., Girvan, E., Horner, R. H., Smolkowsi, K., & Sugai, G. (2018). *A five-point intervention approach for enhancing equity in school discipline*. OSEP Technical Assistance Center for Positive Behavioral Interventions and Supports.

McDaniel, S. C., & Flower, A. (2015). Use of a behavioral graphic organizer to reduce disruptive behavior. *Education and Treatment of Children, 38*, 505–522.

McLaughlin, T. F., & Malaby, J. E. (1976). An analysis of assignment completion and accuracy across time under fixed, variable, and extended token exchange periods in a classroom token economy. *Contemporary Educational Psychology, 1*, 346–355.

McLeskey, J., Barringer, M-D., Billingsley, B., Brownell, M., Jackson, D., Kennedy, M., . . . Ziegler, D. (2017, January). *High-leverage practices in special education*. Council for Exceptional Children and CEEDAR Center.

McMaster, K. N., & Fuchs, D. (2002). Effects of cooperative learning on the academic achievement of students with learning disabilities: An update of Tateyama-Sniezek's review. *Learning Disabilities Research & Practice, 17*, 107–117.

Miller, L. M., Dufrene, B. A., Sterling, H. E., Olmi, D. J., & Bachmayer, E. (2015). The effects of check-in/check-out on problem behavior and academic engagement in elementary school students. *Journal of Positive Behavior Interventions, 17*, 28–38.

Milsom, A. S., & Akos, P. (2003). Counselor preparation: Preparing school counselors to work with students with disabilities. *Counselor Education and Supervision, 43*, 86–95.

Missouri Schoolwide Positive Behavior Support. (2018). *Tier 2 team workbook*. Missouri Department of Elementary and Secondary Education.

Mrachko, A. A., Kostewicz, D. E., & Martin, W. P. (2017). Increasing positive and decreasing negative teacher responses to student behavior through training and feedback. *Behavior Analysis: Research and Practice, 17*, 250–265.

Nelson, J. M., & Harwood, H. (2011). Learning disabilities and anxiety: A meta-analysis. *Journal of Learning Disabilities, 44*, 3–17.

Nelson, J. M., & Manset-Williamson, G. (2006). The impact of explicit, self-regulatory reading comprehension strategy instruction on reading-specific self-efficacy, attributions, and affect of students with reading disabilities. *Learning Disability Quarterly, 29(3)*, 213–230.

Nelson, J. R., & Sugai, G. (1999). School-wide application of positive behavioral supports. In G. Sugai & T. Lewis (Eds.), *Developing positive behavioral support for students with challenging behaviors* (pp. 25–34). Council for Exceptional Children. (ERIC Document Reproduction Service No. 435155)

Nicholls, J. G. (1989). *The competitive ethos and democratic education.* Harvard University Press.

OSEP Technical Assistance Center on Positive Behavioral Interventions and Supports. (2012). *Effective schoolwide interventions*. Office of Special Education Programs.

Park, E., & Blair, K. C. (2020). Check-in/check-out Implementation in schools: A meta-analysis of group design studies. *Education and Treatment of Children, 43*, 361–375.

Payno-Simmons, R. L. (2021). Centering equity in school discipline: The Michigan PBIS Equity Pilot. *Preventing School Failure: Alternative Education for Children and Youth, 65*, 342–353.

Perihan, C., Burke, M., Bowman-Perrott, L., Bicer, A., Gallup, J., Thompson, J., & Sallese, M. (2020). Effects of cognitive behavioral therapy for reducing anxiety in children with high functioning ASD: A systematic review. *Journal of Autism and Developmental Disorders, 50*, 1958–1972.

Raskauskas, J., & Modell, S. (2011). Modifying anti-bullying programs to include students with disabilities. *Teaching Exceptional Children, 44*, 60–67.

Reynolds, C., Skiba, R. J., Graham, S., Sheras, P., Conoley, J. C., & Garcia-Vasquez, E. (2008). Are zero tolerance policies effective in the schools? *American Psychologist, 63*, 852–862.

Richard, J. F., Schneider, B. H., & Mallet, P. (2011). Revisiting the whole-school approach to bullying: Really looking at the whole school. *School Psychology International, 33*, 263–284.

Robbie K., Van Lone, J., Kern, L., & George, H. P. (2021, August). *Using a PBIS framework: Working smarter, not harder in rural schools.* Center on PBIS, University of Oregon.

Rose, C., Monda-Amaya, L. E., & Espelage, D. (2011). Bullying perpetration and victimization in special education: A review of the literature. *Remedial and Special Education, 32*, 114–130.

Rosenberg, M. S., & Jackman, L. A. (2003). Development, implementation, and sustainability of comprehensive schoolwide behavior management systems. *Intervention in School and Clinic, 39*, 10–21.

Safran, S. P., & Oswald, K. (2003). Positive behavior supports: Can schools reshape disciplinary practices? *Exceptional Children, 69*, 362–373.

Scheuermann, B. K., Billingsley, G.M., & Hall, J. A. (2022). *Positive behavioral supports for the classroom* (4th ed.). Pearson.

Scruggs, T. E., & Mastropieri, M. A. (1994). Successful mainstreaming in elementary science classes: A qualitative investigation of three reputational cases. *American Educational Research Journal, 31*, 785–811.

Sideridis, G. D. (2007). Why are students with LD depressed?: A goal orientation model of depression vulnerability. *Journal of Learning Disabilities, 40*, 526–539.

Simonsen, B., Fairbanks, S., Briesch, A., Myers, D., & Sugai, G. (2008). Evidence-based practices in classroom management: Considerations for research to practice. *Education and Treatment of Children, 31*, 351–380.

Stauch, T. A., & Plavnick, J. B. (2020). Teaching vocational and social skills to adolescents with autism using video modeling. *Education and Treatment of Children, 43*, 137–151.

Sugai, G., & Horner, R. H. (2020). Sustaining and scaling positive behavioral interventions and supports: Implementation drivers, outcomes, and considerations. *Exceptional Children, 86*, 120–136.

Sullivan, A. M., Johnson, B., Owens, L., & Conway, R. (2014). Punish them or engage them?: Teachers' views of unproductive student behaviours in the classroom. *Australian Journal of Teacher Education, 39*, 43–56.

Tauber, R. T. (2007). *Classroom management: Sound theory and effective practice.* Praeger.

Todd, A. W., Campbell, A. L., Meyer, G. G., & Horner, R. H. (2008). The effects of a targeted intervention to reduce problem behaviors: Elementary school implementation of Check-In/Check-Out. *Journal of Positive Behavior Interventions, 10*, 46–55.

Troup, D. L., McLaughlin, T. F., Neyman, J., & Schuler, H. (2014). The use of online typing programs in combination with public posting with and without consequences to increase the typing fluency and accuracy for seven high school students with severe behavior disorders. *Journal of Education and Human Development, 3*, 181–201.

Twyman, J. S., Johnson, H., Buie, J. D., & Nelson, C. M. (1994). The use of a warning procedure to signal a more intrusive timeout contingency. *Behavioral Disorders, 19*, 243–253.

U.S. Department of Education. (2017). *School climate and discipline.* https://ed.gov/policy/gen/guid/school-discipline/index.html

Van Camp, A. M., Wehby, J. H., Martin, B. L. N., Wright, J. R., & Sutherland, K. S. (2020). Increasing opportunities to respond to intensify academic and behavioral interventions: A meta-analysis. *School Psychology Review, 49*, 31–46.

Watling, R., & Schwartz, I. S. (2004). Understanding and implementing positive reinforcement as an intervention strategy for children with disabilities. *American Journal of Occupational Therapy, 58*, 113–116.

Wentzel, K. R. (2021). *Motivating students to learn* (5th ed.). Routledge.

Whalon, K. J., Conroy, M. A., Martinez, J. R., & Werch, B. L. (2015). School-based peer-related social competence interventions for children with autism spectrum disorder: A meta-analysis and descriptive review of single case research design studies. *Journal of Autism and Developmental Disorders, 45*, 1513–1531.

Wheeler, J. J., & Richey, D. D. (2014). *Behavior management: Principles and practices of positive behavior supports* (3rd ed.). Pearson.

Wolters, C. A., Denton, C. A., York, M. J., & Francis, D. J. (2014). Adolescents' motivation for reading: Group differences and relation to standardized achievement. *Reading and Writing, 27*, 503–533.

Zheng, C., Erickson, A. G., Kingston, N. M., & Noonan, P. M. (2014). The relationship among self-determination, self-concept, and academic achievement for students with learning disabilities. *Journal of Learning Disabilities, 47*, 462–474.

Zimmerman, B., & Kitsantas, A. (2007). Reliability and validity of Self-Efficacy for Learning Form (SELF) scores of college students. *Journal of Psychology, 215*, 157–163.

Chapter 9

Abbott, M., Greenwood, C. R., Buzhardt, J., Wills, H. P., & Terry, B. (2011). Peer-mediated approaches. In R. W. O'Connor & P. F. Vadasy (Eds.), *Handbook of reading interventions* (pp. 279–299). Guilford Press.

Bambara, L. M., Thomas, A., Chovanes, J., & Cole, C. L. (2018). Peer-mediated intervention: Enhancing the social conversational skills of adolescents with autism spectrum disorder. *Teaching Exceptional Children, 15*, 7–17.

Barber, A. B., Saffo, R. W., Gilpin, A. T., Craft, L. D., & Goldstein, H. (2016). Peers as clinicians: Examining the impact of Stay Play Talk on social communication in young preschoolers with autism. *Journal of Communication Disorders, 59*, 1–15.

Bene, K. Banda, D. R., & Brown, D. (2014). A meta-analysis of peer-mediated instructional arrangements and autism. *Review Journal of Autism and Developmental Disorders, 1*, 135–142.

Bowman-Perrott, L., Davis, H., Vannest, K., Williams, L., Greenwood, C., & Parker, R. (2013). Academic benefits of peer tutoring: A meta-analytic review of single-case research. *School Psychology Review, 42*, 39–55.

Bowman-Perrott, L., deMarin, S., Mahadevan, L., & Etchells, M. (2016). Assessing the academic, social, and language production outcomes of English language learners engaged in peer tutoring: A systematic review. *Education and Treatment of Children, 39*, 359–388.

Campe, S., Denner, J., Green, E., & Torres, D. (2020). Pair programming in middle school: Variations in interactions and behaviors. *Computer Science Education, 30*, 22–46.

Carter, E. W., Asmus, J., Moss, C. K., Biggs, E. E., Bolt, D. M., Born, T. L., . . . Weir, K. (2016). Randomized evaluation of peer support arrangements to support the inclusion of high school students with severe disabilities. *Exceptional Children, 82*, 209–233.

Carter, E. W., Cushing, L. S., & Kennedy, C. H. (2009). *Peer support strategies for improving all students social lives and learning.* Paul H. Brooks.

Carter, E. W., Moss, C. K., Asmus, J., Fesperman, E., Cooney, M., Brock, M. E., . . . Vincent, L. B. (2015). Promoting inclusion, social connections, and learning through peer support arrangements. *Teaching Exceptional Children, 48*, 9–18.

Carter, E. W., Moss, C. K., Hoffman, A., Chung, Y., & Sisco, L. (2011). Efficacy and social validity of peer support arrangements for adolescents with disabilities. *Exceptional Children, 78*, 107–125.

Cihak, D. F., Fahrenkrog, C. D., Ayres, K. M., & Smith, C. (2010). The use of video modeling via a video iPod and a system of least prompts to improve transitional behaviors for students with autism spectrum disorders in the general education classroom. *Teaching Exceptional Children, 12*, 103–115.

Collins, T. A., Gresham, F. M., & Dart, E. H. (2016). The effects of peer-mediated check-in/check-out on the social skills of socially neglected students. *Behavior Modification, 40*, 568–588.

Dart, E. H., Collins, T. A. , Klingbeil, D. A., & McKinley, L. E. (2014). Peer management interventions: A meta-analytic review of single case research. *School Psychology Review, 43*, 367–384.

Dunn, M. E., Shelnut, J., Ryan, J. B., & Katsiyannis, A. (2017). A systematic review of peer-mediated interventions on the academic achievement of students with emotional/behavioral disorders. *Education and Treatment of Children, 40*, 497–524.

Favazza, P. C., Ostrosky, M., & Mouzourou, C. (2016). *The making friends program: Supporting acceptance in your K–2 classroom.* Brookes.

Foss, E., Guha, M. L., Papadatos, P., Clegg, T., Yipp, J., & Walsh, G. (2013). Cooperative inquiry extended: Creating technology with middle school students with differences. *Journal of Special Education Technology, 28(3)*, 33–46.

Frederickson, N. L., & Turner, J. (2003). Utilizing the classroom peer group to address children's social needs: An evaluation of the Circle of Friends intervention approach. *Journal of Special Education, 36*, 234–245.

Frederickson, N. L., Warner, J., & Turner, J. (2005). "Circle of Friends": An exploration of impact over time. *Educational Psychology in Practice, 21*, 197–217.

Fuchs, D., & Fuchs, L. S. (2005). Peer-assisted learning strategies: Promoting word recognition, fluency, and reading comprehension in young children. *Journal of Special Education, 39*, 34–44.

Fuchs, D., Fuchs, L., Mathes, P. G., & Martinez, E. A. (2002). Preliminary evidence on the social standing of students with learning disabilities in PALS and no-PALS classrooms. *Learning Disabilities Research & Practice, 17*, 205–215.

Gillies, R. M. (2016). Cooperative learning: Review of research and practice. *Australian Journal of Teacher Education, 41*, 39–54.

Harris, K. R., & Meltzer, L. (Eds.). (2015). *The power of peers in the classroom.* Guilford Press.

Hassani, S., Alves, S., Avramidis, E., & Schwab, S. (2021). The Circle of Friends intervention: A research synthesis. *European Journal of Special Education*. [Epub ahead of print]

Higgins, T. S. (1982). *A comparison of two methods of practice on the spelling performance of learning disabled adolescents*. Unpublished doctoral dissertation, Georgia State University, Atlanta, GA.

Hochman, J. M., Carter, E. W., Bottema-Beutel, K., Harvey, M. N., & Gustafson, J. R. (2015). Efficacy of peer networks to increase social connections among high school students with and without autism spectrum disorder. *Exceptional Children, 82*, 96–116.

Hughes, E. M., & Solari, E. (2020). Peer assisted learning strategies. *Current Practice Alerts, 29*, 1–4.

Hurley, E. A., Allen, B. A., & Boykin, W. (2009). Culture and the interaction of student ethnicity with reward structure in group learning. *Cognition and Instruction, 27*, 121–146.

Jenkins, J. R., & Jenkins, L. M. (1981). *Cross age and peer tutoring: Help for students with learning problems*. Council for Exceptional Children.

Jimenez, B. A., Browder, D. M., Spooner, F., & Dibiase, W. (2012). Peer-mediated embedded instruction for students with moderate intellectual disability. *Exceptional Children, 78*, 301–217.

Johnson, D. W., & Johnson, R. T. (1986). Mainstreaming and cooperative learning strategies. *Exceptional Children, 52*, 553–561.

Johnson, D. W., & Johnson, R. T. (2009). An educational psychology success story: Social interdependence theory: Cooperative learning. *Educational Researcher, 38*, 365–379.

Johnson, D. W., & Johnson, F. (2017). *Joining together: Group theory and group skills* (12th ed). Allyn & Bacon.

Johnson, D. W., Johnson, R. T., Dudley, B., Ward, M., & Magnuson, D. (1995). The impact of peer mediation training on the management of school and home conflicts. *American Educational Research Journal, 32*, 829–844.

Johnson, D. W., Johnson, R. T., & Holubec, E. J. (2008). *Cooperation in the classroom*. Interaction Book Company.

Kagan, S., & Kagan, M. (2009). Kagan Cooperative Learning. Kagan Publishing.

Kamps, D., Greenwood, C., Arreage-Mayer, C., Veerkamp, M. B., Utler, C., Tapia, Y., . . . Bannister, H. (2008). The efficacy of classwide peer tutoring in middle schools. *Education and Treatment of Children, 31*, 119–152.

Kamps, D., Thiemann-Bourque, K., Heitzman-Powell, L., Schwartz, I., Rosenberg, N., Mason, R., & Cox, S. (2015). A comprehensive peer network intervention to improve social communication of children with autism spectrum disorders: A randomized trial in kindergarten and first grade. *Journal of Autism and Developmental Disorders, 45*, 1809–1824.

Kearns, D. M., Fuchs, D., Fuchs, L. S., McMaster, K. L., & Sáenz, L. (2015). Peer-assisted learning strategies to improve students' word recognition and reading comprehension. In K. R. Harris & L. Meltzer (Eds.), *The power of peers in the classroom* (pp. 143–187). Guilford Press.

Kerr, M. M., & Nelson, C. M. (2002). *Strategies for addressing behavior problems in the classroom* (4th ed.). Merrill/Prentice Hall.

Kerr, M. M., & Nelson, C. M. (2010). *Strategies for addressing behavior problems in the classroom* (6th ed.). Merrill/Prentice Hall.

Leung, K. C., Marsh, H. W., Craven, R. G., Yeung, A. S., & AbdulJabbar, A. S. (2013). Domain specificity between peer support and self-concept. *Journal of Early Adolescence, 33*, 227–244.

Maheady, L., & Gard, J. (2010). Classwide peer tutoring: Practice, theory, research, and personal narrative. *Intervention in School and Clinic, 46*, 71–78.

Maheady, L., Mallette, B., & Harper, G. F. (2006). Four classwide peer tutoring models: Similarities, differences, and implications for research and practice. *Reading & Writing Quarterly: Overcoming Learning Difficulties, 22*, 65–89.

Marshak, L., Mastropieri, M. A., & Scruggs, T. E. (2011). Curriculum enhancements for inclusive secondary social studies classes. *Exceptionality, 19*, 61–74.

Mastropieri, M. A., & Scruggs, T. E. (1993). *A practical guide for teaching science to students with special needs in inclusive settings*. Pro-Ed.

Mastropieri, M. A., Scruggs, T. E., & Bohs, K. (1994). Mainstreaming an emotionally handicapped student in science: A qualitative investigation. In T. E. Scruggs & M. A. Mastropieri (Eds.), *Advances in learning and behavioral disabilities* (Vol. 8, pp. 131–146). JAI Press.

Mastropieri, M. A., Scruggs, T. E., & Graetz, J. (2005). Cognition and learning in inclusive high school chemistry classes. In T. E. Scruggs & M. A. Mastropieri (Eds.), *Cognition and learning in diverse settings: Advances in learning and behavioral disabilities* (Vol. 18, pp. 107–118). Elsevier.

Mastropieri, M. A., Scruggs, T. E., Mantzicopoulos, P. Y., Sturgeon, A., Goodwin, L., & Chung, S. (1998). "A place where living things affect and depend upon each other": Qualitative and quantitative outcomes associated with inclusive science teaching. *Science Education, 82*, 163–179.

Mastropieri, M. A., Scruggs, T. E., & Marshak, L. (2008). Training teachers, parents, and peers to implement effective teaching strategies for content area learning. In T. E. Scruggs & M. A. Mastropieri (Eds.), *Advances in learning and behavioral disabilities: Vol. 21. Personnel preparation* (pp. 209–321). Emerald.

Mastropieri, M. A., Scruggs, T. E., Mohler, L. J., Beranek, M. L., Spencer, V., Boon, R. T., & Talbott, E. (2001). Can middle school students with serious reading difficulties help each other and learn anything? *Learning Disabilities Research & Practice, 16*, 18–27.

Mastropieri, M. A., Scruggs, T. E., Spencer, V., & Fontana, J. (2003). Promoting success in high school world history: Peer tutoring versus guided notes. *Learning Disabilities Research & Practice, 18*, 52–65.

Mathes, P. G., Fuchs, D., Fuchs, L. S., Henley, A. M., & Sanders, A. (1994). Increasing strategic reading practice with Peabody Classwide Peer Tutoring. *Learning Disabilities Research & Practice, 9*, 44–48.

McDuffie, K. A., Mastropieri, M. A., & Scruggs, T. E. (2009). Differential effects of co-teaching and peer-mediated instruction: Results for content learning and student-teacher interactions. *Exceptional Children, 75*, 493–510.

McLeskey, J., Waldron, N., Spooner, F., & Algozzine, B. (Eds.). (2014). *Handbook of effective inclusive schools: Research and practice*. Routledge.

McMaster, K. L., Fuchs, D., & Fuchs, L. S. (2006). Research on peer-assisted learning strategies: The promise and limitations of peer-mediated instruction. *Reading & Writing Quarterly: Overcoming Learning Difficulties, 22*, 5–25.

McMaster, K. L., Kung, S., Han, I., & Cao, M. (2008). Peer-assisted learning strategies: A "Tier 1" approach to promoting English learners' response to intervention. *Exceptional Children, 74*, 194–214.

McMaster, K. N., & Fuchs, D. (2002). Effects of cooperative learning on the academic achievement of students with learning disabilities: An update of Tateyama-Sniezek's review. *Learning Disabilities Research & Practice, 17*, 107–117.

McMaster, K. N., & Fuchs, D. (2005). *Cooperative learning: Use caution*. Current Practice Alerts, Division for Research and Division for Learning Disabilities, Council for Exceptional Children, Issue 11. http://s3.amazonaws.com/cmi-teaching-ld/alerts/8/uploaded_files/original_alert11.pdf?1301000897

Meyer, A., Rose, D. H., & Gordon, D. (2014). *Universal design for learning: Theory & practice.* CAST Professional Publishing.

Meyer, L. E., & Ostrosky, M. M. (2016). Impact of affective intervention on the friendships of kindergarteners with disabilities. *Topics in Early Childhood Special Education*, *35*, 200–210.

Moeyaert, M., Klingbeil, D. A., Rodabaugh, E., & Turan, M. (2021). Three-level meta-analysis of single-case data regarding the effects of peer tutoring on academic and social-behavioral outcomes for at-risk students and students with disabilities. *Remedial and Special Education*, *42*, 94–106.

Myles, B. (2007). *Priming* [Council for Exceptional Children blog]. http://cecblog.typepad.com/cec/

Norland, J. J. (2005). *English language learners' interactions with various science curriculum features.* Unpublished doctoral dissertation, George Mason University, Fairfax, VA.

O'Conner, E. (2016). The use of "Circle of Friends" strategy to improve social interactions and social acceptance: A case study of a child with Asperger's syndrome and other associated needs. *Support for Learning*, *31*, 138–147.

O'Connor, R. E., & Jenkins, J. R. (1996). Cooperative learning as an inclusion strategy: A closer look. *Exceptionality*, *6*, 29–51.

O'Connor, R. E., & Jenkins, J. R. (2014). Cooperative learning for students with learning disabilities: Advice and caution derived from evidence. In H. L. Swanson, K. R. Harris, & S. Graham (Eds.), *Handbook of learning disabilities* (pp. 507–525). Guilford Press.

Ok, M. W., & Rao, K. (2019). Digital tools for the inclusive classroom: Google chrome as assistive and instructional technology, *Journal of Special Education Technology, 34(3)*, 204–211.

Okilwa, N. S. A., & Shelby, L. (2010). The effects of peer tutoring on academic performance of students with disabilities in grades 6 through 12: A synthesis of the literature. *Remedial and Special Education*, *31*, 450–463.

Oortwijn, M. B., Boekaerts, M., & Vedder, P. (2008). The impact of a cooperative learning experience on pupils' popularity, noncooperativeness, and interethnic bias in multiethnic elementary schools. *Educational Psychology*, *28*(2), 1–11.

Powell, S. R., & Fuchs, L. S. (2015). Peer-assisted learning strategies in mathematics. In K. R. Harris & L. Meltzer (Eds.). (2015). *The power of peers in the classroom* (pp. 188–223). Guilford Press.

Regan, K., Evmenova, A. S., Mastropieri, M. A., & Scruggs, T. E. (2015). Peer interactions in the content areas: Using differentiated instruction strategies. In K. R. Harris & L. Meltzer (Eds.), *The power of peers in the classroom* (pp. 33–68). Guilford Press.

Richards-Tutor, C., Aceves, T., & Reutebuch, C. (2015). Peer-supported instruction for English learners. In K. R. Harris & L. Meltzer (Eds.), *The power of peers in the classroom* (pp. 251–287). Guilford Press.

Scruggs, T. E., & Mastropieri, M. A. (1998). Peer tutoring and students with special needs. In K. Topping & S. Ehly (Eds.), *Peer-assisted learning* (pp. 165–182). Erlbaum.

Scruggs, T. E., Mastropieri, M. A., & Marshak, L. (2012). Peer-mediated instruction in inclusive secondary social studies learning: Direct and indirect learning effects. *Learning Disabilities Research and Practice*, *27*, 12–20.

Sindelar, P. T. (1982). The effects of cross-age tutoring on the comprehension skills of remedial reading students. *Journal of Special Education*, *16*, 199–206.

Slavin, R. E. (1991). Synthesis of research on cooperative learning. *Educational Leadership*, *48*(5), 71–82.

Slavin, R. E. (2015). Cooperative learning in elementary schools. *Education 3-13: International Journal of Primary, Elementary and Early Years Education*, *43*, 5–14.

Souvignier, E., & Kronenberger, J. (2007). Cooperative learning in third graders' jigsaw groups for mathematics and science with and without questioning training. *British Journal of Educational Psychology*, *77*, 755–771.

Spencer, V., Scruggs, T.E., & Mastropieri, M.A. (2003). Content area learning in middle school social studies classrooms and students with emotional or behavioral disorders: A comparison of strategies. *Behavioral Disorders*, *28*, 77–93.

Spencer, V. G. (2006). Peer tutoring and students with emotional or behavioral disorders: A review of the literature. *Behavioral Disorders*, *31*, 204–222.

Steinbrenner, J. R., Hume, K., Odom, S. L., Morin, K. L., Nowell, S. W., Tomaszewski, B., . . . Savage, M. N. (2020). *Evidence-based practices for children, youth, and young adults with autism.* University of North Carolina at Chapel Hill, Frank Porter Graham Child Development Institute, National Clearinghouse on Autism Evidence and Practice Review Team.

Stevahn, L., Johnson, D. W., Johnson, R. T., & Schultz, R. (2002). Effects of conflict resolution training integrated into a high school social studies curriculum. *Journal of Social Psychology*, *142*, 305–331.

Stevens, R. J., & Slavin, R. E. (1991). When cooperative learning improves the achievement of students with mild disabilities: A response to Tateyama-Sniezek. *Exceptional Children*, *57*, 276–280.

Tateyama-Sniezek, K. M. (1990). Cooperative learning: Does it improve the academic achievement of students with handicaps? *Exceptional Children*, *56*, 426–437.

Thanh, P., Thi, H., Gillies, R., & Renshawn, P. (2008). Cooperative learning (CL) and academic achievement of Asian students: A true story. *International Education Studies*, *1*, 82–88.

Tomlinson, C. (2014). *The differentiated classroom: Responding to the needs of all learners* (2nd ed.). Association for Supervision and Curriculum Development.

Travers, H., & Carter, E. W. (2021). A systematic review of how peer-mediated interventions impact students without disabilities. *Remedial and Special Education*, *18*, 1–18.

Tsao, L., Odom, S. L., Vuysse, V., Skinner, M., West, T., & Vitztum-Komanecki, J. (2008). Social participation of children with disabilities in inclusive preschool programs: Program typology and ecological features. *Exceptionality*, *16*, 125–140.

Van Ryzin, M. J., Roseth, C. J., & McClure, H. (2020). The effects of cooperative learning on peer relations, academic support, and engagement among students of color. *The Journal of Educational Research, 113(4)*, 283–291.

Watts, G. W., Bryant, D. P., & Carroll, M. L. (2019). Students with emotional-behavioral disorders as cross-age tutors: A synthesis of the literature. *Behavioral Disorders*, *44*, 131–147.

Watts, G. W., Bryant, D. P., & Roberts, G. J. (2020). Effects of cross-age tutors with EBD for kindergarteners at risk of mathematics disabilities. *Journal of Emotional and Behavioral Disabilities*, *28*, 244–256.

Wexler, J., Reed, D. K., Pyle, N., Mitchell, M., & Barton, E. E. (2015). A synthesis of peer-mediated academic interventions for secondary struggling learners. *Journal of Learning Disabilities*, *48*, 451–470.

Ziegler, M., Mathews, A., Mayberry, M., Owen-Deschryver, J., & Carter, E. W. (2020). From barriers to belonging: Promoting inclusion and relationships through the peer to peer program. *Teaching Exceptional Children*, *52*, 426–434.

Chapter 10

Adamson, R. M., & Lewis, T. J. (2017). A comparison of three opportunity-to-respond strategies on the academic engaged time among high school students who present challenging behavior. *Behavioral Disorders*, *42*(2), 41–51.

Baddeley, A., Eysenck, M. W., & Anderson, M. C. (2020). *Memory* (3rd ed.). Psychology Press.

Barkley, R. A. (Ed.). (2015). *Attention deficit hyperactivity disorder: A handbook of assessment and treatment* (4th ed.). Guilford Press.

Beckman, A., Mason, B. A., Wills, H. P., Garrison-Kane, L., & Huffman, J. (2019). Improving behavioral and academic outcomes for students with autism spectrum disorder: Testing an app-based self-monitoring intervention. *Education and Treatment of Children*, *42*(2), 225–244.

Beirne-Smith, M., Patton, J. M., & Hill, S. (2005). *Introduction to intellectual disabilities* (7th ed.). Prentice Hall.

Bjorklund, D. F., & Causey, K. B. (2017). *Children's thinking: Cognitive development and individual differences* (6th ed). SAGE.

Bowman-Perrott, L., Davis, H., Vannest, K., Williams, L., Greenwood, C., & Parker, R. (2013). Academic benefits of peer tutoring: A meta-analytic review of single-case research. *School Psychology Review*, *42*, 39–55.

Brigham, F. J., Scruggs, T. E., & Mastropieri, M. A. (2011). Science education and students with learning disabilities. *Learning Disabilities Research & Practice*, *26*(4), 223–232.

Burchers, S., & Burchers, B. E. (2007). *Vocabulary cartoons II: SAT word power.* New Monic Books.

Chang, Z., Ghiradi, L. Quinn, P. D., Asherson, P., D'Onofrio, B. M., & Larsson, H. (2019). Risks and benefits of attention-deficit/hyperactivity disorder medication on behavioral and neuropsychiatric outcomes: A qualitative review of pharmacoepidemiology studies using linked prescription databases. *Biological Psychiatry*, *86*(5), 335–343.

Ciullo, S., & Reutebuch, C. (2013). Computer-based graphic organizers for students with LD: A systematic review. *Learning Disabilities Research & Practice*, *28*(40), 196–210.

Craik, F. I. M., & Lockhart, R. S. (1972). Levels of processing: A framework for memory research. *Journal of Verbal Learning and Verbal Behavior*, *11*(6), 671–684.

Crossairt, A., Hall, R. V., & Hopkins, B. L. (1973). The effects of experimenter's instructions, feedback, and praise on teacher praise and student attending behavior. *Journal of Applied Behavior Analysis*, *6*(1), 89–100.

Dexter, D. D., Park, Y. J., & Hughes, C. A. (2011). A meta-analytic review of graphic organizers and science instruction for adolescents with learning disabilities: Implications for the intermediate and secondary science classroom. *Learning Disabilities Research & Practice*, *26*(4), 204–213.

Dunlosky, J., & Bjork, R. A. (Eds.). (2008). *Handbook of metamemory and memory.* Taylor & Francis.

Evans, S. W., Owens, J. S., & Bunford, N. (2014). Evidence-based psychosocial treatments for children and adolescents with attention-deficit/hyperactivity disorder. *Journal of Clinical Child and Adolescent Psychology*, *43*, 527–551.

Fried, R., Petty, C., Farone, S. V., Hyder, L. L., Day, H., & Biederman, J. (2016). Is ADHD a risk factor for high school dropout?: A controlled study. *Journal of Attention Disorders*, *20*, 383–389.

Gable, R. A., Hester, P. H., Rock, M. L., & Hughes, K. G. (2009). Back to basics: Rules, praise, ignoring, and reprimands revisited. *Intervention in School and Clinic*, *44*(4), 195–205.

Ghetti, S., Mirandola, C., Angelini, L., Cornoldi, C., & Ciaramelli, E. (2011). Development of subjective recollection: Understanding of and introspection on memory states. *Child Development*, *82*(6), 1954–1969.

Greene, G. (1999). Mnemonic multiplication fact instruction for students with learning disabilities. *Learning Disabilities Research & Practice*, *14*(3), 141–148.

Hall, C., Kent, S. C., McCulley, L., Davis, A., & Wanzek, J. (2013). A new look at mnemonics and graphic organizers in the secondary social studies classroom. *Teaching Exceptional Children*, *46*, 47–55.

Hamilton, K. A., & Yao, M. Z. (2018). Blurring boundaries: Effects of device features on metacognitive evaluations. *Computers in Human Behavior*, *89*, 213–220.

Hammond, Z. (2015a). *3 tips to make any lesson more culturally responsive.* https://www.cultofpedagogy.com

Hammond, Z. (2015b). *Culturally responsive teaching and the brain.* Corwin Press.

Hammond, Z. (2020). The power of protocols for equity. *Deeper Discussions*, *77*(7), 45–50.

Harmon, M. (2020). *Remember 1,600 vocabulary words.* Carolina Hawk Creations.

Haydon, T., Musti-Rao, S., & Alteer, P. (2017). Comparing choral responding and a choral responding plus mnemonic device during geography lessons for students with mild to moderate disabilities. *Education and Treatment of Children*, *40*(1), 77–96.

Heward, W. L., Alber-Morgan, S. R., & Konrad, M. (2022). *Exceptional children: An introduction to special education* (12th ed.). Pearson.

Higbee, K. (2008). *Your memory: How it works and how to improve it* (2nd ed.). Hachette Books.

Holifield, C., Goodman, J., Hazelkorn, M., & Heflin, L. J. (2010). Using self-monitoring to increase attending to task and academic accuracy in children with autism. *Focus on Autism and Other Developmental Disabilities*, *25*(4), 230–238.

Joseph, L. M., & Eveleigh, E. L. (2011). A review of the effects of self-monitoring on reading performance of students with disabilities. *Journal of Special Education*, *45*(1), 43–53.

Kennedy, M. J., & Romig, J. E. (2021). Cognitive load theory: An applied introduction for special and general educators. *Teaching Exceptional Children.* [Epub ahead of print]

Kerr, M. M., & Nelson, C. M. (2010). *Strategies for addressing behavior problems in the classroom* (6th ed.). Merrill/Prentice Hall.

Kuder, S. J. (2017). Vocabulary instruction for secondary students with reading disabilities: An updated research review. *Learning Disability Quarterly*, *40*(3), 155–164.

Lerner, J. W., & Johns, B. (2015). *Learning disabilities and related disabilities: Strategies for success* (13th ed.). Cengage Learning.

Levin, J., & Nolan, J. F. (2022). *Principles of classroom management: A professional decision making model* (8th ed.). Pearson.

Lucangeli, D., Galderisi, D., & Cornoldi, C. (1995). Specific and general transfer effects following metamemory training. *Learning Disabilities Research and Practice*, *10*(1), 11–21.

Maheady, L., & Gard, J. (2010). Classwide peer tutoring: Practice, theory, research, and personal narrative. *Intervention in School and Clinic*, *46*, 71–78.

Marshak, L., Mastropieri, M. A., & Scruggs, T. E. (2011). Curriculum enhancements in inclusive secondary social studies classrooms. *Exceptionality*, *19*(2), 61–74.

Massuti, R., Moreira-Maia, C. R., Campani, F., Sonego, M., Amaro, J., Akutagava-Martins, G. C., . . . Rohde, L. A. (2021). Assessing undertreatment and overtreatment/misuse of ADHD medications in children and adolescents across continents: A systematic review and meta-analysis. *Neuroscience and Biobehavioral Reviews*, *128*, 64–73.

Mastropieri, M. A., Scruggs, T. E., Evmenova, A., & Regan, K. (2018). Memory-enhancing strategies for students with learning disabilities: Lessons learned from 20 years of experimental research. In G. D. Sideridis, K. Bonanno-Sotiropoulos, & T.A. Citro (Eds.), *Paving the pathway for educational success: Effective classroom strategies for students with learning disabilities* (pp. 45–62). Rowman & Littlefield.

Mastropieri, M. A., Scruggs, T. E., & Graetz, J. (2005). Cognition and learning in inclusive high school chemistry classes. In T. E. Scruggs & M. A. Mastropieri (Eds.), *Cognition and learning in diverse settings: Advances in learning and behavioral disabilities* (Vol. 18, pp. 107–118). Elsevier.

Mastropieri, M. A., Scruggs, T. E., Mantzicopoulos, P., Sturgeon, A., Goodwin, L., & Chung, S. (1998). "A place where living things affect and depend on each other": Qualitative and quantitative outcomes associated with inclusive science teaching. *Science Education, 82*, 163–179.

Mastropieri, M. A., Scruggs, T. E., Regan, K., Evmenova, A., & Fontana, J. (2018). Mnemonic strategies: What are they? How can I use them? And how effective are they? In G. D. Sideridis, K. Bonanno-Sotiropoulos, & T. A. Citro (Eds.), *Paving the pathway for educational success: Effective classroom strategies for students with learning disabilities* (pp. 63–76). Rowman & Littlefield.

Mastropieri, M. A., Scruggs, T. E., & Whedon, C. (1997). Using mnemonic strategies to teach information about U.S. presidents: A classroom-based investigation. *Learning Disability Quarterly, 20*, 13–21.

Mautone, J. A., Marshall, S. A., Sharman, J., Eiraldi, R. B., Jawad, A. F., & Power, T. J. (2012). Development of a family-school intervention for young children with attention deficit hyperactivity disorder. *School Psychology Review, 41*, 447–466.

Mayer, R. E., Hegarty, M., Mayer, S. Y., & Campbell, J. (2005). When passive media promote active learning: Static diagrams versus animation in multimedia instruction. *Journal of Experimental Psychology: Applied, 11*, 256–265.

Meyer, A., Rose, D. H., & Gordon, D. (2014). *Universal design for learning: Theory and practice.* CAST.

McLeskey, J., Barringer, M-D., Billingsley, B., Brownell, M., Jackson, D., Kennedy, M., . . . Ziegler, D. (2017, January). *High-leverage practices in special education.* Council for Exceptional Children & CEEDAR Center.

Ninci, J., Rispoli, M., Burke, M. D., & Neely, L. C. (2018). Embedding interests of individuals with autism spectrum disorder: A quality review. *Review Journal of Autism and Developmental Disorders, 5*, 15–28.

Ormrod, J. E., Anderman, E. M., & Anderman, L. (2019). *Educational psychology: Developing learners* (10th ed.). Pearson.

Overton, T. (2016). *Assessing learners with special needs: An applied approach* (8th ed.). Pearson.

Peterson, D. J., & Mulligan, N. W. (2010). Enactment and retrieval. *Memory and Cognition, 38*, 233–243.

Pfiffner, L. J., & DuPaul, G. J. (2015). Treatment of ADHD in school settings. In R. A. Barkley (Ed.), *Attention-deficit hyperactivity disorder: A handbook of diagnosis and treatment* (4th ed., pp. 596–629). Guilford Press.

Radvansky, G. A. (2021). *Human memory* (4th ed.). Pearson.

Re, A., De Franchis, V., & Cornoldi, C. (2010). Working memory control deficit in kindergarten ADHD children. *Child Neuropsychology, 16*(2), 134–144.

Redl, F. (1965). *Controls from within: Techniques for the treatment of the aggressive child.* Free Press.

Reid, R., & Johnson, J. (2012). *Teacher's guide to ADHD.* Guilford Press.

Reid, R., Lienemann, T. O., & Hagaman, J. L. (2013). *Strategy instruction for students with learning disabilities* (2nd ed.). Guilford Press.

Reid, R., Trout, A. L., & Schartz, M. (2005). Self-regulation interventions for children with attention deficit hyperactivity disorder. *Exceptional Children, 71*(4), 361–377.

Rice, M. F., & Dunn, W. (2020). Supporting children's writing in inclusive classrooms with arts-based strategies. *Teaching Exceptional Children, 52*, 147–156.

Rosenbloom, R., Wills, H. P., Mason, R., Huffman, J. M., & Mason, B. A. (2019). The effects of a technology-based self-monitoring intervention on on-task, disruptive, and task completion behaviors for adolescents with autism. *Journal of Autism and Developmental Disorders, 49*, 5047–5062.

Ryan, J. B., Katsiyannis, A., Losinski, L., Reid, R., & Ellis, C. (2014). Review of state medication policies/guidelines regarding psychotropic medications in public schools. *Journal of Child and Family Studies, 23*(4), 704–715.

Schulze, M. A. (2016). Self-management strategies to support students with ASD. *Teaching Exceptional Children, 48*, 225–231.

Scruggs, T. E., & Mastropieri, M. A. (2013). Teaching students with high-incidence disabilities. In B. G. Cook & M. Tankersley (Eds.), *Research-based practices in special education* (pp. 342–352). Pearson.

Scruggs, T. E., Mastropieri, M. A., Berkeley, S. L., & Marshak, L. (2010). Mnemonic strategies: Evidence-based practice and practice-based evidence. *Intervention in School and Clinic, 46*(2), 79–86.

Scruggs, T. E., Mastropieri, M. A., Brigham, F. J., & Marshak, M. (2017). Science and social studies. In J. M. Kauffman, D. P. Hallahan, & P. C. Pullen (Eds.), *Handbook of special education* (2nd ed., pp. 571–585). Taylor & Francis.

Scruggs, T. E., Mastropieri, M. A., McLoone, B. B., Levin, J. R., & Morrison, C. (1987). Mnemonic facilitation of learning disabled students' memory for expository prose. *Journal of Educational Psychology, 79*(1), 27–34.

Sheng, L., Byrd, C. T., McGregor, K. K., Zimmerman, H., & Bludau, K. (2015). List memory in young adults with language learning disability. *Journal of Speech, Language, and Hearing Research, 58*(2), 336–344.

Slattery, L., Crosland, K., & Iovannone, R. (2016). An evaluation of a self-management intervention to increase on-task behavior with individuals diagnosed with attention-deficit/hyperactivity disorder. *Journal of Positive Behavior Interventions, 18*(3), 168–179.

Smith, J. L. M., Saez, L., & Doabler, C. (2016). Using explicit and systematic instruction to support working memory. *Teaching Exceptional Children, 50*, 250–257.

Sprich, S. E., Safren, S. A., Finkelstein, D., Remmert, J. E., & Hammerness, P. (2016). A randomized controlled trial of cognitive behavioral therapy for ADHD in medication treated adolescents. *Journal of Child Psychology Psychiatry, 57*, 1218–1226.

Stefanelli, S., & Alloway, T. P. (2020). Mathematical skills and working memory profile of children with borderline intellectual functioning. *Journal of Intellectual Disabilities, 24*, 358–366.

Stichter, J. P., Conroy, M. A., O'Donnell, R., & Reichow, B. (2017). Current issues and trends in the education of children and youth with autism spectrum disorders. In J. M. Kauffman, D. P. Hallahan, & P. C. Pullen (Eds.), *Handbook of special education* (2nd ed., pp. 394–410). Routledge.

Sullivan, G. S., Mastropieri, M. A., & Scruggs, T. E. (1995). Reasoning and remembering: Coaching thinking with students with learning disabilities. *Journal of Special Education, 29*, 310–322.

Terrill, C., Scruggs, T. E., & Mastropieri, M. A. (2004). SAT vocabulary instruction for high school students with learning disabilities. *Intervention in School and Clinic, 39*, 288–294.

Therrien, W. J., Taylor, J. C., Hosp, J. L., Kaldenberg, E. R., & Gorsh, J. (2011). Science instruction for students with learning disabilities: A meta-analysis. *Learning Disabilities Research & Practice, 26*, 188–203.

Torres-Acosta, N., O'Keefe, J. H., O'Keefe, C. L., & Lavie, C. J. (2020). Cardiovascular effects of ADHD therapies. *Journal of the American College of Cardiology, 76*(7), 858–866.

Uberti, H. Z., Scruggs, T. E., & Mastropieri, M. A. (2003). Keywords make the difference! Mnemonic instruction in inclusive classrooms. A classroom application. *Teaching Exceptional Children, 35*(3), 56–61.

Van Laarhoven, T., Carreon, A., Bonneau, W., & Largerhausen, A. (2018). Comparing mobile technologies for teaching vocational skills to individuals with autism spectrum disorders and/or intellectual disabilities using universally designed prompting systems. *Journal of Autism and Developmental Disabilities, 48*, 2561–2529.

Vaughn, S., & Swanson, E. A. (2015). Special education research advances knowledge in education. *Exceptional Children, 82*(1), 11–24.

Weinstein, Y., Madan, C. R., & Sumeracki, M. A. (2018). Teaching the science of learning. *Cognitive Research: Principles and Implications, 3*(2), 1–17.

White, P. J., O'Reilly, M., Streusand, W., Levine, A., Sigafoos, J., Lancioni, G., . . . Aguilar, J. (2011). Best practices for teaching joint attention: A systematic review of the intervention literature. *Research in Autism Spectrum Disorders, 5*(4), 1283–1295.

Wills, H. P., & Mason, B. A. (2014). Implementation of a self-monitoring application to improve on-task behavior: A high-school pilot study. *Journal of Behavioral Education, 23*, 421–434.

Zisimopoulos, D. A. (2010). Enhancing multiplication performance in students with moderate intellectual disabilities using pegword mnemonics paired with a picture fading technique. *Journal of Behavioral Education, 19*(2), 117–133.

Chapter 11

Balint-Langel, K., Yuan, C., & Youjia, H. (2020). Teaching the Calendar application on a mobile device to young adults with intellectual and developmental disabilities. *Journal of Special Education Technology, 37*(1), 11–21.

Boyle, J. R. (2007). The process of note taking: Implications for students with mild disabilities. *The Clearing House, 80*, 227–232.

Boyle, J. R. (2010). Note-taking skills of middle school students with and without learning disabilities. *Journal of Learning Disabilities, 43*, 530–542.

Boyle, J. R., & Forchelli, G. A. (2014). Differences in the note-taking skills of students with high achievement, average achievement, and learning disabilities. *Learning and Individual Differences, 35*, 9–14.

Boyle, J. R., Forchelli, G. A., & Cariss, K. (2015). Note taking interventions to assist students with disabilities in content area classes. *Intervention in School and Clinic, 59*, 186–195.

Boyle, J. R., & Joyce, R. L. (2019). Smartpen technology for note taking in inclusive English/language arts classes. *Reading and Writing Quarterly, 35*, 525–538.

Boyle, J. R., & Rivera, T. Z. (2012). Note-taking techniques for students with disabilities: A systematic review of the research. *Learning Disability Quarterly, 35*(3), 131–143.

Boyle, J. R., Rosen, S. M., & Forchelli, G. (2014). Exploring metacognitive strategy use during note-taking for students with learning disabilities, *Education, 44*(2), 161–180.

Boyle, J. R., & Weishaar, M. (2001). The effects of strategic note taking on the recall and comprehension of lecture information for high school students with learning disabilities. *Learning Disabilities Research and Practice, 16*, 133–141.

Bryan, T., & Burstein, K. (2004). Improving homework completion and academic performance: Lessons from special education. *Theory into Practice, 43*, 213–219.

Carter, C. J., Bishop, J., & Kravits, S. L. (2011). *Keys to effective learning: Study skills and habits for success* (6th ed.). Merrill/Prentice Hall.

Deshler, D. D., & Schumaker, J. B. (2006). *Teaching adolescents with disabilities: Accessing the general education curriculum.* Corwin Press.

Dorminy, K. P., Luscre, D., & Gast, D. L. (2009). Teaching organizational skills to children with high functioning autism and Asperger's syndrome. *Education and Training in Developmental Disabilities, 44*, 538–550.

Englert, C. S., Mariage, T. V., Okolo, C. M., Shankland, R. K., Moxley, K. D., Courtad, C. A., . . . Chen, H. Y. (2009). The learning-to-learn strategies of adolescents with disabilities: Highlighting, note taking, planning, and writing expository texts. *Assessment for Effective Intervention, 34*, 147–161.

Goldenberg, C. (2013). Unlocking the research on English learners: What we know and don't know about effective instruction. *American Educator, 37*(2), 4–11.

Graham, S., Collins, A. A., & Rigby-Wills, H. (2017). Writing characteristics of students with learning disabilities and typically achieving peers: A meta-analysis. *Exceptional Children, 83*(2), 199–218.

Hampshire, P. K., Butera, G. D., & Bellini, S. (2016). Self-management and parents as interventionists to improve homework independence in students with autism spectrum disorders. *Preventing School Failure, 60*(1), 22–34.

Hampshire, P. K., Butera, G. D., & Hourcade, J. J. (2014). Homework plans: A tool for promoting independence. *Teaching Exceptional Children, 46*, 158–168.

Hoover, J. J., & Patton, J. R. (2006). *Teaching study skills to students with learning problems: A teacher's guide for meeting diverse needs* (2nd ed.). Pro-Ed.

Houser, D., Maheady, L., Pomerantz, D., & Jabot, M. (2015). The effects of the Radical Raceway on homework completion and accuracy of 9th grade social studies inclusion class. *Journal of Behavioral Education, 24*(4), 402–417.

Hughes, C. A., Ruhl, K. L., Schumaker, J. B., & Deshler, D. D. (2002). Effects of instruction in an assignment completion strategy on the homework performance of students with learning disabilities in general education classes. *Learning Disabilities Research & Practice, 17*, 1–18.

Jakulski, J., & Mastropieri, M. A. (2004). Homework for students with disabilities. In T. E. Scruggs & M. A. Mastropieri (Eds.), *Research in secondary schools: Advances in learning and behavioral disabilities* (Vol. 17, pp. 77–122). Elsevier.

Joyce, R. L., & Boyle, J. R. (2020). Improving note-taking skills for students with disabilities through a Smartpen intervention. *Journal of Special Education Technology*, 35, 225–235.

King-Sears, M. E., Evmenova, A. S., & Johnson, T. M. (2017). Using technology for accessible chemistry homework for students with and without learning disabilities. *Learning Disabilities Research & Practice, 32*(2), 121–131.

Konrad, M., Joseph, L. M., & Itoi, M. (2011). Using guided notes to enhance instruction for all students. *Intervention in School and Clinic, 46*, 131–140.

Langberg, J. M., Epstein, J. N., Ginio-Herrera E., Becker, S. P., Vaughn, A. J., & Altaye, M. (2011). Materials organization, planning, and homework completion in middle-school students with ADHD: Impact on academic performance. *School Mental Health, 3*, 93–101.

MacArthur, C. A. (2012). Strategies instruction. In K. R. Harris, S. Graham, T. Urdan, A. G. Bus, S. Major, & H. L. Swanson (Eds.), *APA educational psychology handbook* (Vol. 3, pp. 379–401). American Psychological Association.

MacArthur, C. A. (2016). Instruction in evaluation and revision. In C. A. MacArthur, S. Graham, & J. Fitzgerald (Eds.), *Handbook of writing research* (2nd ed., pp. 272–287). Guilford Press.

Mastropieri, M. A., & Scruggs, T. E. (2002). *Effective instruction for special education* (3rd ed.). Prentice Hall/Merrill.

McLeskey, J., Barringer, M-D., Billingsley, B., Brownell, M., Jackson, D., Kennedy, M., . . . Ziegler, D. (2017, January) *High-leverage practices in special education.* Council for Exceptional Children & CEEDAR Center.

Miller, L. (2003). Developing listening skills with authentic materials. *ESL Magazine*, *6*(2), 16–18.

Muchnick, C. C. (2011). *The everything guide to study skills*. F+WMedia.

Ness, B. M., Sohlberg, M. M., & Albin, R.W. (2011). Evaluation of a second-tier classroom-based assignment completion strategy for middle school students in a resource context. *Remedial and Special Education*, *32*, 406–416.

Ok, M. W., & Rao, K. (2019). Digital tools for the inclusive classroom: Google Chrome as Assistive and Instructional Technology. *Journal of Special Education Technology*, *34*(3), 204–211.

O'Melia, M. C., & Rosenberg, M. S. (1994). Effects of cooperative homework teams on the acquisition of mathematics skills by secondary students with mild disabilities. *Exceptional Children*, *60*, 538–548.

Paulsen, K., & Sayeski, K. L. (2013). Using study skills to become independent learners in secondary content classes. *Intervention in School and Clinic*, *49*(1), 39–45.

Reid, R., Lienemann, T. O., & Hagaman, J. L. (2013). *Strategy instruction for students with learning disabilities* (2nd ed.). Guilford Press.

Spooner, L., & Woodcock, J. (2010). *Teaching children to listen: A practical approach to developing children's listening skills.* Continuum.

Suritsky, S. K., & Hughes, C. A. (1996). Notetaking strategy instruction. In D. D. Deshler, E. S. Ellis, & B. K. Lenz (Eds.), *Teaching adolescents with learning disabilities: Strategies and methods* (2nd ed., pp. 267–312). Love.

Vatterott, C. (2018). *Rethinking homework: Best practices that support diverse needs* (2nd ed.). Association of Supervision and Curriculum Development.

Vaughn, S., & Bos, C. (2019). *Strategies for teaching students with learning and behavior problems* (10th ed.). Pearson.

Vorderman, C., Barker, G., Moran, A., Senker, C., & Sommer, S. (2016). *Help your kids with study skills: A unique step-by-step visual guide.* DK Publishing.

Wiener, J., & Daniels, L. (2016). School experiences of adolescents with attention-deficit/hyperactivity disorder. *Journal of Learning Disabilities*, *49*(6), 567–581.

Wong, L. (2015). *Essential study skills* (8th ed.). Wadsworth.

Zibreg Hargis, D., Patti, A. L., Maheady, L., Budin, S., & Rafferty, L. (2016). Using interdependent group contingencies with randomly selected criteria and rewards to enhance homework performance in an eighth-grade classroom. *Journal of Evidence-Based Practices for Schools*, *15*(2), 172–192.

Chapter 12

Albus, D. A., Lazarus, S. S., Thurlow, M. L., Larson, E. D., & Liu, K. K. (2020). Text-to-speech accommodation policies in 2018–19 (NCEO Report 417). University of Minnesota, National Center on Educational Outcomes.

Aston, C., & Brown, D. L. (2021). Progress or setback: Revisiting the current state of assessment practices of black children. *Contemporary School Psychology*, *25*, 140–148.

Banks, T., & Eaton, I. (2014) Improving test-taking performance of secondary at-risk youth and students with disabilities. *Preventing School Failure: Alternative Education for Children and Youth*, *58*(4), 207–213.

Baron, J. B. (1990). Performance assessment: Blurring the edges among assessment, curriculum, and instruction. In A. B. Champaign, B. E. Lovitts, & B. J. Callinger (Eds.), *Assessment in the service of instruction* (pp. 127–148). American Association for the Advancement of Science.

Berkeley, S., & Riccomini, P. J. (2017). Academic progress monitoring. In J. M. Kauffman, D. P. Hallahan, & P. C. Pullen (Eds.), *Handbook of special education* (2nd ed., pp. 218–232). Taylor & Francis.

Bernstein, B. (2018). *Crush your test anxiety.* Familius.

Boyle, J. R. (2013). Strategic note-taking for inclusive middle school science classrooms. *Remedial and Special Education*, *34*, 78–90.

Brookhart, S. M. (2013). *How to create and use rubrics for formative assessment and grading.* Association of Supervision and Curriculum Development.

Brookhart, S. M. (2009). *Grading* (2nd ed.). Pearson.

Bursuck, W. D., Polloway, E. A., Plante, L., Epstein, M. H., Jayanthi, M., & McConeghy, J. (1996). Report card grading and adaptations: A national survey of classroom practices. *Exceptional Children*, *62*, 301–318.

California Department of Education. (2015). *California alternate performance assessment*. http://www.cde.ca.gov/ta/tg/sr/capa.asp

Carey, M. D., Mannell, R. H., & Dunn, P. K. (2011). Does a rater's familiarity with a candidate's pronunciation affect the rating in oral proficiency interviews? *Language Testing*, *28*, 201–219.

Carman, R. A., & Adams, W. R. (1991). *Study skills: A student's guide for survival* (2nd ed.). Wiley.

Cawthon, S. W. (2008). Accommodations use for statewide standardized assessments: Prevalence and recommendations for students who are deaf or hard of hearing. *Journal of Deaf Studies and Deaf Education*, *13*, 55–76.

Center for Parent Information and Resources. (2020, March). *Supports, modifications, and accommodations for students with disabilities.* https://www.parentcenterhub.org/accommodations/

Christiansen, J., & Vogel, J. R. (1998). A decision model for grading students with disabilities. *Teaching Exceptional Children*, *31*, 30–35.

Cizek, G. J., & Burg, S. S. (2006). *Addressing test anxiety in a high-stakes environment.* Corwin Press.

Clark, A. K., & Karvonen, M. (2020). Constructing and evaluating a validation argument for a next-generation alternate assessment. *Educational Assessment*, *25*(1), 47–64.

Cleveland, R. E. (2018). Using digital portfolios: Reflection, assessment and employment. *TechTrends*, *62*(3), 276–285.

College Board. (2015). *Students with disabilities: The steps to receive test accommodations.* http://sat.collegeboard.org/register/for-students-with-disabilities

Conderman, G., & Hedin, L. (2012). Purposeful assessment practices for co-teachers. *Teaching Exceptional Children*, *44*(4), 18–27.

Connolly, A. J. (2007). *KeyMath 3 Diagnostic Assessment—revised*, Pearson.

Crawford, L., Helwig, R., & Tindal, G. (2004). Writing performance assessments: How important is extended time? *Journal of Learning Disabilities*, *37*, 132–142.

Deno, S. (2016). Data-based decision-making. In S. R. Jimerson, M. K. Burns, & A. M. VanDerHayden (Eds.), *Handbook of response to intervention: The science and practice of multi-tiered systems of support* (2nd ed., pp. 9–28). Springer.

Deshler, D. D., & Schumaker, J. B. (2006). *Teaching adolescents with disabilities: Accessing the general education curriculum.* Corwin Press.

Educational Testing Service. (2018). *Testing accommodations available for test takers with disabilities or health-related needs.* https://www.ets.org/gre/revised_general/register/disabilities/accommodations

Evans, C. (2021). *A culturally responsive classroom assessment framework.* National Center for the Improvement of Educational Assessment. https://www.nciea.org/blog/classroom-assessment/culturally-responsive-classroom-assessment-framework

Feldman, E., Kim, J., & Elliott, S. N. (2011). The effects of accommodations on adolescents' self-efficacy and test performance. *Journal of Special Education*, *45*, 77–88.

Fuchs, D., & Fuchs, L. S. (1989). Effects of examiner familiarity on Black, Caucasian, and Hispanic children: A meta-analysis. *Exceptional Children*, *55*, 303–308.

Fuchs, D., Fuchs, L. S., & Compton, D. C. (2012). Smart RTI: A next-generation approach to multi-level prevention. *Exceptional Children*, *78*, 263–279.

Fuchs, D., Fuchs, L. S., & Power, M. H. (1987). Effects of examiner familiarity of LD and MR students' language performance. *Remedial and Special Education*, *8*(4), 47–52.

Fuchs, L. S. (1994). *Connecting performance assessment to instruction.* Council for Exceptional Children.

Fuchs, L. S. (2008). *Progress monitoring within a multi-level prevention system.* http://www.rtinetwork.org/essential/assessment/progress/mutlilevelprevention

Fuchs, L. S., & Fuchs, D. (2008). The role of assessment within the RTI framework. In D. Fuchs, L. S. Fuchs, & S. Vaughn (Eds.), *Response to intervention: A framework for reading educators* (pp. 27–50). International Reading Association.

Fuchs, L. S., Fuchs, D., & Capizzi, A. M. (2006). Identifying appropriate test accommodations for students with learning disabilities. *Focus on Exceptional Children*, *37*, 1–8.

Fuchs, L. S., Fuchs, D., Eaton, S. B., Hamlett, C. L., & Karns, K. M. (2000). Supplementing teacher judgments of mathematics test accommodations with objective data sources. *School Psychology Review*, *29*, 65–85.

Fuchs, L. S., Fuchs, D., Hamlett, C. L., Phillips, N. B., & Bentz, J. (1994). Classwide curriculum-based measurement: Helping general educators meet the challenge of student diversity. *Exceptional Children*, *60*, 518–537.

Gajria, M., Salend, S. J., & Hemrick, M. A. (1994). Teacher acceptability of testing modifications for mainstreamed students. *Learning Disabilities Research & Practice*, *9*, 236–243.

Gandhi, A. G., Ogut, B., Stein, L., Bzura, R., & Danielson, L. (2017). Enhancing accessibility for students with decoding difficulties on large-scale reading assessments. *Journal of Learning Disabilities*, *51*(6), 540–551.

Ganske, K. (2014). *Word journeys: Assessment-guided phonics, spelling, and vocabulary instruction* (2nd ed.). Pearson.

Gelbart, W. R. (2018). Students with learning disabilities and computer-based high-stakes testing. *Intervention in School and Clinic*, *53*(5), 308–312.

Gollnick, D. M., & Chinn, P. C. (2021). *Multicultural education in a pluralistic society* (11th ed.). Pearson.

Graham-Day, J. K., Fishley, K. M., Konrad, M., Peters, M. T., & Ressa, V. A. (2014). Formative instructional practices: How core content teachers can burnout ideas from IDEA. *Intervention in School and Clinic*, *50*(2), 69–75.

Gregg, N., & Nelson, J. M. (2012). Meta-analysis on the effectiveness of extra time as a test accommodation for transitioning adolescents with learning disabilities: More questions than answers. *Journal of Learning Disabilities*, *45*, 128–138.

Hammill, D. D., & Larsen S. C. (2009). *Test of Written Language—4 (TOWL-4)*. Pro-Ed.

Harry, B., & Klingner, J. K. (2014). *Why are so many minority students in special education?: Understanding race and disability in schools* (2nd ed.). Teachers College Press.

Haynes, P. (2011). *The effect of test-wiseness on self-efficacy and mathematic performance of middle school students with learning disabilities.* Unpublished doctoral dissertation, Virginia Commonwealth University, Richmond.

Hoover, J. J., & Klingner, J. (2011). Promoting cultural validity in the assessment of bilingual special education students. In M. Basterra, E. Trumbull, & G. Solano-Flores (Eds.), *Cultural validity in assessment* (pp. 143–167). Routledge.

Hosp, M. K., Hosp, J. L., & Howell, K. W. (2016). *The ABCs of CBM: A practical guide to curriculum-based measurement* (2nd ed.). Guilford Press.

Hughes, C. (1996). Memory and test-taking strategies. In D. D. Deshler, E. S. Ellis, & B. K. Lenz (Eds.), *Teaching adolescents with learning disabilities: Strategies and methods* (2nd ed., pp. 209–266). Love Publishing.

Hughes, C. A., Rule, K. L., Deshler, D., & Schumaker, J. B. (1993). Test-taking strategy instruction for adolescents with emotional and behavioral disorders. *Journal of Emotional and Behavioral Disorders*, *1*, 189–198.

Hughes, C. A., Schumaker, J. B., Deshler, D. D., & Mercer, C. D. (1988). *The test-taking strategy.* Edge Enterprises.

Jamgochian, E. M., & Ketterlin-Geller, L. R. (2015). The 2% transition: Supporting access to state assessments for students with disabilities. *Teaching Exceptional Children*, *48*(1), 28–35.

Jayanthi, M., Epstein, M. H., Polloway, E. A., & Bursuck, W. D. (1996). A national survey of general education teachers' perceptions of testing adaptations. *Journal of Special Education*, *30*, 99–115.

Johnson, E., Kimball, L., Brown, S. O., & Anderson, D. (2001). A statewide review of the use of accommodations in large-scale, high-scale, high-stakes assessments. *Exceptional Children*, *67*, 251–264.

Johnson, R. L., Penny, J. A., & Gordon, B. (2009). *Assessing performance: Designing, scoring and validating performance tasks.* Guilford Press.

Jung, L. A., & Guskey, T. R. (2010). Grading exceptional learners. *Educational Leadership*, *67*(5), 31–35.

Jones, F. G., Gifford, D., Yovanoff, P., Al Otaiba, S., Levy, D., & Allor, J. (2018). Alternate assessment formats for progress monitoring students with intellectual disabilities and below average IQ: An exploratory study. *Focus on Autism and Other Developmental Disabilities*, *34*(1), 41–51.

Kaufman, A. S., & Kaufman, N. L. (2014). *Kauffman Test of Educational Achievement—Third Edition* (KTEA-3). Pearson.

Kaufman, A., & Kaufman, N. (2018). *Kauffman Assessment Battery for Children—Second Edition Normative Update* (KABC-II NU). Pearson.

Kearns, J., Burdge, M. D., & Clayton, J. (2006). How students demonstrate academic performance in portfolio assessment. In D. M. Browder & F. Spooner (Eds.), *Teaching language arts, math, and science to students with significant cognitive disabilities* (pp. 277–293). Brookes.

Kesselman-Turkel, J., & Peterson, F. (2004). *Test-taking strategies.* University of Wisconsin Press.

Kettler, R. J. (2015). Adaptations and access to assessment of Common Core content. *Review of Research in Education*, *39*(1), 295–330.

Kurth, J., Gross, M., Lovinger, S., & Catalano, T. (2012). Grading students with significant disabilities in inclusive settings: Teacher perspectives. *Journal of International Association of Special Education*, *12*(1), 41–57.

Lai, S. A., Berkeley, S. (2012). High-stakes test accommodations: Research and practice. *Learning Disability Quarterly*, *35*(3), 158–169.

Laitusis, C., Buzick, H., Stone, E., Hansen, E., & Hakkinen, M. (2012). *Smarter Balanced Assessment Consortium: Literature review of testing accommodations and accessibility tools for students with disabilities.* Educational Testing Service.

Lazarus, S. S., Thurlow, M. L., Lail, K. E., & Christensen, L. (2009). A longitudinal analysis of state accommodation policies: Twelve years of change. *Journal of Special Education*, *43*, 67–80.

Lewandowski, L. J., Lovett, B. J., Parolin, R., Gordon, M., & Codding, R. S. (2007). Extended time accommodations and the mathematics performance of students with and without ADHD. *Journal of Psychoeducational Assessment*, *25*, 17–28.

Lindstrom, J. H. (2017). High stakes testing and accommodations. In J. M. Kauffman, D. P. Hallahan, & P. C. Pullen, (Eds.), *Handbook of special education* (2nd ed., pp. 447–460). Taylor & Francis.

Lovett, B. J. (2010). Extended time testing accommodations for students with disabilities: Answers to five fundamental questions. *Review of Educational Research*, *80*, 611–638.

Lucangeli, D., & Scruggs, T. E. (2003). Test anxiety, perceived competence, and academic achievement in secondary school students. In T. E. Scruggs & M. A. Mastropieri (Eds.), *Identification and assessment: Advances in learning and behavioral disabilities* (pp. 223–230). Elsevier Science.

Mastropieri, M. A., & Scruggs, T. E. (2002). *Effective instruction for special education* (3rd ed.). Pro-Ed.

McLeskey, J., Barringer, M-D., Billinglsey, B., Brownell, M., Jackson, D., Kennedy, M., . . . Ziegler, D. (2017, January). *High-leverage practices in special education.* Council for Exceptional Children & CEEDAR Center.

McMaster, K. L., Bresina, B. C., Fuchs, L. S., & Fuchs, D. (2022). Using data in research and practice: Intensifying and strengthening the effectiveness of academic instruction. In T. W. Farmer, E. Talbott, K. L. McMaster, D. L. Lee, & T. C. Aceves (Eds.), *Handbook of special education research* (Vol. 1, pp. 37–50). Routledge.

Meyer, N. K., & Bouck, E. C. (2017). Read-aloud accommodations, expository text, and adolescents with learning disabilities. *Learning Disabilities: A Multidisciplinary Journal*, *22*(1), 34–47.

Meyer, A., Rose, D. H., & Gordon, D. (2014). *Universal design for learning: Theory and practice.* CAST.

Munoz, M. A., & Guskey, T. R. (2015). Standards-based grading and reporting will improve education. *Phi Delta Kappan*, *96*(7), 64–68.

Munk, D., & Bursuck, W. D. (1998). Report card adaptations for students with disabilities: Types and acceptability. *Intervention in School and Clinic*, *33*, 306–308.

Munk, D., & Bursuck, W. D. (2001). Preliminary findings on personalized grading plans for middle school students with learning disabilities. *Exceptional Children*, *67*, 211–234.

Munk, D., & Bursuck, W. D. (2003). Grading students with disabilities. *Educational Leadership*, *61*(2), 38–43.

Polloway, E. A., Epstein, M. H., Bursuck, W. D., Roderique, T. W., McConeky, J. L., & Jayanthi, M. (1994). Classroom grading: A national survey of policies. *Remedial and Special Education*, *15*, 162–170.

Quenemoen, R. F., & Thurlow, M. (2017). Standards-based reform and students with disabilities. In J. M. Kauffman, D. P. Hallahan, & P. C. Pullen (Eds.), *Handbook of special education* (2nd ed., pp. 203–217). Taylor & Francis.

Rao, K., Torres, C., & Smith, S. J. (2021). Digital tools and UDL-based instructional strategies to support students with disabilities online. *Journal of Special Education Technology*, *36*(2), 105–112.

Regan, K., Evmenova, A. S., Hutchison, A., Day, J., Stephens, M., Verbiest, C., & Gafurov, B. (2021). Steps for success: Making instructional decisions for students' essay writing. *Teaching Exceptional Children*, *54*(3), 202–212.

Ritter, S., & Idol-Maestas, L. (1986). Teaching middle school students to use a test-taking strategy. *Journal of Educational Research*, *79*, 350–357.

Rogers, C. M., Thurlow, M. L., Lazarus, S. S., & Liu, K. K. (2019). A summary of the research on effects of test accommodations: 2015–2016 (NCEO Report 412). University of Minnesota, National Center on Educational Outcomes.

Roid, G. H. (2003). *Stanford-Binet Intelligence Scale* (5th ed.). Rolling Meadows, IL: Riverside Publishing.

Salend, S. J. (1995). Modifying tests for diverse learners. *Intervention in School and Clinic*, *31*, 84–90.

Salend, S. J. (2008). Determining appropriate testing accommodations: Complying with NCLB and IDEA. *Teaching Exceptional Children*, *40*(4), 14–22.

Salend, S. J. (2009). *Classroom testing and assessment for all students: Beyond standardization*. Sage.

Salend, S. J. (2011). Creating student-friendly tests. *Educational Leadership*, *69*(3), 52–58.

Salend, S. J. (2016). *Creating inclusive classrooms: Effective, differentiated, and reflective practices* (8th ed.). Pearson.

Salvia, J., Ysseldyke, J., & Witmer, S. (2016). *Assessment in special and inclusive education* (13th ed.). Cengage Learning.

Schirmer, B. R., & Bailey, J. (2000). Writing assessment rubric: An instructional approach with struggling writers. *Teaching Exceptional Children*, *33*, 52–58.

Scruggs, T. E., & Mastropieri, M. A. (1988). Are learning disabled students "test-wise"?: A review of recent research. *Learning Disabilities Focus*, *3*, 87–97.

Scruggs, T. E., & Mastropieri, M. A. (1992). *Teaching test-taking skills: Helping students show what they know.* Brookline Books.

Scruggs, T. E., Mastropieri, M. A., Bakken, J. P., & Brigham, F. J. (1993). Reading vs. doing: The relative effectiveness of textbook-based and inquiry-oriented approaches to science education. *Journal of Special Education*, *27*, 1–15.

Segool, N. K., Carlson, J. S., Goforth, A. N., von der Embse, N., & Barterian, B. (2013). Heightened test anxiety among. Young children: Elementary school students' anxious responses to high stakes testing. *Psychology in the Schools*, *50*, 489–499.

Shapiro, E. S. (2010). *Academic skills problems* (4th ed.). Guilford Press.

Songlee, D. H. (2007). *Effects of test-taking strategy instruction on high-functioning adolescents with autism spectrum disorder.* Unpublished doctoral dissertation, University of Nevada, Las Vegas.

State of Georgia, Department of Education. (2021, June). *2021–2022 Accessibility and accommodations manual.* https://www.gadoe.org/Curriculum-Instruction-and-Assessment/Assessment/Documents/For%20Educators/2021-2022%20_Accessibility_and_Accommodations_Manual.pdf

State of Massachusetts, Department of Elementary and Secondary Education. (2021). *Accessibility and accommodations manual for the 2021–2022 MCAS tests/retests.* https://www.doe.mass.edu/mcas/accessibility/default.html

State of New York, Department of Education. (2019). *Testing accommodations for students with disabilities: Policy and tools to guide decision-making and implementation.* http://www.nysed.gov/state-assessment/accommodations-testing

Stembridge, A. (2020). *Culturally responsive education in the classroom: an equity framework for pedagogy.* Routledge.

Stufft, D. L., Bauman, D., & Ohlsen, M. (2009). Preferences and attitudes toward accommodations of traditional assessment in secondary social studies classrooms. *Social Studies Research and Practice*, *4*, 87–98.

Szarko, J. E., Brown, A. J., & Watkins, M. W. (2013). Examiner familiarity effects for children with autism spectrum disorders. *Journal of Applied School Psychology*, *29*, 37–51.

Thompson, S. J., Johnstone, C. J., & Thurlow, M. L. (2002). *Universal design applied to large scale assessments* (Synthesis Report 44). University of Minnesota, National Center on Educational Outcomes. http://education.umn.edu/NCEO/OnlinePubs/Synthesis44.html

Tortorelli, L. S., & Bruner, L. (2022). The Word Nerds project: Findings from a research-practice partnership focused on spelling instruction. *Journal of Research in Reading*. {Epub ahead of print}

Training and Technical Assistance Center at the George Mason University (2021). *Virginia Alternative Assessment Program (VAAT).* Retrieved from ttaconline.org/vaap

U.S. Department of Education. (2012). *More local freedom: Flexibility and waivers.* http://www2.ed.gov/nclb/freedom/local/flexibility/index.html

Vavrus, L. (1990). Put portfolios to the test. *Instructor*, *100*(1), 48–53.

von der Embse, N., Barterian, J., & Segool, N. (2013). Test anxiety interventions for children and adolescents: A systematic review of treatment studies from 2000–2010. *Psychology in the Schools, 50*(1), 57–71.

von der Embse, N., Jester, D., Roy, D., & Post, J. (2018). Test anxiety effects, predictors, and correlates. A 30-year meta-analytic review. *Journal of Affective Disorders, 227*, 483–493.

Wakeman, S., Thurlow, M., Reyes, E., & Kearns, J. (2021). Fair and equitable grading for all students in inclusive settings. *Inclusive Practices.* [Epub ahead of print]

Wechsler, D. (2014). *Wechsler Intelligence Scale for Children*, (5th ed.). Pearson.

Wesson, C. L., & King, R. P. (1996). Portfolio assessment and special education students. *Teaching Exceptional Children, 28*(2), 44–48.

William & Mary Training & Technical Assistance Center. (2015). *Inclusive grading and progress-monitoring practices.* https://education.wm.edu/centers/ttac/documents/packets/inclusivegrading.pdf

Wilkenson, G. S., & Robertson, G. J. (2017). *Wide Range Achievement Test–5* (WRAT5) (5th ed.). Pearson.

Woodcock, R. W. (2011). *Woodcock Reading Mastery Tests—3rd ed.* (WRMT-III). Pearson.

Woodcock, R. W., Johnson, M. B., & Mather, N. (2015) *Woodcock-Johnson IV, Tests of Achievement*. Riverside Insights.

Woods-Groves, S., Hughes, C. A., Therrien, W. J., Hua, Y., Hendrickson, J. M., & Shaw, J. W. (2012). Effectiveness of an essay writing strategy for post-secondary students with developmental disabilities. *Education and Training in Autism and Developmental Disabilities, 47*(2), 210–222.

Wren, D. G., & Benson, J. (2004). Measuring test anxiety in children: Scale development and internal construct validation. *Anxiety, Stress, and Coping, 17*, 227–240.

Chapter 13

Adams, M. J. (1990). *Beginning to read.* MIT Press.

Al Otaiba, S., Folsom, J. S., Wanzek, J., Greulich, L., Waesche, J., Schatschneider, C., & Connor, C. M. (2016). Professional development to differentiate kindergarten Tier 1 instruction: Can already effective teachers improve student outcomes by differentiating tier 1 instruction? *Reading and Writing Quarterly, 32*(5), 454–476.

Allor, J. H., Chard, D. J. (2011). Comprehensive approach to improving reading fluency for students with disabilities. *Focus on Exceptional Children, 43*(5), 1–12.

Alves, K. D., Kennedy, M. J., Brown, T. S., & Solis, M. (2014). Story grammar instruction with third and fifth grade students with learning disabilities and other struggling readers. *Learning Disabilities: A Contemporary Journal*, 13, 73–93.

Anderson, R. C., Hiebert, E. H., Scott, J. A., & Wilkinson, I. A. G. (1985). *Becoming a nation of readers: The report of the commission on reading.* National Academy of Education, Commission on Education and Public Policy.

Archer, A. L., Gleason, M. M., & Vachon, V. (2005). REWARDS intermediate: Multisyllabic word reading strategies. Sopris West.

Bakken, J. P., & Whedon, C. K. (2002). Teaching text structure to improve reading comprehension. *Intervention in School and Clinic, 37*, 229–233.

Behavioral Research and Teaching. (2005). *Oral reading fluency: 90 years of measurement.* http://brt.uoregon.edu

Berkeley, S., Mastropieri, M. A., & Scruggs, T. E. (2011). Reading comprehension strategy instruction and attribution retraining for secondary students with learning and other mild disabilities. *Journal of Learning Disabilities, 44*, 18–32.

Berkeley, S., Scruggs, T. E., & Mastropieri, M. A. (2010). Reading comprehension instruction for students with learning disabilities, 1995–2006: A meta-analysis. *Remedial and Special Education, 31*, 423–436.

Berninger, V., & Amtmann, D. (2003). Preventing written expression disabilities through early and continuing assessment and intervention for handwriting and/or spelling problems: Research into practice. In H. L. Swanson, K. Harris, & S. Graham (Eds.), *Handbook of learning disabilities* (pp. 345–363). Guilford Press.

Best, S. J., Heller, K. W., & Bigge, J. L. (2010). *Teaching individuals with physical or multiple disabilities* (6th ed.). Prentice Hall.

Blachman, B. A., Schatschneider, C., Fletcher, J. M., Murray, M. S., Munger, K. A., & Vaughn, M. G. (2014). Intensive reading remediation in grade 2 or 3: Are there effects a decade later? *Journal of Educational Psychology, 106*, 46–57.

Boardman, A., Vaughn, S., Buckley, P., Reutebuch, C., Roberts, G., & Klingner, J. (2016). Collaborative strategic reading for students with learning disabilities in upper elementary classrooms. *Exceptional Children,* 82, 409–427.

Bowman-Perrott, L., Burke, M. D., Zhang, D., & Zaini, S. (2014). Direct and collateral effects of peer tutoring on social and behavioral outcomes: A meta-analysis of single-case research. *School Psychology Review, 43*, 260–285.

Bowman-Perrott, L., Davis, H., Vannest, K., Williams, L., Greenwood, C., & Parker, R. (2013). Academic benefits of peer tutoring: A meta-analytic review of single-case research. *School Psychology Review, 42*, 39–55.

Boykin, A., Evmenova, A., Regan, K., & Mastropieri, M. A. (2019). The impact of a computer-based graphic organizer with embedded self-regulated learning strategies on the argumentative writing of students in inclusive cross-curricula settings. *Computers & Education, 137,* 78–90

Browder, D. M. (2015). What should we teach students with moderate and severe developmental disabilities? In B. Bateman, J. Lloyd, & M. Tankersley (Eds.), *Enduring issues in special education: Personal perspectives* (pp. 52–72). Routledge.

Browder, D. M., Root, J. R., Wood, L., & Allison, C. (2017). Effects of a story-mapping procedure using the iPad on the comprehension of narrative texts by students with autism spectrum disorder. *Focus on Autism and Other Developmental Disabilities, 32*(4), 243–255.

Browder, D. M., Wakeman, S. Y., Spooner, F., Ahlgrim-Delzell, L., & Algozzine, B. (2006). Research on reading instruction for individuals with significant cognitive disabilities. *Exceptional Children, 72*, 392–408.

Burks, M. (2004). Effects of classwide peer tutoring on the number of words spelled correctly by students with LD. *Intervention in School and Clinic, 39*, 301–304.

Bursuck, W. D., & Damer, M. (2015). *Teaching reading to students who are at risk or have disabilities: A multi-tier, RTI approach* (3rd ed.). Pearson.

Carnine, D., Silbert, J., Kameénui, E. J., Slocum, T. A., & Travers, P. A. (2017). *Direct instruction reading* (6th ed.). Pearson.

Catts, H. W., & Petscher, Y. (2022). A cumulative risk and resilience model of dyslexia. *Journal of Learning Disabilities, 55*(3), 171–184.

Chard, D. J., Vaughn, S., & Tyler, B. (2002). A synthesis of research on effective interventions for building reading fluency with elementary students with learning disabilities. *Journal of Learning Disabilities, 35*, 386–406.

Ciullo, S. P., & Reutebuch, C. (2013). Computer-based graphic organizers for students with LD: A systematic review of literature. *Learning Disabilities Research & Practice, 28*, 196–210.

Clemens, N. H., Widales-Benitez, O., Kestian, J., Peltier, C., D'Abreu, A., Myint, A., & Marbach, J. (2018). Progress monitoring in the elementary grades. In P. C. Pullen & M. J. Kennedy (Eds.), *Handbook of response to intervention and multi-tiered systems of support* (2nd ed., pp. 175–197). Routledge.

Coleman, M. B., & Heller, K. W. (2009). Assistive technology considerations. In K. W. Heller, P. E. Forner, P. A. Alberto, S. J. Best, & M. N. Schwartzman (Eds.), *Understanding physical, health, and multiple disabilities* (2nd ed., pp. 139–155). Prentice Hall.

Coyne, M. D., Simmons, D. C., Kameénui, E. J., & Stoolmiller, M. (2004). Teaching vocabulary during shared storybook readings: An examination of differential effects. *Exceptionality*, *12*, 145–162.

Cuenca-Carlino, Y., Gozur, M., Jozwik, S., & Krissinger, E. (2018). The impact of self-regulated strategy development on the writing performance of English learners. *Reading & Writing Quarterly*, *34*(3), 248–262.

Daniel, J., & Williams, K. (2021). Self-questioning strategy for struggling readers: A synthesis. *Remedial and Special Education*, *42*(4), 248–261.

Datchuk, S. (2015). Teaching handwriting to elementary students with learning disabilities. *Teaching Exceptional Children*, *48*(1), 19–27.

Datchuk, S., & Kubina, R. M. (2013). A review of teaching sentence-level writing skills to students with writing difficulties and learning disabilities. *Remedial and Special Education*, *34*, 180–192.

De La Paz, S. (2007). Best practices in teaching writing to students with special needs. In S. Graham, C. MacArthur, & J. Fitzgerald (Eds.), *Best practices in writing instruction* (pp. 163–178). Guilford Press.

Deshler, D. D., & Schumaker, J. (2006). *Teaching adolescents with disabilities: Accessing the general education curriculum.* Corwin Press.

Division for Learning Disabilities. (2007). *Thinking about response to intervention and learning disabilities: A teacher's guide.* Author.

Dowling, D. (1995). *303 dumb spelling mistakes and what you can do about them.* National Textbook Company.

Echevarria, J. J., & Graves, A. (2015). *Sheltered content instruction: Teaching English learners with diverse abilities* (5th ed.). Pearson.

Ehri, L. C., Nunes, S. R., Willows, D. M., Schuster, B. V., Yaghoub-Zadeh, Z., & Shanahan, T. (2001). Phonemic awareness instruction helps children learn to read: Evidence from the National Reading Panel's meta-analysis. *Reading Research Quarterly*, *36*, 250–287.

Ellis, E. (1996). Reading strategy instruction. In D. Deshler, E. S. Ellis, & B. Lenz (Eds.), *Teaching adolescents with learning disabilities: Strategies and methods* (2nd ed., pp. 61–125). Love.

Engelmann, S. E., Osborne, S., & Hanner, S. (2008). *Reading mastery signatures grade 4 and 5.* Science Research Associates.

Englert, C. S., & Mariage, T. V. (1996). A sociocultural perspective: Teaching ways-of-thinking and ways-of-talking in a literacy community. *Learning Disabilities Research & Practice*, *11*, 157–167.

Ennis, R. P., Jolivette, K., & Boden, L. J. (2013). STOP and DARE: Self-regulated strategy development for persuasive writing with E/BD in a residential facility. *Education and Treatment of Children*, *36*(3), 81–99.

Espin, C., Chung, S., Foegen, A., & Campbell, H. (2018). Curriculum-based measurement for secondary-school students. In P. C. Pullen & M. J. Kennedy (Eds.), *Handbook of response to intervention and multi-tiered system of support* (2nd ed., pp. 291–315). Routledge.

Evmenova, A. S., & Regan, K. (2012). *Project WeGotIT!: Writing efficiently with graphic organizers: Teachers integrating technology.* Technology and Media Services for Individuals with Disabilities Stepping-Up Technology Implementation Grant, Office of Special Education.

Evmenova, A. S., & Regan, K. (2019). Supporting the writing process with technology for students with disabilities. *Intervention in School and Clinic*, *55*(2), 78–85.

Evmenova, A. S., Regan, K., Boykin, A., Good, K., Hughes, M., MacVittie, N., . . . Chirinos, D. (2016). Emphasizing planning for essay writing with a computer-based graphic organizer. *Exceptional Children*, *82*, 170–191.

Evmenova, A. S., Regan, K., & Hutchison, A. (2018). *Project WEGO-RIITE!: Writing efficiently with graphic organizers: Responsive instruction while implementing technology effectively.* Technology and Media Services for Individuals with Disabilities Stepping-Up Technology Implementation Grant, Office of Special Education.

Evmenova, A. S., Regan, K., & Hutchison, A. (2020). AT for writing: Technology-based graphic organizer with embedded supports. *Teaching Exceptional Children*, *52*(4), 266–269.

Fletcher, D., & Abood, D. (1988). An analysis of the readability of product warning labels: Implications for curriculum development for persons with moderate and severe mental retardation. *Education and Training in Mental Retardation*, *23*, 224–227.

Foorman, B. R. (2007). Primary prevention in classroom reading instruction. *Teaching Exceptional Children*, *39*(5), 24–30.

Fossett, B., Smith, V., & Mirenda, P. (2003). Facilitating oral language and literacy development during general education activities. In D. L. Ryndak & S. Alper (Eds.), *Curriculum and instruction for students with significant disabilities in inclusive settings* (2nd ed., pp. 173–205). Allyn & Bacon.

Foxworth, L. L., Mason, L. H., & Hughes, C. A. (2017). Improving narrative writing skills of secondary students with disabilities using strategy instruction. *Exceptionality*, *25*(4), 217–234.

Fountas, I. C., & Pinnell, G. S. (2013). *The Fountas & Pinnell leveled book list, K–8+* (2013–2015 ed.). Heinemann.

Fuchs, D., Fuchs, L. S., & Compton, D. C. (2012). Smart RTI: A next-generation approach to multi-level prevention. *Exceptional Children*, *78*, 263–279.

Fuchs, D., Fuchs, L. S., & Vaughn, S. (2014). What is intensive instruction and why is it important. *Teaching Exceptional Children*, *46*(4), 13–18.

Gerber, M., & Richards-Tutor, M. M. (2011). Teaching spelling to students with learning disabilities. In R. O'Connor & P. Vadasy (Eds.), *Handbook of reading interventions* (pp. 113–137). Guilford Press.

Fuchs, L. S., & Fuchs, D. (2007). The role of assessment in the three-tier approach to reading instruction. In D. Haager, J. Klingner, & S. Vaughn (Eds.), *Evidence-based reading practices for response to intervention* (pp. 29–42). Brookes.

Gersten, R., & Dimino, J. (1993). Visions and revisions: A special education perspective on the whole language controversy. *Remedial and Special Education*, *14*(4), 5–13.

Gillespie, A., & Graham, S. (2014). A meta-analysis of writing interventions for students with learning disabilities. *Exceptional Children*, *80*, 454–473.

Goodman, K. (2014). *What's whole in whole language in the 21st century?* Garn Press.

Graham, S. (1999). Handwriting and spelling instruction for students with learning disabilities: A review. *Learning Disability Quarterly*, *22*, 78–98.

Graham, S. (2010). Want to improve children's writing?: Don't neglect their handwriting. *American Educator*, *33*(4), 20–40.

Graham, S., Bollinger, A., Booth Olson, C., D'Aoust, C., MacArthur, C., McCutchen, D., & Olinghouse, N. (2012). *Teaching elementary school students to be effective writers: A practice guide* (NCEE 2012-4058). National Center for Education Evaluation and Regional Assistance, Institute of Education Sciences, U.S. Department of Education. http://ies.ed.gov/ncee/wwc/publications_reviews.aspx#pubsearch

Graham, S., & Harris, K. (2007). Best practices in teaching planning. In S. Graham, C. MacArthur, & J. Fitzgerald (Eds.), *Best practices in writing instruction* (pp. 119–140). Guilford.

Graham, S., & Harris, K.R. (2005). *Writing better: Effective strategies for learning difficulties.* Brookes.

Graham, S., & Harris, K. (2011). Writing and students with disabilities. In J. M. Kauffman & D. P. Hallahan (Eds.), *Handbook of special education* (pp. 422–433). Routledge.

Graham, S., Harris, K. R., & Chorzempa, B. F. (2002). Contribution of spelling instruction to the spelling, writing, and reading of poor spellers. *Journal of Educational Psychology, 94*, 669–686.

Graham, S., Harris, K. R., & Fink, B. (2000). Is handwriting causally related to learning to write?: Treatment of handwriting problems in beginning writers. *Journal of Educational Psychology, 92*, 620–633.

Graham, S., Harris, K. R., & Loynachan, C. (1994). The spelling for writing list. *Journal of Learning Disabilities, 27*, 210–214.

Graham, S., Harris, K. R., & Loynachan, C. (1996). The directed spelling thinking activity: Application with high-frequency words. *Learning Disabilities Research & Practice, 11*, 34–40.

Graham, S., Harris, K. K., & Santangelo, T. (2015). Research-based writing practices and the common core: Meta-analysis and meta-synthesis. *Elementary School Journal, 115*(4), 498–522.

Graham, S., & Hebert, M. (2011). Writing to read: A meta-analysis of the impact of writing and writing instruction on reading. *Harvard Educational Review, 81*, 710–744.

Graham, S., & Perin, D. (2007). A meta-analysis of writing instruction for adolescent students. *Journal of Educational Psychology, 99*, 445–476.

Graham, S., & Santangelo, T. (2014). Does spelling instruction make students better spellers, readers, and writers?: A meta-analytic review. *Reading & Writing: An Interdisciplinary Journal, 27*, 1703–1743.

Graham, S., & Weintraub, N. (1996). A review of handwriting research: Progress and prospects from 1980 to 1994. *Educational Psychology Review, 8*, 7–87.

Graves, D. H. (2003). *Writing: Teachers and children at work.* Heinemann.

Gregg, N. C., Coleman, C., Davis, M., & Chalk, J. C. (2007). Timed essay writing: Implications for high-stakes tests. *Journal of Learning Disabilities, 40*, 306–318.

Hall, T. E., Meyer, A., & Rose, D. H. (Eds.). (2012). *Universal design for learning in the classroom: Practical applications.* Guilford Press.

Harris, K. K., & Graham, S. (1992). *Helping young writers master the craft: Strategy instruction and self-regulation in the writing process.* Brookline Books.

Harris, K. K., Graham, S., Aitken, A. A., Barkel, A., Houston, J., & Ray, A. (2017). Teaching spelling, writing, and reading for writing: Powerful evidence-based practices. *Teaching Exceptional Children, 49*(4), 262–272.

Harris, K. K., Graham, S., Mason, L. H., & Friedlander, B. (2008). *Powerful writing strategies for all students.* Brookes.

Hasbrouck, J., & Tindal, G. (2017). *An update to compiled ORF norms* (Technical Report No. 1702). Behavioral Research and Teaching, University of Oregon. https://www.brtprojects.org/wp-content/uploads/2017/10/TechRpt_1702ORFNorms_Fini.pdf

Hauth, C., Mastropieri, M. A., Scruggs, T. E., & Regan, K. (2013). Can students with emotional and behavioral disabilities improve on planning and writing in the content areas of civics and mathematics? *Behavioral Disorders, 38*, 154–170.

Hebert, M., Bohaty, J. J., Nelson, J. R., & Brown, J. (2016). The effects of text structure instruction on expository reading comprehension: A meta-analysis. *Journal of Educational Psychology, 108*(5), 609–629.

Heller, K. W. (2010). Writing instruction and adaptations. In S. J. Best, K. W. Heller, & J. L. Bigge (Eds.), *Teaching individuals with physical or multiple* disabilities (6th ed., pp. 407–431). Pearson.

Heller, K. W., & Alberto, P. A. (2010). Reading instruction and adaptations. In S. J. Best, K. W. Heller, & J. L. Bigge (Eds.), *Teaching individuals with physical or multiple* disabilities (6th ed., pp. 375–406). Pearson.

Hirshorn, E. A., Dye, M. W. G., Hauser, P., Supalla, T. R., & Bavelier, D. (2015). The contribution of phonological knowledge, memory, and language background to reading comprehension in deaf populations. *Frontiers in Psychology, 6*, 1153. http://www.ncbi.nlm.nih.gov/pmc/articles/PMC4548088/

Idol-Maestas, L. (1985). Getting ready to read: Guided probing for poor comprehenders. *Learning Disability Quarterly, 8*, 243–254.

Isaacson, S., & Gleason, M. M. (1997). Mechanical obstacles to writing: What can teachers do to help students with learning problems? *Learning Disabilities Research & Practice, 12*, 188–194.

Johnson, P. H. (1992). Understanding reading disability: A case study approach. In T. Heir & T. Latus (Eds.), *Special education at century's end: Evolution of theory and practice since 1970* (pp. 275–304). Harvard Education Press.

Joseph, L. M., Alber-Morgan, S., Cullen, J., & Rouse, C. (2016). The effects of self-questioning on reading comprehension: A literature review. *Reading and Writing Quarterly, 32*, 152–173.

Joseph, L. M., Konrad, M., Cates, G., Vajcner, T., Eveleigh, E., & Fishley, K. M. (2012). A meta-analytic review of the cover-copy-compare and variations of this self-management procedure. *Psychology in the Schools, 49*, 122–136.

Joseph, L. M., & Schisler, R. (2009). Should adolescents go back to the basics?: A review of teaching word reading skills to middle and high school students. *Remedial and Special Education, 30*, 131–147.

Kearns, D. M., Fuchs, D., Fuchs, L. S., McMaster, K. L., & Sáenz, L. (2015). Peer-assisted learning strategies to improve students' word recognition and reading comprehension. In K. R. Harris & L. Meltzer (Eds.), *The power of peers in the classroom* (pp. 143–187). Guilford Press.

Klingner, J. K., Vaughn, S., & Boardman, A. (2007). *Teaching reading comprehension to students with reading difficulties.* Guilford Press.

Klingner, J. K., Vaughn, S. Boardman, A., & Swanson, E. (2012). *"Now I get it": Boosting comprehension with collaborative strategic reading.* Jossey-Bass.

Kourea, L., Gibson, L., & Werunga, R. (2018). Culturally responsive reading instruction for students with learning disabilities. *Intervention in School and Clinic, 53*, 153–162.

Kubina, R., & Hughes, C. A. (2007). *Fluency instruction* (DLD-DR Current Practice Alerts, Alert 15). Council for Exceptional Children, Division for Learning Disabilities.

Larwin, K. H., Dawson, D., Erickson, M., & Larwin, D. (2012). Impact of guided notes on achievement in K–12 and special education students. *International Journal of Special Education, 27*, 108–119.

Lee, J., & Yoon, S. Y. (2017). The effects of repeated reading on reading fluency for students with reading disabilities: A meta-analysis. *Journal of Learning Disabilities, 50*(2), 213–224.

Lenz, B. K., & Hughes, C. A. (1990). A word identification strategy for adolescents with learning disabilities. *Journal of Learning Disabilities, 23*, 149–163.

Lerner, J., & Johns, B. (2015). *Learning disabilities and related mild disabilities: Strategies for success* (13th ed.). Cengage.

Life Span Institute. (2002). *Reading fluency tables.* University of Kansas.

Losinski, M., Cuenca-Carlino, Y., Zablocki, M., & Teagarden, J. (2014). Examining the efficacy of self-regulated strategy development for students with emotional and behavioral disorders: A meta-analysis. *Behavior Disorders, 40*(1), 52–67.

Maheady, L., & Gard, J. (2010). Classwide peer tutoring: Practice, theory, research, and personal narrative. *Intervention in School and Clinic, 46*, 71–78.

Marschark, M. (2010). *Raising and educating a deaf child: A comprehensive guide to the choices, controversies, and decisions faced by parents and educators* (3rd ed.). Oxford University Press.

Mastropieri, M. A., & Scruggs, T. E. (1991). *Teaching students ways to remember: Strategies for learning mnemonically.* Brookline Books.

Mastropieri, M. A., & Scruggs, T. E. (1997). Best practices in promoting reading comprehension in students with learning disabilities: 1976 to 1996. *Remedial and Special Education, 18*, 197–213.

Mastropieri, M. A., & Scruggs, T. E. (2014). Intensive instruction to improve writing for students with emotional and behavioral disorders. *Behavioral Disorders, 48*, 78–83.

Mastropieri, M. A., Scruggs, T. E., Cerar, N. I., Allen-Bronaugh, D., Thompson, C., Guckert, M., . . . Cuenca-Sanchez, Y. (2014). Fluent persuasive writing with counterarguments for students with emotional disturbance. *Journal of Special Education, 48*, 17–31.

Mastropieri, M. A., Scruggs, T. E., Cerar, N. I., Guckert, M., Thompson, C., Allen-Bronaugh, D., . . . Cuenca-Carlino, Y. (2015). Strategic persuasive writing instruction for students with emotional and behavioral disabilities. *Exceptionality, 23*, 147–169.

Mastropieri, M. A., Scruggs, T. E., Cuenca-Sanchez, Y., Irby, N., Mills, S., Mason, L., & Kubina, R. (2010). Persuading students with emotional disabilities to write: A design study. In T. E. Scruggs & M. A. Mastropieri (Eds.), *Literacy and learning: Advances in learning and behavioral disabilities* (Vol. 23, pp. 237–268). Emerald.

Mastropieri, M. A., Scruggs, T. E., & Graetz, J. (2003). Reading comprehension for secondary students. *Learning Disability Quarterly, 26*, 103–116.

Mastropieri, M. A., Scruggs, T. E., Mills, S., Irby, N., Cuenca-Sanchez, Y., Bronaugh, D. A., . . . Regan, K. (2009). Teaching students with emotional disabilities to write fluently. *Behavioral Disorders, 35*, 19–40.

Mastropieri, M. A., Scruggs, T. E., Mohler, L. J., Beranek, M. L., Spencer, V., Boon, R. T., & Talbott, E. (2001). Can middle school students with serious reading difficulties help each other and learn anything? *Learning Disabilities Research & Practice, 16*, 18–27.

McLaughlin, T. F., Weber, K. P., & Derby, K. M. (2013). Classroom spelling interventions for students with learning disabilities. In H. L. Swanson, K. R. Harris, & S. Graham (Eds.), *Handbook of research in learning disabilities* (2nd ed., pp. 439–447). Guilford Press.

McMaster, K. L., & Fuchs, D. (2016). Classwide intervention using peer-assisted learning strategies. In S. R. Jimerson, M. K. Burns, & A. M. VanDerHeyden (Eds.), *Handbook of response to intervention: The science and practice of multi-tiered systems of support* (pp. 253–268). Springer Science + Business Media.

Mercer, C. D., Mercer, A. R., & Pullen, P. C. (2011). *Teaching students with learning problems* (8th ed.). Pearson.

Meyer, A., Rose, D. M., & Gordon, D. (2014). *Universal design for learning: Theory and practice.* CAST.

Montague, M. (1998). Research on metacognition in special education. In T. E. Scruggs & M. A. Mastropieri (Eds.), *Advances in learning and behavioral disabilities* (Vol. 12, pp. 151–184). JAI Press.

Morphy, P., & Graham, S. (2012). Word processing programs and weaker writers/readers: A meta-analysis of research findings. *Reading and Writing, 25*, 641–678.

National Governors Association (NGA) Center for Best Practices & Council of Chief State School Officers (CCSSO). (2010). *Common Core State Standards: English/language arts.* Author.

National Institute for Direct Instruction. (2015). *Reading mastery signature edition.* http://www.nifdi.org/programs/reading/reading-mastery

National Reading Panel. (2000). *Report of the National Reading Panel. Teaching children to read: An evidence-based assessment of the scientific research literature on reading and its implications for reading instruction.* U.S. Department of Health and Human Services.

O'Connor, R. E., White, A., & Swanson, H. L. (2007). Repeated reading versus continuous reading: Influences on reading fluency and comprehension. *Exceptional Children, 74*, 31–46.

O'Shea, L. J., Sindelar, P. T., & O'Shea, D. (1987). The effects of repeated readings and attentional cues on the reading fluency and comprehension of learning disabled readers. *Learning Disabilities Research, 2*, 103–109.

Ogle, D. M. (1986). K-W-L: A teaching model that develops active reading of expository text. *The Reading Teacher, 39*, 564–570.

Orsosco, M. J., & O'Connor, R. E. (2014). Culturally responsive instruction for English language learners with learning disabilities. *Journal of Learning Disabilities, 47*, 515–531.

Palincsar, A. S., & Brown, A. L. (1984). Reciprocal teaching of comprehension fostering and comprehension monitoring activities. *Cognition and Instruction, 1*, 117–175.

Paratore, J. R., & Doughtery, S. (2011). Home differences and reading difficulty. In A. McGill-Franzen & R. L. Allington (Eds.), *Handbook of reading disability research* (pp. 93–109). Routledge.

Pennington, R., Flick, A., & Smith-Wehr, K. (2018). The use of response prompting and frames for teaching sentence writing to students with moderate intellectual disability. *Focus on Autism and Other Developmental Disabilities, 33*. 142–149.

Powell, S. R., & Fuchs, L. A. (2015). Intensive intervention in mathematics. *Learning Disabilities Research and Practice, 30*, 182–192.

Pressley, M. (2006). *Reading instruction that works: The case for balanced teaching* (3rd ed.). Guilford Press.

Pressley, M., & Allington, R. L. (2015). *Reading instruction that works: The case for balanced teaching* (4th ed.). Guilford Press.

Pressley, M., & Rankin, J. (1994). More about whole language methods of reading instruction for students at-risk for early reading failure. *Learning Disabilities Research & Practice, 9*, 156–168.

Pullen, P. C., & Cash, D. B. (2017). *Reading.* In J. M. Kauffman, D. P. Hallahan, & P. C. Pullen (Eds.), *Handbook of special education* (2nd ed., pp. 523–536). Taylor & Francis.

Pullen, P. C., & Lloyd, J. (2008). *Phonics instruction* (DLD-DR Current Practice Alerts, Alert 12). Council for Exceptional Children, Division for Learning Disabilities.

Reed, D. K., Wexler, J., & Vaughn, S. (2012). *RTI for reading at the secondary level: Recommended literacy practices and remaining questions.* Guilford Press.

Regan, K., & Berkeley, S. (2012). Effective reading and writing instruction: A focus on modeling. *Intervention in School and Clinic, 47*, 276–282.

Regan, K., Berkeley, S., Hughes, M., & Kirby, S. (2014). Effects of computer-assisted instruction for struggling elementary readers with disabilities. *Journal of Special Education, 48*, 106–119.

Regan, K., Evmenova, A., Boykin, A., Sacco, D., Good, K., Ahn, S. Y., . . . Hughes, M. D. (2017). Supporting struggling writers with class-wide teacher implementation of a computer-based graphic organizer. *Reading and Writing Quarterly: Overcoming Learning Difficulties, 33*(5), 428–448.

Regan, K., Evmenova, A. S., Good, K., Leggit, A., Gafurov, G., & Mastropieri, M. (2018). Persuasive writing with mobile-based graphic organizers in inclusive classrooms across the curriculum. *Journal of Special Education Technology, 33*(1), 3–14.

Regan, K., Evmenova, A., MacVittie, N. P., Leggett, A., Ives, S., Schwartzer, J., . . . Rybicki-Newman, M. (2019). A case of early adopters of technology in a social studies classroom. *Contemporary Issues in Technology and Teacher Education, 19*(3), 439–468.

Reid, R., Gonzalez, J. E., Nordness, P. D., Trout, A., & Epstein, M. H. (2004). A meta-analysis of the academic status of students with emotional/behavioral disturbance. *Journal of Special Education, 38*, 130–143.

Ridge, A. D., & Skinner, C. H. (2011). Using the TELLS prereading procedure to enhance comprehension levels and rates in secondary students. *Psychology in the Schools*, *48*, 46–58.

Roberts, C. A., Leko, M. M., & Wilkerson, K. L. (2013). New directions in reading instruction for adolescents with significant cognitive disabilities. *Remedial and Special Education*, *34*(5), 305–317.

Roberts, G., Vaughn, S., Fletcher, J., Stuebing, K., & Barth, A. (2015). Effects of a response-based, tiered framework for intervening with struggling readers in middle school. *Reading Research Quarterly*, *48*(3), 237–254

Rosenshine, B., & Meister, C. (1994). Reciprocal teaching: A review of the research. *Review of Educational Research*, *64*, 479–530.

Routman, R. (1991). *Invitations: Changing as teachers and learners K–12*. Heinemann.

Rudenga, E. A. V. (1992). *Incompatibility?: Ethnographic case studies of learning disabled students in a whole language classroom.* Unpublished doctoral dissertation, Purdue University, West Lafayette, IN.

Santangelo, T., & Graham, S. (2016). A comprehensive meta-analysis of handwriting instruction. *Educational Psychology Review*, *28*, 225–265.

Schirmer, B. R., & McGough, S. M. (2005). Teaching reading to children who are deaf: Do the conclusions of the National Reading Panel apply? *Review of Educational Research*, *75*, 83–117.

Shaywitz, S. (2003). *Overcoming dyslexia.* Knopf.

Shefter, H. (1989). *6 minutes a day to perfect spelling.* Pocket Books.

Shippen, M. E., Houchins, D. E., Steventon, C., & Sartor, D. (2005). A comparison of two direct instruction reading programs for urban middle school students. *Remedial and Special Education*, *26*, 175–182.

Snider, V. E. (1997). Transfer of decoding skills to a literature basal. *Learning Disabilities Research & Practice*, *12*, 54–62.

Solis, M., Miciak, J., Vaughn, S., & Fletcher, J. M. (2014). Why intensive intervention matter: Longitudinal studies of adolescents with reading disabilities and poor reading comprehension. *Learning Disability Quarterly*, *37*(4), 218–229.

Spear-Swerling, L. (2005). *Spelling and students with learning disabilities.* LD OnLine. http://www.ldonline.org/article/5587/

Spector, J. E., & Cavanaugh, B. J. (2015). The conditions of beginning reading instruction for students with autism spectrum disorder. *Remedial and Special Education*, *36*, 337–346.

Speece, D. L., MacDonald, V., Kilsheimer, L., & Krist, J. (1997). Research to practice: Preservice teachers reflect on reciprocal teaching. *Learning Disabilities Research & Practice*, *12*, 177–187.

Spencer, V. G., Scruggs, T. E., & Mastropieri, M. A. (2003). Content area learning in middle school social studies classrooms and students with emotional or behavioral disorders: A comparison of strategies. *Behavioral Disorders*, *28*, 77–93.

Squires, K. E., Wolter, J. A., Houchins, D. E., & Oaks, W. P. (2016). The effects of orthographic pattern intervention on spelling performance of students with reading disabilities: A best evidence synthesis. *Remedial and Special Education*, *37*(6), 357–369.

St. Martin, K., Vaughn, S., Troia, G., Fien, & H., Coyne, M. (2020). *Intensifying literacy instruction: Essential practices.* MiMTSS Technical Assistance Center, Michigan Department of Education.

Stahl, S. A. (1992). Saying the "p" word: Nine guidelines for exemplary phonics instruction. *The Reading Teacher*, *45*, 618–625.

Stahl, S. A., Duffy-Hester, A. M., & Dougherty-Stahl, K. A. (2006). Everything you wanted to know about phonics (and were afraid to ask). In L. M. Morrow, K. A. Dougherty-Stahl, & M. C. McKenna (Eds.), *Reading research at work: Foundations of effective practice* (pp. 126–156). Guilford Press.

Staubitz, J. E., Cartledge, G., & Yurick, A. L. (2005). Repeated reading for students with emotional or behavioral disorders: Peer- and trainer-mediated instruction. *Behavioral Disorders*, *31*, 51–64.

Stecker, P. M. (2007). Tertiary intervention: Using progress monitoring with intensive services. *Teaching Exceptional Children*, *39*(5), 50–57.

Stevens, E. A., Park, S., & Vaughn, S. (2018). A review of summarizing and main idea interventions for struggling readers in grades 3 through 12: 1978–2016. *Remedial and Special Education*, *40*, 131–140.

Stevens, E. A., Walker, M. A., & Vaughn, S. (2017). The effects of reading fluency interventions on the reading fluency and reading comprehension performance of elementary students with learning disabilities: A synthesis of the research from 2001 to 2014. *Journal of Learning Disabilities*, *50*, 576–590.

Stewart, D. A., & Kluwin, T. N. (2001). *Teaching deaf and hard of hearing students: Content, strategies, and curriculum.* Allyn & Bacon.

Strong, G. K., Torgerson, C. J., Torgerson, D., & Hulme, C. (2011). A systematic meta-analytic review of evidence for the effectiveness of the "Fast ForWord" language intervention program. *52*, 224–235.

Suggate, S. P. (2016). A meta-analysis of the long-term effects of phonemic awareness, phonics, fluency, and reading comprehension interventions. *Journal of Learning Disabilities*, *49*, 77–96.

Suid, M. (1981). *Demonic mnemonics.* Dell Publishing.

Temple, C., Ogle, D., Crawford, A., & Freppon, P. (2018). *All children read: Teaching for literacy in today's diverse classrooms* (5th ed.). Pearson.

Therrien, W. J. (2004). Fluency and comprehension gains as a result of repeated reading: A meta-analysis. *Remedial and Special Education*, *25*, 252–261.

Troia, G. A. (2004). Migrant students with limited English proficiency: Can Fast ForWord Language make a difference in their language skills and academic achievement? *Remedial and Special Education*, *25*, 353–366.

Vaughn, S., & Denton, D. (2008). Tier 2: The role of intervention. In D. Fuchs, L. S. Fuchs, & S. Vaughn (Eds.), *Response to intervention: A framework for reading educators* (pp. 51–70). International Reading Association.

Vaughn, S., Martinez, L. R., Williams, K. J., Miciak, J., Fall, A.-M., & Roberts, G. R. (2019). Efficacy of a high school extensive reading intervention for English learners with reading difficulties. *Journal of Educational Psychology*, *111*(3), 373–386.

Vaughn, S., & Roberts, G. (2007). Secondary interventions in reading: Providing additional instruction for students at risk. *Teaching Exceptional Children*, *39*(5), 40–46.

Vaughn, S., Roberts, G., Schnakenberg, J. B., Fall, A-M., Vaughn, M. G., & Wexler, J. (2015). Improving reading comprehension for high school students with disabilities: Effects for comprehension and school retention. *Exceptional Children*, *82*, 117–131.

Vaughn, S., & Wanzek, J. (2014). Intensive interventions in reading for students with reading disabilities: Meaningful impacts. *Learning Disabilities Research and Practice*, *29*, 46–53.

Vaughn, S., Wexler, J., Leroux, A., Roberts, G., Denton, C., Barth, A., & Fletcher, J. M. (2012). Effects of intensive reading intervention for eighth-grade students with persistently inadequate response to intervention. *Journal of Learning Disabilities*, *45*, 515–525.

Wanzek, J., Al Otaiba, S., & Petscher, Y. (2014). Oral reading fluency development for children with emotional disturbance or learning disabilities. *Exceptional Children*, *80*, 187–204.

Williams, K. A., Austin, C. R. , & Vaughn, S. (2018). A synthesis of spelling interventions for secondary students with disabilities. *Journal of Special Education*, *52*(1), 3–15.

Williams, K. A., Walker, M. A., Vaughn, S., & Wanzek, J. (2017). A synthesis of reading and spelling interventions and their effects on spelling outcomes for students with learning disabilities. *Journal of Learning Disabilities*, *50*(3), 286–297.

Wissick, C. A., & Gardner, J. E. (2011). Technology and academic instruction: Considerations for students with high incidence cognitive disabilities. In J. M. Kauffman & D. P. Hallahan (Eds.), *Handbook of special education* (pp. 484–500). Routledge.

Wooten, D. A., Liang, L. A., & Cullinan, B. E. (Eds.). (2018). *Children's literature in the reading program: Engaging young readers in the 21st century* (5th ed.) Guilford Press.

Wordplay. (2012). *Some useful mnemonics.* http://www.fun-with-words.com

Young, C., Mohr, K. A. J., & Rasinski, T. (2014). Reading Together: A successful reading fluency intervention. *Literacy Research and Instruction*, *54*, 67–81.

Zumbrunn, S., & Bruning, R. (2013). Improving the writing and knowledge of emergent writers: The effects of self-regulated strategy development. *Reading and Writing*, *26*, 91–110.

Chapter 14

Avant, M. J. T., & Heller, K. W. (2011). Examining the effectiveness of Touch Math with students with physical disabilities. *Remedial and Special Education*, *32*, 309–321.

Aydemir, T. (2015). A review of articles about Touch Math. *Procedia: Social and Behavioral Sciences*, *174*, 1812–1819.

Barnett, J. E. H., & Cleary, S. (2015). Review of evidence-based mathematics interventions for students with autism. *Education and Training in Autism and Developmental Disabilities*, *50*, 172–185.

Barth, J., Eglash, R., & Barkley, C. (2014). *Math is a verb: Activities and lessons from cultures around the world.* National Council for Teachers of Mathematics.

Benavides-Varela, S., Callegher, Z. C., Fagiolini, B., Leo, I., Altoe, G., & Lucangeli, D. (2020). Effectiveness of digital-based interventions for children with mathematical learning difficulties: A meta-analysis. *Computers & Education*, *157*, 1–15.

Berteletti, I., Lucangeli, D., Piazza, M., Dehaene, S., & Zorzi, M. (2010). Numerical estimation in preschoolers. *Developmental Psychology*, *46*, 545–551.

Bley, N. S. (2019). *Teaching mathematics to students with learning disabilities* (5th ed.). Pro-Ed.

Bouck, E. C., Park., J., & Nickell, B. (2017). Using the concrete-representational-abstract approach to support students with intellectual disability to solve change-making problems. *Research in Developmental Disabilities*, *60*, 24–36.

Bouck, E. C., Park, J., Satsangi, R., Cwiakala, K., & Levy, K. (2019). Using virtual-abstract instructional sequence to support acquisition of algebra. *Journal of Special Education Technology*, *34*(4), 253–268.

Bottge, B. A., Rueda, E., Grant, T. S., Stephens, A. C., & LaRoque, P. T. (2010). Anchoring problem-solving and computation instruction in context-rich learning environments. *Exceptional Children*, *4*, 417–437.

Bottge, B. A., Toland, M. D., Gassaway, L., Butler, M., Choo, S., Griffen, A. K., & Xin, M. (2015). Impact of enhanced anchored instruction in inclusive math classrooms. *Exceptional Children*, *81*, 158–175.

Browder, D. (2015). What should we teach students with moderate and severe developmental disabilities? In B. Bateman, J. Lloyd, & M. Tankersley (Eds.), *Enduring issues in special education: Personal perspectives* (pp. 52–73). Routledge.

Bryant, D. P., Bryant, B. R., Roberts, G., Vaughn, S., Pfannenstiel, K. H., Porterfield, J., & Gersten, R. (2011). Early numeracy intervention for first grade students with math difficulties. *Exceptional Children*, *78*, 7–23.

Butler, F. M., Miller, S. P., Lee, K., & Pierce, T. (2001). Teaching mathematics to students with mild-to-moderate mental retardation: A review of the literature. *Mental Retardation*, *39*, 20–31.

Case, L. P., Harris, K. R., & Graham, S. (1992). Improving the mathematical problem-solving skills of students with learning disabilities: Self-regulated strategy development. *Journal of Special Education*, *26*, 1–19.

Carpenter, T. P., Fennema, E., Frankie, M. L., Levi, L., Empson, S. B., & Lindquist, M. M. (2014). *Children's mathematics: Cognitively guided instruction* (2nd ed.). Heinemann.

Cathcart, W. G., Pothier, V. M., Vance, J. H., & Bezuk, N. S. (2015). *Learning mathematics in elementary and middle schools: A learner-centered approach* (6th ed.). Pearson.

Cox, S. K., & Jimenez, B. A. (2020). Mathematical interventions for students with autism spectrum disorder: Recommendations for practitioners. *Research in Developmental Disabilities*, *105*, 1–9.

Dennis, M. S. (2015). Effects of Tier 2 and Tier 3 mathematics interventions for 2nd graders with mathematics difficulties. *Learning Disabilities Research and Practice*, *30*, 29–42.

Ennis, R. P., & Losinski, M. L. (2020). SRSD fractions: Using self-regulated strategy development model strategies to support students' conceptual and procedural fraction knowledge. *Education and Treatment of Children*, *43*(1), 85–94.

Ennis, R.P., & Losinski, M. (2019). SRSD fractions: Helping students at risk for disabilities add/subtract fractions with unlike denominators. *Journal of Learning Disabilities*, *52*, 399–412.

Fuchs, D., Fuchs, L. S., & Compton, D. C. (2012). Smart RTI: A next-generation approach to multi-level prevention. *Exceptional Children*, *78*, 263–279.

Fuchs, L. S., Fuchs, D., & Hollenbeck, K. N. (2007). Extending responsiveness to intervention to mathematics at first and third grades. *Learning Disabilities Research & Practice*, *22*, 13–24.

Fuchs, L. S., Fuchs, D., Seethaler, P. M., & Craddock, C. (2020) Improving language comprehension to enhance word-problem solving. *Reading & Writing Quarterly*, *36*(2), 142–156.

Fuchs, L. S., Malone, A. S., Seethaler, P. M., Powell, S. R., & Fuchs, D. (2017). Intervention to improve arithmetic, word-problem, and fraction performance in students with mathematics disabilities. In J. M. Kauffman, D. P. Hallahan, & P. C. Pullen (Eds.), *Handbook of special education* (2nd ed., pp. 558–570). Routledge.

Fuchs, L.S., Newman-Gonchar, R., Schumacher, R., Dougherty, B., Bucka, N., Karp, K. S., . . . Morgan, S. (2021). *Assisting students struggling with mathematics: intervention in the elementary grades* (WWC 2021006). National Center for Education Evaluation and Regional Assistance, Institute of Education Sciences, U.S. Department of Education. https://ies.ed.gov/ncee/wwc/Docs/PracticeGuide/WWC2021006-Math-PG.pdf

Fuchs, L. S., Powell, S. R., Seethaler, P. M., Cirino, P. T., Fletcher, J. M., Fuchs, D., . . . Zumeta, R. O. (2009). Remediating number combination and word problems deficits among students with math difficulties: A randomized control trial. *Journal of Educational Psychology*, *101*, 561–576.

Geary, D. C. (2013). Learning disabilities in mathematics: Recent advances. In H. L. Swanson, K. Harris, & S. Graham (Eds.), *Handbook of learning disabilities* (pp. 199–212). Guilford Press.

Gilsdorf, T. E. (2012). *Introduction to cultural mathematics: With case studies from the Otomies and Inca.* Wiley.

Ginsburg, H. P. (1997). Mathematics learning disabilities: A view from developmental psychology. *Journal of Learning Disabilities*, *30*, 20–33.

Ginsburg, H. P. (1998a). Mathematics learning disabilities: A view from developmental psychology. In D. Rivera (Ed.), *Mathematics education for students with learning disabilities* (pp. 22–58). Pro-Ed.

Ginsburg, H. P. (1998b). Toby's math. In R. J. Sternberg & T. Ben-Zeev (Eds.), *The nature of mathematical thinking* (pp. 175–202). Erlbaum.

Greene, G. (1999). Mnemonic multiplication fact instruction for students with learning disabilities. *Learning Disabilities Research and Practice, 14*, 141–148.

Hall, T. E., Meyer, A., & Rose, D. H. (Eds.). (2012). *Universal design for learning in the classroom: Practical applications*. Guilford Press.

Heller, K. W. (2010). Mathematics instruction and adaptations. In S. J. Best, K. W. Heller, & J. L. Bigge (Eds.), *Teaching individuals with physical or multiple disabilities* (6th ed., pp. 456–493). Pearson.

Hodges, C., Moore, S., Lockee, B., Trust, T., & Bond, A. (2020, March 27). The difference between emergency remote teaching and online learning. *EDUCAUSE Review*. https://er.educause.edu/articles/2020/3/the-difference-between-emergency-remote-teaching-and-online-learning

Hunt, J. H., & Little, M. E. (2014). Intensifying interventions for students by identifying and remediating conceptual understandings in mathematics. *Teaching Exceptional Children, 46*(6), 187–196.

Hutchinson, N. L. (1993). Effects of cognitive strategy instruction on algebra problem solving of adolescents with learning disabilities. *Learning Disability Quarterly, 16*, 34–63.

Impecoven-Lind, L. S., & Foegen, A. (2010). Teaching algebra to students with learning disabilities. *Intervention in School and Clinic September, 46*, 31–37.

IRIS Center (2018). *MTSS/RTI: Mathematics*. Peabody College at Vanderbilt University. Retrieved from https://iris.peabody.vanderbilt.edu/module/rti-math/

Janvier, C. (1987). *Problems of representation in the teaching and learning of mathematics*. Erlbaum.

Jimenez, B., Browder, D. M., & Saunders, A. (2012). *Early Numeracy: A skill building math program for students with moderate and severe disabilities*. Attainment Company.

Jimenez, B. A., & Staples, K. (2015). Access to the Common Core State Standards in mathematics through early numeracy skill building for students with significant intellectual disability. *Education and Training in Autism and Developmental Disabilities, 50*, 17–30.

Joseph, G. G. (2011). *The crest of the peacock: Non-European roots of mathematics* (3rd ed.). Princeton University Press.

Khalifa, A. K., & Saad, M. A. E. (2021). The effectiveness of Touch Math on improving early mathematics ability of kindergarten children with mild to borderline intellectual functioning in an inclusion classroom. *Journal of Intellectual Disability Diagnosis and Treatment, 9*, 189–194.

Kilpatrick, J. (1985). Doing mathematics without understanding it: A commentary on Higbee and Kunihira. *Educational Psychologist, 20*(2), 65–68.

Kit, M., Terzioglu, N. K., Atkas, B., & Yikmisi, A. (2018). Effectiveness of Touch Math technique: Meta-analysis study. *European Journal of Special Education Research, 3*, 100–111.

Kong, J. E., Yan, C., Serceki, A., & Swanson, H. L. (2021). Word-problem-solving interventions for students with learning disabilities: A selective meta-analysis of the literature. *Learning Disability Quarterly, 44*, 244–260.

Lafay, A., Osaka, H. P., & Valat, M. (2019). Effects of interventions with manipulatives on immediate learning, maintenance, and transfer in children with mathematics learning disabilities: A systematic review. *Education Research International, 2019*, 1–21.

Lambert, R., & Schuck, R. (2021), "The wall between us": Teaching math to students with disabilities during the COVID spring of 2020. *Asia-Pacific Education Researcher, 30*, 289–298.

Lang, C., Mastropieri, M. A., Scruggs, T. E., & Porter, M. (2004). The effects of self-instructional strategies on problem solving in algebra for students with special needs. In T. E. Scruggs & M. A. Mastropieri (Eds.), *Research in secondary schools: Advances in learning and behavioral disabilities* (Vol. 17, pp. 27–54). Elsevier.

Lang, H., & Pagliaro, C. (2007). Factors predicting recall of mathematics terms by deaf students: Implications for teaching. *Journal of Deaf Studies and Deaf Education, 12*, 449–460.

Losinski, M., Ennis, R. P., & Shaw, A. (2021). Using SRSD to improve the fraction computations of students with and at-risk for EBD. *Behavioral Disorders, 46*(2), 108–119.

Lott, J. W., & Lott, C. J. (2014). *Mathematics lessons learned from across the world*. National Council for Teachers of Mathematics.

Maccini, P., & Hughes, C. (2000). Effects of a problem-solving strategy on the introductory algebra performance of secondary students with learning disabilities. *Learning Disabilities Research & Practice, 15*, 10–21.

Martin, T. S. (2007). *Mathematics teaching today: Improving practice, improving student learning*. National Council of Teachers of Mathematics.

Marzocchi, G. M., Lucangeli, D., De Meo, T., Fini, F., & Cornoldi, C. (2002). The disturbing effect of irrelevant information on arithmetic problem solving in inattentive children. *Developmental Neuropsychology, 21*, 73–92.

Mastropieri, M. A., & Scruggs, T. E. (1991). *Teaching students ways to remember: Strategies for learning mnemonically*. Brookline Books.

Mastropieri, M. A., & Scruggs, T. E. (2014). *Mnemonic math facts*. Graduate School of Education, George Mason University.

Mastropieri, M. A., Scruggs, T. E., Hauth, C., & Allen-Bronaugh, D. (2012). Instructional interventions for students with mathematics learning disabilities. In B. Y. L. Wong (Ed.), *Learning about learning disabilities* (4th ed., pp. 217–241). Elsevier Science.

McLeskey, J., Barringer, M-D., Billingsley, B., Brownell, M., Jackson, D., Kennedy, M., . . . Ziegler, D. (2017, January) *High-leverage practices in special education*. Council for Exceptional Children and CEEDAR Center.

Mercer, C. D., Mercer, A. R., & Pullen, P. C. (2011). *Teaching students with learning problems* (8th ed.). Pearson.

Mercer, C. D., & Miller, S. P. (1992). Teaching students with learning problems in math to acquire, understand, and apply basic math facts. *Remedial and Special Education, 13*, 19–35.

Meyer, A., Rose, D. M., & Gordon, D. (2014). *Universal design for learning: Theory and practice*. CAST.

Miller, S. P., & Mercer, C. D. (1993). Using a graduated word problem sequence to promote problem-solving skills. *Learning Disabilities Research & Practice, 8*, 169–174.

Montague, M. (2008). Self-regulation strategies to improve mathematical problem solving for students with learning disabilities. *Learning Disability Quarterly, 31*, 37–44.

Montague, M., Enders, C., & Dietz, S. (2011). Effects of cognitive strategy instruction on math problem solving of middle school students with learning disabilities. *Learning Disability Quarterly, 34*, 262–272.

Montague, M., & Jitendra, A. (Eds.). (2006). *Teaching mathematics to middle school students with learning difficulties*. Guilford Press.

Montague, M., & Warger, C. (2015). *Solve it! A practical approach to teaching mathematical problem solving skills* (3rd ed.). Exceptional Innovations.

Nasir, N. A., & Cobb, P. (2007). *Improving access to mathematics: Diversity and equity in the classroom*. Teachers College Press.

National Center on Intensive Intervention (NCII). (2016a). *Computation of fractions: Considerations for instruction*. Office of Special Education, U.S. Department of Education.

National Center on Intensive Intervention (NCII). (2016b). *Principles for designing intervention in mathematics*. Office of Special Education, U.S. Department of Education.

National Center on Intensive Intervention (NCII). (2016c). *Sample fraction addition and subtraction concepts. Activities 1–3*. Office of Special Education, U.S. Department of Education.

National Council of Teachers of Mathematics (NCTM). (2000). *Principles and standards for school mathematics.* Author.

National Council of Teachers of Mathematics (NCTM). (2011). *Making it happen.* Author.

National Governors Association (NGA) Center for Best Practices & Council of Chief State School Officers (CCSSO). (2010). *Common Core State Standards: Mathematics*. Author.

National Mathematics Advisory Panel. (2008). *Foundations for success: The final report of the National Mathematics Advisory Panel.* U.S. Department of Education.

Nelson, G., & McMaster, K. L. (2018). Effects of early numeracy interventions for students in preschool and early elementary: A meta-analysis. *Journal of Educational Psychology*, *111*(6), 1001–1022.

Patton, J. R., Cronin, M. E., Bassett, D. S., & Koppel, A. E. (1998). A life skills approach to mathematics instruction: Preparing students with learning disabilities for the real-life math demands of adulthood. In D. Rivera (Ed.), *Mathematics education for students with learning disabilities* (pp. 201–218). Pro-Ed.

Powell, S. R., & Fuchs, L. S. (2012). Early numerical competencies and students with mathematics difficulty. *Focus on Exceptional Children*, *44*(5), 1–16.

Powell, S. R., & Fuchs, L. S. (2015). Intensive intervention in mathematics. *Learning Disabilities Research and Practice*, *30*, 182–192.

Powell, S. R., & Fuchs, L. S. (2018). Effective word problem instruction: Using schemas to facilitate mathematical reasoning. *Teaching Exceptional Children*, *51*(1), 31–42.

Powell, S. R., Fuchs, L. S., Cirino, P. T., Fuchs, D., Compton, D. L., & Changas, P. C. (2015). Effects of a multitier support system on calculation, word problem, and prealgebraic performance among at-risk learners. *Exceptional Children*, *81*, 443–470.

Pushparajan, V. (2011). *An algorithm a day* [Blog]. http://analgorithmaday.blogspot.com/search?q=division

Quintessential Education. (2016). *A maths tuition pedagogy*. http://qeducation.sg/a-maths-tuition/

Reid, R., Gonzalez, J. E., Nordness, P. D., Trout, A., & Epstein, M. H. (2004). A meta-analysis of the academic status of students with emotional/behavioral disturbance. *Journal of Special Education*, *38*, 130–143.

Riccomini, P. J., Stocker, J. D., & Mornao, S. (2017). Implementing an effective mathematics fact fluency practice activity. *Teaching Exceptional Children*, *49*(5), 318–327.

Riccomini, P. J., & Witzel, B. S. (2010). *Response to intervention in math.* Corwin Press.

Rivera, D. P., & Smith, D. D. (1987). Influence of modeling on acquisition and generalization of computational skills: A summary of research findings from three sites. *Learning Disability Quarterly*, *10*, 69–80.

Rosenblum, L. P., & Amato, S. (2004). Preparation in and use of the Nemeth Braille Code for Mathematics by teachers of students with visual impairments. *Journal of Visual Impairment & Blindness*, *98*, 484–495.

Sayeski, K. L., & Paulsen, K. J. (2010). Mathematics reform curricula and special education: Identifying intersections and implications for practice. *Intervention in School and Clinic*, *46*, 13–21.

Schiro, M. S. (2004). *Oral storytelling and teaching mathematics: Pedagogical and multicultural perspectives.* Sage.

Shiah, R. L., Mastropieri, M. A., Scruggs, T. E., & Fulk, B. J. M. (1994–1995). The effects of computer assisted instruction on the mathematical problem solving of students with learning disabilities. *Exceptionality*, *5*, 131–161.

Shin, M., & Bryant, D. P. (2015). Fraction interventions for students struggling to learn mathematics: A research synthesis. *Remedial and Special Education*, 374–387.

Simon, R., & Hanrahan, J. (2004). An evaluation of the Touch-Math method for teaching addition to students with learning disabilities in mathematics. *European Journal of Special Needs Education*, *19*, 191–209.

Staudacher, C., & Turner, S. (1998). *Practical mathematics for consumers* (2nd ed.). Globe Fearon.

Stein, M., Kinder, D., Silbert, J., & Carnine, D. (2018). *Designing effective mathematics instruction* (5th ed.). Pearson.

Stewart, D. A., & Kluwin, T. N. (2001). *Teaching deaf and hard of hearing students: Content, strategies, and curriculum.* Allyn & Bacon.

Strickland, T. K. (2021). Algebra instruction for students with learning disabilities in the era of common core. *Intervention in School and Clinic*, *57*(5), 306–315.

Strickland, T. K., & Maccini, P. (2010). Strategies for teaching algebra to students with learning disabilities: Making research to practice connections. *Intervention in School and Clinic*, *46*, 38–45.

Tucker, B. F., Singleton, A. H., & Weaver, T. L. (2006). *Teaching mathematics to all children: Designing and adapting instruction to meet the needs of diverse learners* (2nd ed.). Merrill/Prentice Hall.

Uberti, H., Mastropieri, M. A., & Scruggs, T. E. (2004). Check it off: Individualizing a math algorithm for students with disabilities via self-monitoring checklists. *Intervention in School and Clinic*, *39*, 269–275.

Van Luit, J. E. H., & Schopman, E. A. M. (2000). Improving early numeracy of young children with special educational needs. *Remedial and Special Education*, *21*, 27–40.

Whitby, P. J. S. (2013). The effects of Solve It! on the mathematical word problem solving ability of adolescents with autism spectrum disorders. *Focus on Autism and Other Developmental Disabilities*, *28*, 78–88.

Xin, Y. P., Jitendra, A. K., & Deatline-Buchman, A. (2005). Effects of mathematical word problem solving instruction on middle school students with learning problems. *Journal of Special Education*, *39*, 181–192.

Zaslavsky, C. (1995). *The multicultural math classroom: Bringing in the world.* Heinemann.

Zaslavsky, C. (1999). *Africa counts: Number and pattern in African cultures* (3rd ed.). Lawrence Hill.

Zisimopoulos, D. A. (2010). Enhancing multiplication performance in students with moderate intellectual disabilities using pegword mnemonics paired with a picture fading technique. *Journal of Behavioral Education*, *19*, 117–133.

Chapter 15

Aceves, T. C., & Orosco, M. J. (2014). *Culturally responsive teaching* (Document No. IC-2). University of Florida, Collaboration for Effective Educator, Development, Accountability, and Reform Center. http://ceedar.education.ufl.edu/tools/innovation-configurations/

Albert, L. R., & Ammer, J. J. (2004). Lesson planning and delivery. In B. K. Lenz, D. D. Deshler, & B. R. Kissam (Eds.), *Teaching content to all: Evidence-based inclusive practices in middle and secondary schools* (pp. 195–220). Allyn & Bacon.

American Printing House for the Blind. (2006). *Adapting science for students with visual impairments: Advance preparation checklist*. https://www.aph.org/app/uploads/2020/07/7-00001-00.pdf

Bakken, J. P., Mastropieri, M. A., & Scruggs, T. E. (1997). Reading comprehension of expository science material and students with learning disabilities: A comparison of strategies. *Journal of Special Education*, *31*, 300–324.

Batshaw, M. L., Roizen, N. J., & Pellegrino, L. (2019). *Children with disabilities* (8th ed.). Brookes.

Berkeley, S., King-Sears, M. E., Hott, B. L., & Bradley-Black, K. (2014). Are history textbooks more "considerate" after 20 years? *Journal of Special Education*, *47*, 217–230.

Berkeley, S., Marshak, L., Mastropieri, M. A., & Scruggs, T. E. (2011). Improving student comprehension of social studies text: A self-questioning strategy for inclusive middle school classes. *Remedial and Special Education*, *32*, 105–113.

Best, R. M., Rowe, M., Ozuru, Y., & McNamara, D. S. (2005). Deep-level comprehension of science texts: The role of the reader and the text. *Topics in Language Disorders*, *25*, 65–83.

Boyle, J. R., & Weishaar, M. (1997). The effects of expert-generated versus student-generated cognitive organizers on the reading comprehension of students with learning disabilities. *Learning Disabilities Research & Practice*, *12*, 228–251.

Brigham, F. J., Scruggs, T. E., & Mastropieri, M. A. (2011). Science education and students with learning disabilities. *Learning Disabilities Research and Practice*, *26*, 223–232.

Browder, D. (2015). What should we teach students with moderate and severe disabilities? In B. Bateman, J. W. Lloyd, & M. Tankersley (Eds.), *Enduring issues in special education: Personal perspectives* (pp. 52–73). Routledge.

Bulgren, J. A. (2004). Effective content area instruction for all students. In T. E. Scruggs & M. A. Mastropieri (Eds.), *Research in secondary schools: Advances in learning and behavioral disabilities* (Vol. 17, pp. 147–174). Elsevier.

Bulgren, J. A., Deshler, D. D., & Schumaker, J. B. (1993). *The content enhancement series: The concept mastery routine.* Edge Enterprises.

Bulgren, J. A., Graner, P. S., & Deshler, D. D. (2013). Literacy challenges and opportunities for students with learning disabilities in social studies and history. *Learning Disabilities Research and Practice*, *28*, 17–27.

Burgstahler, S. (2012). *Making science labs accessible to students with disabilities.* University of Washington. https://www.washington.edu/doit/making-science-labs-accessible-students-disabilities

Capin, P. & Vaughn, S. (2017). Improving reading and social studies learning for secondary students with reading disabilities. *Teaching Exceptional Children*, *49*(4), 249–261.

Carreon, A., Smith, S. J., Mosher, M., Rao, K., & Rowland, A. (2022). A review of virtual reality intervention research for students with disabilities in K–12 settings. *Journal of Special Education Technology*, *37*(1), 82–99.

Chiappetta, E. L., & Koballa, T. R. (2014). *Science instruction in the middle and secondary schools: Developing fundamental knowledge and skills for teachers* (8th ed.). Merrill/Prentice Hall.

Conderman, G., & Hedin, L. (2017). Differentiating study guides. *Intervention in School and Clinic*, *53*(1), 19–27.

Contant, T. L., Bass, J. E., & Carin, A. A. (2018). *Teaching science through inquiry and investigation* (13th ed.). Pearson.

Courtade, G., Jimenez, B., Root, J., & Pennington, R. (2021). Planning for effective inclusive instruction in core content. In J. McLeskey, F. Spooner, B. Algozzine, & N. L. Waldron (Eds.), *Handbook of effective inclusive elementary schools: Research and practice* (2nd ed., pp. 286–301). Routledge.

De La Paz, S. (2005). Effects of historical reasoning instruction and writing strategy mastery in culturally and academically diverse middle school classrooms. *Journal of Educational Psychology*, *97*(2), 139–156.

De La Paz, S., & Wissinger, D. R. (2017). Improving the historical knowledge and writing of students with or at risk for LD. *Journal of Learning Disabilities*, *50*(6), 658–671.

Deshler, D. D., Ellis, E. S., & Lenz, B. K. (1996). *Teaching adolescents with learning disabilities: Strategies and methods* (2nd ed.). Love Publishing.

Deshler, D. D., & Schumaker, J. B. (1988). An instructional model for teaching students how to learn. In J. L. Graden, J. E. Zins, & M. J. Curtis (Eds.), *Alternative instructional delivery systems: Enhancing instructional options for all students* (pp. 391–411). National Association of School Psychologists.

Deshler, D. D., & Schumaker, J. B. (2006). *Teaching adolescents with disabilities: Accessing the general education curriculum.* Corwin Press.

Dion, M., Hoffman, K., & Matter, A. (2000). *Teacher's manual for adapting science experiments for blind and visually impaired students.* Worcester Polytechnic Institute and Visual Impairment Knowledge Center. https://www.perkinselearning.org/content/teacher%E2%80%99s-manual-adapting-science-experiments-blind-and-visually-impaired-students

Driver, R., Asoko, H., Leach, J., Mortimer, E., & Scott, P. (1994). Constructing scientific knowledge in the classroom. *Educational Researcher*, *23*(7), 5–12.

Echevarria, J., & Graves, A. (2015). *Sheltered content instruction: Teaching English language learners with diverse abilities* (5th ed.). Pearson.

Ferretti, R. P., & Fan, Y. (2016). Argumentative writing. In C. A. MacArthur, S. Graham, & J. Fitzgerald (Eds.), *Handbook of writing research* (pp. 301–315). Guilford Press.

Ferretti, R. P., MacArthur, C. D., & Okolo, C. M. (2001). Teaching for historical understanding in inclusive classrooms. *Learning Disability Quarterly*, *24*, 59–71.

Fry, E. (1977). Fry's readability graph: Clarifications, validity, and extension to Level 17. *Journal of Reading*, *21*, 242–252.

Furtak, E. M., Seidel, T., Iverson, H., & Briggs, D. C. (2012). Experimental and quasi-experimental studies of inquiry-based science teaching: A meta-analysis. *Review of Educational Research*, *82*, 300–329.

Gildroy, P., & Deshler, D. D. (2008). Effective learning strategy instruction. In R. Morris & N. Mather (Eds.), *Evidence-based practices for students with learning and behavioral challenges* (pp. 288–301). Routledge.

Gillies, R. M. (2015). *Collaborative learning: Developments in research and practice.* Nova Science.

Good, T. L., & Lavigne, A. L. (2017). *Looking in classrooms* (11th ed.). Routledge.

Grossen, B., & Burke, M. D. (1998). Instructional design that accommodates special learning needs in science. *Information Technology and Disabilities*, *5*, 2.

Hebert, M., Bohaty, J. J., Nelson, J. R., & Brown, J. (2016). The effects of text structure instruction on expository reading comprehension: A meta-analysis. *Journal of Educational Psychology*, *108*, 609–629.

Hock, M. F., Bulgren, J. A., & Brasseur-Hock, I. F. (2017). Strategic instruction model: The less addressed aspects of effective instruction for high school students with learning disabilities. *Learning Disabilities Research & Practice*, *32*(3), 166–179.

Horton, S. V., Boone, R. A., & Lovitt, T. C. (1990). Teaching social studies to learning disabled high school students: Effects of a hypertext study guide. *British Journal of Educational Technology*, *21*, 118–131.

Jimenez, B. A., Browder, D. M., Spooner, F., & Dibiase, W. (2012). Inclusive inquiry science using peer-mediated embedded instruction for students with moderate intellectual disability. *Exceptional Children*, *78*, 301–317.

Jimenez, B. A., Lo, Y., & Saunders, A. F. (2014). The additive effects of scripted lessons plus guided notes on science quiz scores of students with intellectual disability and autism. *Journal of Special Education*, *47*, 231–244.

Kang, H., Barton, A. C., Tan, E., Simpkins, S. D., Rhee, H., & Turner, C. (2019). How do middle school girls of color develop STEM identities?: Middle school girls' participation in science activities and identification with STEM careers. *Science Education*, *103*, 418–439.

Kennedy, M. J., Rodgers, W. J., Romig, J. E., Mathews, H. M., & Peeples, K. N. (2018). Introducing the content acquisition podcast professional development process: Supporting vocabulary instruction for inclusive middle school science teachers. *Teacher Education and Special Education*, *41*(2), 140–157.

Kennedy, M. J., Thomas, C. N., Meyer, J. P., Alves, K. D., & Lloyd, J. W. (2014). Using evidence-based multimedia to improve vocabulary performance of adolescents with LD: A UDL approach. *Learning Disability Quarterly*, *37*, 71–86.

King-Sears, M. E., & Johnson, T. M. (2020). Universal design for learning chemistry instruction for students with and without learning disabilities. *Remedial and Special Education*, *41*(4), 207–218.

King-Sears, M. E., Mercer, C. D., & Sindelar, P. T. (1992). Toward independence with keyword mnemonics: A strategy for science vocabulary instruction. *Remedial and Special Education*, *13*, 22–33.

King-Sears, M. E., & Mooney, J. F. (2004). Teaching content in an academically diverse class. In B. K. Lenz, D. D. Deshler, & B. R. Kissam (Eds.), *Teaching content to all: Evidence-based inclusive practices in middle and secondary schools* (pp. 221–257). Allyn & Bacon.

Knight, V. F., Smith, B. R., Spooner, F., & Browder, D. (2012). Using explicit instruction to teach science descriptors to students with autism spectrum disorder. *Journal of Autism and Developmental Disorders*, *42*, 378–389.

Knight, V. F., Wood, L., McKissick, B. R., & Kuntz, E. M. (2020). Teaching science content and practices to students with intellectual disability. *Remedial and Special Education*, *41*(6), 327–340.

Lee, T. T. H., & So, W. W. M. (2015). Inquiry learning in a special education setting: Managing the cognitive loads of intellectually disabled students. *European Journal of Special Needs Education*, *30*, 156–172.

Lenz, B. K., & Adams, G. (2006). Planning practices that optimize curriculum access. In D. D. Deshler & J. B. Schumaker (Eds.), *Teaching adolescents with disabilities: Accessing the general education curriculum* (pp. 35–78). Corwin Press.

Lenz, B. K., Bulgren, J., Kissam, B. R., & Taymans, J. (2004). SMARTER planning for academic diversity. In B. K. Lenz, D. D. Deshler, & B. R. Kissam (Eds.), *Teaching content to all: Evidence-based inclusive practices in middle and secondary schools* (pp. 47–77). Allyn & Bacon.

Lenz, B. K., Deshler, D. D., & Kissam, B. R. (Eds.). (2004). *Teaching content to all: Evidence-based inclusive practices in middle and secondary schools.* Allyn & Bacon.

Linan-Thompson, S., Lara-Martinez, J. A., & Cavazos, L. O. (2018). Exploring the intersection of evidence-based practices and culturally and linguistically responsive practices. *Intervention in School and Clinic*, *54*(1), 6–13.

Lubin, J., & Polloway, E. A. (2016). Mnemonic instruction in science and social studies for students with learning problems: A review. *Learning Disabilities*, *14*(2), 207–224.

MacArthur, C. A., Ferretti, R. P., & Okolo, C. M. (2002). On defending controversial viewpoints: Debates of sixth graders about the desirability of early 20th century American immigration. *Learning Disabilities Research & Practice*, *17*, 160–172.

Maheady, L., Sacca, M. K., & Harper, G. F. (1988). Classwide peer tutoring with mildly handicapped high school students. *Exceptional Children*, *55*, 52–59.

Marchand-Martella, N. E., Martella, R. C., Modderman, S. L., Petersen, H. M., & Pan, S. (2013). Key areas of effective adolescent literacy programs. *Education and Treatment of Children*, *36*, 161–184.

Marino, M. T., Gotch, C., Israel, M., Vasquez, E. III, Basham, J. D., & Becht, K. (2013). UDL in the middle school science classroom: Can video games and alternative text heighten engagement and learning for students with learning disabilities? *Learning Disability Quarterly*, *37*(2), 87–99.

Marshak, L., Mastropieri, M. A., & Scruggs, T. E. (2011). Curriculum enhancements for inclusive secondary social studies classes. *Exceptionality*, *19*, 61–74.

Mastropieri, M. A., & Scruggs, T. E. (1993). *A practical guide for teaching science to students with special needs in inclusive settings.* Pro-Ed.

Mastropieri, M. A., Scruggs, T. E., Boon, R., & Carter, K. B. (2001). Correlates of inquiry learning in science: Constructing concepts of density and buoyancy. *Remedial and Special Education*, *22*, 130–138.

Mastropieri, M. A., Scruggs, T. E., & Graetz, J. (2005). Cognition and learning in inclusive high school chemistry classes. In T. E. Scruggs & M. A. Mastropieri (Eds.), *Cognition and learning in diverse settings: Advances in learning and behavioral disabilities* (Vol. 18, pp. 107–118). Elsevier Science.

Mastropieri, M. A., Scruggs, T. E., Mantzicopoulos, P. Y., Sturgeon, A., Goodwin, L., & Chung, S. (1998). "A place where living things affect and depend on each other": Qualitative and quantitative outcomes associated with inclusive science teaching. *Science Education*, *82*, 163– 179.

Mastropieri, M. A., Scruggs, T. E., & Marshak, L. (2008). Training teachers, parents, and peers to implement effective teaching strategies for content area learning. In T. E. Scruggs & M. A. Mastropieri (Eds.), *Advances in learning and behavioral disabilities: Vol. 21. Personal preparation* (pp. 311–329). Emerald.

Mastropieri, M. A., Scruggs, T. E., Norland, J., Berkeley, S., McDuffie, K., Tornquist, E. H., & Conners, N. (2006). Differentiated curriculum enhancement in inclusive middle school science: Effects on classroom and high-stakes tests. *Journal of Special Education*, *40*, 130–137.

Mastropieri, M. A., Scruggs, T. E., Spencer, V., & Fontana, J. (2003). Promoting success in high school world history: Peer tutoring versus guided notes. *Learning Disabilities Research & Practice*, *18*, 52–65.

Mastropieri, M. A., Sweda, J., & Scruggs, T. E. (2000). Putting mnemonic strategies to work in an inclusive classroom. *Learning Disabilities Research & Practice*, *15*, 69–74.

Mayer, R. E. (2009). *Multimedia learning* (2nd ed.). Cambridge.

McCormick, S., & Cooper, J. O. (1991). Can SQ3R facilitate learning disabled students' literal comprehension of expository test?: Three experiments. *Reading Psychology*, *12*, 239–271.

McLeskey, J., Barringer, M-D., Billingsley, B., Brownell, M., Jackson, D., Kennedy, M., . . . Ziegler, D. (2017, January). *High-leverage practices in special education*. Council for Exceptional Children and CEEDAR Center.

Melber, L., & Heller, K. W. (2010). Science and social studies instruction and adaptations. In S. J. Best, K. W. Heller, & J. L. Bigge (Eds.), *Teaching individuals with physical or multiple disabilities* (6th ed., pp. 432–455). Pearson.

National Council for the Social Studies. (2013). *College, career, and civic life (C3) framework for social studies state standards.* Author.

National Governors Association (NGA) Center for Best Practices & Council of Chief State School Officers (CCSSO). (2010). *Common Core State Standards: Mathematics*. Author.

National Research Council. (2013). *Next generation science standards: For states, by states.* National Academies Press.

O'Connor, R. E., Beach, K. D., Sanchez, V. M., Bocian, K. M., & Flynn, L. J. (2015). Building BRIDGES: A design experiment to improve reading and United States history knowledge of poor readers in eighth grade. *Exceptional Children*, *81*, 399–425.

O'Connor, R., & Goodwin, V. (2011). Teaching older students to read. In R. O'Connor & P. Vadasy (Eds.), *Handbook of reading interventions* (pp. 380–412). Guilford Press.

O'Dea, R. E., Lagisz, M., Jennions, M. D., & Nakagawa, S. (2018). Gender differences in individual variation in academic grades fail to fit expected patterns for STEM. *Nature Communications*, *9*, 1–8.

Okolo, C. M., Bouck, E., Heutsche, A., Courtad, C., & Englert, C. S. (2011). Technology in the social studies for students with disabilities. In T. Lintner & W. Schweder (Eds.), *Practical strategies for teaching K–12 social studies in inclusive classrooms* (pp. 67–87). Information Age.

Okolo, C. M., Englert, C. S., Bouck, E. C., Heutsche, A., & Wang, H. (2011). The Virtual History Museum: Learning American history in diverse eighth grade classrooms. *Remedial and Special Education*, *32*, 417–428.

Okolo, C. M., & Ferretti, R. P. (2014). History instruction for students with learning disabilities. In H. L. Swanson, K. Harris, & S. Graham (Eds.), *Handbook of learning disabilities* (2nd ed., pp. 463–488). Guilford Press.

Parker, W. C., & Beck, T. A. (2017). *Social studies in elementary education* (15th ed.). Pearson.

Parker, W. C., & Beck, T. A. (2021). *Social studies in elementary education* (16th ed.). Pearson.

Pence, L. E., Workman, H. J., & Riecke, P. (2003). Effective laboratory experiences for students with disabilities: The role of a student laboratory assistant. *Journal of Chemical Education*, *80*, 295–298.

Pyle, N., Vasquez, A. C., Lignugaris-Kraft, B., Gillam, S. L., Reutzel, D. R., Olszewski, A., & Pyle, D. (2017). Effects of expository text structure interventions on comprehension: A meta-analysis. *Reading Research Quarterly*, *52*, 469–501.

Regan, K., Evmenova, A., Mastropieri, M. A., & Scruggs, T. E. (2015). Peer interactions in the content areas: Using differentiated instruction strategies. In K. R. Harris & L. Meltzer (Eds.), *The power of peers: Enhancing learning, development, and social skills* (pp. 33–68). Guilford Press.

Reid, R., Lienemann, T. O, & Hagaman, J. L. (2013). *Strategy instruction for students with learning disabilities* (2nd ed.). Guilford Press.

Rizzo, K. L., & Taylor, J. C. (2016). Effects of inquiry-based instruction on science achievement for students with disabilities: An analysis of the literature. *Journal of Science Education*, *19*(1), 1–16.

Rule, A. C., Stefanich, G. P., Boody, R. M., & Peiffer, B. (2011). Impact of adaptive materials on teachers and their students with visual impairments in secondary science and mathematics classes. *International Journal of Science Education*, *33*, 865–887.

Schumaker, J. B., Deshler, D. D., Alley, G. R., Warner, M. M., & Denton, P. H. (1982). Multipass: A learning strategy for improving reading comprehension. *Learning Disability Quarterly*, *5*, 295–304.

Schumaker, J. B., & Fisher, J. B. (2021). 35 years on the road from research to practice: A review of studies on four content enhancement routines for inclusive subject-area classes, Part I. *Learning Disabilities Research & Practice*, *36*(3), 242–257.

Scruggs, T. E., & Mastropieri, M. A. (1994). Refocusing microscope activities for special students. *Science Scope*, *17*, 74–78.

Scruggs, T. E., & Mastropieri, M. A. (1995a). Science education for students with behavior disorders. *Education and Treatment of Children*, *3*, 322–334.

Scruggs, T. E., & Mastropieri, M. A. (1995b). Science and mental retardation: An analysis of curriculum features and learner characteristics. *Science Education*, *79*, 251–271.

Scruggs, T. E., & Mastropieri, M. A. (2002). *Teaching tutorial: Mnemonic instruction.* Division for Learning Disabilities, Council for Exceptional Children. http://s3.amazonaws.com/cmi-teaching-ld/assets/attachments/53/Mnemonics_tutorial.pdf?1304625439

Scruggs, T. E., & Mastropieri, M. A. (2007). Science learning in special education: The case for constructed vs. instructed learning. *Exceptionality*, *15*, 57–74.

Scruggs, T. E., & Mastropieri, M. A. (2011). Maximizing social studies learning for all with peer tutoring and learning strategies information. In T. Lintner (Ed.), *Practical strategies for teaching K–12 social studies in inclusive classrooms* (pp. 35–46). Information Age.

Scruggs, T. E., & Mastropieri, M. A. (2013a). Science and social studies. In H. L. Swanson, K. Harris, & S. Graham (Eds.), *Handbook of learning disabilities* (2nd ed., pp. 448–462). Guilford Press.

Scruggs, T. E., & Mastropieri, M. A. (2013b). Teaching students with high incidence disabilities. In B. Cook & M. Tankersley (Eds.), *Research-based practices in special education* (pp. 342–352). Pearson.

Scruggs, T. E., & Mastropieri, M. A. (2015). What makes special education special? In B. Bateman, J. Lloyd, & M. Tankersley (Eds.), *Enduring issues in special education: Personal perspectives* (pp. 22–36). Routledge.

Scruggs, T. E., Mastropieri, M. A., Bakken, J. P., & Brigham, F. J. (1993). Reading vs. doing. The relative effectiveness of textbook-based and inquiry-oriented approaches to science education. *Journal of Special Education*, *27*, 1–15.

Scruggs, T. E., Mastropieri, M. A., Brigham, F. J., & Marshak-Milman, L. M. (2017). Science and social studies. In J. Kauffman, D. P. Hallahan, & P. G. Pullen (Eds.), *Handbook of special education* (2nd ed., pp. 571–585). Routledge.

Scruggs, T. E., Mastropieri, M. A., & Marshak, L. (2012). Peer-mediated instruction in inclusive secondary social studies learning: Direct and indirect learning effects. *Learning Disabilities Research and Practice*, *27*, 12–20.

Scruggs, T. E., Mastropieri, M. A., & Okolo, C. (2008). Science and social studies for students with disabilities. *Focus on Exceptional Children*, *41*(2), 1–24.

Scruggs, T. E., Mastropieri, M. A., & Wolfe, S. (1995). Scientific reasoning of students with mental retardation: Investigating preconceptions and conceptual change. *Exceptionality*, *5*, 223–244.

Simpkins, P. M., Mastropieri, M. A., & Scruggs, T. E. (2009). Differentiated curriculum enhancements in inclusive 5th grade science classes. *Remedial and Special Education*, *30*, 300–308.

Slocum, T. A. (2004). Direct instruction: The big ideas. In D. J. Moran & R. W. Malott (Eds.), *Evidence-based educational methods* (pp. 81–94). Elsevier Academic Press.

Sormunen, K., Juuti, K., & Lavonen, J. (2020). Maker-centered project-based learning in inclusive classes: Supporting students' active participation with teacher-directed reflective discussions. *International Journal of Science and Mathematics Education*, *18*, 691–712.

Spencer, V. G., Scruggs, T. E., & Mastropieri, M. A. (2003). Content area learning in middle school social studies classrooms and students with emotional or behavioral disorders: A comparison of strategies. *Behavioral Disorders*, *28*, 77–93.

Stevenson, K. T., Szczytko, R. E., Carrier, S. J., & Peterson, M. N. (2021). How outdoor science education can help girls stay engaged with science. *International Journal of Science Education*, *43*, 1090–1111.

Sullivan, G. S., Mastropieri, M. A., & Scruggs, T. E. (1995). Reasoning and remembering: Coaching thinking with students with learning disabilities. *Journal of Special Education*, *29*, 310–322.

Swanson, E., Hairrell, A., Kent, S., Ciullo, S., Wanzek, J. A., & Vaughn, S. (2014). A synthesis and meta-analysis of reading interventions using social studies content for students with learning disabilities. *Journal of Learning Disabilities*, *47*, 178–195.

Tomlinson, C. A., & Imbeau, M. B. (2010). *Leading and managing a differentiated classroom*. Association for Supervision and Curriculum Development.

VanUitert, V. J., Kennedy, M. J., Romig, J. E., & Carlisle, L. M. (2020). Enhancing science vocabulary knowledge of students with learning disabilities using explicit instruction and multimedia. *Learning Disabilities, 18*(1), 3–25.

Williams, J. P., & Pau, L. S. (2013). Teaching text structure to improve reading comprehension. In H. L. Swanson, K. R. Harris, & S. Graham (Eds.), *Handbook of learning disabilities* (2nd ed., pp. 361–374). Guilford Press.

Chapter 16

Aldosiry, N., Albarbi, A. A., & Alrusaiyes, R. (2021). Practices to prepare students with disabilities for the transition to new educational settings. *Children and Youth Services Review, 120*, 1–7.

Bakken, J. P. (2020). Special education services for students with disabilities: An introduction. In J. P. Bakken & F. E. Obiakor (Eds.), *Advances in special education: Vol. 35. Special education transition services for students with disabilities* (pp. 1–14). Emerald.

Bakken, J. P., & Obiakor, F. E. (Eds.). (2020). *Advances in special education: Vol. 35. Special education transition services for students with disabilities*. Emerald.

Bodine, M. (2020, July 2). Helping children with special needs transition to kindergarten. *Edutopia.* https://www.edutopia.org/article/helping-children-special-needs-transition-kindergarten

Bouck, E. C., & Park, J. Special education transition services for students who are deaf/hard of hearing. (2020) In J. P. Bakken & F. E. Obiakor (Eds.), *Advances in special education: Vol. 35. Special education transition services for students with disabilities* (pp. 53–68). Emerald.

Carter, E. W., Clark, N. M., Cushing, L. S., & Kennedy, C. H. (2005). Moving from elementary to middle school: Supporting a smooth transition for students with severe disabilities. *Teaching Exceptional Children, 37*(3), 8–14.

Cavendish, W., Connor, D. J., Olander, L., & Hallaran, A. (2020). Preparing for their future: Perspectives of high school students with learning disabilities about transition planning. *Exceptionality,* 28(5), 349–361.

Cease-Cook, J., Test, D. W., & Scroggins, L. (2013). Effects of the CD-Rom version of the self-advocacy strategy on quality of contributions in IEP meetings of high school students with intellectual disability. *Education and Training in Autism and Developmental Disabilities, 48*, 258–268.

Center for Autism Research and The Children's Hospital of Philadelphia. (2020). *Transition from preschool to school age services.* carautismroadmap.org.

Chiu, M.M., & Chow, B.W.Y. (2015). International comparisons of student achievement. In R.V. Nata (Ed.), *Progress in Education* (vol. 32, pp. 93–108). Nova Science.

Chen, C., Farmer, T. W., Hamm, J. B., Brooks, D. S., Lee, D., Norwalk, K., . . . Rizzo, K. (2020). Emotional and behavioral risk configurations, students with disabilities, and perceptions of the middle school ecology. *Journal of Emotional and Behavioral Disorders, 28*, 59–182.

Diegelmann, K. M., & Test, D. W. (2018). Effects of a self-monitoring checklist as a component of the Self-Directed IEP. *Education and Training in Autism and Developmental Disabilities, 53*, 73–83.

Erickson, J., Peterson, R. L., & Lembeck, P. (2013, May). *Middle school to high school transition. Strategy brief.* Student Engagement Project, University of Nebraska. http://k12engagement.unl.edu

Felmlee, D., McMillan, C., Rodis, P. I., & Osgood, D. W. (2018). Falling behind: Lingering costs of the high school transition for youth, friendships, and grades. *Sociology of Education, 91*, 159–182.

Glago, K., Mastropieri, M. A., & Scruggs, T. E. (2009). Improving problem solving of elementary students with mild disabilities. *Remedial and Special Education, 30*(6), 372–380.

Griffin, M. M., Taylor, J. L., Urbano, R. C., & Hodapp, R. M. (2014). Involvement in transition planning meetings among high school students with autism spectrum disorders. *Journal of Special Education, 47*, 256–264.

Johnson, D. R., Stout, K. E., & Thurlow, M. L. (2009). Diploma options and perceived consequences for students with disabilities. *Exceptionality, 17*, 119–134.

Kellems, R. (2018). Inclusion in general education: Strategies for embedding transition into academic content. In M. E. Morningstar & B. Clavenna-Deane, *Your complete guide to transition planning and services* (pp. 135–146). Brookes.

Langel, O. K. B. (2018). *Evaluating the effects of the self-advocacy strategy on student participation in educational meetings for middle school students with disabilities.* Unpublished doctoral dissertation, University of Iowa, Iowa City.

Lindstrom, L., Doreen, B., & Miesch, J. (2011). Waging a living: Career development and long-term employment outcomes for young adults with disabilities. *Exceptional Children, 77*, 423–434.

Lipscomb, S., Haimson, J., Liu, A. Y., Burghardt, J., Johnson, D. R., & Thurlow, M. L. (2017). Preparing for life after high school: The characteristics and experiences of youth in special education: Findings from the National Longitudinal Transition Study 2012. Comparisons with other youth: Full report (NCEE 2017-4016). U.S. Department of Education, Institute of Educational Sciences.

Madaus, J. W., Banerjee, M., Merchant, D., & Keenan, W. R. (2011). Transition to postsecondary education. In J. Kauffman, D. P. Hallahan, & J. Lloyd (Eds.), *Handbook of special education* (pp. 691–704). Routledge.

McGahee, D. W., King-Sears, M. E., & Evmenova, A. S. (2021). High school students with learning disabilities: Requesting accommodations in role-play. *Learning Disabilities Research & Practice, 36*(2), 82–95.

Miltenberger, R. G., Zerger, H., Novotny, M., & Hayes, R. (2017). Teaching community living skills to people with intellectual and developmental disabilities. In K. Shogren, M. Wehmeyer, & N. Singh (Eds.), *Handbook of positive psychology in intellectual and developmental disabilities* (pp. 297–309). Springer.

Morningstar, M. E., & Clavenna-Deane, B. (2018). *Your compete guide to transition planning and services.* Brookes.

National Center for Education Statistics. (2018). *The condition of education.* Author.

Office of Special Education and Rehabilitative Services. (2015). Rethinking the high school diploma. *Education Next,* 48–53. http://educationnext.org/files/ednext_XV_1_forum.pdf

Office of Special Education and Rehabilitative Services. (2020). *A transition guide to postsecondary education and employment for students and youth with disabilities*. Author.

Renaud, L. (2018). *Practical life skills: Independent living.* Classroom Complete.

Rojewski, J. W., & Gregg, N. (2011). Career choice patterns and behaviors of work-bound youth with high incidence disabilities. In J. Kauffman, D. P. Hallahan, & J. Lloyd (Eds.), *Handbook of special education* (pp. 584–593). Routledge.

Scanlon, D., Patton, J. R., & Raskind, M. (2011). Transition to daily living for persons with high incidence disabilities. In J. Kauffman, D. P. Hallahan, & J. Lloyd (Eds.), *Handbook of special education* (pp. 594–607). Routledge.

Schloss, M. A., & Gunter, P. L. (2011). Career and technical education. In J. Kauffman, D. P. Hallahan, & J. Lloyd (Eds.), *Handbook of special education* (pp. 470–483). Routledge.

Shogren, K. A. (2013). Self-determination and transition planning. Baltimore: Brookes.

Shogren, K. A., Raley, S. K., Burke, K. M., & Wehmeyer, M. L. (2019). *The self-determined learning model teacher's guide.* Kansas University Center on Developmental Disabilities.

Shogren, K. A., Wehmeyer, M. L., Palmer, S. B., Rifenbark, G. G., & Little, T. D. (2015). Relationships between self-determination and postschool outcomes for youth with disabilities. *Journal of Special Education*, *48*, 256–257.

Sitlington, P. L., Neubert, D. A., & Clark, G. M. (2010). *Transition education and services for students with disabilities* (5th ed.). Prentice Hall.

Strnadová, I., & Cumming, T. M. (2016). *Lifespan transitions and disability.* Routledge.

Suk, A. L., Sinclair, T. E., Osmani, K. J., & Willaims-Diehm, K. (2020). Transition planning: Keeping cultural competence in mind. *Career Development and Transition for Exceptional Individuals*, *43*(2), 122–127.

Test, D. W., & Neale, M. (2004). Using the self-advocacy strategy to increase middle graders' IEP participation. *Journal of Behavioral Education*, *13*, 135–145.

Test, D. W., Fowler, C. H., Wood, W. M., Brewer, D. M., & Eddy, S. (2005). A conceptual framework of self-advocacy for students with disabilities. *Remedial and Special Education*, *26*, 43–54.

Test, D. W., Mazzotti, V. L., Mustian, A. L., Fowler, C. H., Kortering, L., & Kohler, P. (2009). Evidence-based secondary transition predictors for improving postschool outcomes for students with disabilities. *Career Development for Exceptional Individuals*, *32*, 160–181.

Trainor, A. A., Newman, L., Garcia, E., Woodley, H. H., Traxler, R. E., & Deschene, N. D. (2019). Postsecondary education-focused transition planning experiences of English learners with disabilities. *Career Development and Transition for Exceptional Learners with Disabilities. 42*(1), 43–55.

U.S. Department of Education (2021). *43rd Annual report to Congress on the Implementation of the Individuals with Disabilities Education Act.* Washington, DC: Author. Retrieved from https://sites.ed.gov/idea/2020-annual-report-congress-idea/

Van Reusen, A. K., Bos, C. A., Schumaker, J. B., & Deshler, D. D. (1994). *The self-advocacy strategy for education and transition planning.* Edge Enterprises.

Wehmeyer, M. (2020). The importance of self-determination to the quality of life of people with intellectual disability: A perspective. *Journal of Environmental Research and Public Health*, *17*, 7121.

Wehmeyer, M. L., Shogren, K. A., Palmer, S. B., Williams-Diehm, K. L., Little, T. D., & Boulton, A. (2012). The impact of the self-determined learning model of instruction on student self-determination. *Exceptional Children*, *78*, 135–153.

Weiss, M. P., & Fagella-Luby, M. (2020). Transition services for students with learning disabilities. In J.P. Bakken & F.E. Obiakor (Eds.), *Advances in special education services: Vol. 35. Special education transition services for students with disabilities* (pp. 15–34). Emerald.

Wilt, C. L., Hirano, K., & Morningstar, M. E. (2021). Diverse perspectives on transition to adulthood among families: A qualitative exploration. *Journal of Disability Policy Studies*, *32*(1), 24–35.

GLOSSARY

3-W, 2-What, 2-How strategy: Story grammar strategy consisting of seven questions applied to written composition. Students answer each question as they plan and compose their story (see Chapter 13 for the questions used in this strategy).

AAC: Alternative and augmentative communication techniques used with some individuals with cerebral palsy and other disabilities include communication boards containing pictures or words of commonly asked questions and responses, and computerized devices using synthesized speech.

AAIDD: American Association on Intellectual and Developmental Disabilities supports a classification system for intellectual disabilities based on the level of support needed, with severe and profound intellectual disability requiring more extensive and pervasive support.

ABA: Applied Behavior Analysis involves the use of reinforcement (e.g., praise, tokens, edible reinforcers) for displaying appropriate behaviors (e.g., sitting, attending, responding) and carefully recording student behaviors on charts that are used in decision making.

Academic engaged time: Amount of time students spend actively participating in learning activities.

Acoustic reconstructions: *Also called* the keyword method, it is best used when the information to be learned is unfamiliar. Such terms as *nepenthe* and *carnelian* are excellent candidates because they are unfamiliar, and similar-sounding keywords can be created, such as *Neptune* or *carnation*.

Acquisition: Simple accuracy-level criteria, such as 9 out of 10 correct responses to listing 10 letters of the alphabet.

Acronym: Word formed from the first letters of the words to be remembered. An example is "FARM-B," which is used to remember the names of the classes of vertebrate animals (F—fish, A—amphibian, R—reptile, M—mammal, B—bird). A picture showing vertebrate animals on a farm can help enforce this concept.

Acrostics: Word created from each first letter of the words to be remembered; the words are arranged to make a sentence. For example, "My Dear Aunt Sally," is an acrostic that reminds students to *m*ultiply and *d*ivide before they *a*dd and *s*ubtract in a math sentence.

Activating prior knowledge: Eliciting from students what they already know prior to introducing new content.

Activities-oriented approach: Approach to learning in which students undertake specific projects, experiments, or other activities to enhance their understanding of the subject. With this approach, adaptations may focus on physical activities as well as reading and writing requirements.

ADA: American with Disabilities Act was signed into federal law in 1990 and mandated that individuals with disabilities should be provided with "reasonable accommodations" in the workplace and that such individuals could not be discriminated against. ADA also included protections for individuals enrolled in colleges and universities. Adults with disabilities attending universities are also entitled to appropriate modifications in classes.

Adaptive behavior scales: Assessments of how well individuals are able to perform daily living skills, self-help care, communication skills, and social skills.

ADHD: Attention-deficit/hyperactivity disorder is a chronic condition including attention difficulty, hyperactivity, and impulsiveness; may be concurrent with a learning disability.

Adjunct aids: Useful text enhancements such as study guides, outlines, guided notes, partial outlines, and highlighting and underlining.

Adventitious: Disabilities that are acquired later in life.

Affect: Person's emotional mood and feelings.

AIDS: Acquired immunodeficiency syndrome is a viral infection that destroys some white blood cells impacting the body's immune system's ability to protect itself.

Algebra tiles: Manipulatives that use differently colored and sized pieces to represent algebra concepts such as dark-colored pieces to represent positive integers and lighter-colored pieces to represent negative numbers. Tiles can be placed together to represent equations.

Allocate: Designating time or resources for learning a certain subject (by, for example, scheduling a specific amount of time per day to reading instruction).

Alternative and augmentative communication (AAC): Systems designed with specialized devices to help individuals communicate who otherwise may be unable to. Techniques include communication boards containing pictures or words of commonly asked questions and responses to questions and computerized devices using synthesized speech.

Alternative teaching: Type of teaching where one teacher leads the larger group while the other teacher (often, the special education teacher) provides additional practice or strategies to students who may require additional support.

American Sign Language (ASL): Visual-spatial language, unlike English, that is not phonologically based and has own rules of semantics, syntax, pragmatics, and vocabulary. Each sign has three parts: hand shape, location, and movement.

Anoxia: Lack of oxygen to the brain, at any time, including during birth, that causes brain damage and may result in intellectual disabilities, depending on the extent of the damage.

Antecedent: What happens to a person before a target behavior has occurred.

Aphasia: Difficulty speaking (expressive aphasia) or comprehending (receptive aphasia) language.

Application: Applying learned skills or content to relevant contexts.

Applied behavior analysis: Use of reinforcement (e.g., praise, tokens, edible reinforcers) for displaying appropriate behaviors (e.g., sitting, attending, responding) and carefully recording student behaviors on charts that are used in decision making.

AT: Assistive technology is any device ranging from high technology (computers) to low technology (pencil grips) to assist students in learning.

At risk: Student who faces circumstances that could impede well-being and academic success.

Attention-deficit/hyperactivity disorder (ADHD): Chronic condition including attention difficulty, hyperactivity, and impulsiveness; may be concurrent with a learning disability.

Attribution training: Training in which students are taught to attribute success to their own efforts and academic strategies and to attribute failure to their lack of effort or failure to use appropriate strategies.

Authentic literature: Books used during whole-language instruction; examples include picture books, informational books, and chapter books.

Autism spectrum disorders (ASD): Serious developmental disorder that impairs the ability to communicate and interact. Common symptoms include difficulty with communication, difficulty with social interactions, obsessive interests, and repetitive behaviors.

AWARE strategy: Learning strategy initially developed for college students with learning disabilities, it can be adapted for students in secondary settings. Each letter in the acronym represents a step in the strategy (see Chapter 11).

AYP: Adequate yearly progress was established to set annual goals for students in grades 3 through 8 in basic academic skills.

Basal textbooks: Used in traditional approaches to reading instruction at each grade level from kindergarten through middle school; contain short stories and comprehension questions designed to meet certain grade-level criteria. Some emphasize phonics; others highlight literature-based stories. Most include workbooks and worksheets that provide supplemental practice on comprehension and specific word study skills.

Base-10 blocks: Manipulatives used to teach mathematics concepts, including place value, counting, number sense, addition, subtraction, multiplication, and division.

Business-as-usual (BAU): Business as usual consists of normal or traditional teaching methods in contrast with experimental or innovative teaching methods in research.

Bent-finger strategy: Strategy for calculating the ×9 facts. Using this strategy, students hold their two hands, palms down, in front of them. They then count from left to right on their fingers by the number of the fact and bend down the relevant finger.

Bound morpheme: Parts of words that depend on other words and cannot stand alone, as in *-er* in the word *teacher*.

Braille: System of raised dots that are read with fingertips or by ear using audio recordings for individuals who are referred to as totally blind.

Brainstorming: Strategy for activating prior knowledge. Before a lesson, students are presented with a topic and asked to generate as many ideas as possible that are related or similar to the topic.

Cataracts: Clouding of the lens in the eye, which can lead to visual impairments.

CEC: Council for Exceptional Children is the major professional special education organization.

Choral responding: Technique that prompts students to respond to questions together when a specific signal is given (e.g., a raised finger or dropped hand); the teacher should monitor whether all students are responding promptly and accurately.

Circle of Friends: Strategy used to build a network of social support within an inclusive classroom community for a "focus student" with a disability and/or those students without a disability who may feel isolated or excluded.

Classwide peer tutoring: Type of tutoring where all students in the class are divided into pairs of students, who then alternate roles of tutor and tutee to master basic academic skills; the most significant feature is the dramatic increase in engaged time on-task and opportunities to respond.

Cleft palate: Physical impairment in which the upper part of the oral cavity is split.

Code-emphasis approach: Students are taught the sound–symbol relationships among letters and are provided sufficient practice in decoding specific word patterns in reading passages before being presented with reading selections containing unfamiliar words. Individual sounds and words are introduced systematically and practiced in isolation and in word lists, sentences, paragraphs, short stories, and accompanying workbook activities.

Cognitive conflict: Not easily predictable or explainable at first. A discrepant event, often used in teaching science, represents, a conflict that occurs when things or experiments behave differently than expected.

Coloboma: Parts of the retina that are improperly formed, resulting in visual impairments.

Common Core Math Standards (CCMS): Academic benchmarks for what students should know and be able to do in math.

Common Core State Standards (CCSS): Statewide effort to provide a clear and consistent framework in English, language arts/literacy, and mathematics to prepare students for college and the workforce after graduation from high school.

Concept maps: Spatially organized maps that show relationships among events, actions, people, and places in texts to reinforce understanding.

Concepts: Ranging from simple to complex, learning when applied to a novel example. For example, a dog may be initially learned as an individual's dog but is considered learned when it can be applied to all examples of dogs.

Conductive: Damage to the outer or middle ear along the passageway resulting in a hearing loss.

Congenital: Disabilities that are present at birth.

Consultant: Outside person who works with individuals as needed. Special education teachers frequently provide consultative services to general education teachers.

Content enhancement: Strategies that are used to further increase content learning; incorporate effective instructional design and make use of graphic organizers—including study guides, charts, diagrams, outlines, visual-spatial displays, mnemonics, and imagery—to promote learning and comprehension.

Contingent observation timeout: Timeout where the student is seated nearby and can still observe group activities.

Continuum of services: Range of services and programs from least to most restrictive.

Contracting: Establishing a written agreement that formalizes the behaviors a student agrees to exhibit and the positive consequences that will result.

Cooperative learning: Students assigned to small groups that work collaboratively to complete group activities.

Corporal punishment: Paddling or some other method of inflicting physical pain upon a student. Professional organizations and others have long advocated against its use because it is almost never more effective than alternatives and is almost certain to promote resentment and anger in the student.

Corrective feedback: Providing students with immediate feedback when oral reading errors occur so that comprehension will improve.

Co-teaching: Type of teaching where special and general education teachers collaborate and share instructional responsibilities.

Creative and talented: Creatively gifted and talented youth often excel in the visual or performing arts. These individuals typically show outstanding abilities at young ages in particular areas.

Criterion-referenced testing: Form of testing where student performance is compared with predetermined specified criteria, usually considered as meeting minimal competency, for example a written test for a driver's license, in which individuals either pass or fail to meet a certain criterion.

Critical thinking: Use of active reasoning to acquire novel concepts, ideas, or solutions or to evaluate or analyze information to reach a justifiable conclusion.

Cross-age tutoring: Type of tutoring where older students serve as tutors for younger students in need of supplemental instruction or practice. The roles of tutor and tutee are clearly established and do not alternate.

Curriculum-based assessment: Any procedure that evaluates student performance in relation to the school curriculum, such as weekly spelling tests.

Curriculum-based measurement: Frequent, direct measurements of critical school behaviors, which could include timed (e.g., 1- to 5-minute) tests of performance on reading, math, and writing skills; formative in nature, it allows teachers to make instructional decisions about teaching and curriculum while learning is taking place.

Cyberbullying: Harassing messages or malicious rumors sent using a computer or cell phone.

Daily Progress Report: Daily written reports containing how students' individual daily goals and target expectations were met each period during the school day.

Data-based decision making: Decisions that rely on progress monitoring, which involves collecting multiple performance measures over time, in order to (1) determine whether progress is appropriate and, if progress is not appropriate, (2) help identify more effective programs. It also can help determine whether individual students are not responding appropriately to different levels of instruction and may need to be evaluated for learning disabilities.

Data-based individualization: Data collected through progress monitoring to make individual instructional decisions.

dB: Decibels are units of measure of acoustic or sound volume.

DD Act: Developmental Disabilities Assistance and Bill of Rights Acts provide for the development of employment-related training activities for adults with disabilities.

Decoding: Decoding is the practice of using letter-sound relationships to read words.

Demonstration Plus Permanent Model: Strategy that demonstrates how to complete a particular type of problem, for example, subtraction with regrouping or long division, and provides a model, with steps, written on a student's page or somewhere easily accessible for future reference.

Diabetic retinopathy: Insufficient blood flow to the retina, causing visual impairments.

Differentiated instruction: Making adjustments in the delivery of instruction to meet the individual needs of all learners in inclusive classrooms.

Diplegia: Paralysis of corresponding parts on both sides of the body, typically affecting the legs more severely than the arms.

Direct appeals: Asking students personally to follow class rules more carefully, which can be successful in improving appropriate behavior.

Direct assessment measures: Measures in fidelity of implementation that include checklists of intervention components, conducted by a person qualified to observe classroom procedures. The observer records the elements of effective implementation of the intervention and calculates the percentage of steps completed appropriately.

Direct instruction: Direct instruction includes flexible small-group or one-to-one structured, teacher-directed lessons, with use of direct questioning, student responding, teacher feedback and praise, and careful recording and monitoring of progress toward predetermined objectives.

Discrimination learning: Determining how one stimulus is either the same as or different from another stimulus.

DISSECT strategy: Strategy that provides students with tools they can use independently when they encounter unfamiliar words. Each letter in DISSECT stands for one of the steps in the procedure (see Chapter 13).

DOE: Department of Education is a department of the executive branch of the U.S. government responsible for allocating resources and monitoring the implementation of federal legislation.

Down syndrome: Genetic disorder based on a chromosomal anomaly. It is sometimes referred to as trisomy 21 because the 21st pair of chromosomes divides into three (trisomy) instead of a single pair of chromosomes.

Dysgraphia: Extreme difficulty with writing.

Dyslexia: Type of specific learning disability characterized as a severe difficulty with learning to read and spell despite adequate opportunity and instruction.

EAHCA: Education for All Handicapped Children Act is federal legislation passed in 1975 which specified that all children, including those with disabilities, were entitled to free and appropriate public education.

EAI: Enhanced anchored instruction is a math problem-based learning approach, providing the problem in a video format.

EBPs: Evidence-based practices are instructional practices based on rigorous research that have been subjected to review by experts.

Engaged: Time students are actively participating in learning activities.

English learners (ELs): Students who may have reduced language and vocabulary in speaking, reading, and writing skills in English due to reduced previous exposure to English.

Episodic memory: Memory of previous personal experiences and events.

ESEA: Elementary and Secondary Education Act is federal legislation enacted in 1965 showing commitment to equal opportunity for all students.

Every Student Succeeds Act (ESSA): Replacing the No Child Left Behind Act, in this new legislation, the highly qualified teacher requirement was eliminated and replaced with state certificate and licensure requirements. States can choose their own academic standards and can develop their own accountability systems to identify and support struggling schools, not necessarily based solely on federally mandated testing.

Everyday memory: Memory for information encountered in everyday experience.

Evidence based: See Scientifically based.

Evidence-based practice (EBPs): Instructional methods proven to be effective scientifically.

Exclusionary: Standard that learning problems are not the result of sensory, motor, intellectual, emotional, or sociocultural influences.

Exclusionary timeout: Timeout when the student is removed from the activity.

Extrinsic motivation: Participation in an activity in anticipation of an external reward.

FAPE: Free, appropriate public education is a rule under the Individuals with Disabilities Education Act specifying that all children, including those with disabilities formerly excluded from school, are entitled to a free, appropriate public education.

Fidelity of implementation: Degree to which instruction is delivered in the way it was intended.

Fluency: Combination of accuracy criteria with specified amounts of time (e.g., 90% accuracy within 2 minutes, or 90 out of 100 letters correct in 5 minutes).

FOIL: Strategy to teach algebraic notation and conventions in order to compute algebraic equations. The acronym stands for first terms, outer terms × inner terms, and last terms.

Formative assessment: Assessment used at frequent intervals prior to or during instruction so that student progress can be evaluated and teachers can make instructional decisions (e.g., provide feedback, reteach concepts, group students based on knowledge). Its purpose is to continuously check for student understanding and adjust or retain instruction, as needed.

Fragile X syndrome: Most common inherited cause of intellectual disabilities; caused by a mutation on the X chromosome and affects only males.

Framed outlines: Partially completed outlines in which students complete missing information as they study; can be used by students before they are required to complete an entire outline independently.

Free, appropriate public education (FAPE): Rule under the Individuals with Disabilities Education Act specifying that all children, including those with disabilities formerly excluded from school, are entitled to a free, appropriate public education.

Free morpheme: Part of a word that can stand alone, as in *teach* in the word *teacher.*

Functional math: Aspects of mathematics that serve individuals in their daily living, including using a calendar, writing checks, keeping checking and savings bank accounts, calculating household expenses, filling out income tax forms, and paying bills—skills that are important for all students to acquire.

Generalization: Ability to transfer previous learning to novel situations.

Gifted, creative, and talented: Individuals with special gifts, creativity, and/or talents may be extraordinary in intellectual ability, specialized academic areas, music, or the arts.

Glaucoma: Disease of the eye resulting from excessive pressure on the eyeball, causing visual impairments.

HAART: Highly active antiretroviral therapy is a combination of therapies that have proven very effective in reducing HIV/AIDS symptoms.

Hemiplegia: Paralysis in either the left or right side of the body.

Hidden gifted: Gifted, creative, and talented students who remain unidentified or "hidden" for a variety of reasons, including those who are underachievers or are underidentified due to language or cultural differences.

High-interest low-reading level (hi-lo): Books that provide exciting, age-appropriate content for elementary and high school students who read below grade level.

High-leverage practices (HLPs): Foundational skills or evidence-based practices used frequently in classrooms that have shown to increase student success.

Hydrocephaly: Enlargement of the head due to an interference in the flow of cerebral spinal fluid.

Hz: Hertz measures tones with different pitches or frequencies.

IDEA: The Education for All Handicapped Children Act—federal legislation passed in 1975, now known as the Individuals with Disabilities Education Act, or IDEA—specified that all children, including those with disabilities formerly excluded from school, were entitled to a free, appropriate public education (FAPE).

Identification: Responses such as pointing to the correct answer (e.g., on a communication board) and answering matching, multiple-choice, or true/false tests.

IEP: Individualized Education Program required for students who have been referred to special education, which details their special learning needs and mandates appropriate services; short- and long-term goals and objectives for students are also explicitly listed.

IFSP: Individualized Family Service Plan is a written legal document developed by a multidisciplinary team that identifies supports and services for infants and toddlers with disabilities (younger than age 3), and their families.

Imagery: Process of visualizing content from reading, which may be a useful substitute when illustrations are unavailable.

Inclusion: Students with disabilities that are served primarily in the general education classroom, under the responsibility of the general classroom teacher.

Indirect methods of fidelity assessment: Assessment that includes teacher self-reports of implementation, more general rating scales, teacher interviews, and permanent products of teacher and student work.

Individualized education program (IEP): Plan required for students who have been referred to special education, which details their special learning needs and mandates appropriate services; short- and long-term goals and objectives for students are also explicitly listed.

Individuals with Disabilities Education Act (IDEA): Formerly the Education for All Handicapped Children Act, federal legislation passed in 1975 specifying that all children, including those with disabilities formerly excluded from school, were entitled to a free, appropriate public education.

Inquiry-based model: Using either the text- or activities-oriented approach, students use their knowledge or experiences to invent, discover, or construct new knowledge. Adaptations may focus on supports or enhancements to promote the thinking and reasoning process in students with disabilities.

In-school suspension: Type of punishment when a student must attend a specific suspension room in the school and is not allowed in the regularly assigned classroom.

InTASC: Interstate New Teacher Assessment and Support Consortium developed teaching standards for teacher preparation.

Intellectual functioning: General mental abilities to think, problem-solve, reason, learn, and comprehend. Assessments typically measure vocabulary, common knowledge, short-term memory, and ability to solve mazes and jigsaw puzzles.

Intrinsic motivation: Participation in an activity purely out of curiosity, desire to succeed, or desire to contribute.

IPLAN and SHARE: Strategies that teach students to use more effective communication skills to use in education and transition meetings after completing a self-advocacy strategy. Each letter in the acronyms represent specific strategy steps (see Chapter 16).

ISC: Intermittent self-catheterization is a procedure used with children lacking bladder control who use a catheter, attached to a bag, to collect their urine.

IT FITS: Strategy that helps students with learning difficulties remember important information from science textbooks. Each letter in the acronym represents the steps in creating mnemonic keyword strategies (see Chapter 15).

ITBS: Iowa Tests of Basic Skills is a norm-referenced achievement test.

Joint attention: Ability of an individual to coordinate attention between a desired object and a person in a social context; for example, the ability to follow an adult's eye gaze directed to a specific object.

Keyword method: Method used to strengthen the connection between a new word and its associated information. Students are first provided a "keyword," which is a word that is familiar to the learner but that sounds like the new word and is easily pictured.

K-W-L: Strategy used to access prior knowledge before reading expository chapters or units of instruction; students ask and answer three questions based on the three letters K, W, and L (see Chapter 13 for the steps).

Language: System of communicating ideas.

Language delay: Slower onset or sequence of language skills.

Language difference: When difficulties presented in a student's second language also occur in the student's first language.

Larynx: Hollow muscular organ containing the vocal cords in humans.

Learning disabilities: Category that refers to a disorder in one or more of the basic psychological processes involved in understanding or using spoken or written language, which can result in difficulties in reading, writing, listening, speaking, thinking, spelling, or mathematics.

Least-restrictive environment (LRE): Setting least removed from the general education classroom where students with disabilities must be educated.

LEAs: Local education agencies, for example a town, city or county school district who oversee school districts' policies and procedures.

Letter strategies: Strategies used for remembering lists of things. For example, the HOMES strategy prompts recall of the names of the Great Lakes (H—Huron, O—Ontario, etc.). To ensure these are effective, students are asked to rehearse the names represented by the letters.

Life-centered career objectives: Objectives designed around basic competencies that are subdivided according to the needs of targeted students. Each area is then subdivided into more specific-level competencies and objectives that also contain

Long-term memory: Memory that holds information from short-term memory if that content has been rehearsed or remembered by using any other strategy to facilitate long-term recall.

LRE: Least restrictive environment is the setting least removed from the general education classroom where students with disabilities must be educated.

Mainstreaming: First movement devoted to the placement of students with disabilities within the general education classroom.

Meta-analysis: Form of literature review that synthesizes outcomes quantitatively from a number of studies.

Metacognition: Awareness of one's own cognitive processes and how they can be enhanced to increase learning.

Metamemory: Process of knowing when, where, and how to remember.

Microcephaly: Cranial malformation involving a very small skull that is associated with some forms of intellectual disability.

Morpheme: Smallest units of language that carry meaning or function; for example, the word *teacher* contains two morphemes.

Morphology: Meaningful structure of words, as expressed in morphemes.

Motivation: Degree to which students desire to succeed in school and other activities.

MTSS: Multilevel system of intervention designed to address different learning needs, reduce disability identification, and provide evidence for the appropriate identification of learning disabilities; also referred to as *response to intervention*.

Multicultural education: Appreciation of all cultures that is fostered and taught.

MultiPass: Learning strategy used for reading science and social studies textbooks similar to that in the SQ3R strategy—Survey, Question, Read, Recite, and Review; students are taught to review textbook reading materials three times to (1) survey, (2) size up, and (3) sort out.

Multi-tiered systems of support (MTSS): Multilevel system of intervention designed to address different learning needs, reduce disability identification, and provide evidence for the appropriate identification of learning disabilities; also referred to as *response to intervention*.

NCLB: No Child Left Behind Act was a reauthorization of the 1965 ESEA Act, not written specifically for students with disabilities, but nevertheless contained implications for students with disabilities.

Negative attributions: When students relate things that happen to them to forces outside of their own control, for example, that they were picked on or treated unfairly, which caused them to misbehave.

Neuromotor impairments: Abnormality of, or damage to, the brain, spinal cord, or nervous system acquired at or before birth and often result in complex motor problems that can affect several body systems.

Norm-referenced testing: Testing in which student performance is compared with the performance of other students who are the same age or grade level. Students receive scores such as "85th percentile," which means that the student scored higher than 85% of other students who are the same age or grade level on that particular test.

Number line: Lines with marks to represent quantity, including real and whole numbers, rational numbers, and positive and negative numbers.

Occupational surveys: Commercially available surveys that help develop a more comprehensive transition plan in the postsecondary vocational and educational areas.

One teach, one assist: Type of co-teaching where one teacher assumes more responsibility for delivering instruction and the other teacher assists individual students, enhances instruction, or observes individual students to improve instructional decision making.

Onset-rime: Sounds that precede the first vowel in a syllable (onset), followed by the remaining sounds, which are common patterns or word families (rime); these materials provide instruction and practice with phonemic awareness skills.

Operational definition: Description of a characteristic; for example, for "on-task" behavior the student's eyes are directed toward the teacher or on instructional materials and is engaged in an appropriate way.

Orthopedic impairments: Disability relating to a bone, joint, or muscle.

Overlearning: Questioning and practice after learning has been achieved is referred to as overlearning that can be an effective strategy for promoting long-term memory.

Paired associates: Type of factual learning where one item is associated with another, as in a U.S. state with its respective capital (e.g., Boston is the capital of Massachusetts).

Parallel teaching: Method of teaching when a class is divided into skill or ability groups and each teacher leads one group.

Paraplegia: Paralysis of the legs.

PARC: Pennsylvania Association for Retarded Children, now known as the ARC of Pennsylvania is a state advocacy organization for people with intellectual and developmental disabilities.

PASS: Acronym of a strategy meaning to Prioritize instruction, Adapt instruction, Systematically teach in inclusive settings using the SCREAM variables, and Systematically evaluate the outcomes of inclusive instruction.

PBIS: Positive behavior interventions and supports are implemented in RTI systems to facilitate positive behavior, model that uses universal intervention (or Tier 1) for social skills, which might include schoolwide instruction of all students in positive social behaviors; targeted intervention (Tier 2), which could be small-group instruction on specific social skills; and intensive (Tier 3) intervention, which could include individualized and comprehensive instruction in social skills.

PCS: Picture Communication System is part of a communication board using pictures to facilitate communication.

PECS: Picture exchange communication system teaches students to use pictures and symbols to initiate communication and respond to communication from others.

Peer assistance: Pairing students for the purpose of having one student available to assist another student when necessary; can be helpful in promoting success in inclusive classrooms. Also called *peer support*.

Peer social initiation: Procedures intended to enlist peer assistance in promoting social interaction with withdrawn students, including children with autism; may also be referred to as *peer-mediated instruction* (PMI), in which the peer receives training and coaching from an adult to support the learning goal(s) of a student with autism or other needs.

Peer tutoring: Peer-mediated strategy that involves students functioning as tutors and/or tutees to enable one-to-one instruction and practice. Flexible tutoring configurations are formed across and within grade levels and content areas.

Pegword method: Strategy using rhyming words for numbers that is useful in learning numbered or ordered information. For example, to remember that insects have six legs, picture an insect crawling on sticks (pegword for *six*). To remember that spiders have eight legs, picture a spider spinning a web on a gate (pegword for *eight*).

Performance assessment: Type of assessment, usually curriculum based, that requires students to engage in a process or construct some product, often on real-world tasks; includes such diverse outcomes as playing a piece on a piano, writing a persuasive essay, or conducting a science experiment.

Phonemes: Smallest sound units, such as /t/ and /l/.

Phonemic awareness: Instruction and practice in listening and using sounds in isolation initially, then sound blending and sound segmentation, for the purpose of learning that words are composed of individual sounds that can be combined and separated to create new words.

Phonology: Ability to blend and segment the sounds that individual letters or groups of letters make to form words.

PIC: Pictogram Ideogram Communication is part of a communication board or computerized program using pictures and symbols to facilitate communication.

Pictorial or mimetic reconstructions: Strategy best used for information that is both familiar and concrete and does not need to be transformed into familiar forms. For example, a U.S. history text states that World War I soldiers stationed in unhealthy trenches were more likely to die from disease than from battle wounds. Because students are probably already familiar with *trench* and *disease*, it is not necessary to create keywords; rather, simply picture *sick soldiers* in *trenches* to demonstrate the relation. Students can simply think back to the picture and retrieve the answer.

Picture exchange communication system (PECS): System that teaches students to use pictures and symbols to initiate communication and respond to communication from others.

Portfolio assessment: Type of assessment, usually curriculum based, that consists of student products and other relevant information collected over time and displayed in a portfolio.

Positive behavioral interventions and supports (PBIS): Implemented in RTI systems to facilitate positive behavior, model that uses universal intervention (or Tier 1) for social skills, which might include schoolwide instruction of all students in positive social behaviors; targeted intervention (Tier 2), which could be small-group instruction on specific social skills; and intensive (Tier 3) intervention, which could include individualized and comprehensive instruction in social skills.

Postlingual: Individuals who acquire deafness after age 2 or by the time language has developed.

POW + TREE strategy: Strategy for persuasive writing in which each letter in the acronym represents a strategy step for composing persuasive essays (see Chapter 13).

Pragmatics: Use of language in the context of social situations; for example, students typically speak to teachers in a different manner than they would speak to classmates.

Prelingual: Deafness occurring before a child has developed language.

Prereferral assistance team: Teams that assist teachers in implementing classroom interventions to help individual struggling students; may also be referred to as *multidisciplinary teams*, *student study teams*, *general education assistance teams*, *prereferral intervention teams*, *problem-solving teams*, or *teacher assistance teams* and may vary in the way they are implemented.

Primary reinforcers: Tangible rewards such as snacks or drinks.

Problem-solving approach: Implemented by many school districts, in this approach, at Tier 1, the teacher may confer with a student's parents to help resolve a learning or behavioral problem. If the problem is not resolved, at Tier 2, the teacher may meet with the school-identified assistance team to identify the problem and plan an intervention. If the student does not succeed at this level, the agency staff may be called in to redesign and coordinate the implementation of Tier 3, which in many cases may include special education.

Production: Responses such as writing, saying, computing, orally spelling, and exhibiting appropriate behavior.

Progress monitoring: Collection of multiple performance measures over time in order to (1) determine whether progress is appropriate and, if progress is not appropriate, (2) help identify more effective programs; can also help determine whether individual students are not responding appropriately to different levels of instruction and may need to be evaluated for learning disabilities.

Proximity: Moving physically closer to students who are beginning to demonstrate off-task or disruptive behavior, which can, in many instances, help to minimize classroom behavior problems.

Quadriplegia: Paralysis in both the arms and legs.

RAP strategy: Reading comprehension strategy is based on the steps represented by each letter in RAP (see Chapter 13).

Reciprocal teaching: Reading comprehension strategy that includes summarizing, predicting, questioning, and clarifying. Students assume the role of teacher during instruction and take the lead on asking questions.

Reconstructive elaborations: Procedures for reconstructing information into more meaningful and memorable forms. Three types of reconstructions are acoustic (or keyword), symbolic, and mimetic.

Reinforcement: During reading tasks, refers to providing rewards or positive comments to students to encourage and motivate them.

Relationship charts: See Semantic maps.

Reliability: Measures that seek to determine that a test is consistent in what it measures.

Repeated reading: Rereading a passage until fluent, effortless reading is achieved by struggling students. As their familiarity with the passage increases, their fluency and comprehension should also increase.

Response cost: System where previously earned points are withdrawn for serious misbehavior; make certain that students are informed of the possible consequence ahead of time and that the procedure produces the desired results.

Response to intervention (RTI): Multilevel system designed to address different learning needs, reduce disability identification, and provide evidence for the appropriate identification of learning disabilities.

Retinitis pigmentosa: Degeneration of the retina, causing visual impairments.

Retinopathy of prematurity: Excessive oxygen given to premature infants, resulting in visual impairments.

RTI: Response-to-intervention is a multilevel system designed to address different learning needs, reduce disability identification, and provide evidence for the appropriate identification of learning disabilities.

Rule learning: Type of factual learning that involves social behavior, English language, mathematics, and other subject areas. For example, one social behavior rule includes "Raise your hand before speaking."

Same-age tutoring: Students tutor students of the same age. Students who are more skilled in a particular area can tutor less-skilled students. In other cases, pairs of students can alternate roles.

Scaffolded supports: Supports that can be used in guided practice that include modeling, think-alouds, prompting, and immediate feedback.

Scaffolding: Practice used by teachers that provides more supports for students as they are introduced to a new skill, then gradually removes supports as they master the skill.

Schizophrenia: Serious mental disorder affecting the ability to interpret reality normally.

Schoolwide screening measures: Type of measures that are easy to implement and score yet still provide a general picture of academic achievement in a particular area, such as reading. They may be brief and may be administered to all students at all grade levels and are used to indicate which students may require additional evaluation to determine if further assistance is needed.

Scientifically based: Research that employs rigorous and systematic procedures, experimental or quasi-experimental research designs, and reliable, valid measures and that has been subjected to review by experts, for example, in peer-reviewed journals.

Scope and sequence: Breadth and depth of content to be covered.

SCREAM variables: Strategy of instruction with each letter representing the following: Structure, Clarity, Redundancy, Enthusiasm, Appropriate rate, and Maximized engagement through questioning and feedback.

Seclusionary timeout: Timeout where a student is removed from the instructional setting to another setting, such as a timeout room.

Section 504: Section 504 is a component of The Vocational Rehabilitation Act of 1973. This federal legislation is intended to prevent discrimination against individuals with disabilities by any institution that receives federal funds.

Selective mutism: Failure to speak in selected circumstances.

Self-advocacy: Skills relevant to transition that include being aware of legal rights, requesting accommodations, requesting assistance from doctors and others, using job-related social skills, planning for the future and making informed choices, and seeking accommodations whenever needed.

Self-advocacy strategy (SAS): Steps to assist students in acquiring self-advocacy skills for transition. In this strategy, students evaluate and plan for transition to areas such as independent living, consumer skills, citizenship skills, employment skills, family-living skills, and recreational and leisure skills. Students describe their strengths, areas to improve, and preferred accommodations; share; actively listen and discuss; and identify goals.

Self-determination instruction: Teaching individuals how to increase control of their own lives and destinies.

Self-determination skills: Components of self-determination skills, a construct associated with personal values and characteristics, such as autonomy, independence, intrinsic motivation, self-advocacy, and self-efficacy. These skills help students to become advocates for themselves and how to become knowledgeable about themselves with respect to learning strengths, needs, preferences, interests, and rights and responsibilities. This knowledge can be used to request accommodations that promote more success in school, jobs, independent living, and postsecondary education.

Self-Determined Learning Model of Instruction: Using this curriculum material, teachers and students work together to learn how to solve problems, set goals, and learn what they need to do to meet these goals. Four components used throughout this problem-solving process include setting goals, identifying problems, identifying plans, and evaluating.

Self-esteem: General term for the regard in which individuals hold themselves. Generally, students who feel good about who they are and what they can do are more successful than students who do not feel good about themselves.

Self-instruction and self-monitoring: Components of cognitive-behavioral interventions. Self-instruction teaches students to implement steps for completing tasks. Self-monitoring teaches students to monitor their behaviors such as on-task behavior and task completion.

Self-recording: Strategy used in teaching students how to monitor and evaluate their own behavior.

Self-regulated strategy development (SRSD): Model for promoting higher-level cognitive skills and self-regulated use of cognitive strategies especially for writing.

Self-regulation: Use of cognitive strategies to learn and remember more efficiently in order to enhance performance. See also Self-instruction.

Self-stimulating behaviors: Self-stimulating behaviors or stimming refer to repetitive behaviors such as rocking, hand flapping; atypical speech patterns, such as repeating the words of other people over and over again (echolalia) or using no tone inflection, a high pitch, or gibberish; and disruptive behavior, sometimes including self-injury exhibited by some students.

Semantic maps: Spatially organized, as well as semantically organized, representation of a topic to help facilitate memory.

Semantic memory: Memory for facts and concepts about the world.

Semantics: Meanings of words used in language.

Sensitivity: Characteristics of screening measures identifying students who are at risk for academic difficulties in the area being measured.

Sensorineural: Inner-ear damage, causing hearing impairments.

Serial list: Learning information with respect to a specific sequence such as the letters of the alphabet.

Sheltered content instruction: Approach to teaching English learners that integrates language and content instruction.

Short-term memory: Memory that holds information only briefly.

Sight words: Words that are used frequently at various grade levels. Some of these irregular words cannot be easily decoded using phonics skills, including such words as *the*, *a*, *is*, *to*, and *once*.

SMARTER: Content enhancement strategy in which each letter in the acronym represents a strategy step (see Chapter 15).

Social skills: Behaviors used to work and socialize with other people; necessary for successful functioning in school, in society, and on the job.

SPACE strategy: Strategy designed to help students think about more details that need to be included in their narrative stories and involves steps based on each letter in the acronym (see Chapter 13).

Special Friends: Program that provides kindergarten students in inclusive classrooms exposure to disability-related themes and gives frequent opportunities to interact with students with mild to severe disabilities.

Specific learning disabilities (SLD): Category that refers to a disorder in one or more of the basic psychological processes involved in understanding or using spoken or written language, which can result in difficulties in reading, writing, listening, speaking, thinking, spelling, or mathematics.

Specificity: Characteristic of screening measures indicating that students who perform acceptably on the measure are unlikely to have academic problems in that area.

Speech: System of forming and producing sounds that are the basis of language.

Standard-treatment-protocol approach: In this approach, Tier 1 could include some specific, evidence-based reading practice in the general education classroom, perhaps including classwide peer tutoring in reading, explicit instruction in reading skills and subskills where needed, and monitoring of student progress. For students who do not succeed in this program, Tier 2 might include standard small-group instruction in reading. For students who do not succeed on this level, Tier 3 might include highly intensive, individualized instruction based on the student's individual needs. In many cases, Tier 3 may include special education identification and placement.

Standardized: Tests that all students take under the same, or standard, conditions. The information that comes from the test results, then, assumes standardized testing conditions were applied. Standardized administration procedures are published in test manuals and are expected to be closely followed for the test scores to be meaningful.

STAR: Strategy for solving algebraic problems in which each letter represents a step (see Chapter 14).

Station teaching: Smaller groups of students move through several independent workstations for new information, review, or practice while the teachers monitor different stations.

STEM: Acronym for science, technology, engineering, and mathematics.

Stimming: Repetitive student behaviors such as rocking and hand flapping; atypical speech patterns, such as repeating the words of other people over and over again (echolalia) or using no tone inflection, a high pitch, or gibberish; and disruptive behavior, sometimes including self-injury.

Structural analysis: Ability to examine the structures of words and break them into pronounceable syllables; involves examining a word by familiar word parts, such as the prefix, suffix, or syllables.

Stuttering: Common fluency disorder that interferes with a person's ability to speak fluently during which individuals may repeat, extend, or block sounds, syllables, or words.

Summative testing: Tests given at the end of a particular educational period following instruction. Achievement tests given at the end of a school year are good examples. The purpose of summative testing is to fully identify the range of knowledge and skills learned and how much has been accomplished throughout the educational period.

Suspension: Not allowing a student to return to school for a specified time period as a punishment for serious misbehavior.

Symbolic reconstructions: Information that is reconstructed into a symbolic picture, rather than a *keyword* (acoustic) picture. For example, to demonstrate the U.S. policy of neutrality before World War I, a picture could be shown of Uncle Sam (symbol for U.S. policy) watching the war in Europe and exclaiming, "It's not my fight!"

Syntax: Grammatical structure of language concerned with such things as word order and noun–verb agreement.

Task analysis: Process of taking a large task or assignment, breaking it into subcomponent smaller tasks, and estimating task completion time for each subcomponent.

TBI: Traumatic brain injury is the result of an external head injury that impedes learning along the continuum from mild to severe disabilities and may result in physical, cognitive, attention, memory, problem-solving, sensory, and psychosocial difficulties.

T-Chart: Way of displaying expectations during cooperative learning activities that employs two columns in the shape of a *T*.

Team-teaching: Type of co-teaching during which teachers take turns presenting and leading classroom activities and share responsibilities equally.

TELLS strategy: Strategy for activating prior knowledge where each letter represents a step (see Chapter 13).

Test-taking skills: Skills to increase student familiarity and understanding of various test formats, such as multiple choice, short answer, essay, fill-in-the-blank, separate answer sheets, and computerized formats. Practice should include exposure to all relevant formats, and such general skills as using time wisely and test preparation skills.

Text enhancements: Illustrations, maps, diagrams, visual-spatial displays, semantic feature analysis charts, mnemonic pictures, and other adjunct aids developed to accompany text materials to increase comprehension.

Text-oriented (or content-oriented) approach: Method in which students learn content information from science and social studies textbooks adopted by many school districts. With this approach, adaptations may focus on teacher presentations and students' independent learning from textbooks.

Think-alouds: Teacher modeling of the thought processes used to solve a problem; for example, "Here's how I think as I try to solve this problem using the following steps . . . "

THINK–STOP–DARE strategy: Strategy designed for writing persuasive essays. Each letter in the strategy represents a step (see Chapter 13).

Timeout: Type of separation of a student from the routine classroom environment, usually for a violation of class rules.

Token systems: System in which students who follow class rules are awarded points at the end of specified time periods, such as class periods. The points are symbolic representations that can later be exchanged for a reinforcer of value.

Total communication: Using speech (lip) reading, gestures, and sign language or both oral and manual methods. Teachers using total communication rely on the structure of the English language and speak while signing during communications with students who are Deaf.

Touch Math: Commercially available materials that represent quantity by dots on each of the numbers 1–9 found to be effective with students with a variety of disabilities, including physical disabilities, intellectual or learning disabilities, hearing impairments, and autism.

Tourette syndrome: Tic disorder characterized by involuntary muscular movements, vocalizations, and/or inappropriate verbal outbursts that appear to have biological bases that interact with other factors and may contribute to emotional disturbances.

Transition: Process of planning for changes throughout a student's life.

Transition activities: Students moving from one location, subject, or group to another during which academic engaged time may be lost.

Transition coordinator: Person responsible for facilitating transition planning, ensuring all relevant school personnel are informed of transition objectives and methods, and working with interested parties to connect postsecondary goals with appropriate curriculum decisions. General education teachers may help to ensure transition goals are being addressed when appropriate in the general education classroom.

Transition programs: Programs that help prepare students for changes they will undertake throughout their school years and beyond. Examples of transitions can include changing grade levels or moving from kindergarten to elementary school to middle school to high school to college or vocational training; changing placement from special education to general education settings; obtaining a job; joining recreational activities; or moving to new living arrangements or to a new community.

Traumatic brain injury (TBI): Type of physical and cognitive disability that is the result of an external injury that impedes learning along the continuum from mild to severe disabilities and may result in physical, cognitive, attention, memory, problem-solving, sensory, and psychosocial difficulties.

TRAVEL: Strategy that is an acronym for the steps used in developing cognitive organizers to improve student comprehension and recall of text content (see Chapter 15).

Twice-exceptional: Students with a learning disability who are also gifted.

Types and levels of learning: Guidelines for planning instructional adaptations for differentiated instruction. Types of learning include discriminations, facts, rules, procedures, and concepts, as well as problem solving/critical thinking. Levels of learning include—in order of complexity—initial acquisition, fluency, application, and generalization.

Universal design for learning (UDL): Principles that involve developing materials or structuring the environment to improve accessibility for all learners.

Validity: Extent to which a particular test measures what it is intended to measure; often evaluated by comparing different tests of the same skills or abilities.

Visual acuity: How well an individual sees letters and numbers from a specified distance.

Vocabulary instruction: Providing students with practice in learning specific vocabulary words that will be encountered in the readings.

Whole language: Approach that emphasizes meaning and integrates all literacy tasks within reading instruction. A basic tenet of this approach is that the immersion of children in a literature-enriched environment promotes literacy.

Working memory: Information actively processed in short-term memory (e.g., solving a two-part math problem).

WWC: What Works Clearinghouse is a federally funded source for scientifically-based educational practices.

NAME INDEX

SUBJECT INDEX